C000279135

STREI

Lancashire

Blackburn, Blackpool, Burnley, Lancaster, Preston, Southport

www.philips-maps.co.uk

First published in 1997 by

Philip's, a division of
Octopus Publishing Group Ltd
www.octopusbooks.co.uk
2-4 Heron Quays, London E14 4JP
An Hachette Livre UK Company

Fourth colour edition 2008
First impression 2008
LANDA

ISBN-13   978-0-540-09194-2 (pocket)

© Philip's 2008

Ordnance Survey

This product includes mapping data licensed from
Ordnance Survey® with the permission of the
Controller of Her Majesty's Stationery Office.
© Crown copyright 2008. All rights reserved.
Licence number 100011710.

Data for the speed cameras provided by
PocketGPSWorld.com Ltd.

Ordnance Survey and the OS Symbol are
registered trademarks of Ordnance Survey, the
national mapping agency of Great Britain

Printed by Toppan, China

Contents

II   List of mobile speed cameras

III   Key to map symbols

IV   Key to map pages

VI   Route planning

X   Administrative and Postcode boundaries

1   Street maps at 2⅔ inches to 1 mile

226   Street maps at 1⅓ inches to 1 mile

244   Index of towns, villages, streets, hospitals, industrial
estates, railway stations, schools, shopping centres,
universities and places of interest

Digital Data

The exceptionally high-quality mapping found in this atlas is available as digital data in TIFF
format, which is easily convertible to other bitmapped (raster) image formats.

The index is also available in digital form as a standard database table. It contains all the details
found in the printed index together with the National Grid reference for the map square in which
each entry is named.

For further information and to discuss your requirements, please contact james.mann@philips-
maps.co.uk

Mobile speed cameras

The vast majority of speed cameras used on Britain's roads are operated by safety camera partnerships. These comprise local authorities, the police, Her Majesty's Court Service (HMCS) and the Highways Agency.

This table lists the sites where each safety camera partnership may enforce speed limits through the use of mobile cameras or detectors. These are usually set up on the roadside or a bridge spanning the road and operated by a police or civilian enforcement officer. The speed limit at each site (if available) is shown in red type, followed by the approximate location in black type.

Mike Harrington / Alamy

A6
40 Broughton, Garstang Rd (north of M55)
30, 40 Chorley, Bolton Rd
30 Fulwood, Garstang Rd (south of M55)
30 Fulwood, Garstang Rd, north of Blackpool Rd
30 Lancaster, Greaves Rd
50 Lancaster, Scotforth Rd nr Burrow Lane Bailrigg
30 Preston, North Rd
30 Preston, Ringway

A56
30 Colne, Albert Rd
30 Colne, Burnley Rd
30 Nelson, Leeds Rd

A59
60 Gisburn, Gisburn Rd
50 Hutton, Liverpool Rd
30 Preston, New Hall Lane

A65
40, 60 Lancaster, Cowan Bridge

A570
40 Scarisbrick, Southport Rd, Brook House Farm

A581
40 Ulnes Walton, Southport Rd

A583+A5073
30 Blackpool, Whitegate Drive/Waterloo Rd

A583+B5266
30 Blackpool, Church St / Newton Drive

A584
30 Blackpool, Promenade
30 Lytham, West / Central Beach
30, 50 Warton, Lytham Rd

A584+A587
30 Blackpool, Promenade/ Fleetwood Rd

A587
30 Blackpool, East / North Park Drive
30 Cleveleys, Rossall Rd/ Crescent East

A588
60 Pilling, Head Dyke Lane
60 Wyre, Lancaster Rd, Cockerham at Gulf Lane

A666
30, 50 Darwen, Blackburn Rd
30 Darwen, Bolton Rd nr Cross St
30 Darwen, Duckworth St

A671
30 Read, Whalley Rd

A674
30 Cherry Tree, Preston Old Rd

A675
50 Belmont, Belmont Rd (south of village)
50 Darwen, Belmont Rd, north of Belmont Village
30, 60 Withnell, Bolton Rd (Dole Lane to Calf Hey Bridge)

A680
40, 60 Edenfield, Rochdale Rd

A682
60 Barrowford, Gisburn Rd nr Moorcock Inn
30 Brierfield, Colne Rd
40 Crawshawbooth, Burnley Rd
60 Gisburn, Gisburn Rd
60 Gisburn, Long Preston Rd

A683
30 Lancaster, Morecambe Rd

A5073
30 Blackpool, Waterloo Rd

A5085
30 Lane Ends, Blackpool Rd

A5209
30 Newburgh, Course Lane/ Ash Brow

A6062
30 Blackburn, Livesey Branch Rd

A6068
50 Barrowford, Barrowford Rd

A6114
30 Burnley, Casterton Avenue

A6177
50 Haslingden, Grane Rd West of Holcombe Rd
40, 50 Hyndburn, Haslingden Rd /Elton Rd

B5192
30 Kirkham, Preston St

B5251
30 Chorley, Pall Mall

B5242
30 Scarisbrick, Bescar Brow Lane

B5254
30 Lostock Hall, Leyland Rd/Watkin Lane
30 South Ribble, Leyland Rd

B5256
30 Leyland, Turpin Green Lane

B5269
40 Goosnargh, Whittingham Lane

B6231
30 Oswaldtwistle, Union Rd

B6243
50 Longridge, Preston Rd

UNCLASSIFIED
60 Belmont, Egerton Rd
30 Blackburn, East Park Rd
30 Blackburn, Revidge Rd nr Pleckgate
30 Blackburn, Whalley Old Rd, west of Railway Bridge
30 Blackpool, Dickson Rd, Queens St to Pleasant St
30 Briercliffe, Burnley Rd
30 Darwen, Lower Eccleshill Rd
60 Galgate, Bay Horse Rd
30 Nelson, Netherfield Rd
30 Preston, Lytham Rd
30 Preston, St Georges Rd
30 St Annes, Church Rd to Albany Rd, nr High School

Key to map symbols

III

(22a)	**Motorway** with junction number		◆	**Ambulance station**
	Primary route – dual/single carriageway		◆	**Coastguard station**
	A road – dual/single carriageway		◆	**Fire station**
	B road – dual/single carriageway		◆	**Police station**
	Minor road – dual/single carriageway		✚	**Accident and Emergency entrance to hospital**
	Other minor road – dual/single carriageway		Ⓗ	**Hospital**
	Road under construction		✚	**Place of worship**
	Tunnel, covered road		ℹ	**Information Centre** (open all year)
③⓪ ③⓪	**Speed cameras** - single, multiple		🛒	**Shopping Centre**
	Rural track, private road or narrow road in urban area		Ⓟ	**Parking**
	Gate or obstruction to traffic (restrictions may not apply at all times or to all vehicles)		Ⓟ&Ⓡ	**Park and Ride**
	Path, bridleway, byway open to all traffic, road used as a public path		PO	**Post Office**
	Pedestrianised area		Ⅹ	**Camping site**
DY7	**Postcode boundaries**		⛺	**Caravan site**
	County and unitary authority boundaries		⚑	**Golf course**
	Railway, tunnel, railway under construction		✕	**Picnic site**
	Tramway, tramway under construction		Prim Sch	**Important buildings, schools, colleges, universities and hospitals**
	Miniature railway			**Built up area**
Walsall	**Railway station**			**Woods**
	Private railway station		River Medway	**Water name**
South Shields	**Metro station**			**River, weir, stream**
	Tram stop, tram stop under construction			**Canal, lock, tunnel**
	Bus, coach station			**Water**
				Tidal water

Acad	**Academy**	Inst	**Institute**	Recn Gd	**Recreation Ground**
Allot Gdns	**Allotments**	Ct	**Law Court**		
Cemy	**Cemetery**	L Ctr	**Leisure Centre**	Resr	**Reservoir**
C Ctr	**Civic Centre**	LC	**Level Crossing**	Ret Pk	**Retail Park**
CH	**Club House**	Liby	**Library**	Sch	**School**
Coll	**College**	Mkt	**Market**	Sh Ctr	**Shopping Centre**
Crem	**Crematorium**	Meml	**Memorial**	TH	**Town Hall/House**
Ent	**Enterprise**	Mon	**Monument**	Trad Est	**Trading Estate**
Ex H	**Exhibition Hall**	Mus	**Museum**	Univ	**University**
Ind Est	**Industrial Estate**	Obsy	**Observatory**	W Twr	**Water Tower**
IRB Sta	**Inshore Rescue Boat Station**	Pal	**Royal Palace**	Wks	**Works**
		PH	**Public House**	YH	**Youth Hostel**

Church	**Non-Roman antiquity**
ROMAN FORT	**Roman antiquity**
94	**Adjoining page indicators and overlap bands** The colour of the arrow and the band indicates the scale of the adjoining or overlapping page (see scales below)
164	

■ The small numbers around the edges of the maps identify the 1 kilometre National Grid lines

■ The dark grey border on the inside edge of some pages indicates that mapping does not continue onto the adjacent page

The scale of the maps on the pages numbered in blue is 4.2 cm to 1 km • 2⅔ inches to 1 mile • 1: 23810

0 — ¼ — ½ — ¾ — 1 mile
0 — 250m — 500m — 750m — 1 kilometre

The scale of the maps on pages numbered in green is 2.1 cm to 1 km • 1⅓ inches to 1 mile • 1: 47620

0 — ¼ — ½ — ¾ — 1 mile
0 — 250m 500m 750m — 1 kilometre

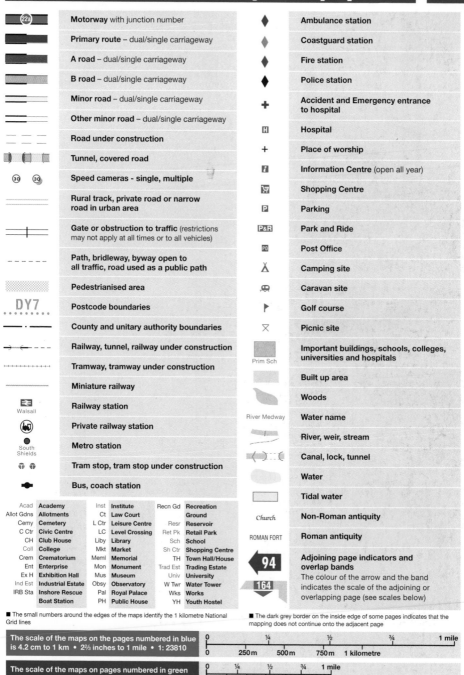

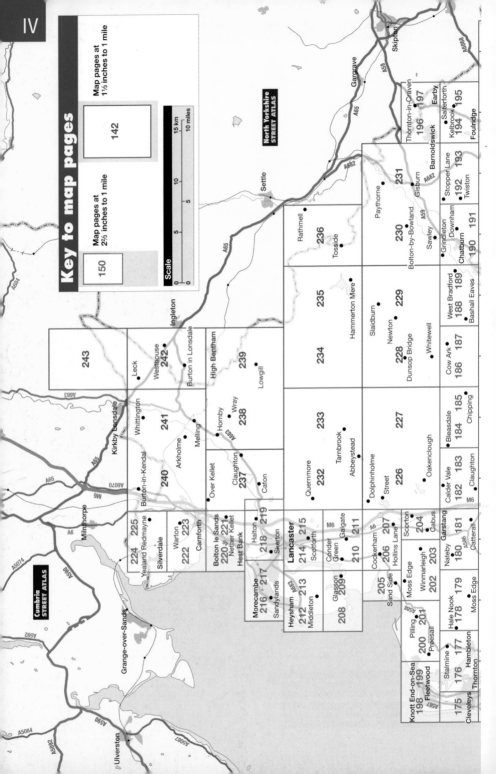

IV

Key to map pages

Map pages at 2⅓ inches to 1 mile

150

Map pages at 1½ inches to 1 mile

142

Scale

| 0 | 5 | 10 | 15 km |
| 0 | 5 | 10 miles |

North Yorkshire STREET ATLAS

Cumbria STREET ATLAS

Skipton

Gargrave

Thornton-in-Craven 196 197 Earby

Salterforth 195
Kelbrook 194
Foulridge

Barnoldswick

Stopper Lane 192 193 Twiston

Paythorne 231

Gisburn

Bolton-by-Bowland 230
Sawley

Grindleton 190 191
Downham
Chatburn

Rathmell 236
Tosside

Hammerton Mere 235

Slaidburn
Newton 229
Dunsop Bridge 228
Whitewell

West Bradford 188 189
Bashall Eaves

Cow Ark 186 187

Settle

Ingleton

Leck

Westhouse 242
Burton in Lonsdale

High Bentham 239

Lowgill

Wray 238
Hornby

234

Bleasdale 184 185
Chipping

227

Calder Vale 182 183
Claughton

Tarnbrook 233
Abbeystead

Quermore 232

Dolphinholme 226
Street
Oakenclough

243

Whittington 241
Arkholme
Melling

Over Kellet 240

Claughton 237
Caton

Kirkby Lonsdale

Burton-in-Kendal

Milnthorpe

Grange-over-Sands

Ulverston

Yealand Redmayne 224 225
Silverdale

Warton 222 223
Carnforth

Bolton le Sands 220 221
Nether Kellet
Hest Bank

Halton 218 219
Skerton

Lancaster 214 215
Scotforth

Conder Green 210 211
Galgate M6

Glasson 208 209

Morecambe 216 217
Sandylands

Heysham 212 213
Middleton

Cockerham 206 207
Hollins Lane

Sand Side 205

Moss Edge 202 203
Winmarleigh

Nateby 180 181
Garstang
Catterall

Scorton 204
Cabus

Knott End-on-Sea 198 199
Fleetwood

Stalmine 176 177
Hambleton
Thornton

Cleveleys 175

Pilling 200 201
Preesall

Hale Nook 178 179
Moss Edge

West Yorkshire STREET ATLAS

Greater Manchester STREET ATLAS

Cheshire STREET ATLAS

Liverpool and Merseyside STREET ATLAS

Manchester · Salford · Stretford · Oldham · Denton · Ashton-under-Lyne · Stalybridge · Rochdale · Littleborough · Todmorden · Heywood · Bury · Prestwich · Urmston · Irlam · Farnworth · Bolton · Leigh · Wigan · Ashton-in-Makerfield · Newton-le-Willows · St Helens · Kirkby · Bootle · Litherland · Liverpool · Wallasey

Colne · Nelson · Brierfield · Burnley · Padiham · Barrowford · Trawden · Wycoller · Laneshaw Bridge · Cornholme · Worsthorne · Haggate · Hurstwood · Holme Chapel · Portsmouth · Sharneyford · Bacup · Broadley · Whitworth · Syke · Shawforth · Nun Hills · Crawshawbooth · Rawtenstall · Waterfoot · Helmshore · Edenfield · Ramsbottom · Summerseat · Greenmount · Edgworth

Clitheroe · Whalley · Read · Barrow · Pendleton · Great Harwood · Clayton-le-Moors · Rishton · Accrington · Goodshaw Fold · Rising Bridge · Haslingden · Belmont · Egerton · Horwich · Blackrod · Adlington · Rivington · Limbrick · Cadshaw · Belgrave · Darwen · Hoddlesden · Belthorn · Oswaldtwistle · Dalsfield · York · Wilpshire · Sunny Bower · Mellor · Blackburn · Cherry Tree · Ewood · Abbey Village · Higher Wheelton · Brinscall · Knowley · Chorley · Coppull · Standish · Billinge · Orrell · Skelmersdale · Digmoor · Rainford · Rainford Junction · Longshaw

Hesketh Lane · Knowle Green · Whitechapel · Inglewhite · Longridge · Ribchester · Goosnargh · Grimsargh · Samlesbury · Balderstone · Ribbleton · Nab's Head · Gregson Lane · Brindle · Whittle-le-Woods · Euxton · Shaw Green · Eccleston · Mawdesley · Parbold · Hoscar · Appley Bridge · Stanley · Aughton · Bickerstaffe · Maghull · Lydiate

St Michael's on Wyre · Great Eccleston · Inskip · Catforth · Barton · Broughton · Cottam · Fulwood · Preston · Bamber Bridge · Lostock Hall · Leyland · Croston · Holmeswood · Rufford · Tarlscough · Burscough · Westhead · Ormskirk · Downholland Cross · Haskayne · Great Altcar

Whin Lane End · Elswick · Singleton · Thistleton · Weeton · Great Plumpton · Wrea Green · Clifton · Freckleton · Warton · Bottom of Hutton · Hutton · New Longton · Much Hoole · Tarleton · Sollom · Bescar · Bispham Green · Halsall · Shirdley Hill · Churchtown · Brown Edge · Marshside · Southport · Ainsdale · Birkdale · Blowick · High Park

Norbreck · Poulton-le-Fylde · Bispham · Blackpool · Stalmining · Sandham's Green · Moss Side · Lytham St Anne's · Lytham · St Annes · Formby · Hightown · Ince Blundell · Kirkby

Barley · Newchurch in Pendle · Higham · Fence · Walk Mill · Love Clough · Walker Fold · Hurst Green · Great Mitton · Bilsborrow

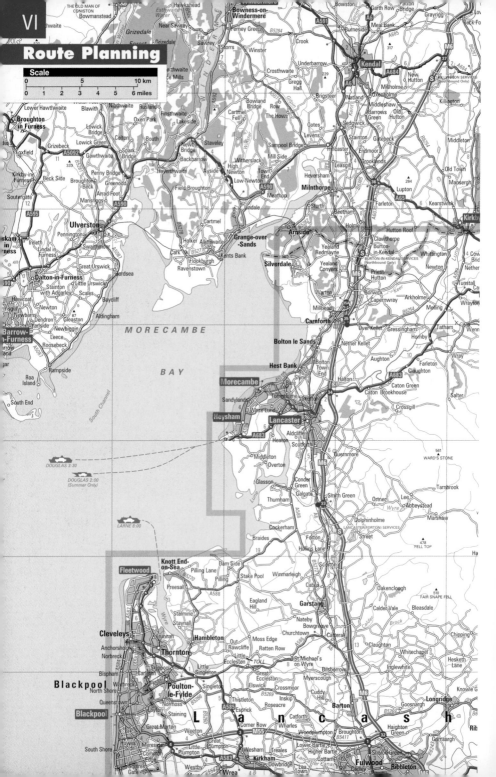

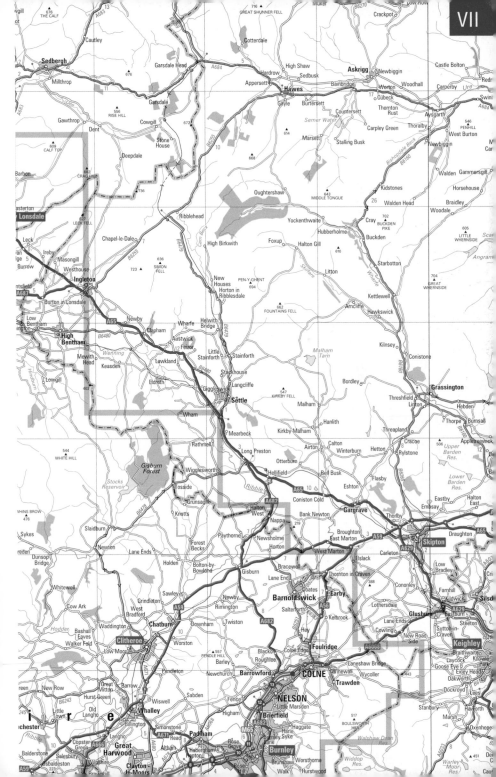

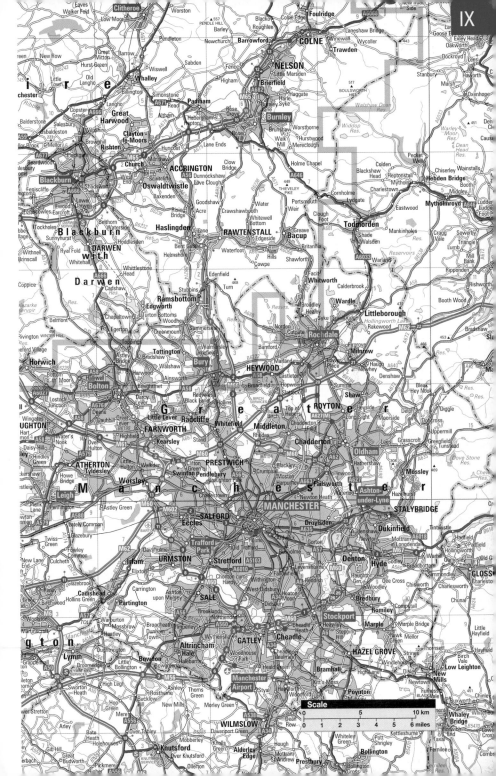

Major administrative and
Postcode boundaries

County and unitary
authority boundaries

District boundaries

Postcode boundaries

Area covered by this atlas

Scale

| 0 | 5 | 10 | 15 km |

| 0 | 5 | 10 miles |

Cumbria

LA10

North Yorkshire

LA7

Burton-in-
Kendal

Silverdale

LA5   LA6   Burton in
Lonsdale

Carnforth

Hornby   High
Bentham

Morecambe LA4

Caton

Heysham   LA1   Lancaster   LA2

LA3   Lancaster

Overton

Glasson   Galgate

Dolphinholme   BD24

Slaidburn   Tosside

BD23

Fleetwood   Scorton   Dunsop
Bridge

Gisburn

FY7   Pilling   Barnoldswick   Earby

FY6   Garstang   BB7   BB18

Cleveleys   FY5   Hambleton   Wyre   Chipping   Ribble Valley   BB9   Pendle   BB8   BD22

FY2   Great   PR3   Clitheroe   Colne   Trawden

Poulton-le-   Eccleston   Bilsborrow   L a n c a s h i r e   Nelson

Blackpool   Fylde   BB12   HX7

Blackpool   FY1   FY3   Longridge   Whalley   BB6   Padiham   BB10   Bradford

Fylde   Preston   Burnley

FY4   Fulwood   PR2   Mellor   BB1   Great   BB11   Burnley

FY8   Warton   PR4   Preston   PR1   Blackburn   Harwood   BB5   Holme Chapel

Lytham   Kirkham   PR5   BB2   Hyndburn   OL14

St Anne's   South Ribble   Bamber Bridge   Accrington   BB4   OL13

Walmer   Darwen   Haslingden   Bacup   Calderdale

Bridge   Leyland   PR25   BB3   Rossendale

Banks   Tarleton   PR26   Brinscall   Blackburn   OL12

Southport   Croston   Chorley   PR6   with   BL10   Whitworth

PR9   Eccleston   Chorley   Darwen   BL7   Ramsbottom   OL10

PR8   Ainsdale   PR7   Belmont   BL8   BL9   Rochdale

L40   WN1   Adlington   BL6

Burscough   BL6   Bury

West Lancashire   WN6   Standish   Horwich   Bolton   Bury   Oldham

Haskayne   Parbold   WN2

Formby   Ormskirk   WN8   Wigan

L37   L39   Skelmersdale   Orrell   SD

Aughton   WN5

Hightown   L38   L31   Maghull   WA11   Salford   SJ

L29   WN5

Sefton   L33   St Helens   Manchester   Tameside

Liverpool   Warrington   Trafford   Stockport

Knowsley

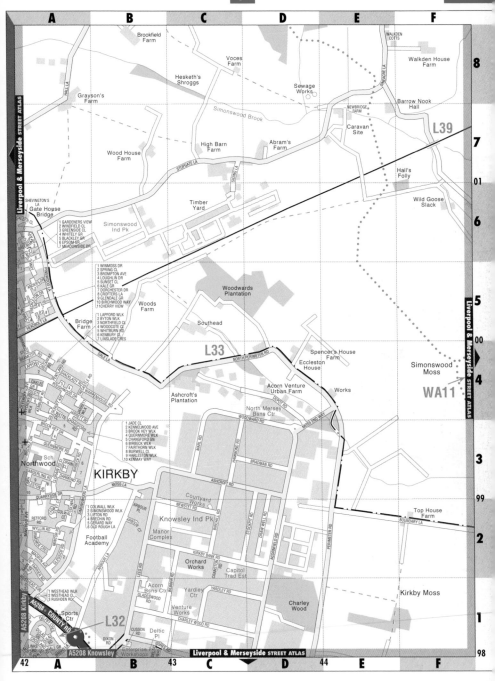

Brookfield Farm

Voces Farm

Hesketh's Shroggs

Walkden House Farm

WALKDEN COTTS

Grayson's Farm

Sewage Works

Simonswood Brook

Barrow Nook Hall

NEWBRIDGE FARM

Caravan Site

L39

Wood House Farm

High Barn Farm

Abram's Farm

Hall's Folly

Wild Goose Slack

Gate House Bridge

SHEVINGTON'S LA

Timber Yard

Simonswood Ind Pk

1 GARDENERS VIEW
2 WINDFIELD CL
3 GREENSIDE CL
4 WHITELY GR
5 BLACKLEY GR
6 EPSOM GR
7 MEADOWSIDE DR

1 WINMOSS DR
2 SPRING CL
3 BROMPTON AVE
4 LOUGHLIN DR
5 SUNSET CL
6 KALE GR
7 DORCHESTER DR
8 CROFTERS LA
9 GLENDALE GR
10 BIRCHWOOD WAY
11 CHERRY VIEW

Woodwards Plantation

Woods Farm

Bridge Farm

1 LAPFORD WLK
2 BYTON WLK
3 NORTHFIELD CL
4 WOODCOTE CL
5 WHITBURN RD
6 KENBURY CL
7 LINSLADE CRES

Southead

L33

NORTH PERIMETER RD

Spencer's House Farm

Eccleston House

Simonswood Moss

WA11

Ashcroft's Plantation

Acorn Venture Urban Farm

North Mersey Bsns Ctr

Works

WOODWARD RD

1 JADE CL
2 KENNELWOOD AVE
3 BROOK HEY WLK
4 GUERNMORE WLK
5 CHANGFORD GN
6 BIRBECK WLK
7 FAIRTHORN WLK
8 BURWELL CL
9 HARLESTON WLK
10 KENMAY WAY

Sch Northwood

KIRKBY

MOSS LA

Courtyard Works

NEWSTET RD

Knowsley Ind Pk

1 COLWALL WLK
2 SIMONSWOOD WLK
3 LITTON RD
4 BRECHIN RD
5 GERARD WAY
6 OLD ROUGH LA

Football Academy

Manor Complex

KIRKBY BANK RD

Orchard Works

Capitol Trad Est

Top House Farm

BOUNDARY LA

Kirkby Moss

1 WESTHEAD WLK
2 WESTHEAD CL
3 RUSHDEN RD

L32

Acorn Bsns Ctr

Yardley Ctr

YARDLEY RD

Venture Works

CHARLEY WOOD RD

Charley Wood

Sports Ctr

CUSSON RD

Deltic Pl

DIXON RD

A5208 Knowsley

Enterprise Workshops

42 A   B   43   C   D   44   E   F   98

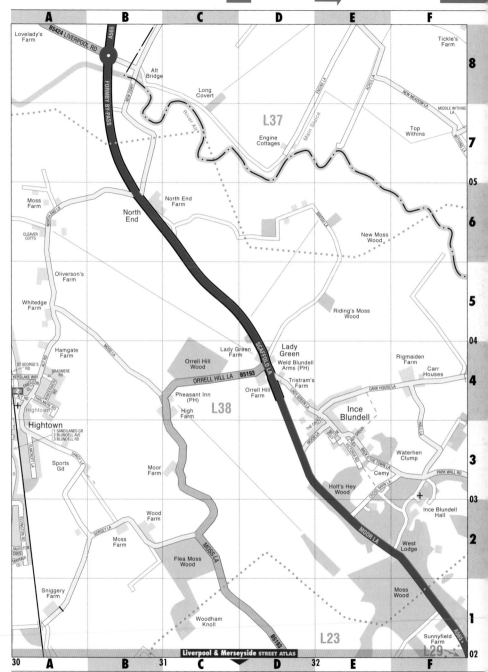

	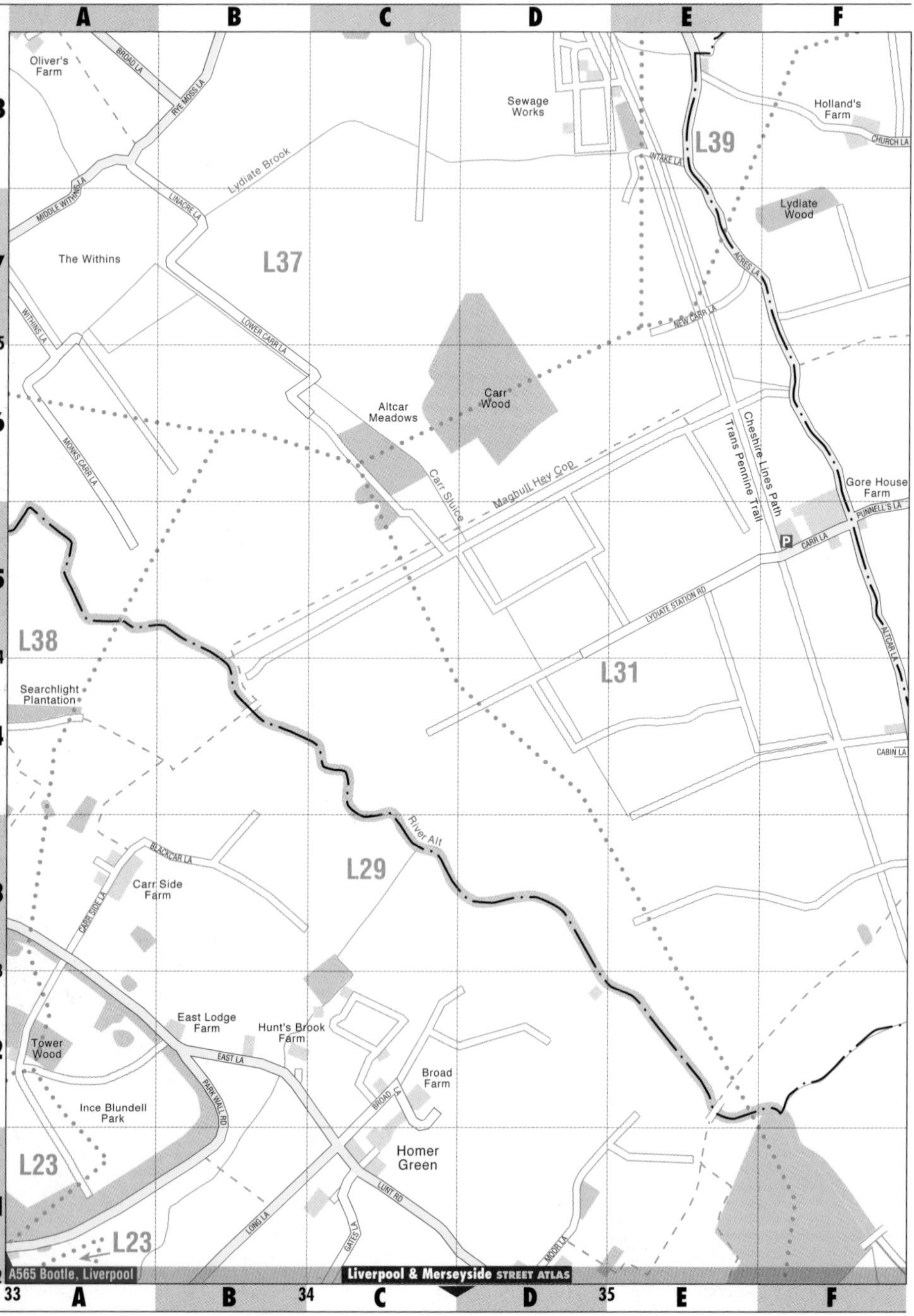 A	B	C	D	E	F

Oliver's Farm

Sewage Works

Holland's Farm

8

CHURCH LA

L39

BROAD LA

RYE MOSS LA

Lydiate Brook

Lydiate Wood

MIDDLE WITHINS LA

LINACRE LA

L37

The Withins

7

LOWER CARR LA

WITHINS LA

NEW CABIN LA

MOSS LA

05

Altcar Meadows

Carr Wood

Cheshire Lines Path

MONKS CARR LA

6

Carr Sluice

Maghull Hey Cop

Trans Pennine Trail

Gore House Farm

PUNNELL'S LA

Gore House Farm

P CABIN LA

5

LYDIATE STATION RD

LYDIATE LA

L38

L31

04

Searchlight Plantation

CABIN LA

4

BLACKCAR LA

River Alt

L29

CARR SIDE LA

Carr Side Farm

3

03

East Lodge Farm

Hunt's Brook Farm

Tower Wood

EAST LA

PARK WALL RD

Broad Farm

2

Ince Blundell Park

BROAD LA

Homer Green

L23

LUNT RD

1

LONG LA

GATES LA

MOOR LA

L23

02

33	A		B	34	C		D	35	E		F

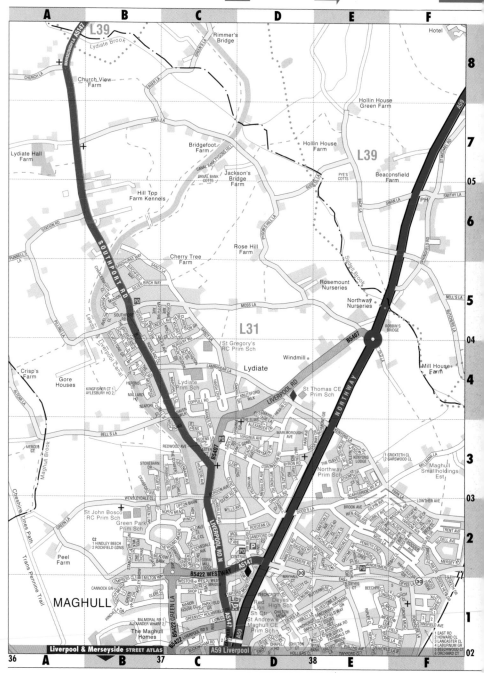

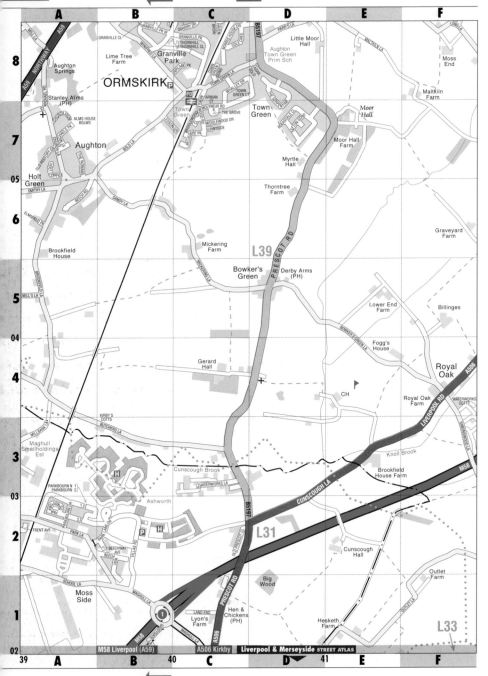

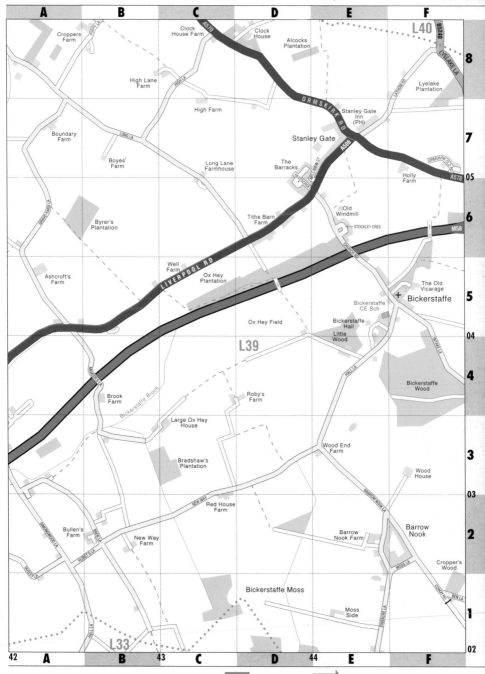

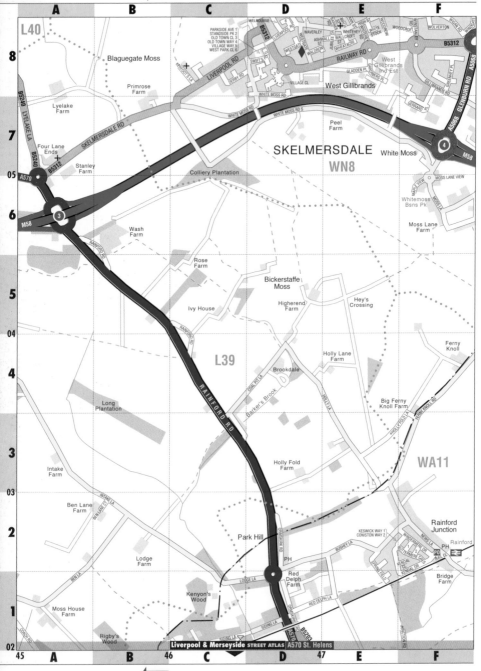

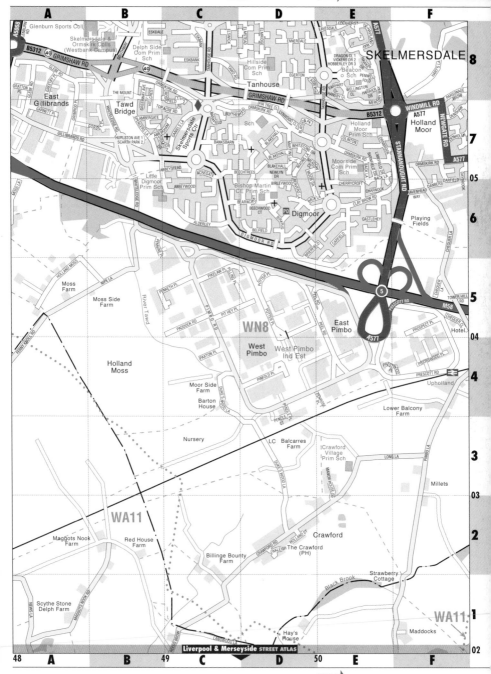

A7
1 DENHOLME
2 FIELDVIEW
3 MEADOWFIELD

E5
1 COSGATE CL
2 MIDDLECOT CL
3 THE ORCHARDS

F7
1 THIRLMERE AVE
2 LATIMER CL
3 BYRON CL
4 WINCHESTER CL

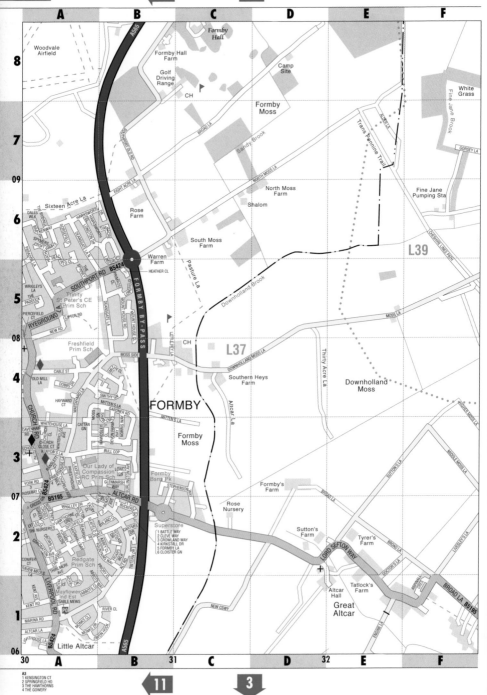

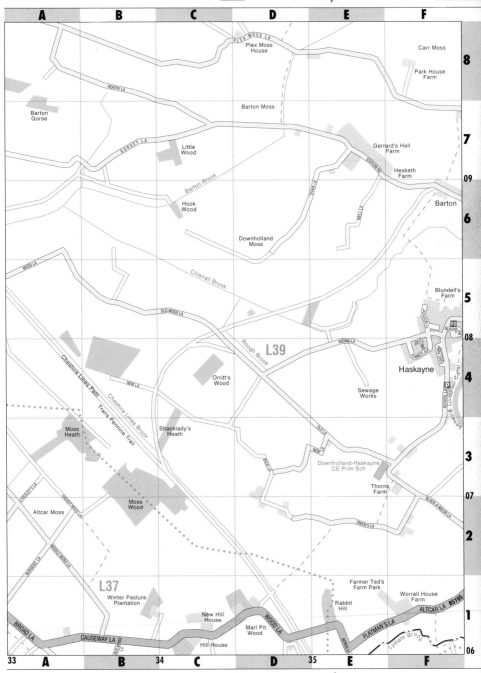

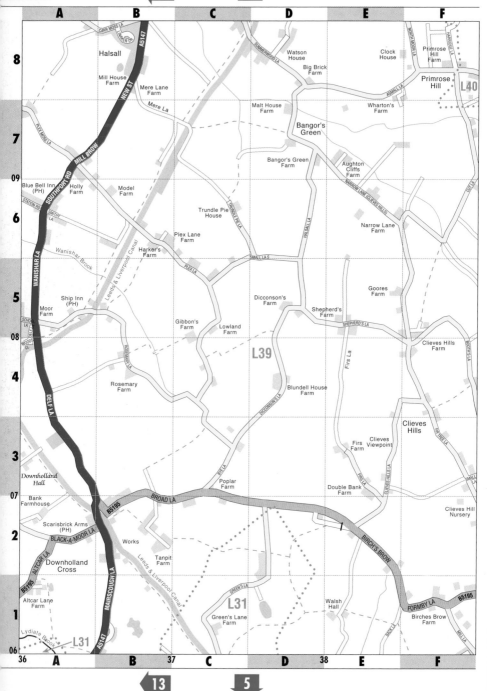

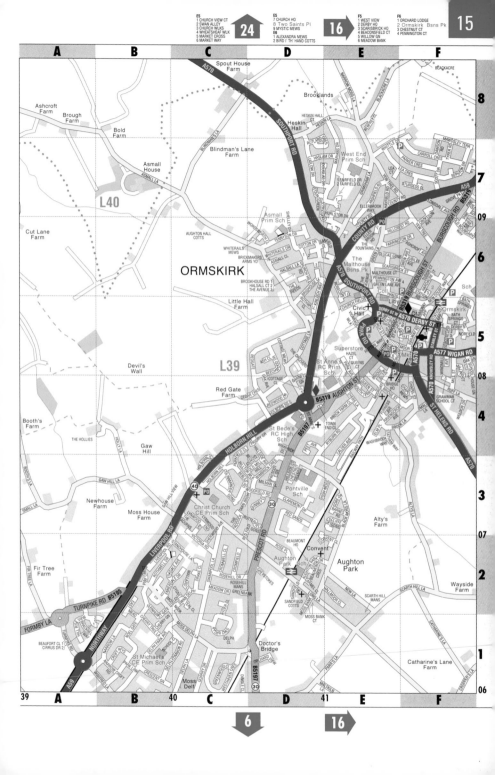

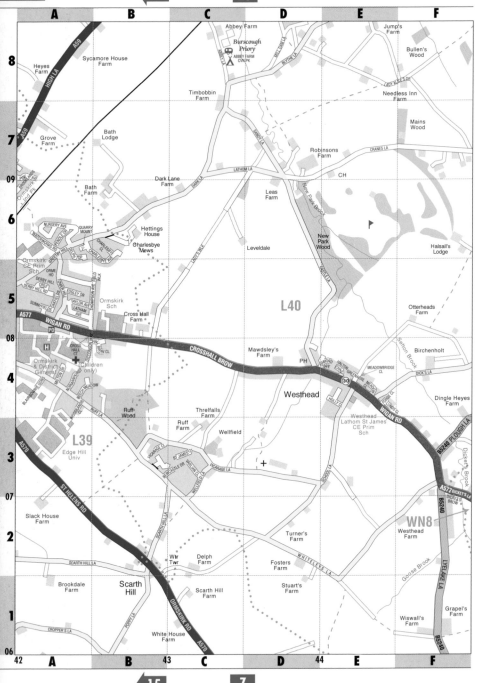

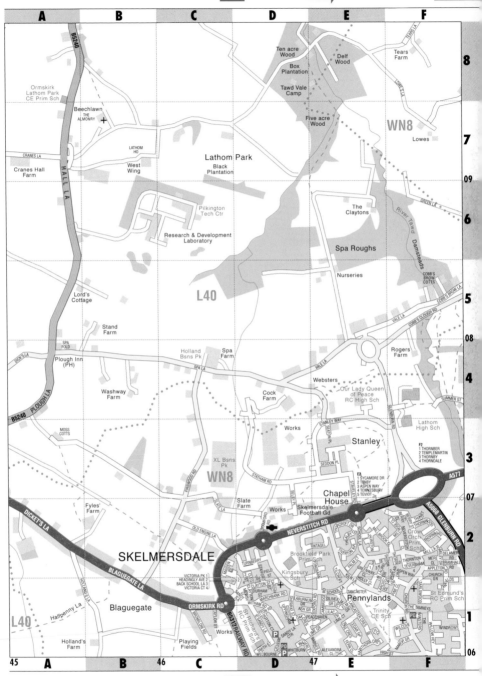

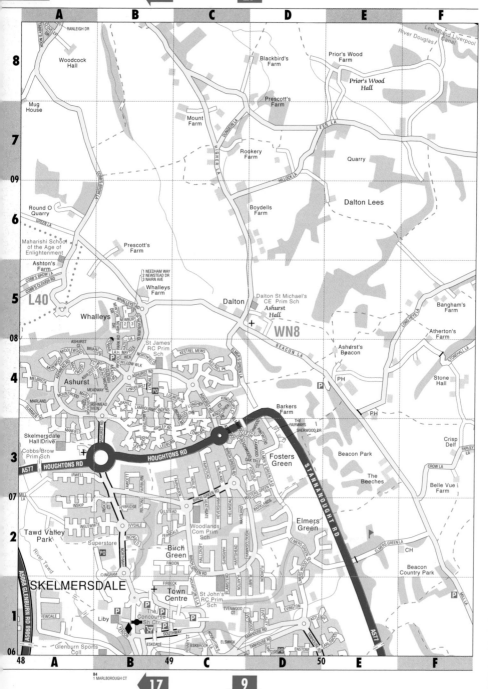

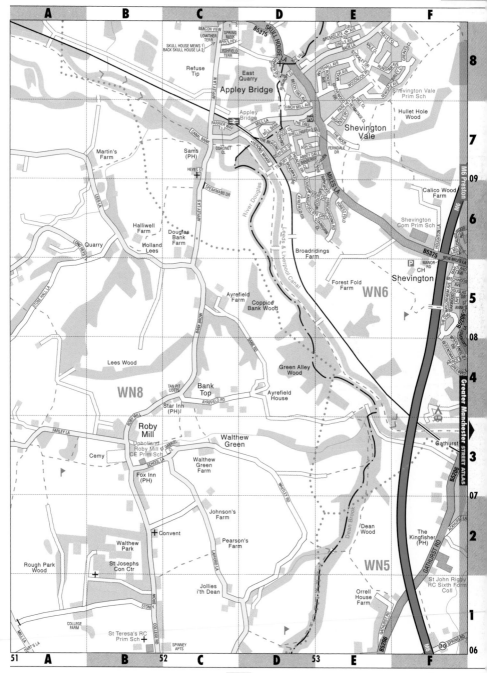

Appley Bridge

Shevington Vale

Hullet Hole Wood

Shevington Vale Prim Sch

Calico Wood Farm

Shevington

WN6

Martin's Farm

Sams (PH)

HEYES ST

Refuse Tip

East Quarry

SPEAKMANS DR

APPLEY LA

FARRER WAY

CORONET

CANAL BANK

APPLEY LA

Quarry

Holland Lees

Halliwell Farm

Douglas Bank Farm

River Douglas

Leeds & Liverpool Canal

Broadridings Farm

Forest Fold Farm

Ayrefield Farm

Coppice Bank Wood

Green Alley Wood

Lees Wood

WN8

TAN PIT COTTS

Bank Top

Star Inn (PH)

Ayrefield House

Ayrefield Rd

BANK BROW

BANK RD

ROBY MILL

Roby Mill

FARLEY LA

Cemy

Fox Inn (PH)

Upholland Roby Mill CE Prim Sch

SCHOOL LA

ST GABRIEL

Walthew Green

Walthew Green Farm

Johnson's Farm

Convent

Pearson's Farm

Walthew Park

St Josephs Con Ctr

Rough Park Wood

STONE FARM LA

LONG FEET RD

LEES LA

COLLEGE FARM

MILL LEA

HART'S LA

MONK

STONE

COLLEGE RD

St Teresa's RC Prim Sch

SPINNEY APTS

Jollies i'th Dean

WN5

Dean Brook

Dean Wood

Orrell House Farm

The Kingfisher (PH)

St John Rigby RC Sixth Form Coll

Gathurst

GATHURST RD

M6

B5206

B5206

SPRING RD

M6 Preston

B5375

Greater Manchester STREET ATLAS

51

52

53

06

07

08

09

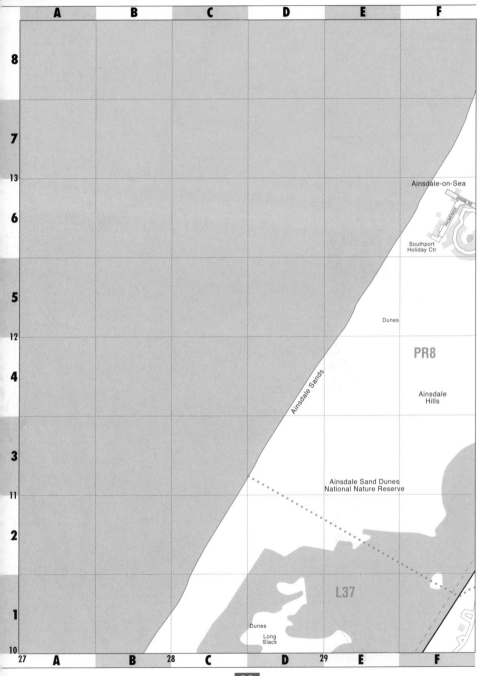

Ainsdale-on-Sea

SHORE RD

PROMENADE

Southport
Holiday Ctr

Dunes

PR8

Ainsdale
Hills

Ainsdale Sands

Ainsdale Sand Dunes
National Nature Reserve

L37

Dunes

Long
Slack

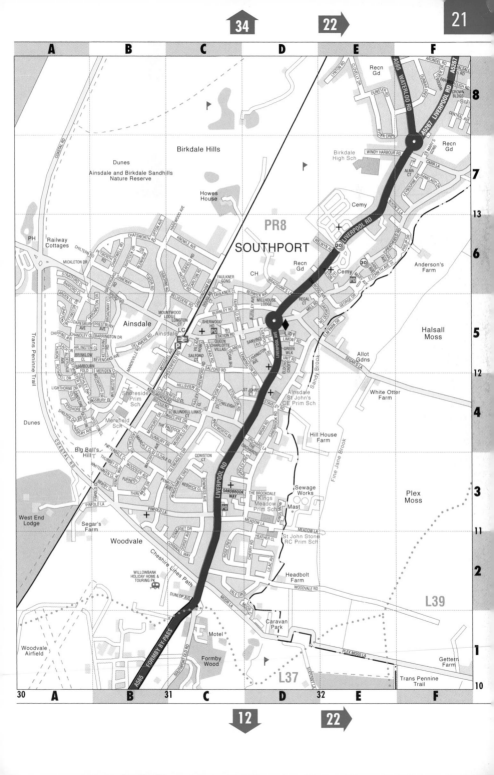

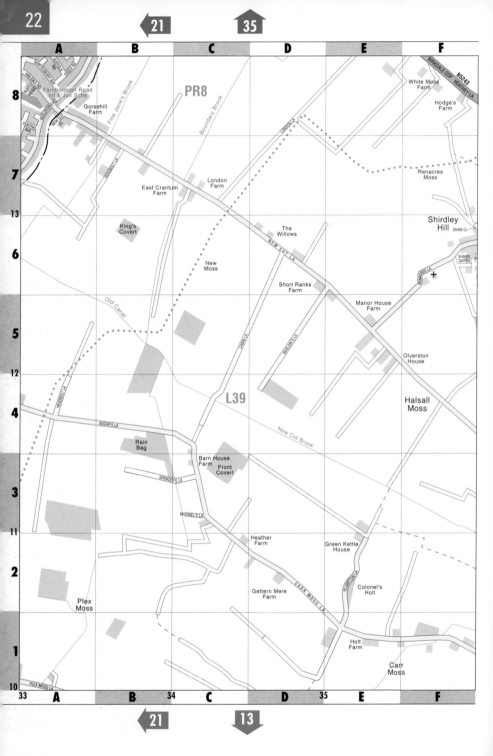

PR8

Farnborough Road Inf & Jun Schs

Gorsehill Farm

White Moss Farm

Hodge's Farm

B5243

BIRKDALE COP

HEATHEY LA

Fine Jane's Brook

Boundary Brook

LONDON LA

Renacres Moss

East Crantum Farm

London Farm

Shirdley Hill

SHAW CL

King's Covert

The Willows

NEW CUT LA

SHAWS GARTH

RENACRES LA

New Moss

Short Ranks Farm

Manor House Farm

Old Canal

CABIN LA

BARLOW'S LA

Olverston House

Halsall Moss

L39

MENDALL LA

SEGAR'S LA

New Cut Brook

Rain Bag

Barn House Farm

Front Covert

SPENCER'S LA

MICHAEL'S LA

Heather Farm

Green Kettle House

CARR MOSS LA

PLUMPTONS LA

Colonel's Holt

Plex Moss

Gettern Mere Farm

Holt Farm

Carr Moss

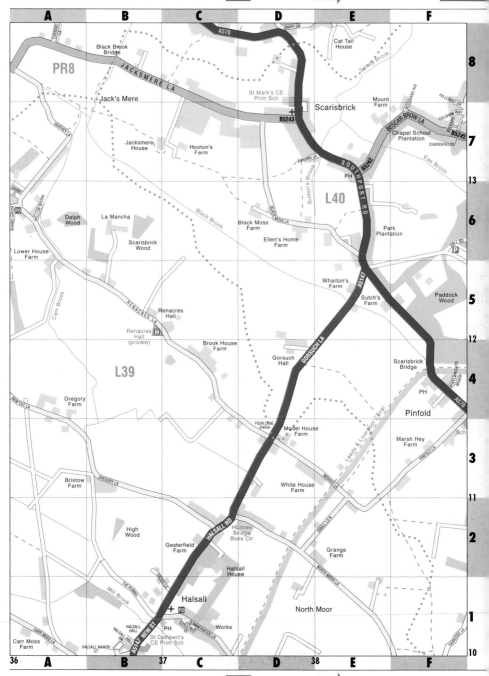

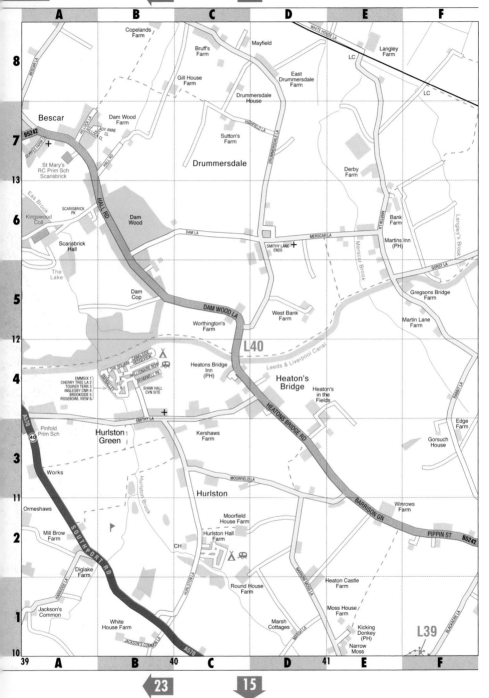

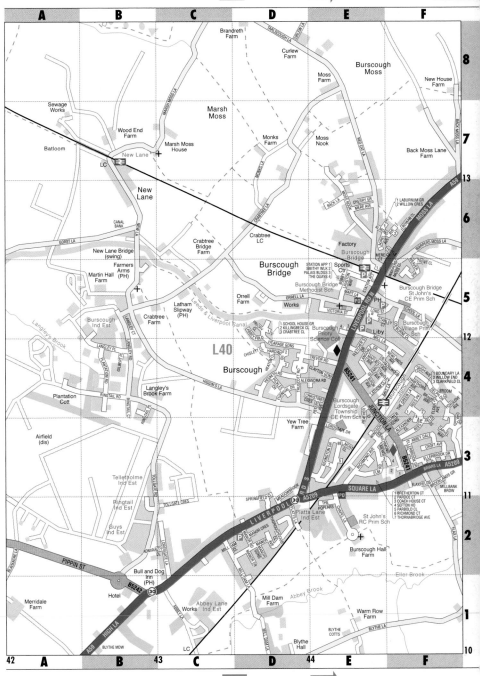

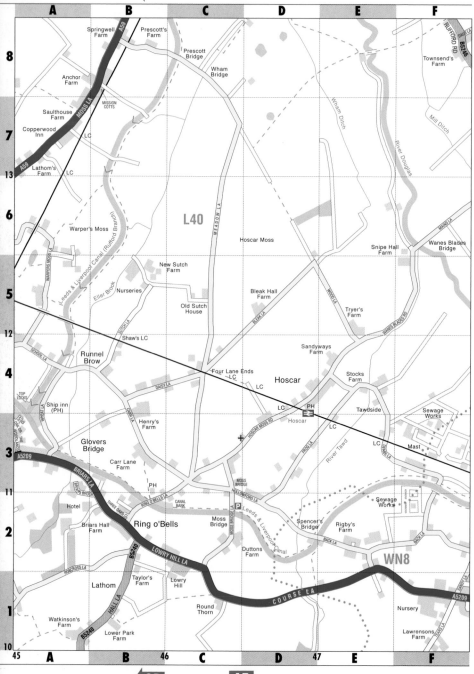

A **B** **C** **D** **E** **F**

8

Springwell Farm
Prescott's Farm
Prescott Bridge
Wham Bridge
Anchor Farm
Townsend's Farm
RUFFORD RD
B5246

MISSION COTTS
MOSS LA
A59

7

Saulthouse Farm
Copperwood Inn
LC
Wham Ditch
River Douglas
Mill Ditch

13

Lathom's Farm
LC
A59

6

Warper's Moss
L40
Hoscar Moss
Snipe Hall Farm
Wanes Blades Bridge

WAPPERS MOSS LA
Leeds & Liverpool Canal (Rufford Branch)
Eller Brook
MEADOW LA
MOSS LA
WANES BLADES RD
MAINS LA

5

New Sutch Farm
Nurseries
Old Sutch House
Bleak Hall Farm
Tryer's Farm

STICKLA
BLEAK LA

12

Shaw's LC
Runnel Brow
Sandyways Farm
Stocks Farm

SCHOOL LA
DAISY LA
CARR LA

4

Four Lane Ends LC
LC
Hoscar
Four Lane Ends

TOP LOCKS
Ship inn (PH)
Henry's Farm
LC
PH
Hoscar
LC
Tawdside
Sewage Works
Mast

3

Glovers Bridge
Carr Lane Farm
PH
MOSS BRIDGE
FROG LA
River Tawd
LC
A5209
BRIARS LA
BENGAL BROOK
THREE GMES G.
RING O'BELLS LA
CANAL BANK
HOLLENGFORD LA

11

Hotel
Briars Hall Farm
Ring o'Bells
Moss Bridge
Spencer's Bridge
Rigby's Farm
Sewage Works
P
Leeds & Liverpool Canal
BACK LA
BACK LA

2

Duttons Farm
WN8
B5240
LOWRY HILL LA
MOSS BRIDGE

Lathom
Taylor's Farm
Lowry Hill
COURSE LA
Nursery
A5209
HALL LA
HORCROSS LA
TEES LA

1

Watkinson's Farm
Round Thorn
Lawrensons Farm
B5240
Lower Park Farm

10

45 **A** **B** **46** **C** **D** **47** **E** **F**

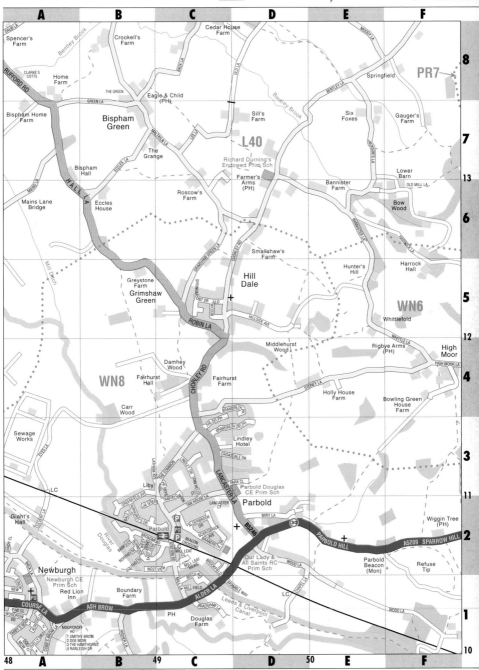

27 41

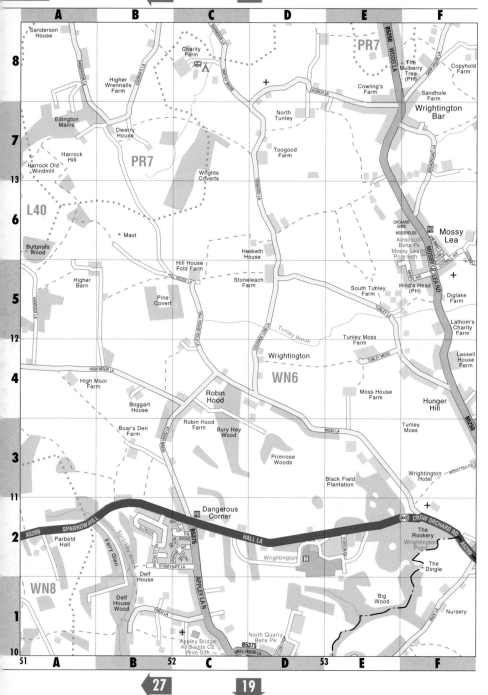

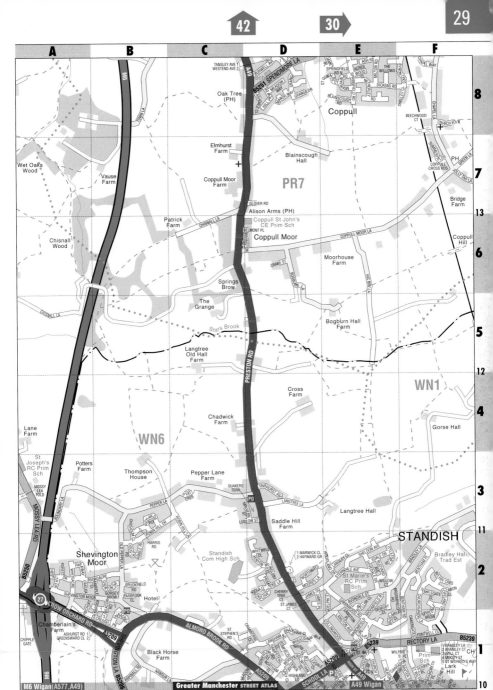

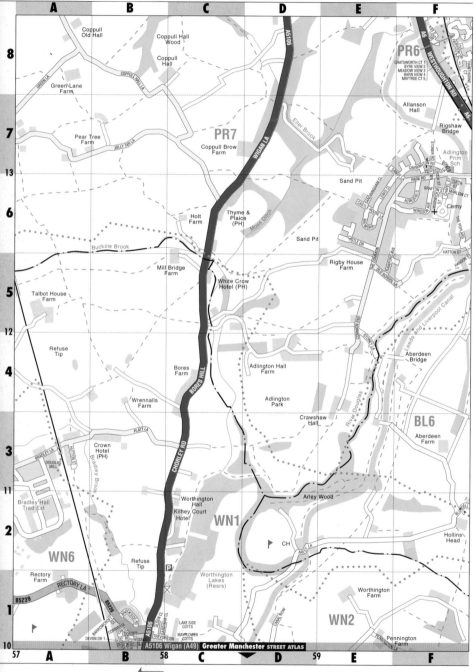

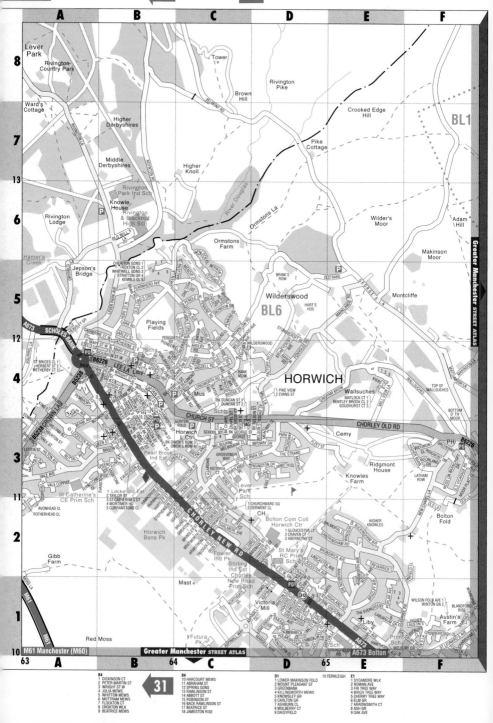

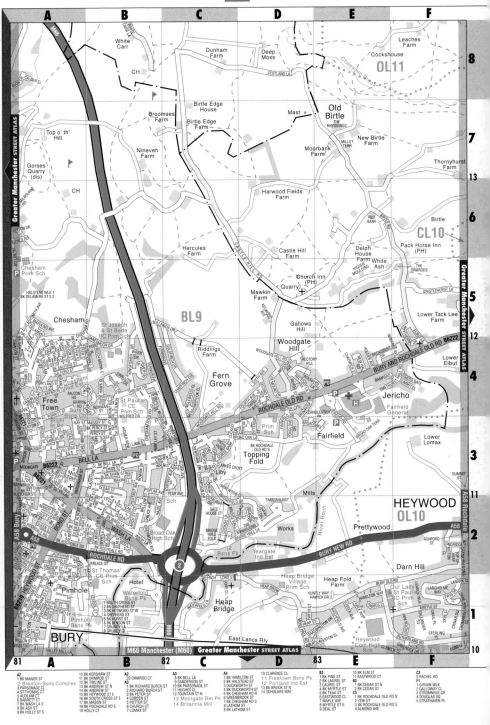

A2	10 BK KERSHAW ST	**A2**	**A3**
1 BK MANOR ST	11 BK ORMROD ST	20 ORMROD CT	8 BK BELL LA
2 Brenton Bsns Complex	12 BK TINLINE ST		9 SANDERSON ST
3 PARSONAGE ST	13 BK ANDREW ST N	**A3**	10 BK PARSONAGE ST
4 ST THOMAS CT	14 BK ANDREW ST	1 BK RICHARD BURCH ST	11 HUGHES CL
5 AUDLUM CT	15 BK HEYWOOD ST E	2 RICHARD BURCH ST	12 FOUNTAIN ST N
6 BARRETT CT	16 BK SOUTH CROSS ST E	3 BK PETER ST	13 Moorgate Ret Pk
7 BK WASH LA S	17 BK MASON ST	4 COBDEN ST	14 Britannia Mill
8 BK ASH ST	18 BK ROCHDALE RD S	5 POTTER ST	
9 BK HOLLY ST S	19 HOLLY CT	6 CHURCH CT	
		7 LOMAX ST	

A4	10 CLARENCE CL	**B2**	10 BK ELM ST	**C3**
1 BK HAMILTON ST	11 Freetown Bsns Pk	1 BK PINE ST	11 EASTWOOD CT	5 RACHEL HO
2 BK HALSTEAD ST	12 Portland Ind Est	2 BK LAUREL ST	**B3**	**F1**
3 DUCKWORTH ST	13 BK BROOK ST N	3 LAUREL ST	1 BK CEDAR ST N	1 GIRVAN WLK
4 BK DUCKWORTH ST	14 SCHOLARS WAY	4 BK MYRTLE ST	2 BK CEDAR ST	2 GALLOWAY CL
5 BK CHESHAM RD N		5 BK TEAK ST	**C3**	3 STRONNESS GR
6 GREENBROOK ST		6 EASTWOOD CL	1 BK ROCHDALE OLD RD N	4 DOUGLAS SQ
7 BK CHESHAM RD S		7 MAPLE AVE	2 YEW ST	5 STRATHAVEN PL
8 LATHOM ST		8 MYRTLE ST S	3 BK ROCHDALE OLD RD S	
9 BK LATHOM ST		9 DEAL ST	4 ALMOND AVE	

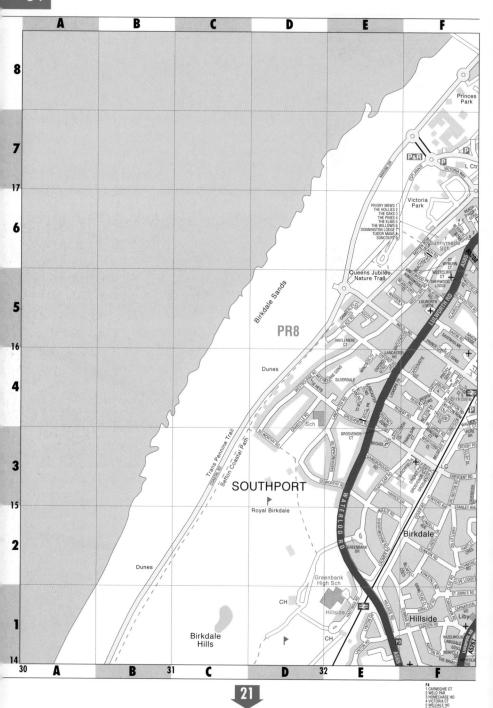

SOUTHPORT

Birkdale Sands

PR8

Dunes

Silverdale

Trans Pennine Trail

Sefton Coastal Path

Royal Birkdale

Dunes

Birkdale Hills

Greenbank High Sch

Hillside

Victoria Park

Queens Jubilee Nature Trail

PRIORY MEWS 1
THE HOLLIES 2
THE OAKS 3
THE PINES 4
THE WILLOWS 5
DONNINGTON LODGE 6
TUDOR MANS 8
SUNCOURT 9

Sunnymede Sch

Birkdale

Hillside

Princes Park

F4
1 CARNEGHIE CT
2 WELD PAR
3 HOMECHASE HO
4 VICTORIA CT
5 WELDALE HO
6 OXFORD CT

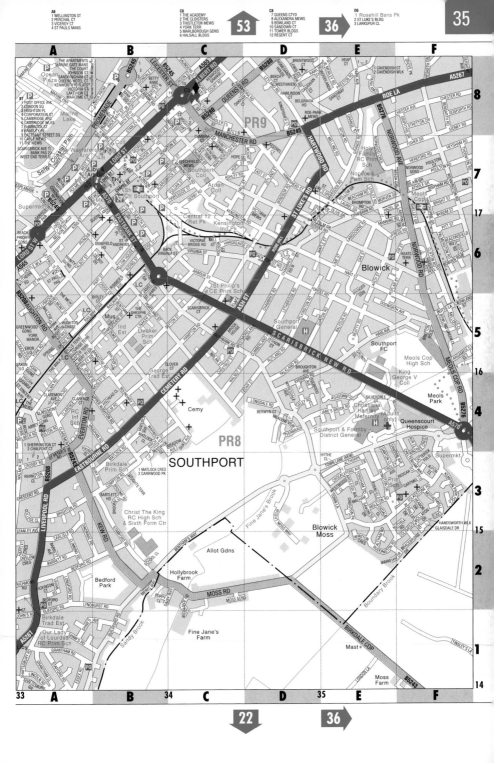

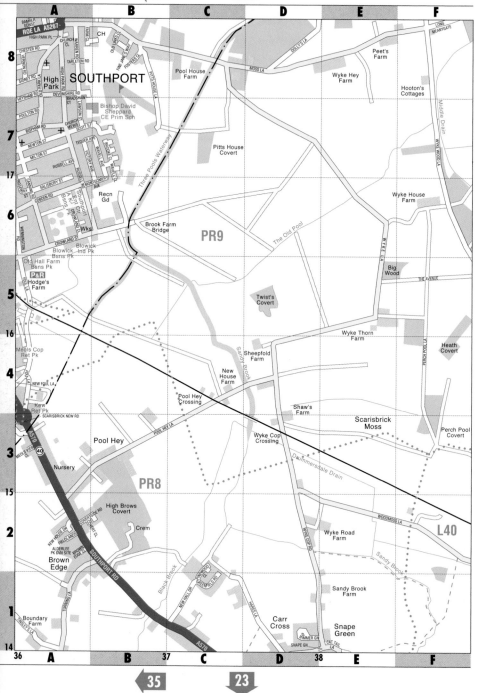

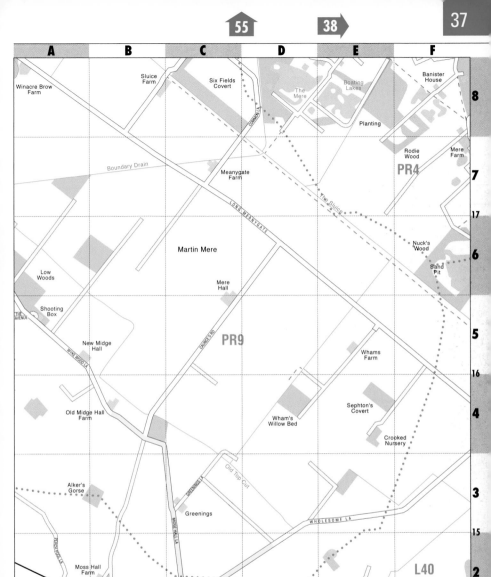

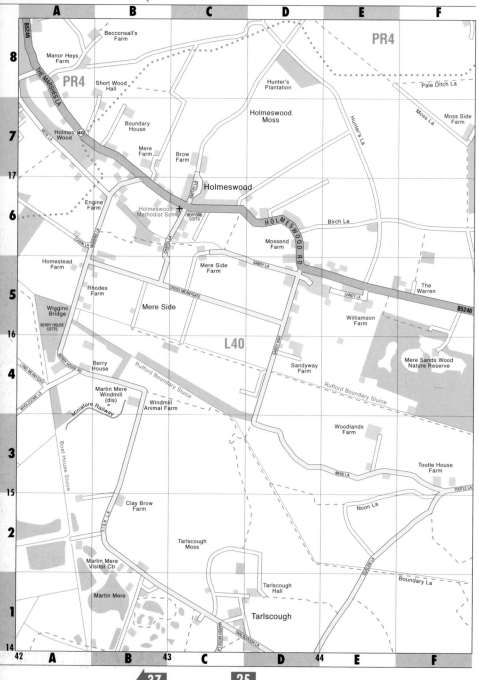

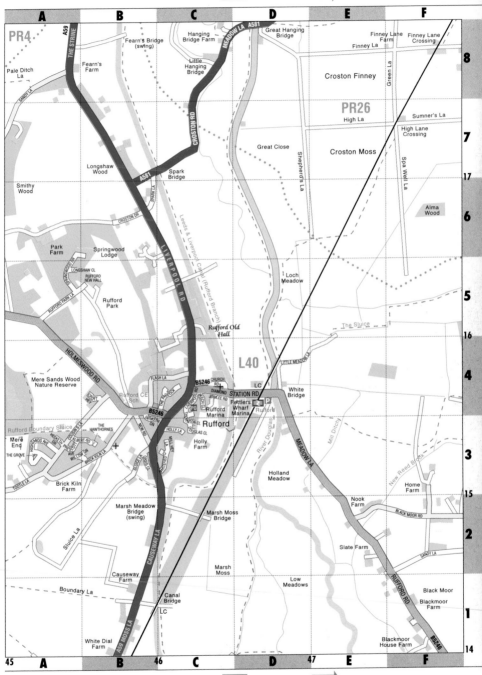

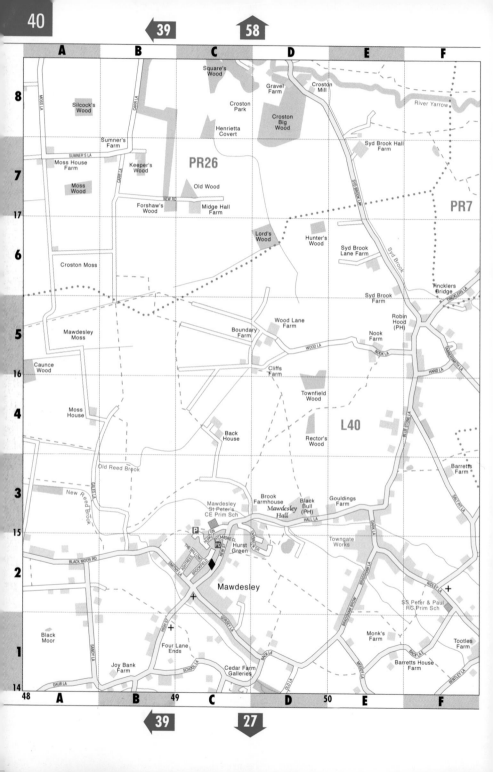

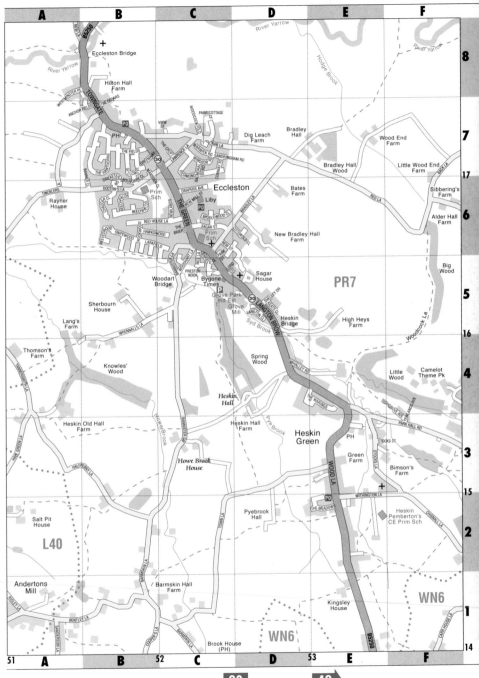

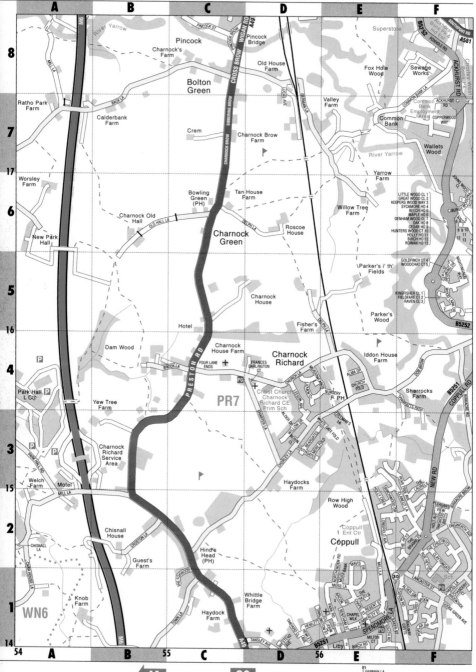

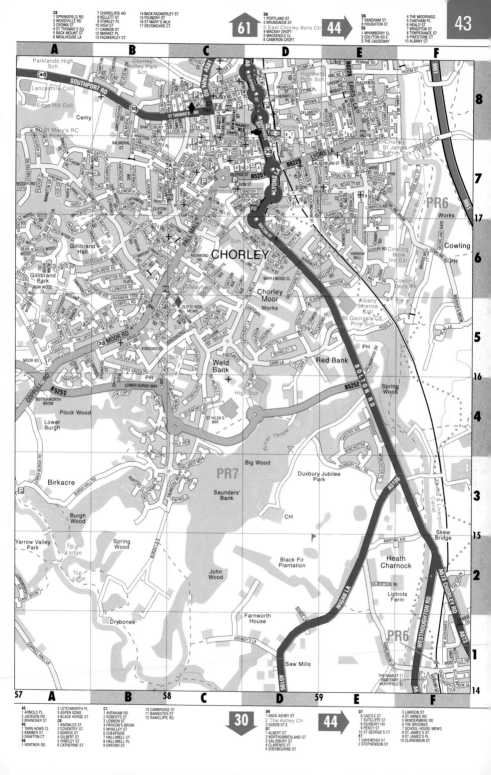

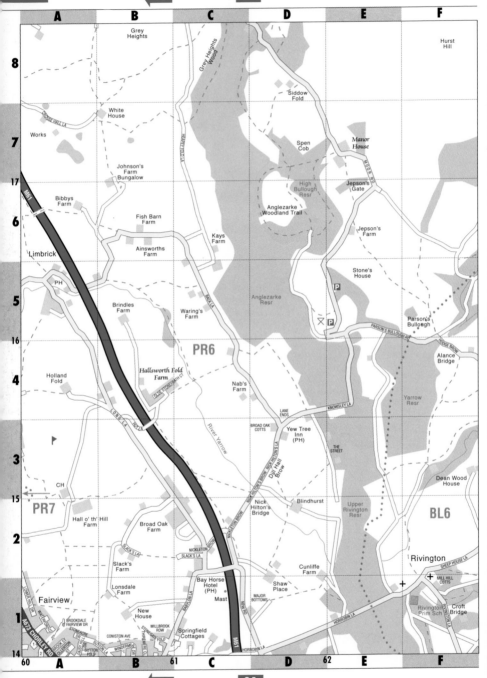

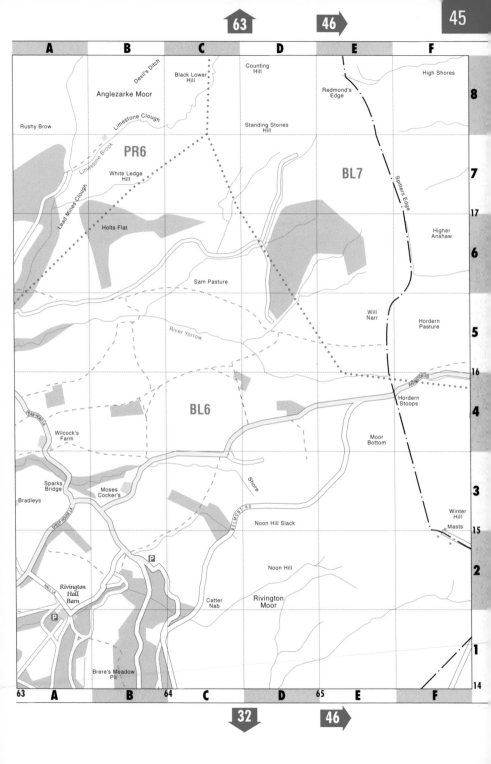

63 46

A B C D E F

Rushy Brow

Devil's Ditch

Anglezarke Moor

Black Lower Hill

Counting Hill

High Shores

Redmond's Edge

8

Limestone Clough

PR6

White Ledge Hill

Standing Stones Hill

BL7

Spitlers Edge

7

17

Limestone Brook

Lead Mines Clough

Holts Flat

Higher Anshaw

6

Sam Pasture

Will Narr

Hordern Pasture

5

River Yorrow

BL6

RIVINGTON RD

16

Hordern Stoops

4

F|AN HA'D LA

Wilcock's Farm

Moor Bottom

Sparks Bridge

Moses Cocker's

Shore

Winter Hill Masts

3

Bradleys

BELMONT RD

15

SHEEP HOUSE LA

Noon Hill Slack

P

Noon Hill

2

HALL LA

Rivington Hall Barn

P

Catter Nab

Rivington Moor

Brere's Meadow Pit

1

14

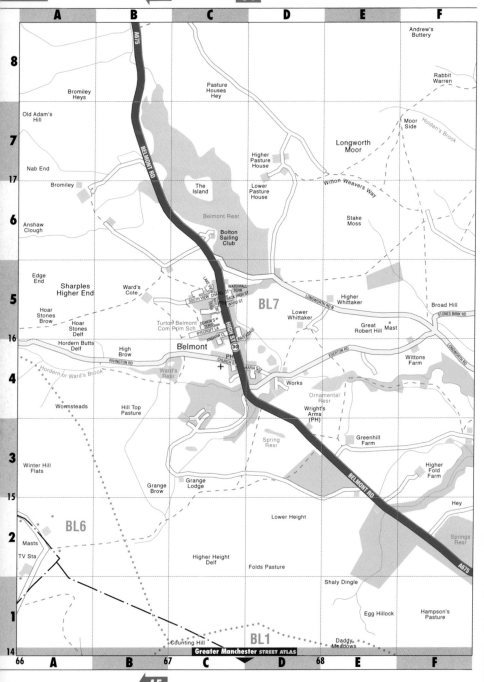

A B C D E F

8

Andrew's Buttery

Bromiley Heys

Pasture Houses Hey

Rabbit Warren

Old Adam's Hill

Moor Side

Holden's Brook

7

Longworth Moor

Nab End

17

Higher Pasture House

Bromiley

The Island

Lower Pasture House

Witton Weavers Way

6

Belmont Resr

Anshaw Clough

Ward's Cote

Stake Moss

Bolton Sailing Club

Edge End

Sharples Higher End

WATERFALL TERR

BL7

Broad Hill

5

LAKE VIEW TERR CHURCH ST

BACK HIGH ST

Higher Whittaker

STONES BANK RD

LONGWORTH RD

Hoar Stones Brow

SOUTH VIEW TERR

WARD ST

Lower Whittaker

Hoar Stones Delf

Turton Belmont Com Prim Sch

DEAKIN'S TERR

RYECROFT

LONGWORTH RD N

Great Robert Hill

Mast

Hordern Butts Delf

High Brow

MISHAM CL

HIGH ST

BRO'DALE

Belmont

16

Wittons Farm

RIVINGTON RD

PH

Hordern or Ward's Brook

Ward's Resr

CHURCH ST

MARIA RD

30

EGERTON RD

4

Wormsteads

Hill Top Pasture

Works

Ornamental Resr

Wright's Arms (PH)

Greenhill Farm

Higher Fold Farm

3

Winter Hill Flats

Spring Resr

Grange Brow

Grange Lodge

Hey

15

Lower Height

BL6

Springs Resr

2

Masts

TV Sta

Higher Height Delf

Folds Pasture

A675

Shaly Dingle

1

Counting Hill

BL1

Egg Hillock

Daddy Meadows

Hampson's Pasture

14

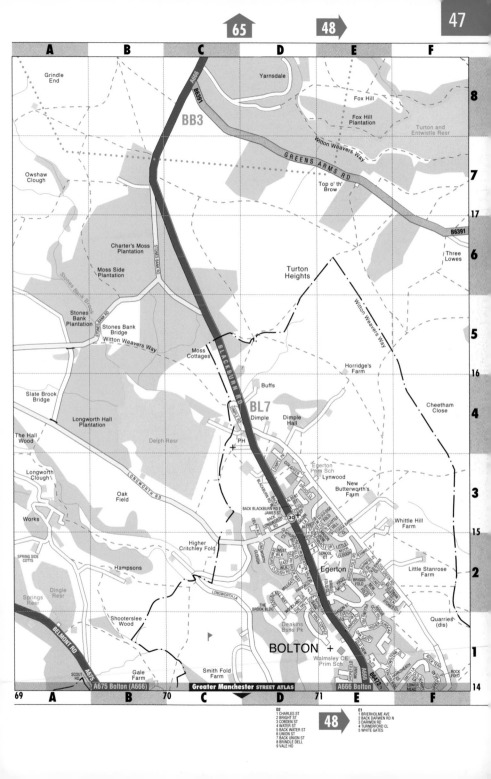

A B C D E F

8

7

17

6

5

16

4

3

15

2

1

14

Grindle End

Yarnsdale

Fox Hill

Fox Hill Plantation

Turton and Entwistle Resr

BB3

Witton Weavers Way

GREENS ARMS RD

B6391

Owshaw Clough

Top o' th' Brow

Three Lowes

Charter's Moss Plantation

Turton Heights

Moss Side Plantation

Stones Bank Brook

Witton Weavers Way

Stones Bank Plantation

Stones Bank Bridge

Witton Weavers Way

Moss Cottages

Horridge's Farm

Cheetham Close

Slate Brook Bridge

Buffs

Longworth Hall Plantation

Delph Resr

BL7

Dimple

Dimple Hall

The Hall Wood

PH

Egerton Prim Sch

Lynwood

New Butterworth's Farm

Longworth Clough

Oak Field

Whittle Hill Farm

Works

BACK BLACKBURN RD
JAMES ST

Higher Critchley Fold

WEST WLK

Egerton

Little Stanrose Farm

SPRING SIDE COTTS

Hampsons

Quarries (dis)

Dingle Resr

LONGWORTH LA

THE BROOK BLDG

Deakins Bsns Pk

BOLTON

Springs Resr

BELMONT RD

Shooterslee Wood

Gale Farm

Smith Fold Farm

Walmsley CE Prim Sch

SCOUT RD

A675

A675 Bolton (A666)

Greater Manchester STREET ATLAS

A666 Bolton

69 A 70 B C 71 D E F

D2
1 CHARLES ST
2 BRIGHT ST
3 COBDEN ST
4 WATER ST
5 BACK WATER ST
6 UNION ST
7 BACK UNION ST
8 BRINDLE DELL
9 VALE HO

E1
1 BRIERHOLME AVE
2 BACK DARWEN RD N
3 DARWEN RD
4 TURNERFORD CL
5 WHITE GATES

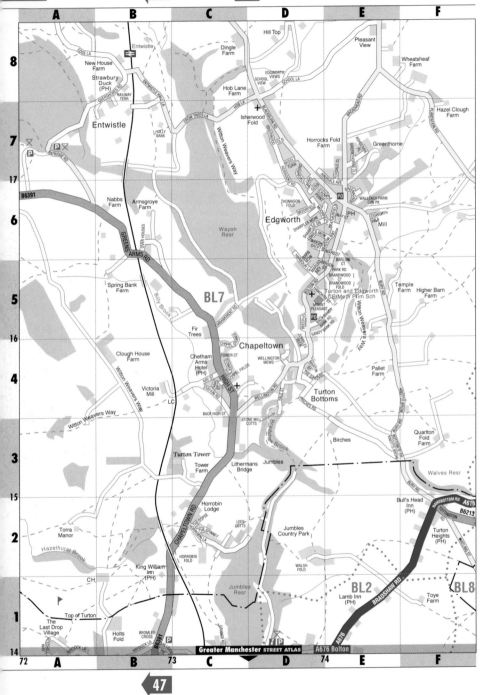

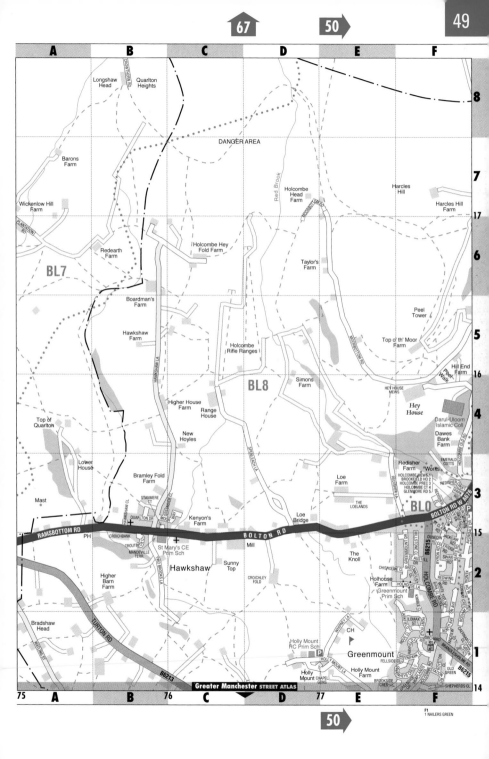

Greater Manchester STREET ATLAS

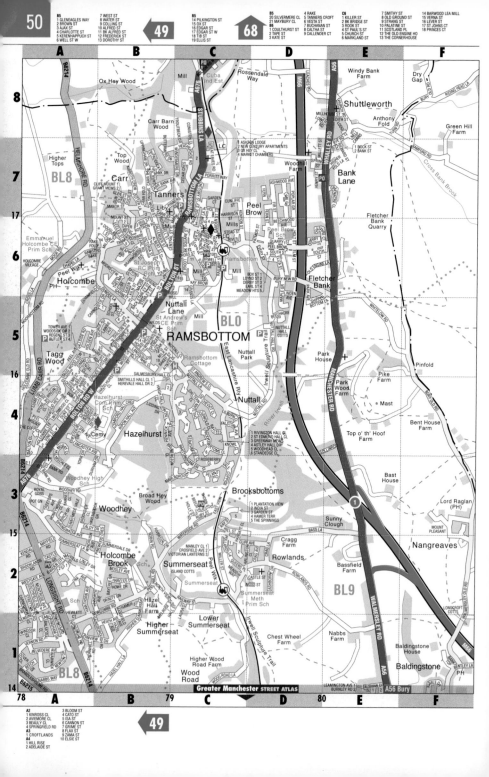

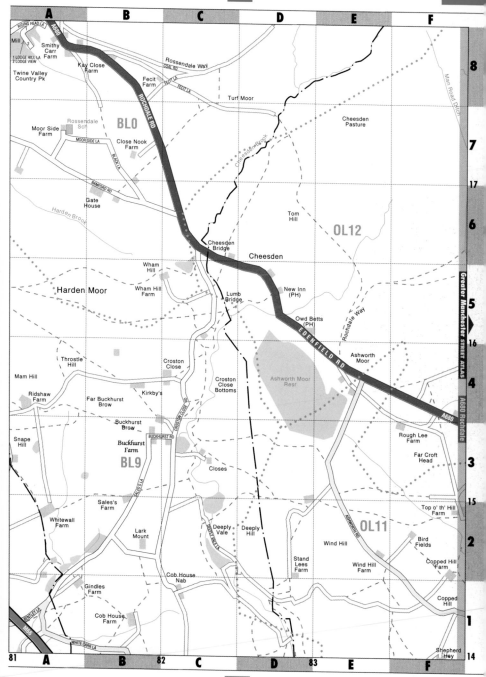

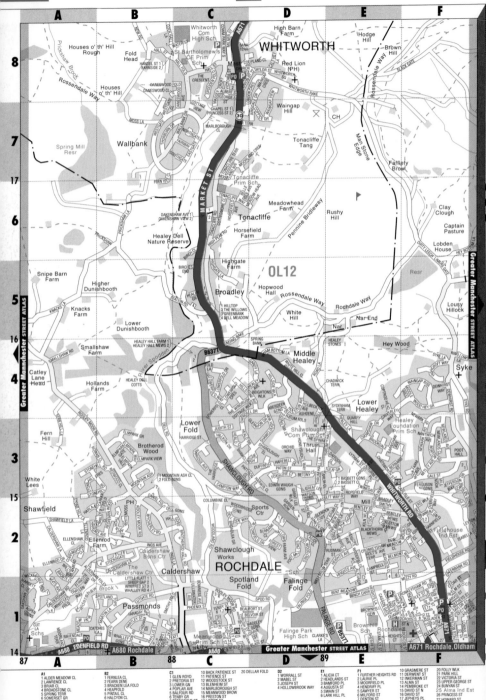

F2
1 CROSBY ST
2 PAVILION CL
3 JOY PL
4 WINDERMERE ST
5 JACOB BRIGHT MEWS

F3
1 NOOK TERR
2 BACK NOOK TERR

WHITWORTH

OL12

Healey Dell
Nature Reserve

ROCHDALE

Greater Manchester STREET ATLAS

Greater Manchester STREET ATLAS

Greater Manchester STREET ATLAS

A1
1 ALDER MEADOW CL
2 LAWRENCE CL
3 BRIAR CL
4 BROADSTONE CL
5 SPRING TERR
6 SOMERSET GR

B2
1 FERNLEA CL
2 FEARN DENE
3 BRACKEN LEA FOLD
4 HEAPFOLD
5 PINTAIL CL
6 HALCYON CL

C1
1 GLEN ROYD
2 PRETORIA ST
3 LOWER GN
4 POPLAR AVE
5 BALFOUR RD
6 TENBY GR
7 TRENGROVE ST
8 AIR HILL TERR
9 BENTINCK ST

10 BACK PATIENCE ST
11 PATIENCE ST
12 WOODSTOCK ST
13 BLENHEIM ST
14 MARLBOROUGH ST
15 MEANWOOD BROW
16 PRESTON ST
17 LISBON ST
18 RUSHEY HILL VIEW
19 DELLAR ST

20 DELLAR FOLD

D2
1 WORRALL ST
2 MABEL ST
3 JOSEPH ST
4 HOLLOWBROOK WAY

E1
1 ALICIA CT
2 HEADLANDS ST
3 BAMFORD PL
4 AUGUSTA ST
5 SWAIN ST
6 LARK HILL PL

F1
1 FURTHER HEIGHTS RD
2 LAURIE PL
3 MOORFIELD PL
4 HENDRIFF PL
5 SAWYER ST
6 MILFORD ST
7 DENTON ST
8 INDUSTRY RD
9 HENLEY ST

10 GRASMERE ST
11 DERWENT ST
12 INKERMAN ST
13 ALMA ST
14 PEMBROKE CT
15 DAVID ST
16 DAVID ST
17 JEPHY'S PL
18 TAYLORS PL
19 WELLINGTON ST

20 FOLLY WLK
21 PARK HILL
22 VICTORIA ST
23 UPPER GEORGE ST
24 BIRTWISTLE ST
25 Alma Ind Est
26 PRINCESS ST
27 HOWARD ST

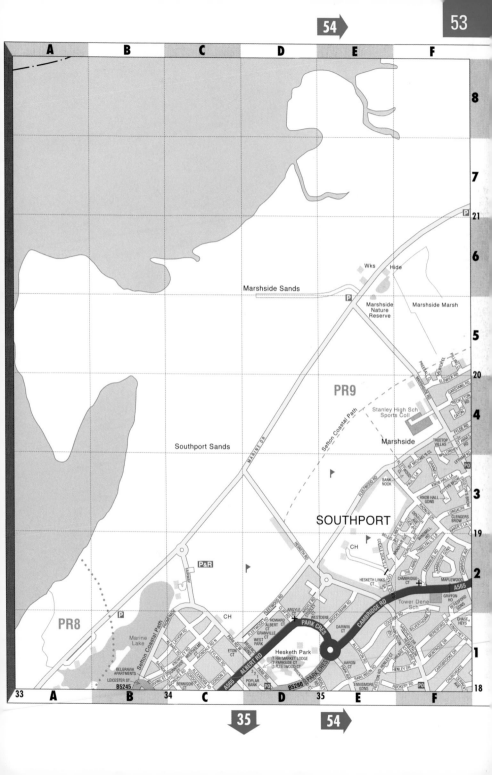

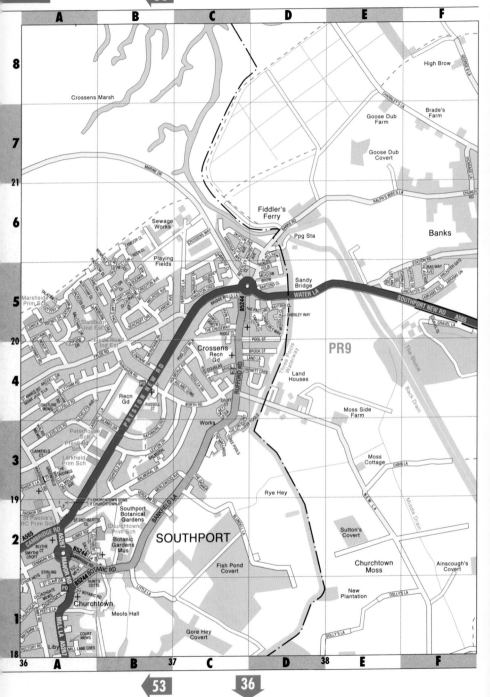

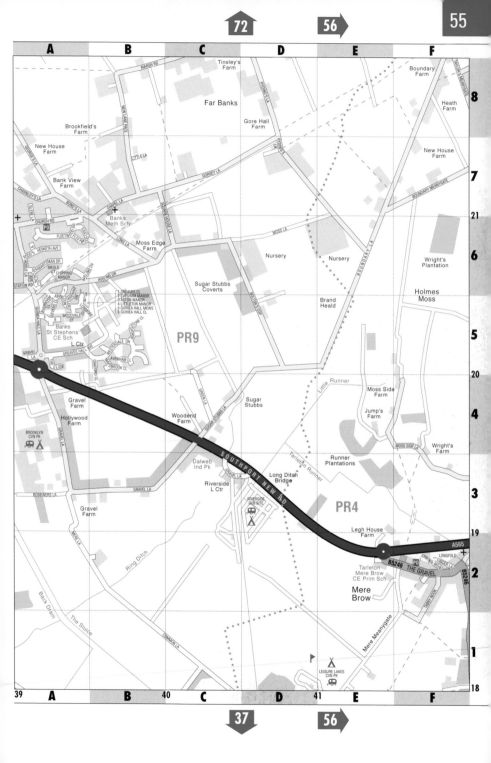

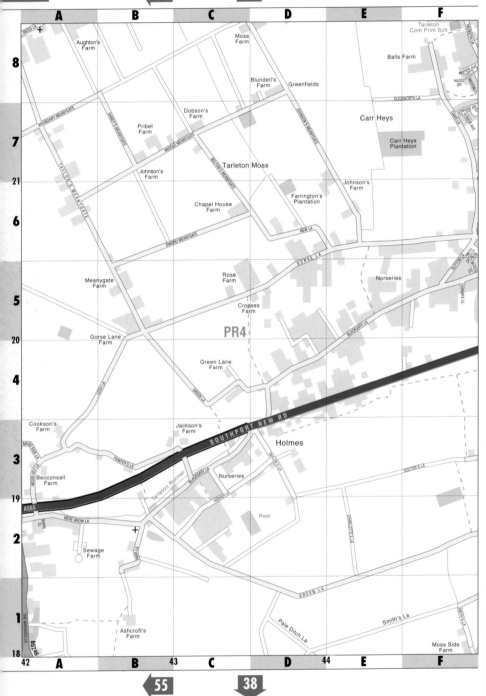

A B C D E F

8

7

21

6

5

20

4

3

19

2

1

18

Moss La
Aughton's Farm
Moss Farm
Blundell's Farm
Greenfields
Tarleton Com Prim Sch
Balls Farm
Duckworth La
Boundary Meanygate
Dandy's Meanygate
Pribet Farm
Dobson's Farm
Johnson's Meanygate
Carr Heys
Carr Heys Plantation
Taylor's Meanygate
Middle Meanygate
Johnson's Farm
Bruer's Meanygate
Tarleton Moss
Chapel House Farm
Farrington's Plantation
Johnson's Farm
Sword Meanygate
New La
Gorse La
Meanygate Farm
Rose Farm
Nurseries
Crosses Farm
PR4
Gorse Lane Farm
Blackgate La
Green Lane Farm
Green La
Legill La
Cookson's Farm
Jackson's Farm
Southport New Rd
Holmes
Moss Side La
Hunter's La
Tarleton Runner
Blackgate La
Nurseries
Ends La
Doctor's La
Becconsall Farm
Mere Brow La
Barn Cl
Resr
Charlotte La
A565
Sewage Farm
La Rue
Green La
The Marshes La
B5246
Ashcroft's Farm
Pale Ditch La
Smith's La
Smith's La
Moss Side Farm

42 A B 43 C D 44 E F 18

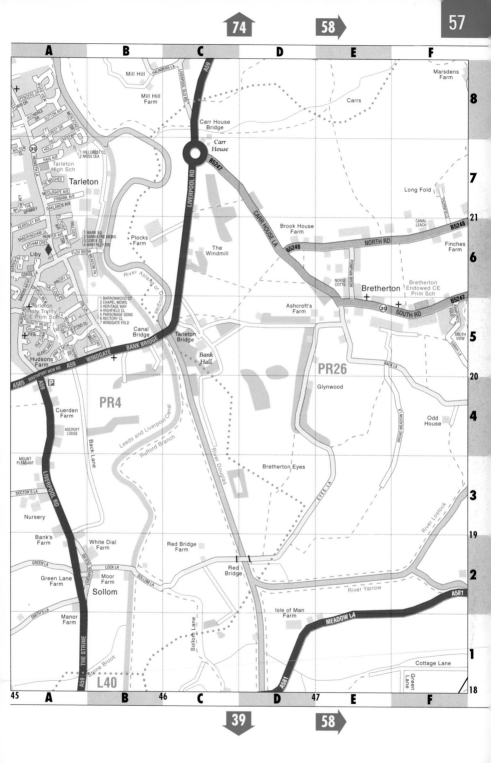

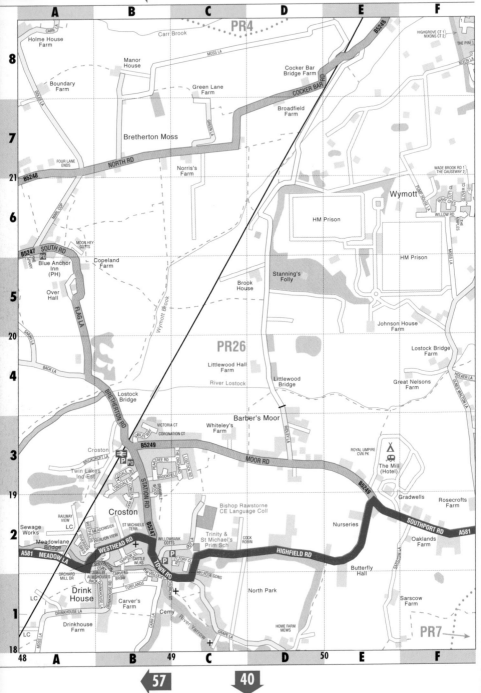

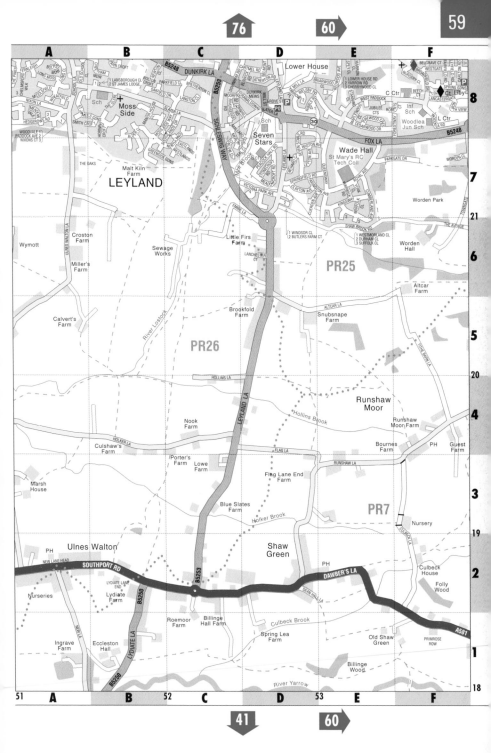

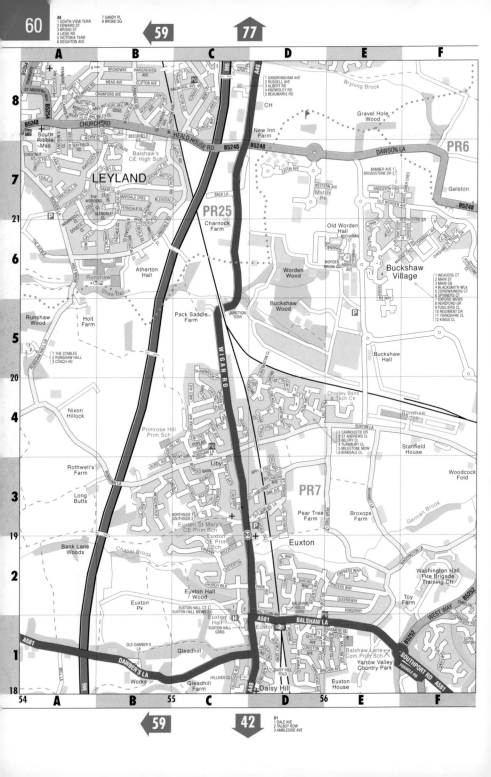

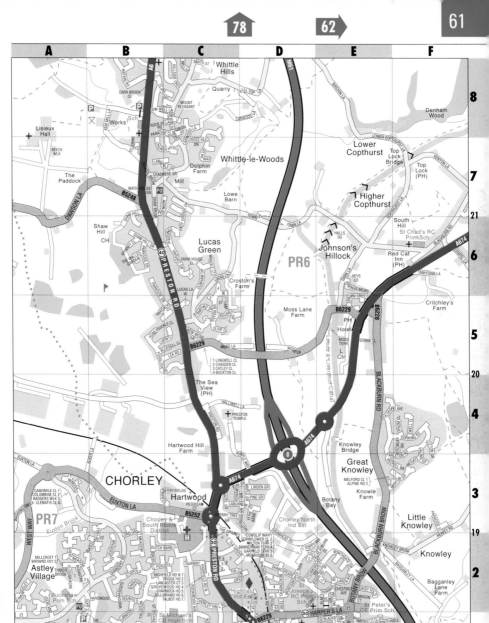

D1
1 PRESTON ST
2 VICTORIA TERR
3 VICARAGE ST
4 WESTWELL RD
5 INGLE CL
6 RUSSELL SQ W
7 WHINFIELD AVE
8 MAYFIELD RD
9 BRIERCLIFFE RD

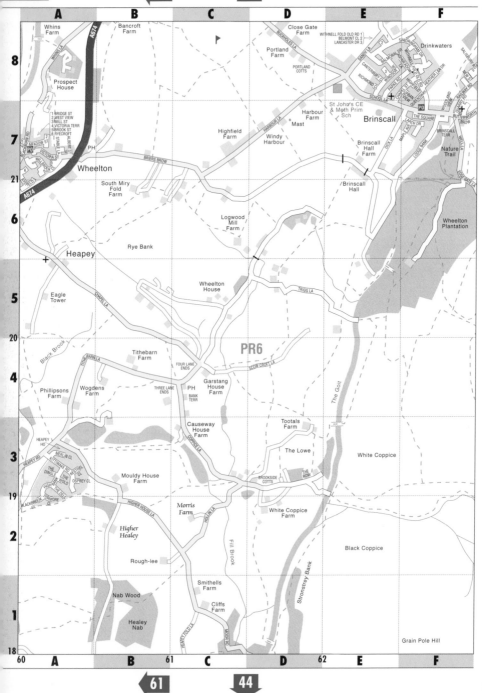

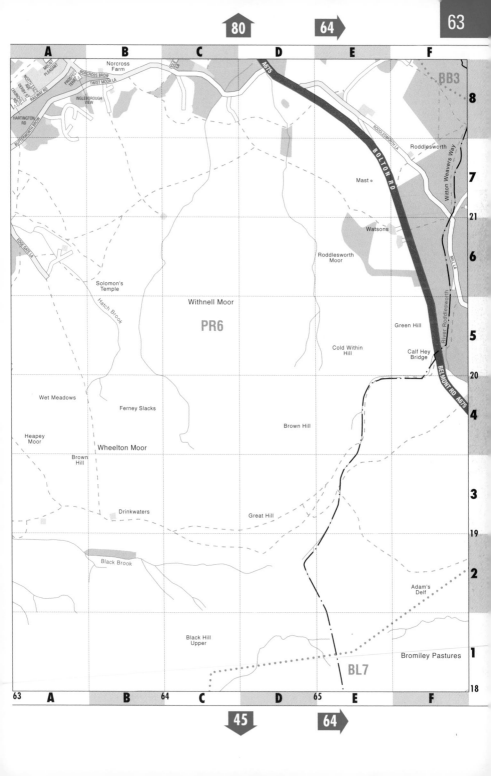

63
81

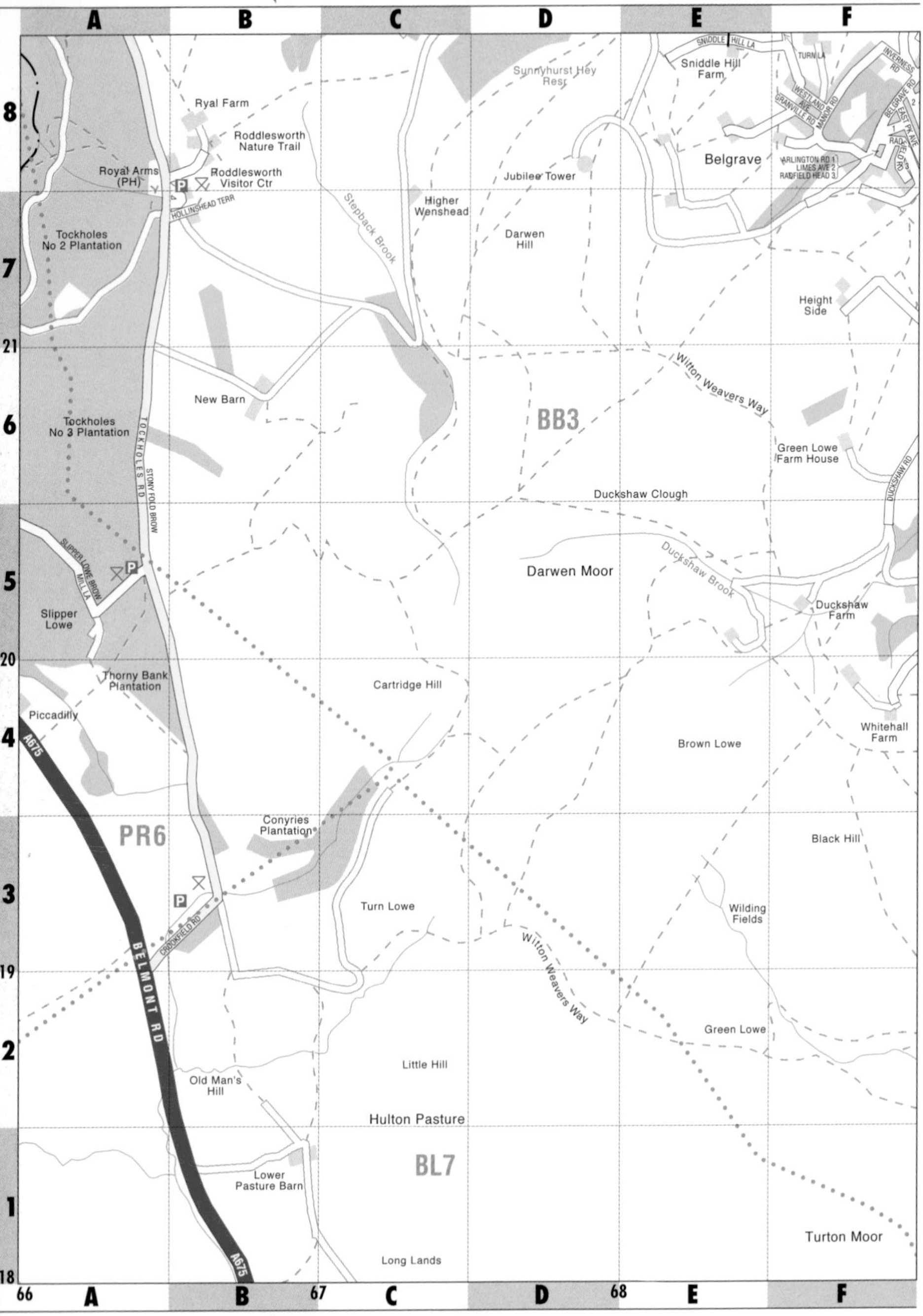

	A	B	C	D	E	F

8

Ryal Farm

Sunnyhurst Hey Rest

SNIDDLE HILL LA

Sniddle Hill Farm

TURN LA

Roddlesworth Nature Trail

Jubilee Tower

Belgrave

ARLINGTON RD 1
LIMES AVE 2
RADFIELD HEAD 3

Royal Arms (PH)

Roddlesworth Visitor Ctr

HOLLINSHEAD TERR

Higher Wenshead

Darwen Hill

7

Tockholes No 2 Plantation

Stepback Brook

Height Side

21

New Barn

BB3

Wilton Weavers Way

6

Tockholes No 3 Plantation

TOCKHOLES RD

STONY FOLD BROW

Duckshaw Clough

Green Lowe Farm House

DUCKSHAW RD

5

SLIPPER LOWE BRIDLEWAY

MILL LA

Darwen Moor

Duckshaw Brook

Duckshaw Farm

Slipper Lowe

20

Thorny Bank Plantation

Cartridge Hill

Whitehall Farm

Piccadilly

4

A675

Brown Lowe

Conyries Plantation

Black Hill

PR6

3

Turn Lowe

Wilding Fields

CROOKED EDGE RD

BELMONT RD

19

Wilton Weavers Way

Green Lowe

2

Old Man's Hill

Little Hill

Hulton Pasture

BL7

1

Lower Pasture Barn

Turton Moor

18

A675

Long Lands

63
46

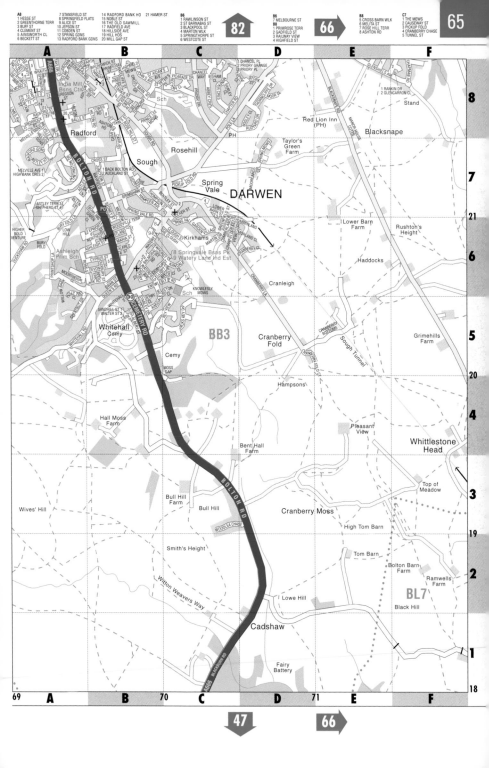

A8
1 HESSE ST
2 GREENTHORNE TERR
3 BUFF ST
4 CLEMENT ST
5 AINSWORTH CL
6 BECKETT ST

7 STANSFIELD ST
8 SPRINGFIELD FLATS
9 ALICE ST
10 JEPSON ST
11 COBDEN ST
12 SPRING GDNS
13 RADFORD BANK GDNS

14 RADFORD BANK HO
15 NOBLE ST
16 THE OLD SAWMILL
17 RADFIELD AVE
18 HILLSIDE AVE
19 HILL HOS
20 MILL GAP ST

21 HAMER ST

82

B6
1 RAWLINSON ST
2 ST BARNABAS ST
3 BLACKPOOL ST
4 MARTON WLK
5 SPRINGTHORPE ST
6 WESTCOTE ST

66

D6
7 MELBOURNE ST

D8
1 PRIMROSE TERR
2 GADFIELD ST
3 RAILWAY VIEW

B8
5 CROSS BARN WLK
6 MELITA ST
7 ROSE HILL TERR
8 ASHTON RD

C7
1 THE MEWS
2 CAUSEWAY ST
3 PICKUP FOLD
4 CRANBERRY CHASE
5 TUNNEL ST

65

Radford
Rosehill
Sough
Spring Vale
DARWEN
Kirkhams
8 Springvale Bsns Pk
9 Watery Lane Ind Est
Whitehall
BB3
Cranleigh
Cranberry Fold
Hampsons
Hall Moss Farm
Bent Hall Farm
Bull Hill Farm
Bull Hill
Smith's Height
Witton Weavers Way
Cadshaw
Fairy Battery
Wives' Hill
Lowe Hill
Cranberry Moss
High Tom Barn
Tom Barn
Bolton Barn Farm
BL7
Black Hill
Ramwells Farm
Top of Meadow
Whittlestone Head
Pleasant View
Grimehills Farm
Sough Tunnel
Cranberry Bottoms
Haddocks
Rushton's Height
Lower Barn Farm
Taylor's Green Farm
Red Lion Inn (PH)
Blacksnape
Stand
1 RANKIN DR
2 GLENCARRON CL

47

66

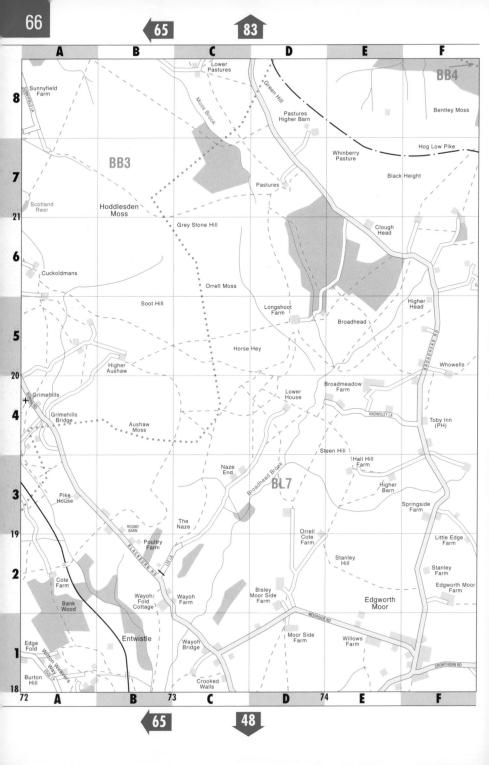

BB4

Bentley Moss

Hog Low Pike

Sunnyfield
Farm

BB3

Lower
Pastures

Moss Brook

Green Hill

Pastures
Higher Barn

Whinberry
Pasture

Black Height

Pastures

Hoddlesden
Moss

Scotland
Resr

Grey Stone Hill

Clough
Head

Cuckoldmans

Orrell Moss

Soot Hill

Longshoot
Farm

Broadhead

Higher
Head

Horse Hey

BROADHEAD RD

Higher
Aushaw

Whowells

Grimehills

Broadmeadow
Farm

Lower
House

Grimehills
Bridge

Aushaw
Moss

KNOWSLEY LA

Toby Inn
(PH)

Steen Hill

Hall Hill
Farm

Pike
House

Naze
End

BL7

Higher
Barn

Springside
Farm

ROUND
BARN

The
Naze

Orrell
Cote
Farm

Little Edge
Farm

BLACKBURN RD

Poultry
Farm

Stanley
Hill

Stanley
Farm

Cote
Farm

Wayoh
Fold
Cottage

Wayoh
Farm

Bisley
Moor Side
Farm

Edgworth Moor
Farm

Bank
Wood

Edgworth
Moor

MOORSIDE RD

Moor Side
Farm

Willows
Farm

Edge
Fold

Entwistle

Wayoh
Bridge

CROWTHORN RD

Burton
Hill

Witton Weavers Way

Crooked
Walls

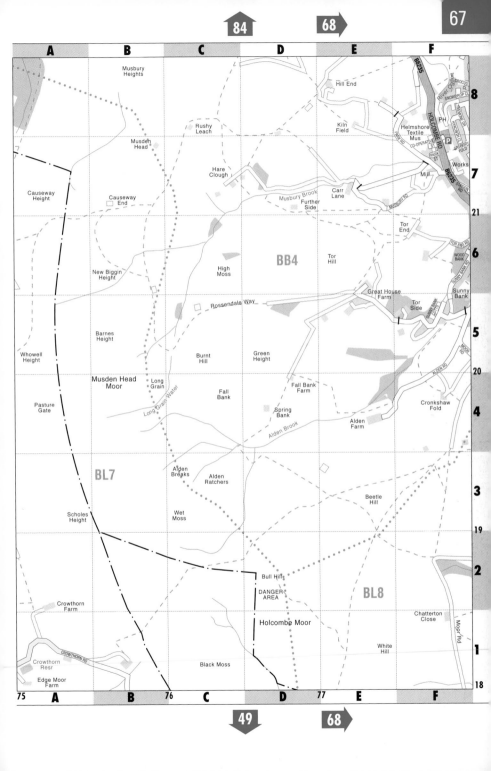

Musbury
Heights

Hill End

RIVER OGDEN
CROCUS
CL

B6235

SNOWDROP CL

8

Rushy
Leach

Kiln
Field

Helmshore
Textile
Mus

PH

HOLCOMBE RD

PARK ST

HAZELHURST RD

SUNNYHURST
APERBURY
FOLD

CO-OPERATIVE

Musden
Head

Works

Hare
Clough

Mill

7

B6235 STATION RD

Causeway
Height

Causeway
End

Musbury Brook

Further
Side

Carr
Lane

MUSBURY RD

21

Tor
End

TOR END RD

BB4

Tor
Hill

6

WOOD
BANK

New Biggin
Height

High
Moss

SUNNY BANK RD

Sunny
Bank

Rossendale Way

Great House
Farm

Tor
Side

SUNNY BANK RD

5

Barnes
Height

Burnt
Hill

Green
Height

ALDER RD

20

Whowell
Height

Musden Head
Moor

Long
Grain

Fall
Bank

Fall Bank
Farm

Spring
Bank

Cronkshaw
Fold

MOOR RD

Pasture
Gate

Long Grain Water

Alden Brook

Alden
Farm

4

Alden
Breaks

Alden
Ratchers

Beetle
Hill

3

BL7

Scholes
Height

Wet
Moss

19

Bull Hill

DANGER
AREA

BL8

2

Crowthorn
Farm

Holcombe Moor

Chatterton
Close

Moor Rd

CROWTHORN RD

Crowthorn
Resr

Black Moss

White
Hill

1

Edge Moor
Farm

18

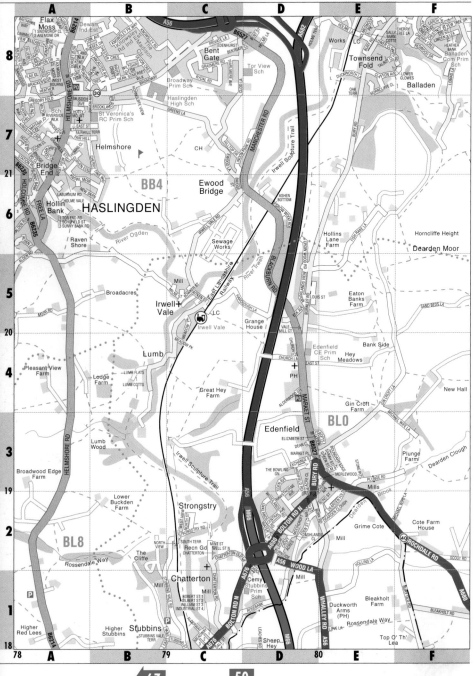

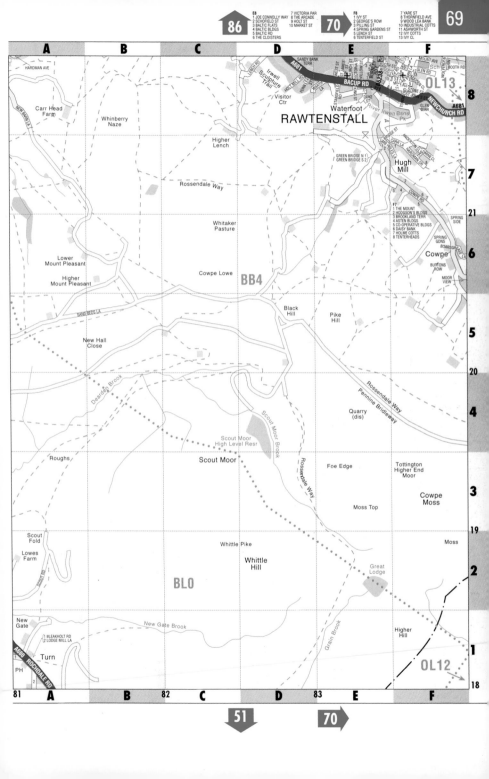

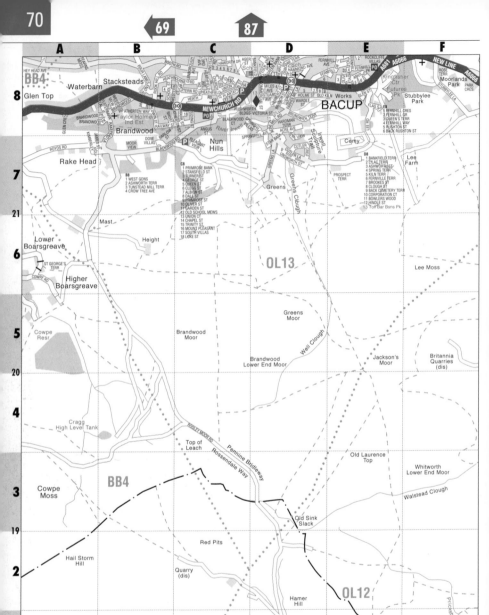

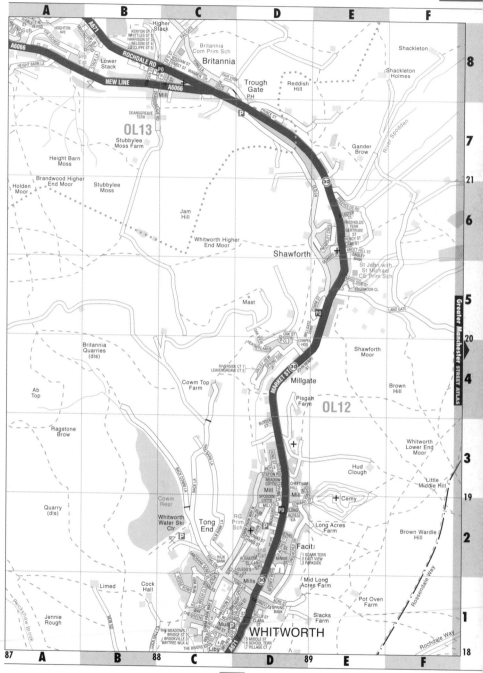

92

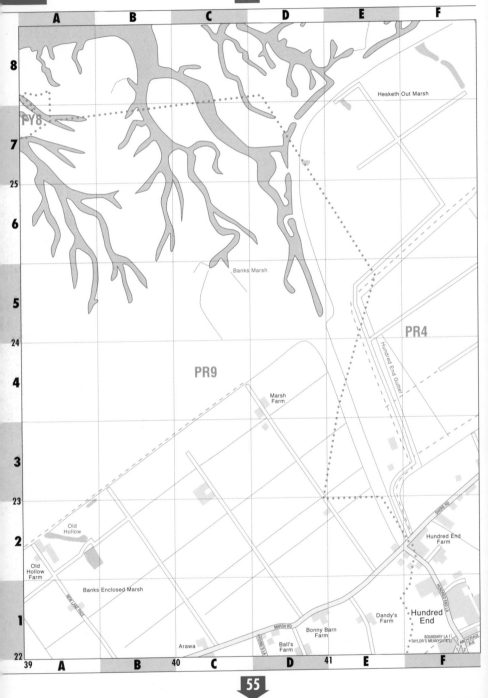

8

PY8

7

25

6

Hesketh Out Marsh

Banks Marsh

5

PR4

24

PR9

Hundred End Gutter

4

Marsh
Farm

3

23

SHORE RD

Old
Hollow

2

Hundred End
Farm

Old
Hollow
Farm

Banks Enclosed Marsh

NEW LANE ENCE

Dandy's
Farm

Hundred
End

1

MARSH RD.

Bonny Barn
Farm

BOUNDARY LA 1
TAYLOR'S MEANYGATE 2

ANCHORAGE
AVE

22

Arawa

Ball's
Farm

39   A   B   40   C   D   41   E   F

55

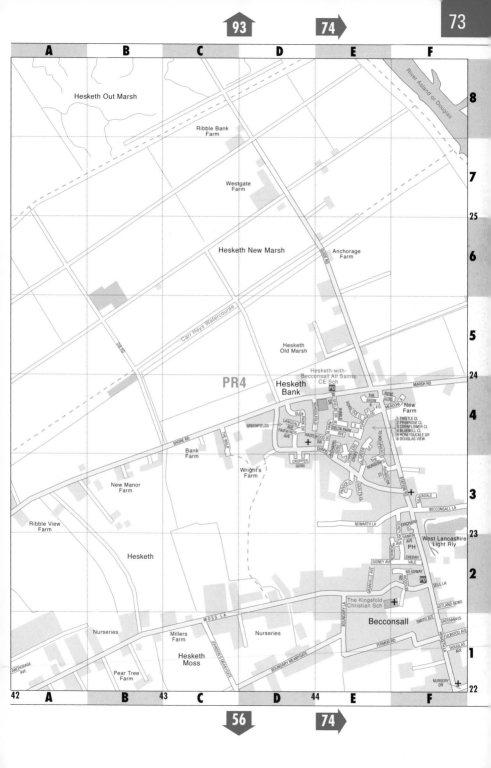

8

Hesketh Out Marsh

Ribble Bank
Farm

River Asland or Douglas

7

Westgate
Farm

25

Hesketh New Marsh

Anchorage
Farm

6

DIB RD

Carr Heys Watercourse

Hesketh
Old Marsh

5

Hesketh-with-
Becconsall All Saints
CE Sch
PO

MARSH RD

24

PR4

Hesketh
Bank

ROSE
GDNS

New
Farm

THE
MEADOW

THE
BROW

SHORE RD

THE WLK

GREENFIELDS

LANGDALE
AVE

FAIRWINDS
AVE

GLEN
PARK DR

HAZELWOOD
DR

RIBBLE
FIELDS

DELTA PARK
AVE

1 THISTLE CL
2 PRIMROSE CL
3 CORNFLOWER CL
4 BLUEBELL CL
5 HONEYSUCKLE GR
6 DOUGLAS VIEW

4

Bank
Farm

Wright's
Farm

CROPPER
GDNS

CHAPEL RD

THE
NURSERIES

STATION RD

SVERDALE

3

New Manor
Farm

PARKSIDE
CHARLES CL

BECCONSALL LA

NEWARTH LA

Ribble View
Farm

ORCHARD

West Lancashire
Light Rly

23

Hesketh

RANKIN
AVE

PH

CHERRY
VALE

SIDNEY AVE

MEADWAY
PO

MILL LA

2

GRANVILLE AVE

BOUNDARY LA

The Kingsfold
Christian Sch

ASTLAND GDNS

Becconsall

SMITH AVE

GREENWAYS

FULWOOD AVE

1

MOSS LA

Nurseries

Millers
Farm

Nurseries

FERMOR RD

DOUGLAS
AVE

ANCHORAGE
AVE

Hesketh
Moss

Pear Tree
Farm

BOUNDARY MEANYGATE

NURSERY
DR

22

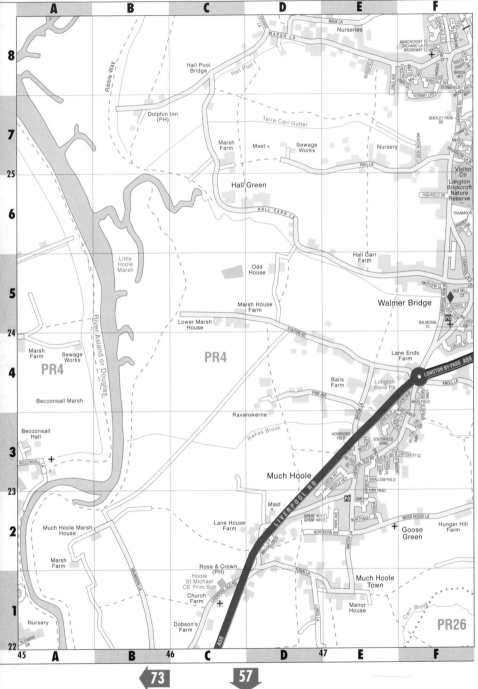

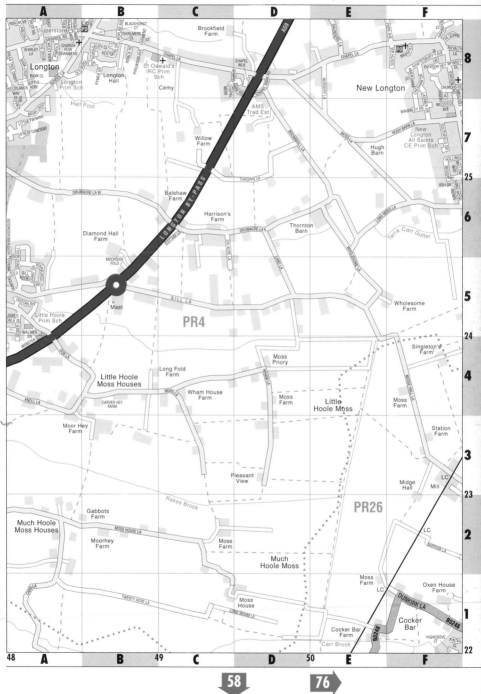

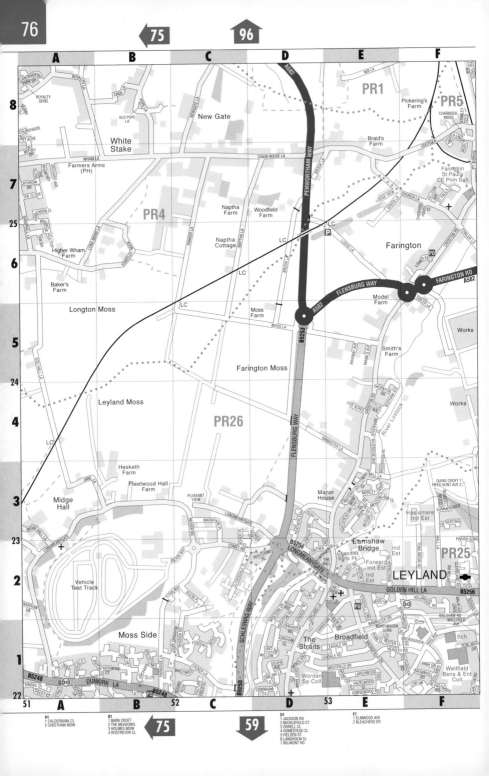

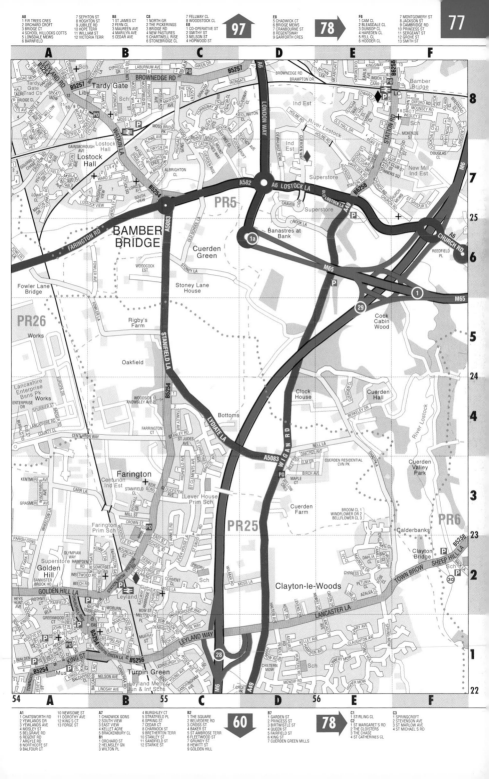

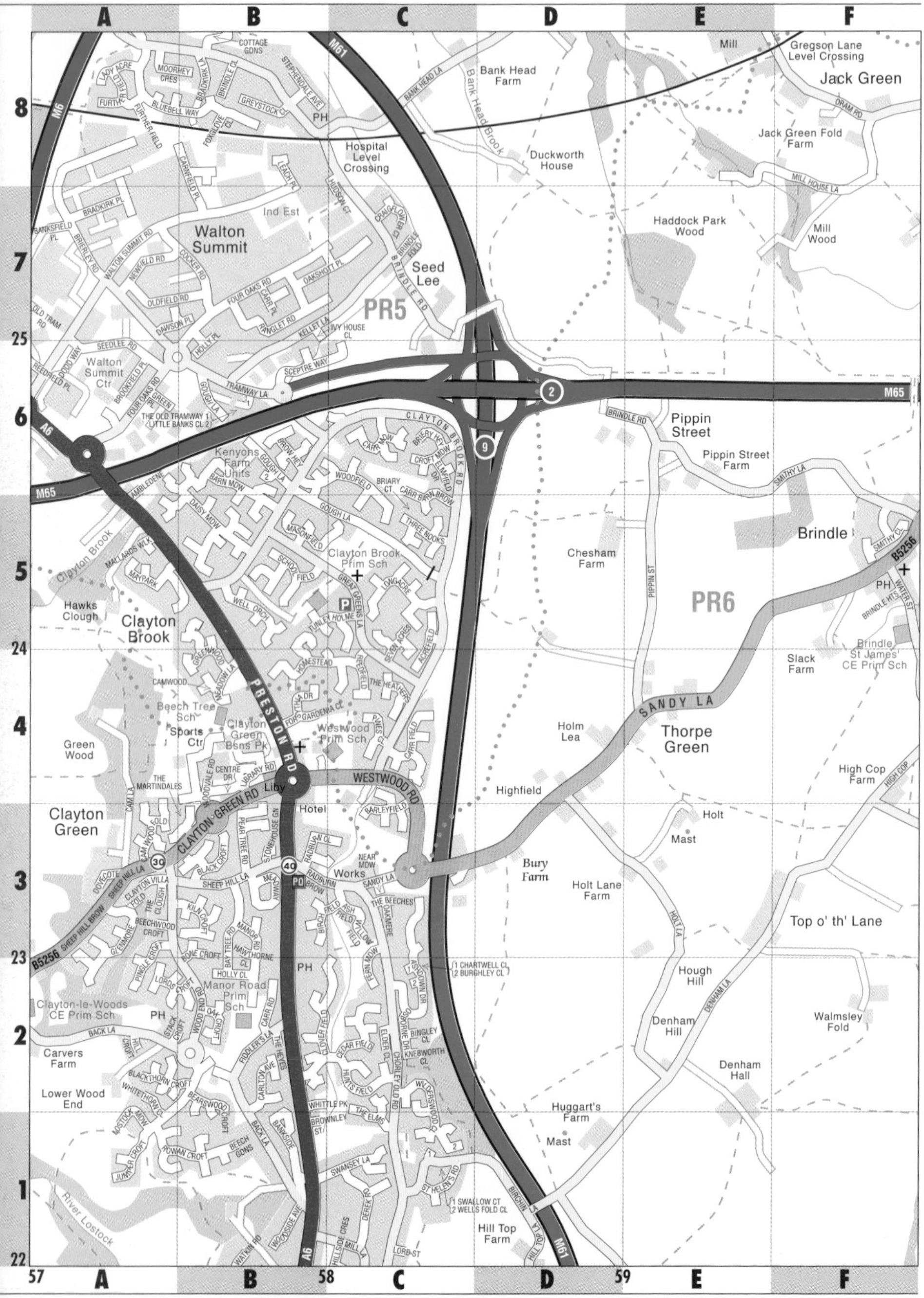

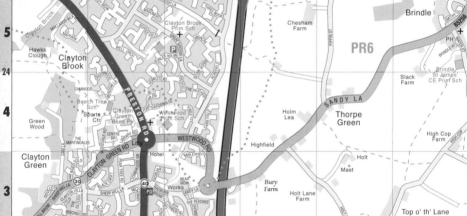

A
B
C
D
E
F
8
7
25
6
5
24
4
3
23
2
1
22
57
58
59
M6
M61
M65
A6
B5256
PR5
PR6
Mill
Gregson Lane
Level Crossing
Jack Green
ORAM RD
Jack Green Fold
Farm
MILL HOUSE LA
Haddock Park
Wood
Mill
Wood
Bank Head
Farm
Bank Head Brook
BANK HEAD LA
Duckworth
House
Hospital
Level
Crossing
COTTAGE
GDNS
STEPHENDALE AVE
LADY ACRE
MOORHEY
CRES
BRADKIRK LA
BRINDLE CL
FURTH
BLUEBELL WAY
GREYSTOCK CL
FOXGLOVE CL
FURTHER FIELD
PH
CARNFIELD PL
LEACH PL
HUDSON CT
Ind Est
Walton
Summit
BRADKIRK PL
BANKSFIELD
PL
BRIERLEY RD
WALTON SUMMIT RD
NEWFIELD RD
COCKER RD
OLDFIELD RD
FOUR OAKS RD
CARR PL
OAKSHOTT PL
RINGLET RD
DAWSON PL
HOLLY PL
KELLET LA
IVY HOUSE
CL
CRAIGFLOWER CT
BRINDLE FOLD
BRINDLE RD
Seed
Lee
OLD TRAM
RD
SEEDLEE RD
DOOD WAY
REEDFIELD PL
Walton
Summit
Ctr
BROOKFIELD PL
FOUR OAKS RD
GREEN
GOUGH LA
THE OLD TRAMWAY 1
LITTLE BANKS CL 2
TRAMWAY LA
SCEPTRE WAY
2
9
CLAYTON BROOK RD
BRINDLE RD
Pippin
Street
Pippin Street
Farm
SMITHY LA
Kenyons
Farm
Units
BROW HEY
CARR MDW
BRIERY HEY
CROFT MDW
ELMFIELD
BRIARY
CT
CARR BARN BROW
AMBLEDENE
BARN MDW
WOODFIELD
GOUGH LA
THREE NOOKS
DAISY MDW
MASONFIELD
Clayton Brook
Clayton Brook
Prim Sch
SCHOOL FIELD
GREAT GREENS LA
LONGACRE
MALLARDS WLK
MAYPARK
WELL ORCH
TUNLEY HOLME
SEVEN ACRES
ACREFIELD
Hawks
Clough
Clayton
Brook
Brindle
SMITHY CL
PH
BRINDLE HTS
WATER ST
Chesham
Farm
PIPPIN ST
Brindle
St James'
CE Prim Sch
Slack
Farm
HOMESTEAD
REDFIELD
THE HEATHERS
CAMWOOD
MEADOW LA
GREENWOOD
Beech Tree
Sch
FORTH DR
GARDENIA CL
PINES CL
CARR FIELD
PRESTON RD
Sports
Ctr
Clayton
Green
Bsns Pk
Westwood
Prim Sch
SANDY LA
Holm
Lea
Thorpe
Green
Green
Wood
THE
MARTINDALES
CENTRE
DR
WOODVALE RD
LIBRARY RD
Liby
WESTWOOD RD
Highfield
High Cop
Farm
HIGH COP LA
Clayton
Green
CAM LA
CLAYTON-GREEN RD
Hotel
BARLEYFIELD
Holt
Mast
CAM WOOD FOLD
PEAR TREE RD
STONEHOUSE GN
RADBURN CL
BLACK CROFT
SHEEP HILL LA
MEADWAY
NEAR
MDW
Works
SANDY LA
Bury
Farm
Holt Lane
Farm
30
40
PO
RADBURN BROW
DOVECOTE
SHEEP HILL LA
CLAYTON VILLA FOLD
THE CLOUGH
KILN CROFT
BIRCH FIELD
ASH FIELD
WILLOW FIELD
THE BEECHES
OAKMERE
HOLT LA
Top o' th' Lane
SHEEP HILL BROW
BEECHWOOD CROFT
GLENMORE
PINGLE CROFT
LORDS CROFT
BAY TREE RD
MANOR RD
HAWTHORNE CL
HOLLY CL
FERN MDW
ASHDOWN DR
1 CHARTWELL CL
2 BURGHLEY CL
Hough
Hill
DENHAM LA
Manor Road
Prim
Sch
PH
Clayton-le-Woods
CE Prim Sch
PH
BACK LA
HILL CROFT
STACK CROFT
WOOD END RD
OAK CROFT
CARR RD
FIDDLER'S LA
THE HEYES
CLOVER FIELD
CEDAR FIELD
ELDER CL
OSBORNE DR
BINGLEY CL
KNEBWORTH CL
CHORLEY OLD RD
Denham
Hill
Walmsley
Fold
Carvers
Farm
Denham
Hall
Lower Wood
End
BLACKTHORN CROFT
WHITETHORN CL
BEARSWOOD CROFT
CARLTON AVE
HUNTS FIELD
WHITTLE PK
THE ELMS
WILDERSWOOD CL
Huggart's
Farm
Mast
LOSTOCK MDW
ROWAN CROFT
BEECH GDNS
BACK LA
BANKSIDE
BROWNLEY ST
JUNIPER CROFT
SWANSEY LA
ST HELEN'S RD
River Lostock
WOODSIDE AVE
HILLSIDE CRES
DEREK RD
1 SWALLOW CT
2 WELLS FOLD CL
BIRCHIN LA
Hill Top
Farm
WATKIN RD
MILL LA
LORD ST
HILL TOP LA

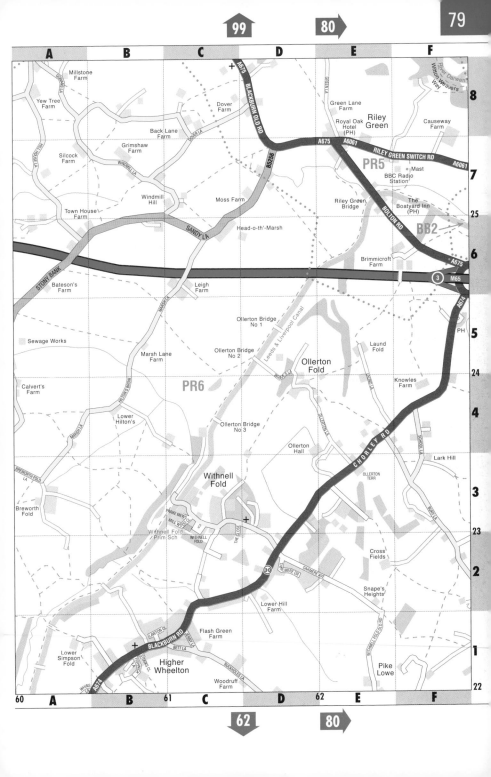

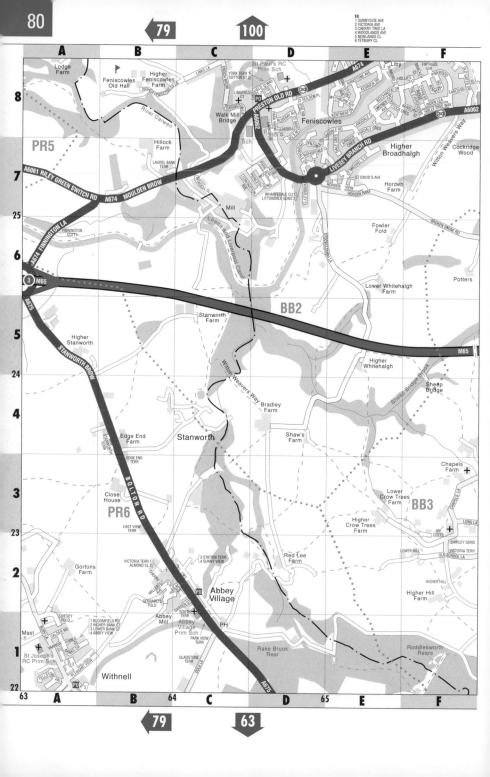

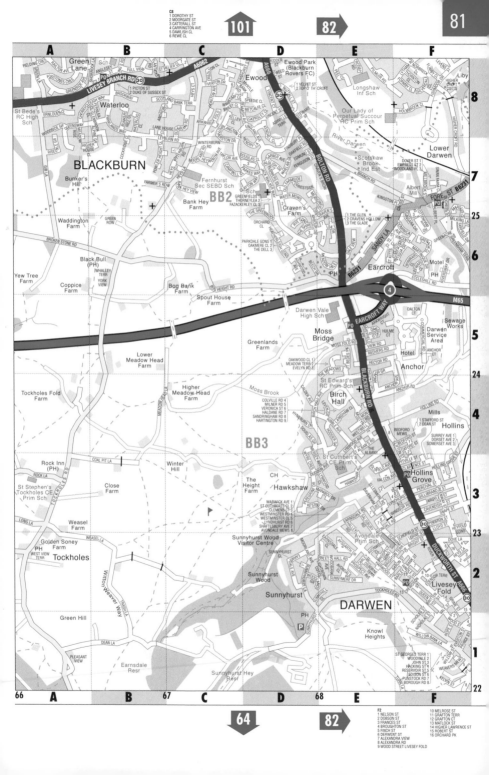

81 102

Map labels

A B C D E F

BLACKBURN

BB2

BB1

BB3

DARWEN

Blackamoor

Higher House Farm

Blackamoor

St James CE Prim Sch

NEW MEADOW CL

FOSSE BANK CT

Guide

Copster Hill Cl

School La

The Old School Ho

PH

Walker Office Park

Blackhill Farm

Sough Pits

Scar Edge

Aspinall Fold

Walker Park Ind Est

Syke Mill

Rann

Belthorn

Dog Inn (PH)

Belthorn Prim Sch

Wood Bank Farm

Pulford Farm

Davy Field Bridge

Davy Field Brook

Woodhead Farm

New Waterside Paper Mill

Bank Fold

Nursery Nook

Lower Grimshaw Farm

Higher Grimshaw Farm

Waterside Brook

Works

Goose House Bridge

Manor House Farm

Eccleshill Cotts

Shaw Fold

Waterside

Victoria Bldgs

Chapels

Darwen Moorland High Sch

Pot House

Harwood Fold

Duke of York Inn (PH)

Shorey Bank

Sch

Brocklehead Farm

St Paul's Terr

Clifton Terr

DARWEN

Cemy

Harwood's Farm

Hoddlesden St Paul's CE Prim Sch

Marsh House

Mast

Hoddlesden

Ranken Arms (PH)

M65

B6231 B6232 A6077

Index A1

A1
1 JAMES ST
2 VARLEY ST
3 WELLINGTON FOLD
4 ARCH ST
5 THE GREEN
6 JAMES ST W
7 ASHWORTH TERR
8 HESSE ST
9 BELGRAVE SQ
10 THE CIRCUS
11 WILLIAM ST
12 BK DUCKWORTH ST
13 PEMBROKE CT
14 STUART CL
15 MIDVILLE PL
16 SOUTH ST
17 GREEN ST E
18 CROFT ST
19 PARLIAMENT ST
20 CHURCH BANK ST
21 CHURCH TERR
22 VICTORIA ST
23 BATH ST
24 FOUNDRY ST
25 HARDMAN WAY
26 COCHRAN ST
27 LOWER CROSS ST
28 FRANKLIN ST

C1
1 ABBEY PL
2 WELL SPRINGS
3 DERWENT CL

81 65

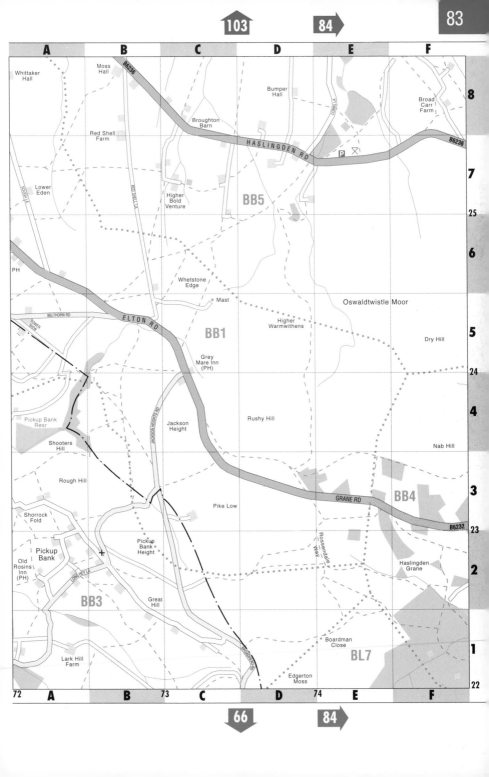

83 104

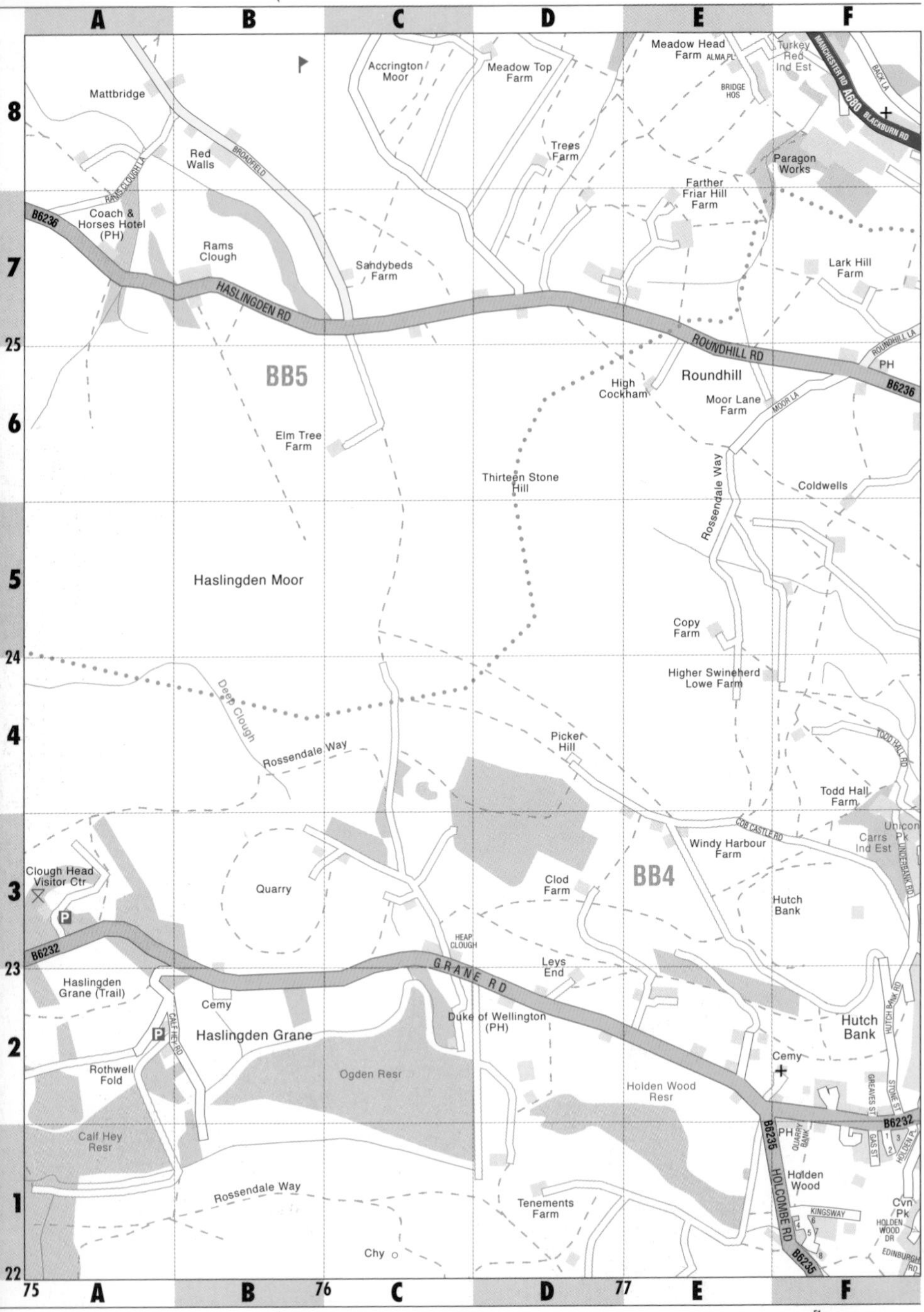

Mattbridge

Accrington Moor

Meadow Top Farm

Meadow Head Farm ALMA PL

Turkey Red Ind Est

MANCHESTER RD

BOX LD

A680

BLACKBURN RD

Red Walls

BROADFIELD

Trees Farm

BRIDGE HOS

Paragon Works

RAMSCLOUGH LA

Coach & Horses Hotel (PH)

B6236

Rams Clough

Sandybeds Farm

Farther Friar Hill Farm

Lark Hill Farm

HASLINGDEN RD

ROUNDHILL RD

ROUNDHILL LA

PH

B6236

25

BB5

High Cockham

Roundhill

Moor Lane Farm

MOOR LA

Elm Tree Farm

6

Coldwells

Thirteen Stone Hill

Rossendale Way

Haslingden Moor

Copy Farm

5

24

Deep Clough

Higher Swineherd Lowe Farm

Rossendale Way

4

Picker Hill

TODD HALL RD

Todd Hall Farm

COL CASTLE RD

Unicorn Ind Est

Carrs Ind Est

Windy Harbour Farm

BB4

DUNCKENHALDS RD

Clough Head Visitor Ctr

P

Quarry

Clod Farm

Hutch Bank

3

B6232

HEAP CLOUGH

Leys End

GRANE RD

Hutch Bank

23

Haslingden Grane (Trail)

Cemy

Duke of Wellington (PH)

CALF HEY RD

GREAVES ST

P

Haslingden Grane

Cemy

STONE ST

DAY ST

2

Rothwell Fold

Ogden Resr

Holden Wood Resr

B6232

PH

B6235

Calf Hey Resr

Holden Wood

Cvn Pk

Rossendale Way

HOLCOMBE RD

KINGSWAY

HOLDEN WOOD DR

1

Tenements Farm

EDINBURGH

B6235

22

Chy

75 76 77

F1
1 WARBURTON ST
2 MUSBURY VIEW
3 WARBURTON BLDGS
4 MUSBURY MEWS
5 GRANGE PARK WAY
6 MILLERS VALE
7 GRANGE HTS
8 WILLOW HEY

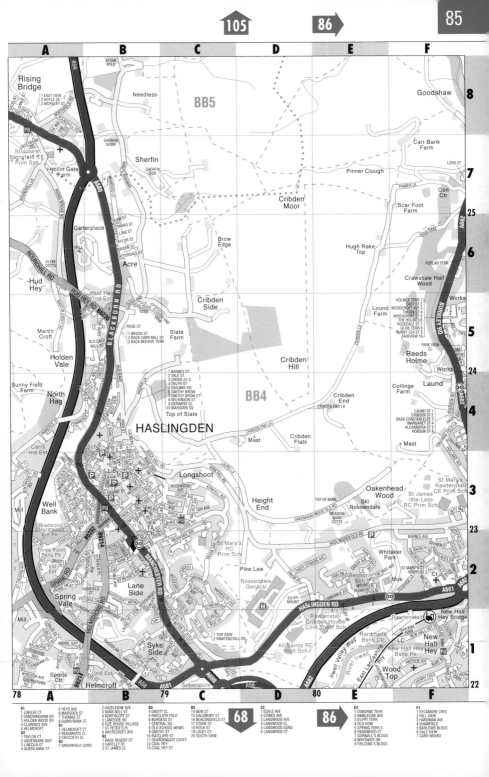

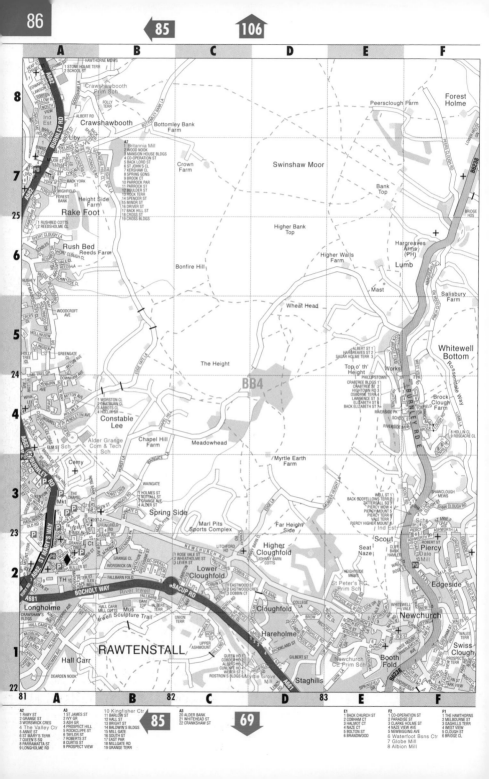

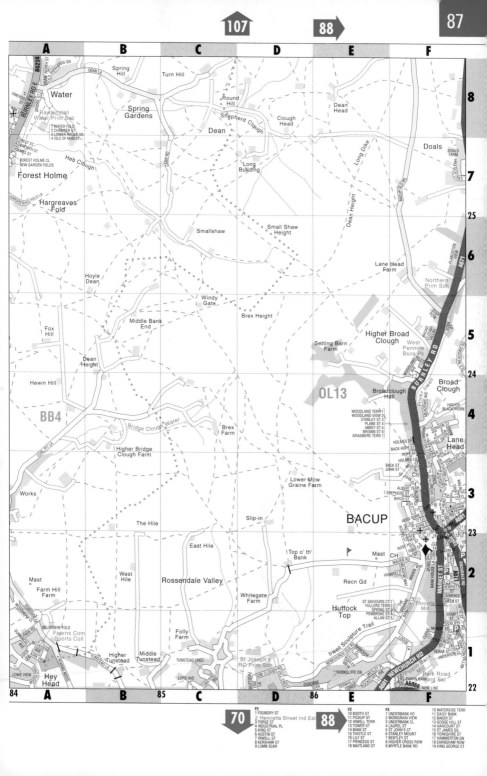

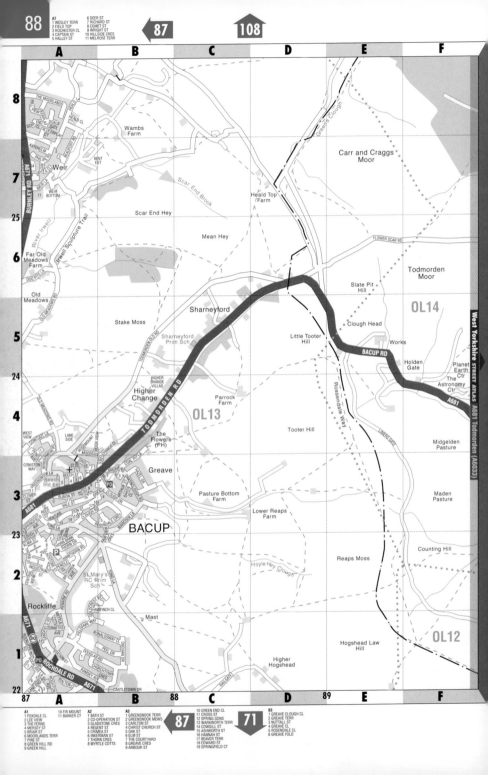

110

90

E6
1 HARDAKER CT
2 CLIFTON CT
3 WHITEHALL CT
4 CONWAY CT
5 TWEED ST

LYTHAM
ST ANNE'S

FY8

St Anne's

St Anne's Pier

Pleasure Island

Mayfield
Prim Sch.

The
Burlington-on-the-sea
Ch.

SEATON
CRES

ELWOOD
GRANGE

NORWOOD RD

BURLINGTON CT 1
TUDOR CT 2

CLIFTON
GRANGE

PIER

NICOLL CT 1
DARLEY CT 2
PIERPOINT 3
BRAIDWOOD CT 4

PARKVIEW
FLATS

ASHTON
GARDEN

PORRITT
CT

St ANDREWS

VERNON
LODGE

CLAREMONT CT 1
DEVERE GDNS 2
POPLAR CT 3
SCHOLARS CT 4
COLLEGE CT 5
LINKS CT 6
ALPINE LODGE 7
THE SPINNAKERS 8
QUAY WEST 9
HILLCLIFFE 10

NORTON CT 1
TARLETON LODGE 2

FAIRHAVEN
LA

WIMBORNE

CLIFTON DR S

A584

Lancashire
Coastal Way

Liby

1 EATON CT
2 KENILWORTH CT
3 RUSSELL CT

CH

Sch

29

28

27

26

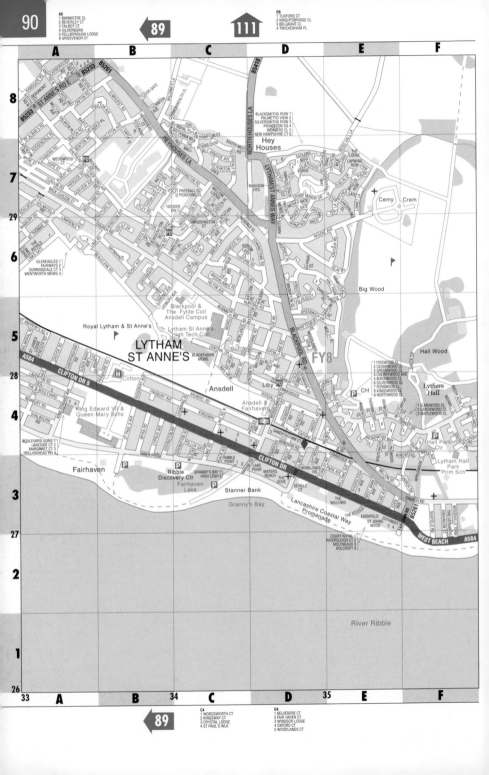

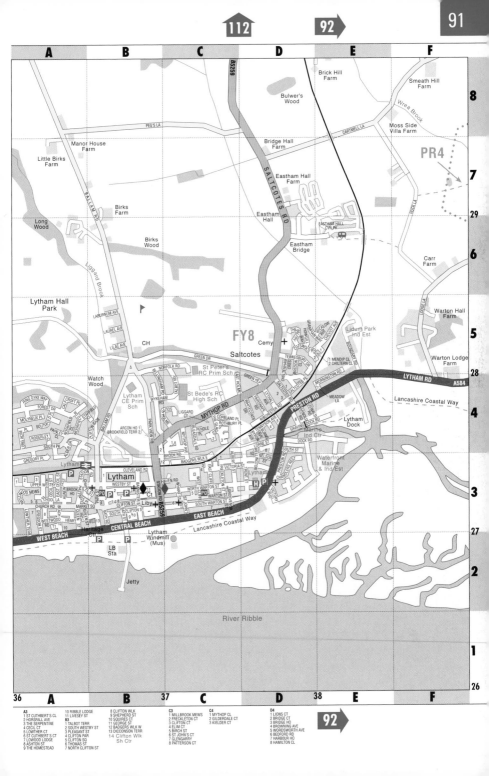

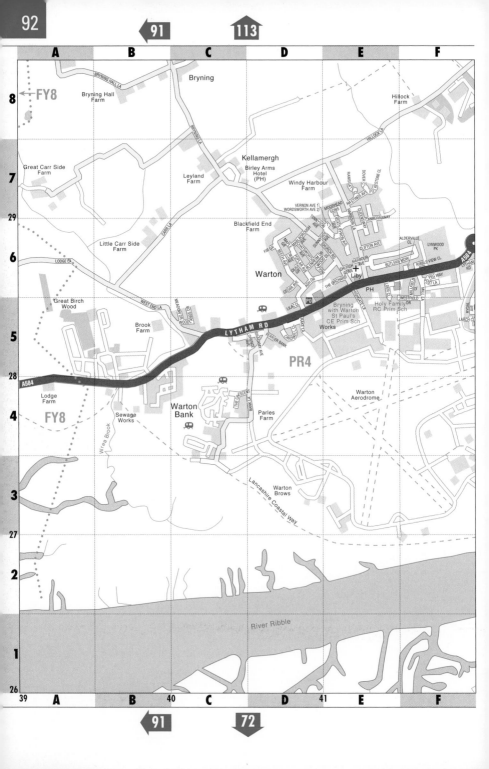

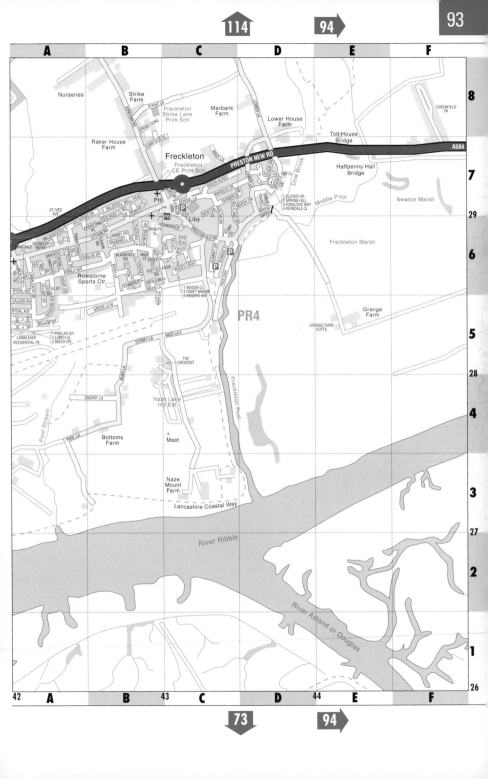

Freckleton

Nurseries
Strike Farm
Freckleton Strike Lane Prim Sch
Marbank Farm
Lower House Farm
Greenfield Pk

Raker House Farm
Toll House Bridge

Freckleton
Freckleton CE Prim Sch
PRESTON NEW RD
Halfpenny Hall Bridge
A584

St Ives Ave
Middle Pool
Newton Marsh

Freckleton Marsh

PR4

Rowstorne Sports Ctr

1 MASON CL
2 CROFT MANOR
3 ANSBRO AVE

Grange Farm

GRANGE FARM COTTS

1 CLOVER DR
2 SPRING HILL
3 FOXGLOVE WAY
4 FERNDALE CL

LAMALEACH RESIDENTIAL PK

1 POPLAR DR
2 LARCH CL
3 BEECH DR

Pool Stream

Bottoms Farm

Mast

Naze Lane Ind Est

The Crescent

Stoney La

Cherry La

Pool La

Naze Mount Farm

Lancashire Coastal Way

Freckleton Pool

River Ribble

River Asland or Douglas

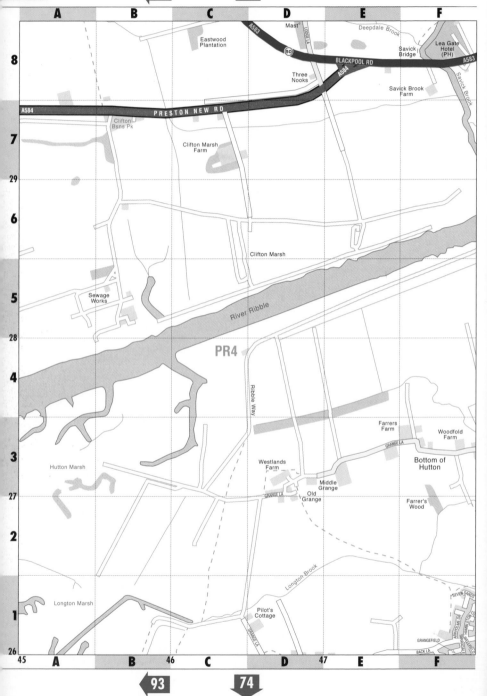

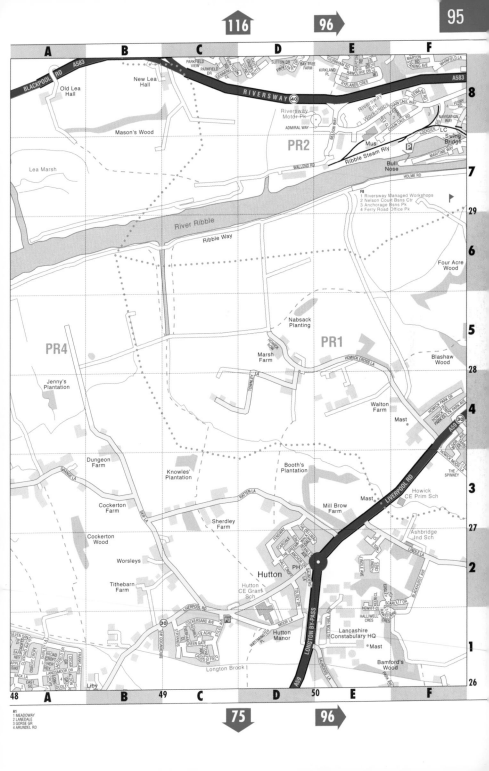

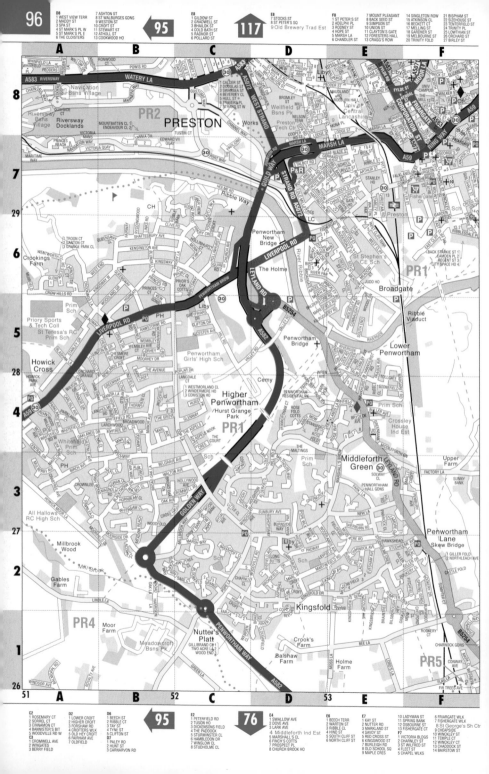

D8
1 WEST VIEW TERR
2 MADDY ST
3 SPA ST
4 ST MARK'S PL W
5 ST MARK'S PL E
6 THE CLOISTERS

7 ASHTON ST
8 ST WALBURGES GDNS
9 WESTON ST
10 CROFT ST
11 STEWART ST
12 ATHOLL ST
13 COOKWOOD HO

E8
1 GILDOW ST
2 GRADWELL ST
3 BHALOK ST
4 COLD BATH ST
5 RADNOR ST
6 POLLARD ST

E8
1 STOCKS ST
8 ST PETER'S SQ
9 Old Brewery Trad Est

F8
1 ST PETER'S ST
2 ADELPHI PL
3 RODNEY ST
4 HOPE ST
5 MARSH LA
6 CHANDLER ST

7 MOUNT PLEASANT
8 BACK SEED ST
9 SIMPSON ST
10 UNION ST
11 CLAYTON'S GATE
12 FORESTERS HALL
13 CRAGG'S ROW

14 SINGLETON ROW
15 ATKINSON CL
16 BECKETT CT
17 MELLING ST
18 GARDNER ST
19 MELBOURNE ST
20 TRINITY FOLD

21 BISPHAM ST
22 SIZEHOUSE ST
23 TENTERFIELD CT
24 TRINITY PL
25 LOWTHIAN ST
26 ORCHARD ST
27 BIRLEY ST

← 95   ↑ 117   F ↑

C2
1 ROSEMARY CT
2 SORREL CT
3 CINNAMON CT
4 BANNISTER'S BIT
5 WOODVILLE RD W

C3
1 CROMWELL AVE
2 WINGATES
3 BERRY FIELD

D2
1 LOWER CROFT
2 HIGHER CROFT
3 FORSHAW RD
4 CROFTERS WLK
5 OLD HEY CROFT
6 FAIRHAM AVE
7 OLDFIELD

D6
1 BEECH ST
2 RIBBLE CT
3 TAY ST
4 TYNE ST
5 CLIFTON ST

D7
1 PALEY RD
2 HUNT ST
3 CARNARVON RD

E2
1 PETERFIELD RD
2 TUSON HO
3 DICKENSONS FIELD
4 THE PADDOCK
5 STURMINSTER CL
6 HAMBLEDON CL
7 WINSLOW CL
8 STUDHOLME CL

E4
1 SWALLOW AVE
2 DOVE AVE
3 LARK AVE
4 Middleforth Ind Est
5 MARSHALL'S CL
6 FINCH'S COTTS
7 PROSPECT PL
8 CHURCH BROOK HO

E6
1 BEECH TERR
2 WARTON ST
3 RIBBLE CL
4 HIND ST
5 SOUTH CLIFF ST
6 NORTH CLIFF ST

E7
1 KAY ST
2 NUTTER RD
3 MARKLAND ST
4 SAVOY ST
5 RED CROSS ST
6 KINGSWOOD ST
7 BURLEIGH RD
8 OLD SCHOOL SQ
9 MAPLE CRES

10 LADYMAN ST
11 SPRING BANK
12 OSBOURNE ST
13 FISHERGATE CT

F7
1 VICTORIA BLDGS
2 CHANLEY ST
3 ST WILFRED ST
4 FLEET ST
5 CHAPEL WLKS

F6
1 FRIARGATE WLK
2 FISHERGATE WLK
3 St GEORGE'S Sh Ctr
4 CHEAPSIDE
5 WINCKLEY CT
6 TEMPLE CT
7 WINCKLEY CT
8 CHADDOCK ST
9 BAIRSTOW ST

← 95   ↓ 76   F

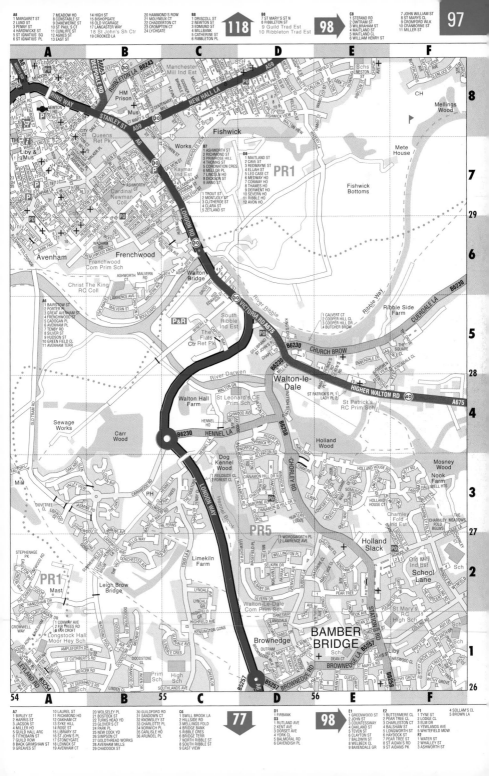

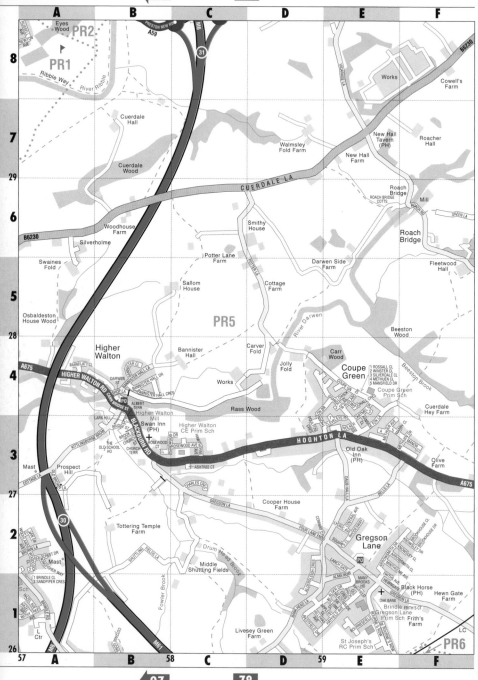

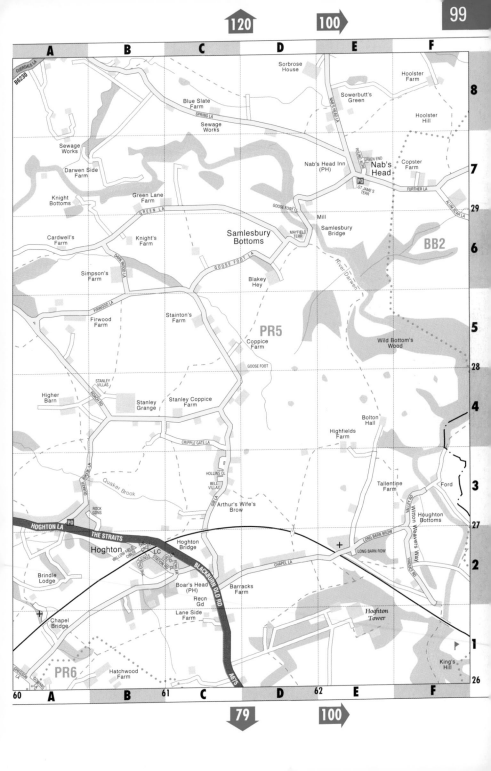

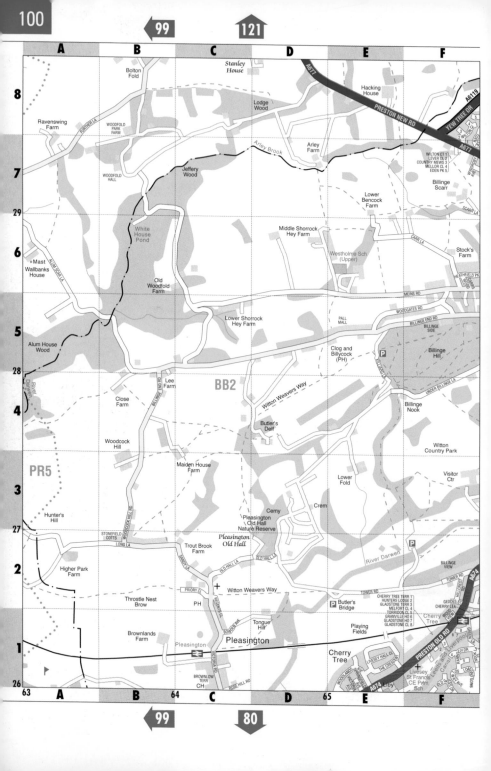

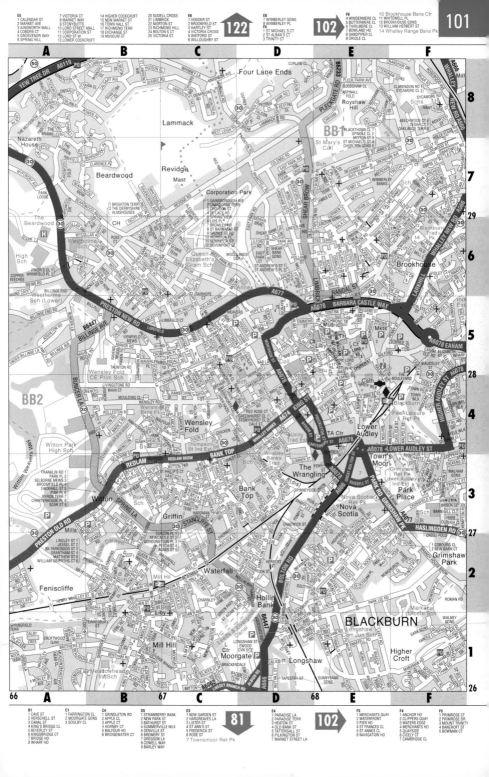

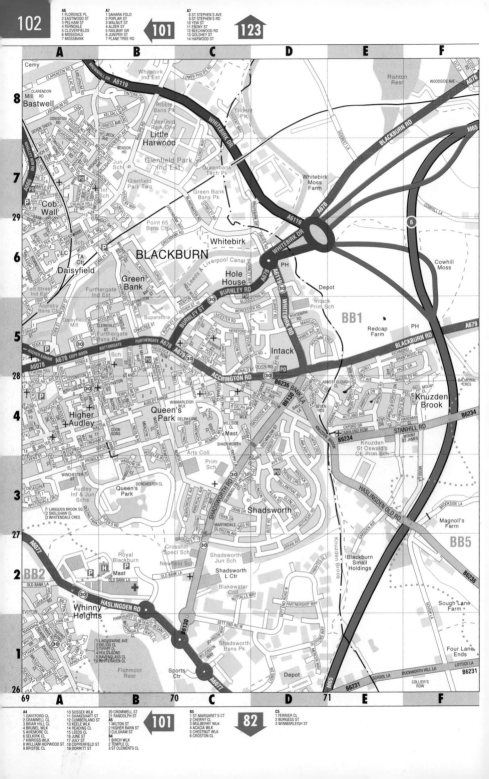

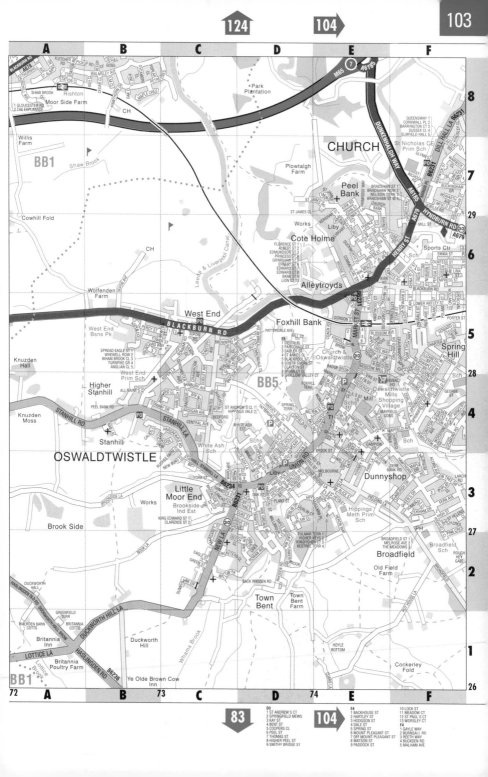

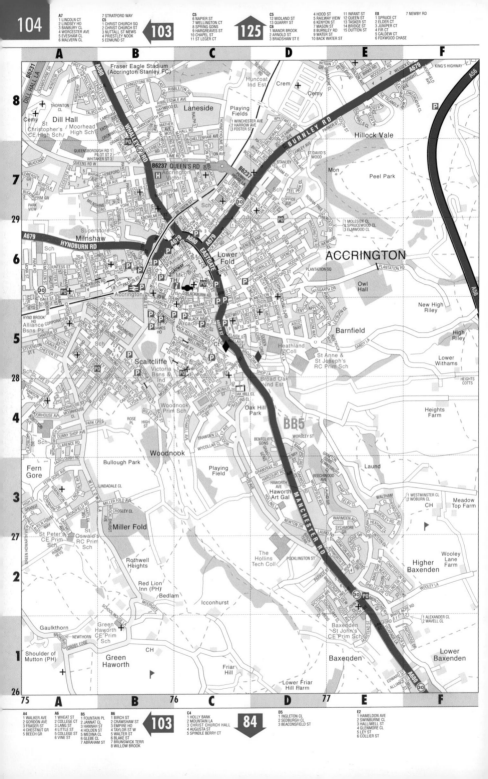

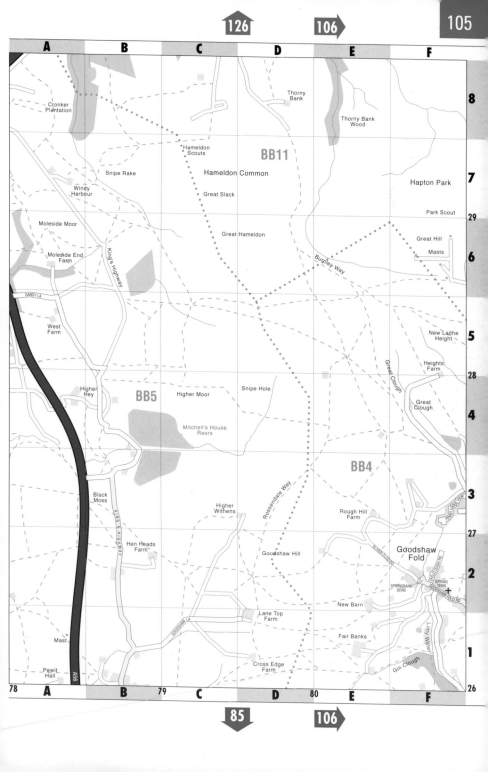

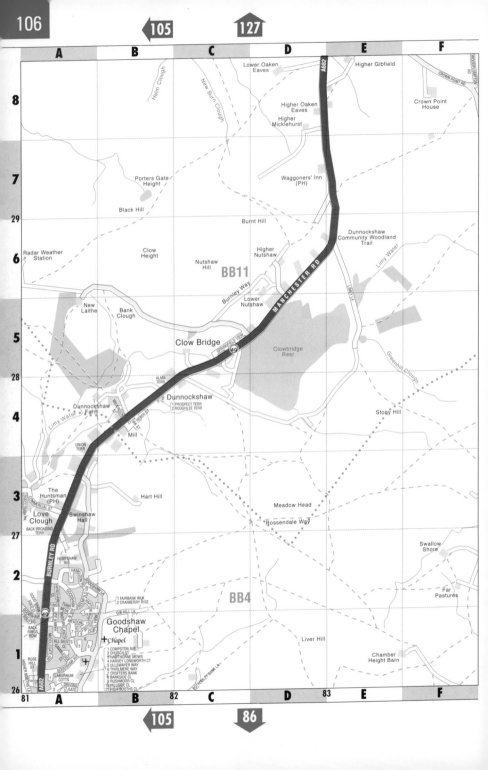

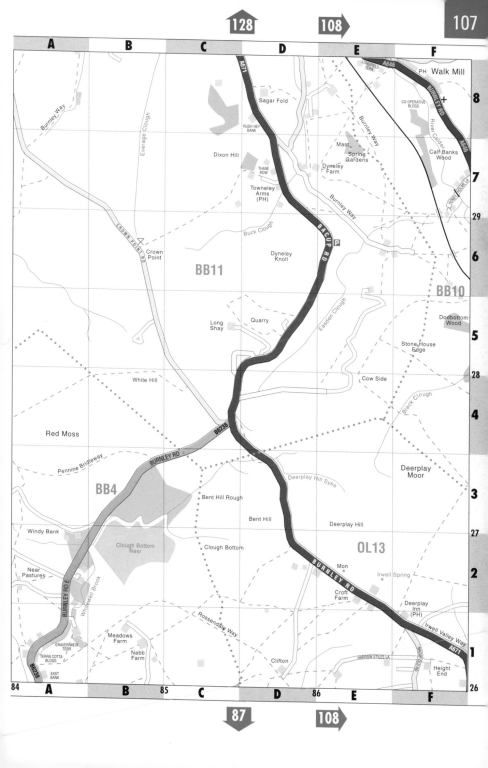

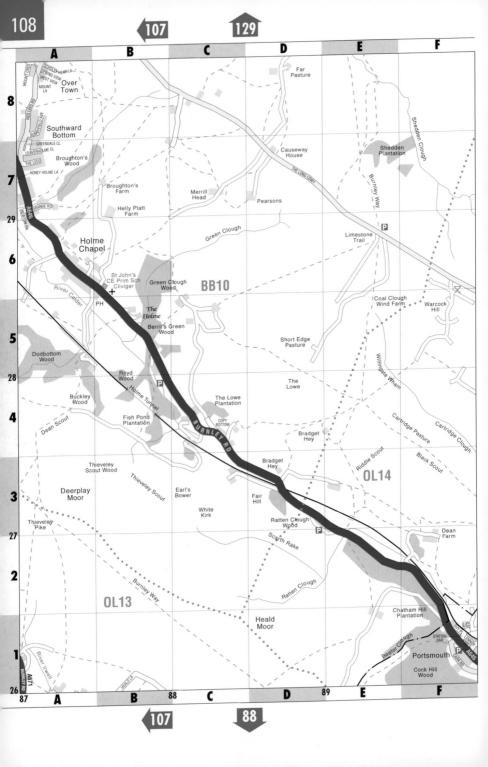

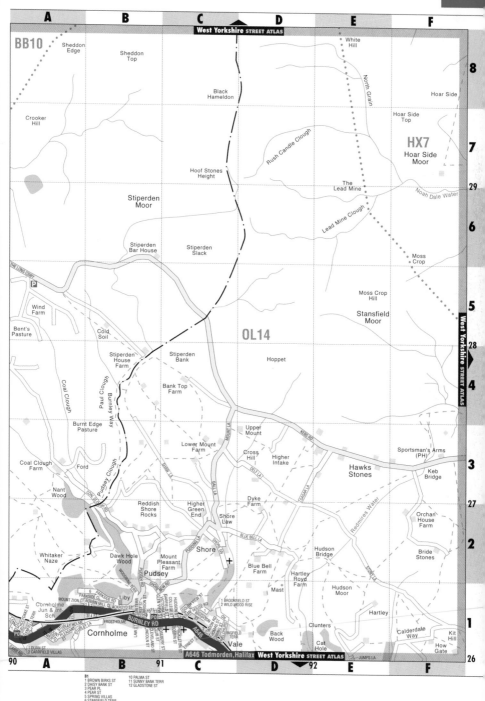

BB10

Sheddon Edge

Sheddon Top

White Hill

North Grain

Hoar Side

Black Hameldon

Hoar Side Top

Crooker Hill

Rush Candle Clough

HX7

Hoar Side Moor

7

Hoof Stones Height

The Lead Mine

Noah Dale Water

29

Stiperden Moor

Lead Mine Clough

6

Stiperden Bar House

Stiperden Slack

Moss Crop

THE LONG CDWY

Moss Crop Hill

OL14

Stansfield Moor

5

Wind Farm

28

Bent's Pasture

Cold Soil

Stiperden House Farm

Stiperden Bank

Hoppet

4

Coal Clough

Paul Clough

Burnley Way

Bank Top Farm

Burnt Edge Pasture

Lower Mount Farm

Upper Mount

KEBB RD

Sportsman's Arms (PH)

3

Coal Clough Farm

Ford

Pudsey Clough

Cross Hill

Higher Intake

Hawks Stones

Keb Bridge

Nant Wood

COAL CLOUGH RD

Reddish Shore Rocks

Higher Green End

Dyke Farm

Redmires Water

Orchan House Farm

27

Whitaker Naze

Dawk Hole Wood

Mount Pleasant Farm

Shore Law

Shore

Blue Bell Farm

Hartley Royd Farm

Hudson Bridge

Bride Stones

2

Pudsey

BLUE BELL LA

Mast

Hudson Moor

Hartley

Liby

Cornholme Jun & Inf Sch

BURNLEY RD

Cornholme

Vale

1 BROOKFIELD ST
2 WILD WOOD RISE

Back Wood

Clunters

Cat Hole

Hartley

Calderdale Way

Kit Hill

How Gate

1

A646 Todmorden, Halifax

JUMPS LA

26

90 A B 91 C D 92 E F

B1
1 BROWN BIRKS ST
2 DAISY BANK ST
3 PEAR PL
4 PEAR ST
5 SPRING VILLAS
6 STANSFIELD TERR
7 CORNHOLME TERR
8 OAKLEIGH TERR
9 GEM APARTMENTS
10 PALMA ST
11 SUNNY BANK TERR
12 GLADSTONE ST

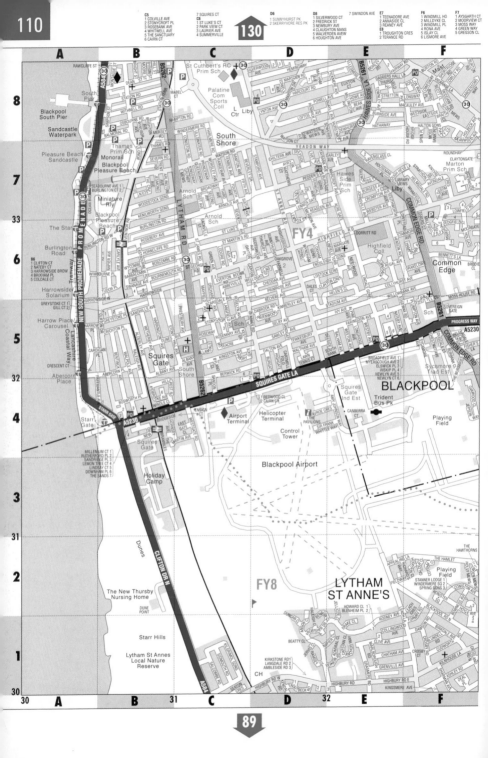

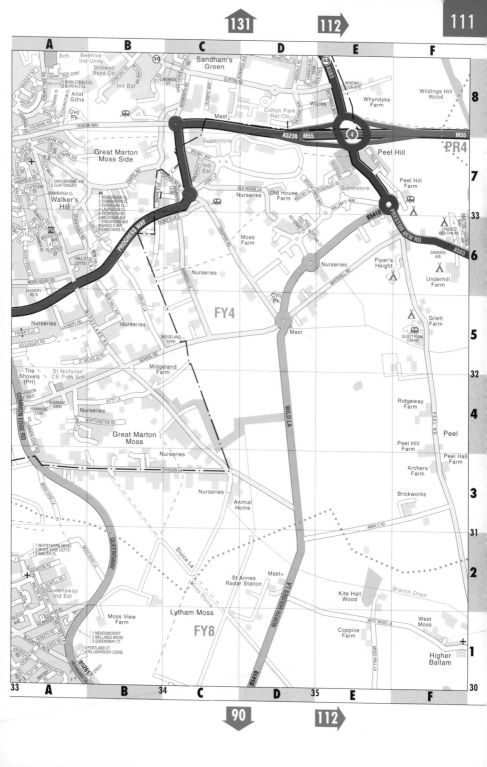

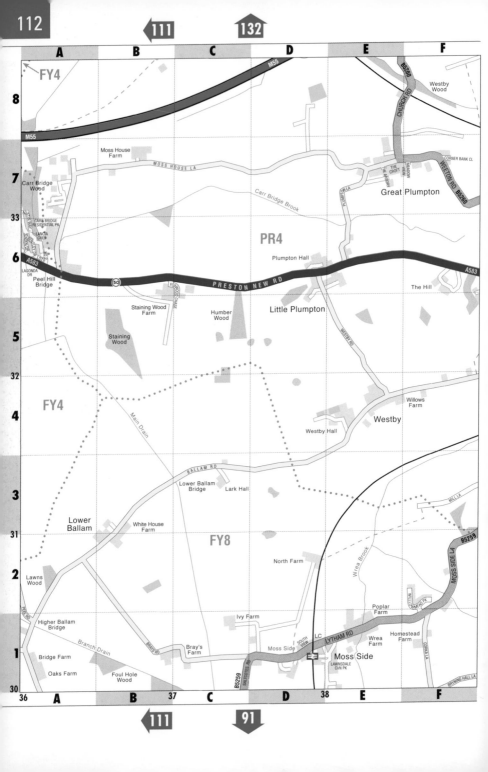

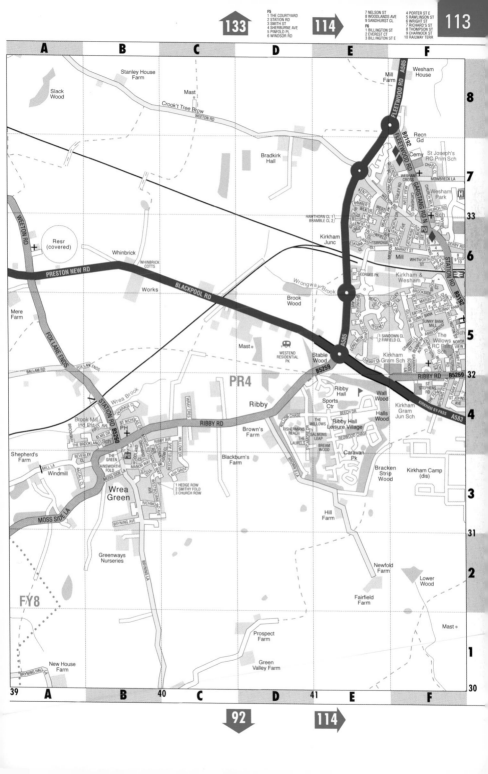

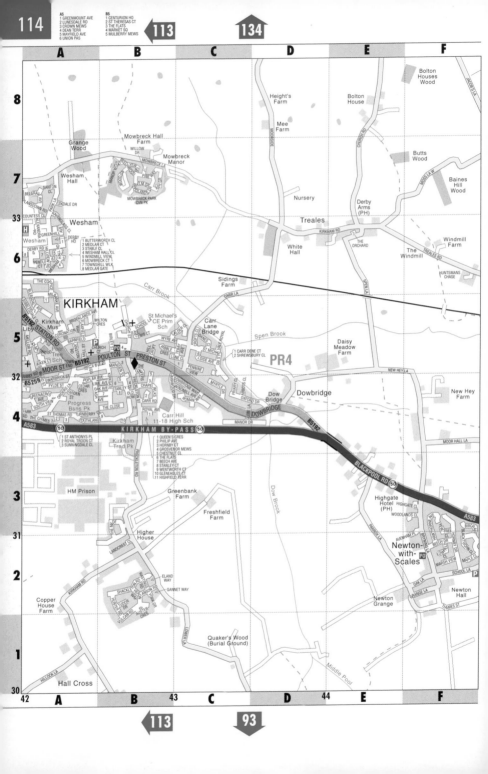

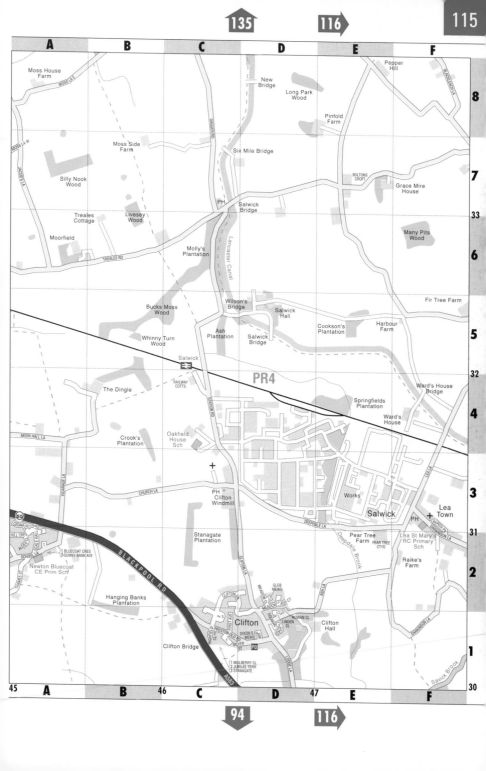

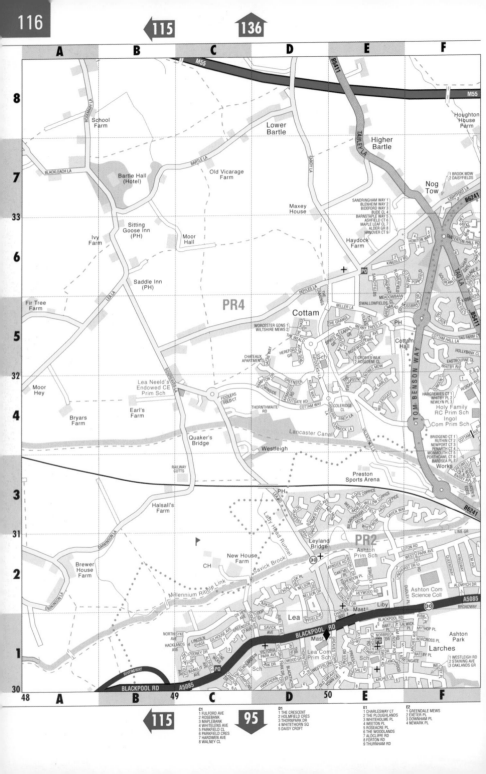

A **B** **C** **D** **E** **F**

M55

School Farm

Lower Bartle

Houghton House Farm

B5411

TABLEY LA

Higher Bartle

8

Bartle Hall (Hotel)

Old Vicarage Farm

Nog Tow

7

BARTLE LA

BLACKLEACH LA

SANDY LA

B6241

Maxey House

SANDRINGHAM WAY 1
BLENHEIM WAY 2
BIDEFORD WAY 3
BUDE CL 4
BARNSTAPLE CT 6
ASHFIELD CT 6
MAPLE LEAF CL 7
ALDER GR 8
HANOVER CT 9

33

Sitting Goose Inn (PH)

Moor Hall

Haydock Farm

HONITON WAY

Ivy Farm

Saddle Inn (PH)

PO

KINGSLEY RD

6

LEA LA

Fir Tree Farm

Cottam Hall

PR4

Cottam

PH

5

WORCESTER GDNS 1
WILTSHIRE MEWS 2

THE BELD

THE GRANGE

MERRY TREES LA

HOLLYBANK CL

EASTBOURNE CL

WHITBY AV

Moor Hey

CHATEAUX APARTMENTS

Hereford DR

2 CROMER WLK
3 ROSEACRE CL

HARGREAVES CT 1
WHITBY PL 2
NEWLYN PL 3

REDGRAVE

32

TOM BENSON WAY

COTTAM HALL LA

Lea Neeld's Endowed CE Prim Sch

FIDDLERS FOLD CT

THORNTHWAITE RD

Earl's Farm

GREENSIDE

OUTGATE RD

COTTAM WAY

COLERIDGE LA

FINCH LA

Holy Family RC Prim Sch
Ingol Com Prim Sch

4

Bryars Farm

Quaker's Bridge

Lancaster Canal

VALENTINES LA

BRIDGEND CT 1
RUTHIN CT 2
NEWPORT CT 3
PENARTH CT 4
MONMOUTH CT 5
PORTHCAWL CT 6
BARDSEA PL A

Works

Westleigh

Preston Sports Arena

B6241

RAILWAY COTTS

3

Halsall's Farm

PH

PR2

31

LADY HEAD RUNNEL

Leyland Bridge

Ashton Prim Sch

LIME GR

Brewer House Farm

New House Farm

CH

SAVICK BROOK

30

LYTHAM RD

Ashton Com Science Coll

ALDWYCH AV

2

Millennium Ribble Link

Liby

Mast

A5085
BROADWAY

RIVERWAY

Lea

BLACKPOOL RD

Mast

30

Ashton Park

Larches

1

NORTH SYKE AVE
HACKLANDS LA

LINCOLN CHASE

GILNOW AVE

VICTORIA PARK AVE

Lea Com Prim Sch

BARTLE CL
WICK PL

MYTHOP PL

NORCROSS PL

NATEBY PL

1 WESTLEIGH AV
2 STAINING AVE
3 OAKLANDS AVE

30

BLACKPOOL RD
A5085

LARCHES LA

48 **A** **49** **B** **C** **50** **D** **E** **F**

C1
1 FULFORD AVE
2 ROSEBANK
3 MAPLEBANK
4 WHITELENS AVE
5 PARKFIELD CL
6 PARKFIELD CRES
7 HARDWEN AVE
8 WALNEY CL

D1
1 THE CRESCENT
2 HOLMFIELD CRES
3 THORNPARK DR
4 WHITETHORN SQ
5 DAISY CROFT

E1
1 CHARLESWAY CT
2 THE PLOUGHLANDS
3 WHITEHOLME PL
4 WEETON PL
5 ROSEACRE PL
6 THE WOODLANDS
7 ALDCLIFFE RD
8 FORTON RD
9 THURNHAM RD

E2
1 GREENDALE MEWS
2 EXETER PL
3 DOWNHAM PL
4 NEWARK PL

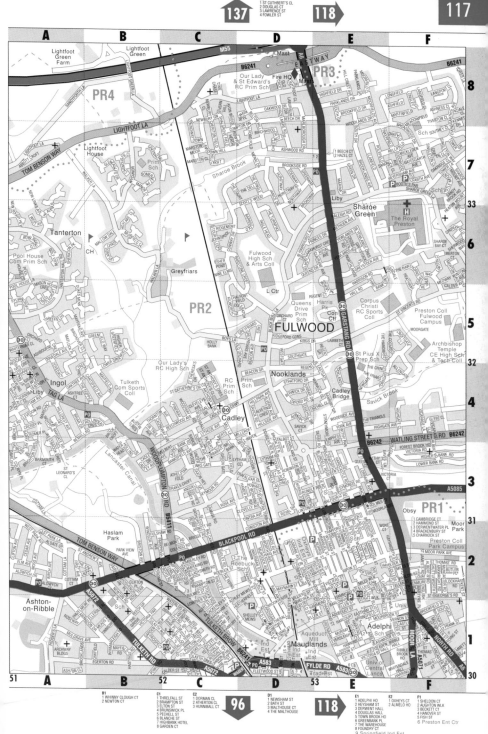

D3
1 ST CUTHBERT'S CL
2 DOUGLAS CT
3 LAWRENCE ST
4 FOWLER ST

137 118

B1
1 WHINNY CLOUGH CT
2 NEWTON CT

C1
1 THRELFALL ST
2 BRAMPTON ST
3 ELTON ST
4 BRUNSWICK PL
5 PECHELL ST
6 BLANCHE ST
7 HIGHBANK HOTEL
8 GARDEN CT

C2
1 DORMAN CL
2 ATHERTON CL
3 HUNNIBALL CT

D1
1 NEWSHAM ST
2 BATH ST
3 MALTHOUSE CT
4 THE MALTHOUSE

E1
1 ADELPHI HO
2 HEYSHAM ST
3 DERWENT HALL
4 DOUGLAS HALL
5 TOWN BROOK HO
6 GREENBANK PL
7 THE WAREHOUSE
8 FOUNDRY CT
9 Springfield Ind Est

E2
1 OXHEYS CT
2 ALMELO HO

F1
1 SHELDON CT
2 AUGHTON WLK
3 BECKETT CT
4 HANOVER ST
5 FISH ST
6 Preston Ent Ctr

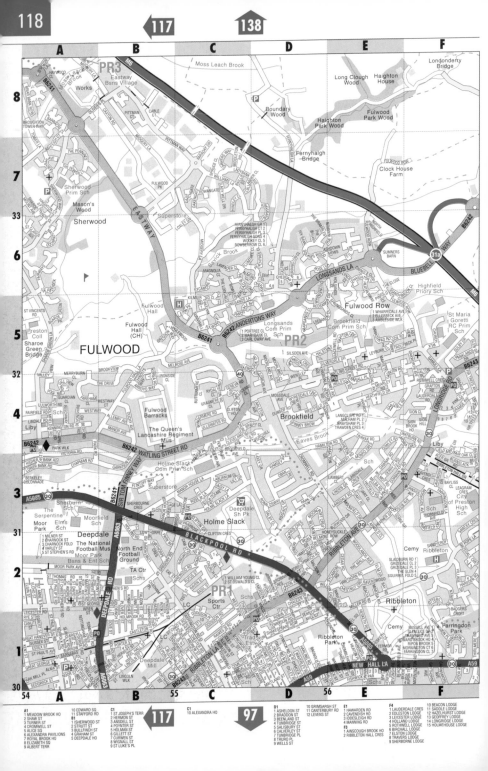

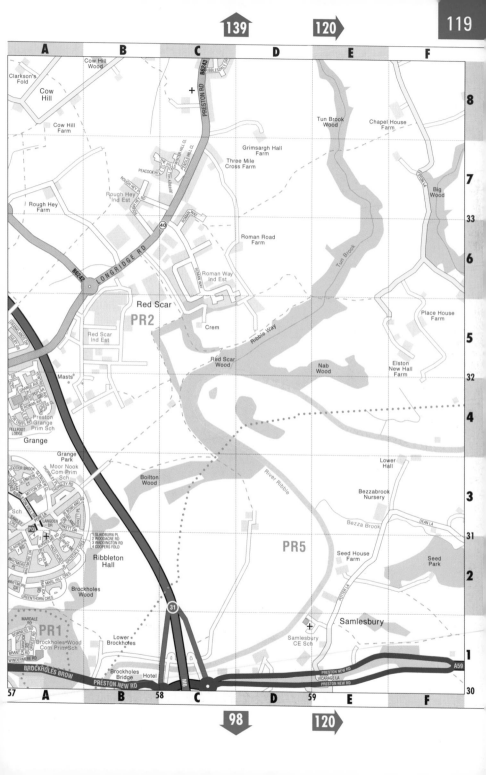

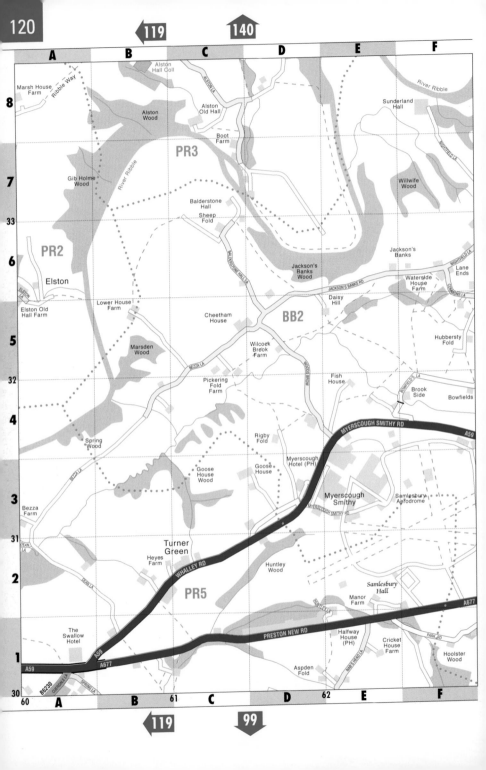

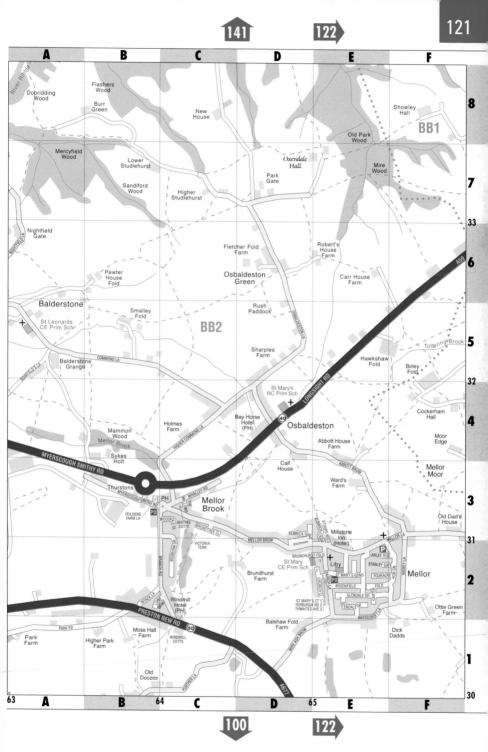

121
142

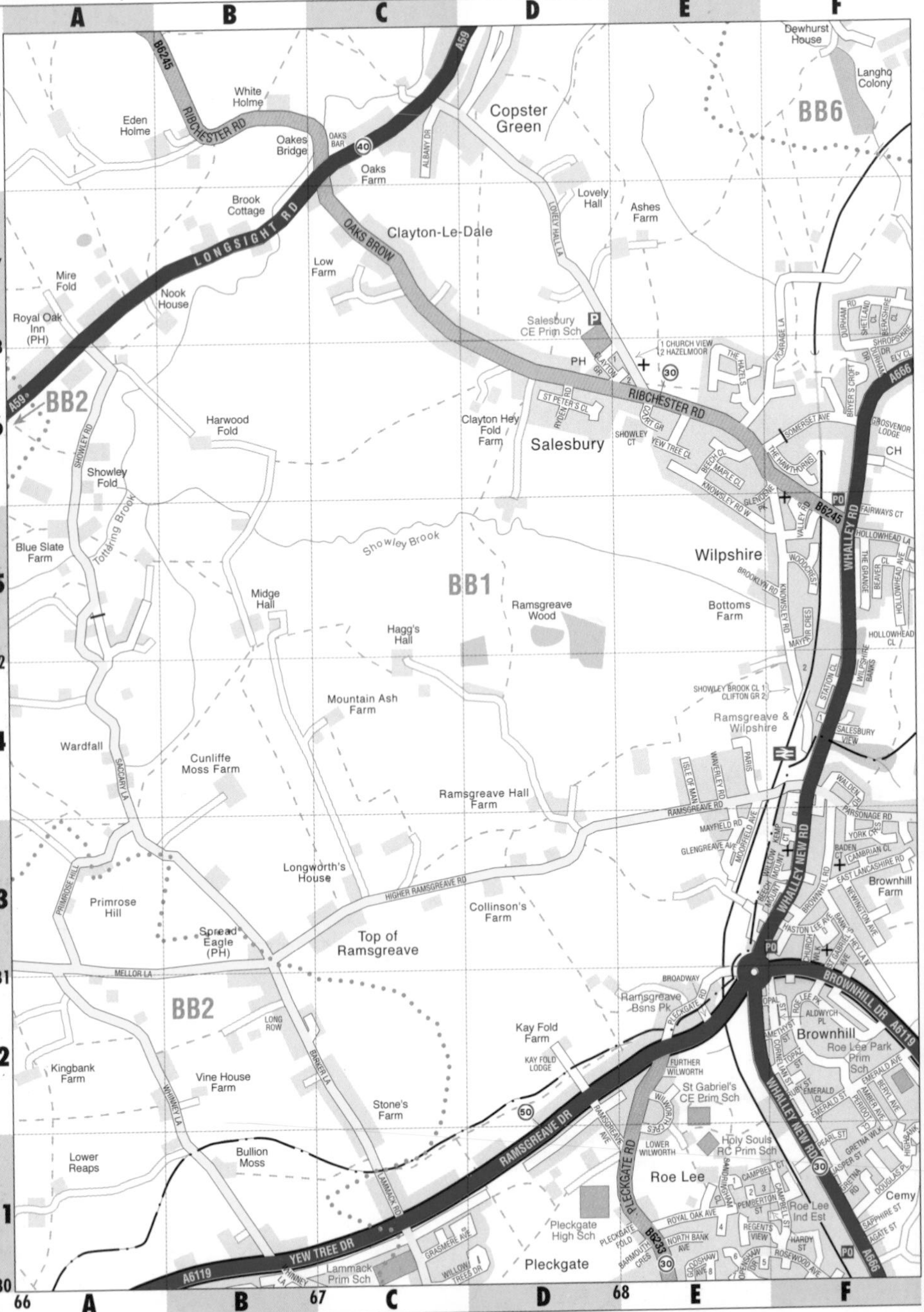
A
B
C
D
E
F
8
7
33
6
5
32
4
3
31
2
1
30
66
67
68
B6245
A59
RIBCHESTER RD
White Holme
Eden Holme
Oakes Bridge
OAKS BAR
40
Oaks Farm
ALBANY DR
Copster Green
Dewhurst House
Langho Colony
BB6
Brook Cottage
LONGSIGHT RD
OAKS BROW
Clayton-Le-Dale
Lovely Hall
LOVELY HALL LA
Ashes Farm
Low Farm
Mire Fold
Nook House
Royal Oak Inn (PH)
Salesbury CE Prim Sch
1 CHURCH VIEW
2 HAZELMOOR
PH
30
THE HAZELS
VICARAGE LA
DURHAM RD
SHETLAND CL
BERKSHIRE CL
SHROPSHIRE DR
ELY CL
A666
A59
BB2
ST PETER'S CL
RYDEN RD
RIBCHESTER RD
Harwood Fold
Clayton Hey Fold Farm
Salesbury
SHOWLEY CT
YEW TREE CL
BEECH CL
MAPLE CL
KNOWSLEY RD W
GLENDENE PK
THE HAWTHORNS
SOMERSET AVE
BRYER'S CROFT
GROSVENOR LODGE
CH
SHOWLEY RD
Showley Fold
Tottering Brook
Blue Slate Farm
Showley Brook
B6245
PO
FAIRWAYS CT
HOLLOWHEAD LA
WHALLEY RD
VALLEY RD
Wilpshire
WOODCREST
BROOKLYN RD
KNOWSLEY RD
THE GRANGE
BEAVER CL
HOLLOWHEAD AVE
BB1
Midge Hall
Ramsgreave Wood
Bottoms Farm
Hagg's Hall
MAYFAIR CRES
HOLLOWHEAD CL
WILPSHIRE BANKS
STATION CL
SHOWLEY BROOK CL 1
CLIFTON GR 2
Mountain Ash Farm
Ramsgreave & Wilpshire
SALESBURY VIEW
Wardfall
Cunliffe Moss Farm
SACCARY LA
ISLE OF MAN
WAVERLEY RD
PARIS
Ramsgreave Hall Farm
RAMSGREAVE RD
WALDEN
PARSONAGE RD
YORK CL
MAYFIELD RD
MOORFIELD AVE
GLENGREAVE AVE
WHALLEY NEW RD
BADEN CT
CAMBRIAN CL
EAST LANCASHIRE RD
Brownhill Farm
PRIMROSE HILL
Longworth's House
HIGHER RAMSGREAVE RD
BROWNHILL RD
NEWINGTON AVE
Primrose Hill
Collinson's Farm
HASTON LEE AVE
Spread Eagle (PH)
Top of Ramsgreave
CHURCH WLK
PO
MELLOR LA
BROADWAY
BROWNHILL DR
A6119
BB2
Ramsgreave Bsns Pk
PLECKGATE RD
ALDWYCH PL
LONG ROW
Kay Fold Farm
Brownhill
Roe Lee Park Prim Sch
KAY FOLD LODGE
FURTHER WILWORTH
Kingbank Farm
Vine House Farm
BARKER LA
St Gabriel's CE Prim Sch
WHALLEY NEW RD
Stone's Farm
50
RAMSGREAVE DR
RAMSGREAVE AVE
WHINNEY LA
LOWER WILWORTH
Holy Souls RC Prim Sch
Lower Reaps
Bullion Moss
PLECKGATE RD
Roe Lee
CAMPBELL CT
PEMBERTON ST
Roe Lee Ind Est
30
Cemy
LAMMACK RD
ROYAL OAK AVE
REGENTS VIEW
HARDY ST
SAPPHIRE ST
Pleckgate High Sch
PLECKGATE FOLD
NORTH BANK AVE
B6233
ROSEWOOD AVE
YEW TREE DR
GRASMERE AVE
Pleckgate
BARMOUTH CRES
GOODSHAW AVE
30
PO
A666
A6119
WHINNEY LA
Lammack Prim Sch
WILLOW TREES DR

E1
1 BLENHEIM CL
2 OUTRAM LA
3 HAYDOCK ST
4 CHATSWORTH CL
5 THORNWOOD CL
6 PENSHAW CL
7 HILL VIEW
8 GOODSHAW CL

121
101

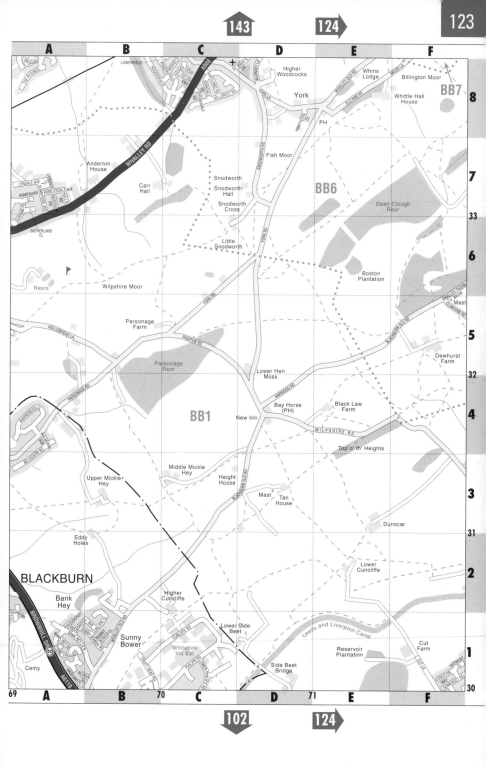

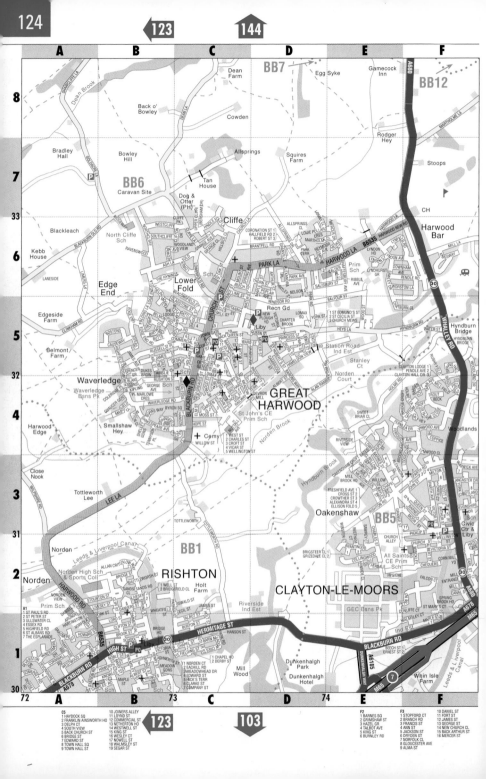

BB7

Dean Farm

Egg Syke

Gamecock Inn

BB12

A680

8

Back o' Bowley

Cowden

Rodger Hey

Stoops

CH

7

Bradley Hall

Bowley Hill

Allsprings

Squires Farm

P

BB6
Caravan Site

Tan House

Dog & Otter (PH)

Cliffe

Harwood Bar

Harwood Bar

33

Blackleach

North Cliffe Sch

Ravenswood

CLIFFE PK's

SOUTHCLIFFE

WOODLAND VIEW

Coronation St 1
Hallfield Rd 2
Robert St 3

Allsprings La

Louie Pullard Cres

Martholm

Park Terr

B6535

HARWOOD NEW RD

Prim Sch

MILL LA

Kebb House

Edge End

Lower Fold

Sch

PARK LA

HARWOOD LA

Lyndon Ho

Dowham Ave

Pendle Rd

Hyndburn Bridge

6

Laneside

Ash La

Park Ave

Nelson St

Salisbury Av

Ribble Av

Worston La

Hyndburn Bridge

Edgeside Farm

Britannia

Windsor Gd

Lomax Sq

York St

Heys La

St Edmund's 1
St Cecilia St 2
Church Mews 3

Pater Ho

5

Belmont Farm

Waverledge

Liby

New Plough

Charter Brook

Station Road Ind Est

Stanley Ct

Clayton Lodge 1
Pendle Ave 2
Clayton Hall Dr 3

Hyndburn Bridge

32

Waverledge Bsns Pk

GREAT HARWOOD

Norden Court

SWEET BRIAR CL

TROUT BECK

4

Harwood Edge

Smallshaw Hey

Byron St

MOSS ST

St John's CE Prim Sch

Norden Brook

Hyndburn Brook

RIVERSIDE VIEW

WOODLANDS

Woodlands

Coppice

3

Close Nook

Tottleworth Lee

LEE LA

Cmry

1 WEST ST
2 CHARLES ST
3 CROFT ST
4 VICAR ST
5 WELLINGTON ST

MILL HO

Freshfield Ave 1
Cross St 2
Crowther St 3
Alexandra St 4
Ellison Fold 5

Oakenshaw

BB5

Civic Ctr & Liby

31

Norden

Leeds & Liverpool Canal

BB1

TOTTLEWORTH

Brigsteer Cl 1
Grizedale Cl 2

All Saints CE Prim Sch

CHEQUERS

Wellington

2

Norden

HARWOOD RD

Norden High Sch & Sports Coll

NORDEN VIEW

RISHTON

Holt Farm

Riverside Ind Est

CLAYTON-LE-MOORS

GEC Bsns Pk

CORN MILL

A678

Prim Sch

A1
1 ST PAUL'S RD
2 ST PETER ST
3 ULLSWATER CL
4 ESSEX RD
5 HIGHFIELD RD
6 ST ALBANS RD
7 THE ESPLANADE

James St

Talbot St

HERMITAGE ST

Hanson St

Mill Wood

Duckenhalgh Park

Dunkenhalgh Hotel

M65

BLACKBURN RD

A6185

7

Whin Isle Farm

1

B6535

HIGH ST

P PO

30

1 WELL ST
2 BRIDGEFIELD CL

1 CHAPEL HO
2 DERBY ST

1 NORDEN CT
2 EACHILL RD
3 MEADOWHEAD DR
4 EDWARD ST
5 NICK'S TERR
6 CLARKE ST
7 COMPANY ST

Mill Wood

BLACKBURN RD

Leeds & Liverpool Canal

30

A678

72

A

73

B

C

74

D

E

F

C5
1 HAYDOCK SQ
2 FRANKLIN AINSWORTH HO
3 DELPH CT
4 SOUTH VIEW
5 BACK CHURCH ST
6 BRIDGE ST
7 EDWARD ST
8 TOWN HALL SQ
9 TOWN HALL ST

10 JOINERS ALLEY
11 LOYND ST
12 COMMERCIAL ST
13 NETHERTON HO
14 WESTWELL ST
15 KING ST
16 WESLEY CT
17 NOWELL ST
18 WALMSLEY ST
19 SEGAR ST

F2
1 BARNES SQ
2 GRIMSHAW ST
3 HAZEL GR
4 ANN ST
5 KING ST
6 BURNLEY RD

F3
1 STOPFORD CT
2 BRANCH RD
3 FRANCIS ST
4 MAY ST
5 JACKSON ST
6 DRYDEN ST
7 NORFOLK CL
8 GLOUCESTER AVE
9 ALMA ST

10 DANIEL ST
11 FORT ST
12 JAMES ST
13 GEORGE ST
14 NEW CHURCH CL
15 BACK ARTHUR ST
16 MERCER ST

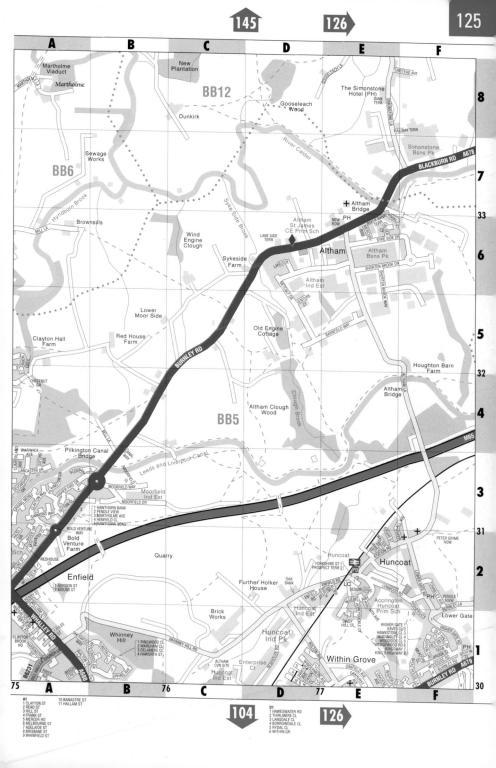

A1
1 CLAYTON ST
2 READ ST
3 HILL ST
4 FRANK ST
5 MERCER HO
6 MELBOURNE ST
7 ADELAIDE ST
8 BRISBANE ST
9 WHINFIELD ST

10 BANASTRE ST
11 HALLAM ST

D1
1 HAWESWATER RD
2 THIRLMERE CL
3 LANGDALE CL
4 BORROWDALE CL
5 RYDAL CL
6 WITHIN GR

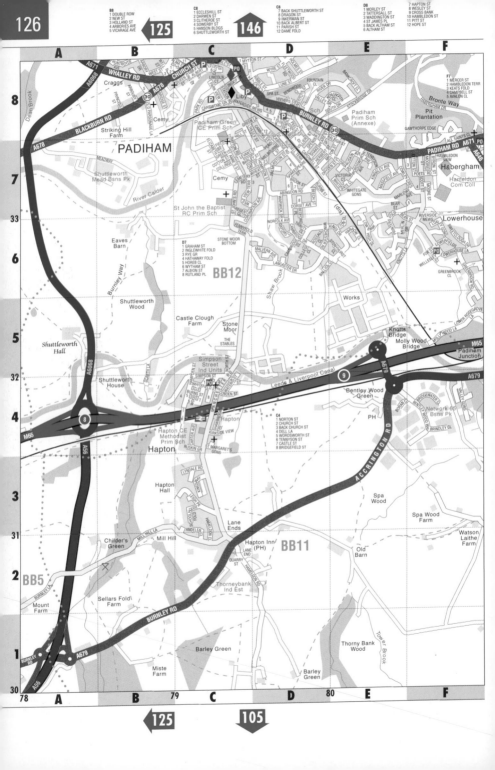

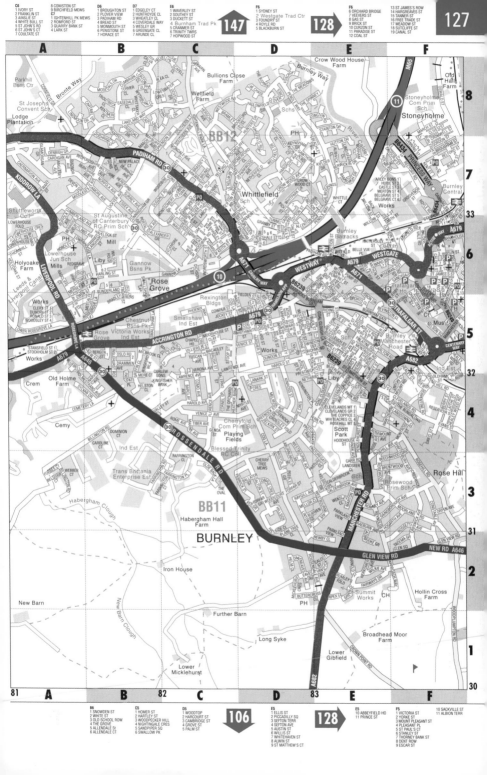

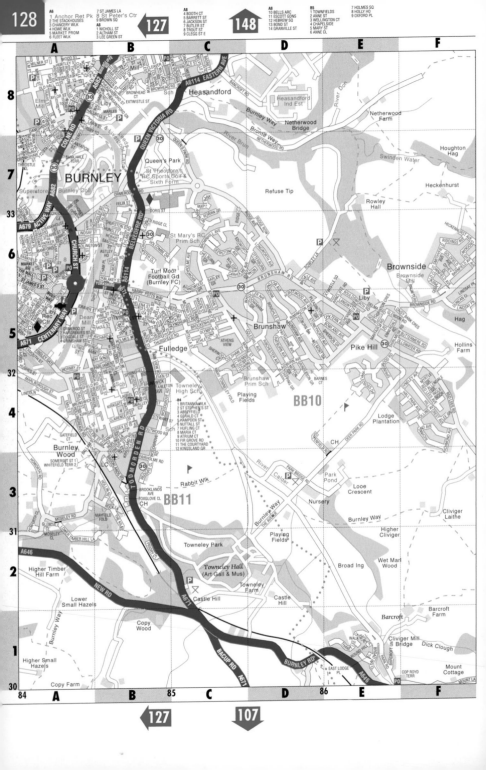

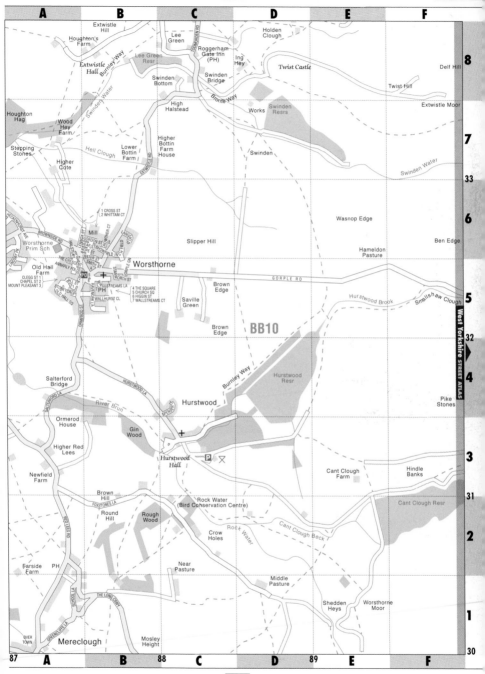

A B C D E F

8

Extwistle Hill
Houghton's Farm
Lee Green
Roggerham Gate Inn (PH)
Holden Clough
Delf Hill
Burnley Way
Lee Green Resr
Extwistle Hall
Swinden Bottom
Swinden Bridge
Ing Hey
Twist Castle
Twist Hill
Extwistle Moor

Bronte Way

7

Houghton Hag
Wood Hey Farm
High Halstead
Works
Swinden Resrs

Swinden Water

Stepping Stones
Hell Clough
Lower Bottin Farm
Higher Bottin Farm House
Swinden

Higher Cote

Swinden Water

33

6

1 CROSS ST
2 WHITTAM CT
Slipper Hill
Wasnop Edge
Ben Edge

Mill
GORDON ST
SMITH ST
LAWES ST
WATER ST
WHITEFIELD INN

Worsthorne Prim Sch
BROWNSIDE RD
HALSTEAD ST

THE CRESCENT
ANNABLY ROAD
Old Hall Farm
CLEGG ST 1
CHAPEL ST 2
MOUNT PLEASANT 3
PH
STONEYCROFT
OLD HALL SQ
PARK LANE
CHURCH ST
SWINDEN GN
WALLHURST CL
FELLSTREAMS LA
Worsthorne
Hameldon Pasture

GORPLE RD

5

4 THE SQUARE
5 CHURCH SQ
6 HIGGIN ST
7 WALLSTREAMS CT
Brown Edge
Saville Green
Hurstwood Brook
Smallshaw Clough

Brown Edge
BB10

32

Salterford Bridge
HURSTWOOD LA
Burnley Way
Hurstwood Resr

4

SALTERFORD LA
River Brun
Ormerod House
Hurstwood
Pike Stones

Higher Red Lees
Gin Wood

3

Newfield Farm
Hurstwood Hall
P
Cant Clough Farm
Hindle Banks

RED LEES RD
Brown Hill
FOXSTONES LA
Rock Water (Bird Conservation Centre)
Cant Clough Resr
31

Round Hill
Rough Wood
Rock Water
Cant Clough Beck

2

Crow Holes

Farside Farm
PH
Near Pasture

Middle Pasture
Shedden Heys
Worsthorne Moor

1

OVER TOWN
THE LONG CSWY
Mereclough
GREENS FIFE LA
VT WOODS
Mosley Height

30

87 A 88 B C 88 C D 89 E F

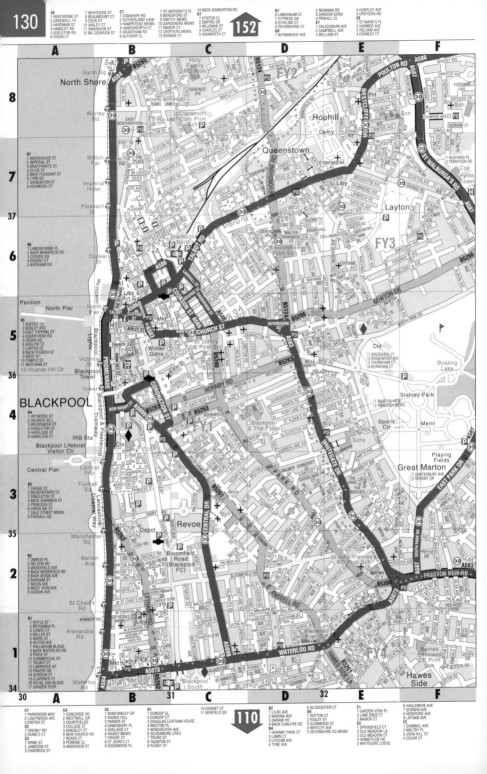

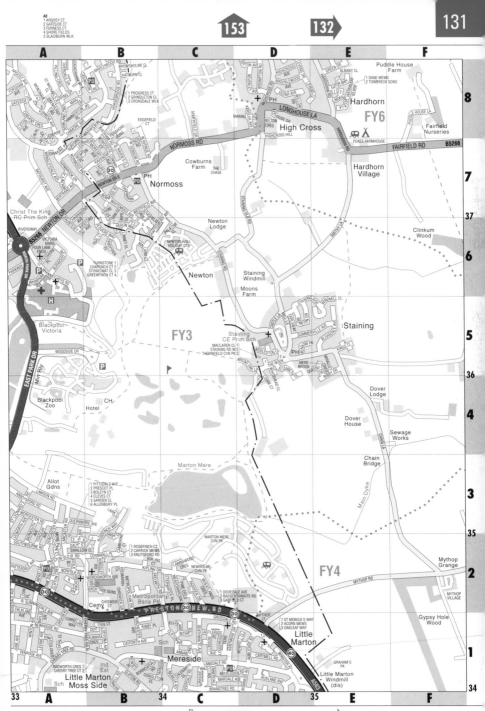

153 132

111 132

A8
1 ARGOSY CT
2 GATESIDE CT
3 FURNESS CT
4 SHORE FIELDS
5 SLAIDBURN WLK

Hardhorn
FY6
Puddle House
Farm
1 DANE MEWS
2 TOWBRECK GDNS
Fairfield
Nurseries
High Cross
FOXES FARMHOUSE
LONGHOUSE LA
NORMOSS RD
FAIRFIELD RD
B5266
Hardhorn
Village
Cowburns
Farm
THE
CHASE
Normoss
PH
PO
Christ The King
RC Prim Sch
37
Clinkum
Wood
RIVERSWAY
Victoria
Mans
FOUR LANE
ENDS
Newton
Lodge
B5266
Staining
Windmill
Moons
Farm
Newton Hall
Holiday Ctr
Newton
Staining
6
TURNSTONE 1
CHAFFINCH CT 2
STONECRAFT CL 3
GREENFINCH CT 4
H
Blackpool
Victoria
FY3
Staining
CE Prim Sch
MACLAREN CL 1
STAINING RD W 2
THORNFIELD CVN PK 3
PH
5
WOODSIDE DR
Mere
Brook
EAST PARK DR
Blackpool
Zoo
CH
Hotel
Dover
Lodge
36
Dover
House
Sewage
Works
Marton Mere
Chain
Bridge
4
Allot
Gdns
1 PITTSDALE AVE
2 PRESCOT PL
3 BOLEYN CT
4 CLEVES CT
5 GARDEN PL
6 ALLENBURY PL
Main Dyke
3
35
Marton Mere
CVN PK
1 ROSEFINCH CT
2 CARRICK MEWS
3 KNUTSFORD RD
Newholme
CVN PK
FY4
Mythop
Grange
2
Sch
Cemy
Metropolitan
Bsns Pk
Ind
Est
1 DOVEDALE AVE
2 BASSENTHWAITE RD
3 GARFIELD CT
Mythop
Village
PRESTON NEW RD
1 ST MONICA'S WAY
2 ACORN MEWS
3 OAKLEAF WAY
Gypsy Hole
Wood
1
GRAHAM'S
PK
Mereside
Sch
Ind
Est
Little
Marton
Little Marton
Little Marton
Windmill
(dis)
34
Moss Side

C1
1 LANGDALE PL
2 CRUMMOCK PL

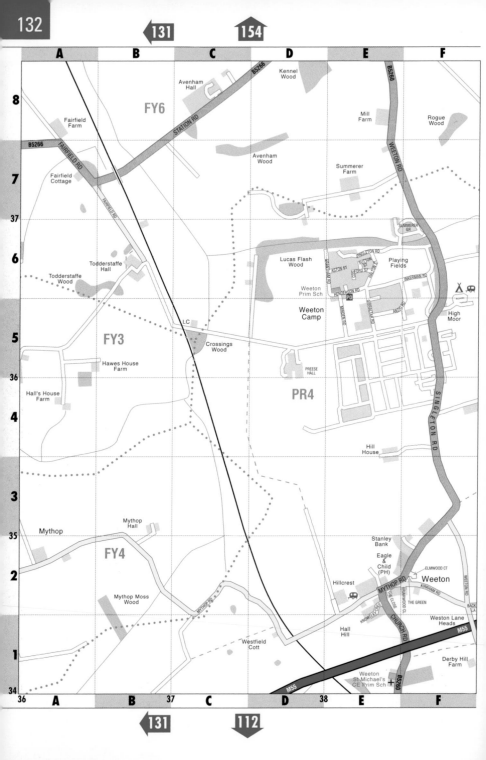

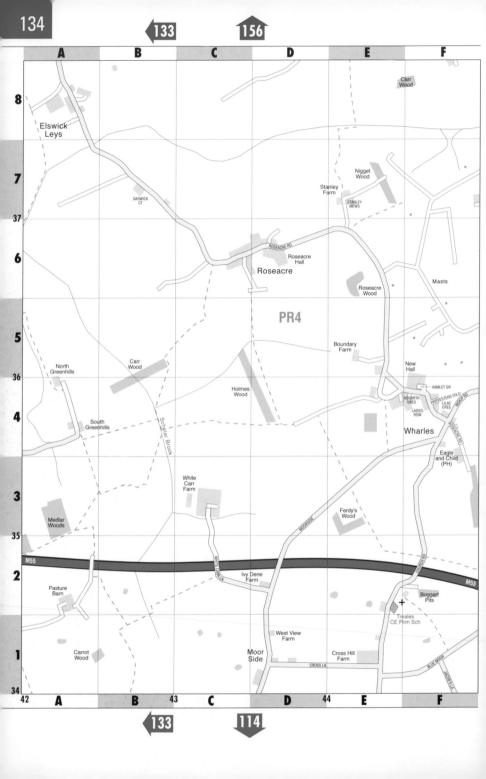

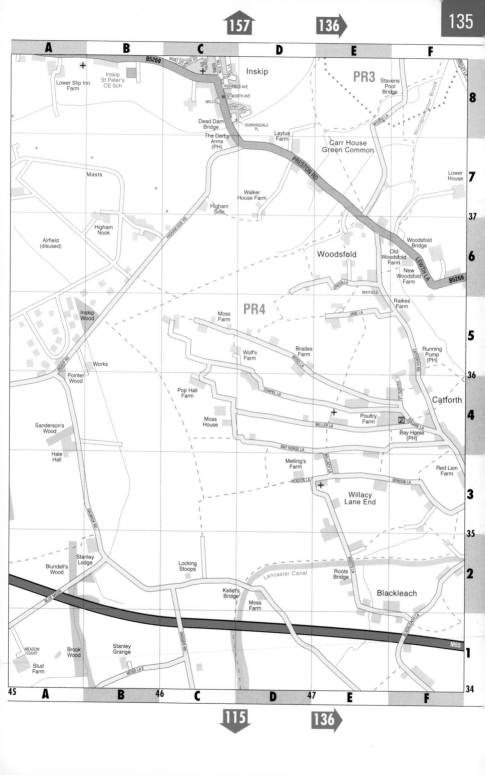

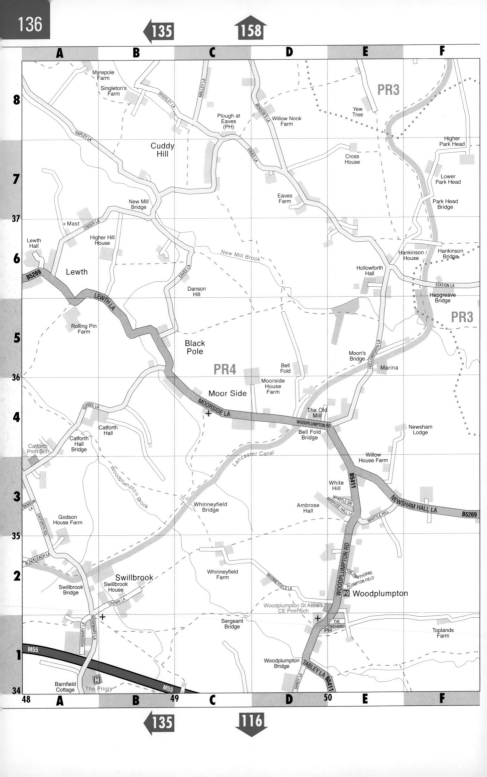

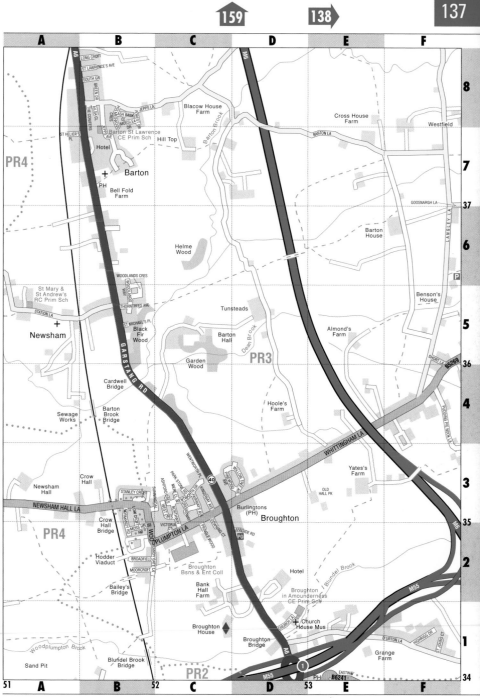

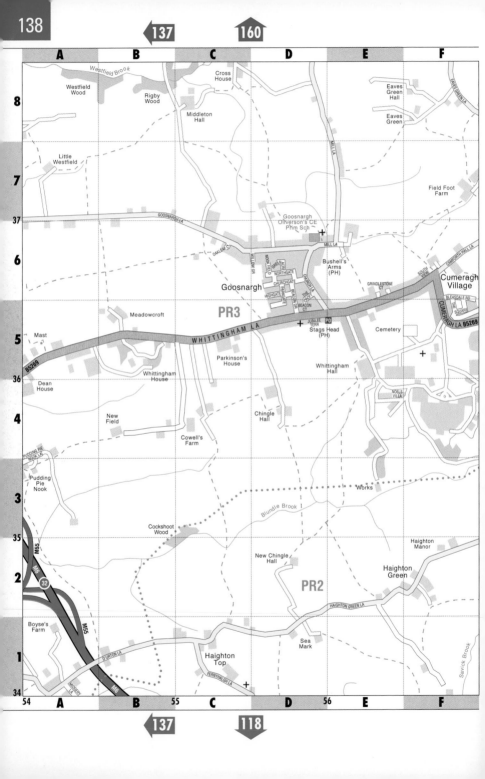

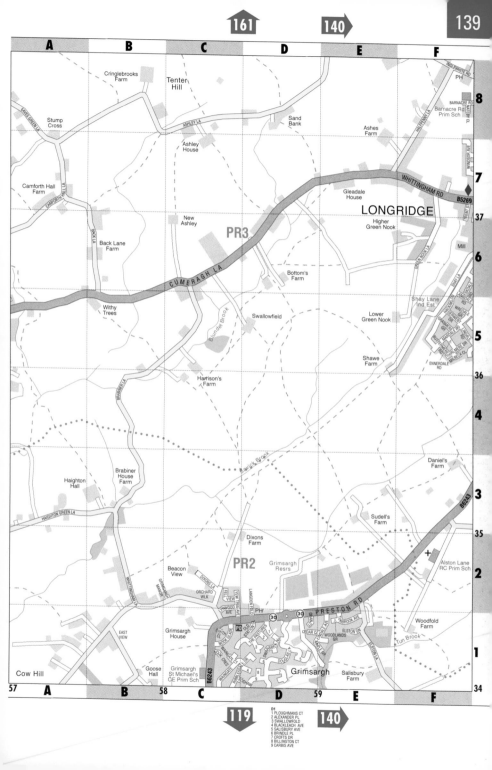

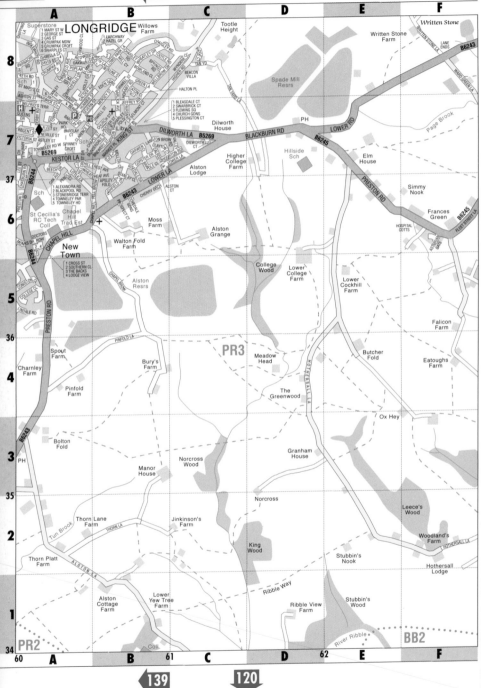

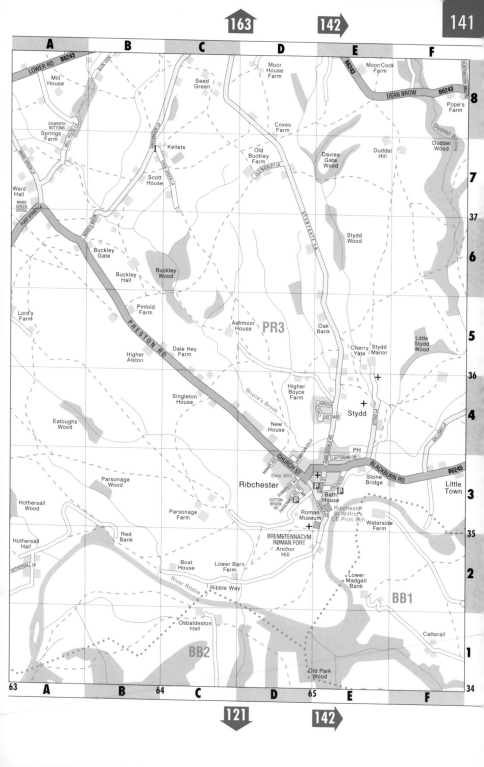

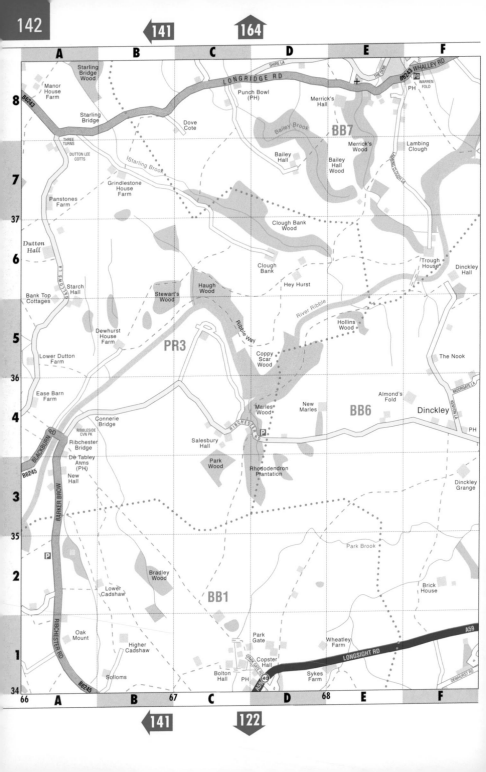

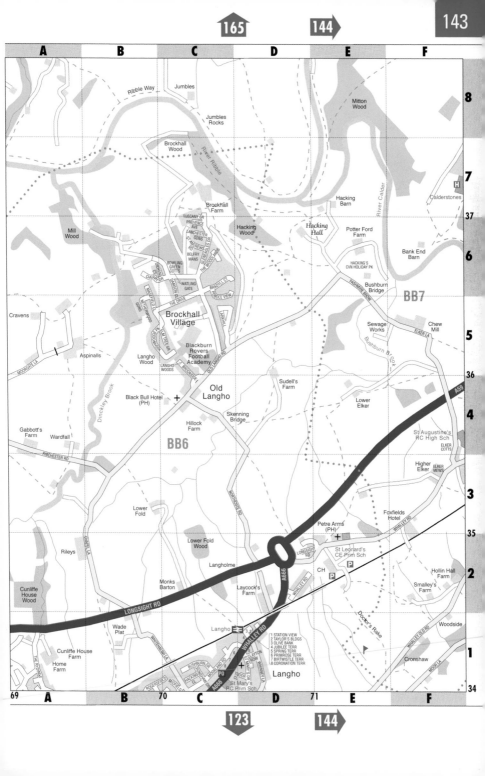

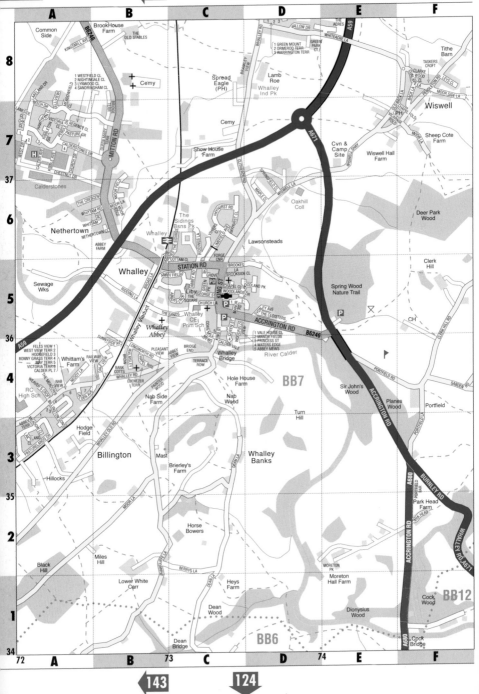

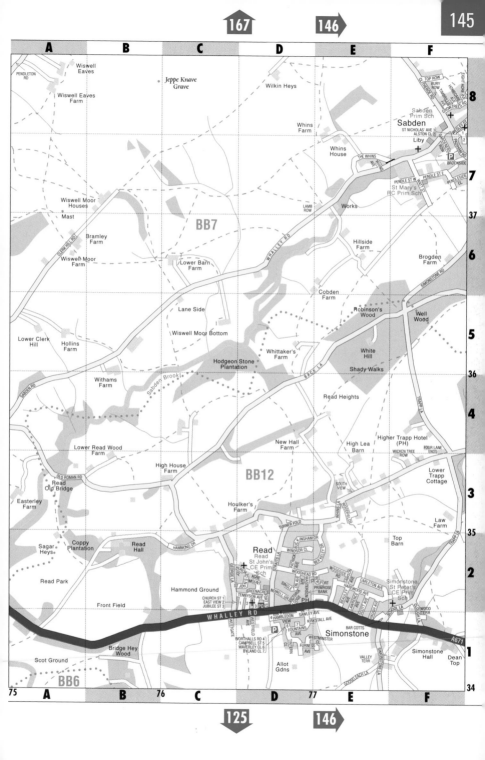

167
146
125
146

A B C D E F

8 7 37 6 5 36 4 3 35 2 1 34

PENDLETON RD

Wiswell Eaves

Wiswell Eaves Farm

Jeppe Knave Grave

Wilkin Heys

Whins Farm

TOP ROW
BURY ROW

Sabden Prim Sch

Sabden

ST NICHOLAS' AVE
ALSTON CL

Liby

Whins House

THE WHINS

BROODNSIDE

PENDLE ST W
PENDLE ST E

St Mary's RC Prim Sch

PENTLESIDE CL

Wiswell Moor Houses

Mast

BB7

Works

LAMB ROW

Bramley Farm

CLERK HILL RD

Wiswell Moor Farm

Lower Barn Farm

WHALLEY RD

Hillside Farm

Brogden Farm

SIMONSTONE RD

Lane Side

Cobden Farm

Robinson's Wood

Well Wood

Lower Clerk Hill

Hollins Farm

Wiswell Moor Bottom

Whittaker's Farm

BECK LA

White Hill

Shady Walks

Hodgeon Stone Plantation

Sabden Brook

Withams Farm

SABDEN RD

Read Heights

Lower Read Wood Farm

New Hall Farm

High Lea Barn

Higher Trapp Hotel (PH)

WICKEN TREE ROW

FOUR LANE ENDS

TRAPP LA

OLD ROMAN RD

High House Farm

BB12

SOUTH VIEW

Lower Trapp Cottage

Read Old Bridge

Easterley Farm

Houlker's Farm

TURNER FOLD

WHINS LA

Law Farm

Sagar Heys

Coppy Plantation

Read Hall

HAMMOND DR

Read St John's CE Prim Sch

INGHAM DR

WINDSOR CL

WOODHEAD RD

Top Barn

TRAPP LA

Read Park

Hammond Ground

Read

PH

Simonstone St Peter's CE Prim Sch

SCHOOL LA

WOOD TERR

Front Field

WHALLEY RD

Simonstone

BAR COTTS

A671

Bridge Hey Wood

Allot Gdns

VALLEY TERR

Simonstone Hall

Dean Top

Scot Ground

BB6

75 A B 76 C D 77 E F

145 168

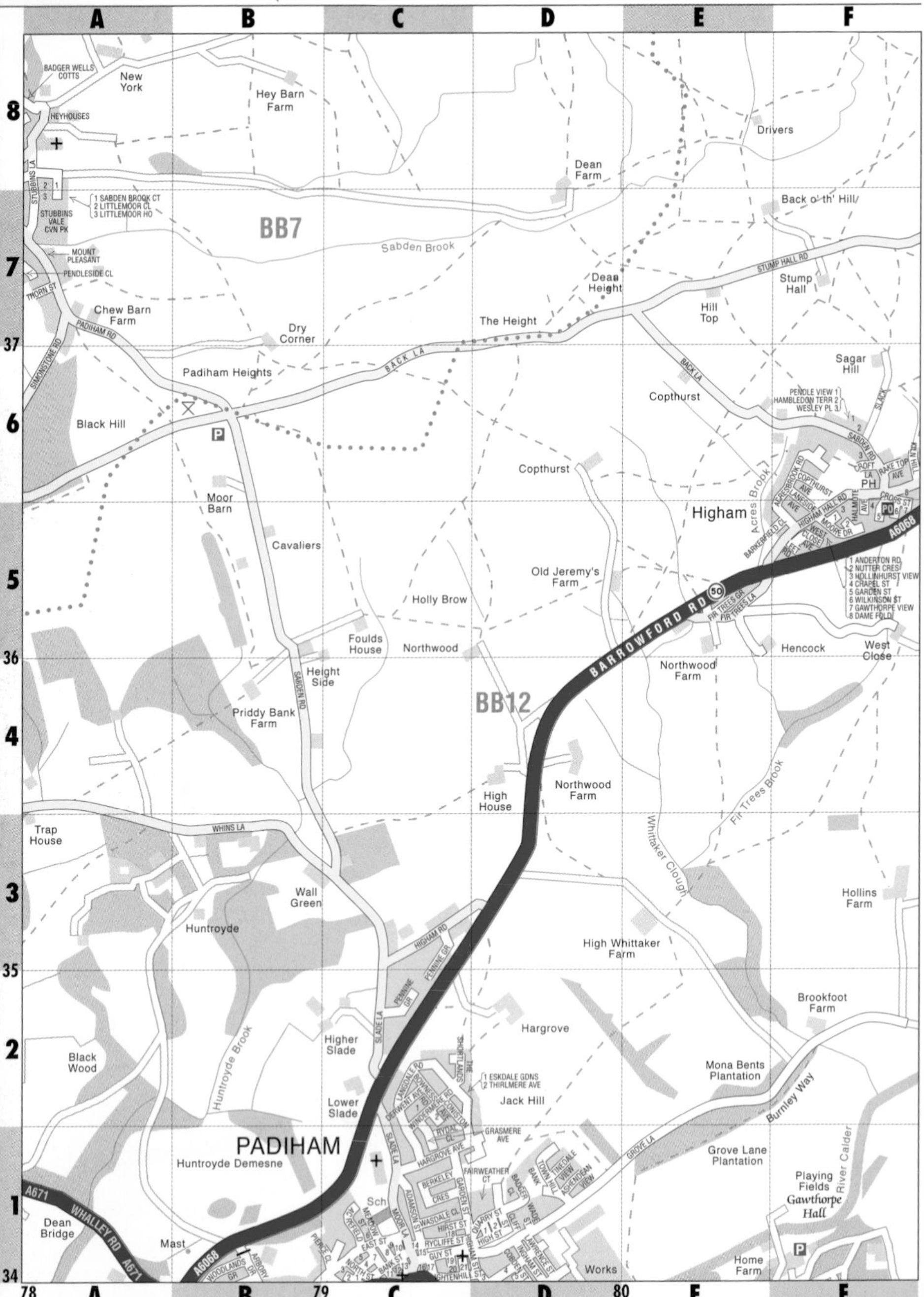

A B C D E F

8

BADGER WELLS COTTS
New York
HEYHOUSES
Hey Barn Farm
Dean Farm
Drivers

1 SABDEN BROOK CT
2 LITTLEMOOR CL
3 LITTLEMOOR RD

Back o' th' Hill

BB7

7

MOUNT PLEASANT
PENDLESIDE CL
Chew Barn Farm
Sabden Brook
Dean Height
Stump Hall
STUMP HALL RD

37

Dry Corner
The Height
Hill Top
Sagar Hill

Padiham Heights
BACK LA

PENDLE VIEW 1
HAMBLEDEN TERR 2
WESLEY PL 3

6

Black Hill
Copthurst

Copthurst

Higham

PH

Moor Barn
Copthurst
1 ANDERTON RD
2 NUTTER CRES
3 CRADEL ST
4 GARDEN ST
5 WILKINSON ST
6 GAWTHORPE VIEW
8 DAME FOLD

5

Cavaliers
Old Jeremy's Farm
Holly Brow
BARROWFORD RD

West Close

36

Foulds House
Northwood
Northwood Farm
Hencock

Height Side

BB12

4

Priddy Bank Farm
Northwood Farm
High House

3

Trap House
WHINS LA
Wall Green
Huntroyde
High Whittaker Farm
Hollins Farm

35

Brookfoot Farm

2

Black Wood
Higher Slade
Hargrove
Mona Bents Plantation
Lower Slade
Jack Hill

1 ESKDALE GDNS
2 THIRLMERE AVE

GRASMERE AVE
FAIRWEATHER CT
Burnley Way

1

A671
WHALLEY RD A671
PADIHAM
Huntroyde Demesne
Sch
Grove Lane Plantation
Playing Fields
Gawthorpe Hall

Dean Bridge
Mast
A6068
Works
Home Farm

34

78 A B 79 C D 80 E F

145 126

C1
1 THE MEWS
2 CHAPEL WLK
3 SPRING GARDENS TERR
4 HALL HILL ST
5 CROSSHILLS
6 ST GILES TERR
7 ST GILES ST
8 ST LEONARD'S ST
9 CLAYBANK FOLD

10 CLAYBANK
11 HAVELOCK ST
12 CHURCH ST
13 GAWTHORPE ST
14 BARBON ST
15 JOHN O' GAUNT ST
16 CENTRAL BLDGS
17 FACTORY LA
18 COPTHURST ST
19 HABERGHAM ST

C1
20 VICTORIA APARTMENTS
21 CLITHEROE ST

D1
1 KAY ST
2 DEAN ST
3 CHIPPING ST
4 PARTRIDGE HILL
5 PARTRIDGE HILL ST

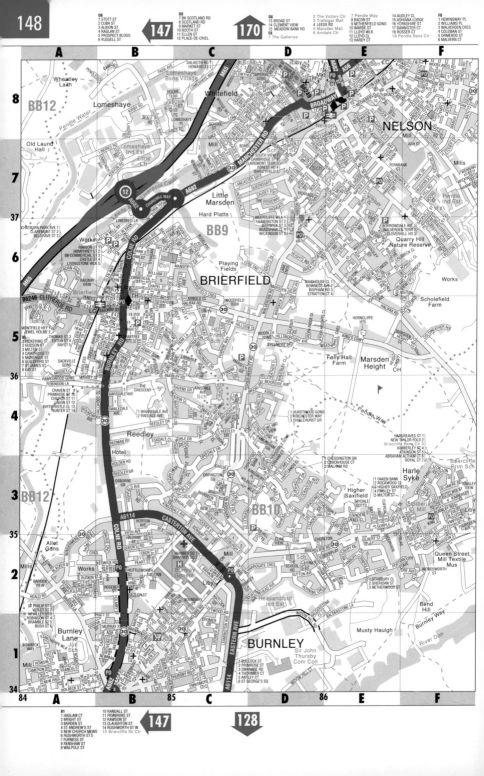

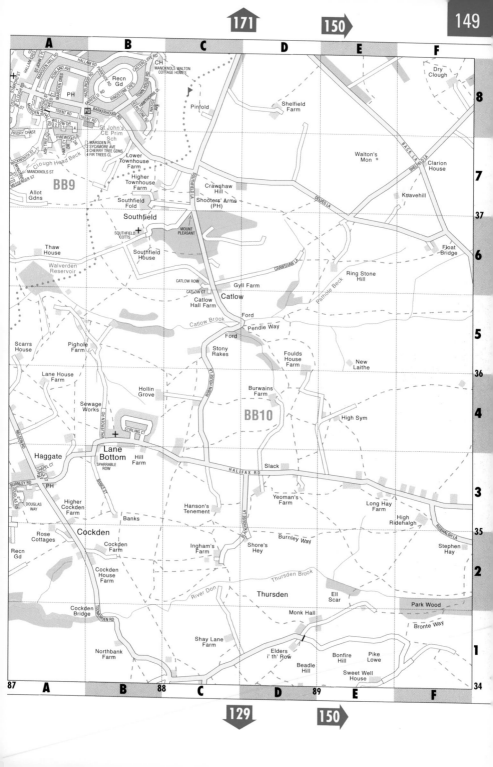

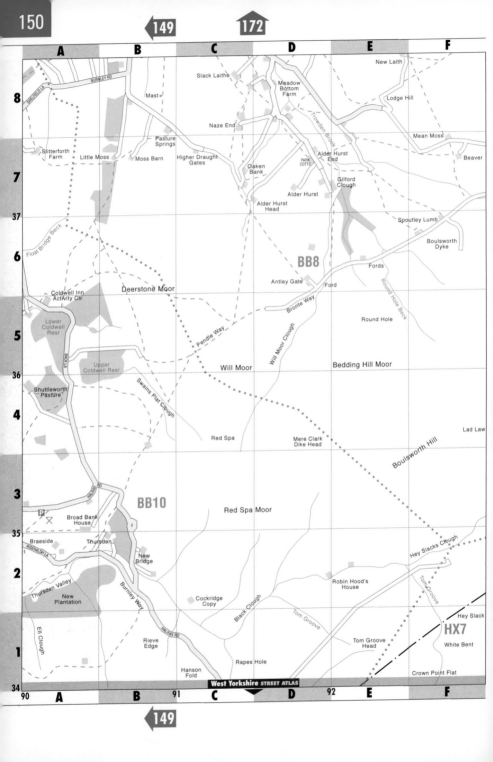

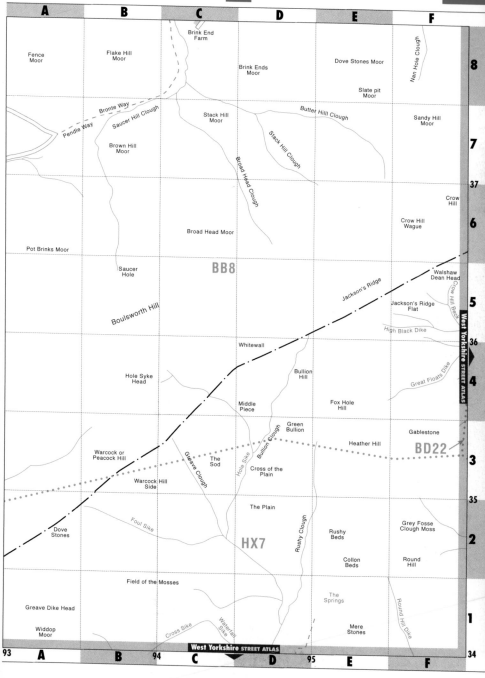

A B C D E F

8

Fence Moor

Flake Hill Moor

Brink End Farm

Brink Ends Moor

Dove Stones Moor

Nan Hole Clough

Slate pit Moor

Bronte Way

Saucer Hill Clough

Pendle Way

Stack Hill Moor

Butter Hilll Clough

Sandy Hill Moor

7

Brown Hill Moor

Stack Hill Clough

Broad Head Clough

37

Crow Hill

Pot Brinks Moor

Broad Head Moor

Crow Hill Wague

6

Saucer Hole

BB8

Walshaw Dean Head

5

Boulsworth Hill

Jackson's Ridge

Jackson's Ridge Flat

Crow Hill Back

West Yorkshire STREET ATLAS

High Black Dike

36

Whitewall

Hole Syke Head

Bullion Hill

Great Floats Dike

4

Middle Piece

Fox Hole Hill

Green Bullion

Gablestone

BD22

Warcock or Peacock Hill

Greave Clough

The Sod

Hole Sike

Bullion Clough

Cross of the Plain

Heather Hill

3

Warcock Hill Side

35

Foul Sike

The Plain

Rushy Clough

Dove Stones

Rushy Beds

Grey Fosse Clough Moss

2

HX7

Collon Beds

Round Hill

Field of the Mosses

Round Hill Dike

Greave Dike Head

The Springs

1

Widdop Moor

Cross Sike

Waterfall Sike

Mere Stones

93 A B 94 C D 95 E F 34

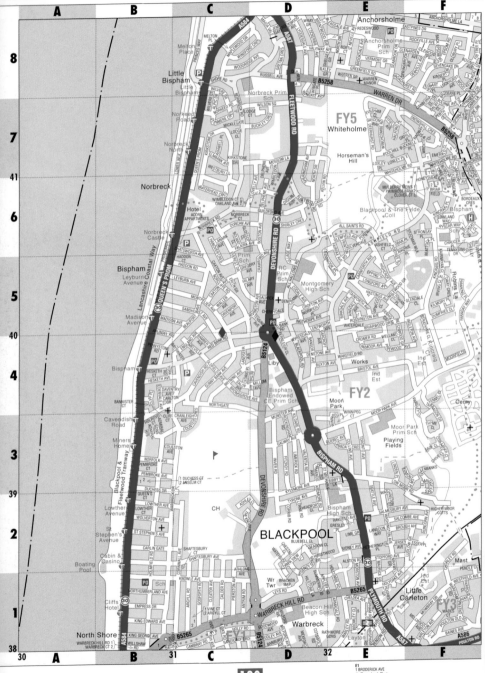

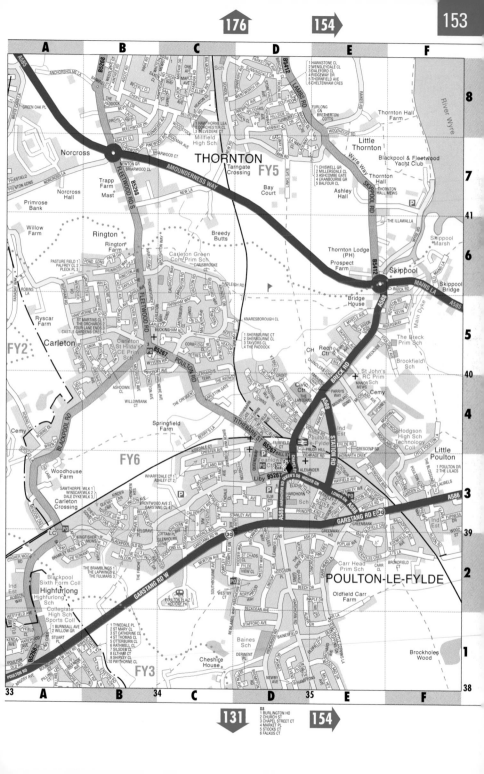

A B C D E F

8

Bank Farm
SHARD LA
A588
Primrose Hill
The Parks
Mill Farm
Bank Wood
Great Toulbrick Farm
Rose Farm
BULL PARK LA
MILL LA
GRANGE RD
Holm Nook
Tarn Brook
Bank House
Shard Riverside Inn
PR3
7

Point Shard
SHARD BRIDGE LA
Rawcliffe Lodge
BOON LA
Shard Bridge
SHARD RD

41

Moors Farm
Shard Bridge Farm
6

Liscoe Farm
A585
A586
Mains Hall
River Wyre
WINDY HARBOUR HOLIDAY CTR
5

FY6
40

Carr Wood
MAINS LA
40
Greenways Nursery
Bankfield Farm
Bankfield Manor
RIVERSIDE CHALET PK
POOL FOOT LA
A585
4

Little Singleton
KEEPERS DR
HOME FARM
Pool Foot Farm House
GARSTANG RD
A586
B5260
FIVE LANE ENDS
GARSTANG NEW RD
3

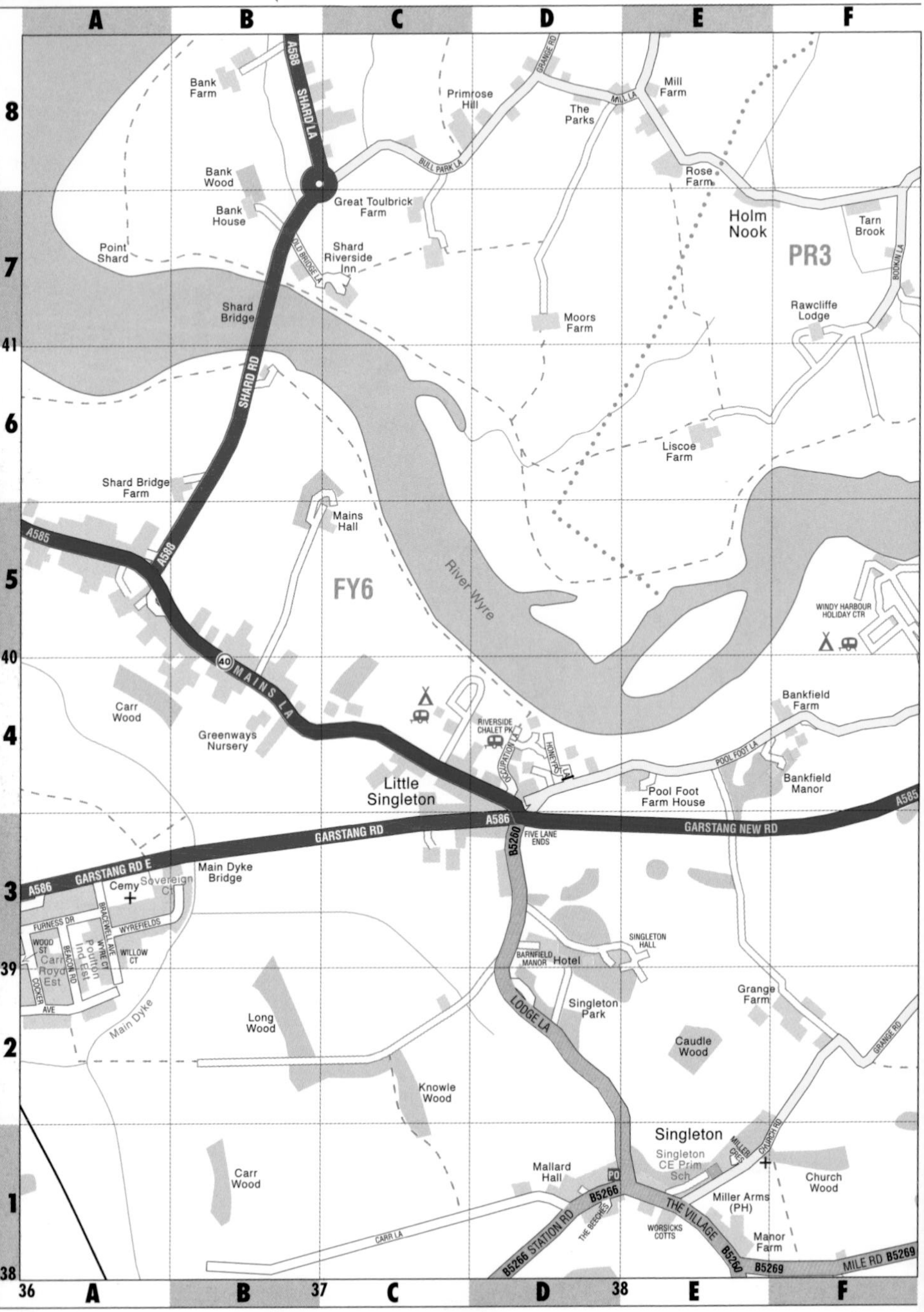

GARSTANG RD E
A586
Cemy
Sovereign Cl
Main Dyke Bridge
SINGLETON HALL
FURNESS DR
BLACK ABBEY LA
WYREFIELDS
WOOD ST
Poulton Ind Est
WILLOW CT
BARNFIELD MANOR Hotel
39

Carr Royd Est
BRACKEN RD
DOCKER
AVE
Main Dyke
Long Wood
Singleton Park
LODGE LA
Grange Farm
GRANGE RD
2

Knowle Wood
Caudle Wood
Singleton
Singleton CE Prim Sch
MILLER LA
CHURCH RD
1

Carr Wood
Mallard Hall
PO
THE BRIDGE
B5266
Miller Arms (PH)
THE VILLAGE
WORBICKS COTTS
Church Wood
Manor Farm
38

B5266 STATION RD
CARR LA
B5266
B5260
MILE RD
B5269
B5269

36 A B 37 C D 38 E F

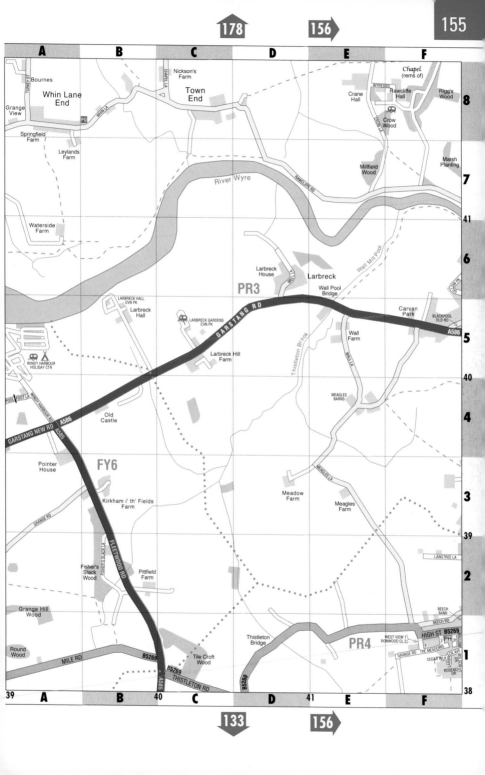

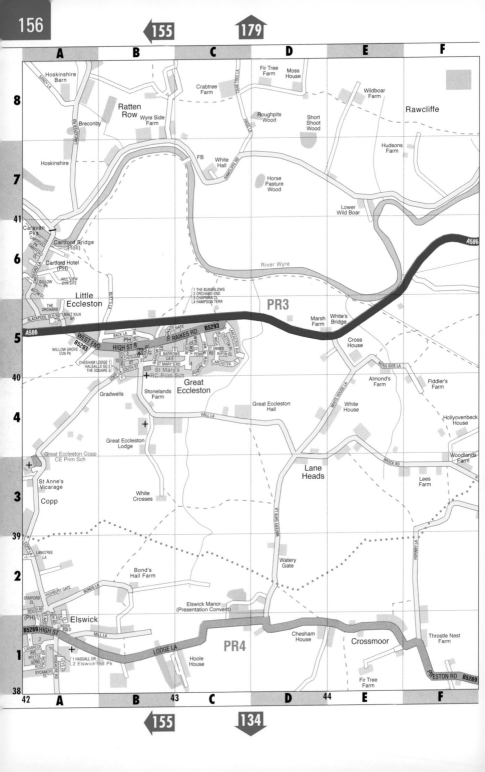

A   B   C   D   E   F

8

Hoskinshire
Barn

Breconby

Ratten
Row

Wyre Side
Farm

Crabtree
Farm

Fir Tree
Farm

Moss
House

Wildboar
Farm

Rawcliffe

7

Hoskinshire

White
Hall

FB

Roughpits
Wood

Short
Shoot
Wood

Horse
Pasture
Wood

Lower
Wild Boar

Hudsons
Farm

41

Caravan Pk

Cartford Bridge
(Toll)

6

Cartford Hotel
(PH)

Little
Eccleston

THE
ORCHARD

MALT KILN
GR

BLACKPOOL OLD RD

1 THE BUNGALOWS
2 ORCHARD END
3 CHAPMAN CL
4 HAMPSON TERR

PR3

River Wyre

A586

Marsh
Farm

White's
Bridge

5

A586   B5293

WEST END

B5293

WILLOW GROVE
CVN PK

HIGH ST

RAIKES RD

BACK LA

PH

B5293

BARROWS
LA E

ST ANNES
RD

PENNY

LANCASTER RD

RIPON CL

LANCASTER LA

Cross
House

40

CHESHAM LODGE 1
HALSALLS SQ 2
THE SQUARE 3

St Mary's
RC Prim Sch

Great
Eccleston

Stonelands
Farm

Almond's
Farm

Fiddler's
Farm

MOSS SIDE LA

Gradwells

Hall La

Great Eccleston
Hall

White
House

WHITE HOUSE LA

Hollyovenbeck
House

4

Great Eccleston
Lodge

Great Eccleston Copp
CE Prim Sch

Lane
Heads

BROCK RD

Lees
Farm

Woodlands
Farm

3

St Anne's
Vicarage

Copp

White
Crosses

WATERY GATE LA

HORNBY LA

39

LANGTREE LA

COPP LA

Bond's
Hall Farm

Watery
Gate

2

STAFFORD
CL

HIGHBURY GATE

BONDS LA

Elswick Manor
(Presentation Convent)

BEECH RD

(PH)

Elswick

LINDEN
FOLD

MILL LA

LODGE LA

PR4

Chesham
House

Crossmoor

Throstle Nest
Farm

1

B5269 HIGH ST

1 HASSALL DR
2 Elswick Ind Pk

Hoole
House

Fir Tree
Farm

PRESTON RD   B5269

LARBRECK
AVE
BRIERIE
GDNS
ROSE
SYCAMORE CL

38

42   A   B   43   C   D   44   E   F

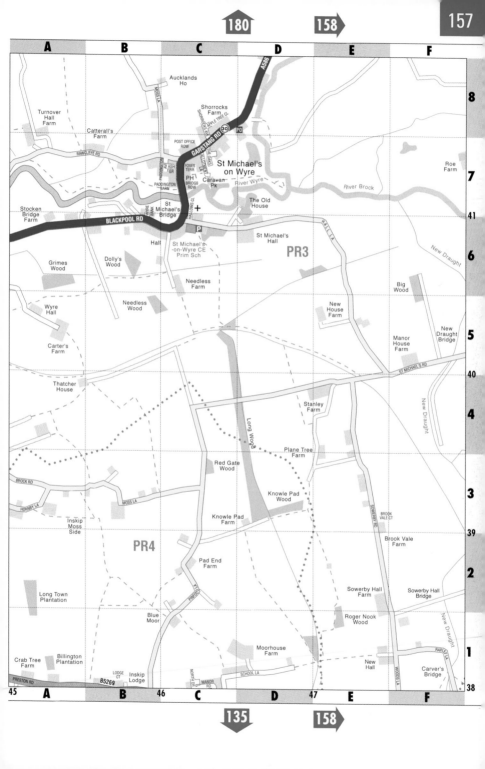

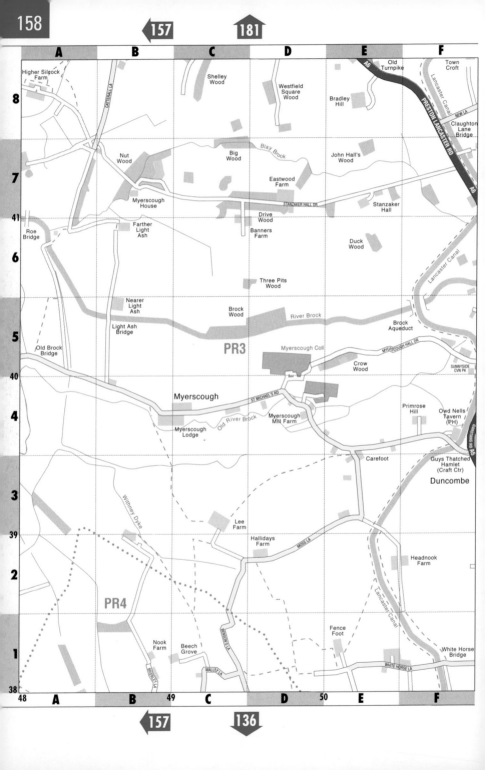

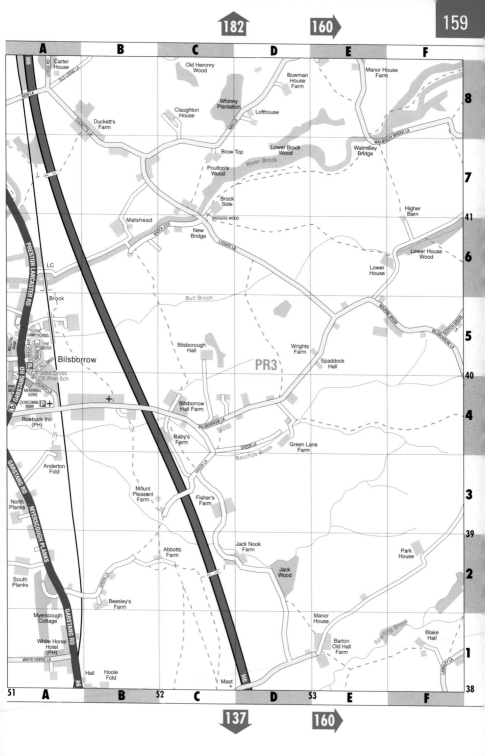

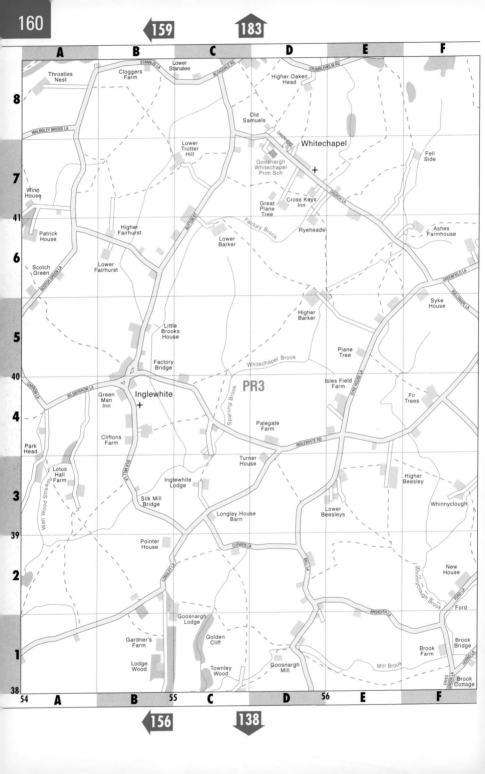

159
183

A **B** **C** **D** **E** **F**

Throstles
Nest

Cloggers
Farm

STANALEE LA

Lower
Stanalee

BLEASDALE RD

CRUMBLEHOLM RD

Higher Oaken
Head

8

WALMSLEY BRIDGE LA

Old
Samuels

OAKENHEAD

Whitechapel

Fell
Side

Lower
Trotter
Hill

Goosnargh
Whitechapel
Prim Sch

7

Wine
House

CHURCH LA

41

Patrick
House

Higher
Fairhurst

BILSBORROW LA

Great
Plane
Tree

Cross Keys
Inn

Factory Brook

Ryeheads

Ashes
Farmhouse

6

Scotch
Green

SCOTCH GREEN LA

Lower
Fairhurst

Lower
Barker

GREENFIELD LA

5

Little
Brooks
House

Higher
Barker

Plane
Tree

BLEASDALE LA

Syke
House

40

Factory
Bridge

Whitechapel Brook

Isles Field
Farm

Fir
Trees

4

CARDERS LA

BILSBORROW LA

Green
Man
Inn

Inglewhite

Sparling Brook

PR3

Palegate
Farm

STYE SHORE LA

INGLEWHITE RD

Park
Head

Cliftons
Farm

SILK MILL LA

Turner
House

Higher
Beesley

3

Well Wood Stream

Lotus
Hall
Farm

Inglewhite
Lodge

Silk Mill
Bridge

Longley House
Barn

Lower
Beesleys

Whinnyclough

39

Pointer
House

LONGLEY LA

CURWEN LA

MILL LA

Whinnyclough Brook

New
House

FORD LA

2

Goosnargh
Lodge

BROADITH LA

Ford

1

Gardner's
Farm

Golden
Cliff

Goosnargh
Mill

Mill Brook

Brook
Farm

Brook
Bridge

Brook
Cottage

Lodge
Wood

Townley
Wood

EAVES GREEN LA

FORD LA

38

54 **A** **B** **55** **C** **D** **56** **E** **F**

156
138

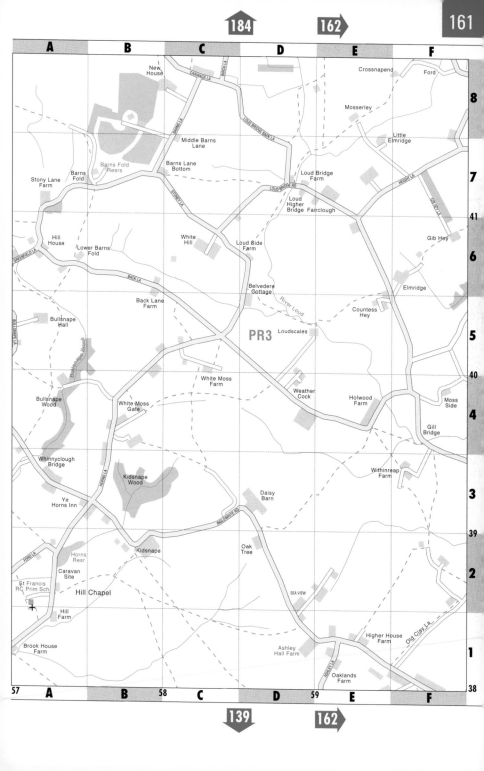

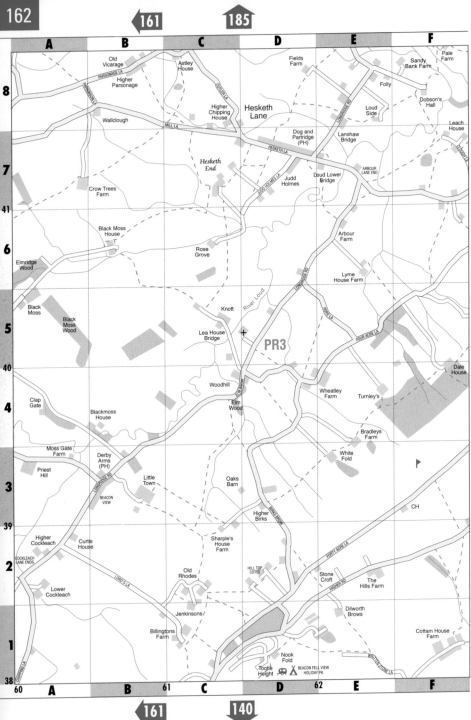

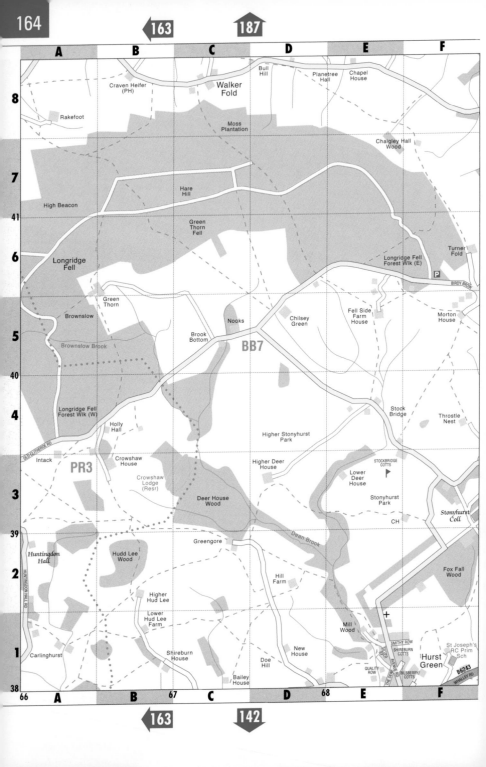

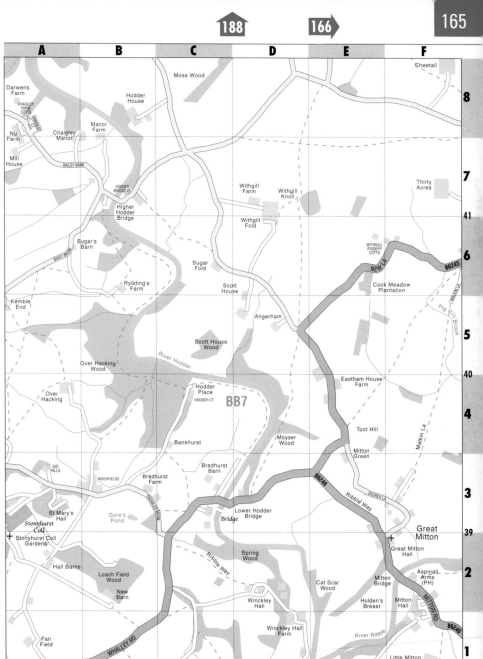

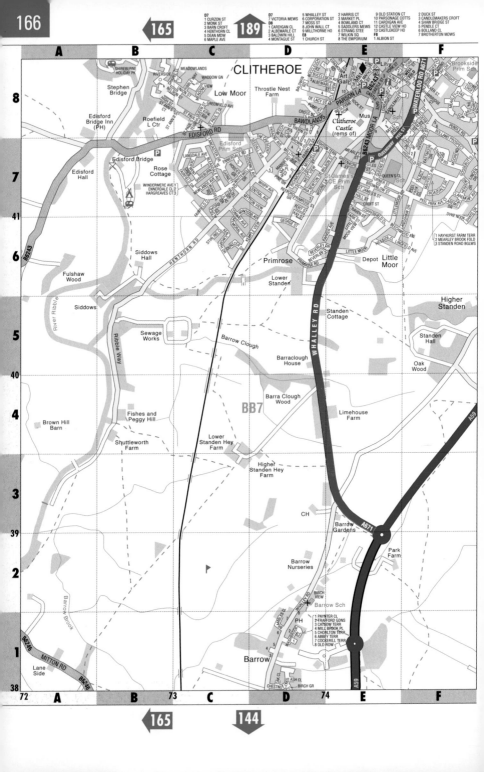

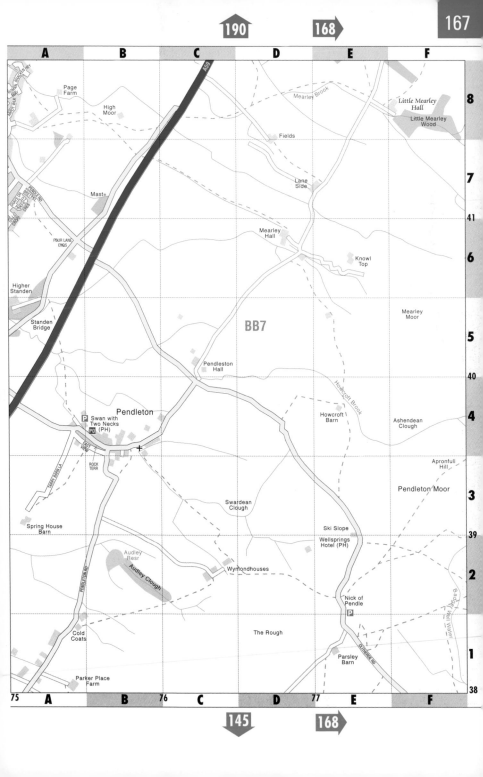

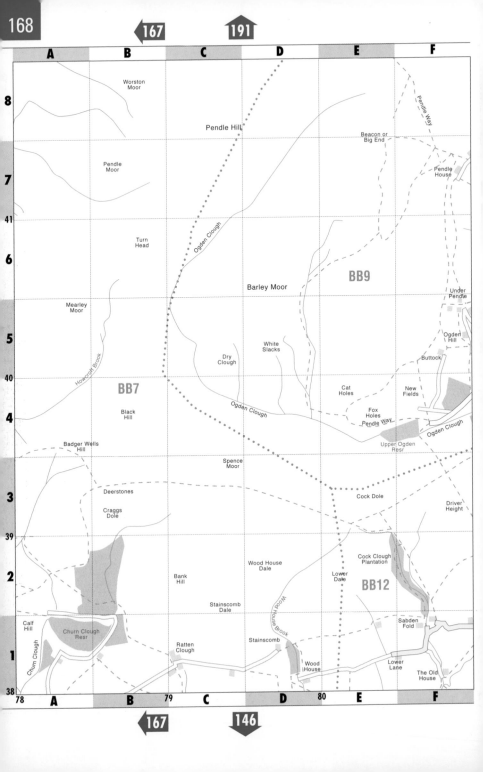

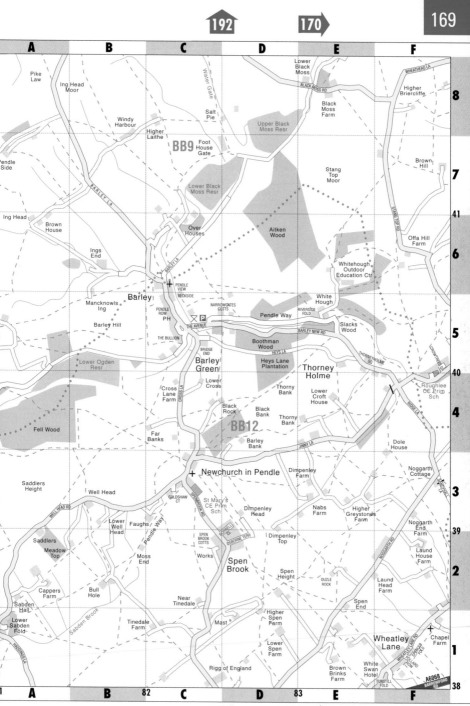

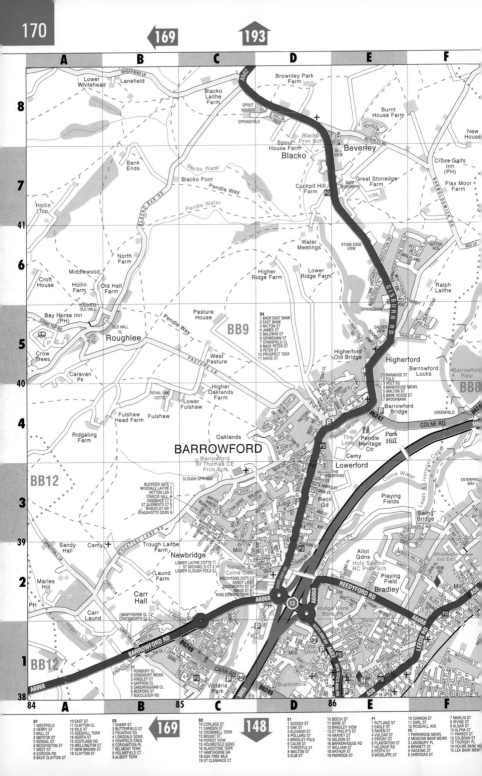

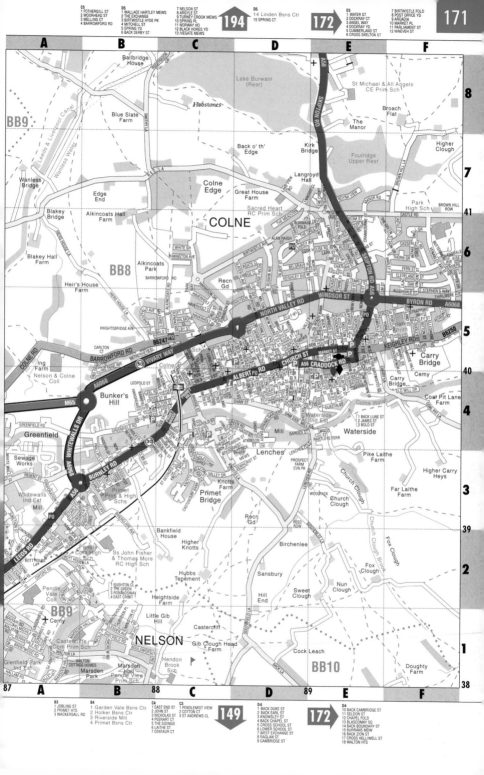

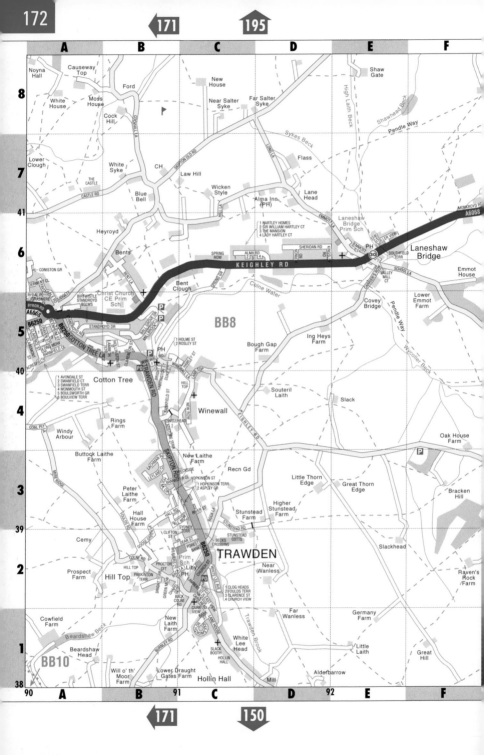

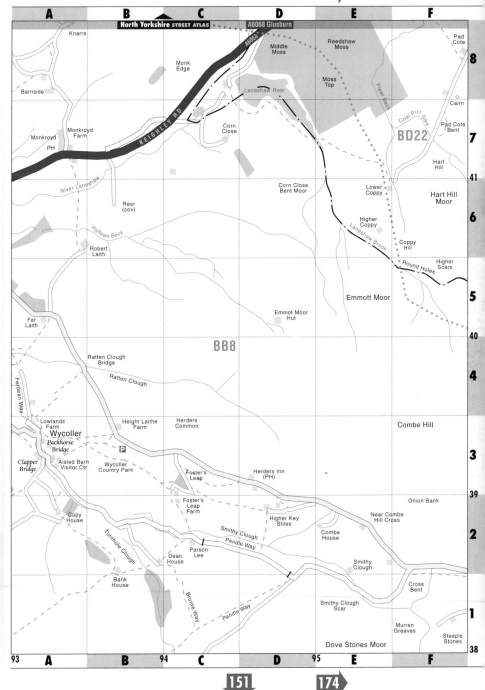

North Yorkshire STREET ATLAS

A6068 Glusburn

A | B | C | D | E | F

8

Knarrs

Barnside

Monk Edge

Middle Moss

Reedshaw Moss

Pad Cote

Moss Top

Cairn

7

Monkroyd
PH

Monkroyd Farm

KEIGHLEY RD

A6068

Corn Close

Laneshaw Resr

Coal Pit Site

Pad Cote Bent

BD22

Hart Hill

41

River Laneshaw

Resr (cov)

Corn Close Bent Moor

Lower Coppy

Hart Hill Moor

6

Hullown Beck

Robert Laith

Higher Coppy

Laneshaw Brook

Coppy Hill

Higher Scars

5

Far Laith

Emmot Moor Hut

Emmott Moor

Round Holes

40

Ferndean Way

BB8

Ratten Clough Bridge

Ratten Clough

4

Lowlands Farm

Wycoller

Packhorse Bridge

Height Laithe Farm

Herders Common

Combe Hill

3

Clapper Bridge

Aisled Barn Visitor Ctr

P

Wycoller Country Park

Foster's Leap

Herders Inn (PH)

39

Copy House

Turnhole Clough

Foster's Leap Farm

Higher Key Stiles

Onion Bank

Near Combe Hill Cross

2

Dean House

Parson Lee

Smithy Clough

Pendle Way

Combe House

Smithy Clough

Cross Bent

Bank House

Brontë Way

Pendle Way

Smithy Clough Scar

Murren Greaves

Steeple Stones

1

38

Dove Stones Moor

93 | A | B | 94 | C | D | 95 | E | F

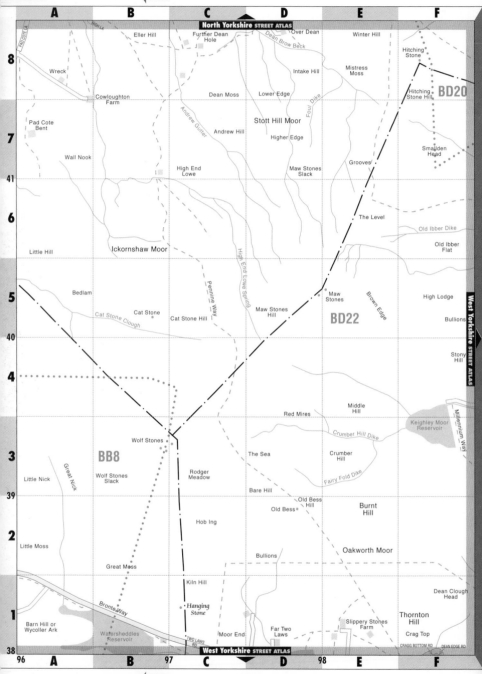

BD20

BD22

BB8

West Yorkshire STREET ATLAS

8

7

41

6

5

40

4

3

39

2

38

A   B   C   D   E   F

96   A   B   97   C   D   E   98   F

Eller Hill
Further Dean Hole
Over Dean
Winter Hill
Hitching Stone
Wreck
Dean Brow Beck
Intake Hill
Mistress Moss
Cowloughton Farm
Dean Moss
Lower Edge
Foul Dike
Hitching Stone Hill
Pad Cote Bent
Stott Hill Moor
Andrew Gutter
Andrew Hill
Higher Edge
Grooves
Smallden Head
Wall Nook
High End Lowe
Maw Stones Slack
The Level
Old Ibber Dike
Little Hill
Ickornshaw Moor
High End Lowe Spring
Old Ibber Flat
Bedlam
Pennine Way
Maw Stones Hill
Maw Stones
Brown Edge
High Lodge
Cat Stone Clough
Cat Stone
Cat Stone Hill
Bullions
Stony Hill
Red Mires
Middle Hill
Keighley Moor Reservoir
Millennium Way
Wolf Stones
Crumber Hill Dike
Crumber Hill
Little Nick
Great Nick
Wolf Stones Slack
The Sea
Fairy Fold Dike
Rodger Meadow
Bare Hill
Old Bess Hill
Burnt Hill
Little Moss
Old Bess
Hob Ing
Oakworth Moor
Great Moss
Bullions
Kiln Hill
Dean Clough Head
Bronte Way
Hanging Stone
Thornton Hill
Barn Hill or Wycoller Ark
Watersheddles Reservoir
Moor End
Far Two Laws
Slippery Stones Farm
Crag Top
Two Laws Rd
CRAGG BOTTOM RD
DEAN EDGE RD

198
176

FLEETWOOD

FY7

Broadwater

Cardinal Allen
RC High
Sch

Playing
Field

Blackpool
& The Fylde Coll
(Nautical)

Larkholme
Prim Sch

Rossall

Rossall
Sq

Caravan
Pk

Camping
Site

Rifle Range

Farmer Parr'
Animal World
(Mus)

Rossall
Sch

Rossall
Sch

ROSSALL LA

B5409

Wyre Way

Fleetwood
Farm

BLUEBELL CL 1
BLACKTHORN CL 2
ELDERBERRY CL 3
CALENDINE CL 4
SPEEDWELL CL 5
KESTREL CL 6

Woodcock
Wood

Westbourne
Rd
Rossall
Beach

Rossall
Beach

Haven
Sch

Northfold
Com Prim
Sch

Westmorland
Ave
Wks

FY5

Jubilee
Gdns

Thornton
Gate

Thornton Cleveleys
Manor Beach
Prim Sch

Beach
Rd

CLEVELEYS

Cleveleys

St Andrew's

Ocean View
Apartments

Grosvenor Ct

B5412

VICTORIA RD

Lauderdale
Ave

St Teresa's
RC Prim Sch

VICTORIA RD W

B5412

Supermarket

Anchorsholme

Anchorsholme

152
176

D2
1 ORION BLDGS
2 SANDRINGHAM LODGE

F4
1 REDWING AVE
2 CURLEW CL
3 WHITECREST AVE
4 BARNFIELD CL
5 CORNWALL MEWS
6 COLCHESTER DR
7 PORTSMOUTH CL

F1
1 TUDOR CL
2 SHERWOOD PL
3 RICHARDS WAY
4 POCHARD PL
5 INGLENOOK CL
6 BUNTING PL
7 SANDPIPER PL
8 THROSTLE WAY
9 REDSTART PL

10 KITTIWAKE CL
11 MOORHEN PL
12 THORNCROSS

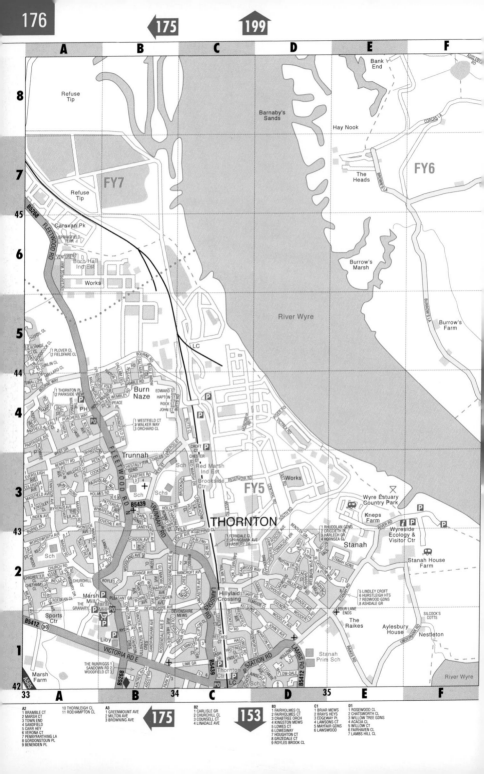

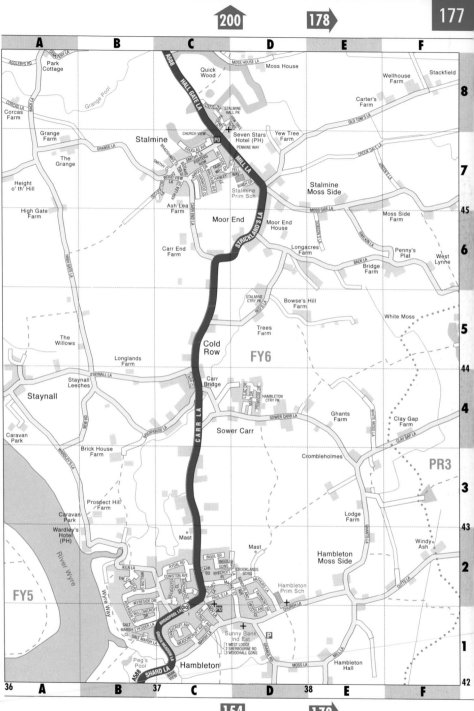

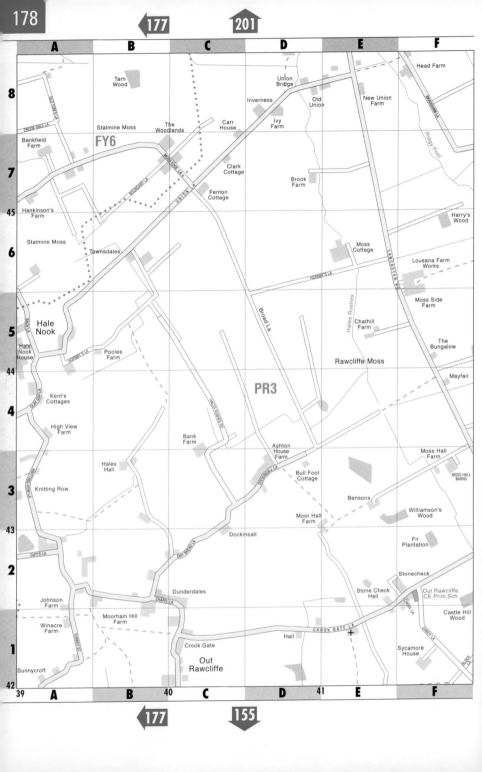

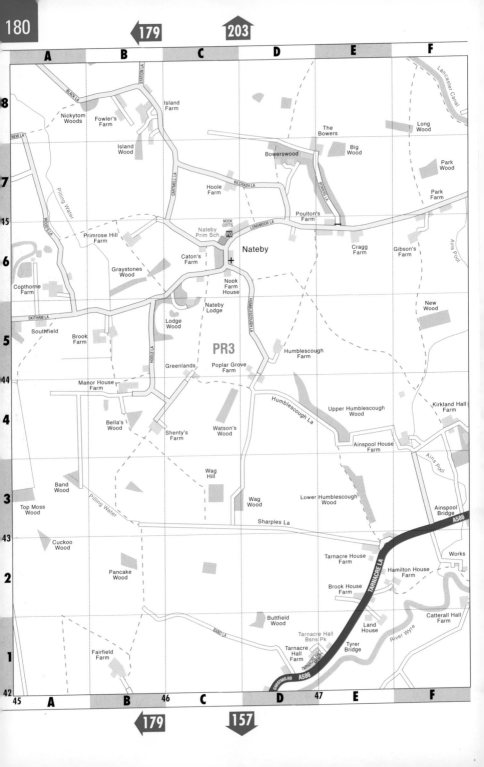

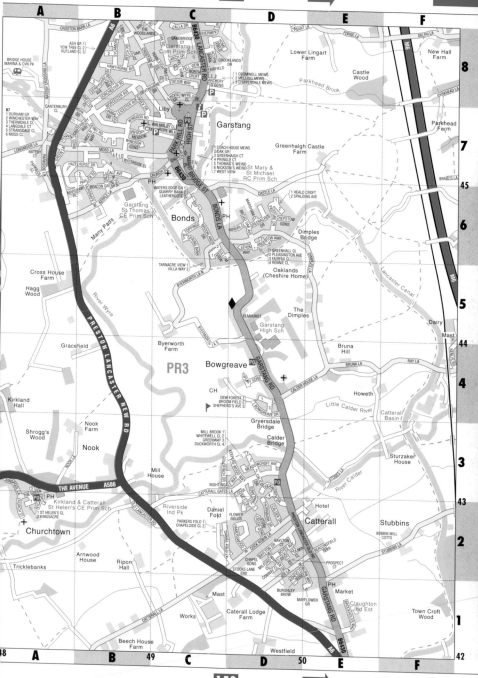

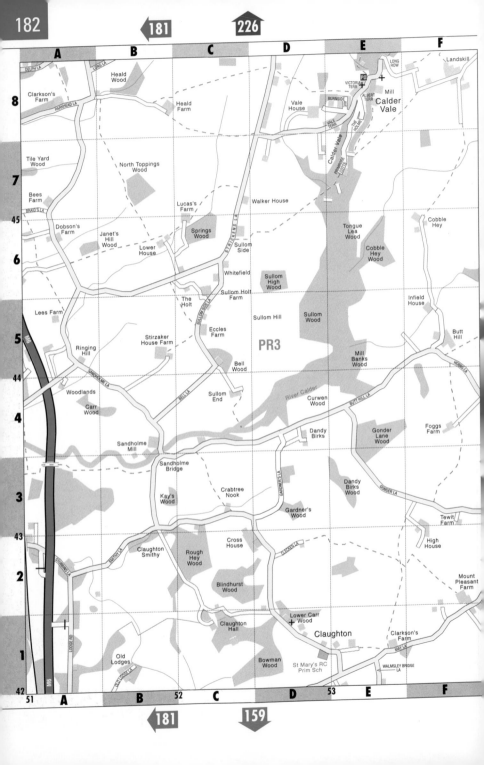

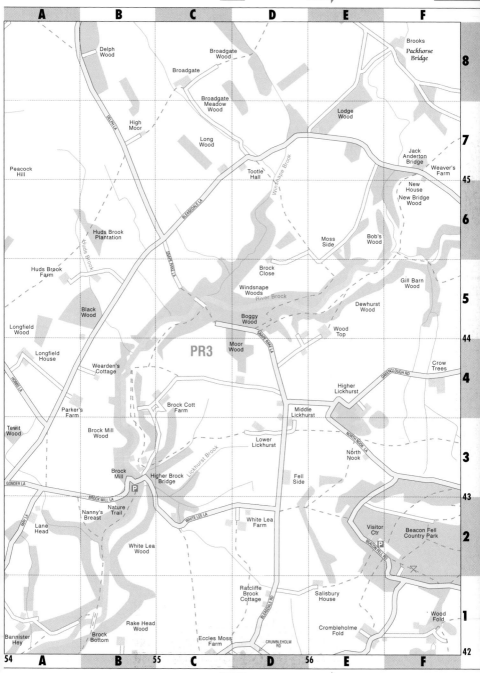

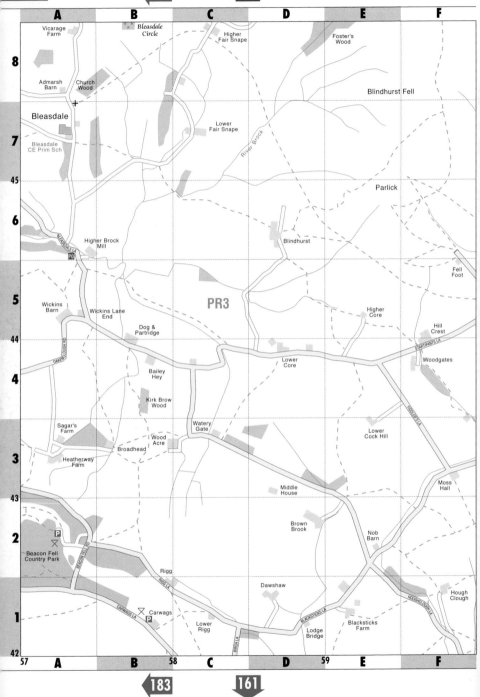

A B C D E F

8

Vicarage
Farm

Bleasdale
Circle

Higher
Fair Snape

Foster's
Wood

Admarsh
Barn

Church
Wood

Blindhurst Fell

Bleasdale

7

Lower
Fair Snape

River Brock

Bleasdale
CE Prim Sch

45

Parlick

6

Higher Brock
Mill

Blindhurst

Fell
Foot

5

Wickins
Barn

Wickins Lane
End

PR3

Higher
Core

Hill
Crest

44

Dog &
Partridge

STARTIFANTS LA

Woodgates

OAKEN CLOUGH RD

4

Bailey
Hey

Lower
Core

FOSTER'S LA

Kirk Brow
Wood

Watery
Gate

3

Sagar's
Farm

Wood
Acre

Broadhead

Lower
Cock Hill

Heatherway
Farm

Moss
Hall

43

Middle
House

2

Beacon Fell
Country Park

Brown
Brook

Nob
Barn

BEACON FELL RD

Rigg

RIGG LA

Dawshaw

HOUGHSLOUGH LA

Hough
Clough

1

Carwags

CARWAGS LA

Lower
Rigg

BIRCH LA

BLACKSTICKS LA

Lodge
Bridge

Blacksticks
Farm

42

57 A B 58 C D 59 E F

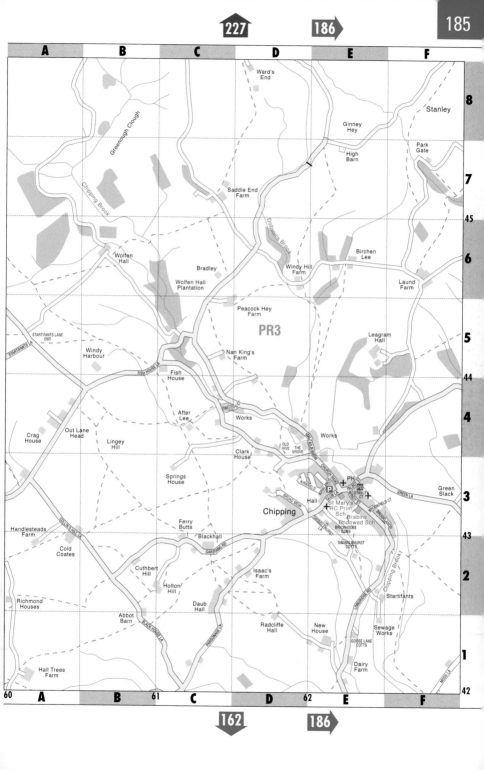

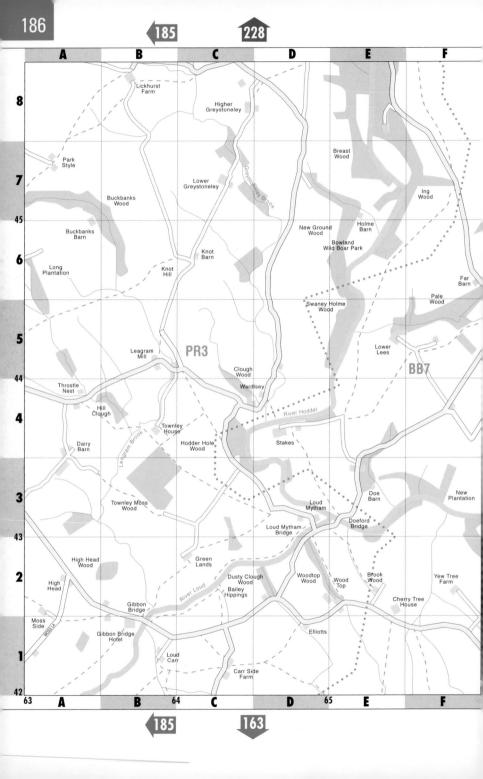

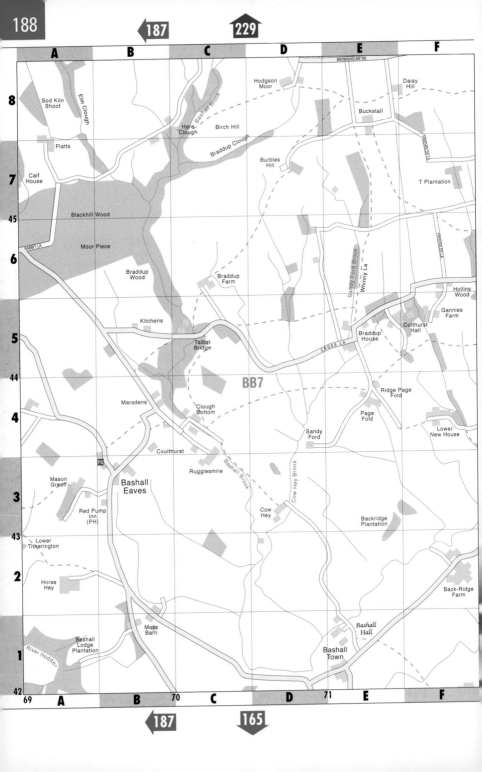

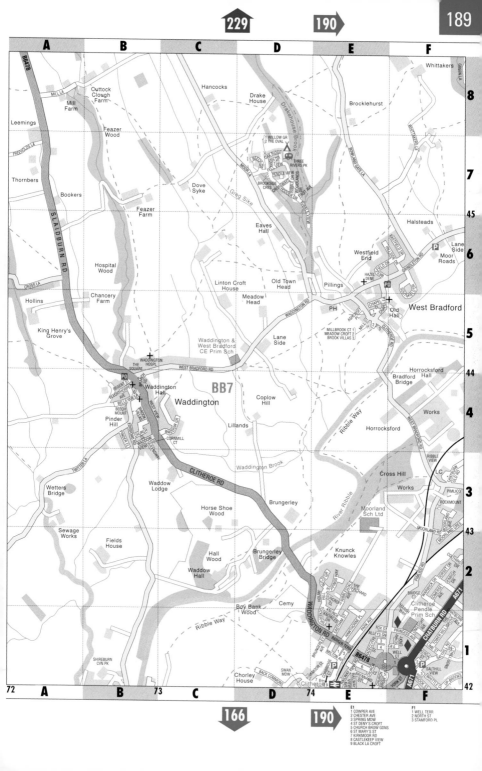

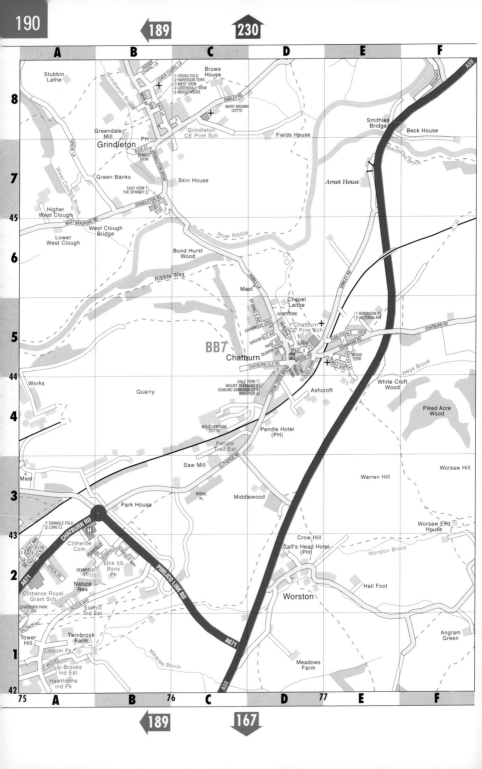

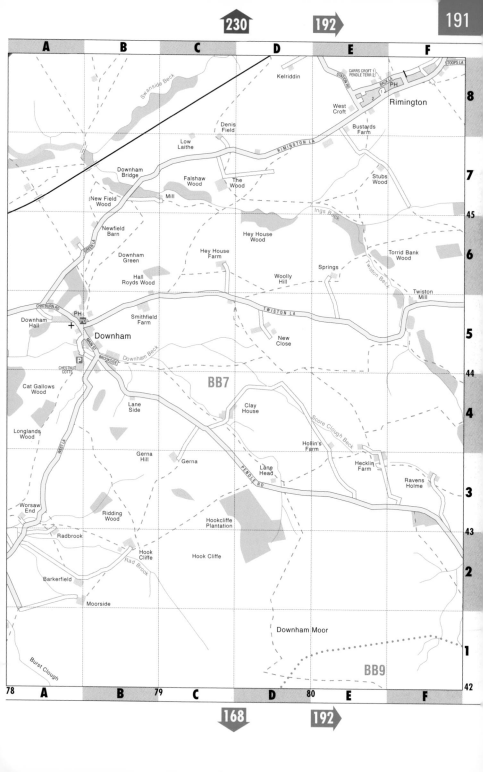

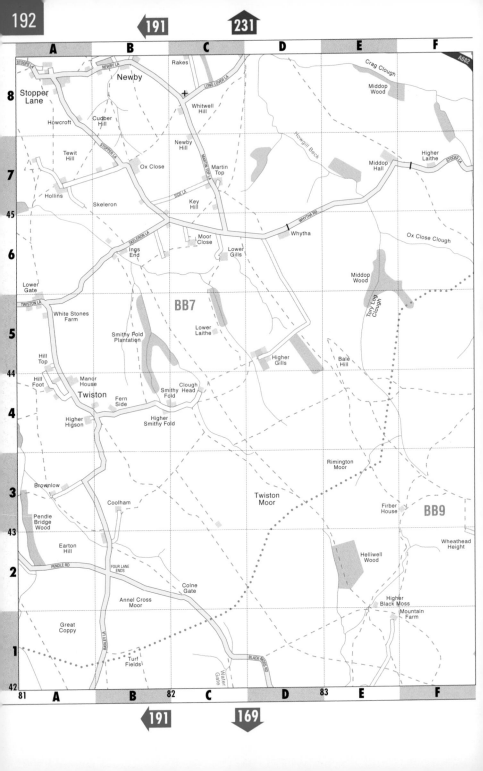

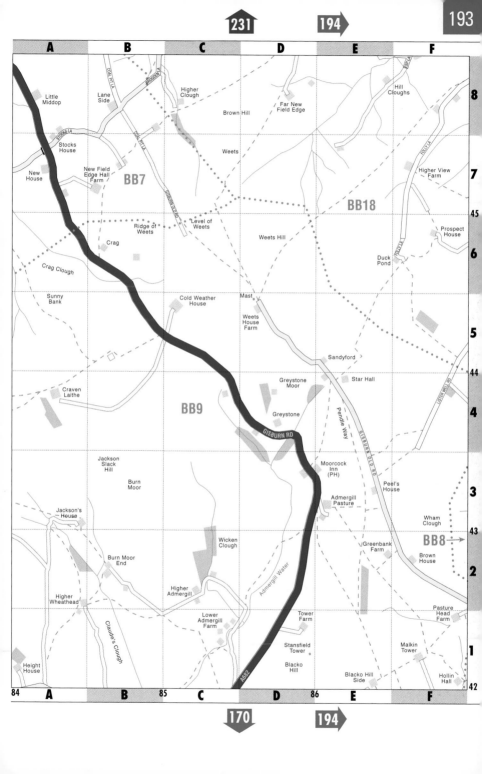

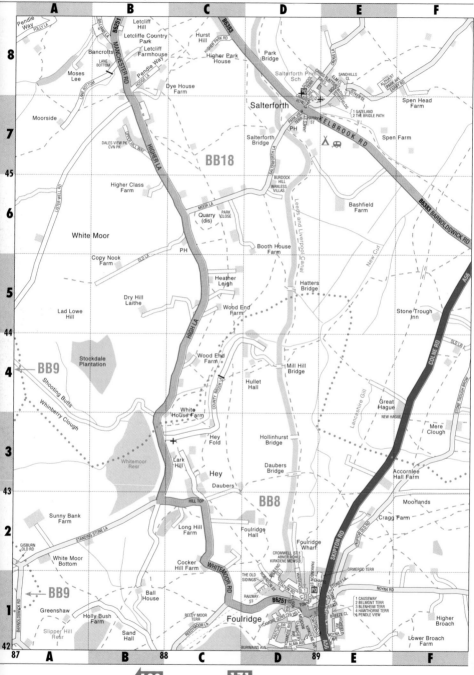

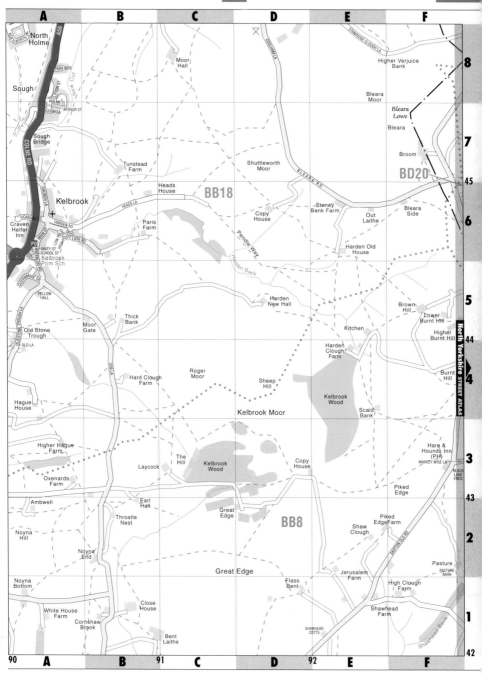

North Holme

Sough

Moor Hall

Higher Verjuice Bank

Bleara Moor

Bleara Lowe

Bleara

Park Side

Sough Bridge

Tunstead Farm

Broom

BD20

Heads House

Shuttleworth Moor

Kelbrook

BB18

Copy House

Steney Bank Farm

Out Laithe

Bleara Side

Craven Heifer Inn

Paris Farm

Pendle Way

Harden Old House

St School
Kelbrook Prim Sch

Harden Beck

Yellow Hall

Harden New Hall

Brown Hill

Lower Burnt Hill

Moor Gate

Thick Bank

Kitchen

Higher Burnt Hill

Old Stone Trough

OLD LA

Harden Clough Farm

Burnt Hill

Hard Clough Farm

Roger Moor

Sheep Hill

Kelbrook Wood

Hague House

Kelbrook Moor

Scald Bank

Higher Hague Farm

The Hill

Kelbrook Wood

Copy House

Hare & Hounds Inn (PH)

WARLEY WISE LA

Oxenards Farm

Laycock

Piked Edge

BLACK LANE ENDS

Ambwell

Earl Hall

Great Edge

BB8

Piked Edge Farm

Noyna Hill

Throstle Nest

Shaw Clough

Noyna End

Pasture

PASTURE BARN

Noyna Bottom

Great Edge

Jerusalem Farm

High Clough Farm

White House Farm

Close House

Flass Bent

Shawhead Farm

Cornshaw Brook

Bent Laithe

SHAWHEAD COTTS

Shawhead Beck

North Yorkshire STREET ATLAS

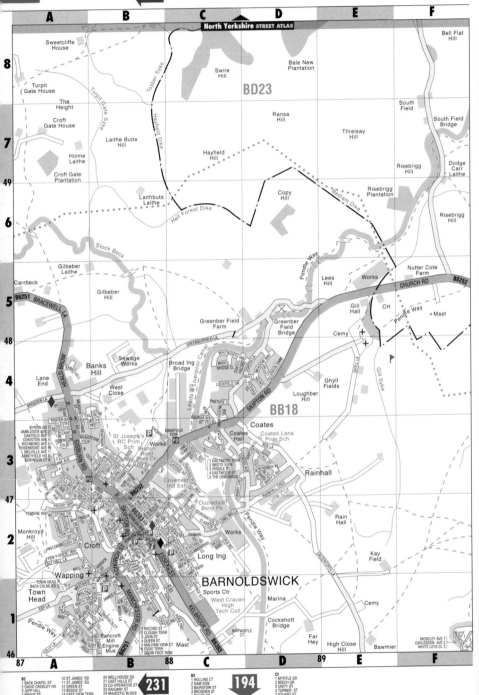

North Yorkshire STREET ATLAS

B2
1 BACK CHAPEL ST
2 DAVID CROSLEY HO
3 JEPP HILL
4 BROOK ST
5 ORCHARD ST
6 GARDEN ST
7 MARKET ST
8 BACK SKIPTON RD
9 FORESTER'S BLDGS

10 ST JAMES' RD
11 ST JAMES' ST
12 GREEN ST
13 BESSIE ST
14 EAST VIEW TERR
15 PLEASANT VIEW
16 FAR EAST VIEW
17 MONTROSE TERR
18 POST OFFICE BLDGS
19 EAST PAR

20 WELLHOUSE SQ
21 EAST HILLS ST
22 CO-OPERATIVE ST
23 RAILWAY ST
24 MAJESTIC BLDGS
25 SUSSEX ST
26 OLD TOWN HALL

B3
1 HOLLINS CT
2 DAM SIDE
3 BAIRSTOW ST
4 BROGDEN ST
5 BRUCE ST
6 CORNMILL TERR
7 NORTH PAR
8 MASONS WAY

C2
1 MYRTLE GR
2 BEECH GR
3 UNITY ST
4 TURNER ST
5 STUART ST
6 CRAVEN ST

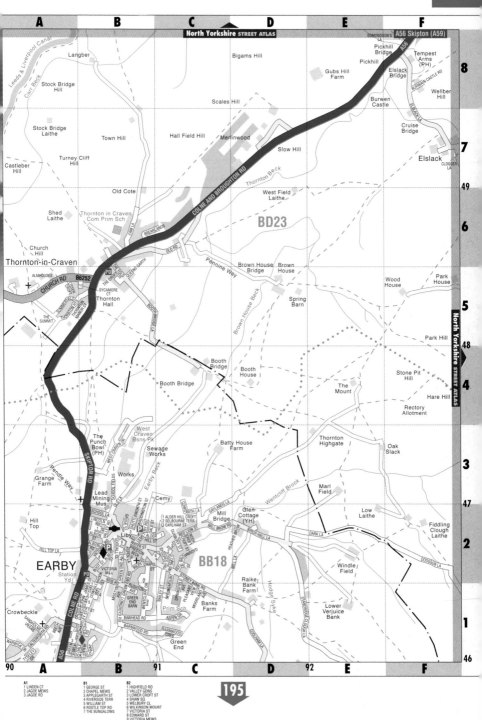

A
B
C
D
E
F
North Yorkshire STREET ATLAS
A56 Skipton (A59)
EDMONDSON'S LA
8
7
49
6
5
48
4
3
47
2
1
46
90
91
92
Leeds & Liverpool Canal
Carr Beck
Langber
Stock Bridge Hill
Bigams Hill
Pickhill Bridge
Pickhill
Tempest Arms (PH)
Gubs Hill Farm
Elslack Bridge
BURWAIN CASTLE RD
Wellber Hill
Burwen Castle
Scales Hill
ELSLACK LA
Cruise Bridge
Stock Bridge Laithe
Town Hill
Hall Field Hill
Merlinwood
Slow Hill
Elslack
CLOGGER LA
Turney Cliff Hill
Castleber Hill
Thornton Beck
COLNE AND BROUGHTON RD
Old Cote
West Field Laithe
Shed Laithe
Thornton in Craven Com Prim Sch
BD23
CAM LA
BREARLANDS
Church Hill
OLD RD
Thornton-in-Craven
Pennine Way
Brown House Bridge
Brown House
Wood House
Park House
ALMHOUSES
CHURCH RD
B6252
PO
THE FOLD
THE CROFT
QUEENS GARTH
SYCAMORE CT
Thornton Hall
Spring Barn
SUMMERFIELD
THORNTON HTS
THORNTON MANOR CT
THE SUMMIT
BOOTH BRIDGE LA
Brown House Beck
Park Hill
Booth Bridge
Booth House
Stone Pit Hill
Booth Bridge
The Mount
Hare Hill
Rectory Allotment
West Craven Bsns Pk
The Punch Bowl (PH)
WEST CRAVEN DR
Sewage Works
Batty House Farm
Thornton Highgate
Oak Slack
SKIPTON RD
Earby Beck
Pendle Way
Grange Farm
Works
SCHOOL FIELDS
Wentcliff Brook
Marl Field
Lead Mining Mus
OLD LA
Cemy
SHUTTLEWORTH ST
WADDINGTON ST
GAYLANDS LA
Glen Cottage (YH)
Low Laithe
Hill Top
SCHOOL LA
LINCOLN RD
1 ALDER HILL CROFT
2 SELBOURNE TERR
3 EARLHAM ST
Mill Bridge
MILL BROW RD
Fiddling Clough Laithe
Liby
P
ALBION ST
VALLEY RD
GROVE ST
ALDER HILL ST
RED LION ST
HEATHER BROW
BIRCH HALL LA
DARK LA
HILL TOP LA
WATER ST
PRESTON BECK
ASPEN LA
DUXBURY ST
BROWNROYD
EARBY
Station Yd
VICTORIA MILL
CHAPEL ST
STOOPES HILL
BB18
MILL LA
Windle Field
DODGSON LA
GREEN END AVE
NEW RD
RUSHTON AVE
STONEY BANK RD
Raike Bank Farm
Hodge Syke
COLNE RD
GREEN END BARN
MOSTYN AVE
LONGROYD RD
WENTCLIFFE DR
BAILEY ST
SPRINGMOUNT
SPRINGFIELD AVE
PLEASANT VIEW
MOORLAND AVE
Banks Farm
STANDRIDGE CLOUGH LA
Lower Verjuice Bank
Crowbeckle
SANDHOLME VILLAS
SALTERFORTH RD
BEECH AVE
BAWHEAD RD
Prim Sch
ASPEN GR
BARNWOOD RD
BARNWOOD CRES
COLLHAM LA
WARWICK DR
TYSELEY GR
A56
BROOK FIELD
Green End

A1
1 LINDEN CT
2 JAGOE MEWS
3 JAGOE RD

B1
1 GEORGE ST
2 CHAPEL MEWS
3 APPLEGARTH ST
4 RIVERSIDE TERR
5 WILLIAM ST
6 ROSTLE TOP RD
7 THE BUNGALOWS

B2
1 HIGHFIELD RD
2 VALLEY GDNS
3 LOWER CROFT ST
4 SHAW SQ
5 WELBURY CL
6 WILKINSON MOUNT
7 VICTORIA ST
8 EDWARD ST
9 VICTORIA MEWS

195

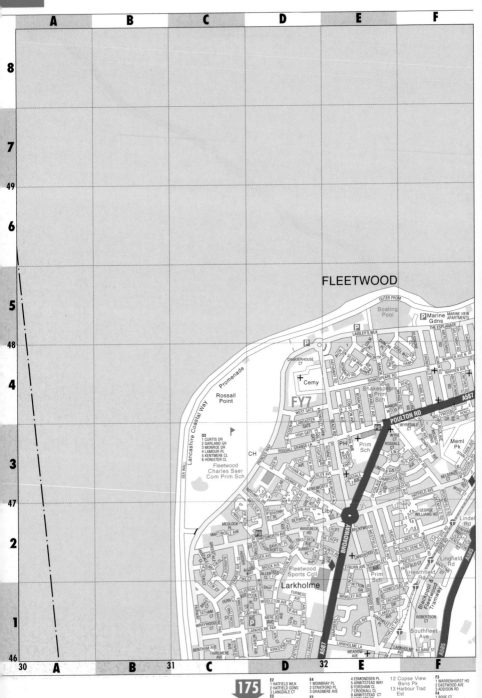

FLEETWOOD

FY7

Marine View Apartments

Boating Pool

Marine Gdns

THE ESPLANADE

OUTER PROM

LAIDLEY'S WLK

CHARTERHOUSE CT

Promenade

Rossall Point

Shakespeare Prim Sch

WEST GATE

POULTON RD

Meml Pk

D3
1 CURTIS DR
2 GARLAND GR
3 MONROE DR
4 LAMOUR PL
5 KENTMERE CL
6 HONISTER CL

Fleetwood Charles Saer Com Prim Sch

CH

Prim Sch

PH

Fleetwood Sports Coll

Larkholme

Liby

BROADWAY

Brentwood

GEORGE WILLIAMS HO

Linden Rd

Lingfield Rd

Prim Sch

Heathfield Rd

Blackpool & Fleetwood Tramway

Southfleet Ave

LARKHOLME LA

MEADOW AVE

175

E2
1 HATFIELD WLK
2 HATFIELD GDNS
3 LANGDALE CT
E3
1 MASONS CT
2 WESTWOOD AVE
3 LONSDALE CRES

E4
1 MOWBRAY PL
2 STRATFORD PL
3 GRASMERE AVE
F2
1 WESTHEAD WLK
2 HATFIELD MEWS
3 GREGSON DR

4 EDMONDSEN PL
5 ARMITSTEAD WAY
6 FORSHAW CL
7 CROOKALL CL
8 ARMITSTEAD CT
9 NOBLETT CT
10 MAYFIELD PL
11 HARBOUR CL

12 Copse View
   Bsns Pk
13 Harbour Trad
   Est

F3
1 WARRENHURST HO
2 EASTWOOD AVE
3 ADDISON RD
F4
1 ROSE CT
2 SEYMOUR ST
3 ALBANY RD
4 WELBECK HO

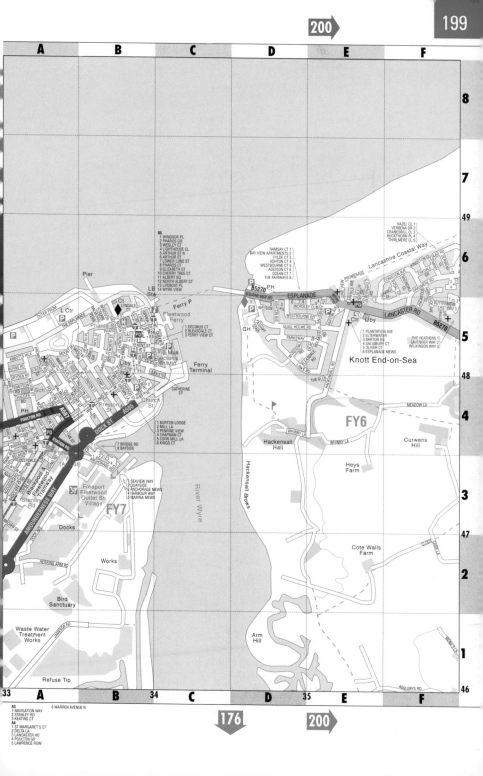

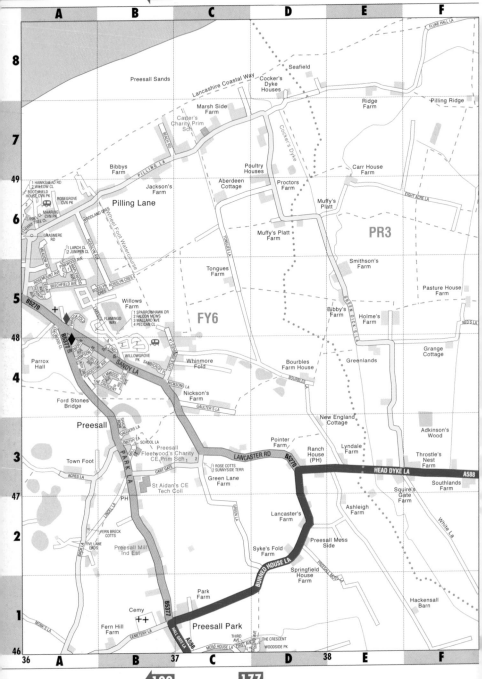

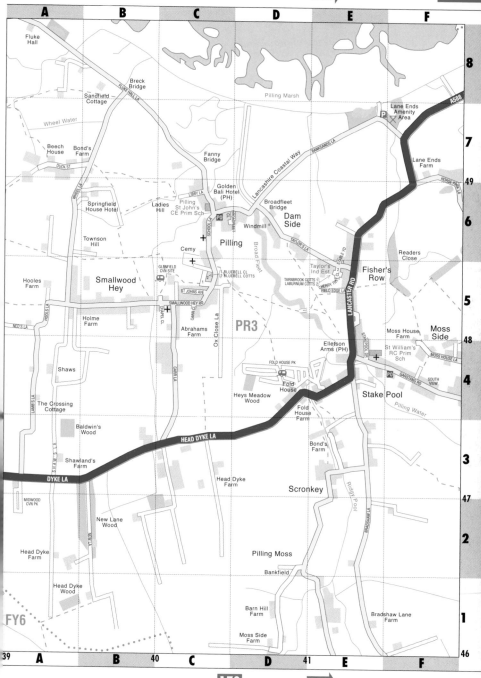

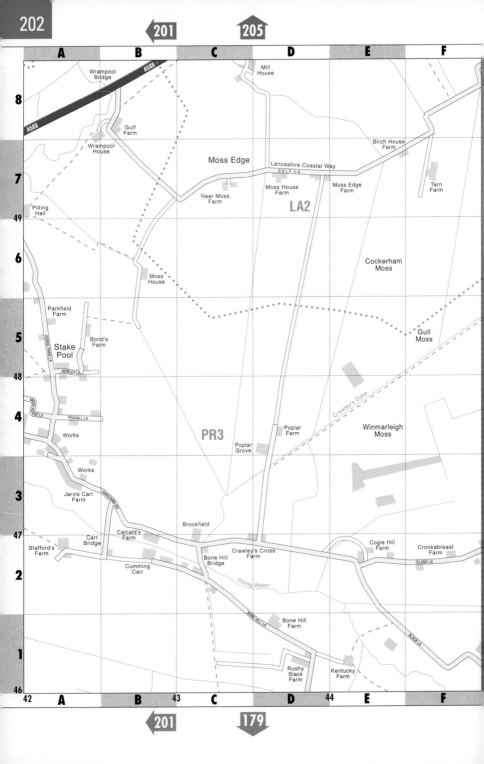

A B C D E F

8

Wrampool
Bridge

A588

Mill
House

Gulf
Farm

7

Wrampool
House

Moss Edge

Birch House
Farm

Lancashire Coastal Way

GULF LA

49

Pilling
Hall

Near Moss
Farm

Moss House
Farm

Moss Edge
Farm

LA2

Tarn
Farm

6

Moss
House

Cockerham
Moss

Parkfield
Farm

5

HORSE PARK LA

Stake
Pool

Bond's
Farm

Gull
Moss

48

MORLEY LA

Crawley's Dyke

MO
ROSE LA

4

PEAHALL LA

Works

PR3

Poplar
Farm

Winmarleigh
Moss

Poplar
Grove

Works

GARSTANG RD

Jarvis Carr
Farm

3

Brookfield

47

Stafford's
Farm

Carr
Bridge

Calcald's
Farm

Cogie Hill
Farm

Crookabreast
Farm

Crawley's Cross
Farm

ISLAND LA

Bone Hill
Bridge

2

Cumming
Carr

Pilling Water

BONE HILL LA

Bone Hill
Farm

BLACK LA

1

Rushy
Slack
Farm

Kentucky
Farm

46

42 A B 43 C D 44 E F

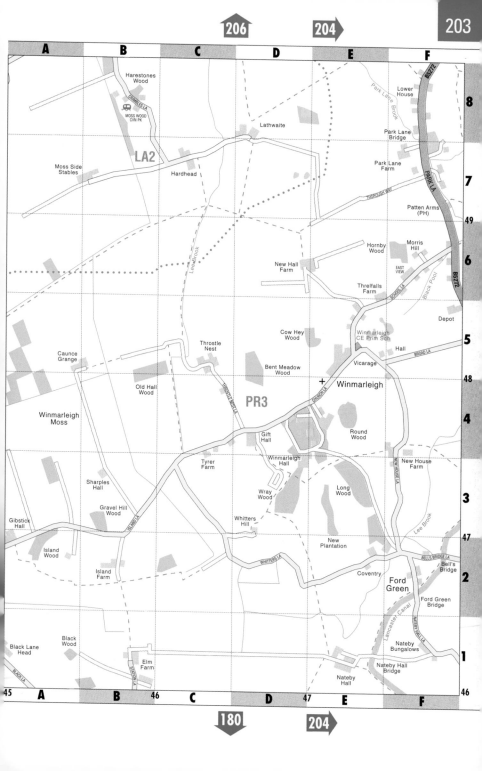

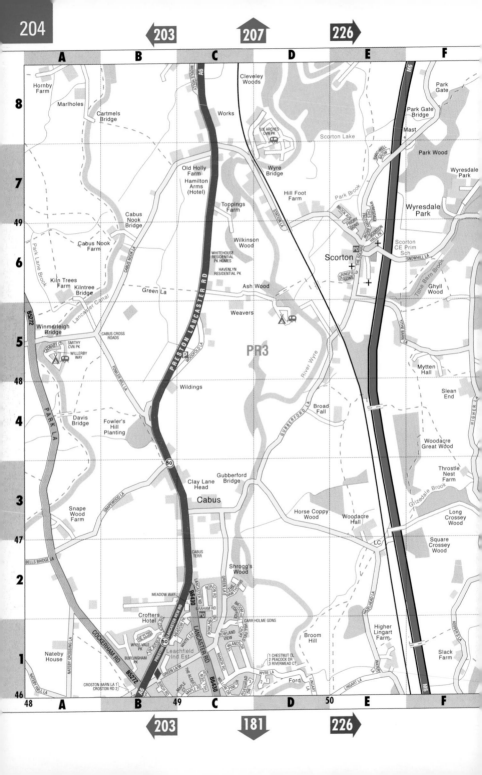

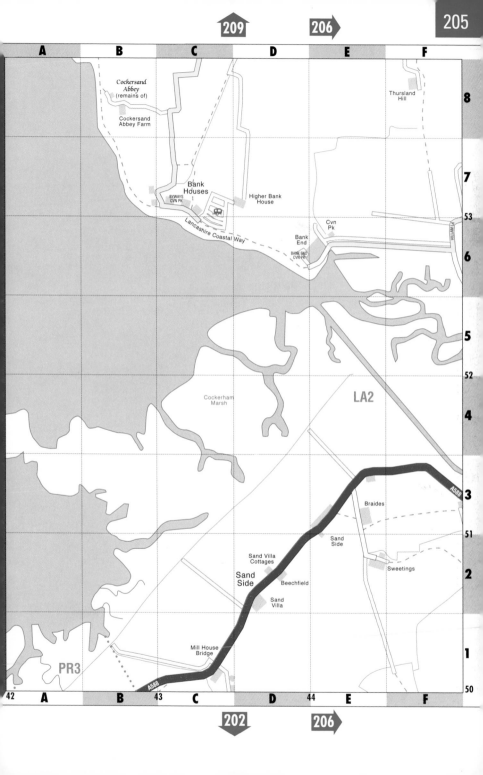

A B C D E F

8

Cockersand Abbey (remains of)

Thursland Hill

Cockersand Abbey Farm

7

53

Bank Houses

BYWAYS CVN PK

Higher Bank House

Cvn Pk

Lancashire Coastal Way

Bank End

BANK END CVN PK

6

Cvn Pk

Cockerham Marsh

LA2

52

5

4

A588

3

Braides

51

Sand Side

Sand Villa Cottages

Sweetings

Sand Side

Beechfield

2

Sand Villa

Mill House Bridge

1

PR3

A588

50

A B C D E F

42 43 44

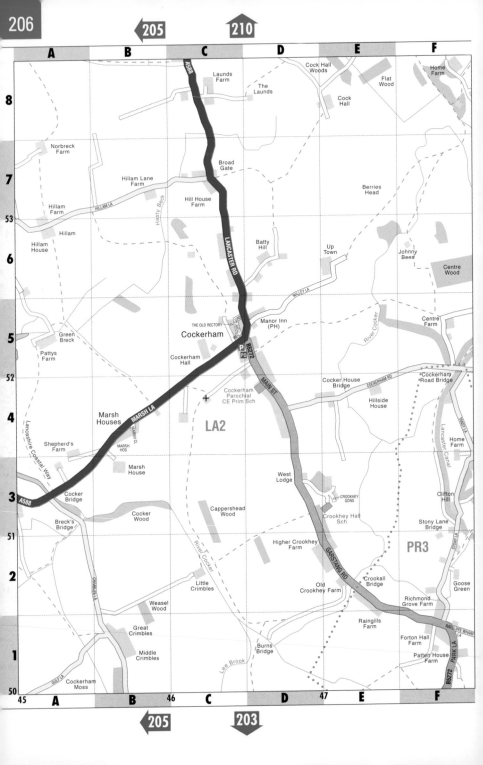

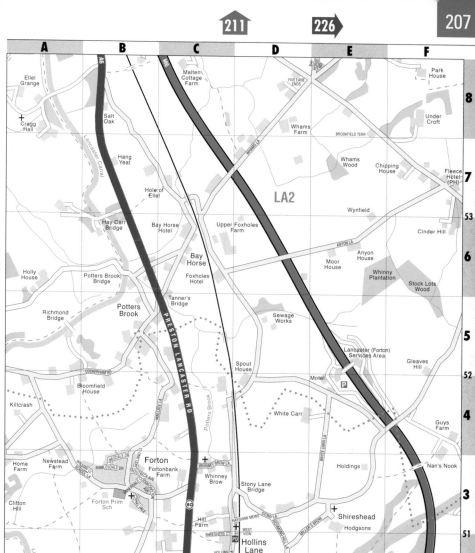

212

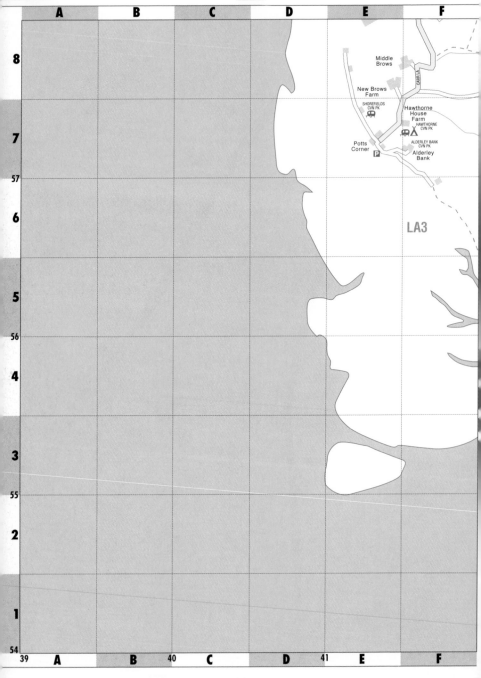

Middle Brows

New Brows Farm

SHOREFIELDS CVN PK

Potts Corner

Hawthorne House Farm

HAWTHORNE CVN PK

ALDERLEY BANK CVN PK

Alderley Bank

CARR LA.

LA3

209
214
209
206

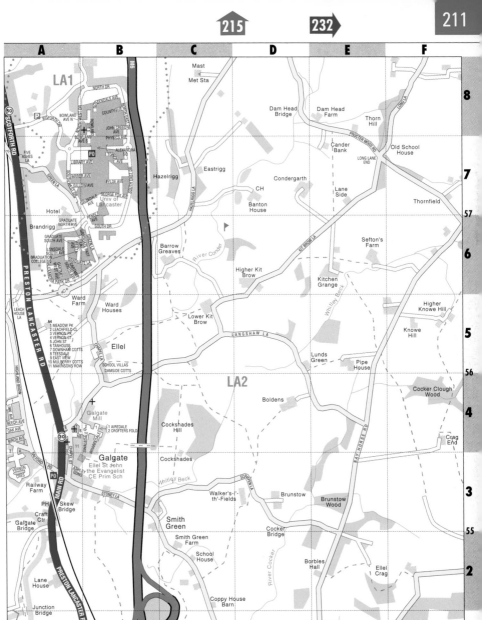

216

E7
1 WEMYSS CL
2 DUNBAR DR
3 TOWER COTTS
4 HEYSHAM RD
5 MIDDLETON WAY

F8
1 STRAWBERRY MEWS
2 BACK KNOWLYS RD
3 KNOWLYS DR
4 KNOWLYS CRES
5 TARNBROOK RD

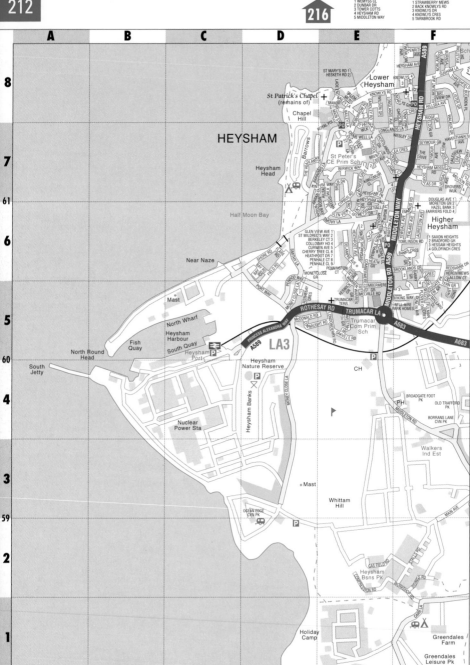

HEYSHAM

LA3

208

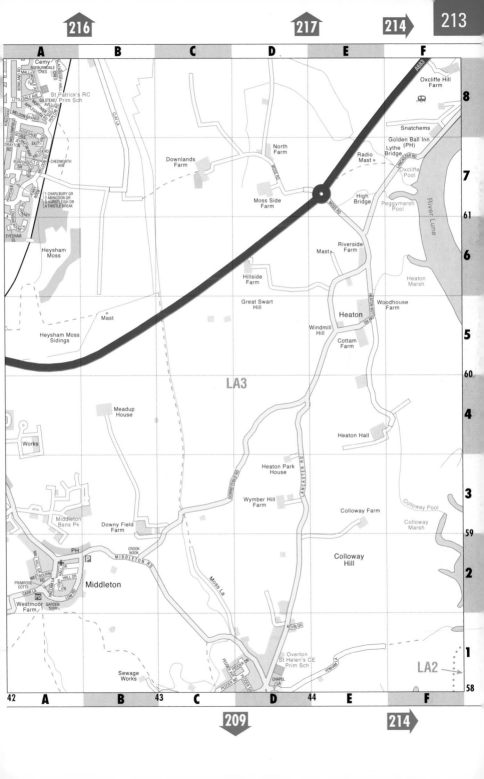

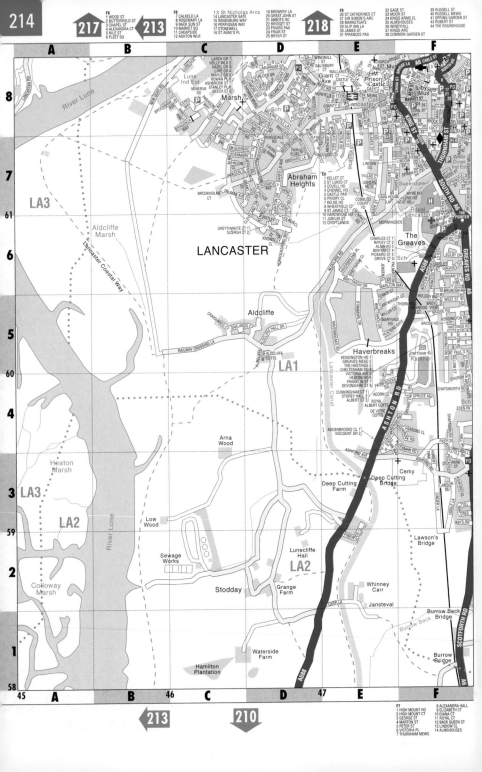

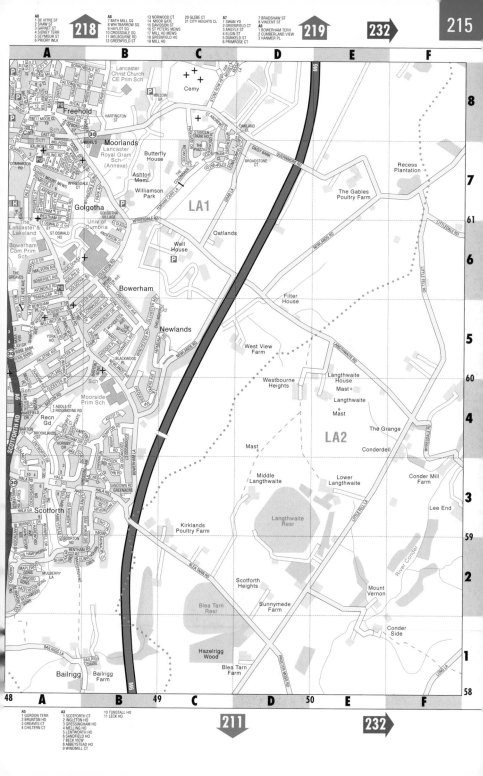

MORECAMBE

Stone Jetty

Morecambe L Pk

Mkt

CENTRAL DR

B5321

Superstore

SPRINGFIELD ST 1
LANCASHIRE ST 2
YORKSHIRE ST 3
BK MARINE RD 4
CLAREMONT CRES 5

1 MARINE CT
2 PALACE CT
3 GARDNER ARC
4 GARDNER BLDGS
5 BK WINTERDYNE TERR

WEST END RD
COACH MEWS

CUMBERLAND VIEW RD 1
CUMBERLAND VIEW CL 2
CRAIG ST 3
NORTON RD 4
SANDYLANDS ARC 5

Heysham
High
Sports
Coll

1 LEVENS CT
2 NORTON DR
3 WILLACY PAR
4 HAWKSWORTH AVE

Sandylands

LA3

Whittam
House

B5273

OXCLIFFE RD

Fanny
House

Cemy

Cvn
Pk

212

213

D2
1 RYDAL GR
2 DREWTON AVE
3 CROOKLEIGH PL
4 DRAYCOMBE CT
5 CROSSDALE AVE

E1
1 KINGSWAY CT
2 KINGSDALE AVE
3 WYRESDALE AVE
4 GRIZEDALE PL

E3
1 CAMBRIDGE RD
2 GRAFTON PL
3 GRAFTON PL
4 BK AVONDALE RD (E)
5 GLOUCESTER DR
6 SUNACRE CT
7 HENLEY MEWS
8 MEARSBECK

F3
1 CLEAVLANDS WLK
2 BUCKINGHAM PL
3 OLDEST BARN MEWS

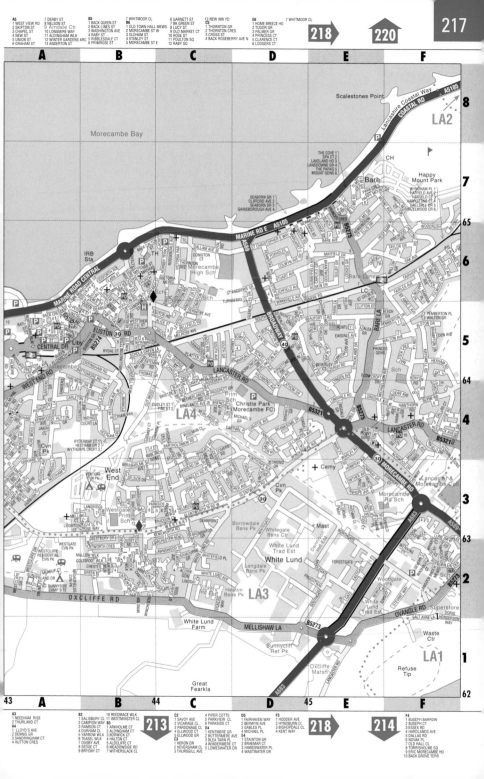

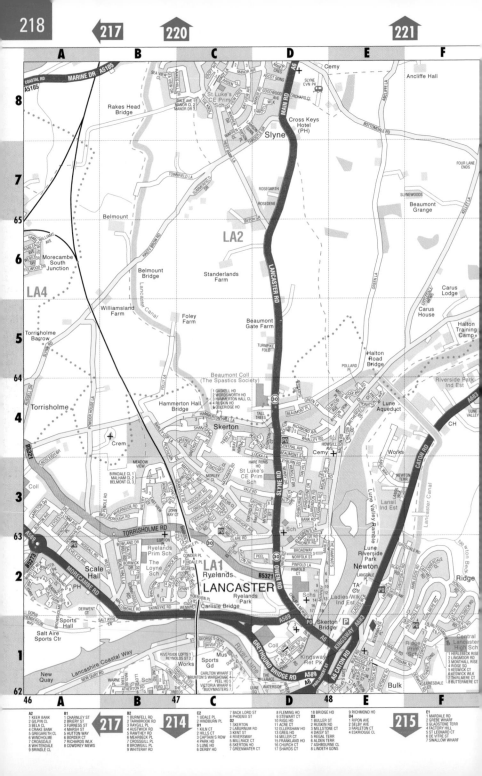

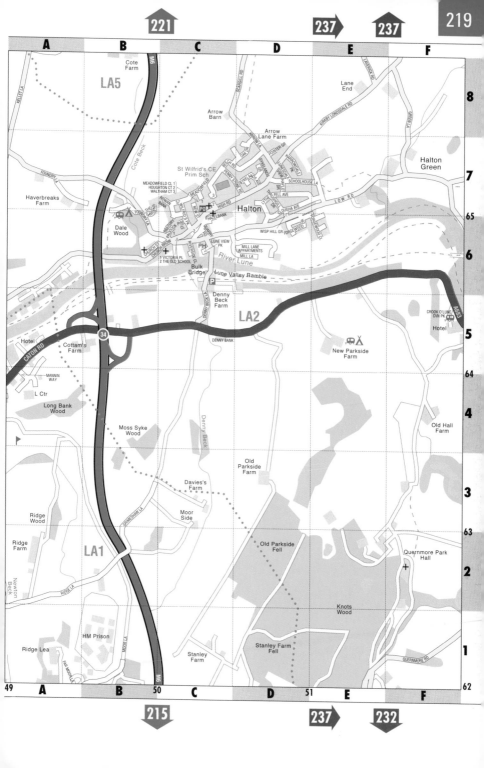

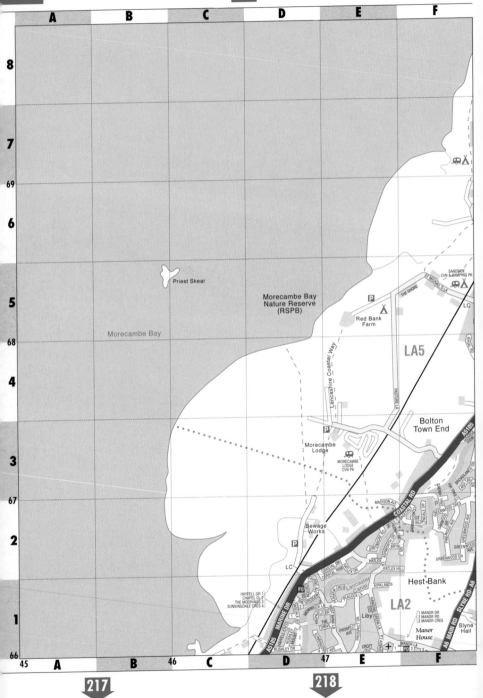

A B C D E F

8

7

69

6

5

Priest Skear

Morecambe Bay
Nature Reserve
(RSPB)

Red Bank
Farm

LA5

68

4

Lancashire Coastal Way

PASTURE LA

Bolton
Town End

A5105

3

Morecambe
Lodge

MORECAMBE
LODGE
CVN PK

67

MADISON AVE

COASTAL RD

BROADLANDS DR

Morecambe Bay

SANDSIDE
CVN & CAMPING PK

THE SHORE

ST MICHAEL'S LA

LC

CHERRY TREE DR

GREENWOOD CRES

GREENWOOD
AVE

GREENWOOD DR

2

Sewage
Works

LC

Hatlex

COASTAL RD
COASTAL RISE

BRYN

WATLEX HILL

Hest Bank

Lancaster Canal

KIRKLANDS

HANGING GREEN LA

1

HAYFELL GR 1
CHAPEL CL 2
THE MOORINGS 3
SUNNINGDALE CRES 4

MARINE DR

A5105

RUSHLEY DR

HAYFELL CRES

MOWBRICK LA

MELD DR
THE CRESCENT
CRES

PEACOCK LA

PLACOCK LA

THE
DRIVE

PROSPECT
AVE

PO

Liby

CROFT
AVE

MANOR LA

LA2

1 MANOR DR
2 MANOR RD
3 MANOR CRES

Manor
House

MANOR RD

A6 MAIN RD

SLYNE RD A6

Slyne
Hall

66

45 A B 46 C D 47 E F

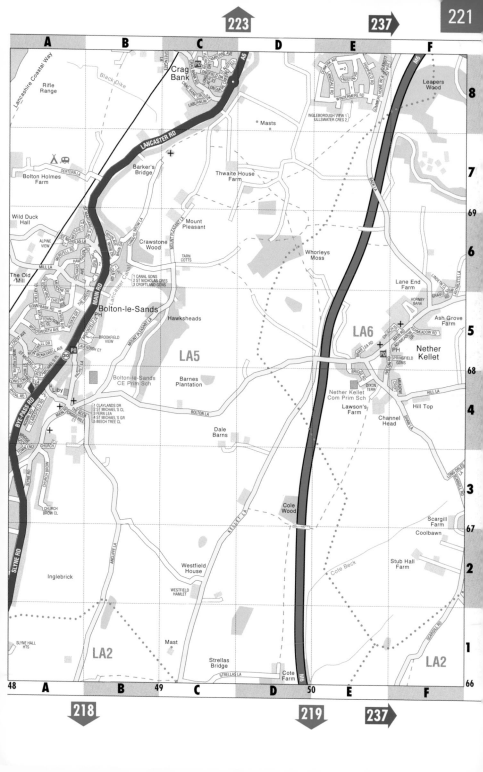

224

Heald Brow

Lancashire Coastal way

Jack Scout

Ridgway Park

Quaker's Stang

Quicksands Pool

Crag Foot

Brown's Houses

Jenny Brown's Point

Morecambe Bay Nature Reserve

LA5

Ings Point

220

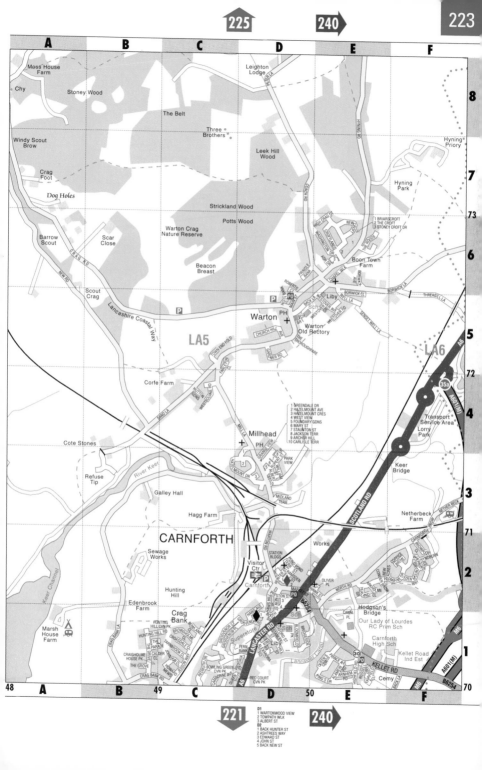

D1
1 WARTONWOOD VIEW
2 TOWPATH WLK
3 ALBERT ST
D2
1 BACK HUNTER ST
2 ASHTREES WAY
3 EDWARD ST
4 JOHN ST
5 BACK NEW ST

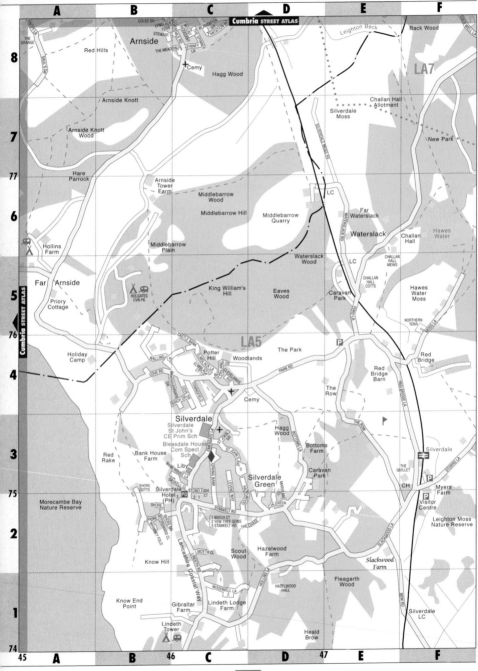

LA7

LA5

Arnside

Red Hills

Cemy

Hagg Wood

Arnside Knott

Arnside Knott Wood

Hare Parrock

Arnside Tower Farm

Middlebarrow Wood

Middlebarrow Hill

Middlebarrow Quarry

Middlebarrow Plain

Middlebarrow Plain

Hollins Farm

Far Arnside

Priory Cottage

Holgates Cvn Pk

Holiday Camp

King William's Hill

Eaves Wood

Waterslack Wood

Silverdale Moss

Challan Hall Allotment

New Park

LC

Far Waterslack

Waterslack

Challan Hall

Hawes Water

LC

Caravan Park

Challan Hall Mews

Challan Hall Cotts

Northern Terr

Hawes Water Moss

LA5

The Park

Potter Hill

Woodlands

Castle Bank

Wallings

Cove Rd

The Row

The Row

Cemy

Silverdale

Silverdale St John's CE Prim Sch

Bleasdale House Com Specl Sch

Red Rake

Bank House Farm

Liby

Hagg Wood

Bottoms Farm

Caravan Park

Silverdale Green

Shore Cotts

Silverdale Hotel (PH)

Shore

Shore

Morecambe Bay Nature Reserve

Know Hill

Scout Wood

Hazelwood Farm

Red Bridge

Red Bridge Barn

The Quillet

Silverdale

CH

Myers Farm

Visitor Centre

Leighton Moss Nature Reserve

Lancashire Coastal Way

Lindeth Cl

Woodwell La

Know End Point

Gibraltar Farm

Lindeth Lodge Farm

Lindeth Tower

Hazelwood Hall

Fleagarth Wood

Heald Brow

Slackwood Farm

Silverdale LC

Leighton Beck

Back Wood

Beech Ct
Yew Tree Gdns
Stankelt Ho

45   46   47

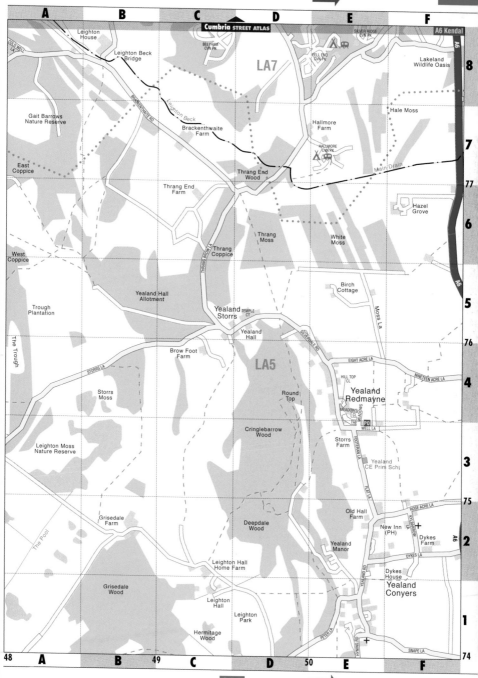

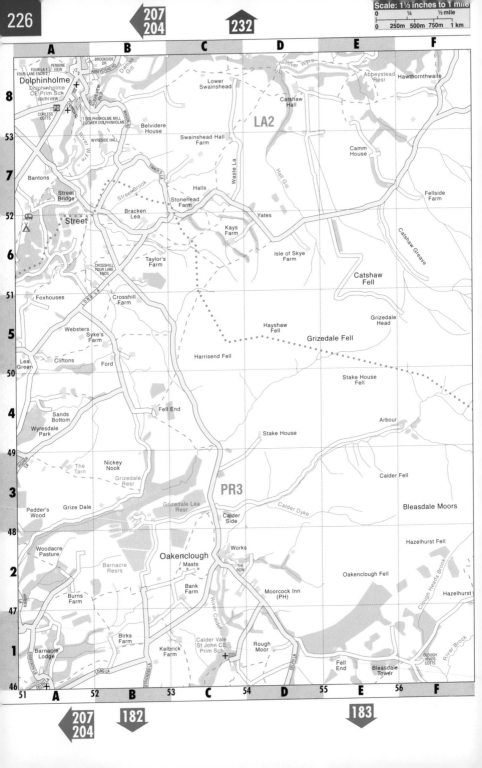

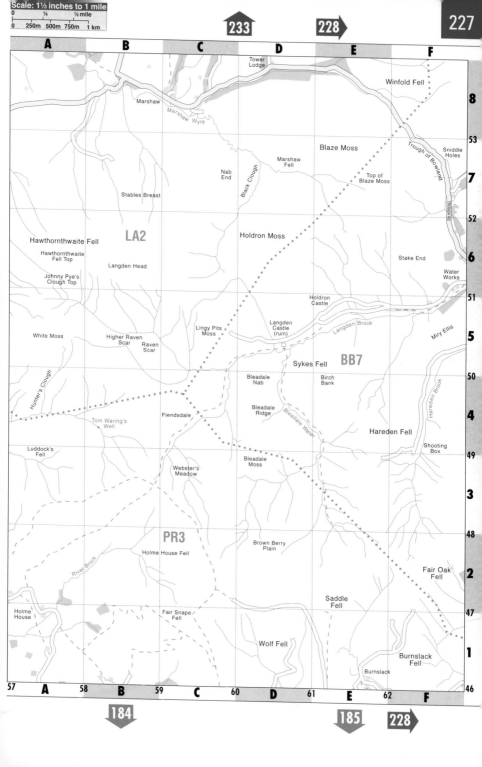

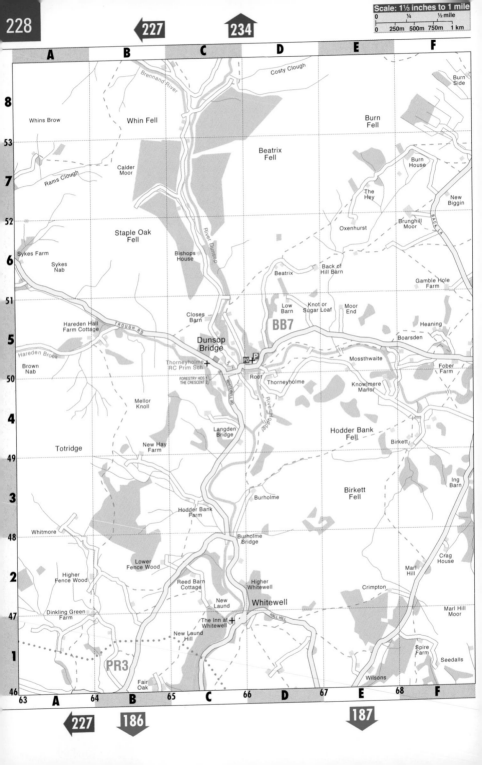

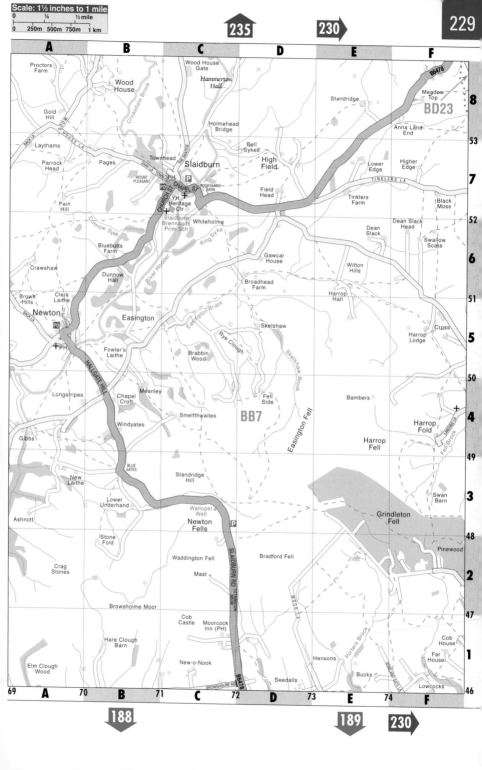

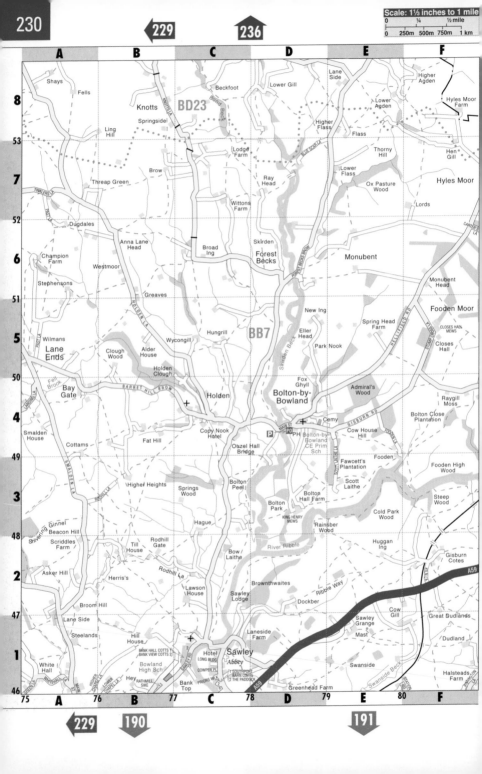

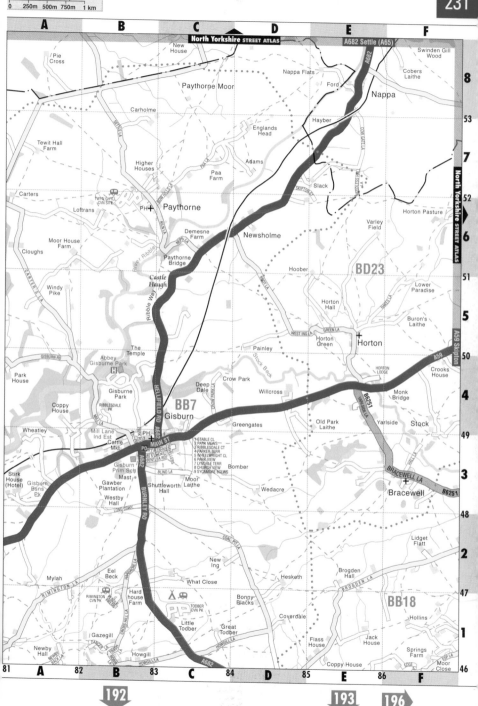

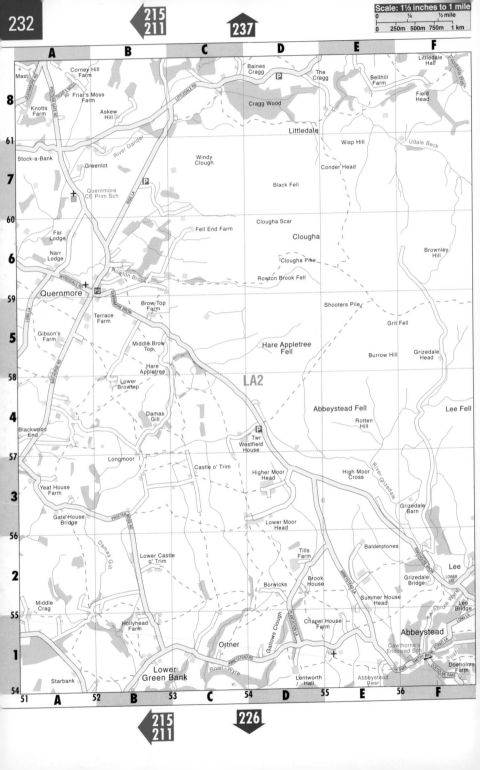

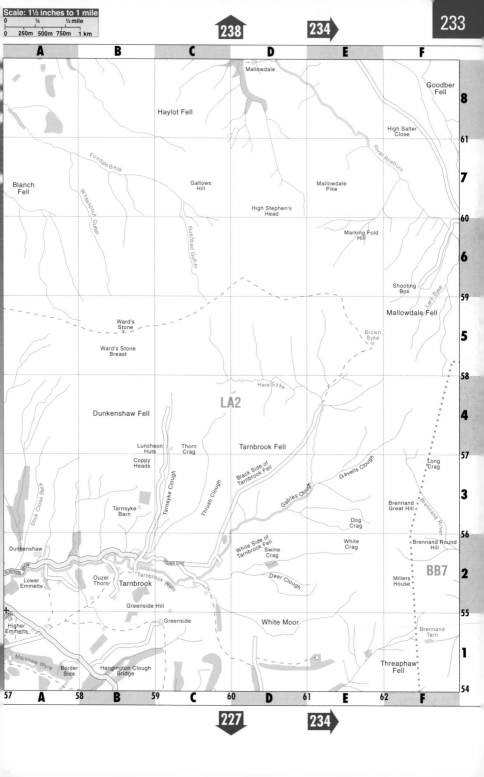

Scale: 1⅓ inches to 1 mile

0   ¼   ½ mile

0   250m 500m 750m 1 km

238
234

Mallowdale

Goodber Fell

Haylot Fell

High Salter Close

Foxdale Beck

Blanch Fell

Gallows Hill

Mallowdale Pike

Whitespout Gutter

High Stephen's Head

River Roeburn

Rushbed Gutter

Marking Fold Hill

Shooting Box

Lary Syke

Mallowdale Fell

Ward's Stone

Brown Syke

Ward's Stone Breast

Hare Syke

LA2

Dunkenshaw Fell

Tarnbrook Fell

Luncheon Huts

Thorn Crag

Coppy Heads

Black Side of Tarnbrook Fell

Gavells Clough

Long Crag

Tarnsyke Clough

Thrush Clough

Gables Clough

Brennand Great Hill

Brennand River

Stick Close Beck

Tarnsyke Barn

Dog Crag

White Crag

Brennand Round Hill

Dunkenshaw

White Side of Tarnbrook Fell

Swine Crag

HIGHER SYKE

Millers House

BB7

FLINTRON BROW

Lower Emmetts

Ouzel Thorn

Tarnbrook

Tarnbrook Wyre

Deer Clough

Greenside Hill

White Crag

Higher Emmetts

Greenside

White Moor

Brennand Tarn

Marshaw Wyre

Border Side

Hangington Clough Bridge

Threaphaw Fell

227
234

A   B   C   D   E   F

8   61   7   60   6   59   5   58   4   57   3   56   2   55   1   54

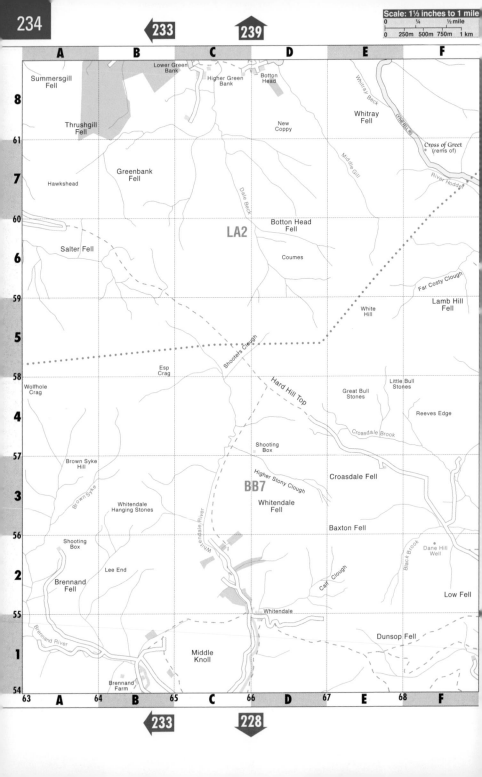

Scale: 1½ inches to 1 mile

0   ¼   ½ mile
0   250m 500m 750m 1 km

Summersgill Fell

Lower Green Bank

Higher Green Bank

Botton Head

Whitray Back

Thrushgill Fell

New Coppy

Whitray Fell

Cross of Greet (rems of)

Greenbank Fell

Middle Gill

River Hodder

Hawkshead

Dale Beck

Salter Fell

LA2

Botton Head Fell

Coumes

Far Costy Clough

Lamb Hill Fell

White Hill

Shooters Clough

Esp Crag

Hard Hill Top

Wolfhole Crag

Little Bull Stones

Great Bull Stones

Reeves Edge

Shooting Box

Croasdale Brook

Brown Syke Hill

Higher Stony Clough

Croasdale Fell

Brown Syke

BB7

Whitendale Fell

Whitendale Hanging Stones

Whitendale River

Baxton Fell

Shooting Box

Black Brook

Dane Hill Well

Lee End

Brennand Fell

Calf Clough

Low Fell

Whitendale

Brennand River

Dunsop Fell

Middle Knoll

Brennand Farm

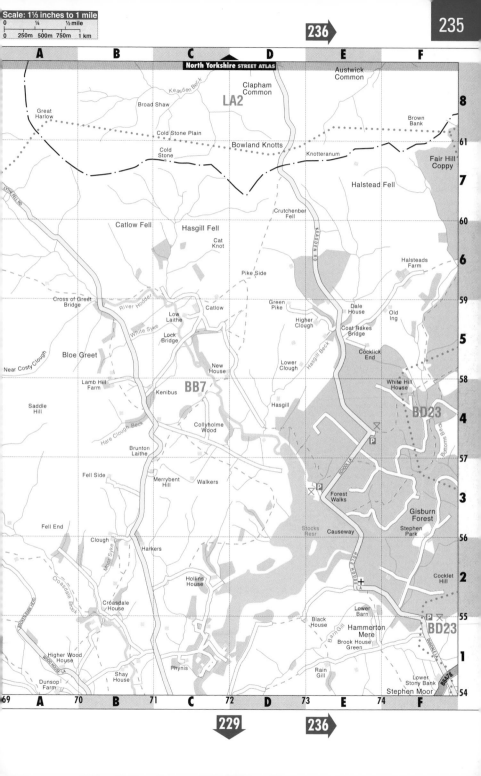

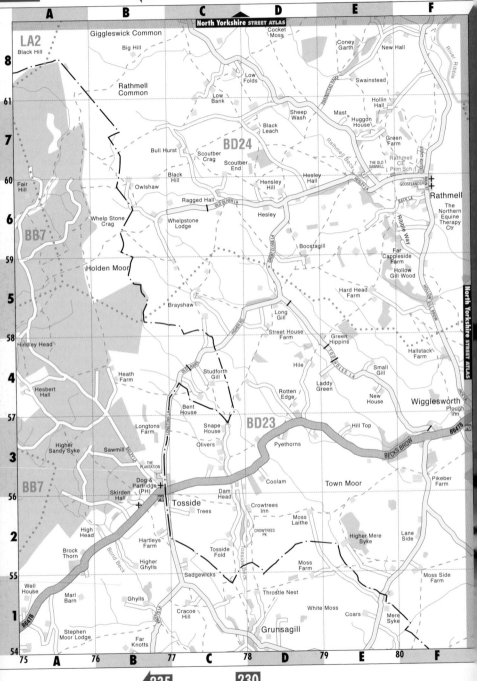

235

North Yorkshire STREET ATLAS

Scale: 1⅓ inches to 1 mile

| 0 | ¼ | ½ mile |
| 0 | 250m | 500m | 750m | 1 km |

LA2 Black Hill

Gigggleswick Common

Big Hill

Cocket Moss

Coney Garth

New Hall

River Ribble

8

Rathmell Common

Low Folds

Swainstead

61

Low Bank

Sheep Wash

Mast

Hollin Hall

Huggon House

7

Black Leach

BD24

Bull Hurst

Scoutber Crag

Scoutber End

Hesley Hall

Green Farm

THE OLD SAWMILL

Rathmell CE Prim Sch

GOOSELANDS LA

60

Fair Hill

Black Hill

Owlshaw

Hensley Hill

Hesley

Rathmell

The Northern Equine Therapy Ctr

Ragged Hall

OLD OLIVER LA

6

BB7

Whelp Stone Crag

Whelpstone Lodge

Hesley

Ribble Way

Far Cappleside Farm

Boostagill

Hollow Gill Wood

59

Holden Moor

Brayshaw

Hard Head Farm

5

Long Gill

Street House Farm

Green Hippins

Hallstack Farm

58

Hindley Head

Heath Farm

Studforth Gill

Hile

Small Gill

4

Hesbert Hall

Bent House

Rotten Edge

Laddy Green

New House

Wigglesworth

Plough Inn

57

Longtons Farm

Snape House

BD23

Hill Top

B6478

PO

3

Higher Sandy Syke

Sawmill

Olivers

Pyethorns

BECKS BROW

Pikeber Farm

THE PLANTATION

BB7

Skirden Hall

Dog & Partridge (PH)

PO

Coolam

Town Moor

56

Dam Head

Tosside

Trees

Crowtrees Inn

Moss Laithe

Lane Side

2

High Head

Hartleys Farm

CROWTREES PK

Higher Mere Syke

Brock Thorn

Higher Ghylls

Tosside Fold

Moss Farm

Moss Side Farm

55

Marl Barn

Ghylls

Sedgewicks

Throstle Nest

Well House

1

Cracoe Hill

White Moss

Coars

Mere Syke

Stephen Moor Lodge

Far Knotts

Grunsagill

B6478

54

75 A **76** B **77** C **78** D **79** E **80** F

235

230

North Yorkshire STREET ATLAS

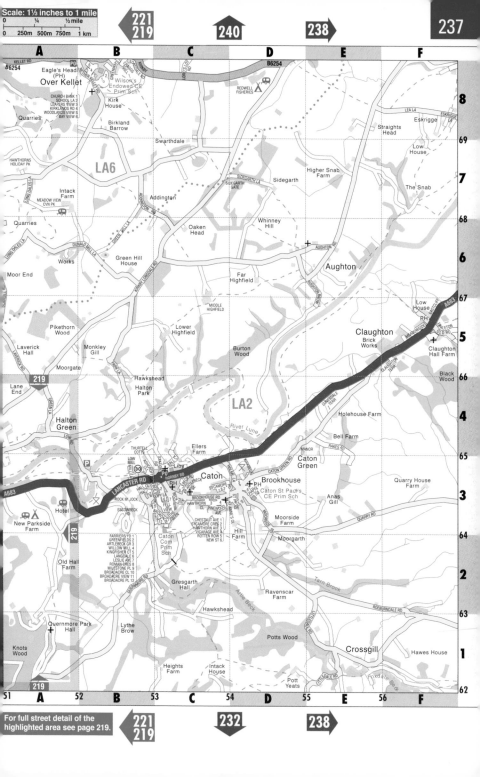

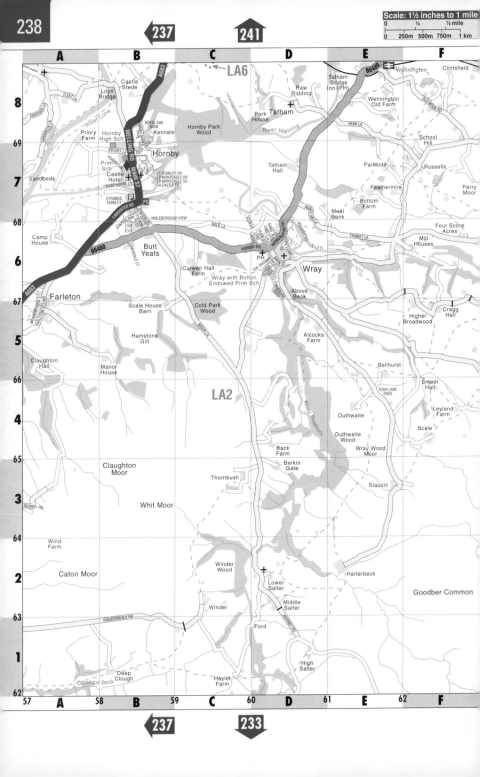

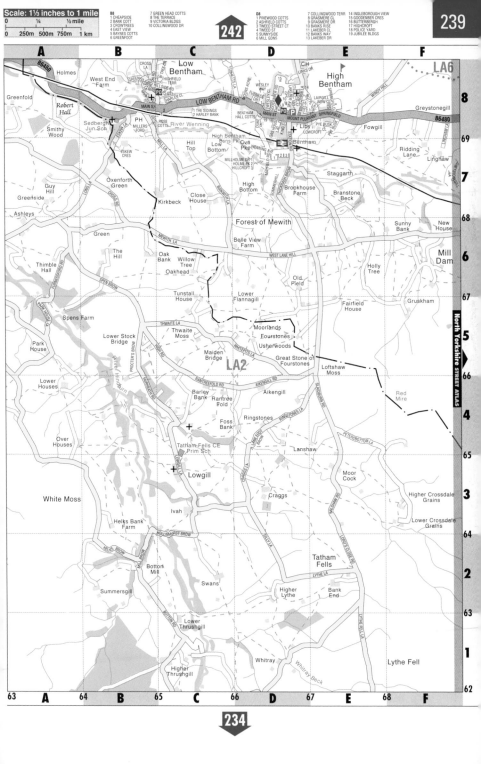

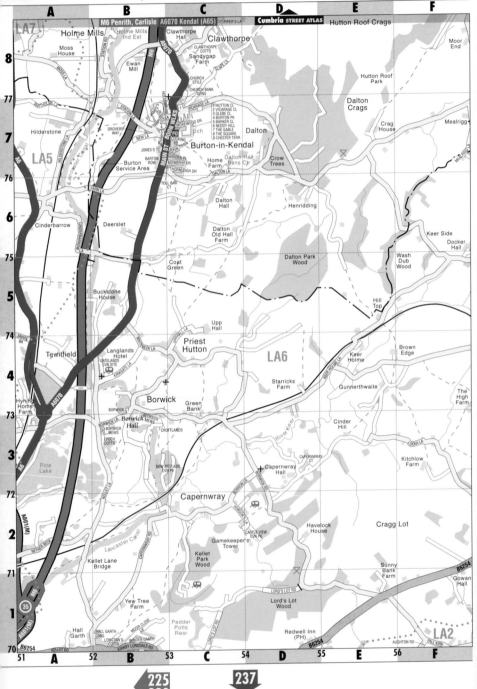

225
223

Scale: 1⅓ inches to 1 mile

0   ¼   ½ mile
0 250m 500m 750m 1 km

Cumbria STREET ATLAS

LA7

A   B   M6 Penrith, Carlisle   A6070 Kendal (A65)   PIPER'S LA   D   E   F

Holme Mills

Moss House

Holme Mills Ind Est

Clawthorpe Hall

Hutton Roof Crags

Moor End

Clawthorpe

Ewan Mill

CLAWTHORPE COTTS

Hutton Roof Park

8

Sandygap Farm

CHURCH STILE

Hilderstone

DROVERS WAY

CHURCH BANK GDNS

Dalton Crags

77

NEW LA

VICARAGE LA

Crag House

Mealrigg

LA5

Burton Service Area

MOCKING

7

3 HUTTON CL
2 VICARAGE CL
1 GLEBE CL
4 BURTON PK
5 BARKER CL
6 NEDDY HILL
7 THE GABLE
8 THE SQUARE
9 CHESTER TERR

Dalton

Burton-in-Kendal

MOREWOOD DR

Home Farm

Dalton Hall Bsns Ctr

Crow Trees

76

Burton Service Area

MOWBRAY DR

THORNLEIGH DR

TOLL BAR CT

DALTON LA

Cinderbarrow

Deerslet

Dalton Hall

Henridding

Keer Side

Docker Hall

6

Dalton Old Hall Farm

75

Coat Green

Dalton Park Wood

Wash Dub Wood

Hill Top

Buckstone House

5

Upp Hall

74

Tewitfield

Langlands Hotel
GATELANDS CVN SITE

PRIEST HUTTON

LA6

Keer Holme

Brown Edge

Borwick

Starricks Farm

Gunnerthwaite

The High Farm

4

Priest Hutton

73

Hyning Home Farm

Borwick Hall

BORWICK CT

BORWICK LA

BEDESIDE

Green Bank

River Keer

Cinder Hill

LOCKA LA

BORWICK MEWS

EPOCH COTTS

CROFTLANDS

Pine Lake

3

NEW ENGLAND CVN PK

Capernwray Hall

Kitchlow Farm

Capernwray CT

72

Capernwray

Havelock House

Cragg Lot

2

CASTLE VIEW CVN PK

Gamekeeper's Tower

Kellet Lane Bridge

Lancaster Canal

Kellet Park Wood

Sunny Bank Farm

71

Gowan Hall

A6(M)

Yew Tree Farm

LORD'S LOT RD

LA2

1

35

Hall Garth

HALL GARTH GDNS

MOOR CLOSE

Pedder Potts Resr

Lord's Lot Wood

Redwell Inn (PH)

B6254

AUGHTON RD

FELL KIRK

LONGTAIN'S COTTS

WINDER GARTH

SUNNY LONSDALE RD

B6254

70

51   A   52   B   53   C   54   D   55   E   56   F

225
223

237

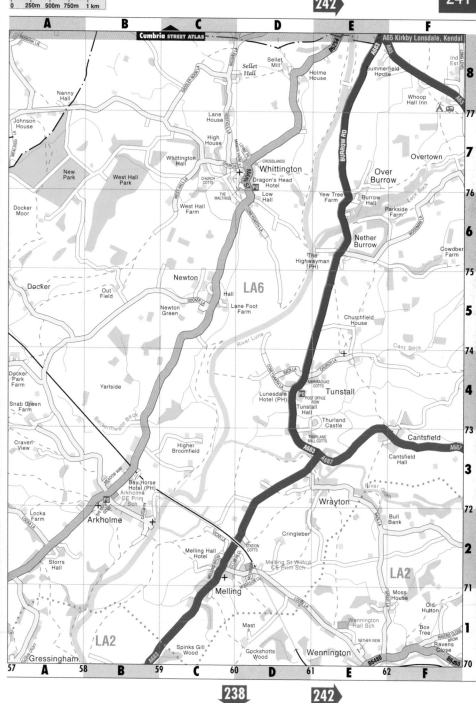

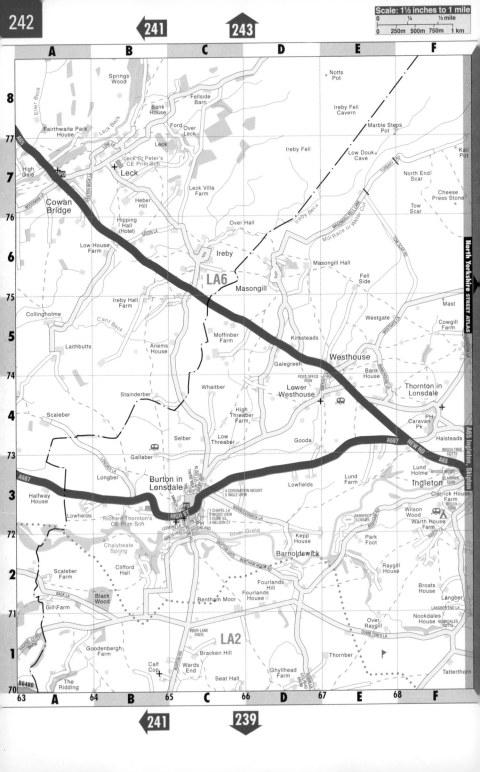

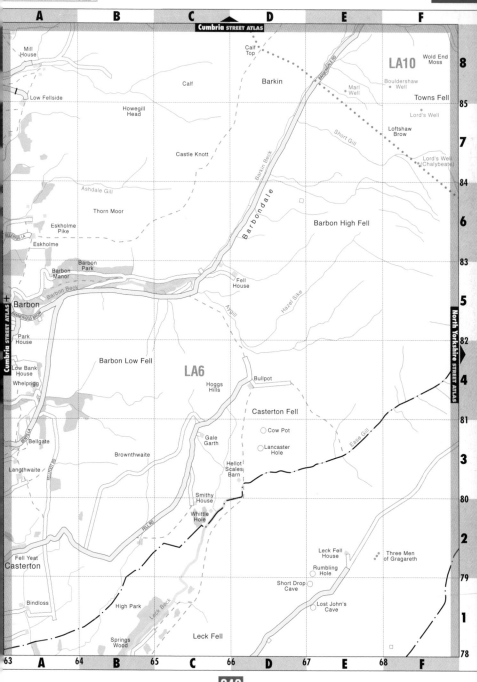

LA10

Wold End Moss

Mill House

Calf Top

Barkin

Bouldershaw Well

Low Fellside

Calf

Marl Well

Towns Fell

Howegill Head

Lord's Well

Loftshaw Brow

Castle Knott

Short Gill

Lord's Well (Chalybeate)

Ashdale Gill

Barkin Beck

Barbondale

Thorn Moor

Barbon High Fell

Eskholme Pike

Eskholme

Barbon Park

Barbon Manor

Barbon Beck

Fell House

Hazel Sike

Barbon

Argill

Park House

North Yorkshire STREET ATLAS

Low Bank House

Barbon Low Fell

Whelprigg

LA6

Hoggs Hills

Bullpot

Casterton Fell

Bellgate

Cow Pot

Ease Gill

Brownthwaite

Gale Garth

Lancaster Hole

Langthwaite

Hellot Scales Barn

Smithy House

Whittle Hole

Leck Fell House

Three Men of Gragareth

Fell Yeat

Rumbling Hole

Casterton

Short Drop Cave

Bindloss

Lost John's Cave

High Park

Leck Beck

Leck Fell

Springs Wood

Index

Place name May be abbreviated on the map

Location number Present when a number indicates the place's position in a crowded area of mapping

Locality, town or village Shown when more than one place has the same name

Postcode district District for the indexed place

Page and grid square Page number and grid reference for the standard mapping

Church Rd 6 Beckenham BR2..........53 C6

Cities, towns and villages are listed in CAPITAL LETTERS   Public and commercial buildings are highlighted in magenta
Places of interest are highlighted in blue with a star ★

Abbreviations used in the index

Acad	Academy	Comm	Common	Gd	Ground	L	Leisure	Prom	Promenade
App	Approach	Cott	Cottage	Gdn	Garden	La	Lane	Rd	Road
Arc	Arcade	Cres	Crescent	Gn	Green	Liby	Library	Recn	Recreation
Ave	Avenue	Cswy	Causeway	Gr	Grove	Mdw	Meadow	Ret	Retail
Bglw	Bungalow	Ct	Court	H	Hall	Meml	Memorial	Sh	Shopping
Bldg	Building	Ctr	Centre	Ho	House	Mkt	Market	Sq	Square
Bsns, Bus	Business	Ctry	Country	Hospl	Hospital	Mus	Museum	St	Street
Bvd	Boulevard	Cty	County	HQ	Headquarters	Orch	Orchard	Sta	Station
Cath	Cathedral	Dr	Drive	Hts	Heights	Pal	Palace	Terr	Terrace
Cir	Circus	Dro	Drove	Ind	Industrial	Par	Parade	TH	Town Hall
Cl	Close	Ed	Education	Inst	Institute	Pas	Passage	Univ	University
Cnr	Corner	Emb	Embankment	Int	International	Pk	Park	Wk, Wlk	Walk
Coll	College	Est	Estate	Intc	Interchange	Pl	Place	Wr	Water
Com	Community	Ex	Exhibition	Junc	Junction	Prec	Precinct	Yd	Yard

Index of towns, villages, streets, hospitals, industrial estates, railway stations, schools, shopping centres, universities and places of interest

Aal–Agn

A

Aalborg Pl LA1 ....214 F7
Aaron Ct PR9 ....53 E1
Abacus St FY1 ...... 130 C2

Abbey Cl
Formby L37 ....12 B2
Up Holland WN8 ....10 C7
Abbey Cres BB3 ....65 C8
Abbeydale LA3 ....217 B2
Abbey Dale
Appley Bridge WN6 .....19 D7
Burscough L40 ....25 F3
Abbeydale Way BB5....103 F5
Abbey Dr WN5 ....10 E6
Abbey Farm BB7 ....144 B6
Abbey Farm Cvn Pk
L40 ....16 C8
Abbeyfield 3 BB11 .....128 B4
Abbeyfield Cl LA1 ..... 215 A3
Abbeyfield Ho
Barnoldswick BB18 .... 196 A3
🔟 Burnley BB11 ....127 E5
Abbey Fields BB7 .....144 C5
Abbey Fold L40 ....25 D5
Abbey Gdns PR8 ....35 A4
Abbey Gisburne Park Hospl
BB7 ....231 B4
Abbey Gr PR6 ....31 B7
Abbey La
Burscough L40 ....25 C1
Ormskirk L40 ....25 C1
Abbey Lane Ind Est L40 ..25 C1
Abbey Mews BB7 ......144 C5
Abbey Pl 1 BB3 ....82 C1
Abbey Rd
Blackpool FY4 .... 110 D5
Whalley BB7 ....144 C5
Abbey St
Accrington BB5 .... 104 C6
Accrington, Scaitcliffe
BB5 .... 104 C5
Bacup OL13 ....87 F4
Preston PR2 ....96 D8
ABBEYSTEAD.........232 F1
Abbeystead WN8 ....9 C7
Abbeystead Dr LA1 .... 215 A3
Abbeystead Ho 3 LA1 .. 215 A3

Abbeystead La LA2 ....232 E2
Abbeystead Rd LA2 ... 232 C1
Abbey Terr
Barrow BB7 ....166 C1
Billington BB7 ....144 A3
Abbey View
Whalley BB7 ....144 C4
Withnell PR6 ....80 A1
ABBEY VILLAGE.........80 C2
Abbey Village Prim Sch
PR6 ....80 C1
Abbeyville FY4.......... 110 C6
Abbey Wlk PR1 ....96 D3
Abbeywood WN8..........9 C7
Abbot Mdw PR1 ....96 D4
Abbots Cl
Formby L37 ....12 A1
Kirkham PR4 ....114 C4
Rawtenstall BB4 ....86 A4
Abbots Croft BB7 .....144 C5
Abbotsford L39 ....15 F5
Abbotsford Ave BB2 .. 101 D1
Abbotsford Rd FY3 ... 131 A3
Abbots Ho 21 LA1 .....214 F8
Abbots Row FY4 ....90 D6
Abbotsway PR1 ....96 C6
Abbots Way
Formby L37 ....12 B1
Lancaster LA1 ....214 C8
Abbott Brow BB2 ......121 E3
Abbott Clough Ave
BB1 ....102 E4
Abbott Clough Cl BB1..102 E4
Abbott Croft PR2 ......117 A7
Abbotts Cl PR5 ....97 F3
Abbott St 14 BL6 ....32 B4
Abbotts Wlk FY7 ...... 199 A5
Abbot Wlk BB7 ....167 A8
Abel St BB11 ....128 A8
Abercorn Pl FY4 ....110 B5
Abercrombie Rd FY7 ..198 F4
Aberdare Cl BB1 ....101 E7
Aberdeen Dr BB1 ......102 A4
Aberdeen Gdns OL12...52 D4
Aberdeen Rd LA1 ..... 215 A4
Abernethy Ct BL6 ....32 D2
Abernethy St BL6 ....32 D2
Abingdon Dr BB2 ..... 117 B1
Abingdon Gr LA3 ..... 213 A7
Abingdon Rd BB12 ....126 D7
Abingdon St FY1 ......130 B5
Abinger St BB10 .... 148 C1
Abington Dr PR9 ....55 A5

Abner Row BB8......... 194 D1
Abraham Altham Ct
BB10 ....148 F3
ABRAHAM HEIGHTS ...214 D7
Abraham St
7 Accrington BB5 .....104 B5
Blackburn BB2.......... 101 E2
11 Horwich BL6.........32 B4
Abram Fold PR9 ....54 F5
Abram Ho PR1...........97 A7
Abrams Gn PR9..........54 F5
Acacia Cl 4 FY5...... 176 D1
Acacia Rd PR2 .... 118 E2
Acacia Wlk 4 BB1.....102 B5
Academy The 1 PR9....35 C8
ACCRINGTON...........104 E6
Accrington Huncoat Prim
Sch BB5 ....125 F2
Accrington Rd
Blackburn BB1 ....102 C4
Burnley BB11 ....127 C5
Hapton BB11 ....126 E3
Whalley BB6, BB7 .....144 E4
Accrington Sta BB5 ...104 B6
Accrington Victoria Hospl
BB5 ....104 B7
Acer Gr PR2 ....118 F3
Ackhurst Bsns Pk & Ind Est
PR7 ....42 F8
Ackhurst La WN5 ....19 F2
Ackhurst Rd PR7 ....42 F8
Ackroyd St OL14 ......109 B1
Acorn Appartments
FY2 ....152 C6
Acorn Ave BB5 ....103 F3
Acorn Bank PR3 ...... 181 C8
Acorn Bsns Ctr L33 .....1 B1
Acorn Cl
Kingsfold PR1 ....96 B2
Lancaster LA1 ....214 F4
Leyland PR25 ....60 A8
Acornfield Rd L33 ......1 D2
Acorn Gdn LA3 ....217 C2
Acorn Mdw LA5 ....221 A4
Acorn Mews FY4........ 131 D1
Acorn St
Bacup OL13 ....87 F2
Blackburn BB1..........102 B4
Clachan The L39 ....15 C1
Acorn Venture Urban
Farm ★ L33.............45 B6
ACRE 85 B6
Acre Ave OL13 ....70 D8

Acre Cl BL0 ....68 D3
Acre Ct 11 LA1.........218 D2
Acrefield
Blackburn BB2..........101 A7
Clayton Brook PR5......78 C5
Newburgh WN8 ....27 A1
Padiham BB12 ....146 C1
Acrefield Dr BB4..........86 A6
Acregate WN8 ....9 C7
Acre Gate FY4 ....110 E7
Acregate La PR1 ....118 D1
Acre Gr
Much Hoole PR4 ....74 F3
Southport PR8 ....34 F3
Acre Mill Rd OL13 ......70 D8
Acre Moss La LA4......217 A4
Acremount BB2 ....145 D2
Acresbrook Rd BB12 ..146 F6
Acresfield
Adlington PR7 ....30 F6
Colne BB8 ....172 A5
Acresfield Cl BL6 ....31 C3
Acres La
Great Altcar L37 ....3 E8
Maghull L31, L39 ....4 E7
Preesall FY6 ....200 A3
Acre St
Burnley BB10...........148 B1
Burnley, Haggate BB10 ..149 A3
Whitworth OL12.........71 D1
Acres The BB6 ....144 E8
Acreswood Cl PR7 ......29 E8
Acre View OL13 ....70 D7
Active Way BB11 ......128 A6
Acton Rd FY4..........130 E1
Adamson St
Blackburn BB2..........101 C5
Padiham BB12 ....146 C1
Ada St
Blackburn BB2..........101 C5
Burnley BB10...........148 B1
Nelson BB9 ....148 E6
Ramsbottom BL0........68 D4
Addenbrooke Cl LA1 ..214 E4
Addington Rd LA2, LA6 ..237 D7
Addington St BB1.......102 A4
Addison Cres FY6 .....130 D6
Addison Ct FY6 ....199 D5
Addison Rd FY7 ....199 A3
Addison St
Accrington BB5 ....104 C7
Blackburn BB2..........101 C5

Adelaide Ave FY5 ..... 153 C8
Adelaide Ct 5 FY1 ... 130 C5
Adelaide La BB5 ....104 C5
Adelaide St W FY1.....130 B4
Adelaide St
7 Accrington, Enfield
BB5 ....125 A1
Accrington, Scaitcliffe
BB5 ....104 C5
5 Adlington PR6........31 A8
Blackpool FY1 ....130 B5
Fleetwood FY7.........199 B5
Preston PR1 ....97 B8
2 Ramsbottom BL0.....50 A4
Rawtenstall BB4 ....86 A7
Adelaide Terr BB2 ....101 C5
ADELPHI...............117 E1
Adelphi Ho 1 PR1 ....117 E1
Adelphi Pl 2 PR1 ......96 F8
Adelphi St
6 Blackpool FY1.......130 B5
Burnley BB11 ....128 A7
Lancaster LA1 ....215 A6
Preston PR1 ....96 F8
Standish WN6 ....29 E2
ADLINGTON..............31 B7
Adlington Ave FY6 .... 153 B3
Adlington Prim Sch
PR7 ....30 F7
Adlington St Pauls CE
Prim Sch PR6 ....31 A7
Adlington South Bsns
Village PR7 ....31 A6
Adlington St BB11 ....128 A6
Adlington Sta PR6 ......31 A7
Admiral Cl PR4 ....110 E1
Admiral Gdns FY2 .....152 B3
Admiral Hts FY7 ....152 B3
Admirals Sound FY5 ..175 C2
Admiralty Cl L40..........95 C7
Admiralty Way PR2 .....95 D7
Adrian St PR1 ....130 B1
Adstone Ave FY5 ......130 F7
Agate St BB1 ....122 F1
Ager St OL13 ....70 C8
Agglebys Rd FY6 ......176 F8
Agnes Ing La LA2 .....238 D2
Agnes St
Blackburn BB2..........101 C3
Preston PR1.............97 A8
Agnew Rd FY7 ....198 F4
Agnew St FY8 ....91 A3

Aiken Ct PR4 114 A5
Aikengill Rd LA2 239 D4
Ailsa Ave FY4 130 F2
Ailsa Cl PR3 137 B8
Ailsa Rd BB1 102 D3
Ailsa Wlk LA3 212 E7
Aindow Ct PR8 34 F3
Ainley Ct 10 FY1 130 C6
Ainscough Brook Ho 1 PR2 118 F3
Ainscouth Bsns Pk WN6 28 F6
AINSDALE 21 B5
Ainsdale Ave
Blackpool FY2 152 E5
Burnley BB10 148 C5
Edgworth BL7 48 E6
Fleetwood FY7 175 D7
Thornton FY5 176 D1
Ainsdale & Birkdale Sandhills Nature Reserve* PR8 21 B7
Ainsdale Cl LA1 218 B3
Ainsdale Dr
Darwen BB3 65 B5
Preston PR2 116 E2
Whitworth OL12 52 D7
AINSDALE-ON-SEA 20 F6
Ainsdale St John's CE Prim Sch PR8 21 D4
Ainsdale Sand Dunes National Nature Reserve* PR8 20 E3
Ainsdale Sta PR8 21 C5
Ainse Rd BL6 31 B3
Ainslie Cl BB6 124 B5
Ainslie Rd PR2 117 E3
Ainslie St 3 BB12 127 C6
Ainspool La PR3 181 A3
Ainsworth Ave BL6 32 E2
Ainsworth Cl 5 BB3 65 A8
Ainsworth Fold PR4 113 B3
Ainsworth Mall 3 BB1 101 E5
Ainsworth St BB1 101 E5
Aintree Cotts BB2 121 C3
Aintree Cres PR8 35 F4
Aintree Dr BB3 82 A7
Aintree Rd
Blackpool FY4 130 D1
Thornton FY5 153 B8
Airdrie Cres BB11 127 D4
Airdrie Pl FY2 152 E6
Aire Cl LA3 217 F3
Airedale LA2 211 B4
Airedale Ave FY3 130 E3
Airedale Ct FY6 153 C4
Airegate L31 5 B2
Airey Hos PR3 163 D1
Airey St BB5 104 D3
Air Hill Terr 8 OL12 52 C1
Airton Garth BB9 170 C3
Aisled Barn Visitor Ctr* BB8 173 A3
Aitken Cl BL0 50 B5
Aitken St
Accrington BB5 104 C7
Haslingden BL0 68 C5
Ajax St 3 BL0 50 B5
A K Bsns Pk PR9 36 A6
Akeman Cl LA3 217 E3
Alamein Rd LA5 223 E1
Alandale Cl PR25 60 B7
Alan Gr LA3 212 F6
Alan Haigh Ct BB8 171 D6
Alan Ramsbottam Way BB6 124 D4
Alaska St BB2 101 E2
Albany Ave FY4 110 B5
Albany Cl FY6 131 E8
Albany Ct 10 PR7 43 E8
Albany Dr
Bamber Bridge PR5 97 D2
Copster Green BB1 122 C8
Albany Rd
Blackburn BB2 101 B6
3 Fleetwood FY7 198 F4
Lytham St Anne's FY8 90 C5
Morecambe LA4 216 F4
Southport PR9 53 C1
Albany Science Coll PR7 43 E5
Albany The BB3 81 E4
Albatros St PR1 118 B1
Albemarle Ct 2 BB7 166 D8
Albemarle St BB7 166 D8
Alberta Cl BB2 101 B8
Albert Ct
Lancaster LA1 214 E4
Southport PR9 53 D1
Albert Ho BB4 86 D1
Albert Mill BB3 81 F7
Albert Pl
Blackburn BB3 81 F7
Southport PR9 35 B8
Albert Rd
Barnoldswick BB18 196 B2
Blackpool FY1 130 C5
Colne BB8 171 D4
Formby L37 2 B8
Fulwood PR2 117 F3
Lancaster LA1 218 D1
Leyland PR25 60 C8
Lytham St Anne's FY8 90 A7
Morecambe LA4 216 F4
Preston PR1 117 F2
Rawtenstall BB4 86 A8
Rufford L40 39 A3
Albert Rd *continued*
Southport PR9 53 D1
Albert Sq 11 FY7 199 B5
Albert St
Accrington BB5 104 C5
Blackburn BB2 101 C2
Bolton BL7 47 D3
Brierfield BB9 148 B5
Burnley BB11 128 B6
Bury BL9 33 A2
3 Carnforth LA5 223 D1
Carnforth, Millhead LA5 223 D3
1 Chorley PR7 43 D7
Church BB5 103 E6
Clayton-le-M BB5 124 F2
Darwen BB3 65 B5
Earby BB18 197 B2
Fleetwood FY7 199 B4
Great Harwood BB6 124 D4
Hoddlesden BB3 82 F1
Horwich BL6 32 B4
Kirkham PR4 113 F6
Lytham St Anne's FY8 91 C3
Nelson BB9 148 D8
Oswaldtwistle BB5 103 E4
Padiham BB12 126 C8
Ramsbottom BL0 50 B6
Rishton BB1 124 B1
Wheelton PR6 62 A7
Whitewell Bottom BB4 86 E5
Whitworth OL12 52 C8
Albert Terr
Bacup OL13 87 F3
9 Barrowford BB9 170 D3
Calder Vale PR3 182 E8
Higher Walton PR5 98 B3
9 Preston PR1 118 A1
Rawtenstall BB4 86 B2
Southport PR8 35 A5
Albion Ave FY3 130 F6
Albion Ct BB11 127 E4
Albion Mews LA1 218 E1
Albion Mill 8 BB4 86 F2
Albion Rd
Blackburn BB2 101 D1
Earby BB18 197 B2
Albion St
Accrington BB5 104 B6
Bacup, Greave OL13 88 A3
7 Bacup, Stacksteads OL13 70 C8
Blackburn BB2 101 C1
Brierfield BB9 148 B5
Burnley BB11 127 E5
Chorley PR7 43 C7
1 Clitheroe BB7 166 F8
Earby BB18 197 B2
Lancaster LA1 218 E1
3 Nelson BB9 148 D8
7 Padiham BB12 126 D7
Albion Terr 11 BB11 127 F5
Albrighton Cl PR5 77 B7
Albrighton Cres PR5 77 B7
Albrighton Rd PR5 77 C7
Albyn Bank Rd PR1 97 B7
Albyn St E PR1 97 B7
Alcester Ave PR1 96 C5
Alconbury Cres FY5 175 C2
Aldate Gr PR2 117 A2
ALDCLIFFE 214 D5
Aldcliffe Cotts LA1 214 D5
Aldcliffe Ct 5 LA4 217 B3
Aldcliffe Hall Dr LA1 214 D5
Aldcliffe Mews LA1 214 D5
Aldcliffe Rd
Lancaster LA1 214 E6
7 Preston PR2 116 E1
Alden Cl
Haslingden BB4 68 A6
Standish WN1 30 B1
Alden Rd BB4, BL8 67 F5
Alden Rise BB4 68 A6
Alden Terr 6 LA1 218 D3
Alder Ave
Bury BL9 33 C3
Rawtenstall BB4 86 B2
Alderbank BL6 31 F3
Alder Bank
Blackburn BB2 101 B4
20 Rawtenstall BB4 86 A3
Alderbrook Dr WN8 27 C2
Alder Cl
Leyland PR26 59 B8
Newton-w-S PR4 115 A2
Thornton FY5 176 C1
Alder Coppice PR2 116 E3
Alder Ct
Fleetwood FY7 198 C2
Lancaster LA1 214 D8
Alderdale Ave PR8 21 A5
Alder Dr
Charnock Richard PR7 42 D3
Gregson Lane PR5 98 E1
Alderfield PR1 96 D3
Alderford Cl BB7 166 C7
Alder Gr
Blackpool FY3 130 E7
Coppull PR7 42 F1
Fulwood PR2 116 F6
Huncoat BB5 125 E2
Lancaster LA1 214 D8
Lytham St Anne's FY8 91 A4
Poulton-le-F FY6 153 D1
Alder Grange Com & Tech Sch BB4 86 A4
Alder Hill Croft BB18 197 C2
Alder Hill St BB18 197 B2
Alder La
Formby L37, L39 12 E7
Moss Edge PR3 179 A1
Parbold WN8 27 C1
Alderlee Pk Cvn Site PR8 36 A2
Alderley WN8 9 C6
Alderley Ave FY4 110 B5
Alderley Bank Cvn Pk LA3 208 F7
Alderley Hts LA1 218 D3
Alderman Foley Dr OL12 52 A2
Alderman Rd LA1 214 F4
Alder Meadow Cl 1 OL12 52 A1
Alderney Cl BB2 101 B1
Alder Rd PR2 119 A4
Aldersleigh Cres PR5 98 D1
Alderson Cres L37 11 F4
Alder St
Bacup OL13 87 F3
4 Blackburn BB1 102 A7
Burnley BB12 127 C7
Rawtenstall BB4 86 B3
Alders The PR3 204 C1
Alderville Cl PR4 92 F6
Alderway BL0 68 C1
Alderwood BB4 86 B2
Alderwood Gr BL0 68 D4
Aldfield Ave PR2 116 C1
Aldingham Ct 2 LA4 217 B3
Aldingham Wlk 11 LA4 217 A5
Aldon Gr PR4 95 A1
Aldon Rd FY6 153 F2
Aldren's La LA1 218 D3
Aldwych Ave FY3 130 E3
Aldwych Ct PR2 117 A2
Aldwych Dr
Bamber Bridge PR5 77 B7
Preston PR2 117 A2
Aldwych Pl BB1 122 F2
Alert St PR2 117 C1
Alexander Cl
Accrington BB5 104 E1
Burscough L40 25 F3
Alexander Ct FY6 153 D3
Alexander Dr L31 5 D3
Alexander Gr BB12 127 B6
Alexander Mews BB2 101 C6
Alexander Pl 2 PR2 139 D1
Alexander St BB9 171 A2
Alexander Wharf L31 5 C1
Alexandra Cl
Clayton-le-M BB5 124 E3
Skelmersdale WN8 17 E1
Alexandra Ct 4 LA1 214 F8
Alexandra Hall 8 LA1 214 F7
Alexandra Ho 10 PR1 118 C1
Alexandra Mews
1 Ormskirk L39 15 E6
8 Southport PR9 35 C8
Alexandra Park Dr LA1 211 A6
Alexandra Pavilions 6 PR1 118 A1
Alexandra Pl BB6 124 D6
Alexandra Rd
Bamber Bridge PR5 97 D3
Blackburn BB2 101 C6
Blackpool FY1 130 B1
Burscough L40 25 D4
Carnforth LA5 223 D1
8 Darwen BB3 81 F2
Formby L37 11 B1
Kirkham PR4 114 A6
Lancaster LA1 218 D3
Longridge PR3 140 A7
Lytham St Anne's FY8 90 A7
Morecambe LA3 216 E3
Southport PR9 35 D8
Thornton FY5 153 C8
Alexandra Sq LA1 211 B7
Alexandra St
Clayton-le-M BB5 124 E3
Preston PR1 97 C7
Alexandra View 7 BB3 81 F2
Alexandra Dr FY8 89 F5
Alexandria St BB4 85 F4
Alford Fold PR2 117 D7
Alfred St
Blackpool FY1 130 C5
Bolton, Egerton BL7 47 D3
Bury BL9 33 A1
Darwen BB3 65 B6
Lancaster LA1 215 A8
10 Ramsbottom BL0 50 B5
Whitworth OL12 71 D2
Algar St 9 BB9 170 F2
Alice Ave PR25 77 A1
Alice Sq 5 PR1 118 A1
Alice St
Accrington BB5 104 D7
Barnoldswick BB18 196 B2
9 Darwen BB3 65 A8
Morecambe LA4 217 C5
Oswaldtwistle BB5 103 E3
Alicia Ct 1 OL12 52 E1
Alicia Dr OL12 52 E1
Alisan Rd FY6 153 B5
Alker La PR7 61 B3
Alker St PR7 43 C7
Alkincoats Rd BB8 171 C5
Allan Critchlow Way BB1 124 B2
Allandale FY4 110 C5
Allandale Ave FY5 175 F4
Allandale Gdns LA1 214 D8
Allan St OL13 87 F1
Allenbury Pl FY3 131 A2
Allenby Ave PR2 118 B4
Allenby Rd FY8 89 E8
Allen Cl
Cleveleys FY5 175 D1
Fleetwood FY7 198 D2
Allen Ct BB10 128 A8
Allendale Ct 6 BB12 127 B6
Allendale Gr BB10 128 F4
Allendale St
5 Burnley BB12 127 B6
Colne BB8 171 F5
Allengate PR2 117 F4
Allen St BB10 128 A8
Allen Way FY7 198 D2
Allerton Cl BB3 82 A2
Allerton Dr BB12 127 D6
Allerton Rd
Bamber Bridge PR5 97 D4
Southport PR9 53 E1
Alleys Gn BB7 189 E1
ALLEYTROYDS 103 E6
Alleytroyds BB5 103 E5
All Hallows RC High Sch PR1 96 A3
All Hallows Rd FY2 152 D5
Alliance Bsns Pk BB5 104 A5
Alliance St BB5 104 F1
Allington Cl PR5 97 E3
Allison Gr BB8 171 F6
Allonby Ave FY5 175 E4
Allotment La PR3 157 C7
All Saints CE Prim Sch BB5 124 F2
All Saints Cl
Padiham BB12 126 F7
Rawtenstall BB4 106 A1
All Saint's Cl BB5 103 B4
All Saints RC High Sch BB4 85 D1
All Saints Rd FY2 152 E6
All Saints' Rd FY8 89 E6
Allsprings Cl BB6 124 D6
Allsprings Dr BB6 124 D6
Alma Ave BB8 194 D1
Alma Cl WN8 10 C7
Alma Ct
Southport PR8 21 F7
Up Holland WN8 10 C7
Alma Dr PR7 42 E4
Alma Hill WN8 10 C7
Alma Hill Est WN8 10 C7
Alma Ho LA1 214 F6
Alma Ind Est 25 OL12 52 F1
Alma Par WN8 10 C7
Alma Pl
Accrington BB5 84 E8
Clitheroe BB7 166 D7
Alma Rd
Lancaster LA1 214 F6
Laneshaw Bridge BB8 172 C6
Southport PR8 35 A4
Up Holland WN8 10 C7
Alma Row PR5 98 E1
Alma St
Bacup OL13 88 A2
Blackburn BB2 101 D5
9 Clayton-le-M BB5 124 F3
Padiham BB12 126 C8
Preston PR1 118 A1
13 Rochdale OL12 52 F1
Alma Terr BB11 106 B4
Alma Wood Cl PR7 43 A6
Almelo Ho 2 PR1 117 E2
Almhouses BD23 197 A5
Almond Ave
Burscough Bridge L40 25 E6
4 Bury BL9 33 C3
Almond Brook Rd WN6 29 C1
Almond Cl
Abbey Village PR6 80 B2
Fulwood PR2 118 D6
Higher Penwortham PR1 96 B3
Almond Cres BB4 68 F8
Almond St BB3 65 A8
Almonry The L40 17 B7
Alms House Bglws L39 6 A7
Almshouses 14 LA1 214 F7
Alnwick Cl BB12 127 E7
Alpha St
Darwen BB3 65 B8
10 Nelson BB9 170 F2
Salterforth BB18 194 E8
Alpic Dr FY5 152 C7
Alpine Ave
Bamber Bridge PR5 77 B7
Blackpool FY4 110 E5
Alpine Cl
Bamber Bridge PR5 77 B7
Hoddlesden BB3 82 E1
Alpine Gr BB2 81 B8
Alpine Hts PR3 181 B6
Alpine Lo FY8 89 E5
Alpine Rd PR6 61 E3
Alpine View LA5 221 A6
Alsop St PR1 117 F2
Alston Ave FY5 175 D4
Alston Cl BB7 145 F7
Alston Ct
Longridge PR3 140 B6
Southport PR8 21 E6
Alston Dr LA4 217 F5
Alston Hall Coll PR3 120 B8
Alston La PR3 140 A2
Alston Lane RC Prim Sch PR3 139 F2
Alston Rd FY2 152 E2
Alston St PR1 118 D1
Altcar La
Formby L37 11 F1
Haskayne L39 14 A2
Maghull L31 4 F5
Runshaw Moor PR25 59 E5
Altcar Rd L37 12 B2
ALTHAM 125 E6
Altham Bsns Pk BB5 125 E6
Altham Cvn Site BB5 125 C1
Altham Ind Est BB5 125 D6
Altham La BB5 125 F4
Altham Rd
Morecambe LA4 217 C3
Southport PR8 35 E2
Altham St James CE Prim Sch BB5 125 D6
Altham St
2 Burnley BB10 128 A8
6 Padiham BB12 126 D8
Altham Wlk LA4 217 C3
Althorp Cl 6 FY1 130 C7
Althorpe Dr PR8 35 E3
Altom St BB1 101 E6
Alton Cl L38 2 F2
Alt Rd
Formby L37 12 B2
Hightown L38 3 A4
Altys La L39 15 F3
Alum Scar La BB2 100 A6
Alvern Ave PR2 117 D4
Alvern Cres PR2 117 D4
Alvina La L33 1 A5
Alwin St 8 BB11 127 E5
Alwood Ave FY3 130 F6
Amber Ave BB1 122 F2
Amberbanks Gr FY1 130 B2
Amber Dr PR6 43 E6
Ambergate
Fulwood PR2 116 F6
Skelmersdale WN8 9 B7
Amberley St BB2 101 C2
Amberwood PR4 113 F5
Amberwood Dr BB2 101 A1
Ambledene PR5 78 A5
Ambleside Ave
Barnoldswick BB18 196 A3
3 Euxton PR7 60 D1
Knott End-on-S FY6 199 F6
2 Rawtenstall BB4 85 E2
Ambleside Cl
Accrington, Hillock Vale BB5 104 E8
Bamber Bridge PR5 97 E2
Blackburn BB1 102 A6
Ambleside Dr BB3 82 C3
Ambleside Rd
Blackpool FY4 131 D1
Fulwood PR2 118 E5
Lancaster LA1 218 F2
Lytham St Anne's FY8 110 E1
Maghull L31 5 D2
Ambleside Wlk PR2 118 E5
Ambleway PR5 97 C4
Ambrose Ave PR7 60 E6
Ambrose Hall La PR4 136 E3
Ambrose St PR25 77 B2
Amelia St BB1 102 B6
Amersham WN8 9 C7
Amersham Cl PR4 75 F8
Amersham Gr BB10 148 D4
Amethyst St BB1 122 F2
Amounderness Way
Cleveleys FY5 175 F4
Fleetwood FY7 199 A3
Thornton FY5 153 C7
Ampleforth Dr PR5 97 A1
AMS Trad Est PR4 75 D7
Amy Johnson Way FY4 110 E4
Amy St OL12 52 B1
Ancenis Ct PR4 114 B5
ANCHOR 81 F5
Anchorage Ave PR4 72 F1
Anchorage Bsns Pk 3 PR2 95 F8
Anchorage Mews FY7 199 B3
Anchorage Rd FY7 199 B3
Anchor Ave BB3 81 F4
Anchor Ct
Darwen BB3 81 F5
Preston PR1 96 F7
Anchor Dr PR4 95 D2
Anchor Fields PR7 41 B7
Anchor Gr BB3 81 E5
Anchor Ho 1 BB1 101 F4
Anchor Rd BB3 81 F4
Anchor Ret Pk 1 BB11 128 A6
ANCHORSHOLME 175 E1
Anchorsholme La
Cleveleys FY5 152 F8
Thornton FY5 153 A8
Anchorsholme La E FY5 175 E1
Anchorsholme La W FY5 175 C1
Anchorsholme Prim Sch FY5 152 E8
Anchor St PR9 35 B7
Anchor Way FY8 110 E1
Ancliffe La LA2, LA5 221 B2
Andelen Cl BB11 126 C3
Anders Dr L33 1 A5

Anderson Cl
Bacup OL13 87 F1
Lancaster LA1 215 B6
Anderson Rd BB1 123 A7
Anderson St 9 FY1 130 C4
ANDERTON 31 C8
Anderton Cl BB4 69 F7
Anderton Cres PR7 60 E7
Anderton La BL6 31 E4
Anderton Prim Sch PR6 31 B8
Anderton Rd
Euxton PR7 60 D1
Higham BB12 146 F5
Anderton St Joseph's RC Prim Sch PR6 31 B8
Anderton St
Adlington PR7 31 A7
Chorley PR7 43 C7
13 Morecambe LA4 217 A5
Andertons Way PR2 118 D5
Anderton Way PR3 181 D6
Andreas Cl PR8 35 B4
Andrew Ave BB4 85 F1
Andrew Cl
Blackburn BB2 81 B8
Ramsbottom BL8 49 F1
Andrew Rd BB9 171 B1
Andrews Cl L37 11 E1
Andrews La L37 11 E1
Andrew St
Bury BL9 33 A2
Preston PR1 118 C1
Andrews Yort L37 11 E1
Anemone Dr BB4 67 F8
Angela St BB2 101 B1
Angelbank BL6 31 F2
Angel Way 3 BB8 171 E5
Anger's Hill Rd FY4 130 F1
Anglesey Ave BB12 127 A7
Anglesey St BB2 81 B8
Angle St BB10 128 A8
Anglezarke Rd PR6 31 A7
Anglezarke Woodland Trail* PR6 44 D6
Anglian Cl BB5 103 C5
Angus St OL13 70 C8
Aniline St PR6 43 E8
Annan Cres FY4 131 C1
Annandale Gdns WN8 10 A7
Annarly Fold BB10 129 A5
Annaside Cl 2 FY4 110 E7
Anna's Rd FY4 111 E3
Anne Ave PR8 21 E6
Anne Cl 6 BB10 128 B5
Annesley Ave FY3 130 E8
Anne St 2 BB11 128 B5
Annie St
Accrington BB5 104 C7
Ramsbottom BL0 50 A4
5 Rawtenstall BB4 86 A2
Annis St PR1 97 C8
Ann St
Barrowford BB9 170 D3
Brierfield BB9 148 B6
4 Clayton-le-M BB5 124 F3
Skelmersdale WN8 8 E8
Ansbro Ave PR4 93 C6
ANSDELL 90 C4
Ansdell & Fairhaven Sta FY8 90 D4
Ansdell Gr
Fulwood PR2 117 C3
Southport PR9 54 A4
Ansdell Prim Sch FY8 90 C5
Ansdell Rd
Blackpool FY1 130 D2
Horwich BL6 32 C4
Ansdell Rd N FY8 90 D4
Ansdell Rd S FY8 90 D3
Ansdell St 3 PR1 118 C1
Ansdell Terr BB2 101 E1
Anselm Ct FY2 152 B3
Anshaw Cl BL7 46 C5
Anson Cl FY8 110 D1
Anson Rd PR4 114 B2
Anstable Rd LA4 217 E5
Anthony Rd LA1 214 E7
Antigua Dr BB3 81 F6
Antley Ct BB10 148 C1
Antrim Rd FY2 152 C1
Anvil Cl WN5 10 D5
Anvil St OL13 70 E8
Anyon La LA2 207 E6
Anyon St BB3 82 B2
Anzio Rd PR4 132 E5
Apartments The PR9 35 B8
Apex Cl BB11 127 E2
Apiary The PR26 58 A6
Appealing La FY8 110 E2
Appleby Bsns Ctr BB1 102 A5
Appleby Cl
Accrington BB5 104 D5
Gregson Lane PR5 98 E1
Appleby Dr BB9 170 D4
Appleby Rd FY2 152 D1
Appleby St
Blackburn BB1 102 A5
Nelson BB9 148 D8
Preston PR1 117 F1
Apple Cl 2 BB2 101 C4
Applecross Dr BB10 128 E4
Apple Ct 3 BB2 101 C4
Applefields PR25 60 B7
Applegarth
Barnoldswick BB18 196 C3
Applegarth *continued*
Barrowford BB9 170 B1
Applegarth Rd LA3 213 A8
Applegarth St 3 BB18 197 B1
Apple Hey WN6 19 C8
Applesike PR4 95 A1
Apple St BB2 101 C4
Appleton Cl FY6 153 A2
Appleton Rd WN8 17 F2
Appletree Cl
Kingsfold PR1 96 C2
Lancaster LA1 215 A3
Apple Tree Cl
Euxton PR7 60 D3
St Michael's on W PR3 157 C8
Appletree Dr LA1 215 A3
Apple Tree Way BB5 103 E5
Applewood Cl FY8 90 F3
APPLEY BRIDGE 19 D8
Appley Bridge All Saints CE Prim Sch WN6 28 C1
Appley Bridge Sta WN6 19 C7
Appley Cl WN6 28 C2
Appley La N WN6 28 C1
Appley La S WN6, WN8 19 C6
Approach Way BB11 127 F2
Apsley Brow L31 5 B1
Apsley Fold PR3 140 B6
Aquaduct Street Ind Est PR1 117 D1
Aqueduct Mill PR1 117 D1
Aqueduct Rd BB2 101 D1
Aqueduct St PR1 117 E1
Aragon Cl L31 5 E3
Arago St BB5 104 C7
Arbories Ave 4 BB12 126 B8
Arbory Dr BB12 126 B8
Arbory The PR4 112 E7
Arbour Ct L33 1 B2
Arbour Dr BB2 81 D6
Arbour La
Kirkby L33 1 B2
Shevington Moor WN6 29 B1
Arbour Lane End PR3 162 E7
Arbour Pl L33 1 B2
Arbour St
9 Bacup OL13 88 A3
Southport PR8 35 C6
Arboury St BB12 126 B8
Arcade BB5 104 C5
Arcade The 8 BB4 69 E8
Arcadia 9 BB8 171 E5
Arcadia Ave L31 5 D3
Archbishop Temple CE High Sch & Tech Coll PR2 117 F5
Archer Hill LA5 223 D3
Archery Ave BB8 194 D1
Archery Gdns PR3 181 C8
Arches The BB7 144 B6
Arch St
Burnley BB11 127 F6
4 Darwen BB3 82 A1
Archway Bldgs PR2 117 A1
Arcon Ho
5 Coppull PR7 42 E1
Lancaster LA1 214 F5
Lytham St Anne's FY8 91 B4
Arcon Rd PR7 42 E1
Ardee Rd PR1 96 D6
Arden Cl
Slyne LA2 218 C8
Southport PR8 21 A5
Arden Coll PR9 35 C7
Ardengate LA1 214 F4
Arden Gn FY7 198 E4
Ardleigh Ave PR8 35 E3
Ardley Rd BL6 32 C4
Ardmore Rd FY2 152 D2
Ardwick St BB10 128 A8
Argameols Cl PR8 35 F5
Argarmeols Gr L37 11 E5
Argarmeols Rd L37 11 E6
Argosy Ave FY3 130 F8
Argosy Ct 1 FY3 131 A8
Argyle Ct PR9 53 D1
Argyle Rd
7 Leyland PR25 77 A1
Poulton-le-F FY6 153 E3
Southport PR9 53 D2
Argyle St
Accrington BB5 104 B6
8 Colne BB8 171 D5
Darwen BB3 81 F3
Heywood OL10 33 F1
3 Lancaster LA1 215 A7
Argyll Ct FY2 152 C1
Argyll Rd
Blackpool FY2 152 C1
Preston PR1 118 A1
Ariel Way FY7 198 E4
ARKHOLME 241 B2
Arkholme Ave FY1 130 D2
Arkholme CE Prim Sch LA6 241 B3
Arkholme Cl LA5 223 E2
Arkholme Ct 1 LA4 217 B3
Arkholme Dr PR4 94 F1
Arkwright Ct
Blackpool FY4 111 C7
Darwen BB3 81 E5
Arkwright Fold BB2 81 C8
Arkwright Rd PR1 117 F2
Arkwright St
Burnley BB12 127 C7
Horwich BL6 32 C2
Arley Gdns BB12 127 F7
Arley La WN1, WN2 30 D2
Arley Rise BB2 121 E2
Arley St PR6 43 D8
Arley Wood Dr PR7 43 A6
Arlington Ave FY4 110 B7
Arlington Cl
Ramsbottom BL9 50 C2
Southport PR8 21 A5
Arlington Rd BB3 64 F8
Armadale Rd FY2 152 E1
Armaside Rd PR4 116 D4
Armitstead Ct 8 FY7 198 F2
Armitstead Way 5 FY7 198 F2
Armstrong St
Horwich BL6 32 C2
Preston PR2 117 B2
Arncliffe Ave BB5 103 F4
Arncliffe Gr BB9 170 C3
Arncliffe Rd
Burnley BB10 128 E5
Morecambe LA3 216 D1
Arndale Cl FY7 198 C2
Arndale Ctr
9 Morecambe LA4 217 A5
6 Nelson BB9 148 E8
Arndale Rd PR3 140 A7
Arnhem Rd
Carnforth LA5 223 E1
Preston PR1 97 D8
Arnian Ct L39 6 C7
Arnold Ave FY4 110 C7
Arnold Cl
Blackburn BB2 102 A1
Brierfield BB9 148 C5
Burnley BB11 127 E2
Fulwood PR2 118 E2
Arnold Pl 1 PR7 43 A5
Arnold Rd FY8 91 D4
Arnold Sch FY4 110 C7
Arnold St 2 BB5 104 C6
Arno St 9 PR1 97 B7
Arnott Rd
Blackpool FY4 130 E1
Fulwood PR2 117 C2
ARNSIDE 224 B8
Arnside Ave
Blackpool FY1 130 D1
Lytham St Anne's FY8 90 C7
Arnside Cl
Clayton-le-M BB5 124 E2
Coupe Green PR5 98 E4
Lancaster LA1 215 B3
Arnside Cres
Blackburn BB2 80 E8
Morecambe LA4 217 C6
Arnside Rd
Broughton PR3 137 D2
Preston PR2 116 E2
Southport PR9 35 C7
Arnside Terr PR9 35 C7
Arran Ave BB1 102 D2
Arran Cl LA3 212 E7
Arran St BB11 127 D5
Arrow La LA2 219 D7
Arrowsmith Cl PR5 98 E2
Arrowsmith Ct 7 BL6 32 E1
Arrowsmith Dr PR5 98 E2
Arrowsmith Gdns FY5 175 E5
Arroyo Way PR2 118 B4
Arthur St N 5 FY7 199 B5
Arthurs La FY6 177 D2
Arthur St
Bacup OL13 88 B3
Barnoldswick BB18 196 A3
Blackburn BB2 101 C4
Brierfield BB9 148 B6
Burnley BB11 127 E6
Clayton-le-M BB5 124 F3
Earby BB18 195 A7
6 Fleetwood FY7 199 B5
Great Harwood BB6 124 D6
10 Nelson BB9 170 E1
Preston PR1 96 E7
Arthur Way BB2 101 C4
Artlebeck Cl LA2 237 C3
Artlebeck Gr LA2 237 C3
Artlebeck Rd LA2 237 C3
Artle Pl LA1 218 C2
Arundel Ave FY2 152 B5
Arundel Cl 7 BB12 127 D7
Arundel Dr FY6 153 C5
Arundel Pl 16 PR1 97 A7
Arundel Rd
4 Longton PR4 95 A1
Lytham St Anne's FY8 90 C4
Southport PR8 21 F8
Arundel St BB1 124 A2
Arundel Way PR25 60 C8
Ascot Cl
Lancaster LA1 215 B4
Southport PR8 34 E5
Ascot Gdns LA2 218 D8
Ascot Rd
Blackpool FY3 130 E6
Thornton FY5 153 B8
Ascot Way BB5 104 D5
Ascroft Lo PR4 57 A4
Ash Ave
Galgate LA2 210 F4
Haslingden BB4 85 C3
Kirkham PR4 114 A4
Ash Bank Cl PR3 137 B8
Ashborne Dr BL9 50 D2
Ashbourne Cl 7 LA1 218 D3
Ashbourne Cres PR2 117 A5
Ashbourne Dr LA1 218 D3
Ashbourne Gr LA3 217 C2
Ashbourne Rd LA1 218 D3
Ashbridge Ind Sch PR4 95 F2
Ashbrook Cl PR4 73 E3
Ashbrook St LA1 214 D8
Ash Brow WN8 27 B1
Ashburn Cl 7 BL6 32 D1
Ashburnham Rd BB8 171 A2
Ashburton Ct 7 FY1 130 B7
Ashburton Rd FY1 130 B7
Ashby St PR7 43 D6
Ash Cl
Appley Bridge WN6 19 D7
Barrow BB7 166 D1
Elswick PR4 156 A1
Ormskirk L39 15 D5
Rishton BB1 103 B8
Ashcombe Gate FY5 153 D7
Ashcombe Pl BL7 48 E7
Ash Coppice PR2 116 D2
Ashcroft LA3 216 E1
Ashcroft Ave L39 15 F6
Ashcroft Cl LA2 237 B3
Ashcroft Pl BB7 189 E5
Ashcroft Rd
Formby L37 11 F1
Kirkby L33 1 C3
Ash Ct PR4 115 D2
Ashdale Cl
Coppull PR7 29 D8
Formby L37 11 C2
Ashdale Gr FY5 176 E2
Ashdale Pl LA1 218 C2
Ashdene OL12 52 D4
Ashdown Cl
Carleton FY6 153 B5
Southport PR8 35 E4
Ashdown Dr PR6 78 C2
Ashdown Mews PR2 118 E6
Ash Dr
Freckleton PR4 93 A5
Poulton-le-F FY6 153 E2
Thornton FY5 176 C1
Warton LA5 223 E6
Warton PR4 92 D6
West Bradford BB7 189 D7
Asheldon St 1 PR1 118 D1
Ashen Bottom BB4 68 D6
Ashendean View BB12 146 D1
Ashfield PR2 117 F8
Ash Field PR6 78 C3
Ashfield Ave
Lancaster LA1 214 D7
Morecambe LA4 217 F6
Ashfield Cl BB9 170 C1
Ashfield Cotts 2 LA2 239 D8
Ashfield Ct
Adlington PR6 31 B8
Blackpool FY2 152 E6
Fulwood PR2 116 F6
Ashfield Rd
Adlington PR6 31 B8
Blackpool FY2, FY5 152 E6
Burnley BB11 127 F6
Chorley PR7 43 B7
Ashfield Rise PR3 181 D2
Ashfields PR26 76 B1
Ashfield Terr WN6 19 C8
Ashford Ave LA1 214 E3
Ashford Cl LA1 214 F3
Ashford Cres PR3 137 C3
Ashford Rd
Lancaster LA1 214 F3
Preston PR2 116 E2
Ashford St
Heywood OL10 33 F2
Nelson BB9 148 E7
Ash Gr
Bamber Bridge PR5 97 F1
Barnoldswick BB18 196 B2
Chorley PR7 43 C5
Darwen BB3 82 B2
Formby L37 11 C1
Garstang PR3 181 B8
8 Horwich BL6 32 E1
Kirkham PR4 114 B7
Lancaster LA1 214 F5
Longton PR4 74 F8
New Longton PR4 75 F6
Orrell WN5 10 F6
Preesall FY6 200 A4
Ramsbottom BL0 49 F3
3 Rawtenstall BB4 86 A3
Skelmersdale WN8 17 D1
St Michael's on W PR3 157 C7
Water BB4 87 A8
Wrea Green PR4 113 C3
Ashgrove PR1 118 E1
Ash Holme PR1 118 C3
Ashiana Lo 15 BB9 148 E8
Ash La
Clifton PR4 115 E2
Great Harwood BB6 124 B6
Longridge PR3 140 B8
Ashlands Cl BL0 68 D2
Ash Lea Gr FY6 177 C7
Ashleigh Ct PR2 118 A7
Ashleigh Mews FY3 130 E4
Ashleigh Prim Sch BB3 65 A6
Ashleigh St
Darwen BB3 65 B6
Preston PR1 97 C7
Ashley Cl
Blackpool FY2 152 D2
Thornton FY5 153 B7
Ashley Ct
Accrington BB5 103 F5
Poulton-le-F FY6 153 C3
Ashley Gdns LA2 211 A3
Ashley Hall Farm PR3 161 D2
Ashley La PR3 139 C8
Ashley Mews PR2 117 C1
Ashley Rd
Lytham St Anne's FY8 110 F1
Skelmersdale WN8 18 B3
Southport PR9 35 C7
Ashley St BB12 127 F7
Ash Mdw PR2 116 E3
Ashmeadow Gr LA6 221 F5
Ashmeadow La PR6 62 F8
Ashmeadow Rd LA6 221 F5
Ashmead Rd WN8 18 A4
Ashmead View WN8 18 A4
Ashmoor St PR1 117 E1
Ashmore Gr FY5 175 D1
Ashmount Dr OL12 52 F2
Ashness Cl
Fulwood PR2 117 F8
Horwich BL6 31 F3
Ash Rd
Coppull PR7 29 E8
Elswick PR4 156 A1
Ash St
Bacup OL13 87 F3
Blackburn BB1 102 A7
Blackpool FY4 110 C6
Burnley BB11 128 B5
Bury BL9 33 A2
Fleetwood FY7 199 A4
Great Harwood BB6 124 C6
Nelson BB9 148 F8
Oswaldtwistle BB5 103 D4
Southport PR8 35 C5
Trawden BB8 172 C2
Ashton Ave FY6 199 D5
Ashton Barns LA2 210 C7
Ashton Cl PR2 96 A8
Ashton Com Science Coll PR2 116 F2
Ashton Ct
Knott End-on-S FY6 199 D5
Lancaster LA1 214 F7
Ashton Dr
Lancaster LA1 218 C2
Nelson BB9 148 F6
Ashton Garden Ct FY8 89 E7
Ashtongate PR2 116 F1
Ashton Ho BB3 65 B8
Ashton La BB3 65 A8
Ashton Meml* LA1 215 B7
ASHTON-ON-RIBBLE 117 A1
Ashton Prim Sch PR2 116 E2
Ashton Rd
Blackpool FY1 130 C3
8 Darwen BB3 65 B8
Lancaster LA1, LA2 214 E4
Morecambe LA4 217 C5
Southport PR8 34 F1
Ashton St
Longridge PR3 140 A8
8 Lytham St Anne's FY8 91 A3
7 Preston PR2 96 D8
Ashton Wlk 12 LA1 214 F8
Ashtree Ct
Fulwood PR2 117 A4
Higher Walton PR5 98 C3
Ashtree Gr PR1 96 B4
Ash Tree Gr
Hest Bank LA5 220 F3
Nelson BB9 149 A7
Ashtrees L40 40 C2
Ashtrees Way 2 LA5 223 D2
Ash Tree Wlk 18 BB9 170 D3
ASHURST 18 A4
Ashurst Cl WN8 18 A4
Ashurst Ct L37 11 E2
Ashurst Gdns WN8 18 B4
Ashurst Rd
Clayton-le-W PR25 77 D1
Shevington Moor WN6 29 B2
Skelmersdale WN8 18 B4
Ashville Terr BB2 81 D8
Ashwall St WN8 8 E8
Ashwell Pl FY5 152 C7
Ashwood WN8 18 C3
Ashwood Ave
Blackburn BB3 81 D6
Ramsbottom BL0 50 D7
Ashwood Cl FY8 90 E4
Ashwood Ct LA1 214 F5
Ashwood Rd PR2 117 D7
Ashworth Cl BB2 101 C5
Ashworth Ct
5 Blackpool FY3 130 D7
Preston, Fishwick PR1 97 B7
Preston, Frenchwood PR1 97 B6
Ashworth Dr LA2 220 E2
Ashworth Gr PR1 97 C6
Ashworth Hospl L31 6 B2
Ashworth La
Newchurch BB4 86 F3
Preston PR1 97 C6
Ashworth Rd
Blackpool FY4 111 C8
Newchurch BB4 86 F2
Ramsbottom OL11 51 E2
Ashworth St
Accrington BB5 104 E2
15 Bacup, Greave OL13 88 A3
3 Bacup, Stacksteads OL13 70 D8
3 Bamber Bridge PR5 97 F2
1 Preston PR1 97 B7
11 Rawtenstall BB4 69 F8
Rishton BB1 124 B1
Water BB4 87 A7
Ashworth Terr
2 Bacup OL13 70 B8

Ashworth Terr *continued*
7 Darwen BB3 . . . 82 A1
Askrigg Cl
Accrington BB5 . . . 104 E5
Blackpool FY4 . . . 111 A7
Asland Cl PR5 . . . 77 F8
Asland Gdns PR9 . . . 54 C4
Asmall Cl L39 . . . 15 D6
Asmall La
Halsall L39, L40 . . . 14 E8
Ormskirk L39, L40 . . . 15 B7
Asmall Prim Sch L39 . . . 15 D6
Aspden St PR5 . . . 97 E1
Aspels Cres PR1 . . . 96 C4
Aspels Nook PR1 . . . 96 C4
Aspels The PR1 . . . 96 C4
Aspendale Cl PR4 . . . 74 F8
Aspen Dr BB10 . . . 128 C7
Aspen Fold BB5 . . . 103 B5
Aspen Gdns
3 Chorley PR7 . . . 43 B6
Rochdale OL12 . . . 52 A1
Aspen Gr
Earby BB18 . . . 197 C1
Formby L37 . . . 11 C1
Aspen La
Earby BB18 . . . 197 B2
Oswaldtwistle BB5 . . . 103 C4
Aspen Way 3 WN8 . . . 17 E2
Aspinall Cl
Horwich BL6 . . . 32 D1
Kingsfold PR1 . . . 96 D2
Aspinall Cres L37 . . . 12 F1
Aspinall Fold BB1 . . . 101 E8
Aspinall Rd WN6 . . . 29 B1
Aspinall St BL6 . . . 32 D1
Aspinall Way BL6 . . . 32 C1
Aspley Gr BB8 . . . 172 C3
Asshawes The PR6 . . . 43 F1
Assheton Pl PR2 . . . 118 E4
Assheton Rd BB2 . . . 101 A5
Astbury Chase BB3 . . . 82 B2
Asten Bldgs 4 BB4 . . . 69 F7
Aster Chase BB3 . . . 82 A7
Aster Ct L31 . . . 5 C3
Astland Gdns PR4 . . . 73 F2
Astland St FY8 . . . 89 E6
Astley Cres PR4 . . . 93 C6
Astley Ct LA1 . . . 214 D6
Astley Ctr The 2 PR7 . . . 43 D6
Astley Gate BB2 . . . 101 E5
Astley Hall* PR7 . . . 61 A1
Astley Hall Dr BL0 . . . 50 C4
Astley Ho BB11 . . . 128 B6
Astley Hts BB3 . . . 65 A7
Astley Rd PR7 . . . 61 C1
Astley St
Chorley PR7 . . . 61 C1
Darwen BB3 . . . 65 A7
Longridge PR3 . . . 140 A7
Astley Terr BB3 . . . 65 A7
ASTLEY VILLAGE . . . 61 A2
Aston Ave FY5 . . . 176 A2
Aston Manor PR9 . . . 55 A5
Aston St PR4 . . . 132 E6
Aston Way PR26 . . . 76 C2
Aston Wlk BB2 . . . 82 A8
Astronomy Ctr The*
OL14 . . . 88 F4
Asturian Gate PR3 . . . 140 F6
Athelstan Fold PR2 . . . 117 C3
Athens View BB10 . . . 128 C5
Atherton Cl 2 PR2 . . . 117 C2
Atherton Rd PR25 . . . 59 D8
Atherton St
Adlington PR7 . . . 31 A6
Bacup OL13 . . . 70 C8
Atherton Way OL13 . . . 70 B8
Athletic St BB10 . . . 128 C5
Athlone Ave FY2 . . . 152 C2
Athole Gr PR9 . . . 35 F7
Athol Gr PR6 . . . 43 E6
Atholl St 12 PR1 . . . 96 D8
Athol St N BB11 . . . 127 D5
Athol St S BB11 . . . 127 D5
Athol St
Nelson BB9 . . . 148 F8
Ramsbottom BL0 . . . 50 C7
Atkinson Cl 15 PR1 . . . 96 F8
Atkinson St
Burnley BB10 . . . 148 F3
Colne BB8 . . . 171 D4
Atlas Rd BB3 . . . 82 B1
Atlas St BB5 . . . 125 A1
Atrium Ct 9 BB11 . . . 128 B4
Aubigny Dr PR2 . . . 117 D4
Auburn Gr FY1 . . . 130 D2
Auckland St BB3 . . . 65 B7
Audenlea FY5 . . . 175 F3
Audenshaw Rd LA4 . . . 217 C4
Audley Cl
Lytham St Anne's FY8 . . . 90 D5
14 Nelson BB9 . . . 148 E8
Audley Inf & Jun Schs
BB1 . . . 102 A3
Audley La BB1 . . . 102 A4
Audley Range BB1 . . . 102 B4
Audley St BB1 . . . 102 A5
Audlum Ct 5 BL9 . . . 33 A2
AUGHTON
Hornby . . . 237 E6
Ormskirk . . . 6 A7
Aughton Brow LA2 . . . 237 E6
Aughton Chase PR8 . . . 35 A5
Aughton Christ Church CE
Prim Sch L39 . . . 15 C3
Aughton Ct LA1 . . . 218 D4
Aughton Hall Cotts L39 . . . 15 C6
Aughton Mews PR8 . . . 35 A5
AUGHTON PARK . . . 15 E2
Aughton Park Dr L39 . . . 15 D2
Aughton Park Sta L39 . . . 15 D2
Aughton Rd
Aughton LA2 . . . 237 E6
Southport PR8 . . . 35 A5
Aughton St Michael's CE
Prim Sch L39 . . . 15 B1
Aughton St
Fleetwood FY7 . . . 199 B5
Ormskirk L39 . . . 15 E4
Aughton Town Green Prim
Sch L39 . . . 6 D8
Aughton Wlk 2 PR1 . . . 117 F1
Augusta Cl OL12 . . . 52 E2
Augusta St
4 Accrington BB5 . . . 104 C4
4 Rochdale OL12 . . . 52 E1
Auster Cres PR4 . . . 114 B2
Austin Cres PR2 . . . 117 B4
Austin Gr FY1 . . . 130 B1
Austins Cl PR25 . . . 60 A8
Austin's La BL6 . . . 32 F1
Austin St
6 Bacup OL13 . . . 87 F2
5 Burnley BB11 . . . 127 E5
Austin Way FY4 . . . 112 A7
Austwick Rd 4 LA1 . . . 218 B2
Austwick Way BB5 . . . 104 E5
Avallon Way BB3 . . . 82 C1
Avalon Cl 5 BB12 . . . 126 F7
Avalon Dr PR4 . . . 93 C7
Avalwood Ave PR4 . . . 75 B8
Avebury Cl
Blackburn BB2 . . . 82 A8
Horwich BL6 . . . 32 F1
Aveling Dr PR9 . . . 55 A6
Avelon Cl L31 . . . 5 B5
AVENHAM . . . 97 A6
Avenham Cl PR9 . . . 55 B5
Avenham Colonnade
PR1 . . . 97 A6
Avenham Ct 19 PR1 . . . 97 A7
Avenham Gr 5 FY1 . . . 130 B6
Avenham La PR1 . . . 97 A7
Avenham Mills 28 PR1 . . . 97 A7
Avenham Pl
Newton-w-S PR4 . . . 114 F2
6 Preston PR1 . . . 97 A6
Avenham Rd
1 Chorley PR7 . . . 43 C7
Preston PR1 . . . 97 A7
Avenham St PR1 . . . 97 A7
Avenham Terr 11 PR1 . . . 97 A6
Avenue Par BB5 . . . 104 D6
Avenue Rd
Hurst Green BB7 . . . 164 E1
Normoss FY3 . . . 131 B7
Avenue The
Adlington PR6 . . . 31 A8
Banks PR9 . . . 54 F5
Barley BB12 . . . 169 C5
Burnley BB10, BB11 . . . 128 D3
Carleton FY6 . . . 153 C4
Churchtown PR3 . . . 181 A3
Fulwood PR2 . . . 117 A6
Garstang PR3 . . . 204 B1
Higher Penwortham PR1 . . . 96 B5
Leyland PR25 . . . 60 A6
Ormskirk L39 . . . 15 D6
Ormskirk L39 . . . 15 E6
Orrell WN5 . . . 10 D3
Preston PR2 . . . 116 D1
Southport PR8 . . . 36 F5
Avery Gdns FY6 . . . 153 B6
Aviemore Cl
5 Blackburn BB1 . . . 102 A4
2 Ramsbottom BL0 . . . 50 A2
Avocet Ct PR26 . . . 76 A1
Avon Ave FY7 . . . 175 D8
Avon Bridge PR2 . . . 117 C8
Avon Cl BB2 . . . 101 D3
Avon Ct BB12 . . . 127 D7
Avondale Ave
Blackburn BB1 . . . 102 E5
Burnley BB12 . . . 127 C7
Avondale Cl BB3 . . . 81 E2
Avondale Cres FY4 . . . 110 F7
Avondale Dr
Bamber Bridge PR5 . . . 77 B8
Ramsbottom BL0 . . . 49 F2
Tarleton PR4 . . . 57 A8
Avondale Mews BB3 . . . 81 E3
Avondale Prim Sch BB3 . . . 81 E2
Avondale Rd
Chorley PR7 . . . 43 C7
Darwen BB3 . . . 81 E3
Lancaster LA1 . . . 215 A6
Lytham St Anne's FY8 . . . 89 C8
Morecambe LA3 . . . 216 E3
Nelson BB9 . . . 148 D7
Southport PR9 . . . 35 B8
Avondale Rd N PR9 . . . 53 C1
Avondale St
Colne BB8 . . . 172 A5
Standish WN6 . . . 29 E2
Avon Dr
Barnoldswick BB18 . . . 196 C3
Bury BL9 . . . 33 A8
Avon Gdns PR4 . . . 116 D5
Avon Gn FY7 . . . 198 E4
Avonhead Cl BL6 . . . 31 F3
Avon Ho 12 PR1 . . . 97 D8
Avon Pl FY1 . . . 130 C8
Avonside Ave FY5 . . . 176 A3
Avon St FY8 . . . 89 E6
Avonwood Cl BB3 . . . 81 E2
Avroe Cres FY4 . . . 110 D4
Axeholme Ct BL6 . . . 31 F3
Aylesbury Ave FY4 . . . 130 D1
Aylesbury Ho L31 . . . 5 B4
Aylesbury Wlk BB10 . . . 148 D3
Ayr Cl PR8 . . . 35 F4
Ayr Ct FY7 . . . 175 E7
Ayrefield Gr WN6 . . . 19 D6
Ayrefield Rd WN8 . . . 19 C4
Ayreshire Cl PR7 . . . 60 F6
Ayr Gr BB11 . . . 127 D3
Ayr Rd BB1 . . . 102 D3
Ayr St LA1 . . . 215 B7
Ayrton Ave FY4 . . . 110 D7
Ayrton St BB8 . . . 171 E5
Ayrton View LA2 . . . 218 E4
Aysgarth Ave PR2 . . . 117 F7
Aysgarth Ct 1 FY4 . . . 110 F7
Aysgarth Dr
Accrington BB5 . . . 104 D6
Darwen BB3 . . . 81 E2
Lancaster LA1 . . . 218 D4
Ays-Garth Rd LA1 . . . 214 D8
Azalea Cl
Clayton-le-W PR25 . . . 77 E2
Fulwood PR2 . . . 118 C6
Azalea Gr LA4 . . . 217 E5
Azalea Rd BB2 . . . 101 B6

B

Babbacombe Ave FY4 . . . 110 B6
Babylon La PR6 . . . 31 B8
Back Albert Rd BB8 . . . 171 D4
Back Albert St
Bury BL9 . . . 33 A2
10 Padiham BB12 . . . 126 C8
Back Alfred St 11 BL0 . . . 50 B5
Back Altham St 5
BB12 . . . 126 D8
Back Andrew St N 13
BL9 . . . 33 A2
Back Andrew St 14 BL9 . . . 33 A2
Back Arthur St 15 BB5 . . . 124 F3
Back Ashburton Rd 14
FY1 . . . 130 C7
Back Ashby St 1 PR7 . . . 43 D6
Back Ash St 8 BL9 . . . 33 A2
Back Atkinson St BB8 . . . 171 C4
Back Avondale Rd (E) 4
LA3 . . . 216 E3
Back Avondale Rd (W)
LA3 . . . 216 E3
Back Bath St PR9 . . . 35 B8
Back Bell La
8 Bury BL9 . . . 33 A3
Bury BL9 . . . 33 B3
Back Benson St BL9 . . . 33 A1
Back Blackburn Rd E
BL7 . . . 47 D3
Back Blackburn Rd W
BL7 . . . 47 D3
Back Bolton Rd BB3 . . . 65 B7
Back Bond St W BL9 . . . 33 A2
Back Bond St BB8 . . . 171 D5
Back Boundary St 14
BB8 . . . 171 D4
Back Bourne's Row PR5 . . . 98 E1
Back Bridge St 2 BL0 . . . 50 C6
Back Broading Terr
BB4 . . . 106 A3
Back Brook St N 13 BL9 . . . 33 A4
Back Brow WN8 . . . 10 C7
Back Brown St BB8 . . . 171 C4
Back Burnley Rd BB5 . . . 104 C6
Back Burton Rd FY4 . . . 130 F1
Back Calton St LA4 . . . 217 B6
Back Cambridge St 10
BB8 . . . 171 D4
Back Canada St BL6 . . . 32 B3
Back Carr Mill St BB4 . . . 85 B5
Back Cedar St N 1 BL9 . . . 33 B3
Back Cedar St 2 BL9 . . . 33 B3
Back Cemetery Terr 9
OL13 . . . 70 D8
Back Chapel St
1 Barnoldswick BB18 . . . 196 B2
4 Colne BB8 . . . 171 D4
Horwich BL6 . . . 32 C3
Back Chesham Rd N 5
BL9 . . . 33 A4
Back Chesham Rd S
BL9 . . . 33 A4
Back Chester St BL9 . . . 33 A4
Back Church St
Barrowford BB9 . . . 170 D3
8 Blackpool FY1 . . . 130 B5
5 Great Harwood BB6 . . . 124 C5
3 Hapton BB12 . . . 126 C4
1 Newchurch BB4 . . . 86 E1
Back Clarendon Rd
FY1 . . . 130 B2
Back Clayton St 9
BB9 . . . 170 D1
Back Club St PR5 . . . 77 E7
Back Colne Rd
Barnoldswick BB18 . . . 196 A1
Trawden BB8 . . . 172 C2
Back Commons BB7 . . . 189 D1
Back Constablelee BB4 . . . 85 F4
Back Cookson St 12
FY1 . . . 130 C6
Back Cowm La OL12 . . . 71 C3
Back Crescent St LA4 . . . 217 A5
Back Crown St BL6 . . . 32 A4
Back Cunliffe Rd 4
FY1 . . . 130 D2
Back Curzon St FY8 . . . 90 A7
Back Darwen Rd N 2
BL7 . . . 47 E1
Back Deal St BL9 . . . 33 B2
Back Delamere St S
BL9 . . . 33 A5
Back Derby St 6 BB8 . . . 171 D5
Back Drinkhouse La
PR26 . . . 58 B1
Back Duckworth St
4 Bury BL9 . . . 33 A4
12 Darwen BB3 . . . 82 A1
Back Duke St 1 BB8 . . . 171 D4
Back Duncan St BL6 . . . 32 C3
Back Earl St 2 BB8 . . . 171 D4
Back East Bank 1
BB9 . . . 170 D4
Back Eaves St FY1 . . . 130 B7
Back Elizabeth St BB4 . . . 86 F4
Back Elm St 10 BL9 . . . 33 B2
Back Emmett St BL6 . . . 32 B3
Back Epsom Rd FY5 . . . 152 F8
Back Fazakerley St 14
PR7 . . . 43 C8
Back Fir St BL9 . . . 33 B2
Back Fletcher St BL9 . . . 33 A2
Back Forest Rd PR8 . . . 35 D6
Back Garston St BL9 . . . 33 A4
Back George St BL6 . . . 32 C3
Back Gisburn Rd BB9 . . . 170 E7
Back Glen Eldon Rd
FY8 . . . 89 E7
Back Green St 7 LA4 . . . 217 B6
Back Grimshaw St 8
PR1 . . . 97 A7
Back Grove Terr 10
LA4 . . . 217 F4
Back Hall St BB8 . . . 171 D4
Back Halstead St 2
BL9 . . . 33 A4
Back Hamilton St 1
BL9 . . . 33 A4
Back Harry St BB9 . . . 170 D3
Back Haslam St BL9 . . . 33 A4
Back Headroomgate Rd
FY8 . . . 89 F8
Back Heys BB5 . . . 103 E3
Back Heywood St E 15
BL9 . . . 33 A2
Back Heywood St W
BL9 . . . 33 A1
Back High St
Belmont BL7 . . . 46 C5
Blackpool FY1 . . . 130 B6
Chapeltown BL7 . . . 48 C4
Back Hill St 17 BB4 . . . 86 A7
Back Holly St S 9 BL9 . . . 33 A2
Back Holly St BL9 . . . 33 A2
Back Hope St OL13 . . . 87 F4
Backhouse St 1 BB5 . . . 103 E4
Back Hunter St 1
LA5 . . . 223 D2
Back Huntley Mount Rd
BL9 . . . 33 B3
Back Hurst St BL9 . . . 33 A1
Back Ingham St E BL9 . . . 33 A1
Back Ingham St BL9 . . . 33 A1
Back Kershaw St 10
BL9 . . . 33 A2
Back Knowlys Rd 2
LA3 . . . 212 F8
Back La
Accrington BB5 . . . 104 E1
Appley Bridge WN6 . . . 19 E8
Bolton Green PR7 . . . 42 B7
Bretherton PR26 . . . 57 E5
Burscough Bridge L40 . . . 25 E6
Carnforth LA5, LA6 . . . 221 E7
Chorley PR6 . . . 44 C5
Clayton Green PR6 . . . 78 A2
Cumeragh Village PR3 . . . 139 B6
Gisburn BB7 . . . 231 C3
Great Eccleston PR3 . . . 156 B5
Greenhalgh PR4 . . . 133 B4
Grindleton BB7 . . . 190 B8
Haskayne, Clieves Hills
L39 . . . 14 E1
Haskayne L39 . . . 13 D3
Higham BB12 . . . 146 E6
Leyland PR25 . . . 60 C7
Longridge PR3 . . . 161 B6
Longton PR4 . . . 74 E8
Maghull L39 . . . 5 E6
Mawdesley L40 . . . 40 D1
Nelson BB10 . . . 149 F7
Newburgh L40, WN8 . . . 26 E2
Newton BB7 . . . 228 F6
Preesall FY6 . . . 200 A2
Rathmell BD24 . . . 236 F6
Rawtenstall BB4 . . . 86 A3
Rimington BB7 . . . 191 E8
Royal Oak L39 . . . 7 B2
Sabden BB12, BB7 . . . 146 C6
Skelmersdale, Digmoor
WN8 . . . 9 D6
Skelmersdale, Holland Moor
WN8 . . . 9 E7
Stalmine FY6 . . . 177 E6
Trawden BB8 . . . 172 B2
Tunstall LA6 . . . 241 D4
Warton LA5 . . . 223 D5
Whitworth OL12 . . . 71 C3
Wiswell BB7 . . . 144 F8
Wray LA2 . . . 238 C6
Wrayton LA6 . . . 241 E2
Back La E L40 . . . 40 F1
Back Lathom St 9 BL9 . . . 33 A4
Back Laurel St 2 BL9 . . . 33 B2
Back Leach St BB8 . . . 171 C4
Back Lee St BB4 . . . 85 B2
Back Lines St 2 LA4 . . . 217 B5
Back Longworth Rd
BL7 . . . 47 D3
Back Lord St
Blackpool FY1 . . . 130 B6
7 Lancaster LA1 . . . 218 D1
5 Rawtenstall BB4 . . . 86 A7
Back Lune St BB8 . . . 171 E4
Back Manor St 1 BL9 . . . 33 A2
Back Marine Rd LA4 . . . 216 F4
Back Mason St 17 BL9 . . . 33 A2
Back Moon Ave 5
FY1 . . . 130 B2
Back Morecambe St
LA4 . . . 217 B6
Back Moss La L40 . . . 25 F7
Back Mount St 5 PR7 . . . 43 C8
Back Myrtle St S BL9 . . . 33 B2
Back Myrtle St 4 BL9 . . . 33 B2
Back Nelson St BL6 . . . 32 D3
Back New St 5 LA5 . . . 223 D2
Back Nook Terr 2
OL12 . . . 52 F3
Back North Cres FY8 . . . 89 E6
Back Oddfellows Terr
BB4 . . . 86 F3
Back Oram St BL9 . . . 33 A4
Back Ormrod St 11 BL9 . . . 33 A2
Back O The Town La L38 . . . 3 E3
Back Owen's Row BL6 . . . 32 C3
Back Oxford St BL9 . . . 33 A1
Back Parkinson St
BB2 . . . 101 B2
Back Parsonage St 10
BL9 . . . 33 A3
Back Patience St 10
OL12 . . . 52 C1
Back Percy St BL9 . . . 33 B3
Back Peter St
8 Barrowford BB9 . . . 170 D4
3 Bury BL9 . . . 33 A3
Back Pine St 1 BL9 . . . 33 B2
Back Pleasant St 5
FY1 . . . 130 B7
Back Queen St
Great Harwood BB6 . . . 124 C5
12 Lancaster LA1 . . . 214 F7
1 Morecambe LA4 . . . 217 B5
Back Railway View PR7 . . . 31 A7
Back Rawlinson St 16
BL6 . . . 32 B4
Back Read's Rd FY1 . . . 130 C4
Back Regent St 1 BB4 . . . 85 B3
Back Rhoden Rd BB5 . . . 103 D2
Back Richard Burch St 1
BL9 . . . 33 A3
Back Rings Row BB4 . . . 106 A1
Back Rochdale Old Rd N 1
BL9 . . . 33 C3
Back Rochdale Old Rd S
3 Bury BL9 . . . 33 C3
Bury, Fairfield BL9 . . . 33 D3
Back Rochdale Rd BL9 . . . 33 B2
Back Rochdale Rd S 18
BL9 . . . 33 A2
Back Roseberry Ave N 4
LA4 . . . 217 C5
Back Rushton St 6
OL13 . . . 70 E8
Back St Anne's Rd W
FY8 . . . 89 E6
Back St George's Sq
FY8 . . . 89 D7
Back St John St OL13 . . . 87 F3
Back Salford St BL9 . . . 33 A4
Back Sandy Bank Rd
BL7 . . . 48 D5
Back School La
Skelmersdale WN8 . . . 17 D2
Up Holland WN8 . . . 10 C7
Back Seed St 8 PR1 . . . 96 F8
Back Shannon St 4
FY1 . . . 130 B3
Back Shaw-Street BL9 . . . 33 B3
Back Shuttleworth St 7
BB12 . . . 126 C8
Back Skipton Rd 8
BB18 . . . 196 B2
Back Skull House La
WN6 . . . 19 C8
Back South Cross St E 16
BL9 . . . 33 A2
Back Spencer St BB4 . . . 86 A7
Back Springfield Rd N
FY8 . . . 89 E6
Back Square St BL0 . . . 50 C6
Back St LA3 . . . 209 D8
Back Stanley St BL0 . . . 50 B5
Back Starkie St PR1 . . . 96 F6
Backs The PR3 . . . 140 A6
Back Sun St 9 LA1 . . . 214 F8
Back Teak St 5 BL9 . . . 33 B2
Back Tinline St 12 BL9 . . . 33 A2
Back Union St 7 BL7 . . . 47 D2
Back Virginia St PR8 . . . 35 C6
Back Warbreck Rd 2
FY1 . . . 130 B6
Back Wash La BL9 . . . 33 B2
Back Wash La S 7 BL9 . . . 33 A2
Back Waterloo Rd 8
FY1 . . . 130 B1
Back Water St
10 Accrington BB5 . . . 104 C6

Back Water St *continued*
5 Bolton BL7 47 D2
Back Wellington St
BB5 104 C5
Back West Cres FY8 89 E6
Back West End Rd N
LA4 216 F4
Back Willow St BB12 127 E6
Back Winterdyne Terr
LA3 216 E4
Back Woodfield Rd 4
FY1 130 B2
Back Wood St BL6 32 C3
Back Wright St BL6 32 B4
Back York St
Clitheroe BB7 166 F8
Rawtenstall BB4 86 A7
Back Zion St 16 BB8 171 D4
Bacon St 8 BB9 148 E8
BACUP 70 E8
Bacup Holy Trinity Stacksteads CE Prim Sch
OL13 70 C8
Bacup Mus* OL13 87 F3
Bacup Old Rd OL13 87 F7
Bacup & Rawtenstall Gram Sch BB4 69 F8
Bacup Rd
Rawtenstall BB4, OL13 69 E8
Rawtenstall, Lower Cloughfold
BB4 86 C2
Todmorden OL14 88 E5
Walk Mill BB11 107 E6
Bacup St Saviour's Com Prim Sch OL13 71 A8
Bacup Thorn Prim Sch
OL13 87 F3
Baden Ct BB1 122 F3
Baden Terr BB2 101 D1
Badge Brow BB5 103 E5
Badger Cl BB12 146 D1
Badger Rd PR26 77 A4
Badgers Cl BB5 104 E8
Badgers Croft PR2 118 F1
Badgers Rake L37 11 C5
Badger St BL9 33 A3
Badgers Way PR5 97 B3
Badgers Wlk PR7 61 A3
Badgers Wlk E FY8 91 C3
Badgers Wlk W 12 FY8 91 B3
Badgers Wood PR3 159 C7
Badger Wells Cotts
BB7 146 A8
Bagganley La
Chorley PR6 61 E1
Great Knowley PR6 61 F2
Bagnold Rd PR1 118 D1
Bagot St FY1 130 B1
Baildon Rd OL12 52 B1
Bailey Bank BB7 165 A7
Bailey Cl BB2 81 C8
Bailey Ct FY3 130 E6
Bailey La
Heysham LA3 212 E8
Tosside BD23 236 B3
Bailey St
Burnley BB11 127 E5
Earby BB18 197 C1
Baillie St
Fulwood PR2 118 C7
Fulwood PR2 118 C7
BAILRIGG 215 A1
Bailrigg Chase LA1 215 B1
Bailrigg La LA1 215 A1
Baines Ave FY3 152 F1
Baines Endowed CE Prim Sch FY4 130 F1
Bainesfield FY6 153 D1
Baines Sch FY6 153 D1
Bairstow St
3 Barnoldswick BB18 196 B3
Blackpool FY1 130 B3
14 Preston PR1 96 F7
Bakers Ct FY4 110 F7
Baker's La PR9 53 F3
Bakers Mews PR4 57 A6
Baker St
12 Bacup OL13 87 F3
Blackburn BB1 102 B4
Burnley BB11 127 E5
Coppull PR7 42 E1
Lancaster LA1 218 D3
4 Leyland PR25 77 B2
Nelson BB9 170 E1
Ramsbottom BL0 50 B5
Bala Cl BB1 101 E6
Balaclava St BB1 101 E6
Balcarres Ct PR25 77 A1
Balcarres Pl PR25 60 A8
Balcarres Rd
Chorley PR7 43 B5
Leyland PR25 60 A8
Leyland PR25 77 B1
Preston PR2 117 C2
BALDERSTONE 121 A5
Balderstone Cl BB10 148 D2
Balderstone Hall La
BB2 120 C6
Balderstone La BB10 148 E2
Balderstone Rd
Freckleton PR4 93 B7
Preston PR1 96 D5
BALDINGSTONE 50 F1
Baldwin Gr FY1 130 D2
Baldwin Hill 3 BB7 166 D8
Baldwin Rd BB7 166 D8
Baldwin's Bldgs 14 BB4 86 A3
Baldwin St
Bacup OL13 70 B8
7 Bamber Bridge PR5 97 E1
5 Barrowford BB9 170 D4
Blackburn BB2 101 C3
Balfour Cl
Brierfield BB9 148 D5
Thornton FY5 153 D7
Balfour Ct 9 PR25 77 A1
Balfour Ho 5 BB2 101 C4
Balfour Rd
Fulwood PR2 117 E3
5 Rochdale OL12 52 C1
Southport PR8 35 E5
Balfour St
Blackburn BB2 101 C4
Great Harwood BB6 124 E5
Leyland PR25 77 A1
Balham Ave FY4 110 E5
BALLADEN 68 F8
Balladen Com Prim Sch
BB4 68 F8
Ballam Rd
Lower Ballam FY8 112 C3
Lytham St Anne's FY8 91 B4
Preston PR2 116 E1
Ballam St BB11 128 A4
Ballantrae Rd BB1 102 D3
Ballater St BB11 127 D3
Balle St BB3 65 A8
Ball Grove Dr BB8 172 B5
Balliol Cl BB12 126 D6
Ball La LA2 237 C3
Ballot Hill Cres PR3 159 A5
Ball's Pl PR8 35 B7
Ball St
Blackpool FY1 130 B1
3 Nelson BB9 170 D1
Poulton-le-F FY6 153 D3
Balmer Gr FY1 130 D3
Balmoral PR7 30 E6
Balmoral Ave
Blackburn BB1 123 A4
Clitheroe BB7 166 C6
Leyland PR25 60 C8
Morecambe LA3 216 E3
Balmoral Cl
Horwich BL6 32 E2
Ramsbottom BL8 50 A1
Southport PR9 54 B3
Walmer Bridge PR4 74 F5
Balmoral Cres BB1 102 F4
Balmoral Ct PR7 43 B8
Balmoral Dr
Brinscall PR6 62 E8
Formby L37 11 E1
Southport PR9 54 B3
Balmoral Pl FY5 153 C8
Balmoral Rd
Accrington BB5 104 D7
5 Bamber Bridge PR5 97 D3
Blackpool FY4 110 B8
Chorley PR7 43 B8
Darwen BB3 65 B6
Eccleston PR7 41 C7
Haslingden BB4 85 A1
Lancaster LA1 215 A7
Lytham St Anne's FY8 90 A5
Maghull L31 5 C1
Morecambe LA3, LA4 216 F3
New Longton PR4 96 A1
Balmoral Terr FY7 199 B5
Balm St BL0 50 A4
Balniel Cl PR7 43 A7
Balshaw Ave PR7 60 D2
Balshaw Cres PR25 76 F2
Balshaw House Gdns
PR7 60 D2
Balshaw La PR7 60 D1
Balshaw Lane Com Prim Sch PR7 60 E1
Balshaw Rd
Leyland PR25 76 F1
Lowgill LA2 239 E3
Balshaw's CE High Sch
PR25 60 B7
Balshaw St 4 PR5 97 E2
Baltic Bldgs 4 BB4 69 E8
Baltic Flats 3 BB4 69 E8
Baltic Rd 5 BB4 69 E8
Baltimore Rd FY8 90 B6
Bamber Ave
Blackpool FY2 152 C4
Buckshaw Village PR7 60 E7
BAMBER BRIDGE 97 E1
Bamber Bridge Sta PR5 77 E8
Bamber Gdns PR9 36 A8
Bambers La FY4 111 C6
Bambers La N FY4 111 C7
Bamber St 2 PR7 43 B5
Bamber's Wlk PR4 113 E7
Bamburgh Cl FY4 111 A7
Bamburgh Dr BB12 127 E7
Bamford Cl BL9 33 E4
Bamford Cres BB5 104 D4
Bamford Pl 3 OL12 52 E1
Bamford Rd BL0 51 B6
Bamfords Fold PR26 57 F5
Bamford St
Burnley BB11 128 A6
Nelson BB9 149 A8
Bampton Dr PR4 116 D4
Bamton Ave FY4 110 C7
Banastre PR7 61 A2
Banastre Rd PR8 35 B5
Banastre St 10 BB5 125 A1
Banbury Ave
Blackpool FY2 152 D1
Oswaldtwistle BB5 103 C4
Banbury Cl
3 Accrington BB5 104 A7
Blackburn BB2 80 F8
Banbury Dr PR2 117 E4
Banbury Rd
Longshaw WN5 10 D2
Lytham St Anne's FY8 90 A6
Morecambe LA3 217 C3
Bancroft Ave FY5 176 C2
Bancroft Fold BB18 196 A1
Bancroft Mill Engine Mus*
BB18 196 B1
Bancroft Rd BB10 128 C8
Bancroft St 4 BB1 101 F5
Band La PR3 180 D1
Bangor Ave FY2 152 D4
BANGOR'S GREEN 14 D7
Bangor St BB1 101 F7
Bank Ave WN5 10 D5
Bank Bottom BB3 82 A1
Bank Bridge PR4 57 B5
Bank Brow WN8 19 C5
Bank Cl
Galgate LA2 210 F3
Longton PR4 75 A8
Bank Cott 2 LA2 239 B8
Bank Cotts BB7 144 B4
Bank Croft PR4 75 A8
Bankcroft Cl BB12 126 E8
Bank End Cvn Pk LA2 205 D6
Bankfield
Burnley BB11 128 A6
Skelmersdale WN8 9 C7
Bankfield Ct FY5 153 B8
Bankfield Gr FY1 130 E3
Bankfield La PR9 54 B2
Bankfield St
Bacup OL13 70 D8
Colne BB8 171 B4
Trawden BB8 172 B4
Bankfield Terr
1 Bacup OL13 70 D8
Barnoldswick BB18 196 C3
BANK FOLD 82 F5
Bank Fold BB9 170 E4
Bank Hall Cotts BB7 230 C1
Bank Hall Terr BB10 128 A7
Bank Head La PR5 98 D1
BANK HEY 123 A2
Bank Hey Cl BB1 123 A1
Bank Hey La N BB1 122 F3
Bank Hey La S BB1 123 A1
Bank Hey St FY1 130 B5
Bank Hey View BB2 81 C7
Bank House La
Bacup OL13 87 F2
Silverdale LA5 224 C3
Westhouse LA6 242 E4
Bankhouse Mews BB9 170 E4
Bankhouse Rd BB9 170 E1
BANK HOUSES 205 C7
Bankhouse St
Burnley BB11 127 F6
Burnley BB11 128 A6
Bank House St BB9 170 E4
Bank La
Blackburn BB1 102 D4
Warton PR4 92 D4
BANK LANE 50 E7
Bank Mdw BL6 32 C4
Bank Mill St 3 BB4 85 B2
Bank Nook PR9 53 F3
Bank Par
Burnley BB11 128 A6
Middleforth Green PR1 96 D3
Preston PR1 97 A6
Bank Pas PR8 35 A7
Bank Pl PR2 117 C1
Bank Rd
Lancaster LA1 218 D3
Up Holland WN8 19 D4
BANKS 54 F6
Banksands La PR3 201 E7
Banksbarn WN8 9 C7
Banks Bridge Cl BB18 196 C4
Banks Cres LA3 212 F6
Banksfield Ave PR2 117 C3
Banksfield Pl PR5 78 A7
BANKS HILL 196 B4
Banks Hill BB18 196 A4
Bankside
Blackburn BB2 101 E2
Clayton Green PR6 78 B1
Hightown L38 2 F3
Parbold WN8 27 B2
Bankside Cl
Bacup OL13 87 E1
Goodshaw Chapel BB4 106 A1
Bankside La OL13 87 F2
Banks Meth Sch PR9 55 B7
Bank Sq PR9 35 B8
Banks Rd
Fulwood PR2 117 C3
Southport PR9 54 D6
Banks Rise 10 LA2 239 D8
Banks St Stephens' CE Sch
PR9 55 A5
Banks St
Blackpool FY1 130 B6
Lane Bottom BB10 149 B3
Bank St
Accrington BB5 104 C5
Adlington PR7 31 A7
14 Bacup OL13 87 F2
Bank Lane BL0 50 E7
Bank St *continued*
Barnoldswick BB18 196 C2
Brierfield BB9 148 B6
Chapeltown BL7 48 C4
Chorley PR7 43 C8
Church BB5 103 E6
Darwen BB3 82 A1
Haslingden BB4 85 B3
11 Nelson BB9 170 E1
Padiham BB12 146 C1
Rawtenstall BB4 86 A2
Trawden BB8 172 C1
Banks Way 12 LA2 239 D8
Bank Terr
Heapey PR6 62 C4
Simonstone BB12 125 E8
Whitworth OL12 52 C8
Bank Top BL9 50 F1
BANK TOP 101 D3
Bank Top
Blackburn BB2 101 C4
Burnley BB11 128 A6
BANK TOP 19 C4
Bank View FY6 177 C1
Bank View Cotts BB7 230 C1
Bankwood WN6 19 E6
Banner Cl PR7 41 B6
Bannerigg Brow LA6 243 A5
Bannerman Terr PR6 61 D2
Bannister Brook Ho
PR25 77 A2
Bannister Cl
Higher Walton PR5 98 B4
Trawden BB8 172 B3
Bannister Ct
Blackpool FY2 152 B4
17 Nelson BB9 148 E8
Bannister Dr PR25 76 E1
Bannister Gn PR7 41 C3
Bannister Hall Cres
PR5 98 B4
Bannister Hall Dr PR5 98 B4
Bannister Hall La PR5 98 B4
Bannister La
Eccleston PR7 41 C5
Hill Dale L40, WN6 27 E6
Leyland PR26 76 E4
Bannister's Bit 4 PR1 96 C2
Bannister St
11 Chorley PR7 43 C7
Lytham St Anne's FY8 91 B3
Bannistre Cl 1 FY8 90 A8
Bannistre Ct PR4 57 A6
Bannistre Mews PR4 57 A6
Barbara Castle Way
BB1 101 E5
Barberry Bank BL7 47 E2
BARBER'S MOOR 58 D3
BARBON 243 A5
Barbondale Rd LA6,
LA10 243 E8
Barbon Pl LA1 218 C2
Barbon St
Burnley BB10 148 C2
14 Padiham BB12 146 C1
Barbrook Cl WN6 29 B2
Barclay Ave
Blackpool FY4 130 F2
Burnley BB11 127 C4
Barclay Ct PR3 140 A7
Barclay Rd PR3 140 A7
Bar Cotts BB12 145 E1
Barcroft Gn BB10 128 E1
Barcroft St BB8 171 C5
Barden Croft BB5 124 F4
Barden Jun Sch BB10 148 A1
Barden La BB10, BB12 148 A2
Barden Pl PR2 118 D4
Barden Rd BB5 103 F4
Barden St 3 BB10 148 B1
Barden View BB10 148 A2
Bardsea Pl PR2 116 F3
Bardsley Cl WN8 10 A7
Bardsway FY5 176 A3
Bardsway Ave FY3 130 F6
BARE 217 E7
Bare Ave LA4 217 E6
Bare La LA4 217 E5
Bare Lane Sta LA4 217 E6
Barford Cl
Southport PR8 21 A6
Up Holland WN8 10 A7
Barford Gr BL6 32 F1
Bargee Cl BB1 101 F3
Barham St 6 FY1 130 B2
Barker Brow BB1, PR7 142 A3
Barker Cl LA6 240 B7
Barker Ct 11 OL13 88 A1
Barkerfield Cl BB12 146 F5
Barkerhouse Rd BB10,
BB9 149 B8
Barker La BB2 122 C2
Barker Terr BB7 189 E1
Barkfield Ave L37 11 E4
Barkfield La L37 11 D4
BARLEY 169 B5
Barley Bank St BB3 81 F2
Barley Cl BB2 101 D5
Barley Cop La LA1 218 B4
Barleydale Rd BB9 170 E5
Barleyfield
Clayton Green PR5 78 C3
Nelson BB9 148 D7
Barley Gr BB10 128 C6
BARLEY GREEN 169 C5
Barley Holme Rd BB4 86 A8
Barley La BB9 169 B7
Barley New Rd BB12 169 E5
Barley St BB12 126 C7
Barley Way 9 BB2 101 D5
Barlow Cres FY3 130 E4
Barlow Ct BL7 48 E5
Barlows Bldgs 5 BB4 85 F1
Barlow's La L39 22 D5
Barlow St
Accrington BB5 104 A6
Bacup OL13 70 B7
Horwich BL6 32 C2
Preston, Maudlands
PR1 117 E1
Preston PR1 117 F2
11 Rawtenstall BB4 86 A3
Barmouth Ave FY3 131 A3
Barmouth Cres BB1 122 E1
Barmouth Ct PR2 117 A3
Barmskin La
Heskin Green PR7 41 B2
Wrightington Bar WN6 28 C8
Barn Acre BL6 31 E1
Barnacre Cl
Fulwood PR2 118 A8
Lancaster LA1 215 B2
Barnacre Rd PR3 140 A8
Barnacre Rd Prim Sch
PR3 139 F8
Barnard Cl BB5 103 C4
Barnbrook St BL9 33 A3
Barn Cl PR4 56 A2
Barn Croft
3 Clitheroe BB7 166 D7
Higher Penwortham PR1 96 B4
1 Leyland PR26 76 B1
Barncroft Dr BL6 32 F3
Barnes Ave BB4 85 F2
Barnes Cl BL0 50 A3
Barnes Ct BB10 128 D4
Barnes Dr
Cleveleys FY5 175 E5
Maghull L31 5 C3
Barnes Rd
Morecambe LA3 216 E3
Ormskirk L39 15 E3
Skelmersdale WN8 17 E1
Barnes Sq 1 BB5 124 F
Barnes St
Accrington BB5 104 C
Burnley BB11 128 A
Church BB5 103 E
Clayton-le-M BB5 124 F
Haslingden BB4 85 B
BARNFIELD 104 E
Barnfield
6 Bamber Bridge PR5 77 A
Kirkham PR4 114 A
Much Hoole PR4 74 E
Barnfield Ave BB10 128 F
Barnfield Bsns Ctr
BB9 148 F
Barnfield Cl
Bolton BL7 47 E
4 Cleveleys FY5 175 F
Colne BB8 172 A
Barnfield Dr WN8 9 E
Barnfield Manor FY6 154 D
Barnfield St
Accrington BB5 104 D
Rochdale OL12 52 F
Barnfield Way BB5 125 E
Barnflatt Cl PR5 98 A
Barn Gill Cl BB1 101 F
Barn Hey PR4 95 A
Barn Hey Dr PR26 76 E
Barn Hey Rd L33 1 A
Barn Mdw
Clayton Brook PR5 78 B
Edgworth BL7 48 D
Barn Meadow Cres
BB1 124 C
Barnmeadow La BB6 124 C
BARNOLDSWICK
Earby 196 C
Ingleton 242 D
Barnoldswick CE Prim Sch
BB18 196 B
Barnoldswick La LA6 242 D
Barnoldswick Rd
Beverley BB8, BB9 170 F
Kelbrook BB18 194 F
Barnsfold PR2 117 D
Barnside
Euxton PR7 60 C
Whitworth OL12 52 B
Barns La PR3 161 C
Barnstaple Way PR4 116 F
Barns The PR4 133 A
Barn View PR6 30 F
Barnwood Cres BB18 197 C
Barnwood Rd BB18 197 B
Baron Rd FY1 130 C
Barons Cl BB3 82 A
Baron St
Darwen BB3 81 F
Rawtenstall BB4 86 D
Barons Way
Blackburn BB3 82 A
Euxton PR7 60 D
Great Harwood BB6 124 D
Barracks Rd BB11 127 D
Barret Hill Brow BB7 230 B
Barret St BB18 197 A
Barrett Ave PR8 35 A
Barrett Ct 6 BL9 33 A
Barrett Rd PR8 35 A
Barrett St 5 BB10 128 A
Barrington Ct BB5 103 B
Barrington Dr PR8 21 B

Barrison Gn L40 24 E2
Barritt Rd BB4 85 F2
Barronwood Ct PR4 57 A5
BARROW 166 D1
Barrowcroft Cl WN1 30 B1
BARROWFORD 170 C4
Barrowford Rd
Barrowford BB9 170 B1
Colne BB8 171 B5
4 Colne BB8 171 C5
Fence BB12 147 C7
Barrowford St Thomas CE Prim Sch BB9 170 C3
Barrowford Sch BB9 170 D3
BARROW NOOK 7 F2
Barrow Nook La L39 7 E2
Barrow Sch BB7 166 D2
Barrows La LA3 212 E7
Barrow's La PR3 156 B5
Barrows La E PR3 156 B5
Barry Ave PR2 117 A3
Barry Gr LA3 212 F6
Barry St BB12 127 C7
Bar St BB10 128 B8
Bar Terr OL12 52 C7
Bartholomew Rd LA4 217 C4
Bartle La PR4 116 C7
Bartle Pl PR2 116 E1
Bartle Rd FY8 90 A8
Bartle St BB11 127 D5
Bartlett Ho PR8 35 B3
BARTON
Fulwood 137 B7
Ormskirk 13 F6
Barton Ave
Blackpool FY1 130 B2
Knott End-on-S FY6 199 E5
Barton Ct LA1 215 A4
Barton Gdns LA1 215 B5
Barton Heys Rd L37 11 D1
Barton La PR3 137 E7
Barton Mans FY8 89 C7
Barton Rd
Lancaster LA1 215 A4
Lytham St Anne's FY8 89 D8
Barton Row LA6 240 B7
Barton St Lawrence CE Prim Sch PR3 137 B7
Bartons Cl PR9 54 D5
Barton Sq FY6 199 E5
Barton St BB2 101 E5
Barwood Lea Mill 14 BL0 50 C6
Bashall Gr PR25 77 B3
BASHALL TOWN 188 E1
Basil St
Colne BB8 171 D4
Preston PR1 118 C2
Basnett St BB10 148 C1
Bassenthwaite Rd FY3 131 C2
Bassett Cl OL12 52 E3
Bassett Gdns OL12 52 E3
Bassett Way OL12 52 E2
Bass La BL9 50 D3
BASTWELL 102 A8
Bastwell Rd BB1 101 F7
Bateman Gr LA4 217 B5
Bateman Rd LA4 217 B5
Bateman St BL6 32 D2
Bates St BB5 124 E3
Bath Ho* PR3 141 E3
Bath Mill La LA1 215 A8
Bath Mill Sq 7 LA1 215 A8
Bath Rd FY8 91 B3
Bath St N PR9 35 B8
Bath Springs L39 15 F5
Bath Springs Ct L39 15 F5
Bath St
Accrington BB5 104 B4
1 Bacup OL13 88 A2
Blackburn BB2 101 C4
Blackpool FY4 130 B1
Colne BB8 171 E5
23 Darwen BB3 82 A1
Lancaster LA1 215 A8
Lytham St Anne's FY8 91 B3
Morecambe LA4 217 A5
Nelson BB9 148 F8
2 Preston PR2 117 D1
Southport PR9 35 B8
Bathurst Ave FY3 131 A7
Bathurst St 3 BB2 101 D5
Batridge Rd BL7 48 A7
Battersby St BL9 33 D3
Battismore Rd LA4 217 B5
Battle Way L37 12 B2
Bawdlands BB7 166 D8
Bawhead Rd BB18 197 B1
Baxendale Gr 9 PR5 97 E1
BAXENDEN 104 E1
Baxenden St John's CE Prim Sch BB5 104 E1
Baxtergate LA4 217 B6
Baxter St WN6 29 F1
Bayard St BB12 127 A6
Bay Cl LA3 212 D6
Baycliffe Cres LA4 217 A5
BAY GATE 230 A4
BAY HORSE 207 C6
Bay Horse Dr LA1 215 B3
Bay Horse La PR4 135 D4
Bay Horse Rd LA2 211 E4
Bayley Fold BB7 166 E8
Bayley St BB5 124 E3
Bayliss Cl PR2 118 F3
Baylton Ct PR3 181 D2
Baylton Dr PR3 181 D2
Baynes Cotts 5 LA2 239 B8
Baynes St BB3 82 F1
Bay Rd
Fulwood PR2 118 E2
Heysham LA3 212 D6
Bayside FY7 199 B4
Bay St BB1 102 A7
Bayswater FY2 152 C4
Bay The FY5 175 C5
Baytree Cl
Bamber Bridge PR5 77 C8
Southport PR9 54 D5
Bay Tree Farm PR2 95 D8
Baytree Gr BL0 50 B2
Bay Tree Rd PR6 78 B3
Baytree Wlk OL12 71 C1
Bay View LA6 237 B8
Bay View Apartments FY6 199 D5
Bay View Ave LA2 218 C8
Bay View Cres LA2 218 C8
Bay View Dr LA3 212 F8
Baywood St BB1 101 F7
BAZIL 209 D6
Bazil Gr LA3 209 D7
Bazil La LA3 209 D7
Bazley Rd FY8 90 D3
Beacham Rd PR8 35 E7
Beach Ave
Cleveleys FY5 175 D3
Lytham St Anne's FY8 90 C3
Beachcomber Dr FY5 175 C3
Beachley Rd PR2 117 A4
Beachley Sq BB12 127 D7
Beachmews PR8 34 F6
Beach Priory Gdns PR8 35 A6
Beach Rd
Cleveleys FY5 175 D3
Fleetwood FY7 198 E3
Lytham St Anne's FY8 89 D7
Pilling Lane FY6 200 B7
Southport PR8 34 F6
Beach St
Lytham St Anne's FY8 91 A3
Morecambe LA4 217 E7
Beacon Ave PR2 117 D5
Beacon Cl BB8 171 C3
Beacon Crossing WN8 27 C2
Beacon Ct PR3 138 D5
Beacon Ctry Pk* WN8 18 F2
Beacon Dr PR3 138 D6
Beacon Fell Ctry Pk* PR3 183 F2
Beacon Fell Rd PR3 183 E2
Beacon Fell View Holiday Pk PR3 162 D1
Beacon Gr
Fulwood PR2 117 D4
Garstang PR3 181 B6
Beacon Hill High Sch FY2 152 D1
Beacon Hts WN8 10 A8
Beacon La L40, WN8 18 D4
Beacon Lo 10 PR2 118 F4
Beacon Rd
Poulton-le-F FY6 154 A3
Shevington Moor WN6 29 B2
Beacon Sch WN8 9 E8
Beaconsfield Ave PR1 118 E1
Beaconsfield Ct 4 L39 15 F5
Beaconsfield Rd PR9 35 F6
Beaconsfield St
3 Accrington BB5 104 D5
Great Harwood BB6 124 C5
16 Haslingden BB4 85 B3
Beaconsfield Terr
Catterall PR3 181 E2
Chorley PR6 61 D2
Beacon St PR7 43 D7
Beacons The WN6 19 D7
Beacon View
Appley Bridge WN6 19 C8
Longridge PR3 162 B3
Standish WN6 29 D1
Beacon View Dr WN8 10 B7
Beacon Villa PR3 140 C8
Beale Cl BB1 102 B1
Beale Rd BB9 148 B8
Beamish Ave BB2 81 D8
Beamont Dr PR1 96 D8
Bean Ave FY4 110 E8
Beardshaw Ave FY1 130 D2
Beardsworth St BB1 102 A7
BEARDWOOD 101 B7
Beardwood BB2 101 A8
Beardwood Brow BB2 101 B7
Beardwood Dr BB2 101 A7
Beardwood Fold BB2 101 A7
Beardwood High Sch BB2 101 A6
Beardwood Hospl The BB2 101 A6
Beardwood Mdw BB2 101 A7
Beardwood Pk BB2 101 B7
Bearncroft WN8 9 D6
Bear St BB12 126 F6
Bearswood Croft PR6 78 B2
Bearwood Way FY5 176 C2
Beatie St BB9 148 B6
Beatrice Ave BB12 127 C7
Beatrice Mews 9 BL6 32 B4
Beatrice Pl BB2 82 A8
Beatrice St 17 BL6 32 B4
Beattock Pl FY2 152 F6
Beatty Ave PR7 43 B6
Beatty Cl FY8 110 D1
Beatty Rd PR8 35 E5
Beauclerk Rd FY8 90 B6
Beaufort L37 12 A2
Beaufort Ave FY2 152 C5
Beaufort Cl
Ormskirk L39 15 A1
Simonstone BB12 145 E2
Beaufort Gr LA4 217 D5
Beaufort Rd
Morecambe LA4 217 E5
Weir OL13 88 A7
Beaufort St
Nelson BB9 148 E7
Rochdale OL12 52 C1
Beauley Ave BB12 145 E2
Beauly Cl 3 BL0 50 A2
Beaumaris Ave BB2 101 A1
Beaumaris Cl 2 BB4 85 B1
Beaumaris Rd PR25 60 C8
Beaumont Ave BL6 32 C4
Beaumont Coll (The Spastics Society) LA1 218 D4
Beaumont Cres L39 15 D2
Beaumont Ct
8 Blackpool FY1 130 C6
Lytham St Anne's FY8 90 A8
Beaumont Gdns FY6 153 A5
Beaumont Ho L39 15 D2
Beaumont Pl LA1 218 D4
Beaumont Rd BL6 32 C4
Beaumont St LA1 218 D4
Beaumont Way BB3 82 C1
Beaver Cl BB1 122 F5
Beavers La WN8 9 D6
Beaver Terr 17 OL13 88 A3
Bebles Rd L39 15 C3
BECCONSALL 73 E1
Becconsall La PR4 73 F3
Beck Ct FY7 198 D1
Beckdean Ave FY6 153 D2
Beckenham Ct BB10 148 D3
Beckett Ct 16 PR1 96 F8
Beckett St 6 BB3 65 A8
Beck Gr FY5 175 E4
Becks Brow BD23 236 F3
Becks Crossing BB8 172 C2
Beckside
Barley BB12 169 C5
Trawden BB8 172 C3
Beck Side LA2 237 C3
Beckside Mews LA6 240 B3
Beck View 7 LA1 215 A3
Beckway Ave FY3 130 F7
Bedale Pl FY5 175 E1
Beddington St 6 BB9 170 D1
Bedford Ave FY5 175 D3
Bedford Cl BB5 103 C4
Bedford Ct PR8 35 A2
Bedford Mews BB3 81 F4
Bedford Pl
Lancaster LA1 215 A4
Padiham BB12 126 D7
Bedford Rd
Blackpool FY1 130 C8
Fulwood PR2 118 A4
6 Lytham St Anne's FY8 91 D4
Southport PR8 35 A2
Bedfordshire Ave BB12 127 B7
Bedford St
6 Barrowford BB9 170 C1
Blackburn BB2 101 C2
Bolton, Egerton BL7 47 D2
Bury BL9 33 A4
Darwen BB3 81 F4
Bedford Terr BB4 68 A8
Beechacre BL0 50 D5
Beecham St LA4 217 B6
Beech Ave
Adlington PR6 31 B8
Bilsborrow PR3 159 A5
Blackpool FY3 130 E5
Darwen BB3 82 B2
Earby BB18 197 A1
Euxton PR7 60 C4
Galgate LA2 210 F4
Horwich BL6 32 E1
Kirkham PR4 114 B4
Leyland PR25 60 A7
Parbold WN8 27 C2
Poulton-le-F FY6 153 D4
Warton PR4 92 D6
Beech Bank PR4 155 F1
Beech Cl
Bacup OL13 88 A3
Clitheroe BB7 166 D8
Oswaldtwistle BB5 103 C2
Rishton BB1 103 B8
Rufford L40 39 C4
Skelmersdale WN8 17 E1
Whitworth OL12 71 C1
Wilpshire BB1 122 E6
Beech Cres BB5 125 A1
Beechcroft
Cleveleys FY5 175 C4
Maghull L31 5 D1
Beech Ct
Fulwood PR2 117 E7
Leyland PR25 59 F8
Silverdale LA5 224 C2
Southport PR9 35 D8
Beech Dr
Formby L37 11 D4
Freckleton PR4 93 A5
Fulwood PR2 117 D8
Haslingden BB4 85 C2
Kirkham PR4 113 E4
Longridge PR3 140 A7
Newton-w-S PR4 114 F2
Poulton-le-F FY6 153 D2
Beech Dr *continued*
Whalley BB7 144 A7
Beeches Ct FY5 176 C1
Beeches The
Blackpool FY3 130 E3
Clayton Green PR6 78 C3
Singleton FY6 154 D1
Tarleton PR4 57 A7
Beechfield
Hill Dale WN8 27 C5
Lancaster LA1 214 D7
Maghull L31 5 E1
Beechfield Ave
Blackpool FY3 130 E3
Knott End-on-S FY6 200 A5
Wrea Green PR4 113 C4
Beechfield Ct PR25 60 B8
Beechfield Gdns PR8 34 F6
Beechfield Mews PR9 35 C7
Beechfield Rd PR25 60 B8
Beechfields PR7 41 B6
Beech Gdns PR6 78 B1
Beech Gr
5 Accrington BB5 104 A4
2 Barnoldswick BB18 196 C2
Blackburn BB3 81 D6
Burnley BB10 148 C4
Chatburn BB7 190 D5
Knott End-on-S FY6 199 E6
Morecambe LA4 217 E5
Preston PR2 117 B1
Ramsbottom BL8 50 A1
Slyne LA2 218 C6
Southport PR9 35 F7
Warton LA5 223 D5
West Bradford BB7 189 D7
Beech Grove Cl BL9 33 B4
Beech Ho PR7 42 F6
Beechill Ct PR5 97 E3
Beech Ind Est OL13 88 A3
Beeching Cl LA1 214 F6
Beech Mdw L39 16 A4
Beech Mount
Blackburn BB1 122 F3
Waddington BB7 189 B4
Beech Rd
Aughton L39 6 A6
Elswick PR4 155 F1
Garstang PR3 181 B8
Halton LA2 219 C7
Leyland PR25 77 A2
Beech St S PR1 96 E6
Beech St
Accrington BB5 104 C5
Bacup OL13 88 A3
Barnoldswick BB18 196 B1
Blackburn BB1 102 A7
Bury BL9 33 B2
Clayton-le-M BB5 124 F1
Clitheroe BB7 166 D8
Edgworth BL7 48 D5
Great Harwood BB6 124 C6
Lancaster LA1 214 D8
10 Nelson BB9 170 E1
Padiham BB12 126 D7
1 Preston PR1 96 D6
Ramsbottom BL0 50 C3
Rawtenstall BB4 86 A3
Beech Terr
Ingleton LA6 242 F3
1 Preston PR1 96 E6
Beechthorpe Ave BB7 189 B4
Beech Tree Ave WN6 19 D8
Beech Tree Cl
Bolton-le-S LA5 221 A4
Nelson BB9 148 E7
Beech Tree Cotts LA6 242 F3
Beechtrees WN8 9 D7
Beech Tree Sch PR5 78 B4
Beechway
Fulwood PR2 118 A4
Higher Penwortham PR1 96 B3
Maghull L31 6 B2
Beechway Ave L31 6 B2
Beech Wlk PR6 61 A7
Beechwood
Kirkham PR4 114 B7
Skelmersdale WN8 18 C3
Beechwood Ave
Accrington BB5 104 D3
Bamber Bridge PR5 97 D4
Burnley BB11 127 F3
Clitheroe BB7 166 E6
Fulwood PR2 117 C4
Ramsbottom BL0 50 D6
Shevington WN6 19 F5
Beechwood Cres WN5 10 E6
Beechwood Croft PR6 78 A3
Beechwood Ct
Blackburn BB1 101 F7
Coppull PR7 29 F8
Maghull L31 5 F1
Skelmersdale WN8 9 D6
Beechwood Dr
Blackburn BB2 80 E8
Formby L37 11 C1
Ormskirk L39 15 D5
Thornton FY5 153 B8
Beechwood Gdns LA1 215 A2
Beechwood Gr FY2 152 E4
Beechwood Mews BB1, BB2 82 A8
Beechwood Rd
12 Blackburn BB1 102 A7
Chorley PR7 43 E6
Beeford Dr WN5 10 E5
Beehive Ind Units FY4 111 B8
Bee La PR1 96 E1
Bee Mill PR3 141 D3
Beenland St 3 PR1 118 D1
Beeston Ave FY6 153 C5
Beetham Ct BB5 124 E2
Beetham Cvn Pk LA5, LA7 225 C8
Beetham Pl FY3 130 E6
Begonia St BB3 82 B1
Begonia View BB3 82 A7
Beightons Wlk OL12 52 D4
Bela Cl 3 LA1 218 A2
Bela Gr FY1 130 D2
Belfield WN8 9 D6
Belfield Rd BB5 104 C4
Belford Ave FY5 175 F4
Belford St BB12 127 F7
Belfry Cl PR7 60 D4
Belfry Cres WN6 29 F2
Belfry Mans BB6 143 C6
Belfry The FY8 91 D5
Belgarth Rd BB5 104 C7
BELGRAVE 64 E8
Belgrave Ave
Higher Penwortham PR1 96 B3
Kirkham PR4 114 A7
Belgrave Cl
Blackburn BB2 101 B3
3 Lytham St Anne's FY8 90 D6
Belgrave Cres BL6 32 D3
Belgrave Ct
Burnley BB12 127 F7
Leyland PR25 59 F8
Belgrave Pl
Poulton-le-F FY6 153 B2
Southport PR8 34 F3
Belgrave Rd
Blackpool FY4 130 E1
Colne BB8 171 D6
Darwen BB3 65 A8
5 Leyland PR25 77 A1
Poulton-le-F FY6 153 B3
Southport PR8 34 F3
Belgrave Sq 9 BB3 82 A1
Belgrave St
Brierfield BB9 148 A6
Burnley BB12 127 F7
Nelson BB9 170 F1
Rising Bridge BB5 85 A8
Rochdale OL12 52 D1
Belgravia Apartments PR9 53 B1
Belgravia Ho PR9 35 D8
Bell-Aire Park Homes LA3 212 F5
Bellamy Ave LA4 217 A3
Belle Field Cl PR1 97 A1
Belle Isle Ave OL12 52 C6
Belle View Pl FY3 130 D5
Belle Vue Ave LA1 215 A5
Belle Vue Dr LA1 215 A5
Belle Vue La BB7 189 B4
Belle Vue Pl BB11 127 E6
Belle Vue St
Blackburn BB2 101 C5
Burnley BB11 127 E6
Bellfield Rd LA4 217 C5
Bellflower Cl PR25 77 E3
Bellingham Rd FY8 91 B4
Bellis Ave PR9 53 F2
Bellis Way PR5 97 B2
Bell La
Bury BL9 33 A3
Claughton PR3 182 C4
Clayton-le-M BB5 125 B4
Bells Arc 10 BB10 128 A8
Bells Bridge La PR3 203 F2
Bell's Cl L31 5 C4
Bells La PR5 98 E3
Bell's La L31 5 B3
Bell St BB4 85 B3
Bell Villas PR5 99 C3
BELMONT 46 C4
Belmont Ave
Blackpool FY1 130 C4
Fulwood PR2 118 D2
Orrell WN5 10 D3
Poulton-le-F FY6 153 B3
Belmont Cl
Brinscall PR6 62 E8
Burscough L40 25 E3
Fulwood PR2 118 D2
Lancaster LA1 218 B3
Belmont Cres PR2 118 D2
Belmont Ct PR3 140 B7
Belmont Dr PR6 61 E1
Belmont Gr BB10 128 D5
Belmont Pl PR7 29 D6
Belmont Rd
Adlington PR6 31 B7
Belmont BB3, BL7 64 A2
Bolton BL7 47 A1
Fleetwood FY7 199 A3
Fulwood PR2 117 C2
Great Harwood BB6 124 B5
Horwich BL6 32 C7
Leyland PR25 59 D8
Lytham St Anne's FY8 90 C5
Rivington BL6 45 C3
Belmont Sch BB4 85 E2
Belmont St PR8 35 A5
Belmont Terr
7 Barrowford BB9 170 D3
Foulridge BB8 194 E1
Belmont Way OL12 52 E2

Belper St BB1 . . . . . 102 A6
Belsfield Dr PR4 . . . . . 73 E4
Belshaw Ct BB11 . . . . . 127 A3
BELTHORN 82 F6
Belthorn Prim Sch BB1 . . . 82 F6
Belthorn Rd BB1 . . . . . 82 E6
Belton Hill PR2 . . . . . 117 D8
Belvedere Ave
Ramsbottom BL8 . . . . . 50 A1
Rawtenstall BB4 . . . . . 87 A1
Belvedere Ct
[1] Lytham St Anne's FY8 . . . . . 90 D4
Thornton FY5 . . . . . 153 C8
Belvedere Dr
Chorley PR7 . . . . . 43 B8
Formby L37 . . . . . 11 F1
Belvedere Fold BB4 . . . . . 87 A1
Belvedere Pk L39 . . . . . 6 C7
Belvedere Rd
Adlington PR6 . . . . . 31 B8
Blackburn BB1 . . . . . 123 A3
Burnley BB10 . . . . . 128 B6
[2] Leyland PR25 . . . . . 77 B2
Southport PR8 . . . . . 21 C5
Thornton FY5 . . . . . 153 C8
Belverdale Gdns FY4 . . . . . 110 F5
Belvere Ave FY4 . . . . . 110 D6
Belvoir St OL12 . . . . . 52 C1
Benbow Cl FY8 . . . . . 110 D2
Bence Rd PR1 . . . . . 97 B6
Bence St BB8 . . . . . 171 E5
Bench Carr OL12 . . . . . 52 E1
Bendwood Cl BB12 . . . . . 126 D8
Benenden Pl [9] FY5 . . . . . 176 A2
Bengal St PR7 . . . . . 61 D1
Bengarth Rd PR9 . . . . . 35 F8
Benjamin Hargreaves CE Prim Sch BB5 . . . . . 104 D5
Ben La
Barnoldswick BB18 . . . . . 196 D3
Rainford L39 . . . . . 8 A1
Ben Lane Ct L39 . . . . . 8 B2
Bennett Ave FY1 . . . . . 130 C4
Bennett Dr WN5 . . . . . 10 D4
Bennett Rd FY5 . . . . . 176 A3
Bennett's La FY4 . . . . . 110 F6
Bennett St [4] BB9 . . . . . 170 F2
Bennington St BB1, BB2 . . . . . 101 F3
Bennison Ct PR9 . . . . . 53 C1
Benson Ave LA4 . . . . . 217 D4
Benson Ho BB1 . . . . . 102 B7
Benson La PR4 . . . . . 135 F3
Benson Rd FY3 . . . . . 152 E1
Benson's La PR4 . . . . . 158 C1
Benson St
Blackburn BB1 . . . . . 102 B7
Bury BL9 . . . . . 33 A1
Edgworth BL7 . . . . . 48 E5
Bentcliffe Gdns BB5 . . . . . 104 D4
Bent Est OL13 . . . . . 88 A7
Bent Gap La BB2 . . . . . 101 C4
BENT GATE 68 C8
Bentgate Cl BB4 . . . . . 68 D8
Bentham Ave
Burnley BB10 . . . . . 148 B3
Fleetwood FY7 . . . . . 198 C1
Bentham Cl BB2 . . . . . 101 B1
Bentham Hall Cotts LA2 . . . . . 239 D8
Bentham Moor Rd LA6 . . . . . 242 D2
Bentham Pl WN6 . . . . . 29 F2
Bentham Rd
Blackburn BB2 . . . . . 101 B1
Ingleton LA6 . . . . . 242 E3
Lancaster LA1 . . . . . 215 A2
Standish WN6 . . . . . 29 F2
Bentham St
Coppull PR7 . . . . . 42 E1
Southport PR8 . . . . . 35 B5
Bentham Sta LA2 . . . . . 239 D7
Bentham's Way PR8 . . . . . 35 C2
Bentinck Ave FY4 . . . . . 110 B5
Bentinck Rd FY8 . . . . . 89 C8
Bentinck St [9] OL12 . . . . . 52 C1
Bent La
Colne BB8 . . . . . 172 B6
Leyland PR25 . . . . . 60 C8
Bentlea Rd BB7 . . . . . 231 B3
Bentley Brook Cl BL6 . . . . . 32 E4
Bentley Dr
Blackpool FY4 . . . . . 112 A6
Kirkham PR4 . . . . . 113 E5
Bentley Gn FY5 . . . . . 176 D2
Bentley La
Bispham Green L40 . . . . . 27 E8
Bury BL9 . . . . . 51 A1
Heskin Green L40, PR7 . . . . . 41 A1
Bentley Mews OL12 . . . . . 52 E2
Bentley Park Rd PR4 . . . . . 74 F7
Bentley St
[7] Bacup OL13 . . . . . 87 F3
Blackburn BB1 . . . . . 102 C5
Darwen BB3 . . . . . 65 C7
Nelson BB9 . . . . . 148 D7
Rochdale OL12 . . . . . 52 E2
Bentley Wood Way BB11 . . . . . 126 F4
Bentmeadows OL12 . . . . . 52 E1
Benton Rd PR2 . . . . . 118 D4
Bents La LA6 . . . . . 243 A3
Bent St
Blackburn BB2 . . . . . 101 D4
Bent St *continued*
Haslingden BB4 . . . . . 68 D8
[4] Oswaldtwistle BB5 . . . . . 103 D3
Bentwood Rd BB4 . . . . . 85 A3
Beresford Dr PR9 . . . . . 53 F1
Beresford Gdns PR9 . . . . . 53 F2
Beresford Rd BB1 . . . . . 101 D7
Beresford St
[8] Blackpool FY1 . . . . . 130 C7
Nelson BB9 . . . . . 148 F6
Bergen St BB11 . . . . . 127 B5
Bergerac Cres FY5 . . . . . 152 F6
Berkeley Cl
Chorley PR7 . . . . . 43 D5
Nelson BB9 . . . . . 148 E7
Berkeley Colonnade PR2 . . . . . 118 A4
Berkeley Cres BB12 . . . . . 146 C1
Berkeley Ct
Heysham LA3 . . . . . 212 E6
Poulton-le-F FY6 . . . . . 153 E3
Berkeley Dr
Clayton-le-W PR5 . . . . . 77 E4
Simonstone BB12 . . . . . 145 E2
Berkeley St
Brierfield BB9 . . . . . 148 A5
Nelson BB9 . . . . . 148 E7
Preston PR1 . . . . . 117 E1
Berkley Cl PR4 . . . . . 113 E5
Berkshire Ave BB12 . . . . . 127 B7
Berkshire Cl BB1 . . . . . 122 F7
Bernard St OL12 . . . . . 52 E3
Berne Ave BL6 . . . . . 32 A3
Berridge Ave BB12 . . . . . 127 A6
Berriedale Rd BB9 . . . . . 171 A1
Berry Cl WN8 . . . . . 17 F2
Berry Field [3] PR1 . . . . . 96 C3
Berry House Cotts L40 . . . . . 38 A5
Berry House Rd L40 . . . . . 38 A4
Berry La PR3 . . . . . 140 A7
Berrys La BB7 . . . . . 144 C2
Berry's La FY6 . . . . . 153 C4
Berry Sq BL6 . . . . . 31 D3
Berry St
Bamber Bridge PR5 . . . . . 77 A8
Brierfield BB9 . . . . . 148 B5
Burnley BB11 . . . . . 127 F4
Preston PR1 . . . . . 97 A7
Skelmersdale WN8 . . . . . 17 F2
Bertha St BB5 . . . . . 104 D6
Bertram Ave LA4 . . . . . 217 A4
Bertrand Ave FY3 . . . . . 131 A7
Berwick Ave
Cleveleys FY5 . . . . . 175 F4
Southport PR8 . . . . . 21 D5
Berwick Dr
Burnley BB12 . . . . . 127 E7
Fulwood PR2 . . . . . 117 D4
Berwick Rd
Blackpool FY4 . . . . . 110 C5
Lytham St Anne's FY8 . . . . . 89 F7
Preston PR1 . . . . . 97 A6
Berwick St PR1 . . . . . 118 E1
Berwick Way LA3 . . . . . 212 E7
Berwyn Ave [2] LA4 . . . . . 217 D5
Berwyn Cl BL6 . . . . . 32 C5
Berwyn Ct PR8 . . . . . 35 D4
Beryl Ave
Blackburn BB1 . . . . . 122 F2
Cleveleys FY5 . . . . . 175 E1
Besant Cl BB1 . . . . . 102 B1
BESCAR 24 A7
Bescar Brow La L40 . . . . . 23 F7
Bescar La L40 . . . . . 37 B1
Bescar La Sta L40 . . . . . 37 B2
Bescot Way [12] FY5 . . . . . 152 F7
Bessie St [13] BB18 . . . . . 196 B2
Best St PR4 . . . . . 113 F5
Bethel Ave FY2 . . . . . 152 D4
Bethel Rd BB1 . . . . . 102 A7
Bethel St
Barnoldswick BB18 . . . . . 196 B3
Colne BB8 . . . . . 171 B4
Bethesda Cl BB2 . . . . . 101 D3
Bethesda Rd FY1 . . . . . 130 B4
Bethesda St
Barnoldswick BB18 . . . . . 196 B2
Burnley BB11 . . . . . 127 F6
Betjeman Cl FY2 . . . . . 152 F6
Betony LA4 . . . . . 217 F6
Betony Cl OL12 . . . . . 52 D3
Bett La PR6 . . . . . 79 C1
Betty Anne Ct PR9 . . . . . 35 B8
Beulah Ave LA4 . . . . . 217 D5
Bevan Pl BB9 . . . . . 170 F2
BEVERLEY 170 E7
Beverley Ave
Longshaw WN5 . . . . . 10 E1
Poulton-le-F FY6 . . . . . 131 D8
Beverley Cl
Clitheroe BB7 . . . . . 166 E6
Preston PR2 . . . . . 96 C8
Southport PR9 . . . . . 54 C5
Wrea Green PR4 . . . . . 113 A3
Beverley Ct
[2] Lytham St Anne's FY8 . . . . . 90 A8
Morecambe LA4 . . . . . 217 E5
Beverley Dr BB7 . . . . . 166 D6
Beverley Gr FY4 . . . . . 110 C7
Beverley Rd BB9 . . . . . 170 E8
Beverley Rd N FY8 . . . . . 90 A8
Beverley Rd S FY8 . . . . . 90 A8
Beverley St
[5] Blackburn BB2 . . . . . 101 B1
Burnley BB11 . . . . . 127 E5
Beverly Cl FY5 . . . . . 153 B8
Bevington Cl BB11 . . . . . 127 E5
Bewcastle Dr L40 . . . . . 16 C3
Bexhill Rd PR2 . . . . . 117 A4
Bexley Ave FY2 . . . . . 130 D8
Bexley Pl FY8 . . . . . 90 E5
Bezza La BB2, PR5 . . . . . 120 C5
Bhailok St [3] PR1 . . . . . 96 E8
Bibby Dr FY3 . . . . . 131 E5
Bibby Rd PR9 . . . . . 54 A1
Bibby's La FY2 . . . . . 152 E3
BICKERSTAFFE 7 F5
Bickerstaffe CE Sch L39 . . . . . 7 E5
Bickerstaffe St [2] FY1 . . . . . 130 B3
Bickerton Rd PR8 . . . . . 34 F4
Bicknell St BB1 . . . . . 101 E6
Bideford Ave FY3 . . . . . 131 A6
Bideford Way PR4 . . . . . 116 F6
Bidston St PR1 . . . . . 97 E8
Bigdale Dr L33 . . . . . 1 A3
Big Fold BL6 . . . . . 31 D2
Bigforth Dr LA1 . . . . . 211 A8
Biggins La LA6 . . . . . 241 C8
Billinge Ave BB2 . . . . . 101 B5
Billinge Cl BB2 . . . . . 101 B5
Billinge End BB2 . . . . . 101 A6
Billinge End Rd
Blackburn BB2 . . . . . 100 F5
Pleasington BB2 . . . . . 100 B4
Billinge Hospl WN5 . . . . . 10 D2
Billinge Side BB2 . . . . . 100 F5
Billinge St BB1 . . . . . 102 B4
Billinge View BB2 . . . . . 100 F2
BILLINGTON 144 B3
Billington Ave BB4 . . . . . 86 A5
Billington Ct [8] PR2 . . . . . 139 D1
Billington Gdns BB7 . . . . . 144 A4
Billington Rd BB11 . . . . . 127 B3
Billington St E [3] PR4 . . . . . 113 F6
Billington St [1] PR4 . . . . . 113 F6
Bilsberry Cotts BB7 . . . . . 164 F1
Bilsborough Hey PR1 . . . . . 96 E2
Bilsborough Mdw PR2 . . . . . 116 E3
BILSBORROW 159 A5
Bilsborrow La
Bilsborrow PR3 . . . . . 159 C4
Inglewhite PR3 . . . . . 160 A4
Binbrook Pl PR7 . . . . . 43 A7
Bingley Ave FY3 . . . . . 130 F6
Bingley Cl PR6 . . . . . 78 C2
Binns St BB4 . . . . . 86 A7
Binyon Ct LA1 . . . . . 214 F6
Binyon Rd LA1 . . . . . 214 F5
Birbeck Rd L33 . . . . . 1 A3
Birbeck Wlk L33 . . . . . 1 A3
Birchall Lo [6] PR2 . . . . . 118 F4
Birch Ave
Burscough L40 . . . . . 25 E4
Clayton-le-W PR25 . . . . . 77 D3
Cleveleys FY5 . . . . . 175 E2
Euxton PR7 . . . . . 60 C4
Galgate LA2 . . . . . 211 A4
Haslingden BB4 . . . . . 85 C3
Higher Penwortham PR1 . . . . . 96 A3
Newton-w-S PR4 . . . . . 114 F3
Preston PR2 . . . . . 117 A2
Birchbank Gdns BB1 . . . . . 102 A7
Birch Cl
Huncoat BB5 . . . . . 125 E2
Maghull L31 . . . . . 5 F1
Whitworth OL12 . . . . . 52 C6
Birch Cres
Gregson Lane PR5 . . . . . 98 E1
Oswaldtwistle BB5 . . . . . 103 F3
Birch Dr LA5 . . . . . 224 C4
Birchenlee La BB8 . . . . . 171 E2
Birches End OL12 . . . . . 52 C5
Birches Rd BL7 . . . . . 48 D4
Birches The L37 . . . . . 11 E5
Birchfield PR4 . . . . . 74 F4
Birch Field PR6 . . . . . 78 B3
Birchfield Ave BL9 . . . . . 33 E1
Birchfield Dr PR3 . . . . . 140 A8
Birchfield Mews [9] BB12 . . . . . 127 C6
Birchfield Way L31 . . . . . 5 B5
Birch Gn L37 . . . . . 11 D4
Birch Gr
Barrow BB7 . . . . . 166 D1
Lancaster LA1 . . . . . 214 D8
Ramsbottom BL0 . . . . . 50 A3
Stalmine FY6 . . . . . 177 D7
BIRCH GREEN 18 C2
Birch Green Rd WN8 . . . . . 18 C3
BIRCH HALL 81 E4
Birch Hall Ave BB3 . . . . . 81 D4
Birch Hall La BB18 . . . . . 197 D2
Birch Ho PR7 . . . . . 42 F6
Birchill Rd L33 . . . . . 1 C2
Birchin La PR6 . . . . . 78 D1
Birchis Brow L39 . . . . . 14 E2
Birch La PR3 . . . . . 184 C1
Birchover Cl PR2 . . . . . 117 A5
Birch Rd
Chorley PR6 . . . . . 61 E2
Coppull PR7 . . . . . 42 E1
Garstang PR3 . . . . . 181 C8
Birch St
[1] Accrington BB5 . . . . . 104 B6
Bacup OL13 . . . . . 87 F3
Fleetwood FY7 . . . . . 199 A4
[5] Lytham St Anne's FY8 . . . . . 91 C3
Skelmersdale WN8 . . . . . 8 E8
Southport PR8 . . . . . 35 B4
Birch Terr BB5 . . . . . 104 D2
Birchtree Ave LA3 . . . . . 216 E1
Birch Tree Gdns FY3 . . . . . 131 B2
Birch Tree Way [4] BL6 . . . . . 32 E1
Birch View BB7 . . . . . 166 D2
Birch Way FY6 . . . . . 153 C4
Birchway Ave FY3 . . . . . 130 E6
Birch Wlk [1] BB1 . . . . . 102 B4
Birchwood PR26 . . . . . 76 C1
Birchwood Ave PR4 . . . . . 95 B1
Birchwood Cl FY8 . . . . . 90 E4
Birchwood Dr
Coppull PR7 . . . . . 42 E2
Fulwood PR2 . . . . . 117 D7
Hambleton FY6 . . . . . 177 C2
Birchwood Way L33 . . . . . 1 A5
Bird i' th' Hand Cotts [2] L39 . . . . . 15 E6
Bird St
Brierfield BB9 . . . . . 148 B5
Preston PR1 . . . . . 96 D6
Birdy Brow BB7 . . . . . 165 A6
BIRKACRE 43 A3
Birkacre Brow PR7 . . . . . 42 F2
Birkacre Rd PR7 . . . . . 42 F4
Birkbeck Pl FY7 . . . . . 198 D2
Birkbeck Way BB10 . . . . . 148 A1
BIRKDALE 34 F2
Birkdale Ave
Blackpool FY2 . . . . . 152 E5
Fleetwood FY7 . . . . . 175 E7
Longton PR4 . . . . . 74 F8
Lytham St Anne's FY8 . . . . . 110 F1
Birkdale Cl
Euxton PR7 . . . . . 60 D4
Lancaster LA1 . . . . . 218 B3
Longton PR4 . . . . . 74 F8
Thornton FY5 . . . . . 153 D8
Birkdale Cop PR8 . . . . . 35 E1
Birkdale Dr PR2 . . . . . 116 E2
Birkdale High Sch PR8 . . . . . 21 E7
BIRKDALE HILLS 21 C7
Birkdale Prim Sch PR8 . . . . . 35 B3
Birkdale Sch for the Hearing Impaired PR8 . . . . . 34 D4
Birkdale Sta PR8 . . . . . 34 F4
Birkdale Trad Est PR8 . . . . . 35 A2
Birkett Dr PR2 . . . . . 119 A3
Birkett Pl PR2 . . . . . 119 A3
Birkett Rd BB5 . . . . . 104 D7
Birkett's Pl LA4 . . . . . 217 C5
Birkey La L37 . . . . . 11 F2
Birklands Ave LA4 . . . . . 217 C4
Birkrig WN8 . . . . . 9 D6
Birks Brow PR3 . . . . . 162 D3
Birkside Way FY4 . . . . . 131 C1
Birk St PR1 . . . . . 96 E7
Birkwith La LA2 . . . . . 239 C7
Birley Cl WN6 . . . . . 19 F8
Birley Ct PR8 . . . . . 35 B5
Birley Pl BB10 . . . . . 128 A8
Birley St
Blackburn BB1 . . . . . 101 F6
Blackpool FY1 . . . . . 130 B5
Kirkham PR4 . . . . . 114 B5
[1] Preston PR1 . . . . . 97 A7
Birleywood WN8 . . . . . 9 D6
Birnam Gn FY7 . . . . . 198 E4
Birtle Rd BL9 . . . . . 33 E6
Birtwistle Ave BB8 . . . . . 171 D6
Birtwistle Cl BB9 . . . . . 148 B5
Birtwistle Ct BB18 . . . . . 196 C1
Birtwistle Fold [7] BB8 . . . . . 171 E5
Birtwistle Hyde Pk [3] BB8 . . . . . 171 D5
Birtwistle St
Accrington BB5 . . . . . 104 C5
[3] Bamber Bridge PR5 . . . . . 77 B7
Great Harwood BB6 . . . . . 124 B5
Birtwistle Standroyd Bglws BB8 . . . . . 172 A5
Birtwistle Terr BB6 . . . . . 143 C1
Bisham Cl BB3 . . . . . 65 C8
Bishopdale Cl
Blackburn BB2 . . . . . 80 D7
[3] Morecambe LA3 . . . . . 217 F3
Bishopdale Rd LA1 . . . . . 214 D7
Bishop David Sheppard CE Prim Sch PR9 . . . . . 36 B7
Bishopgate [15] PR1 . . . . . 97 A8
Bishop Martin CE Prim Sch WN8 . . . . . 9 D6
Bishop Rawstorne CE Language Coll PR26 . . . . . 58 C2
Bishopsgate
Blackpool FY3 . . . . . 153 B1
Lancaster LA1 . . . . . 215 A4
Bishops Gate FY8 . . . . . 90 D7
Bishop St
Accrington BB5 . . . . . 104 C5
Burnley BB10 . . . . . 148 B1
Nelson BB9 . . . . . 148 D8
Bishopstone Cl BB2 . . . . . 82 A8
Bishopsway PR1 . . . . . 96 D3
Bison Pl PR26 . . . . . 76 C2
BISPHAM 152 B5
Bispham Ave PR26 . . . . . 76 E4
Bispham Ct WN5 . . . . . 10 D2
Bispham Endowed CE Jun Sch FY2 . . . . . 152 D4
BISPHAM GREEN 27 B7
Bispham Hall Bsns Pk WN5 . . . . . 10 C2
Bispham High Sch FY2 . . . . . 152 E2
Bispham Hospl FY2 . . . . . 152 F6
Bispham Rd
Blackpool FY2 . . . . . 152 D3
Blackpool, Warbreck FY3 . . . . . 130 E8
Carleton FY5, FY6 . . . . . 153 A6
Cleveleys FY5 . . . . . 175 C2
Bispham Rd *continued*
Cleveleys, Whiteholme FY5 . . . . . 152 F6
Nelson BB9 . . . . . 148 E6
Southport PR9 . . . . . 35 F7
Bispham St [21] PR1 . . . . . 96 F8
Bittern Cl FY3 . . . . . 131 B6
Bivel St BB12 . . . . . 127 D6
Bk Commercial St BB9 . . . . . 148 B6
Bk Dawson St BL9 . . . . . 33 A4
Bk Owen St BB5 . . . . . 104 C7
Bk Scotland Rd [7] BB9 . . . . . 148 D8
Bk Shepherd St BL9 . . . . . 33 A1
Black Abbey St BB5 . . . . . 104 C5
Blackacre La L39, L40 . . . . . 15 E8
BLACKAMOOR 82 B8
Black-A-Moor La L39 . . . . . 14 A2
Blackamoor Rd BB1 . . . . . 82 C8
Blackberry Hall Cres LA3 . . . . . 213 A8
Blackberry Way PR1 . . . . . 96 B2
Blackbrook CL PR6 . . . . . 62 A2
Black Bull La PR2 . . . . . 117 D5
BLACKBURN 101 E1
Blackburn Brow PR6 . . . . . 61 E3
Blackburn Cathedral* BB1 . . . . . 101 E4
Blackburn Coll BB2 . . . . . 101 D5
Blackburn Mus & Art Gall* BB1 . . . . . 101 E5
Blackburn Old Rd
Blackburn BB1 . . . . . 123 D3
Great Harwood BB1, BB6 . . . . . 123 F5
Hoghton PR5 . . . . . 99 C2
Blackburn Rd
Accrington BB5 . . . . . 104 C6
Blackburn BB1 . . . . . 102 E8
Bolton, Egerton BL7 . . . . . 47 C4
Church BB5 . . . . . 103 F6
Clayton-le-M BB5 . . . . . 124 E1
Darwen BB3 . . . . . 81 E4
Edenfield BL0, BB4 . . . . . 68 D5
Edgworth BL7 . . . . . 48 D7
Great Harwood BB6 . . . . . 124 C4
Great Knowley PR6 . . . . . 61 E4
Haslingden BB4, BB5 . . . . . 85 B5
Higher Walton PR5 . . . . . 98 B3
Higher Wheelton PR6 . . . . . 79 C1
Longridge PR3 . . . . . 140 D7
Oswaldtwistle BB5, BB1 . . . . . 103 C5
Padiham BB12 . . . . . 126 A8
Ribchester PR3 . . . . . 141 E3
Rishton BB1 . . . . . 124 A1
Wheelton PR6 . . . . . 61 F6
Whittlestone Head BB3, BL7 . . . . . 66 B2
Blackburn St
Blackburn BB1 . . . . . 101 E6
[5] Burnley BB11 . . . . . 127 F6
Chorley PR6 . . . . . 43 E7
Blackburn Sta BB1 . . . . . 101 F4
Blackburn Trad Pk BB1 . . . . . 101 F6
Blackcar La L29 . . . . . 4 B3
Black Croft PR6 . . . . . 78 B3
Blacker St BB10 . . . . . 148 A2
Blackfen Pl FY2 . . . . . 130 D8
Blackfield Rd PR4 . . . . . 93 B6
Blackgate La
Holmes PR4 . . . . . 56 C3
Tarleton PR4 . . . . . 56 E5
Blackhorse Ave BL6 . . . . . 31 C2
Blackhorse Cl BL6 . . . . . 31 C3
Black Horse St
Blackrod BL6 . . . . . 31 C3
[4] Chorley PR7 . . . . . 43 B6
Black Horse Yd [12] BB8 . . . . . 171 D5
Black House La
Chipping PR3 . . . . . 185 B1
Lane Bottom BB10 . . . . . 149 D3
Blackhurst Ave PR4 . . . . . 95 F2
Blackhurst Ct PR4 . . . . . 75 B8
Blackhurst Rd L31 . . . . . 5 C5
Black La
Nateby PR3 . . . . . 180 A8
Ramsbottom BL0 . . . . . 51 B
Black Lane Croft [9] BB7 . . . . . 189 E1
Black Lane Ends BB8 . . . . . 195 F3
BLACKLEACH 135 F2
Blackleach Ave [4] PR2 . . . . . 139 D
Blackleach La PR4 . . . . . 135 F1
Blackledge Cl WN5 . . . . . 10 E5
Blackley Gr L33 . . . . . 1 A6
Black Moor Rd L40 . . . . . 40 A2
Black Moss La
Ormskirk L39 . . . . . 15 E
Scarisbrick L40 . . . . . 23 D6
Black Moss Rd BB9 . . . . . 169 E8
BLACKO . . . . . 170 D
Blacko Bar Rd BB9 . . . . . 170 B
Blacko Prim Sch BB9 . . . . . 170 D8
BLACK POLE 136 C5
BLACKPOOL 130 A4
Blackpool Airport FY4 . . . . . 110 D3
Blackpool Central Pier* FY1 . . . . . 130 A3
Blackpool & Fleetwood Tramway* FY2 . . . . . 152 B3
Blackpool Lifeboat Visitor Ctr* FY1 . . . . . 130 A4
Blackpool Lights* FY1 . . . . . 130 B

Blackpool North Pier* FY1 130 A5
Blackpool North Sta FY1 130 C6
Blackpool Old Rd
Little Eccleston PR3 156 A5
Poulton-le-F FY6 153 B2
Blackpool Pleasure Beach* FY4 110 B7
Blackpool Pleasure Beach Sta FY4 110 B6
Blackpool Rd
Blackpool FY2 152 D4
Carleton FY6 153 A4
Clifton PR4 94 E8
Longridge PR3 140 A7
Lytham St Anne's FY8 90 D5
Newton-w-S PR4 115 B2
Preston, Larches PR2 116 E1
Preston PR1, PR2 117 C2
St Michael's on W PR3 157 B6
Wrea Green PR4 113 C6
Blackpool Rd N FY8 110 F2
Blackpool Sixth Form Coll FY3 153 A2
Blackpool South Pier* FY4 110 A8
Blackpool South Sta FY4 130 B1
Blackpool St
5 Church BB5 103 E5
3 Darwen BB3 65 B6
Blackpool & The Fylde Coll Ansdell Campus FY8 90 C5
Blackpool & The Fylde Coll Bispham Campus FY2 152 E6
Blackpool & The Fylde Coll Central Campus FY1 130 D4
Blackpool & The Fylde Coll (Nautical) FY7 175 E8
Blackpool & The Fylde Coll (Park Road Campus) FY1 130 C4
Blackpool Twr* FY1 130 B5
Blackpool Victoria Hospl FY3 131 A5
Blackpool Zoo* FY3 131 A4
BLACKROD 31 D2
Blackrod Anglican/Methodist Prim Sch BL6 31 C2
Blackrod Brow BL6 31 B4
Blackrod By-Pass Rd BL6 31 D2
Blackrod Sta BL6 31 E2
Blacksmiths Row FY8 90 D7
Blacksmith Wlk PR7 60 E6
BLACKSNAPE 65 E8
Blacksnape Rd BB3 82 D2
Blacksticks La PR3 184 D1
Blackstone Rd PR6 61 E1
Blackthorn Cl
Blackburn BB1 101 F7
Cleveleys FY5 175 F5
Newton-w-S PR4 114 F2
Preston PR2 116 D1
Rochdale OL12 52 E2
Blackthorn Cres OL13 87 F3
Blackthorn Croft PR6 78 A2
Blackthorn Dr PR1 96 B3
Blackthorn La OL13 87 F3
Blackthorn Mews
Lytham St Anne's FY8 90 C5
Rochdale OL12 52 E2
Blackwood Ct OL13 70 C8
Blackwood Pl LA1 215 B5
Blackwood Rd OL13 70 B7
Blades St LA1 214 E7
BLAGUEGATE 17 B1
Blaguegate La WN8 17 B2
Blainscough Rd PR7 29 E8
Blairgowrie Gdns L39 16 A4
Blair Gr PR9 35 F7
Blair St OL12 52 D1
Blairway Ave FY3 130 F6
Blake Ave PR5 77 A7
Blake Gdns BB6 124 B4
Blakehall WN8 9 D7
Blakeley Cres BB18 196 B3
Blake St 6 BB5 104 B6
Blakewater Coll BB1 102 C2
Blakewater Rd BB1 102 C7
Blakey Moor BB2 101 D5
Blakey St BB11 128 B6
Blakiston St FY7 199 A4
Blanche St 6 PR2 117 C1
Blandford Ave FY5 175 C1
Blandford Cl PR8 34 F5
Blandford Rise BL6 32 F1
Blannel St BB11 127 E6
Blascomay Sq 13 BB8 171 D4
Blashaw La PR1 96 A5
Blaydike Moss PR26 76 B1
Blaydon Ave FY5 175 E4
Blaydon Pk WN8 9 D7
Bleachers Dr 2 PR25 76 E1
Blea Cl BB12 127 B8
Bleakholt Rd BL0 68 F1
Bleak La L40 26 D5
Bleara Rd BB18 195 D7
BLEASDALE 184 A7
Bleasdale Ave
Blackpool FY5 152 E8
Clitheroe BB7 166 C7
Kirkham PR4 114 A5
Poulton-le-F FY6 153 C2
Staining FY3 131 E5
Bleasdale CE Prim Sch PR3 184 A7
Bleasdale Cl
2 Bamber Bridge PR5 77 F8
Leyland PR25 60 B7
Ormskirk L39 6 D7
Bleasdale Ct
Fleetwood FY7 199 C5
Longridge PR3 140 B7
Bleasdale Gr LA3 216 E1
Bleasdale House Com Specl Sch LA5 224 C3
Bleasdale Rd
Cumeragh Village PR3 138 F6
Knott End-on-S FY6 199 D5
Lytham St Anne's FY8 91 C4
Whitechapel PR3 183 D1
Bleasdale St E PR1 118 C1
Bleasedale La PR3 183 C6
Blea Tarn Pl 3 LA4 217 D4
Blea Tarn Rd LA2 215 C2
Blelock St PR1 97 A7
Blenheim Ave
Blackpool FY1 130 D4
Kirkham PR4 113 F5
Blenheim Cl
Bamber Bridge PR5 77 C8
1 Blackburn BB1 122 E1
Blenheim Dr
Thornton FY5 176 C2
Warton PR4 92 D6
Blenheim Pl FY8 110 E1
Blenheim Rd PR8 21 B6
Blenheim St
Colne BB8 172 A5
13 Rochdale OL12 52 C1
Blenheim Terr BB8 194 E1
Blenheim Way PR4 116 E6
Blessed Sacrament RC Prim Sch PR2 118 F3
Blessed Trinity RC Coll BB11 127 C3
Blind La
Burton in L LA6 242 C3
Gisburn BB7 231 C3
Higham BB12 147 A6
Blindman's La L39 15 C7
Bloomfield Ct PR1 117 E2
Bloomfield Grange PR1 96 C2
Bloomfield Pk LA5 223 D1
Bloomfield Rd
Blackpool FY1 130 C2
Withnell PR6 80 A1
Bloomfield Road (Blackpool FC) FY1 130 C2
Bloom St 3 BL0 50 A4
Blossom Ave
Blackpool FY4 110 F7
Oswaldtwistle BB5 103 E5
Blossoms The
Fulwood PR2 118 C6
Poulton-le-F FY6 153 F3
BLOWICK 35 E6
Blowick Bsns Pk PR9 36 A6
Blowick Ind Pk PR9 36 A6
BLOWICK MOSS 35 E3
Blucher St BB8 171 E4
Bluebell Ave BB4 68 A8
Bluebell Cl
Blackpool FY2 152 D2
Cleveleys FY5 175 F5
Hesketh Bank PR4 73 E4
Lucas Green PR6 61 C5
Pilling PR3 201 C5
Bluebell Cotts PR3 201 C5
Bluebell Gr BB11 127 A5
Blue Bell La OL14 109 D2
Blue Bell Pl PR1 97 A7
Bluebell Way
Fulwood PR2 118 F6
Huncoat BB5 125 E2
Walton Summit PR5 78 A8
Bluebell Wood PR25 76 F3
Bluecoat Cres PR4 115 A2
Blue Gates BB7 229 B3
Blue Moor PR4 135 A2
Blue Scar La BB7 230 D7
Bluestone La L31 5 E1
Blue Stone La L40 40 F4
Blundell Ave
Formby L37 11 B4
Hightown L38 2 F3
Southport PR8 34 F2
Blundell Cres PR8 34 F2
Blundell Dr PR8 34 F2
Blundell Gr L38 2 F3
Blundell La
Blackrod BL6 31 A2
Higher Penwortham PR1 96 B6
Southport PR9 54 C2
Blundell Links Ct PR8 21 C4
Blundell Rd
Fulwood PR2 117 E3
Hightown L38 2 F2
Lytham St Anne's FY8 110 F1
Blundell St FY1 130 B3
Blythe Ave FY5 175 E5
Blythe Cotts L40 25 E1
Blythe Ct PR9 54 A2
Blythe La
Burscough L40 25 E1
Ormskirk L40 16 D8
Blythe Mdw L40 25 B1
Blythe Mews PR8 22 A8
Blythewood WN8 9 D7
Boarded Barn PR7 60 C3
Boardman Ave FY1 130 D2
Boardman St BL6 31 D2
Board St BB10 148 A1
Boarsgreave La BB4 69 F6
Bobbin Cl BB5 104 A5
Bobbiners La PR9 55 A3
Bobbin Mill Cl OL14 109 B1
Bobbin Mill Cotts PR3 181 F2
Bobbin St OL14 109 C1
Bobby Langton Way L40 25 E5
Bocholt Way BB4 86 A2
Bodiam Rd BL8 49 F2
Bodie Hill LA2 209 E5
Bodkin La PR3 154 F7
Bodmin Ave PR9 54 B5
Bodmin St PR1 118 D1
Boegrave Ave PR5 77 A8
Bogburn La PR7 29 D6
Bog Height Rd BB3 81 C6
Boland St BB1 102 A7
Bold La L39 6 B7
Bold St
Accrington BB5 104 D6
Bacup OL13 87 F1
Blackburn BB1 101 E6
Bury BL9 33 A3
Colne BB8 171 E4
Fleetwood FY7 199 B5
Morecambe LA3 216 E4
Preston PR1 117 D1
Southport PR9 35 B8
Bold Venture Cotts BB7 190 C4
Bold Venture Way BB5 125 A3
Boleyn Ct FY3 131 A2
Boleyn The L31 5 E3
Bolland Cl 6 BB7 166 F8
Bolland Prospect BB7 166 F7
Bolland St BB18 196 B3
BOLTON 47 D1
Bolton Ave
Accrington BB5 125 D1
Carleton FY6 153 C5
Lancaster LA1 218 D4
BOLTON-BY-BOWLAND 230 D4
Bolton-by-Bowland CE Prim Sch BB7 230 D4
Bolton Cl L37 12 A2
Bolton Com Coll, Horwich Ctr BL6 32 D2
Bolton Croft PR26 59 B8
Bolton Gr BB9 170 D3
BOLTON GREEN 42 C8
Bolton La LA5 221 C4
BOLTON-LE-SANDS 221 B5
Bolton-le-Sands CE Prim Sch LA5 221 B4
Bolton Mdw PR26 59 A8
Bolton Rd
Abbey Village PR6 80 B3
Adlington BL6, PR6 31 D6
Blackburn BB2 101 D2
Blackburn, Ewood BB2 81 E7
Chorley PR6 43 E4
Darwen BB3 65 B7
Darwen, Cadshaw BB3 65 C3
Edgworth BL7 48 D5
Ramsbottom BL8 49 D2
Riley Green PR5, PR6 79 E6
Southport PR8 35 A4
Bolton Rd N BL0 68 D2
Bolton Rd W BL0, BL8 50 A4
Bolton's Cop PR9 55 D5
Boltons Croft PR4 115 E7
Boltons Ct PR1 97 A7
Bolton's Ct 24 BB1 101 E5
Bolton's Meanygate PR4 56 C7
Bolton St
Blackpool FY1 130 B2
Chorley PR7 43 C7
Colne BB8 171 C4
5 Newchurch BB4 86 E1
Ramsbottom BL0 50 B6
BOLTON TOWN END 220 F3
Bombay St BB2 101 C3
Bonchurch St BB1 102 C4
Bond Cl BL6 32 C3
Bondís La PR7 30 F7
BONDS 181 C6
Bonds La
Bonds PR3 181 C6
Elswick PR4 156 A2
Bond's La PR9 55 A7
Bond St
Blackpool FY4 110 B7
13 Burnley BB10 128 A8
Bury BL9 33 A2
Colne BB8 171 D5
Darwen BB3 82 A2
Edenfield BL0 68 E2
Lancaster LA1 215 A8
Nelson BB9 148 D7
Bone Croft PR6 78 B3
Bone Hill La PR3 202 D1
Bonfire Hill Cl BB4 86 B7
Bonfire Hill Rd BB4 86 A7
Bonney St FY5 176 B3
Bonny Grass Terr BB7 144 A4
Bonny St FY1 130 B4
Bonsall St BB2 101 B2
Boome St FY4 110 C6
Boon Town LA6 240 C7
Boon Wlks LA6 240 C7
Booth Bridge La BD23 197 B5
Booth Cres BB4 87 A1
Booth Ct 4 BB10 128 A8
Boothfield House Cvn Pk FY6 200 A6
BOOTH FOLD 86 E1
Boothley Rd FY1 130 D6
Boothman Pl BB9 170 E2
Boothman St BB2 101 D2
Booth Rd OL13 70 B8
Boothroyden FY1 130 B8
Booth's La L39 14 F4
Booth's Par PR2 117 F7
Booth St
Accrington BB5 104 C4
10 Bacup OL13 87 F2
Carnforth LA5 223 D1
Haslingden BB4 85 A4
10 Nelson BB9 148 D8
Rawtenstall BB4 69 E8
Southport PR9 35 B8
Bootle St PR1 118 C1
Boot St BB18 197 B2
Boot Way BB11 128 A5
Borage Cl FY5 176 A5
Boran Ct BB11 126 E4
Bordeaux Cres FY5 152 F6
Border Ct 6 LA1 218 B1
Bores Hill WN1 30 C4
Borough Rd BB3 82 A1
Borrans Lane Cvn Pk LA3 212 F4
Borron La LA6 240 C3
Borrowdale L37 11 F5
Borrowdale Ave
Blackburn BB1 102 C3
Fleetwood FY7 198 E4
Nelson BB9 148 F7
Borrowdale Bsns Pk LA3 217 D3
Borrowdale Cl
4 Accrington BB5 125 D1
Burnley BB10 148 C3
Borrowdale Dr BB10 148 C4
Borrowdale Gr LA4 217 D5
Borrowdale Rd
Blackpool FY4 131 B1
Lancaster LA1 215 A8
Leyland PR25 60 B7
BORWICK 240 B4
Borwick Ave LA5 223 E6
Borwick Cl LA5 223 E6
Borwick Ct
Borwick LA6 240 B4
3 Morecambe LA4 217 B3
Borwick Dr LA1 218 B2
Borwick La LA6 240 B3
Borwick Mews LA6 240 B3
Borwick Rd LA6 240 D3
Bosburn Dr BB2 121 C2
Boscombe Ave LA3 216 E2
Boscombe Rd FY4 110 B6
Bosley Arc 2 FY1 130 B5
Bosley Cl BB3 65 D8
Bostock St 21 PR1 97 A7
Boston Ave FY2 152 D6
Boston Rd
Bacup OL13 87 F3
Lytham St Anne's FY8 90 B6
Bostons BB6 124 B5
Boston St BB9 148 F6
Boston Way FY4 110 F8
Bosworth Dr PR8 21 B4
Bosworth Pl FY4 110 B4
Bosworth St BL6 32 B4
Botanic Gardens Mus* PR9 54 B2
Botanic Rd PR9 54 B2
Botany Bay* PR6 61 E3
Botany Brow PR6 61 E2
Bott House La BB8, BB9 171 A2
Bottomdale Rd LA2 218 E8
Bottomgate BB1 102 B5
Bottomley Bank La BB4 86 B8
Bottomley St BB9 148 E8
BOTTOM OF HUTTON 94 F3
Bottom o' th' Knotts Brow BL7 48 E3
Bottom O' Th' Moor BL6 32 F3
Bottoms La LA5 224 D3
Botton Rd LA2 239 C1
Boulder St 12 BB4 86 A7
Bouldsworth Rd BB10 128 E5
Boulevard PR1 97 B5
Boulevard Gdns FY8 90 A4
Boulevard The
Blackburn BB1 101 E4
Lytham St Anne's FY8 90 A4
Boulsworth Cres BB9 171 B1
Boulsworth Dr BB8 172 C1
Boulsworth Gr BB8 172 A5
Boulview Terr BB8 172 A5
Boundary Cl
Eccleston PR7 41 B6
New Longton PR4 75 F8
Boundary Ct FY3 153 A1
Boundary Edge BL0 68 E3
Boundary La
Becconsall PR4 73 E1
Burscough L40 25 F4
Hale Nook FY6, PR3 178 B7
Holmes PR4, PR9 55 E6
Kirkby L33 1 F2
Shevington Moor WN6 29 A3
Boundary Meanygate
Becconsall PR4 73 D1
Holmes PR4 55 F7
Boundary Prim Sch FY3 130 F8
Boundary Rd
Accrington BB5 104 D7
Fulwood PR2 117 D3
Lancaster LA1 214 F6
Lytham St Anne's FY8 91 E5
Boundary St
Burnley BB10 148 C2
Colne BB8 171 D4
Leyland PR25 77 B2
Southport PR8 35 B4
Bourbles La FY6 200 D4
Bourne Brow PR3 159 E5
Bourne May Rd FY6 199 D5
Bournemouth Rd FY4 110 B6
Bourne Rd FY5 176 B5
Bournesfield PR5 98 E1
Bourne's Row PR5 98 E1
Bourne Way FY5 176 A4
Bovington Ave FY5 152 F8
Bow Brook Rd PR25 77 C1
Bowden Ave BB2 100 C1
Bowden Pl FY8 90 C6
Bowen St BB2 101 B2
Bower Cl BB2 101 B2
BOWERHAM 215 B6
Bowerham Com Prim Sch LA1 215 A6
Bowerham La LA1 215 B3
Bowerham Rd LA1 215 A5
Bowerham Terr 1 LA1 215 A6
Bowers La PR3 180 E7
Bower St
Blackburn BB2 101 B2
Bury BL9 33 C3
Bowers The PR7 43 D4
Bowes Lyon Pl FY8 90 C7
Bowfell Ave LA4 217 D5
Bowfell Cl FY4 131 D1
Bowfield's La BB2 120 F4
BOWGREAVE 181 D4
Bowgreave Cl 1 FY4 111 A6
Bowgreave Dr PR3 181 D4
Bow Hills La BB7 231 C6
BOWKER'S GREEN 6 D5
Bowker's Green La L39 6 E4
Bowker St BL0 68 C5
Bow La
Leyland PR25 77 B1
Preston PR1 96 E7
Bowland Ave
Burnley BB10 128 E5
Chorley PR6 43 D8
Fleetwood FY7 175 D8
Bowland Ave E LA1 211 B8
Bowland Ave N LA1 211 B8
Bowland Ave S LA1 211 B8
Bowland Cl
Crag Bank LA5 223 C1
Longridge PR3 140 B8
Bowland Cres FY3 131 A8
Bowland Ct
4 Clitheroe BB7 166 E8
9 Southport PR9 35 C8
Bowland Dr LA1 218 B2
Bowland Gate La BB7 189 E7
Bowland High Sch BB7 230 B1
Bowland Ho 7 BB1 101 F6
Bowland Pl PR2 119 A3
Bowland Rd
Fulwood PR2 119 A3
Garstang PR3 204 C1
Heysham LA3 213 A8
Bowland View
Brierfield BB9 148 D4
Garstang PR3 204 C1
Glasson LA2 209 E4
Bowland Wild Boar Pk* BB7 186 E6
Bowlers Cl PR2 118 C5
Bowlers Wlk OL12 52 F2
Bowlers Wood 11 OL13 70 D8
Bowlingfield PR2 117 A6
Bowling Gn The BL0 68 D3
Bowling Green Cl
Darwen BB3 65 B7
Southport PR8 35 F5
Bowling Green Cotts BB6 143 C6
Bowling Green Cvn Pk LA5 223 C1
Bowman Ct 5 BB1 101 F5
Bowness Ave
Blackpool FY4 131 D1
Fleetwood FY7 198 C1
Lytham St Anne's FY8 110 F2
Nelson BB9 148 E6
Rochdale OL12 52 C1
Southport PR8 21 C3
Thornton FY5 176 B2
Bowness Cl BB1 102 A6
Bowness Rd
Lancaster LA1 218 E1
Padiham BB12 146 C2
Preston PR1 119 A1
Bowood Ct FY3 131 B7
Bowran St PR1 96 F8
Bow St PR25 77 B2
Bow Wood Cl PR7 43 A6
Boxer Pl PR26 76 C2
Box St BL0 50 D6
Boxwood Dr BB2 80 F8
Boxwood St BB1 101 F8
Boyd Cl WN6 29 F1

Boyes Ave PR3 181 D2
Boyle St BB1 101 F6
Boys La PR2 117 C5
Brabiner La PR2, PR3 139 B4
Brabins Endowed Sch PR3 185 E3
Bracebridge Dr PR8 35 F2
BRACEWELL 231 F3
Bracewell Ave FY6 154 A3
Bracewell Cl BB9 148 E8
Bracewell La BD23 231 F3
Bracewell Rd PR2 118 E5
Bracewell St
Barnoldswick BB18 196 B3
Burnley BB10 148 B1
Nelson BB9 148 F8
Brackenbury Cl 5 PR5 77 A7
Brackenbury Rd PR1, PR2 117 E3
Brackenbury St PR1 117 F2
Bracken Cl
Blackburn BB2 80 F8
Chorley PR6 43 E8
Brackendale BB2 101 C1
Bracken Dr PR4 93 D7
Bracken Gr BB4 68 A8
Bracken Hey BB7 167 A8
Bracken Lea Fold 3 OL12 52 B2
Brackenthaite Rd LA5, LA7 225 B7
Brackenway L37 12 A6
Bracken Way FY2 152 D2
Bracknel Way L39 15 A1
Braconash Rd PR25 76 E2
Bradda Rd BB2 101 E1
Braddon Cl LA4 217 C3
Braddon St 2 PR1 118 D1
Brades Ave FY5 176 D2
Brades La PR4 93 D7
Brade St PR9 54 C4
Bradford Gr LA3 212 F6
Bradford St BB5 104 D6
Bradkirk La PR5 78 B8
Bradkirk Pl PR5 78 A7
BRADLEY 170 E2
Bradley Ct BB7 163 E8
Bradley Fold 5 BB9 170 E1
Bradley Gdns BB12 127 B5
Bradley Hall Rd BB9 170 F1
Bradley Hall Trad Est WN6 30 A2
Bradley La
Eccleston PR7 41 D6
Standish WN6 29 E1
Standish WN6 29 F2
Bradley Pl 8 PR8 35 B7
Bradley Prim Sch BB9 170 E1
Bradley Rd BB9 170 E1
Bradley Rd E BB9 170 E1
Bradley Smithy Cl OL12 52 E2
Bradley St
Colne BB8 171 F5
Southport PR9 35 C8
Bradley View 12 BB9 170 E1
Bradman Rd L33 1 D3
Bradshaw Brow L40 40 E2
Bradshaw Cl
Blackburn BB1 101 E8
Nelson BB9 148 E7
Standish WN6 29 D1
Bradshaw Ct PR9 36 A7
Bradshawgate Dr LA5 224 C4
Bradshaw La
Corner Row PR4 133 D1
Eagland Hill PR3 179 A7
Mawdesley L40 40 E2
Parbold WN8 27 C1
Scronkey PR3 201 E2
Bradshaw Rd BL2, BL7 48 E1
Bradshaw Row BB5 103 F6
Bradshaw St E 3 BB5 104 C6
Bradshaw St W BB5 103 F6
Bradshaws Cl FY6 177 C7
Bradshaw's La PR8 21 D6
Bradshaw St
Church BB5 103 F6
7 Lancaster LA1 215 A7
Nelson BB9 148 D7
Bradwood Ct BB4 85 A2
Bradyll Ct BB6 143 C6
Brady St BL6 32 A4
Braefield Cres PR2 118 F2
Braemar Ave
Southport PR9 53 E2
Thornton FY5 153 C7
Braemar Ct 2 LA4 217 E4
Braemar Dr BL9 33 D2
Braemar Wlk FY2 152 F6
Braeside BB2 101 C6
Braewood Cl BL9 33 C3
Braganza Way LA1 214 C8
Braid Cl PR1 96 D1
Braidhaven WN6 19 E7
Braid's La PR3 182 A7
Braidwood Ct FY8 89 D7
Braintree Ave PR1 96 E2
Braith Cl FY4 110 F8
Braithwaite St 3 FY1 130 B7
Bramble Cl PR4 113 E6
Bramble Ct
Kingsfold PR1 96 E2
1 Thornton FY5 176 A2
Brambles Cl BB7 166 D1
Bramble St BB10 148 A1
Brambles The
Blackburn BB2 101 A8
Blackpool FY8 110 B4
Coppull PR7 42 F2
Fulwood PR2 118 D6
Bramble Way
Burscough L40 25 F4
Parbold WN8 27 C1
Bramblewood PR26 58 B2
Bramblings The FY6 153 B2
Bramcote Cl L33 1 A4
Bramcote Rd L33 1 A4
Bramhall Rd WN8 17 F2
Bramley Ave
Burnley BB12 127 C8
Fleetwood FY7 198 E4
Bramley Cl 8 BB5 103 E5
Bramley Ct WN6 29 E1
Bramley Gdns FY6 153 A2
Bramley View BB7 144 D8
Brampton Ave FY5 175 F4
Brampton Dr
Bamber Bridge PR5 97 E1
Morecambe LA4 217 F5
Brampton St 2 PR2 117 C1
Bramwell Pk L40 24 B4
Bramwell Rd PR4 93 B6
Bramworth Ave BL0 50 B6
Branch Rd
Blackburn BB2, BB3 81 E7
Burnley BB11 128 B4
2 Clayton-le-M BB5 124 F3
Mellor Brook BB2 121 C2
Waddington BB7 189 B4
Branch St
Bacup OL13 70 D8
Nelson BB9 148 F8
Brancker St 3 PR7 43 A5
Brandiforth St PR5 97 F2
Brandlesholme Rd BL8 50 A1
Brandon Cl WN8 10 A7
Brandreth Delph WN8 27 C3
Brandreth Dr WN8 27 C2
Brandreth Pk WN8 27 D4
Brandreth Pl WN6 29 F1
BRANDWOOD 70 B8
Brandwood
Higher Penwortham PR1 96 A4
6 Newchurch BB4 86 E1
Brandwood Ct BL7 48 E5
Brandwood Fold BL7 48 E5
Brandwood Gr BB10 128 C6
Brandwood Pk OL13 70 B8
Brandwood Rd OL13 70 B8
Brandwood St BB3 82 B1
Brandy House Brow BB2 101 F2
Branksome Ave FY5 175 F3
Branksome Dr LA4 217 D4
Branston Rd FY4 130 E1
Branstree Rd FY4 131 C1
Brant Ct FY7 198 C1
Brantfell Dr BB12 127 B8
Brantfell Rd
Blackburn BB1 101 D7
Great Harwood BB6 124 D6
Brant Rd PR1 119 A1
Brantwood BB5 124 E2
Brantwood Ave
Blackburn BB1 102 F5
Morecambe LA4 217 E6
Brantwood Dr
Lancaster LA1 215 A2
Leyland PR25 77 B1
Brassey St BB12 127 C7
Brathay Pl FY7 198 D2
Braxfield Ct FY8 89 D6
Brayshaw Pl PR2 118 E4
Brays Heys 2 FY5 176 C1
Brays Rd FY8 112 B1
Bray St PR2 117 C1
Brazil Cl LA3 217 A2
Brazley Ave BL6 32 E1
Bread St 4 BB12 127 D6
Bream Wood PR4 113 E4
Brearlands BD23 197 B6
Brearley St OL13 70 D8
Brechin Rd L33 1 A2
Breck Cl FY6 153 E5
Breck Dr FY6 153 E5
Breck Prim Sch The FY6 153 F5
Breck Rd
Blackpool FY3 130 E4
Poulton-le-F FY6 153 F6
Breckside Cl FY6 153 E5
Brecon Ave BB5 103 C4
Brecon Cl FY1 130 D3
Brecon Rd BB1 102 C5
Bredon Ave PR7 60 E1
Bredon Cl FY8 91 D5
Bredon Ct L37 11 E4
Breeze Cl
Foulridge BB8 194 E1
Thornton FY5 176 A4
Breeze Mount PR5 77 C8
Breeze Rd PR8 34 E2
Brenbar Cres OL12 71 D1
Brendjean Rd LA4 217 C4
Brendon Wlk FY3 130 F8
Brennand Cl
Bamber Bridge PR5 77 F8
Lancaster LA1 218 A2
Brennand St
Burnley BB10 148 B1
Clitheroe BB7 189 E1
Brentlea Ave LA3 212 E7
Brentlea Cres LA3 212 E7
Brenton Bsns Complex 2 BL9 33 A2
Brent St BB10 148 C3
Brentwood FY7 198 E2
Brentwood Ave
Blackpool FY5 152 D8
Burnley BB11 127 E3
Poulton-le-F FY6 153 C3
Brentwood Cl L38 2 F2
Brentwood Ct PR9 53 D1
Brentwood Rd
Adlington PR6 31 B8
Nelson BB9 171 A1
BRETHERTON 57 E6
Bretherton Cl PR26 59 C8
Bretherton Cotts FY5 153 E8
Bretherton Ct L40 25 F3
Bretherton Endowed CE Prim Sch PR26 57 F5
Bretherton Rd PR26 58 B4
Bretherton Terr 9 PR25 77 B1
Brettarch Dr LA1 214 E5
Brettargh Cl LA1 214 E6
Brettargh Dr LA1 214 E6
Brett Cl BB7 167 A7
Bretton Fold PR8 35 F5
Brewery La
Formby L37 11 F6
19 Lancaster LA1 214 F8
Brewery St
6 Blackburn BB2 101 D5
Longridge PR3 140 B7
Breworth Fold La PR6 79 A3
Briar Ave PR7 60 C4
Briar Bank Row PR2 118 A8
Briar Cl 3 OL12 52 A1
Briarcroft BB3 82 A6
Briar Croft PR4 75 A7
Briarfield BL7 47 D2
Briar Field FY2 152 F6
Briarfield Rd FY6 153 B5
Briar Gr PR2 117 A4
Briar Hill Cl 3 BB1 102 A4
Briar Lea Rd LA6 221 E5
Briar Mews 1 FY5 176 C1
Briar Rd
Blackburn BB1 101 F8
Southport PR8 21 D4
Thornton FY5 176 C1
Briars Brook L40 26 A2
Briarscroft LA5 223 E6
Briars Gn WN8 18 B4
Briars La
Maghull L31 5 E1
Ring o'Bells L40 26 A3
Briar St 5 OL13 88 A1
Briars The
Fulwood PR2 118 D6
Southport PR8 34 F1
Briarwood PR4 93 A6
Briarwood Cl
Leyland PR25 59 E8
Thornton FY5 153 B7
Weeton PR4 132 F2
Briarwood Ct FY5 153 B7
Briarwood Dr FY2 152 E5
Briary Croft L38 2 F3
Briary Ct PR5 78 C5
Brickcroft LA2 210 A4
Brickcroft La PR26 58 B3
Brickhouse Gdns PR3 185 E3
Brickhouse La FY6 177 B4
Brick Kiln La L40 39 B3
Brickmakers Arms Yd L39 15 D6
Brick St
9 Burnley BB11 127 F6
Bury BL9 33 A3
Bridge Ave L39 15 E5
Bridge Bank 4 PR5 97 C6
Bridge Cl
Bamber Bridge PR5 77 A8
6 Newchurch BB4 86 F1
Bridge Croft
Bolton-le-S LA5 221 A4
Clayton-le-M BB5 124 E4
Bridge Ct
3 Bamber Bridge PR5 77 A8
Clitheroe BB7 189 F2
2 Lytham St Anne's FY8 91 D4
BRIDGE END 68 A7
Bridge End
Bamber Bridge PR5 77 C8
Barley BB12 169 C5
Whalley BB7 144 C4
Bridge End Cl BB4 68 A7
Bridge Farm Dr L31 5 F2
Bridgefield Cl BB1 124 B2
Bridgefield Dr BL9 33 C2
Bridgefield St 8 BB12 126 C4
Bridge Gr PR8 35 B6
Bridgehall Dr WN8 10 B7
Bridge Hall Dr BL9 33 C2
Bridge Hall Fold BL9 33 C2
Bridge Hall La BL9 33 D2
Bridge Ho
7 Blackburn BB2 101 B1
18 Lancaster LA1 218 D2
3 Lytham St Anne's FY8 91 D4
Ormskirk L39 15 E4
Rishton BB1 124 B1
Bridge Hos
Accrington BB5 84 E8
Whitewell Bottom BB4 86 F7
Bridge House Marina & Cvn Pk PR3 181 A8
Bridge House Rd FY4 110 F8
Bridge La LA1 214 F8
Bridge Mews
6 Bamber Bridge PR5 77 E8
Ingleton LA6 242 F3
Bridge Mill Ct PR6 43 F6
Bridgemill Rd BB1 101 F4
Bridge Mill Rd BB9 148 C8
Bridgend Ct PR2 116 F3
Bridgend Dr PR8 21 B4
Bridge Rd
3 Bamber Bridge PR5 77 C8
Chatburn BB7 190 D5
Fleetwood FY7 199 B4
Lancaster LA1 214 F5
Lytham St Anne's FY8 90 E4
Morecambe LA4 217 C5
Nether Kellet LA6 221 E4
Preston PR2 117 C2
Bridge Row PR3 157 C7
Bridgeside
Blackpool FY8 110 B4
Carnforth LA5 223 D1
Bridge St
14 Accrington BB5 104 C6
Bamber Bridge PR5 77 E7
Blackburn BB1 101 E4
Brierfield BB9 148 B5
Burnley BB11 128 A6
Bury BL9 33 A3
Church BB5 103 E6
Colne BB8 171 C4
Darwen BB3 82 A1
Garstang PR3 181 C6
6 Great Harwood BB6 124 C5
Haslingden BB4 68 C6
Higher Walton PR5 98 B3
Horwich BL6 32 C4
Newchurch BB4 86 F1
Ormskirk L39 15 E4
Padiham BB12 126 B8
Ramsbottom BL0 50 C6
Rawtenstall BB4 69 E7
Rishton BB1 124 B2
Southport PR8 35 B6
Water BB4 87 A8
Wheelton PR6 62 A7
Whitworth OL12 71 C1
Bridge Terr
6 Preston PR5 97 C6
Whalley BB7 144 B7
Bridget St 22 LA1 214 F8
Bridgewater Ave 7 FY5 152 F7
Bridgewater Cl BB11 126 F4
Bridgewater Ct 6 BB2 101 C4
Bridgeway PR5 77 C8
Bridge Wills La PR9 54 C5
Bridle Path The BB18 194 D7
Bridleway
Lytham St Anne's FY8 90 E7
Newchurch BB4 86 F2
Brief St BB10 128 A8
Briercliffe Ave
Blackpool FY3 130 F2
Colne BB8 171 B3
Briercliffe Bsns Ctr BB10 148 F3
Briercliffe Prim Sch BB10 148 F3
Briercliffe Rd
Burnley BB10 148 C1
Burnley, Harle Syke BB10 148 D2
9 Chorley PR6 61 D1
Briercliffe Sh Ctr 15 BB10 148 B1
Briercliffe St BB8 171 B3
Brier Cres BB9 148 D6
Brier Dr LA3 212 E7
BRIERFIELD 148 C6
Brierfield
New Longton PR4 75 F8
Skelmersdale WN8 9 D6
Brierfield Sta BB9 148 B5
Brier Heights Cl BB9 148 D5
Brierholme Ave 1 BL7 47 E1
Brierley Ave FY3 130 E7
Brierley La PR4 136 B8
Brierley Rd PR5 78 A7
Brierley St PR2 117 D1
Briers Brow PR6 62 B7
Briers The PR7 41 C6
Briery Cl PR2 118 C4
Brieryfield Rd PR1 96 D8
Briery Hey PR5 78 C6
Briery St 2 LA1 218 B1
Brigg Field BB5 124 F4
Briggs Fold BL7 47 E2
Briggs Fold Cl BL7 47 E2
Briggs Fold Rd BL7 47 E2
Briggs Rd PR2 117 C2
Brighouse Cl L39 15 D6
Brighton Ave
Blackpool FY4 110 B8
Cleveleys FY5 175 D2
Lytham St Anne's FY8 89 F7
Brighton Cres PR2 117 A3
Brighton Rd
Burnley BB10 148 C3
Southport PR8 35 A3
Brighton St
Bury BL9 33 B3
7 Chorley PR6 43 E8
Todmorden OL14 109 C1
Brighton Terr
Blackburn BB2 101 B6
Darwen BB3 81 E2
Bright St Mill BL9 33 A3
Bright's Cl BB7 229 A5
Bright St
Blackburn BB1 102 B6
Blackpool FY4 110 B8
2 Bolton BL7 47 D2
2 Burnley BB10 148 B1
Bury BL9 33 A3
Clitheroe BB7 166 F8
Colne BB8 171 D5
Colne, Cotton Tree BB8 172 B5
Darwen BB3 81 F2
Oswaldtwistle BB5 103 D3
Padiham BB12 126 D8
13 Rawtenstall BB4 86 A3
Southport PR9 35 F7
Brightstone Cl PR9 55 B5
Bright Terr BB8 172 B2
Brightwater BL6 31 F2
Brigsteer Cl BB5 124 E2
BRINDLE 78 F5
Brindle Cl
Bamber Bridge PR5 98 A2
9 Lancaster LA1 218 A2
Longridge PR3 140 B7
Walton Summit PR5 78 B8
Brindle Dell 8 BL7 47 D2
Brindle Fold PR5 78 C7
Brindle Gregson Lane Prim Sch PR5 98 E1
Brindle Hts PR6 78 F5
Brindle Pl 6 PR2 139 D1
Brindle Rd
Bamber Bridge PR5 97 F2
Walton Summit PR5, PR6 78 C7
Brindle St James' CE Prim Sch PR6 78 F5
Brindle St
Blackburn BB2 101 C1
Chorley PR7 43 C6
Preston PR1 97 C8
Brindley Cl BB11 126 F4
Brindley St BL6 32 C2
Brinklow Cl PR8 21 A5
Brink's Row BL6 32 D5
BRINSCALL 62 E7
Brinscall Terr PR6 62 F7
Brinwell Bsns Ctr FY4 111 B8
Brinwell Rd FY4 131 B1
Brisbane Pl FY5 152 F7
Brisbane St 8 BB5 125 A1
Bristol Ave
Blackpool FY2 152 E4
Fleetwood FY7 175 C8
Leyland PR25 77 C3
Bristol Cl 9 BB1 102 A4
Bristol St
Burnley BB11 127 D3
Colne BB8 171 E5
Morecambe LA4 217 C4
Bristow Ave PR2 117 B2
BRITANNIA 71 C8
Britannia Ave OL13 88 A2
Britannia Com Prim Sch OL13 71 C8
Britannia Cotts BB5 103 A1
Britannia Dr PR2 96 B7
Britannia Mill
14 Bury BL9 33 A3
1 Rake Foot BB4 86 A7
Britannia Pl 2 FY1 130 B1
Britannia St BB6 124 C5
Britannia Way
Blackpool FY4 111 E8
Haslingden BB4 68 A8
Britannia Wlk
1 Burnley BB11 128 B4
Lytham St Anne's FY8 90 C8
British Commercial Vehicle Mus* PR25 77 A1
British in India Mus* BB8 171 E5
British Lawnmower Mus* PR8 35 B5
Britten Cl BB2 102 A2
Britten St BB3 81 F2
Britwell Cl BB2 82 A8
Brixey St PR1 96 D6
Brixham Pl 4 FY4 110 B6
Brixton Rd PR1 97 B7
Broadacre
Caton LA2 237 C3
Shevington Moor WN6 29 B2
Up Holland WN8 10 A6
Broadacre Cl LA2 237 C3
Broadacre Pl LA2 237 C3
Broadacre View LA2 237 C3
Broadbent Dr BL9 33 E4
BROAD CLOUGH 87 F4
Broad Clough Villas OL13 87 F5
Broad Croft PR4 95 A1
Broadfield
Accrington BB5 84 B8
Broughton PR3 137 B2
BROADFIELD
Leyland 76 E1
Oswaldtwistle 103 F2
Broadfield BB5 103 F2
Broadfield Ave
Blackpool FY4 110 F5
Poulton-le-F FY6 153 F3
Broadfield Ct FY6 153 F3
Broadfield Dr
Kingsfold PR1 96 D2

Broadfield Dr *continued*
Leyland PR25 76 E1
Broadfield Rd BB5 104 A3
Broadfields PR7 61 B2
Broadfield Sch BB5 103 F2
Broadfields Cvn Pk LA3 217 A2
Broadfield St BB5 103 F3
Broadfleet Cl PR3 201 C6
Broadfold Ave BB1 102 B7
BROADGATE 96 E6
Broadgate PR1 96 D6
Broadgate Foot Pk LA3 212 F4
Broadgreen Cl PR25 76 F1
Broadhead Rd
Edgworth BL7 48 E7
Hoddleston BB3, BL7 66 F5
Broadhurst La WN6 28 F7
Broadhurst Rd FY5 152 E8
Broadhurst Way BB9 148 C4
Broad Ing OL12 52 C1
Broad Ing Cl BB10 128 E1
Broadith La PR3 160 E1
Broad La
Formby L37 12 F1
Great Altcar L37, L38 4 A8
Haskayne L39 14 B2
Kirkby L33 1 A1
Maghull, Homer Green L29 4 C2
Southport L37 12 C7
Whalley BB7 144 B5
Winmarleigh PR3 203 F5
Broadlands PR8 34 E3
Broadlands Dr LA5 220 F3
Broadlands Pl FY8 90 F4
Broadlands Sch BB1 82 B8
Broadlea Gr OL12 52 C2
BROADLEY 52 C5
Broadley St BB4 86 A3
Broad Mdw
Bamber Bridge PR5 77 A8
Chipping PR3 185 D3
Broadmead WN8 27 B2
Broad Meadow La PR26 57 F4
Broadness Dr BB9 148 E6
Broad Oak Ave PR3 181 D6
Broad Oak Cl 4 PR6 31 A8
Broad Oak Cotts PR6 44 D3
Broad Oak Gn PR1 96 B3
Broad Oak High Sch BL9 33 B2
Broad Oak Ind Est BB5 104 D4
Broad Oak La
Bury BL9 33 D3
Higher Penwortham PR1 96 B3
Kingsfold PR4 96 B2
Staining FY3 131 D5
Broadoak Rd L31 5 E1
Broad Oak Rd BB5 104 D5
Broadoaks BL9 33 D3
Broad Oak Terr BL9 33 E3
Broadpool La FY6 177 C1
Broadriding Rd WN6 19 E6
Broad Sq 8 PR25 60 A8
Broad St
3 Leyland PR25 60 A8
13 Nelson BB9 148 D8
Broadstone Cl 4 OL12 52 A1
Broadstone Ct LA1 215 C7
Broadstone Dr PR7 60 E7
Broadtree Cl BB2 121 C3
Broadwater Ave FY7 175 F8
Broadwater Gdns FY7 175 E8
Broadway
Accrington BB5 104 B6
Blackburn BB1 122 E2
Blackpool FY4 110 C7
Fleetwood FY7 198 E2
Fulwood PR2 117 D7
Haslingden BB4 68 B8
Horwich BL6 32 D3
Lancaster LA1 218 D2
Leyland PR25 60 B8
Morecambe LA4 217 D5
Nelson BB9 148 D8
Preston PR2 116 F2
Broadway Cl PR8 21 B5
Broadway Cres BB4 68 A8
Broadway Pl
Barrowford BB9 170 D3
Nelson BB9 171 A1
Broadway Prim Sch BB4 68 C8
Broadway St BB2 101 B1
Broadwood Cl PR1 96 B4
Broadwood Dr PR2 117 F7
Broadwood Way FY8 90 E4
Brock Ave FY7 198 D2
Brock Bank BB4 86 F4
Brockbank Ave LA1 214 C8
Brock Cl
Lancaster LA1 218 C3
Morecambe LA3 217 F3
Brock Clough Rd BB4 86 F4
Brockenhurst St BB10 128 C5
BROCKHALL VILLAGE 143 C5
Brockholes Brow PR1, PR2 119 A1
Brockholes Cres FY6 153 E2
Brockholes View PR1 97 C7
Brockholes Way PR3 181 E1
Brockholes Wood Com Prim Sch PR1 119 A1
Brocklebank Rd PR9 53 E2
Brocklehurst Ave BB5 104 B3
Brocklewood Ave FY6 131 D8
Brock Mill La PR3 183 B2
Brock Rd
Chorley PR6 61 D1
Lane Heads PR3, PR4 156 E3
Brock Side PR3 159 C6
Brock St LA1 214 F8
Brockway FY6 153 D2
Brockway Ave FY3 130 F6
Broderick Ave 1 FY2 152 E1
Brodick Rd BB1 102 D3
Brodie Cl FY4 110 F6
Brogden La BB18 231 E2
Brogden St 4 BB18 196 B3
Brogden View BB18 196 A4
Broken Bank Head BB7 235 A2
Broken Banks BB8 171 E4
Broken Stone Rd BB3 81 A6
Bromilow Rd WN8 17 C1
Bromley Cl FY2 152 E1
Bromley Cross BL7 48 B1
Bromley Ct 5 FY2 152 E1
Bromley Gn PR6 61 F4
Bromley Ho BB2 101 C5
Bromley Rd FY8 89 F6
Bromley St
Blackburn BB2 101 C5
Preston PR1 96 D8
Brompton Ave L33 1 A5
Brompton Cl FY8 90 D5
Brompton Rd
Poulton-le-F FY6 131 D8
Southport PR8 35 E7
Bromsgrove Ave FY2 152 C4
Bromsgrove Rd BB10 128 B8
Bronte Ave BB10 128 D6
Bronte Cl OL12 52 A1
Brooden Dr BB9 148 C4
Brook Ave
Maghull L31 5 E2
Morecambe LA3 216 F3
Scorton PR3 204 E7
Brookbank BB9 170 E4
Brook Bldg The BL7 47 D2
Brook Croft PR2 117 B4
Brook Ct 9 BB4 86 A7
Brookdale
Adlington PR6 44 A1
Belmont BL7 46 C5
New Longton PR4 76 A6
Rochdale OL12 52 E3
Brookdale Ave FY5 152 E8
Brookdale Cl PR25 60 B6
Brookdale The PR8 21 D3
Brooke Cl
Accrington BB5 104 E2
Southport PR9 36 B7
Brookes La BB7 144 C5
Brookes St 7 OL13 70 D8
Brooke St PR6 43 E7
Brookes The 6 PR6 43 E7
Brook Farm Cl L39 15 E4
BROOKFIELD 118 D4
Brookfield
Croston PR26 58 B3
Mawdesley L40 40 C2
Mellor BB2 121 E2
Parbold WN8 27 C2
Brookfield Ave
Blackpool FY4 111 A6
Fulwood PR2 118 C4
Thornton FY5 176 C1
Brookfield Cl LA5 221 B5
Brookfield Com Prim Sch PR2 118 E5
Brookfield Ct PR3 185 E3
Brookfield Dr PR2 117 E8
Brookfield Ho BL0 49 F3
Brookfield La L39 6 A5
Brookfield Park Prim Sch WN8 17 D2
Brookfield Pl PR5 78 A6
Brookfield Rd
Shevington Moor WN6 29 B2
Thornton FY5 176 C1
Up Holland WN8 10 B7
Brookfield Sch FY6 153 F5
Brookfield St
2 Blackburn BB1 101 E6
Preston PR1 117 F1
Todmorden OL14 109 C1
Brookfield Terr
Hampson Green LA2 207 E8
Lytham St Anne's FY8 91 B4
Brookfield View LA5 221 B5
Brook Field Way BB18 197 B1
Brookford Cl BB12 127 D8
Brook Gr
Cleveleys FY5 175 E4
Morecambe LA3 216 F3
Brook Hey PR4 74 F8
Brook Hey Dr L33 1 A3
Brook Hey Wlk L33 1 A3
Brook Ho
Lytham St Anne's FY8 91 A3
Southport PR8 35 C5
Brookholme Ct LA1 214 C7
BROOKHOUSE
Blackburn 101 F6
Lancaster 237 D3
Brookhouse Bsns Ctr 10 BB1 101 F6
Brookhouse Cl
Blackburn BB1 101 F6
Gregson Lane PR5 98 F2
Brookhouse Dr PR5 98 F2
Brookhouse Gdns 12 BB1 101 F6
Brookhouse La BB1 101 F6
Brookhouse Prim Sch BB1 101 F7
Brookhouse Rd
Caton LA2 237 C3
Ormskirk L39 15 D6
Brookhouse St PR2 117 D1
Brook La
Charnock Richard PR7 42 C4
Farington PR26, PR4 76 D6
Much Hoole PR4 74 E3
Ormskirk L39 15 E4
Brookland LA6 242 C3
Brookland Cl BB5 124 F4
Brooklands
Chipping PR3 185 F3
Horwich BL6 32 C3
Much Hoole PR4 74 D2
Ormskirk L39 16 A6
Preston PR2 117 A1
Brooklands Ave
Burnley BB11 128 B3
Fulwood PR2 117 E7
Haslingden BB4 68 B7
Kirkham PR4 114 A5
Brooklands Ct LA1 215 A4
Brooklands Dr
Bonds PR3 181 C6
Heysham LA3 212 F6
Orrell WN5 10 D5
Brooklands Gr L40 25 F3
Brooklands Rd
Burnley BB11 128 B3
Lytham St Anne's FY8 90 C6
Ramsbottom BL0 50 A2
Up Holland WN8 10 C7
Brookland St BB4 86 D1
Brooklands Terr BB1 102 A7
Brooklands The PR4 113 B4
Brooklands Way FY4 111 E7
Brookland Terr 3 BB4 69 F7
Brooklyn Ave FY3 130 E8
Brooklyn Cvn Pk PR9 55 A4
Brooklyn Rd BB1 122 F5
Brook Mdw PR4 116 F7
Brook Mill Ind Est PR4 113 B4
Brook Pl PR2 116 D2
Brook Rd
Lytham St Anne's FY8 91 C3
Morecambe LA3 216 F3
Brook St N PR2 117 D3
BROOKSBOTTOMS 50 C3
Brooksbottoms Cl BL0 50 C4
Brookshaw St BL9 33 A4
Brookside
Brockhall Village BB6 143 C5
Coppull PR7 42 F1
Downham BB7 191 B5
Euxton PR7 60 C2
Hurlston Green L40 24 B4
Kirkham PR4 113 F6
Sabden BB7 145 F7
Thornton FY5 176 C3
BROOK SIDE 103 A3
Brook Side L31 5 E1
Brookside Cl
Leyland PR26 76 E3
Ramsbottom BL0 50 A3
Whalley BB7 144 C5
Brookside Cotts PR6 62 D3
Brookside Cres
Ramsbottom BL8 49 E1
West Bradford BB7 189 D7
Brookside Ctr FY5 176 C3
Brookside Dr LA2 226 A8
Brookside Ind Est BB5 103 C3
Brookside La BB5 103 B3
Brookside Prim Sch BB7 166 F8
Brookside Rd
Fulwood PR2 117 D7
Southport PR8 35 C2
Standish WN1 30 B1
Brookside St BB5 103 C3
Brookside View BB5 103 B4
Brooks Rd L37 11 D2
Brook St
Adlington PR6 44 A1
4 Barnoldswick BB18 196 B2
Blackburn BB2 101 B2
Blackpool FY4 130 E1
Bury BL9 33 A3
Clitheroe BB7 189 F1
Colne BB8 171 D5
Earby BB18 197 B2
Fleetwood FY7 175 E8
Haslingden BB4 85 B5
Higher Walton PR5 98 B3
Kirkham PR4 113 F6
Lancaster LA1 214 E7
Nelson BB9 148 E8
Oswaldtwistle BB5 103 E4
Padiham BB12 126 D7
Preston PR1 117 E2
Rishton BB1 124 B1
Southport PR9 54 D4
Wheelton PR6 62 A7
Brooks Way L37 11 D2
Brook Vale Ct PR3 157 E3
Brookview PR2 118 B5
Brook Villas
Waddington BB7 189 B4
West Bradford BB7 189 E5
Brookville OL12 71 C1
Brookway
Blackburn BB2 81 B8
Longton PR4 74 F8
Wrea Green PR4 113 A4
Broom Cl
Burscough L40 25 F4
Clayton-le-W PR25 77 E3
Broome Cl PR8 35 B3
Broome Rd PR8 35 B3
Broom Field PR3 181 D4
Broomfield Ho WN6 29 E2
Broomfield Mill St PR1 117 F1
Broomfield Pl
Blackburn BB2 101 B3
Standish WN6 29 E1
Broomfield Rd
Fleetwood FY7 198 F2
Standish WN6 29 E2
Broomflat Cl WN6 29 E1
Broom Hill Coppice PR3 204 C2
Broomholme WN6 19 D7
Brotherod Hall Rd OL12 52 C2
Brothers St BB2 101 A1
Brotherston Dr BB2 81 C8
Brotherton Mdws 7 BB7 166 F8
Brougham St BB12 127 F7
Brough Ave FY2 152 F2
BROUGHTON 137 D3
Broughton Ave
Blackpool FY3 130 E7
Southport PR8 35 D4
Broughton Bsns & Ent Coll PR3 137 C2
Broughton Cl BB2 102 A1
Broughton Gr LA3 217 C3
Broughton in Amounderness CE Prim Sch PR3 137 D1
Broughton St
1 Burnley BB12 127 D6
4 Darwen BB3 81 F2
Preston PR1 117 E2
Broughton Tower Way PR2 118 A8
Broughton Way FY6 153 C6
Brow Cl PR3 156 A6
Brow Edge BB4 86 D1
Browfoot Cl LA5 223 F2
Browgate BB7 190 F8
Browgill Pl 8 LA1 218 B2
Browhead Ct BB10 128 B8
Browhead Rd BB10 128 B8
Brow Hey PR5 78 B6
Brown Birks Rd BB5 104 E8
Brown Birks St 1 OL14 109 B1
BROWNEDGE 97 D1
BROWN EDGE 36 A2
Brownedge Cl PR5 97 D1
Brown Edge Cl PR8 36 A2
Brownedge La PR5 97 E1
Brownedge Rd PR5 77 B8
Brownedge Wlk PR5 97 D1
BROWNHILL 122 F2
Brownhill Ave BB10 128 C6
Brownhill Dr BB1 123 A1
Brownhill La PR4 75 D7
Brown Hill La BB8 171 F7
Brownhill Rd
Blackburn BB1 122 F3
Leyland PR25 76 F1
Brown Hill Row BB8 171 F7
Brownhill Sch OL12 52 E1
Brownhill View OL12 52 E1
Browning Ave
4 Lytham St Anne's FY8 91 D4
Oswaldtwistle BB5 103 C5
3 Thornton FY5 176 A3
Browning Cl BB8 171 D6
Browning Cres PR1 118 D2
Browning Rd PR1 118 D2
Browning St BB3 82 F1
Brown La
Bamber Bridge PR5 98 A2
Higher Walton PR5 98 A3
Brownley St
Chorley PR6 43 E7
Clayton Green PR6 78 B1
BROWNLOW 10 C1
Brownlow La WN5 10 C1
Brownlow Rd BL6 32 C5
Brownlow St
Blackburn BB1 102 D4
Clitheroe BB7 166 E7
Brownlow Terr BB2 100 C1
Brownroyd BB18 197 C2
Brown St E BB8 171 D5
Brown St W BB8 171 C4
Browns Hey PR7 61 A2
BROWNSIDE 128 F6
Brownside Mill BB10 128 F6
Brownside Rd BB10 128 F5
Brown's La
Kirkham PR4 113 D3
Thornton FY6 176 E7
Brown Sq 9 BB11 128 A6
Brown St
Accrington BB5 104 B5
Bacup OL13 87 F4
Bamber Bridge PR5 77 F8
Blackburn BB1 101 E5
Blackrod BL6 31 D2
Burnley BB11 127 F6
Chorley PR6 43 D8
Clitheroe BB7 166 D7
Fleetwood FY7 199 A3
2 Ramsbottom BL0 50 B5
Thornton FY5 176 B3
Brows Cl L37 11 E3
Browsholme LA1 218 A2
Browsholme Ave
Burnley BB10 128 C6
Fulwood PR2 118 F3
Browsholme Cl
Crag Bank LA5 223 C1
Normoss FY3 131 B8
Browsholme Hall* BB7 187 E7
Browsholme Rd BB7 229 C1
Brows La L37 11 E3
Brow The PR4 73 E4
Brow View BB10 128 B8
Broxton Ave WN5 10 F7
Broyd View LA1 214 F5
Bruce St
5 Barnoldswick BB18 196 B3
Blackburn BB1 102 B6
Burnley BB11 127 D5
Bruna La PR3 181 E4
Brundhurst Fold BB2 121 E2
Brunel Dr BB1 102 A4
Brunel St
Burnley BB12 127 C7
Horwich BL6 32 C2
Brunel Way FY4 111 C7
Brunel Wlk BB1 101 F4
Brungerley Ave BB7 189 E1
Brun Gr FY1 130 E1
BRUNSHAW 128 D5
Brunshaw Ave BB10 128 D5
Brunshaw Prim Sch BB10 128 D4
Brunshaw Rd BB10 128 D6
Brun St BB11 127 F6
Brunswick Ave BL6 32 E2
Brunswick Dr BB8 171 A3
Brunswick Pl 4 PR2 117 C1
Brunswick Rd LA3 216 E3
Brunswick St
Blackburn BB2 101 D4
3 Blackpool FY1 130 B4
Burnley BB11 128 A4
2 Chorley PR6 43 D8
Darwen BB3 65 B8
Nelson BB9 148 E7
Brunswick Terr
7 Accrington BB5 104 B6
Bacup OL13 70 D8
Brun Terr BB10 128 F5
Brunton Ho 2 LA1 215 A5
Brunton Rd LA1 214 F6
Brunton's Warehouse LA1 218 C1
Brush St BB11 127 C5
Brussels Rd BB3 82 C1
Bryan Rd FY3 130 D5
Bryan St BB2 101 E2
Brydeck Ave PR1 96 E4
Bryer's Croft BB1 122 F6
Bryer St 25 LA1 214 F8
Bryn Gr LA2 220 E2
BRYNING 92 C8
Bryning Ave
Blackpool FY2 152 C4
Wrea Green PR4 113 B3
Bryning Fern La PR4 113 F4
Bryning Hall La
Moss Side FY8 112 F1
Warton PR4 92 B8
Wrea Green FY8, PR4 113 A1
Bryning La
Newton-w-S PR4 114 F2
Wrea Green PR4 113 B2
Bryning with Warton St Paul's CE Prim Sch PR4 92 D6
Bryony Cl
Cleveleys FY5 175 F5
Orrell WN5 10 D5
Bryony Ct 9 LA3 217 B2
Buccleuch Ave BB7 166 D8
Buccleuch Cl BB7 166 D8
Buccleuch Rd 7 BB9 170 C1
Buccleuch St BB11 127 E5
Buchanan Ct PR7 60 E6
Buchanan St
Blackpool FY1 130 C6
Chorley PR6 43 D7
7 Ramsbottom BL0 50 B6
Buckden Cl FY5 175 C1
Buckden Gate BB9 170 C3
Buckden Pl LA3 212 F8
Buckden Rd 4 BB5 103 F4
Buckfast Dr L37 12 B2
Buckholes La PR6 79 C1
Buckhurst Rd BL9 51 C3
Buckingham Ave
Horwich BL6 32 E2
Kingsfold PR1 96 E2
Buckingham Cl BB4 85 A1
Buckingham Dr BB12 145 D2
Buckingham Gr
Church BB5 103 F7
Formby L37 11 E1
Morecambe LA3 216 F3
Buckingham Pl 2 LA3 216 F3
Buckingham Rd
Lytham St Anne's FY8 90 D4
Maghull L31 5 C1
Morecambe LA3, LA4 216 F3
Buckingham St PR6 43 D7
Buckingham Way FY6 153 C5
Bucklands Ave PR2 117 D2

Buckley Cres FY5 152 D7
Bucknell Pl FY5 152 F7
Buckshaw Hall Cl PR7 61 B2
Buckshaw Prim Sch PR7 61 A2
BUCKSHAW VILLAGE 60 E6
Buck St
  Burnley BB11 127 E5
  Colne BB8 171 E5
  Grindleton BB7 190 B7
Buckthorn Pl FY6 199 F6
Buckton Cl PR6 61 C6
Bude Cl PR4 116 F6
Buffalo Rd PR26 77 A4
Buff St 3 BB3 65 A8
Bulcock St BB10 148 C1
BULK 218 E1
Bulk Rd LA1 218 E1
Bulk St LA1 214 F8
Bull Cop L37 12 B3
Bullens La L40 23 E7
Buller Ave PR1 96 E4
Buller St
  1 Lancaster LA1 218 D3
  Rawtenstall BB4 86 A2
Bullfinch Dr BL9 33 B5
Bullfinch St 3 PR1 118 B1
Bullion The BB12 169 C5
Bullough Cl BB5 104 A5
Bull Park La FY6 154 C8
Bullsnape La PR3 161 A5
Bull St BB11 128 A6
Bulmer St PR2 117 C2
Buncer La BB2 101 A4
Bungalows The
  Burnley BB11 127 F4
  7 Earby BB18 197 B1
  Great Eccleston PR3 156 C5
BUNKER'S HILL 171 B4
Bunkers Hill Cl BB2 81 B8
Bunker St PR4 93 C6
Bunting Pl 6 FY5 175 F1
Bunyan St 24 OL12 52 F1
Buoymasters LA1 218 C1
Burbank Cl FY4 110 F5
Burdett St BB11 127 D5
Burdock Hill BB18 194 D6
Burdock Wlk LA3 217 B2
Burford Cl
  Blackburn BB2 80 E8
  Blackpool FY3 131 A7
Burford Dr LA3 213 A7
Burgate FY4 110 D5
Burgess Ave FY4 110 E7
Burgess Gdns L31 5 C2
Burgess' La L37 13 A2
Burgess St
  2 Blackburn BB1 102 C5
  6 Haslingden BB4 85 B3
Burgh Hall Rd PR7 43 A3
Burgh La PR7 43 C4
Burgh La S PR7 43 B2
Burghley Brow PR3 181 D1
Burghley Cl PR6 78 C2
Burghley Ct 4 PR25 77 B1
Burgh Mdws PR7 43 C4
Burgh Wood Way PR7 43 A6
Burgundy Cres FY5 152 F7
Burholme Cl PR2 119 A2
Burholme Pl PR2 119 A2
Burholme Rd PR2 119 A2
Burleigh Rd 7 PR1 96 E7
Burleigh St BB12 127 F7
Burlingham Pk PR3 204 B1
Burlington Ave
  Formby L37 12 B3
  Morecambe LA4 217 D5
Burlington Ct
  Blackpool FY4 110 B7
  Lytham St Anne's FY8 89 C8
Burlington Ctr The FY8 89 E6
Burlington Gdns PR25 60 B8
Burlington Gr LA4 217 D5
Burlington Ho 1 FY6 153 D3
Burlington Rd
  Blackpool FY4 110 B6
  Southport PR8 34 F3
Burlington Rd W FY4 110 A6
Burlington St
  Blackburn BB2 101 C5
  Chorley PR7 43 D7
  Nelson BB9 148 C7
Burnage Gdns FY4 110 D7
Burnedge Cl OL12 71 D2
Burned House La FY6 200 D2
Burneside Cl LA4 217 C4
Burnfell Rd 1 LA1 218 B2
Burn Gr FY5 175 E4
Burn Hall Ind Est FY7 176 A6
Burnham Cl BB11 127 E5
Burnham Ct
  Blackpool FY3 130 E5
  Morecambe LA3 216 E1
Burnham Gate BB11 127 E5
Burnham Trad Pk 4 BB11 127 E6
BURNLEY 128 A7
Burnley Ave PR8 21 D5
Burnley Barracks Sta BB12 127 E6
Burnley Central Sta BB12 127 F7
Burnley Cl BB1 102 B5
Burnley Coll BB11 128 A7
Burnley General Hospl BB10 148 C2
Burnley La BB11, BB5 126 A2
BURNLEY LANE 148 A1
Burnley Manchester Road Sta BB11 127 F5
Burnley Rd
  Accrington, Hillock Vale BB5 104 D8
  8 Accrington, Lower Fold BB5 104 C6
  Baldingstone BL9 50 E1
  Blackburn BB1 102 C6
  Brierfield BB9, BB10 148 B5
  Burnley BB10, BB11 128 D1
  Burnley, Harle Syke BB10 148 F3
  Clayton-le-M BB5 125 C5
  Colne BB8, BB9 171 B3
  Edenfield BL0 68 D5
  Gisburn BB7 231 B3
  Hapton BB11, BB5 126 B1
  Holme Chapel BB10 108 C4
  Padiham BB12 126 D8
  Rawtenstall BB4 85 F5
  Rawtenstall, Goodshaw Fold BB4 106 A2
  Southport PR8 21 C5
  Todmorden OL14 108 C4
  Trawden BB8 172 B1
  Weir BB11, BB4 107 C3
  Whalley BB6 144 F3
Burnley Rd E
  Rawtenstall BB4 69 E8
  Water BB4 107 A2
  Whitewell Bottom BB4 86 F4
Burnley St BB1 102 C5
BURNLEY WOOD 128 A4
BURN NAZE 176 B4
Burnsall Ave
  Blackpool FY3 153 A1
  Heysham LA3 212 F8
Burnsall Cl BB10 148 E3
Burnsall Pl
  Barrowford BB9 170 C3
  Fulwood PR2 118 E4
Burnsall Rd 2 BB5 103 F4
Burns Ave
  Lytham St Anne's FY8 91 D4
  Oswaldtwistle BB5 103 D5
  Thornton FY5 176 A3
Burns Cl WN5 10 D1
Burns Dr BB5 104 E2
Burnside
  Edenfield BL0 68 D2
  Parbold WN8 27 B2
Burnside Ave
  Blackpool FY4 110 E8
  Calder Vale PR3 182 E8
  Fleetwood FY7 198 C2
  Fulwood PR2 118 F3
Burnside Way PR1 96 D3
Burnslack Rd PR2 118 F3
Burns Pl FY4 110 F8
Burns Rd FY7 199 A5
Burns St
  Burnley BB12 127 F7
  Hapton BB12 126 C4
  Nelson BB9 170 D1
  Padiham BB12 126 D7
  Preston PR1 118 D2
Burns Way BB6 124 B4
Burns Wlk BB3 82 B1
Burrans Mdw 15 BB8 171 D4
Burrell Ave BB8 171 D6
Burrington Cl PR2 118 D6
Burrow Heights La LA2 210 F8
Burrow Rd
  Over Burrow LA6 241 E7
  Preston PR1 118 A1
Burrow's La FY6 176 F5
BURSCOUGH 25 D4
BURSCOUGH BRIDGE 25 D5
Burscough Bridge Methodist Sch L40 25 E5
Burscough Bridge St John's CE Prim Sch L40 25 F5
Burscough Bridge Sta L40 25 E5
Burscough Ind Est L40 25 B5
Burscough Junc Sta L40 25 F4
Burscough Lordsgate Township CE Prim Sch L40 25 E3
Burscough Priory Science Coll L40 25 E5
Burscough Rd L39 15 F7
Burscough St L39 15 F6
Burscough Village Prim Sch L40 25 F5
Burton Ave LA1 218 A3
Burton Ct FY7 175 C8
Burton Gdns BB9 148 B5
Burton Hill LA6 242 C3
BURTON-IN-KENDAL 240 C7
BURTON IN LONSDALE 242 C3
Burton Lo FY7 199 B4
Burton Morewood CE Prim Sch LA6 240 C7
Burton Pk LA6 240 B7
Burton Rd
  Blackpool FY4 130 F1
  Low Bentham LA2 239 B8
Burton St
  Burnley BB11 128 B5
  Rishton BB1 124 C1
Burwain Castle Rd BD23 197 F8
Burwain Fold BB8 171 D6
Burwains Ave BB8 194 D1
Burwell Ave
  Coppull PR7 29 D8
  Formby L37 11 D1
Burwell Cl
  Kirkby L33 1 A3
  Rochdale OL12 52 D4
Burwen Cl BB11 127 D3
Burwood Cl PR1 96 F2
Burwood Dr
  Blackpool FY3 131 A6
  Fulwood PR2 118 E3
BURY 33 A1
Bury Bsns Ctr BL9 33 A4
Bury Fold BB3 65 A6
Bury Fold La BB3 65 A6
Bury La PR6 79 F3
Bury New Rd
  Heywood BL9, OL10 33 E2
  Ramsbottom BL0 50 D6
Bury Old Rd
  Edenfield BL0 68 F1
  Heywood BL9, OL10 33 E1
  Nangreaves BL0, BL9 50 F4
Bury Rd
  Edenfield BL0 68 D3
  Edgworth BL7 48 E5
  Haslingden BB4 85 B3
  Rawtenstall BB4 68 E7
  Southport PR8 35 B3
Bury & Rochdale Old Rd BL9 33 F4
Bury Row BB7 145 F8
Bury St
  Darwen BB3 82 A1
  Oswaldtwistle BB5 103 D3
Buseph Barrow 1 LA4 217 F4
Buseph Ct 2 LA4 217 F4
Buseph Dr LA4 217 F4
Bushburn Dr BB6 143 C1
Bushby's La L37 11 C2
Bushby's Pk L37 11 D2
Bushell Pl PR1 97 A6
Bushell St PR1 117 F1
Bushey La WA11 8 E2
Bush La
  Freckleton PR4 93 B5
  Freckleton PR4 93 B6
Bush St BB10 148 B1
Bussel Rd PR1 96 E2
Butcher Brow PR5 97 E5
Butchers La L39 6 B3
Bute Ave FY1 130 B7
Bute Rd BB1 102 D3
Bute St BB11 127 D3
Butler Pl PR1 117 F2
Butler Rd FY1 130 B3
Butlers Farm Ct PR25 59 D7
Butlers Mdw PR4 92 E6
Butler St
  Blackpool FY1 130 C6
  7 Burnley BB10 128 A8
  Preston PR1 96 F7
  Ramsbottom BL0 50 A5
  Rishton BB1 124 C1
Butterbergh 16 LA2 239 D8
Buttercross Cl BB11 127 D2
Butterfield Gdns L39 15 D3
Butterfield St
  2 Barrowford BB9 170 D3
  2 Lancaster LA1 214 F8
Butterlands PR1 97 F8
Buttermere Ave
  Chorley PR7 43 B6
  Colne BB8 171 F6
  Fleetwood FY7 198 C2
  2 Morecambe LA4 217 D4
Buttermere Cl
  1 Bamber Bridge PR5 97 E2
  5 Blackburn BB1 101 F6
  Formby L37 11 D3
  Fulwood PR2 118 C4
  Maghull L31 5 E1
Buttermere Cres WA11 8 F2
Buttermere Ct LA1 218 F1
Buttermere Dr
  Knott End-on-S FY6 199 F5
  Oswaldtwistle BB5 103 D5
  Ramsbottom BL0 50 B7
Buttermere Rd
  Burnley BB10 128 F5
  Lancaster LA1 218 F1
  Longridge PR3 139 F5
Butterwick Fields BL6 31 F3
Butterworth Brow
  Brinscall PR6 63 A7
  Chorley PR7 43 A4
Butterworth Cl PR4 114 A6
Butt Hill La PR3 182 E4
Buttons Row BB4 69 F6
Button St PR3 160 C6
Butts
  Barnoldswick BB18 196 B2
  Great Harwood BB6 124 B5
Butts Cl FY5 176 C4
Butts Gr BB7 189 E2
Butts La
  Freckleton PR4 93 C6
  High Bentham LA2 239 E8
  Southport PR8 35 F5
Butt's La PR3 156 B5
Butts Mount BB6 124 C5
Butts Rd FY5 176 C4
BUTT YEATS 238 B6
Buxton Ave FY2 152 D4
Buxton St
  Accrington BB5 104 A5
  Morecambe LA4 217 C4
  Whitworth OL12 71 D3
Bye La L39 14 C3
Bye-Pass Rd LA5 221 A4
Bye Rd BL0 50 E8
Byerworth La N PR3 181 C5
Byerworth La S PR3 181 C4
Byfield Ave FY5 152 E7
Bygone Times* PR7 41 C5
Byland Cl
  Blackpool FY4 110 C5
  Formby L37 12 B2
  Read BB12 145 D1
Bymbrig Cl PR5 77 E8
Byre View PR6 30 F8
Byrom St
  Blackburn BB2 101 D4
  Southport PR9 35 F7
Byron Ave
  Bolton-le-S LA5 221 A5
  Lytham St Anne's FY8 91 D4
  Thornton FY5 176 A3
  Warton PR4 92 E6
Byron Cl
  Accrington BB5 104 E2
  Formby L37 11 F4
  8 Orrell WN5 10 F7
  Oswaldtwistle BB5 103 C5
  Tarleton PR4 56 F5
Byron Cres PR7 29 F8
Byron Gr BB18 196 A3
Byron Rd
  Colne BB8 171 F5
  Maghull L31 5 D3
  Morecambe LA3 216 E3
  Ramsbottom BL8 49 F2
Byron Sq BB6 124 B4
Byron St
  Blackpool FY4 130 B1
  Chorley PR6 43 D8
  Fleetwood FY7 199 A5
  Padiham BB12 126 F7
Byron Terr BB2 101 B3
Byton Wlk L33 1 A4
Byways Cvn Pk LA2 205 C7

C

Cabin End Row BB1 102 E4
Cabin La
  Halsall Moss L39 22 C5
  Holmeswood L40 38 A6
  Maghull L31 4 F4
  Southport PR9 54 F3
Cable Ct PR2 118 B8
Cable Mews 10 PR8 35 B7
Cable St
  Formby L37 12 A4
  Lancaster LA1 214 F8
  Southport PR8 35 B7
CABUS 204 C3
Cabus Cross Roads PR3 204 B5
Cabus Nook La PR3 204 B6
Cabus Terr PR3 204 C2
Cadby Ave FY3 130 F3
CADLEY 117 C4
Cadley Ave PR2 117 B3
Cadley Cswy PR2 117 C4
Cadley Dr PR2 117 B3
Cadogan Pl 5 PR1 97 A6
Cadogan St BB9 170 D2
CADSHAW 65 D1
Cadshaw Cl BB1 101 E8
Cadwell Rd L31 5 B5
Caernarfon Cl FY5 176 D2
Caernarvon Ave BB12 127 A7
Caernarvon Cl BL8 49 F1
Caernarvon Rd BB4 85 A1
Cage La PR4 76 B8
Cairn Ct 6 FY4 110 C5
Cairndale Dr PR25 60 B6
Cairn Gr FY4 110 C4
Cairns Cl BB9 170 C3
Cairnsmore Ave PR1 118 F1
Cairo St BB12 127 D6
Caister Cl WN8 9 E8
Calcott St BB11 127 E2
Caldbeck Cl BB9 148 E6
Caldbeck Rd LA1 218 F1
Calder Ave
  Billington BB7 144 A4
  Chorley PR7 43 B5
  Cleveleys FY5 175 F2
  Darwen BB3 81 D4
  Fleetwood FY7 198 D3
  Freckleton PR4 93 A5
  Fulwood PR2 117 F6
  Longridge PR3 140 A8
  Ormskirk L39 15 E4
  Whalley BB7 144 A7
Calderbank Cl 1 PR26 76 A1
Calder Banks BB1 101 F7
Calderbrook Ave BB11 127 E3
Calderbrook Pl BB11 127 E3
Calder Cl
  Bury BL9 33 A8
  Crag Bank LA5 223 B1
  Kirkby L33 1 A6
  Kirkham PR4 114 C5
  Lytham St Anne's FY8 110 F2
  Nelson BB9 170 D1
Calder Ct BB5 125 E6
Calder Dr
  Catterall PR3 181 D2
  Maghull L31 5 F2
Calder House La PR3 181 D4
Calder Pl
  Billington BB7 144 A4
  Great Harwood BB6 124 E6
Calder Rd
  Blackpool FY2 152 C1
  Rawtenstall BB4 86 A4
  Withnell PR6 80 A1
CALDERSHAW 52 C2
Caldershaw Bsns Ctr OL12 52 B2
Caldershaw Ctr The OL12 52 B2
Caldershaw La OL12 52 A2
Caldershaw Prim Sch OL12 52 A1
Caldershaw Rd OL11, OL12 52 A1
Calder St
  Blackburn BB1 101 F7
  Burnley BB11 127 F6
  Colne BB8 171 C4
  Nelson BB9 170 D1
  Padiham BB12 126 C8
  Preston PR2 117 C1
Calderstones Dr BB7 144 A7
Calderstones Hospl BB7 144 A7
Calder Terr BB9 148 B8
CALDER VALE 182 E8
Calder Vale
  Barrowford BB9 170 D2
  Whalley BB7 144 C4
Caldervale Ave FY6 153 C3
Calder Vale Rd BB12 127 F6
Calder Vale St John CE Prim Sch PR3 226 C1
Calder View BB9 170 E5
Calder Way LA3 217 F2
Caldew Ct 5 BB5 104 E8
Caldicott Way FY6 153 C6
Caldy Dr BL8 50 A3
Caleb St 6 BB9 170 E1
Caledonian Ave 1 FY3 130 E7
Calendar St 1 BB1 101 E5
Calendine Cl FY5 175 F5
Calfcote La PR3 140 B7
Calf Croft Pl FY8 91 A4
Calf Hall La BB18 196 A2
Calf Hall Rd BB18 196 A2
Calf Hey BB5 124 F4
Calf Hey La OL12 52 D8
Calf Hey Rd BB4 84 B2
Calgary Ave BB2 101 B8
Calico Cl BB5 103 B4
Calico Dr PR3 181 D3
Calico St BB2 101 D1
Calico Wood Ave WN6 19 F6
Calkeld La 7 LA1 214 F8
Calla Dr PR3 181 C8
Callander Cl PR2 118 C7
Callander Sq OL10 33 F1
Callender Ct 9 BL0 50 B6
Callender St BL0 50 B6
Callon St PR1 97 E8
Caltha Dr BB3 82 A7
Caltha St 8 BL0 50 B6
Calva Cl BB12 127 B8
Calverley St 6 PR1 118 D1
Calverley Way OL12 52 E4
Calvert Ct PR5 97 D5
Calvert Pl FY3 131 A7
Cambell's Ct FY8 89 E7
Camberley Cl PR8 34 E5
Camborne Ave LA5 221 C8
Camborne Ct FY3 131 B2
Camborne Pl PR4 93 B6
Cambray Rd FY1 152 C1
Cambrian Cl BB1 122 F3
Cambrian Ct PR9 35 D8
Cambrian Way BB4 85 B1
Cambridge Arc 5 PR8 35 B7
Cambridge Ave
  Lancaster LA1 215 B5
  Southport PR9 53 F2
Cambridge Cl
  7 Blackburn BB1 101 F4
  Padiham BB12 126 D6
  Preston PR1 117 E2
Cambridge Ct
  Preston PR1 117 F2
  Southport PR9 53 F2
Cambridge Dr
  Blackburn BB1 102 E4
  Garstang PR3 181 B7
  Padiham BB12 126 D6
Cambridge Gdns
  Darwen BB3 82 C1
  Southport PR9 53 F2
Cambridge Rd
  9 Bamber Bridge PR5 77 F8
  Blackpool FY1 130 D5
  Cleveleys FY5 175 C3
  Fleetwood FY7 198 E3
  Formby L37 11 D1
  Lytham St Anne's FY8 90 E3
  1 Morecambe LA3 216 E3
  Orrell WN5 10 F8
  Skelmersdale WN8 17 E1
  Southport PR9 53 E2
Cambridge St
  Accrington BB5 104 D6
  Blackburn BB1 101 F4

Cambridge St *continued*
4 Brierfield BB9 148 B5
3 Burnley BB11 127 D5
10 Chorley PR7 43 C7
9 Colne BB8 171 D4
Darwen BB3 82 C1
Great Harwood BB6 124 D5
Haslingden BB4 85 B1
Nelson BB9 148 D7
Preston PR1 117 E2
Cambridge Wlk PR1 117 E2
Cambridge Wlks 6 PR8 35 B7
Cam Cl 1 PR5 77 F8
Camden Pl PR1 96 F6
Camden Rd FY3 130 E6
Camden St
11 Barrowford BB9 170 D3
Nelson BB9 148 D7
Camellia Dr PR25 77 E2
Camelot Theme Pk* PR7 41 F4
Cameron Ave FY3 130 E7
Cameron Croft 6 PR6 43 D8
Cameron St BB10 148 A1
Camforth Hall La PR3 139 A7
Cam La
Clayton Green PR6 78 A4
Thornton-in-C BD23 197 B6
Camms View BB4 68 A8
Camomile Cl PR7 61 A3
Campbell Ave 2 FY3 130 E7
Campbell Cl BB2 81 C7
Campbell St
Blackburn BB1 122 F1
4 Padiham BB12 126 F7
Preston PR1 97 B8
Read BB12 145 D1
Rochdale OL12 52 E2
Campion Cl FY5 175 F5
Campion Ct BB5 103 E4
Campion Dr
Haslingden BB4 68 A8
Preston PR2 116 C1
Campions The PR2 116 C1
Campion Way
2 Morecambe LA3 217 B2
Rochdale OL12 52 C3
Camp St BB10 148 E3
Cam St PR1 118 C2
Camwood PR5 78 B4
Camwood Dr PR5 97 B1
Cam Wood Fold PR6 78 A3
Canada Cres FY2 152 E3
Canada St BL6 32 B3
Canal Bank
Appley Bridge WN6 19 C7
Burscough Bridge L40 25 B6
Ring o'Bells L40 26 C2
Canal Bank Cotts L31 5 C7
Canal Bank Pygons Hill L31 5 C7
Canal Gdns LA5 221 B6
Canal Leach PR26 57 F6
Canal Mews BB9 148 D8
Canal Pl LA5 223 E1
Canal Row WN2 30 D1
Canalside
Blackburn BB1 101 F3
Hurlston Green L40 24 B4
Canal Side BB9 170 D2
Canalside Craft Ctr* LA2 211 A3
Canal St
Adlington PR7 31 A6
3 Blackburn BB2 101 B1
19 Burnley BB11 127 F6
Church BB5 103 E6
Clayton-le-M BB5 124 F2
Canal Way BB5 125 B3
Canal Wlk PR6 43 F8
Canberra Cl FY5 152 F7
Canberra Ct FY4 110 E4
Canberra La PR4 116 E4
Canberra Rd PR25 60 B8
Canberraway PR4 92 E6
Candlemakers Croft 3 BB7 166 F8
Candlemakers Ct BB7 166 E8
Candlestick Pk BL9 33 D4
Cann Bridge St PR5 98 B4
Canning Rd PR9 36 A6
Canning St
Burnley BB12 127 F7
Padiham BB12 126 D7
Cannock Ave FY3 130 E8
Cannock Gn L31 5 B1
Cannon Hill PR2 117 C1
Cannon St
Accrington BB5 104 B5
11 Chorley PR7 43 C8
10 Nelson BB9 170 F1
Preston PR1 96 F7
6 Ramsbottom BL0 50 A4
Canon Cl WN6 29 F2
Canon St BL9 33 A4
Canterbury Ave
Blackpool FY3 130 F3
Lancaster LA1 215 B5
Canterbury Cl
Brinscall PR6 62 E8
Carleton FY6 153 C5
Formby L37 11 F5
Garstang PR3 181 A7
Morecambe LA3 217 B2
Southport PR8 34 F4
Canterbury Rd 11 PR1 118 D1
Canterbury St
Blackburn BB2 101 E4
Chorley PR6 43 E6
Canterbury Way PR3 181 B7
Cantlow Fold PR8 21 A4
CANTSFIELD 241 F3
Cantsfield Ave PR2 117 B4
Canute St PR1 118 A1
CAPERNWRAY 240 C2
Capernwray Ct LA6 240 D3
Capernwray Rd LA6 240 B2
Cape St BB4 86 A2
Capesthorne Dr PR7 43 B3
Capilano Pk L39 6 C8
Capitol Trad Est L33 1 C2
Capitol Way PR5 97 C5
Capstan Cl FY8 110 E1
Captain's Row 3 LA1 218 D1
Captain St
Horwich BL6 32 B4
4 Weir OL13 88 A7
Carawood Cl WN6 19 D7
Carbis Ave 9 PR2 139 D1
Carcroft Ave FY2 152 D4
Cardale PR4 95 D2
Cardiff St WN8 17 D1
Cardigan Ave
Burnley BB12 127 A7
11 Clitheroe BB7 166 E8
Oswaldtwistle BB5 103 C4
Cardigan Cl 1 BB7 166 D8
Cardigan Pl FY4 110 A5
Cardigan Rd PR8 34 F1
Cardigan St
Preston PR2 117 D1
Rochdale OL12 52 E3
Cardinal Allen RC High Sch FY7 175 E8
Cardinal Gdns FY8 90 D6
Cardinal Newman Coll PR1 97 B7
Cardinal Pl FY5 175 E3
Cardinal St BB10 148 B1
Cardwell Cl PR4 92 D5
Cardwell Pl BB2 101 E5
Cardwell St BB12 126 D7
Carfax Fold OL12 52 B2
Carfax Rd L33 1 A4
Carfield WN8 9 E6
Carham Rd BB1 101 E8
Carholme Ave BB10 128 C6
Caribou The LA2 209 F5
Carisbrooke Ave FY4 111 A7
Carisbrooke Cl FY6 153 C6
Carisbrooke Dr PR9 53 F1
CARLETON 153 A5
Carleton Ave
Blackpool FY3 152 F1
Fulwood PR2 118 D4
Simonstone BB12 145 E2
Carleton Dr PR1 96 A4
Carleton Gate FY6 153 C4
Carleton Gdns FY6 153 B5
Carleton Green Com Prim Sch FY6 153 C6
Carleton Rd
Colne BB8 171 A3
Great Knowley PR6 61 F3
Carleton St Hilda's CE Prim Sch FY6 153 B5
Carleton St
Morecambe LA4 217 A4
Nelson BB9 148 E7
Carleton Way FY6 153 B5
Carley St BB3 81 E2
Carlin Gate FY2 152 B2
Carlinghurst Rd BB2 101 D4
Carlisle Ave
Fleetwood FY7 198 D1
Higher Penwortham PR1 96 A4
Carlisle Gr 1 FY5 176 B2
Carlisle Ho 35 PR1 97 A7
Carlisle Pl 3 PR6 31 A8
Carlisle Rd
Accrington BB5 104 D7
Southport PR8 35 A2
Carlisle St
Blackburn BB1 101 F4
Preston PR1 97 A8
Rochdale OL12 52 E3
Carlisle Terr LA5 223 D3
Carl Oway Ave PR2 118 C5
Carl's Way L33 1 A6
Carlton Ave
Clayton Green PR6 78 B2
Up Holland WN8 10 A7
Carlton Cl BL6 31 D2
Carlton Ct BB8 171 B5
Carlton Dr PR1 97 B5
Carlton Gdns BB1 101 E6
Carlton Gr
Blackpool FY2 152 B4
6 Horwich BL6 32 D1
Carlton Pl BB7 166 F7
Carlton Rd
Blackburn BB1 101 E6
Burnley BB11 127 E5
Leyland PR25 59 F8
Lytham St Anne's FY8 89 F7
Southport PR8 21 C6
Carlton St
3 Bacup OL13 88 A3
Brierfield BB9 148 B5
Preston PR2 96 D8
Carlton Wharf LA1 218 C1
Carluke St BB1 102 C5
Carlyle Ave FY4 110 B6
Carlyle Gr LA4 217 E6
Carlyle St BB10 148 C3
Carmel Cl L39 15 D2
Carnaby Cl PR3 204 A5
Carnarvon Rd
Blackburn BB2 101 B5
3 Preston PR1 96 D7
Southport PR8 34 F1
Carneghie Ct 1 PR8 34 F4
Carnfield Pl PR5 78 B8
CARNFORTH 223 C2
Carnforth Ave FY2 152 E5
Carnforth Brow LA5 223 F2
Carnforth Christ Church CE Prim Sch LA5 223 D1
Carnforth Cl BB2 102 A1
Carnforth Dr BL8 50 A2
Carnforth High Sch LA5 223 E1
Carnforth Sta LA5 223 D2
Carnoustie Cl
Fulwood PR2 117 B7
Southport PR8 34 F4
Carnoustie Ct PR1 96 A6
Carnoustie Dr
Euxton PR7 60 D4
Ramsbottom BL0 50 B5
Caroline Cl LA3 212 F8
Caroline Ct BB11 127 B4
Caroline St
6 Blackpool FY1 130 B3
Preston PR1 97 C8
CARR 50 B7
Carradice Cl BB9 148 D8
Carradon Dr WN6 29 E1
Carr Bank Ave BL0 50 B7
Carr Bank Dr BL0 50 B7
Carr Bank Rd BL0 50 B7
Carr Barn Brow PR5 78 C6
Carr Bridge Residential Pk FY4 112 A6
Carr Brook Cl PR6 61 B8
Carr Cl
Cold Row FY6 177 C4
Poulton-le-F FY6 153 E2
Smallwood Hey PR3 201 C5
CARR CROSS 36 D1
Carr Dene Ct PR4 114 C5
Carr Dr PR4 113 E7
Carr End La FY6 177 C6
Carr Field PR5 78 C4
Carrfield Villas OL14 109 A1
Carr Fold BL0 50 B7
Carr Gate FY5 175 C4
CARR HALL 170 B2
Carr Hall Dr BB9 170 C1
Carr Hall Gdns BB9 170 B1
Carr Hall Rd BB9 170 B1
Carr Hall St BB4 85 A5
Carr Head BB8 172 C2
Carr Head La FY6 153 E2
Carr Head Prim Sch FY6 153 E2
Carr Hey 5 FY5 176 A2
Carr Hill 11-18 High Sch PR4 114 B4
Carr Holme Gdns PR3 204 C1
CARR HOUSE GREEN COMMON 135 E7
Carr House La
Bretherton PR26 57 D6
Heskin Green WN6 41 F1
Ince Blundell L38 3 E4
Lancaster LA1 214 E7
Wrightington Bar WN6 28 F8
Carrick Mews FY3 131 B2
Carrier's Row BB8 172 E6
Carrington Ave 4 BB2 81 C8
Carrington Gr LA4 217 E5
Carrington Rd
Adlington PR7 30 F7
Chorley PR7 43 C7
Carr La
Blackburn BB2 100 F6
Chorley PR7 43 D5
Cold Row FY6 177 C6
Croston PR26 40 B8
Heysham LA3 212 E7
Kirkham PR4 114 C6
Lancaster LA2 214 E2
Leyland PR25 77 A3
Maghull L31 4 F5
Middleton LA3 212 F1
Much Hoole PR4, PR5 75 A1
Rawtenstall BB4 69 F7
Rawtenstall, Hall Carr BB4 86 A1
Ring o'Bells L40 26 B3
Singleton FY6 154 C1
Smallwood Hey PR3 201 C4
Southport PR8 21 F7
Tarleton PR4 56 F7
Warton PR4 92 B6
Carr Mdw PR5 78 C6
Carr Mill St BB4 85 B5
Carr Moss La
Halsall L39 14 B8
Southport L39 22 D2
Carr Mount 7 BB4 85 F1
Carroll Cres L39 15 F7
Carrol St PR1 118 B1
Carron La PR3 160 A4
Carr Pl PR5 78 B7
Carr Rd
Barnoldswick BB18 196 A3
Barrowford BB9 170 C1
Blackpool FY5 152 D6
Burnley BB11 127 E3
Clayton Green PR6 78 B2
Carr Rd *continued*
Colne BB8 171 E6
Darwen BB3 65 B8
Fleetwood FY7 199 A4
Hambleton FY6 177 C2
Horwich BL6 32 B5
Kirkham PR4 114 B4
Rawtenstall BB4 85 F1
Water BB4 87 C7
Carr Royd Est FY6 154 A3
Carr's Cres L37 11 E1
Carr's Cres W L37 11 D1
Carrs Croft BB7 191 E8
Carrside BB9 148 B8
Carr Side La L29 4 A3
Carrs Ind Est BB4 85 A4
Carr St
Bamber Bridge PR5 77 E8
Blackburn BB1 101 E6
Chorley PR6 61 E1
Preston PR1 97 B7
Ramsbottom BL0 50 B7
Carrs Wood BB2 100 F6
Carr View BB8 172 C1
Carrwood Dr PR4 114 B4
Carrwood Gdns LA2 210 F3
Carrwood Gn BB12 126 C8
Carrwood Hey BL0 50 A4
Carrwood Pk PR8 35 B4
Carrwood Rd PR5 97 B3
Carrwood Way PR5 97 B2
CARRY BRIDGE 171 F5
Carry La BB8 171 E4
Carshalton Rd FY1 130 B8
Carsluith Ave FY3 130 F3
Carson Rd FY4 131 A1
Carter Ave BB11 126 C4
Carter Fold BB2 121 E2
Carter's Charity Prim Sch FY6 200 C7
Carter's La BB7 231 A5
Carter St
Accrington BB5 104 B4
7 Blackpool FY1 130 B5
Burnley BB12 127 C7
Carterville Cl FY4 111 A7
Cartford Cl PR3 156 A6
Cartford Cvn Pk PR4 156 A6
Cartford La PR3 156 A6
Cartford Pk PR3 156 A6
Cart Gate FY6 200 B3
Cartmel Ave
Accrington BB5 104 A3
Fleetwood FY7 198 D1
Maghull L31 5 E2
Cartmel Cl PR8 35 F3
Cartmel Dr
Burnley BB12 127 B8
Coupe Green PR5 98 E4
Formby L37 12 B2
Cartmell Fold FY4 110 D5
Cartmell La
Lytham St Anne's FY8 91 E8
Nateby PR3 180 C7
Cartmell Rd
Blackpool FY4 131 D1
Lytham St Anne's FY8 89 F5
Cartmel Pl
Morecambe LA4 217 D4
Preston PR2 116 E2
Cartmel Rd
Blackburn BB2 101 A3
Lancaster LA1 218 F2
Leyland PR25 59 D8
Cartmel South Ave LA1 211 A6
Cartmel West Ave LA1 211 A6
Cartwright Ct LA1 214 E5
Carus Ave BB3 82 E1
Carus Pk LA6 241 B2
Carvel Way L40 25 F3
Carver Hey Farm PR4 75 B4
Carvers Brow PR26 58 B1
Carwags La PR3 161 C8
Carwood Gr BL6 32 D1
Carwood La PR6 61 C8
Caryl Rd FY8 89 D8
Caspian Way LA1 214 E4
Casserley Rd BB8 171 F6
Casson Gate OL12 52 E1
Castercliff Bank BB8 171 C3
Castercliffe Com Prim Sch BB9 171 B1
Castercliffe Rd BB9 149 B8
CASTERTON 243 A2
Casterton PR7 60 C2
Casterton Ave BB10 148 C3
Casterton Prim Sch BB10 148 C3
Castle Ave FY6 153 B6
Castle Bank LA5 224 C4
Castle Cl BB8 171 E6
Castle Cres BL6 32 C5
Castlecroft Ave BL6 31 D2
Castle Ct
Colne BB8 171 F6
Lancaster LA1 214 E8
Castle Dr
Adlington PR7 30 E6
Formby L37 11 F1
Castle Fold PR1 96 F2
Castle Gardens Cres FY6 153 B5
Castlegate FY1 130 B1
Castle Gate BB7 166 E8
Castle Gr BL0 50 A2
Castlehey WN8 9 E6
Castle Hill LA1 214 E8
Castle Hill Rd BL9 33 D5
Castle House La PR7 30 E6
Castlekeep Ho 13 BB7 166 E8
Castlekeep View 8 BB7 189 E1
Castle La
Bonds PR3 181 D6
Staining FY3 131 D5
Westhead L40 16 E5
Castle Mount PR2 117 F7
Castle Par 5 LA1 214 E8
Castle Park Mews LA1 214 E8
Castle Pk
Hornby LA2 238 B7
Lancaster LA1 214 E8
Castle Rd BB8 172 A7
Castlerigg Dr BB12 127 B8
Castlerigg Pl FY4 131 C1
Castle St
Blackburn BB1 102 B5
Brierfield BB9 148 B6
Burnley BB12 127 F7
6 Chorley PR7 43 D7
Clitheroe BB7 166 E8
7 Hapton BB12 126 C4
Nelson BB9 148 F8
Preston PR1 117 F1
Ramsbottom BL9 50 D2
Southport PR9 35 B8
Castle The BB8 172 A7
Castleton Rd PR1 118 B1
Castletown Dr OL13 88 B1
Castle View
Barnoldswick BB18 196 B1
Clitheroe BB7 166 E8
Castle View Cvn Pk LA6 240 D2
Castle View Ho 12 BB7 166 E8
Castle Wlk
Higher Penwortham PR1 96 C7
Southport PR8 35 A6
Castle Wlks PR26 58 B2
Catches La OL11 52 B1
CATFORTH 135 F4
Catforth Ave FY4 131 B1
Catforth Prim Sch PR4 136 A4
Catforth Rd
Catforth PR4 135 F5
Preston PR2 116 E1
Catharine's La L39 15 F1
Cathedral Dr LA3 217 B2
Cathedral RC Prim Sch The LA1 215 A7
Catherine Cl PR4 113 F7
Catherine Ct FY7 199 C4
Catherine St E BL6 32 B4
Catherine St W BL6 32 B5
Catherine St
6 Chorley PR7 43 C6
Kirkham PR4 113 F6
5 Preston PR1 97 B8
Cathrow Dr PR4 76 A7
Cathrow Way FY5 176 D2
Catley Cl PR6 61 C5
CATLOW 149 C5
Catlow Ct BB10 149 C5
Catlow Hall St BB5 103 E4
Catlow Row BB10 149 C6
Catlow Terr BB7 166 D1
CATON 237 C3
Caton Ave FY7 198 D1
Caton Cl
Longridge PR3 140 B8
Southport PR9 53 F4
Caton Com Prim Sch LA2 237 C3
Caton Dr PR25 77 E2
Caton Gr FY3 130 F7
CATON GREEN 237 D3
Caton Green Rd LA2 237 D3
Caton Rd LA1 218 F4
Caton St Paul's CE Prim Sch LA2 237 D3
Cato St 4 BL0 50 A4
Cat Tail La PR8 36 E1
Cattan Gn L37 12 B3
CATTERALL 181 E2
Catterall Cl FY1 130 D7
Catterall Gates La PR3 181 C3
Catterall La PR3 181 C1
Catterall St 3 BB2 81 C8
Catterick Fold PR8 35 F3
Cattle St BB6 124 C5
Caunce Ave PR9 55 A6
Caunce's Rd PR9 37 C5
Caunce St FY1, FY3 130 D6
Causeway
Foulridge BB8 194 D1
Great Harwood BB6 124 B5
Causeway Ave PR2 117 C4
Causeway Croft BB7 189 F1
Causeway Head BB4 68 A8
Causeway La
Haskayne L37 13 B1
Rufford L40 39 B2
Causeway St 2 BB3 65 C7
Causeway The
3 Chorley PR6 43 E8
Southport PR9 54 C5
Wymott PR26 58 F6
Causey Foot BB9 148 D7

Cavalry Way BB11 127 D6
Cavell Cl BB1 102 B1
Cavendish Cres PR2 118 F3
Cavendish Ct
Bolton-le-S LA5 221 A5
Southport PR9 35 E8
Cavendish Dr PR2 118 F3
Cavendish Mans FY5 175 C4
Cavendish Pl
6 Bamber Bridge PR5 97 D3
Blackburn BB2 101 B3
Cavendish Rd
Blackpool FY2 152 C4
Lytham St Anne's FY8 89 D8
Morecambe LA3 216 E3
2 Preston PR1 118 E1
Southport PR8 34 F3
Cavendish St
Barnoldswick BB18 196 B1
1 Chorley PR6 43 E7
Darwen BB3 81 F3
Lancaster LA1 214 D8
Cavendish Wlk PR9 35 E8
Cave St
1 Blackburn BB2 101 B1
2 Preston PR1 97 D8
Cavour St BB12 127 F7
Cawsey The PR1 97 A2
Cawthorne's Endowed Sch LA2 232 F1
Cawthorne St LA1 214 E8
Caxton Ave FY2 152 C5
Caxton Rd PR2 118 B8
Cecil Ct FY8 91 A3
Cecilia Rd BB2 101 A2
Cecilia St PR1 118 D1
Cecil St
Barnoldswick BB18 196 B3
Blackpool FY1 130 C7
4 Lytham St Anne's FY8 91 A3
Oswaldtwistle BB5 103 E4
Rishton BB1 124 C2
Cedar Ave
5 Bamber Bridge PR5 77 B8
Cleveleys FY5 175 E2
Euxton PR7 60 C4
Fleetwood FY7 175 E8
Haslingden BB4 85 C3
Horwich BL6 32 E1
Knott End-on-S FY6 200 A5
Poulton-le-F FY6 131 D8
Preston PR2 117 A2
Rawtenstall BB4 85 E2
Warton PR4 92 D6
Cedar Cl
Garstang PR3 181 B8
Grimsargh PR2 139 D1
Newton-w-S PR4 115 A3
Rishton BB1 103 B8
Cedar Cres
Kirkham PR4 114 A4
Ormskirk L39 15 D4
Ramsbottom BL0 50 C7
Cedar Ct
Blackburn BB1 101 F7
7 Leyland PR25 77 B1
Cedar Dr L37 11 C1
Cedar Farm Galleries* L40 40 C1
Cedar Field PR6 78 C2
Cedar Gr
Longton PR4 95 A1
Orrell WN5 10 F6
Skelmersdale WN8 17 E1
Cedar Ho PR7 42 F6
Cedar Rd
Chorley PR6 61 D2
Fulwood PR2 118 E2
Lancaster LA1 214 D8
Cedars Cl BB18 196 A1
Cedars Inf Sch BB1 101 F8
Cedar Sq 5 FY1 130 B5
Cedar St
Accrington BB5 104 D6
Blackburn BB1 101 F8
Burnley BB11 128 B5
Bury BL9 33 B3
Morecambe LA4 216 F4
Rochdale OL12 52 F1
Southport PR8 35 D4
Cedars The
Chorley PR7 43 B4
Eccleston PR7 41 B7
New Longton PR4 75 F8
Cedar Way PR1 96 B3
Cedar Wlk PR4 155 F1
Cedarwood Cl FY8 90 E4
Cedarwood Dr PR25 59 E8
Cedarwood Pl LA1 215 C7
Cedric Pl FY2 152 C4
Celia St BB10 128 C5
Cemetery La
Burnley BB11 127 A4
Preesall Park FY6 200 B1
Cemetery Rd
Darwen BB3 65 B5
Earby BB18 197 B2
Padiham BB12 126 C7
Preston PR1 118 C1
Ramsbottom BL0 50 A4
Southport PR8 35 C4
Cemetery View PR7 31 A6
Centaur Ct 7 BB8 171 C4
Centenary Mill PR1 97 C8
Centenary Way BB11 128 A5
Central 12 Ret Pk PR9 35 C6
Central Ave
Clitheroe BB7 166 D7
Edenfield BL0 68 D2
Gregson Lane PR5 98 E2
Kirkham PR4 113 F6
Lancaster LA1 218 D4
Oswaldtwistle BB5 103 C4
Southport PR8 21 F8
Central Ave N FY5 175 F3
Central Beach FY8 91 B3
Central Bldgs 16 BB12 146 C1
Central Dr
Blackpool FY1 130 C3
Higher Penwortham PR1 96 A4
Lytham St Anne's FY8 90 C5
Morecambe LA4 217 A5
Central Lancaster High Sch LA1 218 F1
Central Rd FY5 176 D3
Central Sq
7 Haslingden BB4 85 B3
Maghull L31 5 D2
Central St BL0 50 C6
Central View OL13 88 A2
Centre Dr PR6 78 B4
Centurian Way BB1 82 B6
Centurion Ct BB1 82 B7
Centurion Ho 1 PR4 114 B5
Centurion Ind Est PR25 77 B3
Centurion Way PR25, PR26 77 A4
Ceres Way LA1 214 C8
Chadderton Ct 22 PR1 97 A8
Chaddock St 29 PR1 97 A7
Chadfield Rd FY1 130 D2
Chad St BB8 171 A2
Chadwick Ct 5 PR5 77 E8
Chadwick Gdns 1 PR5 77 A7
Chadwick St
Blackburn BB2 101 D3
3 Blackpool FY1 130 C3
Bury BL9 33 E4
Chadwick Terr OL12 52 D4
Chaffinch Cl FY5 175 F5
Chaffinch Ct FY3 131 B6
Chaffinch Dr BL9 33 C4
Chaigley Ct BB7 165 A8
Chaigley Farm Cotts BB7 165 A8
Chaigley Rd PR3 140 B8
Chain Caul Rd PR2 95 F8
Chain Caul Way PR2 95 F8
Chain House La PR4 76 D7
Chain La FY3, FY4 131 E4
Chalfont Ct PR8 35 A3
Chalfont Field PR2 117 C5
Challan Hall Cotts LA5 224 E5
Challan Hall Mews LA5 224 E5
Challenge Way BB1 102 C7
Chamber St BB4 87 A8
Chambres Rd PR8 35 D5
Chambres Rd N PR8 35 D6
Champagne Ave FY5 152 F7
Chancel Pl BB3 65 C8
Chancel Way BB3 65 C8
Chancery Cl PR7 42 F1
Chancery Rd PR7 61 B2
Chancery Wlk 3 BB11 128 A6
Chandler Bsns Pk PR25 76 E2
Chandlers Croft PR4 73 E4
Chandlers Ford FY6 153 E4
Chandlers Rest FY8 91 D3
Chandler St 6 PR1 96 F8
Chandley Cl PR8 21 A5
Change Cl OL13 88 B4
Changford Gn L33 1 A3
Changford Rd L33 1 A3
Channel Way PR2 96 C8
Channing Rd FY8 90 C4
Chanters Way BB3 82 A5
Chapel Alley L37 11 F3
Chapel Brow
Leyland PR25 77 B2
Longridge PR3 140 B5
Chapel Cl
Clitheroe BB7 166 B8
Hest Bank LA2 220 D1
Kirkham PR4 113 F7
Overton LA3 209 C8
Pilling PR3 201 C5
Trawden BB8 172 B2
West Bradford BB7 189 E5
Whalley BB7 144 C5
Chapel Ct BB10 149 A3
Chapel Fields BL7 48 C4
Chapel Fold
12 Colne BB8 171 D4
Wiswell BB7 144 F7
Chapel Gdns
Catterall PR3 181 D2
Hesketh Bank PR4 73 E4
Ramsbottom BL8 49 E1
Chapel Grange BL7 48 C4
Chapel Hill
Longridge PR3 140 A6
Salterforth BB18 194 D7
Chapel Hill La BB4 86 B4
Chapel Hill Trad Est PR3 140 A6
Chapel Ho
Burnley BB11 127 C5
Maghull L31 5 D1
Rishton BB1 124 C1
Chapel Hos OL12 71 D4
CHAPEL HOUSE 17 E2
Chapel House Rd BB9 148 E7
Chapelhouse Wlk L37 12 A3
Chapel La
Banks PR9 55 B7
Burscough L40 25 E2
Burton in L LA6 242 C3
Catforth PR4 135 D4
Coppull PR7 42 F1
Formby L37 11 F3
Galgate LA2 211 B5
Hoghton PR5 99 D2
Holmeswood L40 38 B6
Langho BB6 143 B2
Longton PR4 75 C8
New Longton PR4 75 E8
Out Rawcliffe PR3 178 B2
Overton LA3 209 D8
Parbold WN8 27 D1
Ramsbottom BL8 50 A6
West Bradford BB7 189 E5
Wheelton PR6 62 B5
Chapel Mdw PR4 75 C8
Chapel Mdws PR4 57 A5
Chapel Mews
2 Earby BB18 197 B1
Ormskirk L39 15 F4
Chapel Park Rd PR4 75 D8
Chapel Rd
Blackpool FY4 111 B7
Fulwood PR2 118 A4
Hesketh Bank PR4 73 E4
Chapel Rise BB7 144 B4
CHAPELS 82 A3
Chapels BB3 82 A3
Chapels Brow BB3 82 A3
Chapelside 4 BB10 128 B5
Chapelside Cl PR3 181 D2
Chapels La BB3 80 F3
Chapel Sq LA2 237 D3
Chapel St
10 Accrington BB5 104 C5
Adlington PR7 30 F6
14 Bacup OL13 70 C8
Barnoldswick BB18 196 B2
Belmont BL7 46 C5
Belthorn BB1 82 F6
Blackburn BB2 101 D4
Blackpool FY1 130 B4
Blackrod BL6 31 D2
Bolton, Egerton BL7 47 D3
Brierfield BB9 148 B6
Brinscall PR6 62 F8
Burnley BB11 128 A6
Chorley PR7 43 C8
Clayton-le-M BB5 124 E3
Colne BB8 171 D4
Coppull PR7 42 E1
Darwen BB3 65 A8
Earby BB18 197 B2
Foulridge BB8 194 E1
Galgate LA2 211 A3
Great Eccleston PR3 156 B5
Haslingden BB4 85 B3
Higham BB12 146 F5
Horwich BL6 32 C3
3 Lancaster LA1 214 F8
Longridge PR3 140 B7
Lytham St Anne's FY8 91 A3
3 Morecambe LA4 217 A5
Nelson BB9 148 E8
Newchurch BB4 86 E1
Ormskirk L39 15 F4
Oswaldtwistle BB5 103 E4
Poulton-le-F FY6 153 D3
Preston PR1 96 F7
Rawtenstall BB4 86 A8
Rishton BB1 124 C1
Slaidburn BB7 229 C7
Southport PR8 35 B7
Whitworth OL12 52 C8
Worsthorne BB10 129 A5
Chapel Street Ct 3 FY6 153 D3
Chapel The BB4 86 A3
CHAPELTOWN 48 D4
Chapeltown Rd BL7 48 C2
Chapel View
Goodshaw Chapel BB4 106 A1
Overton LA3 209 D8
Chapel Way PR7 29 F8
Chapel Wlk
Coppull PR7 42 E1
Longton PR4 75 D8
2 Padiham BB12 146 C1
Warton LA5 223 E6
Chapel Wlks
Kirkham PR4 114 B4
5 Preston PR1 96 F7
Chapel Yd PR5 97 D5
Chapman Cl PR3 156 C5
Chapman Ct
Barnoldswick BB18 196 B3
Fleetwood FY7 199 B4
Chapman Rd
Fulwood PR2 118 A3
Hoddlesden BB3 82 F1
Chapter Rd BB3 65 C8
Chardonnay Cres 2 FY5 152 F7
Charlbury Gr LA3 213 A7
Charles Ave PR8 21 E6
Charlesbye Ave L39 16 B6
Charlesbye Cl L39 16 B6
Charles Cl PR4 73 E3
Charles Cres PR5 98 C3
Charles Ct
4 Blackpool FY3 130 D7
Lancaster LA1 214 F6
Charles La BB4 85 A2
Charles St
Blackburn BB2 101 D2
Blackpool FY1 130 C6
1 Bolton, Egerton BL7 47 D2
Clayton-le-M BB5 124 E2
Colne BB8 171 E5
Darwen BB3 82 A2
Great Harwood BB6 124 C4
Lancaster LA1 214 F6
Morecambe LA4 217 C5
Nelson BB9 170 E2
Newchurch BB4 86 F2
Oswaldtwistle BB5 103 E3
Charleston Ct 3 PR5 97 E2
Charles Way PR2 116 E1
Charlesway Ct 1 PR2 116 E1
Charlesworth Cl L31 5 B5
Charley Wood Rd L33 1 C1
Charlotte Pl 33 PR1 97 A7
Charlotte's La PR4 56 E2
Charlotte St
Blackburn BB1 101 E6
Burnley BB11 127 F5
Preston PR1 97 A7
4 Ramsbottom BL0 50 B5
Charnley Cl PR1 96 C2
Charnley Ct PR5 97 F2
Charnley Fold Bglws PR5 97 F3
Charnley Fold Ind Est PR5 97 F3
Charnley Fold La PR5 97 F3
Charnley Rd FY1 130 C4
Charnley's La PR9 54 E7
Charnley St
Blackburn BB2 101 C2
1 Lancaster LA1 218 B1
2 Preston PR1 96 F7
Charnock Ave PR1 96 E2
Charnock Brow PR7 42 C7
Charnock Fold PR1 118 A2
Charnock Gdns PR1 96 F1
CHARNOCK GREEN 42 C6
Charnock Ho PR7 61 C2
Charnock Moss PR5 76 F8
CHARNOCK RICHARD 42 D4
Charnock St
Chorley PR6 43 D7
9 Kirkham PR4 113 F6
8 Leyland PR25 77 B1
Preston PR1 117 F2
Charnocks The PR6 61 A1
Charnwood Ave FY3 131 A7
Charnwood Cl BB2 101 A8
Charter Brook BB6 124 D5
Charterhouse Ct FY7 198 D4
Charterhouse Pl BB2 101 B3
Charter La PR7 42 D3
Charter St BB5 104 A5
Chartwell Cl PR6 78 C2
Chartwell Rd PR8 21 B6
Chartwell Rise 5 PR5 77 C8
Chasden Cl PR6 61 C5
Chase Cl PR8 34 F4
Chase Heys PR9 54 A1
Chase The
Burnley BB12 127 D8
Cottam PR4 116 D5
3 Leyland PR25 77 C2
Normoss FY3 131 C7
Silverdale LA5 224 D2
Thornton FY5 176 A4
CHATBURN 190 C5
Chatburn Ave
Burnley BB10 128 D5
Clitheroe BB7 189 F1
Chatburn CE Prim Sch BB7 190 D5
Chatburn Cl
Great Harwood BB6 124 E5
Normoss FY3 131 B8
Rawtenstall BB4 86 A4
Chatburn Gdns OL10 33 F2
Chatburn Old Rd BB7 190 D5
Chatburn Park Ave BB9 148 A6
Chatburn Park Dr
Brierfield BB9 148 A6
Clitheroe BB7 190 A2
Chatburn Rd
Chatburn BB7 190 F5
Clitheroe BB7 190 A3
Fulwood PR2 118 F4
Longridge PR3 140 A7
Chatburn St BB2 101 C5
Chateaux Apartments PR4 116 D5
Chatham Ave FY8 110 E1
Chatham Cres BB8 171 E6
Chatham Pl
5 Chorley PR6 43 E8
Preston PR1 118 B2
Chatham St
Colne BB8 171 E6
Nelson BB9 170 D1
Chatsworth Ave
Blackpool FY2 152 C6
Fleetwood FY7 198 D2
Warton PR4 92 D6
Chatsworth Cl
Barrowford BB9 170 B1
4 Blackburn BB1 122 E1
Chorley PR7 43 B8
2 Thornton FY5 176 D1
Chatsworth Ct PR6 43 F1
Chatsworth Rd
Bamber Bridge PR5 97 D3
Lancaster LA1 214 F4
Chatsworth Rd *continued*
1 Leyland PR25 77 A1
Lytham St Anne's FY8 89 D7
Morecambe LA4 216 F4
Southport PR8 21 B6
Chatsworth St
Preston PR1 97 D8
Rochdale OL12 52 E3
Chatteris Pl FY5 175 C1
CHATTERTON 68 C1
Chatterton BL0 68 C2
Chatterton Dr BB5 104 E2
Chatterton Old La BL0 68 C2
Chatterton Rd BL0 68 C1
Chaucer Ave FY5 175 F2
Chaucer Cl PR7 41 B6
Chaucer Gdns BB6 124 B4
Chaucer Pl FY2 152 F6
Chaucer Rd FY7 199 A4
Chaucer St PR1 118 D2
Cheam Ave PR7 43 D6
Cheapside
Blackpool FY1 130 B5
6 Chorley PR7 43 C7
Formby L37 12 A2
11 Lancaster LA1 214 F8
1 Low Bentham LA2 239 B8
9 Preston PR1 96 F7
Cheddar Ave FY4 110 D6
Cheddar Dr PR2 118 D6
Chedworth Ave LA3 213 A7
CHEESDEN 51 D6
Cheetham Hill OL12 71 D3
Cheetham Mdw PR26 59 B8
Cheetham St BB2 101 C5
Chelburn Gr BB10 128 C6
Chelford Ave FY3 130 E8
Chelford Cl PR1 96 F2
Chelmsford Cl LA1 215 B5
Chelmsford Gr PR7 43 B7
Chelmsford Pl PR7 43 B7
Chelmsford Wlk PR26 59 A8
Chelsea Ave FY2 152 E1
Chelsea Ct 3 FY2 152 E1
Chelsea Mews
4 Blackpool FY2 152 E1
Lancaster LA1 218 D2
Chelston Dr BB4 68 A7
Cheltenham Ave BB5 104 C8
Cheltenham Cres
Lytham St Anne's FY8 91 D5
Thornton FY5 153 D8
Cheltenham Dr WN5 10 D2
Cheltenham Rd
Blackburn BB2 101 C5
Blackpool FY1 130 B7
Lancaster LA1 214 F5
Cheltenham Way PR8 35 F3
Chelwood Cl FY6 200 A5
Chennel Ho 4 LA1 214 E8
Chepstow Gdns PR3 181 D6
Chepstow Rd FY3 130 F8
Chequer Cl WN8 9 F5
Chequer La WN8 9 F6
Chequers BB5 124 F2
Chequers Ave LA1 215 B4
Chequers Way FY5 176 D2
Cheriton Field PR2 117 C7
Cheriton Gdns BL6 32 B5
Cheriton Pk PR8 35 E3
Cherries The PR7 60 D3
Cherry Ave BL9 33 C3
Cherry Cl
2 Blackburn BB1 102 B5
Fulwood PR2 118 D6
Kirkham PR4 113 E5
Cherryclough Way BB2 81 B8
Cherry Cres
Oswaldtwistle BB5 103 D2
Rawtenstall BB4 68 F8
Cherrycroft WN8 9 E6
Cherry Ct FY3 131 A7
Cherrydale FY2 152 D5
Cherry Dr BB6 143 C6
Cherryfields PR7 60 D4
Cherryfold Com Prim Sch BB11 127 D4
Cherry Gn L39 15 B1
Cherry Gr
Abbey Village PR6 80 B2
Burscough Bridge L40 25 E6
Longridge PR3 140 A7
Cherry La PR4 93 B4
Cherry Lea BB2 100 F2
Cherry Orch PR3 140 B6
Cherry Rd PR8 21 D2
Cherry St BB1 102 B5
CHERRY TREE 100 E1
Cherry Tree Cl
Fisher's Row PR3 201 E5
Hest Bank LA5 220 F2
Heysham LA3 212 E6
Knott End-on-S FY6 200 A6
Cherry Tree Ct
Blackpool FY4 131 B1
10 Fleetwood FY7 199 B5
Standish WN6 29 D2
Cherry Tree Dr LA1 214 F4
Cherry Tree Gdns
Blackpool FY4 111 A8
Nelson BB9 149 A8
Cherry Tree Gr PR6 61 C3
Cherry Tree La
3 Blackburn BB2 80 E8
Hurlston Green L40 24 B4
Ormskirk L39 15 B1
Rawtenstall BB4 68 F8

herry Tree Mews
BB11 127 D3
herry Tree Rd FY4 131 A1
herry Tree Rd N FY4 131 A1
herry Trees PR5 97 C3
herry Tree Sta BB2 100 F1
herry Tree Terr BB2 100 F1
herry Tree Way
Haslingden BB4 68 B7
5 Horwich BL6 32 E1
herry Vale PR4 73 F2
herry View L33 1 A5
herry Wood PR1 96 A3
herrywood Ave
Cleveleys FY5 175 C1
Lytham St Anne's FY8 90 E4
herrywood Cl PR25 59 E8
heryl Dr FY5 153 B8
HESHAM 33 A5
hesham Cres BL9 33 A3
hesham Dr PR4 75 F8
hesham Fold Rd BL9 33 B3
hesham Ind Est BL9 33 A4
hesham Lo PR3 156 B5
hesham Prim Sch BL9 33 A5
hesham Rd BL9 33 A5
hesham St PR3 156 B5
heshire Ct
Buckshaw Village PR7 60 F6
Ramsbottom BL0 50 D6
heshire House Cl
PR26 76 F7
heshire Lines Path
L39 12 F6
hesmere Croft PR1 96 B5
hesmere Dr PR1 96 B5
hessington Gn BB10 148 D3
hester Ave
Chorley PR7 43 E4
Cleveleys FY5 175 E2
2 Clitheroe BB7 189 E1
Poulton-le-F FY6 153 C4
Southport PR9 35 F8
hesterbrook PR3 141 E4
hester Cl
Blackburn BB1 102 A3
Garstang PR3 181 B7
Morecambe LA3 217 B2
hester Cres BB4 68 B8
hester Ct FY5 176 C3
hester Dr BL0 50 A4
hesterfield Cl PR8 21 C4
hesterfield Rd
Blackpool FY1 130 C7
Southport PR8 21 C5
hester Pl
Adlington PR6 31 A8
Great Eccleston PR3 156 C5
Lancaster LA1 215 A5
hester Rd
Blackpool FY3 130 D6
Preston PR1 118 C1
Southport PR9 35 F8
hester St
Accrington BB5 104 A5
Blackburn BB1 102 A4
Bury BL9 33 A4
hester Terr LA6 240 B7
hestnut Ave
Blackpool FY4 110 F5
Bolton-le-S LA5 221 A5
Bury BL9 33 B2
Caton LA2 237 C3
Chorley PR6 61 E2
Euxton PR7 60 C4
Higher Penwortham PR1 96 A4
hestnut Bsns Pk
BB11 127 B5
hestnut Cl
Bamber Bridge PR5 97 E2
Blackpool FY2 152 D2
Garstang PR3 204 D1
Halsall L39 23 C1
Kirkham PR4 114 B5
hestnut Cotts BB7 191 A5
hestnut Cres
Barrow BB7 166 D1
Fulwood PR2 118 E2
Longton PR4 74 F8
hestnut Ct
Leyland PR25 60 A7
3 Ormskirk L39 15 F6
hestnut Dr
Barnoldswick BB18 196 A1
Fulwood PR2 117 D7
Morecambe LA4 217 F6
Rawtenstall BB4 68 F8
Whalley BB7 144 A7
hestnut Gdns
Blackburn BB1 101 F7
Thornton FY5 176 B3
hestnut Gr
4 Accrington BB5 104 A4
Clayton-le-M BB5 125 A4
Darwen BB3 65 A5
Lancaster LA1 214 D8
hestnut Grange L39 15 D3
hestnut Rise BB11 127 F4
hestnut St PR8 35 C5
hestnuts The PR7 42 F2
hestnut Way L37 11 C1
hestnut Wlk 5 BB1 102 B5
hethams Cl FY5 176 A2
hevassut Cl BB9 170 C1
heviot Ave
Burnley BB10 128 E5
Cleveleys FY5 175 F4
Lytham St Anne's FY8 91 E5

Cheviot Cl
Horwich BL6 32 C5
Ramsbottom BL0 50 C4
Cheviot St PR1 96 C8
Chew Gdns FY6 153 B3
Chichester Cl
Burnley BB10 128 B6
Thornton FY5 176 A2
Chicken St BB2 101 C4
Chiddlingford Ct FY1 130 D3
Childrey Wlk BB2 82 A8
Chilgrove Ave BL6 31 D1
Chiltern Ave
Blackpool FY4 110 D7
Burnley BB10 128 E5
Euxton PR7 60 D1
Poulton-le-F FY6 153 C3
Chiltern Cl
Horwich BL6 32 C5
Lytham St Anne's FY8 91 D5
Ramsbottom BL0 50 C4
Chiltern Ct 4 LA1 215 A5
Chiltern Mdw PR25 77 D1
Chiltern Rd
Ramsbottom BL0 50 C4
Southport PR8 21 B6
Chilton Cl L31 5 D1
Chilton Ct L31 5 D1
Chilton Mews L31 5 D1
Chimes The
Kirkham PR4 114 A4
Tarleton PR4 57 A5
China St
Accrington BB5 103 F6
Lancaster LA1 214 F8
Chindit Cl L37 11 D2
Chindits Way PR2 118 B4
Chines The PR2 117 E4
Chingford Bank BB10 148 D3
Chingle Cl PR2 118 E6
Chippendale Mews
PR3 181 C8
CHIPPING 185 D3
Chipping Ave PR8 21 A5
Chipping Gr
Burnley BB10 128 D4
Normoss FY3 131 A8
Chipping La PR3 140 A8
Chipping Manor PR9 55 A6
Chipping St 3 BB12 146 D1
Chirk Dr FY5 176 D2
Chisacre Dr WN6 19 D7
Chisholm Cl WN6 29 B2
Chisholme Cl BL8 49 F2
Chislehurst Ave FY4 130 D1
Chislehurst Gr BB10 148 D4
Chislehurst Pl FY8 90 E5
Chislett Cl L40 25 D4
Chisnall Ave WN6 28 F6
Chisnall La
Coppull PR7 29 C6
Heskin Green PR7 41 F2
Wrightington Bar WN6 29 A5
Chiswell Gr FY5 153 D8
Chiswick Ct FY3 131 B2
Chiswick Gr FY3 131 B2
Chive Cl FY2 152 F3
Chorcliffe Ho 7 PR7 43 C8
CHORLEY 43 C6
Chorley All Saints CE Prim
Sch PR7 43 B5
Chorley Astley Park Sch
PR7 43 B8
Chorley Bsns & Tech Ctr
PR7 60 E4
Chorley Cl PR9 54 F5
Chorley Hall Rd PR7 61 C2
Chorley La PR7 42 D3
CHORLEY MOOR 43 D6
Chorley New Rd BL6 32 C2
Chorley New Road Prim
Sch BL6 32 D2
Chorley North Ind Est
PR6 61 D3
Chorley Old Rd
Clayton Green PR6 78 C2
Horwich BL6 32 E3
Whittle-le-W PR6 61 C8
Chorley Rd
Adlington PR6 31 A8
Bamber Bridge PR5 97 D3
Blackpool FY3 152 F2
Blackrod BL6, PR7 31 B5
Hill Dale L40, WN8 27 D6
Ollerton Fold BB2, PR6 79 E4
Parbold WN8 27 C4
Standish WN1 30 C3
Chorley St James CE Prim
Sch PR6 43 E7
Chorley Southlands High
Sch PR7 43 A5
Chorley & South Ribble
District Hospl PR7 61 C2
Chorley St PR6 31 B8
Chorley Sta PR6 43 D8
Chorley West Bsns Pk
PR7 42 F8
Chorlton Cl BB10 148 D2
Chorlton Gdns BB1 101 F7
Chorlton St BB1 101 F7
Chorlton Terr BB7 166 D1
Christ Church CE Prim Sch
BB8 172 B5
Christ Church Charnock
Richard CE Prim Sch
PR7 42 D4
Christ Church Hall 3
BB5 104 C4

Christ Church Sq 1
BB5 104 C5
Christ Church St
2 Accrington BB5 104 C5
4 Bacup OL13 88 A3
Preston PR1 96 E7
Christiana Hartley
Maternity Hospl PR8 35 E4
Christian Rd PR1 96 E7
Christie Ave LA4 217 D4
Christie Park (Morecambe
FC) LA4 217 D4
Christines Cres L40 25 E4
Christleton Cl BB10 148 F3
Christ The King RC High
Sch & Sixth Form Ctr
PR8 35 B3
Christ The King RC Maths
& Computing Coll
PR1 97 B6
Christ The King RC Prim
Sch
Blackpool FY3 131 A7
Burnley BB11 127 E3
Chromolyte Ind Est PR8 35 B5
CHURCH 103 E7
Church Alley BB5 124 F2
Church Ave
Accrington BB5 104 E2
Higher Penwortham PR1 96 C6
Lancaster LA1 214 F4
Preston PR1 97 E8
Church Bank
Church BB5 103 E7
Over Kellet LA6 237 B8
Church Bank Gdns
LA6 240 C7
Church Bank St 20 BB3 82 A1
Church Brook Ho 8
PR1 96 E4
Church Brow
Bolton-le-S LA5 221 A3
Clitheroe BB7 189 E1
Halton LA2 219 C6
Walton-le-D PR5 97 E5
Church Brow Cl LA5 221 A3
Church Brow Gdns 5
BB7 189 E1
Church Cl
Clitheroe BB7 189 E1
Dolphinholme LA2 226 A8
Formby L37 12 A3
Freckleton PR4 93 A6
Mellor BB2 121 E2
Ramsbottom BL0 50 B5
Read BB12 145 D2
Southport PR9 36 A8
Waddington BB7 189 B4
Church Close Ct L37 12 A3
Church Cotts LA6 241 C7
Church Ct
Bolton-le-S LA5 221 A3
6 Bury BL9 33 A3
Edenfield BL0 68 D4
Kirkham PR4 114 A5
16 Lancaster LA1 218 D2
Preston PR1 118 C2
Church Dr
Lytham St Anne's FY8 90 F3
Orrell WN5 10 D5
Whalley BB7 144 A7
Churchfield PR2 117 F6
Churchfields
Bescar L40 23 F7
Southport PR8 34 F3
Church Fields L39 15 E5
Church Fold
Charnock Richard PR7 42 E4
Coppull PR7 29 F8
Churchgate
Goosnargh PR3 138 D6
Southport PR9 53 F1
Churchgate Mews PR9 54 A1
Church Gdns
Longridge PR3 140 B7
Warton PR4 92 E6
Church Gn
Formby L37 11 C2
Skelmersdale WN8 17 F1
Church Gr LA3 209 E8
Church Hall BB5 103 F7
Church Hill
Nether Kellet LA6 221 F5
Whittle-le-W PR6 61 C7
Church Hill Ave LA5 223 D5
Church Hill Rd
Blackburn BB1 102 A7
Ormskirk L39 15 D6
Church Ho 7 L39 15 E5
Church House Mus
PR3 137 D1
Churchill Ave
Rishton BB1 103 A8
Southport PR9 53 F2
Churchill Cl 2 FY5 176 B2
Churchill Ct FY3 130 D6
Churchill Dr PR2 118 D4
Churchill Rd
Barrowford BB9 170 B1
Brinscall PR6 63 A8
Fulwood PR2 118 C4
Churchill St OL11, OL12 52 C1
Churchill Way
Burnley BB9 148 B7
Leyland PR25 77 A2
Nelson BB9 148 B8
Church La
Accrington BB5 125 A1

Church La *continued*
Aughton L39 6 A7
Bilsborrow PR3 159 A4
Broughton PR3 137 D1
Charnock Richard PR7 42 D4
Edenfield BL0 68 D4
Farington PR4, PR26 76 F7
Goosnargh PR3 138 D6
Great Harwood BB6 124 C6
Great Mitton BB7 165 E3
Hambleton FY6 177 D1
Kelbrook BB18 195 A6
Maghull L31 5 A8
Mellor BB2 121 E2
Morecambe LA4 217 B6
Newchurch BB4 86 E1
Newton-w-S PR4 115 B3
12 Padiham BB12 146 C1
Tunstall LA6 241 E4
Whalley BB7 144 C5
Whitechapel PR3 160 E7
Winmarleigh PR3 203 E4
Wrightington Bar WN6 28 D8
Churchlands La WN6 29 F2
Church Mdws BB8 171 D5
Church Mews
Bamber Bridge PR5 77 F7
Great Harwood BB6 124 D5
Southport PR9 36 A7
Church & Oswaldtwistle
Sta BB5 103 E5
Church Pk
Overton LA3 209 D8
Salwick PR4 115 F3
Church Raike PR3 185 E3
Church Rd
Bamber Bridge PR5 77 E7
Banks PR9 55 A6
Bickerstaffe L39 7 E6
Formby L37 12 A4
Kirkham PR4 113 F7
Leyland PR25 60 A8
Lytham St Anne's FY8 90 B6
Lytham St Anne's, Lytham
FY8 90 F3
Rufford L40 39 C4
Shuttleworth BL0 50 E8
Singleton FY6 154 F1
Skelmersdale WN8 17 F1
Tarleton PR4 57 A5
Thornton FY5 176 A2
Thornton-in-C BD23 197 A5
Walton Summit PR5 77 F6
Warton PR4 92 E6
Weeton PR4 132 F1
Wharles PR4 134 F2
Church Row
Preston PR1 97 A7
Wrea Green PR4 113 B4
Church Row Chambers
PR4 75 A8
Churchside PR4 75 F8
Church Sq BB10 129 B5
Church St
Accrington BB5 104 C5
Adlington PR7 31 A7
Bacup OL13 70 C8
Barnoldswick BB18 196 B2
Barrowford BB9 170 D4
Belmont BL7 46 C4
Blackburn BB1 101 E5
Blackpool FY1 130 C5
Blackrod BL6 31 C2
Brierfield BB9 148 B5
Burnley BB11 128 A6
Burnley, Harle Syke
BB10 148 F2
Bury BL9 33 A3
Chorley PR7 43 C7
Church BB5 103 E6
Churchtown PR3 181 A2
Clayton-le-M BB5 124 F2
1 Clitheroe BB7 166 E8
Colne BB8 171 D5
Croston PR26 58 B1
Darwen BB3 82 A1
Fleetwood FY7 199 B4
Garstang PR3 181 C7
Goodshaw Chapel BB4 106 A1
Great Harwood BB6 124 C5
Halton LA2 219 B6
2 Hapton BB12 126 C4
Haslingden BB4 85 B4
Higher Walton PR5 98 B3
Horwich BL6 32 C3
Kirkham PR4 114 B5
Lancaster LA1 214 F8
Leyland PR25 77 B2
Longridge PR3 140 B7
Morecambe LA4 217 B6
Newchurch BB4 86 E1
Ormskirk L39 15 E5
Orrell WN5 10 E5
Oswaldtwistle BB5 103 D3
Padiham BB12 126 C8
2 Poulton-le-F FY6 153 D3
Preston PR1 97 A7
5 Ramsbottom BL0 50 C6
Rawtenstall BB4 69 E8
Read BB12 145 D2
Ribchester PR3 141 D3
Rishton BB1 124 A1
Slaidburn BB7 229 C7
Southport PR9 35 C7
Standish WN6 29 E1
Trawden BB8 172 C2
Up Holland WN8 10 C7
Whittington LA6 241 C7

Church St *continued*
Whitworth OL12 52 C8
Church Stile LA6 240 C8
Church Terr
21 Darwen BB3 82 A1
Higher Walton PR5 98 B3
CHURCHTOWN
Catterall 181 A2
Southport 54 A1
Churchtown Cres OL13 88 B1
Churchtown Ct PR9 54 A2
Churchtown Gdns PR9 54 A2
Churchtown Prim Sch
PR9 54 B2
Church View
Aughton L39 6 A7
Gisburn BB7 231 B3
Salesbury BB1 122 E6
Stalmine FY6 177 C7
Tarleton PR4 57 A5
Trawden BB8 172 C2
Church View Ct 1 L39 15 E5
Churchward Sq BL6 32 C2
Church Way
Formby L37 11 C2
Nelson BB9 148 D6
Church Wlk
Blackburn BB1 122 F3
Euxton PR7 60 C2
Fulwood PR2 118 F5
Kirkham PR4 113 F7
Tarleton PR4 57 A6
Church Wlks 3 L39 15 E5
Churton Gr WN6 29 B2
Cicely Ct 6 BB1 101 F4
Cicely La BB1 101 F5
Cicely St BB1 101 F4
Cinderbarrow La LA5,
LA6 240 A6
Cinder La
Lancaster LA1 214 F3
Lewth PR4 136 A6
Mere Brow PR4 55 F2
Cinnamon Brow WN8 10 C6
Cinnamon Ct 3 PR1 96 C2
Cinnamon Hill Dr N
PR5 97 D3
Cinnamon Hill Dr S
PR5 97 D3
Cintra Ave PR2 117 D3
Cintra Terr PR2 117 D3
Circus The 10 BB3 82 A1
Cirrus Dr L39 15 A1
City Ct PR1 97 A8
City Heights Cl 21 LA1 215 A8
City of Preston High Sch
PR2 118 F3
City Space Ho PR1 96 F6
City Views PR1 97 A7
Clairane Ave PR2 117 E6
Clairville PR8 34 F5
Clancut La PR7 42 F2
Clanfield PR2 117 E7
Clara St
Preston PR1 97 C7
Whitworth OL12 71 D1
Clare Ave BB8 171 A2
Claremont Ave
Chorley PR7 43 B7
Clitheroe BB7 166 F7
Southport PR8 35 A4
Claremont Com Prim Sch
FY1 130 C8
Claremont Cres LA4 216 F4
Claremont Ct
Blackpool FY1 130 C7
Lytham St Anne's FY8 89 E5
Claremont Dr
Clitheroe BB7 166 F7
Ormskirk L39 15 D3
Claremont Gdns PR8 35 A4
Claremont Pl FY8 89 E8
Claremont Rd
Accrington BB5 104 B8
Blackpool FY1 130 C8
Chorley PR7 43 B5
Morecambe LA4 216 F4
Southport PR8 35 A4
Claremont St
Brierfield BB9 148 A6
Burnley BB12 127 D6
Colne BB8 172 A5
Claremont Terr BB9 148 D7
Claremount Ave PR25 60 B8
Clarence Ave
Cleveleys FY5 175 D3
4 Haslingden BB4 85 A1
Knott End-on-S FY6 199 E5
Clarence Cl 10 BL9 33 A4
Clarence Ct
15 Blackpool FY4 130 B1
5 Morecambe LA4 217 E6
Southport PR8 35 A4
Clarence High Sch L37 11 F6
Clarence Pk BB2 101 B7
Clarence Rd
Accrington BB5 104 A4
Southport PR8 35 A4
Clarence St
Barnoldswick BB18 196 C1
Blackburn BB1 101 D6
Burnley BB11 128 B4
4 Chorley PR7 43 D7
Colne BB8 172 A5
Darwen BB3 81 F3

Clarence St *continued*
Lancaster LA1 . . . . 215 A7
Leyland PR25 . . . . 77 B2
Longridge PR3 . . . . 140 A8
Morecambe LA4 . . . . 217 B5
Oswaldtwistle BB5 . . . . 103 C3
Rawtenstall BB4 . . . . 86 A7
Rochdale OL12 . . . . 52 D2
Trawden BB8 . . . . 172 C2
Clarendon Gr L31 . . . . 5 C5
Clarendon Rd
Blackburn BB1 . . . . 101 F8
Blackpool FY1 . . . . 130 B2
Lancaster LA1 . . . . 218 D3
Lytham St Anne's FY8 . . . . 90 A8
Clarendon Rd E
Blackburn BB1 . . . . 102 A8
Morecambe LA4 . . . . 216 F4
Clarendon Rd N FY8 . . . . 89 F8
Clarendon Rd W LA3 . . . . 216 E4
Clarendon St
Accrington BB5 . . . . 104 D6
Bury BL9 . . . . 33 A4
[10] Chorley PR6 . . . . 43 E7
Colne BB8 . . . . 172 B5
Preston PR1 . . . . 97 A6
Clare Rd LA1 . . . . 218 C2
Clare St
Blackpool FY1 . . . . 130 B1
Burnley BB11 . . . . 127 D6
Claret St BB5 . . . . 104 A5
Clarke Holme St [3] BB4 . . . . 86 F2
Clarke's Cotts L40 . . . . 27 A8
Clarkes Croft BL9 . . . . 33 C3
Clarke's La OL12 . . . . 52 E1
Clarke St BB1 . . . . 124 B1
Clarke Wood Cl BB7 . . . . 144 F8
Clarkfield Cl L40 . . . . 25 F3
Clarkfield Dr LA4 . . . . 217 D5
Clarksfield Rd LA5 . . . . 221 A4
Clark St
Morecambe LA4 . . . . 217 B6
Poulton-le-F FY6 . . . . 153 F3
Clarrick Terr LA6 . . . . 242 F3
CLAUGHTON
Catterall 182 D1
Hornby 237 E5
Claughton Ave PR25 . . . . 77 E1
Claughton Dr LA1 . . . . 215 A3
Claughton Ind Est PR3 . . . . 181 E1
Claughton Mans [5]
FY4 . . . . 110 D8
Claughton St [13] BB10 . . . . 148 B1
Claughton Terr LA2 . . . . 237 F5
CLAWTHORPE 240 C8
Clawthorpe Cotts LA6 . . . . 240 C8
Claybank [10] BB12 . . . . 146 C1
Claybank Fold [9]
BB12 . . . . 146 C1
Clay Brow Rd WN8 . . . . 9 E6
Clayburn Cl PR6 . . . . 61 E2
Clay Gap La FY6, PR3 . . . . 177 F4
Clay La LA3 . . . . 213 B8
Claylands Dr LA5 . . . . 221 A4
Claypool Prim Sch BL6 . . . . 32 F1
Claypool Rd BL6 . . . . 32 E1
Clay St BB11 . . . . 127 C5
Clayton Ave
Leyland PR25 . . . . 59 D7
Rawtenstall BB4 . . . . 68 E8
CLAYTON BROOK 78 A5
Clayton Brook Ho BB5 . . . . 125 A1
Clayton Brook Prim Sch
PR5 . . . . 78 B5
Clayton Brook Rd PR5 . . . . 78 C6
Clayton Cl [11] BB9 . . . . 170 D1
Clayton Cres FY4 . . . . 110 E6
Clayton Ct PR3 . . . . 140 B7
Claytongate
Blackpool FY4 . . . . 111 A7
Coppull PR7 . . . . 42 F2
Claytongate Dr PR1 . . . . 97 A2
Clayton Gdns L40 . . . . 25 E4
Clayton Gr BB1 . . . . 122 D6
CLAYTON GREEN 78 A3
Clayton Green Bsns Pk
PR6 . . . . 78 B4
Clayton Green Rd PR6 . . . . 78 B3
Claytonhalgh PR3 . . . . 141 E3
Clayton Hall Dr BB5 . . . . 124 F4
CLAYTON-LE-DALE 122 C7
CLAYTON-LE-MOORS 124 E2
Clayton-le-Moors Ind Est
BB5 . . . . 124 F1
CLAYTON-LE-WOODS 77 D2
Clayton-le-Woods CE Prim Sch
Clayton Green PR6 . . . . 78 A2
Clayton-le-W PR6 . . . . 77 F2
Clayton-le-Woods Manor
Road Prim Sch PR6 . . . . 78 B2
Clayton Lo BB5 . . . . 124 F4
Clayton Mews WN8 . . . . 17 D1
Clayton Row BB6 . . . . 143 D1
Clayton's Gate [11] PR1 . . . . 96 F8
Clayton St
[1] Accrington BB5 . . . . 125 A1
[6] Bamber Bridge PR5 . . . . 97 E1
Barnoldswick BB18 . . . . 196 C2
Blackburn BB2 . . . . 101 E4
Colne BB8 . . . . 171 E4
Great Harwood BB6 . . . . 124 C5
[18] Nelson BB9 . . . . 170 D1
[7] Oswaldtwistle BB5 . . . . 103 E5
Clayton St *continued*
Skelmersdale WN8 . . . . 17 D1
Clayton Street Ind Units
BB9 . . . . 170 D1
Clayton Villa Fold PR6 . . . . 78 A3
Clayton Way
Blackburn BB2 . . . . 81 D7
Clayton-le-M BB5 . . . . 125 A3
Cleator Ave FY2 . . . . 152 C1
Cleaver Cotts L38 . . . . 3 A6
Cleaver St
Blackburn BB1 . . . . 101 F5
Burnley BB10 . . . . 128 B8
Clecken La PR3 . . . . 182 D2
Clegg Ave FY5 . . . . 175 D3
Clegg's Ct OL12 . . . . 71 C2
Clegg St E [9] BB10 . . . . 128 A8
Clegg St
[6] Bacup OL13 . . . . 70 C8
Brierfield BB9 . . . . 148 B5
Burnley BB10 . . . . 128 A8
Haslingden BB4 . . . . 85 B3
Kirkham PR4 . . . . 114 A5
Nelson BB9 . . . . 148 E6
Skelmersdale WN8 . . . . 17 D1
Whitworth OL12 . . . . 71 C2
Worsthorne BB10 . . . . 129 A5
Clematis Cl PR7 . . . . 61 A3
Clematis St BB2 . . . . 101 B6
Clemens Ct BB3 . . . . 81 E3
Clementina St OL12 . . . . 52 F1
Clements Dr BB9 . . . . 148 C4
Clement St
Accrington BB5 . . . . 104 C5
[4] Darwen BB3 . . . . 65 A8
Clement View [14] BB9 . . . . 148 D8
Clengers Brow PR9 . . . . 54 A3
Clent Ave L31 . . . . 5 C3
Clent Gdns L31 . . . . 5 C3
Clent Rd L31 . . . . 5 C3
Clerk Hill Rd BB7 . . . . 144 F5
Clerkhill St BB1 . . . . 102 B5
Clery St BB12 . . . . 127 A5
Clevedon Rd
Blackpool FY1 . . . . 130 B7
Fulwood PR2 . . . . 117 A4
Cleveland Ave PR2 . . . . 118 C4
Cleveland Cl BL0 . . . . 50 C3
Cleveland Dr LA1 . . . . 214 D7
Cleveland Rd
Leyland PR25 . . . . 76 F2
Lytham St Anne's FY8 . . . . 91 B3
Clevelands Ave
Morecambe LA3 . . . . 216 F3
Silverdale LA5 . . . . 224 C4
Clevelands Gr
Burnley BB11 . . . . 127 E4
Morecambe LA3 . . . . 216 F3
Clevelands Mt BB11 . . . . 127 E4
Clevelands Rd BB11 . . . . 127 F4
Cleveland St
Chorley PR7 . . . . 43 C8
Colne BB8 . . . . 171 F6
[2] Coppull PR7 . . . . 42 E1
Todmorden OL14 . . . . 109 B1
Clevelands Wlk [1] LA3 . . . . 216 F3
CLEVELEYS 175 C3
Cleveleys Ave
Cleveleys FY5 . . . . 175 D3
Fulwood PR2 . . . . 117 C4
Lancaster LA1 . . . . 218 A2
Southport PR9 . . . . 54 A4
Cleveleys Rd
Accrington BB5 . . . . 104 B8
Blackburn BB2 . . . . 101 F1
Coupe Green PR5 . . . . 98 E3
Southport PR9 . . . . 54 A3
Cleves Ct FY3 . . . . 131 A2
Cleves The L31 . . . . 5 E3
Cleve Way L37 . . . . 12 B2
CLIEVES HILLS 14 F3
Clieves Hills La L39 . . . . 14 E3
Clieves Viewpoint*
L39 . . . . 14 E3
Clifden Ct L37 . . . . 11 F3
Cliff Ave BL9 . . . . 50 C2
Cliff Bank Hamlet BB4 . . . . 86 E2
Cliff Ct FY2 . . . . 152 B4
CLIFFE 124 C6
Cliffe Ct PR1 . . . . 97 D8
Cliffe Dr PR6 . . . . 61 B8
Cliffe La BB6 . . . . 124 C6
Cliffe Pk BB6 . . . . 124 C6
Cliffe St BB9 . . . . 170 E1
Cliff Mount BL0 . . . . 50 B7
Clifford Ave
Longton PR4 . . . . 95 A1
Morecambe LA4 . . . . 217 D6
Clifford Rd
Blackpool FY1 . . . . 130 C7
Southport PR8 . . . . 35 A2
Clifford St
Barnoldswick BB18 . . . . 196 C2
Chorley PR7 . . . . 43 D8
Colne BB8 . . . . 171 E5
Cliff Pl FY2 . . . . 152 B4
Cliff Rd PR9 . . . . 53 D1
Cliff St
Colne BB8 . . . . 171 B3
Padiham BB12 . . . . 146 D1
Preston PR1 . . . . 96 E6
Rishton BB1 . . . . 124 B2
Cliffs The LA3 . . . . 216 D2
CLIFTON 115 D1
Clifton Ave
Accrington BB5 . . . . 104 C7
Blackpool FY4 . . . . 131 C1
Leyland PR25 . . . . 60 B8
Clifton Ave *continued*
Preston PR2 . . . . 117 A2
Warton PR4 . . . . 92 E6
Clifton Bsns Pk PR4 . . . . 94 B7
Clifton Cl FY5 . . . . 176 C1
Clifton Cres
Blackpool FY3 . . . . 131 A2
Preston PR1 . . . . 118 C2
Clifton Ct
[1] Blackpool FY4 . . . . 110 B6
[3] Lytham St Anne's, Lytham
FY8 . . . . 91 C3
[2] Lytham St Anne's, St Annes
FY8 . . . . 89 E6
Clifton Dr
Blackpool FY4 . . . . 110 B5
Blackrod BL6 . . . . 31 C3
Great Harwood BB6 . . . . 124 C6
Higher Penwortham PR1 . . . . 96 C5
Lytham St Anne's FY8 . . . . 90 D3
Morecambe LA4 . . . . 217 E5
Clifton Dr N FY8 . . . . 110 B2
Clifton Dr S FY8 . . . . 89 E5
Clifton Gate FY8 . . . . 91 B4
Clifton Gdns FY8 . . . . 90 C6
Clifton Gn PR4 . . . . 115 D2
Clifton Gr
Chorley PR7 . . . . 43 B7
Preston PR1 . . . . 118 C3
Wilpshire BB1 . . . . 122 F4
Clifton Grange FY8 . . . . 89 D7
Clifton Ho PR2 . . . . 118 C4
Clifton Hospl FY8 . . . . 90 B5
Clifton La PR4 . . . . 115 D2
Clifton Lo FY8 . . . . 89 E5
Clifton Par [4] FY8 . . . . 91 B3
Clifton Pk Ret Ctr FY4 . . . . 111 D8
Clifton Pl
Freckleton PR4 . . . . 93 B6
Fulwood PR2 . . . . 117 B2
Clifton Prim Sch FY8 . . . . 90 C6
Clifton Rd
Blackpool FY4 . . . . 111 C8
Brierfield BB9 . . . . 148 C4
Burnley BB12 . . . . 127 C7
Fleetwood FY7 . . . . 199 A3
Formby L37 . . . . 12 A5
Southport PR8 . . . . 35 F6
Clifton Sq [5] FY8 . . . . 91 B3
Clifton St
Accrington BB5 . . . . 104 A4
Blackpool FY1 . . . . 130 B5
Burnley BB12 . . . . 127 F6
Colne BB8 . . . . 171 D5
Darwen BB3 . . . . 81 F4
Earby BB18 . . . . 195 A8
Lytham St Anne's FY8 . . . . 91 B3
[5] Preston PR1 . . . . 96 D6
Rishton BB1 . . . . 124 B1
Trawden BB8 . . . . 172 C2
Clifton Terr BB3 . . . . 82 E2
Clifton Windmill*
PR4 . . . . 115 C3
Clifton Wlk [8] FY8 . . . . 91 B3
Clifton Wlk Sh Ctr [14]
FY8 . . . . 91 B3
Clinkham Rd BB6 . . . . 124 A5
Clinning Rd PR8 . . . . 35 A2
Clinton Ave FY1 . . . . 130 C4
Clinton St BB1 . . . . 102 A6
Clippers Quay [2] BB1 . . . . 101 F4
CLITHEROE 166 D8
Clitheroe Castle*
BB7 . . . . 166 E8
Clitheroe Castle Mus*
BB7 . . . . 166 E8
Clitheroe Com Hospl
BB7 . . . . 190 A3
Clitheroe Pendle Prim Sch
BB7 . . . . 189 F1
Clitheroe Pl FY4 . . . . 111 A8
Clitheroe Rd
Brierfield BB9 . . . . 148 A5
Chatburn BB7 . . . . 190 C3
Knowle Green PR3 . . . . 163 C1
Lytham St Anne's FY8 . . . . 90 C6
Sabden BB7 . . . . 167 E1
Waddington BB7 . . . . 189 C3
West Bradford BB7 . . . . 189 F5
Whalley BB7 . . . . 144 C7
Clitheroe Royal Gram Sch
Clitheroe BB7 . . . . 189 F1
Clitheroe BB7 . . . . 190 A2
Clitheroes La PR4 . . . . 93 B6
Clitheroe St
[3] Padiham BB12 . . . . 126 C8
Preston PR1 . . . . 97 C7
Clitheroe Sta BB7 . . . . 189 E1
Clive Ave FY8 . . . . 110 E1
Clive Lo PR8 . . . . 34 F2
Clive Rd
Higher Penwortham
PR1 . . . . 96 B6
Southport PR8 . . . . 34 F2
Clive St BB12 . . . . 127 F8
Clockhouse Ave BB10 . . . . 148 D3
Clockhouse Ct BB10 . . . . 148 D3
Clockhouse Gr BB10 . . . . 148 D3
Clod La BB4 . . . . 68 C8
Clods Carr La FY6 . . . . 199 F2
Clogger La BD23 . . . . 197 F7
Clog Heads BB8 . . . . 172 C2
Cloister Dr BB3 . . . . 82 C1
Cloister Gn L37 . . . . 12 B2
Cloisters LA3 . . . . 217 C2
Cloisters The
Blackpool FY3 . . . . 130 E5
Formby L37 . . . . 11 F3
Cloisters The *continued*
[2] Leyland PR25 . . . . 77 C2
[6] Preston PR2 . . . . 96 D8
[6] Rawtenstall BB4 . . . . 69 E8
[2] Southport PR9 . . . . 35 C8
Tarleton PR4 . . . . 57 A6
Whalley BB7 . . . . 144 D5
Clone Primet High Sch
BB8 . . . . 171 B3
Clone Primet Prim Sch
BB8 . . . . 171 B3
Clorain Cl L33 . . . . 1 A3
Clorain Rd L33 . . . . 1 A3
Closes Hall Mews BB7 . . . . 230 F5
Close The
Banks PR9 . . . . 55 A5
Clayton-le-M BB5 . . . . 124 F4
Cleveleys FY5 . . . . 175 D2
Cleveleys, Rossall Beach
FY5 . . . . 175 D4
Fulwood PR2 . . . . 118 E6
Garstang PR3 . . . . 204 B1
Ince Blundell L38 . . . . 3 E3
Kirkham PR4 . . . . 114 B4
New Longton PR4 . . . . 76 A7
Rising Bridge BB5 . . . . 85 A8
Weeton PR4 . . . . 132 E2
Withnell Fold PR6 . . . . 79 C3
Clougha Ave
Halton LA2 . . . . 219 D7
Lancaster LA1 . . . . 215 B6
Clough Acre PR7 . . . . 61 A2
Clough Ave
Bamber Bridge PR5 . . . . 97 B3
Burscough L40 . . . . 25 F4
Clough Bank BB7 . . . . 190 D5
Clough End Rd BB4 . . . . 85 B5
Clough End View BB4 . . . . 85 B5
Cloughfield PR1 . . . . 96 D1
CLOUGHFOLD 86 D2
Clough Gdns BB4 . . . . 85 B5
Clough Heads Cotts
PR3 . . . . 226 F1
Clough Head Visitor Ctr*
BB4 . . . . 84 A3
Clough La
Hesketh Lane PR3 . . . . 163 A7
Simonstone BB12 . . . . 145 F1
Clough Rd
Bacup OL13 . . . . 88 A3
Nelson BB9 . . . . 149 A8
Clough Springs BB9 . . . . 170 C3
Clough St
[8] Bacup OL13 . . . . 70 D8
Burnley BB11 . . . . 127 D5
Darwen BB3 . . . . 65 C6
[5] Newchurch BB4 . . . . 86 F1
Clough Terr BB18 . . . . 196 B1
Clough The
Clayton Green PR6 . . . . 78 A3
Darwen BB3 . . . . 65 C6
Cloughwood Cres WN6 . . . . 19 D6
Clovelly Ave
Blackpool FY5 . . . . 152 D6
Fulwood PR2 . . . . 117 D3
Clovelly Dr
Higher Penwortham
PR1 . . . . 96 A5
Newburgh WN8 . . . . 27 A1
Skelmersdale WN8 . . . . 18 A8
Southport PR8 . . . . 21 E8
Clover Ave FY8 . . . . 111 A1
Clover Cres BB12 . . . . 127 D8
Clover Ct
Blackpool FY2 . . . . 152 F6
Southport PR8 . . . . 35 C5
Clover Dr PR4 . . . . 93 D7
Cloverfield PR1 . . . . 96 B4
Clover Field PR6 . . . . 78 B2
Cloverfields [5] BB1 . . . . 102 A6
Cloverhill Ho BB9 . . . . 148 F7
Clover Hill Rd BB9 . . . . 148 F7
Clover Mews FY3 . . . . 130 E6
Clover Rd PR7 . . . . 43 A5
Clover St OL13 . . . . 88 A3
Clover Terr BB3 . . . . 82 A3
CLOW BRIDGE 106 C5
Club La PR3 . . . . 185 E3
Club St
Bamber Bridge PR5 . . . . 77 F7
Todmorden OL14 . . . . 109 B1
Clucas Gdns L39 . . . . 15 E6
Clydesdale Pl PR26 . . . . 76 C2
Clyde St
Blackburn BB2 . . . . 101 B3
[4] Blackpool FY1 . . . . 130 B7
Preston PR2 . . . . 96 C8
Clyffes Farm Cl L40 . . . . 24 A7
Coach Ho PR7 . . . . 60 A5
Coach House Ct L40 . . . . 25 E3
Coach House Mews
PR3 . . . . 181 C7
Coach Mews LA4 . . . . 216 F4
Coach Rd
Bickerstaffe L39 . . . . 7 F1
Church BB5 . . . . 103 E5
Warton LA5 . . . . 223 D7
Coal Clough La BB11 . . . . 127 E4
Coal Clough Rd OL14 . . . . 109 B2
Coal Hey [12] BB4 . . . . 85 B3
Coal Hey St [13] BB4 . . . . 85 B3
Coal Pit La
Accrington BB5 . . . . 103 F4
Bacup OL13 . . . . 88 B3
Barnoldswick BB7 . . . . 193 B7
Colne BB8 . . . . 171 F4
Gisburn BB7 . . . . 231 D2
Rawtenstall BB4 . . . . 87 A4
Coal Pit La *continued*
Skelmersdale L39 . . . . 8 D
Tockholes BB3 . . . . 81 E
Coal Rd BL0 . . . . 51 C
Coal St [12] BB11 . . . . 127 F
Coastal Dr LA2 . . . . 220 E
Coastal Rd
Hest Bank LA2, LA5 . . . . 220 F
Morecambe LA4 . . . . 217 F
Southport, Birkdale PR8 . . . . 34 C
Southport, Woodvale PR8 . . . . 21 A
Coastal Rise LA2 . . . . 220 E
Coastline Mews PR9 . . . . 54 A
COATES . . . . 196 C
Coates Ave BB18 . . . . 196 C
Coates Fields BB18 . . . . 196 C
Coates La BB18 . . . . 196 D
Coates Lane Prim Sch
BB18 . . . . 196 D
Cobbis Brow Cotts L40 . . . . 17 F
Cobbled Court Yd LA1 . . . . 214 F
Cobb's Brow La L40,
WN8 . . . . 18 E
Cobbs Brow Prim Sch
WN8 . . . . 18 A
Cobb's Clough Rd L40 . . . . 17 F
Cobbs La BB5 . . . . 83 E
Cob Castle Rd BB4 . . . . 84 E
Cobden Ct [4] BB1 . . . . 101 E
Cobden Ho BB4 . . . . 86 D
Cobden Rd PR9 . . . . 36 A
Cobden St
Barnoldswick BB18 . . . . 196 E
[3] Bolton, Egerton BL7 . . . . 47 D
Britannia OL13 . . . . 71 E
Burnley, Harle Syke
BB10 . . . . 148 F
Burnley, Heasandford
BB10 . . . . 128 E
[4] Bury BL9 . . . . 33 A
Chorley PR6 . . . . 61 E
[11] Darwen BB3 . . . . 65 A
Hapton BB12 . . . . 126 C
Nelson BB9 . . . . 148 C
Padiham BB12 . . . . 146 D
Cobham Ct [2] BB4 . . . . 86 E
Cobham Rd BB5 . . . . 104 D
Cob La BB8, BB18 . . . . 195 E
Cob Moor Ave WN5 . . . . 10 D
Cob Moor Rd WN5 . . . . 10 D
Cobourg Cl BB2 . . . . 101 F
COB WALL . . . . 102 A
Cob Wall BB1 . . . . 102 A
Cochran St [26] BB3 . . . . 82 A
COCKDEN . . . . 149 E
Cocker Ave FY6 . . . . 154 A
COCKER BAR . . . . 75 F
Cocker Bar Rd PR26 . . . . 58 D
COCKERHAM . . . . 206 C
Cockerham Parochial CE
Prim Sch LA2 . . . . 206 D
Cockerham Rd
Forton LA2, PR3 . . . . 207 B
Garstang PR3 . . . . 204 E
Cockerham Wlk FY3 . . . . 131 A
Cockerill St BB4 . . . . 85 E
Cockerill Terr BB7 . . . . 166 D
Cocker La PR26 . . . . 76 C
Cocker Rd PR5 . . . . 78 E
Cockersand Ave PR4 . . . . 95 C
Cockersand Dr LA1 . . . . 215 A
Cocker Sq [3] FY1 . . . . 130 E
Cocker St
Blackpool FY1 . . . . 130 B
Darwen BB3 . . . . 65 C
Cocker Trad Est FY1 . . . . 130 C
Cockhall La OL12 . . . . 71 C
Cock Hall La OL12 . . . . 52 C
Cockhill La BB8 . . . . 172 E
Cocking Yd LA6 . . . . 240 C
Cockleach Lane Ends
PR3 . . . . 162 A
Cockle Dick's La PR9 . . . . 53 E
Cockridge Cl BB2 . . . . 81 B
Cock Robin PR26 . . . . 58 C
Cock Robin La PR3 . . . . 181 D
Codale Ave FY2 . . . . 152 D
Coddington St BB1 . . . . 102 E
Coe La PR4 . . . . 57 A
Cog La BB11 . . . . 127 D
Cog St BB11 . . . . 127 D
Colbran St
Burnley BB10 . . . . 128 E
[12] Nelson BB9 . . . . 170 F
Colburne Cl L40 . . . . 25 F
Colchester Ave LA1 . . . . 215 B
Colchester Dr [6] FY5 . . . . 175 F
Colchester Rd
Blackpool FY3 . . . . 130 F
Southport PR8 . . . . 35 F
Coldale Ct [5] FY4 . . . . 110 E
Cold Bath St [4] PR1 . . . . 96 F
COLD ROW . . . . 177 C
Coldstream Pl BB2 . . . . 101 E
Coldweather Ave BB9 . . . . 148 E
Cold Well La LA7 . . . . 224 F
Colebatch PR2 . . . . 117 D
Cole Cres L39 . . . . 6 C
Coleman St [4] BB9 . . . . 148 F
Colenso Rd
Blackburn BB1 . . . . 101 D
Fulwood PR2 . . . . 117 C
Coleridge Ave FY5 . . . . 176 A
Coleridge Cl
Colne BB8 . . . . 171 D
Cottam PR4 . . . . 116 E
Coleridge Dr BB5 . . . . 104 E
Coleridge Ho LA2 . . . . 218 C

Coleridge Pl BB6 124 B4
Coleridge Rd
Blackpool FY1 130 D6
Longshaw WN5 10 D1
Ramsbottom BL8 49 F2
Coleridge St BB2 101 C3
Coles Dr LA5 224 B8
Coleshill Ave BB10 128 D5
Colesville Ave FY5 176 B1
Colinmander Gdns L39 15 C3
Colin St
Barnoldswick BB18 196 B3
Burnley BB11 127 D5
Colinton WN8 9 E7
Colldale Terr BB4 85 B2
College Ave
Cleveleys FY5 175 C1
Formby L37 11 E4
College Cl
Formby L37 11 D4
Longridge PR3 140 A5
Padiham BB12 126 D6
Southport PR8 35 A3
College Croft BD24 236 F7
College Ct
5 Accrington BB5 104 A6
4 Blackpool FY1 130 C4
Preston PR1 117 F2
College Farm WN8 19 A1
College Gate FY5 175 C5
College La BB4 86 D2
College Path L37 11 D5
College Rd WN8 10 B8
College St
2 Accrington BB5 104 A6
Todmorden OL14 109 C1
Collegiate High Sch Sports Coll FY3 153 A1
Collier's Row BB1 102 F1
Colliers St BB5 103 E5
Collier St 6 BB5 104 E2
Collinge Fold La BB4 85 F4
Collinge St
Padiham BB12 126 C7
Rawtenstall BB4 85 F4
Collingham Pk LA1 215 A2
Colling St 9 BL0 50 B5
Collingwood BB5 124 E2
Collingwood Ave
Blackpool FY3 130 E6
Lytham St Anne's FY8 110 E1
Collingwood Dr 10 LA2 239 B8
Collingwood Pl FY3 130 E6
Collingwood Rd PR7 43 B7
Collingwood St
Colne BB8 171 C4
Standish WN6 29 E1
Collingwood Terr 7 LA2 239 D8
Collins Ave FY2 152 E3
Collins Dr BB5 104 E2
Collin's Hill La PR3 185 A3
Collinson St PR1 118 C1
Collins Rd PR5 97 F1
Collins Rd N PR5 97 F2
Collisdene Rd WN5 10 E6
Collison Ave PR7 43 C8
Colloway Ho LA3 212 E6
Collyhurst Ave FY4 110 E6
Colman Ct PR1 96 D6
Colnbrook WN6 29 B1
COLNE 171 C6
Colne & Broughton Rd BD23 197 C6
COLNE EDGE 171 C7
Colne La BB8 171 E4
Colne Lord Street Sch BB8 171 C5
Colne Rd
Barnoldswick BB18 196 A1
Barrowford BB8, BB9 170 F4
Brierfield BB9 148 B6
Burnley BB10, BB11 128 A8
Burnley, Burnley Lane BB10 148 B3
Kelbrook BB18 195 A7
Trawden BB8 172 B2
Colne Sta BB8 171 C4
Colonnade The LA1 215 C7
Colthirst Dr BB7 190 A2
Colt House Cl PR25 60 A7
Coltsfoot Dr PR6 61 D2
Coltsfoot Wlk LA3 217 B2
Columbia Way BB2 101 B8
Columbine Cl
Chorley PR7 61 A3
Rochdale OL12 52 C3
Colville Ave 1 FY4 110 C5
Colville Rd BB3 81 E4
Colville St BB10 128 A8
Colwall Cl L33 1 A2
Colwall Rd L33 1 A2
Colwall Wlk L33 1 A2
Colwyn Ave
Blackpool FY4 130 E1
Morecambe LA4 217 D6
Colwyn Pl PR2 117 A3
Colyton Cl PR6 43 E8
Colyton Rd PR6 43 E8
Colyton Rd E 2 PR6 43 E8
Combermere Gr LA3 212 E5
Combermere Rd LA3 212 E6
Comer Gdns L31 5 C3
Comet Rd PR26 76 C2
Comet St 8 OL13 88 A7
Commerce St
Bacup OL13 87 F2
Commerce St *continued*
Haslingden BB4 85 A4
Commercial Rd
Chorley PR7 61 C1
Darwen BB3 81 F5
Great Harwood BB6 124 C5
Nelson BB9 148 E8
Commercial St
Bacup OL13 70 D8
Barnoldswick BB18 196 B2
10 Blackpool FY1 130 B1
Brierfield BB9 148 B6
Church BB5 103 E6
12 Great Harwood BB6 124 C5
Oswaldtwistle BB5 103 D3
Rawtenstall BB4 106 A3
Rishton BB1 124 B1
Common Bank Employment Area PR7 42 F8
Common Bank La PR7 42 F8
COMMON EDGE 110 F6
Common Edge Rd FY4 110 F6
Common End PR7 30 E5
Common Garden St 38 LA1 214 F8
Common La PR9 55 C1
Commonside FY8 90 D4
Commons La BB2 121 B5
Common The
Adlington PR7 30 E5
Parbold WN8 27 C3
Commonwealth Cl FY8 90 C8
Como Ave BB11 127 C4
Company St BB1 124 B1
Compley Ave FY6 153 C2
Compley Gn FY6 153 C2
Compression Rd LA3 212 E2
Compston Ave BB4 106 A1
Compton Cl FY6 153 C5
Compton Gn PR2 117 D7
Compton Rd PR8 35 B3
Comrie Cres BB11 127 D3
Concorde Ho 1 FY1 130 C4
Concourse Sh Ctr The WN8 18 B1
Conder Ave FY5 175 F2
Conder Brow LA5 223 E2
CONDER GREEN 210 C5
Conder Green Rd LA2 210 F3
Conder Pl LA1 218 C2
Conder Rd PR2 116 E1
Conder Side Cvn Pk LA2 210 A4
Condor Gr
Blackpool FY1 130 D3
Lytham St Anne's FY8 89 E8
Condor Way PR1 97 A2
Conduit St BB9 170 D1
Coneygarth La
Tunstall LA6 241 D4
Whittington LA6 241 D6
Congleton Cl FY4 131 B1
Congress St PR7 61 C1
Conifer Ct L37 12 A2
Conifers The
Barton PR3 137 B8
Hambleton FY6 177 B2
Kirkham PR4 114 B5
Maghull L31 5 C3
Conisber Cl BL7 47 E1
Coniston Ave
Accrington BB5 103 F4
Adlington PR6 31 B8
Barnoldswick BB18 196 A3
Carleton FY6 153 B4
Euxton PR7 60 D1
Fleetwood FY7 198 E4
Hambleton FY6 177 C2
Knott End-on-S FY6 199 F6
Lytham St Anne's FY8 110 F2
Orrell WN5 10 F7
Padiham BB12 146 C2
Preston PR2 117 D2
Thornton FY5 176 B1
Coniston Cl
Longridge PR3 140 A5
Ramsbottom BL0 50 C7
Coniston Cres FY5 176 B1
Coniston Ct
Morecambe LA4 217 C6
Southport PR8 21 C3
Coniston Dr
Bamber Bridge PR5 97 E2
Darwen BB3 82 C2
Coniston Gr BB8 172 A6
Coniston Ho PR1 96 B4
Coniston Rd
Blackburn BB1 102 A8
Blackpool FY4 110 C7
Blackrod BL6 31 D3
Bolton-le-S LA5 221 A4
Carnforth LA5 221 E8
Chorley PR7 43 B6
Formby L37 11 D2
Fulwood PR2 118 C4
Lancaster LA1 218 E2
Maghull L31 5 E2
Morecambe LA4 217 C6
Coniston St 8 BB12 127 C6
Coniston Way
Bacup OL13 88 A4
Croston PR26 58 B3
Rainford WA11 8 F2
Rishton BB1 123 F1
Connaught Dr FY5 176 D2
Connaught Rd
Heysham LA3 212 D5
Lancaster LA1 215 B5
Connaught Rd *continued*
Preston PR1 96 E5
Consett Ave FY5 175 E5
Constable Ave
Bamber Bridge PR5 77 A7
Burnley BB11 127 F3
CONSTABLE LEE 86 B4
Constable Lee Cres BB4 86 A4
Constable St 8 PR1 97 A8
Convent Cl
Bamber Bridge PR5 97 D1
Leyland PR25 77 C2
Ormskirk L39 15 E2
Convent Cres FY3 131 A8
Conway Ave
Bamber Bridge PR5 97 A1
Blackburn BB1 101 E7
Cleveleys FY5 175 D2
Clitheroe BB7 166 C6
Leyland PR25 60 C8
Normoss FY3 131 B7
Conway Cl
Catterall PR3 181 D2
Euxton PR7 60 E1
Haslingden BB4 85 B1
Ramsbottom BL0 50 B6
Conway Cres
Barnoldswick BB18 196 C3
Ramsbottom BL8 49 F2
Conway Ct
Gregson Lane PR5 98 D2
4 Lytham St Anne's FY8 89 E6
Conway Dr
Bury BL9 33 D2
Fulwood PR2 117 C6
Oswaldtwistle BB5 103 B4
Conway Gr BB10 148 C3
Conway Ho 7 PR1 97 D8
Conway Rd
Eccleston PR7 41 C7
Rawtenstall BB4 86 C2
Conyers Ave PR8 34 F3
Cooke St BL6 32 D4
Cook Gdns BB1 102 B4
Cook Green La PR3 141 C7
Cook House Rd BB8 171 E6
Cookson Cl PR4 93 B6
Cookson Rd FY5 176 B3
Cookson St FY1 130 C5
Cook St BL9 33 A2
Cookwood Ho 13 PR1 96 D8
Coolham La BB18 197 D1
Coolidge Ave LA1 214 D7
Coombes The PR2 117 F5
Cooperage The BB5 103 D3
Co-operation St
2 Bacup OL13 88 A2
1 Newchurch BB4 86 F2
Rawtenstall, Cloughfold BB4 86 B2
4 Rawtenstall, Crawshawbooth BB4 86 A7
Co-operative Bldgs
5 Rawtenstall BB4 69 F7
Walk Mill BB10 107 F8
Co-operative St
1 Bamber Bridge PR5 77 E8
22 Barnoldswick BB18 196 B2
Haslingden BB4 67 F7
Cooper Ct FY5 175 D3
Cooper Hill Cl PR5 97 D5
Cooper Hill Dr PR5 97 D5
Cooperís La PR7 28 B8
Cooper Rd PR1 96 D8
Coopers Cl 5 BB5 103 D3
Coopers Fold PR2 119 A2
Cooper St
Bacup OL13 87 F4
Burnley BB11 128 A5
Horwich BL6 32 B4
Nelson BB9 170 E1
Cooper's Way FY1 130 D7
Coop St FY1 130 B3
Coote La PR4, PR5 76 F7
Copeland Dr WN6 29 F2
Copeland Pl FY8 91 C4
Cop La PR1 96 C4
Cop Lane CE Prim Sch PR1 96 C3
COPP 156 A3
Copperas La BL6 31 B1
Copper Beech Cl PR4 74 E3
Copper Beeches
Blackburn BB2 101 A6
Kingsfold PR1 96 D2
Copperfield Cl BB10 128 F6
Copperfield St BB1 101 F3
Copperwood Way PR7 42 F7
Coppice Ave BB5 104 D7
Coppice Brow LA5 223 F2
Coppice Cl
Chorley PR6 61 E1
Nelson BB9 171 A2
Coppice Dr
Longshaw WN5 10 D2
Whitworth OL12 52 D7
Coppice La PR6 62 C3
Coppice Leys L37 11 E3
Coppice Sch The PR5 97 F1
Coppice St BL9 33 C3
Coppice The
Blackburn BB2 101 A7
Burnley BB11 127 E4
Clayton-le-M BB5 124 F4
Fulwood PR2 117 B4
Kirkham PR4 114 A6
Longton PR4 75 A7
Coppice The *continued*
Morecambe LA4 217 E5
Ramsbottom BL0 50 A4
Coppingford Cl OL12 52 A2
Coppins Gn FY6 153 E1
Copp La PR3, PR4 156 A2
COPPULL 42 E2
Coppull Cross Rds PR7 29 F7
Coppull Ent Ctr PR7 42 E2
Coppull Hall La PR7 30 B8
COPPULL MOOR 29 D6
Coppull Moor La PR7 29 E6
Coppull Parish CE Prim Sch PR7 42 F1
Coppull Prim Sch PR7 42 E1
Coppull Rd
Chorley PR7 43 A4
Maghull L31 5 C4
Coppull St John's CE Prim Sch PR7 29 D6
Cop Royd Terr BB10 128 F1
Copse Cl BB1 101 F7
Copse Rd FY7 198 F2
Copse The
Accrington BB5 103 F5
Chapeltown BL7 48 C2
Chorley PR7 43 B4
Copse View Bsns Pk 12 FY7 198 F2
Copster Dr PR3 140 B7
COPSTER GREEN 122 D8
Copster Hill Cl BB1 82 D8
Cop The FY5 175 D6
Copthurst Ave BB12 146 F6
Copthurst La PR6 61 F7
Copthurst St 18 BB12 146 C1
Coptrod Head Cl OL12 52 E4
Copy Bottom BB10 108 C4
Copy La LA2 237 C3
Copy Nook BB1 102 A5
Coral Cl FY4 131 A1
Corbridge Cl
Blackpool FY4 111 A7
Carleton FY6 153 C5
Corbridge Ct BB7 189 E1
Corcas La FY6 176 F8
Cordwainers Ct PR7 60 E6
Coriander Cl FY2 152 F3
Corka La FY8 112 F1
Cork Rd LA1 215 B5
Cork St BL9 33 A2
Corlass St 10 BB9 170 D3
Corless Cotts LA2 226 A8
Cornbrook WN8 9 E7
Corncroft PR1 96 C3
Cornel Gr BB11 127 C4
Cornelian St BB1 122 F2
Cornelian Way FY3 131 A1
Corner Bank Cl PR4 112 F7
Cornerhouse The 13 BL0 50 C6
CORNER ROW 133 E2
Corners The FY5 175 C4
Cornfield PR4 116 E6
Cornfield Cl PR4 73 E4
Cornfield Gr BB12 127 A8
Cornfield St BB3 82 B2
Cornflower Cl PR6 61 D2
Cornford Rd FY4 111 B8
Cornhill Arc BB5 104 B6
CORNHOLME 109 B1
Cornholme BB10 148 E2
Cornholme Jun & Inf Sch OL14 109 A1
Cornholme Terr 7 OL14 109 B1
Cornmill Ct
Altham BB5 125 E6
Waddington BB7 189 B4
Corn Mill La FY7 199 B4
Corn Mill Lo L31 5 C2
Corn Mill Mews BB7 144 C5
Cornmill Pl BB18 196 B3
Cornmill Terr 6 BB18 196 B3
Corn Mill Yd BB5 124 F2
Corn Mkt LA1 214 F8
Cornthwaite Rd PR2 117 E3
Cornwall Ave
Blackburn BB1 102 E4
Blackpool FY2 152 C2
Buckshaw Village PR7 60 F6
Cleveleys FY5 175 F4
Cornwall Cres WN1 30 B1
Cornwall Mews 5 FY5 175 F4
Cornwall Pl
Blackpool FY3 131 B2
Church BB5 103 F7
Cornwall Rd BB1 124 A1
Cornwall Way PR8 21 C2
Corona Ave L31 5 C5
Coronation Ave
Blackburn BB2 80 C7
Formby L37 12 A2
Forton PR3 207 B3
Padiham BB12 126 C7
Coronation Cres 5 PR1 97 B7
Coronation Ct PR26 58 B3
Coronation Gr BB4 86 E1
Coronation Mount LA6 242 C3
Coronation Pl 6 BB9 170 D3
Coronation Rd
Brierfield BB9 148 C5
Cleveleys FY5 175 C2
Kirkham PR4 114 A5
Lytham St Anne's FY8 90 C4
Maghull L31 5 D3
Coronation St
Barnoldswick BB18 196 C2
Blackpool FY1 130 B4
Great Harwood BB6 124 D6
Coronation Terr BB6 143 C1
Coronation Way LA1 218 E4
Coronation Wlk PR8 35 A7
Coronet Cl WN6 19 C7
Corporation Ct 10 OL13 70 D8
Corporation St
Accrington BB5 104 A5
11 Blackburn BB2 101 E5
Blackpool FY1 130 B5
Chorley PR6 61 D1
6 Clitheroe BB7 166 D8
Colne BB8 171 A3
Preston PR1 96 F8
4 Southport PR8 35 B7
Corpus Christi RC Sports Coll PR2 117 E5
Corranstone Cl BL6 32 B3
Corrib Rd FY2 152 D2
Corringham Rd LA4 217 B5
Corston Gr BL6 31 D1
Corwen Cl BB1 101 E7
Cosford St PR4 132 E6
Cosgate Cl 1 WN5 10 E5
COTE HOLME 103 D6
Cotman Cl OL13 71 B8
Cotswold Ave PR7 60 D1
Cotswold Cl
Eccleston PR7 41 D6
Ramsbottom BL0 50 C4
Cotswold Dr BL6 32 C5
Cotswold Rd
Blackpool FY2 152 D1
Chorley PR7 43 C6
Lytham St Anne's FY8 91 D5
Cottage Cl L39 15 D4
Cottage Fields PR7 43 B5
Cottage Gdns PR5 78 B8
Cottage La
Bamber Bridge PR5 97 F3
Ormskirk L39 15 D5
Cottage Mews L39 15 D5
Cottage Mus* LA1 214 E8
Cottage View OL12 52 C7
Cottage Wlk OL12 52 C4
COTTAM 116 D5
Cottam Ave PR2 117 A4
Cottam Cl
Lytham St Anne's FY8 110 F2
Whalley BB7 144 C5
Cottam Ct PR2 117 A2
Cottam Gn PR4 116 F6
Cottam Hall La PR2 116 F5
Cottam La PR2 117 A2
Cottam Pl FY6 153 C2
Cottam Prim Sch PR4 116 D5
Cottam St PR7 43 C6
Cottam Way PR4 116 D4
Cottesloe Pl BB9 170 C3
Cottesmore Cl OL12 52 C6
Cottesmore Pl FY3 131 A6
Cottom Croft BB5 124 F4
Cotton Ct
2 Colne BB8 171 C3
Preston PR1 97 A8
Cotton Dr L39 15 D6
Cotton Hall St BB3 82 A2
Cotton Spinners Ct BB3 82 B1
Cotton St
Accrington BB5 104 B5
Burnley BB12 127 D7
Padiham BB12 126 C7
COTTON TREE 172 B4
Cotton Tree La BB8 172 A5
Cottys Brow PR9 53 F3
Coudray Rd PR9 53 E1
Coulston Ave FY2 152 B3
Coulston Rd LA1 215 B6
Coultate St 7 BB12 127 C6
Coulter Beck La LA6 242 A7
Coulthurst St 1 BL0 50 B6
Coulton Rd BB9 148 B7
Counsell Ct 3 FY5 176 B2
Countess Cl PR4 114 A7
Countess Cres FY2 152 C3
Countess Rd BB3 82 A7
Countess St BB5 104 A6
Countessway 3 PR5 97 E1
Countess Way PR7 60 D2
Country Mews BB2 100 F8
County Ave LA1 211 B8
County Brook La BB8, BB18 194 C4
County Cl PR26 77 A4
County Rd
Kirkby L33 1 A1
Ormskirk L39 15 E6
County St LA1 214 E8
Coupe Gn PR5 98 E4
COUPE GREEN 98 E4
Coupe Green Prim Sch PR5 98 E4
Coupland Cl OL12 52 C8
Courage Low La WN6 28 D5
Course La L40, WN8 26 D1
Courtfield L39 15 D7
Courtfield Ave FY2 130 D8
Courtfields 3 FY1 130 C4
Court Gr BB1 122 E6
Courtgreen L39 15 D7
Court Hey L31 5 E1
Court Mews PR9 54 A1

Court Rd PR9 35 C8
Court Royal FY8 90 E3
Court The
Fulwood PR2 117 C7
Higher Penwortham PR1 96 C4
Southport PR9 35 B8
Courtyard The
7 Bacup OL13 88 A3
11 Burnley BB11 128 B4
Cleveleys FY5 175 D1
1 Kirkham PR4 113 F5
Courtyard Works L33 1 C2
Cousin's La L40 39 A3
Cove Dr LA5 224 C4
Covell Ho 3 LA1 214 E8
Coventry St 2 PR7 43 C6
Cove Rd LA5 224 B4
Coverdale Dr BB2 80 D7
Coverdale Rd LA1 214 D8
Coverdale Way 4 BB12 127 D7
Covert Cl PR8 36 A2
Covertside Rd PR8 36 A2
Covert The FY5 175 F4
Cove The
Cleveleys FY5 175 C4
Lytham St Anne's FY8 90 D3
Morecambe LA4 217 E7
Coveway Ave FY3 130 E6
Cowan Brae BB1 101 D6
COWAN BRIDGE 242 A7
COW ARK 187 C8
Cowdrey Mews 8 LA1 218 B1
Cowell Way 8 BB2 101 D5
Cowes Ave 2 BB4 85 C2
Cowgarth La BB18 197 C2
Cow Gate La BD23 231 E7
Cowgill St
14 Bacup OL13 88 A3
Earby BB18 197 B1
COW HILL 119 A8
Cowhill La BB1 102 F7
Cow La BB11 127 F6
Cowley Cres BB12 126 E7
Cowley Rd
Blackpool FY4 110 F8
Fulwood PR2 118 E4
COWLING 43 F6
Cowling Brow PR6 43 E7
Cowling Brow Ind Est PR6 43 F6
Cowling Bsns Pk PR6 43 F6
Cowling La PR25 76 D1
Cowling Rd PR6 43 F6
Cowm Park Way N OL12 71 D2
Cowm Park Way S OL12 71 C1
Cowm St OL12 71 E5
COWPE 69 F6
Cowper Ave 1 BB7 189 E1
Cowpe Rd BB4 69 F7
Cowper Pl BB7 230 C1
Cowper St
Blackburn BB1 101 F7
Burnley BB11 127 C5
Cowslip Way PR6 61 D2
Cowtoot La OL13 88 A4
Cow Well La PR6 61 B8
Coxfield Gr WN6 19 D7
Cox Green Cl BL7 47 D3
Cox Green Rd BL7 47 E2
Coyford Dr PR9 54 A4
Crabtree Ave
Bacup OL13 88 A1
Higher Penwortham PR1 96 A3
Newchurch BB4 86 F2
Crabtree Bldgs BB4 86 F4
Crabtree Cl L40 25 D4
Crabtree La L40 25 D6
Crabtree Orch 3 FY5 176 B3
Crabtree Rd FY5 176 B3
Crabtree St
Blackburn BB1 102 B5
Brierfield BB9 148 B5
Colne BB8 171 C4
Whitewell Bottom BB4 86 F4
Cracoe Gill BB9 170 C3
Craddock Rd BB8 171 E5
Crag Ave BL9 50 D2
CRAG BANK 221 C8
Crag Bank Cres LA5 221 C8
Crag Bank La LA5 223 B1
Crag Bank Rd LA5 221 C8
CRAG FOOT 222 F8
Cragg Bottom Rd BD22 174 F1
Cragg Row BB18 194 D7
Craggs Hill LA6 237 B8
Craggs La LA2 239 D3
Cragg's Row 13 PR1 96 F8
Cragg St
1 Blackpool FY1 130 B3
Colne BB8 171 C5
Crag La BL9 50 D2
Crag Rd
Lancaster LA1 218 F1
Warton LA5 223 A6
Craigflower Ct PR5 78 C7
Craigholme House Pk LA5 223 B1
Craiglands Ave LA3 216 D2
Craiglands Ct LA1 214 C5
Craig St LA3 216 D3
Crail Pl OL10 33 F1
Crake Ave FY7 198 C2
Crake Bank 4 LA1 218 A2
Crambe Hts BB3 82 A7
Cranberry Bottoms BB3 65 E5
Cranberry Chase 4 BB3 65 C7
Cranberry Cl BB3 65 D6
CRANBERRY FOLD 65 D5
Cranberry Fold Ct BB3 65 D5
Cranberry La BB3 65 D6
Cranberry Rise BB4 106 A2
Cranborne Cl
Horwich BL6 32 F1
Standish WN6 29 D1
Cranborne St 10 PR1 97 C8
Cranborne Terr BB2 101 C6
Cranbourne Dr
Chorley PR6 43 E7
Church BB5 104 A8
Cranbourne Gr FY5 153 E7
Cranbourne St
7 Bamber Bridge PR5 77 E8
Chorley PR6 43 D7
Colne BB8 171 E6
Cranbrook Ave
Blackpool FY2 152 E5
Oswaldtwistle BB5 103 C4
Cranbrook St BB2 101 D2
Cranbury Ct FY5 175 D3
Cranesbill Cl FY6 199 F6
Cranes La L40 16 E7
Crane St PR7 29 D6
Cranfield View BB3 65 C6
Crangle Fold BB7 190 A2
Crank Rd WN5 10 D1
Crankshaw St 22 BB4 86 A3
Cranleigh Ave FY2 152 C3
Cranleigh Cl BL6 31 D1
Cranmer St 5 BB11 127 E6
Cranshaw Dr BB1 101 F8
Cranston Rd L33 1 C2
Cranwell Ave LA1 215 B5
Cranwell Cl 2 BB1 102 A4
Cranwell Ct PR4 113 F5
Craven Cl PR2 117 F7
Craven Cnr 8 FY5 152 F7
Craven Ct BL6 32 D2
Cravendale Ave BB9 170 F3
Craven Dr PR5 77 D7
Craven St E BL6 32 D2
Craven's Ave BB2 81 E7
Craven's Brow BB2 81 E7
Cravens Hollow BB2 81 D6
Cravens Hollows BB2 81 E6
Craven St
Accrington BB5 104 A5
6 Barnoldswick BB18 196 C2
Brierfield BB9 148 B5
Burnley BB11 128 A5
Bury BL9 33 C3
Clitheroe BB7 166 E7
Colne BB8 172 A5
Nelson BB9 148 C8
Rawtenstall BB4 85 F2
Cravenwood Cl BB5 103 F5
CRAWFORD 9 E2
Crawford Ave
Adlington PR7 30 E5
Blackpool FY2 152 D5
Chorley PR7 43 B7
Leyland PR25 60 B8
Maghull L31 5 B3
Preston PR1 118 F1
Crawford Rd WN8 9 D2
Crawford St BB9 170 E1
Crawford Village Prim Sch WN8 9 E3
CRAWSHAWBOOTH 86 A8
Crawshawbooth Prim Sch BB4 86 A8
Crawshaw Dr BB4 86 A6
Crawshaw Grange BB4 86 A7
Crawshaw La BB10 149 D6
Crawshaw's Bldgs BB4 86 A1
Crawshaw St 2 BB5 104 B6
Crediton Ave PR9 54 B5
Crediton Cl 5 BB2 81 C8
Crescent Ave
Cleveleys FY5 175 D2
Formby L37 11 E1
Crescent Ct FY4 110 A5
Crescent E FY5 175 D2
Crescent Gn L39 15 B1
Crescent Rd
Poulton-le-F FY6 153 E4
Southport PR8 34 F3
Crescent St PR1 118 C1
Crescent The
Bamber Bridge PR5 77 C8
Bamber Bridge, School Lane PR5 97 F2
Blackburn BB2 100 E1
Blackpool FY4 110 B7
Burnley BB10 148 B4
Carleton FY6 153 C4
Chorley PR7 61 C2
Clitheroe BB7 166 D7
Colne BB8 171 E6
Dunsop Bridge BB7 228 C5
Fleetwood FY7 175 E8
Freckleton PR4 93 C5
Hest Bank LA2 220 D1
Horwich BL6 32 E1
Lytham St Anne's FY8 89 E6
Preesall FY6 200 B4
Preesall Park FY6 200 D1
Preston, Ashton-on-R PR2 117 B2
Crescent The *continued*
1 Preston, Lea PR2 116 D1
Southport PR9 54 C3
Warton PR4 92 C4
Whalley BB7 144 A6
Whitworth OL12 52 C8
Worsthorne BB10 129 A5
Crescent W FY5 175 D2
Cressell Pk WN6 29 B1
Cresswood Ave FY5 175 D1
Crestway
Blackpool FY3 130 F6
Tarleton PR4 57 A8
Creswell Ave PR2 116 F3
Creswick Ave BB11 127 F3
Creswick Cl BB11 127 F3
Crewdson St BB3 81 F2
Crewgarth Rd LA3 217 B2
Cribden End La BB4 85 D4
Cribden La BB4 85 E5
CRIBDEN SIDE 85 C5
Cribden St BB4 85 F4
Criccieth Cl 3 BB4 85 B1
Criccieth Pl FY5 176 D2
Crichton Pl FY4 110 B5
Cricketers Cl BB5 103 C2
Cricketers Gn PR7 41 B6
Cricket Path
Formby L37 11 F5
Southport PR8 34 F3
Crimbles La LA2 206 B2
Crimea St 5 OL13 88 A2
Crime Well La LA3 212 E7
Crinan Sq OL10 33 F1
Cringle Way BB7 190 A2
Cripple Gate WN6 29 A2
Cripple Gate La PR5 99 C4
Critchley Cl PR4 74 F3
Croasdale 7 LA1 218 A2
Croasdale Ave
Burnley BB10 148 E2
Fulwood PR2 118 E4
Croasdale Cl LA5 223 C1
Croasdale Dr
Cleveleys FY5 175 F4
Clitheroe BB7 166 F7
Parbold WN8 27 C3
Croasdale Sq BB1 102 A3
Croasdale Wlk FY3 131 B8
Crockleford Ave PR8 35 E3
Crocus Cl BB4 67 F8
Crocus Field PR25 60 A7
CROFT 196 B2
Croft Acres BL0 68 D2
Croft Ave
Burscough L40 25 F3
Orrell WN5 10 D5
Slyne LA2 218 C8
Croft Bank PR1 96 C3
Croft Cl BB4 86 A5
Croft Ct
Fleetwood FY7 198 E2
Freckleton PR4 93 B6
Southport PR9 54 C4
Thornton FY5 176 C4
Crofters Bank BB4 106 A1
Crofters Fold
Galgate LA2 211 B4
Morecambe LA3 216 E1
Crofters Gn
Euxton PR7 60 C3
Preston PR1 117 E2
Crofters La L33 1 A5
Crofters Mdw PR26 76 E3
Crofters Mews 12 FY1 130 C7
Crofters Wlk
4 Kingsfold PR1 96 D2
Lytham St Anne's FY8 90 E7
Croft Field L31 5 E1
Croftgate PR2 117 F5
Croft Head Rd BB1 123 B1
Croft Hey L40 39 B4
Croft Heys L39 15 B1
Croft Ho FY6 153 D4
Croft La BB12 146 F6
Croftland Gdns LA5 221 B6
Croftlands
Borwick LA6 240 B3
12 Lancaster LA1 214 E8
Orrell WN5 10 D4
1 Ramsbottom BL0 50 A3
Warton LA5 223 E6
Croft Manor PR4 93 C6
Croft Mdw PR5 78 C6
Crofton Ave FY2 152 D5
Croft Pk PR25 77 D1
Croft Rd PR6 43 E7
Crofts Cl PR4 114 C5
Crofts Dr 7 PR2 139 D1
Croftson Ave L39 15 F7
Croft St
Bacup OL13 87 F3
Burnley BB11 128 A5
Bury BL9 33 A2
Clitheroe BB7 166 E7
18 Darwen BB3 82 A1
Earby BB18 197 C2
Great Harwood BB6 124 C4
Morecambe LA4 217 C5
Preston PR1 96 E8
Crofts The PR4 95 A1
Croft The
Blackburn BB1 101 D7
Burton in L LA6 242 C3
Caton LA2 237 C3
Cleveleys FY5 175 D2
Colne BB8 171 E7
Eccleston PR7 41 C7
Croft The *continued*
Euxton PR7 60 B3
Fleetwood FY7 198 E2
Garstang PR3 204 B1
Goosnargh PR3 138 D6
Great Plumpton PR4 112 E7
Hoghton PR5 99 B2
Lytham St Anne's FY8 111 B1
Maghull L31 5 B5
Orrell WN5 10 D3
Poulton-le-F FY6 153 D2
Thornton-in-C BD23 197 B5
Warton LA5 223 E6
Croft Way FY5 153 C8
Croftwood Terr BB2 101 A1
Croichbank BL8 49 B2
Croichley Fold BL8 49 D2
Cromarty Sq OL10 33 F1
Crombleholme Rd PR1 118 E1
Cromer Ave BB10 148 C1
Cromer Gr BB10 148 C1
Cromer Pl
Blackburn BB1 101 E7
Fulwood PR2 117 A4
Cromer Rd
Blackpool FY2 152 E4
Lytham St Anne's FY8 111 A1
Southport PR8 34 E2
Cromfield L39 15 C2
Cromford Wlk 9 PR1 97 C8
Crompton Ave FY4 110 F7
Crompton Ct 23 PR1 97 A8
Crompton Pl BB2 101 C5
Crompton St PR1 118 C1
Cromwell Ave 1 PR1 96 C3
Cromwell Cl L39 15 C2
Cromwell Mews PR3 181 C8
Cromwell Rd
Blackpool FY1 130 C7
Fulwood PR2 118 D3
Higher Penwortham PR1 96 C3
Lancaster LA1 214 E6
Cromwell St
Accrington BB5 104 B8
20 Blackburn BB1 102 A4
Burnley BB12 127 F8
Foulridge BB8 194 D1
4 Preston PR1 118 A1
Cromwell Terr 12 BB9 170 D3
Cromwell Way PR1 96 F1
Cronkeyshaw Ave OL12 52 E2
Cronkeyshaw Rd OL12 52 F1
Cronkshaw St BB10 128 A7
Cronshaw Dr BB6 143 C1
Crookall Cl 7 FY7 198 F2
Crook Dale La FY6 177 E7
Crooked La 19 PR1 97 A8
Crooked Shore OL13 87 F3
Crookfield Rd BL7 64 B3
Crook Gate La PR3 178 E1
Crookhalgh Ave BB10 128 F6
Crookhey Gdns LA2 206 E3
Crookhey Hall Sch LA2 206 E3
Crookings La PR1 96 A6
Crooklands Dr PR3 181 C8
Crooklands Gdns FY6 177 D2
Crookleigh Pl 3 LA3 216 D2
Crook Nook LA3 213 B2
Crook O'Lune Cvn Pk LA2 219 F5
Crook St
Adlington PR7 30 F7
Chorley PR7 43 B5
Preston PR1 97 B8
Cropper Gdns PR4 73 D3
Cropper Rd FY4 111 C6
Cropper Rd N FY4 111 C7
Cropper's La L39 16 A1
Cropton Rd L37 11 F3
Crosby Cl BB3 65 B6
Crosby Ct FY8 110 F1
Crosby Gr FY3 130 F3
Crosby Pl PR2 117 A4
Crosby Rd
Blackburn BB2 101 E1
Lytham St Anne's FY8 110 F1
Southport PR8 35 A3
Crosby St 1 OL12 52 F2
Crosfield Ave BL9 50 C2
Crosier Wlk PR4 116 E5
Crosland Rd L32 1 A1
Crosland Rd N FY8 90 A8
Crosland Rd S FY8 90 A8
Crosley Cl BB5 104 B3
Cross Bank 9 BB12 126 D8
Cross Barn Gr BB3 65 B8
Cross Barn La L38 3 E3
Cross Barn Wlk 5 BB3 65 B8
Cross Bldgs 19 BB4 86 A7
Cross Brow PR7 42 C8
Crossdale Ave 5 LA3 216 D2
Crossdale Sq 10 LA1 215 A8
Cross Edge BB5 104 A1
Crosse Hall La PR6 43 F7
Crosse Hall St PR6 43 F7
CROSSENS 54 C4
Crossens Way PR9 54 C6
Cross Field PR4 95 C1
Crossfield Rd WN8 9 C8
Crossfield St BB2 101 F3
Cross Flatts Cres BB18 194 E8
Cross Fold
Blackburn BB1 101 F2
Grindleton BB7 190 B8
Cross Gates BB6 124 C5
CROSSGILL 237 E1
Crossgill Pl 7 LA1 218 B2
Cross Gn L37 12 A2
Cross Green Cl L37 12 A2
Cross Green Rd PR2 117 E6
Cross Hagg St BB8 171 C4
Crosshall Brow L40 16 C4
Cross Hall Ct L39 16 A4
Cross Halls PR1 96 C3
Cross Helliwell St 17 BB8 171 D4
Cross Hill Ct LA5 221 A4
Cross Hill Four Lane Ends PR3 226 B6
Cross Hill La BB7 231 B1
Crosshill Rd BB2 101 B5
Crosshills 5 BB12 146 C1
Crosshill Specl Sch BB1 102 C2
Cross Hos PR7 42 C8
Crossings The PR5 99 B2
Cross Keys Dr PR6 61 C7
Cross La
Barley Green BB12 169 C4
Halsall L39 23 C1
Low Bentham LA2 239 B8
Orrell WN5 10 D3
Ramsbottom BL8 50 A6
Salterforth BB18 194 E8
Treales PR4 134 D1
Waddington BB7 188 E5
Crossland Rd FY4 130 E1
Crosslands LA6 241 D7
Crossland St BB5 104 A5
Crossley Fold BB11 127 D4
Crossley House Ind Est PR1 96 E4
Cross Meanygate L40 38 C5
CROSSMOOR 156 E1
Cross Rd LA2 239 B7
Cross St N BB4 85 B5
Cross St S BB4 85 B4
Cross St W BB8 171 B4
Cross School St 5 BB8 171 D4
Cross Skelton St 6 BB8 171 E5
Cross St
Accrington BB5 104 C5
11 Bacup OL13 88 A3
Blackburn BB3 81 F7
Blackpool FY1 130 B7
Brierfield BB9 148 B5
Burnley, Harle Syke BB10 148 F3
Chorley PR7 61 C1
Clayton-le-M BB5 124 E3
Clitheroe BB7 166 D8
Darwen BB3 65 B7
Earby BB18 197 A1
Fleetwood FY7 199 B5
Great Harwood BB6 124 D5
Higham BB12 146 F6
3 Leyland PR25 77 B2
Longridge PR3 140 A6
Lytham St Anne's FY8 89 D8
3 Morecambe LA4 217 C5
Nelson BB9 148 D8
Oswaldtwistle BB5 103 D4
Preston PR1 96 F7
Ramsbottom BL0 50 C6
18 Rawtenstall BB4 86 A7
Southport PR8 35 B6
Standish WN6 29 E1
Worsthorne BB10 129 B6
Cross Swords Cl PR7 43 A5
Cross The L38 3 E4
Cross Way FY5 175 D4
Crossways BB7 189 D7
CROSTON 58 B2
Croston Ave PR6 31 A8
Croston Barn La PR3 181 A8
Croston Cl 6 BB1 102 B5
Croston Close Rd BL9, OL12 51 C4
Croston Dr L40 39 B6
Croston La PR7 42 B2
Croston Rd
Croston L40, PR26 39 C7
Farington PR26 76 F6
Garstang PR3 181 B8
Leyland PR26 76 E4
Croston's Brow PR9 53 F3
Croston St BB1 102 C5
Croston Sta PR26 58 B3
Crowborough Cl BL6 32 F1
Crowder Ave FY5 176 B2
Crowell Way PR5 97 E3
Crow Foot Row BB18 196 B1
Crow Hills Rd PR1 96 A6
Crow La
Ramsbottom BL0 50 C6
Skelmersdale WN8 18 F3
Town End PR3 155 E8
Crowland Cl PR9 36 A6
Crowland St PR9 36 A6
Crowland Way L37 12 B2
Crowle St PR1 97 D8
Crown Bldgs PR8 21 F8
Crown Cl L37 12 A2
Crowndale BL7 48 D7
Crownest Ind Est BB18 196 C3
Crownest Rd BB18 196 C3
Crown Gdns BL7 48 D6
Crown La
Fleetwood FY7 199 B4
Horwich BL6 32 A4

Crown La *continued*
Swillbrook PR4 ... 136 B2
Crownlee PR1 ... 96 A3
Crown Mews 3 PR4 ... 114 A5
Crown Point BL7 ... 48 D6
Crown Point Rd BB11 ... 127 E1
Crown St
Accrington BB5 ... 104 A5
3 Chorley PR7 ... 43 C8
Darwen BB3 ... 65 A8
Leyland PR25 ... 77 B3
Preston PR1 ... 96 F8
Crown Way BB8 ... 171 C5
Crow Orchard Prim Sch WN8 ... 17 F2
Crow Orchard Rd WN6 ... 29 A1
Crow Park La BB7 ... 231 C4
Crowshaw Dr OL12 ... 52 E3
Crowther Ct BB10 ... 129 B6
Crowther St
Burnley BB11 ... 128 B4
Clayton-le-M BB5 ... 124 E3
Crowthorn Rd BL7 ... 67 A1
Crow Tree Ave 4 OL13 ... 70 B8
Crowtrees 3 LA2 ... 239 B8
Crow Trees Brow BB7 ... 190 D4
Crow Trees Gdns BB7 ... 190 D5
Crowtrees Gr BB9 ... 169 F5
Crow Trees La BL7 ... 48 C7
Crowtrees Pk BD23 ... 236 D2
Crowtrees Rd BB7 ... 145 F8
Crow Wood Ave BB12 ... 127 D7
Crow Wood Ct BB12 ... 127 E7
Crow Wood Rd BB4 ... 68 D6
Croxteth Cl L31 ... 5 E3
Croxton Wlk 8 BL6 ... 32 B4
Croyde Cl PR9 ... 54 B5
Croyde Rd FY8 ... 90 A5
Croydon Rd 5 FY3 ... 130 E7
Croydon St BB2 ... 101 C5
Crummock Pl 2 FY4 ... 131 C1
Crummock Rd PR1 ... 119 A1
Crumpax Ave PR3 ... 140 A8
Crumpax Croft PR3 ... 140 A8
Crumpax Gdns PR3 ... 140 A7
Crumpax Mdw PR3 ... 140 A8
Crystal Gr FY8 ... 89 E8
Crystal Lo 3 FY8 ... 90 C4
Crystal Mews FY1 ... 130 B1
Crystal Rd
Blackpool FY1 ... 130 B1
Thornton FY5 ... 176 B5
Cuba Ind Est BL0 ... 50 C8
Cuba St 2 BB9 ... 148 D8
Cub St PR26 ... 77 A4
Cuckoo Brow BB1 ... 101 D8
Cuckoo La
Bury, Heap Bridge BL9 ... 33 C2
Bury, Topping Fold BL9 ... 33 C3
Cuckstool La BB12 ... 147 E6
CUDDY HILL ... 136 B7
Cudworth Rd FY8 ... 110 F1
Cuerdale La PR5 ... 98 D6
Cuerdale St BB10 ... 148 E3
Cuerden Ave PR25 ... 59 D7
Cuerden Church Sch PR5 ... 77 F8
Cuerden Cl PR5 ... 77 E4
CUERDEN GREEN ... 77 C6
Cuerden Green Mills 7 PR5 ... 77 B7
Cuerden Residential Cvn Pk PR25 ... 77 E3
Cuerden Rise PR5 ... 77 C7
Cuerden St
Chorley PR6 ... 43 E7
Colne BB8 ... 171 B3
Cuerden Valley Pk* PR5 ... 77 F3
Cuerden Way PR5 ... 77 D7
Culbeck La PR7 ... 59 F2
Culshaw St
3 Blackburn BB1 ... 102 A5
Burnley BB10 ... 128 C5
Culshaw Way L40 ... 23 F7
Culvert La WN8 ... 27 A2
Cumberland Ave
Blackpool FY1 ... 130 D4
Burnley BB12 ... 127 A6
Clayton-le-M BB5 ... 125 A3
Cleveleys FY5 ... 175 E4
Leyland PR25 ... 59 E7
Cumberland Cl BB3 ... 65 C6
Cumberland Rd PR8 ... 35 D5
Cumberland St
12 Blackburn BB1 ... 102 A4
5 Colne BB8 ... 171 E5
Nelson BB9 ... 170 E1
Cumberland View 2 LA1 ... 215 A6
Cumberland View Cl LA3 ... 216 D3
Cumberland View Rd LA3 ... 216 D3
Cumbria Ct PR9 ... 35 C7
Cumbrian Ave FY3 ... 130 E7
Cumbrian Way BB12 ... 127 B8
Cumeragh La PR3 ... 139 C6
CUMERAGH VILLAGE ... 138 F6
Cummins Ave L37 ... 11 E5
Cunliffe Ave BL0 ... 50 A4
Cunliffe Cl BB1 ... 123 B1
Cunliffe Ct BB5 ... 124 F2
Cunliffe Ho BB4 ... 86 D1
Cunliffe La BB7 ... 144 F8
Cunliffe Rd
Blackburn BB1 ... 123 C1
Blackpool FY1 ... 130 D2
Cunliffe St
Chorley PR7 ... 43 D7
11 Preston PR1 ... 97 A8
Ramsbottom BL0 ... 50 C7
Cunnery Mdw PR25 ... 77 E1
Cunningham Ave PR7 ... 43 A6
Cunningham Ct LA1 ... 214 E5
Cunningham Gr BB12 ... 127 B6
Cunscough La L31, L39 ... 6 D3
Curate St
Chorley PR6 ... 61 E1
Great Harwood BB6 ... 124 C5
Curlew Cl
Blackburn BB1 ... 101 E8
2 Cleveleys FY5 ... 175 F4
Leyland PR25 ... 59 C7
Oswaldtwistle BB5 ... 103 D3
Curlew Gdns BB11 ... 127 C5
Curlew Gr LA3 ... 212 F5
Curlew La L40 ... 38 E2
Curteis St BL6 ... 32 B4
Curtis Dr 1 FY7 ... 198 D3
Curtis St 8 BB4 ... 86 A3
Curven Edge BB4 ... 68 A7
Curve St OL13 ... 87 F1
Curwen Ave LA3 ... 212 E6
Curwen La PR3 ... 160 C2
Curwen St 7 PR1 ... 118 C1
Curzon Pl BB2 ... 101 C3
Curzon Rd
Lytham St Anne's FY8 ... 90 A7
Poulton-le-F FY6 ... 153 E3
Southport PR8 ... 35 E5
Curzon St
10 Burnley BB11 ... 127 F6
1 Clitheroe BB7 ... 166 D7
Colne BB8 ... 171 E4
Cusson Rd L33 ... 1 B1
Custom House La FY7 ... 199 C5
Customs Way PR2 ... 96 C8
Cutgate Rd OL12 ... 52 B1
Cuthbert FY8 ... 90 E3
Cut La
Haskayne L39, L40 ... 14 F6
Rishton BB1 ... 123 F1
Rochdale OL12 ... 52 A1
Cutler Cl BB2 ... 101 C5
Cutler Cres OL13 ... 70 D7
Cutler La
Bacup OL13 ... 70 D7
Hesketh Lane PR3 ... 162 C8
Cutt Cl PR26 ... 58 F6
Cutts La FY6 ... 177 F2
Cyclamen Cl PR25 ... 77 E2
Cygnet Cl L39 ... 15 C2
Cygnet Ct L33 ... 1 A2
Cypress Ave FY5 ... 175 E2
Cypress Cl
Clayton-le-W PR25 ... 77 E2
Fulwood PR2 ... 119 A4
Cypress Gr
Bamber Bridge PR5 ... 77 B8
7 Blackpool FY3 ... 130 D7
Cypress Rd PR8 ... 35 F6
Cypress Ridge BB2 ... 80 F8
Cyprus Ave FY8 ... 90 B4
Cyprus Rd LA3 ... 212 E7
Cyprus St BB3 ... 65 B6

D

Dacre Way PR4 ... 116 D5
Daffodil Cl
Haslingden BB4 ... 68 A8
Rochdale OL12 ... 52 E3
Dagger Rd PR4 ... 115 C8
Daggers Hall La FY4 ... 110 E8
Daggers La FY6 ... 200 B3
Dahlia Cl
Blackburn BB3 ... 82 B7
Clayton-le-W PR25 ... 77 E2
Rochdale OL12 ... 52 D3
Dailton Rd WN8 ... 10 A7
Daisy Bank
11 Bacup OL13 ... 87 F3
Lancaster LA1 ... 215 D7
6 Rawtenstall BB4 ... 69 F7
Daisy Bank Cl PR25 ... 76 D1
Daisy Bank Cres BB10 ... 128 E5
Daisy Bank St 2 OL14 ... 109 B1
Daisy Croft PR2 ... 95 D8
DAISYFIELD ... 102 A6
Daisyfield 9 BL6 ... 32 D1
Daisyfield Mill BB1 ... 102 A5
Daisyfield Prim Sch BB1 ... 102 A6
Daisyfields PR4 ... 116 F7
Daisyfield St BB3 ... 81 E5
Daisy Fold PR6 ... 61 E2
DAISY HILL ... 60 D1
Daisy Hill BB4 ... 86 A3
Daisy Hill Ct BB5 ... 125 E1
Daisy Hill Dr PR6 ... 31 A8
Daisy Hill Fold PR7 ... 60 D1
Daisy La
Blackburn BB1 ... 101 F6
Preston PR1 ... 118 C3
Ring o'Bells L40 ... 26 B4
Daisy Mdw PR5 ... 78 B5
Daisy St
Blackburn BB1 ... 102 A6
Colne BB8 ... 171 D4
4 Lancaster LA1 ... 218 D3
Daisy Way PR8 ... 35 C2
Dalby Cl
Blackpool FY5 ... 152 F7
Preston PR1 ... 118 D3
Dalby Cres BB2 ... 101 A1
Dalby Lea BB2 ... 101 A1
Dale Ave
1 Euxton PR7 ... 60 D1
Longton PR4 ... 74 E8
Slyne LA2 ... 218 C8
Dale Cl
Burnley BB12 ... 127 D6
Maghull L31 ... 5 C2
Parbold WN8 ... 27 B2
Dale Cres BB2 ... 80 E7
Dalecrest WN5 ... 10 D1
Dale Dyke Wlk FY6 ... 153 B3
Daleford Cl FY5 ... 153 C8
Dalegarth Cl FY4 ... 131 C1
Dalehead Rd PR25 ... 60 B7
Dale La L33 ... 1 B4
Dale Mill BB4 ... 86 F2
Dale St E BL6 ... 32 D2
Dale St W BL6 ... 32 D2
Dales Ct FY4 ... 110 D6
Dalesford BB4 ... 85 B1
Dale St
Accrington BB5 ... 104 A6
Bacup OL13 ... 87 F3
8 Bacup, Stacksteads OL13 ... 70 C8
Blackburn BB2 ... 101 D4
Blackpool FY1 ... 130 B3
Brierfield BB9 ... 148 A5
Burnley BB12 ... 127 D6
Colne BB8 ... 171 C5
Earby BB18 ... 197 B2
Haslingden BB4 ... 85 B3
Lancaster LA1 ... 215 A7
Nelson BB9 ... 148 C8
4 Oswaldtwistle BB5 ... 103 E4
Preston PR1 ... 97 B8
Ramsbottom BL0 ... 68 C1
Dales The BB6 ... 123 A8
Dale Street Mews 7 FY1 ... 130 B3
Dalesview Cres LA3 ... 212 F7
Dales View Pk Cvn Pk BB18 ... 194 B7
Dalesway BB9 ... 170 C3
Dales Wlk L37 ... 12 A6
Dale Terr BB7 ... 190 D5
Dale View
Billington BB7 ... 144 B4
Blackburn BB2 ... 81 E6
Chorley PR7 ... 43 C4
Earby BB18 ... 197 A1
6 Rawtenstall BB4 ... 85 F1
Dalewood Ave FY4 ... 130 E1
Dalglish Dr BB2 ... 81 D7
Dalkeith Ave FY3 ... 131 A2
Dalkeith Rd BB9 ... 148 C8
Dallam Ave LA4 ... 217 C6
Dallam Dell FY5 ... 176 B4
Dallas Ct LA4 ... 217 F4
Dallas Rd
Lancaster LA1 ... 214 E7
5 Morecambe LA4 ... 217 F4
Dallas St PR1 ... 117 E2
Dall St BB11 ... 128 A4
Dalmore Rd PR2 ... 117 A3
DALTON
Burton-in-Kendal ... 240 D7
Skelmersdale ... 18 C5
Dalton Ave FY4 ... 110 D5
Dalton Cl
Blackburn BB1 ... 102 B5
Ramsbottom BL0 ... 50 A4
Dalton Ct BB3 ... 81 F5
Dalton Hall Bsns Ctr LA6 ... 240 C7
Dalton La LA6 ... 240 C7
Dalton Rd
Lancaster LA1 ... 215 A8
Morecambe LA3 ... 216 D3
Dalton St Michael's CE Prim Sch WN8 ... 18 D5
Dalton Sq LA1 ... 214 F8
Dalton St
Burnley BB11 ... 127 D3
Lytham St Anne's FY8 ... 89 D8
Nelson BB9 ... 170 E1
Dalweb Ind Pk PR9 ... 55 C3
Dame Fold
Higham BB12 ... 146 F6
12 Padiham BB12 ... 126 C8
Damfield La L31 ... 5 C1
Dam Head Rd BB18 ... 196 B2
Dam La L40 ... 24 C6
DAM SIDE ... 201 D6
Dam Side
2 Barnoldswick BB18 ... 196 B3
Colne BB8 ... 171 D4
Damside Cotts LA2 ... 211 B5
Damside St LA1 ... 214 F8
Damson Cl BB6 ... 143 C6
Dam Top BB4 ... 86 B2
Dam Wood La L40 ... 24 C5
Danbers WN8 ... 9 F6
Dancer La BB7 ... 231 B1
Dandy Row BB3 ... 82 C3
Dandy's Meanygate PR4 ... 56 A8
Dandy Wlk BB1 ... 101 E4
Dane Mews FY6 ... 131 E8
Danesbury Pl 4 FY1 ... 130 C5
Danes Cl PR4 ... 114 C5
Danes Dr PR5 ... 97 D1
Daneshouse Rd BB10 ... 128 A8
Danesmoor Dr BL9 ... 33 B4
Dane St BB10 ... 128 A7
Danesway
Adlington PR7 ... 43 F1
Bamber Bridge PR5 ... 97 D1
Higher Penwortham PR1 ... 96 A4
Daneswood Ave OL12 ... 52 C8
Daneswood Cl OL12 ... 52 C8
Daneswood Fold OL12 ... 52 C8
Daneway PR8 ... 21 B6
Danewerke St 9 PR1 ... 97 A8
DANGEROUS CORNER ... 28 C2
Daniel Fold OL12 ... 52 B2
Daniel Fold La PR3 ... 181 D2
Daniell St BB1 ... 124 A2
Daniels La WN8 ... 9 C7
Daniel St
10 Clayton-le-M BB5 ... 124 F3
Whitworth OL12 ... 71 D2
Daniel Street Ind Est OL12 ... 71 D2
Danson Gdns 3 FY2 ... 130 D8
Danvers St BB1 ... 124 B2
Danvers Way PR2 ... 118 C7
Daram Ho 3 FY1 ... 130 D2
Darbishire Rd FY7 ... 198 F4
Daresbury Ave PR8 ... 21 A5
Darfield WN8 ... 9 F7
Darkinson La
Preston PR4 ... 116 B2
Salwick PR4 ... 115 F1
Dark La
Blackrod BL6 ... 31 B3
Earby BB18 ... 197 E2
Johnson's Hillock PR6 ... 61 E6
Maghull L31 ... 5 E1
Mawdesley L40 ... 40 E3
Newchurch BB4 ... 86 E1
Ormskirk L40 ... 16 C6
Darkwood Cres BB7 ... 190 D5
Dark Wood La PR5 ... 99 B6
Darley Ave FY4 ... 110 E7
Darley Ct FY8 ... 89 D7
Darley St BL6 ... 32 B5
Darlington St PR7 ... 42 E1
Darmond Rd L33 ... 1 A3
Darnbrook Rd BB18 ... 196 A2
DARN HILL ... 33 F2
Darnley St BB10 ... 128 C5
Dartford Cl 1 BB1 ... 102 A4
Dartmouth Cl PR4 ... 113 F5
Dart St PR2 ... 96 C8
Darul-Uloom Islamic Coll BL8 ... 49 F4
DARWEN ... 81 E2
Darwen Cl PR3 ... 140 B7
Darwen Ent Ctr BB3 ... 82 A2
Darwen L Ctr BB3 ... 82 A1
Darwen Moorland High Sch BB3 ... 82 B3
Darwen Rd 3 BL7 ... 47 E1
Darwen St Barnabas CE Prim Sch BB3 ... 65 C6
Darwen St Peter's CE Prim Sch BB3 ... 65 B8
Darwen St
Blackburn BB2 ... 101 E4
Higher Walton PR5 ... 98 B4
2 Padiham BB12 ... 126 C8
Preston PR1 ... 97 C7
Darwen Sta BB3 ... 82 A1
Darwen Vale High Sch BB3 ... 81 E5
Darwen View PR5 ... 97 E5
Darwin Ct PR9 ... 53 E1
Darwin St BB10 ... 148 A2
Daub Hall La PR5 ... 98 E3
Daub La L40 ... 40 A1
Dauntesey Ave FY3 ... 131 A6
Davenham Rd
Darwen BB3 ... 81 E3
Formby L37 ... 11 F3
Davenport Ave FY2 ... 152 C5
Daventry Ave FY2 ... 152 B4
David Crosley Ho 2 BB18 ... 196 B2
David St N 15 OL12 ... 52 F1
Davidson St 15 LA1 ... 215 A8
David St
Bacup OL13 ... 70 D8
11 Barrowford BB9 ... 170 D4
Burnley BB11 ... 127 F4
16 Rochdale OL12 ... 52 F1
Davies Rd BB1 ... 102 D6
Davis St PR3 ... 140 A8
Davitt Cl 4 BB4 ... 85 B3
Davy Field Brow BB1 ... 82 B6
Davy Field Rd BB1 ... 82 B6
Dawber Delph WN6 ... 19 D8
Dawber's La PR7 ... 59 E2
Dawlish Ave FY3 ... 130 F8
Dawlish Cl BB2 ... 81 C8
Dawlish Dr PR9 ... 54 A5
Dawlish Lo FY8 ... 89 D7
Dawlish Pl PR2 ... 117 A3
Dawnay Rd PR2 ... 118 E3
Dawson Ave
Simonstone BB12 ... 145 E2
Southport PR9 ... 54 C5
Dawson Gdns L31 ... 5 C2
Dawson La PR6, PR7 ... 60 E7
Dawson Pl PR5 ... 78 A7
Dawson Rd
Lytham St Anne's FY8 ... 110 F1
Ormskirk L39 ... 15 F7
Dawson Sq BB11 ... 128 A7
Dawson St BL9 ... 33 A4
Dawson Wlk PR1 ... 117 F1
Daybrook WN8 ... 9 F7
Dayfield WN8 ... 10 B7
Day St BB9 ... 148 E7
Dayton Pl FY4 ... 110 C6
Deakins Bsns Pk BL7 ... 47 D1
Deakins Mill Way BL7 ... 47 D2
Deakin's Terr BL7 ... 46 C5
Deal Pl FY8 ... 110 F1
Deal St 9 BL9 ... 33 B2
DEAN ... 87 C8
Dean Brow PR3 ... 141 F8
Dean Cl
Edenfield BL0 ... 68 D3
Up Holland WN8 ... 10 C7
Deancroft Ave LA3 ... 216 E2
Dean Ct
Bamber Bridge PR5 ... 97 E1
Fleetwood FY7 ... 175 D8
Dean Edge Rd BD22 ... 174 F1
Deanfield BB7 ... 190 B2
Deanfield Ct BB7 ... 190 A2
Deanfield Dr BB7 ... 190 B2
Deanfield Way BB7 ... 190 B2
Dean Fold BB4 ... 87 A8
Dean Hall La PR7 ... 59 D2
Dean Head La BL6 ... 45 A4
Dean La
Billington BB6, BB7 ... 144 C1
Samlesbury PR5 ... 119 F3
Tockholes BB3 ... 81 B1
Water BB4 ... 87 B8
Dean Mdw 5 BB7 ... 166 D7
Dean Mill BB11 ... 128 A5
Deanpoint LA3 ... 217 C3
Dean Rd
Haslingden, Helmcroft BB4 ... 85 B1
Haslingden, Helmshore BB4 ... 68 B8
Deans Ct L37 ... 11 F5
Deansgate
Blackpool FY1 ... 130 B5
Morecambe LA4 ... 217 B5
Deansgate La L37 ... 12 B5
Deansgate La N L37 ... 12 A6
Deansgrave BB4 ... 85 B1
Deansgreave Rd OL13 ... 71 B7
Deansgreave Terr OL13 ... 71 B7
Deans La L40, WN8 ... 26 E3
Dean St
Bamber Bridge PR5 ... 97 E1
Blackpool FY4 ... 110 B8
Burnley BB11 ... 127 E6
Darwen BB3 ... 81 F4
2 Padiham BB12 ... 146 D1
Trawden BB8 ... 172 C2
Dean Terr 4 PR4 ... 114 A5
Dean Wood Ave WN5 ... 10 E8
Dean Wood Cl PR7 ... 43 A6
Dearden Clough BL0 ... 68 E2
Dearden Fold BL0 ... 68 E2
Deardengate BB4 ... 85 B3
Deardengate Croft 11 BB4 ... 85 B3
Dearden Nook BB4 ... 86 A1
Dearden Way WN8 ... 10 A7
Deben Cl WN6 ... 29 D1
Deborah Ave PR2 ... 118 A7
Decimus Ct FY7 ... 199 C5
DEEPDALE ... 118 A2
Deepdale Ave FY6 ... 153 B5
Deepdale Ct BB9 ... 170 C3
Deepdale Dr BB10 ... 148 C4
Deepdale Gn BB9 ... 170 C3
Deepdale Ho 5 PR1 ... 118 B1
Deepdale Inf Sch PR1 ... 118 B2
Deepdale Jun Sch PR1 ... 118 B2
Deepdale La PR4 ... 115 E3
Deepdale Mill PR1 ... 118 B1
Deepdale Mill St PR1 ... 118 B1
Deepdale Rd
Blackpool FY4 ... 131 C1
Fleetwood FY7 ... 199 A3
Preston PR1 ... 118 B2
Deepdale Sh Pk PR1 ... 118 C3
Deepdale St PR1 ... 97 B8
Deeply Vale La BL9, OL11 ... 51 C2
Deer Chace BB12 ... 147 D8
Dee Rd LA1 ... 218 B2
Deerfold PR7 ... 61 B2
Deerhurst Rd FY5 ... 152 E7
Deer Park La LA2 ... 238 B7
Deer Park Rd BB10 ... 128 E4
Deer Pk BB5 ... 104 E8
Deerplay Cl BB10 ... 148 E2
Deerplay Ct OL13 ... 88 A8
Deerplay Dr OL13 ... 88 A8
Deer St 6 OL13 ... 88 A7
Deerstone Ave BB10 ... 128 C6
Deerstone Rd BB9 ... 149 B8
Deeside FY4 ... 110 E5
Dee St FY8 ... 89 E6
Deganwy Ave BB1 ... 101 E7
De-Haviland Way WN8 ... 9 E8
Deighton Ave 6 PR25 ... 60 A8
Deighton Cl WN5 ... 10 E6
Deighton Rd PR7 ... 43 B6
De Lacy Ho BB2 ... 101 C5
De Lacy St
Clitheroe BB7 ... 166 D8
Preston PR2 ... 117 D2
Delamere Ave LA3 ... 212 E6
Delamere Cl
Accrington BB5 ... 125 B1
Blackburn BB2 ... 101 B2

Delamere Pl PR6 43 D8
Delamere Rd
Burnley BB10 148 F3
Skelmersdale WN8 17 F2
Southport PR8 21 B5
Delamere St BL9 33 A5
Delamere Way WN8 10 A7
Delany Dr PR4 93 A6
Delaware Rd 8 FY3 152 E1
Delaware St PR1 118 D1
Delfby Cres L32 1 A1
Delf La
Haskayne L39 14 A4
Todmorden OL14 109 D3
Delius Cl BB2 102 A1
Dellar Fold 20 OL12 52 C1
Dellar St 19 OL12 52 C1
Dellfield La L31 5 E1
Dell Gdns OL12 52 B2
Dell La 4 BB12 126 C4
Dell Mdw OL12 52 C5
Dell Rd OL12 52 B3
Dell Side Way OL12 52 C2
Dell The
Appley Bridge WN6 19 D7
Blackburn BB2 81 D6
Fulwood PR2 117 D7
Knowley PR6 62 A3
Up Holland WN8 10 B7
Wrea Green PR4 113 B3
Dellway The PR4 95 D2
Delma Rd BB10 128 E5
Delph App BB1 102 C4
Delph Ave BL7 47 D3
Delph Brook Way BL7 47 D2
Delph Cl
Blackburn BB1 102 C4
Ormskirk L39 15 C1
Delph Common Rd L39 15 C1
Delph Ct 3 BB6 124 C5
Delph Dr L40 25 F4
Delphene Ave FY5 152 D6
Delphinium Way BB3 82 A7
Delph La
Blackburn, Queen's Park BB1 102 C4
Blackburn, Shadsworth BB1 102 C3
Charnock Green PR7 42 D6
Coppull PR7 42 E5
Formby L37 11 C3
Garstang PR3 181 F8
Oakenclough PR3 183 B7
Ormskirk L39 15 C1
Delph Lane Est BB1 102 C4
Delph Mount
Great Harwood BB6 124 B6
Nelson BB9 148 D6
Delph Park Ave L39 15 B1
Delph Rd BB6 124 C5
Delphside Cl WN5 10 D5
Delph Side Com Prim Sch WN8 9 C8
Delphside Rd WN5 10 D5
Delph St
Darwen BB3 82 B3
Haslingden BB4 85 B4
Delph The WN8 27 C3
Delph Top L39 16 A6
Delph Way PR6 61 C7
Delta La 2 FY7 199 A4
Delta Park Ave PR4 73 E4
Delta Park Dr PR4 73 E4
Deltic Pl L33 1 B1
Deltic Way L33 1 B1
Delves La BB10 149 E7
Demming Cl PR2 95 C8
Denbigh Ave
Cleveleys FY5 175 E1
Southport PR9 53 F3
Denbigh Cl PR25 77 B1
Denbigh Dr BB7 189 F2
Denbigh Gr BB12 127 A7
Denby Cl PR5 97 C3
Denebank FY2 152 D5
Dene Bank Rd BB5 103 E3
Denefield Ho PR8 35 B6
Dene The
Blackburn BB2 101 B7
Hurst Green BB7 142 E8
Deneway Ave FY3 130 F6
Denford Ave
Leyland PR25 60 B8
Lytham St Anne's FY8 90 A4
Denham La PR6 78 E2
Denham Way FY7 198 F2
Denham Wood Cl PR7 42 F6
Denholme
Skelmersdale WN8 9 F7
1 Up Holland WN8 10 A7
Denholme Gr FY2 152 E5
Denis St LA1 215 A8
Denmark Rd
Lytham St Anne's FY8 90 D4
Southport PR9 54 A2
Denmark St LA1 214 D7
Dennis Gr 2 LA4 217 A4
Dennison Ind Est LA3 217 E2
Denny Ave LA1 218 C2
Denny Bank LA2 219 C5
Denny Beck La LA2 219 C5
Denshaw WN8 9 F7
Denstone Ave FY2 152 D4
Dent Dale BB5 104 D5
Dentdale Cl BB2 80 D7
Denton St
Barnoldswick BB18 196 A3
7 Rochdale OL12 52 F1
Dent Row 8 BB11 127 F5
Dent St BB8 171 B3
Denville Ave FY5 152 F8
Denville Rd
Blackburn BB2 101 D5
Preston PR1 118 C1
Denville St 5 BB2 101 D5
Depot Rd
Blackpool FY3 152 E1
Kirkby L33 1 D4
Derbe Rd FY8 89 F5
Derby Cl BB3 65 B5
Derby Cres PR4 135 C8
Derby Ct L37 11 E5
Derby Hill PR4 133 A1
Derby Hill Cres L39 16 A5
Derby Hill Rd L39 16 A5
Derby Ho
Kirkham PR4 114 A6
6 Lancaster LA1 218 D1
2 Ormskirk L39 15 F5
Derby Pl PR6 31 A8
Derby Rd
Blackpool FY1 130 B7
Cleveleys FY5 175 C3
Formby L37 11 E5
Fulwood PR2 117 E3
Garstang PR3 181 B7
Kirkham PR4 114 A6
Lancaster LA1 218 D1
Longridge PR3 140 A7
Lytham St Anne's FY8 90 C5
Poulton-le-F FY6 153 D4
Skelmersdale WN8 8 C8
Southport PR9 35 C7
Derby St W L39 15 E5
Derbyshire Almshouses The BB2 101 B6
Derbyshire Ave PR3 181 B8
Derby Sq PR1 97 D8
Derby St
Accrington BB5 104 C6
Blackburn BB1 102 A6
Brinscall PR6 63 A8
Burnley BB11 127 F5
Clitheroe BB7 166 F8
Colne BB8 171 D5
Horwich BL6 32 D1
Leyland PR25 77 B2
7 Morecambe LA4 217 A5
Nelson BB9 170 E1
Ormskirk L39 15 F5
Preston PR1 97 A8
Ramsbottom BL0 50 D6
Rishton BB1 124 C1
Derek Rd PR6 78 C1
Derham St BB2 101 E3
Derry Rd PR2 118 E3
Dertern La LA5 221 A7
Derwent Ave
Burnley BB10 148 A2
Fleetwood FY7 198 D2
Formby L37 11 D2
Morecambe LA4 217 C5
Padiham BB12 146 C2
Southport PR9 53 F1
Derwent Cl
Colne BB8 172 A6
3 Darwen BB3 82 C1
Freckleton PR4 93 A6
Haslingden BB4 85 B4
Horwich BL6 32 C2
Knott End-on-S FY6 199 F6
Maghull L31 5 F2
Rishton BB1 123 F1
Derwent Cres BB7 166 C7
Derwent Ct LA1 218 A2
Derwent Dr
Freckleton PR4 93 A6
Longridge PR3 139 F5
Derwent Hall 3 PR1 117 E1
Derwent Ho 9 PR1 97 D8
Derwent Pl
Blackpool FY5 152 D8
Poulton-le-F FY6 153 D1
Derwent Rd
Chorley PR7 43 B5
Lancaster LA1 215 B8
Lytham St Anne's FY8 111 A1
Orrell WN5 10 F8
Derwent St
6 Darwen BB3 81 F2
11 Rochdale OL12 52 F1
Derwentwater Pl PR1 117 F2
Dever Ave PR25 76 D1
Devere Gdns FY8 89 E5
De Vitre Cotts LA1 214 E4
De Vitre St 7 LA1 218 E1
Devona Ave FY4 131 B1
Devon Ave
Fleetwood FY7 198 E3
Oswaldtwistle BB5 103 B6
Up Holland WN8 10 B6
Devon Cl PR5 97 D3
Devon Cres BB4 68 B8
Devon Dr WN1 30 B1
Devon Farm Way L37 12 B3
Devon Gr BB12 127 A7
Devon Pl
1 Church BB5 103 E5
Lancaster LA1 215 A4
Devonport Cl PR5 97 E3
Devonport Ct BB2 101 C5
Devonport Rd BB2 101 C5
Devonport Way PR6 43 E8
Devon Rd BB1 102 C5
Devonshire Ave FY5 176 B2
Devonshire Ct
9 Blackpool FY3 130 D7
17 Chorley PR7 43 C8
Devonshire Dr
Clayton-le-M BB5 125 A3
Garstang PR3 181 B8
Devonshire Ho FY3 130 D6
Devonshire Mews FY5 176 B1
Devonshire Pl PR1 118 E1
Devonshire Prim Sch FY3 130 D6
Devonshire Rd
Blackpool FY2 152 D2
Burnley BB10 128 A8
Chorley PR7 43 C7
Fulwood PR2 118 A4
Lytham St Anne's FY8 89 D7
Morecambe LA3 216 F3
Rishton BB1 124 A1
Southport PR9 36 A8
Devonshire Sq FY3 130 D5
Devonshire Square Mews 5 FY3 130 D5
Devonshire St
Accrington BB5 104 B7
Lancaster LA1 214 F5
Devon St
Blackpool FY4 130 D1
Colne BB8 171 E6
Darwen BB3 65 B6
Devron Mill BB6 124 D4
Dewan Ind Est BB4 68 B8
Dewberry Fields WN8 10 B7
Dew Forest PR3 181 D4
Dewhirst Rd OL12 52 F4
Dewhirst Way OL12 52 F4
Dewhurst Ave FY4 110 E8
Dewhurst Cl BB3 65 C6
Dewhurst Clough Rd BL7 47 D2
Dewhurst Ct BL7 47 D3
Dewhurst Ind Est PR2 117 D1
Dewhurst Rd BB6 142 F1
Dewhurst Row PR5 77 D7
Dewhurst St
Blackburn BB1 102 A4
Colne BB8 171 D3
Darwen BB3 65 B6
Preston PR2 117 D1
Dew Meadow Cl OL12 52 E2
Dexter Way WN8 10 B6
Deycroft Ave L33 1 A4
Deycroft Wlk L33 1 A4
Deyes Ct L31 5 E1
Deyes End L31 5 E1
Deyes High Sch L31 5 D1
Deyes La
Maghull L31 5 D1
Maghull, Moss Side L31 5 F1
Diamond Jubilee Rd L40 39 C4
Diana Ct 10 LA1 214 F7
Dianne Rd FY5 176 D2
Dibbs Pocket PR4 93 D7
Dib Rd PR4 73 B5
Dicconson's La L39 14 D4
Dicconson Terr 13 FY8 91 B3
Dicconson Way L39 16 A5
Dickens Ave BB18 196 A3
Dickens Ct BB6 143 C6
Dickensons Field 3 PR1 96 E2
Dickens Rd PR7 29 E8
Dickens St BB1 102 A3
Dicket's Brow L40 16 F3
Dicket's La L40, WN8 17 A2
Dickie's La FY4 111 B7
Dickie's La S FY4 111 C6
Dickinson Cl
Blackburn BB2 101 C3
Formby L37 11 F2
Dickinson Ct
1 Horwich BL6 32 B4
Southport PR8 35 A2
Dickinson Rd L37 11 F2
Dickinson St W BL6 32 B4
Dick La PR6 62 E7
Dick's La L40 16 F4
Dickson Ave PR1 118 D2
Dickson Hey PR4 75 F8
Dickson Rd FY1 130 B7
Dickson St W BL6 32 B4
Dickson St
Burnley BB12 127 C6
Colne BB8 171 E6
8 Preston PR1 97 B7
Didsbury St BB1 102 C5
Digham Ave FY5 152 D6
DIGMOOR 9 D6
Digmoor Dr WN8 9 C7
Digmoor Rd WN8 9 D6
DILL HALL 104 A8
Dill Hall La BB5 103 F7
Dilworth Bottoms PR3 141 A8
Dilworth Ct PR3 140 C7
Dilworth La PR3 140 C7
Dimmock St BB2 101 C2
Dimple Pk BL7 47 D3
Dimple Rd BL7 47 C4
Dimples La PR3 181 E5
DINCKLEY 142 F4
Dinckley Gr FY1 130 D3
Dinckley Sq BB2 101 B6
Dinely St BB5 103 F6
Dingle Ave
Appley Bridge WN6 19 E8
Dingle Ave *continued*
Blackpool FY3 130 F8
Up Holland WN8 10 C8
Dingle Cl L39 15 C1
Dingle Rd WN8 10 B7
Dingle The
Fulwood PR2 117 D7
Knowley PR6 62 A3
Dinmore Ave FY3 131 A8
Dinmore Pl FY3 131 A7
Dinorwic Rd PR8 35 A2
Dirty Leech OL12 52 F6
Disraeli St BB10 148 A2
Ditchfield L37 12 A2
Division La FY4 111 C3
Dixey St BL6 32 A3
Dixon Rd
Kirkby L33 1 B1
Longridge PR3 140 B7
Dixon's Farm Mews PR4 115 D1
Dixons La PR2 139 C2
Dixon St
Barrowford BB9 170 C3
Blackburn BB2 101 C4
Horwich BL6 32 B3
DOALS 87 F7
Doals Farm OL13 87 F7
Doals Gate OL13 88 A8
Dobbin Cl BB4 86 C2
Dobbin Ct BB4 86 C2
Dobbin La BB4 86 C2
Dob Brow PR7 42 F4
Dobbs Dr L37 12 A4
Dob La PR4 75 A4
Dobs La LA2 209 E3
Dobson Ave FY8 89 E8
Dobson Cl WN6 28 E2
Dobson Rd FY3 131 B7
Dobson's La FY6 177 E6
Dobson St 2 BB3 81 F2
Dock Ave FY7 199 A2
DOCKER 241 A5
Docker La LA6 241 C5
Docker Park Farm* LA6 241 A4
Dockinsall La PR3 178 D3
Dockray Ct 2 BB8 171 E5
Dockray St BB8 171 E5
Dockray Yd 4 BB8 171 E5
Dock Rd FY8 91 D4
Dock St
Blackburn BB1 102 A5
Fleetwood FY7 199 B4
Docky Pool La FY4 111 A6
Doctor's La
Eccleston PR7 41 B6
Great Altcar L37 12 E2
Sollom PR4 56 F3
Doctors Row PR3 140 A6
Dodd's La L31 5 D2
Dodd Way PR5 78 A6
Dodgeons Cl FY6 153 C2
Dodgson La BB18 197 F2
Dodgson Pl PR1 118 C1
Dodgson Rd PR1 118 C1
Dodney Dr PR2 116 C1
Dodworth Ave PR8 35 E5
Doeholme Rake LA2 232 F1
Doe Mdw WN8 27 A1
Dog Pits La OL13 88 A6
Dole La
Abbey Village PR6 80 C1
Chorley PR7 43 C8
Doles La PR26 58 A7
Dolls House & Fleetwood Mus The* FY7 199 C5
Dolly's La PR9 36 D8
DOLPHINHOLME 226 A8
Dolphinholme CE Prim Sch LA2 226 A8
Dolphinholme Mill LA2 226 A8
Dombey St BB1 102 A4
Dominica Ave BB3 81 F6
Dominion Ct BB11 127 B4
Dominion Rd BB2 101 C8
Doncaster Rd FY3 131 A3
Donnington Lo PR8 34 F6
Donnington Rd
Carleton FY6 153 C6
Lytham St Anne's FY8 89 F7
Donshort Mews 2 BB9 170 C1
Don St FY8 89 E7
Doodstone Ave PR5 97 B1
Doodstone Cl PR5 97 B1
Doodstone Dr PR5 97 B1
Doodstone Nook PR5 97 B1
Dora St BL0 50 A4
Dorchester Ave
Bamber Bridge PR5 97 B2
Oswaldtwistle BB5 103 C4
Dorchester Cl
Blackburn BB1 102 B3
Thornton FY5 153 C8
Dorchester Dr L33 1 A5
Dorchester Gdns LA3 217 C2
Dorchester Rd
Blackpool FY1 130 B8
Garstang PR3 181 B8
Up Holland WN8 10 A7
Doric Gn WN5 10 D3
Doris Henderson Way LA1 217 F1
Doris St
Burnley BB11 128 B7
Chorley PR6 61 D1
Dorking Rd PR6 61 F4
Dorman Cl 1 PR2 117 C2
Dorman Rd PR2 118 E3
Dorothy Ave 11 PR25 77 A1
Dorothy St
1 Blackburn BB2 81 C8
13 Ramsbottom BL0 50 B5
Dorrington Rd LA1 214 F5
Dorritt Rd FY4 110 E6
Dorritt St 19 BB1 102 A4
Dorset Ave
3 Bamber Bridge PR5 97 D3
Cleveleys FY5 175 D4
Darwen BB3 81 F3
Padiham BB12 126 D7
Southport PR8 21 C2
Dorset Dr
Blackburn BB1 102 E4
Clitheroe BB7 189 F2
Haslingden BB4 68 A8
Dorset Rd
Lytham St Anne's FY8 89 F8
Preston PR1 118 A1
Rishton BB1 124 A1
Standish WN1 30 B1
Dorset St
10 Blackpool FY4 130 D1
Burnley BB12 127 A6
Dotcliffe Rd BB18 195 A6
Double Row 1 BB12 126 B8
Doughty St BB8 171 D4
Douglas Ave
Becconsall PR4 73 F1
Blackpool FY3 130 D7
Heysham LA3 212 F7
Horwich BL6 32 C5
Stalmine FY6 177 C7
Up Holland WN8 10 B7
Douglas Cl
Bamber Bridge PR5 77 F7
Blackburn BB2 81 D7
Horwich BL6 32 C5
Rufford L40 39 C3
Douglas Ct
2 Fulwood PR2 117 D3
Southport PR8 21 C5
Douglas Dr
Freckleton PR4 93 B6
Heysham LA3 212 F7
Maghull L31 5 F2
Ormskirk L39 15 D7
Orrell WN5 10 F7
Shevington WN6 19 F5
Douglas Gr BB3 81 D4
Douglas Hall 4 PR1 117 E1
Douglas Ho PR7 43 D5
Douglas La PR2 139 D1
Douglas Leatham Ho 3 FY1 130 D1
Douglas Mill WN6 30 A3
Douglas Pl
Blackburn BB1 122 F1
Fleetwood FY7 198 D3
Douglas Rd
Bacup OL13 88 A1
Burnley BB10 149 A3
Fulwood PR2 117 D3
Shevington Moor WN6 29 B2
Southport PR9 54 C4
Douglas Rd N PR2 117 D3
Douglas Sq 4 OL10 33 F1
Douglas St
Colne BB8 171 E6
Lytham St Anne's FY8 89 D6
Preston PR2 96 C8
Ramsbottom BL0 50 B6
Douglas View
Adlington PR7 31 A6
Hesketh Bank PR4 73 E4
Douglas Way BB10 149 A3
Doultons The PR5 97 C3
Dove Ave 2 PR1 96 E4
Dove Cl FY5 175 F1
Dovecote PR6 78 A3
Dovedale Ave
Blackpool FY3 131 C2
Fulwood PR2 117 A5
Maghull L31 5 C2
Thornton FY5 176 B3
Dovedale Cl
Burnley BB10 148 C4
Fulwood PR2 117 A4
Leyland PR25 60 A6
Dovedale Dr
Burnley BB12 127 C8
Standish WN6 29 E2
Dovedale Gdns PR3 140 B6
Dove Dr BL9 33 B4
Dove La BB3 81 F2
Dover Cl
Blackburn BB1 102 C4
Ramsbottom BL8 50 A1
Warton PR4 92 E7
Dover Ct FY1 130 D2
Dover Gdns FY6 153 B5
Dover La PR5, PR6 79 C8
Dover Rd
Blackpool FY1 130 E2
Lytham St Anne's FY8 89 F8
Southport PR8 34 F2
Dover St
Accrington BB5 104 A4
Blackburn BB3 81 F7
Nelson BB9 170 E1
Dove St
Lytham St Anne's FY8 89 D6
Preston PR1 118 B1
Dovestone Dr FY6 153 B3

Dovetree Cl PR5 97 A3
Dove Tree Ct FY4 131 B1
Dove Villas OL13 70 B7
DOWBRIDGE 114 D4
Dowbridge PR4 114 C4
Dowbridge Way PR4 114 C5
Downes Gr LA4 217 D4
Downeyfield Rd LA3 213 C3
Downfield Cl BL0 50 B6
DOWNHAM 191 B5
Downham Ave
Great Harwood BB6 124 F6
Rawtenstall BB4 86 A4
Downham Cotts 7 LA2 211 A4
Downham Dr BB5 104 A3
Downham Gr BB10 128 D5
Downham Pl
Lytham St Anne's FY8 90 C6
3 Preston PR2 116 E2
Downham Rd
Chatburn BB7 190 E5
Leyland PR25 76 D1
Downham St BB2 101 C4
Downham Wlk WN5 10 D1
DOWNHOLLAND CROSS 14 A2
Downholland-Haskayne CE Prim Sch L39 13 E3
Downholland Moss La L37 12 C4
Downing Ct PR3 137 C3
Downing St PR1 97 E8
Downley Cl OL12 52 B2
Downs The FY6 153 D4
Dowry St BB5 104 C6
Dragon Cl WN8 9 E8
Dragon St 8 BB12 126 C8
Drake Cl
Lytham St Anne's FY8 110 E1
Ormskirk L39 15 C2
Drakelowe Ave FY4 110 F6
Drakes Croft PR2 117 C3
Drakes Hollow PR5 97 D4
Drammen Ave BB11 127 B5
Draperfield PR7 43 A4
Drapers Ave PR7 41 C6
Draw Well Rd L33 1 D2
Draycombe Ct 4 LA3 216 D2
Draycombe Dr LA3 216 E2
Draycot Ave FY3 130 F8
Drayton Rd LA3 213 A7
Drewitt Cres PR9 54 D4
Drew St BB11 127 B5
Drewton Ave 2 LA3 216 D2
DRINK HOUSE 58 A1
Drinkhouse La PR26 58 A1
Drinkhouse Rd PR26 58 B1
Driscoll St 1 PR1 97 B8
Driver St 16 BB4 86 A7
Drive The
Bacup OL13 87 F2
Brockhall Village BB6 143 C5
Crag Bank LA5 223 B1
Edenfield BL0 68 D3
Fulwood PR2 118 B4
Hest Bank LA2 220 E1
Heysham LA3 212 F7
Longton PR4 75 A8
Walton-le-D PR5 97 F5
Driving Gate BB4 106 A1
Dronsfield Rd FY7 198 F4
Drovers Way
Burton-in-K LA6 240 B7
Lytham St Anne's FY8 90 E7
Drovers Wlk LA3 212 F7
Druids Cl BL7 47 D3
Drumacre La E PR4 75 D6
Drumacre La W PR4 75 A6
Drumhead Rd PR6 61 D2
DRUMMERSDALE 24 C7
Drummersdale La L40 24 D7
Drummond Ave FY3 130 E7
Dry Bread La PR3 178 C2
Dryburgh Ave FY3 130 F3
Dryden Gr BB6 124 C4
Dryden Rd FY7 199 A4
Dryden St
6 Clayton-le-M BB5 124 F3
Padiham BB12 126 E7
Dryfield La BL6 32 A5
Duchess Ct FY2 152 B3
Duchess Dr FY2 152 B3
Duchess St BB3 81 F7
Duchy Ave PR2 118 B4
Ducie Pl PR1 118 F1
Ducie St BL0 50 B7
Ducketts La PR3 159 B8
Duckett St 3 BB11 127 E6
Duckshaw Rd BB3 64 F6
Duck St
2 Clitheroe BB7 166 F8
Smallwood Hey PR3 201 A7
Wray LA2 238 D6
Duckworth Cl PR3 181 D3
Duckworth Dr PR3 181 D3
Duckworth Hall BB5 103 A2
Duckworth Hall Brow BB5 103 A1
Duckworth Hill La BB5 103 B1
Duckworth La
Rawtenstall BB4 68 E8
Tarleton PR4 56 F8
Duckworth St
Barrowford BB9 170 D2
Blackburn BB2 101 D3
3 Bury BL9 33 A4
Duckworth St *continued*
Church BB5 103 E6
Darwen BB3 81 F2
Duddle La PR5 97 D2
Duddon Ave
Darwen BB3 81 E3
Fleetwood FY7 198 D2
Maghull L31 5 F2
Duddon Cl LA3 217 F3
Dudley Ave
Blackpool FY2 152 D1
Oswaldtwistle BB5 103 C4
Dudley Cl PR4 95 A1
Dudley Pl PR2 116 F2
Dudley St
Brierfield BB9 148 C5
Colne BB8 171 F5
Morecambe LA4 217 C4
Duerden St BB9 148 D7
Duffins Cl OL12 52 D3
Dugdale Ct FY4 110 F5
Dugdale La BB7, BD23 235 F1
Dugdale Rd BB12 127 C7
Dugdales Cl FY4 111 E7
Dugdale St BB11 128 A5
Duke Ave PR8 35 C4
Duke of Sussex St BB2 81 B8
Duke St Prim Sch PR7 43 C6
Dukes Brow
Blackburn BB2 101 C6
Great Harwood BB6 124 B5
Dukes Ct BB2 101 B6
Dukes Dr BB3 82 F1
Dukes Mdw PR2 117 A5
Duke St
Bamber Bridge PR5 77 E7
Blackburn BB2 101 D5
Blackpool FY1 130 B1
Burnley BB10 148 F3
Burton in L LA6 242 C3
Chorley PR7 43 C6
Clayton-le-M BB5 125 A2
Colne BB8 171 D4
Colne, Cotton Tree BB8 172 B5
Formby L37 11 F2
Great Harwood BB6 124 B5
Heysham LA3 212 E7
High Bentham LA2 239 D8
Lancaster LA1 218 C1
Oswaldtwistle BB5 103 D3
Preston PR1 97 B7
Ramsbottom BL0 50 A4
Rawtenstall BB4 69 E8
Rochdale OL12 52 F1
Southport PR8 35 B5
Dukes Way L37 11 F2
Duke's Wood La WN8 9 D3
Dulas Gn L32 1 A1
Dulas Rd L32 1 A1
Dumbarton Cl 2 FY4 111 A6
Dumbarton Rd LA1 215 A7
Dumb Tom's La LA2, LA6 242 E1
Dumfries Cl FY2 152 F5
Dunald Mill La LA2, LA6 237 B6
Dunbar Cl FY4 111 A6
Dunbar Cres PR8 21 F8
Dunbar Dr
Fulwood PR2 117 D4
2 Heysham LA3 212 E7
Dunbar Rd
Fulwood PR2 116 F3
Southport PR8 34 F1
Duncan Ave FY2 152 C6
Duncan Cl
Brownside BB10 128 F5
Lytham St Anne's FY8 110 D1
Duncan Pl FY7 198 E4
Duncan St
Burnley BB12 127 A5
Horwich BL6 32 C3
DUNCOMBE 158 F3
Duncombe Terr PR3 159 A4
Duncroft Cl BB7 189 E2
Dundas St BB8 171 C4
Dundee Cl OL10 33 F1
Dundee Dr BB1 102 A4
Dundee La BL0 50 B6
Dundee St LA1 215 A7
Dunderdale Ave BB9 148 C7
Dunderdale St PR3 140 B7
Dundonald St PR1 97 D8
Dundonnell Rd BB9 171 A1
Dunedin Rd BL8 49 F2
Dunelt Ct 2 FY1 130 C2
Dunelt Rd FY1 130 D2
Dune Point FY8 110 B2
Dunes Ave FY4 110 B5
Dunes Dr L37 11 C4
Dunes Ho FY8 89 F5
Dungeon La WN8 18 C7
Dunham Dr PR6 61 C6
Dunkeld St 5 LA1 215 A7
Dunkenhalgh Way
Church BB5 103 E7
Clayton-le-M BB5 124 E1
Dunkenshaw Cres LA1 215 B2
Dunkirk Ave
Carnforth LA5 221 E8
Fulwood PR2 117 C3
Dunkirk La
Leyland PR26 59 C8
New Longton PR26 76 A1
Dunkirk Mews PR25 59 D8
Dunkirk Rd PR8 34 F2
Dunlin Ave LA3 212 F5
Dunlin Cl FY5 176 A5
Dunlin Dr FY8 90 E7
Dunlop Ave PR8 21 C2
Dunmail Ave 1 FY3 130 F2
Dunmore St PR1 97 B8
Dunnock La PR4 116 E4
DUNNOCKSHAW 106 B4
Dunnockshaw Community Woodland Trail* BB11 106 E6
DUNNYSHOP 103 E3
Dunny Shop Ave BB5 104 A4
Dunoon Cl PR2 116 F4
Dunoon Dr BB1 102 D3
Dunoon St BB11 127 D5
Dunrobin Dr PR7 60 D1
Dunscar Dr PR6 61 E1
DUNSOP BRIDGE 228 C5
Dunsop Cl
3 Bamber Bridge PR5 77 F8
1 Blackpool FY1 130 D1
Dunsop Ct 2 FY1 130 D1
Dunsop Gdns LA3 217 F2
Dunsop Rd PR2 118 D4
Dunsop St BB1 101 F7
Dunster Ave BB5 103 C5
Dunster Gr BB7 166 C6
Dunster Rd PR8 21 E8
Dunvegan Cl 3 FY4 111 A6
Durban Ct FY5 175 C4
Durban Gr BB11 127 E4
Durham Ave
Burnley BB12 127 B7
Cleveleys FY5 175 E3
Lancaster LA1 215 A4
Lytham St Anne's FY8 89 E7
Durham Cl
Blackburn BB1 101 F4
Leyland PR25 59 E7
4 Morecambe LA3 217 B2
Durham Dr
Buckshaw Village PR7 60 E6
Oswaldtwistle BB5 103 F3
Ramsbottom BL0 50 B3
Wilpshire BB1 122 F6
Durham Gr 1 PR3 181 B7
Durham Rd
Blackpool FY1 130 D5
Darwen BB3 81 F2
Wilpshire BB1 122 F7
Durham St
Accrington BB5 104 D7
Skelmersdale WN8 17 D2
Durley Rd FY1 130 D2
Durn St OL14 109 A1
D'urton La PR2, PR3 137 F1
Dutch Barn Cl PR7 61 B2
Dutton Brook Ho PR3 141 D3
Dutton Ct 1 FY3 130 D5
Duttonfield Cl PR26 76 E3
Dutton Lee Cotts PR3 142 A7
Dutton Rd FY3 130 D5
Dutton St 15 BB5 104 C6
Duttons Way BB1 102 D1
Duxbury Cl L31 5 E3
Duxbury Dr BL9 33 C2
Duxbury Hall Rd PR7 43 E3
Duxbury Ho 8 PR6 43 D7
Duxbury Jubilee Pk* PR7 43 D3
Duxbury St
Darwen BB3 65 B6
Earby BB18 197 C2
Dyers La L39 15 E4
Dyer St PR4 113 F5
Dyke La PR3 201 A3
Dyke Nook BB7 166 F6
Dykes La LA5 225 F2
Dymock Rd PR1 118 D1
Dymock Rd N PR1 118 D1
Dyneley Ave BB10 128 F4
Dyneley Rd BB1 102 C7
Dyson St BB2 101 E2

E

Eachill Gdns BB1 103 B8
Eachill Rd BB1 124 B1
Eager La L31 5 B8
EAGLAND HILL 179 C7
Eagle Brow Cl FY5 176 B4
Eagle St
Accrington BB5 104 B5
Blackburn BB1 102 C4
2 Nelson BB9 170 F1
Oswaldtwistle BB5 103 C2
Eagles The FY6 153 E5
Eagleton Way PR1 97 A2
Eagley Bank OL12 71 E6
Eagley Rd BB9 148 C4
Ealand Chase BL6 31 F3
Ealing Gr PR6 61 F3
Eamont Ave PR9 54 B5
Eamont Pl FY7 198 D2
Eanam BB1 101 F5
Eanam Old Rd BB1 101 F5
EARBY 197 A2
Earby Lead Mining Mus* BB18 197 B2
Earby Rd BB18 194 F8
Earby Springfield Prim Sch BB18 197 C1
EARCROFT 81 E6
Earcroft Way BB3 81 E5
Eardley Rd LA3 212 E8
Earhart Cl WN8 9 E8
Earlesdon Ave BB18 196 F1
Earlham St BB18 197 C2
Earl Rd BL0 50 B6
Earls Ave PR5 77 E8
Earls Dr BB3 82 E1
Earl St
Barnoldswick BB18 196 C2
Blackburn BB1 101 E6
Burnley BB10 128 B8
Clayton-le-M BB5 124 F2
Colne BB8 171 D4
Great Harwood BB6 124 B5
Lancaster LA1 218 D1
11 Nelson BB9 170 F1
Preston PR1 96 F8
Ramsbottom BL0 50 D6
Earlsway FY3 131 D5
Earls Way PR7 60 D2
Earlswood WN8 18 E1
Earnsdale Ave BB3 81 D2
Earnsdale Cl BB3 81 E2
Earnsdale Rd BB3 81 E3
Earnshaw Ave OL12 52 E3
EARNSHAW BRIDGE 76 E2
Earnshaw Dr PR25 76 D1
Earnshaw Rd OL13 87 F3
Earnshaw Row 18 OL13 87 F3
Easby Cl L37 12 A2
Easdale Ave LA4 217 E5
Easedale Cl
Burnley BB12 127 B8
Hest Bank LA5 220 F2
Easedale Dr PR8 21 B4
EASINGTON 229 B5
Easington LA1 218 A2
Easington Cres FY3 131 B8
East Ave BB18 196 B2
East Bank
2 Barrowford BB9 170 D4
Water BB4 107 A1
Eastbank Ave FY4 111 A7
East Bank Ave BB4 85 B2
East Bank Rd FY8 89 E5
Eastbank St PR8 35 B6
Eastbank Street Sq 9 PR8 35 B7
East Beach FY8 91 C3
East Boothroyden FY1 130 B8
Eastbourne Cl PR2 116 F5
Eastbourne Rd
Blackpool FY4 110 B6
Southport PR8 35 A3
East Cecil St FY8 91 A3
East Chorley Business Ctr 3 PR6 43 D8
Eastcliff LA2 237 F5
East Cliff PR1 96 F6
East Cliffe FY8 91 C3
East Cliff Rd PR1 96 F6
Eastcott Cl BB2 82 A8
East Cres BB5 104 B8
East Croft BB9 171 B2
East Ct FY5 175 D5
East Dene WN8 27 B2
East End St 1 BB8 171 C4
Eastern Ave BB10 148 C1
Eastfield Dr
Longton PR4 95 A1
West Bradford BB7 189 F6
Eastgate
Accrington BB5 104 C6
Fulwood PR2 117 E4
Morecambe LA3 217 E2
Ribchester PR3 141 E4
Whitworth OL12 52 C7
East Gate BB4 85 B3
East Gate Cl FY8 110 C4
EAST GILLIBRANDS 9 A8
Eastham Hall Cvn Pk FY8 91 E6
Eastham Pl BB11 128 B6
Eastham St
Burnley BB10 128 B5
Clitheroe BB7 189 E1
Lancaster LA1 215 A7
Preston PR1 117 E1
East Hills St 21 BB18 196 B2
East Holme FY8 91 C4
East La L29 4 B2
East Lancashire Rd BB1 122 F3
East Lancashire Rly* BL0 50 C5
Eastlands
Heysham LA3 213 A7
Leyland PR26 59 C7
East Leigh WN8 18 D1
East Lodge Pl BB10 128 E1
East Mead
Blackpool FY3 130 F3
Ormskirk L39 15 B2
East Meade L31 5 C2
Eastmoor Dr BB7 166 F7
East Mount WN5 10 F6
Easton Cl PR2 118 D6
East Par
19 Barnoldswick BB18 196 B2
17 Rawtenstall BB4 86 A3
East Park Ave
Blackburn BB1 101 D7
Darwen BB3 64 F8
East Park Ct BB1 101 D6
East Park Dr FY3 131 A5
East Park Rd BB1 101 D6
EAST PIMBO 9 E5
Eastpines Dr FY5 152 F8
East Rd
Fulwood PR2 118 A3
Lancaster LA1 215 A8
Maghull L31 5 F1
East Rd *continued*
Thornton FY5 176 D3
Eastside FY4 110 F8
East Sq PR4 95 A1
East St
Bamber Bridge PR5 77 E7
Blackburn BB2 101 C3
Blackburn, Feniscowles BB2 80 D8
Brierfield BB9 148 C5
Edenfield BL0 68 D4
Farington PR25 77 B2
Hapton BB12 126 C4
Haslingden BB4 68 A7
Leyland PR25 77 B1
Morecambe LA3 216 E4
10 Nelson BB9 170 D1
Padiham BB12 146 C1
13 Preston PR1 97 A8
Rawtenstall BB4 85 F5
Southport PR9 35 D7
East Terr PR7 60 D4
East Topping St 3 FY1 130 B5
East View
Bacup OL13 87 F2
3 Bamber Bridge PR5 77 A7
Fulwood PR2 118 F5
9 Galgate LA2 211 A4
Grimsargh PR2 139 B1
Grindleton BB7 190 B7
4 Low Bentham LA2 239 B8
Pendleton BB7 167 B4
9 Preston, Frenchwood PR5 97 C6
Preston PR1 97 A8
Ramsbottom BL0 50 C3
Ramsbottom, Chatterton BL0 68 C1
Read BB12 145 D2
Rising Bridge BB5 85 A8
Trawden BB8 172 C2
Whitworth OL12 71 D2
Winmarleigh PR3 203 F6
East View Ct LA1 218 B3
East View Terr
Abbey Village PR6 80 B3
14 Barnoldswick BB18 196 B2
East Ward Com Prim Sch BL9 33 B2
Eastway
Freckleton PR4 93 A6
Fulwood PR2 118 B6
Maghull L31 5 E1
East Way PR6 43 D8
Eastway Bsns Village PR2 118 B8
East Wlk BL7 47 D2
Eastwood Ave
Blackpool FY3 130 E8
2 Fleetwood FY7 198 F3
Eastwood Cl 6 BL9 33 B2
Eastwood Cres BB4 86 C2
Eastwood Ct 11 BL9 33 B2
Eastwood Rd PR25 76 F1
Eastwood St
Barnoldswick BB18 196 C3
2 Blackburn BB1 102 A6
Rawtenstall BB4 86 C2
Eastwood Terr BB18 196 C3
Eaton Ave
Blackpool FY1 130 C1
Leyland PR7 60 D7
Eaton Ct FY8 89 F6
Eaton Pl PR4 113 F5
Eaton Way FY6 131 E8
Eaves Ave BB11 127 D2
Eaves Cl BB5 125 F1
Eavesdale WN8 9 E8
Eaves Green La PR3 138 F8
Eaves Green Rd PR7 43 B5
Eavesham Cl PR1 97 A1
Eaves La
Chorley PR6 43 E8
Cuddy Hill PR4 136 D7
Fulwood PR2 117 E3
Eaves Rd FY8 111 A1
Eaves St FY1 130 B7
Eaveswood Cl PR5 97 E1
Ebenezer Terr BB7 144 B4
Ebony St 11 BB1 102 A7
Ebor Lo PR8 35 A5
Ebor St BB10 148 B2
Ecclesgate Rd FY4 111 A5
Eccleshill Cotts BB3 82 C4
Eccleshill Gdns BB3 82 C4
Eccleshill Rd BB3 81 F6
Eccleshill St 1 BB12 126 C8
Eccles La L40 27 B7
Eccles Rd L37 11 D1
Eccles St
Accrington BB5 104 B7
Blackburn BB2 101 E3
Preston PR1 118 C1
Ramsbottom BL0 50 B6
ECCLESTON 41 C6
Eccleston Prim Sch PR7 41 B6
Eccleston Rd FY1 130 D1
Eckersley Cl BB2 81 D8
Eckroyd Cl BB9 148 D6
Eclipse Rd BB2 80 D8
Ecroyd Rd PR2 117 C2
Ecroyd St
Leyland PR25 77 A1

Ecroyd St *continued*
Nelson BB9 148 C8
Edale Ave 1 BB4 85 C2
Edale Cl PR25 60 A7
Edale Ct PR1 117 F1
Edale Dr WN6 29 E2
Eddington Rd FY8 90 B4
Eddleston Cl FY3 131 D5
Edelston Rd 5 FY1 130 C6
Eden Ave
Edenfield BL0 68 D3
Fleetwood FY7 198 D2
Lytham St Anne's FY8 90 E3
Morecambe LA4 217 F5
Southport PR9 53 F2
Eden Cl BB9 170 D4
Eden Ct BL0 68 D2
EDENFIELD 68 D3
Edenfield
Lytham St Anne's FY8 90 E3
Much Hoole PR4 74 F4
Edenfield Ave FY6 153 F2
Edenfield CE Prim Sch
BL0 68 D4
Edenfield Cl PR8 35 E3
Edenfield Rd
Ramsbottom OL11, OL12 51 E4
Rochdale OL12 52 A1
Edenfield St OL11, OL12 52 C1
Eden Gdns PR3 140 B8
Eden Gr LA5 221 B6
Eden Hall PR1 117 E1
Edenhurst
Haslingden BB4 68 D8
Skelmersdale WN8 9 E8
Edenhurst Cl L37 11 C2
Edenhurst Dr L37 11 C2
Eden Mount Way LA5 223 F2
Eden Pk
Blackburn BB2 101 A8
Lancaster LA1 214 F4
Edensor Terr BB3 81 F2
Eden St
Accrington BB5 104 A5
Blackburn BB1 102 A5
9 Blackpool FY1 130 C6
Edenfield BL0 68 D2
Leyland PR25 60 A8
Edenvale Ave FY2 152 B4
Edenvale Cres LA1 218 C3
Edenvale Rd LA1 218 C3
Edenway PR2 117 D7
Edgar St W 17 BL0 50 B5
Edgar St
Accrington BB5 104 B6
Huncoat BB5 125 E2
Nelson BB9 170 F2
16 Ramsbottom BL0 50 B5
Edgecott Cl LA3 213 A7
EDGE END 124 B6
Edge End BB6 124 B5
Edge End Ave BB9 148 D6
Edge End La
Burnley BB9 148 D6
Great Harwood BB6 124 B6
Edge End Rd BB6 124 B5
Edge End Terr BB2 80 B3
Edgefield PR7 61 B2
Edgefield Ct FY3 131 B8
Edge Gate La PR6 63 A6
Edge Hall Rd WN5 10 E5
Edgehill Cl PR2 117 D4
Edge Hill Coll PR7 43 A8
Edgehill Cres PR25 76 E2
Edgehill Dr PR2 117 D4
Edge Hill Univ L39 16 A3
Edge La
Barnoldswick BB18 231 F1
Britannia OL13 71 C8
Entwistle BL7 48 A8
Rawtenstall BB4 86 D3
Edgeley Ct 1 BB12 127 D7
Edgemoor Cl OL12 71 E5
EDGESIDE 86 F2
Edgeside BB6 124 B5
Edgeside La BB4 86 F2
Edgeware Rd BB2 101 C6
Edgeway Pl 3 FY5 176 C1
Edgeway Rd FY4 110 E5
Edge Yate La BB4 86 B5
Edgley Ct PR4 95 E2
Edgley Dr L39 16 A5
EDGWORTH 48 D6
Edgworth Gr BB10 128 C6
Edgworth Vale BL7 48 E6
Edgworth Views BL7 48 D8
Edinburgh Cl PR25 77 C1
Edinburgh Dr BB5 103 F3
Edinburgh Rd
Formby L37 11 E1
Haslingden BB4 84 F1
Edisford Prim Sch
BB7 166 C7
Edisford Rd
Clitheroe BB7 166 C8
Waddington BB7 189 B4
Edison St BB3 81 F1
Edith St
Barnoldswick BB18 196 B3
Blackburn BB1 102 A4
Nelson BB9 148 F8
Shuttleworth BL0 50 E8
Edleston Lo 2 PR2 118 F4
Edleston St BB5 103 F4
Edmondsen Pl 4 FY7 198 F2
Edmondson's La BD23 197 F8
Edmondson St BB18 196 B3
Edmonton Dr BB2 101 A8
Edmonton Pl FY2 152 F3
Edmund Gennings Ct
BB7 190 D5
Edmundson St
Blackburn BB2 101 C5
Church BB5 103 E6
Edmund St
5 Accrington BB5 104 C5
Blackburn BB2 81 D7
Burnley BB10 148 B1
Darwen BB3 82 B1
3 Preston PR1 97 B8
Edward Cl PR4 57 A5
Edward Ct BB5 103 E6
Edward Sq 10 PR1 118 A1
Edward St
Accrington BB5 104 E1
18 Bacup OL13 88 A3
Bamber Bridge PR5 77 E8
Barnoldswick BB18 196 C3
Blackpool FY1 130 B5
Burnley BB11 128 A6
3 Carnforth LA5 223 D2
Chorley PR6 43 D7
Church BB5 103 E6
Darwen BB3 82 A2
8 Earby BB18 197 B2
7 Great Harwood BB6 124 C5
Haslingden BB4 85 B6
Horwich BL6 32 A3
Lancaster LA1 215 A8
2 Leyland PR25 60 A8
Lytham St Anne's FY8 89 F7
Morecambe LA4 217 A5
Nelson BB9 170 F2
Preston PR1 96 F8
Rawtenstall BB4 86 A8
Rishton BB1 124 B1
Thornton FY5 176 B4
Walton-le-D PR5 97 C5
Whitworth OL12 71 D2
Edward VII Quay PR2 96 B7
Edwell Ave FY4 110 D8
Edwinstowe Rd FY8 90 D6
Edwin Waugh Gdns
OL12 52 D3
Egan St PR1 97 A8
Egbert St PR1 118 A1
EGERTON 47 E2
Egerton WN8 9 D8
Egerton Gr PR7 43 B6
Egerton Lo BL7 47 E1
Egerton Prim Sch BL7 47 D3
Egerton Rd
Belmont BL7 46 E4
Blackpool FY1 130 B7
Leyland PR25 76 F2
Preston PR2 117 B1
Egerton Vale BL7 47 D2
Egremont Ave FY5 175 D5
Egypt Mount BB4 85 D2
Egypt Terr 3 BB4 85 E2
Eider Cl FY5 175 F5
Eidsforth La PR3 226 A1
Eidsforth Rd LA4 217 B6
Eight Acre Ave BB7 145 F8
Eight Acre La
Formby L37 12 B6
Preesall PR3 200 F6
Yealand Redmayne LA5 225 E4
Eildon Dr FY6 153 D1
Elaine Ave FY4 130 F1
Eland Way PR4 114 B2
Elbow La L37 11 F3
Elbow St PR7 43 C7
Elbut La BL9 33 F5
Elcho St PR1 118 A2
Elder Ave L40 25 F4
Elderberry Cl FY5 175 F5
Elderbrook Cl PR4 73 E4
Elder Cl
Clayton Green PR6 78 C2
Fulwood PR2 118 D6
Warton PR4 92 E6
Elder Ct 2 BB5 104 E8
Elder St BB9 170 F2
Elderwood Ave FY5 153 B7
Eldon Ct FY8 89 F7
Eldon Gr LA3 212 F7
Eldon Ho PR6 43 D7
Eldon Prim Sch PR1 117 E2
Eldon Rd BB1 101 D7
Eldons Croft PR8 21 D5
Eldon St
Chorley PR6 43 D7
Preston PR1, PR2 117 D2
Eldwick St BB10 148 C1
Eleanor St
Blackburn BB1 101 F5
3 Nelson BB9 170 E1
Electricity St BB5 104 B6
Elgar Cl BB2 102 A2
Elgin Cres BB11 127 D4
Elgin Pl FY3 131 A7
Elgin St
4 Lancaster LA1 215 A7
Preston PR1 118 A2
Elijah St 4 PR1 97 D8
Elim Ct 4 FY8 91 C3
Elim Gdns BB2 101 C1
Elim Pl BB2 101 C1
Elim View BB10 148 D2
Elizabeth Ave PR8 21 E6
Elizabeth Cl FY3 131 D5
Elizabeth Ct
Blackpool FY3 130 D6
9 Lancaster LA1 214 F7
Poulton-le-F FY6 153 D3
Elizabeth Dr BB4 68 A8
Elizabeth Ho BB3 82 B1
Elizabeth Sq 8 PR1 118 A1
Elizabeth St
Accrington BB5 103 F5
Blackburn BB1 101 F5
Blackpool FY1 130 C6
Burnley BB11 128 A5
Edenfield BL0 68 D3
9 Fleetwood FY7 199 B5
Nelson BB9 170 E1
Padiham BB12 126 C7
Preston PR1 96 F8
Whitewell Bottom BB4 86 F4
Eliza St
Burnley BB10 128 B5
Ramsbottom BL0 50 D6
Elker Cotts BB7 143 F4
Elker La BB7 143 F5
Elker Mews BB7 143 F3
Elkfield Dr FY3 153 A1
Elkin Rd LA4 217 D5
Elland Pl FY1 130 B1
Elland Rd BB9 148 C6
ELLEL 211 B5
Ellel Hall Gdns LA2 210 F3
Ellel St John the Evangelist CE Prim Sch
LA2 211 A3
Ellen Ct PR1 117 F2
Ellenrod Dr OL12 52 A2
Ellenrod La OL12 52 A2
Ellenshaw Cl
Darwen BB3 82 B1
Rochdale OL12 52 A2
Ellenshaw St BB3 82 B1
Ellen St
Bamber Bridge PR5 97 E1
Darwen BB3 65 A7
11 Nelson BB9 148 D8
Preston, Maudlands PR1 117 E1
Preston PR1 117 F2
Ellerbeck Ave PR2 118 E5
Ellerbeck Cl BB10 148 E3
Ellerbeck Rd
Accrington BB5 104 B7
Cleveleys FY5 175 C2
Darwen BB3 82 B1
Eller Brook Cl PR6 43 F1
Ellerbrook Dr L40 25 F3
Eller Brook Ho L39 15 E6
Ellerbrook Way L39 15 E6
Ellerigg La LA6 243 A6
Ellershaw Ho 12 LA1 218 D2
Ellerslie Rd PR2 117 B1
Ellesmere Ave
Colne BB8 171 F5
Thornton FY5 176 D1
Ellesmere Gr LA4 217 A3
Ellesmere Rd
Blackpool FY4 130 E1
Darwen BB3 81 E3
Morecambe LA4 216 F4
Elletson St FY6 153 D4
Elliott Ave BB3 65 B6
Elliott Cl PR1 117 E2
Elliott St
Burnley BB10 128 C5
Preston, Adelphi PR1 117 E1
Preston PR1 117 E2
Elliott Wlk PR1 117 E2
Ellis Dr LA4 217 E6
Ellisland FY4 131 C1
Ellison Fold BB5 124 E3
Ellison Fold La BB3 82 C1
Ellison Fold Terr BB3 82 B1
Ellison St
Accrington BB5 104 B6
Darwen BB3 82 A2
Ellis St
Barnoldswick BB18 196 B2
1 Burnley BB11 127 E5
19 Ramsbottom BL0 50 B5
Ellwood Ave
Lancaster LA1 218 E4
Morecambe LA3 217 C2
Ellwood Ct 4 LA3 217 C2
Ellwood Gr 5 LA3 217 C2
Elm Ave
Blackpool FY3 130 E5
Galgate LA2 210 F4
Poulton-le-F FY6 153 D3
Preston PR2 117 A2
Warton PR4 92 D6
Elmbank Ave FY5 152 C7
Elm Brow PR3 162 C4
Elm Cl
Barnoldswick BB18 196 A1
Haslingden BB4 85 B3
Rishton BB1 103 B8
Salterforth BB18 194 E8
Elmcroft La L38 3 A3
Elm Ct
Poulton-le-F FY6 153 D3
Skelmersdale WN8 17 E1
Elmdale Cl L37 11 D2
Elm Dr
3 Bamber Bridge PR5 97 F1
Formby L37 11 D1
Elmers Gn WN8 18 D2
ELMERS GREEN 18 D2
Elmer's Green La WN8 18 C4
Elmers Wood Rd WN8 18 D2
Elmfield Dr PR5 78 C6
Elmfield Hall BB5 103 F7
Elmfield St BB5 103 F7
Elm Gr
Chorley PR6 61 E2
Clayton-le-W PR25 77 D3
Darwen BB3 82 B3
Fulwood PR2 118 E2
6 Horwich BL6 32 E1
Kirkham PR4 114 B7
Morecambe LA4 217 E7
Skelmersdale WN8 17 E1
Elmhurst PR3 181 D5
Elmhurst Rd FY8 90 B8
Elm Mill BB10 128 A8
Elm Park Dr PR8 21 E5
Elmpark Gate OL12 52 B3
Elmpark Gr OL12 52 B3
Elmpark Vale OL12 52 B3
Elmpark View OL12 52 B3
Elmpark Way OL12 52 B3
Elm Pl L39 15 E4
Elm Rd
Burscough L40 25 E3
Southport PR8 35 B4
Elmridge WN8 9 D8
Elmridge Cres FY2 152 F3
Elms Ave
Cleveleys FY5 175 E2
Lytham St Anne's FY8 90 E3
Elms Ct LA4 217 E7
Elmsdale Cl LA1 218 C2
Elms Dr
Morecambe LA4 217 E7
Wrea Green PR4 113 B4
Elmsfield Pk L39 6 A6
Elmside Cl FY5 176 D2
Elmslack Ct LA5 224 C4
Elmslack La LA5 224 C4
Elmsley St PR1 117 E2
Elmslie Gdns FY3 130 E3
Elms Rd LA4 217 E7
Elms Sch PR1 118 A3
Elm St
6 Bacup OL13 88 A3
Blackburn BB1 102 A7
Burnley BB10 128 A8
Bury BL9 33 B2
Colne BB8 171 E6
Edenfield BL0 68 E3
Fleetwood FY7 199 A4
Great Harwood BB6 124 C4
Haslingden BB4 85 B3
9 Nelson BB9 170 E1
Ramsbottom BL0 50 D6
Rawtenstall BB4 86 A3
Rochdale OL12 52 F1
Whitworth OL12 71 D2
Elmstead WN8 9 D8
Elms The
Clayton Green PR6 78 C1
Maghull L31 5 D3
Southport, Birkdale PR8 34 F6
Southport, Blowick PR8 35 C5
Elmswood Cl FY8 90 F4
Elm Tree Gr BB6 143 C5
Elmwood
Chorley PR7 61 B1
Longridge PR3 140 A8
Skelmersdale WN8 18 C3
Elmwood Ave
1 Leyland PR25 76 E1
Preesall FY6 200 B4
Elmwood Cl BB5 104 D6
Elmwood Ct PR4 132 F2
Elmwood Dr
Higher Penwortham PR1 96 B4
Thornton FY5 176 C1
Elmwood Gdns LA1 215 A2
Elmwood St BB11 127 D5
Elsby Ave FY5 153 C8
Elsie St 10 BL0 50 A4
Elsinore Cl FY7 198 F5
ELSLACK 197 F7
Elslack La BD23 197 F7
Elson Rd L37 11 D1
ELSTON 120 A6
Elston Ave FY3 131 A8
Elston Gn PR2 139 E1
Elston La PR2 119 F7
Elston Lo 7 PR2 118 F4
ELSWICK 156 A1
Elswick WN8 9 C8
Elswick Gdns BB2 121 D3
Elswick Gn PR9 54 A5
Elswick Ind Pk PR4 156 A1
ELSWICK LEYS 134 A8
Elswick Lo BB2 121 E3
Elswick Pl
Blackpool FY4 110 E5
Lytham St Anne's FY8 90 B8
Elswick Rd
Leyland PR25 59 D8
Preston PR2 116 E1
Southport PR9 53 F4
Elswick St BB3 82 B1
Elsworth Cl L37 2 C8
Elterwater FY6 199 E5
Elterwater Pl
Blackpool FY3 131 C2
Lancaster LA1 218 E1
Eltham Ct FY3 153 B1
Elton Rd BB1, BB4 83 B5
Elton St 3 PR2 117 C1
Elvaston Rd FY6 153 C6
Elvington Rd L38 3 A2
Elwood Grange FY8 89 C8
Ely Cl
Darwen BB3 82 C1
Wilpshire BB1 122 F6
Ely Mews PR9 54 A2
Embankment Rd BL7 48 C5
Emerald Ave BB1 122 F2
Emerald Cl
Blackburn BB1 122 F2
Blackpool FY5 152 F7
Emerald Cotts BL8 49 F3
Emerald St BB1 122 F2
Emerson Ave FY4 110 D7
Emerson Cl L38 3 A4
Emerson Rd PR1 118 D2
Emerson St LA1 215 A4
Emesgate La LA5 224 C3
Emily St
Bamber Bridge PR5 77 A8
Blackburn BB1 102 A6
Burnley BB11 128 A4
Emlsett Rd PR5 97 E3
Emmanuel Christian Sch
OL12 52 D2
Emmanuel Holcombe CE Prim Sch BL8 50 A6
Emmanuel Rd PR9 53 F2
Emmanuel St PR1, PR2 117 E2
Emma St BB5 103 F6
Emmaus Rd LA3 212 F6
Emmett St
Horwich BL6 32 B3
Preston PR1 117 F1
Emmott Ct BB8 172 E6
Emmott La BB8 172 D6
Emmsix L40 24 B4
Emnie La PR26, PR25 59 C7
Empire Gr 2 FY3 130 D7
Empire Ho 3 BB5 104 B6
Empire St BB6 124 D6
Emporium The 8 BB7 166 E8
Empress Ave PR2 117 E4
Empress Cl L31 5 B1
Empress Dr FY2 152 B1
Empress St
Accrington BB5 103 F6
Blackburn BB3 81 F7
Colne BB8 171 E5
Empress Way PR7 60 E2
Endcliffe Rd LA4 217 C5
Endeavour Cl PR2 96 B7
Enderley Ct FY5 176 C1
Ending Rake OL12 52 C4
Endsleigh Gdns FY4 110 E6
Endsleigh Gr LA1 218 A3
End St BB8 171 B4
ENFIELD 125 A2
Enfield Cl PR7 41 C5
Enfield Rd
Accrington BB5 125 E2
Blackpool FY1 130 C7
Engel Cl BL0 50 A5
Engine La L37 3 E8
England Ave
Blackburn BB2 81 D8
Blackpool FY2 152 C4
English Martyrs' Pl
PR1 117 F2
English Martyrs RC Prim Sch PR1 117 E1
Ennerdale WN8 9 D8
Ennerdale Ave
Blackburn BB1 102 C3
Fleetwood FY7 198 C1
Maghull L31 5 E2
Morecambe LA4 217 D4
Ennerdale Cl
Clitheroe BB7 166 C7
Formby L37 11 D3
Forton PR3 207 B3
Knott End-on-S FY6 199 F6
Lancaster LA1 218 F2
Leyland PR25 60 A7
Oswaldtwistle BB5 103 D5
Ennerdale Dr
Ormskirk L39 15 B2
Walton-le-D PR5 97 E5
Ennerdale Rd
Blackpool FY4 131 C1
Burnley BB10 128 E5
Chorley PR7 43 A6
Clitheroe BB7 166 C7
Formby L37 11 E3
Longridge PR3 139 F5
Ennismore Gdns PR9 53 E1
Ennismore St BB10 148 C1
Enoch Brow BB2 80 C8
Ensign Ct FY8 110 C4
Enstone WN8 18 D1
Enterprise Ct BB5 125 D1
Enterprise Dr PR26 77 A4
Enterprise Way
Fleetwood FY7 176 A6
Nelson BB8 170 F3
Enterprise Workshops
L33 1 B1
Entwisle Rd BB5 104 B8
ENTWISTLE 48 B7
Entwistle Hall La BL7 48 B8
Entwistle St BB3 82 A1
Entwistle Sta BL7 48 B8
Ephraim St PR1 97 C7
Epoch Cotts LA6 240 B3
Epping Ave BB5 125 B1
Epping Cl FY2 152 E5
Epping Pl PR6 43 D8
Epsom Cl PR6 61 F4
Epsom Croft PR6 31 B7
Epsom Gr L33 1 A6

Epsom Rd FY5 152 F8
Epsom Way BB5 104 D5
Epworth St BB3 65 B6
Equity St BB3 65 A8
Erdington Rd FY1 130 C3
Eric Morecambe Ho 9 LA4 217 F4
Ericson Dr PR8 35 B5
Erith Gr FY2 152 C5
Ermine Cl BB2 82 A8
Ermine Pl LA3 217 E3
Ernest St
 Britannia OL13 71 C8
 Church BB5 103 E6
 Clayton-le-M BB5 124 F1
 Todmorden OL14 109 C1
Ernlouen Cl BB2 81 A8
Erskine Rd PR6 61 E1
Escar St 9 BB11 127 F5
Escott Gdns 11 BB10 128 A8
Escowbeck Ho LA2 237 B3
Esher Pond PR2 117 C6
Eshton Terr BB7 166 D7
Esk Ave
 Edenfield BL0 68 D5
 Fleetwood FY7 198 D2
Eskbank WN8 9 C8
Eskbrook WN8 18 C1
Eskdale WN8 9 B8
Eskdale Ave
 Fleetwood FY7 198 D1
 Ormskirk L39 15 C2
Eskdale Cl
 Blackpool FY4 130 F1
 Burnley BB10 148 B4
 Formby L37 11 D2
 Fulwood PR2 117 F8
Eskdale Cres BB2 80 E8
Eskdale Ct FY5 175 D1
Eskdale Dr
 Formby L37 11 D2
 Kirkham PR4 114 A7
 Maghull L31 5 E2
Eskdale Gdns BB12 146 C2
Eskdale Gr FY6 199 F6
Eskdale Pl LA4 217 D4
Eskdale Rd
 Leyland PR25 60 C7
 Longridge PR3 139 F6
Eskew Cres LA2 239 B7
Eskew La LA2 239 B8
Eskham Cl PR4 113 E6
Eskrigge Cl 4 LA1 218 D4
Eskrigge La LA2 238 A8
Esp La BB18 231 F1
Esplanade
 Knott End-on-S FY6 199 D6
 Preston PR1 97 B5
 Southport PR8 34 F7
Esplanade Mews FY6 199 E5
Esplanade The
 Fleetwood FY7 199 A5
 Rishton BB1 103 A8
ESPRICK 133 D5
Essex Ave
 Burnley BB12 127 B7
 Heywood BL9 33 E1
Essex Cl BB2 101 D3
Essex Pl FY2 152 F2
Essex Rd
 3 Morecambe LA4 217 F4
 4 Rishton BB1 124 A1
 Southport PR8 22 A8
 Standish WN1 30 B1
Essex St
 Accrington BB5 104 D6
 Barnoldswick BB18 196 B2
 Colne BB8 171 E4
 Darwen BB3 82 C1
 Horwich BL6 32 D1
 Nelson BB9 170 E1
 Preston PR1 118 A1
Essie Terr BB18 196 B1
Essington Ave LA4 217 A4
Est Bank Rd BL0 50 A3
Esther St BB1 102 C5
Esthwaite Gdns LA1 218 F1
Ethel St
 Barnoldswick BB18 196 C2
 Whitworth OL12 71 D2
Ethersall Rd BB9 148 E6
Eton Ave BB5 104 C7
Eton Cl BB12 126 E6
Eton Ct PR9 53 C1
Eton Pk PR2 118 C5
Eton Way WN5 10 F8
Ettington Dr PR8 21 A5
Ettrick Ave FY7 198 D3
Europa Dr PR26 77 A4
Europa Way LA1 214 C8
Euston Gr LA4 217 B5
Euston Rd LA4 217 B5
Euston St PR1 96 E7
EUXTON 60 D2
Euxton Balshaw La Sta PR7 60 D1
Euxton CE Prim Sch PR7 60 C2
Euxton Ct FY4 110 E8
Euxton Hall Ct PR7 60 C2
Euxton Hall Gdns PR7 60 C1
Euxton Hall Hospl PR7 60 C1
Euxton Hall Mews PR7 60 C2
Euxton La
 Chorley PR7 61 B3
 Euxton PR7 60 E4
Euxton St Mary's RC Prim Sch PR7 60 C3
Evans St
 Burnley BB11 127 F4
 Horwich BL6 32 D4
 Preston PR2 117 D1
Evanstone Cl BL6 32 B3
Evelyn Rd BB3 81 E5
Evelyn St BB10 148 A1
Evenwood WN8 18 D1
Evenwood Ct WN8 18 C1
Everard Cl L40 23 F7
Everard Rd PR8 35 D4
Everest Cl FY8 111 A1
Everest Ct 2 PR4 113 F6
Everest Dr FY2 152 C5
Everest Rd FY8 111 A2
Evergreen Ave
 Horwich BL6 32 B3
 Leyland PR25 60 A7
Evergreen Cl PR7 43 B5
Evergreens The
 Blackburn BB2 80 F8
 Cottam PR4 116 E4
 Formby L37 11 D4
 Horwich BL6 32 E1
Eversham Cl PR9 55 A5
Eversholt Cl BB12 147 D7
Eversleigh Ave FY5 176 A3
Eversleigh St PR1 117 E1
Eversley WN8 18 D1
Everton BB2 102 A1
Everton Rd
 Blackpool FY4 110 C6
 Southport PR8 35 A4
Everton St BB3 81 F1
Every St
 Brierfield BB9 148 B6
 Burnley BB11 127 E5
 Nelson BB9 148 D8
 Ramsbottom BL0 50 D6
Evesham Ave PR1 96 E2
Evesham Cl
 5 Accrington BB5 104 A7
 Blackpool FY5 152 E7
 Heysham LA3 213 A6
 Hutton PR4 95 C1
Evesham Manor PR9 55 A6
Evesham Rd
 Lytham St Anne's FY8 90 A5
 Normoss FY3 131 B7
Eve St BB9 171 A2
Evington WN8 18 D1
Ewell Cl PR6 61 F4
EWOOD 81 D8
Ewood BB2 101 D1
EWOOD BRIDGE 68 C6
Ewood Cvn Site BB2 101 D1
Ewood La BB4 68 C7
Ewood Park (Blackburn Rovers FC) BB2 81 D8
Exchange St
 Accrington BB5 103 F5
 18 Blackburn BB1 101 E5
 Blackpool FY1 130 B6
 Colne BB8 171 D4
 Darwen BB3 82 A2
 Edenfield BL0 68 D3
Exchange The 2 BB8 171 D5
Exe St PR1 118 B2
Exeter Ave LA1 215 B6
Exeter Dr FY5 176 A2
Exeter Pl 2 PR2 116 E2
Exeter St
 Blackburn BB2 101 D2
 3 Blackpool FY4 130 C1
Exmoor Cl PR9 54 B6
Exmouth St BB11 128 A5
Exton St BB9 148 A5
Extwistle Rd BB10 129 B7
Extwistle Sq BB10 128 E5
Extwistle St
 Burnley BB10 128 B8
 Nelson BB9 148 D7
Eyes La
 Bretherton PR26 57 E3
 Newburgh WN8 27 A3

F

FACIT 71 D2
Factory Brow
 Blackrod BL6 31 D3
 Scorton PR3 204 E6
Factory Hill
 Horwich BL6 32 D4
 5 Lancaster LA1 218 E1
Factory La
 Adlington PR6 31 B8
 Barrowford BB9 170 D4
 Middleforth Green PR1 96 F3
 17 Padiham BB12 146 C1
Factory St BL0 50 C7
Fairacres WN6 29 B1
Fairbairn Ave BB12 127 C8
Fairbairn St BL6 32 B3
Fairbank Gr LA4 217 A3
Fairbank Wlk BB4 106 A2
Fairburn WN8 18 B3
Fairclough Rd
 Accrington BB5 104 A3
 Thornton FY5 176 A3
Fair Elms LA1 214 D7
Fairfax Ave FY2 152 E5
Fairfax Cl PR3 181 D6
Fairfax Pl PR5 97 D2
Fairfax Rd PR2 118 E4
FAIRFIELD 33 E3
Fairfield PR3 181 C8
Fairfield Ave
 Newchurch BB4 86 F2
 Normoss FY3 131 B7
 Poulton-le-F FY6 153 D3
Fairfield Cl
 Carnforth LA5 223 E1
 Clitheroe BB7 166 C7
 Lancaster LA1 214 E8
 Ormskirk L39 15 E7
Fairfield Com Prim Sch BL9 33 D3
Fairfield Ct
 Fleetwood FY7 198 F2
 Poulton-le-F FY6 153 D4
Fairfield Dr
 Burnley BB10 148 C3
 Bury BL9 33 D3
 Clitheroe BB7 166 C7
 Ormskirk L39 15 E7
 Preston PR2 117 B2
Fairfield General Hospl BL9 33 E4
Fairfield Gr LA3 216 E2
Fairfield Rd
 Blackpool FY1 130 C8
 Fulwood PR2 118 A4
 Lancaster LA1 214 E8
 Leyland PR25 59 F8
 Morecambe LA3 216 E2
 Nelson BB9 149 B8
 Poulton-le-F FY6 131 F7
 Southport PR8 21 C5
Fairfield St
 Accrington BB5 103 F4
 5 Bamber Bridge PR5 77 B7
Fairham Ave 6 PR1 96 D2
FAIRHAVEN 90 A3
Fairhaven WN8 18 C3
Fairhaven Ave FY7 175 D7
Fairhaven Cl 6 FY5 176 D1
Fair Haven Ct 2 FY8 90 D4
Fairhaven La FY8 89 E5
Fairhaven Lake* FY8 90 C3
Fairhaven Rd
 Blackburn BB2 101 F1
 Leyland PR25 76 D1
 Lytham St Anne's FY8 89 F5
 Middleforth Green PR1 96 E5
 Southport PR9 54 B4
Fairhaven Way 1 LA4 217 D5
Fairheath Rd LA2 239 B4
Fair Hill BB4 68 A7
Fairhill Terr BB4 68 A7
Fairholme Rd BB11 128 B3
Fairholmes Cl 1 FY5 176 B3
Fairholmes Ct 2 FY5 176 B3
Fairholmes Way FY5 176 B3
Fairhope Ave
 Lancaster LA1 218 C3
 Morecambe LA4 217 F6
Fairhope Ct BB2 101 C6
Fairhurst Ave WN6 29 D3
Fairhurst Ct FY5 175 D3
Fairhurst's Dr WN8 27 B2
Fairhurst St FY1 130 C6
Fairlawn Rd FY8 90 F3
Fairlea Ave LA4 217 F6
Fairlie WN8 18 C3
Fairmont Dr FY6 177 D2
Fair Oak Cl PR2 118 F3
Fairsnape Ave PR3 140 B7
Fairsnape Dr PR3 181 B6
Fairsnape Rd FY8 91 D4
Fairstead WN8 18 C3
Fairthorn Wlk L33 1 A3
FAIRVIEW 44 A1
Fairview BB4 85 F5
Fair View OL13 71 C8
Fairview Ave FY8 90 A7
Fairview Cl PR4 74 F5
Fair View Cres OL13 88 B3
Fairview Dr
 Adlington PR6 44 A1
 Adlington PR6, PR7 30 F8
Fair View Rd BB11 128 B5
Fairway
 Chorley PR7 61 C2
 Fleetwood FY7 198 C1
 Higher Penwortham PR1 96 B6
 Poulton-le-F FY6 153 A2
 Southport PR9 53 C2
 Whitworth OL12 52 C7
Fair Way FY6 177 C7
Fairway Gdns FY6 199 D5
Fairway Rd FY4 110 E8
Fairways
 Fulwood PR2 118 A6
 Horwich BL6 32 C3
 Lytham St Anne's FY8 90 A6
Fairways Ave PR3 137 C3
Fairways Ct
 Formby L37 11 C5
 Wilpshire BB1 122 F5
Fairways Dr BB11 127 E2
Fairways The
 Knott End-on-S FY6 199 D5
 Skelmersdale WN8 18 D3
Fairweather Ct BB12 146 D1
Fairwinds Ave PR4 73 D4
Falcon Ave BB3 81 E3
Falcon Cl
 Blackburn BB1 101 D8
 Bury BL9 33 B4
Falcon Ct BB5 124 F2
Falcon Dr FY6 153 B2
Falcon Ho BL9 33 A4
Falcon Mews FY6 200 B4
Falcon St PR1 118 B2
FALINGE FOLD 52 D1
Falinge Fold OL12 52 D1
Falinge Park High Sch OL12 52 D1
Falinge Rd OL12 52 E1
Falkirk Ave FY2 152 C6
Falkland WN8 18 C3
Falkland Ave FY4 130 F2
Falkland Rd PR8 35 D5
Falkland St PR1 96 F7
Falkus Ct 6 FY6 153 D3
Fallbarn Cres BB4 86 A1
Fallbarn Fold BB4 86 B2
Fall Barn Rd BB4 86 B2
Fall Kirk LA2 240 F1
Fallowfield Cl PR4 113 E6
Fallowfield Dr
 Burnley BB12 127 D8
 Rochdale OL12 52 D2
Fallowfield Rd FY8 90 C6
Falmouth Ave
 Fleetwood FY7 175 C8
 Haslingden BB4 85 C2
Falmouth Rd FY1 130 C2
Falshaw Dr BL9 50 E1
Falstone Ave BL0 50 C4
Faraday Ave BB7 166 D8
Faraday Dr PR2 118 C7
Faraday Rise OL12 52 B1
Faraday St BB12 127 D7
Faraday Way FY2, FY6 153 A6
FAR ARNSIDE 224 A5
FAR BANKS 55 C8
Far Croft PR5 97 A1
Far East View 16 BB18 196 B2
Fareham Cl
 Bamber Bridge PR5 97 F3
 Fulwood PR2 118 A4
Fareham Dr PR9 55 A5
Far Field PR1 96 D3
Farfield Dr BB3 81 F6
Farholme La OL13 70 D8
Faringdon Ave FY4 110 E5
FARINGTON
 Bamber Bridge 76 F6
 Leyland 77 B3
Farington Ave PR25 59 D7
Farington Gate PR25 77 B2
Farington Prim Sch PR25 77 B3
Farington Rd PR5, PR26 77 A6
Farington St Paul's CE Prim Sch PR26 76 F7
Far La PR1 96 C2
FARLETON 238 A6
Farleton Cl LA5 223 C5
Farleton Ct 3 LA1 218 D4
Farleton Old Rd LA2 238 A5
Farley La
 Skelmersdale WN8 18 F3
 Up Holland WN8 19 A3
Farm Ave
 Adlington PR6 31 A8
 Bacup OL13 87 F4
Farm Cl
 Southport PR9 36 A8
 Thornton FY5 176 B2
Farmdale Dr L31 5 E1
Farmdale Rd LA1 215 B5
Farmend Cl PR4 75 B8
Farmer Parr's Animal World (Mus)* FY7 175 F7
Farmer's Row BB2 81 B7
Farmer Ted's Farm Pk* L39 13 E1
Farm House Cl
 Blackburn BB1 102 C4
 Lucas Green PR6 61 C6
Farm Meadow Rd WN5 10 E5
FAR MOOR 10 E4
Far Moor La LA1 215 C8
Farnborough Rd PR8 21 F8
Farnborough Road Inf & Jun Schs PR8 22 A8
Farnell Pl FY4 110 D6
Farnham Way FY6 153 C5
Farnlea Dr LA4 217 E5
Far Nook PR6 61 B7
Farnworth Rd FY5 176 D1
Faroes Cl BB2 101 F1
Farrer Ave LA1 211 A7
Farrer St BB9 148 C7
Farrier Rd L33 1 A2
Farriers Fold LA3 212 F7
Farriers Way
 Buckshaw Village PR7 60 E6
 Poulton-le-F FY6 153 E4
Farriers Yd LA2 237 C3
Farrier Way WN6 19 C7
Farringdon Cl PR1 118 F1
Farringdon Cres PR1 118 F1
Farringdon La PR2 118 F3
Farringdon Pl PR1 118 F1
Farrington Cl
 1 Blackburn BB2 101 C1
 Burnley BB11 127 C3
Farrington Ct
 Burnley BB11 127 C3
 Leyland PR25 77 C4
Farrington Dr L39 15 E6
Farrington Pl BB11 127 C3
Farrington Rd
 Britannia OL13 71 B8
 Burnley BB11 127 B3
Farrington St PR7 43 C8
Farthings The PR7 60 F1
Faulkner Cl PR8 21 C6
Faulkner Gdns PR8 21 C6
Faulkner's La PR3 207 B1
Favordale Rd BB8 172 A5
Fawcett WN8 18 B3
Fawcett Cl BB2 101 D3
Fawcett Rd L31 5 D3
Fayles Gr FY4 131 A1
Fazackerley Cl BB2 81 D7
Fazackerley St PR2 117 C1
Fazakerley St 13 PR7 43 C8
Fearn Dene 2 OL12 52 B2
Fearnhead Ave BL6 32 B5
Fearns Com Sports Coll OL13 87 A1
Fearns Moss
 Bacup OL13 70 A8
 Rawtenstall BB4, OL13 87 A1
Fecit La BL0 51 C8
Fecitt Brow BB1 102 D4
Fecitt Rd BB2 101 B6
Federation St BB18 196 A3
Feilden Pl BB2 80 D8
Feildens Farm La BB2 121 B3
Feilden St BB2 101 D5
Felgate Brow FY3 130 E5
Felix St BB11 128 B7
Fellborough Lo 5 FY8 90 A8
Fell Brow PR3 140 B6
Fell Cl 5 PR5 77 F8
Fell End Cvn Pk LA7 225 E8
Fellery St PR7 43 C8
Fellfoot Lo PR2 119 A4
Fellfoot Rd LA6 243 A3
Fellgate LA3 217 E2
Fell Rd
 Casterton LA6 243 B2
 Morecambe LA4 217 F4
Fellside Cl BL8 49 F1
Fellside View LA3 212 F7
Fellstone Vale PR6 80 A1
Fells View BB7 144 A4
Fellview PR9 54 D6
Fell View
 Burnley BB10 148 D3
 Caton LA2 237 C3
 Chorley PR6 43 E6
 Garstang PR3 181 C8
 Grimsargh PR2 139 C2
 Weir OL13 88 A8
 West Bradford BB7 189 D7
 Whalley BB7 144 A7
Fell View Cl PR3 181 C8
Fell Way FY6 177 D7
Fellway Cl 7 PR5 77 C8
Felstead WN8 18 B2
Felstead St PR1 97 D8
Feltons WN8 18 B2
Felton Way PR4 74 F3
Fenber Ave FY4 110 C7
FENCE 147 E7
Fencegate BB12 147 D7
Fengrove PR4 75 A8
Fenham Carr La LA1 215 C7
FENISCLIFFE 101 A2
Feniscliffe Dr BB2 101 A2
FENISCOWLES 80 D8
Feniscowles Prim Sch BB2 80 C8
Fennel Cl FY2 152 F4
Fenney Ct WN8 18 C1
Fennyfold Terr BB12 126 C6
Fensway PR4 95 D2
Fenton Ave BB18 196 D3
Fenton Rd
 Blackpool FY1 130 C6
 Fulwood PR2 118 C4
Fenton St LA1 214 E8
Fenwick St BB11 127 D3
Ferguson Gdns OL12 52 F3
Ferguson Rd FY1 130 E2
Ferguson St BB2 81 D7
Fermor Rd
 Becconsall PR4 73 E1
 Preston PR1 118 E1
Fern Ave BB5 103 F3
Fern Bank
 Carnforth LA5 223 D1
 Chorley PR6 61 D3
 Lancaster LA1 215 A5
 Maghull L31 5 E1
 Nelson BB9 148 E7
Fernbank Ave BB18 196 A3
Fernbank Ct BB9 148 E7
Fern Breck Cotts FY6 200 A2
Fern Cl
 2 Bamber Bridge PR5 77 B8
 Skelmersdale WN8 17 E1
Ferncliffe Dr LA3 216 D2
Fern Ct FY7 198 C1
Ferndale
 4 Blackburn BB1 102 A6
 Fulwood PR2 117 E6
 Skelmersdale WN8 18 C2
Ferndale Ave FY4 110 D7
Ferndale Cl
 Freckleton PR4 93 D7
 Leyland PR25 60 B7
 Thornton FY5 176 C2
Ferndale Dr WN6 19 E7
Ferndale St BB10 128 C8
FERN GORE 104 A3
Fern Gore Ave BB5 104 A3
Fern Gr FY1 130 C3
Ferngrove BL9 33 B4
FERN GROVE 33 C4
Fernhill Ave OL13 70 E8

Fernhill Cl OL13 70 E8
Fernhill Cres 1 OL13 70 E8
Fernhill Dr OL13 70 E8
Fernhill Gr 2 OL13 70 E8
Fern Hill La OL12 52 A3
Fernhill Pk OL13 70 E8
Fernhills BL7 47 E2
Fernhill Way 4 OL13 70 E8
Fernhurst Ave FY4 130 D1
Fernhurst Gate L39 15 B1
Fernhurst Sec SEBD Sch BB2 81 C7
Fernhurst St BB2 81 D8
Fern Isle Cl OL12 52 B6
Fern Lea
Bolton-le-S LA5 221 A4
Nelson BB9 148 E8
Fernlea Ave
Barnoldswick BB18 196 B2
Oswaldtwistle BB5 104 A3
Fernlea Cl
Blackburn BB2 81 B8
1 Rochdale OL12 52 B2
Fernlea Dr BB5 124 F4
Fern Lea St BB4 69 D8
Fernleigh
10 Horwich BL6 32 D1
Leyland PR26 59 A8
Fernleigh Cl
Blackpool FY2 152 D4
Garstang PR3 181 C8
Fernley Rd PR8 35 A5
Fern Mdw PR6 78 C2
Fern Rd BB11 127 E4
Fernside Way OL12 52 A1
Fern St
Bacup OL13 87 F3
Colne BB8 171 F6
Newchurch BB4 86 F1
Ramsbottom BL0 50 D7
Ferns The
3 Bacup OL13 88 A1
Bamber Bridge PR5 97 C3
Britannia OL13 71 A8
Kirkham PR4 113 F4
Preston PR2 117 C2
Fernstone Cl BL6 32 A3
Fern Terr BB4 85 A3
Fernview Dr BL0 50 A1
Fernville Terr 6 OL13 70 D8
Fernwood Ave FY5 153 B8
Fernwood Cl FY8 90 E4
Fernyhalgh Ct PR2 118 D6
Fernyhalgh Gdns PR2 118 D6
Fernyhalgh Gr PR2 118 D6
Fernyhalgh La PR2 118 D7
Fernyhalgh Pl PR2 118 D6
Ferny Knoll Rd WA11 8 F4
Ferrier Bank PR4 92 D5
Ferrier Cl 1 BB1 102 C5
Ferrier Ct BB1 102 C5
Ferry Rd PR2 95 F8
Ferry Road Office Pk 4 PR2 95 F8
Ferryside La PR9 54 C5
Ferry View Ct FY7 199 C5
Ffrances Pas 31 LA1 214 F8
FIDDLER'S FERRY 54 D6
Fiddlers Fold Ct PR4 116 C4
Fiddler's La
Chipping PR3 184 F4
Clayton Green PR6 78 B2
Fidler La PR26 76 F5
Field Cl L40 25 F3
Field Edge La PR3 201 E5
Fielden St
Burnley BB11 127 D5
Chorley PR6 43 E8
5 Leyland PR25 76 D1
Fieldfare Cl
Middleforth Green PR1 96 E3
Thornton FY5 176 A5
Fieldfare Ct PR7 42 F5
Fieldfare Way OL13 88 A1
Fieldhouse Ave FY5 176 D2
Fieldhouse Ind Est OL12 52 F2
Fieldhouse Rd OL12 52 F2
Fielding Cres BB2 101 A1
Fielding La
Great Harwood BB6 124 B5
Oswaldtwistle BB5 103 E3
Fielding Pl PR6 31 B8
Fielding Rd FY1 130 D8
Fielding's Bldgs 9 BB4 85 E2
Fielding St BB1 124 C1
Fieldings The
Fulwood PR2 117 D3
Maghull L31 5 B4
Fieldlands PR8 36 A2
Field Maple Dr PR2 118 F3
Field Rd LA3 212 D6
Fieldsend LA3 213 A7
Fields End BB6 123 C8
Fieldside Ave PR7 60 C1
Fieldside Cl PR5 97 C3
Fields Rd BB4 85 C1
Field St
Blackburn BB2 101 B2
Blackpool FY1 130 C2
Padiham BB12 126 C7
Skelmersdale WN8 17 D2
Fields The PR7 41 B7
Field Top 2 OL13 88 A7
Fieldview 2 WN8 10 A7
Fieldway FY8 110 E2
Field Wlk L39 16 B5
Fife Cl PR6 43 E6
Fife St
Accrington BB5 104 A4
Barrowford BB9 170 C1
Fifth Ave
Blackpool FY4 110 C7
Burnley BB10 148 B3
Bury BL9 33 D4
Filberts Cl PR2 117 C3
Filberts The PR2 117 C3
File St PR7 43 C7
Filey Pl
Blackpool FY1 130 B6
Fulwood PR2 117 A4
Filey Rd FY8 111 A1
Filton Gr LA3 217 E3
Finch Cl BB1 101 E6
Finches The FY6 153 B2
Finch La
Appley Bridge WN6 28 B1
Cottam PR4 116 E4
Finchley Rd FY1 130 B8
Finch Mill Ave WN6 19 D7
Finch's Cotts 6 PR1 96 E4
Finch St 5 BB3 81 F2
Findon WN8 18 C2
Fine Jane's Way PR9 36 B8
Finney Park Dr PR2 95 D8
Finnington Cotts BB2 80 A6
Finnington La BB2 80 A6
Finsbury Ave
Blackpool FY1 130 D2
Lytham St Anne's FY8 90 B4
Finsbury Pl BB2 81 D7
Finsley Gate BB11 128 A5
Finsley St BB10 148 E3
Finsley View BB10 148 F3
Firbank
1 Bamber Bridge PR5 97 D1
Euxton PR7 60 C2
Firbank Ave PR4 57 A7
Firbank Rd LA1 218 E1
Firbeck WN8 18 C1
Fir Cl FY7 198 C2
Fir Cotes L31 5 E1
Fircroft WN6 29 A2
Fir Ct 4 BB5 104 E8
Firfield Cl PR4 113 E5
Fir Gr
Blackpool FY1 130 E2
Warton PR4 92 D6
Fir Grove Rd 10 BB11 128 B4
Fir Mount 10 OL13 88 A1
Firs Cl L37 11 D5
Firs Cres L37 11 D5
Firshill Cl FY5 153 B8
Firs La L39 14 E3
Firs Link L37 11 D4
Fir St
Burnley BB10 128 B5
Bury BL9 33 A2
Haslingden BB4 85 B3
Nelson BB9 148 F8
Ramsbottom BL0 50 D7
Southport PR8 35 F6
First Ave
Blackpool FY4 110 C7
Church BB5 104 A8
Clifton PR4 115 C1
Poulton-le-F FY6 153 E3
Preesall Park FY6 200 C1
Preston PR2 117 A2
West Bradford BB7 189 D7
Wrea Green PR4 113 B4
First Terr LA3 209 B5
Firswood Cl FY8 90 E4
Firswood Rd L40, WN8 17 C3
Fir Tree Ave PR2 117 B4
Firtree Cl PR7 43 C3
Fir Tree Cl
Hest Bank LA5 220 F2
Much Hoole PR4 74 E3
Skelmersdale WN8 9 D7
Fir Tree La
Haskayne L39 14 F3
Ormskirk L39 15 A2
Fir Tree Pl FY5 152 F8
Fir Trees Ave
Bamber Bridge PR5 77 A8
Fulwood PR2 119 A4
Fir Trees Cl BB9 149 A8
Fir Trees Cres 1 PR5 77 A8
Firtrees Dr BB2 80 F8
Fir Trees Gr BB12 146 E5
Fir Trees La BB12 146 E5
Fir Trees Pl PR2 118 F4
Fir Trees Rd PR5 97 A1
Fir Tree Way 3 BL6 32 E1
Firwood WN8 18 D3
Firwood Cl PR3 140 A8
Firwood La PR5 99 B5
Fisher Dr
Orrell WN5 10 E7
Southport PR9 35 F7
Fishergate PR1 96 F7
Fishergate Ct 13 PR1 96 E7
Fishergate Ctr PR1 96 F7
Fishergate Hill PR1 96 E6
Fishergate Wlk 7 PR1 96 F7
Fishermans Cl L37 11 E6
Fishermans Reach PR4 113 D4
Fishermans Way FY7 175 C8
Fisher's La FY4 111 A5
FISHER'S ROW 201 E5
Fisher's Slack La FY6 155 B2
Fisher St FY1 130 C6
Fish House La PR3 185 B5
Fish La L40 38 B2
Fishmoor Dr BB2 81 F8
Fish Rake La BL0, BB4 68 E6
Fish St 5 PR1 117 F1
FISHWICK 97 C8
Fishwick La PR6 79 B1
Fishwick Par PR1 97 D8
Fishwick Prim Sch PR1 118 E1
Fishwick Rd PR1 97 C8
Fishwick View PR1 97 D8
Fitchfield PR1 96 F2
Fitzgerald St PR1 118 C1
Fitzroy Rd FY2 152 D3
Fitzroy St PR1 96 E7
Five Acres PR26 76 E4
Five Ashes La LA2 210 F7
Five Lane Ends
Hampson Green LA2 207 D8
Preesall FY6 200 A2
Singleton FY6 154 D3
Flag La
Bamber Bridge PR1 96 F1
Bretherton PR26 58 A5
Chorley PR6 43 F5
Runshaw Moor PR26, PR7 59 D4
Flag St OL13 70 E8
Flakefleet Ave FY7 198 E1
Flamingo Way FY6 200 B5
Flamstead WN8 18 C1
Flare Rd LA3 212 D6
Flash La L40 39 B4
Flatfield Way L31 5 E1
Flat La LA5 225 E3
Flatman's La L39 13 E1
Flats Ret Pk The PR5 97 C5
Flats The
Chorley PR7 43 B6
Kirkham PR4 114 B4
3 Kirkham PR4 114 B5
Flax Cl BB4 68 A8
Flaxfield Rd L37 12 A3
Flaxfields L40 25 F3
Flaxfield Way PR4 114 A5
Flax La L40 25 F2
FLAX MOSS 68 A8
Flax Moss Cl BB4 68 A8
Flax St 8 BL0 50 A4
Flaxton WN8 18 C1
Fleetgreen LA1 218 C3
Fleet La LA2 238 A8
Fleet Sq 6 LA1 214 F8
Fleet St
Blackpool FY1 130 C4
Chorley PR7 43 C7
Horwich BL6 32 D3
Longridge PR3 140 A7
Lytham St Anne's FY8 89 D8
Nelson BB9 170 E1
4 Preston PR1 96 F7
Fleet Street La PR3 141 A6
Fleet Wlk 6 BB11 128 A6
FLEETWOOD 198 E5
Fleetwood Charles Saer Com Prim Sch FY7 198 D3
Fleetwood Chaucer Com Prim Sch FY7 199 A4
Fleetwood Cl
Blackburn BB2 101 F1
Southport PR9 53 F3
Fleetwood Cres PR9 55 A6
Fleetwood Ct PR9 53 D1
Fleetwood Dr PR9 55 A6
Fleetwood Flakefleet Prim Sch FY7 198 E2
Fleetwood Hospl FY7 199 B5
Fleetwood Old Rd PR4 133 E3
Fleetwood Rd
Blackpool FY5 152 D7
Burnley BB10 148 C2
Carleton FY6 153 B5
Esprick PR4 133 D5
Fleetwood FY7 175 E8
Kirkham PR4 113 F7
Padiham BB12 126 D8
Southport PR9 53 E3
Fleetwood Rd N FY5 176 B3
Fleetwood Rd S FY5 153 B7
Fleetwood Sports Coll FY7 198 D2
Fleetwood St
6 Leyland PR25 77 B2
Preston PR2 117 D1
Fleming Ho 8 LA1 218 D2
Fleming Sq
Blackburn BB2 101 E4
Longridge PR3 140 B7
Flensburg Way PR26 76 D4
Fletcher Ave PR4 57 A6
FLETCHER BANK 50 D6
Fletcher Rd
Preston PR1 118 C1
Rishton BB1 103 A8
Fletcher's Dr L40 25 E4
Fletcher St
Blackburn BB2 101 D3
Bury BL9 33 A2
Nelson BB9 148 F7
Fletton Cl OL12 52 E2
Fletton Mews OL12 52 E2
Flett St PR2 117 C1
Flimby WN8 18 D1
Flimby Cl BB2 81 F8
Flintoff Way PR1 118 B3
Flintron Brow LA2 233 A2
Flip Rd BB4 85 A2
Flockton Ct 7 BL6 32 B4
Floodgates Rd L38 2 F5
Flordon WN8 18 D2
Florence Ave
Burnley BB11 127 C4
Warton PR4 92 D5
Florence Pl 1 BB1 102 A6
Florence St
Blackburn BB1 102 A6
Blackpool FY4 111 A6
Burnley BB11 127 C5
Church BB5 103 E6
Flowerfield PR4 116 E6
Flower Fields PR3 181 D2
Flower Scar Rd OL13 88 E6
Flowers Cl BB2 81 D7
Floyd Rd PR2 118 E3
Floyer St PR1 97 B7
Fluke Hall La PR3 201 B8
Flyde Road Ind Est PR9 54 B4
Fold BB9 170 E5
Fold Gdns OL12 52 B3
Fold House Pk PR3 201 D4
Fold La OL12 52 C4
Folds BL6 31 C3
Foldside PR4 93 C7
Folds St BB12 127 F8
Fold The BD23 197 B5
Fold View BL7 47 E1
Folkestone Cl
Cleveleys FY5 175 F4
Warton PR4 92 E7
Folkestone Rd
Lytham St Anne's FY8 89 F8
Southport PR8 35 F3
Folly La
Barnoldswick BB8 193 F7
Lancaster LA1, LA2 218 B4
Folly Terr BB4 86 B8
Folly Wlk 20 OL12 52 F1
Folly Wood Dr PR7 43 A6
Fontwell Cl WN6 29 F1
Fooden La BB7 230 E4
Footeran La LA5 225 E3
Foot Mill Cres OL12 52 D2
Foot Wood Cres OL12 52 D2
Forbes Ct BB11 127 A3
FORD GREEN 203 F2
Fordham Cl PR8 35 E3
Ford La
Goosnargh PR3 160 F2
Silverdale LA5 224 E5
Fordside Ave BB5 124 E4
Ford St
Barrowford BB9 170 E4
Burnley BB10 148 B1
Lancaster LA1 218 B1
Fordstone Ave FY6 200 A4
Fordway Ave FY3 130 F6
Foregate PR2 117 E4
Foreside BB9 170 E5
Fore St BB3 81 F7
Forest Ave BB12 147 E8
Forest Bank
Rawtenstall BB4 86 A7
Trawden BB8 172 C2
Forest Bank Rd BB4 86 A7
FOREST BECKS 230 D6
Forest Becks Brow BB7 230 D6
Forest Brook Ho PR2 117 F3
Forest Cl PR5 97 C3
Forest Dr
Lytham St Anne's FY8 90 F4
Shevington Moor WN6 29 A2
Skelmersdale WN8 18 C3
Forester Dr BB12 147 D8
Forester's Bldgs 9 BB18 196 B2
Foresters Hall 12 PR1 96 F8
Forest Fold WN6 19 E6
Forest Gate FY3 130 E5
Forest Gr PR3 137 B8
Forest Ho BB9 148 D7
FOREST HOLME 87 A7
Forest Holme Cl BB4 87 A7
Forest La BB9 170 B2
FOREST OF MEWITH 239 D6
Forest Pk LA1 214 C7
Forest Rd PR8 35 D6
Forestry Hos BB7 228 C5
Forest St
Burnley BB11 128 B6
Nelson BB9 170 D1
Water BB4 87 A7
Forest View
14 Barrowford BB9 170 D3
Brierfield BB9 148 A5
Rochdale OL12 52 D2
Forestway PR25 59 F8
Forest Way PR2 117 F6
Forfar Gr BB11 127 D3
Forfar St BB11 127 D3
Forge Cl L40 16 E4
Forge Cnr BB7 144 C5
Forge La PR3 181 E8
Forge St
3 Bacup OL13 87 F2
13 Leyland PR25 77 A1
Forgewood Cl LA2 219 E6
Forgewood Dr LA2 219 D6
FORMBY 11 E3
Formby Ave FY7 175 D7
Formby Bridge L37 11 E2
Formby Bsns Pk L37 12 B3
Formby By-Pass
Formby L37 12 B5
Formby By-Pass *continued*
Hightown L37, L38 3 B8
Formby Cl BB2 81 F8
Formby Cres PR4 74 F8
Formby Fields L37 12 A2
Formby Gdns L37 11 F4
Formby High Sch L37 11 E4
Formby La
Formby L37 12 B2
Haskayne L39 14 F1
Formby Pl PR2 116 E2
Formby Point Cvn Pk L37 11 B1
Formby Rd FY8 110 F1
Formby St L37 11 E2
Formby Sta L37 11 E2
Forrest Ct 4 FY3 130 E8
Forrester Cl PR25 76 E1
Forrestside BB2 81 D7
Forrest St BB1 102 A5
Forshaw Ave
Blackpool FY3 130 F8
Lytham St Anne's FY8 89 D8
Forshaw Cl 6 FY7 198 F2
Forshaw Rd 3 PR1 96 D2
Forsythia Dr PR6 78 B4
Fort Ave PR3 141 D3
FORTON 207 B3
Forton Primary Sch PR3 207 B3
Forton Rd 8 PR2 116 E1
Fort St
Accrington BB5 104 B6
Blackburn BB1 102 A5
11 Clayton-le-M BB5 124 F3
Clitheroe BB7 166 D7
Read BB12 145 D2
Fort Street Ind Est BB1 102 A6
Forty Acre La PR3 163 B5
Forward Ind Est PR25 76 E2
Foscote Rd L33 1 A4
Foss Ct LA3 217 E2
Fossdale Moss PR26 76 C1
Fosse Bank Ct BB2 82 A8
Fosse Cl BB2 82 A8
Fosse Ct LA3 217 E3
Foster Croft PR1 96 C6
Foster Ct
Bury BL9 33 D4
Chorley PR6 61 E1
Fosterfield Pl PR6 61 E1
Foster Rd
Barnoldswick BB18 196 A3
Formby L37 11 D2
Fosters Cl PR9 36 B8
FOSTERS GREEN 18 D3
Fosters Green Rd WN8 18 D3
Foster St
Accrington BB5 104 C7
Chorley PR6 61 E1
Fothergill St 1 BB8 171 C5
Fouldrey Ave FY6 153 F5
Foulds Cl BB8 171 C3
Foulds Rd BB8 172 B3
Foulds Terr BB8 172 C2
Foul La PR8, PR9 36 A5
FOULRIDGE 194 D1
Foulridge Wharf* BB8 194 D2
Foundary Gdns LA5 223 D3
Foundry Ct 8 PR1 117 E1
Foundry La LA2 219 B6
Foundry St
1 Bacup OL13 87 F2
Blackburn BB2 101 D4
3 Burnley BB11 127 F6
15 Chorley PR7 43 C8
24 Darwen BB3 82 A1
Haslingden BB4 85 B2
Rawtenstall BB4 85 F1
Fountain Cl BB12 126 D8
Fountain Pl 1 BB5 104 B5
Fountain St N 12 BL9 33 A3
Fountains Ave
Blackburn BB1 102 B8
Read BB12 145 D1
Fountains Cl PR7 43 D5
Fountains Sq 3 BB9 170 D3
Fountains Reach PR5 97 D1
Fountain St
Accrington BB5 104 A5
Barnoldswick BB18 196 C2
Bury BL9 33 A2
Colne BB8 171 D4
Darwen BB3 65 A8
Nelson BB9 170 E1
Fountains The
Barrowford BB9 170 D3
Ormskirk L39 15 E6
Fountains Way
Formby L37 12 B2
Oswaldtwistle BB5 103 B5
Fouracre BB2 121 E2
Four Acre La PR3 162 E5
Fourfields PR5 97 E2
Four La LA2 226 A8
FOUR LANE ENDS 101 D8
Four Lane Ends
Barley BB7 192 B2
Blackpool FY3 131 A6
Bretherton PR26 58 A7
Burton in L LA2 242 C1
Carleton FY6 153 B5
Charnock Richard PR7 42 C4
Clitheroe BB7 167 A6
Dolphinholme LA2 226 A8
Gregson Lane PR5 98 D2

Four Lane Ends continued
Halsall L39 23 D3
Halton LA2 218 F7
Heapey PR6 62 C4
Morecambe LA3 216 D1
Simonstone BB12 145 F4
Thornton FY5 176 E1
Wray LA2 238 E4
Four Lanes End Rd OL13 70 B8
Four Oaks Rd PR5 78 B7
Fourth Ave
Blackpool FY4 110 C7
Bury BL9 33 D4
Fowler Ave PR26 77 B6
Fowler Cl PR5 99 C2
Fowler Height Cl BB2 81 B7
Fowler Hill La PR3 204 B5
Fowler Ind Pk BL6 32 C2
Fowler La
Farington PR26 76 F6
Leyland PR5, PR26 77 B5
Fowler St 4 PR2 117 D3
Foxcote PR7 61 C2
Foxcroft BB12 127 D8
Foxdale Ave FY3 130 D7
Foxdale Cl
1 Bacup OL13 88 A1
Edgworth BL7 48 E7
Southport PR8 35 E3
Foxdale Gr PR1 118 D3
Foxdale Pl LA1 218 C2
Foxen Dole La BB12 147 A5
Foxes Farmhouse FY6 131 E7
Foxes Terr PR3 157 C7
Foxfield Ave LA4 217 C3
Foxfield Cl BB5 103 D4
Foxfield Dr BB4 86 F4
Foxfields FY6 177 C8
Foxfold WN8 18 D3
Foxglove Ave L40 25 F4
Foxglove Cl
Burnley BB11 128 B3
Hesketh Bank PR4 73 E4
Standish WN6 29 D2
Walton Summit PR5 78 B8
Foxglove Ct OL12 52 D3
Foxglove Dr
Bury BL9 33 D3
Lucas Green PR6 61 C5
Foxglove Way PR4 93 D7
Fox Gr LA3 216 E3
Foxhall Rd FY1 130 B3
Foxhall Sq 8 FY1 130 B3
FOXHILL BANK 103 D5
Foxhill Bank Brow BB5 103 E5
Foxhill Cl L37 11 C3
Foxhill Dr BB4 86 F4
Foxhill Terr BB5 103 E4
Foxhole Rd
Chorley PR7 42 F8
Euxton PR7 60 F1
Foxholes Rd
Horwich BL6 32 D4
Morecambe LA4 217 D6
Foxhouse La L31 5 F1
Foxhouse St BB2 101 C5
Fox Ind Est 2 FY2 152 E1
Fox La
Coupe Green PR5 98 E3
Leyland PR25 59 E7
Fox Lane Ends PR4 113 A5
Fox St
Accrington BB5 104 B6
Clitheroe BB7 189 E1
Horwich BL6 32 C2
Padiham BB12 126 F6
Preston PR1 96 F7
Foxstones Cres BB2 81 A8
Foxstones La BB10 129 B2
Foxwell Cl BB4 85 C2
Foxwood Chase
6 Accrington, Hillock Vale BB5 104 E8
Little Plumpton PR4 112 C6
Foxwood Cl WN5 10 E5
Foxwood Dr PR4 113 E5
Foxwood The PR7 42 C1
Frailey Cl PR8 21 C4
Frances Darlington Ct PR7 42 D4
Frances St 3 BB3 81 F2
France St
Blackburn BB2 101 D4
Church BB5 103 E6
Francis Ave BB9 170 E5
Francis St
Blackburn BB2 101 B1
Blackpool FY1 130 B6
Burnley BB10 148 A1
3 Clayton-le-M BB5 124 F3
Colne BB8 171 B3
Preston PR2 117 C1
Frankland Ho 15 LA1 218 D2
Franklands PR4 95 A1
Franklands Dr PR2 119 A5
Franklands Fold PR4 75 A8
Franklin Ainsworth Ho 2 BB6 124 C5
Franklin Rd BB2 101 B3
Franklin St
2 Burnley BB12 127 C6
Clitheroe BB7 166 D7
28 Darwen BB3 82 A1
Lancaster LA1 214 F5
Frank St
4 Accrington BB5 125 A1
Frank St continued
Barnoldswick BB18 196 B2
Preston PR1 117 F1
Fraser Ave PR1 96 E5
Fraser Eagle Stadium (Accrington Stanley FC) BB5 104 B8
Fraser St
3 Accrington BB5 104 A4
Burnley BB10 148 B1
Frazer Gr 13 FY4 130 B1
FRECKLETON 93 C7
Freckleton CE Prim Sch PR4 93 C7
Freckleton Ct FY8 91 C3
Freckleton Dr L33 1 A5
Freckleton Rd
Kirkham PR4 114 B3
Southport PR9 53 F4
Freckleton St
Blackburn BB2 101 E4
Blackpool FY1 130 C3
Kirkham PR4 114 B4
2 Lytham St Anne's FY8 91 C3
Freckleton Strike Lane Prim Sch PR4 93 B8
Frederick Row BB1 102 B5
Frederick St
Accrington BB5 104 A6
Barnoldswick BB18 196 A3
5 Blackburn BB2 101 E3
2 Blackpool FY4 110 D8
Chorley PR6 43 E7
Darwen BB3 82 A2
Oswaldtwistle BB5 103 E4
12 Ramsbottom BL0 50 B5
Fredora Ave FY3 131 A2
FREEHOLD 215 A8
Freeholds La BB7 188 F6
Freeholds Rd OL12 71 E6
Freeholds Terr OL12 71 E6
Free La BB4 68 A6
Freeman Cl BB1 102 C4
Freeman's La PR7 42 E3
Freemantle Ave FY4 110 B4
Freeport Fleetwood Outlet Sh Village FY7 199 A3
FREE TOWN 33 A4
Freetown Bsns Pk 11 BL9 33 A4
Free Trade St 16 BB11 127 F6
Freightway LA3 217 E2
French Cl BB2 101 B4
French Rd BB2 101 B4
FRENCHWOOD 97 B6
Frenchwood Ave
Lytham St Anne's FY8 90 F3
Preston PR1 97 B6
Frenchwood Com Prim Sch PR1 97 B6
Frenchwood Knoll PR1 97 B6
Frenchwood St 4 PR1 97 A6
FRESHFIELD 11 E5
Freshfield Ave BB5 124 E3
Freshfield Ct L37 11 E4
Freshfield Cvn Pk L37 11 B6
Freshfield Gdns L37 11 E4
Freshfield Prim Sch L37 12 A4
Freshfield Rd L37 11 E4
Freshfields PR2 116 D3
Freshfield Sta L37 11 E5
Friargate PR1 96 F8
Friargate Wlk 6 PR1 96 F7
Friar's Moss Rd LA2 232 A8
Friar's Pas 23 LA1 214 F8
Friar St 24 LA1 214 F8
Friars The PR2 117 E4
Friars Wlk L37 12 B2
Friary Cl PR4 114 C4
Friday St PR6 43 D8
Frieldhurst Rd OL14 109 C1
Frinton Gr FY2 152 E6
Friths Ave PR5 98 E1
Frith's Ct PR5 98 F1
Frobisher Dr FY8 110 D1
Frog La L40 26 D3
Frome St PR1 118 D1
Froom St PR6 43 F8
Frostholme OL14 109 B1
Fryent Cl BL6 31 D2
Fryer Cl PR1 96 D1
Fry St BB9 148 F8
Fulford Ave 1 PR2 116 C1
Fulham St BB9 170 F2
FULLEDGE 128 C5
Fullers Terr OL13 87 F1
Full View BB2 81 B8
Fulmar Cres LA3 212 F5
Fulmars The FY6 153 B2
Fulmar Terr BB5 103 E3
Fulshaw Rd PR2 117 B2
FULWOOD 117 D5
Fulwood Ave
Becconsall PR4 73 F1
Blackpool FY3 130 F8
Southport PR8 35 D4
Fulwood & Cadley Prim Sch PR2 117 D4
Fulwood Dr LA4 217 F6
Fulwood Hall Hospl PR2 118 C5
Fulwood Hall La PR2 118 B4
Fulwood High Sch & Arts Coll PR2 117 D6
Fulwood Hts PR2 118 C5
Fulwood Pk PR2 118 B7
FULWOOD ROW 118 E5
Fulwood Row PR2 118 E6
Funchal Ave L37 11 D1
Furlong Cres FY3 153 A1
Furlong Gn FY5 153 E8
Furlong La FY6 153 D5
Furness Ave
Blackburn BB1 102 B8
Fleetwood FY7 198 D1
Formby L37 11 F3
Normoss FY3 131 A8
Ormskirk L39 15 E4
Read BB12 145 D1
Furness Cl
Chorley PR7 43 D5
Southport PR8 21 B3
Furness Ct 3 FY3 131 A8
Furness Dr
High Bentham LA2 239 D8
Poulton-le-F FY6 154 A3
Furnessford Rd LA2 239 A6
Furness Rd LA3 216 D2
Furness St
7 Burnley BB10 148 B1
3 Lancaster LA1 218 B1
Furnival Dr L40 25 D4
Further Ends Rd PR4 93 B6
Further Field PR5 78 A8
Furthergate BB1 102 B5
Furthergate Bsns Pk BB1 102 B5
Furthergate Ind Est BB1 102 B5
Further Heights Rd 1 OL12 52 F1
Further La BB2, PR5 100 A8
Further Wilworth BB1 122 E2
Fushetts La LA2 239 D8
Fusiliers Cl PR7 60 F6
Futura Pk BL6 32 C1
Futures Pk OL13 70 E8
Fylde Ave
Lancaster LA1 211 B7
Leyland PR26 76 E4
Fylde Coast Hospl FY3 130 F7
Fylde Ct FY6 199 D5
Fylde Rd
Lytham St Anne's FY8 90 D5
Poulton-le-F FY6 153 E4
Preston PR1, PR2 117 D1
Southport PR9 54 B4
Fylde Road Ind Est PR1 117 D1
Fylde St
Kirkham PR4 114 A4
Preston PR1 96 E8
Fylde View Cl FY6 153 D2

G

Gabbot St PR7 31 A7
Gable Mews L37 12 A1
Gables Pl 3 LA4 217 D5
Gables The PR4 116 E4
Gable The LA6 240 B7
Gadfield St 2 BB3 65 B8
Gadsby St FY1 130 B2
Gage St 32 LA1 214 F8
Gaghills Rd BB4 86 F1
Gaghills Terr 3 BB4 86 F1
Gainsborough Ave
Bamber Bridge PR5 77 A7
Blackburn BB2 101 C6
Burnley BB11 127 F3
Morecambe LA4 217 D6
Gainsborough Rd
Blackpool FY1 130 D4
Ramsbottom BL0 50 B1
Southport PR8 34 E3
Gaisgill Ave LA4 217 B3
Gait Barrows Nature Reserve* LA7 225 A7
Gales La L40 40 A3
Gale St OL12 52 F3
GALGATE 211 B3
Galgate Mill LA2 211 B4
Galleries The 1 BB9 148 E8
Gallery The L37 11 F3
Galligreaves St BB2 101 D3
Galligreaves Way BB2 101 D3
Gall La OL14 109 C3
Galloway Cl 2 OL10 33 F1
Galloway Cres FY2 152 F5
Galloway Dr WN8 10 B6
Galloway Rd FY7 198 F5
Gallows La PR3 142 A6
Galway Ave FY2 152 D3
Gamble Rd FY5 176 B4
Gambleside Cl BB4 106 A1
Game St BB6 124 C5
Gamull La PR2 118 F5
Gandy La OL12 52 D4
Gannet Way PR4 114 B2
Gannow Bsns Pk BB12 127 B6
Gannow La BB12 127 C6
Gantley Ave WN5 10 D3
Gantley Cres WN5 10 D3
Gantley Rd WN5 10 D4
Ganton Cl PR8 35 E3
Ganton Ct PR1 96 A6
Garbett St BB5 104 A4
Garden Ave PR4 113 B4
Garden City BL0 50 A2
Garden Cl
Blackpool FY3 131 A2
Poulton-le-F FY6 153 F3
Garden Ct
8 Preston PR2 117 C1
Garden Ct continued
Ramsbottom BL0 50 C7
Gardeners Mews 10 FY1 130 C7
Gardeners Row BB7 145 F7
Gardeners View L33 1 A6
Gardenia Cl PR6 78 B4
Garden Pl LA6 240 C7
Garden Row OL12 52 D2
Gardens Gr LA4 217 A4
Garden St
Abbey Village PR6 80 C2
Accrington BB5 104 B7
11 Bacup OL13 70 C8
1 Bamber Bridge PR5 77 B7
6 Barnoldswick BB18 196 B2
Blackburn BB2 101 C4
Brierfield BB9 148 B5
Colne BB8 171 D4
Great Harwood BB6 124 C4
Higham BB12 146 F5
Kirkham PR4 114 A4
Lytham St Anne's FY8 89 E6
Nelson BB9 148 E8
Oswaldtwistle BB5 103 D4
Padiham BB12 146 C1
Preston PR1 96 F7
Ramsbottom BL0 50 C6
Ramsbottom, Brooksbottoms BL0 50 C3
Gardens The
Edgworth BL7 48 D4
Halton LA2 219 B6
Garden Terr
17 Blackpool FY4 130 B1
Chorley PR7 61 C1
Middleton LA3 213 A2
Garden Vale Bsns Ctr 1 BB8 171 B4
Garden View Pl 1 FY4 130 E1
Garden Wlk
Cleveleys FY5 175 D5
Preston PR2 117 B1
Gardinar Cl WN1 30 B1
Gardiners Pl WN8 8 E8
Gardner Arc LA3 216 E4
Gardner Bldgs LA3 216 E4
Gardner Rd
Formby L37 12 B4
Lancaster LA1 218 D2
Morecambe LA3 216 E3
Warton LA5 223 D5
Gardner's La PR3 182 D3
Gardner St 18 PR1 96 F8
Garfield Ave LA1 214 D7
Garfield Ct FY3 131 C2
Garfield Dr LA4 217 F4
Garfield St
Accrington BB5 104 D5
Fleetwood FY7 199 B5
Todmorden OL14 109 C1
Garfield Terr PR6 61 D2
Garforth Cres 9 PR5 77 E8
Garland Gr 2 FY7 198 D3
Garner Ave BB2 81 D7
Garnet Cl 4 FY5 152 F7
Garnet St 3 LA1 215 A8
Garnett Gn L39 15 D4
Garnett Pl WN8 9 A7
Garnett Rd BB7 166 C7
Garnett St
Barrowford BB9 170 D2
Darwen BB3 82 B1
6 Morecambe LA4 217 B6
Ramsbottom BL0 50 B5
Garrick Gr FY3 130 E7
Garrick Par PR8 35 A6
Garrick St BB9 170 F2
Garrison Rd PR2 118 B3
Garsdale Ave BB10 148 B4
Garsdale Cl PR5 97 E5
Garsdale Rd PR2 118 E4
Garsden Ave BB1 102 E3
Gars End LA2 238 D6
GARSTANG 181 C7
Garstang Cl FY6 153 C3
Garstang Com Prim Sch PR3 181 C8
Garstang High Sch PR3 181 D5
Garstang New Rd FY6 154 E3
Garstang Rd
Bilsborrow PR3 159 A4
Bowgreave PR3 181 D4
Catterall PR3 181 E1
Chipping PR3 185 C2
Cockerham LA2, PR3 206 E2
Fisher's Row PR3 202 B3
Fulwood PR1, PR2, PR3 117 E5
Little Eccleston PR3, FY6 155 D5
Newsham PR3 137 B4
Singleton FY6 154 C3
Southport PR9 54 A5
St Michael's on W PR3 157 C7
Garstang Rd E FY6 153 E3
Garstang Rd N PR4 113 F7
Garstang Rd S PR4 113 F6
Garstang Rd W FY3, FY6 153 B2
Garstang St Thomas' CE Prim Sch PR3 181 B6
Garstang St BB3 82 A2
Gars The LA2 238 D6
Garstone Croft PR2 117 D6
Garston St BL9 33 A4
Garswood Cl
Brierfield BB12 147 F2
Maghull L31 5 E3
Garton Ave FY4 110 D6
Gas Field Rd LA3 212 E2
Gas House La LA2 239 D8
Gaskell Cl LA5 224 C3
Gaskell Cres FY5 176 A2
Gaskell Ho LA1 218 C4
Gaskell Rd PR1 96 E5
Gaskell St PR6 43 E8
Gas St
Adlington PR7 31 A6
Bacup OL13 87 F2
8 Burnley BB11 127 F6
Haslingden BB4 84 F1
Longridge PR3 140 A8
Gas Terr PR25 77 B2
Gatefield Ct BB11 128 A4
Gategill Gr WN5 10 D3
Gate Ho PR1 96 E7
Gate House Ct BL9 33 C2
Gateland BB18 194 D8
Gatelands Cvn Site LA6 240 B4
Gatesgarth Ave PR2 117 F7
Gateside Ct 2 FY3 131 A8
Gateside Dr FY3 130 F8
Gates La L29 4 C1
Gate St BB1 102 A5
Gateway Cl FY5 153 D7
Gathurst La WN6 19 F4
Gathurst Rd
Fulwood PR2 117 C2
Orrell WN5 10 E8
Gaulter's La FY6 200 C4
Gaw Hill La L39 15 B3
Gaw Hill View L39 15 B3
Gawthorpe Edge BB12 126 F8
Gawthorpe Hall* BB12 146 F1
Gawthorpe Rd BB12 127 D7
Gawthorpe St 13 BB12 146 C1
Gawthorpe View BB12 146 F5
Gaydon Way FY5 152 E7
Gaylands La BB18 197 C2
Gayle Way 1 BB5 103 F4
Gaythorne Ave PR1 97 F8
GEC Bsns Pk BB5 124 E2
Geddes St BB2 100 F2
Geldof Dr FY1 130 C8
Gem Apartments 9 OL14 109 B1
General St FY1 130 B6
Geneva Rd PR2 118 C4
Genoa St BB11 127 C4
Geoffrey Lo 13 PR2 118 F4
Geoffrey St
Bury BL9 33 A4
Chorley PR6 61 D1
Preston PR1 97 C8
Ramsbottom BL0 50 A4
George Ave
Blackpool FY4 130 F1
Great Harwood BB6 124 B4
George Dr PR8 21 E5
George Fox Ave LA1 211 B7
George La BB12 145 C2
George Rd BL0 50 B5
George St W BB2 101 D4
George's La
Banks PR9 55 A7
Horwich BL6 32 E5
George's Rd PR1 96 F7
George's Row 2 BB4 69 F8
George St
Accrington BB5 103 F4
4 Bacup OL13 70 C8
Barnoldswick BB18 196 C4
Blackburn BB2 101 E4
Blackpool FY1 130 C6
Burnley BB11 127 F5
Chorley PR7 43 C7
13 Clayton-le-M BB5 124 F3
Clitheroe BB7 166 D6
Darwen BB3 82 A2
1 Earby BB18 197 B1
Great Harwood BB6 124 C5
Haslingden BB4 85 B3
Horwich BL6 32 C3
3 Lancaster LA1 214 F7
Leyland PR25 77 B2
Longridge PR3 140 A8
11 Lytham St Anne's FY8 91 B3
Morecambe LA4 217 C5
Oswaldtwistle BB5 103 E5
Preston PR1 97 B7
Rishton BB1 124 B1
Whalley BB7 144 C5
Whitworth OL12 52 C8
George Terr WN5 10 D5
George Trad Est PR8 35 B4
George Williams Ho FY7 198 F2
Georgian Pl L37 11 E1
Gerald Ct 4 BB11 128 B4
Gerard Way L33 1 A2
German La
Bolton Green PR7 42 D7
1 Coppull PR7 42 E1
Gerrard Pl WN8 8 F7
Gerrard's Fold PR6 80 B2
Gerrard St
Lancaster LA1 214 D7
Preston PR1 96 E7

Gerrard's Terr FY6 . . . . . . 153 C4
Gertrude St
Nelson BB9 . . . . . . 171 A2
Shawforth OL12 . . . . . . 71 E6
Ghants La FY6 . . . . . . 177 E2
Ghyll La BB18 . . . . . . 196 E4
Ghyll Mdws BB18 . . . . . . 196 D4
Gibfield Rd BB8 . . . . . . 171 A3
Gib Hey La PR3 . . . . . . 161 F7
Gib Hill La BB4 . . . . . . 106 B2
Gib Hill Rd BB9 . . . . . . 171 B1
Gib La
Blackburn BB2 . . . . . . 81 A7
Hoghton PR5 . . . . . . 99 C3
Gibraltar Rd PR4 . . . . . . 132 E5
Gibraltar St BB2 . . . . . . 101 B6
Gibson St BB9 . . . . . . 170 F2
Giddygate La L31 . . . . . . 6 B1
Gidlow Ave PR6 . . . . . . 31 A7
Gifford Way BB3 . . . . . . 82 B2
Gilbert Pl L40 . . . . . . 25 B4
Gilbertson Rd PR7 . . . . . . 43 E2
Gilbert St
Burnley BB10 . . . . . . 148 E2
4 Chorley PR7 . . . . . . 43 C6
Ramsbottom BL0 . . . . . . 68 C1
Rawtenstall BB4 . . . . . . 86 D1
Gildabrook Rd FY4 . . . . . . 110 D5
Gilderdale Ct 2 FY8 . . . . . . 91 C4
Gildow St 1 PR1 . . . . . . 96 E8
Gilescroft Ave L33 . . . . . . 1 A4
Giles St
Clitheroe BB7 . . . . . . 166 E7
Nelson BB9 . . . . . . 170 E1
Gilett Farm Cvn Pk
FY4 . . . . . . 111 F5
Gilhouse Ave PR2 . . . . . . 116 C1
Gillcroft PR7 . . . . . . 41 B7
Gill Ct FY4 . . . . . . 110 B5
Giller Cl PR1 . . . . . . 96 F2
Giller Dr PR1 . . . . . . 96 F2
Giller Fold PR1 . . . . . . 96 F2
Gillett St 6 PR1 . . . . . . 118 C1
Gillhead Brow LA2 . . . . . . 242 D1
Gillians La BB18 . . . . . . 194 B8
Gillibrand Cl PR1 . . . . . . 96 C1
Gillibrand Ho PR7 . . . . . . 61 C2
Gillibrand Prim Sch
PR7 . . . . . . 43 B6
Gillibrands Rd WN8 . . . . . . 9 A7
Gillibrand St
Chorley PR7 . . . . . . 43 C7
Darwen BB3 . . . . . . 81 F3
Walton-le-D PR5 . . . . . . 97 D5
Gillibrand Wlks PR7 . . . . . . 43 C7
Gillies St
Accrington BB5 . . . . . . 104 C6
Blackburn BB2 . . . . . . 101 F3
Gillison Cl LA6 . . . . . . 241 C2
Gill La PR4 . . . . . . 75 C5
Gill Nook PR4 . . . . . . 75 A5
Gillow Ave LA1 . . . . . . 211 A7
Gillow Ct LA1 . . . . . . 214 F5
Gillow Pk PR3 . . . . . . 155 F6
Gillow Rd PR4 . . . . . . 113 F5
Gills Croft BB7 . . . . . . 167 A7
Gill St
Burnley BB12 . . . . . . 127 E6
Colne BB8 . . . . . . 171 B3
Nelson BB9 . . . . . . 170 D1
Gilpin Ave L31 . . . . . . 5 E2
Gilpin Cl 2 LA1 . . . . . . 218 A2
Gilstead Ave LA3 . . . . . . 213 A8
Gin Bow PR7 . . . . . . 43 D6
Gin Croft La BL0 . . . . . . 68 E4
Gingham Brow BL6 . . . . . . 32 E4
Girvan Gr BB11 . . . . . . 127 D5
Girvan Wlk 1 OL10 . . . . . . 33 F1
GISBURN 231 C4
Gisburn Ave FY8 . . . . . . 90 C6
Gisburn Bsns Pk BB7 . . . 231 A3
Gisburn Gr
Blackpool FY3 . . . . . . 130 E7
Burnley BB10 . . . . . . 128 D5
Gisburn Old Rd
Barnoldswick BB7,
BB9 . . . . . . 193 C7
Blacko BB9 . . . . . . 193 E4
Gisburn Prim Sch BB7 . . . 231 B3
Gisburn Rd
Barnoldswick BB18 . . . . . . 196 A3
Barrowford BB9 . . . . . . 170 E5
Blacko BB9 . . . . . . 193 D4
Bolton-by-B BB7 . . . . . . 230 E4
Fulwood PR2 . . . . . . 118 E4
Gisburn Road Com Prim
Sch BB18 . . . . . . 196 B2
Gisburn St
Barnoldswick BB18 . . . . . . 196 B3
Blackburn BB2 . . . . . . 101 C4
Gladden Pl WN8 . . . . . . 8 E8
Glades The FY8 . . . . . . 91 C4
Gladeswood Rd L33 . . . . . . 1 B1
Glade The
Blackburn BB2 . . . . . . 81 E6
Morecambe LA4 . . . . . . 217 E5
Gladeway FY5 . . . . . . 153 D7
Gladstone Cl BB2 . . . . . . 100 F1
Gladstone Cres 3 OL13 . . . 88 A2
Gladstone Ho BB2 . . . . . . 100 F1
Gladstone Rd PR9 . . . . . . 35 F6
Gladstone St
Bacup OL13 . . . . . . 88 A2
Blackburn BB1 . . . . . . 102 B6
Blackpool FY4 . . . . . . 130 C1
Gladstone St *continued*
Bury BL9 . . . . . . 33 B3
Great Harwood BB6 . . . . . . 124 C5
12 Todmorden OL14 . . . . . . 109 B1
Gladstone Terr
Abbey Village PR6 . . . . . . 80 C1
16 Barrowford BB9 . . . . . . 170 D3
Blackburn BB2 . . . . . . 100 F1
3 Lancaster LA1 . . . . . . 218 E1
Trawden BB8 . . . . . . 172 B4
Gladstone Way FY5 . . . . . . 175 F1
Glaisdale Dr PR8 . . . . . . 35 F3
Glamis Dr
Chorley PR7 . . . . . . 43 B8
Southport PR9 . . . . . . 54 B3
Glamis Rd PR25 . . . . . . 60 C8
Glamorgan Gr BB12 . . . . . . 127 A7
GLASSON 209 F5
Glasson Cl BB2 . . . . . . 101 F1
Glasson Dock & Lune
Estuary Nature Trail*
LA2 . . . . . . 210 B5
Glastonbury Ave FY1 . . . . . . 130 E2
Glebe Cl
6 Accrington BB5 . . . . . . 104 B5
Burton-in-K LA6 . . . . . . 240 C7
Fulwood PR2 . . . . . . 117 F4
Maghull L31 . . . . . . 5 B1
Standish WN6 . . . . . . 29 F1
Glebe Cotts BB4 . . . . . . 85 A6
Glebe Ct 20 LA1 . . . . . . 215 A8
Glebe La
Banks PR9 . . . . . . 55 A7
Kirkham PR4 . . . . . . 114 C4
Glebelands PR4 . . . . . . 57 A5
Glebe Pl PR8 . . . . . . 35 B7
Glebe Rd
Skelmersdale WN8 . . . . . . 9 A8
Standish WN6 . . . . . . 29 F1
Glebe St
Burnley BB11 . . . . . . 128 B4
Great Harwood BB6 . . . . . . 124 C5
Glebe The PR26 . . . . . . 59 B8
Gleb Mews PR4 . . . . . . 115 D2
Gledhill Way BL7 . . . . . . 48 A1
Gledstone View BB18 . . . . . . 196 A3
Glegside Rd L33 . . . . . . 1 A2
Glenapp Ave FY4 . . . . . . 111 A6
Glenarden Ave FY5 . . . . . . 152 F8
Glenavon Dr OL12 . . . . . . 52 D3
Glenbeck Cl BL6 . . . . . . 32 D1
Glenborough Ave OL13 . . . . 70 C8
Glenbrook Cl BB2 . . . . . . 81 B8
Glenburn Rd
Skelmersdale WN8 . . . . . . 17 F2
Skelmersdale WN8 . . . . . . 18 A1
Glenburn Sports Coll
WN8 . . . . . . 9 B8
Glencarron Cl BB3 . . . . . . 65 F8
Glencoe Ave
Blackpool FY3 . . . . . . 153 A1
Hoddlesden BB3 . . . . . . 82 E1
Glencoe Cl OL10 . . . . . . 33 F1
Glen Cottage (Youth
Hostel)* BB18 . . . . . . 197 D2
Glencourse Dr PR2 . . . . . . 118 D5
Glencoyne Dr PR9 . . . . . . 54 B5
Glen Cres OL13 . . . . . . 70 A8
Glencroft PR7 . . . . . . 60 C3
Glencross Pl FY4 . . . . . . 110 E7
Glendale Ave PR5 . . . . . . 97 C1
Glendale Cl
Blackpool FY2 . . . . . . 152 F5
Burnley BB11 . . . . . . 128 A3
Leyland PR25 . . . . . . 60 B7
Poulton-le-F FY6 . . . . . . 153 C3
Glendale Cres PR5 . . . . . . 97 C1
Glendale Dr BB2 . . . . . . 121 E2
Glendale Gr
Fulwood PR2 . . . . . . 118 D2
Kirkby L33 . . . . . . 1 A5
Glendale Way L37 . . . . . . 11 F2
Glendene Pk BB1 . . . . . . 122 E5
Glenden Foot OL12 . . . . . . 52 D2
Glendor Rd BB10 . . . . . . 128 E5
Glen Dr WN6 . . . . . . 19 E8
Gleneagles FY8 . . . . . . 90 A6
Gleneagles Ave BB3 . . . . . . 82 E1
Gleneagles Ct
Blackburn BB1 . . . . . . 102 C3
Kirkham PR4 . . . . . . 114 B4
Gleneagles Dr
Brockhall Village BB6 . . . . 143 C6
Euxton PR7 . . . . . . 60 D4
Fulwood PR2 . . . . . . 117 B7
Higher Penwortham PR1 . . . . 96 A6
Lancaster LA1 . . . . . . 215 C7
Morecambe LA4 . . . . . . 217 D6
Southport PR8 . . . . . . 21 C3
Gleneagles Way 1 BL0 . . . 50 B5
Glen Eldon Rd FY8 . . . . . . 89 E7
Glenfield Ave FY2 . . . . . . 152 E6
Glenfield Cl BB1 . . . . . . 102 B7
Glenfield Cvn Site
PR3 . . . . . . 201 C5
Glenfield Park Ind Est
Blackburn BB1 . . . . . . 102 B7
Nelson BB9 . . . . . . 171 A1
Glenfield Park One
BB1 . . . . . . 102 B8
Glenfield Park Two
BB1 . . . . . . 102 B7
Glenfield Rd BB9 . . . . . . 171 A1
Glengarry 7 FY8 . . . . . . 91 C3
Glen Garth BB18 . . . . . . 196 D3
Glen Gdns OL12 . . . . . . 52 F2
Glen Gr PR2 . . . . . . 118 F5
Glengreave Ave BB1 . . . . . . 122 E3
Glenholme Gdns FY6 . . . . . . 153 C2
Glenluce Cres BB1 . . . . . . 102 D3
Glenluce Dr PR1 . . . . . . 97 F8
Glenmarsh Way L37 . . . . . . 12 B3
Glenmere Cres FY5 . . . . . . 152 C7
Glenmore PR6 . . . . . . 78 A3
Glenmore Ave FY5 . . . . . . 176 B2
Glenmore Cl 4 BB5 . . . . . . 104 E2
Glenmore Rd BL0 . . . . . . 49 F2
Glenpark Dr PR9 . . . . . . 54 B4
Glen Park Dr PR4 . . . . . . 73 D4
Glen Rd BB4 . . . . . . 69 F8
Glenrose Terr PR8 . . . . . . 35 A5
Glenroy Ave BB8 . . . . . . 171 D6
Glen Royd 1 OL12 . . . . . . 52 C1
Glenroyd Cl FY3 . . . . . . 130 E3
Glenroyd Dr L40 . . . . . . 25 E4
Glenshiels Ave BB3 . . . . . . 65 E8
Glenside WN6 . . . . . . 28 B2
Glen Sq BB11 . . . . . . 127 F2
Glen St
Bacup OL13 . . . . . . 70 E8
Blackpool FY3 . . . . . . 130 E4
Burnley BB11 . . . . . . 127 E6
Colne BB8 . . . . . . 171 D6
Ramsbottom BL0 . . . . . . 50 B7
Glen Terr BB4 . . . . . . 69 F8
Glen The
Blackburn BB2 . . . . . . 81 E6
Caton LA2 . . . . . . 237 C3
Fulwood PR2 . . . . . . 118 F2
Knott End-on-S FY6 . . . . . . 199 E4
GLEN TOP 70 A8
Glentworth Rd E LA4 . . . . 217 D3
Glentworth Rd W LA4 . . . . 217 C3
Glen View PR3 . . . . . . 141 B8
Glen View Ave LA3 . . . . . . 212 E6
Glenview Cl PR2 . . . . . . 119 A3
Glen View Cres LA3 . . . . . . 212 E6
Glenview Ct PR2 . . . . . . 119 A3
Glen View Dr LA3 . . . . . . 212 E6
Glen View Rd BB11 . . . . . . 127 E2
Glen View St OL14 . . . . . . 109 B1
Glenway PR1 . . . . . . 96 C4
Glen Way BB9 . . . . . . 148 B6
Glenwood St 3 FY3 . . . . 130 D5
Global Way BB3 . . . . . . 82 A5
Globe La BL7 . . . . . . 47 D3
Globe Mill 7 BB4 . . . . . . 86 F2
Glossop Cl FY2 . . . . . . 152 C6
Gloucester Ave
Accrington BB5 . . . . . . 104 A7
Blackpool FY1 . . . . . . 130 D4
8 Clayton-le-M BB5 . . . . . . 124 F3
Cleveleys FY5 . . . . . . 175 D3
Horwich BL6 . . . . . . 32 D2
Lancaster LA1 . . . . . . 215 A4
Leyland PR25 . . . . . . 77 C3
Gloucester Ct
5 Blackpool FY1 . . . . . . 130 D4
Horwich BL6 . . . . . . 32 D2
Gloucester Dr 5 LA3 . . . . 216 E3
Gloucester Rd
Blackburn BB1 . . . . . . 102 D5
Chorley PR7 . . . . . . 43 C6
Lytham St Anne's FY8 . . . . . . 90 D4
Rishton BB1 . . . . . . 103 A8
Southport PR8 . . . . . . 34 F5
Glover Cl PR26 . . . . . . 58 F6
Glover Rd PR7 . . . . . . 29 D7
GLOVERS BRIDGE 26 B3
Glover's Ct 23 PR1 . . . . . . 97 A7
Glover St
Horwich BL6 . . . . . . 32 B4
Preston PR1 . . . . . . 97 A7
Glynn St BB5 . . . . . . 103 F7
Godiva St BB10 . . . . . . 148 A1
Godley St BB11 . . . . . . 128 B6
Godwin Ave 7 FY3 . . . . . . 130 E3
Goe La PR4 . . . . . . 93 B6
Goitside BB9 . . . . . . 170 E1
Goit St
Blackburn BB2 . . . . . . 101 C2
Newchurch BB4 . . . . . . 86 F1
Golbourne Cl FY7 . . . . . . 198 D2
Golbourne St PR1 . . . . . . 118 B1
Goldacre La BB6 . . . . . . 124 A7
Goldburn Cl PR2 . . . . . . 116 F6
Goldcrest Ave OL13 . . . . . . 88 A2
Goldcrest Dr PR5 . . . . . . 98 A2
GOLDEN HILL 77 A2
Golden Hill 9 PR25 . . . . . . 77 B2
Golden Hill La PR25 . . . . . . 76 F2
Golden Hill PRU PR25 . . . . . . 76 E2
Golden Way PR1 . . . . . . 96 C3
Goldfield Ave BB10 . . . . . . 128 F6
Goldfinch Cres LA3 . . . . . . 212 F5
Goldfinch Ct PR7 . . . . . . 42 F5
Goldfinch Dr
Bury BL9 . . . . . . 33 C4
Catterall PR3 . . . . . . 181 C3
Goldfinch St PR1 . . . . . . 118 B1
Goldhey St 13 BB1 . . . . . . 102 A7
Goldsboro Ave FY3 . . . . . . 130 F3
Goldshaw Ct BB12 . . . . . . 169 C3
Goldstone Dr FY5 . . . . . . 152 F7
Goldthread Works 27
PR1 . . . . . . 97 A7
Golf Rd L37 . . . . . . 11 E5
Golf View PR2 . . . . . . 117 A6
GOLGOTHA 215 B7
Golgotha Rd LA1 . . . . . . 215 A6
Golgotha Village LA1 . . . . . . 215 B7
Gollinrod BL9 . . . . . . 50 E4
Gonder La PR3 . . . . . . 182 E3
Gooch St BL6 . . . . . . 32 C2
Goodall Cl BB18 . . . . . . 197 B2
Goodenber Cres 15
LA2 . . . . . . 239 D8
Goodenber Rd LA2 . . . . . . 239 D8
Goodier St PR1 . . . . . . 97 C8
GOODSHAW 85 F8
Goodshaw Ave
Blackburn BB1 . . . . . . 122 E1
Goodshaw Chapel BB4 . . . 106 A1
Goodshaw Ave N BB4 . . . 106 A2
GOODSHAW CHAPEL 106 B1
Goodshaw Chapel*
BB4 . . . . . . 106 B1
Goodshaw Cl BB1 . . . . . . 101 E8
GOODSHAW FOLD 105 F2
Good Shaw Fold Cl
BB4 . . . . . . 106 A2
Goodshaw Fold Rd
BB4 . . . . . . 105 F2
Goodshaw La
Accrington BB5 . . . . . . 105 C1
Goodshaw Chapel BB4 . . . . 106 B2
Good St PR1 . . . . . . 96 E7
Goodwood Ave
Blackpool FY2 . . . . . . 152 D1
Fulwood PR2 . . . . . . 117 F7
Slyne LA2 . . . . . . 218 D8
Goodwood Ct
Blackpool FY1 . . . . . . 130 C4
Lancaster LA1 . . . . . . 215 B4
Goodwood Pl 9 FY1 . . . . 130 C5
Goodwood Rd LA1 . . . . . . 215 B4
Goosebutts La BB7 . . . . . . 166 F7
Goose Cote Hill BL7 . . . . . . 47 E1
Goose Foot PR5 . . . . . . 99 D5
Goose Foot Cl PR5 . . . . . . 99 D7
Goose Foot La PR5 . . . . . . 99 C6
Goose Green Ave PR7 . . . . . . 42 F1
Goose Green La BB8 . . . . . . 172 B2
Goose Hill St 13 OL13 . . . . . . 87 F3
Goose House La BB3 . . . . . . 82 A3
Gooselands BD24 . . . . . . 236 F6
Goose Lane Cotts PR3 . . . 185 E1
Gooseleach La BB12 . . . . . . 145 E1
GOOSNARGH 138 C6
Goosnargh La PR3 . . . . . . 138 B7
Goosnargh Oliverson's CE
Prim Sch PR3 . . . . . . 138 D6
Goosnargh Whitechapel
Prim Sch PR3 . . . . . . 160 D7
Gordale Cl
Barnoldswick BB18 . . . . . . 196 A2
Blackpool FY4 . . . . . . 111 A8
Gordon Ave
2 Accrington BB5 . . . . . . 104 A4
Maghull L31 . . . . . . 5 C3
Southport PR9 . . . . . . 53 C1
Thornton FY5 . . . . . . 176 B2
Gordon Rd
Fleetwood FY7 . . . . . . 198 F3
Lytham St Anne's FY8 . . . . . . 90 D4
8 Nelson BB9 . . . . . . 170 D1
Gordon St
Bacup OL13 . . . . . . 87 F4
14 Blackpool FY4 . . . . . . 130 B1
Burnley BB12 . . . . . . 127 F7
Chorley PR6 . . . . . . 43 D7
Church BB5 . . . . . . 103 E5
Clayton-le-M BB5 . . . . . . 125 A2
Colne BB8 . . . . . . 171 F5
Darwen BB3 . . . . . . 82 A3
Preston PR1 . . . . . . 117 E1
Rawtenstall BB4 . . . . . . 85 F2
Southport PR9 . . . . . . 35 C8
Worsthorne BB10 . . . . . . 129 B6
Gordonstoun Cres WN5 . . . 10 F7
Gordonstoun Pl
Blackburn BB2 . . . . . . 101 C3
8 Thornton FY5 . . . . . . 176 A2
Gordon Terr 1 LA1 . . . . . . 215 A5
Gordon Way OL10 . . . . . . 33 F1
Gore Cl BL9 . . . . . . 33 C1
Gore Dr L39 . . . . . . 15 E3
Gores La L37 . . . . . . 11 F5
Gores Rd L33 . . . . . . 1 B1
Goring St PR7 . . . . . . 43 D7
Gornall's Bldgs 7 BB4 . . . . 85 E2
Gorple Gn BB10 . . . . . . 129 B5
Gorple Rd BB10 . . . . . . 129 D5
Gorple St BB10 . . . . . . 148 E3
Gorrell Cl BB12 . . . . . . 169 D2
Gorse Ave FY5 . . . . . . 175 F3
Gorse Bank BL9 . . . . . . 33 C3
Gorse Cl
Great Knowley PR6 . . . . . . 61 E5
Tarleton PR4 . . . . . . 57 A6
Gorsefield L37 . . . . . . 12 A6
Gorse Gr
Fulwood PR2 . . . . . . 118 E3
Haslingden BB4 . . . . . . 68 A8
3 Longton PR4 . . . . . . 95 A1
Gorse La PR4 . . . . . . 56 D5
Gorse Rd
Blackburn BB2 . . . . . . 101 B5
Blackpool FY3 . . . . . . 130 E4
Gorse St BB1 . . . . . . 102 B6
Gorse Way L37 . . . . . . 11 C4
Gorsewood Rd PR25 . . . . . . 76 E1
Gorsey Brow WN6 . . . . . . 29 B2
Gorsey La
Banks PR9 . . . . . . 55 C7
Haskayne L39 . . . . . . 13 B7
Hightown L38 . . . . . . 3 B2
Mawdesley L40 . . . . . . 40 C1
Gorsey Pl WN8 . . . . . . 9 B7
Gorst La L40, PR9 . . . . . . 25 A6
Gorsuch La L39, L40 . . . . . . 23 D4
Gorton Fold BL6 . . . . . . 32 C3
Gorton St FY1 . . . . . . 130 C6
Gosforth Rd
Blackpool FY2 . . . . . . 152 C1
Southport PR9 . . . . . . 35 F8
Goudhurst Ct BL6 . . . . . . 32 E4
Gough La
Clayton Brook PR5 . . . . . . 78 C5
Walton Summit PR5 . . . . . . 78 B6
Goulding Ave PR25 . . . . . . 77 B1
Goulding St PR7 . . . . . . 43 D6
Gowans La PR6 . . . . . . 79 A8
Gower Ct PR26 . . . . . . 76 D3
Gower Gdns L40 . . . . . . 25 F3
Gower Gr PR4 . . . . . . 75 A5
Gowery The 4 L37 . . . . . . 12 A3
Goyt St FY8 . . . . . . 89 F7
Grab La LA1 . . . . . . 215 C7
Graburn Rd L37 . . . . . . 11 F4
Gracamy Ave PR4 . . . . . . 92 D5
Grace St BL6 . . . . . . 32 B3
Graduate East La LA1 . . . 211 A6
Graduate La LA1 . . . . . . 211 A6
Graduate North Ave
LA1 . . . . . . 211 A6
Graduate South Ave
LA1 . . . . . . 211 A6
Graduation College Sq
LA1 . . . . . . 211 A6
Gradwell St 2 PR1 . . . . . . 96 E8
Grafton Ave
Accrington BB5 . . . . . . 104 E2
Burnley BB10 . . . . . . 148 B5
Grafton Ct
3 Chorley PR7 . . . . . . 43 B5
12 Darwen BB3 . . . . . . 81 F2
Grafton Dr PR8 . . . . . . 21 A5
Grafton Gdns BB5 . . . . . . 104 E3
Grafton Pl 3 LA3 . . . . . . 216 E3
Grafton Rd
Fulwood PR2 . . . . . . 118 F4
2 Morecambe LA3 . . . . . . 216 E3
Grafton St
Adlington PR7 . . . . . . 30 F6
Blackburn BB2 . . . . . . 101 D2
Blackpool FY1 . . . . . . 130 C7
Clitheroe BB7 . . . . . . 166 F8
Nelson BB9 . . . . . . 170 F1
Preston PR1 . . . . . . 96 E6
Grafton Terr 11 BB3 . . . . . . 81 F2
Grafton Villas OL13 . . . . . . 87 F1
Graham Ave
Appley Bridge WN6 . . . . . . 28 C2
Bamber Bridge PR5 . . . . . . 77 C8
Graham Rd PR3 . . . . . . 204 C2
Graham's Pk FY4 . . . . . . 131 E1
Graham St
Hoddlesden BB3 . . . . . . 82 F1
Lancaster LA1 . . . . . . 214 F6
6 Morecambe LA4 . . . . . . 217 A5
1 Padiham BB12 . . . . . . 126 D7
4 Preston PR1 . . . . . . 118 B1
Grammar School Ct
L39 . . . . . . 15 F4
Grammar School La
PR4 . . . . . . 113 F5
Grampian Way FY8 . . . . . . 91 D5
Granary The FY5 . . . . . . 176 A2
Granby Ave FY3 . . . . . . 130 E8
Granby Cl PR9 . . . . . . 53 F3
Granby St BB12 . . . . . . 127 D6
Grand Manor Dr FY8 . . . . . . 90 D7
Grane Pk BB4 . . . . . . 85 A2
Grane Rd BB4 . . . . . . 84 C2
Grane St BB4 . . . . . . 85 B2
GRANGE 119 A4
Grange PR7 . . . . . . 29 D8
Grange Ave
Barrowford BB9 . . . . . . 170 F5
Fulwood PR2 . . . . . . 118 F4
Great Harwood BB6 . . . . . . 124 C6
Rawtenstall BB4 . . . . . . 86 B3
Southport PR9 . . . . . . 35 E8
Thornton FY5 . . . . . . 176 B2
Grange Cl
Great Harwood BB6 . . . . . . 124 C6
Knott End-on-S FY6 . . . . . . 199 F6
Oswaldtwistle BB5 . . . . . . 104 A3
Rawtenstall BB4 . . . . . . 86 B2
Grange Cres BB4 . . . . . . 86 A2
Grange Ct 13 FY1 . . . . . . 130 C7
Grange Dr
Coppull PR7 . . . . . . 29 D8
Coupe Green PR5 . . . . . . 98 E4
Euxton PR7 . . . . . . 60 C4
Grange Farm Cotts PR4 . . . 93 E5
Grangefield PR4 . . . . . . 94 F1
Grange Gdns FY6 . . . . . . 153 D2
Grange Hts 7 BB4 . . . . . . 84 F1
Grange La
Accrington BB5 . . . . . . 104 C5
Formby L37 . . . . . . 11 E5
Hutton PR4 . . . . . . 94 D3
Newton-w-S PR4 . . . . . . 114 F2
Stalmine FY6 . . . . . . 177 B7
Grange Park Cl PR1 . . . . . . 96 A6
Grange Park Way 5
BB4 . . . . . . 84 F1
Grange Pl PR2 . . . . . . 118 F4
Grange Rd
Blackburn BB2 . . . . . . 101 B2
Blackpool FY3 . . . . . . 130 F7
Bolton BL7 . . . . . . 48 C1
Elswick PR4 . . . . . . 155 F1
Fleetwood FY7 . . . . . . 198 D3
Fulwood PR2 . . . . . . 117 C3
Hambleton FY6 . . . . . . 177 D1
Hightown L38 . . . . . . 2 E6
Holme Chapel BB10 . . . . . . 108 A7
Leyland PR25 . . . . . . 76 D2

Grange Rd *continued*
Lytham St Anne's FY8 89 E7
Rawtenstall BB4 86 B2
Singleton FY6 155 A3
Southport PR9 35 E7
Whitworth OL12 71 D3
Grange St
Accrington BB5 104 C5
Barnoldswick BB18 196 A3
Burnley BB11 127 E5
Clayton-le-M BB5 124 E3
Morecambe LA4 217 E6
2 Rawtenstall BB4 86 A2
Grange Terr 19 BB4 86 A3
Grange The
Arnside LA5 224 A8
Cottam PR4 116 E5
Lytham St Anne's FY8 90 E3
Southport PR9 54 C3
Wilpshire BB1 122 F5
Grange View
Carnforth LA5 223 D3
Hest Bank LA5 220 F3
Grange View Rd LA6 221 F6
Granings The PR4 116 D6
Granny's Bay FY8 90 C3
Grant Cl LA1 214 D7
Grant Dr PR4 75 A5
Grantham Cl PR8 35 A1
Grantham Rd
5 Blackpool FY1 130 C7
Southport PR8 35 A1
Weeton Camp PR4 132 E6
Grantham St BB2 101 B2
Grant Mews BL0 50 B7
Granton Cl L37 11 E3
Granton Wlk PR2 117 A4
Grant Rd BB2 101 B3
Grants La BL0 50 C6
Grant St
Accrington BB5 104 A6
Burnley BB11 127 E5
Granville Ave
Becconsall PR4 73 E2
Maghull L31 5 C2
Granville Cl L39 6 B8
Granville Ct
Chorley PR6 61 E1
Southport PR9 53 D1
Granville Gdns BB5 104 D3
Granville Ho
Blackburn BB2 100 F1
Formby L37 11 E4
GRANVILLE PARK 6 B8
Granville Pk L39 6 C8
Granville Pk W L39 6 B8
Granville Rd
Accrington BB5 104 D3
Blackburn BB2 101 B5
Blackpool FY1 130 D5
Brierfield BB9 148 C6
Chorley PR6 61 E1
Darwen BB3 64 F8
Great Harwood BB6 124 D6
Lancaster LA1 218 C3
Morecambe LA3 216 E3
Southport PR8 34 D4
Granville St
Adlington PR6 31 A7
Burnley, Harle Syke BB10 148 F2
14 Burnley, Stoneyholme BB10 128 A8
Colne BB8 171 E5
Haslingden BB4 68 A7
Grape La PR26 58 C1
Grasmere Ave
Blackburn BB1 122 C1
3 Fleetwood FY7 198 E4
Leyland PR25 77 A3
Orrell WN5 10 F8
Padiham BB12 146 C1
Thornton FY5 176 B2
Up Holland WN8 10 B7
Grasmere Cl
Accrington, Hillock Vale BB5 104 E8
Bamber Bridge PR5 97 D2
Colne BB8 172 A5
Euxton PR7 60 E1
Fulwood PR2 118 C4
8 High Bentham LA2 239 D8
Rishton BB1 124 A1
Grasmere Dr 9 LA2 239 D8
Grasmere Gr
Longridge PR3 139 F5
Whittle-le-W PR6 61 B7
Grasmere Rd
Blackpool FY1 130 D2
Formby L37 11 D3
Haslingden BB4 68 C8
Hightown L38 3 A4
Knott End-on-S FY6 199 F6
Lancaster LA1 215 A8
Lytham St Anne's FY8 110 E1
Maghull L31 5 D2
Morecambe LA4 217 E6
Grasmere St
Burnley BB10 148 A2
10 Rochdale OL12 52 F1
Grasmere Terr
Bacup OL13 87 F4
Chorley PR7 43 B5
Grasscroft Cl FY7 198 D2
Grassington Dr
Burnley BB10 148 D3
Bury BL9 33 D1
Grassington Pl 4 FY5 152 F8
Grassington Rd FY8 90 C7
Gratton Pl WN8 9 A8
Gravel Cl PR9 54 F5
Gravel La
Banks PR9 54 F5
Banks PR9 55 B3
Gravel The PR4 55 F2
Graver Weir Terr BB4 107 A1
Grave-Yard La L39 7 A6
Graving Dock Rd FY8 91 D4
Gravners Field FY5 176 D2
Grayrigg Dr LA4 217 B3
Grays Pl LA3 216 E2
GREAT ALTCAR 12 E1
Great Arley Sch FY5 176 B3
Great Avenham St 3 PR1 97 A6
Great Bolton St BB2 101 E3
Great Close La BD23, BD24 236 D6
Great Croft Cl BB18 196 A3
Great Eaves Rd BL0 50 C7
GREAT ECCLESTON 156 C4
Great Eccleston Copp CE Prim Sch PR3 156 A3
Great Flatt OL12 52 B1
Great George St
Colne BB8 171 D5
Preston PR1 118 A1
Great Gill PR4 75 A5
Great Greens La PR5 78 C5
Great Hanover St PR1 118 A1
GREAT HARWOOD 124 D4
Great Harwood Prim Sch BB6 124 B5
Great Hay PR4 74 E2
Great Hey PR4 74 E2
Great House Barn* BL6 31 F8
Great John St 20 LA1 214 F8
GREAT KNOWLEY 61 E3
Great Lee OL12 52 D3
Great Lee Wlk OL12 52 D2
GREAT MARTON 130 F3
GREAT MARTON MOSS 111 B4
GREAT MARTON MOSS SIDE 111 B7
Great Mdw
Bamber Bridge PR5 77 A8
Chorley PR7 61 A2
GREAT MITTON 165 F2
Great Park Dr PR25 77 A2
GREAT PLUMPTON 112 E7
Great Shaw St PR1 96 F8
Great Stone of Fourstones* LA2 239 D5
Great Stones Cl BL7 47 E2
Great Townley St PR1 97 D8
Great Tunstead PR4 75 A7
Great Wood Cl PR7 42 F6
Great Wood Prim Sch LA4 217 E5
GREAVE 88 B3
Greave Cl
4 Bacup OL13 88 B3
Rawtenstall BB4 86 A4
Greave Clough Cl 1 OL13 88 B3
Greave Clough Dr OL13 88 B3
Greave Cres 8 OL13 88 A3
Greave Fold 6 OL13 88 B3
Greave Rd OL13 88 B3
Greaves Cl
Appley Bridge WN6 19 F8
Banks PR9 55 A6
Greaves Ct 3 LA1 215 A5
Greaves Dr LA1 214 F6
Greaves Hall Ave PR9 55 A5
Greaves Mdw PR1 96 E2
Greaves Mead LA1 214 F5
Greaves Rd LA1 214 F6
Greaves St
Great Harwood BB6 124 C4
Haslingden BB4 84 F2
9 Preston PR1 97 A7
Greaves The LA1 215 A6
Greaves Town La PR2 116 E1
Greave Terr 2 OL13 88 B3
Grebe Cl FY3 131 B7
Grebe Wharf 2 LA1 218 E1
Greenacre
Blackburn BB3 81 F6
Westhead L40 16 E4
Green Acre PR3 138 D6
Greenacre Cl BL0 50 E7
Greenacre Ct LA1 215 B3
Greenacre Pk LA2 220 E2
Greenacre Rd LA2 220 E2
Greenacres
Chorley PR7 43 C5
Edgworth BL7 48 E6
Fulwood PR2 117 B7
Read BB12 145 D2
Green Acres PR4 93 C7
Greenacres Ave PR4 114 A4
Greenacres Dr PR3 181 D6
Greenacre St BB7 166 E7
Greenacres The PR4 95 D2
Green Ave FY4 110 C6
Greenbank
3 Horwich BL6 32 D1
Ormskirk L39 15 C2
Poulton-le-F FY6 153 E3
Whitworth OL12 52 C5
GREEN BANK 102 B6
Green Bank
Bacup OL13 70 D8
Barnoldswick BB18 196 D4
Greenbank Ave
Maghull L31 5 C3
Orrell WN5 10 D3
Preston PR1 117 D2
Green Bank Bsns Pk BB1 102 C7
Greenbank Dr
Fence BB12 147 E8
Southport PR8 34 E2
Greenbank High Sch PR8 34 E1
Greenbank Pk BB4 86 B2
Greenbank Pl 6 PR1 117 E1
Greenbank Prim Sch OL12 52 F1
Greenbank Rd
Blackburn BB1 102 B6
Middleforth Green PR1 96 E4
Rochdale OL12 52 F2
Greenbanks FY2 152 F3
Greenbank St
Preston, Maudlands PR1 117 D2
Preston PR1 117 E1
Rawtenstall BB4 86 B2
Greenbank Tech Pk BB1 102 C7
Greenbank Terr BB3 81 F6
Greenbank Way BB1 102 C6
Greenbarn Way BL6 31 D1
Greenberfield La BB18 196 C4
Greenbriar Cl FY3 152 F1
Green Bridge N BB4 69 E7
Green Bridge S BB4 69 E7
Greenbrook Cl
Bury BL9 33 A4
Padiham BB12 126 F6
Greenbrook Rd BB12 126 F6
Greenbrook St 6 BL9 33 A4
Green Cl BB11 127 E2
Greencliffe La BB10 129 A1
Greencroft PR1 96 D3
Greendale Ave BB4 86 E2
Greendale Cl
Fleetwood FY7 198 C2
Holme Chapel BB10 108 A7
Greendale Dr LA5 223 D3
Greendale Mews 1 PR2 116 E2
Greendale View BB7 190 B8
Green Dick's La PR3 200 E5
Green Dr
Bamber Bridge PR5 97 C1
Barton PR3 137 B8
Cleveleys FY5 175 C5
Clitheroe BB7 190 A2
Fulwood PR2 117 E7
Higher Penwortham PR1 96 B5
Lytham St Anne's FY8 91 C5
Poulton-le-F FY6 131 E8
Green End PR5 99 E7
Green End Ave BB18 197 B2
Green End Barn BB18 197 B1
Green End Cl 10 OL13 88 A3
Green End Rd BB18 197 B1
GREENFIELD 171 A4
Greenfield Ave
Chatburn BB7 190 D5
Clitheroe BB7 166 C8
Parbold WN8 27 B2
Greenfield Cl PR9 54 A3
Green Field Cl 10 PR1 97 A6
Greenfield Ct 2 LA1 215 A7
Greenfield Dr PR5 77 A8
Greenfield Gdns 1 BB4 85 B2
Greenfield Ho 18 LA1 215 A8
Greenfield La PR3 161 A6
Greenfield Pk PR4 93 F8
Greenfield Rd
Adlington PR6 31 A8
Blackpool FY5 152 E8
Burnley BB10 128 D4
Chorley PR6 43 E8
Colne, Bunker's Hill BB8 171 B4
Colne, Greenfield BB8 171 A4
Fleetwood FY7 198 F2
Southport PR8 36 C1
Greenfields
Blackburn BB2 81 D7
Caton LA2 237 C3
Hesketh Bank PR4 73 D4
Greenfields Cres PR4 113 E6
Greenfield St
Darwen BB3 65 C6
Haslingden BB4 85 B3
12 Lancaster LA1 215 A8
Rawtenstall BB4 86 A3
Greenfield Terr
Oswaldtwistle BB5 103 A1
Todmorden OL14 109 A1
Greenfield View BB3 82 A7
Greenfield Way PR2 117 B5
Greenfinch Ct FY3 131 B6
Greenfold Dr BB4 106 A2
Greenfoot 6 LA2 239 B8
Greenfoot La LA2 239 B8
Greenford Cl WN5 10 D6
Greenford Rd PR8 21 C4
Greengate FY5 176 D2
Green Gate
Fulwood PR2 117 C3
Hutton PR4 95 C1
Greengate Cl
6 Burnley BB12 127 D7
Greengate Cl *continued*
Bury BL9 33 C2
Rawtenstall BB4 86 A5
Greengate La LA5 221 C8
Greenhaigh Ct PR3 181 C7
GREENHALGH 133 C5
Greenhalgh La
Adlington PR6 31 B8
Greenhalgh PR4 133 D4
Greenhall Cl PR3 181 D6
Greenham Ave L33 1 A6
Greenhaven WN8 10 B7
GREEN HAWORTH 104 B1
Green Haworth CE Prim Sch BB5 104 B1
Greenhead Ave BB1 102 B7
Green Head Cotts 7 LA2 239 B8
Greenhead La BB12 147 D5
Green Hey
Lytham St Anne's FY8 91 D4
Much Hoole PR4 74 E3
Greenhey Pl WN8 8 F8
Greenheys Ave FY6 153 B4
Greenheys Cres BL8 49 F1
Green Heys Dr L31 5 F1
Greenhill BB6 124 B5
Green Hill 9 OL13 88 A1
Greenhill Ave PR4 114 A6
Green Hill La LA2, LA6 237 B6
Greenhill Pl 2 FY1 130 C6
Green Hill Rd 8 OL13 88 A1
Greenholme Ave LA4 217 B3
Green Howarth View BB5 104 A3
Greenhurst Cl BB2 101 D4
Greenings La PR9 37 C3
Green La
Banks PR9 55 C4
Bilsborrow PR3 159 B2
Bispham Green L40 27 B7
Blackburn BB2 101 A1
Bretherton PR26 58 C7
Chipping PR3 185 F3
Coppull PR7 30 A8
Cowan Bridge LA6 242 B6
Downham BB7 191 B6
Farington PR26 76 E7
Formby L37 11 F5
Freckleton PR4 93 B6
Garstang PR3 181 A7
Grindleton BB7 190 A7
Halton LA2 219 F8
Holmes PR4 56 C4
Horton BD23 231 E5
Horwich BL6 32 B5
Kingsfold PR4 96 C1
Lancaster, Bailrigg LA1, LA2 211 A7
Lancaster LA1, LA2 218 E6
Longridge PR3 140 B8
Maghull L31 5 A2
Maghull L31 5 C1
Morecambe LA3 217 B2
Ormskirk L39 15 E6
Orrell WN5 10 D3
Padiham BB12 126 C8
Preesall FY6 200 C2
Riley Green PR5 79 E8
Samlesbury Bottoms PR5 99 B7
Skelmersdale L40 18 A6
Skelmersdale L40, WN8 17 F6
Sollom PR4 56 D1
Woodsfold PR4 135 E6
Green La E PR3 204 C2
Greenland Ave WN6 29 E1
Greenland La PR6 31 D5
Greenlands Cres PR2 118 E3
GREEN LANE 81 A8
Green Lane Ave L39 15 E6
Green La The L40 25 F4
Green La W
Freckleton PR4 93 B5
Garstang PR3 204 B1
Greenlea Cl WN5 10 D5
Greenlea Dr LA4 217 D5
Green Link L31 5 B2
Greenloon's Dr L37 11 C3
Greenloon's Wlk L37 11 C2
Green Mdw BB8 172 B2
Greenmead Cl PR4 116 E5
Green Meadow La FY6 177 C1
Greenmoor La PR3 141 B7
GREENMOUNT 49 E1
Green Mount BB6 144 D8
Greenmount Ave
1 Kirkham PR4 114 A5
1 Thornton FY5 176 A3
Greenmount Cl BL8 49 F2
Greenmount Dr BL8 49 F2
Greenmount Prim Sch BL8 49 F2
Green Nook La PR3 139 F6
Green Oak Pl FY5 153 A8
Greenock Cl BB11 127 D4
Greenock Dr OL10 33 F1
Greenock St BB11 127 D4
Greenpark Cl BL8 49 F1
Green Park Cl BB2 101 C2
Green Park Ct BB7 144 D8
Green Park Dr L31 5 B1
Green Park Prim Sch L31 5 B2
Green Pk BB7 144 C5
Green Pl PR5 78 A6
Green Rd BB8 171 D4
Green Ridge Cl BB9 148 D5
Green Row BB3 81 B6
Green St E 17 BB3 82 A1
Greens Arms Rd BB3, BL7 47 E7
Greenset Cl LA1 218 C4
Greenside
Cottam PR4 116 D4
Euxton PR7 60 C3
Ribchester PR3 141 E3
Greenside Ave
Blackburn BB2 81 A8
Preston PR2 116 C1
Greenside Cl
Hawkshaw BL8 49 B3
Kirkby L33 1 A6
Greenside Dr BL8 49 F1
Greenside Gdns PR26 59 B7
Greens La
Bacup, Greave OL13 88 A3
Bacup, Nun Hills OL13 70 D7
Haslingden BB4 68 C7
Green's La
Haskayne L31 14 C1
Stalmine FY6 177 F7
Greenslate Ave WN6 19 E8
Greenslate Ct WN5 10 E3
Greenslate Rd WN5 10 E3
Greensnook La OL13 88 A3
Greensnook Mews 2 OL13 88 A3
Greensnook Terr 1 OL13 88 A3
Green St
Adlington PR6 31 B8
12 Barnoldswick BB18 196 B2
Burnley BB10 148 B1
Chorley PR7 43 A5
Darwen BB3 82 A1
Edenfield BL0 68 E3
Great Harwood BB6 124 B5
Lancaster LA1 218 E1
Lytham St Anne's FY8 91 A3
Morecambe LA4 217 B6
Oswaldtwistle BB5 103 C2
Padiham BB12 126 C7
Rawtenstall BB4 86 A3
Greens The OL12 71 C1
Greenstone Ave BL6 32 B3
Greensward Cl WN6 29 B1
Greensway PR3 137 C3
Green The
Adlington PR6 43 F2
Bispham Green L40 27 B8
Bolton-le-S LA5 221 B5
Churchtown PR3 181 A2
Colne BB8 171 F6
5 Darwen BB3 82 A1
Eccleston PR7 41 C6
Fulwood PR2 118 F2
Hesketh Bank PR4 73 E3
Nelson BB9 171 B2
Parbold WN8 27 B2
Ramsbottom BL8 49 F1
Silverdale LA5 224 D2
Weeton PR4 132 F2
Wrea Green PR4 113 B3
Greenthorn Cres PR2 119 A2
Greenthorne Cl BL7 48 E7
Greenthorne Terr 2 BB3 65 A8
Greenvale WN6 19 F4
Greenville Dr L31 5 C1
Greenwater Ct 7 LA1 218 D2
Greenway
Catterall PR3 181 D3
Eccleston PR7 41 B7
Fulwood PR2 117 D7
Higher Penwortham PR1 96 B4
Horwich BL6 32 F3
Green Way 4 FY4 110 F7
Greenway Ave WN8 9 B8
Greenway Cl WN8 17 E2
Greenway Ho FY6 153 E3
Greenway Mews BL0 50 C4
Greenways
Becconsall PR4 73 F1
Lytham St Anne's FY8 90 B6
Orrell WN5 10 D3
Over Kellet LA6 237 B8
Greenway St BB3 81 F3
Greenwich Dr FY8 90 D5
Green Wlk
Blackrod BL6 31 D1
Earby BB18 197 A1
Southport PR8 21 D5
Greenwood PR5 78 B4
Greenwood Ave
Blackpool FY1 130 E2
Hest Bank LA5 220 F2
Horwich BL6 32 D1
Greenwood Cl
Lytham St Anne's FY8 90 E4
Ormskirk L39 15 C1
Greenwood Cres LA5 220 F2
Greenwood Ct PR25 77 A1
Greenwood Dr LA5 220 F2
Greenwood Gdns PR8 35 A5
Greenwood Rd WN6 29 E2
Greenwood St
1 Bamber Bridge PR5 97 E1
Preston PR1 97 B7
Greenwood The BB2 81 D7
Greetby Hill L39, L40 16 A6
Greetby Pl WN8 9 A8
Gregareth Cl 5 LA1 218 A2

Greg Ho 13 LA1 218 D2
Gregory Ave FY2 152 C5
Gregory Fold BB4 68 A7
Gregory La L39 23 B3
Gregory Mdw PR3 181 B7
Gregory Pl FY8 91 A3
Gregory's Ct LA1 215 A4
Gregson Cl 5 FY4 110 F7
Gregson Dr 3 FY7 198 F2
Gregson La
7 Blackburn BB2 101 D5
Gregson Lane PR5 98 E1
Higher Walton PR5 98 C2
GREGSON LANE 98 E2
Gregson Rd LA1 215 A7
Gregson's Ave L37 11 E5
Gregson St
Darwen BB3 65 A8
Lytham St Anne's FY8 91 A3
Gregson Way PR2 118 B5
Grenada Cl BB3 81 F6
Grenfell Ave FY3 130 E7
Grenville Ave
Bamber Bridge PR5 97 D2
Lytham St Anne's FY8 110 E1
Gresham Rd FY5 175 D1
Gresham St BB4 86 F1
Gresley Ave BL6 32 B3
Gresley Ct LA1 214 F6
Gresley Pl FY2 152 E2
GRESSINGHAM 241 A1
Gressingham Dr LA1 215 A4
Gressingham Ho 3 LA1 215 A3
Gressingham Wlk LA1 215 B3
Greta Heath LA6 242 C3
Greta Pl
Fleetwood FY7 198 D3
Lancaster LA1 218 C2
Gretdale Ave FY8 89 E8
Gretna Cres FY5 152 D8
Gretna Rd BB1 122 F1
Gretna Wlk BB1 122 F1
Greyfriars Ave PR2 117 D5
Greyfriars Cres PR2 117 D5
Greyfriars Dr PR1 96 C5
Greyfriars Rd PR8 21 B6
Grey Heights View PR6 43 E8
Greyhound Bridge Rd LA1 218 D1
Grey St
Barrowford BB9 170 D3
Burnley BB10 128 A8
Greystock Ave PR2 117 E6
Greystock Cl PR5 78 B8
Greystock Pl PR2 117 E6
Greystoke Ave BB2 80 E8
Greystoke Ct FY4 110 B5
Greystoke Pl FY4 110 B5
Greystokes L39 15 D2
Greystonegill La LA2 239 F7
Greystones PR26 76 B1
Greystones Dr BB12 147 E8
Greythwaite Ct LA1 214 D6
Greywood Ave BL9 33 B2
GRIFFIN 101 C3
Griffin Cl
Burnley BB11 127 B5
Bury BL9 33 B4
Huncoat BB5 125 F1
Griffin Ho BL9 33 A4
Griffin Park Prim Sch BB2 101 B3
Griffin St BB2 101 B3
Griffiths Dr PR9 35 F8
Griffon Ho PR9 53 F2
Grimeford La BL6, PR6 31 C5
GRIMEFORD VILLAGE 31 D6
Grimeshaw La LA1 219 B3
Grime St
Chorley PR7 43 D6
Darwen BB3 81 F2
7 Ramsbottom BL0 50 A4
Grimrod Pl WN8 9 A7
GRIMSARGH 139 D1
Grimsargh Manor PR2 139 C2
Grimsargh St Michael's CE Sch PR2 139 C1
Grimsargh St 10 PR1 118 D1
GRIMSHAW GREEN 27 B5
Grimshaw Green La L40, WN8 27 C6
Grimshaw La L39 15 E7
GRIMSHAW PARK 101 F2
Grimshaw Pk BB2 101 F3
Grimshaw Pl PR1 97 A7
Grimshaw Rd WN8 9 D8
Grimshaw Ret Pk BB2 101 F3
Grimshaw St
Accrington BB5 104 A5
6 Barrowford BB9 170 D4
Burnley BB11 128 A5
Church BB5 103 E6
2 Clayton-le-M BB5 124 F2
Darwen BB3 65 B7
Great Harwood BB6 124 C5
Preston PR1 97 A7
Grindlestone Ct PR3 138 E6
Grindlestone Hirst BB8 171 C3
GRINDLETON 190 B7
Grindleton Brow BB7 190 B7
Grindleton CE Prim Sch BB7 190 C8
Grindleton Cl FY3 131 B8
Grindleton Gr BB10 128 D5
Grindleton Rd
1 Blackburn BB2 101 C4
Grindleton BB7 190 B7
West Bradford BB7 189 F6
Gringley Rd LA4 217 C3
Grinstead Cl PR8 34 F1
Grisedale Ave BB1 102 C2
Grisedale Cl L37 11 E3
Grisedale Dr BB12 127 B8
Grisedale Pl PR7 43 B5
Gristlehurst La BL9 33 F5
Grizedale Ave
Garstang PR3 181 B7
Lancaster LA1 211 B7
Poulton-le-F FY6 153 C3
Grizedale Cl
Clayton-le-M BB5 124 E2
Fulwood PR2 118 F2
Grizedale Cres PR2 119 A2
Grizedale Ct
Blackpool FY3 130 E5
8 Thornton FY5 176 B3
Grizedale Pl
Fulwood PR2 118 F2
4 Morecambe LA3 216 E1
Grizedale Rd
Blackpool FY4 131 C1
Lancaster LA1 218 F2
Grosvenor Cl PR8 34 E3
Grosvenor Ct
Carnforth LA5 223 C1
Cleveleys FY5 175 C2
6 Lytham St Anne's FY8 90 A8
Southport PR8 34 E3
Grosvenor Gdns PR8 34 F3
Grosvenor Lo BB1 122 F6
Grosvenor Mews PR4 114 B4
Grosvenor Park Prim Sch LA3 217 F2
Grosvenor Pl
Carnforth LA5 223 C1
Preston PR2 117 B2
Southport PR8 34 F3
Grosvenor Rd
Carnforth LA5 223 D1
Chorley PR7 43 B6
Morecambe LA3 216 D3
Southport PR8 34 E4
Grosvenor St
Blackpool FY1 130 C5
Burnley BB12 127 F7
Colne BB8 171 F5
Lytham St Anne's FY8 91 C3
Preston PR1 97 B7
Grosvenor Way
5 Blackburn BB1 101 E5
Horwich BL6 32 C3
Grouse St OL12 52 F1
Grove Ave
Adlington PR6 31 A7
Longton PR4 74 F8
Grove Cres PR6 31 A7
Grove Ct
Lancaster LA1 214 F6
Oswaldtwistle BB5 103 C3
Grove La BB12 146 E1
Grove Mead L31 5 F1
Grove Mill PR7 41 C5
Grove Park Ind Est PR7 41 C5
Grove Pk
Ormskirk L39 15 F7
Southport PR9 35 F8
Grove Rd
Preston PR5 97 C6
Up Holland WN8 10 C8
Grove St
Accrington BB5 104 A6
Bacup OL13 88 A3
12 Bamber Bridge PR5 77 F8
Barrowford BB9 170 D3
Blackburn BB2 101 E2
4 Burnley BB11 127 D5
Earby BB18 197 B2
Leyland PR25 59 D8
Lytham St Anne's FY8 89 F7
Morecambe LA4 216 F4
Nelson BB9 148 E8
Oswaldtwistle BB5 103 D3
Southport PR8 35 A4
Grove Terr PR8 35 A5
Grove The
Appley Bridge WN6 28 C2
Bilsborrow PR3 159 A5
4 Burnley BB12 127 B6
Chipping PR3 185 D4
Chorley PR7 61 C2
Cleveleys FY5 175 E3
Clitheroe BB7 189 F1
Crag Bank LA5 223 B1
Higher Penwortham PR1 96 B4
Lancaster LA1 215 A7
Ormskirk L39 6 C7
Oswaldtwistle BB5 103 E5
Preston PR2 117 B1
Rufford L40 39 A3
Whalley BB7 144 C5
Grovewood PR8 34 E5
Grovewood Dr WN6 19 E8
Grovewood Ho PR7 61 C2
Grundy Cl
Bury BL9 33 A1
Southport PR8 35 E5
Grundy La BL9 33 A1
Grundy Mews FY4 110 C7
Grundy's La PR7 43 D1
Grundy St 7 PR25 77 B2
GRUNSAGILL 236 D1
Guardian Cl PR2 118 A4
Gubberford La PR3 204 D4
Guernsey Ave
Blackburn BB2 101 F1
Buckshaw Village PR7 60 F6
GUIDE 82 D8
Guide La BB12 147 A7
Guide Rd PR4 73 E6
Guildford Ave
Blackpool FY2 152 D6
Great Knowley PR6 61 E4
Guildford Rd
30 Preston PR1 97 A7
Southport PR8 22 A8
Guildford St 6 BB9 148 B5
Guildford Way FY6 153 C6
Guild Hall Arc 5 PR1 97 A7
Guildhall St PR1 96 F7
Guild Row 7 PR1 97 A7
Guild Trad Est 9 PR1 97 B8
Guild Way PR1 96 D7
Guinea Hall Cl PR9 55 A5
Guinea Hall La PR9 55 A5
Guinea Hall Mews PR9 55 A5
Gulf La LA2, PR3 202 D7
Gummers Howe Wlk LA5 221 E8
Gurney St BB2 101 B3
Gutter La BL0 50 B7
Guys Ind Est L40 25 B2
Guy St BB12 146 C1
Guys Thatched Hamlet (Craft Ctr)* PR3 158 F3
Guysyke BB8 171 C4
Gynn Ave FY1 130 B8
Gynn Sq FY1 130 B8

H

HABERGHAM 126 F7
Habergham Dr BB12 126 F8
Habergham St 19 BB12 146 C1
Hackensall Rd FY6 199 E5
Hacking Cl BB6 143 C1
Hacking Dr PR3 139 F5
Hacking's Cvn Holiday Pk BB7 143 E6
Hacking St
Bury BL9 33 A2
Darwen BB3 81 F1
5 Nelson BB9 170 F2
Hacklands Ave PR2 116 C1
Haddings La BB12 147 A8
Haddon Ct FY2 152 C5
Haddon Pl PR2 117 D3
Haddon Rd FY2 152 C5
Hadlee Terr LA1 218 B1
Hadleigh Rd FY6 153 C6
Hadrian Rd LA3 217 E3
Hadstock Ave L37 11 D1
HAGGATE 149 A3
Hagg La PR3 156 C8
Hagg St BB8 171 C4
Haig Ave
Lancaster LA1 214 D8
Leyland PR25 76 F1
Preston PR2 117 D2
Southport PR8 35 E5
Tarleton PR4 57 A7
Haigh Cl PR7 43 A7
Haigh Cres
Chorley PR7 43 B7
Maghull L31 5 C4
Haigh Ct PR8 35 F6
Haigh Hall Cl BL0 50 B4
Haighton Ct PR2 118 A7
Haighton Dr PR2 118 E6
HAIGHTON GREEN 138 E2
Haighton Green La PR2 138 E2
HAIGHTON TOP 138 C1
Haig Rd FY1 130 B1
Hail St BL0 50 A4
Hala Cres LA1 215 A3
Hala Gr LA1 215 A3
Hala Hill LA1 215 B3
Hala Rd LA1 215 A3
Hala Sq LA1 215 A3
Halcyon Cl 6 OL12 52 B2
Haldane Rd BB3 81 E4
Haldane St BB10 148 B2
Halden Rd LA3 216 E3
Hale Carr Gr LA3 216 E1
Hale Carr La LA3 216 E1
HALE NOOK 178 A5
Hales Rushes Rd PR3 178 C4
Hale St BB11 128 A4
Half Acre PR5 77 A8
Half Acre La BL6 31 C2
Halford Pl FY5 152 E7
Halfpenny La
Heskin Green PR7 41 B3
Longridge PR3 139 F8
Halifax Rd
Brierfield BB9 148 C5
Lane Bottom BB10 149 D3
Nelson BB9, BB10 148 E5
Southport PR8 21 C5
Halifax St FY3 130 F3
Hallam Cres BB9 149 A8
Hallam La LA3 213 A2
Hallam Rd BB9 149 A8
Hallam St 11 BB5 125 A1
Hallam Way FY4 111 E7
Hall Ave FY4 130 C1
Hallbridge Gdns WN8 10 B8
Hall Brow Cl L39 16 B4
HALL CARR 86 A1
Hall Carr La PR4 74 D6
Hall Carr Mill Cotts BB4 86 B2
Hall Carr Rd BB4 86 A1
Hall Cl
Caton LA2 237 B3
Rawtenstall BB4 86 A6
Hall Coppice The BL7 47 E1
Hallcroft WN8 18 C2
Hall Croft PR4 95 D2
HALL CROSS 114 A1
Hall Dr
Caton LA2 237 B3
Middleton LA3 213 A2
Morecambe LA4 217 E4
Halley Rd BB3 81 E3
Halley St 5 OL13 88 A7
Hallfield Rd BB6 124 D6
Hall Fold OL12 52 C8
Hall Garth Gdns LA6 240 B1
Hall Gate PR7 61 A2
Hallgate Hill BB7 229 B4
Hall Gate La FY6 177 C8
Hall Gdns OL12 52 C2
Hall Gn WN8 10 B7
Hall Gr LA3 213 A2
Hall Greaves Cl LA3 209 D8
HALL GREEN 10 A7
Hall Green Cl WN8 10 B7
Hall Green La L40, PR7 41 A3
Hall Hill BB7 228 D1
Hall Hill St 4 BB12 146 C1
Halliwell Cres PR4 95 E1
Halliwell Ct 7 PR7 43 C7
Halliwell Hts PR5 97 F3
Halliwell La PR6 61 C4
Halliwell Pl 8 PR7 43 C7
Halliwell St
3 Accrington BB5 104 E2
Chorley PR7 43 C7
Hall La
Appley Bridge WN6 28 D2
Bickerstaffe L39 7 E4
Bispham Green L40, WN8 27 A6
Bracewell BD23 231 F3
Great Eccleston PR3 156 C4
Ince Blundell L38 3 F3
Kirkby L33 1 A8
Leyland PR25 76 F2
Longton PR4 74 E7
Maghull, Lydiate L31 5 B7
Mawdesley L40 40 D3
Orrell WN5 10 F4
Rivington BL6 45 A2
Skelmersdale L40 17 A6
St Michael's on W PR3 157 E6
Hall Mdws BB8 172 C3
Hallmoor Cl L39 15 E2
Hallmore Cvn Pk LA7 225 E7
Hallows Cl PR3 157 C6
Hallows Farm Ave OL12 52 D2
Hallows St BB10 148 A2
Hall Park Ave BB10 128 F4
Hall Park Ctr FY8 90 F4
Hall Park Dr FY8 90 E6
Hall Pk
Haslingden BB4 85 A6
Lancaster LA1 214 F4
Hall Rd
Bescar L40 23 F6
Bescar L40 24 B6
Fulwood PR2 117 E5
Middleforth Green PR1 96 E3
Trawden BB8 172 B3
Hallsall Dr LA4 217 F6
Hall's Cotts FY4 111 A6
Hall St
Bacup OL13 87 F3
Blackburn BB2 101 E2
Burnley BB11 128 A6
Clitheroe BB7 166 E7
Colne BB8 171 D4
Haslingden BB4 85 B2
Morecambe LA4 217 B6
Preston PR2 117 C1
Ramsbottom BL0 50 C2
12 Rawtenstall BB4 86 A3
Southport PR9 35 C7
Whitworth OL12 52 B8
Whitworth OL12 52 C8
Worsthorne BB10 129 A5
Hallwell St BB10 128 A8
Hallwood Cl BB10 148 B4
Hallwood Rd PR7 43 A5
Halmot Ct 3 BB4 86 E1
Halmote Ave BB12 146 F5
HALSALL 23 C1
Halsall Bldgs 6 PR9 35 C8
Halsall Ct L39 15 D6
Halsall Hall L39 23 B1
Halsall Hall Dr L39 23 B1
Halsall La
Formby L37 11 F3
Haskayne L39 14 D6
Ormskirk L39 15 D6
Halsall Manor Ct L39 23 B1
HALSALL MOSS 22 F4
Halsall Rd
Halsall L39 23 C2
Southport PR8 22 A8
Halsalls Sq PR3 156 B5
Halsbury St PR1 97 B6
Halstead Cl BB9 170 D4
Halstead La BB9 170 D4
Halstead Rd PR2 118 E5
Halstead St
Burnley BB11 127 F5
Bury BL9 33 A4
Worsthorne BB10 129 A6
Halstead Wlk BL9 33 A5
HALTON 219 D7
Halton Ave
Clayton-le-W PR25 77 D1
Cleveleys FY5 175 E4
Halton Chase L40 16 E4
Halton Ct 4 LA4 217 B3
Halton Gdns
Blackpool FY4 110 F8
Cleveleys FY5 175 F4
HALTON GREEN 219 F7
Halton Pl
Fulwood PR2 118 F4
Longridge PR3 140 B8
Halton Rd
Lancaster LA1 218 E4
Maghull L31 5 D3
Nether Kellet LA6 221 E5
Halton St PR4 132 E6
Hambledon Dr 6 PR1 96 E2
Hambledon St 10 BB12 126 D8
Hambledon Terr
Higham BB12 146 F6
2 Padiham BB12 126 F7
Hambledon View
Padiham BB12 126 F7
Read BB12 145 D1
HAMBLETON 177 C1
Hambleton Cl PR4 94 F1
Hambleton Ctry Pk FY6 177 D4
HAMBLETON MOSS SIDE 177 E2
Hambleton Prim Sch FY6 177 D2
Hameldon App BB11 127 D5
Hameldon Ave 1 BB5 104 E2
Hameldon Cl BB11 126 C2
Hameldon Com Coll BB12 126 F7
Hameldon Rd
Goodshaw Chapel BB4 106 A2
Hapton BB11 126 D2
Hameldon View BB6 124 D5
Hamer Ave
Blackburn BB1 102 D5
Goodshaw Chapel BB4 106 A1
Hamer Rd PR2 117 D3
Hamer St
21 Darwen BB3 65 A8
Ramsbottom BL0 50 B2
Rawtenstall BB4 86 A2
Hamerswood Dr PR3 181 D2
Hamer Terr BL0 50 C3
Hamilton Cl 8 FY8 91 D4
Hamilton Ct 6 FY1 130 B4
Hamilton Dr LA1 218 A3
Hamilton Gr PR2 118 E3
Hamilton Rd
Barrowford BB9 170 C1
Chorley PR7 43 C7
Fulwood PR2 118 D4
Morecambe LA4 218 A6
Nelson BB8 171 A2
Hamilton St BB2 101 D2
Hamilton Way OL10 33 E1
Hamlet Cl BB2 101 C3
Hamlet Gr PR4 134 F4
Hamlet Rd FY7 198 F4
Hamlet The
Adlington PR7 43 F1
Lytham St Anne's FY8 110 F2
Hammerton Gn 17 OL13 87 F3
Hammerton Hall Cl LA1 218 C4
Hammerton Hall La LA1 218 C4
HAMMERTON MERE 235 E1
Hammerton Pl FY3 131 A8
Hammerton St
Bacup OL13 87 F4
Burnley BB11 127 F5
Hammond Ave OL13 70 D8
Hammond Ct PR1 117 E1
Hammond Dr BB12 145 C2
Hammond Rd L33 1 C3
Hammond's Row 20 PR1 97 A8
Hammond St
Nelson BB9 148 F7
Preston, Adelphi PR1 117 E2
Preston, Maudlands PR1 117 E1
Preston PR1 117 F2
Hampden Ave BB3 65 B7
Hampden Rd PR25 77 A2
Hampden St
5 Burnley BB11 128 B4
Hapton BB12 126 C4
Hampsfell Dr LA4 217 B3
Hampshire Cl BB1 123 A7
Hampshire Pl FY4 110 F6
Hampshire Rd
Bamber Bridge PR5 97 E3
Rishton BB1 124 A1
Hampson Ave PR25 77 D1
Hampson Cotts LA2 211 B1
Hampson Gr FY6 200 A4
HAMPSON GREEN 211 D1
Hampson La LA2 211 C1
Hampson St BL6 32 B4
Hampson Terr PR3 156 C5
Hampstead Cl FY8 90 E6

Hampstead Mews 3 FY1 ... 130 C7
Hampstead Rd
Fulwood PR2 ... 118 D2
Standish WN6 ... 29 D1
Hampton Cl PR7 ... 43 B8
Hampton Ct FY8 ... 90 C8
Hampton Pl FY5 ... 175 E3
Hampton Rd
Blackpool FY4 ... 110 C8
Formby L37 ... 11 E1
Morecambe LA3 ... 216 E3
Southport PR8 ... 35 C5
Hampton St PR2 ... 117 C2
Hamptons The FY6 ... 153 D1
Hanbury St PR2 ... 117 C1
Hancock St BB2 ... 101 C3
Handbridge The PR2 ... 117 E5
Handel St OL12 ... 52 B8
Hand La L40 ... 40 F5
Handley Rd 4 FY1 ... 130 C6
Handshaw Dr PR1 ... 97 A2
Handsworth Ct 4 FY1 ... 130 C7
Handsworth Rd FY1 ... 130 C7
Handsworth Wlk PR8 ... 35 F3
Hanging Green La LA2 ... 220 E1
Hanley Cl FY6 ... 177 C7
Hanmer Pl 3 LA1 ... 215 A6
Hannah Ct PR7 ... 60 E6
Hannah St
3 Accrington BB5 ... 104 B5
16 Bacup OL13 ... 88 A3
Darwen BB3 ... 65 B8
Hanover Cres FY2 ... 152 C5
Hanover Ct PR2 ... 116 F6
Hanover St
Colne BB8 ... 171 D5
Morecambe LA4 ... 217 B5
4 Preston PR1 ... 117 F1
Hansby Cl WN8 ... 9 E8
Hanson Bldgs 5 BB12 ... 126 C8
Hanson St
Adlington PR7 ... 30 F5
Great Harwood BB6 ... 124 C4
Rishton BB1 ... 124 C1
Hanstock Cl WN5 ... 10 E5
Hants La L39 ... 15 E6
Happy Mount Ct LA4 ... 217 F7
Happy Mount Dr LA4 ... 217 E7
HAPTON ... 126 B4
Hapton CE Methodist Prim Sch BB11 ... 126 C4
Hapton Rd BB12 ... 126 C7
Hapton St
7 Padiham BB12 ... 126 D8
Thornton FY5 ... 176 B4
Hapton Sta BB11 ... 126 C4
Hapton Way BB4 ... 106 A2
Harbour Ave PR4 ... 92 E6
Harbour Cl 11 FY7 ... 198 F2
Harbour Ho 7 FY8 ... 91 D4
Harbour La
Brinscall PR6 ... 62 D7
Edgworth BL7 ... 48 D5
Warton PR4 ... 92 E6
Harbour Trad Est 13 FY7 ... 198 F2
Harbour Way FY7 ... 199 B3
Harbury Ave PR8 ... 21 A4
Harcles Dr BL0 ... 50 B2
Harcourt Mews 10 BL6 ... 32 B4
Harcourt Rd
Accrington BB5 ... 104 D3
Blackburn BB2 ... 101 C6
Blackpool FY4 ... 110 D8
Lancaster LA1 ... 218 C3
Harcourt St
14 Bacup OL13 ... 87 F3
2 Burnley BB11 ... 127 D5
Preston PR1 ... 117 E1
Hardacre La
Lucas Green PR6 ... 61 C5
Rimington BB7 ... 231 B2
Hardacre St L39 ... 15 F6
Hardaker Ct 1 FY8 ... 89 E6
Hardcastle Rd PR2 ... 117 E3
Harden Rd BB18 ... 195 A6
HARDHORN ... 131 E8
Hardhorn Ct FY6 ... 153 D3
Hardhorn Rd FY6 ... 153 D2
HARDHORN VILLAGE ... 131 E7
Hardhorn Way FY6 ... 153 D2
Harding Rd L40 ... 25 D4
Harding St PR6 ... 31 B8
Hard Knott Rise LA5 ... 221 E8
Hardlands Ave 4 LA4 ... 217 F4
Hardman Ave BB4 ... 86 A1
Hardman Cl
Blackburn BB1 ... 102 F4
Rawtenstall BB4 ... 69 F7
Hardman Dr BB4 ... 69 F7
Hardmans Bsns Ctr BB4 ... 85 E1
Hardman St
Blackburn BB2 ... 101 C3
3 Blackpool FY1 ... 130 C6
Hardman Terr OL13 ... 70 D8
Hardman Way 25 BB3 ... 82 A1
Hardsough La BL0 ... 68 D5
Hardwen Ave 7 PR2 ... 116 C1
Hardwicke Ho 10 LA1 ... 214 E8
Hardwicke St 4 PR1 ... 97 A8
Hardy Ave
Barnoldswick BB18 ... 196 A3
Brierfield BB9 ... 148 B6
Hardy Cl PR2 ... 95 F8
Hardy Ct 13 BB9 ... 148 E8
Hardy Dr PR7 ... 43 A7
Hardy St
Blackburn BB1 ... 122 F1
Brierfield BB9 ... 148 B6
Harebell Cl
Blackburn BB2 ... 80 D8
Formby L37 ... 11 F1
Rochdale OL12 ... 52 D3
Hare Clough Cl BB2 ... 101 F3
Hareden Brook Cl BB1 ... 101 F3
Hareden Cl 4 PR5 ... 77 F8
Hareden Rd PR2 ... 118 F2
Harefield Rise BB12 ... 127 D7
HAREHOLME ... 86 D1
Hareholme La BB4 ... 86 D2
Hare Runs Ho LA1 ... 218 D3
Hares La PR8 ... 36 D1
Harestone Ave PR7 ... 43 A5
Harewood PR7 ... 61 B2
Harewood Ave
Blackpool FY3 ... 153 A1
Lancaster LA1 ... 215 A3
Morecambe LA3 ... 216 E2
Simonstone BB12 ... 145 E2
Southport PR8 ... 21 C6
Harewood Cl FY6 ... 153 C5
Harewood Rd PR1 ... 118 C2
Hargate Ave OL12 ... 52 A2
Hargate Cl BL9 ... 50 C2
Hargate Rd FY5 ... 176 C2
Hargher St BB11 ... 127 D5
Hargreaves Ave PR25 ... 60 B8
Hargreaves Ct
Clitheroe BB7 ... 166 C7
Fulwood PR2 ... 116 F4
Whitewell Bottom BB4 ... 86 F6
Hargreaves Dr BB4 ... 85 F2
HARGREAVES FOLD ... 87 A7
Hargreaves Fold La BB4 ... 87 A7
Hargreaves La 2 BB2 ... 101 E3
Hargreaves Rd BB5 ... 103 C4
Hargreaves St
9 Accrington BB5 ... 104 C5
14 Burnley BB11 ... 127 F6
Burnley, Harle Syke BB10 ... 148 F3
Colne BB8 ... 171 B4
Haslingden BB4 ... 85 B3
Hoddlesden BB3 ... 82 F1
Nelson BB9 ... 148 C7
Southport PR8 ... 35 C6
Thornton FY5 ... 176 B3
Whitewell Bottom BB4 ... 86 E5
Hargrove Ave
Burnley BB12 ... 127 D7
Padiham BB12 ... 146 C1
Harington Cl L37 ... 11 D3
Harington Gn L37 ... 11 D3
Harington Rd L37 ... 11 D4
Harland St PR2 ... 117 D3
Harland Way OL12 ... 52 B2
Harlech Ave FY1 ... 130 D1
Harlech Cl BB4 ... 85 B1
Harlech Dr
Leyland PR25 ... 77 C1
Oswaldtwistle BB5 ... 103 C4
Harlech Gr FY5 ... 176 D2
Harleston Rd L33 ... 1 A3
Harleston Wlk L33 ... 1 A3
HARLE SYKE ... 148 F3
Harley Bank LA2 ... 239 C8
Harley Cl LA2 ... 239 C8
Harley Rd FY3 ... 130 E4
Harley St BB12 ... 127 C6
Harling Rd PR1 ... 118 D1
Harling St BB12 ... 127 B6
Harold Ave
8 Blackpool FY4 ... 111 A6
Burnley BB11 ... 127 C4
Harold St
Burnley BB11 ... 127 D5
Colne BB8 ... 171 C4
Harold Terr PR5 ... 77 A8
Harperley PR7 ... 61 B2
Harpers La BB12 ... 147 D8
Harper's La PR6 ... 61 D1
Harper St BB18 ... 196 A3
Harridge Ave OL12 ... 52 C3
Harridge La
Halsall L39 ... 14 F8
Hurlston L39, L40 ... 24 A1
Harridge St OL12 ... 52 C3
Harridge The OL12 ... 52 C3
Harrier Ct LA1 ... 214 E8
Harrier Dr
Blackburn BB1 ... 101 D8
Skelmersdale WN8 ... 9 E8
Harriet St BB11 ... 127 E5
Harrington Ave FY4 ... 110 B5
Harrington Rd
Chorley PR7 ... 43 B8
Morecambe LA3 ... 216 E3
Harrington St
Accrington BB5 ... 125 A1
Preston PR1 ... 117 F1
Harris Ave FY1 ... 130 D1
Harris Cl OL10 ... 33 E1
Harris Ct 2 BB7 ... 166 E8
Harris Mus & Art Gallery* PR1 ... 97 A7
Harrison Ave FY5 ... 176 B2
Harrison Cres
Blackrod BL6 ... 31 C3
Morecambe LA3 ... 216 D1
Harrison Dr BB8 ... 171 C6
Harrison La PR4 ... 96 B2
Harrison Rd
Adlington PR7 ... 31 A6
Harrison Rd *continued*
Chorley PR7 ... 43 C6
Fulwood PR2 ... 117 E6
Harrison St
Barnoldswick BB18 ... 196 C1
Blackburn BB2 ... 101 D4
Blackpool FY1 ... 130 C3
Britannia OL13 ... 71 B8
Burnley BB10 ... 148 F2
Horwich BL6 ... 32 B4
Ramsbottom BL0 ... 50 C7
Todmorden OL14 ... 109 B1
Harrison Terr BB7 ... 190 B8
Harrison Trading Est PR1 ... 118 C1
Harris Pk PR2 ... 117 E5
Harris Prim Sch PR2 ... 117 B7
Harris Rd WN6 ... 29 B3
Harris St
Fleetwood FY7 ... 199 A4
2 Preston PR1 ... 97 A7
Harrock La
Appley Bridge WN6 ... 28 A5
Hill Dale L40, WN6 ... 27 F6
Harrock Rd PR25 ... 77 D1
Harrod Dr PR8 ... 34 E3
Harrogate Cres BB10 ... 148 D2
Harrogate Rd FY8 ... 90 C7
Harrogate Way PR9 ... 54 C6
HARROP FOLD ... 229 F4
Harrop Pl PR2 ... 118 E4
Harrow Ave
Accrington BB5 ... 104 C7
Fleetwood FY7 ... 198 F3
Harrow Cl
Orrell WN5 ... 10 F8
Padiham BB12 ... 126 E6
Harrowdale Pk LA2 ... 219 D7
Harrow Dr BB1 ... 102 B3
Harrow Gr LA4 ... 217 F4
Harrow Pl
Blackpool FY4 ... 110 A5
Lytham St Anne's FY8 ... 90 E5
Harrowside FY4 ... 110 B6
Harrowside Brow 3 FY4 ... 110 B6
Harrowside W FY4 ... 110 A5
Harrow St BB5 ... 103 E4
Harrow Stiles La OL13 ... 107 E1
Harry Potts Way BB10 ... 128 B5
Harry St
Barrowford BB9 ... 170 D3
Salterforth BB18 ... 194 D7
Harsnips WN8 ... 18 C2
Harswell Cl WN5 ... 10 E5
Hartford Ave FY1 ... 130 D2
Hartington Rd
Brinscall PR6 ... 63 A8
Darwen BB3 ... 81 E4
Preston PR1 ... 96 D7
Hartington St
Brierfield BB9 ... 148 B5
Colne, Cotton Tree BB8 ... 172 B5
Lancaster LA1 ... 215 B8
Rishton BB1 ... 124 A1
Hartland WN8 ... 18 C2
Hartland Ave PR9 ... 54 B5
Hartlands Cl BB10 ... 148 D3
Hartley Ave BB5 ... 104 A3
Hartley Cres PR8 ... 34 F2
Hartley Dr BB9 ... 149 A7
Hartley Homes BB8 ... 172 C6
Hartley Rd PR8 ... 34 F2
Hartley St
3 Blackburn BB1 ... 101 E6
2 Burnley BB11 ... 127 C5
Colne BB8 ... 171 D5
Earby BB18 ... 197 B1
Great Harwood BB6 ... 124 D6
2 Haslingden BB4 ... 85 B3
Horwich BL6 ... 32 B3
Nelson BB9 ... 148 E7
2 Oswaldtwistle BB5 ... 103 E4
Rochdale OL12 ... 52 B1
Hartleys Terr BB8 ... 171 E4
Hartmann St BB5 ... 104 A6
Hartshead WN8 ... 18 C2
Hart's Hos BL6 ... 32 D5
Hart's La WN8 ... 9 F8
Hart St
Blackburn BB1 ... 101 F4
Burnley BB11 ... 128 A6
Southport PR8 ... 35 E6
HARTWOOD ... 61 C3
Hartwood Gn PR6 ... 61 C3
Hartwood Rd PR9 ... 35 D7
Harvest Dr PR6 ... 61 C6
Harvesters Fold PR4 ... 134 F4
Harvey Longworth Ct BB4 ... 106 A1
Harvey St
14 Nelson BB9 ... 170 E1
Oswaldtwistle BB5 ... 103 D4
Harvington Dr PR8 ... 21 B5
Harwich Rd FY8 ... 111 A1
Harwin Cl OL12 ... 52 D3
Harwood Ave FY8 ... 89 E8
HARWOOD BAR ... 124 F6
Harwood Cl FY6 ... 177 C7
Harwood Gate BB1 ... 102 B6
Harwood La BB6 ... 124 E6
Harwood New Rd BB6 ... 124 E6
Harwood Rd
Rishton BB1 ... 124 A2
Wilpshire BB1 ... 123 D4
Harwood's La BB3 ... 82 E1
Harwood St
14 Blackburn, Cob Wall BB1 ... 102 A7
Blackburn, Green Bank BB1 ... 102 B6
Darwen BB3 ... 81 E2
Hasbury Dr FY5 ... 176 C2
Hasgill Ct LA1 ... 218 C1
HASKAYNE ... 13 F4
Haskoll St BL6 ... 32 D1
Haslam Ct 1 BB10 ... 148 B1
Haslam Dr L39 ... 15 D7
Haslam St BL9 ... 33 A4
Haslemere Ave 6 FY3 ... 130 E3
Haslemere Ind Est PR25 ... 76 F3
HASLINGDEN ... 85 B4
HASLINGDEN GRANE ... 84 B2
Haslingden Grane (Trail)* BB4 ... 84 A2
Haslingden High Sch BB4 ... 68 B8
Haslingden Old Rd
Blackburn BB1, BB5 ... 102 E3
Rawtenstall BB4 ... 85 E2
Haslingden Prim Sch BB4 ... 85 B2
Haslingden Rd
Blackburn BB1, BB2 ... 102 B2
Oswaldtwistle BB5 ... 83 D7
Rawtenstall BB4 ... 85 E2
Haslingden St James CE Prim Sch BB4 ... 85 B3
Haslow Pl FY3 ... 130 F7
Hassall Dr PR4 ... 156 A1
Hassett Cl PR1 ... 96 E6
Hastings Ave
Blackpool FY2 ... 152 E5
Warton PR4 ... 92 E7
Hastings Cl
Blackburn BB1 ... 102 C4
Thornton FY5 ... 176 C1
Hastings Pl FY8 ... 91 A3
Hastings Rd
Kirkham PR4 ... 114 B2
Lancaster LA1 ... 214 F5
Leyland PR25 ... 77 B2
Preston PR2 ... 117 B1
Southport PR8 ... 34 E1
Thornton FY5 ... 176 C1
Hastings The LA1 ... 214 F5
Haston Lee Ave BB1 ... 122 F3
Hasty Brow Rd LA2 ... 218 B6
Hatfield Ave
Fleetwood FY7 ... 198 F3
Morecambe LA4 ... 217 F6
Hatfield Cl FY5 ... 176 C2
Hatfield Ct LA4 ... 217 F6
Hatfield Gdns 2 FY7 ... 198 E2
Hatfield Mews 2 FY7 ... 198 F2
Hatfield Rd
Accrington BB5 ... 104 D7
Fulwood PR2 ... 118 E3
Southport PR8 ... 21 C6
Hatfield Wlk 1 FY7 ... 198 E2
Hathaway FY4 ... 110 E8
Hathaway Fold 4 BB12 ... 126 D7
Hathaway Rd
Fleetwood FY7 ... 198 E4
Lancaster LA1 ... 218 C3
Hatlex Dr LA2 ... 220 E2
Hatlex Hill LA2 ... 220 E2
Hatlex La LA2 ... 220 E2
Hattersley St BB11 ... 127 E6
Hatton St PR7 ... 30 F6
Haugh Ave BB12 ... 145 E2
Haugh St BB10 ... 148 B2
Haunders La PR4 ... 74 B1
Havelock Cl BB2 ... 101 D3
Havelock Rd
Bamber Bridge PR5 ... 77 E7
Middleforth Green PR1 ... 96 E5
Havelock St
Blackburn BB2 ... 101 C2
5 Blackpool FY1 ... 130 B4
Burnley BB12 ... 127 B6
Lancaster LA1 ... 215 A6
Oswaldtwistle BB5 ... 103 D3
11 Padiham BB12 ... 146 C1
Preston, Adelphi PR1 ... 117 E2
Preston, Maudlands PR1 ... 117 D2
Preston PR1 ... 117 F2
Havenbrook Gr BL0 ... 50 A3
Haven Brow L39 ... 6 C8
Havenlyn Residential Pk PR3 ... 204 C6
Haven Rd FY8 ... 91 C3
Haven Sch FY5 ... 175 E4
Haven St BB10 ... 128 C5
Haven Wlk L31 ... 5 C4
HAVERBREAKS ... 214 E5
Haverbreaks Pl LA1 ... 214 E6
Haverbreaks Rd LA1 ... 214 E5
Haverholt Cl BB8 ... 171 C5
Haverholt Rd BB8 ... 171 C5
Haverthwaite Ave LA3 ... 212 F7
Havre Pk BB18 ... 196 C2
Hawarden Ave LA4 ... 217 C5
Hawarden Rd 1 PR1 ... 118 E1
Hawarden St BB9 ... 148 E7
Hawes Dr BB8 ... 171 F6
HAWES SIDE ... 130 F1
Hawes Side La FY4 ... 110 E8
Hawes Side Prim Sch FY4 ... 110 E7
Hawesside St PR9 ... 35 C7
Hawes Terr BB10 ... 148 B2
Haweswater Ave PR7 ... 43 B6
Haweswater Gr L31 ... 5 F2
Haweswater Pl 3 LA4 ... 217 E4
Haweswater Rd 1 BB5 ... 125 D1
Hawfinch Cl OL13 ... 88 A2
Hawick Gr OL10 ... 33 E1
Hawk Cl BL9 ... 33 B4
Hawker Dr WN8 ... 9 E8
Hawkeshead Cl BB2 ... 101 B4
Hawkhurst Ave PR2 ... 117 D6
Hawkhurst Cres PR2 ... 117 D6
Hawkhurst Rd
Middleforth Green PR1 ... 96 E5
Preston PR1 ... 118 B1
Hawking Pl FY2 ... 152 F5
Hawkins Cl PR1 ... 117 E1
Hawkins St
Blackburn BB2 ... 101 B2
Preston PR1 ... 117 E1
Hawksbury Dr PR1 ... 96 D2
Hawksclough WN8 ... 18 D2
Hawks Gr BB4 ... 86 A1
HAWKSHAW
Darwen ... 81 D3
Ramsbottom ... 49 C2
Hawkshaw Ave BB3 ... 81 E3
Hawkshaw Bank Rd BB1 ... 101 D8
Hawkshaw Cl BL8 ... 49 B3
Hawkshaw La BL8 ... 49 B5
Hawkshaw St BL6 ... 32 B3
Hawkshead PR1 ... 96 E3
Hawkshead Ave PR7 ... 60 D1
Hawkshead Cl L31 ... 5 E2
Hawkshead Dr LA4 ... 217 C3
Hawkshead Rd
Fulwood PR2 ... 118 E5
Knott End-on-S FY6 ... 199 F6
Hawkshead St
Blackburn BB2 ... 101 B4
Southport PR8, PR9 ... 35 D7
Hawkshead Terr FY4 ... 111 D8
Hawksheath Cl BL7 ... 47 E1
Hawksley St BL6 ... 32 D2
HAWKS STONES ... 109 E3
Hawk St
Burnley BB11 ... 128 A6
Carnforth LA5 ... 223 E2
Hawkstone Cl
Huncoat BB5 ... 125 F1
Thornton FY5 ... 153 D8
Hawkstone Ct LA4 ... 217 F6
Hawkswood PR7 ... 41 B6
Hawkswood Gdns BB9 ... 148 A4
Hawksworth Ave LA3 ... 216 E2
Hawksworth Cl L37 ... 12 A6
Hawksworth Dr L37 ... 12 A6
Hawksworth Gr LA3 ... 216 D2
Hawksworth Rd BB5 ... 104 B8
Hawley Gn OL12 ... 52 D2
Hawley St
Colne BB8 ... 171 C4
Colne, Cotton Tree BB8 ... 172 C5
Haworth Art Gallery* BB5 ... 104 D3
Haworth Ave
Accrington BB5 ... 104 D3
Ramsbottom BL0 ... 50 A2
Rawtenstall BB4 ... 85 F2
Haworth Dr OL13 ... 70 C8
Haworth St
Accrington BB5 ... 125 B1
Edgworth BL7 ... 48 D5
Oswaldtwistle BB5 ... 103 E4
Rishton BB1 ... 124 B1
Haws Ave LA5 ... 223 D1
Haws Hill LA5 ... 223 D1
Hawthorn Ave
Burscough L40 ... 25 F4
Caton LA2 ... 237 C3
Darwen BB3 ... 82 C2
Edenfield BL0 ... 68 D2
Fleetwood FY7 ... 175 E8
Orrell WN5 ... 10 F6
Oswaldtwistle BB5 ... 103 F3
Ramsbottom BL0 ... 50 A2
Hawthorn Bank BB5 ... 125 A3
Hawthorn Cl
Caton LA2 ... 237 C3
Kirkham PR4 ... 113 E6
Langho BB6 ... 123 D8
Leyland PR26 ... 76 D2
New Longton PR4 ... 76 A7
Whalley BB7 ... 144 A7
Hawthorn Cres
Preston PR2 ... 116 D1
Skelmersdale WN8 ... 17 E1
Hawthorn Dr BB1 ... 103 B8
Hawthorne Ave
Burnley BB10 ... 148 C5
Garstang PR3 ... 181 B8
Higher Walton PR5 ... 98 C3
Horwich BL6 ... 32 E1
Newton-w-S PR4 ... 114 F3
Hawthorne Cl
Barrowford BB9 ... 170 B1
Clayton Green PR6 ... 78 B3
Nelson BB9 ... 149 B8
Hawthorne Cres L37 ... 12 A2
Hawthorne Ct PR6 ... 30 F8
Hawthorne Cvn Pk LA3 ... 208 F7
Hawthorne Dr BB18 ... 196 C4

Hawthorne Gr
17 Barrowford BB9 170 D3
Carleton FY6 153 B5
Southport PR9 35 F7
Hawthorne Ind Pk BB7 190 A1
Hawthorne Lea FY5 153 C8
Hawthorne Mdws BB4 106 A1
Hawthorne Pl BB7 189 E1
Hawthorne Rd
Burnley BB11 127 F4
Thornton FY5 153 C8
Hawthorne St BB1 101 F8
Hawthornes The L40 39 B3
Hawthorne Terr BB8 194 E1
Hawthorn Gdns BB5 125 A3
Hawthorn Rd
Bacup OL13 88 A2
Blackpool FY1 130 C7
Bolton-le-S LA5 221 A6
Fulwood PR2 118 E2
Morecambe LA4 217 F4
Hawthorns Holiday Pk LA6 237 A7
Hawthorns Jun Sch BB1 101 F8
Hawthorns The
Bilsborrow PR3 159 A5
Eccleston PR7 41 B7
3 Formby L37 12 A3
Fulwood PR2 117 F6
Garstang PR3 204 C2
Lancaster LA1 215 A2
Lytham St Anne's FY8 110 F2
Newburgh WN8 27 A1
1 Newchurch BB4 86 F1
Wilpshire BB1 122 F6
Woodplumpton PR4 136 E2
Haxey Wlk BL6 31 F3
Haydock Ave PR25 60 A8
Haydock Gr LA3 216 D1
Haydock La BL7 48 A1
Haydock Rd LA1 215 B3
Haydocks La PR4 116 D5
Haydock Sq 1 BB6 124 C5
Haydock St
6 Bamber Bridge PR5 97 E2
3 Blackburn BB1 122 E1
Burnley BB10 148 C1
Haydon Ave PR5 77 A7
Hayfell Ave LA4 217 C3
Hayfell Cres LA2 220 D1
Hayfell Gr LA2 220 D1
Hayfield BB2 101 A7
Hayfield Ave
Blackpool FY2 152 E2
Gregson Lane PR5 98 E1
Poulton-le-F FY6 153 E3
Hayfield Cl
Gregson Lane PR5 98 E1
Ramsbottom BL8 49 F1
Hayfield Rd L39 15 E7
Hayfields BB18 194 E8
Hayhurst Cl BB7 144 C6
Hayhurst Farm Terr BB7 166 F7
Hayhurst Rd BB7 144 C6
Hayhurst St BB7 166 F7
Haylemere Ct PR8 34 E5
Hayling Pl PR2 117 A4
Haylot Dr LA2 219 D7
Haylot Sq 9 LA1 215 A8
Haymans Gn L31 5 E1
Haymarket FY8 90 B6
Haymarket Lo PR9 53 D1
Hayshaw Mews PR3 207 D3
Haysworth St PR1 117 F2
Hayward Ct L37 12 A4
Hayward Gr WN6 29 D2
Haywood Cl
Accrington BB5 104 B8
Fulwood PR2 118 A8
Haywood Rd BB5 104 B8
Hazel Ave
Bamber Bridge PR5 98 A1
Bury BL9 33 B2
Clayton-le-M BB5 124 F2
Darwen BB3 82 B2
Fleetwood FY7 175 F8
Ramsbottom BL0 50 B1
Hazelbank LA2 219 C6
Hazel Bank LA3 212 F7
Hazelbank Gdns L37 11 E5
Hazel Cl
Bamber Bridge PR5 97 F1
Blackburn BB2 101 C4
Higher Penwortham PR1 96 B3
Knott End-on-S FY6 199 F6
Hazel Coppice PR2 116 E3
Hazel Ct
Fulwood PR2 117 E7
Ormskirk L39 15 E5
Hazel Dene BB7 189 E6
Hazeldene Ave 2 BB4 85 B2
Hazeldene Rd FY7 198 F2
Hazel Gr
Bacup OL13 88 B3
Bamber Bridge PR5 98 A1
Blackburn BB1 102 F5
Blackpool FY3 130 E5
Chorley PR6 61 C3
Clayton-le-M BB5 125 A2
Clitheroe BB7 166 C7
Fulwood PR2 119 A4
Lancaster LA1 214 D8
Hazel Gr *continued*
Longridge PR3 140 B8
Rawtenstall BB4 85 F4
Southport PR8 35 E7
Tarleton PR4 56 F8
Hazel Hall La BL0 50 B1
Hazelhead La PR3 204 E2
HAZELHURST 50 B4
Hazelhurst Cl BL0 50 B4
Hazelhurst Com Prim Sch BL0 50 A4
Hazelhurst Dr PR3 181 A7
Hazelhurst Lo 12 PR2 118 F4
Hazelhurst Rd PR2 119 A2
Hazel La WN8 18 B4
Hazelmere Rd
Fulwood PR2 117 D8
Preston PR2 117 A1
Hazelmoor BB1 122 E6
Hazel Mount BL7 47 E2
Hazelmount Ave LA5 223 D3
Hazelmount Cres LA5 223 D3
Hazelmount Dr LA5 223 C3
Hazelrigg La LA2 211 C7
Hazel St
Ramsbottom BL0 50 A4
Rising Bridge BB5 85 A8
Hazels The
Coppull PR7 42 E1
Wilpshire BB1 122 E6
Hazelwood
Silverdale LA5 224 C2
Southport PR8 34 F1
Hazelwood Ave L40 25 E4
Hazelwood Cl
Blackburn BB1 123 A1
Leyland PR25 76 E1
Hazelwood Dr
Hesketh Bank PR4 73 E4
Morecambe LA4 217 F6
Hazelwood Gdns LA1 215 A2
Hazelwood Hall LA5 224 D1
Hazelwood Rd BB9 149 A8
Hazlehurst Cl L37 11 C2
Hazlewood Cl FY5 176 A2
Headbolt La
Kirkby L33 1 A5
Southport, Hillside PR8 22 B7
Southport L39 22 A4
Head Dyke La PR3 201 C3
Headfort Cl FY2 152 D2
Headingley Cl BB5 125 F1
Headingly Ave WN8 17 D1
Headlands St 2 OL12 52 E1
Headlands The LA3 212 D7
Headley Rd PR25 76 E1
Headroomgate Rd FY8 89 F8
Heads La BB18 195 B6
Heald Brow BB18 196 A4
Heald Cl
Rochdale OL12 52 C3
Weir OL13 88 A8
Heald Croft PR3 181 D6
Heald Dr OL12 52 C3
Heald House Rd PR25 60 C7
Heald La OL13 88 A8
Heald Rd BB10, BB12 148 A2
Heald St
Blackpool FY3 130 D6
6 Chorley PR6 43 E8
Healdwood Cl BB12 147 F3
Healdwood Dr BB12 147 F3
Healey Ave OL12 52 D4
Healey Ct BB11 127 F5
Healey Dell Cotts OL12 52 B4
Healey Dell Nature Reserve* OL12 52 B6
Healey Foundation Prim Sch OL12 52 E3
Healey Gr OL12 52 C5
Healey Hall Farm OL12 52 C4
Healey Hall Mews OL12 52 C4
Healey La OL12 52 E3
Healey Mount BB11 127 F4
Healey Row BB11 127 F5
Healey St FY3 130 D7
Healey Stones OL12 52 E4
Healey Wood Rd BB11 127 F4
Healey Wood Road Ind Est BB11 127 F5
Heaning Ave
Accrington BB5 104 D8
Blackburn BB1 102 D4
Heanor Dr PR8 35 F3
HEAP BRIDGE 33 C1
Heap Bridge Village Prim Sch BL9 33 D1
Heap Brow BL9 33 D1
Heap Clough BB4 84 C3
Heap Ct PR9 35 E8
HEAPEY 62 A6
Heapey Fold La PR6 44 C7
Heapey Ho PR6 62 A3
Heapey Rd PR6 61 F2
Heapfold 4 OL12 52 B2
Heaplands BL8 49 F1
Heap St
Brierfield BB9 148 A5
Burnley BB10 148 B1
Bury BL9 33 D1
Rawtenstall BB4 86 A8
Worsthorne BB10 129 B6
Heapworth Ave BL0 50 B6
Heartwood Cl BB2 101 A8
HEASANDFORD 128 C8
Heasandford Ind Est
Burnley BB10 148 D2
Heasandford Ind Est *continued*
Burnley, Heasandford BB10 128 D8
Heasandford Prim Sch BB10 128 B8
Heath Ave BL0 50 B1
Heathbourne Rd OL13 70 C8
HEATH CHARNOCK 43 F2
Heather Bank
Burnley BB11 127 C4
Rawtenstall BB4 68 F8
Heather Brow BB18 197 D2
Heather Cl
Brierfield BB9 148 D4
Burscough L40 25 E4
Chorley PR6 43 E8
Formby L37 12 B5
Haslingden BB4 68 A8
Horwich BL6 32 B4
Southport PR8 21 D2
Thornton FY5 176 B1
Heatherfield BL7 48 E6
Heatherfield Pl PR2 117 C1
Heather Gr PR2 118 E3
Heatherlands OL12 71 D4
Heatherlea Cl WN8 10 C7
Heather Lea Dr PR6 62 F8
Heatherlea Rd BB12 147 D7
Heatherleigh PR26 76 D3
Heatherleigh Gdns BB2 81 D6
Heatherside Rd BL0 50 C7
Heathers The
Clayton Brook PR5 78 C4
Knott End-on-S FY6 199 F5
Heatherway PR2 118 E6
Heatherways L37 12 A6
Heathey La L39, PR8 23 A7
Heathfield PR6 43 F1
Heathfield Ave OL13 70 C8
Heathfield Cl L37 12 A6
Heathfield Dr PR2 118 E4
Heathfield Pk BB2 100 F6
Heathfield Rd
Bacup OL13 70 C8
Fleetwood FY7 198 E2
Southport PR8 21 F6
Heathfoot Ave LA3 212 E6
Heathfoot Dr LA3 212 E6
Heathgate
Fence BB12 147 D8
Skelmersdale WN8 18 C2
Heath Gr LA3 212 E6
Heath Hill Dr OL13 70 C8
Heathland WN8 10 B7
Heathland Coll BB5 104 D5
Heathrow Pl PR7 43 A7
Heath St BB10 128 B8
Heathway PR2 117 F5
Heathway Ave FY3 130 E6
Heathy La L39 13 B8
Heatley Cl BB2 101 D3
Heatley St PR1 96 F8
HEATON 213 E5
Heaton Bottom Rd LA3 213 E5
Heaton Bsns Pk LA3 217 C2
Heaton Cl
Bamber Bridge PR5 97 D4
Burscough L40 25 D4
Carleton FY6 153 C5
Morecambe LA3 217 E3
Thornton FY5 153 C8
Up Holland WN8 10 A7
Heaton Ho LA1 214 F5
Heaton Mount Ave PR2 117 F7
Heaton Pl PR1 118 E1
Heaton Rd
Lancaster LA1 214 F5
Lytham St Anne's FY8 90 A8
HEATON'S BRIDGE 24 D4
Heatons Bridge Rd L40 24 D3
Heaton St
3 Blackburn BB2 101 E4
Leyland PR25 76 E2
Standish WN6 29 E1
Heaviley Gr BL6 32 A5
Hebden Ave FY1 130 D1
Heber St BB11 106 B4
Hebrew Rd BB10 128 A8
Hebrew Sq 12 BB10 128 A8
Heckenhurst Ave BB10 129 A6
Hector Rd BB3 81 E5
Hedge Row PR4 113 B3
Hedge Rows OL12 71 C1
Hedgerows Rd PR26 59 A8
Hedgerow The BB2 101 A8
Hedgeview L40 24 B4
Heeley Rd FY8 89 E8
Height Barn La OL13 71 A8
Height Croft BB9 148 E5
HEIGHT END 85 D3
Height La PR3 161 F7
Heights Ave OL12 52 E2
Heights Cl OL12 52 E2
Heights Cotts BB5 104 F4
Heights Ct OL12 52 E1
Heightside Ave BB4 86 E2
Height Side La BB4 86 B7
Heightside Mews BB4 86 E2
Heights La OL12 52 E1
Heights Rd BB9 148 D6
Heights The BL6 32 D1
Helena St BB10 128 B5
Helen's Cl FY4 110 E6
Helks Brow LA2 239 B2
Hellifield PR2 117 F7
Hellifield Rd
Bolton-by-B BB7 230 E5
Gisburn BB7 231 C4
Helm Cl BB11 127 D2
HELMCROFT 85 B1
Helmcroft 5 BB4 85 A1
Helmcroft Ct 1 BB4 85 B1
Helmn Way BB9 170 F2
Helmsdale WN8 18 C2
Helmsdale Cl BL0 50 A4
Helmsdale Rd
Blackpool FY4 110 F7
Nelson BB9 171 A1
HELMSHORE 68 B7
Helmshore Prim Sch BB4 68 A7
Helmshore Rd
Haslingden BB4 68 A7
Ramsbottom BL0, BL8, BB4 68 A3
Helmshore Textile Mus* BB4 67 F8
Helmside Ave LA4 217 C3
Helmsley Gn 2 PR25 77 B1
Helston Cl
Burnley BB11 127 B4
Southport PR9 54 B5
Helton Cl BB9 170 D4
Helvellyn Dr BB12 127 C8
Hemingway FY4 110 D8
Hemingway Pl 1 BB9 148 F8
Hempshaw Ave BB4 106 A2
Hemp St OL13 87 F1
Henderson Rd
Fleetwood FY7 198 F2
Weeton Camp PR4 132 E6
Henderson St PR1 117 E2
Hendon Brook Sch BB8 171 C1
Hendon Pl PR2 116 E2
Hendon Rd BB9 148 F8
Hendriff Pl 4 OL12 52 F1
Hendry La BB2 81 D7
Henfield Cl BB5 125 A3
Henley Ave FY5 175 D2
Henley Ct
7 Blackpool FY2 152 E1
Southport PR9 53 E1
Henley Dr PR9 53 F1
Henley Mews 7 LA3 216 E3
Henley St 9 OL12 52 F1
Hennel Ho PR5 97 C4
Hennel La PR5 97 C3
Henrietta St
Bacup OL13 87 F2
Blackburn BB2 101 C5
Preston PR1 97 B8
Henrietta Street Ind Est 2 OL13 87 F2
Henry Gdns BB9 148 B5
Henry St
Accrington BB5 104 D3
Bank Lane BL0 50 D7
Blackpool FY1 130 C2
Church BB5 103 F6
Clayton-le-M BB5 125 A2
Colne BB8 171 C4
Lancaster LA1 214 F7
Lytham St Anne's FY8 91 A3
2 Nelson BB9 170 D1
Rawtenstall BB4 85 F2
Rishton BB1 124 B1
Henry Whalley St BB2 101 A2
Henson Ave FY4 110 E6
Henthorn Cl 4 BB7 166 D7
Henthorne St 1 FY1 130 C6
Henthorn Rd BB7 166 C6
Henwick Hall Ave BL0 50 B4
Herbert St
Bacup OL13 70 D8
Blackburn BB2 101 D2
Burnley BB11 127 E5
Horwich BL6 32 B4
Leyland PR25 77 A1
Padiham BB12 126 D7
Preston PR1 118 B1
Herb Gdns The LA6 241 B3
Hereford Ave
8 Blackpool FY3 130 E3
Burnley BB12 127 B7
Garstang PR3 181 B8
Hereford Cl BB5 104 B7
Hereford Dr BB7 166 F7
Hereford Gr
Buckshaw Village PR7 60 F6
Cottam PR4 116 D5
Up Holland WN8 10 B6
Hereford Rd
Blackburn BB1 102 C5
Nelson BB8, BB9 171 A2
Southport PR9 35 F7
Hereford St BB9 148 C8
Herevale Hall Dr BL0 50 B4
Heriot Cl FY5 175 F1
Heritage The PR25 76 F3
Heritage Way
Cleveleys FY5 175 F1
Tarleton PR4 57 A5
Herkomer Ave BB11 127 E2
Herlebeck Rise LA1 218 F2
Hermitage Cl WN6 19 E7
Hermitage St BB1, BB5 124 C1
Hermitage The FY5 175 F2
Hermitage Way FY8 90 D6
Hermon Ave FY5 175 E1
Hermon St 2 PR1 118 C1
Hern Ave PR5 77 A8
Heron Cl
Blackburn BB1 101 D8
Cleveleys FY5 175 F5
Heron Ct BB11 127 C5
Heron Dr 1 LA4 217 C3
Heron Mews LA3 212 F6
Herons Ct L31 5 B4
Herons Wharf WN6 19 D7
Heronsyke LA1 218 D4
Heron Way
Blackpool FY3 131 B6
Kirkham PR4 114 B2
Oswaldtwistle BB5 103 E3
Herring Arm Rd FY7 199 A2
Herschel Ave BB12 127 C8
Herschell St
2 Blackburn BB2 101 B1
Preston PR1 97 B6
Hertford St BB2 101 C2
Hesketh Ave
Banks PR9 55 A6
Blackpool FY2 152 B4
HESKETH BANK 73 D4
Hesketh Cl
Darwen BB3 65 C6
Fulwood PR2 118 E1
Hesketh Ct
Blackpool FY2 152 B4
Great Harwood BB6 124 E6
Hesketh Dr
Maghull L31 5 F1
Rufford L40 39 A3
Shevington Moor WN6 29 A2
Southport PR9 53 F1
Hesketh Gn L40 39 B4
Hesketh La
Becconsall PR4 73 F1
Hesketh Lane PR3 162 D7
Tarleton PR4 57 A7
HESKETH LANE 162 D8
Hesketh Links Ct PR9 53 E2
Hesketh Lo L37 11 E3
Hesketh Pl FY7 199 B5
Hesketh Rd
Burscough L40 25 D4
Fulwood PR2 118 E1
Heysham LA3 212 E8
Longridge PR3 140 A8
Lytham St Anne's FY8 111 A1
Southport PR9 53 D2
Hesketh St
Great Harwood BB6 124 C5
Preston PR2 117 C1
Hesketh-with-Becconsall All Saints CE Sch PR4 73 E4
Heskin Cl L31 5 D4
HESKIN GREEN 41 E3
Heskin Hall Ct L39 15 D8
Heskin La L39 15 D8
Heskin Pemberton's CE Prim Sch PR7 41 E2
Hesley La BD24 236 E6
Hessam Hts LA3 212 F5
Hesse St 1 BB3 65 A8
HEST BANK 220 F1
Hest Bank La LA2 218 C7
Hest Bank Rd LA4 217 E6
Hester Cl L38 2 F4
Hestham Ave LA4 217 B4
Hestham Cres LA4 217 B4
Hestham Dr LA4 217 B4
Hestham Par LA4 217 B4
Hetherington Pl FY2 152 E2
Hetton Lea BB9 170 C3
Heversham WN8 18 C2
Heversham Ave PR2 117 F7
Heversham Cl
Lancaster LA1 215 B3
2 Morecambe LA4 217 C3
Hewart Dr BL9 33 C3
Hewart St BB12 127 A7
Hewitt Bsns Pk WN5 10 E4
Hewitt Cl PR4 95 E
Hewitt St 8 PR25 77 B2
Hewlett Ave PR7 42 D1
Hewlett Ct BL8 50 A1
Hewlett St PR7 42 D1
Hewngate PR5 98 E
Hexham Ave FY5 175 E4
Hexham Cl BB5 104 E3
Hexham Rd LA4 217 F5
HEY 194 C3
Hey Bottom La OL12 52 F6
Heycrofts View BL0 68 E3
Heydon Cl L37 11 D3
Hey End PR4 75 F8
Heyescroft L39 7 D6
Heyes Rd WN5 10 E6
Heyes St WN6 19 C2
Heyes The PR6 78 B2
Heyfold Gdns BB3 81 F3
HEY HEAD 87 A
Hey Head Ave BB4 70 A8
Heyhead St BB9 148 C8
Hey House Mews BL8 49 F4
Heyhouses BB7 146 A
HEY HOUSES 90 D
Heyhouses Ct FY8 90 B8
Heyhouses Endowed CE Prim Sch FY8 89 F
Heyhouses La FY8 90 C
Heyhurst Rd BB2 101 D
Heymoor Ave BB6 124 D
Heys BB5 103 D
Heys Ave 5 BB4 85 A
Heys Cl
Blackburn BB2 81 C
Rawtenstall BB4 86 C

Heys Ct
Blackburn BB2 81 C8
Oswaldtwistle BB5 103 E3
HEYSHAM 212 D7
Heysham Ave LA3 212 F8
Heysham Bsns Pk LA3 212 E2
Heysham Cres BB2 101 F1
Heysham Hall Dr LA3 212 E6
Heysham Hall Gr LA3 212 E7
Heysham High Sports Coll LA3 216 F3
Heysham Mossgate Rd LA3 212 F7
Heysham Nature Reserve* LA3 212 D4
Heysham Pk LA3 212 E7
Heysham Port Sta LA3 212 C5
Heysham Rd
4 Heysham LA3 212 E7
Morecambe LA3 216 D2
Southport PR9 35 F7
Heysham St 2 PR1 117 E1
Heys Hunt Ave PR25 77 A2
Heys La
Barley Green BB12 169 D5
Blackburn BB2, BB3 81 C7
Darwen BB3 81 F2
Great Harwood BB6 124 E5
Oswaldtwistle BB5 103 E3
Heys Lo PR6 61 E6
Heys St
Bacup OL13 87 F1
Haslingden BB4 85 A3
Rawtenstall BB4 86 C1
Thornton FY5 176 B3
Hey St BB9 170 E1
Heys The
Coppull PR7 42 F2
Parbold WN8 27 C3
Southport PR8 34 D4
HEYWOOD 33 F2
Heywood Cl L37 11 E3
Heywood Com High Sch OL10 33 E1
Heywood Rd PR2 116 E2
Heywood St
1 Blackpool FY1 130 B4
Bury BL9 33 A1
Great Harwood BB6 124 C4
Heyworth Ave BB2 81 C7
Hibbert Terr LA1 214 F3
Hibson Rd
Nelson BB9 148 D8
Nelson, Little Marsden BB9 148 D7
Hic Bibi La PR7 29 E6
Hickory St BB1 101 F7
Hickson Ave L31 5 C3
Hick's Terr BB1 124 B1
Hidings Court La LA4 217 B4
Hiers House La BB8 171 B5
Higgin's La L40 25 C4
Higgin St
Burnley BB10 128 B5
Colne BB8 171 D5
Worsthorne BB10 129 B5
HIGHAM 146 E5
Higham Gr FY3 130 F2
Higham Hall Rd BB12 146 F5
Higham Rd BB12 146 C3
Higham Side Rd PR4 135 C6
Higham St BB12 146 D1
Highbank BB1 122 F1
High Bank PR6 62 A3
Highbank Ave FY4 111 A8
High Bank Cres BB3 65 A7
Highbank Hotel 7 PR2 117 C1
Highbanks L31 5 C3
High Barn La OL12 71 C3
HIGH BENTHAM 239 E8
High Bentham Bsns Pk LA2 239 D7
High Bentham Com Prim Sch LA2 239 D8
High Booths Cl BB4 106 A1
Highbury Ave
Blackpool FY3 130 E8
Fleetwood FY7 198 F3
Highbury Gate PR4 156 A2
Highbury Pl BB1 101 D6
Highbury Rd FY8 110 E1
Highbury Rd E FY8 110 E1
Highbury Rd W FY8 110 D1
High Cl BB12 126 E6
High Cop PR6 78 F4
High Crag Ct LA5 223 E6
Highcroft 17 LA2 239 D8
Highcroft Ave FY2 152 E5
Highcroft Way OL12 52 F4
HIGH CROSS 131 D8
Highcross Ave FY6 131 D8
Highcross Hill FY6 131 D8
Highcross Rd FY6 153 D1
High Ct LA4 217 F5
Highdale LA3 213 A7
Higher Antley St BB5 104 A5
HIGHER AUDLEY 102 A4
Higher Audley St BB1 101 F4
Higher Austin's BL6 32 F1
HIGHER BALLAM 111 F1
Higher Bank Rd PR2 117 F3
Higher Bank St
Blackburn BB2 101 B6
Withnell PR6 80 A1
Higher Barn BL6 32 F3
Higher Barn St 2 BB1 102 A5
HIGHER BARTLE 116 E7
HIGHER BAXENDEN 104 F2
Higher Blackthorn OL13 87 F4
HIGHER BOARSGREAVE 70 A6
Higher Bold Venture BB3 65 A6
Higher Booths La BB4 106 A1
HIGHER BROAD CLOUGH 87 F5
HIGHER BROADHALGH 80 E7
Higherbrook Cl BL6 32 D1
HIGHER CHANGE 88 B4
Higher Change Villas OL13 88 B4
Higher Chapel La BB7 230 A1
Higher Church St BB3 82 B1
HIGHER CLOUGHFOLD 86 D2
Higher Cockcroft 14 BB1 101 E5
Higher Commons La BB2 121 C4
HIGHER COPTHURST 61 E7
HIGHER CROFT 101 F1
Higher Croft PR1 96 C2
Higher Croft Cotts BB3 81 F8
Higher Croft Rd BB2, BB3 81 F8
Higher Cross Row 8 OL13 87 F3
Higher Cswy BB9 170 D3
Higher Dunscar BL7 47 E1
Higher Eanam BB1 102 A5
HIGHER END 10 D3
Higher Feniscowles La BB2 80 B8
Higherfield BB6 123 C8
Higher Firs Dr BB5 125 A3
Higher Fold La BL0 50 E7
Higher Furlong PR4 74 F6
Higher Gate BB5 125 F1
Highergate Cl BB5 125 F2
Higher Gate Rd BB5 125 F1
Higher Gn FY6 153 E3
Higher Greenfield PR2 117 B5
Higher Heys BB5 103 E3
HIGHER HEYSHAM 212 F6
Higher Hill BB3 80 F2
Higher House Cl BB2 81 A7
Higher House La PR6 62 B2
Higher Knowles BL6 32 E2
Higher La
Haslingden BB4 85 B4
Holmes PR4 56 C3
Salterforth BB18 194 B7
Scorton PR3 204 F4
Skelmersdale WN8 18 C7
Up Holland WN8 10 C7
Higher Lawrence St 14 BB3 81 F2
Higher London Terr BB3 82 B2
Higher Mdw PR25 77 E1
Higher Mill St BB4 86 A3
Higher Moor Cotts FY2 152 F2
Higher Moor Rd FY3 153 A2
Higher Moss La L37 13 A2
Higher Moulding BL9 33 E5
Higher Park Rd BB18 194 C8
Higher Peel St 8 BB5 103 D3
HIGHER PENWORTHAM 96 C4
Higher Perry St BB3 82 B2
Higher Ramsgreave Rd BB1 122 C3
Higher Rd
Knowle Green PR3 163 B3
Longridge PR3 162 E2
Tosside BD23 236 C5
Higher Reedley Rd BB9, BB10 148 D5
Higher Row BL9 33 B3
Higher Saxifield BB10 148 E3
Higher South St BB3 82 A1
HIGHER STANDEN 166 F5
HIGHER STANHILL 103 B4
HIGHER SUMMERSEAT 50 B1
Higher Summerseat BL0 50 B2
Higher Syke LA2 233 C2
Higher Tentre BB11 128 B5
Higher View WN8 10 C6
HIGHER WALTON 98 B4
Higher Walton CE Prim Sch PR5 98 C3
Higher Walton Mill PR5 98 B4
Higher Walton Rd PR5 97 E4
Higher Waterside BB3 82 E3
HIGHER WHEELTON 79 B1
Higher Witton Rd BB2 101 B4
Highfield
Bacup OL13 87 F2
Brinscall PR6 62 F8
Great Harwood BB6 124 B5
Rawtenstall BB4 86 A7
Highfield Ave
Bamber Bridge PR5 97 C1
Burnley BB10 148 B3
Foulridge BB8 194 E1
Fulwood PR2 118 C4
Inskip PR4 135 C8
Leyland PR25 77 C3
Highfield Cl
Adlington PR6 31 A7
Clifton PR4 115 C1
Oswaldtwistle BB5 103 F3
Highfield Cl *continued*
Tarleton PR4 57 A5
Highfield Cres
5 Barrowford BB9 170 D3
Morecambe LA4 216 F4
Nelson BB9 170 E3
Highfield Ct
Darwen BB3 82 D1
Haslingden BB4 85 A2
Highfield Dr
Fulwood PR2 117 E8
Hest Bank LA2 220 D1
Kingsfold PR1 96 D2
Longridge PR3 140 B6
Longton PR4 74 F6
Highfield Gdns BB2 101 E2
Highfield Gr PR5 97 C2
Highfield Humanities Coll FY4 110 E6
Highfield Ind Est PR7 61 D2
Highfield La L40 24 D7
Highfield Mews BB3 65 B8
Highfield Pk
Haslingden BB4 85 A1
Maghull L31 5 F1
Highfield Prim Sch PR6 43 E8
Highfield Priory Sch PR2 118 F5
Highfield Rd
Adlington PR6 31 A7
Blackburn BB2 101 E3
Blackpool FY4 110 E6
Blackrod BL6 31 E1
Carnforth LA5 221 E8
Clitheroe BB7 166 F7
Croston PR26 58 D2
Darwen BB3 82 B1
1 Earby BB18 197 B2
Edenfield BL0 68 D3
Ormskirk L39 15 E7
Rawtenstall BB4 86 D1
5 Rishton BB1 124 A1
Southport PR9 54 B3
Highfield Rd N
Adlington PR6 31 A8
Chorley PR7 61 C2
Highfield Rd S PR7 61 C1
Highfield St
4 Darwen BB3 65 B8
Haslingden BB4 85 A2
Highfield Terr
Kirkham PR4 114 B4
Low Bentham LA2 239 C8
High Fold BB18 195 A6
HIGHFURLONG 153 A2
Highfurlong Sch FY3 153 A2
Highgale Gdns PR5 77 C7
Highgate
Blackpool FY4 110 D5
Goosnargh PR3 138 D6
Higher Penwortham PR1 96 B5
Nelson BB9 148 D7
High Gate FY7 198 D3
Highgate Ave PR2 117 E4
Highgate Cl
Fulwood PR2 117 F4
Newton-w-S PR4 114 F3
Highgate Cres WN6 19 E7
Highgate La
Warton PR4 92 E6
Whitworth OL12 52 C5
High Gate La FY6 177 A6
Highgate Pl FY8 90 D6
Highgate Rd
Maghull L31 5 D3
Up Holland WN8 10 B7
High Gn PR25 76 F1
Highgrove Ave PR7 41 F3
Highgrove Cl LA4 217 A4
Highgrove Ct PR26 58 F8
Highgrove Rd LA1 214 F4
High La
Bickerstaffe L39 7 C8
Laneshaw Bridge BD22 174 A8
Ormskirk L39, L40 16 A8
Salterforth BB18 194 C5
Highland Ave PR1 96 B4
Highland Brow LA2 211 A4
Highland Dr PR7 60 E6
Highland Lo WN6 29 D1
Highland Rd BL6 32 E1
High Lea PR6 31 A8
High Legh FY8 90 C3
High Mdw PR5 97 B2
Highmeadow WN8 10 A6
Highmoor BB9 148 F6
HIGH MOOR 27 F4
High Moor La WN6 28 B4
Highmoor Pk BB7 166 F8
High Moss L39 15 E3
High Mount Ct 2 LA1 214 F7
High Mount Ho 1 LA1 214 F7
HIGH PARK 36 A8
High Park Pl PR9 36 A8
High Park Rd PR9 36 A8
High Peak Rd OL12 52 C6
High Rd
Halton LA2 219 C7
Lowgill LA2 239 C5
Highrigg Dr PR3 137 F1
Highsands Ave L40 39 A3
High St
Accrington BB5 104 B4
Belmont BL7 46 C5
Blackburn BB1 101 E5
Blackpool FY1 130 B6
Brierfield BB9 148 B5
Burton in L LA6 242 C3
High St *continued*
Chapeltown BL7 48 C4
10 Chorley PR7 43 C8
Clitheroe BB7 166 B8
Colne BB8 171 E5
Darwen BB3 82 A1
Elswick PR4 155 F1
Fleetwood FY7 199 B4
Garstang PR3 181 C7
Great Eccleston PR3 156 B5
Haslingden BB4 85 B4
Horwich BL6 32 B4
Lancaster LA1 214 F7
Mawdesley L40 40 B1
Nelson BB9 148 D7
Oswaldtwistle BB5 103 F3
Padiham BB12 146 D1
14 Preston PR1 97 A8
Rishton BB1 124 B1
Skelmersdale WN8 17 E1
Standish WN6 29 E1
HIGHTOWN 2 F3
Hightown BB4 86 E4
Hightown Rd BB4 86 F4
Hightown Sta L38 3 A4
Highways Ave PR7 60 D1
Highwoods Pk BB6 143 B5
Higson St BB2 101 D5
Hilary Ave FY2 152 C5
Hilary St BB10 148 A1
Hilbre Cl PR9 53 F1
Hilbre Dr PR9 53 F1
Hilderstone La LA5 240 A7
Hildrop Rd 7 BB9 170 F1
Hillam La LA2 206 B7
Hillary Cres L31 5 D1
Hillary Ct L37 11 E2
Hillbrook Rd PR25 76 F2
HILL CHAPEL 161 A2
Hill Cl WN6 19 E8
Hillcliffe FY8 89 E5
Hill Cres PR4 115 A2
Hillcrest
Blackpool FY3 130 D5
Maghull L31 5 F1
Skelmersdale WN8 9 B8
Hill Crest OL13 87 D1
Hillcrest Ave
Bolton-le-S LA5 221 A5
Fulwood PR2 117 A4
Hill Crest Ave
Burnley BB10 128 F4
Fulwood PR2 117 E8
Longridge PR3 140 A7
Hillcrest Cl PR4 57 A8
Hillcrest Dr
Bescar L40 23 F7
Longridge PR3 140 A7
Tarleton PR4 57 A8
Hillcrest Rd
Blackburn BB2 100 F2
Blackpool FY4 110 B4
Langho BB6 123 C8
Ormskirk L39 15 E6
Hillcroft
Fulwood PR2 117 C7
High Bentham LA2 239 D7
Hill Croft
Clayton Green PR6 78 A2
Kirkham PR4 114 B5
HILL DALE 27 D5
Hilldean WN8 10 C8
Hill End La BB4 86 C1
Hill Field Croft PR3 204 C1
Hill Hos 19 BB3 65 A8
Hill House Fold La WN6 28 C5
Hill House La
Appley Bridge WN6 28 C5
Jack Green PR6 79 A7
Hillingdon Rd BB10 148 D3
Hillingdon Rd N BB10 148 D3
Hillkirk Dr OL12 52 C3
Hill La
Blackrod BL6 31 C2
Colne BB8 172 C7
Nether Kellet LA6 221 F4
Hillmount Ave LA3 212 F8
Hillock Cl L40 24 A7
Hillock La
Bescar L40 24 A7
Skelmersdale WN8 18 D7
Warton PR4 92 E8
Hillocks The PR26 58 B1
HILLOCK VALE 104 E8
Hillpark Ave
Fulwood PR2 117 D4
Gregson Lane PR5 98 D1
Hill Pl BB9 148 D6
Hill Rd
Higher Penwortham PR1 96 C5
Lancaster LA1 218 D3
Leyland PR25 77 C1
Hill Rd S PR1 96 D3
Hill Rise
Haslingden BB4 85 C1
1 Ramsbottom BL0 50 A4
Hill Rise View L39 15 A1
Hillsborough Ave BB9 148 D5
Hills Ct 2 LA1 218 D1
Hillsea Ave LA3 212 F8
HILLSIDE 34 F1
Hillside
Burnley BB11 127 D3
Tarleton PR4 57 A6
Hill Side LA1 214 E8
Hillside Ave
Blackburn BB1 102 D4
Blackrod BL6 31 E1
Bolton BL7 48 B1
Burnley BB10 148 C5
18 Darwen BB3 65 A8
Farington PR26 76 F7
Fulwood PR2 117 D4
Hill Dale WN8 27 D5
Horwich BL6 32 C4
Kirkham PR4 114 C5
Ormskirk L39 15 D3
Preesall FY6 200 B4
Hillside Cl
Blackburn BB1 102 C4
Blackpool FY3 130 E6
Brierfield BB9 148 C5
Burnley BB11 127 D2
Clitheroe BB7 166 E6
Euxton PR7 60 C1
Goodshaw Chapel BB4 106 A1
Great Harwood BB6 124 C6
Thornton FY5 153 D8
Hillside Com Prim Sch WN8 9 D8
Hillside Cres
Horwich BL6 32 C4
Weir OL13 87 F7
Whittle-le-W PR6 61 C8
Hillside Ct L39 15 D3
Hillside Dr
Newchurch BB4 86 E2
Stalmine FY6 177 C7
West Bradford BB7 189 F6
Hillside Gdns BB3 65 A7
Hillside Rd
Haslingden BB4 85 C3
Low Bentham LA2 239 C8
2 Preston PR1 97 C6
Ramsbottom BL0 50 A5
Southport PR8 34 E1
Hillside Sch PR3 140 D7
Hillside Sta PR8 34 E1
Hillside View BB9 148 C5
Hillside Way OL12 71 C1
Hillside Wlk
Blackburn BB1 102 C4
Rochdale OL12 52 D4
Hill St
3 Accrington, Enfield BB5 125 A1
Accrington, Scaitcliffe BB5 104 C5
Barnoldswick BB18 196 C2
Blackburn BB1 102 B5
Blackpool FY4 130 B1
Brierfield BB9 148 B5
Carnforth LA5 223 D1
Colne BB8 171 D4
Fence BB9 147 F6
Oswaldtwistle BB5 103 D5
Padiham BB12 126 C8
Preston PR1 96 F8
Ramsbottom BL9 50 C3
Rawtenstall BB4 86 A7
Southport PR9 35 B7
Hills The PR2 119 C7
Hillstone Ave OL12 52 D4
Hillstone Cl BL8 49 F2
Hillsview Rd PR8 21 C4
Hilltop OL12 52 C5
HILL TOP 172 B2
Hill Top
Barrowford BB9 170 D4
Colne, Cotton Tree BB8 172 C4
Foulridge BB8 194 C2
New Longton PR4 76 A6
Trawden BB8 172 B2
Hill Top Cl
Freckleton PR4 93 D7
Yealand Redmayne LA5 225 E4
Hill Top Cotts PR3 162 D2
Hilltop Dr BB4 68 C7
Hill Top La
Earby BB18 197 A2
Whittle-le-W PR6 61 D8
Hilltop Wlk L39 15 C3
Hill View
Beverley BB9 170 E7
7 Blackburn BB1 122 E1
2 Rawtenstall BB4 85 F1
Hill View Cvn Site PR3 156 A6
Hill View Dr PR7 29 D8
Hillview Rd PR4 114 A6
Hill View Rd PR3 204 C1
Hill Wlk PR25 77 A2
Hillylaid Rd FY5 176 D2
Hilmont Terr BB1 101 F7
Hilmore Rd LA4 217 A5
Hilstone La FY2 152 D1
Hilton Ave
6 Blackpool FY1 130 B1
Horwich BL6 32 A3
Lytham St Anne's FY8 90 C6
Hilton Ct FY8 89 E5
Hilton Rd BB3 65 B8
Hilton's Brow PR6 79 B4
Hilton St BB3 65 A8
Hinchley Gn L31 5 B1
Hindburn Ave L31 5 F2
Hindburn Pl 2 LA1 218 C2
Hinde St LA1 218 E1
Hindis Head Ave WN6 28 F6
Hindle Fold La BB6 124 C6

Hindle St
Accrington BB5 104 B6
12 Bacup OL13 70 D8
Darwen BB3 81 F2
Haslingden BB4 85 B3
Hindley Beech 1 L31 5 C2
Hindley Cl PR2 118 C7
Hindley Ct 3 BB9 170 C1
Hindley St 5 PR7 43 C6
Hind St
Burnley BB10 148 B2
4 Preston PR1 96 E6
Hinton St BB10 128 B5
Hippings La BB4 86 F1
Hippings Meth Prim Sch BB5 103 E3
Hippings Vale BB5 103 D4
Hippings Way BB7 189 E2
Hirst St
Padiham BB12 146 C1
Todmorden OL14 109 B1
Hoarstones Ave BB12 147 D7
Hobart Pl FY5 152 F8
Hobart St BB11 128 B6
Hobberley Dr WN8 9 E8
Hobbs La PR3 183 A4
Hobcross La L40 26 A2
Hob Gn BB2 121 F2
Hob La BL7 48 C7
Hobson's La LA6 240 C2
Hobson St BB4 85 F4
Hockley Pl FY3 130 F7
Hodder Ave
Blackpool FY1 130 D1
Chorley PR7 43 B5
Fleetwood FY7 198 D2
Maghull L31 5 F2
1 Morecambe LA3 217 F3
Hodder Bridge Ct BB7 165 B7
Hodder Brook PR2 119 A3
Hodder Cl
6 Bamber Bridge PR5 77 F8
Fleetwood FY7 198 C2
Hodder Ct BB7 165 C4
Hodder Dr
Lytham St Anne's FY8 90 C7
West Bradford BB7 189 D7
Hodder Gr
Clitheroe BB7 166 C7
Darwen BB3 81 E4
Hodder Pl
Blackburn BB1 101 F6
Lancaster LA1 215 B5
Hodder St
Accrington BB5 104 D6
1 Blackburn BB1 101 E6
Burnley BB10 148 C3
Longridge PR3 140 B7
Hodder Way FY6 153 D2
HODDLESDEN 82 F1
Hoddlesden Fold BB3 82 F1
Hoddlesden Rd BB3 82 E1
Hoddlesden St Paul's CE Prim Sch BB3 82 F1
Hodge Bank Bsn Pk BB9 170 D2
Hodge Brow BL6 44 F4
Hodgefield BB7 144 A4
Hodge La BB18 194 B8
Hodge St PR8 35 B7
Hodgson Ave PR4 93 A5
Hodgson High Sch Tech Coll FY6 153 F3
Hodgson Pl FY6 153 D2
Hodgson Rd FY1 130 C8
Hodgson's Bldgs 2 BB4 69 F7
Hodgson St
Darwen BB3 82 B1
3 Oswaldtwistle BB5 103 E4
Hodson St
Bamber Bridge PR5 97 E1
Southport PR8 35 C6
Hogarth Ave BB11 127 F3
Hogarth Cres PR4 134 F4
Hoggs Hill La L37 11 F1
Hogg's La PR7 43 E5
HOGHTON 99 B2
Hoghton Ave OL13 71 A8
Hoghton Cl
Lancaster LA1 214 D6
Lytham St Anne's FY8 110 F2
Hoghton Gr PR9 35 C8
Hoghton La PR5 98 D3
Hoghton Pl 3 PR9 35 B7
Hoghton Rd
Leyland PR25 76 D1
Longridge PR3 140 C7
Hoghton St
8 Bamber Bridge PR5 77 A8
Southport PR9 35 C7
Hoghton Twr* PR5 99 E1
Hoghton View PR1 97 C6
Holbeck Ave
Blackpool FY4 110 F8
Morecambe LA4 217 F4
Rochdale OL12 52 D4
Holbeck St BB10 148 A1
Holborn Dr L39 15 C3
Holborn Hill L39 15 C4
HOLCOMBE 50 A6
HOLCOMBE BROOK 50 B2
Holcombe Brook Prim Sch BL0 50 A2
Holcombe Ct BL0 49 F2
Holcombe Dr BB10 128 B6
Holcombe Gr PR6 61 E1
Holcombe Lee BL0 50 A4
Holcombe Mews BL0 49 F3
Holcombe Old Rd BL8, BL0 50 A5
Holcombe Prec BL0 49 F3
Holcombe Rd
Blackpool FY2 152 E1
Haslingden BB4 67 F8
Ramsbottom BL8 49 F2
Holcombe Village BL8 50 A6
Holcroft FY8 90 E3
Holcroft Pl FY8 90 F4
HOLDEN 230 C4
Holden Ave
Bury BL9 33 E4
Ramsbottom BL0 50 A5
Holden Cl BB9 170 C1
Holden Fold BB3 82 B3
Holden La BB7 230 B5
Holden Pl BB4 84 F1
Holden Rd
Brierfield BB9 148 A5
Burnley, Reedley BB10 148 B3
Holden St
4 Accrington BB5 104 B5
Adlington PR7 30 F7
Belthorn BB1 82 F6
Blackburn BB2 101 C4
Burnley BB11 127 F5
Clitheroe BB7 166 F8
HOLDEN VALE 85 A5
Holden Way LA1 214 F5
Holden Wood Dr BB4 84 F1
HOLE HOUSE 102 C6
Hole House La BB7 235 E2
Hole House St BB1 102 C5
Holgate FY4 110 F6
Holgate Dr WN5 10 E6
Holgates Cvn Pk LA5 224 B5
Holgate St
Burnley BB10 148 F3
Great Harwood BB6 124 C5
Holhouse La BL8 49 F2
Holker Bsns Ctr 2 BB8 171 B4
Holker Cl
Coupe Green PR5 98 E3
Lancaster LA1 214 D6
Holker La PR26 59 B4
Holker St
Colne BB8 171 B4
Darwen BB3 65 B8
Holland Ave
Bamber Bridge PR5 97 E2
Rawtenstall BB4 85 F3
Holland Bsns Pk L40 17 C4
Holland Ct WN8 9 D2
Holland Ho WN8 10 C6
Holland House Ct PR5 97 E3
Holland House Rd PR5 97 E3
Holland Lo 4 PR2 118 F4
HOLLAND MOOR 9 F7
Holland Moor Prim Sch WN8 9 E7
Holland Moss WN8 9 A5
Holland Pl BB9 170 E2
Holland Rd PR2 117 C1
Holland's La WN8 17 A1
HOLLAND SLACK 97 E2
Holland St
Accrington BB5 103 F6
Blackburn BB1 101 D6
3 Burnley BB12 126 B8
Holliers Cl L31 5 E1
Hollies Cl
Blackburn BB2 80 F8
Catterall PR3 181 D2
Hollies Rd BB1 123 A7
Hollies The
Ormskirk L39 15 A4
Southport PR8 34 F6
HOLLIN BANK 68 A6
Hollin Bank BB9 148 B6
Hollin Bridge St BB2 101 D2
Hollin Cl BB4 86 F4
Hollin Fold BB9 170 D8
Hollin Gr BB4 86 A4
Hollingreave Dr BB4 86 A5
Hollingreave Rd BB11 128 A4
Hollings PR4 75 F7
Hollington St BB8 172 B5
HOLLIN HALL 172 C1
Hollin Hall BB8 172 C1
Hollinhead Cres PR2 117 B4
Hollin Hill BB11 128 B3
Hollinhurst Ave PR1 96 C6
Hollinhurst Brow LA2 239 C2
Hollinhurst Ct PR1 96 C6
Hollinhurst View BB12 146 F5
Hollin La
Knowley PR6 62 C2
Rawtenstall BB4 86 A4
Hollin Mill St BB9 148 B6
HOLLINS 81 F4
Hollins Ave BB10 128 F4
Hollins Cl
Accrington BB5 104 C4
Hoghton PR5 99 C3
Hollins Ct 1 BB18 196 B3
Hollins Gr PR2 117 B3
HOLLINS GROVE 81 F3
Hollins Grove St BB3 81 F3
Hollinshead Ho FY8 90 A4
Hollinshead St PR7 43 C8
Hollinshead Terr BB3 64 B7
Hollins Hill PR3 207 C2
Hollins La
Accrington BB5 104 D3
Edenfield BL0 68 E2
Hollins Lane PR3 207 C2
Runshaw Moor PR26 59 C4
Silverdale LA5 224 D1
HOLLINS LANE 207 D2
Hollins Rd
Barnoldswick BB18 196 A2
Darwen BB3 81 F4
Nelson BB9 171 A2
Preston PR1 118 B2
Hollin St BB2 101 C2
Hollins Tech Coll The BB5 104 D2
Hollinview Cl BB4 86 A5
Hollin Way
Rawtenstall, Constable Lee BB4 86 A4
Rawtenstall, Rush Bed BB4 86 A6
Hollinwood Dr BB4 86 A5
Hollowbrook Way 4 OL12 52 D2
Hollowell La BL6 32 D1
Hollowford La L40 26 D2
Hollowforth La PR4 136 E5
Hollow Gill Brow BD23, BD24 236 F5
Hollowhead Ave BB1 122 F5
Hollowhead Cl BB1 122 F5
Hollowhead La BB1 123 A5
Hollowrane LA6 240 C7
Holly Ave BB4 85 C1
Holly Bank
1 Accrington BB5 104 C4
Entwistle BL7 48 B7
Fulwood PR2 117 C5
Warton LA5 223 D5
Hollybank Cl PR2 116 F5
Hollybrook Rd PR8 35 A5
Holly Cl
Clayton Green PR6 78 B2
Skelmersdale WN8 17 E1
Thornton FY5 176 C3
Westhead L40 16 E4
Holly Cres PR7 42 E2
Holly Ct
Blackburn BB1 101 F7
19 Bury BL9 33 A2
Holly Fold La L39, WA11 8 E3
Holly Gr
Longridge PR3 140 A8
Tarleton PR4 57 A7
Holly Ho
8 Burnley BB11 128 B5
Chorley PR7 42 F6
Holly La
Ormskirk L39 15 B4
Rufford L40 39 C3
Skelmersdale L39, WA11 8 E4
Holly Mews FY8 110 F2
Holly Mount BB4 68 A7
Holly Mount La BL8 49 E1
Holly Mount RC Prim Sch BL8 49 D1
Holly Pl PR5 78 B6
Holly Rd
Blackpool FY1 152 C1
Thornton FY5 176 B3
Holly St
Blackburn BB1 101 F7
Burnley BB10 128 B5
Bury BL9 33 A2
Nelson BB9 148 F8
Oswaldtwistle BB5 103 D4
Ramsbottom BL0 50 C3
Holly Terr BB1 101 F8
Holly Tree Cl
Darwen BB3 65 A6
Rawtenstall BB4 85 F5
Holly Tree Way BB2 80 F8
Holly Wlk LA1 214 D8
Hollywood Ave
Blackpool FY3 130 E5
Higher Penwortham PR1 96 C3
Hollywood Gr FY7 198 F4
Holman St 5 PR1 118 C1
Holmbrook Cl BB2 81 F8
Holmby St BB10 148 B2
Holmdale Ave PR9 54 C4
Holme Ave FY7 175 D8
Holme Bank BB4 85 F1
Holme Bank Mews 14 BB9 170 F2
Holmebrook Dr BL6 32 D1
HOLME CHAPEL 108 A6
Holme Cl BB18 195 A7
Holme Cotts 7 BB4 69 F7
Holme Cres BB8 172 B3
Holme End BB12 147 F4
Holmefield Ave FY5 175 E2
Holmefield Cl FY5 175 E2
Holmefield Ct 8 BB9 170 D3
Holmefield Gdns 15 BB9 170 D3
Holmefield Gr L31 5 C1
Holmefield Rd
Knott End-on-S FY6 199 E5
Lytham St Anne's FY8 90 A7
Holme Hill BB7 189 E2
Holmehouse Lo 15 PR2 118 F4
Holme House Rd OL14 109 C1
Holme La
Caton LA2 237 D3
Haslingden BB4 68 D8
Rawtenstall BB4 68 E8
Holme Lea BB5 124 F4
HOLME MILLS 240 A8
Holme Mills Ind Est LA6 240 B8
Holme Pk LA2 239 D7
Holme Rd
Bamber Bridge PR5 77 E8
Burnley BB12 127 E7
Clayton-le-M BB5 124 E4
Higher Penwortham PR1, PR2 96 C7
HOLMES 56 D3
Holmes Ct PR1 117 E3
Holmes Dr OL13 87 F4
Holmes La OL13 87 F3
HOLME SLACK 118 C3
Holme Slack Com Prim Sch PR1 118 C3
Holme Slack La PR1 118 C3
Holmes Mdw 3 PR26 76 B1
Holmes Rd FY5 176 B3
Holmes Sq 7 BB11 128 B5
Holmes St
Burnley BB11 128 B5
Padiham BB12 126 D8
Rawtenstall BB4 86 B3
Water BB4 87 A7
Holme St
Accrington BB5 104 C6
Bacup OL13 70 D8
Barrowford BB9 170 D2
Colne, Cotton Tree BB8 172 B5
Darwen BB3 65 A8
Nelson BB9 148 E8
Holmes Terr BB4 85 F5
Holmes The BB4 85 F5
Holmestrand Ave BB11 127 B4
HOLMESWOOD 38 C6
Holmeswood PR4 114 A5
Holmeswood Cres PR3 137 B8
Holmeswood Meth Sch L40 38 C6
Holmeswood Pk BB4 68 E8
Holmeswood Rd L40 38 D6
Holme Terr
Haslingden BB4 68 D8
Nelson BB9 148 C8
Holme The PR3 182 E8
Holme Vale BB4 68 A6
Holmfield Cres 2 PR2 116 D1
Holmfield Pk L37 11 D4
Holmfield Rd
Blackpool FY2 152 B2
Fulwood PR2 118 A4
HOLM NOOK 154 E7
Holmrook Rd PR1 118 B1
Holmsley St BB10 128 B5
Holmwood Cl L37 11 D3
Holmwood Dr L37 11 D4
Holmwood Gdns L37 11 D4
Holroyd Ct FY2 152 B3
Holsands Cl PR2 118 E6
Holstein Ave OL12 52 D4
Holstein St PR1 97 A8
Holst Gdns BB2 102 A1
Holt Ave PR7 42 F2
Holt Brow PR25 60 A6
Holt Coppice L39 6 A7
HOLT GREEN 6 A7
Holtís Terr OL12 52 E2
Holt La PR6 78 E3
Holt Mill Rd BB4 69 D8
Holt St W BL0 50 B5
Holts La FY6 153 F2
Holt Sq BB9 170 E5
Holt St
Orrell WN5 10 D5
Ramsbottom BL0 50 D6
9 Rawtenstall BB4 69 E8
Rishton BB1 124 C1
Whitworth OL12 71 C1
Holy Cross RC High Sch PR7 43 C4
Holy Family RC Prim Sch
Blackpool FY1 130 C8
Fulwood PR2 116 F4
Southport PR9 35 E7
Warton PR4 92 E6
Holyoake Ave FY2 152 E1
Holyoake St
Burnley BB12 127 A6
Todmorden OL14 109 A1
Holy Saviour RC Prim Sch BB9 170 E2
Holy Souls RC Prim Sch BB1 122 E1
Holy Trinity CE Prim Sch
Burnley BB11 127 E5
Southport PR9 35 C8
Holy Trinity RC Prim Sch BB9 148 C5
Holy Trinity Sch BB3 82 A1
Homeacre Ave BB7 145 F8
Home Breeze Ho 1 LA4 217 E6
Homechase Ho 3 PR8 34 F4
Home Farm Cl LA2 238 D6
Home Farm Mews PR26 58 D1
Home Field PR3 181 C8
Homefylde Ho 4 FY3 130 E3
Homelinks Ho FY8 90 D3
Homer Ave PR4 56 F7
HOMER GREEN 4 C1
Homer St 1 BB11 127 C5
Homesands Ho PR9 35 D8
Homestead PR5 78 B4
Homestead Cl 4 PR25 76 D1
Homestead Dr FY7 198 E1
Homestead The 9 FY8 91 A3
Homestead Way FY7 198 E1
Homewood Ave LA4 217 F6
Homfray Ave LA3 217 E3
Homfray Gr LA3 217 E3
Honey Hole BB2 101 E2
Honey Holme La BB10 107 F7
Honey Moor Dr FY5 176 B4
Honeypot La FY6 154 D4
Honeysuckle Cl PR6 61 B5
Honeysuckle Ct BB5 125 E1
Honeysuckle Gr PR4 73 E4
Honeysuckle Pl FY2 152 F6
Honeysuckle Row PR2 118 E2
Honeysuckle Way OL12 52 D3
Honeywood Cl BL0 50 A3
Honister Ave FY3 130 F2
Honister Cl 6 FY7 198 D3
Honister Rd
Burnley BB10 148 B3
Lancaster LA1 218 F2
Honister Sq FY8 110 F2
Honiton Ave BB2 81 C8
Honiton Way PR4 116 F6
Hoodhouse St BB11 127 E4
Hood St 4 BB5 104 C6
HOOHILL 130 E8
Hoo Hill Ind Est FY3 130 E8
Hoo Hill La FY3 130 E8
Hookwood Ave FY5 175 D1
Hoole La
Banks PR9 55 A6
Nateby PR3 180 B5
Hoole St Michael CE Prim Sch PR4 74 C1
Hools La PR3 201 A5
Hope Cl FY5 176 B4
Hope La PR3 162 E5
Hope St N BL6 32 B5
Hope Sq PR9 35 D7
Hope St
Accrington BB5 104 B5
Adlington PR6 31 B8
Bacup OL13 87 F4
Blackburn BB2 101 D5
Brierfield BB9 148 B5
Chorley PR7 61 C1
Darwen BB3 81 F1
Great Harwood BB6 124 C4
Haslingden BB4 85 B2
Horwich BL6 32 B4
Lancaster LA1 215 A7
Lytham St Anne's FY8 90 A7
Morecambe LA4 217 C4
Nelson BB9 148 D8
12 Padiham BB12 126 D8
4 Preston PR1 96 F8
Ramsbottom BL0 50 B5
Rawtenstall BB4 86 C1
Southport PR9 35 C7
Worsthorne BB10 129 B6
Hope Terr
10 Bamber Bridge PR5 77 A8
Blackburn BB2 101 C6
Hopkinson St BB8 172 B3
Hopkinson Terr BB8 172 C3
Hopton Rd FY1 130 B2
Hopwood Ave BL6 32 C4
Hopwood St
Accrington BB5 104 B4
4 Bamber Bridge PR5 77 E8
Bamber Bridge PR5 77 F
7 Burnley BB11 127 E
Preston PR1 97 A8
Horace St 7 BB12 127 D
Horden Rake BB2 80 E
Horden View BB2 80 E
Hordley St BB12 127 A
Horeb Cl 5 BB12 126 D
Hornbeam Cl PR1 96 B
HORNBY 238 B
Hornby Ave
Fleetwood FY7 175 D
Fulwood PR2 118 E
Hornby Bank
Hornby LA2 238 B
Nether Kellet LA6 221 F
Hornby Croft PR26 59 B
Hornby Ct
4 Blackburn BB2 101 C
Kirkham PR4 114 B
Lancaster LA1 218 C
Hornby Dr
Lancaster LA1 215 A
Newton-w-S PR4 114 F
Hornby Hall Cl LA2 238 B
Hornby High Sch LA2 238 B
Hornby La PR4 156 F
Hornby Park Ct 1 FY3 130 D
Hornby Rd
Blackpool FY1 130 C
Caton LA2 237 C
Chorley PR6 43 E
Longridge PR3 140 B
Lytham St Anne's FY8 89 E
Southport PR9 54 A
Wray LA2 238 D
Wray LA2 238 D
Hornby St Margaret's CE Prim Sch LA2 238 B
Hornby's La
Hale Nook PR3 178 A
Moss Edge PR3 178 D

rnby St
urnley BB11 128 A5
swaldtwistle BB5 103 E3
rnby Terr LA4 217 C6
rnchurch Dr PR7 43 A7
rncliffe Cl BB4 68 E8
rncliffe Hts BB9 148 E5
rncliffe Rd FY4 110 B6
rncliffe View BB4 68 B8
rne St BB5 104 C7
rning Cres BB10 148 D2
rnsea Cl
ulwood PR2 117 A4
hornton FY5 176 D2
rnsey Ave FY8 110 B4
rns La PR3 161 B3
rridge Fold BL7 47 E3
rrobin Fold BL7 48 C2
rrobin La
hapeltown BL7 48 C2
ivington PR6, BL6 44 E1
rrocks Fold PR4 74 E3
rrocksford Way
A1 214 D6
rrocks Rd BL7 48 D6
rsebridge Rd FY3 131 B8
rsefield Ave OL12 52 C6
rse Park La PR3 202 A5
rsfall Ave 2 FY8 91 A3
rsfall Cl BB5 104 B7
rsfield Cl BB8 171 F5
RTON 231 E5
rton Ave BB10 148 B3
rton Lo BD23 231 E4
RWICH 32 D4
rwich Bsns Pk BL6 32 B2
rwich Heritage Ctr*
L6 32 C4
rwich L Ctr* BL6 32 C3
rwich Parish CE Prim
ch BL6 32 C4
SCAR 26 D4
scar Moss Rd L40 26 D3
scar Sta L40 26 D4
spital Cotts PR3 140 F6
sticle La LA6 241 C7
thersall La PR3 140 D4
ughclough La PR3 184 F1
ugh La PR25 77 A1
ughton Ave 6 FY4 110 D8
ughton Cl PR1 96 C3
ughton Ct
alton LA2 219 C7
7 Thornton FY5 176 B3
ughton La WN6 19 F6
ughton Rd PR1 96 C3
ughton's La WN8 18 C1
ughtons Rd WN8 18 B3
ughton St 8 PR6 43 D8
uldsworth Rd PR2 117 E3
unds Hill 2 FY1 130 B4
unds Hill Ctr 12
Y1 130 B5
useman Pl FY4 110 E7
ve Ave FY7 175 C8
ve Cl BL8 49 F1
ve Rd FY8 89 F6
ward Brook Ho PR1 118 F1
ward Cl
ccrington BB5 103 F5
ytham St Anne's FY8 110 E1
Maghull L31 5 F1
ward Ct PR9 53 D1
ward Dr PR4 56 F7
ward Mews LA5 223 C1
ward Rd PR7 43 C5
wards La WN5 10 F7
ward St
Blackpool FY1 130 C6
Burnley BB11 127 D5
Nelson BB9 148 C8
Rishton BB1 124 A1
7 Rochdale OL12 52 F1
warth Ave BB5 103 F7
warth Cres FY6 153 E3
warth Rd PR2 117 D3
wden Hts FY6 153 B3
we Ave FY4 110 E8
we Croft BB7 166 F8
we Dr BL0 50 B2
we Gr PR7 43 A7
wells Cl L31 5 D2
we Wlk 4 BB11 128 A6
wgill Ave LA1 218 E4
wgill Cl BB9 148 F6
wgill La BB7 231 C1
wgills The PR2 118 A7
wgill Way FY8 91 D5
wick CE Prim Sch
R1 95 F3
WICK CROSS 96 A5
wick Cross La PR1 95 E5
wick Moor La PR1 96 A3
wick Park Ave PR1 95 F4
wick Park Cl PR1 95 F4
wick Park Dr PR1 95 F4
wick Row PR2 95 D5
worth Cl BB11 128 A3
worth Rd BB11 128 A3
wsin St BB10 148 A1
ylake Cl PR2 117 B6
yle Ave FY8 110 F2
yle Bottom BB5 103 E1
yles La PR4 116 D6
yle St
Bacup OL13 70 E8
Rising Bridge BB5 85 A8
Whitworth OL12 71 D3

Hozier St BB1 102 C5
Hubert Pl LA1 214 D8
Hubie St BB12 127 F7
Huck La FY8 91 E7
Hudcar La BL9 33 A4
HUD HEY 85 A6
Hud Hey Ind Est BB4 85 B5
Hud Hey Rd BB4 85 B5
Hud Rake BB4 85 B4
Hudson Cl BB2 101 B8
Hudson Ct PR5 78 C8
Hudson Rd FY1 130 D2
Hudson St
Accrington BB5 104 C4
2 Brierfield BB9 148 B5
Burnley BB11 127 D5
9 Preston PR1 97 A6
Todmorden OL14 109 C1
Hufling Ct 7 BB11 128 B4
Hufling La BB11 128 B4
Hugh Barn La PR4 75 F7
Hugh Bsns Pk BB4 69 F8
Hughes Ave BL6 32 A4
Hughes Cl 11 BL9 33 A3
Hughes Gr FY2 152 E1
Hughes St BB11 128 A5
Hugh La PR26 76 D3
HUGH MILL 69 F7
Hugh Rake BB4 85 F6
Hullet Cl WN6 19 E8
Hull Rd FY1 130 B4
Hull St
Burnley BB11 128 B5
Preston PR2 96 C8
Hulme Ave FY5 176 C2
Hulme Ct BB3 81 E5
Hulmes Bridge Bsns Ctr
L39 23 D2
Hulme St PR8 35 A7
Hulton Dr BB9 148 E6
Humber Ave 2 FY3 130 E8
Humber Sq BB10 148 C2
Humber St PR3 140 A7
Humblescough La
PR3 180 D5
Humphrey St BB9 148 B6
HUNCOAT 125 E2
Huncoat Ind Est BB5 125 C1
Huncoat Ind Pk BB5 125 D1
Huncoat Sta BB5 125 E2
HUNDRED END 72 F1
Hundred End La PR4,
PR9 72 F1
Hungerford Rd FY8 89 F5
HUNGER HILL 28 F4
Hunniball Ct 3 PR2 117 C2
Hunslet St
Burnley BB11 128 B6
Nelson BB9 148 F7
Hunstanton Cl PR7 60 D5
Hunter Ave PR4 57 A6
Hunter Rd PR4 114 B2
Hunters Chase WN5 10 E1
Hunters Dr BB12 127 D8
Hunters Fold PR4 75 A5
Hunters Gate LA1 214 E5
Hunters Gn BL0 49 F3
Hunter's La PR4 56 B3
Hunters Lo
Bamber Bridge PR5 97 D3
Blackburn BB2 100 F1
Hunters Rd PR25 77 D1
Hunter St
Brierfield BB9 148 B5
Carnforth LA5 223 D2
Hunters Wood Ct PR7 42 F6
Hunt Fold Dr BL8 49 F1
Huntingdon Gr L31 5 C4
Huntingdon Hall Rd
PR3 164 A2
Huntingdon Rd FY5 175 C1
Hunting Hill Cvn Pk
LA5 223 C1
Hunting Hill Rd LA5 223 B1
Huntington Dr BB3 65 A7
Huntís Cotts PR9 54 A1
Huntley Ave 4 FY3 130 E7
Huntley Cl LA4 217 E5
Huntley La PR5 120 D2
Huntley Mount Rd BL9 33 B3
Huntley St BL9 33 B3
Huntly Way OL10 33 E1
Hunt Rd L31 5 D1
Huntroyde Ave BB12 126 B8
Huntroyde Cl 2 BB12 127 D7
Hunts Field PR6 78 C2
Huntsmans Chase PR4 114 F6
Hunt St 2 PR1 96 D7
HURLSTON 24 C3
Hurlston Ave WN8 9 C8
Hurlston Dr L39 15 E7
HURLSTON GREEN 24 B3
Hurlston La L40 24 C1
Hurn Gr PR7 43 A7
Hurst Brook PR7 42 F1
Hurst Cres BB4 86 B3
Hurstdene Cl FY6 153 F3
Hurstead St BB5 104 E1
Hurst Gn L40 40 C2
HURST GREEN 164 F1
Hurst La BB4 86 B3
Hurstleigh Dr LA3 213 A7
Hurstleigh Hts FY5 176 E2
Hurstmere Ave FY4 110 E8
Hurst Pk PR1 96 C4
Hurst's La L39 7 B2
Hurst St BL9 33 A2
Hurstway PR2 117 D7

Hurstway Cl PR2 117 D7
HURSTWOOD 129 C4
Hurstwood L37 11 E5
Hurstwood Ave
Blackburn BB2 101 A1
Burnley BB10 128 D5
Hurstwood Dr FY2 152 D2
Hurstwood Ent Pk BB4 85 A2
Hurstwood Gdns BB9 148 D4
Hurstwood La BB10 129 B4
Hurtley St BB10 128 A8
HUTCH BANK 84 F2
Hutch Bank Rd BB4 84 F2
Hutchinson Ct BB3 82 A2
Hut La PR6 44 B3
Huttock End La OL13 70 D8
HUTTOCK TOP 87 E2
HUTTON 95 D2
Hutton CE Gram Sch
PR4 95 D2
Hutton Cl LA6 240 C7
Hutton Cres 4 LA4 217 A4
Hutton Ct WN8 17 D1
Hutton Dr BB12 127 E7
Hutton Gdns LA5 223 C4
Hutton Gr LA4 217 A4
Hutton Hall Ave PR4 95 E1
Hutton Rd WN8 17 D1
Hutton St
Blackburn BB1 102 B5
Standish WN1 30 A3
Hutton Way
5 Lancaster LA1 218 B1
Ormskirk L39 15 E5
Huyton Rd BL6, PR7 31 A6
Huyton Terr PR6 31 B6
Hyacinth Ave BB5 125 E2
Hyacinth Cl BB4 67 F8
Hyatt Cres WN6 29 C3
Hydeaway Ct LA4 217 B4
Hyde Rd
Blackpool FY1 130 B2
Morecambe LA4 217 F4
Hygiene BB5 124 E2
Hynd Brook Ho BB5 104 A5
Hyndburn Bridge BB5 124 F5
Hyndburn Cl
Carnforth LA5 223 F2
2 Morecambe LA3 217 F3
Hyndburn Dr BB3 81 D4
Hyndburn Park Prim Sch
BB5 104 A6
Hyndburn Rd
Accrington BB5 104 A6
Church BB5 103 F6
Great Harwood BB6 124 F5
Hyndburn St BB5 103 F6
Hyning Rd LA5 223 E8
Hynings The BB6 124 B6
Hythe Cl
Blackburn BB1 102 C4
Southport PR8 35 E3

I

Ibbison Ct FY1 130 C3
Icconhurst Cl BB5 104 E2
Ice St BB1 101 E7
Iddesleigh Rd 3 PR1 118 E1
Iddon Ct 6 FY1 130 C6
Idlewood Pl FY5 152 F8
Idstone Cl BB2 82 A8
Ightenhill Cty Prim Sch
BB12 127 C6
Ightenhill Park La
BB12 127 C8
Ightenhill Pk Mews 1
BB12 127 C7
Ightenhill St BB12 146 C1
Ilex Mill BB4 86 A2
Ilford Rd FY4 130 E1
Ilkley Ave
Lytham St Anne's FY8 90 C6
Southport PR9 54 C6
Ilkley Gr FY5 152 E8
Illawalla The FY5 153 E6
Illingworth Rd PR1 118 E1
Ilway PR5 97 E3
Imam Muhammad Zakariya
Sch PR1 96 F7
Imperial Gdns BB9 148 D8
Imperial St 2 FY1 130 B7
INCE BLUNDELL 3 E4
Ince Cres L37 11 D3
Ince La PR7 41 C6
Inchfield WN8 18 B2
Inch Field BB10 129 B6
India Mill Bsns Ctr BB3 65 A8
India St
Accrington BB5 103 F6
Darwen BB3 65 B8
Ramsbottom BL0 50 C3
Industrial Cotts 10 BB4 69 F8
Industrial Pl 4 OL13 87 F2
Industrial St
Bacup OL13 88 A2
Ramsbottom BL0 68 C1
Industry Rd 8 OL12 52 F1
Industry St
Darwen BB3 82 B2
Whitworth OL12 71 D2
Infant St 11 BB5 104 C6
Infirmary Cl BB2 101 D2
Infirmary Rd BB2 101 D2
Infirmary St BB2 101 E2
Ing Dene Ave BB8 171 B4
Ing Dene Cl BB8 171 B4

Ingfield Terr OL14 109 C1
Ingham St
Barrowford BB9 170 D3
Bury BL9 33 A1
Padiham BB12 146 D1
Inglby Cl BB1 102 D5
Ingleborough Dr BB18 196 A2
Ingleborough Rd LA1 218 B3
Ingleborough View
Brinscall PR6 63 A8
Carnforth LA5 221 E8
14 High Bentham LA2 239 D8
Hornby LA2 238 B6
Ingleborough Way
PR25 77 C2
Ingleby Cl
Cleveleys FY5 175 F5
Standish WN6 29 D2
Ingle Cl 5 PR6 61 D1
Ingle Head PR2 117 D6
Inglehurst Rd BB11 127 B5
Ingle Nook BB10 128 F4
Inglenook Cl 5 FY5 175 F1
Inglesby Cnr L40 24 B4
INGLETON 242 F3
Ingleton Ave FY2 152 F4
Ingleton Cl 1 BB5 104 D5
Ingleton Dr LA1 215 A4
Ingleton Ho 2 LA1 215 A3
Ingleton Rd
Fulwood PR2 118 E4
Southport PR8 35 E3
Ingle View LA6 242 C3
Ingleway FY5 175 F3
Ingleway Ave FY3 130 F6
INGLEWHITE 160 B4
Inglewhite WN8 18 A2
Inglewhite Fold 2
BB12 126 D7
Inglewhite Rd PR3 161 C3
Inglewood Cl
Bury BL9 33 C4
Fleetwood FY7 198 C1
Warton PR4 92 D6
Inglewood Gr FY2 152 E5
INGOL 117 A4
Ingol Com Prim Sch
PR2 116 F4
Ingol Gdns FY6 177 C2
Ingol Gr FY6 177 C2
Ingol La FY6 177 D2
Ingot St PR1 96 D8
Ingram WN8 18 B2
Ings Ave
Barnoldswick BB18 196 B3
Rochdale OL12 52 B2
Ings La OL12 52 C2
Ingthorpe Ave FY2 152 D5
Inkerman Rd PR4 132 F6
Inkerman St
6 Bacup OL13 88 A2
Blackburn BB1 101 E6
9 Padiham BB12 126 C8
Preston PR2 117 D2
12 Rochdale OL12 52 F1
Inner Prom FY8 90 B3
INSKIP 135 D8
Inskip WN8 18 A2
Inskip Ct WN8 18 B2
Inskip Pl
Blackpool FY4 110 E5
Lytham St Anne's FY8 90 A8
Inskip Rd
Leyland PR25 76 D2
Preston PR2 116 E1
Southport PR9 54 A4
Wharles PR4 135 A5
Inskip St Peter's CE Sch
PR4 135 B8
Inskip St BB12 126 C8
Institute St BB12 126 D8
INTACK 102 D5
Intack La BB2 121 B2
Intack Prim Sch BB1 102 D5
Intack Rd PR4 75 B8
Intake Cres BB8 171 F6
Intake La
Maghull L39 4 E8
Skelmersdale L39 8 B2
Inverness Rd BB3 64 F8
Inver Rd FY2 152 D3
Ipswich Pl FY5 175 C2
Ipswich Rd PR2 118 D2
IREBY 242 C6
Ireby Rd LA6 242 C3
Irene Pl BB2 101 B5
Irene St BB10 128 C5
Iris St BL0 50 B6
Irongate PR5 77 C8
Ironside Cl PR2 118 B4
Iron St
Blackburn BB2 101 E3
Horwich BL6 32 C2
Irton Rd PR9 35 E8
Irvin Ave PR9 54 C5
Irvine St 8 BB9 170 F2
Irving Cl FY2 152 F5
Irving Pl BB2 101 B5
Irving St PR9 53 B1
Irvin St PR1 118 B1
Irwell WN8 18 A3
Irwell Rd WN5 10 F7
Irwell St
7 Bacup OL13 87 F2
Burnley BB12 127 A6
Longridge PR3 140 B7
Longridge PR3 140 B8
Lytham St Anne's FY8 89 F7

Irwell St *continued*
Ramsbottom BL0 50 C6
Irwell Terr 12 OL13 87 F2
IRWELL VALE 68 C5
Irwell Vale Rd BB4, BL0 68 C6
Irwell Vale Sta BL0 68 C5
Isabella St
Longridge PR3 140 A8
Rochdale OL12 52 F2
Isa St 5 BL0 50 A4
Isherwood Fold BL7 48 D7
Isherwood St
Blackburn BB2 101 D1
Preston PR1 118 C1
Island Cotts BL9 50 C2
Island La PR3 203 B3
Islay Cl 5 FY4 110 F6
Islay Rd FY8 90 E6
Isle of Man BB1 122 E4
Isle of Man St BB4 87 A7
Isleworth Dr PR7 43 B7
Islington BB2 101 E3
Islington Cl BB10 148 D3
Ivan St BB10 148 B2
Ivegate
Colne BB8 171 D5
Foulridge BB8 194 E1
Ivegate Mews 13 BB8 171 D5
Ivinson Rd BB3 82 B3
Ivory St 1 BB12 127 C6
Ivy Ave
Blackpool FY4 110 E5
Haslingden BB4 85 C3
Ivy Bank PR2 118 D6
Ivybridge WN8 18 B2
Ivy Cl
Clayton-le-W PR25 77 E2
13 Rawtenstall BB4 69 F8
Ring o'Bells L40 26 A3
Ivy Cotts
12 Rawtenstall BB4 69 F8
Tockholes BB3 80 F3
Ivydale WN8 18 B2
Ivy Gdns FY5 176 A4
Ivy Gr 2 BB4 86 A3
Ivy House Cl PR5 78 B7
Ivy Pl OL14 108 F1
Ivy St
Blackburn BB2 101 E2
Burnley BB10 148 B1
Nelson BB8 171 A2
Ramsbottom BL0 49 F3
1 Rawtenstall BB4 69 F8
Southport PR8 35 D6
Ivy Terr BB3 65 B6

J

j2 Bsns Pk BL9 33 C2
Jackdaw Rd BL8 49 F2
JACK GREEN 78 F8
Jack La BD23 236 F4
Jacks Key Dr BB3 65 C5
Jacksmere La L40, PR8 23 B8
Jackson Cl
Haskayne L39 13 F5
Lancaster LA1 214 C7
Jackson Heights Rd
BB1 83 B4
Jackson Rd
2 Chorley PR7 43 A5
1 Leyland PR25 76 D1
Jackson's Banks Rd
BB2 120 E6
Jackson's Common La
L40 24 B1
Jackson's La L40 27 E7
Jackson St
8 Bamber Bridge PR5 77 F8
Blackpool FY3 130 E7
6 Burnley BB10 128 A8
Chorley PR7 43 D6
5 Clayton-le-M BB5 124 F3
Jackson Terr LA5 223 D3
Jack Walker Way BB2 81 D7
Jacob Brigth Mews 5
OL12 52 F2
Jacob's La PR4 115 A7
Jacob St BB5 104 C5
Jacson St 3 PR1 97 A7
Jade Cl L33 1 A3
Jagoe Mews 2 BB18 197 A1
Jagoe Rd 3 BB18 197 A1
Jamea Al Kauthar LA1 214 F5
James Ave
Blackpool FY4 130 F1
Great Harwood BB6 124 B5
Jameson Rd FY7 199 A1
Jameson St 2 FY1 130 C3
James Pl
Coppull PR7 29 E8
Standish WN6 29 D2
James St W 6 BB3 82 A1
James Sq WN6 29 D2
James St
Bacup OL13 70 B7
Bamber Bridge PR5 97 E1
Barnoldswick BB18 196 B1
4 Barrowford BB9 170 D4
Belthorn BB1 82 F6
Blackburn BB1 101 E5
Bolton BL7 47 D3
Burnley BB10 148 A1
Bury BL9 33 A1

James St *continued*
12 Clayton-le-M BB5 . . . . . . 124 F3
Colne BB8 . . . . 171 E4
1 Darwen BB3. . . . . 82 A1
Earby BB18 . . . . 197 B1
Great Harwood BB6 . . . . . . 124 B5
Haslingden BB4. . . . . 85 A2
Horwich BL6 . . . . 31 F3
Huncoat BB5 . . . . 125 E2
30 Lancaster LA1 . . . . 214 F8
Morecambe LA4. . . . . 217 C5
Oswaldtwistle BB5 . . . . . . 103 D3
Preston PR1. . . . . 97 B7
Rawtenstall BB4 . . . . 86 A2
Rishton BB1. . . . . 124 C1
Salterforth BB18 . . . . 194 D7
Whitworth OL12. . . . . 71 D2
Jameston Rise 18 BL6. . . . . 32 B4
Jane La
Catforth PR4 . . . . 135 E5
Leyland PR26. . . . . 76 A3
Jane's Brook Rd PR8 . . . . . 35 E4
Jane's Mdw PR4. . . . . 57 A5
Jane St OL12 . . . . 71 E6
Janice Dr PR2. . . . . 117 D7
Janine Cl LA4 . . . . 217 A4
Jannat Cl 2 BB5 . . . . 104 B5
Jarrett Rd L33. . . . . 1 A4
Jarrett Wlk L33. . . . . 1 A4
Jarvis St OL12 . . . . 52 F1
Jasmine Rd PR5 . . . . 97 A3
Jasper St BB1 . . . . 122 F1
Jefferson Cl LA1. . . . . 214 D7
Jefferson Way OL12. . . . . . . 52 F3
Jeffrey Ave PR3 . . . . 140 B7
Jeffrey Hill Cl PR2. . . . . . 119 C7
Jeffrey Sq FY1. . . . . 130 D3
Jellicoe Cl FY8 . . . . 110 E1
Jem Gate FY5 . . . . 152 D8
Jemmett St PR1 . . . . 117 E2
Jenny La
Blackpool FY4 . . . . 111 C7
Higher Wheelton PR6 . . . . . . 79 C1
Jenny Nook LA3 . . . . 213 A7
Jenny St BB9. . . . . 148 D6
Jensen Cl LA1. . . . . 214 E6
Jensen Dr FY4. . . . . 112 A6
Jepheys Pl 17 OL12 . . . . 52 F1
Jepheys St OL12. . . . . 52 F1
Jepp Hill 3 BB18. . . . . 196 B2
Jepps Ave PR3 . . . . 137 B7
Jepps La PR3. . . . . 137 B8
Jepson St 10 BB3. . . . . 65 A8
Jepson Way FY4 . . . . 110 F4
JERICHO. 33 F4
Jericho Rd BL9 . . . . 33 E4
Jersey Ave FY2. . . . . 152 E2
Jersey Fold PR7 . . . . 60 E6
Jersey St BB2 . . . . 101 B1
Jervis Cl FY8 . . . . 110 D1
Jesmond Ave FY4. . . . . 110 B7
Jesmond Ct FY8 . . . . 89 F8
Jesmond Gr LA4. . . . . 217 D3
Jessel St BB2. . . . . 101 B2
Jesson Way LA5 . . . . 223 C1
Jevington Way LA3 . . . . . . 213 A7
Jewel Holme BB9. . . . . 148 A5
Jib Hill Cotts BB10. . . . . . 148 D2
Jinny La BB12 . . . . 169 E4
Jobling St 1 BB8. . . . . 171 B3
Jockey St BB11 . . . . 127 C5
Joe Connolly Way 1
BB4 . . . . 69 E8
Joe La PR3. . . . . 181 D2
John Creed Ave LA1 . . . . . 211 B8
John Cross CE Prim Sch
PR3 . . . . 159 A4
John Henry St OL12. . . . . . . 71 D4
John Hill St 3 FY4 . . . . . . 130 F2
John Kay Ct LA1. . . . . 218 B3
Johnny Barn Cl BB4 . . . . . . 86 D2
Johnny Barn Cotts BB4 . . . 86 D2
John o' Gaunt St 15
BB12 . . . . 146 C1
Johnson Cl
Crag Bank LA5. . . . . 223 C1
Lancaster LA1 . . . . 214 C7
Johnson New Rd BB3. . . . . 82 E2
Johnson Rd
Blackpool FY4 . . . . 130 F2
Darwen BB3. . . . . 82 D4
JOHNSON'S HILLOCK. 61 E6
Johnson's Meanygate
PR4 . . . . 56 D7
Johnson St PR9 . . . . 35 B8
Johnson Way BB1 . . . . 102 C1
Johnspool PR2 . . . . 117 C6
John St
2 Bamber Bridge PR5 . . . . . 97 E1
Barnoldswick BB18 . . . . . . 196 B1
Barrowford BB9. . . . . 170 E4
Blackpool FY1 . . . . 130 B2
Brierfield BB9 . . . . 148 B6
4 Carnforth LA5. . . . . 223 D2
Church BB5 . . . . 103 E7
Clayton-le-M BB5. . . . . 124 F3
2 Colne BB8. . . . . 171 C4
Coppull PR7 . . . . 42 E1
Darwen BB3. . . . . 81 F1
Earby BB18 . . . . 197 B1
6 Galgate LA2 . . . . 211 A4
Haslingden BB4. . . . . 85 B3
Leyland PR25. . . . . 77 A1
Newchurch BB4. . . . . 86 F1
Oswaldtwistle BB5 . . . . . . 103 D3

John St *continued*
Thornton FY5. . . . . 176 B4
Whitworth OL12. . . . . 71 D2
Johnston Cl BB2. . . . . 101 C5
Johnston St BB2. . . . . 101 C5
Johnsville Ave FY4. . . . . . 110 E7
Johns Wood Cl PR7. . . . . . . 42 F6
John Wall Ct 8 BB7 . . . . 166 D8
John William St 7 PR1 . . . 97 C8
Joiners Alley 10 BB6. . . . . 124 C5
Joiner's Row BB2. . . . . 101 E3
Jolly Tar La PR7 . . . . 30 B7
Jonathan Cl BB4. . . . . 68 A8
Jones' Gr FY7 . . . . 199 B5
Jones St BL6 . . . . 32 B4
Jones's Yd LA6 . . . . 240 B7
Joseph St
Barrowford BB9. . . . . 170 D2
Darwen BB3. . . . . 82 B1
3 Rochdale OL12. . . . . 52 D2
Joyce Ave FY4 . . . . 130 F2
Joy Pl 3 OL12. . . . . 52 F2
Joy St
Ramsbottom BL0 . . . . 50 B6
Rochdale OL12. . . . . 52 F2
Jubilee Almshouses
PR26 . . . . 58 B1
Jubilee Ave
Ormskirk L39. . . . . 15 F6
Orrell WN5. . . . . 10 D4
Preesall FY6 . . . . 200 A4
Preston PR2. . . . . 116 D1
Jubilee Bldgs 19 LA2 . . . 239 D8
Jubilee Cl
Darwen BB3. . . . . 82 D1
Haslingden BB4. . . . . 85 A1
Jubilee Ct
1 Haslingden BB4 . . . . 85 A1
11 Lancaster LA1 . . . . 214 E8
Jubilee Cts PR25 . . . . 59 E8
Jubilee Dr
Cleveleys FY5 . . . . 175 C4
Skelmersdale WN8 . . . . 8 E8
Jubilee La FY4 . . . . 111 B5
Jubilee La N FY4 . . . . 111 B6
Jubilee Pl PR6. . . . . 61 D1
Jubilee Rd
9 Bamber Bridge PR5 . . . . . 77 A8
Church BB5 . . . . 103 F7
Formby L37 . . . . 11 D1
Haslingden BB4. . . . . 85 A1
Walmer Bridge PR4. . . . . 74 F4
Jubilee St
Accrington BB5 . . . . 125 A1
Blackburn BB1. . . . . 101 E4
Burnley BB10. . . . . 148 F3
Darwen BB3. . . . . 82 A1
Oswaldtwistle BB5 . . . . . . 103 E4
Read BB12. . . . . 145 D2
Jubilee Terr
Clifton PR4. . . . . 115 C1
Freckleton PR4 . . . . 93 C7
Goosnargh PR3 . . . . 138 D5
Langho BB6 . . . . 143 D1
Jubilee Trad Est PR1 . . . . . 117 E1
Jubilee Way
Croston PR26. . . . . 58 B3
Lytham St Anne's FY8 . . . . . . 90 C8
Judd Ho PR1 . . . . 96 E6
Judd Holmes La PR3. . . . 162 D7
Judeland PR7 . . . . 61 A2
Jude St BB9. . . . . 148 D8
Jud Falls BB7 . . . . 165 A3
Judge Fields BB8. . . . . . . 171 D6
Judges Lodgings Mus*
LA1. . . . . 214 E8
Judith St OL12. . . . . 52 C3
Julia Mews 4 BL6. . . . . 32 B4
Julia St BL6 . . . . 32 B4
July St 17 BB1. . . . . 102 A4
Jumbles Beck BL7 . . . . 48 D4
Jumbles Ctry Pk* BL7 . . . . 48 D2
Junction La L40 . . . . 25 E3
Junction Rd
Preston PR2. . . . . 96 D7
Rainford WA11 . . . . 8 F1
Junction St
Brierfield BB9 . . . . 148 B6
Burnley BB12. . . . . 127 E6
Burnley, Whittlefield
BB12. . . . . 127 E7
Colne BB8 . . . . 171 A3
Darwen BB3. . . . . 65 B7
Junction Terr PR7 . . . . 60 C5
June Ave FY4. . . . . 131 A1
June St 16 BB1 . . . . 102 A4
June's Wlk PR4. . . . . 75 A5
Juniper Cl FY6 . . . . 200 A5
Juniper Croft PR6 . . . . 78 A1
Juniper Ct 3 BB5 . . . . 104 E8
Juniper St 6 BB1 . . . . 102 A7
Juno St BB9. . . . . 170 F2
Jutland St PR1 . . . . 97 A8

K

Kairnryan Cl FY2 . . . . 152 F5
Kale Gr L33 . . . . 1 A5
Kane St PR2. . . . . 117 C1
Kateholm OL13 . . . . 88 A7
Kate St 3 BL0. . . . . 50 B6
Kay Brow BL0 . . . . 50 C6
Kay Fold Lo BB1. . . . . 122 D2
Kay Gdns BB11 . . . . 128 B5
Kayley La BB7 . . . . 190 E5
Kaymar Ind Est PR1. . . . . . . 97 C7

Kay St
Blackpool FY1 . . . . 130 B4
8 Brierfield BB9. . . . . 148 B5
Bury BL9 . . . . 33 A3
Chapeltown BL7. . . . . 48 C4
Clitheroe BB7 . . . . 166 D6
Darwen BB3. . . . . 82 B1
3 Oswaldtwistle BB5. . . . . 103 D3
1 Padiham BB12 . . . . 146 D1
1 Preston PR1. . . . . 96 E7
Ramsbottom BL0, BL9 . . . . . 50 C3
Rawtenstall BB4 . . . . 86 A2
Kayswell Rd LA4. . . . . 217 F5
Kearsley Ave PR4 . . . . 57 A6
Keasden Ave FY4 . . . . 110 D7
Keasden Rd BB7 . . . . 235 E6
Keating Ct 3 FY7. . . . . . . 199 A3
Keats Ave
Bolton-le-S LA5 . . . . 221 A5
Longshaw WN5 . . . . 10 D1
Rochdale OL12. . . . . 52 A1
Warton PR4 . . . . 92 E6
Keats Cl
Accrington BB5 . . . . 104 E2
Blackpool FY2 . . . . 152 F6
Colne BB8 . . . . 171 D6
Eccleston PR7 . . . . 41 D5
Thornton FY5. . . . . 176 A2
Keats Fold 3 BB12 . . . . . . 126 F7
Keats Rd BL8 . . . . 49 F2
Keats Terr PR8. . . . . 35 F6
Keats Way PR4 . . . . 116 D4
Kebs Rd OL14. . . . . 109 D3
Keele Cl FY5. . . . . 176 A2
Keele Wlk BB1. . . . . 101 F4
Keen Cl PR4 . . . . 95 E2
Keepers Gate FY8. . . . . 90 D7
Keeper's Hey FY5. . . . . . . 176 A4
Keeper's La PR3 . . . . 204 F1
Keepers Wood Way
Catterall PR3. . . . . 181 D3
Chorley PR7. . . . . 42 F6
Keer Bank 1 LA1. . . . . 218 A2
Keer Holme La LA6 . . . . . . 240 E4
Keighley Ave BB8. . . . . . . 171 D6
Keighley Rd
Colne BB8 . . . . 171 F5
Laneshaw Bridge BB8 . . . . . 172 D6
Trawden BB8. . . . . 172 C4
Keirby Wlk BB11. . . . . 128 A6
Keith Gr FY5. . . . . 175 D1
Keith St BB12. . . . . 127 C6
KELBROOK. 195 A6
Kelbrook Dr BB11. . . . . 127 E3
Kelbrook Prim Sch
BB18 . . . . 195 A6
Kelbrook Rd BB18 . . . . 194 E7
Kelk Beck Cl L31 . . . . 5 F2
KELLAMERGH. 92 D7
Kellet Acre 4 PR5. . . . . 77 A7
Kellet Ave PR25. . . . . 77 D1
Kellet Ct 1 LA1 . . . . 214 E8
Kellet La
Bolton-le-S LA5, LA2 . . . . . 221 C3
Borwick LA6. . . . . 240 B3
Walton Summit PR5. . . . . 78 B7
Kellet Rd
Carnforth LA5 . . . . 223 E1
Over Kellet LA6 . . . . 240 A1
Kellet Road Ind Est
LA5. . . . . 223 F1
Kellett St 8 PR7 . . . . 43 C8
Kelley Cl BB2. . . . . 81 C8
Kelmarsh Cl FY3. . . . . 131 B2
Kelne Ho 7 LA1 . . . . 214 E8
Kelsall Ave BB1. . . . . 102 B8
Kelsey St LA1. . . . . 214 E8
Kelso Ave FY5 . . . . 175 D1
Kelsons Ave FY5. . . . . 176 C2
Kelswick Dr BB9. . . . . 148 E6
Kelverdale Rd FY5 . . . . . . 152 F8
Kelvin Rd FY5 . . . . 152 D6
Kelvin St BB3. . . . . 81 F1
Kelwood Ave BL9 . . . . 33 D5
Kemble Cl BL6. . . . . 32 B5
Kem Mill La PR6. . . . . 61 B8
Kemp Ct BB1 . . . . 122 F3
Kemple View BB7 . . . . 166 D6
Kemp St FY7 . . . . 199 B4
Kempstone BB7 . . . . 190 D5
Kempton Ave FY3. . . . . . . 130 E3
Kempton Park Fold
PR8 . . . . 35 F3
Kempton Rd LA1. . . . . 215 B4
Kempton Rise BB1. . . . . . . 101 F3
Kenbury Cl L33 . . . . 1 A4
Kenbury Rd L33 . . . . 1 A4
Kendal Ave
Barrowford BB9. . . . . 170 D4
Blackpool FY3 . . . . 153 A1
Cleveleys FY5 . . . . 175 D4
Kendal Cl WA11. . . . . 8 F2
Kendal Dr
Maghull L31. . . . . 5 E2
Morecambe LA4. . . . . 217 F4
Rainford WA11 . . . . 8 F2
Kendall Cl BB2 . . . . 81 D8
Kendal Rd
Lytham St Anne's FY8 . . . . 110 D1
Ramsbottom BL0 . . . . 50 A2
Kendal Rd W BL0. . . . . 49 F2
Kendal Row BB1. . . . . 82 F6
Kendal St
Blackburn BB1. . . . . 101 E6
Clitheroe BB7 . . . . 189 F1
5 Nelson BB9. . . . . 170 D1
Preston PR1. . . . . 96 E8
Kendal Way PR8 . . . . 21 B3

Kenilworth Ave FY7 . . . . . . 198 E3
Kenilworth Cl BB12 . . . . . . 126 E8
Kenilworth Ct FY8 . . . . 89 F6
Kenilworth Dr
Clitheroe BB7 . . . . 166 C6
Earby BB18 . . . . 195 A8
Kenilworth Gdns FY4 . . . . 110 B7
Kenilworth Pl
Fleetwood FY7. . . . . 198 E3
Lancaster LA1 . . . . 215 A5
Kenilworth Rd
Lytham St Anne's FY8 . . . . . . 89 F6
Morecambe LA3. . . . . 217 C3
Southport PR8 . . . . 21 B4
Kenlis Rd PR3 . . . . 181 F4
Kenmay Way L33 . . . . 1 A3
Kenmure Pl PR1 . . . . 117 F2
Kennedy Cl LA1. . . . . 214 D6
Kennedy Ho FY1. . . . . 130 B1
Kennelwood Ave L33. . . . . . . 1 A3
Kennet Dr PR2. . . . . 117 F8
Kennett Dr PR25. . . . . 77 B2
Kennington Prim Sch
PR2 . . . . 118 A4
Kennington Rd PR2 . . . . . . 118 A4
Kensington Ave PR1 . . . . . . 96 B6
Kensington Cl BL8 . . . . 50 A1
Kensington Ct
1 Formby L37 . . . . 12 A3
Morecambe LA4. . . . . 217 E6
Kensington Dr BL6. . . . . 32 D3
Kensington Gdns PR5. . . . . . 97 C1
Kensington Ho LA1 . . . . . . 214 F5
Kensington Ind Pk PR9. . . . . 35 C6
Kensington Pl BB11. . . . . 127 D4
Kensington Rd
Blackpool FY3 . . . . 130 E4
Chorley PR7. . . . . 43 B7
Cleveleys FY5 . . . . 175 C3
Formby L37 . . . . 11 E1
Lancaster LA1 . . . . 214 F5
Lytham St Anne's FY8 . . . . . . 90 D4
Morecambe LA4. . . . . 217 B5
Southport PR9. . . . . 35 C6
Kensington St BB9. . . . . . 148 C7
Kent Ave
2 Bamber Bridge PR5 . . . . . 97 D3
Cleveleys FY5 . . . . 175 E4
Formby L37 . . . . 12 A1
Kent Ct BB9 . . . . 170 D4
Kent Dr
Blackburn BB1. . . . . 102 E4
Clayton-le-W PR25 . . . . 77 D1
Kent Ho LA1. . . . . 214 F7
Kentmere Ave
Bamber Bridge PR5. . . . . 97 E1
Leyland PR25. . . . . 77 A3
Kentmere Cl
Burnley BB12. . . . . 127 B8
5 Fleetwood FY7 . . . . 198 D3
Kentmere Dr
Blackburn BB2. . . . . 80 E8
Blackpool FY4 . . . . 131 C1
Longton PR4 . . . . 75 B8
Kentmere Gr 1 LA4 . . . . . 217 D4
Kentmere Rd LA1. . . . . 218 E1
Kenton Cl L37 . . . . 11 F6
Kent Rd
Blackpool FY1 . . . . 130 C3
Formby L37 . . . . 12 A1
Southport PR8. . . . . 35 A4
Kent's Cl PR4. . . . . 113 E7
Kent St
Blackburn BB1. . . . . 101 F4
Burnley BB12. . . . . 127 F7
Fleetwood FY7. . . . . 199 B5
3 Lancaster LA1 . . . . 218 D2
Preston PR1. . . . . 117 F2
Kent Way 4 LA3. . . . . 217 F3
Kent Wlk BB4. . . . . 68 A8
Kenwood Ave LA4. . . . . 217 A4
Kenwood Grange PR9. . . . . . 35 C8
Kenworthys Flats PR9. . . . . 35 B8
Kenwyn Ave FY3. . . . . 130 E3
Kenyon Bsns Ctr BB9 . . . . 148 B7
Kenyon La
Dinckley BB6 . . . . 142 F4
Whittle-le-W PR6. . . . . 61 F7
Kenyon Rd
Morecambe LA4. . . . . 217 F5
Nelson BB9 . . . . 148 B7
Standish WN6 . . . . 29 D2
Kenyons Farm Units
PR5 . . . . 78 B6
Kenyons La L31. . . . . 5 E3
Kenyon's La L37 . . . . 12 A3
Kenyons Lo L31. . . . . 5 E3
Kenyon St
6 Accrington BB5 . . . . . . 104 C6
Blackburn BB1. . . . . 102 C5
Britannia OL13. . . . . 71 B8
Bury BL9 . . . . 33 A3
Ramsbottom BL0 . . . . 50 C6
Rawtenstall BB4 . . . . 86 A3
Keppel Pl BB11 . . . . 127 E6
Kepple La PR3. . . . . 181 B6
Kerenhappuch St 5
BL0. . . . . 50 B5
Kerfoot's La WN8 . . . . 8 C8
Kerr Pl PR1. . . . . 96 D8
Kershaw Cl 7 BB4. . . . . 86 A7
Kershaw St
8 Bacup OL13 . . . . 87 F2
Bury BL9 . . . . 33 A2
Chorley PR6. . . . . 61 E1
Church BB5 . . . . 103 E7
Kerslake Way L38. . . . . 3 A4
Kerslea Ave FY3 . . . . 131 D8

Kerton Row PR8 . . . . 34 F4
Keston Gr FY4 . . . . 110 C5
Kestor La PR3 . . . . 140 A7
Kestrel Cl
Blackburn BB1. . . . . 101 D8
Cleveleys FY5 . . . . 175 F5
Knowley PR6 . . . . 62 A3
Kestrel Ct PR9. . . . . 35 D7
Kestrel Dr
Bury BL9 . . . . 33 B4
Darwen BB3. . . . . 81 D3
Kestrel Mews WN8. . . . . 18 C4
Kestrel Pk WN8. . . . . 18 C4
Kestrel Terr BB5 . . . . 103 E3
Keswick Cl
Accrington BB5 . . . . 125 D1
Maghull L31. . . . . 5 E2
Southport PR8. . . . . 21 C3
Keswick Ct LA1. . . . . 218 F1
Keswick Dr BB2 . . . . 80 E8
Keswick Gr
Heysham LA3. . . . . 212 E5
Knott End-on-S FY6 . . . . . . 199 F5
Keswick Rd
Blackpool FY1 . . . . 130 C3
Burnley BB10. . . . . 148 B2
Lancaster LA1 . . . . 218 F1
Lytham St Anne's FY8 . . . . . . 89 E8
Keswick Way WA11 . . . . 8 F2
Keswick Wlk LA1 . . . . 218 F1
Kettering Rd PR8 . . . . 21 B5
Kevin Ave FY6 . . . . 153 F5
Kevin Gr LA3 . . . . 213 D1
Kew Gdns
Higher Penwortham
PR1. . . . . 96 B5
Leyland PR25. . . . . 77 B3
Kew Gr FY5. . . . . 175 D
Kew House Dr PR8. . . . . 36 A2
Kew Rd
Formby L37 . . . . 11 D1
Nelson BB9 . . . . 170 F2
Southport PR8. . . . . 35 B3
Kew Ret Pk PR8 . . . . 36 A4
Kew Woods Prim Sch
PR8 . . . . 35 F3
Keynsham Gr BB12. . . . . . 127 D7
Keystone Ct FY4 . . . . 111 D6
Key View BB3. . . . . 65 C5
Khyber St BB8. . . . . 171 C4
Kibble Cres BB10 . . . . 148 C
Kibble Gr BB9 . . . . 148 D
Kibboth Crew BL0 . . . . 50 B
Kidbrooke Ave FY4. . . . . . . 110 B
Kidder St BB2 . . . . 81 D
Kiddlington Cl PR5 . . . . 77 D
Kiddrow La BB12 . . . . 127 A
Kidsgrove PR2. . . . . 116 F
Kielder Ct 3 FY8. . . . . 91 C
Kielder Dr BB12 . . . . 127 E
Kiers Ct BL6. . . . . 32 E
Kilbane St FY7. . . . . 198 F
Kilburn Rd WN5 . . . . 10 C
Kilcrash La PR3. . . . . 180 D
Kildale Cl L31 . . . . 5 C
Kildare Ave FY5. . . . . 176 A
Kildare Rd FY2 . . . . 152 D
Kildonan Ave 6 FY4. . . . . . 111 A
Kilgrimol Gdns FY8 . . . . . 110 C
Kilkerran Cl PR6. . . . . 43 D
Killer St 1 BL0. . . . . 50 C
Killiard La BB2 . . . . 100 E
Killingbeck Cl L40 . . . . 25 D
Killington St BB10 . . . . . . 148 C
Killingworth Mews 4
BL6. . . . . 32 D
Killon St BL9 . . . . 33 A
Kilmory Pl FY2 . . . . 152 F
Kilmuir Cl PR2. . . . . 118 C
Kiln Bank OL12 . . . . 71 C
Kilnbank Ave LA4 . . . . 217 A
Kiln Bank La OL12 . . . . 71 C
Kiln Cl BB7. . . . . 190 A
Kiln Croft PR6 . . . . 78 B
Kiln Ct 1 LA1 . . . . 218 D
Kilngate PR5 . . . . 97 C
Kiln Hill BB12 . . . . 146 F
Kilnhouse La FY8 . . . . 111 A
Kiln House Way BB5 . . . . 104 A
Kiln La
Hambleton FY6 . . . . 177 E
Paythorne BB7. . . . . 231 C
Rimington BB7. . . . . 230 F
Skelmersdale WN8 . . . . 17 E
Wray LA2. . . . . 238 D
Kiln St
Nelson BB9 . . . . 148 D
Ramsbottom BL0 . . . . 50 B
Kilns The BB11 . . . . 128 B
Kiln Terr 5 OL13 . . . . 70 B
Kiln Wlk OL12 . . . . 52 B
Kilruddery Rd PR1 . . . . 96 B
Kilsby Cl PR5. . . . . 97 B
Kilworth Ht PR2 . . . . 117 C
Kimberley Ave FY4. . . . . . . 110 B
Kimberley Cl BB10 . . . . . . 148 B
Kimberley Rd PR2 . . . . . . 117 C
Kimberley St
Bacup OL13 70
Burnley BB10. 148
Coppull PR7 42
Kimberly Cl PR4 93
Kimble Cl BL8 49
Kime St BB12. 127
Kincardine Ave 7
FY4. 111
Kincraig Ct FY2. 152
Kincraig Pl FY2. 152

Kincraig Prim Sch FY2...152 F6
Kincraig Rd FY2...152 F5
Kinder Cnr FY6...153 B3
King Edward Ave
Blackpool FY2...152 B1
Lytham St Anne's FY8...90 A4
King Edward St BB5...103 C3
King Edward Terr BB9...170 D2
King Edward VII & Queen Mary Inf Sch FY8...90 A4
King Edward VII & Queen Mary Sch FY8...90 B4
Kingfisher Bank BB11...127 C4
Kingfisher Cl
Blackburn BB1...101 E8
Chorley PR7...42 F5
Kingfisher Ct
Caton LA2...237 C3
Maghull L31...5 B4
Oswaldtwistle BB5...103 E3
Preston PR1...96 D8
Southport PR9...35 D8
Kingfisher Ctr
Bacup OL13...70 E8
10 Rawtenstall BB4...86 A3
Kingfisher Dr
Bury BL9...33 B4
Poulton-le-F FY6...153 B2
Kingfisher Mews FY6...153 B2
Kingfisher Pk WN8...18 C4
Kingfisher St PR1...118 B1
Kingfisher Way
Bamber Bridge PR5...98 A2
Fleetwood FY7...198 E3
King George Ave FY2...152 B1
King George Ct 19 OL13...87 F3
King George V Coll PR8...35 E5
King Henry Mews BB7...230 D3
King La BB7...166 E8
Kingsacre PR3...181 A3
Kings Arc 37 LA1...214 F8
Kings Arms Cl 34 LA1...214 F8
Kings Ave BB4...86 A1
Kingsbarn Cl PR2...118 D7
Kingsbridge Cl PR1...96 E2
King's Bridge Cl 4 BB2...101 B1
Kingsbridge Ct 6 BB2...101 B1
King's Bridge St BB2...101 B1
Kingsbridge Wharf BB2...101 B1
Kingsbury Cl PR8...21 B4
Kingsbury Ct WN8...18 C4
Kingsbury Pl BB10...148 D3
Kingsbury Prim Spec Sch WN8...17 D1
Kings Cl
Buckshaw Village PR7...60 F6
Formby L37...11 E2
Staining FY3...131 E5
King's Cl FY6...153 E3
Kingscote Dr FY3...130 E7
Kings Cres PR25...77 A1
King's Cres LA3...216 E3
King's Croft PR5...97 D5
King's Cswy BB9...148 E5
Kings Ct
Fleetwood FY7...199 B4
Leyland PR25...77 A1
King's Ct 12 PR25...77 A1
Kingsdale Ave
Burnley BB10...148 C3
Fulwood PR2...118 D5
2 Morecambe LA3...216 E1
Kingsdale Cl
Leyland PR25...60 B6
Walton-le-D PR5...97 F5
Kingsdale Rd LA1...214 D7
Kings Dr
Fulwood PR2...117 D5
Hoddlesden BB3...82 F1
Padiham BB12...126 E6
King's Dr LA5...223 E1
KINGSFOLD...96 D2
Kingsfold Christian Sch The PR4...73 E2
Kingsfold Dr PR1...96 D2
Kingsfold Prim Sch PR1...96 D2
Kingshaven Dr PR1...96 E2
Kings Hey Dr PR9...53 F1
King's Highway
Accrington BB5...105 B2
Huncoat BB5...104 F8
Kingshotte Gdns BB9...170 C3
Kingsland Gr
Blackpool FY1...130 D3
12 Burnley BB11...128 B4
Kingsland Rd BB11...128 B4
Kingslea PR7...30 F8
Kingsley Ave BB12...126 E7
Kingsley Cl
Blackburn BB2...80 D7
Church BB5...103 F7
Maghull L31...5 C5
Thornton FY5...176 A3
Kingsley Ct 5 FY1...130 C4
Kingsley Dr PR7...43 A5
Kingsley Rd
Blackpool FY3...131 B2
Cottam PR4...116 E6
Laneshaw Bridge BB8...172 D6
Kingsley St BB9...170 F2
Kings Mdw PR8...21 D3
Kingsmead
Blackburn BB1...102 D4
Chorley PR7...43 C5
Kings Meadow Prim Sch PR8...21 D3
Kingsmede FY4...110 E6
Kingsmere Ave FY8...110 F1
Kingsmill Ave BB7...144 A8
Kingsmuir Ave PR2...118 D4
Kingsmuir Cl LA3...212 E7
Kings Rd
Cleveleys FY5...175 C2
Formby L37...11 E2
King's Rd
Accrington BB5...104 B7
Blackburn BB2...101 B1
Lytham St Anne's FY8...89 E5
King's Sq FY1...130 C5
King St
Accrington BB5...104 B6
5 Bacup OL13...87 F2
6 Bamber Bridge PR5...77 B7
Barnoldswick BB18...196 B2
Blackburn BB2...101 D4
Blackpool FY1...130 C5
Brierfield BB9...148 A5
Burnley, Harle Syke BB10...148 F3
Carnforth LA5...223 D1
Chorley PR7...43 D6
5 Clayton-le-M BB5...124 F2
Clitheroe BB7...166 E8
Colne BB8...171 E5
Fleetwood FY7...199 A4
15 Great Harwood BB6...124 C5
Haslingden BB4...85 B4
High Bentham LA2...239 D8
Horwich BL6...32 A4
Lancaster LA1...214 F8
Leyland PR25...77 A1
Longridge PR3...140 B7
Morecambe LA4...217 B5
Padiham BB12...126 C8
Ramsbottom BL0...50 C6
Rawtenstall BB4...69 E8
Southport PR8...35 A6
Whalley BB7...144 C5
Whitworth OL12...71 D3
Kingston Ave
Accrington BB5...104 A4
Blackpool FY4...110 C5
Kingston Cl FY6...199 F6
Kingston Cres
Haslingden BB4...68 A7
Southport PR9...54 C5
Kingston Dr FY8...90 D6
Kingston Mews 4 FY5...176 B3
Kingston Pl BB3...81 F7
King Street Terr BB9...148 A5
Kingsway
Accrington BB5...104 A8
Bamber Bridge PR5...77 E8
Blackburn BB3...82 A7
Blackpool FY4...110 C7
Burnley BB11...128 A6
Cleveleys FY5...175 C2
Euxton PR7...60 E2
Great Harwood BB6...124 F6
Hapton BB11...126 C3
Haslingden BB4...84 F1
Heysham LA3...213 A8
Higher Penwortham PR1...96 B6
Huncoat BB5...125 F1
Lancaster LA1...218 E1
Leyland PR25...59 E7
Lytham St Anne's FY8...90 C4
Preston PR2...116 F2
Southport PR8...35 A7
Kingsway Ave PR3...137 C3
Kingsway Ct
2 Lytham St Anne's FY8...90 C4
1 Morecambe LA3...216 E1
Kingsway Ret Pk LA1...218 E1
Kingsway W PR1...96 B6
King's Wlk FY5...175 D5
Kingswood PR7...43 B5
Kingswood Cl FY8...90 E4
Kingswood Coll L40...24 A6
Kingswood Ho PR8...34 F5
Kingswood Pk PR8...34 F5
Kingswood Rd PR25...77 A2
Kingswood St 6 PR1...96 E7
King William St BB1...101 E5
Kinloch Way L39...15 D6
Kinnerton Pl FY5...152 F8
Kinross Cl
Blackburn BB1...102 A4
1 Ramsbottom BL0...50 A2
Kinross Cres FY4...131 A1
Kinross St BB11...127 D4
Kinross Wlk 7 BB1...102 A4
Kintbury Rd FY8...89 F4
Kintour Rd FY8...90 E6
Kintyre Cl FY4...110 F7
Kintyre Way LA3...212 E7
Kipling Dr FY3...131 B2
Kipling Pl BB6...124 B4
Kirby Dr PR4...93 B6
Kirby Rd
Blackburn BB2...101 D1
Blackpool FY1...130 B2
Nelson BB9...148 B8
Kirby's Cotts L31...6 B3
Kirk Ave BB7...166 C8
Kirkbeck Cl LA2...237 D3
KIRKBY...1 B3
Kirkby Ave
Clayton-le-W PR25...77 E1
Cleveleys FY5...175 E4
Kirkby Bank Rd L33...1 C2
Kirkby Lonsdale Rd LA2...219 D7
Kirkby Lonsdale Rd
Caton LA2, LA6...237 B6
Over Kellet LA6...240 B1
Kirkdale Ave
Lytham St Anne's FY8...89 F7
Newchurch BB4...86 E1
Kirkdale Cl BB3...65 C6
Kirkdale Gdns WN8...10 A7
Kirkdale Rd BB6...123 C8
Kirkdene Ave BB8...194 D1
Kirkdene Mews BB8...194 D1
Kirkes Rd LA1...215 A7
Kirkfell Dr BB12...127 C8
Kirkfield PR3...185 D3
Kirkgate
Burnley BB11...128 B4
Kirkham PR4...114 B4
Kirkgate La LA6...240 B4
KIRKHAM...114 A5
Kirkham Ave FY1...130 E2
Kirkham By-Pass PR4...114 B4
Kirkham Cl PR25...76 D1
Kirkham Gram Jun Sch PR4...113 F4
Kirkham Gram Sch PR4...113 F5
Kirkham Mus* PR4...114 A5
Kirkham Rd
Freckleton PR4...93 B8
Kirkham PR4...114 E6
Southport PR9...54 A4
Weeton PR4...132 F2
Kirkham St PR1...96 E8
Kirkham Trad Pk PR4...114 B4
Kirkham & Wesham Prim Sch PR4...113 F5
Kirkham & Wesham Sta PR4...113 F6
Kirk Head PR4...74 E2
Kirkhill Ave BB4...85 C3
Kirk Hill Rd BB4...85 C3
Kirk Ho BB5...103 E6
Kirklake Bank L37...11 C2
Kirklake Rd L37...11 D2
Kirkland & Catterall St Helen's CE Prim Sch PR3...181 A2
Kirkland Pl PR2...95 E8
Kirklands
Chipping PR3...185 E3
Hest Bank LA2...220 E1
Kirklands Rd LA6...237 B8
Kirklees Rd PR8...34 F1
Kirkmoor Cl BB7...189 D1
Kirkmoor Rd BB7...166 E8
Kirk Rd BB5...103 E7
Kirkside View BB11...126 C4
Kirkstall Ave
Blackpool FY1...130 E2
Read BB12...145 D1
Kirkstall Cl PR7...43 D5
Kirkstall Dr
Barnoldswick BB18...196 D3
Chorley PR7...43 D5
Formby L37...12 B2
Kirkstall Rd
Chorley PR7...43 D5
Southport PR8...34 F2
Kirkstone Ave
Blackburn BB2...80 E8
Fleetwood FY7...198 D1
Kirkstone Dr
Blackpool FY5...152 C7
Morecambe LA4...217 D5
Kirkstone Rd FY8...110 D1
Kirk View BB4...87 A1
Kirton Cres FY8...90 C6
Kirton Pl FY5...175 E1
Kit Brow La LA2...211 D6
Kittiwake Cl 10 FY5...175 F1
Kittiwake Rd PR6...62 A3
Kittlingborne Brow PR5...98 A3
Kitty La FY4...111 B4
Knacks La OL12...52 A5
Knaresboro Ave FY3...130 F3
Knaresborough Cl FY6...153 D5
Knebworth Cl PR6...78 C2
Knight Cres BB3...82 A6
Knighton Ave BB2...101 C8
Knightsbrdige Cl PR4...113 E6
Knightsbridge Ave
Blackpool FY4...110 D6
Colne BB8...171 B5
Knightsbridge Cl
Kirkham PR4...113 E6
2 Lytham St Anne's FY8...90 D6
Knights Cl FY5...175 F1
Knightscliffe Cres WN6...19 D6
Knitting Row La PR3...178 A3
Knob Hall Gdns PR9...53 F3
Knob Hall La PR9...53 F3
Knoll La PR4...75 A4
Knoll The LA2...218 C8
Knot Acre PR4...76 A8
Knot La
Paythorne BB7, BD23...231 D5
Walton-le-D PR5...97 F5
KNOTT END-ON-SEA...199 E5
Knott Hill St OL12...71 E6
Knott La LA5...224 A8
KNOTTS...230 B8
Knotts Brow BL7...48 F4
Knotts Dr BB8...171 C3
Knotts La
Bolton-by-B BB7, BD23...230 B8
Colne BB8...171 D3
Padiham BB12...126 E6
Knotts Mount BB8...171 C3
Knott St BB3...82 A1
Knotwood Ct BB5...103 E5
Knowe Hill Cres LA1...215 B3
Knowl Cl BL0...50 C4
Knowle Ave
Blackpool FY2...152 C1
Cleveleys FY5...175 E1
Southport PR8...21 C6
KNOWLE GREEN...163 C1
Knowle La BB3...82 A3
Knowles Brow BB7...165 B3
Knowlesly Mdws BB3...65 C6
Knowlesly Rd BB3...65 B6
Knowles Rd FY8...89 E7
Knowles St
1 Chorley PR7...43 C6
Preston PR1...97 D8
Rishton BB1...124 B1
Knowles Wood Dr PR7...43 A6
Knowle The FY2...152 C2
KNOWLEY...61 F2
Knowley Brow PR6...61 E2
Knowl Gap Ave BB4...85 A1
Knowl Mdw BB4...68 A6
Knowlmere St BB5...104 B7
Knowlys Ave LA3...212 F8
Knowlys Cres 4 LA3...212 F8
Knowlys Dr 3 LA3...212 F8
Knowlys Gr LA3...212 F8
Knowlys Rd LA3...212 E8
Knowsley Ave
Blackpool FY3...130 E3
Leyland PR25...77 C4
Knowsley Cl
Gregson Lane PR5...98 F2
Lancaster LA1...214 D6
Knowsley Cres
Shawforth OL12...71 E6
Thornton FY5...176 C2
Weeton PR4...132 E2
Knowsley Dr PR5...98 F2
Knowsley Gate FY7...198 D4
Knowsley Gr 5 BL6...32 D1
Knowsley Ind Pk L33...1 C2
Knowsley La
Edgworth BL7...66 E4
Rivington PR6...44 E4
Knowsley Park Way BB4...68 B8
Knowsley Rd
Haslingden BB4...68 B8
Leyland PR25...60 C8
Ormskirk L39...15 F5
Southport PR9...53 C1
Wilpshire BB1...122 F5
Knowsley Rd Ind Est BB4...68 B8
Knowsley Rd W BB1...122 E5
Knowsley Road Ind Est BB4...85 B1
Knowsley St
3 Colne BB8...171 D4
32 Preston PR1...97 A7
Knox Gr FY1...130 D3
Knunck Knowles Dr BB7...189 E1
Knutsford Rd FY3...131 B2
Knutsford Wlk L31...5 D4
KNUZDEN BROOK...102 F4
Knuzden Brook BB1...102 D4
Knuzden St Oswald's CE Prim Sch BB1...102 E4
Korea Rd PR2...118 B4
Kumara Cres FY4...131 B1
Kyan St BB10...148 B2
Kylbarrow La LA5...225 F2
Kylemore Ave FY2...152 D3
Kyston Cl 1 FY1...130 D7

L

Laburnum Ave
Bamber Bridge PR5...77 B8
Lytham St Anne's FY8...91 B5
Laburnum Cl
Burnley BB11...127 D3
Preston PR1...118 C3
Laburnum Cotts PR3...201 E5
Laburnum Dr
Fulwood PR2...117 D8
Oswaldtwistle BB5...103 F3
Skelmersdale WN8...17 D1
Laburnum Gr
Burscough Bridge L40...25 E6
Horwich BL6...32 E1
Lancaster LA1...214 D8
Maghull L31...5 F1
Southport PR8...35 F7
Laburnum Pk LA5...221 C8
Laburnum Rd
Blackburn BB1...102 A8
Chorley PR6...61 D3
Haslingden BB4...68 A7
2 Lancaster LA1...218 D2
Laburnum St
6 Blackpool FY3...130 D7
Haslingden BB4...85 A3
Lacey Ct 19 BB4...85 B3
Lachman Rd BB8...172 B3
Lacy Ave PR1...96 E2
Ladbrooke Gr BB11...127 E2
Lade End LA3...212 E8
Ladies Row PR4...134 F4
Ladies Wlk LA1...218 E2
Ladies Wlk Ind Est LA1...218 E2
Lady Acre PR5...78 A8
Lady Alice's Dr L40...16 E8
Lady Anne Cl L40...24 B7
Ladybank Ave PR2...118 D7
Ladybower La FY6...153 B3
Lady Cl BB3...82 A6
Lady Crosse Dr PR6...61 C7
LADY GREEN...3 D4
Lady Green Ct L38...3 E3
Lady Green La L38...3 D4
Lady Hartley Ct BB8...172 D6
Lady Hey Cres PR2...116 C1
Ladyman St 10 PR1...96 E7
Lady Pl PR5...97 E4
Ladysmith Ave BL9...33 A5
Ladysmith Rd PR2...117 C2
Lady St PR1...96 F8
Lady's Wlk L40...16 C6
Lady Well Dr PR2...118 C7
Ladywell St PR1...96 E8
Lafford La
Up Holland, Roby Mill WN8...19 C2
Up Holland WN8...10 C8
Lagonda Dr FY4...111 F6
Lagonda Way FY4...111 F6
Laidley's Wlk FY7...198 E5
Lairgill Row LA2...239 E8
Laister Ct 7 LA4...217 E6
Laithbutts La LA6...221 F5
Laithe St
Burnley BB11...127 F4
6 Colne BB8...171 C4
Lake Ave LA4...216 F4
Lakeber Ave LA2...239 D8
Lakeber Cl 11 LA2...239 D8
Lakeber Dr 13 LA2...239 D8
Lake Gr LA4...216 F4
Lakeland Cl
Billington BB7...144 A3
Forton PR3...207 B3
Lakeland Dr BB7...144 A8
Lakeland Gdns PR7...43 A5
Lakeland Ho LA4...217 E7
Lakeland Way BB12...127 B8
Lakeland Wildlife Oasis* LA7...225 F8
Lake Point FY8...90 D3
Lake Rd
Lytham St Anne's FY8...90 C4
Morecambe LA3...216 F3
Lake Rd N FY8...90 C4
Lakes Dr WN5...10 E6
Lakeside FY6...200 B5
Lakeside Ave WN5...10 E3
Lake Side Cotts WN1...30 C1
Lake View BL7...46 C5
Lakeview Ct PR9...35 B8
Lake View Rd BB8...171 D7
Lakeway FY3...130 F6
Lakewood Ave FY5...175 D1
Lamaleach Dr PR4...93 A6
Lamaleach Residential Pk PR4...93 A5
Lambert Cl PR2...118 E3
Lambert Rd
Fulwood PR2...118 E3
Lancaster LA1...218 C3
Lamberts Mill Footwear Mus* BB4...86 B2
Lambert St BB8...172 C2
Lambeth Cl
Blackburn BB1...102 A4
Horwich BL6...32 D3
Lambeth Ct PR2...117 E5
Lambeth St
Blackburn BB1...102 A4
Colne BB8...172 B5
Lambing Clough La BB7...142 E7
Lambourne WN8...18 B4
Lambridge Cl LA4...217 B3
Lamb Row BB7...145 E7
Lambshear La L31...5 C4
Lambs Hill Cl 7 FY5...176 D1
Lamb's La PR3...201 A4
Lambs Rd FY5...153 D8
Lambton Gates BB4...86 C2
Lamlash Rd BB1...102 D4
LAMMACK...101 C8
Lammack Prim Sch BB1...122 C1
Lammack Rd BB1...101 C8
Lamour Pl 4 FY7...198 D3
Lanark Ave FY2...152 C6
Lanark Cl OL10...33 F1
Lanark St BB11...127 D4
Lancambe Ct LA1...218 A2
Lancashire Coll PR7...43 A8
Lancashire Constabulary HQ PR4...95 E1
Lancashire Dr PR7...60 F6
Lancashire Enterprise Bsns Pk PR26...77 A4
Lancashire Fire & Rescue HQ PR2...117 D8
Lancashire Rd PR26...77 A4
Lancashire St LA4...216 E4
LANCASTER...214 C6

Lancaster Ave
Accrington BB5 .... 104 B7
Clayton-le-W PR25 .... 77 E1
Great Eccleston PR3 ..... 156 C5
Haslingden BB4 .... 68 B8
Horwich BL6 .... 32 D2
Lytham St Anne's FY8 ...... 89 F4
Ramsbottom BL0 .... 50 A4
Thornton FY5 .... 176 C2
Lancaster Castle*
LA1 .... 214 E8
Lancaster Christ Church
CE Prim Sch LA1 .... 215 B8
Lancaster City Mus*
LA1 .... 214 F8
Lancaster Cl
Adlington PR6 .... 31 B7
Great Eccleston PR3 ..... 156 C5
Knott End-on-S FY6 ...... 199 F5
Maghull L31 .... 5 F1
Southport PR8 .... 34 E4
Lancaster Cres WN8 ...... 17 E1
Lancaster Ct
Chorley PR7 .... 61 C2
Parbold WN8 .... 27 C2
Lancaster Dallas Road Com
Prim Sch LA1 .... 214 E7
Lancaster Dr
Banks PR9 .... 54 F5
Brinscall PR6 .... 62 E8
Clayton-le-M BB5 .... 125 A3
Clitheroe BB7 .... 166 C7
Padiham BB12 .... 126 D6
Lancastergate PR25 .... 59 F8
Lancaster Gate
Banks PR9 .... 54 F5
Fleetwood FY7 .... 198 D4
14 Lancaster LA1 .... 214 F8
Nelson BB9 .... 148 D7
Lancaster Gdns PR8 ...... 34 E4
Lancaster Girls' Gram Sch
LA1 .... 214 F7
Lancaster Ho
3 Fleetwood FY7 .... 199 A4
Southport PR8 .... 34 E4
Lancaster La
Clayton-le-W PR25 .... 77 E2
Parbold WN8 .... 27 C3
Lancaster & Lakeland
Nuffield Hospl The
LA1 .... 215 A7
Lancaster Lane Com Prim
Sch PR25 .... 77 D1
Lancaster Maritime Mus*
LA1 .... 218 C1
Lancaster & Morecambe
Coll LA1 .... 217 F3
Lancaster & Morecambe
Coll (Annexe) LA4 ...... 217 B5
Lancaster Pl
Adlington PR6 .... 31 A8
Blackburn BB2 .... 101 B5
Lancaster Rd
Blackpool FY3 .... 131 A3
Caton LA2 .... 237 B3
Cockerham LA2 .... 206 C6
Crag Bank LA5 .... 221 B7
Fisher's Row PR3 .... 201 E5
Formby L37 .... 11 E1
Garstang PR3 .... 204 C1
Hornby LA2 .... 238 B7
Knott End-on-S FY6 ...... 199 F5
Lancaster LA3 .... 213 D3
Morecambe LA4 .... 217 C5
Morecambe, Torrisholme
LA4 .... 217 F4
Moss Edge PR3 .... 178 E6
Preesall FY6 .... 200 C3
Preston, Adelphi PR1 ...... 96 F8
Preston, Avenham PR1 ..... 97 A8
Ratten Row PR3 .... 156 A8
Slyne LA2 .... 218 D6
Southport PR8 .... 34 E4
Lancaster Rd N PR1 ...... 117 F1
Lancaster Road Prim Sch
LA4 .... 217 D4
Lancaster Royal Gram Sch
LA1 .... 215 A8
Lancaster Royal Gram Sch
(Annexe) LA1 .... 215 B7
Lancaster St
Blackburn BB2 .... 101 C4
Colne BB8 .... 171 D5
Coppull PR7 .... 42 F1
Oswaldtwistle BB5 ...... 103 C3
Lancaster Sta LA1 .... 214 E8
Lancaster Steiner Sch
LA1 .... 218 B1
Lancaster Way 17 PR1 .... 97 A8
Lanchester Ct PR25 .... 59 D6
Lanchester Gdns BB6 ... 143 C6
Lancia Cres FY4 .... 112 A6
Lancing Pl BB2 .... 101 C3
Landcrest Cl PR4 .... 114 B2
Land End L31 .... 6 C1
Land Gate OL12 .... 71 F5
Landing La BB7 .... 229 F4
Land La
New Longton PR4 .... 75 D5
Southport PR9 .... 54 D4
Landless St BB9 .... 148 A5
Landseer Ave FY2 .... 152 C4
Landseer Cl BB11 .... 127 E3
Landseer St PR1 .... 118 C1
Landsmoor Dr PR4 .... 95 A1
LANE BOTTOM 149 B3
Lane Bottom BB18 .... 194 B8
Lanedale PR4 .... 75 A8
Lane End BB11 .... 126 C2
Lane End Rd
Bacup OL13 .... 88 A1
Britannia OL13 .... 71 A8
LANE ENDS 230 A5
Lane Ends
Burnley BB9 .... 148 D6
Longridge PR3 .... 140 F8
Rivington PR6 .... 44 D4
Lane Ends Ct 2 FY4 ..... 130 E1
Lanefield Dr FY5 .... 175 C4
Lane Foot Brow LA2 ..... 239 D4
LANE HEAD 87 F4
Lane Head LA2 .... 238 D6
Lane Head La OL13 .... 87 F3
LANE HEADS 156 D3
Lane Ho BB8 .... 172 C1
Lane House Cl BB2 .... 81 B8
LANESHAW BRIDGE 172 F6
Laneshaw Bridge Prim Sch
BB8 .... 172 E6
Laneshaw Cl BB3 .... 81 E4
LANESIDE 104 C8
Laneside
Altham BB5 .... 125 D6
Great Harwood BB6 ...... 124 A6
LANE SIDE 85 B2
Lane Side OL13 .... 88 A4
Laneside Ave
Accrington BB5 .... 104 B8
Higham BB12 .... 146 F6
Laneside Cl BB7 .... 144 A7
Laneside Ho 5 BB4 .... 85 B2
Laneside Rd BB4 .... 85 C2
Lane Side Terr BB5 ...... 125 D6
Lane The
Carleton FY6 .... 153 A3
Sunderland LA3 .... 209 A5
Lane Top
Colne, Cotton Tree
BB8 .... 172 C5
Fence BB12 .... 147 D7
Langber End La LA6 ..... 242 F1
Langcliffe Rd PR2 .... 118 E4
Langdale LA2 .... 237 C3
Langdale Ave
Clitheroe BB7 .... 166 C7
Croston PR26 .... 58 B3
Formby L37 .... 11 D2
Hesketh Bank PR4 .... 73 D4
Rawtenstall BB4 .... 85 E2
Langdale Bsns Pk LA3 .. 217 D3
Langdale Cl
3 Accrington BB5 ...... 125 D1
Bamber Bridge PR5 .... 97 D1
Blackburn BB2 .... 80 E8
Formby L37 .... 11 D2
Freckleton PR4 .... 93 A6
Thornton FY5 .... 176 B2
Langdale Cres PR2 ...... 118 E3
Langdale Ct
Cleveleys FY5 .... 175 F1
3 Fleetwood FY7 .... 198 E2
4 Garstang PR3 .... 181 B7
Higher Penwortham PR1 .... 96 C4
Langdale Dr
Burscough L40 .... 25 E4
Maghull L31 .... 5 E2
Langdale Gdns PR8 .... 34 F1
Langdale Gr PR6 .... 61 B7
Langdale Pl
1 Blackpool FY4 .... 131 C1
Lancaster LA1 .... 218 E2
Langdale Prep Sch
FY2 .... 152 B1
Langdale Rd
Blackburn BB2 .... 80 E8
Blackpool FY4 .... 131 C1
Carnforth LA5 .... 221 E8
Fulwood PR2 .... 118 E3
Lancaster LA1 .... 218 E2
Leyland PR25 .... 60 B6
Longridge PR3 .... 139 F5
Lytham St Anne's FY8 .... 110 D1
Morecambe LA4 .... 217 D5
Padiham BB12 .... 146 C2
Langdale Rise BB8 .... 171 F6
Langden Brook Mews
LA3 .... 217 F2
Langden Brook Sq
BB1 .... 102 A3
Langden Cres PR5 .... 77 F8
Langden Dr PR2 .... 119 A3
Langden Fold PR2 .... 139 D1
Langdon Way FY2 .... 152 E2
Langfield BB10 .... 129 B6
Langfield Ave FY4 .... 110 C5
Langfield Cl PR2 .... 117 F8
Langford St BB5 .... 104 E1
Langham Ave BB5 .... 104 B8
Langham Rd
Blackburn BB1 .... 101 D7
Standish WN6 .... 29 D1
Langham St BB12 .... 127 B6
LANGHO 143 D1
Langholm Cl 6 PR25 ...... 76 D1
Langholme Cl BB9 .... 170 C1
Langholme Rd PR1 .... 96 B4
Langholme St BB9 .... 148 E6
Langholme Way OL10 ...... 33 F1
Langho St BB2 .... 101 C1
Langho Sta BB6 .... 143 C1
Langho Woods BB6 ...... 143 C5
Langley Cl
Hightown L38 .... 2 F2
Langley Cl *continued*
Standish WN6 .... 29 E2
Langley Ct L40 .... 25 B5
Langley La PR3 .... 137 F6
Langley Pl L40 .... 25 B4
Langley Rd
Burscough L40 .... 25 B4
Lancaster LA1 .... 215 A7
Langport Cl PR2 .... 117 F8
Langridge Way LA4 ...... 217 B3
Langroyd Rd BB8 .... 171 E6
Langsford Cl BB18 ...... 196 C2
Langshaw Dr BB7 .... 166 F6
Langshaw La LA2 .... 211 D5
Lang St
3 Accrington BB5 ...... 104 A6
Blackpool FY1 .... 130 C6
Langstone Cl BL6 .... 32 B3
Langthwaite Rd LA1,
LA2 .... 215 E5
Langton Ave WN6 .... 29 E1
Langton Brow
Eccleston PR7 .... 41 D5
Longridge PR3 .... 140 B7
Langton Cl
Blackburn BB2 .... 81 C8
Eccleston PR7 .... 41 D5
Lancaster LA1 .... 218 E4
Leyland PR26 .... 59 C8
Langton Pl WN6 .... 29 E1
Langton Rd PR4 .... 114 A5
Langton St PR1 .... 96 D7
Langtree WN8 .... 18 B3
Langtree La
Elswick PR4 .... 155 F2
Standish WN6 .... 29 D3
Langwood FY7 .... 198 E2
Langwood Ave 3 BB4 ..... 85 C2
Langwood Cl 4 BB4 .... 85 C2
Langwood Ct 6 BB4 .... 85 C2
Langwood Gdns 5 BB4 .... 85 C2
Langwood La WA11 .... 9 C1
Langwyth Rd BB10 .... 128 E5
Lansborough Cl PR26 ..... 59 B8
Lansbury Pl 3 BB9 ...... 170 F2
Lansdowne Cl
Burnley BB11 .... 127 F4
Ramsbottom BL0 .... 50 B5
Lansdowne Gr LA4 .... 217 E7
Lansdowne Pl 1 FY1 .... 130 B6
Lansdowne Rd
Lytham St Anne's FY8 ...... 90 D5
Morecambe LA4 .... 217 E7
Southport PR8 .... 35 E6
Lansdowne St BB2 .... 101 B3
Lansdown Hill PR2 ...... 117 C7
Lansdown Rd PR4 .... 114 A7
Lansil Ind Est LA1 .... 218 E3
Lansil Way LA1 .... 218 E3
Lansil Wlk LA1 .... 218 E3
Lanterns The FY6 .... 153 D4
Lapford Cres L33 .... 1 A4
Lapford Wlk L33 .... 1 A4
Lappet Gr PR4 .... 116 E5
Lapwing Row FY8 .... 90 E7
Lapwings The FY6 .... 153 B2
LARBRECK 155 E6
Larbreck Ave PR4 .... 156 A1
Larbreck Gardens Cvn Pk
PR3 .... 155 C5
Larbreck Hall Cvn Pk
PR3 .... 155 B5
Larbreck Rd FY3 .... 130 E7
Larch Ave PR6 .... 61 E2
Larch Cl
Blackburn BB2 .... 80 F8
Freckleton PR4 .... 93 A5
Knott End-on-S FY6 ...... 200 A5
Rawtenstall BB4 .... 68 F8
Skelmersdale WN8 .... 17 E1
Larch Dr PR6 .... 62 F7
LARCHES 116 F1
Larches Ave PR2 .... 116 F1
Larches La PR2 .... 116 E1
Larches The BB1 .... 101 F7
Larchgate PR2 .... 118 C7
Larch Gate PR5 .... 98 E2
Larch Gr
Bamber Bridge PR5 .... 97 F1
Garstang PR3 .... 181 C8
Lancaster LA1 .... 214 D8
Larch Rd BB5 .... 103 F3
Larch St
Blackburn BB1 .... 102 A7
Burnley BB12 .... 127 C7
Bury BL9 .... 33 B2
Nelson BB9 .... 148 F8
Southport PR8 .... 35 E6
Larchway PR3 .... 140 B8
Larch Way L37 .... 11 D4
Larchwood
Higher Penwortham
PR1 .... 96 B4
Lancaster LA1 .... 215 B4
Preston PR2 .... 116 E1
Larchwood Cl FY8 .... 90 F4
Larchwood Cres PR25 ..... 76 E1
Largs Rd BB1 .... 102 C3
Lark Ave 3 PR1 .... 96 E4
Lark Cl FY3 .... 131 B3
Lark Ct FY7 .... 198 D1
Larkfield PR7 .... 41 B6
Larkfield Cl BL8 .... 49 F1
Larkfield Ct PR9 .... 54 A3
Larkfield La PR9 .... 54 A3
Larkfield Prim Sch PR9 ... 54 A3
Larkhill
Brockhall Village BB6 .... 143 C5
Larkhill *continued*
Skelmersdale WN8 .... 18 B4
Lark Hill
Blackburn BB1 .... 101 F6
Higher Walton PR5 .... 98 B3
Rawtenstall BB4 .... 86 A3
Larkhill Ave BB10 .... 148 C5
Larkhill Gr L38 .... 2 F3
Larkhill La L37 .... 11 C4
Lark Hill Pl 6 OL12 .... 52 E1
Larkhill Rd PR1 .... 97 B7
Larkhill St
Blackpool FY1 .... 130 C6
Preston PR1 .... 97 B7
LARKHOLME 198 D1
Larkholme Ave FY7 .... 198 E1
Larkholme La FY7 .... 198 E1
Larkholme Par FY7 ...... 198 D1
Larkholme Prim Sch
FY7 .... 175 D8
Larkspur Cl
Blackburn BB2 .... 80 D8
3 Southport PR8 .... 35 D6
Lark St
4 Burnley BB12 .... 127 C7
Colne BB8 .... 171 E6
Darwen BB3 .... 65 B5
Last Drop Village The*
BL7 .... 48 A1
Latham Ave
9 Blackpool FY3 .... 130 E3
Ormskirk L39 .... 16 A5
Latham Cres PR4 .... 57 A6
Latham Rd BL6 .... 31 C3
Latham Row BL6 .... 32 F3
Latham St
Burnley BB10 .... 148 B1
Preston PR1 .... 97 A6
LATHOM 26 B1
Lathom Ave
Morecambe LA4 .... 217 D4
Parbold WN8 .... 27 B3
Lathom Cl L40 .... 25 E4
Lathom Dr L31 .... 5 E3
Lathom Gr LA4 .... 217 D4
Lathom High Sch WN8 .... 17 F3
Lathom Ho L40 .... 17 B7
Lathom La L40 .... 16 C7
LATHOM PARK 17 C7
Lathom Rd
Bickerstaffe L39 .... 7 F8
Southport PR9 .... 53 C1
Lathom St 8 BL9 .... 33 A4
Lathom Way PR3 .... 181 D6
Latimer Cl 2 WN5 .... 10 F7
Latimer Dr PR4 .... 75 F7
Lauderdale Ave FY5 ...... 175 D1
Lauderdale Cres 1
PR2 .... 118 F4
Lauderdale Rd PR2 ...... 118 F4
Lauderdale St PR1 .... 96 E6
LAUND 85 F4
Laund Gate BB12 .... 147 D8
Laund Gr BB5 .... 104 D3
Laund Hey View BB4 ...... 85 B1
Laund La
Haslingden BB4 .... 85 C3
Ollerton Fold PR6 .... 79 E4
Laund Rd BB5 .... 104 D3
Laundry Rd N FY4 .... 111 A5
Laund St BB4 .... 85 F4
Laund The PR26 .... 76 A1
Laura St BL0 .... 50 C2
Laurel Ave
Blackpool FY1 .... 130 E2
Burscough Bridge L40 ..... 25 E6
Darwen BB3 .... 82 B2
Euxton PR7 .... 60 B3
Fleetwood FY7 .... 175 F8
Lytham St Anne's FY8 ...... 91 B5
Laurel Bank LA1 .... 214 D7
Laurel Bank Ave PR2 .... 117 C3
Laurel Bank Terr BB2 ..... 80 B7
Laurel Dr
Skelmersdale WN8 .... 17 E2
Thornton FY5 .... 153 B8
Laurel Gr PR8 .... 35 E7
Laurel St
4 Bacup OL13 .... 87 F3
Burnley BB11 .... 128 B4
3 Bury BL9 .... 33 B2
10 Preston PR1 .... 97 A7
Laurels The
Coppull PR7 .... 42 F3
Kirkham PR4 .... 113 D4
Poulton-le-F FY6 .... 153 F3
Laureston Ave LA3 .... 212 F6
Laurie Pl 2 OL12 .... 52 F1
Laurier Ave 3 FY4 ...... 110 C6
Laurier Rd BB10 .... 148 B2
Lauriston Cl 4 FY4 ..... 111 A6
Lavender Cl PR2 .... 118 C6
Lavender Gr PR7 .... 43 C5
Lavender Hill BB4 .... 68 F8
Lavender Way FY6 .... 199 F5
Laverick Rd LA2 .... 237 A5
Laverton Cl BL9 .... 33 E1
Laverton Rd FY8 .... 90 A4
Lawley Rd BB2 .... 101 A5
Lawn Ct 2 FY1 .... 130 D4
Lawns Ave WN5 .... 10 C5
Lawnsdale Cvn Pk FY8 ... 112 E1
Lawn St BB10 .... 128 A8
Lawns The PR9 .... 53 F2
Lawnswood Ave
Lancaster LA1 .... 215 A3
Poulton-le-F FY6 .... 153 C2
Lawnswood Cres FY3 ... 131 C2
Lawnswood Dr LA3 ...... 217 C2
Lawn Tennis Ct FY4 ...... 110 D5
Lawnwood Ave PR7 .... 43 A5
Lawrence Ave
Bamber Bridge PR5 .... 97 D2
Burnley BB11 .... 127 C4
Lytham St Anne's FY8 ...... 90 A6
Preston PR1 .... 97 B5
Simonstone BB12 .... 145 E2
Lawrence Cl 2 OL12 ...... 52 A1
Lawrence La PR7 .... 41 C7
Lawrence Rd
Chorley PR7 .... 43 B
Higher Penwortham PR1 .... 96 B5
Lawrence Row 5 FY7 ... 199 A4
Lawrence St
Blackburn BB2 .... 101 C4
12 Blackpool FY4 .... 130 B1
3 Fulwood PR2 .... 117 D3
Padiham BB12 .... 146 D1
Whitewell Bottom BB4 ..... 86 F4
Lawrie Ave BL0 .... 50 B5
Lawson Ave BL6 .... 32 C4
Lawson Cl LA1 .... 214 F3
Lawson Gdns LA2 .... 218 C8
Lawson Pl LA2 .... 218 C8
Lawson Rd
Blackpool FY3 .... 131 A3
Lytham St Anne's FY8 .... 111 A2
Lawsons Ct 4 FY5 ...... 176 C1
Lawsons Rd FY5 .... 176 C2
Lawson St
3 Chorley PR6 .... 43 E7
Preston PR1 .... 96 F8
Rawtenstall BB4 .... 86 A8
Southport PR9 .... 36 A7
Law St
Newchurch BB4 .... 86 F1
Todmorden OL14 .... 109 B1
Lawswood
Formby L37 .... 11 E5
6 Thornton FY5 .... 176 C1
Lawton Cl PR6 .... 79 B1
Laxey Gr PR1 .... 118 D1
Laxey Rd BB2 .... 101 E1
Laycock Gate FY3 .... 130 D6
LAYTON 130 E7
Layton Prim Sch FY3 ..... 130 E8
Layton Rd
Blackpool FY3 .... 130 E6
Preston PR2 .... 116 E1
Layton Sta FY2 .... 152 E1
Lazenby Ave FY7 .... 198 C2
LEA 116 D1
Lea Bank BB4 .... 86 D2
Lea Bank Mews 15
BB9 .... 170 F2
Leach Cres FY8 .... 110 F2
Leaches Rd BL0 .... 50 D8
Leachfield Cl 2 LA2 .... 211 A4
Leachfield Ind Est PR3 .. 204 B1
Leachfield Rd LA2 .... 210 F4
Leach House La LA2 ..... 211 A5
Leach La FY8 .... 110 E1
Leach Pl PR5 .... 78 B8
Leach St
Blackburn BB2 .... 101 E2
Colne BB8 .... 171 C4
Lea Com Prim Sch
PR2 .... 116 D1
Lea Cres L39 .... 15 F7
Leacroft BB3 .... 82 A6
Lea Ct L39 .... 15 E7
Leadale PR2 .... 116 D2
Leadale Cl WN6 .... 29 D1
Leadale Gn PR25 .... 76 E1
Leadale Rd PR25 .... 76 E1
Lead Mines Clough*
PR6 .... 45 A
Lea Dr BB2 .... 81 E6
Leaford Ave FY3 .... 130 E8
Leafy Cl PR25 .... 60 B7
Leagram Cres PR2 ...... 119 A3
Lea La
Cottam PR4 .... 116 B5
Gressingham LA2 .... 237 F8
Heysham LA3 .... 212 E6
Leamington Ave
Baldingstone BL9 .... 50 E1
Burnley BB10 .... 148 C1
Southport PR8 .... 21 D
Leamington Rd
Blackburn BB2 .... 101 B6
Blackpool FY1 .... 130 D5
Lytham St Anne's FY8 ...... 89 F6
Morecambe LA4 .... 217 D2
Southport PR8 .... 21 D5
Leamington St BB9 ...... 148 E
Lea Mount Dr BL9 .... 33 D4
Leander Gdns FY6 ...... 153 D2
Lea Neeld's Endowed CE
Prim Sch PR4 .... 116 C4
Leapers View LA6 .... 237 B8
Lea Rd
Lucas Green PR6 .... 61 C5
Preston PR2, PR4 .... 116 D1
Lea St Mary's RC Primary
Sch PR4 .... 115 F
Leaside Cl OL12 .... 52 D
Leathercote PR3 .... 181 C
LEA TOWN .... 115 F
Leavengreave Ct OL12 .... 71 D
Leaverholme Cl BB10 ... 108 A
Leaver St BB12 .... 127 A
Leavesley Rd FY1 .... 130 D
Lea Way Cl FY5 .... 153 D
Lebanon St BB10 .... 128 C
LECK .... 242 B

Leckhampton Rd FY1 130 B8
Leck Ho 11 LA1 215 A3
Leckonby St PR3 156 B5
Leck St Peter's CE Prim Sch LA6 242 B7
Ledburn WN8 18 B3
Ledbury Ave FY8 90 B5
Ledbury Rd FY3 131 B7
Ledson Gr L39 6 B7
LEE 232 F2
Lee Brook Cl BB4 86 A4
Leebrook Rd BB4 85 F4
Leeds Cl 15 BB1 102 A4
Leeds Rd
Blackpool FY1 130 D5
4 Nelson BB9 148 E8
Nelson, Bradley BB9 170 F1
Lee Gr BB10 128 F4
Lee Green St 3 BB10 128 A8
Leehouse Dr FY6 131 D8
Leeís St OL13 71 C8
Leek St PR1 97 E8
Lee La
Bispham Green L40 27 C7
Great Harwood BB1 124 B3
Horwich BL6 32 B4
Whittlestone Head BL7 66 B2
Leeming La LA6 242 C3
Lee Rd
Bacup OL13 70 E8
Blackpool FY4 111 B8
Nelson BB9 170 F2
LEES 187 B6
Leesands Cl PR2 118 E5
Lees Cotts BL7 48 C2
Lees Ct LA3 212 E7
Lees La WN8 18 E7
Leeson Ave PR7 42 D4
Lees Rd
Adlington PR6 31 B8
Kirkby L33 1 B2
Lee St
Accrington BB5 104 C6
Bacup OL13 87 F2
Barrowford BB9 170 D3
Burnley BB10 128 A8
Longridge PR3 140 A7
Rawtenstall BB4 86 A4
Lees The BB10 108 A7
Leeswood WN8 18 B3
Leet Rd BB12 146 F5
Lee View 2 OL13 88 A1
Leeward Cl BB3 81 F6
Leeward Rd PR2 95 F8
Legh La PR4 56 B4
Leicester Ave
Cleveleys FY5 175 E3
Garstang PR3 181 B7
Horwich BL6 32 A3
Leicester Gate FY5 175 E3
Leicester Lo 3 PR2 118 F4
Leicester Rd
Blackburn BB1 102 C5
Blackpool FY1 130 D5
Preston PR1 118 A1
Leicester St PR9 35 B8
Leigh Brow PR5 97 B2
Leigh Pk BB11 126 C3
Leigh Row PR7 43 C7
Leighton Ave
Fleetwood FY7 198 D3
Maghull L31 5 D2
Leighton Ct LA4 217 A3
Leighton Dr LA1 214 D7
Leighton Hall* LA5 225 C1
Leighton Moss Nature Reserve* LA5 225 A3
Leighton Moss Visitor Ctr* LA5 224 F2
Leighton St PR1 96 E8
Leinster Rd LA1 215 A5
Leisure Lakes Cvn Pk PR4 55 E1
Leith Ave FY5 175 D2
Lemonius St BB5 104 C4
Lemon Tree Ct FY8 110 B4
LENCHES 171 D3
Lenches Fold BB8 171 D4
Lenches Rd BB8 171 D3
Lench Rd BB4 69 D8
Lench St 5 BB4 69 F8
Lendel Cl L37 11 E3
Lennon St 3 PR7 43 C7
Lennox Ct FY4 110 D6
Lennox Gate FY4 110 D7
Lennox Rd OL14 109 A1
Lennox St
18 Preston PR1 97 A7
Worsthorne BB10 129 A6
Lennox Wlk OL10 33 F1
Lenton Ave L37 11 D4
Lentworth Ave FY2 152 D5
Lentworth Dr LA1 215 A4
Lentworth Ho 5 LA1 215 A3
Leo Case Ct 5 PR1 97 D8
Leonard St
Barnoldswick BB18 196 B2
Nelson BB9 148 E7
Leonard Terr BB3 82 E3
Leopold Gr FY1 130 B5
Leopold Rd BB2 101 B6
Leopold St BB8 171 B4
Leopold Way BB2 82 A8
Lesley Rd PR8 35 E7
Leslie Ave
Caton LA2 237 C3
Thornton FY5 176 C2
Letchworth Dr PR7 43 B6
Letchworth Pl 2 PR7 43 B6
Letcliffe Ctry Pk* BB18 194 B8
Lethbridge Rd PR8 35 D5
Letitia St BL6 32 A3
Levant St BB12 126 C7
Leven Ave FY7 198 D3
Leven Gr BB3 81 E4
Levens Cl
Banks PR9 55 A5
Blackburn BB2 81 F8
Lancaster LA1 214 D7
Poulton-le-F FY6 131 E8
Levens Ct LA3 216 E2
Levens Dr
Clayton-le-W PR25 77 D2
Morecambe LA3 216 E2
Poulton-le-F FY6 153 D1
Levensgarth Ave PR2 117 F8
Levens Gr FY1 130 D3
Levens St 12 PR1 118 D1
Leven St BB11 128 B4
Levens Way LA5 224 C3
Lever Cl BB2 100 F8
Lever Ct FY8 90 A7
Lever House La PR25 77 C2
Lever House Prim Sch PR25 77 C3
Lever Park Ave BL6 32 B5
Lever Park Sch BL6 32 C3
Lever St
Blackpool FY3 130 E4
16 Ramsbottom BL0 50 C6
Rawtenstall BB4 86 B2
Levine Ave FY4 131 A1
Lewis Cl PR7 30 E6
Lewis Ct PR9 35 D8
Lewis Dr OL10 33 F1
Lewis St BB6 124 D5
Lewis Textile Mus* BB1 101 E5
Lewtas St FY1 130 B6
LEWTH 136 A6
Lewth La PR4 136 B5
Lex St PR1 97 C8
Lexton Dr PR9 54 B3
Leybourne Ave PR8 21 F7
Leyburn Ave
Blackpool FY2 152 C5
Fleetwood FY7 198 E2
Leyburn Cl
Accrington BB5 104 E5
Fulwood PR2 118 E5
Leyburn Rd
Blackburn BB2 81 C7
Lancaster LA1 218 D3
Leycester Dr LA1 218 A3
Ley Ct LA1 214 D8
Leyfield PR1 96 E2
Leyfield Cl FY3 153 A1
Leyfield Rd PR25 59 F8
LEYLAND 76 F2
Leyland Cl
Southport PR9 54 E5
Trawden BB8 172 B3
Leyland La
Leyland PR25 76 D2
Runshaw Moor PR26, PR25 59 D4
Leyland Meth Inf Sch PR25 77 B1
Leyland Meth Jun Sch PR25 77 B1
Leyland Rd
Burnley BB11 128 B6
Middleforth Green PR1 96 E3
Southport PR9 53 C1
Leyland St Andrew's CE Inf Sch PR25 59 F8
Leyland St James CE Prim Sch PR26 59 B8
Leyland St Mary's RC Prim Sch PR25 76 F1
Leyland St Mary's RC Tech Coll PR25 59 E7
Leyland St BB5 103 F5
Leyland Sta PR25 77 B2
Leylands The FY8 90 F2
Leyland Way
Leyland PR25 77 C1
Ormskirk L39 15 F5
Leys Cl
Elswick PR4 156 A1
Wiswell BB7 144 F8
Leys Rd FY2 152 D1
Ley St 5 BB5 104 E2
Leyster St LA4 217 C5
Leyton Ave PR25 59 D7
Leyton St OL12 52 F2
Libby La PR3 201 C6
Library Ave LA1 211 A7
Library Mews FY4 110 E7
Library Rd PR6 78 B4
Library St
Chorley PR7 43 C7
Church BB5 103 E6
15 Preston PR1 97 A7
Lichen Cl PR7 42 D4
Lichfield Ave LA4 217 D6
Lichfield Rd
Blackpool FY1 130 C8
Chorley PR7 43 C6
Preston PR2 116 F2
Liddesdale Rd BB9 171 B2
Liddington Cl BB2 82 A8
Liddington Hall Dr BL0 50 B4
Lidget Ave PR2 116 C1
Lidgett BB8 172 A5
Lidum Park Ind Est FY8 91 E5
Liege Rd 4 PR25 60 A8
Lifeboat Pl 13 FY7 199 B5
Lifeboat Rd L37 11 B1
Lifton Rd L33 1 A2
Liggard Ct FY8 91 C4
Lightbown Ave FY3 130 E3
Lightbown Cotts BB3 81 E2
Lightbown St BB3 82 A3
Lightburne Ave FY8 89 F5
Lightfoot Cl PR2 117 D8
Lightfoot Green La PR4 117 B8
Lightfoot La PR2, PR4 117 B7
Lighthorne Dr PR8 21 A4
Lighthouse Cl 4 FY7 199 B5
Lighthouse La L37 12 A1
Lighthurst Ave PR7 43 C6
Lighthurst La PR7 43 D5
Lightwood Ave
2 Blackpool FY4 130 C1
Lytham St Anne's FY8 90 D3
Lilac Ave
1 Blackpool FY1 130 D2
Haslingden BB4 85 B3
Kingsfold PR1 96 F2
Lytham St Anne's FY8 91 B5
Southport PR8 21 D2
Lilac Cl PR4 92 D5
Lilac Cres PR4 134 F4
Lilac Dr FY6 177 D4
Lilac Gr
Abbey Village PR6 80 C2
Clitheroe BB7 166 C7
Darwen BB3 82 B3
Knott End-on-S FY6 199 E5
Preston PR1 118 C3
Skelmersdale WN8 17 E1
Lilac Rd BB1 102 A8
Lilac St BB8 171 F6
Lilacs The
Poulton-le-F FY6 153 F3
Thornton FY5 176 A3
Lilac Terr 2 OL13 70 D8
Lilburn Cl BL0 50 C4
Lilford Cl PR4 57 A5
Lilford Rd BB1 101 D6
Lily Gr
Lancaster LA1 215 A5
Preston PR1 118 C3
Lily St
16 Bacup OL13 87 F2
Blackpool FY1 130 C5
Darwen BB3 82 B1
Nelson BB9 148 F6
Lima Rd FY8 90 B6
Lima St BL9 33 B3
LIMBRICK 44 A6
Limbrick BB1 101 E6
Limbrick Rd PR6 43 E7
Lime Ave
Galgate LA2 211 A4
Kirkham PR4 114 B4
Oswaldtwistle BB5 103 D2
Limebrest Ave FY5 153 D8
Lime Chase PR2 117 C8
Limechase Cl 9 FY4 111 A6
Lime Cl PR1 96 B4
Lime Ct WN8 17 E1
Limefield BB2 101 B5
Limefield Ave
Brierfield BB9 148 C6
Whalley BB7 144 C6
Limefield Ct BB2 101 B5
Limefield Dr WN8 9 E7
Limefield St BB5 104 D5
Lime Gr
Blackpool FY2 152 E2
Chorley PR7 43 C5
Garstang PR3 181 B8
Lancaster LA1 214 D8
Longridge PR3 140 A8
Lytham St Anne's FY8 89 D8
Poulton-le-F FY6 153 E2
Preston PR2 116 F2
Ramsbottom BL0 50 D7
Skelmersdale WN8 17 E1
Thornton FY5 176 C1
Lime Rd
Accrington BB5 104 C7
Haslingden BB4 85 C3
Limerick Rd FY2 152 D3
Limers Gate
Rochdale OL12 52 F5
Todmorden OL14 88 E4
Limers La BB6 124 A6
Limes Ave
Darwen BB3 65 A8
Euxton PR7 60 C4
Morecambe LA3 216 E3
Lime St
Blackburn BB1 101 E6
Clitheroe BB7 189 F1
Colne BB8 171 E6
Great Harwood BB6 124 C6
Nelson BB9 148 C8
Southport PR8 35 E6
Limestone Trail* BB10 108 E6
Lime Tree Gr BB4 86 A4
Lime Tree Way L37 11 C2
Limewood Cl
Accrington BB5 104 D6
Bridge End BB4 68 A7
Limey La BB11 106 E6
Limont Rd PR8 21 D5
Linacre La L37 4 B7
Linadale Ave 4 FY5 176 B2
Linaker Dr L39 14 B8
Linaker Prim Sch PR8 35 B5
Linaker St PR8 35 B5
Lina St BB5 103 F6
Linby St BB10 128 B5
Lincoln Ave
Cleveleys FY5 175 E3
Fleetwood FY7 198 E3
Lincoln Chase PR2 116 C1
Lincoln Cl
Blackburn BB1 102 B4
Morecambe LA4 217 D3
Lincoln Ct
1 Accrington BB5 104 A7
Blackpool FY1 130 C4
Padiham BB12 126 C8
Lincoln Ho 7 PR1 97 B7
Lincoln Pk BB7 190 A1
Lincoln Pl BB4 85 A3
Lincoln Rd
Blackburn BB1 102 B4
Blackpool FY1 130 C5
Earby BB18 197 B2
Lancaster LA1 214 E7
Southport PR8 35 A1
Lincoln St
Burnley BB11 128 A4
3 Haslingden BB4 85 A3
Preston PR1 118 B1
Todmorden OL14 109 B1
Lincoln Way
Clitheroe BB7 190 A2
Garstang PR3 181 B7
Lincoln Wlk PR1 118 B1
Lindadale Ave BB5 104 A3
Lindadale Cl BB5 104 A3
Lindale Ave PR2 139 E1
Lindale Cres BB10 148 A2
Lindale Gdns FY4 110 E6
Lindale Rd
Fulwood PR2 118 A4
Longridge PR3 139 F5
Lindbeck Ct FY4 111 C8
Lindbeck Rd FY4 131 C1
Lindbergh Ave LA1 214 E4
Lindel La FY6 200 B2
Lindel Rd FY7 198 F2
Linden Ave
Blackburn BB1 101 D6
Cleveleys FY5 175 F3
Orrell WN5 10 E6
Ramsbottom BL0 50 D6
Linden Bsns Ctr 14 BB8 171 D5
Linden Cl
Bamber Bridge PR5 97 B1
Barrowford BB9 170 B1
Cleveleys FY5 175 F2
Clifton PR4 115 D1
Edenfield BL0 68 D2
Linden Cres BB3 82 C2
Linden Ct
1 Earby BB18 197 A1
Orrell WN5 10 E6
Linden Dr
Bamber Bridge PR5 97 B1
Clitheroe BB7 166 F7
Linden Fold PR4 156 A1
Linden Gn FY5 175 F2
Linden Gr
Chorley PR6 61 D3
Fulwood PR2 118 E3
Garstang PR3 181 C8
Orrell WN5 10 E6
Linden Lea
Blackburn BB2 80 F8
Rawtenstall BB4 68 F8
Linden Mews FY8 110 F2
Linden Pl FY2 152 E3
Linden Rd
Colne BB8 171 D5
Earby BB18 197 B1
Lindens WN8 18 B4
Linden St BB10 128 B5
Lindens The FY6 200 B4
Linden Wlk WN5 10 E6
Linderbreck La FY6 131 E8
Lindeth Cl
Nether Kellet LA6 221 F6
Silverdale LA5 224 C2
Lindeth Gdns 8 LA1 218 D3
Lindeth Rd LA5 224 C2
Lindholme WN8 18 C3
Lindisfarne Ave BB2 101 F1
Lindisfarne Cl BB12 127 E7
Lindle Ave PR4 95 E2
Lindle Cl PR4 95 E2
Lindle Cres PR4 95 E2
Lindle La PR4 96 A2
Lindley Ave WN5 10 C5
Lindley Croft FY5 176 E2
Lindley Dr WN8 27 C3
Lindley St
Bamber Bridge PR5 77 B8
Blackburn BB2 101 B2
Lindon Park Rd BB4 68 C7
Lindow Cl 13 LA1 214 F7
Lindow Sq LA1 214 E7
Lindow St LA1 214 F7
Lindred Rd BB9 148 B7
Lindsay Ave
Blackpool FY3 130 E3
Leyland PR25 77 B1
Lytham St Anne's FY8 90 B6
Poulton-le-F FY6 153 D2
Lindsay Ct
Blackpool FY8 110 B4
Morecambe LA3 217 C2
Lindsay Dr PR7 43 A7
Lindsay Pk BB10 128 F5
Lindsay St
Burnley BB11 128 A6
Horwich BL6 32 D1
Lindsey Ho 2 BB5 104 A7
Linedred La BB9 148 B7
Lines St LA4 217 B5
Linfield Terr FY4 110 E6
Lingart La PR3 204 D1
Lingdales L37 12 B5
Lingfield Ave BB7 166 E6
Lingfield Cl LA1 215 B3
Lingfield Ct BB2 80 C8
Lingfield Rd FY7 198 F2
Lingfield Way BB2 80 D8
Lingham La LA2 239 F8
Lingmoor Dr BB12 127 A8
Lingmoor Rd LA1 218 F1
Lingwell Cl PR6 61 C5
Link 59 Bsns Pk BB7 190 B2
Links Ave PR9 53 F3
Links Ct FY8 89 E5
Links Dr LA2 239 D8
Links Field PR2 117 C3
Links Gate
Fulwood PR2 117 C3
Lytham St Anne's FY8 90 A6
Thornton FY5 153 D7
Linkside Ave BB9 149 B8
Links La BB2 80 C8
Links Lo FY8 90 A6
Links Rd
Blackpool FY1 130 C8
Higher Penwortham PR1 96 B6
Kirkby L32 1 A1
Knott End-on-S FY6 199 D5
Lytham St Anne's FY8 89 E5
Links The FY5 175 C4
Links View FY8 90 C5
Linley Gr BL0 50 A2
Linnet Cl FY3 131 B6
Linnet Dr BL9 33 B4
Linnet La FY8 90 E7
Linnet St PR1 118 B2
Linslade Cres L33 1 A4
Linton Ave LA3 216 D1
Linton Dr BB11 127 D3
Linton Gdns BB9 170 C3
Linton Gr PR1 96 B5
Linton St PR2 117 D3
Lion Ct BB5 103 E6
Lionel St BB12 127 C6
Lion La BL6 31 C2
Lions Ct 1 FY8 91 D4
Lions Dr BB1 102 D1
Lion St BB5 103 E6
Liptrott Rd PR7 43 A5
Lisbon Dr
Burnley BB11 127 E5
Darwen BB3 82 C1
Lisbon St 17 OL12 52 C1
Lismore Ave 6 FY4 110 F6
Lismore Pk PR8 34 E4
Lister Croft BD23 197 A5
Lister Gr LA3 212 F8
Lister St
Accrington BB5 104 A6
3 Blackburn BB2 101 E3
Lister Well Rd BB18 194 A6
Litchford Ho BB4 86 C2
Little Acre
Longton PR4 75 A8
Thornton FY5 153 D8
LITTLE ALTCAR 12 A1
Little Banks Cl PR5 78 B6
LITTLE BISPHAM 152 C8
Little Brewery La L37 11 F6
LITTLE CARLETON 152 F1
Little Carr La PR7 43 D5
Little Cl
Leyland PR26 76 E3
Middleforth Green PR1 96 C3
Little Coppins La FY6 153 E1
Littledale Ave LA3 213 A8
Littledale Mews LA2 218 F6
Littledale Rd
Crossgill LA2 237 E1
Quernmore LA2 232 C8
Little Digmoor Prim Sch WN8 9 B6
LITTLE ECCLESTON 156 A5
Little Fell La LA2 215 E3
Little Fell Rd LA1, LA2 215 F6
Little Flatt OL12 52 B1
LITTLE HARWOOD 102 B8
Little Hey La L37 12 B4
LITTLE HOOLE MOSS HOUSES 75 B4
Little Hoole Prim Sch PR4 75 A5
LITTLE KNOWLEY 61 F3
Little La
Banks PR9 55 B7
Longridge PR3 140 A7
Southport PR9 54 B1
LITTLE MARSDEN 148 C7
LITTLE MARTON 131 D1
LITTLE MARTON MOSS SIDE 131 B1
Little Meadow La L40 39 D4
LITTLE MOOR 166 E6
Little Moor BB7 166 E6
Littlemoor Cl BB7 146 A8
Little Moor Clough BL7 47 E2

LITTLE MOOR END 103 C3
Littlemoor Ho BB7 146 A7
Littlemoor Rd BB7 166 E7
Little Moor View BB7 166 E6
LITTLE PLUMPTON 112 D5
LITTLE POULTON 153 F4
Little Poulton La FY6 153 F4
Little Queen St BB8 171 C4
LITTLE SCOTLAND 31 B2
Little Scotland BL6 31 B2
LITTLE SINGLETON 154 C4
Little St 4 BB5 104 A6
Little Stones Rd BL7 47 E2
LITTLE THORNTON 153 E7
Little Toms La BB10 148 D3
Littleton Gr WN6 29 E2
Little Tongues La FY6 200 B4
Littleton Manor PR9 55 A5
LITTLE TOWN 141 F3
Little Twining PR4 75 A7
Littlewalk Ct BB5 103 E5
Littlewood FY7 198 E3
Little Wood Cl PR7 42 F6
Littondale Gdns BB2 80 D7
Liverpool Ave PR8 21 D5
Liverpool New Rd PR4 74 F5
Liverpool Old Rd
Much Hoole PR4 74 E3
Sollom PR4 57 B2
Walmer Bridge PR4 74 F5
Liverpool Rd
Bickerstaffe L39 7 C5
Birkdale Hills PR8 21 E6
Blackpool FY1 130 D5
Burnley BB12 127 A6
Formby L37 12 A1
Higher Penwortham PR1 96 B5
Hightown L37 3 A8
Longton PR4 74 F7
Maghull L31 5 D4
Much Hoole PR4 74 D2
Ormskirk L39 15 B2
Preston, Howick Cross PR1, PR4 95 F3
Preston PR1 96 D6
Royal Oak L39 6 F4
Rufford L40 39 C5
Skelmersdale WN8 8 C8
Sollom PR4 57 A3
Southport PR8 35 A3
Liverpool Rd N
Burscough Bridge L40 25 E5
Maghull L31 5 C2
Liverpool Rd S
Burscough L40 25 D2
Maghull L31 5 C1
Livesey Branch Rd BB2 81 B8
LIVESEY FOLD 81 F2
Livesey Fold PR6 80 A1
Livesey Hall Cl BB2 100 E1
Livesey St Francis CE Prim Sch BB2 100 F1
Livesey St
11 Lytham St Anne's FY8 91 A3
Padiham BB12 126 C8
Preston PR1 97 B7
Rishton BB1 124 B2
Livesley's La
Great Altcar L37 12 F2
Haskayne L37 13 A2
Livet Ave FY4 110 D7
Livingstone Rd
Accrington BB5 104 B8
Blackburn BB2 101 B4
Blackpool FY1 130 C4
Livingstone St BB9 148 B5
Livingstone Wlk BB9 148 B6
Lloyd Cl
Lancaster LA1 218 B1
12 Nelson BB9 148 E8
Lloyd's Ave 1 LA4 217 A4
Lloyd St
Darwen BB3 81 F3
Whitworth OL12 71 C1
Lloyd Wlk 11 BB9 148 E8
Lobden Cres OL12 52 D8
Lochinch Cl FY4 111 A6
Locka La
Gressingham LA6 240 F3
Lancaster LA1 218 D4
Locke Ind Est BL6 32 B3
Lockerbie Ave FY5 152 D8
Lockfield Dr BB18 196 C4
Lock Gate BB4 85 C1
Lockhart Rd PR1 117 F2
Lockhurst Ave FY5 152 F8
Lock La PR4 57 B2
Lockside BB2 101 D2
Lockside Rd PR2 95 F8
Lock St 10 BB5 103 E4
Lockwood Ave FY6 153 D4
Lockyer Ave BB12 127 B7
Lodge Bank
Brinscall PR6 62 F7
Horwich BL6 31 F2
Lodge Bank Est BL6 31 F3
Lodge Cl
2 Bamber Bridge PR5 97 F1
Blackpool FY5 152 C7
Freckleton PR4 93 B7
Lodge Ct
Blackpool FY5 152 C7
Inskip PR4 157 B1
Staining FY3 131 D5
Lodge Hill La BL0 51 A8
Lodge La
Bacup OL13 87 F1
Clifton PR4 115 D1
Elswick PR4 156 B1
Farington PR26 76 E6
Lytham St Anne's FY8 91 F5
Melling LA2, LA6 241 D1
Rainford L39, WA11 8 D1
Singleton FY6 154 D2
Lodge Mill La BL0 69 A1
Lodge Pk PR3 181 D3
Lodge Rd
Catterall PR3 182 A1
Orrell WN5 10 E4
Lodges Ct 6 LA4 217 E6
Lodges Gr LA4 217 E6
Lodgeside BB5 124 F3
Lodge St
Accrington BB5 104 C7
Lancaster LA1 214 F8
Preston PR1 96 E8
Ramsbottom BL0 50 C6
Shuttleworth BL0 50 E8
Lodge Terr BB5 103 E5
Lodge The
Great Harwood BB6 124 B5
Lytham St Anne's FY8 90 E7
Lodge View
Farington PR26 76 E7
Longridge PR3 140 A6
Ramsbottom BL0 51 A8
Lodge Wood Cl PR7 43 A6
Lodgings The PR2 118 C5
Lodore Rd FY4 110 C6
Loelands The BL8 49 E3
Lofthouse Way FY7 199 A4
Loftos Ave FY4 110 D8
Logwood St BB1 101 F7
Lois Pl BB2 101 C5
Lomas La BB4 68 F8
Lomax Cl BB6 124 D6
Lomax Sq BB6 124 D5
Lomax St
7 Bury BL9 33 A3
Darwen BB3 82 A2
Great Harwood BB6 124 C5
Ramsbottom BL8 49 F1
Rochdale OL12, OL16 52 F1
LOMESHAYE 148 B8
Lomeshaye Bsns Village BB9 148 C8
Lomeshaye Ind Est BB9 148 B7
Lomeshaye Jun Sch BB9 148 C8
Lomeshaye Pl BB9 148 C8
Lomeshaye Rd BB9 148 D7
Lomeshaye Way BB9 148 C8
Lomond Ave
Blackpool FY3 130 F2
Lytham St Anne's FY8 90 B5
Lomond Cl PR7 60 D4
Lomond Gdns BB2 100 F1
Londonderry Rd LA3 212 E5
London La PR8 22 D8
London Rd
Blackburn BB1 101 E6
Blackpool FY3 130 D6
Preston PR1 97 C6
London Sq 2 PR8 35 B7
London St
Fleetwood FY7 199 B4
Southport PR8, PR9 35 B7
London Terr BB3 82 B2
London Way PR5 97 C3
London Wlk BB1 101 E6
Longacre
Clayton Brook PR5 78 C5
Longton PR4 74 F8
Southport PR9 53 F3
Long Acre Cl LA5 221 C8
Long Acre Pl FY8 91 A4
Long Acres Dr OL12 71 D2
Longacres La OL12 71 D2
Long Barn Brow PR5 99 E2
Long Barn Row PR5 99 E2
Longber La LA6 242 B3
Long Bldg BB7 230 C1
Longbrook Ave PR5 97 E1
Long Butts PR1 96 D2
Long Cl
Clitheroe BB7 190 A2
Leyland PR26 59 A8
Longcliffe Dr PR8 21 C4
Long Copse PR7 60 F1
Long Croft
Barton PR3 137 B8
Longton PR4 95 A1
Longcroft Cotts BL9 50 F1
Long Croft Mdw PR7 61 B2
Long Cswy BB7 231 B2
Long Cswy The BB10 108 D7
Long Dales La
Caton LA6 237 A6
Over Kellet LA6 237 A7
Longfield
Formby L37 12 B5
Fulwood PR2 117 F8
Higher Penwortham PR1 96 B4
Longfield Ave
Coppull PR7 42 E2
Poulton-le-F FY6 153 D4
Longfield Ct BB18 196 B1
Longfield Dr LA5 221 C8
Longfield Manor PR7 43 A5
Longfield Pl FY6 153 D4
Longfield Terr BB10 107 E8
Longfold
Maghull L31 5 E1
Mere Brow PR4 55 F2
Longford Ave FY2 152 E5
Longford Rd PR8 35 A2
Long Gn BB18 197 C2
Longhey WN8 18 C4
Long Hey La BB1, BB3 83 A2
Long Heys La WN8 18 F5
Long Heys or Back La WN8 19 A6
LONGHOLME 86 A2
Longholme Rd 9 BB4 86 A2
Longhouse La FY6 131 D8
LONG ING 196 C2
Long Ing La BB18 196 C2
Long La
Abbeystead LA2 232 F1
Banks PR9 55 B6
Bickerstaffe L39 7 B7
Chorley PR6 44 B4
Formby L37 11 E4
Laneshaw Bridge BB8 172 D7
Low Bentham LA2 239 B7
Maghull L29 4 B1
Oakenclough PR3 226 B1
Ormskirk L39 6 F8
Pleasington BB2 100 B2
Quernmore LA2 232 A5
Skelmersdale WN8 9 E3
Street PR3 226 B5
Tockholes BB3 81 A3
Longlands Ave LA3 212 E8
Longlands Cres LA3 212 F8
Longlands La LA3 212 E7
Longlands Rd LA1 218 C3
Long Lane End LA2 211 E7
Long Level LA6 241 F8
Longley Cl PR2 117 F8
Longley La PR3 160 B2
Long Lover La BB7 192 C8
Long Marsh La LA1 218 B1
Long Mdw
Chorley PR7 43 A5
Colne BB8 172 A5
Kirkham PR4 113 E5
Mellor Brook BB2 121 B2
Much Hoole PR4 74 F4
Longmeadow La
Heysham LA3 213 A7
Thornton FY5 176 C3
Longmeanygate
Leyland, Midge Hall PR26 76 A2
Leyland PR26 76 D2
Long Meanygate
Mere Brow PR9 37 C7
Southport PR9 36 F8
Longmere Cres LA5 221 C8
Longmire Way 10 LA4 217 A5
Longmoor La PR3 180 E6
Long Moss PR26 59 A8
Long Moss La PR4 76 A6
Long Moss Mdws PR4 75 F6
LONGRIDGE 140 A8
Longridge Ave FY4 110 E5
Longridge CE Prim Sch PR3 140 A7
Longridge Community Hospl PR3 140 A7
Longridge Dr OL10 33 F2
Longridge Fell Forest Wlk (E)* BB7 164 F6
Longridge Fell Forest Wlk (W)* PR3 164 A4
Longridge Heath BB9 148 D4
Longridge High Sch PR3 140 A6
Longridge Lo 14 PR2 118 F4
Longridge Rd
Hesketh Lane PR3 162 D6
Hurst Green BB7, PR3 142 D8
Longridge PR3 162 B3
Red Scar PR2 119 B6
Longridge St Wilfrid's RC Prim Sch PR3 140 A8
Long Row
Blackburn BB2 122 B2
Calder Vale PR3 182 E8
Longroyd Rd BB18 197 B1
Longsands Com Prim Sch PR2 118 D5
Longsands La PR2 118 E6
LONGSHAW
Blackburn 101 D1
Orrell 10 E1
Longshaw Ave WN5 10 E1
Longshaw Cl
Longshaw WN5 10 E1
Rufford L40 39 A5
Longshaw Com Jun Sch BB2 101 E1
Longshaw Comm WN5 10 E1
Longshaw Inf Sch BB2 81 E8
Longshaw La BB2 101 D2
Longshaw Old Rd WN5 10 E1
Longshaw St BB2 101 D1
LONGSHOOT 85 C3
Longsight Ave
Accrington, Hillock Vale BB5 104 E8
Clitheroe BB7 189 F1
Longsight Rd
Langho BB6 143 B2
Osbaldeston BB1, BB2 121 E4
Ramsbottom BL0 50 A2
Longstock Hall Moor Hey Sch PR5 97 A1
LONGTON 75 A8
Longton Ave FY5 176 B2
Longton Brickcroft Nature Reserve* PR4 74 F6
Longton Brickcroft Visitor Ctr* PR4 74 F7
Longton Bsns Pk PR4 74 E4
Longton By-Pass PR4 75 C6
Longton Cl BB1 102 C5
Longton Ct PR8 21 C5
Longton Dr
Formby L37 12 A6
Morecambe LA4 217 E4
Longton Prim Sch PR4 75 A8
Longton Rd
Blackpool FY1 130 C5
Burnley BB12 127 E8
Longton's Cotts LA6 240 B1
Longtons La BD23 236 B3
Longton St
Blackburn BB1 102 C5
Chorley PR6 43 E8
Longway FY4 110 F8
Long Wham La PR4 75 D1
Longwood Cl FY8 90 E4
Longworth Ave
Blackrod BL6 31 C3
Burnley BB10 128 D6
Coppull PR7 42 F2
Longworth Clough BL7 47 D2
Longworth La BL7 47 C2
Longworth Rd
Billington BB7 144 B4
Bolton BL7 47 B3
Horwich BL6 32 C4
Longworth Rd N BL7 46 D5
Longworth St
5 Bamber Bridge PR5 97 E2
Chorley PR7 43 B6
Preston PR1 118 C1
Lonmore PR5 97 D3
Lonmore Cl PR9 55 A5
Lonsdale Ave
Fleetwood FY7 198 E3
Morecambe LA4 217 E4
Ormskirk L39 15 F7
Lonsdale Cl PR25 60 A6
Lonsdale Cres 3 FY7 198 E3
Lonsdale Dr PR26 58 B3
Lonsdale Gdns 4 BB9 170 D3
Lonsdale Gr LA4 217 E4
Lonsdale Mews 5 PR5 77 A8
Lonsdale Pl LA1 215 A5
Lonsdale Rd
Blackpool FY1 130 B2
Formby L37 11 F3
Hest Bank LA2 220 D1
Morecambe LA4 217 E4
Preston PR1 118 C1
Southport PR8 35 D4
Lonsdale South Ave LA1 211 A6
Lonsdale St
Accrington BB5 103 F5
Burnley BB12 127 C7
Nelson BB9 170 F1
Lord Ave OL13 87 C1
Lord St W
12 Blackburn BB2 101 E5
Southport PR8 35 A6
Lord's Ave PR5 77 B7
Lord's Close Rd LA2 239 E2
Lord's Cres BB3 82 A6
Lords Croft PR6 78 A2
Lord Sefton Way L37 12 E2
Lordsgate Dr L40 25 E3
Lordsgate La L40 25 C2
Lord's La
Kingsfold PR1 96 E1
Longridge PR3 162 B2
Lord's Lot Rd
Capernwray LA6 240 D1
Over Kellet LA6 240 C1
Lordsome Rd LA3 216 E2
Lord Sq BB1 101 E5
Lord St
Accrington BB5 104 B6
Bacup OL13 87 F2
Blackburn BB2 101 E5
Blackpool FY1 130 B6
Brierfield BB9 148 B5
Burscough Bridge L40 25 E5
Bury BL9 33 A2
Bury, Heap Bridge BL9 33 C1
Chorley PR6 43 D7
Clayton Green PR6 78 C1
Colne BB8 171 C5
Darwen BB3 82 A2
Eccleston PR7 41 C5
Fleetwood FY7 199 B4
Great Harwood BB6 124 C4
Horwich BL6 32 B4
Lancaster LA1 218 D1
Lytham St Anne's FY8 89 E7
Morecambe LA4 217 B6
Oswaldtwistle BB5 103 E4
Preston PR1 97 A8
Rawtenstall BB4 86 A2
Rawtenstall, Crawshawbooth BB4 86 A7
Rishton BB1 124 B1
Southport PR8, PR9 35 B7
Lord Street Mall 10 BB1 101 E5
Lord Street Prim Sch BL6 32 B4
Lord's Wlk PR1 97 A8
Lords Wood Cl PR7 43 A6
Lorne Rd FY2 152 D2
Lorne St
Chorley PR7 43 C7
Darwen BB3 81 F2
Lytham St Anne's FY8 91 D4
Lorne Way OL10 33 F1
Lorraine Ave PR2 117 E3
Lorton Cl
Burnley BB12 127 B8
Fulwood PR2 117 F6
Lostock Gdns FY4 110 E6
LOSTOCK HALL 77 B7
Lostock Hall Com High Sch & Art Coll PR5 97 C1
Lostock Hall Com Prim Sch PR5 97 B1
Lostock Hall Com Prim Sch Avondale Unit PR5 77 B8
Lostock Hall Sta PR5 77 B8
Lostock La PR5 77 D7
Lostock Mdw PR6 78 A1
Lostock Rd PR26 58 C3
Lostock Sq PR5 77 B7
Lostock View PR5 77 B7
Lothersdale Cl BB10 148 D3
Lothian Ave FY7 198 D3
Lothian Pl FY2 152 E5
Lottice La BB5, BB1 103 A1
Lotus Dr FY4 112 A6
Loud Bridge Back La PR3 161 D8
Loud Bridge Rd PR3 161 D7
Loughlin Dr L33 1 A5
Loughrigg Cl BB12 127 B7
Loughrigg Terr FY4 131 C1
Louie Pollard Cres BB6 124 D6
Louise St FY1 130 B3
Louis St BL0 68 D5
Louis William St BB1 82 D8
Loupsfell Dr LA4 217 C4
Lourdes Ave PR5 97 A1
Louvain St BB18 196 A3
Lovat Rd PR1 117 F2
LOVE CLOUGH 106 A3
Loveclough Pk BB4 106 A3
Love Clough Rd BB4 105 F2
Love La BL0 68 E1
Lovely Hall La BB1 122 D7
Low Bank BB12 126 E6
LOW BENTHAM 239 C8
Low Bentham Com Prim Sch LA2 239 B8
Low Bentham Rd LA2 239 C8
Lowcroft
High Bentham LA2 239 E8
Skelmersdale WN8 18 C3
Low Croft PR3 137 B2
Lowcross Rd FY6 153 E2
Lower Alt Rd L38 2 F4
Lower Antley St BB5 103 F5
Lower Ashworth Cl BB2 101 C4
Lower Audley Ind Est BB2 101 F3
Lower Audley St BB1, BB2 101 F4
LOWER BALLAM 112 A3
Lower Bank Rd PR2 117 F3
Lower Bank St PR6 80 A1
Lower Barnes St BB5 124 E4
Lower Barn St BB3 65 C7
LOWER BARTLE 116 D8
LOWER BAXENDEN 104 F1
LOWER BOARSGREAVE 70 A6
Lowerbrook Cl BL6 32 D1
Lower Burgh Rd PR7 43 A4
Lower Burgh Way PR7 43 B4
Lower Carr La L37 4 B7
Lower Chapel La BB7 190 B8
LOWER CLOUGHFOLD 86 C2
Lower Clough Fold BB9 170 C2
Lower Clough St BB9 170 D2
Lower Clowes BB4 68 E8
Lower Clowes Rd BB4 68 E8
Lower Cockcroft 13 BB2 101 E5
LOWER COPTHURST 61 E7
Lower Copthurst La PR6 61 E7
Lower Cribden Ave BB4 85 D2
Lower Croft 1 PR1 96 D2
Lower Croft St 3 BB18 197 B2
Lower Cross St 27 BB3 82 A1
LOWER DARWEN 81 F7
Lower Darwen Prim Sch BB3 82 A6
Lower Dolphinholme LA2 226 A8
Lower East Ave BB18 196 B3
Lower Eccleshill Rd BB3 82 A5
Lowerfield BB6 123 C8
Lower Field PR26 76 F6
Lowerfields BB12 126 F6
Lowerfold BB6 124 C6
LOWER FOLD
Accrington 104 C6
Great Harwood 124 C6
Rochdale 52 C3
Lowerfold Cl OL12 52 C4
Lowerfold Cres OL12 52 C4
Lowerfold Dr OL12 52 C4
Lowerfold Rd BB6 124 C6

Lowerfold Way OL12 . . . . . . 52 C4
LOWERFORD 170 E3
Lowergate BB7 . . . . 166 E8
Lower Gate Rd BB5 . . . . . . 125 F2
Lower Gn
Poulton-le-F FY6 . . . . 153 E3
3 Rochdale OL12 . . . . 52 C1
LOWER GREEN BANK 232 B1
Lower Greenfield PR2 . . . . 117 B5
Lower Hazel Cl BB2 . . . . . 101 C4
LOWER HEALEY 52 E4
Lower Hey PR4 . . . . 95 A1
LOWER HEYSHAM 212 E8
Lower Hill BB3 . . . . 80 F2
Lower Hill Dr PR6 . . . . 44 A1
Lower Hollin Bank St
BB2 . . . . 101 D2
LOWERHOUSE 126 F6
LOWER HOUSE 59 D8
Lowerhouse Cres
BB12 . . . . 127 A6
Lowerhouse Fold
BB12 . . . . 127 A6
Lower House Gn BB4 . . . . . 87 A8
Lowerhouse Jun Sch
BB12 . . . . 127 A6
Lowerhouse La
Burnley, Rose Grove
BB12 . . . . 127 B6
Padiham BB12 . . . . 126 F6
Lower House Rd PR26 . . . . 59 D8
Lower La
Freckleton PR4 . . . . 93 D7
Haslingden BB4 . . . . 85 B4
Kirkham PR4 . . . . 114 C1
Longridge PR3 . . . . 140 B7
Lower Laithe Cotts
BB9 . . . . 170 C2
Lower Laithe Dr BB9 . . . . 170 C3
Lower Lee LA2 . . . . 232 F2
Lower Lune St 7 FY7 . . . . 199 B5
Lower Makinson Fold 1
BL6 . . . . 32 D1
Lower Manor La BB12 . . . . 147 F2
Lower Mdw BL7 . . . . 48 D6
Lower Mead BL7 . . . . 47 F1
Lower Mead Dr BB12 . . . . 147 F2
Lower North Ave BB18 . . . 196 B2
Lower Park St BB18 . . . . . 196 C2
Lower Parrock Rd
BB9 . . . . 170 C1
LOWER
PENWORTHAM 96 E5
Lower Philips Rd BB1 . . . 102 C8
Lower Prom PR9 . . . . 35 B8
Lower Rd
Longridge PR3 . . . . 140 E7
Shuttleworth BL0 . . . . 50 E8
Lower Ridge Cl BB10 . . . . 128 B6
Lower Rook St BB18 . . . . 196 C2
Lower Rosegrove La
BB12 . . . . 127 A5
Lower School St 6
BB8 . . . . 171 D4
LOWER SUMMERSEAT 50 C1
Lower Tentre BB11 . . . . . . 128 B5
LOWER THURNHAM 210 B2
Lower Timber Hill La
BB11 . . . . 128 A2
Lower West Ave BB18 . . . . 196 B2
LOWER WESTHOUSE . . . 242 D4
Lower Wilworth BB1 . . . . . 122 E1
Lower Wlk FY2 . . . . 152 C7
Lowesby Cl PR5 . . . . 97 E3
Lowes Ct
3 Blackpool FY1 . . . . 130 B1
5 Thornton FY5 . . . . 176 B3
Lowes Gn L37 . . . . 12 B3
Lowe's La WN8 . . . . 17 F8
Lowes Rd BL9 . . . . 33 A6
Loweswater Cl BB5 . . . . . . 104 F8
Loweswater Cres
BB12 . . . . 127 B8
Loweswater Dr 5 LA4 . . 217 D4
Lowesway
Blackpool FY4 . . . . 110 F8
6 Thornton FY5 . . . . 176 B3
Lowe View BB4 . . . . 87 A1
Lowfield Cl PR4 . . . . 114 F2
Lowfield Rd FY4 . . . . 110 F7
Low Fold BB18 . . . . 195 A6
LOWGILL 239 C3
Lowgill La LA2 . . . . 239 C3
Low Gn PR25 . . . . 76 F1
Low Hill BB3 . . . . 65 A6
Lowick Cl PR5 . . . . 98 E4
Lowick Dr FY6 . . . . 153 D1
Low La
Leck LA6 . . . . 242 B7
Morecambe LA4 . . . . 217 F5
Lowlands Rd
Bolton-le-S LA5 . . . . 221 A5
Morecambe LA4 . . . . 217 C4
Lowland Way FY2 . . . . 152 F6
Low Mill LA2 . . . . 237 B3
LOW MOOR 166 C8
Low Moor La BB18 . . . . . . 196 B1
Low Moor Rd FY2 . . . . 152 E3
Lowndes St PR1 . . . . 117 E2
Lowood Gr PR2 . . . . 116 D1
Lowood Lo 7 FY8 . . . . 91 A3
Lowood Pl BB2 . . . . 101 A6
Low Rd
Halton LA2 . . . . 237 A4
Middleton LA3 . . . . 213 A2
Lowrey Terr FY1 . . . . 130 B2
Lowry Cl PR5 . . . . 77 A7
Lowry Hill La L40 . . . . 26 B2
Low St LA6 . . . . 242 C3
Lowstead Pl FY4 . . . . 110 E6
Lowstern Cl BL7 . . . . 47 E1
Lowther Ave
Blackpool FY2 . . . . 152 B2
Maghull L31 . . . . 5 F2
Morecambe LA3 . . . . 217 E3
Lowther Cres PR26 . . . . 76 D2
Lowther Ct
Blackpool FY2 . . . . 152 B2
5 Lytham St Anne's FY8 . . . 91 A3
Lowther Dr PR26 . . . . 76 D3
Lowther La BB8 . . . . 194 D1
Lowther Pl BB1 . . . . 102 A8
Lowther Rd
Fleetwood FY7 . . . . 198 F4
Lancaster LA1 . . . . 218 F1
Lowther St
Colne BB8 . . . . 171 E6
Nelson BB9 . . . . 148 C8
Preston PR2 . . . . 117 C1
Lowther Terr
Appley Bridge WN6 . . . . 19 C8
Lytham St Anne's FY8 . . . . . 91 A3
Lowthian St 25 PR1 . . . . 96 F8
Lowthorpe Cres PR1 . . . . . 118 B2
Lowthorpe Pl PR1 . . . . 118 B2
Lowthorpe Rd PR1 . . . . . . 118 B2
Lowthwaite Dr BB9 . . . . . . 148 E6
Lowton Rd FY8 . . . . 90 A8
Loxham Gdns FY4 . . . . 110 D6
Loxley Gdns BB12 . . . . . . 126 F6
Loxley Gn PR2 . . . . 118 C6
Loxley Pl FY5 . . . . 152 E7
Loxley Pl E FY5 . . . . 152 F7
Loxley Rd PR8 . . . . 35 D4
Loxwood Cl PR5 . . . . 97 A3
Loynd St
11 Great Harwood
BB6 . . . . 124 C5
Ramsbottom BL0 . . . . 50 D6
Loyne Pk LA6 . . . . 241 D7
Loyne Sch The LA1 . . . . . . 218 B2
Lubbock St BB12 . . . . 127 C6
Lucas Ave PR7 . . . . 42 D8
LUCAS GREEN 61 C6
Lucas La E PR6 . . . . 61 C6
Lucas La W PR6 . . . . 61 C5
Lucas St BL9 . . . . 33 A3
Lucerne Cl PR2 . . . . 118 C4
Lucerne Rd PR2 . . . . 118 C4
Lucy St
Barrowford BB9 . . . . 170 D3
Lancaster LA1 . . . . 214 F8
8 Morecambe LA4 . . . . 217 B6
Ludlow WN8 . . . . 18 C4
Ludlow Dr L39 . . . . 15 D7
Ludlow Gr FY2 . . . . 152 F2
Ludlow St WN6 . . . . 29 D3
Luke St 18 OL13 . . . . 70 C8
Lulworth WN8 . . . . 18 C4
Lulworth Ave
Blackpool FY3 . . . . 131 A3
Preston PR2 . . . . 117 D2
Lulworth Lo PR8 . . . . 34 F5
Lulworth Pl PR5 . . . . 97 D2
Lulworth Rd
Fulwood PR2 . . . . 118 A4
Southport PR8 . . . . 34 F5
LUMB
Haslingden 68 B4
Rawtenstall 86 F6
Lumb Carr Ave BL0, BL8 . . . 50 A4
Lumb Carr Rd BL0, BL8 . . . 50 A4
Lumb Cotts BL0 . . . . 68 B4
Lumb Flats BL0 . . . . 68 B4
Lumb Holes La BB4 . . . . . . 69 E7
Lumb La BB4 . . . . 86 F4
Lumb Scar 9 OL13 . . . . 87 F2
Lunds Cl L40 . . . . 16 E4
Lunds La PR4 . . . . 74 D1
Lund St
Blackburn BB2 . . . . 101 C4
2 Preston PR1 . . . . 97 A8
Lune Ave L31 . . . . 5 E2
Lune Cl PR4 . . . . 114 C5
Lunedale Ave FY1 . . . . 130 C1
Lune Dr
Clayton-le-W PR25 . . . . 77 E2
Morecambe LA3 . . . . 217 F3
Lune Gr FY1 . . . . 130 C3
Lune Ho
Lancaster, Abraham Heights
LA1 . . . . 214 F7
5 Lancaster LA1 . . . . 218 D1
Lune Ind Est LA1 . . . . 214 C8
Lune Rd
Fleetwood FY7 . . . . 198 F4
Lancaster LA1 . . . . 218 B1
Lunesdale Cl FY8 . . . . 90 C7
Lunesdale Ct
Butt Yeats LA2 . . . . 238 B6
Lancaster LA1 . . . . 218 F1
Lunesdale Dr PR3 . . . . 207 B3
Lunesdale Rd 2 PR4 . . . . 114 A5
Lunesdale Terr LA2 . . . . . 237 E4
Lunesdale View LA2 . . . . . 219 D7
Luneside LA1 . . . . 214 C8
Lune Sq LA1 . . . . 218 D1
Lune St
Colne BB8 . . . . 171 E4
Lancaster LA1 . . . . 218 D1
Longridge PR3 . . . . 140 B8
Padiham BB12 . . . . 126 D8
Preston PR1 . . . . 96 F7
Lune Terr LA1 . . . . 218 D1
Lune Valley LA1 . . . . 218 F4
Lune View FY6 . . . . 199 E6
Lune View Cvn Pk LA2 . . 219 C6
Lune View Pk LA2 . . . . . . 219 C6
Lunt Rd L29 . . . . 4 C1
Lupin Cl
Accrington BB5 . . . . 104 A7
Lucas Green PR6 . . . . 61 B5
Lupin Rd BB5 . . . . 104 B7
Lupton Dr BB9 . . . . 170 D4
Lupton Pl LA1 . . . . 218 B3
Lupton St PR7 . . . . 43 C6
Lutner St BB11 . . . . 128 A5
Luton Rd
Cleveleys FY5 . . . . 175 E1
Preston PR2 . . . . 116 F2
Lutwidge Ave PR1 . . . . . . 118 C1
Lyceum Ave 3 FY3 . . . . . . 130 D4
Lychfield Dr PR5 . . . . 77 E7
Lychgate 24 PR1 . . . . 97 A8
Lyddesdale Ave FY5 . . . . . 152 D8
Lydd Gr PR7 . . . . 43 A7
Lydgate
Burnley BB10 . . . . 148 E2
Chorley PR7 . . . . 43 A5
Lydia St BB5 . . . . 104 B4
LYDIATE 5 D4
Lydiate La
Bilsborrow PR3 . . . . 159 C6
Leyland PR25 . . . . 77 C4
Ulnes Walton PR7 . . . . 59 B1
Lydiate Lane End PR7 . . . . . 59 B2
Lydiate Prim Sch L31 . . . . . 5 C4
Lydiate Station Rd L31 . . . . 4 E5
Lydric Ave PR5 . . . . 98 E2
Lyelake La L40 . . . . 16 F2
Lymbridge Dr BL6 . . . . 31 D1
Lyme Gr FY6 . . . . 199 E5
Lymm Ave LA1 . . . . 218 A3
Lynbridge Cl WN5 . . . . 10 E5
Lyncroft Cres FY3 . . . . 130 E7
Lyndale WN8 . . . . 18 B4
Lyndale Ave
Bamber Bridge PR5 . . . . 97 C2
Haslingden BB4 . . . . 85 B2
Wilpshire BB1 . . . . 123 A7
Lyndale Cl
Leyland PR25 . . . . 60 B6
Rawtenstall BB4 . . . . 86 A7
Wilpshire BB1 . . . . 123 A7
Lyndale Ct FY7 . . . . 199 B5
Lyndale Gr PR5 . . . . 97 C2
Lyndale Rd BB11 . . . . 126 C3
Lyndale Res Cvn Pk
FY4 . . . . 111 F6
Lyndale Terr BB7 . . . . 231 B3
Lynden Ave LA4 . . . . 217 E5
Lyndeth Cl PR2 . . . . 118 E6
Lyndhurst
Maghull L31 . . . . 5 D1
Skelmersdale WN8 . . . . 18 B4
Lyndhurst Ave
Blackburn BB1 . . . . 102 E5
Blackpool FY4 . . . . 130 D1
Lyndhurst Dr PR2 . . . . 116 E2
Lyndhurst Gr BB6 . . . . 124 E6
Lyndhurst Rd
Blackburn BB2 . . . . 101 E2
Burnley BB10 . . . . 128 C5
Darwen BB3 . . . . 81 F3
Southport PR8 . . . . 35 B2
Lyndon Ave BB6 . . . . 124 E6
Lyndon Ct BB6 . . . . 124 E6
Lyndon Ho BB6 . . . . 124 E6
Lynfield Rd BB6 . . . . 124 E6
Lynn Gr 6 FY1 . . . . 130 B7
Lynn Pl PR2 . . . . 118 D2
Lynslack Terr LA5 . . . . 224 B8
Lynthorpe Rd
Blackburn BB2 . . . . 101 E2
Nelson BB9 . . . . 171 A1
Lynton Ave
Blackpool FY4 . . . . 110 D8
Leyland PR25 . . . . 60 C8
Lynton Ct FY7 . . . . 175 C8
Lynton Dr PR8 . . . . 34 E1
Lynton Rd
Accrington BB5 . . . . 103 F4
Southport PR8 . . . . 34 E1
Lynwood Ave
Blackpool FY3 . . . . 130 E8
Clayton-le-M BB5 . . . . 124 F4
Darwen BB3 . . . . 81 E4
Grimsargh PR2 . . . . 139 C2
Ormskirk L39 . . . . 15 C3
Lynwood Cl
Clayton-le-M BB5 . . . . 124 F4
Colne BB8 . . . . 171 D7
Darwen BB3 . . . . 81 E3
Skelmersdale WN8 . . . . 9 D7
Whalley BB7 . . . . 144 A7
Lynwood Dr FY6 . . . . 177 C7
Lynwood End L39 . . . . 15 C3
Lynwood Pk PR4 . . . . 92 F6
Lynwood Rd
Blackburn BB2 . . . . 101 B6
Huncoat BB5 . . . . 125 E2
Lyons La PR6 . . . . 43 D7
Lyons La S PR7 . . . . 43 D7
Lyons Rd PR8 . . . . 35 A5
Lystra Ct FY8 . . . . 89 F5
Lythall Ave FY8 . . . . 91 D4
LYTHAM 91 B3
Lytham CE Prim Sch
FY8 . . . . 91 B4
Lytham Cl
Fulwood PR2 . . . . 117 D3
Lancaster LA1 . . . . 215 C7
Lytham Ct PR7 . . . . 60 D4
Lytham Hall* FY8 . . . . 90 F4
Lytham Hall Park Prim Sch
FY8 . . . . 90 F3
Lytham Heritage Ctr*
FY8 . . . . 91 B3
Lytham Rd
Blackburn BB2 . . . . 101 F1
Blackpool FY1, FY4 . . . . . . 110 C6
Burnley BB10 . . . . 148 C2
Freckleton PR4 . . . . 93 B6
Fulwood PR2 . . . . 117 D3
Moss Side FY8 . . . . 112 E1
Southport PR9 . . . . 54 A4
Warton FY8, PR4 . . . . 92 D5
LYTHAM ST ANNE'S 90 B5
Lytham St Anne's High
Tech Coll FY8 . . . . 90 C5
Lytham St Anne's Local
Nature Reserve*
FY8 . . . . 110 B1
Lytham St Annes Way
FY8 . . . . 90 D7
Lytham St
Chorley PR6 . . . . 43 E7
Rochdale OL12 . . . . 52 E3
Lytham Sta FY8 . . . . 91 A3
Lytham Windmill (Mus)*
FY8 . . . . 91 C2
Lythcoe Ave PR2 . . . . 117 C4
Lythe Fell Ave LA2 . . . . . 219 D7
Lythe Fell Rd LA2 . . . . . . 234 F8
Lythe La LA2 . . . . 239 E2
Lyth Rd LA1 . . . . 218 F2
Lytles Cl L37 . . . . 12 A2
Lytton St BB12 . . . . 126 F7

M

Maaruig Cvn Pk FY6 . . . . 200 A6
Mabel Ct FY4 . . . . 110 B8
Mabel St
Colne BB8 . . . . 171 F5
2 Rochdale OL12 . . . . 52 D2
Maberry Cl WN6 . . . . 19 D7
MacAuley Ave FY4 . . . . . . 110 F8
MacAuley St BB11 . . . . . . 127 C5
Macbeth Rd FY7 . . . . 198 E4
McCall Cl PR4 . . . . 113 A3
McDonald Rd LA3 . . . . 212 D5
Mackay Croft 4 PR6 . . . . . . 43 D8
McKenzie St PR5 . . . . 77 F8
Mackenzie Cl 5 PR6 . . . . . . 43 D8
MacLaren Cl FY3 . . . . 131 D5
MacLeod St BB9 . . . . 148 D8
Maddy St 2 PR1 . . . . 96 D8
Madeley Gdns OL12 . . . . . . 52 C1
Maden Rd OL13 . . . . 87 F2
Maden St BB5 . . . . 103 E6
Maden Way OL13 . . . . 87 F2
Madison Ave
Blackpool FY2 . . . . 152 B5
Hest Bank LA5 . . . . 220 E2
Madison Ctr The BB4 . . . . . 68 B8
Madison Hts FY8 . . . . 90 D7
Madryn Ave L33 . . . . 1 A2
Maesbrook Cl PR9 . . . . 55 B5
Mafeking Ave BL9 . . . . 33 A5
Mafeking Rd PR2 . . . . 117 C2
Magdalen Ave FY5 . . . . . . 175 D1
Maggots Nook Rd WA11 . . . . 9 A1
MAGHULL 5 B1
Maghull La L31 . . . . 6 B1
Maghull Smallholdings Est
L31 . . . . 5 F3
Magnolia Cl PR2 . . . . 118 C6
Magnolia Dr PR25 . . . . 77 E2
Magnolia Rd PR1 . . . . 96 B3
Magpie Cl BB11 . . . . 127 C5
Maharishi School of the
Age of Enlightenment
L40 . . . . 18 A5
Maida Vale FY5 . . . . 152 D8
Maiden Cl
Rawtenstall BB4 . . . . 69 F8
Skelmersdale WN8 . . . . 17 C2
Maiden St BB4 . . . . 85 B6
Main Ave LA3 . . . . 212 F3
Main Cl LA3 . . . . 209 D8
Main Dr
Cold Row FY6 . . . . 177 D4
Poulton-le-F FY6 . . . . 153 E2
Main Rd
Bolton-le-S LA5 . . . . 221 B5
Galgate LA2 . . . . 211 A3
Hest Bank LA2 . . . . 220 F1
Nether Kellet LA6 . . . . 221 F5
Mains La
Bispham Green L40 . . . . 27 A6
Poulton-le-F FY6 . . . . 154 B4
Main Sprit Weind PR1 . . . . 97 A7
Main Sq PR7 . . . . 60 E6
Main St
Bolton-by-B BB7 . . . . 230 D4
Buckshaw Village PR7 . . . . . 60 E6
Burton-in-K LA6 . . . . 240 B7
Cockerham LA2 . . . . 206 D4
Downham BB7 . . . . 191 B5
Gisburn BB7 . . . . 231 C3
Grindleton BB7 . . . . 190 B8
Heysham LA3 . . . . 212 E8
High Bentham LA2 . . . . 239 D8
Hornby LA2 . . . . 238 B7
Kelbrook BB18 . . . . 195 A6
Lancaster LA1 . . . . 218 D2
Low Bentham LA2 . . . . 239 B8
Overton LA3 . . . . 209 D8
Rathmell BD24 . . . . 236 F6
Warton LA5 . . . . 223 D5
Main St continued
Whittington LA6 . . . . 241 D7
Wray LA2 . . . . 238 D6
Mainway LA1 . . . . 218 D2
Mairscough La L39 . . . . 14 B1
Maitland Ave FY5 . . . . 175 D1
Maitland Cl 5 PR1 . . . . 97 C8
Maitland Pl BB4 . . . . 86 A1
Maitland St
18 Bacup OL13 . . . . 87 F2
4 Preston PR1 . . . . 97 C8
1 Preston PR1 . . . . 97 D8
Majestic Bldgs 24
BB18 . . . . 196 B2
Majestic Mews WN5 . . . . . . 10 D5
Major Bottoms PR6 . . . . 44 D1
Major St
Accrington BB5 . . . . 104 B4
Ramsbottom BL0 . . . . 50 B6
Rawtenstall BB4 . . . . 86 A7
Makinson Ave BL6 . . . . 32 E1
Makinson La BL6 . . . . 32 F4
Makinsons Row 11
LA2 . . . . 211 A4
Malcolm Pl FY7 . . . . 198 E4
Malcolm St PR1 . . . . 118 D1
Malden St PR25 . . . . 77 A1
Maldern Ave FY6 . . . . 153 C5
Maldon Pl PR2 . . . . 118 D2
Malham Ave
5 Accrington BB5 . . . . 103 F4
Blackpool FY4 . . . . 110 D8
Malham Cl
Lancaster LA1 . . . . 218 B3
Southport PR8 . . . . 35 E3
Malham Gdns BB1 . . . . 101 F3
Malham Pl PR2 . . . . 118 E4
Malham Rd BB10 . . . . 148 D3
Malham View Cl BB18 . . . 196 A1
Malham View Ct BB18 . . . 196 B1
Malham Wend BB9 . . . . . . 170 C3
Malkin Cl BB9 . . . . 170 E8
Malkin La BB7 . . . . 165 F6
Mallard Ave FY6 . . . . 200 B4
Mallard Cl
Heysham LA3 . . . . 212 F5
Leyland PR25 . . . . 59 D8
Ormskirk L39 . . . . 15 C2
Thornton FY5 . . . . 176 A4
Mallard Ct
Blackpool FY3 . . . . 131 B6
Lancaster LA1 . . . . 214 E8
Mallard Dr BL6 . . . . 32 A3
Mallard Ho L31 . . . . 5 B4
Mallard Pl BB5 . . . . 103 D3
Mallards The PR9 . . . . 54 C3
Mallards Wlk PR5 . . . . 78 A5
Mallee Ave PR9 . . . . 54 A3
Mallee Cres PR9 . . . . 54 A3
Malley La PR4 . . . . 136 C8
Mallom Ave PR7 . . . . 60 E1
Mallory Ave L31 . . . . 5 B4
Mallowdale FY5 . . . . 176 A4
Mallow Dale PR2 . . . . 117 B6
Mallowdale Ave LA3 . . . . . 213 A8
Mallowdale Rd LA1 . . . . . . 218 B2
Mallow Wlk LA3 . . . . 217 B2
Mall The
Burnley BB11 . . . . 128 A6
Fulwood PR2 . . . . 118 E2
Lytham St Anne's FY8 . . . . . 90 C7
Maltby Pl 2 FY4 . . . . 130 F2
Malthouse Bsns Pk The
L39 . . . . 15 E6
Malthouse Ct
Ormskirk L39 . . . . 15 E6
3 Preston PR2 . . . . 117 D1
Malthouse The 4
PR2 . . . . 117 D1
Malthouse Way PR1 . . . . . . 96 D3
Maltings The
Longton PR4 . . . . 74 F8
Middleforth Green PR1 . . . . 96 D4
Thornton FY5 . . . . 176 A4
Whittington LA6 . . . . 241 D7
Malt Kiln Brow PR3 . . . . . 185 E4
Malt Kiln Gr PR3 . . . . 156 A5
Maltkiln La
Bispham Green L40,
WN8 . . . . 27 C7
Ormskirk L39 . . . . 6 E8
Malton Dr PR5 . . . . 77 A7
Malt St BB5 . . . . 104 B7
Malvern Ave
Blackburn BB2 . . . . 101 D1
Blackpool FY1 . . . . 130 D2
Lancaster LA1 . . . . 215 A6
Oswaldtwistle BB5 . . . . 103 E3
Padiham BB12 . . . . 126 D6
Preston PR1 . . . . 97 B6
Stalmine FY6 . . . . 177 C7
Malvern Cl
6 Accrington BB5 . . . . 104 A7
Bamber Bridge PR5 . . . . 77 C8
Horwich BL6 . . . . 32 C5
Malvern Ct 6 BB9 . . . . 148 F8
Malvern Rd
Lytham St Anne's FY8 . . . . . 90 D5
Nelson BB9 . . . . 171 A1
Preston PR1 . . . . 97 B6
Malvern St
Preston PR1 . . . . 97 B5
Standish WN6 . . . . 29 D3
Malvern Way BB4 . . . . 68 A7
Manby Cl PR5 . . . . 98 E3

Manchester Mill Ind Est
PR1 97 C8
Manchester Rd
Accrington BB5 104 D3
Barnoldswick BB18 196 B1
Blackpool FY3 130 D6
Blackrod BL6 31 E1
Burnley BB11 127 E3
Clow Bridge BB11 106 D6
Hapton BB11, BB12 126 C4
Haslingden, Ewood Bridge BB4 68 D7
Haslingden, Lane Side BB4 85 B2
Nelson BB9 148 D7
Preston PR1 97 B7
Ramsbottom BL0, BL9 50 E4
Southport PR9 35 C7
Mancknols St BB9 149 A7
Mancknols Walton Cottage Homes BB9 149 B8
Mandela Ct BB1 101 E6
Mandeville Rd PR8 21 B5
Mandeville Terr BL8 49 B2
Manfield WN8 18 A3
Manion Ave L31 5 B5
Manion Cl L31 5 B5
Manitoba Cl BB2 101 B8
Manley Cl BL9 50 C2
Manner Sutton St BB1 101 F5
Manning Rd
4 Preston PR1 118 E1
Southport PR8 35 E6
Mannin Way LA1 219 A4
Manor Ave
Burscough L40 25 D2
Fulwood PR2 118 B4
Higher Penwortham PR1 96 B4
Ribchester PR3 141 D3
Slyne LA2 218 C8
Manor Brook 1 BB5 104 C6
Manor Cl
Burton in L LA6 242 C3
Coupe Green PR5 98 F3
Slyne LA2 218 C8
Manor Complex L33 1 B2
Manor Cres
Burscough L40 25 D2
Slyne LA2 218 D8
Manorcroft PR4 74 F8
Manor Ct
11 Blackpool FY1 130 C7
3 Blackpool, Hawes Side FY4 130 E1
Caton LA2 237 D4
Fulwood PR2 117 B7
Manor Ctyd LA3 212 E8
Manor Dr
Burscough L40 25 D2
Cleveleys FY5 175 D3
Kirkham PR4 114 C4
Slyne LA2 218 C8
Manor Farm LA6 241 D7
Manor Fields BB7 144 C5
Manor Gdns L40 25 D2
Manor Gr
Higher Penwortham PR1 96 A4
Morecambe LA3 216 F2
Skelmersdale WN8 17 F1
Manor House Cl
Leyland PR26 59 B8
Maghull L31 5 C1
Manor House Cotts BB3 65 E8
Manor House Cres PR1 118 B3
Manor House Dr WN8 9 E3
Manor House La PR1 118 C3
Manor House Park Flats FY5 175 C3
Manor La
Hest Bank LA2 220 F1
Higher Penwortham PR1 96 B4
Manor Lo L37 11 E4
Manor Mews FY6 153 E4
Manor Pk PR2 118 C4
Manor Pl BB5 103 F7
Manor Rd
Blackburn BB2 101 B5
Blackpool FY1 130 D4
Burnley BB12 127 B7
Burscough L40 25 D2
Clayton Green PR6 78 B3
Clitheroe BB7 166 D7
Colne BB8 171 E7
Darwen BB3 64 F8
Fleetwood FY7 198 E4
Garstang PR3 204 C1
Horwich BL6 32 D4
Inskip PR4 135 C8
Shevington WN6 19 F6
Slyne LA2 218 D8
Southport PR9 54 A2
Whalley BB7 144 C5
Wrea Green PR4 113 B4
Manor St
Accrington BB5 104 D7
Bacup OL13 87 F1
Bury BL9 33 A2
Nelson BB9 148 F8
Ramsbottom BL0 50 B7
Manor Way
Coppull PR7 29 D8
Wrea Green PR4 113 B3
Manor Wood
Fleetwood FY7 198 E4
Kirkham PR4 114 B7
Manse Ave WN6 28 F5
Mansell Way BL6 32 D1
Mansergh St BB10 148 C2
Mansfield Ave BL0 50 B2
Mansfield Cres BB9 148 C6
Mansfield Dr PR5 98 E3
Mansfield Gr BB9 148 C6
Mansfield Rd FY3 130 D8
Mansion House Bldgs 3 BB4 86 A7
Mansion St S BB5 104 D6
Mansion The BB8 172 C6
Manston Gr PR7 43 A7
Manx Jane's La PR9 54 A4
Manxman Rd BB2 101 F1
Many Brooks Ho PR5 98 E1
Maple Ave
Blackpool FY3 130 D5
Brinscall PR6 62 F7
Burscough L40 25 E4
7 Bury BL9 33 B2
6 Clitheroe BB7 166 D7
Fleetwood FY7 175 F8
Haslingden BB4 85 C3
Horwich BL6 32 E1
Morecambe LA3 216 E2
Thornton FY5 153 C8
Maplebank 3 PR2 116 C1
Maple Bank BB10 128 C7
Maple Cl
Formby L37 11 C1
Newton-w-S PR4 114 F2
Whalley BB7 144 D6
Wilpshire BB1 122 E6
Maple Cres
9 Preston PR1 96 E7
Rishton BB1 103 B8
Maple Ct
Clayton-le-W PR25 77 D3
Garstang PR3 204 C1
Maple Dr
Bamber Bridge PR5 97 F1
Oswaldtwistle BB5 103 F3
Poulton-le-F FY6 153 E2
Maple Gr
Chorley PR6 61 D3
Fulwood PR2 119 A4
Grimsargh PR2 139 D1
Higher Penwortham PR1 96 B4
Lancaster LA1 214 D8
Ramsbottom BL0 50 D6
Warton PR4 92 D6
Maple Ho PR7 42 F6
Maple Leaf Cl PR2 116 F6
Maple Mews BB3 82 D1
Maple Rd PR3 204 C1
Maple St
Blackburn BB1 102 A7
Clayton-le-M BB5 124 F1
Great Harwood BB6 124 D6
Rishton BB1 124 B1
Southport PR8 35 E6
Maples The PR26 58 F6
Maple View WN8 8 F6
Maplewood
Skelmersdale WN8 18 A4
Southport PR9 53 F2
Maplewood Ave FY6 200 A5
Maplewood Cl
Chorley PR7 43 E6
Leyland PR25 59 E8
Lytham St Anne's FY8 90 F4
Maplewood Dr FY5 152 C8
Maplewood Gdns LA1 215 A2
Marabou Dr BB3 81 E3
Marathon Pl PR26 76 C3
Marble Ave 5 FY5 152 F7
Marble Place Sh Ctr PR8 35 B7
Marble St BB5 103 E4
Marchbank Rd WN8 17 D1
March St BB12 127 F8
Marchwood Rd FY3 131 B8
Marcroft Ave FY4 110 E7
Mardale Ave
Blackpool FY4 131 C1
Morecambe LA4 217 D5
Mardale Cl PR8 21 B4
Mardale Cres PR25 60 B7
Mardale Rd
1 Lancaster LA1 218 E1
Longridge PR3 139 F5
Preston PR1 119 A1
Maresfield Rd PR1 96 E5
Margaret Ct FY8 90 A4
Margaret Rd PR1 96 E4
Margaret St
Blackburn BB1 102 D4
Oswaldtwistle BB5 103 C2
1 Preston PR1 97 A8
Rawtenstall BB4 85 F4
Margate Ave FY4 110 E6
Margate Rd
Fulwood PR2 117 A4
Lytham St Anne's FY8 89 F8
Maria Ct 8 BB11 128 B4
Marians Dr L39 15 E7
Maria Sq BL7 46 D4
Maria St BB3 65 B6
Maricourt Ave BB1 102 D5
Marilyn Ave 4 PR5 77 B8
Marina Ave
2 Blackpool FY1 130 D2
Poulton-le-F FY3 131 D8
Marina Cl PR5 97 A1
Marina Dr
Bamber Bridge PR5 97 A1
Fulwood PR2 117 E7
Marina Gr PR5 97 A1
Marina Mews FY7 199 B3
Marina Rd L37 11 F1
Marine Ave BB11 127 C4
Marine Cres PR7 60 F6
Marine Ct LA3 216 E4
Marine Dr
Hest Bank LA2 220 D1
Lytham St Anne's FY8 90 D3
Southport, Birkdale PR8 34 E7
Southport, Marshside PR8, PR9 53 D4
Marine Gate Mans PR9 35 B8
Marine Ind Ctr FY8 91 D4
Marine Par
Fleetwood FY7 198 C1
Southport PR8 35 A8
Marine Rd E LA4 217 C6
Marine Rd W LA3, LA4 216 F4
Marine Road Central LA4 217 A5
Mariners Cl FY7 198 E1
Mariners Way PR2 96 B8
Marine View Apartments FY7 198 F5
Marino Cl FY5 153 D8
Maritime Ct PR9 35 B8
Maritime St FY7 198 F2
Maritime Way PR2 95 F7
Markazul Uloom Sch BB2 101 F2
Mark Cl PR1 96 F1
Market Ave 2 BB1 101 E5
Market Chambers BL0 50 C7
Market Cross 5 L39 15 E5
Marketgate 28 LA1 214 F8
Market Pl
Adlington PR7 31 A7
12 Chorley PR7 43 C8
3 Clitheroe BB7 166 E8
10 Colne BB8 171 E5
Edenfield BL0 68 D3
Garstang PR3 181 C7
Longridge PR3 140 B7
4 Poulton-le-F FY6 153 D3
Ramsbottom BL0 50 C7
Standish WN6 29 E1
Market Prom 5 BB11 128 A6
Market St W PR1 96 F8
Market Sq
Burnley BB11 128 A6
4 Kirkham PR4 114 B5
10 Lancaster LA1 214 F8
Lytham St Anne's FY8 91 A3
Nelson BB9 148 D8
Market St
Adlington PR7 31 A6
Bacup OL13 87 F2
7 Barnoldswick BB18 196 B2
Blackpool FY1 130 B5
Carnforth LA5 223 D2
Chorley PR7 43 C7
Church BB5 103 E5
Colne BB8 171 E5
Darwen BB3 82 A1
Edenfield BL0 68 D4
Hambleton FY6 177 C2
Kirkham PR4 113 F6
Lancaster LA1 214 F8
Morecambe LA4 217 A5
9 Nelson BB9 148 D8
Preston PR1 96 F8
11 Rawtenstall BB4 69 E8
Southport PR8 35 B7
Standish WN6 29 E1
Whitworth OL12, OL13 71 D4
Market Street La 7 BB2 101 E4
Market Way
8 Blackburn BB1 101 E5
6 Ormskirk L39 15 E5
Market Wlk PR7 43 C8
Markham Dr PR8 35 E2
Markham Rd BB2 101 B3
Markham St PR2 117 C1
Marklands Rd BL6 32 E5
Markland St
3 Preston PR1 96 E7
6 Ramsbottom BL0 50 C6
Mark Rd L38 2 F4
Markross St BB4 86 A2
Mark's Ave PR26 76 E5
Mark Sq PR4 57 A6
Mark St
Bacup OL13 70 C8
Burnley BB10 148 B1
Marland WN8 18 A4
Marl Ave PR1 96 B4
Marlboro Rd FY3 130 E4
Marlborough Ave
Cleveleys FY5 175 D5
Maghull L31 5 D3
Warton PR4 92 D6
Marlborough Cl
Ramsbottom BL0 50 C3
Whitworth OL12 52 C7
Marlborough Ct 1 WN8 18 B4
Marlborough Dr
Bamber Bridge PR5 97 D3
Fulwood PR2 117 D7
Marlborough Gdns
Skelmersdale WN8 18 A4
5 Southport PR9 35 C8
Marlborough Rd
Accrington BB5 104 C7
Lytham St Anne's FY8 110 E1
Morecambe LA3 216 E3
Southport PR9 35 C7
Marlborough St
Burnley BB11 128 A4
Chorley PR6 61 E1
14 Rochdale OL12 52 C1
Marl Cop PR26 58 A6
Marl Croft PR1 96 D2
Marled Hey BL7 48 D5
Marles Ct BB10 128 B8
Marlfield PR4 74 F4
Marlfield Cl PR2 116 F5
Marl Gr WN5 10 D4
Marl Hill Cres PR2 119 A2
Marlhill Rd FY3 131 B8
Marlin St 7 BB9 170 F2
Marlow Ct PR7 30 F6
Marlowe Ave
Accrington BB5 104 E2
Padiham BB12 126 F7
Marlowe Cres BB6 124 B4
Marl Pits BB4 86 B3
Marl Rd L33 1 C3
Marlton Rd BB2 101 D1
Marlton Way LA1 214 E6
Marmaduke Cotts LA6 241 D4
Marple Cl WN6 29 B2
Marquis Cl BB3 81 F7
Marquis Dr PR4 93 C7
Marquis St PR4 113 F5
Marron Cl PR25 59 E8
Marsden Cl PR7 41 B7
Marsden Com Prim Sch BB9 148 D7
Marsden Cres BB9 149 A8
Marsden Ct BB10 148 C3
Marsden Dr BB9 148 D6
Marsden Gr BB9 148 C5
Marsden Hall Rd BB9 149 A8
Marsden Hall Rd N BB9 171 B1
Marsden Hall Road S BB9 149 A8
MARSDEN HEIGHT 148 E5
Marsden Height Cl BB9 148 F5
Marsden Heights Com Coll BB9 148 B6
Marsden Mall 5 BB9 148 E8
Marsden Pl BB9 149 A8
Marsden Rd
Blackpool FY4 110 D8
Burnley BB10 148 C3
Southport PR9 35 E7
Marsden Sq BB4 85 B4
Marsden St
Accrington BB5 104 B4
Blackburn BB2 101 B2
6 Haslingden BB4 85 A3
Kirkham PR4 114 B5
Marsett Cl OL12 52 A1
Marsett Pl PR2 118 E5
MARSH 214 C8
Marshall Ave BB5 125 F2
Marshall Gr PR2 117 A4
Marshallsay L37 12 A2
Marshall's Brow PR1 96 E3
Marshall's Cl
Maghull L31 5 C4
5 Middleforth Green PR1 96 E4
Marsham Cl PR3 181 D6
Marsham Gr BB3 82 C1
Marshaw Pl PR3 181 A6
Marshaw Rd LA1 218 B2
Marsh Brows L37 11 E2
Marsh Cl LA2 206 B4
Marsh Cres LA4 217 F4
Marsh Ct 2 FY5 176 A2
Marshdale Rd FY4 110 F7
Marsh Dr PR4 93 D7
Marshes La The PR4 38 A8
Marsh Gate BB3 82 D1
Marsh Gates PR4 93 D7
Marsh Hos LA2 206 B4
MARSH HOUSE 82 C1
Marsh House La BB3 82 C1
MARSH HOUSES 206 B4
Marsh La
Brindle PR6 79 B5
Cockerham LA2 206 B4
Glasson LA2 209 D3
Hambleton FY6 177 C1
Hightown L37, L38 3 E6
Hurlston L40 24 D1
Longton PR4 74 D8
Preston PR1 96 E7
Withnell Fold PR6 79 A4
Marsh Mill* FY5 176 B2
Marsh Mill FY5 176 B2
Marsh Moss La L40 25 C7
Marsh Rd
Banks PR9 72 D1
Hesketh Bank PR4 73 F4
Thornton FY5 176 A2
MARSHSIDE 53 E4
Marshside Nature Reserve* PR9 53 E5
Marshside Prim Sch PR9 54 A5
Marshside Rd PR9 53 F4
Marsh St
Blackburn BB1 101 E6
Horwich BL6 32 A4
4 Lancaster LA1 218 B1
Marsh Terr BB3 82 A2
Marsh View PR4 114 F2
Marsh Way
Clitheroe BB7 189 F2
Kingsfold PR1 96 C2
Mars St BL7 48 E6
Marston Cl PR2 117 C7
Marston Cres L38 3 A2
Marston Moor PR2 117 C7
Martholme Ave BB5 125 A3
Martholme Cl BB6 124 D6
Martholme La BB6 124 F8
Martin Ave FY8 110 C4
Martin Croft Rd BB4 85 A5
Martindale Ave FY7 198 C2
Martindale Cl BB1 102 C2
Martindales The PR6 78 B3
Martin Dr BB3 65 C6
Martinfield PR2 117 F8
Martin Field Rd PR1 96 E2
Martinfields BB10 148 C4
Martinique Dr BB3 81 F6
Martin La
Drummersdale L40 24 E6
Rochdale OL12 52 B1
Martin Mere* L40 38 B1
Martin Mere Visitor Ctr* L40 38 B2
Martins Ave PR7 43 E2
Martins La WN8 9 D7
Martin St
Burnley BB10 148 B1
Bury BL9 33 D3
Edgworth BL7 48 D4
Martin Top La BB7 192 C7
Mart La L40 25 E5
Martland Ave WN6 19 F5
Marton Dr
Blackpool FY4 110 D8
Burnley BB11 127 E3
Morecambe LA4 217 F6
Marton Fold FY4 111 A4
Marton Mere Cvn Pk FY3, FY4 131 C2
Marton Pl LA4 217 F6
Marton Prim Sch FY4 110 F7
Marton Rd PR2 95 F8
Marton St 4 LA1 214 F7
Marton View FY3 130 E4
Marton Wlk 4 BB3 65 B6
Marwick Cl WN6 29 D2
Mary Ave PR8 21 E6
Marybank Cl PR2 118 C5
Mary Brown Cotts BB7 190 C8
Maryland Cl LA5 224 D2
Mary St E BL6 32 B4
Mary St W
Horwich BL6 32 A4
Longridge PR3 140 A8
Mary St
Blackburn BB1 102 A4
5 Burnley BB10 128 B5
Carnforth LA5 223 D3
Colne BB8 171 C4
Lancaster LA1 214 F8
Ramsbottom BL0 50 B5
Rishton BB1 124 B1
Mary Towneley Fold BB10 128 C4
Maryvale Ho LA1 214 E5
Masefield Ave
Padiham BB12 126 E7
Thornton FY5 176 A3
Masefield Cl
Brockhall Village BB6 143 B5
Great Harwood BB6 124 B4
Masefield Pl PR5 97 D2
Mason Cl PR4 93 C6
Masonfield PR5 78 B5
Masonfield Cres LA1 215 D7
MASONGILL 242 D6
Masongill Fell La LA6 242 E7
Mason Hill View PR2 118 A4
Mason House Cres PR2 117 A5
Mason Row BL7 47 E2
Masons Ct 1 FY7 198 E3
Mason St
7 Accrington BB5 104 C6
Bolton BL7 47 E1
Bury BL9 33 A2
Chorley PR6 61 E2
Colne BB8 171 D5
Horwich BL6 32 B3
Oswaldtwistle BB5 103 D3
Masons Way 8 BB18 196 B3
Masonwood PR2 118 A6
Massam's La L37 11 F6
Massey Croft OL12 52 C8
Massey La BB9 148 A5
Massey St
Brierfield BB9 148 A4
Bury BL9 33 B3
Masterson Ave BB12 145 D2
Matcham Ct 11 FY1 130 B5
Matchmoor La BL6 32 F4
Mather Ave BB5 104 B8
Mather St FY3 130 D7
Mathias Ct LA4 217 B6
Matlock Ave PR8 35 B4
Matlock Cl PR8 35 B4
Matlock Cres PR8 35 B4
Matlock Ct BL6 32 E4
Matlock Gr BB10 148 C2
Matlock Pl PR2 117 A5
Matlock Rd PR8 35 B4
Matlock St 13 BB3 81 F2

Matrix Pk PR7 .....60 D7
Matterdale Rd PR25 .....60 B7
Matthew Cl BB8 .....171 E4
Matthews Ct FY4 .....110 D7
Matthew St BB2 .....101 B2
Matthias St LA4 .....217 B6
Mattock Cres LA4 .....217 F5
Maudland Bank PR1 .....96 E8
Maudland Ho PR1 .....96 E8
Maudland Rd
Blackpool FY1 .....130 C2
Preston PR1 .....96 E8
MAUDLANDS 117 D1
Maudsley St
Accrington BB5 .....104 C6
Blackburn BB1 .....101 F5
Maud St
Barrowford BB9 .....170 D2
Chorley PR7 .....43 B6
Maureen Ave 3 PR5 .....77 B8
Maurice Gr FY2 .....152 E1
Maurice St BB9 .....148 D8
Mavis Dr PR7 .....42 E2
Mavis Rd BB2 .....101 A5
MAWDESLEY 40 C2
Mawdesley St Peter's CE Prim Sch L40 .....40 C3
Mawdsley Cl L37 .....12 B3
Mawdsley Terr L39 .....15 F7
Maxwell Gr FY2 .....152 E2
Maxwell St BL9 .....33 B3
Maybank Cl PR9 .....54 A1
May Bell Ave FY5 .....175 F3
Maybury Ave BB12 .....127 B7
Maybury Cl 21 BL0 .....50 B5
Maycroft Ave FY6 .....153 B5
Mayfair BL6 .....32 D3
Mayfair Cl
Haslingden BB4 .....68 A7
Hightown L38 .....2 F2
Lytham St Anne's FY8 .....90 D6
Mayfair Cotts WN1 .....30 C1
Mayfair Cres BB1 .....122 F5
Mayfair Ct FY1 .....130 E2
Mayfair Dr FY5 .....153 C8
Mayfair Gdns 5 FY5 .....176 C1
Mayfair Rd
Blackpool FY1 .....130 E2
Burnley BB10 .....128 E5
Nelson BB9 .....171 A1
Mayfayre Ave L31 .....5 B5
Mayfield
Darwen BB3 .....65 B7
Woodsfold PR4 .....135 E6
Mayfield Ave
Adlington PR6 .....31 A7
Bamber Bridge PR5 .....77 C8
Blackpool FY4 .....110 C5
Clitheroe BB7 .....166 F7
Formby L37 .....11 C1
Fulwood, Ingol PR2 .....117 B4
Fulwood PR2 .....117 A5
Haslingden BB4 .....85 A1
5 Kirkham PR4 .....114 A5
Lancaster LA1 .....218 C3
Oswaldtwistle BB5 .....103 F4
Thornton FY5 .....176 A4
Mayfield Cl
Middleforth Green PR1 .....96 E4
Ramsbottom BL0 .....50 A2
Mayfield Ct L37 .....11 F5
Mayfield Dr LA4 .....217 E6
Mayfield Fold BB11 .....128 B3
Mayfield Gdns BB5 .....103 F4
Mayfield Pl 10 FY7 .....198 F2
Mayfield Prim Sch FY8 .....89 E8
Mayfield Rd
Blackburn BB1 .....122 E3
8 Chorley PR6 .....61 D1
High Bentham LA2 .....239 D7
Leyland PR25 .....60 A7
Lytham St Anne's FY8 .....89 E8
Preston PR2 .....117 B1
Ramsbottom BL0 .....50 A2
Up Holland WN8 .....10 B7
Mayfield Sch PR7 .....43 C6
Mayfield St BB2 .....101 E3
Mayfield Terr PR5 .....99 D5
Mayflower Ave PR1 .....96 A3
Mayflower Cres PR7 .....60 F7
Mayflower Gr PR3 .....181 E1
Mayflower Ind Est L37 .....12 A1
Mayflower St BB2 .....101 B2
Mayhall Ct L31 .....5 D2
May La
Bilsborrow PR3 .....159 C8
Claughton PR3 .....182 E1
Maylands Pl BB9 .....170 C3
Maylands Sq LA4 .....217 C4
Maynard St PR1, PR2 .....117 D2
Mayo Dr PR4 .....57 A6
Mayor Ave FY1 .....130 C2
Maypark PR5 .....78 A5
Mayson St BB1 .....101 E4
May St
Barrowford BB9 .....170 D2
Blackburn BB1 .....102 A4
Edgworth BL7 .....48 E6
Nelson BB9 .....170 F2
May Terr BB7 .....144 A4
May Tree Cl BB10 .....148 E3
Maytree Ct PR6 .....30 F8
Maytree Wlk WN8 .....18 B4
Mayville Rd BB9 .....148 B6
Mead Ave PR25 .....60 B8
Meadow Ave
Fleetwood FY7 .....198 E1
Knott End-on-S FY6 .....200 A6
Meadow Ave continued
Southport PR8 .....35 C4
Meadoway
Accrington BB5 .....104 A7
Longton PR4 .....74 F8
Tarleton PR4 .....57 A5
Meadow Bank
Kingsfold PR1 .....96 C3
Maghull L31 .....5 B2
6 Ormskirk L39 .....15 F5
Meadow Bank Ave BB10 .....148 B5
Meadow Bank Cotts BB4 .....85 E3
Meadow Bank Mews 2 BB9 .....170 F2
Meadow Bank Rd 15 BB9 .....148 D8
Meadowbarn Cl PR4 .....116 E5
Meadowbridge Cl L40 .....16 E4
Meadowbrook
Blackpool FY3 .....131 C2
Burscough L40 .....25 D2
Meadowbrook Cl BL9 .....33 C4
Meadow Brook Ho 1 PR1 .....118 A1
Meadow Brow PR9 .....54 D5
Meadow Cl
Billington BB7 .....144 A3
Blackburn BB1 .....102 B4
Blackpool FY2 .....152 D2
Burnley BB10 .....148 C4
Clifton PR4 .....115 D2
Foulridge BB8 .....194 D1
Huncoat BB5 .....125 F1
Skelmersdale WN8 .....9 D7
Westhead L40 .....16 E4
Wrea Green PR4 .....113 B3
Meadow Clough WN8 .....18 B4
Meadow Cotts OL12 .....71 D3
Meadow Court Rd LA4 .....217 C3
Meadow Cr PR4 .....113 F6
Meadow Cres FY6 .....153 A3
Meadowcroft
Blackburn BB3 .....82 A6
Euxton PR7 .....60 B3
Formby L37 .....11 F2
Lytham St Anne's FY8 .....111 A1
Skelmersdale WN8 .....18 B4
Meadow Croft
Nether Kellet LA6 .....221 F4
West Bradford BB7 .....189 E5
Meadowcroft Ave
Catterall PR3 .....181 D3
Cleveleys FY5 .....175 E2
Hambleton FY6 .....177 C1
Meadowcroft Bsns Pk PR4 .....96 B1
Meadowcroft Cl BB4 .....86 A5
Meadowcroft Gr LA3 .....216 E1
Meadowcroft Rd PR25 .....59 D7
Meadow Ct
11 Oswaldtwistle BB5 .....103 E4
Preston PR1 .....96 E6
Treales PR4 .....135 A1
Meadow Dr
Bolton-le-S LA5 .....221 A5
Ormskirk L39 .....15 C2
Warton PR4 .....92 C5
Meadow Edge BB9 .....170 F5
Meadowfield
Fulwood PR2 .....117 F8
Halton LA2 .....219 C7
3 Up Holland WN8 .....10 A7
Meadow Field PR1 .....96 E2
Meadowfield Cl
Halton LA2 .....219 C7
Whalley BB7 .....144 A7
Meadowfields BB2 .....81 D7
Meadow Gdns BB1 .....124 B1
Meadow Head Ave OL12 .....52 D6
Meadow Head Cl BB2 .....101 A1
Meadowhead Dr BB1 .....124 B1
Meadowhead Inf Sch BB2 .....101 B1
Meadowhead Jun Sch BB2 .....81 B8
Meadow Head La
Longton PR4 .....74 F7
Tockholes BB3 .....81 B4
Meadow Ho 7 PR1 .....97 A8
Meadow Hts BL0 .....50 D6
Meadow La
Clayton Brook PR5 .....78 B4
Croston PR26 .....57 E1
Hesketh Bank PR4 .....73 F4
Hoscar L40 .....26 C6
Knott End-on-S FY6 .....199 F4
Lytham St Anne's FY8 .....91 E4
Maghull L31 .....5 F1
Rufford L40 .....39 D3
Southport PR8 .....21 D3
Meadowland Cl PR26 .....76 E3
Meadowlands
Charnock Richard PR7 .....42 D4
Clitheroe BB7 .....166 C8
Meadow Pk
Galgate LA2 .....210 F4
Garstang PR3 .....204 C1
Haslingden BL0 .....68 C4
Kirkham PR4 .....113 E6
Staining FY3 .....131 D5
Tarleton PR4 .....57 B6
Meadow Reach PR1 .....96 B2
Meadow Rise BB2 .....81 A8
Meadows Ave
Bacup OL13 .....87 F4
Meadows Ave continued
Cleveleys FY5 .....175 F2
Haslingden BB4 .....85 C2
Meadows Cl LA5 .....225 E4
Meadows Dr BB4 .....106 A1
Meadowside
Claughton LA2 .....237 F5
Croston PR26 .....58 A2
Grindleton BB7 .....190 C8
Lancaster LA1 .....214 F7
Walmer Bridge PR4 .....75 A5
Meadowside Ave BB5 .....124 E3
Meadowside Dr
Gregson Lane PR5 .....98 E1
Kirkby L33 .....1 A6
Meadowside Rd 6 LA4 .....217 B3
Meadow St
Accrington BB5 .....104 C6
Adlington PR7 .....31 A6
Barnoldswick BB18 .....196 A4
17 Burnley BB11 .....127 F6
Darwen BB3 .....65 B6
Great Harwood BB6 .....124 C4
Lancaster LA1 .....214 D8
Leyland PR25 .....77 A1
Padiham BB12 .....146 C1
Preston PR1 .....97 A8
Wheelton PR6 .....62 A7
Meadows The
Arnside LA5 .....224 C8
Bamber Bridge PR5 .....97 F3
Billington BB7 .....144 A4
Burnley BB12 .....127 D8
Cleveleys FY5 .....175 F2
Colne BB8 .....171 D6
Darwen BB3 .....81 E5
Elswick PR4 .....155 F1
Heskin Green PR7 .....41 E2
Hollins Lane PR3 .....207 C2
2 Leyland PR26 .....76 B1
Maghull L31 .....5 D1
Oswaldtwistle BB5 .....103 F3
Whitworth OL12 .....71 C1
Yealand Redmayne LA5 .....225 E3
Meadow Terr BB3 .....81 E5
Meadow Vale
Blackburn BB2 .....81 E6
Leyland PR26 .....59 A8
Meadow View
Adlington PR6 .....30 F8
Clitheroe BB7 .....166 C8
Farleton LA2 .....238 A6
Great Plumpton PR4 .....112 F7
Lancaster LA1 .....218 B3
Orrell WN5 .....10 E8
Rochdale OL12 .....52 A1
Southport PR8 .....35 D4
Meadow View Cvn Pk LA6 .....237 A7
Meadow Way
Arkholme LA6 .....241 B3
Bacup OL13 .....87 F2
Barnoldswick BB18 .....196 D4
Blackrod BL6 .....31 E1
Coppull PR7 .....29 D8
Edgworth BL7 .....48 E6
Garstang PR3 .....204 C2
Ramsbottom BL9 .....50 C2
Meads Rd PR2 .....117 B1
Meadup Ct LA3 .....217 A2
Meadway
Becconsall PR4 .....73 F2
Blackpool FY4 .....130 F1
Clayton Green PR6 .....78 B3
Higher Penwortham PR1 .....96 A5
Padiham BB12 .....126 B7
Ramsbottom BL0 .....68 C1
Skelmersdale WN8 .....18 A4
Meadway Cl BL6 .....32 D3
Meagles Barns PR3 .....155 E4
Meagles La PR3, PR4 .....155 E3
Mealhouse La 6 PR7 .....43 C8
Mealrigg La LA6 .....241 A7
Meanwood Ave FY4 .....110 F7
Meanwood Brow 15 OL12 .....52 C1
Meanwood Com Prim Sch OL12 .....52 C1
Meanygate PR5 .....97 E1
Mearbeck Pl 6 LA1 .....218 B2
Mearley Brook Fold BB7 .....166 F7
Mearley Rd PR2 .....118 E4
Mearley St BB7 .....166 E7
Mearley Syke BB7 .....166 F8
Mearsbeck 8 LA3 .....216 E3
Meath Rd PR1 .....96 D6
Mede The PR4 .....114 B3
Medina Cl 5 BB5 .....104 B5
MEDLAR 133 F4
Medlar Cl PR4 .....113 E6
Medlar Ct PR4 .....114 A6
Medlar Gate PR4 .....114 A6
Medlar La PR4 .....133 E4
Medlar-with-Wesham CE Prim Sch PR4 .....113 F6
Medley St OL12 .....52 F1
Medlock Ave FY7 .....198 D2
Medlock Pl FY7 .....198 D2
Medway PR2 .....117 F6
Medway Ave FY7 .....175 D8
Medway Cl PR5 .....97 B1
Medway Dr BL6 .....32 D3
Medway Ho 6 PR1 .....97 D8
Meeting House La LA1 .....214 E8
Meins Croft BB2 .....101 A6
Meins Rd BB2 .....100 F6
Melba Rd PR2 .....118 E3
Melbert Ave PR2 .....117 C3
Melbourne Ave
Blackpool FY5 .....152 F7
Fleetwood FY7 .....175 E8
Melbourne Cl BL6 .....32 C3
Melbourne Ct 1 FY5 .....152 F8
Melbourne Gr BL6 .....32 C3
Melbourne Rd 11 LA1 .....215 A8
Melbourne St
6 Accrington BB5 .....125 A1
7 Darwen BB3 .....65 B6
2 Newchurch BB4 .....86 F1
Oswaldtwistle BB5 .....103 D3
Padiham BB12 .....126 D7
19 Preston PR1 .....96 F8
Melbreck WN8 .....18 A4
Melbury Dr BL6 .....32 F1
Meldon Grange LA3 .....213 A8
Meldon Rd LA3 .....213 A7
Meldreth Cl L37 .....11 C1
Melford Cl PR6 .....61 F3
Melford Dr WN5 .....10 D3
Melfort Cl BB2 .....100 F1
Melia Cl BB4 .....85 F2
Melita St 6 BB3 .....65 B8
MELLING 241 C1
Melling Brow LA6 .....241 C2
Melling Cl PR6 .....31 B7
Melling Ct
3 Colne BB8 .....171 C5
Morecambe LA4 .....217 A3
Melling Ho 4 LA1 .....215 A3
Melling Mews PR3 .....181 C8
Melling Rd
Hornby LA2 .....238 B7
Southport PR9 .....35 E7
Melling St Wilfrid CE Prim Sch LA6 .....241 D2
Mellings Ave WN5 .....10 E1
Mellings Fold 3 PR1 .....97 C6
Melling's La FY8 .....111 A1
Melling St 17 PR1 .....96 F8
Mellings Wood FY8 .....111 A1
Mellishaw La LA3 .....217 D1
MELLOR 121 F2
MELLOR BROOK 121 C3
Mellor Brow BB2 .....121 D2
Mellor Cl
Blackburn BB2 .....100 F8
Burnley BB11 .....127 D3
Standish WN6 .....29 E2
Mellor Ct PR3 .....140 B7
Mellor La BB2 .....121 F3
Mellor Pl 6 PR1 .....97 B7
Mellor Rd
Kirkham PR4 .....114 A5
Leyland PR25 .....76 D2
Mellors Cl PR8 .....35 F5
Mellwood Ave FY3 .....152 F1
Melrose Ave
Blackpool FY3 .....130 E8
Burnley BB11 .....127 D4
Fulwood PR2 .....118 C5
Morecambe LA4 .....217 C5
Oswaldtwistle BB5 .....103 F3
Southport PR9 .....54 B5
Melrose Gdns PR26 .....58 C2
Melrose St
10 Darwen BB3 .....81 F2
Lancaster LA1 .....215 A7
Ramsbottom BL0 .....50 B2
Melrose Terr 11 OL13 .....88 A7
Melrose Way PR7 .....43 D5
Melton Gr FY8 .....90 E3
Melton Pl
Blackpool FY5 .....152 C8
Leyland PR25 .....77 B1
Melville Ave
Barnoldswick BB18 .....196 A3
Darwen BB3 .....65 A7
Melville Dr BB2 .....101 D5
Melville Gdns BB3 .....65 A8
Melville Rd
Blackpool FY2 .....152 C4
Heysham LA3 .....212 E5
Melville St
Burnley BB10 .....148 C1
Darwen BB3 .....65 A8
Memorial Gdns PR3 .....159 A4
Memory Cl PR4 .....93 B7
Menai Dr PR2 .....117 D7
Mendip Cl
Horwich BL6 .....32 C5
Lytham St Anne's FY8 .....91 E5
Mendip Rd PR25 .....77 D1
Menivale Cl PR9 .....54 B5
Meols Cl L37 .....11 E2
Meols Cop High Sch PR8 .....35 F5
Meols Cop Rd PR8, PR9 .....35 F4
Meols Cop Retail Pk PR9 .....36 A4
Meols Cop Sta PR9 .....35 F7
Meols Ct PR9 .....55 A6
Meolsgate Ave PR4 .....57 A7
Meols View Cl PR8 .....36 A3
Mercer Cres BB4 .....68 A8
Mercer Ct
Adlington PR7 .....43 F1
Maghull L31 .....5 A3
Mercer Dr BB6 .....124 E6
Mercer Ho 5 BB5 .....125 A1
Mercer Rd PR5 .....97 A1
Mercer's La L39 .....7 B4
Mercer St
16 Clayton-le-M BB5 .....124 F3
Great Harwood BB6 .....124 D5
Mercer St continued
1 Padiham BB12 .....126 F7
Preston PR1 .....97 C8
Mercer Way BB1 .....102 D1
Merchants Ho 4 BB1 .....101 F4
Merchants Landing BB1 .....101 F3
Merchants Quay 1 BB1 .....101 F3
Merclesden Ave BB9 .....171 B1
Mercury Way WN8 .....9 E8
Mere Ave
Burscough Bridge L40 .....25 E6
Fleetwood FY7 .....198 D1
Mere Brook FY3 .....131 E5
MERE BROW 55 E2
Mere Brow La PR4 .....56 A2
Mere Cl
Broughton PR3 .....137 C3
Skelmersdale WN8 .....17 F2
MERECLOUGH 129 A1
Mere Ct
Burnley BB11 .....127 B4
Burscough Bridge L40 .....25 E5
Meredith St BB9 .....148 E7
Merefell Rd LA5 .....221 A6
Merefield PR7 .....61 A1
Merefield Sch PR8 .....21 B4
Merefold BL6 .....31 F3
Mere Fold PR7 .....42 D3
Mere La
Banks PR9 .....55 A2
Holmeswood PR4 .....38 A7
Rufford L40 .....38 E3
Mereland Cl WN5 .....10 E6
Mereland Rd FY3 .....131 A2
Mere Park Ct FY3 .....131 A2
Merepark Dr PR9 .....54 B4
Mere Rd
Blackpool FY3 .....130 D5
Formby L37 .....11 D2
Mere Sands Wood Nature Reserve* L40 .....38 F4
MERESIDE 131 C1
Mereside Cl PR4 .....74 F7
Mereside Prim Sch FY4 .....131 C1
Meres Way PR8 .....35 B2
Merewood WN8 .....18 A4
Meriden Cl PR8 .....21 B5
Merlecrest Dr PR4 .....57 A8
Merlewood BL0 .....68 E3
Merlewood Ave PR9 .....54 B3
Merlin Cl PR6 .....62 A3
Merlin Ct BB5 .....103 D3
Merlin Dr BB5 .....103 D3
Merlin Gr
Leyland PR25 .....59 C8
Padiham BB12 .....126 E6
Merlin Rd BB2 .....101 B6
Merlyn Rd FY5 .....175 E1
Merrick Ave PR1 .....97 F8
Merrilox Ave L31 .....5 D3
Merryburn Cl PR2 .....118 A4
Merry Trees La PR4 .....116 E5
Merscar La L40 .....24 D6
Mersey Ave
Darwen BB3 .....81 D3
Formby L37 .....11 E6
Maghull L31 .....5 F2
Mersey Rd
Blackpool FY4 .....110 B8
Fleetwood FY7 .....198 F4
Orrell WN5 .....10 F7
Mersey St
4 Bacup OL13 .....88 A1
Burnley BB12 .....127 A6
Longridge PR3 .....140 B8
Preston PR2 .....96 C8
Merton Ave PR2 .....117 F6
Merton Ct PR2 .....117 F6
Merton Gr PR6 .....61 F3
Merton St
Burnley BB12 .....127 F7
4 Nelson BB9 .....170 D1
Messenger St BB9 .....149 A7
Meta St BB2 .....101 E2
Metcalf Dr BB5 .....125 D6
Metcalfe Cl BB2 .....81 D8
Metcalfe St BB12 .....127 B5
Mete St PR1 .....97 D8
Methuen Ave
Coupe Green PR5 .....98 E3
Fulwood PR2 .....117 E6
Methuen Cl PR5 .....98 E3
Methuen Dr PR5 .....98 F3
Metropolitan Bsns Pk FY3 .....131 B2
Metropolitan Dr FY3 .....131 B2
Mettle Cote OL13 .....88 A1
Mewith La LA2 .....239 C6
Mews The
1 Darwen BB3 .....65 C7
Lancaster LA1 .....215 B6
Morecambe LA4 .....217 E5
1 Padiham BB12 .....146 C1
Southport, Birkdale PR8 .....35 A4
Southport PR8 .....35 A5
11 Southport PR8 .....35 B7
Mexford Ave FY2 .....130 D8
Meyler Ave FY3 .....130 E8
Michael Pl 4 LA4 .....217 D5
Michaels Cl L37 .....11 E3
Michael's La L39 .....22 C3
Michaelson Ave LA4 .....217 E4

Michael Wife La
Edenfield BL0 68 F2
Edenfield BL0 68 F3
Mickering La L39 6 C5
Mickleden Ave PR2 117 F7
Mickleden Rd FY4 131 C1
Micklefield Ct 2 PR25 76 D1
Micklegate FY5 152 C7
Micklehurst Cres
BB11 127 D2
Mickleton Dr PR8 21 A5
Middlecot Cl 2 WN5 10 E5
Middlefield PR26 59 A8
Middleforth Gn PR1 96 E4
MIDDLEFORTH GREEN 96 E3
Middleforth Ind Est 4
PR1 96 E4
Middlegate LA3 217 E2
Middlegate Gn BB4 106 A1
MIDDLE HEALEY 52 D4
Middle Hey PR4 74 E3
Middle Highfield LA2 237 C5
Middle Hill OL12 52 F4
Middle Holly PR3 204 C8
Middle Meanygate PR4 56 C7
Middle Moss La
Great Altcar L37 12 F3
Haskayne L37 13 A2
Middlesex Ave BB12 127 B7
Middle St
Blackpool FY1 130 B3
Colne BB8 171 C4
Lancaster LA1 214 F8
Whitworth OL12 71 D1
MIDDLETON 213 B2
Middleton Ave FY7 198 D1
Middleton Bsns Pk
LA3 213 A3
Middleton Dr BB9 170 E6
Middleton Rd
Fulwood PR2 118 C7
Heysham LA3 212 E5
Middleton LA3 213 B2
Middleton Way LA3 212 F6
Middle Turn BL7 48 D7
Middle Withins La L37,
L38 4 A7
Middlewood WN8 18 A4
Middlewood Cl
Eccleston PR7 41 C6
Ormskirk L39 6 C7
Middlewood Dr L39 6 C7
Middlewood Rd L39 6 C7
Midfield BB6 123 C8
MIDGE HALL 76 A3
Midge Hall La
Bescar PR9 37 C3
Leyland PR4, PR5 75 F4
Midgeland Rd FY4 111 B5
Midgeland Terr FY4 111 C5
Midgery La PR2 118 B7
Midgley St BB8 171 E4
Midhurst Dr PR8 21 B4
Midland St
12 Accrington BB5 104 C5
Nelson BB9 170 E1
Midland Terr LA5 223 D3
Midsummer St BB2 101 C5
Midville Pl 15 BB3 82 A1
Midwood Cvn Pk PR3 201 A2
Milbanke Ave PR4 114 A5
Milbeck Cl PR3 139 F5
Milbourne Rd BL9 33 A6
Milbourne St FY1 130 C5
Milbrook Cl BB11 127 B5
Milburn Ave FY5 175 F5
Mildred Cl FY5 176 A3
Mile End Cl BB8 194 D1
Mile End Row BB2 101 B6
Mile Rd FY6 155 A1
Miles Ave OL13 70 D8
Miles La
Appley Bridge WN6 19 E6
Shevington WN6 19 F6
Miles St PR1 117 F2
Milestone Mdw PR7 60 D4
Mile Stone Mdw PR7 60 D4
Milestone Pl LA2 237 C3
Miles Wlk PR1 117 E2
Miletas Pl FY8 90 C4
Milford Ave FY2 152 D1
Milford Cl
Catterall PR3 181 D2
Formby L37 11 C1
Milford St
Colne BB8 171 C5
6 Rochdale OL12 52 F1
Milking La BB3 82 A6
Milking Stile La LA1 214 D8
Milk St BL0 50 B5
Millar Barn La BB4 69 F8
Millar's Pace PR9 54 B5
Millbank
Fulwood PR2 117 C3
4 Preston PR1 97 B8
Mill Bank WN6 19 D7
Millbank Brow L40 25 F3
Millbank La L31, L39 5 F3
Millbrook BB12 147 E8
Mill Brook PR3 181 D3
Millbrook Cl
Oswaldtwistle BB5 103 D2
Skelmersdale WN8 17 E2
Wheelton PR6 62 A7
Millbrook Ct
Colne BB8 172 B5
West Bradford BB7 189 E5
Mill Brook Ho BB5 124 E3
Millbrook Mews 1 FY8 91 C3
Mill Brook Pl BB7 166 D1
Mill Brook Row PR6 44 B1
Millbrook St BB3 81 F7
Millbrook Way PR1 96 C3
Mill Brow
Haskayne L39 14 A7
Lowgill LA2 239 B2
Mill Brow Rd BB18 197 C2
Mill Cl PR4 135 C8
Millcombe Way PR5 97 E3
Mill Cotts BB3 82 F3
Millcroft
Chorley PR7 61 A2
Fulwood PR2 117 D4
Millcroft Ave WN5 10 D5
Mill Ct PR3 140 B8
Mill Dam Cl L40 25 C2
Mill Dam La L40 16 D8
Milldyke Cl 2 FY4 110 F6
Millenium Ct FY8 110 B4
Mill Entrance BB5 124 F2
Miller Ave PR6 80 B2
Miller Cl BB5 103 C5
Miller Cres FY6 154 E1
Miller Ct
Lancaster, Haverbreaks
LA1 214 E5
14 Lancaster LA1 218 D2
Miller Field PR2 116 E3
MILLER FOLD 104 B3
Miller Fold Ave BB5 104 B3
Miller Ho 4 PR1 97 A7
Miller La
Catforth PR4 135 E4
Cottam PR4 116 E5
Miller Rd PR1, PR2 118 E2
Miller's Brow PR3 207 E3
Millers Cl FY8 90 D7
Millers Ct L39 15 F5
Millersdale Cl FY5 153 E7
Millers Ford LA2 239 B8
Millersgate PR4 116 E4
Millers Nook WN8 10 B7
Miller St
4 Blackpool FY1 130 B1
11 Preston PR1 97 C8
Ramsbottom BL9 50 C2
Millers Vale 6 BB4 84 F1
Millet Terr BL9 33 E7
Millett St BL0 50 D7
Mill Field
Clayton-le-M BB5 124 F4
Parbold WN8 27 C1
Millfield Cl PR4 92 F6
Millfield High Sch FY5 153 C8
Millfield Rd
Blackpool FY4 110 F6
Chorley PR7 61 C1
Millfold OL12 71 D2
Mill Gap St 20 BB3 65 A8
MILLGATE 71 D4
Millgate BL7 47 D2
Mill Gate
Fulwood PR2 117 D3
15 Rawtenstall BB4 86 A3
Millgate Rd 18 BB4 86 A3
Millgate Terr OL12 71 E5
Mill Gdns 6 LA2 239 D8
Mill Gn BB8 171 D4
Millgreen Cl WN8 10 A7
Millham St BB1 101 E6
Mill Haven PR2 117 D3
MILLHEAD 223 D4
Mill Hey Ave FY6 153 E1
Mill Hey La L40 39 C3
MILL HILL 101 C1
Mill Hill
Oswaldtwistle BB5 103 E4
Preston PR1 96 E8
Mill Hill Bridge St BB2 101 B2
Mill Hill Cotts BL6 44 F1
Mill Hill Gr LA3 213 A2
Mill Hill La BB11 126 B3
Mill Hill St BB2 101 B2
Mill Hill Sta BB2 101 B2
Mill Ho 19 LA1 215 A8
Millholme Dr LA2 239 D7
Mill Ho Mews 17 LA1 215 A8
Mill House La
Jack Green PR6 78 F8
Longridge PR3 141 A8
Millhouse Lo PR8 21 D5
Millhouse St BL0 50 E8
Mill House View WN8 10 C7
Millington Ave FY4 110 E8
Millionaire Row L40 24 B4
Mill La
Appley Bridge WN6 19 D7
Bacup OL13 88 B3
Becconsall PR4 73 F2
Blackburn BB2 101 E4
Bolton Green PR7 42 A8
Bolton-le-S LA5 221 A6
Burscough L40 25 E4
Carnforth LA5 223 D4
Caton LA2 237 B3
Clayton Green PR6 78 C1
Coppull PR7 42 E2
Darwen BB3 64 A5
Earby BB18 197 D2
Elswick PR4 156 B1
Fleetwood FY7 199 B4
Fulwood PR2 117 C4
Mill La continued
Gisburn BB7 231 B4
Goosnargh PR3 138 E6
Great Harwood BB6 125 A6
Halton LA2 219 D6
Hambleton FY6 177 E1
Haskayne L39 14 F1
Hesketh Lane PR3 162 C8
Heskin Green PR7 42 A2
Horwich BL6 32 D4
Leyland, Earnshaw Bridge
PR26 76 E3
Leyland PR25 59 D8
Low Bentham LA2 239 C7
Parbold WN8 27 C1
Skelmersdale, Elmers Green
WN8 18 F1
Skelmersdale, Pennylands
WN8 17 F2
Skelmersdale, Tawd Valley
Park WN8 18 A3
Southport PR9 54 A1
Staining FY3 131 D5
Stalmine FY6 177 D7
Up Holland WN8 10 A8
Waddington BB7 189 A8
Walton-le-D PR5 97 D5
Warton PR4 92 F6
Wrea Green PR4 113 A3
Mill Lane Appartments
LA2 219 D6
Mill Lane Cres PR9 54 A1
Mill Lane Ind Est BB7 231 B3
Mill Leat Cl WN8 27 C2
Mill Leat Mews WN8 27 C2
Mill Lo PR4 75 F8
Mill Nook OL12 52 F3
Millom Ave FY2 152 D4
Millom Cl FY7 175 C8
Millrace Ct 5 LA1 218 D2
Millrace The LA1 218 D1
Mill Rd
Orrell WN5 10 D5
Southport PR8 21 D5
Millrose Cl WN8 17 F2
Mill Row BB4 85 F5
Mills St OL12 71 D1
Mill St
Accrington BB5 104 F1
Adlington PR6 31 B8
Bacup OL13 87 F3
Barnoldswick BB18 196 A2
Barrowford BB9 170 D4
Church BB5 103 F6
Clayton-le-M BB5 124 F2
4 Coppull PR7 42 E1
Great Harwood BB6 124 C5
Haslingden BB4 85 B5
Kirkham PR4 114 A5
Lancaster LA1 215 A8
Leyland PR25 77 B3
Leyland, Seven Stars
PR25 59 D8
Ormskirk L39 15 F5
Oswaldtwistle BB5 103 D3
Padiham BB12 126 C8
Preesall FY6 200 B3
Preston PR1 96 D8
Ramsbottom BL0 50 A4
Southport PR8 35 C6
West Bradford BB7 189 E5
Wheelton PR6 62 A7
Millstone Ct 3 LA1 218 D3
Mill The
Leyland PR26 76 D2
Preston PR1 96 F8
Millthorne Ave BB7 166 D7
Millthorne Ho 9 BB7 166 D8
Mill View PR4 93 B7
Mill View Ct L39 7 E7
Mill View La BL6 32 E4
Millwood Cl BB2 101 A1
Mill Wood Cl PR6 79 C3
Millwood Glade PR7 61 B1
Millwood Rd PR5 97 B3
Mill Yd BL9 33 A3
Milman Cl L39 15 D3
Milner Rd
Darwen BB3 81 E4
Lytham St Anne's FY8 90 E4
Milner St
Burnley BB10 128 A8
Preston PR1 118 A2
Whitworth OL12 52 C8
Milne St BL0 68 C5
MILNSHAW 104 A6
Milnshaw Gdns BB5 104 B7
Milnshaw La BB5 104 B6
Milnthorpe Ave FY5 175 D5
Milton Ave
Blackpool FY3 130 F5
Clitheroe BB7 189 E1
2 Thornton FY5 176 A3
Milton Cl
Bamber Bridge PR5 97 D2
Darwen BB3 82 C1
Great Harwood BB6 124 B4
Haslingden BB4 68 A7
Milton Cres
Kirkham PR4 114 A5
Poulton-le-F FY6 131 D8
Milton Ct PR7 42 E1
Milton Dr L39 16 A4
Milton Gr
Barnoldswick BB18 196 A3
Longshaw WN5 10 D1
Orrell WN5 10 F6
Milton Pl FY2 152 F6
Milton Rd
Colne BB8 171 D5
Coppull PR7 29 E8
Milton St
3 Barrowford BB9 170 D4
1 Blackburn BB1 102 A5
3 Brierfield BB9 148 B5
Burnley, Harle Syke
BB10 148 F3
Clayton-le-M BB5 124 F3
Fleetwood FY7 199 A4
Nelson BB9 170 D1
Oswaldtwistle BB5 103 E4
Padiham BB12 126 E7
Ramsbottom BL0 50 B6
Southport PR9 36 A7
Milton Terr PR6 61 D2
Milton Way L31 5 B1
Mimosa Cl PR7 61 A3
Mimosa Rd PR2 118 E2
Mincing La BB2 101 E4
Minden Rd PR4 132 E5
Minehead Ave BB10 148 D2
Minerva Rd LA1 214 C8
Minnie St OL12 71 D2
Minnie Terr BB2 101 C6
Minor St 15 BB4 86 A7
Minstead Ave L33 1 A2
Minster Cres BB3 65 C8
Minster Dr LA3 217 B2
Minster Pk PR4 116 E5
Minstrel Wlk FY6 153 D4
Mint Ave BB9 170 D4
Mintholme Ave PR5 98 E2
Mintor Rd L33 1 A2
Mint St BL0 68 C2
Mire Ash Brow BB2 121 D1
Mire Ridge BB8 172 A3
Mirfield Gr 11 FY4 130 D1
Miry La WN8 27 D2
Mission Cotts L40 26 B8
Mitcham Rd FY4 111 B8
Mitchell St
Burnley BB12 127 C6
Clitheroe BB7 166 D7
4 Colne BB8 171 D5
Mitella St BB10 128 C5
Mitre St BB11 127 E6
Mitten's La L37 12 B3
Mitton Ave
Barrowford BB9 170 F6
Rawtenstall BB4 86 A4
Mitton Cl
Blackburn BB2 101 C1
Heywood OL10 33 F2
Mitton Dr PR2 119 A3
Mitton Gr BB10 128 D5
Mitton Hos BB9 170 F6
Mitton Rd
Great Mitton BB7 165 F2
Whalley BB7 144 B7
Mitton St BB1 101 F7
Mizpah St BB10 128 C5
Mizzy Rd OL12 52 F1
Moira Cres PR2 118 F4
Moleside Cl BB5 104 D6
Mollington Rd BB2 101 B7
Molly Wood La BB11 126 F5
Molyneaux FY8 90 E3
Molyneux Ct 21 PR1 97 A8
Molyneux Dr FY4 110 D7
Molyneux Pl FY8 91 A4
Molyneux Rd L39 6 C7
Mona Pl PR1 96 E8
Monarch Cres FY8 90 B8
Monarch St BB5 103 E4
Mona Rd BB2 101 E1
Moneyclose Gr LA3 212 D5
Money Close La LA3 212 D4
Monk Hall St BB10 128 A7
Monkroyd Ave BB18 196 A2
Monkroyd Rd BB8 172 F7
Monks Carr La L37, L38 4 A6
Monks Cl L37 12 A1
Monks Dr
Formby L37 12 A1
Longridge PR3 140 A6
Withnell PR6 80 A1
Monks Gate FY8 90 D7
Monks La L40 25 D7
Monk's La FY6 200 A1
Monk St
Accrington BB5 104 A6
2 Clitheroe BB7 166 D7
Monkswell Ave LA5 221 A5
Monkswell Dr LA5 221 A5
Monks Wlk PR1 96 C6
Monkswood Ave LA4 217 E5
Monmouth Ct PR2 116 F3
Monmouth Rd BB1 102 C5
Monmouth St
5 Burnley BB12 127 D6
Colne BB8 172 A5
Monomer Rd FY5 176 C4
Monroe Dr 3 FY7 198 D3
Montague Cl
Blackburn BB2 101 D4
Normoss FY3 131 A8
Montague Rd BB11 127 E5
Montague St
Blackburn BB2 101 D5
Blackpool FY4 110 B8
5 Brierfield BB9 148 B5
4 Clitheroe BB7 166 D8
Colne BB8 171 E6
Montagu Mews L37 11 E5
Montagu Rd L37 11 E5
Montcliffe Rd PR6 61 E1
Monteagle Dr LA2 238 B7
Monteagle Sq LA2 238 B7
Montfield Hey BB9 148 A5
Montford Ct BB12 147 F6
Montford Rd BB9 147 F6
Montgomery Ave PR9 36 B6
Montgomery Cl BB5 104 E2
Montgomery Gr BB12 127 C7
Montgomery High Sch
FY2 152 D5
Montgomery St 7 PR5 77 F8
Monthall Rise LA1 218 F1
Montjoly St PR1 97 C7
Monton Rd BB3 81 E4
Montpelier Ave FY2 152 C5
Montreal Ave FY1 130 D4
Montreal Rd BB2 101 C8
Montrose Ave
Blackpool FY1 130 C3
Ramsbottom BL0 50 A2
Montrose Cl PR6 43 E6
Montrose Cres LA3 212 E7
Montrose Dr PR9 53 F1
Montrose St
Blackburn BB2 101 C3
Brierfield BB9 148 B6
Burnley BB11 127 F4
Montrose Terr 17
BB18 196 B2
MONUBENT 230 E6
Moody La L40 40 E1
Moody St WN6 29 E1
Moon Ave 7 FY1 130 B2
Moon Bay Wharf LA3 212 D6
Moons Acre LA2 239 D8
Moon St PR5 77 E8
Moor Ave
Appley Bridge WN6 19 E8
Higher Penwortham PR1 96 A4
Moorbottom Rd BL8 49 E5
Moorbrook Sch PR2 117 E3
Moorbrook St PR1 117 E1
Moor Cl
Darwen BB3 65 D8
Lancaster LA1 215 A8
Southport PR8 21 D2
Moor Close La LA6 240 B1
Moorcroft
Blackburn BB3 82 A6
Broughton PR3 137 B2
Edenfield BL0 68 D2
Moorcroft Cres PR2 118 D3
Moorcroft Ho WN8 27 A1
Moor Dr WN8 9 D7
Moor Edge BB7 144 B6
Moore Dr BB12 146 F5
Moorend BB7 166 F7
MOOR END 177 D6
Moor End Prim Sch
BB5 103 D4
Moores La WN6 29 D2
Moore St
Blackpool FY4 130 B1
Colne BB8 171 C5
Nelson BB9 148 F7
Padiham BB12 126 F7
Preston PR1 97 C7
Moore Tree Dr FY4 111 A8
Moorfield BL7 48 D6
Moor Field
New Longton PR4 76 A7
Whalley BB7 144 B6
Moorfield Ave
Accrington, Hillock Vale
BB5 104 F8
Blackburn BB1 122 E3
Blackpool FY3 130 E6
Carleton FY6 153 B4
Moorfield Cl
Clayton-le-M BB5 125 B3
Fulwood PR2 117 E8
Preston PR1 96 A2
Moorfield Dr
Clayton-le-M BB5 125 B3
Fulwood PR2 118 E3
Lytham St Anne's FY8 91 A4
Moorfield Ind Est BB5 125 B3
Moorfield La L40 24 C3
Moorfield Pl 3 OL12 52 F1
Moorfield Rd PR25 59 C8
Moorfields
Blackpool FY2 152 F4
Chorley PR6 61 E1
Moorfields Ave PR2 117 E8
Moorfield Sch PR1 118 A3
Moorfield Way BB5 125 B3
MOORGATE 101 D1
Moorgate
Accrington BB5 104 B2
Blackpool FY4 110 F6
Bury BL9 33 A3
Fulwood PR2 117 F5
Ormskirk L39 15 E4
Moor Gate 14 LA1 215 A8
Moorgate Gdns 2
BB2 101 C1
Moorgate La BB6 143 A5
Moorgate Rd BB18 196 A1
Moorgate Ret Pk 13
BL9 33 A3
Moorgate St BB2 101 C1
Moor Hall La PR4 114 F4
Moor Hall St PR1 117 E2
Moorhead Gdns PR4 92 E7
Moorhead High Sch
BB5 104 A7
Moorhead St 2 BB8 171 C5
Moorhen Pl 11 FY5 175 F1

Moor Hey Cotts PR26 58 A6
Moorhey Cres
Higher Penwortham PR1 96 B5
Walton Summit PR5 78 A8
Moorhey Dr PR1 96 B5
Moorhouse Ave BB5 104 A4
Moorhouse Cl BB5 104 A4
Moorhouses L38 2 F3
Moorhouse St
Accrington BB5 104 A4
1 Blackpool FY1 130 B7
Burnley BB11 127 C5
Moorings The
Burnley BB12 127 E7
4 Chorley PR6 43 E8
Hest Bank LA2 220 D1
Maghull L31 5 B4
Moor La
Billington BB6, BB7 144 B2
Butt Yeats LA2 238 C5
Clitheroe BB7 166 E8
Darwen BB3 82 B3
Haslingden BB4 84 F6
Hutton PR4 95 D1
Ince Blundell L38, L23 3 E2
Lancaster LA1 215 A8
Langho BB6 123 E8
Maghull L29 4 D1
Padiham BB12 146 C1
Preston PR1 117 F1
Salterforth BB18 194 C6
Southport PR8 21 C2
Waddington BB7 229 D2
West Bradford BB7 189 D7
Whalley BB7 144 B6
Wiswell BB7 144 F7
Moorland Ave
Blackburn BB2 80 D7
Clitheroe BB7 189 F3
Darwen BB3 81 D2
Earby BB18 197 C1
Fulwood PR2 118 D4
Poulton-le-F FY6 153 E4
Whitworth OL12 52 C7
Moorland Cl BB9 170 F6
Moorland Cres
Clitheroe BB7 189 F2
Fulwood PR2 118 D4
Whitworth OL12 52 C7
Moorland Dr
Brierfield BB9 148 D4
Horwich BL6 32 F3
Moorland Gate PR6 43 F6
Moorland Gdns FY6 153 E4
Moorland Rd
Blackburn BB2 81 C7
Burnley BB11 127 F3
Clitheroe BB7 189 F2
Langho BB6 143 C1
Lytham St Anne's FY8 90 A7
Poulton-le-F FY6 153 F4
Moorland Rise BB4 85 C2
MOORLANDS 215 B7
Moorlands PR1 117 E3
Moorland Sch Ltd BB7 189 E3
Moorlands Ct BB3 65 D7
Moorlands Gr LA3 216 E3
Moorland St OL12 52 E1
Moorlands Terr 6 OL13 88 A1
Moorlands The OL13 88 A8
Moorlands View BL0 68 D5
Moorland Terr OL12 52 A1
Moorland View BB9 148 E6
Moor Nook Com Prim Sch PR2 119 A3
Moor Park Ave
Blackpool FY2 152 E4
Preston PR1 118 A2
Moor Park Bsns & Ent Sch PR1 118 A2
Moor Park Prim Sch FY2 152 E3
Moor Platt Cl BL6 32 F3
Moor Rd
Barber's Moor PR26 58 D3
Chorley PR7 43 B5
Haslingden BB4 67 F5
Orrell WN5 10 E6
Ramsbottom BL8 50 A6
Rivington PR6 44 E7
Moorside
Melling LA6 241 D2
Wharles PR4 134 D3
MOOR SIDE
Broughton 136 C4
Kirkham 134 D1
Moorside Ave
Blackburn BB1 102 D4
Brierfield BB9 148 D4
Fulwood PR2 118 F3
Horwich BL6 32 C4
Moorside Cl LA6 241 D2
Moorside Com Prim Sch WN8 9 E7
Moorside Cres OL13 88 A4
Moorside Dr
Clayton-le-M BB5 125 A2
Preston PR1 96 B2
Moorside Fold PR4 75 B5
Moorside La PR4 136 C4
Moor Side La
Ramsbottom BL0 51 A7
Wiswell BB7 144 F8
Moorside Prim Sch LA1 215 B4
Moorside Rd
Caton LA2 237 D3
Edgworth BL7 66 D1
Moor St
Clayton-le-M BB5 124 F3
Kirkham PR4 114 A5
23 Lancaster LA1 214 F8
Ormskirk L39 15 F5
Moorsview BL0 50 B6
Moorthorpe Cl BB3 65 A6
Moor View
Bacup, Brandwood OL13 70 B7
Bacup, Greave OL13 88 A4
Rawtenstall BB4 69 F6
Salterforth BB18 194 E8
Moorview Cl BB10 148 E2
Moorview Ct 2 FY4 110 F7
Moorway FY6 153 F4
Moor Way BL8 49 C3
Moray Cl BL0 50 A4
MORECAMBE 216 E5
Morecambe Bay Com Prim Sch LA4 217 B5
Morecambe Bay Nature Reserve (RSPB)* LA5 220 D5
Morecambe High Sch LA4 217 C6
Morecambe Lodge Cvn Pk LA5 220 E3
Morecambe Rd
Blackburn BB2 101 F1
Lancaster LA3, LA1 218 A2
Morecambe Rd Sch LA3 217 F3
Morecambe St E 5 LA4 217 B6
Morecambe St W 2 LA4 217 B6
Morecambe Sta LA4 217 A5
Moresby Ave FY3 131 B7
Moreton Dr
Poulton-le-F FY6 153 D2
Staining FY3 131 D5
Moreton Gn LA3 212 F7
Moreton Pk BB7 144 E2
Moreton St BB5 104 B6
Morewood Dr LA6 240 C7
Morland Ave
Bamber Bridge PR5 77 A7
Kirkham PR4 113 F7
Morley Ave BB2 101 A1
Morley Cl LA1 218 C3
Morley Croft PR26 76 E3
Morley La PR3 202 A5
Morley Rd
Blackpool FY4 130 E1
Lancaster LA1 218 C3
Southport PR9 35 E8
Morley St 1 BB12 126 D8
Morningside LA1 214 E7
Mornington Ct PR1 118 F1
Mornington Rd
Adlington PR6 31 B8
Higher Penwortham PR1 96 B5
Lytham St Anne's FY8 91 E4
Preston PR1 118 F1
Southport PR9 35 C7
Morris Cl PR25 60 A8
Morris Cres PR2 118 D2
Morris Ct PR2 118 D2
Morris La L39 23 E3
Morrison St PR6 61 D2
Morris Rd
Chorley PR6 61 E1
Fulwood PR2 118 D2
Up Holland WN8 10 A7
Morse St BB10 128 D5
Morston Ave FY2 152 E1
Mortimer Gr LA3 213 A8
Mortimer Ho BL6 32 B3
Morton St 22 BB1 101 E5
Mort St BL6 32 B4
Morven Gr PR8 35 E7
Moscow Mill St BB5 103 E5
Mosedale Dr BB12 127 B8
Moseley Ave BB18 196 F1
Moseley Cl BB11 128 A2
Moseley Rd BB11 128 A3
Mosley Ave BL0 50 B2
Mosley St
Barnoldswick BB18 196 B2
Blackburn BB2 101 E2
4 Leyland PR25 77 A1
Nelson BB9 148 D8
Preston PR1 97 C8
Southport PR8 35 B4
Mosman Pl BB9 170 C3
Moss Acre Rd PR1 96 E2
Moss Ave
Orrell WN5 10 D3
Preston PR2 117 A2
Mossbank 7 BB1 102 A6
Moss Bank
Coppull PR7 42 E1
Ormskirk L39 15 D2
Moss Bank Ct L39 15 D2
Moss Bank Pl FY4 110 F8
Mossbourne Rd FY6 153 C2
MOSS BRIDGE 81 E5
Moss Bridge L40 26 C3
Moss Bridge La L40 26 C2
Moss Bridge Pk PR5 77 C8
Mossbrook Dr PR4 116 F5
Moss Cl
Chorley PR6 43 E8
6 Garstang PR3 181 B7
Moss Cl *continued*
Haslingden BB4 68 A8
Moss Cotts L40 17 A3
Mossdale 6 BB1 102 A6
Mossdale Ave PR2 118 D4
Moss Delph La L39 15 C1
Moss Dr BL6 32 F3
MOSS EDGE 179 A3
Moss Edge Cotts FY8 111 A2
Moss Edge La
Blackpool FY4 111 A3
Hale Nook FY6, PR3 178 C7
Lytham St Anne's FY8 111 B2
Moss End Way L33 1 D3
Mossfield Cl
Bamber Bridge PR5 77 B8
Bury BL9 33 B3
Mossfield Rd PR6 43 E8
Mossfields WN6 28 F6
Moss Fold Rd BB3 81 E5
Moss Gate BB1 102 B6
Mossgate Pk LA3 212 F5
Mossgate Prim Sch LA3 216 E1
Moss Gdns PR8 35 C2
Mossgiel Ave PR8 21 B5
Moss Gn L37 12 B4
Moss Hall Barns PR3 178 F3
Moss Hall La FY8 90 E7
Moss Hall Rd
Accrington BB5 104 C8
Bury BL9 33 D1
Moss Hey La PR4 56 A3
Mosshill Cl L31 5 C3
Moss House La
Fisher's Row PR3 202 A4
Great Plumpton PR4 112 C7
Much Hoole PR4 75 B2
Stalmine FY6 177 D8
Moss House Rd
Blackpool FY4 111 A6
Broughton PR4 137 B2
Moss La
Appley Bridge WN6 28 E3
Bamber Bridge PR5 77 B8
Banks PR9 55 D6
Becconsall PR4 73 C1
Bickerstaffe L39 7 F2
Blackburn BB1, BB5 102 F3
Bretherton PR26 58 C8
Burscough L40 26 A7
Catforth PR4 135 D5
Chipping PR3 186 A1
Clayton-le-W PR25 77 D2
Coppull PR7 42 E1
Croston PR26 40 A8
Duncombe PR3 158 D2
Farington PR26 76 D5
Formby L37, L39 12 E5
Garstang PR3 181 B7
Glasson LA2 209 E1
Hambleton FY6 177 D1
Hightown L38, L23 3 C2
Holme Mills LA5 240 A8
Horwich BL6 31 F2
Inskip PR4 157 B3
Kingsfold PR1 96 E1
Kirkby L33 1 B3
Leyland PR25 77 C2
Lucas Green PR6 61 D5
Maghull L31 5 E2
Maghull, Lydiate L31 5 D5
New Longton PR4 75 E7
Silverdale LA5 224 F5
Skelmersdale WN8 8 F6
Southport PR9 36 D8
St Michael's on W PR3 157 B8
Walmer Bridge PR4 75 C4
Whitworth OL12 52 B7
Wymott PR26 58 F5
Moss La E PR4 115 A8
Mosslands PR25 76 D1
Moss Lane View WN8 8 F6
Moss La W PR4 114 F7
Mosslawn Rd L32 1 A1
Moss Lea PR4 57 A7
Mosslea Dr PR3 137 B8
Moss Nook
Burscough Bridge L40 25 E6
Ormskirk L39 15 C2
Mossom La FY5 152 D7
Moss Pl LA1 218 E4
Moss Rd
Lancaster LA3 213 E7
Orrell WN5 10 D3
Southport PR8 35 C2
Moss Side
Barnoldswick BB18 196 C2
Formby L37 12 B4
MOSS SIDE
Leyland 59 B8
Lytham St Anne's 112 E1
Maghull 6 A1
Pilling 201 F5
Moss Side La
Lane Heads PR3 156 E5
Mere Brow PR4 55 F4
Stalmine FY6 177 E7
Wrea Green PR4 113 A3
Moss Side Prim Sch PR26 76 B1
Moss Side St OL12 71 E5
Moss Side Sta FY8 112 D1
Moss Side Way PR26 59 C8
Moss St
Bamber Bridge PR5 77 B8
Blackburn BB1 102 A6
7 Clitheroe BB7 166 D8
Moss St *continued*
Great Harwood BB6 124 C4
Preston PR1 96 E8
Ramsbottom BL9 50 D2
Moss Terr PR6 61 E5
Moss View
Maghull L31 5 F1
Ormskirk L39 15 E4
Mossway PR4 75 F7
Moss Way 3 FY4 110 F7
Moss Wood Cl PR7 43 A6
Moss Wood Cvn Pk PR3 203 B8
MOSSY LEA 28 F6
Mossy Lea Fold WN6 29 A3
Mossy Lea Rd WN6 28 F5
Mostyn Ave BB18 197 B1
Mostyn St BB3 81 E4
Motherwell Cres PR8 35 F3
Mottram Cl PR6 61 C5
Mottram Mews 6 BL6 32 B4
Mottram St BL6 32 B4
Moulden Brow BB2 80 B7
Moulding Cl BB2 101 B4
Mounsey Rd PR5 77 F8
Mountain Ash OL12 52 B3
Mountain Ash Cl OL12 52 B3
Mountain La 2 BB5 104 C4
Mountain Rd PR7 29 E8
Mount Ave
Lancaster LA1 218 D3
Morecambe LA4 217 F7
Rawtenstall BB4 69 F8
Mountbatten Cl PR2 96 B7
Mountbatten Rd PR7 43 B6
Mount Carmel Prep Sch L39 15 D2
Mount Carmel RC High Sch BB5 104 A4
Mount Cres
Holme Chapel BB10 108 A8
Orrell WN5 10 F6
Mountfield Ct WN5 10 F7
Mount Gdns LA4 217 E7
Mount House Cl L37 12 B5
Mount House Rd L37 12 B5
Mount La
Burnley BB10 128 F1
Holme Chapel BB10 108 A8
Todmorden OL14 109 C3
Mount Pleasant
Adlington PR6 31 A8
Arnside LA5 224 C8
16 Bacup OL13 70 C8
Blackburn BB1 101 F5
Brinscall PR6 63 A8
Chatburn BB7 190 D5
Edgworth BL7 48 D5
High Bentham LA2 239 D8
Nangreaves BL9 50 F3
Nelson BB10 149 C6
7 Preston PR1 96 F8
Rawtenstall BB4 85 E2
Sabden BB7 146 A7
Slaidburn BB7 229 B7
Sollom PR4 57 A3
Whittle-le-W PR6 61 C8
Worsthorne BB10 129 A5
Mount Pleasant La LA5 221 B5
Mount Pleasant Prim Sch BB5 124 F2
Mount Pleasant St
3 Burnley BB11 127 F5
2 Horwich BL6 32 D1
6 Oswaldtwistle BB5 103 E4
Todmorden OL14 109 A1
Mount Rd
Burnley BB11 127 F4
Fleetwood FY7 199 A5
Mount St James BB1 102 F4
Mountside Cl OL12 52 F2
Mount St
Accrington BB5 104 B4
13 Barrowford BB9 170 D3
Blackpool FY1 130 B6
Brierfield BB9 148 B5
Clayton-le-M BB5 125 A2
Fleetwood FY7 199 A4
Great Harwood BB6 124 C4
Horwich BL6 32 D2
Preston PR1 96 F7
Ramsbottom BL0 50 B6
Rawtenstall BB4 85 E2
Southport PR9 35 D7
Mount Terr BB4 86 A2
Mount The
Blackburn BB2 101 C6
1 Rawtenstall BB4 69 F7
Skelmersdale WN8 9 B8
Mount Trinity 3 BB1 101 F5
Mountwood WN8 18 A4
Mountwood Lo PR8 21 C5
Mount Zion Ct OL14 109 A1
Mowbray Ave BB2 101 F2
Mowbray Dr
Blackpool FY3 152 F1
Burton-in-K LA6 240 C7
Mowbray Pl 1 FY7 198 E4
Mowbray Rd FY7 198 E4
Mowbreck Ct PR4 114 A6
Mowbreck La PR4 114 B7
Mowbreck Park Cvn Pk PR4 114 B7
Mowbrick La LA2 220 D1
Mowgrain View 2 OL13 87 F3
MUCH HOOLE 74 D3
MUCH HOOLE MOSS HOUSES 75 A2
Muirfield PR1 96 A6
Muirfield Cl
Euxton PR7 60 D4
Fulwood PR2 117 B6
Muirfield Dr PR8 21 C4
Mulberry Ave PR1 96 A3
Mulberry Cl PR4 115 C1
Mulberry Cotts 10 LA2 211 A4
Mulberry Ct 8 BL6 32 D1
Mulberry La LA1 215 A2
Mulberry Mews
Blackpool FY2 152 F6
5 Kirkham PR4 114 B5
Mulberry St BB1 102 B5
Mulberry Wlk 3 BB1 102 B5
Mulgrave Ave PR2 117 A1
Mullion Cl PR9 54 B5
Muncaster Rd PR1 117 F2
Munro Ave WN5 10 E6
Munro Cres PR2 118 E3
Munster Ave FY2 152 D3
Murchison Gr FY5 175 E1
Murdock Ave PR2 117 D2
Murdock St BB2 101 B4
Murray Ave PR26 76 E5
Murray St
Burnley BB10 148 B1
Leyland PR25 77 B1
Preston PR1 117 E1
Musbury Cres BB4 86 A1
Musbury Mews 4 BB4 84 F1
Musbury Rd BB4 67 F7
Musbury View 2 BB4 84 F1
Musden Ave BB4 68 A7
Museum of Lancashire* PR1 97 B8
Museum St 19 BB1 101 E5
MYERSCOUGH 158 C4
Myerscough Ave
Blackpool FY4 110 F5
Lytham St Anne's FY8 89 D8
Myerscough Coll PR3 158 D5
Myerscough Hall Dr PR3 158 E5
Myerscough Planks PR3 159 A2
MYERSCOUGH SMITHY 120 E3
Myerscough Smithy Rd BB2 120 E4
Myers St
Barnoldswick BB18 196 B1
Burnley BB10 128 A8
Myndon St LA1 218 D3
Myra Ave LA4 217 C4
Myra Rd FY8 90 B4
Myrtle Ave
Blackpool FY3 130 D5
Burnley BB11 127 D4
Cleveleys FY5 175 F5
Poulton-le-F FY6 153 E5
Myrtle Bank Rd
9 Bacup OL13 87 F3
Blackburn BB2 81 C8
Myrtle Cotts 8 OL13 88 A2
Myrtle Dr PR4 114 C4
Myrtle Gdns BL9 33 B2
Myrtle Gr
1 Barnoldswick BB18 196 C2
Burnley BB10 128 F4
Haslingden BB4 85 A1
Morecambe LA3 216 F3
Southport PR9 35 E7
Myrtle Grove Mill BB4 86 D1
Myrtle St N BL9 33 B2
Myrtle St S 8 BL9 33 B2
Mystic Mews 9 L39 15 E5
MYTHOP 132 A3
Mythop Ave FY8 91 C4
Mythop Cl 1 FY8 91 C4
Mythop Ct FY4 131 D1
Mythop Pl PR2 116 F1
Mythop Rd
Lytham St Anne's FY8 91 C4
Weeton FY4, PR4 132 C2
Mythop Village FY4 131 F2
Mytton St BB12 126 D8
Mytton View BB7 166 D7

N

Naarian Ct BB1 101 F7
Nabbs Fold BL8 49 F3
Nabbs Way BL8 50 A1
Nab La
Blackburn BB2 101 D5
Oswaldtwistle BB5 103 B4
Nab Rd PR6 61 E1
NAB'S HEAD 99 E7
Nab's Head La PR5 99 E8
Naburn Dr WN5 10 E5
Nab View BB7 144 A4
Nab Wood Dr PR7 43 A6
Nailers Gn BL8 49 F1
Nairn Ave WN8 18 B5
Nairn Cl
Blackpool FY4 111 A7
Standish WN6 29 D1
Nairne St BB11 127 D5
Nancy St BB3 82 B1
NANGREAVES 50 F2

Nansen Rd
Blackburn BB2 101 B3
Fleetwood FY7 199 A3
Nantwich Ave OL12 52 F3
Napier Ave
Blackpool FY4 110 B6
Tarleton PR4 56 F8
Napier Cl FY8 110 E1
Napier St
6 Accrington BB5 104 C5
Nelson BB9 148 E7
Napier Terr PR8 35 A5
Naples Rd BB3 82 C1
NAPPA 231 E8
Naptha La PR4 76 C6
Narcissus Ave BB4 68 A8
Nares Rd BB2 101 B3
Nares St PR2 117 C1
Narrow Croft Rd L39 15 B1
Narrowgates Cotts BB12 169 C5
Narrow La
Leyland PR5 75 F2
Ormskirk L39 15 B1
Narrow Lane (Clieves Hills) L39 14 E6
Narrow Moss La L39, L40 15 E8
Narvik Ave BB11 127 B4
Nasmyth St BL6 32 C3
NATEBY 180 D6
Nateby Ave FY4 110 E5
Nateby Cl
Longridge PR3 139 F8
Lytham St Anne's FY8 90 B7
Nateby Crossing La PR3 181 A8
Nateby Ct
2 Blackpool FY4 110 B6
Garstang PR3 181 A7
Nateby Hall La PR3 203 F1
Nateby Pl PR2 116 F1
Nateby Prim Sch PR3 180 C6
National Football Mus The* PR1 118 B2
Nave Cl BB3 82 C1
Navena Ave FY7 198 E2
Navigation Bsns Village PR2 96 A8
Navigation Ho 6 BB1 101 F3
Navigation Way
Blackburn BB1 101 F3
1 Fleetwood FY7 199 A3
Preston PR2 96 A7
Naylorfarm Ave WN6 19 F5
Naylor's Terr BL7 46 C5
Naze Ct
Freckleton PR4 93 B6
4 Newchurch BB4 86 E1
Naze La PR4 93 B6
Naze La E PR4 93 C5
Naze Lane Ind Est PR4 93 C4
Naze Rd BB4 86 E1
Naze View Ave 4 BB4 86 F2
Neales Fold PR9 54 D5
Neapsands Cl PR2 118 D5
Neargates PR7 42 D3
Near Mdw PR6 78 C3
Neath Cl
Bamber Bridge PR5 97 E3
Blackburn BB1 101 E7
Neddy Hill LA6 240 B7
Neddy La BB7 144 A4
Nedens Gr L31 5 C3
Nedens La L31 5 C3
Ned's La
Smallwood Hey PR3 201 A5
Stalmine FY6 177 D5
Needham Ave LA4 217 A3
Needham Rise 1 LA4 217 A3
Needham Way WN8 18 B5
Needless Hall La BD23 231 E7
Nell Carrs BL0 50 E8
Nell La PR5 77 E4
Nell's La L39 5 F5
NELSON 148 E8
Nelson Ave PR25 77 B1
Nelson & Colne Coll
Barrowford BB9 170 D2
Colne BB8 171 A5
Nelson Court Bsns Ctr 2 PR2 95 F8
Nelson Cres PR2 116 D2
Nelson Ct
Burton in L LA6 242 C3
Fleetwood FY7 198 F3
Southport PR8 34 F4
Nelson Dr PR2 116 D2
Nelson Gdns PR4 135 C8
Nelson Rd
2 Blackpool FY1 130 B2
Burnley BB10 149 A4
Chorley PR7 43 C7
Fleetwood FY7 198 F3
Nelson Sq BB11 127 F5
Nelson St
Accrington BB5 104 C5
3 Bamber Bridge PR5 77 E8
Britannia OL13 71 C8
Clitheroe BB7 166 B8
7 Colne BB8 171 D5
1 Darwen BB3 81 F2
Great Harwood BB6 124 D6
Horwich BL6 32 D3
7 Kirkham PR4 113 F5
Nelson St *continued*
Lancaster LA1 214 F8
Lytham St Anne's FY8 91 D3
8 Morecambe LA4 217 A5
Southport PR8 35 A6
Nelson Sta BB9 148 E8
Nelson Terr
Church BB5 103 F6
Preston PR1 96 D8
Nelson Way PR2 95 E8
Nene Cl PR25 60 B7
Neps La BB7 231 C6
Neptune Ct FY4 111 D6
Neptune St BB11 127 F6
Neptune Way BB3 82 B6
Nesswood Ave FY4 110 E6
Neston St PR1 97 E8
Nether Beck LA6 240 A2
NETHER BURROW 241 E6
Netherby St BB11 127 E4
Netherfield Cl BB12 127 D7
Netherfield Gdns 9 BB9 148 E8
Netherfield Rd BB9 148 E8
Netherheys Cl BB8 171 B5
NETHER KELLET 221 F5
Nether Kellet Com Prim Sch LA6 221 E4
Nether Kellet Rd LA6 237 B8
Netherlands Rd LA4 217 C4
Netherley Rd PR7 29 E8
Netherton Ho 13 BB6 124 C5
NETHERTOWN 144 A6
Nethertown Cl BB7 144 B6
Nether View LA2 241 E1
Netherwood Gdns BB6 143 B5
Netherwood Rd BB10 128 D7
Netherwood St BB10 148 E2
Nethway Ave FY3 130 F6
Netley Ave OL12 52 F3
Network 65 Bsns Pk BB11 126 F4
Neverstitch Cl WN8 17 F2
Neverstitch Rd WN8 17 D2
Nevett St PR1 97 D8
Neville Ave FY5 175 E1
Neville Dr FY5 153 B8
Neville St PR3 140 A7
Nevill St PR8 35 B7
Nevy Fold Ave BL6 32 F3
New Acres
Carnforth LA5 223 F2
Newburgh WN8 27 A1
Newark Pl
Fulwood PR2 117 D8
4 Preston PR2 116 E2
Newark Rd OL12 52 F3
Newark Sq OL12 52 F3
Newark St BB5 103 F5
Newarth La PR4 73 E3
New Bank Rd BB2 101 B6
New Barn BB4 68 B6
New Barn Ct BB1 101 F2
New Barn La BB4 69 A8
New Bath St BB8 171 E6
Newbeck Cl BL6 32 D1
Newbigging Ave 5 BB4 86 F2
New Bonny St FY1 130 B4
NEWBRIDGE 170 C2
Newbridge Farm L33 1 E7
New Briggs Fold BL7 47 E2
New Brown St 17 BB9 170 D1
New Brunswick St BL6 32 B3
NEWBURGH 27 A2
Newburgh CE Prim Sch WN8 27 A1
Newburn Cl WN8 18 B5
Newbury Ave 3 FY4 110 D8
Newbury Cl PR2 117 C8
New Bury Cl BB5 103 C3
Newbury Gn PR2 117 C8
Newbury Rd
Lytham St Anne's FY8 90 A4
Skelmersdale WN8 18 B5
NEWBY 192 B8
Newby Ave
Fleetwood FY7 198 D1
Poulton-le-F FY6 153 D1
Newby Back La BB7 231 A1
Newby Cl
Burnley BB11 127 E2
Southport PR8 21 B3
Newby Ct L37 11 F3
Newby Dr
Clayton-le-W PR25 77 E2
Lancaster LA1 218 D3
Skelmersdale WN8 18 B5
Newby La BB7 192 B8
Newby Pl
Blackpool FY4 131 B1
Fulwood PR2 118 D4
Newby Rd 7 BB5 104 E8
New Carr La L31 4 E7
Newcastle Ave
Blackpool FY3 130 D4
Cleveleys FY5 175 F4
Newcastle St BB2 101 C3
New Century Apartments BL0 50 C7
New Chapel La BL6 32 F2
New Chapel St BB2 101 B2
NEWCHURCH 86 F1
Newchurch Cl BB2 101 F2
New Church Cl 14 BB5 124 F3
New Church Ho 6 FY1 130 C4
NEWCHURCH IN PENDLE 169 C3
New Church Mews 5 BB10 148 B1
Newchurch Old Rd OL13 87 E1
Newchurch Rd
Bacup OL13 70 C8
Rawtenstall BB4 86 C2
New Cock Yd 23 PR1 97 A7
Newcombe Rd BL0 50 B2
New Court Dr BL7 47 E3
New Court Way L39 15 F5
Newcroft LA5 223 E6
New Cswy L37, L38 3 B8
New Cut Cl PR8 22 A8
New Cut La L39, PR8 22 D6
New England Cvn Pk LA6 240 B3
Newfield Ct FY8 89 F6
Newfield Dr
Blackburn BB2 82 A8
Nelson BB9 148 E8
Newfield Rd PR5 78 A7
Newfield Sch BB1 102 C2
New Fold WN5 10 C4
New Foul La PR8 36 A4
New Garden Fields BB4 87 A7
New Garden St 1 BB2 101 E3
NEWGATE 10 A6
Newgate
Fulwood PR2 117 E4
Morecambe LA3 217 E2
NEW GATE 76 C8
Newgate Ave WN6 19 E8
Newgate La PR4 76 C8
Newgate Rd WN8 9 F7
New Ground Ct BB10 148 C3
New Hague BB18 194 F3
New Hall Ave FY4 111 B5
New Hall Ave N FY4 111 B6
New Hall Dr PR8 36 C1
NEW HALL HEY 85 F1
New Hall Hey Bsns Pk BB4 85 F1
New Hall Hey Rd BB4 85 F1
New Hall La PR1 97 C8
New Hall Rd BL9 33 E4
New Hall St BB10, BB12 148 A1
New Hampshire Ct FY8 90 D7
Newhaven Dr PR3 181 D2
New Hey La PR4 114 E5
Newholme Cvn Pk FY3 131 C2
New House La PR3 203 F3
Newhouse Rd
Accrington BB5 125 D1
Blackpool FY4 130 F2
New House St BB8 171 E5
Newington Ave BB1 122 F3
New Inn Yd 13 LA4 217 B6
New La
Burscough Bridge L40 25 B6
Burton-in-K LA6 240 B7
Duncombe PR3 158 F8
Eagland Hill PR3 179 D7
Great Mitton BB7 165 E6
Haskayne L39 13 E3
Middleforth Green PR1 96 E3
Ormskirk L39 15 E2
Oswaldtwistle BB5 103 C2
Smallwood Hey PR3 201 B2
Southport PR9 54 E3
Tarleton PR4 56 D6
Thornton FY5 153 C7
Ulnes Walton PR7 59 A1
NEWLANDS 215 C5
Newlands PR7 41 C6
Newlands Ave
Blackpool FY3 130 F2
Burscough L40 25 F4
Clitheroe BB7 166 C7
Higher Penwortham PR1 96 B5
Lancaster LA1 215 B5
Rochdale OL12 52 F3
Newlands Cl
5 Blackburn BB2 80 E8
Rochdale OL12 52 F3
Newlands Rd
Lancaster LA1 215 C5
Lytham St Anne's FY8 90 C5
Morecambe LA4 217 C4
Quernmore LA1 215 E6
Newlands Way FY6 153 C1
NEW LANE 25 B6
New Lane Head PR26 59 A2
New Lane Pace PR9 55 B8
New Lane Sta L40 25 B7
New Line OL13 71 B8
New Line Ind Est OL13 71 A8
New Links Ave PR2 117 A6
NEW LONGTON 75 F8
New Longton All Saints CE Prim Sch PR4 75 F7
Newlyn Ave
Blackpool FY4 110 E5
Maghull L31 5 E1
Newlyn Ct FY4 110 E5
Newlyn Dr WN8 9 D7
Newlyn Pl PR2 116 F5
Newman Gr FY5 175 E5
Newman Rd 2 FY1 130 D8
Newman St BB10 148 B1
Newmarket Ave LA1 215 B3
Newmarket St LA4 217 E7
New Market St
15 Blackburn BB1 101 E5
Chorley PR7 43 C8
Clitheroe BB7 166 E8
Colne BB8 171 D5
New Market The FY1 130 B1
New Meadow Cl BB1 82 A8
New Meadow La L37 3 F8
New Miles La WN6 19 F5
New Mill Ind Est PR5 77 F7
New Mill St
Blackburn BB1 101 F6
Eccleston PR7 41 C6
New Moss La PR6 61 C5
New Oxford St BB8 171 E6
New Palace Ct BB12 127 B7
New Park St 2 BB2 101 D5
New Pastures 4 PR5 77 C8
New Plough Yd BB6 124 D5
Newport Ct PR2 116 F3
Newport St BB9 170 E1
New Quay Rd LA1 214 B8
New Rd
Adlington PR6 31 D8
Bamber Bridge PR5 97 B1
Blackpool FY8 110 B4
Burnley BB11 128 B2
Coppull PR7 42 F3
Croston PR26 40 B7
Earby BB18 197 B2
Formby L37 12 A5
Ingleton LA6 242 F4
Lancaster LA1 214 F8
Newchurch BB4 86 F2
Rufford L40 39 B3
Silverdale LA5 224 F1
Staynall FY6 177 B4
Thornton FY5 153 C7
Warton LA5 223 A6
Whitworth OL12 71 B1
New Rough Hey PR2 116 F6
New Row
Altham BB5 125 E6
Trawden BB8 172 C4
New Row Cotts PR3 163 D1
New Scotland Rd BB9 170 E1
NEWSHAM 137 A5
Newsham Hall La PR4 136 F3
Newsham Pl LA1 215 A5
Newsham Rd LA1 215 A5
Newsham St 1 PR2 117 D1
NEWSHOLME 231 D6
News La WA11 8 F2
Newsome St 10 PR25 77 A1
New South Prom FY4 110 A6
New St
Blackrod BL6 31 D2
Brinscall PR6 62 F8
2 Burnley BB12 126 B8
Carnforth LA5 223 D2
Caton LA2 237 D3
Colne BB8 171 B3
Eccleston PR7 41 C6
Halsall L39 14 B8
Halton LA2 219 C6
14 Haslingden BB4 85 B3
Lancaster LA1 214 F8
Mawdesley L40 40 C2
4 Morecambe LA4 217 A5
Nelson BB9 170 F1
Rochdale OL12 52 E2
Newstead Dr WN8 18 B5
Newstet Rd L33 1 C2
New Taylor Fold BB10 148 F3
Newthorn BB5 104 A1
NEWTON
Blackpool 131 C6
Lancaster 218 E2
Slaidburn 229 A5
Whittington 241 C5
Newton Ave
Poulton-le-F FY6 153 C2
Preston PR1 98 A8
Newton Bluecoat CE Prim Sch PR4 115 A2
Newton Cl
Freckleton PR4 93 C7
Leyland PR26 59 B8
Newton Ct
Blackpool FY3 130 E5
2 Preston PR2 117 B1
Newton Dr
Accrington BB5 104 D3
Blackpool FY3 130 E5
Holme Chapel BB10 108 A7
Ramsbottom BL8 50 A1
Skelmersdale WN8 18 B5
Newton Dr E FY3 131 B7
NEWTON FELLS 229 C3
Newton Gr FY5 153 D7
Newton Hall Holiday Ctr FY3 131 C6
Newton Ho PR1 97 A8
Newton Pl FY3 131 A7
Newton Rd
Lytham St Anne's FY8 90 A7
Preston PR2 117 B2
Newton St
Blackburn BB1 102 B5
Burnley BB12 127 C7
Clitheroe BB7 166 D7
Darwen BB3 82 B2
Oswaldtwistle BB5 103 C5
2 Preston PR1 97 B8
Southport PR9 36 A7
Newton Terr LA1 218 E3
NEWTON-WITH-SCALES 114 F2
Newtown BB18 196 B2
NEW TOWN 140 A6
Newtown St BB8 171 E5
New Way
Royal Oak L39 7 C2
Whitworth OL12 71 C1
New Wellington Cl BB2 101 C1
New Wellington Gdns BB2 101 C1
New Wellington St BB2 101 C1
Nib La PR1 76 E8
Nicholas St
Burnley BB11 128 A5
Burnley, Harle Syke BB10 148 E3
3 Colne BB8 171 C4
Darwen BB3 81 F1
Nicholl St 1 BB10 128 A8
Nicholson Cres LA4 217 E5
Nichol St PR7 61 C1
Nickey La BB2 121 F2
Nick Hilton's Brow PR6 44 D3
Nick Hilton's La PR6 44 D3
Nickleton Brow PR6 44 C2
Nicksons La FY6 200 B4
Nickson's Weind PR3 181 C7
Nicola Cl OL13 88 A7
Nicoll Ct FY8 89 D7
Nightfield La BB2 120 F6
Nightingale Cl
Blackburn BB1 102 B1
Whalley BB7 144 A7
Nightingale Cres 4 BB11 127 C5
Nightingale Dr FY6 153 B2
Nightingale Rd BL6 31 C3
Nightingale St 2 PR6 31 A8
Nightingale Way
Catterall PR3 181 D3
Chorley PR7 42 F5
Nile Cl PR2 95 E8
Nile St
5 Lancaster LA1 214 F8
12 Nelson BB9 170 D1
Preston PR1 97 A7
Nimes St PR1 97 D8
Nine Elms PR2 117 C6
Nineteen Acre La LA5 225 F4
Nineveh St 12 BB8 171 E5
Nipe La WN8 9 B5
Nithside FY4 131 C1
Niton Cl BB4 85 C1
Nixon La PR26 59 A8
Nixons Ct PR26 58 F8
Nixons La WN8 9 D7
Nixon's La PR8 21 E7
Noble St
15 Darwen BB3 65 A8
Great Harwood BB6 124 C4
Rishton BB1 124 B1
Noblett Ct 9 FY7 198 F2
Noblett St BB1 101 F5
Noel Gate L39 15 B1
Noel Jones Ct FY8 89 E7
Noel Rd LA1 218 C3
Noel Sq PR2 118 E1
Noggarth Rd BB12 169 F2
NOG TOW 116 F7
Nolan St PR8 35 C5
NOOK 181 B3
Nook Cotts PR3 180 C6
Nook Cres PR2 139 C1
Nook Croft BB18 197 C2
Nookdales Cotts LA6 242 F1
Nook Farm Ave OL12 52 F3
Nookfield PR26 76 A1
Nook Field PR3 138 D6
Nookfield Cl FY8 91 A4
Nook Glade PR2 139 C1
Nook La
Bamber Bridge PR5 77 D6
Blackburn BB2 100 F1
Churchtown PR3 181 A3
Mawdesley L40 40 E5
Oswaldtwistle BB5 103 B2
NOOKLANDS 117 D4
Nooklands PR2 117 E4
Nook Terr
Blackburn BB2 101 A1
1 Rochdale OL12 52 F3
Nook The
Appley Bridge WN6 19 E7
Bolton-le-S LA5 221 A4
Staining FY3 131 D5
Noon Sun St OL12 52 F1
Noor St PR1 118 A1
Nora St BB9 170 D3
NORBRECK 152 B6
Norbreck Cl BB2 81 F8
Norbreck Ct FY5 152 C6
Norbreck Dr PR2 116 E1
Norbreck Prim Sch FY5 152 D8
Norbreck Rd FY5 152 C7
Norburn Cres L37 11 F2
Norbury Cl PR9 54 C5
Norcliffe Rd FY2 152 C5
Norcote Lo L37 11 E4
NORCROSS 153 A7
Norcross Brow PR6 63 B8
Norcross La FY5 153 A7
Norcross Pl PR2 116 F1
NORDEN 124 A2
Norden Ct BB6 124 E5
Norden Ct BB1 124 B1

Norden High Sch & Sports Coll BB1 124 A2
Norden View BB1 124 A2
Norfield L39 15 F5
Norfolk Ave
Blackpool FY2 152 B3
Burnley BB12 127 B7
Cleveleys FY5 175 E3
Morecambe LA3 216 E2
Padiham BB12 126 D6
Norfolk Cl
7 Clayton-le-M BB5 124 F3
Leyland PR25 59 E7
Norfolk Gr
Accrington BB5 104 A7
Southport PR8 34 F1
Norfolk Rd
Bamber Bridge PR5 97 D4
Blackpool FY3 131 A2
Longshaw WN5 10 E1
Lytham St Anne's FY8 91 C5
Preston PR1 118 A1
Southport PR8 34 F1
Norfolk St
Accrington BB5 104 D7
Blackburn BB2 101 C2
Colne BB8 171 E5
Darwen BB3 82 B1
Lancaster LA1 218 D2
Nelson BB9 170 D1
Rishton BB1 124 A1
Norham Cl BB12 127 E7
Norkeed Rd FY5 152 C7
Norland Dr LA3 212 F8
Norman Cl FY5 175 F1
Normandie Ave FY2 152 D3
Normandy Rd PR4 137 B3
Normanhurst L39 16 A4
Norman Rd BB5 103 C5
Norman St
Blackburn BB2 101 C3
Burnley BB10 128 A7
Bury BL9 33 B4
Normington Cl L31 5 C4
NORMOSS 131 B7
Normoss Ave FY3 131 A7
Normoss Rd FY3 131 C7
Norris House Dr L39 6 C8
Norris St
3 Chorley PR7 43 C6
Darwen BB3 82 B1
Fulwood PR2 117 D3
Preston PR1 117 E2
Norris Way L37 12 B3
Norse Cotts PR26 57 E6
North Albert St 12 FY7 199 B5
North Albion St FY7 199 A4
Northall PR4 74 E2
Northam Cl
Southport PR9 54 A5
Standish WN6 29 D1
North Ave
Barnoldswick BB18 196 B2
Blackpool FY3 130 D7
Ramsbottom BL8 49 F1
North Bank Ave BB1 122 E1
Northbrook Gdns PR25 76 E1
Northbrook Prim Sch PR25 76 F1
Northbrook Rd PR25 76 F1
North Church St FY7 199 B5
Northcliffe BB6 124 B6
North Cliffe Sch BB6 124 B6
North Cliff St 6 PR1 96 E6
North Clifton St 7 FY8 91 B3
Northcote Rd
Langho BB6 143 C3
Preston PR1 96 D7
Northcote St
Darwen BB3 65 B6
4 Haslingden BB4 85 B2
8 Leyland PR25 77 A1
North Cres FY8 89 E6
North Croft PR3 181 C8
North Ct
Blackpool FY5 152 E8
Cleveleys FY5 175 D5
Northdene WN8 27 B2
North Dr
Appley Bridge WN6 28 C2
Blackpool FY5 152 D6
Cleveleys FY5 175 E2
Inskip PR4 157 C1
Kirkham PR4 113 F6
Lancaster LA1 211 B8
North Dunes L38 2 F4
North East Ave PR6 63 A8
North East Dr LA1 211 B8
NORTH END 3 B6
Northenden Rd PR7 42 E1
North End Football Gd (Preston North End FC) PR1 118 B2
North End La L38 3 A6
Northern Ave PR4 74 E2
Northern Equine Therapy Ctr The* BD24 236 F6
Northern Prim Sch OL13 87 F6
Northern Terr LA5 224 F5
Northfield WN8 18 B4
Northfield Ave FY1 130 B8
Northfield Cl L33 1 A4
Northfield Rd
Blackburn BB1 101 E7
Rising Bridge BB5 85 A8
Northfleet Ave FY7 198 E2
Northfold Com Prim Sch FY5 175 E4
Northgate
Blackburn BB2 101 E5
Blackpool FY2 152 C4
Goosnargh PR3 138 D6
Leyland PR25 77 B2
Lytham St Anne's FY8 89 D6
Morecambe LA3 217 E2
Whitworth OL12 52 C7
Northgate Cl BL6 32 C1
Northgate Dr PR6 61 E2
North Gr 1 PR5 77 C8
NORTH HAG 85 A4
North Highfield PR2 118 E6
NORTH HOLME 195 A8
North Houses La FY8 111 D1
Northlands
Fulwood PR2 117 E6
Leyland PR26 59 C7
Northleach Ave PR1 96 F2
Northleach Dr PR8 21 A5
North Meade L31 5 C2
North Meadowside PR4 75 A6
North Mersey Bsns Ctr L33 1 D4
North Moor La L39 23 E2
North Moss La L37 12 D7
North Nook La PR3 183 E3
North Par 7 BB18 196 B3
North Park Ave BB9 170 C1
North Park Dr FY3 130 F5
North Perimeter Rd L33 1 D4
North Prom FY8 89 D7
North Quarry Bsns Pk WN6 28 D1
North Rd
Blackburn BB1 102 C3
Bretherton PR26 58 B7
Carnforth LA5 223 E2
Lancaster LA1 214 F8
Preston PR1 117 F1
Rawtenstall BB4 86 C2
Southport PR9 54 C4
North Ribble St 7 PR5 97 C6
North Road Prim Sch LA5 223 D1
NORTH SHORE 130 B8
Northside PR7 60 C3
North Sq
Blackpool FY3 130 D6
Cleveleys FY5 175 D5
North St
Barnoldswick BB18 196 B1
Burnley BB10 148 A1
Burnley, Harle Syke BB10 148 F3
Chorley PR7 61 D2
2 Clitheroe BB7 189 F1
Colne BB8 171 E6
Fleetwood FY7 199 B5
Hapton BB12 126 C5
Haslingden BB4 85 C1
Morecambe LA4 217 B5
14 Nelson BB9 170 D1
Newchurch BB4 86 E1
Padiham BB12 146 C1
Preston PR1 96 F8
Ramsbottom BL0 68 C2
Rawtenstall BB4 86 A2
Southport PR9 35 C8
Water BB4 87 A8
Whitworth OL12 71 C1
North Syke Ave PR2 116 C1
Northumberland Ave
Blackpool FY2 152 B1
Cleveleys FY5 175 F5
Northumberland Cl BB3 65 C6
Northumberland St
2 Chorley PR7 43 D7
Morecambe LA4 217 A5
North Union View PR5 76 F8
North Vale PR6 43 F1
North Valley Rd BB8 171 D5
North Valley Ret Pk BB8 171 D5
North View
Kirkham PR4 113 F5
Leyland PR25 59 F8
Ramsbottom BL0 50 B2
Ramsbottom, Strongstry BL0 68 C2
Rawtenstall BB4 86 A8
North View Cl PR3 156 C5
North Warton St FY8 91 C3
Northway
Broughton PR3 137 C3
Fleetwood FY7 198 D1
Fulwood PR2 117 D7
Maghull L31, L39 5 E4
Ormskirk L39 15 A1
Skelmersdale WN8 18 B2
Northway Prim Sch L31 5 E3
Northways WN6 29 D2
North West Bsns Coll PR9 35 B7
North West Dr LA1 211 A8
NORTHWOOD 1 A3
Northwood Cl
Burnley BB12 127 D7
Lytham St Anne's FY8 90 E4
Northwood Way FY6 153 D2
Norton Ave LA3 216 D3
Norton Ct FY8 89 F4
Norton Dr LA3 216 E2
Norton Gr LA3 216 D2
Norton Pl LA3 216 D2
Norton Rd
Garstang PR3 204 C2
Morecambe LA3 216 D2
Rochdale OL12 52 F3
Norton St 1 BB12 126 C4
Norton Vale FY5 176 D2
Norway Ho 11 BB8 171 D5
Norwich Pl
Blackpool FY2 152 D5
24 Preston PR1 97 A7
Norwich St BB1 101 F7
Norwood Ave
Becconsall PR4 73 F2
Blackburn BB2 101 E2
Blackpool FY3 130 E8
Southport PR9 35 E7
Norwood Cl PR6 31 A8
Norwood Cres PR9 35 E7
Norwood Ct 13 LA1 215 A8
Norwood Dr LA4 217 F3
Norwood Gdns PR9 35 F7
Norwood Prim Sch PR9 35 E7
Norwood Rd
Lytham St Anne's FY8 89 C8
Southport PR8, PR9 35 F6
Notre Dame Gdns BB1 102 A6
Nottingham Rd PR1 118 A1
Nottingham St BB1 102 A4
Novak Pl 6 LA4 217 F4
NOVA SCOTIA 101 E3
Nova Scotia Ret Pk BB2 101 E3
Nowell Gr BB12 145 D2
Nowell St 17 BB6 124 C5
Noyna Ave BB8 194 E1
Noyna Rd BB8 194 E1
Noyna St BB8 171 E6
Noyna View BB8 171 E7
NUN HILLS 70 C7
Nun's St LA1 215 A8
Nurseries The
Blackpool FY4 110 F5
Formby L37 12 A2
Hesketh Bank PR4 73 E3
Nursery Ave L39 16 A6
Nursery Cl
Coppull PR7 42 E4
Leyland PR25 59 F8
Nursery Dr
Becconsall PR4 73 F1
Formby L37 11 F2
Nursery La PR4 75 E8
Nursery Nook BB3 82 D5
Nursery Rd L31 5 C4
Nuthall Rd PR8 35 F3
NUTTALL 50 C4
Nuttall Ave
Great Harwood BB6 124 C4
Horwich BL6 32 A3
Nuttall Cl BL0 50 C5
Nuttall Hall Cotts BL0 50 D5
Nuttall Hall Rd BL0 50 D5
Nuttall La BL0 50 C4
NUTTALL LANE 50 C5
Nuttall Rd
Blackpool FY1 130 D2
Ramsbottom BL0 50 D4
Nuttall St Mews 3 BB5 104 C5
Nuttall St
Accrington BB5 104 C5
3 Bacup OL13 88 B3
Blackburn BB2 101 D1
Blackburn, Ewood BB2 81 D8
6 Burnley BB11 128 B4
Bury BL9 33 A1
Rawtenstall BB4 86 B3
Nuttalls Way BB1 102 C2
Nutter Cres BB12 146 F5
Nutter Rd
Accrington BB5 104 C7
Cleveleys FY5 175 D3
2 Preston PR1 96 E7
NUTTER'S PLATT 96 C1

O

Oak Ave
Blackpool FY4 110 D8
Euxton PR7 60 D3
Galgate LA2 210 F4
Higher Penwortham PR1 96 B3
9 Horwich BL6 32 E1
Kirkham PR4 114 B4
Longridge PR3 140 A7
Morecambe LA4 217 F6
Ormskirk L39 15 D4
Ramsbottom BL0 50 A2
Rising Bridge BB5 85 A8
Thornton FY5 153 C8
Oak Bank
Accrington BB5 125 D2
Gregson Lane PR5 98 E1
Oakbank Dr BB5 103 E5
Oak Cl
Barrow BB7 166 D1
Rishton BB1 103 B8
Whalley BB7 144 A7
Whitworth OL12 71 D4
Oak Cres WN8 17 D1
Oak Croft PR6 78 B2
Oakdene Ave BB5 125 E1
Oak Dr
Burscough L40 25 F3
Chorley PR6 61 C3
Freckleton PR4 93 A5
Halton LA2 219 D7
Oaken Bank BB10 148 E3
Oaken Cl OL13 88 B3
OAKENCLOUGH 226 C2
Oakenclough Rd
Bacup OL13 88 B3
Bleasdale PR3 183 F4
Oakeneaves Ave BB11 127 D2
Oakengate PR2 118 C7
Oakengates WN6 29 F1
Oakenhead Cl PR3 160 D7
Oakenhead St PR1 118 E1
OAKENHEAD WOOD 85 E3
Oakenhead Wood Old Rd BB4 85 E3
Oakenhurst Rd BB2 101 D4
OAKENSHAW 124 E3
Oakenshaw Ave OL12 52 C6
Oakenshaw Croft BB5 124 E3
Oakenshaw View OL12 52 C6
Oakfield
Fulwood PR2 117 F7
Preston PR2 117 B1
Oakfield Ave
Barnoldswick BB18 196 A3
Clayton-le-M BB5 124 E3
Huncoat BB5 125 E1
Oakfield Cl BL6 32 F2
Oakfield Cres BB5 103 F4
Oakfield Dr
Formby L37 11 D4
Leyland PR26 59 B8
Oakfield House Sch PR4 115 C4
Oakfield Rd
Blackburn BB2 81 D7
Hightown L38 2 F2
Oakfields L39 16 A5
Oakford Cl PR9 55 B5
Oakgate Cl PR4 56 F5
Oak Gates BL7 47 E1
Oak Gn L39 15 F5
Oak Gr
Darwen BB3 82 B2
Garstang PR3 181 C7
New Longton PR4 76 A6
Oakgrove FY4 110 D6
Oakham Ct
12 Preston PR1 97 A7
Southport PR9 35 C8
Oakhill Cl L31 5 D2
Oak Hill Cl BB5 104 C4
Oakhill Coll BB7 144 D6
Oakhill Cottage La L31 5 D4
Oakhill Dr L31 5 D4
Oakhill Rd L31 5 D3
Oak Ho PR7 42 F6
Oakhurst Ave BB5 125 E1
Oak La
Accrington BB5 104 D5
Newton-w-S PR4 114 F2
Oakland Ave FY5 152 D6
Oakland Cl LA1 215 D8
Oakland Glen PR5 97 A3
Oaklands Ave
Barrowford BB9 170 D3
Tarleton PR4 57 A7
Oaklands Ct LA1 214 C5
Oaklands Dr
Higher Penwortham PR1 96 A4
Rawtenstall BB4 85 E2
Oaklands Gr PR2 116 F1
Oaklands Rd BL0 68 D2
Oakland St
4 Bamber Bridge PR5 97 E1
Nelson BB9 148 E8
Oaklands Terr BB1 101 F7
Oaklea WN6 29 A2
Oakleaf Cl PR3 138 C6
Oakleaf Ct FY5 175 D4
Oakleaf Way FY4 131 D1
Oaklee Gr L33 1 A4
Oakleigh WN8 9 D2
Oakleigh Terr 8 OL14 109 B1
Oakley Rd
Morecambe LA3 216 D2
Rawtenstall BB4 85 F2
Oakley St BB4 85 E2
Oakmere PR6 78 C3
Oakmere Ave PR6 79 D2
Oakmere Cl BB2 81 D6
Oakmoor Ave FY2 152 E4
Oak Rd PR3 181 B8
Oak Ridge BB7 189 D7
Oakridge Cl PR2 117 F7
Oaks Bar BB1 122 C8
Oaks Brow BB1 122 C7
Oaksfield BB3 81 E5
Oakshaw Dr OL12 52 A1
Oakshott Pl PR5 78 B7
Oak St
Accrington BB5 104 C5
5 Bacup OL13 88 A3
Blackburn BB1 101 F7
Brierfield BB9 148 B6
Burnley BB12 127 C6
Clayton-le-M BB5 124 F1
Clow Bridge BB11 106 B4
Colne BB8 171 F6
Fleetwood FY7 199 A4
Great Harwood BB6 124 C6
2 Nelson BB9 170 E1
Oswaldtwistle BB5 103 D3
Preston PR1 97 A7
Ramsbottom BL0 50 B5
Southport PR8 35 E6
Whitworth OL12 71 D5
Oaks The
Bamber Bridge PR5 97 B3
Blackpool FY3 130 E3
Chorley PR7 43 B4
Leyland PR26 59 A7
Poulton-le-F FY6 153 D4
Southport PR8 34 F6
St Michael's on W PR3 157 C7
Oak Terr
Barnoldswick BB18 196 C3
Rawtenstall BB4 68 E8
Oaktree Ave
Clayton-le-W PR25 77 D4
Fulwood PR2 117 A4
Oaktree Cl PR2 117 A4
Oak Tree Ct WN8 18 D3
Oak Tree Dr PR4 113 E4
Oak View
Leyland PR25 76 E2
Whitworth OL12 71 D4
Oakville Rd LA3 212 E5
Oakway PR3 140 A8
Oakwood WN8 18 D3
Oakwood Ave
Bamber Bridge PR5 97 C4
Blackburn BB1 123 B1
Lytham St Anne's FY8 90 E4
Shevington WN6 19 F5
Southport PR8 21 D6
Oakwood Cl
Blackpool FY4 110 F4
Burnley BB10 148 D3
Darwen BB3 81 E5
Thornton FY5 176 D2
Oakwood Dr
Fulwood PR2 117 D8
Southport PR8 21 E5
Oakwood Gdns LA1 215 A2
Oakwood Gr LA5 220 F2
Oakwood Rd
Accrington BB5 104 D3
Chorley PR7 43 B6
Coppull PR7 42 F2
Oakwood View PR7 43 B4
Oakworth Ave PR2 118 F5
Oasis Cl L40 39 B3
Oat St BB12 126 D7
Oban Cres PR1 118 D3
Oban Ct PR2 139 D1
Oban Dr BB1 102 C3
Oban Pl FY2 152 E6
Oban St BB10 128 C8
Observatory Rd BB2 102 A2
Occupation La
Singleton FY6 154 D4
Stalmine FY6 177 C7
Ocean Bvd FY4 110 A7
Ocean Ct FY6 199 D5
Ocean Edge Cvn Pk LA3 212 D3
Ocean Plaza PR8 35 A8
Ocean View Apartments FY5 175 C2
Ocean Way FY5 175 C3
Odell Way PR5 97 E3
Off Botanic Rd PR9 54 A1
Offerton St BL6 32 A3
Off Mount Pleasant St 7 BB5 103 E4
Ogden Cl BB4 68 A7
Ogden Dr BB4 68 A7
O'Hagan Ct BB9 148 B6
Old Acre L38 2 F3
Old Back La BB7 144 F7
Old Bank La
Blackburn, Shadsworth BB1, BB2 102 B2
Blackburn, Whinny Heights BB2 102 A2
Old Bank St 4 BB2 101 E4
OLD BIRTLE 33 E7
Old Boundary Way L39 15 F6
Old Brewery Trad Est 9 PR1 96 E8
Old Bridge La FY6 154 B7
Old Bridge Way PR6 61 D1
Old Buckley La PR3 141 D7
Oldbury Pl FY5 152 F8
Old Carr Mill St BB4 85 B5
Old Clitheroe Rd PR3 163 E3
Old Cock Yd PR1 97 A7
Old Croft PR2 117 D8
Old Dawber's La PR7 60 B1
Olde Back La BB11 127 C3
Old Engine Ho The 12 BL0 50 C6
Old Engine La
Ramsbottom BL0 50 D6
Skelmersdale WN8 17 C2
Oldest Barn Mews 3 LA3 216 F3
Olde Stoneheath Ct PR6 44 B4
Old Farmside BB2 81 D7
Oldfield
7 Kingsfold PR1 96 D2
Much Hoole PR4 74 F4
Oldfield Ave
Blackpool FY2 152 C4
Darwen BB3 81 E3
Oldfield Carr La FY6 153 E1
Oldfield Cl FY6 153 E1
Oldfield Cres FY6 153 E3
Oldfield Rd PR5 78 A7
Old Forge FY8 90 D7

Old Gates Dr BB2 80 F8
Old Gn BL8 49 F1
Old Greaves Town La PR2 116 E1
Old Greenwood La BL6 32 D1
Old Ground St 8 BL0 50 C6
Old Hall Cl
  Bamber Bridge PR5 77 E8
  7 Morecambe LA4 217 F4
  Roughlee BB9 170 B5
Old Hall Dr
  Bamber Bridge PR5 77 E8
  Huncoat BB5 125 F1
Old Hall Farm Bsns Pk PR9 36 A5
Old Hall La
  Charnock Green PR7 42 B6
  Pleasington BB2 100 C2
Old Hall Pk PR3 137 E3
Old Hall Sq BB10 129 A5
Old Hall St BB10 128 A8
Oldham St
  Burnley BB11 127 F4
  3 Morecambe LA4 217 B6
Old Hey Croft 5 PR1 96 D2
Old Hive PR3 185 D4
Old House La FY4 111 D7
Old Kiln OL13 70 D8
Old La
  Bispham Green L40 27 D8
  Earby BB18 197 B2
  Formby L37 11 F6
  Haskayne L39 13 E3
  Horwich BL6 32 F2
  Kelbrook BB18 194 F4
  Maghull L31 5 E4
  Salterforth BB18 194 B5
  Shawforth OL12, OL13 71 E6
Old Lancaster La PR2 117 D1
Old Lancaster Rd PR3 181 B2
OLD LANGHO 143 C4
Old Langho Rd BB6 143 C5
Old Laund St BB12 147 E8
Old Links Cl PR9 36 B8
Old Lodge La PR3 159 A8
Old Lord's Cres BL6 32 B5
Old Lostock La PR5 77 E7
Old Mains La FY6 153 F6
Old Market Ct 9 LA4 217 B6
Old Meadow Ct 3 FY3 130 E3
Old Meadow La 2 FY3 130 E3
Old Meadows Rd OL13 88 A5
Old Mill Ct PR4 74 F5
Old Mill Dr BB8 171 F4
Old Mill Hill L39 15 D3
Old Mill Ind Est PR5 97 F2
Old Mill La
  Formby L37 11 F4
  Hill Dale L40 27 F6
Old Mill St BB1 101 F6
Old Millstones PR1 96 D7
Old Mill Terr PR6 61 E1
Old Moor Rd LA2 238 F8
Old Moss La L39 13 C5
Old Nab Rd BB6 123 E8
Old Oak Gdns PR5 97 B2
Old Oliver La BD24 236 C6
Old Orch PR2 117 D5
Old Park La PR9 36 A8
Old Parsonage La BB12 126 B8
Old Penny Gdns LA4 217 E4
Old Pepper La WN6 29 B2
Old Pope La PR4 76 B8
Old Prescot Cl L31 6 C2
Old Quarry La BL7 47 F1
Old Raike BD23 236 C4
Old Rake BL6 32 E5
Old Rd BD23 197 C6
Old Rectory Gn L39 6 A7
Old Rectory The LA2 206 C5
Old Roman Rd BB12, BB7 145 A3
Old Rough La L33 1 A2
Old Row
  Barrow BB7 166 D1
  Kirkham PR4 114 B4
  4 Rawtenstall BB4 85 E2
Old Sawmill The
  16 Darwen BB3 65 A8
  Rathmell BD24 236 E7
Old Sch Mews 8 BB4 85 B3
Old School Cl PR26 59 A8
Old School Dr PR4 75 B8
Old School Ho The
  Blackburn BB1 82 D8
  Darwen BB3 82 B1
  Higher Walton PR5 98 B3
Old School La
  Adlington PR7 30 E5
  Bamber Bridge PR5 77 C6
  Euxton PR7 60 D3
  Tockholes BB3 80 F2
Old School Mews
  12 Bacup OL13 70 C8
  Chorley PR7 43 C5
Old School Row 3 BB12 127 B6
Old School Sq 8 PR1 96 E7
Old School The LA2 219 C6
Old Sidings The BB8 194 D1
Old St BB4 86 F1
Old Stables The BB7 144 B8
Old Station Cl PR2 139 D1
Old Station Ct 9 BB7 166 E8
Old Stone Trough La BB18 195 A5
Old Swan Cl BL7 47 E2
Old Swan Cotts BL7 47 E2
Old TH 26 BB18 196 B2
Old Tom's La FY6 177 E8
Old Town Cl WN8 8 D8
Old Town Ct L37 11 E4
Old Town Hall Mews 1 LA4 217 B6
Old Town La L37 11 E4
Old Town Way WN8 8 D8
Old Trafford Pk LA3 212 F4
Old Tram Rd PR1, PR5 97 A4
Old Tramway The PR5 78 B6
Old Vicarage 16 PR1 97 A8
Old Vicarage Ct FY8 89 F5
Old Vicarage Rd BL6 32 F3
Old Will's La BL6 32 B6
Old Worden Ave PR7 60 E7
Olivant St BB12 127 C7
Olive Bank BB6 143 D1
Olive Cl PR6 61 C5
Olive Gr
  Blackpool FY3 130 E5
  Skelmersdale WN8 17 E1
  Southport PR8 35 E7
  Warton PR4 92 D6
Olive La BB3 82 B2
Oliver Ct FY6 199 E5
Olive Rd LA1 218 D2
Oliver Pl LA5 223 E2
Olivers Pl PR2 118 A8
Oliver's Pl PR2 118 B8
Oliver St 10 OL13 70 C8
Olive St OL13 70 E8
Olive Terr BB4 85 F5
OLLERTON FOLD 79 D5
Ollerton La PR6 79 E4
Ollerton Rd FY8 90 D5
Ollerton St PR6 44 A1
Ollerton Terr PR6 79 E3
Olympian Way PR25 77 A2
Olympia St BB10 128 C5
Olympic Way FY4 111 C8
Omerod St BB4 87 A8
Omrod Pl 1 FY1 130 B2
Onchan Dr OL13 88 B1
Onchan Rd BB2 101 E1
One Ash Cl OL12 52 F2
Onslow Cres PR8 35 A2
Onslow Rd FY3 130 F7
Ontario Cl BB2 101 A8
Oozebooth Terr BB1 101 E7
Oozehead La BB2 101 B5
Opal Cl 6 FY5 152 F7
Opal St BB1 122 F2
Openshaw Dr BB1 101 E8
Openshaw St BL9 33 A1
Oporto Cl BB11 127 E5
Oram Rd PR5 78 F8
Oram St BL9 33 A4
Orange St BB5 104 B8
Orchard Ave
  Blackpool FY4 110 C6
  Bolton-le-S LA5 221 A6
  New Longton PR4 76 A7
  Poulton-le-F FY6 153 E1
Orchard Bridge 6 BB11 127 F6
Orchard Cl
  Becconsall PR4 73 F3
  Blackburn BB2 81 D6
  Euxton PR7 60 D3
  Freckleton PR4 93 A6
  Fulwood PR2 117 A5
  Silverdale LA5 224 B2
  Slyne LA2 218 D8
  Thornton FY5 176 B4
  Wrea Green PR4 113 B3
Orchard Croft 2 PR5 77 A8
Orchard Ct
  Fulwood PR2 117 D5
  Leyland PR25 59 D7
  Maghull L31 5 F1
  Orrell WN5 10 D3
Orchard Dr
  Fleetwood FY7 198 E1
  Lucas Green PR6 61 C5
  Oswaldtwistle BB5 103 F5
Orchard End PR3 156 C5
Orchard Gdns
  Mossy Lea WN6 28 F6
  Much Hoole PR4 74 E3
Orchard Grange PR1 96 A5
Orchard La
  Lancaster LA1 214 D7
  Longton PR4 74 F8
  Southport PR8 21 D4
Orchard Lo 1 L39 15 F6
Orchard Mill Dr PR26 58 B2
Orchard Pk 16 BB3 81 F2
Orchard Pl PR4 74 E3
Orchard Rd FY8 89 E6
Orchard St
  5 Barnoldswick BB18 196 B2
  Great Harwood BB6 124 C4
  1 Leyland PR25 77 B1
  26 Preston PR1 96 F8
Orchards The
  Barnoldswick BB18 196 C3
  Carleton FY6 153 B5
  3 Orrell WN5 10 E5
  Overton LA3 209 D8
  Southport PR8 21 D4
Orchard The
  Barrowford BB9 170 E6
  Burnley BB11 127 C4
  Clitheroe BB7 189 E2
  Croston PR26 58 C3
  Kirkham PR4 114 E6
  Leyland PR26 76 B1
  Little Eccleston PR3 156 A5
  Ormskirk L39 15 D5
  Warton PR4 92 E6
  Woodplumpton PR4 136 E1
  Wray LA2 238 D6
Orchard View L39 15 D1
Orchard Wlk
  Grimsargh PR2 139 C2
  Ramsbottom BL8 49 F1
Orchid Cl WN8 10 B6
Orchid Way OL12 52 D3
Ord Ave FY4 130 F1
Orders La PR4 114 A4
Ordnance St BB1 102 A5
Ord Rd PR2 117 C2
Oregon Ave FY3 130 E8
Oriole Cl 9 BB1 101 F6
Orion Bldgs 1 FY5 175 D2
Orkney Cl BB1 102 D3
Orkney Rd 1 FY1 130 C2
Orme Ho L39 16 A5
Ormerod Rd BB10, BB11 128 B7
Ormerod St
  Accrington BB5 104 B5
  Burnley BB11 128 A5
  Colne BB8 171 C4
  Haslingden BB4, BB5 85 B7
  5 Nelson BB9 148 F8
  Rawtenstall BB4 86 A2
  Thornton FY5 176 B4
  Worsthorne BB10 129 A5
Ormerod Terr
  Barrow BB6 144 D8
  Foulridge BB8 194 E1
Orme St 1 FY1 130 C3
Ormond Ave
  Blackpool FY1 130 B8
  Westhead L40 16 E4
Ormonde Cres L33 1 A2
Ormond St BL9 33 A3
Ormont Ave FY5 175 E2
Ormrod Ct 20 BL9 33 A2
Ormrod St BL9 33 A2
Ormrods The BL9 33 F5
Ormsby Cl WN6 29 E2
ORMSKIRK 15 C6
Ormskirk Bsns Pk 2 L39 15 F6
Ormskirk CE Prim Sch L39 16 A6
Ormskirk Coll L39 15 E6
Ormskirk & District General Hospl L39 16 A4
Ormskirk Ind Pk L39 16 A6
Ormskirk Lathom Park CE Prim Sch L40 17 A8
Ormskirk Old Rd L39 7 F7
Ormskirk Rd
  Bickerstaffe L39 7 E7
  Preston PR1 97 A8
  Rainford WA11 8 D1
  Skelmersdale, Tanhouse WN8 9 D7
  Skelmersdale WN8 17 C1
  Up Holland WN8 10 A7
Ormskirk Sch L39 16 B5
Ormskirk Sta L39 15 F5
Ormston Ave BL6 32 C5
Orms Way L37 11 E3
Orpen Ave BB11 127 F3
Orpington Sq BB10 148 C3
ORRELL 10 E6
Orrell Cl 3 PR25 76 D1
Orrell Gdns WN5 10 F6
Orrell Hill La L38 3 C4
Orrell Holgate Prim Sch WN5 10 E5
Orrell La L40 25 D5
Orrell Newfold Com Prim Sch WN5 10 D4
ORRELL POST 10 E7
Orrell Rd WN5 10 E7
Orrell Sta WN5 10 E4
Orrell Water Pk* WN5 10 E4
Orrest Rd PR1 119 A1
ORTNER 232 C1
Orton Ct BB9 170 D4
Orwell Cl L37 11 D1
OSBALDESTON 121 D4
OSBALDESTON GREEN 121 D6
Osbaldeston La BB2 121 D5
Osbert Croft PR4 95 A1
Osborne Ave FY5 175 F1
Osborne Cres LA3 216 F3
Osborne Dr PR6 78 C2
Osborne Gr
  Burnley BB10 148 B3
  Cleveleys FY5 175 D5
  Morecambe LA4 217 A3
Osborne Rd
  Bamber Bridge PR5 97 D3
  Blackburn BB2 101 B6
  Cleveleys FY5 175 D5
  Formby L37 11 E1
  Lytham St Anne's FY8 89 F5
  Morecambe LA3, LA4 216 F3
  Southport PR8 21 B6
Osborne St 12 PR1 96 E7
Osborne Terr
  Bacup OL13 70 D8
  Darwen BB3 81 E2
  1 Rawtenstall BB4 85 E2
  Spen Brook BB12 169 D2
  Whitewell Bottom BB4 86 F4
Osborne Way BB4 85 A1
Osbourne Rd FY4 110 B8
Osbourne Way PR1 118 A1
Oscar St 4 FY4 130 F2
Oslo Rd BB11 127 B5
Osprey Cl
  Blackburn BB1 101 D8
  Knowley PR6 62 A3
Oswald Rd
  Lytham St Anne's FY8 91 D4
  Preston PR2 117 C1
Oswald St
  Accrington BB5 104 D6
  Blackburn BB1 101 E6
  Burnley BB12 127 F8
  Oswaldtwistle BB5 103 D3
  Rishton BB1 124 C2
OSWALDTWISTLE 103 B3
Oswaldtwistle Mills Shopping Village* BB5 103 E4
Otley Rd FY8 90 B7
Ottawa Cl BB2 101 A8
Otterburn Cl FY3 153 B1
Otterburn Gr BB10 128 D6
Otterburn Rd BB2 81 C7
Otters Cl PR2 118 F2
Ottershaw Gdns BB1 101 E8
Ottery Cl PR9 54 A5
Otway St PR1 117 E2
Oulton Cl L31 5 B4
Our Lady & All Saints RC Prim Sch WN8 27 C2
Our Lady of Compassion RC Prim Sch L37 12 A3
Our Lady of Lourdes RC Prim Sch
  Carnforth LA5 223 E1
  Southport PR8 35 A1
Our Lady of Perpetual Succour RC Prim Sch BB2 81 E8
Our Lady of the Assumption RC Prim Sch FY4 110 F5
Our Lady Queen of Peace RC High Sch WN8 17 F4
Our Lady & St Anselm's RC Prim Sch OL12 71 D2
Our Lady & St Edward's RC Prim Sch PR2 117 D8
Our Lady & St Gerard's RC Prim Sch PR5 77 A8
Our Lady & St Hubert's RC Prim Sch BB6 124 E6
Our Lady & St John RC Arts Coll BB1 102 C3
Our Lady & St Paul's RC Prim Sch OL10 33 F1
Our Lady's RC Coll LA1 218 D1
Our Lady's RC High Sch PR2 117 C4
Our Lady Star of the Sea RC Prim Sch FY8 89 F6
Ousby Ave 7 LA3 217 B2
Ousby Rd LA3 217 B2
Ouseburn Rd BB2 81 C8
Outer Prom FY7 198 E5
Outgate Rd PR4 116 D4
Out La PR26 58 C2
Outlet La L31, L39 6 F1
Outlook The L38 2 F4
Out Moss La LA4 217 B4
Outram Ho PR5 97 D1
Outram La 2 BB1 122 E1
Outram Way PR5 77 E8
OUT RAWCLIFFE 178 C1
Out Rawcliffe CE Prim Sch PR3 178 F2
Outterside St PR7 31 A6
Outwood Rd BB11 128 B4
Ouzledale Bsns Pk BB18 196 C2
Ouzle Rock BB12 169 E2
Oval The
  Burnley BB11 127 C3
  Shevington WN6 19 F5
  West Bradford BB7 189 D7
Ovangle Rd LA3 217 F2
OVER BURROW 241 E7
Overdale Gr FY3 131 A8
Overdell Dr OL12 52 C4
Overfield Way OL12 52 F2
Over Hos BL7 48 B6
OVER KELLET 237 A8
Overshores Rd BL7 48 B8
OVERTON 209 D8
Overton Rd PR2 95 E8
Overton St Helen's CE Prim Sch LA3 213 D1
OVERTOWN 241 F7
OVER TOWN 108 A8
Over Town BB10 129 A1
Ovington Dr PR8 35 E3
Owen Ave L39 15 F6
Owen Ct BB5 124 F3
Owen Rd LA1 218 D2
Owen's La L39 13 E2
Owen's Row BL6 32 C3
Owens St PR6 43 E7
Owen St
  Accrington BB5 104 C7
  Burnley BB12 127 A5
  Darwen BB3 82 A3
  Preston PR1 97 B8
Owlet Hall Rd BB3 81 E2
Owsten Ct BL6 31 F3
Owtram St 2 PR1 97 C8
Oxcliffe Ave LA3 216 D1
Oxcliffe Gr LA3 216 D1
Oxcliffe Rd LA3 216 F2
Oxendale Rd FY5 176 D2
Oxenholme Ave FY5 175 D4
Oxenhurst Rd FY3 131 A8
Oxford Ave BB5 125 A3
Oxford Cl
  Blackburn BB1 101 F4
  Padiham BB12 126 D6
Oxford Ct
  4 Lytham St Anne's FY8 90 D4
  6 Southport PR8 34 F4
Oxford Dr
  Blackburn BB1 102 E4
  Kirkham PR4 114 C4
Oxford Gdns PR8 34 E4
Oxford Mews PR7 60 E6
Oxford Pl
  9 Burnley BB11 128 B5
  Lancaster LA1 218 C3
Oxford Rd
  Bamber Bridge PR5 77 F8
  Blackpool FY1 130 D5
  Burnley BB11 128 B5
  Cleveleys FY5 175 D3
  Fleetwood FY7 198 E3
  Fulwood PR2 117 D4
  Lytham St Anne's, Ansdell FY8 90 D4
  Lytham St Anne's FY8 89 E8
  Nelson BB9 171 A2
  Orrell WN5 10 F8
  Skelmersdale WN8 17 E1
  Southport PR8 34 E4
Oxford St
  Accrington BB5 104 B6
  Adlington PR7 31 A6
  Brierfield BB9 148 B5
  Bury BL9 33 A1
  Carnforth LA5 223 D1
  9 Chorley PR7 43 C7
  Colne BB8 171 E5
  Darwen BB3 81 F4
  Lancaster LA1 218 D3
  Morecambe LA4 217 B6
  Preston PR1 97 A6
Oxford Way
  Fleetwood FY7 198 E3
  Rochdale OL12 52 E2
Ox Hey BB5 124 F4
Ox Hey Ave PR2 116 C1
Oxhey Cl BB10 128 F6
Ox Hey Cl BL0 50 C7
Oxheys Ct 1 PR1 117 E2
Oxheys Ind Est PR1 117 D2
Oxheys St PR1 117 D2
Oxhill Pl FY5 152 F7
Oxhouse Rd WN5 10 D4
Oxley Cl PR4 113 F5
Oxley Rd PR1 118 D1
Oxley Rd N PR1 118 D1
Ox St 15 BL0 50 B5
Oystercatcher Gate FY8 90 E7

P

Paa La BB7 231 C7
Packet La LA5 221 A4
Pad Cote La BD22 174 A8
Paddington Ave PR3 157 C7
Paddington Barn PR3 157 C7
Paddock Ave PR26 59 A8
Paddock Dr FY3 131 C2
Paddock La BB1 102 D4
Paddock Rd WN8 9 C5
Paddock St 9 BB5 103 E4
Paddock The
  Blackburn BB2 101 A8
  Carleton FY6 153 C5
  Formby L37 12 A5
  Fulwood PR2 118 A6
  4 Kingsfold PR1 96 E2
  Ormskirk L39 15 C3
  Oswaldtwistle BB5 103 E4
  Ramsbottom BL0 50 B7
  Rufford L40 39 C4
  Sawley BB7 230 C1
  Southport PR8 21 C4
  Thornton FY5 153 B8
Paddock Top Mews BB8 171 D3
Padgate Pl BB11 127 B4
PADIHAM 126 B7
Padiham Green CE Prim Sch BB12 126 C8
Padiham Prim Sch BB12 126 D8
Padiham Prim Sch Annexe BB12 126 E8
Padiham Rd
  Burnley BB12 127 E6
  Burnley, Habergham BB12 127 B7
  3 Burnley, Whittlefield BB12 127 D6
  Padiham BB12 126 F7
  Sabden BB7 146 A7

adstow Cl PR9 .... 54 A5
adway PR1 .... 96 D2
age Ct L37 .... 11 F3
agefield Cres BB7 ..... 167 A7
ages Ct PR5 .... 77 B7
aignton Rd BB1 .... 101 D7
ainley Cl FY8 .... 91 A4
ainter Wood BB7 .... 144 B4
aisley St BB11 .... 127 D5
alace Ct LA3 .... 216 E4
alace Gdns BB12 .... 127 B7
alace Rd PR8 .... 34 E5
alace St
Burnley BB12 .... 127 C7
Bury BL9 .... 33 A2
alais Bldgs L40 .... 25 E5
alatine Ave LA1 .... 215 A5
alatine Cl FY3 .... 131 C6
alatine Com Sports Coll
FY4 .... 110 C8
alatine Rd
Blackburn BB2 .... 101 C5
Blackpool FY1 .... 130 C4
Cleveleys FY5 .... 175 D4
Southport PR8 .... 34 F5
alatine Sq BB11 .... 127 E5
alatine St 10 BL0 .... 50 C6
aley Rd 1 PR1 .... 96 D7
alfrey Cl FY6 .... 153 B6
alladium Bldgs 7
FY1 .... 130 B1
all Mall
Blackburn BB2 .... 100 E5
Chorley PR7 .... 43 C6
alma St 10 OL14 .... 109 B1
almaston Cl LA1 .... 214 E6
alm Ct WN8 .... 17 E2
alm Dr FY6 .... 153 B6
almer Ave FY1 .... 130 C2
almer Gr 3 LA4 .... 217 E6
almer St BB1 .... 101 D6
almerston Cl BL0 .... 50 C4
almerston Rd PR9 .... 35 F6
almerston St BB12 ..... 126 D7
almetto View FY8 .... 90 D7
alm Gr PR8 .... 35 E6
alm St
Blackburn BB1 .... 102 A7
5 Burnley BB11 .... 127 D5
ankhurst Cl BB1 .... 102 B1
ansy St N BB5 .... 104 B7
ansy St S BB5 .... 104 B7
anton St BL6 .... 32 D1
arade The LA5 .... 223 B1
aradise Cl PR6 .... 61 C8
aradise La
1 Blackburn BB2 .... 101 E4
Formby L37 .... 12 A6
Leyland PR26 .... 76 B1
aradise St
Accrington BB5 .... 104 B5
Barrowford BB9 .... 170 E5
Blackburn BB2 .... 101 D4
11 Burnley BB11 .... 127 F6
Knowley PR6 .... 61 F3
2 Newchurch BB4 .... 86 F2
Ramsbottom BL0 .... 50 C7
aradise Terr 2 BB2 ..... 101 E4
aragon Way LA1 .... 214 C8
ARBOLD 27 D2
arbold Cl
Blackpool FY3 .... 152 F1
Burscough L40 .... 25 E3
arbold Douglas CE Prim
Sch WN8 .... 27 D3
arbold Hill WN8 .... 27 E2
arbold Sta WN8 .... 27 C2
ardoe Cl PR4 .... 73 E3
ardoe Ct L40 .... 25 F3
aris BB1 .... 122 E4
arish Gdns PR25 .... 77 A2
arish St 11 BB12 .... 126 C8
ark Ave
Barnoldswick BB18 .... 196 B1
Barrowford BB9 .... 170 C1
Blackburn BB1 .... 101 D6
Burnley BB11 .... 127 E4
Chatburn BB7 .... 190 D5
Clitheroe BB7 .... 189 E1
Euxton PR7 .... 60 D2
Fleetwood FY7 .... 198 F3
Formby L37 .... 11 F1
Great Harwood BB6 .... 124 D6
Haslingden BB4 .... 85 B1
Lancaster LA1 .... 215 B7
Longshaw WN5 .... 10 E1
Lytham St Anne's FY8 ...... 90 E3
Maghull L31 .... 5 D3
Much Hoole PR4 .... 74 E2
New Longton PR4 .... 75 F8
Ormskirk L39 .... 15 E5
Preston PR1 .... 118 B2
Ramsbottom BL0 .... 50 D6
Salterforth BB18 .... 194 E8
Southport PR9 .... 35 E8
arkbourn L31 .... 6 A2
arkbourn Dr L31 .... 6 A2
arkbourn N L31 .... 6 A2
arkbourn Sq L31 .... 6 A2
ark Bridge Rd BB10 .... 128 D3
ark Cl
Fulwood PR2 .... 118 D3
Hightown L37 .... 2 E8
Middleforth Green PR1 ..... 96 D4
Parbold WN8 .... 27 D3
Salterforth BB18 .... 194 C6
ark Cotts BB8 .... 150 D7
Park Cres
Accrington BB5 .... 104 A4
Bacup OL13 .... 70 F8
Blackburn BB2 .... 101 C6
Haskayne L39 .... 13 F4
Haslingden BB4 .... 85 C1
Morecambe LA4 .... 217 E7
Southport PR9 .... 53 D1
Stalmine FY6 .... 177 C8
Park Ct LA1 .... 214 F3
Parkdale Gdns BB2 .... 81 D6
Park Dr
Brierfield BB9 .... 148 C5
Nelson BB9 .... 148 F7
Preston PR2 .... 116 D1
Parke Mews PR6 .... 79 C3
Parker Ave BB7 .... 166 E6
Parker Cres L39 .... 15 F7
Parke Rd PR6 .... 62 E8
Parker La
Burnley BB11 .... 128 A5
New Longton PR4 .... 76 C6
Parkers Fold PR3 .... 181 C2
Parker St
Accrington, Higher Baxenden
BB5 .... 104 E2
Accrington, Hillock Vale
BB5 .... 104 E8
3 Blackpool FY1 .... 130 C5
Burnley BB11 .... 128 A6
Burnley, Harle Syke
BB10 .... 148 F3
Bury BL9 .... 33 A2
Chorley PR7 .... 61 C1
Colne BB8 .... 171 C5
Lancaster LA1 .... 215 A8
11 Nelson BB9 .... 170 F2
Preston PR2 .... 117 D2
Rishton BB1 .... 124 C2
Parkers Wood Cl PR7 ..... 43 A6
Parker Terr BB7 .... 231 B3
Parkes Way BB2 .... 81 D7
Park Farm Cl PR4 .... 74 F8
Park Farm Rd BB2 .... 80 D8
Parkfield Ave PR2 .... 117 B2
Parkfield Cl
Leyland PR26 .... 59 C8
Ormskirk L39 .... 15 C4
5 Preston PR2 .... 116 C1
Parkfield Cres 6 PR2 ... 116 C1
Parkfield Dr
Lancaster LA1 .... 215 A6
Preston PR2 .... 95 C8
Parkfield Gr L31 .... 5 C1
Parkfield View PR2 .... 95 C8
Parkfoot Lodges LA6 ..... 242 E3
Parkgate PR3 .... 138 D5
Parkgate Dr
Lancaster LA1 .... 215 C7
Leyland PR25 .... 59 F7
Park Gate Rd BB1 .... 142 D1
Park Hall L Ctr PR7 .... 42 A4
Park Hall Rd PR7 .... 41 F3
Park Head BB7 .... 144 F2
Parkhead La PR3 .... 182 A8
Park Hey Dr WN6 .... 19 E7
Park High Sch BB8 .... 171 F6
PARK HILL 8 D2
Park Hill
Barnoldswick BB18 .... 196 C1
21 Rochdale OL12 .... 52 F1
Parkhill Bsns Ctr
BB12 .... 127 A8
Park Hill Rd PR3 .... 181 C7
Park Ho
4 Lancaster LA1 .... 218 D1
Longridge PR3 .... 140 A7
Park House La LA2 .... 239 A5
Parkinson La PR3 .... 162 B8
Parkinson St
Blackburn BB2 .... 101 C2
Burnley BB11 .... 128 A4
Foulridge BB8 .... 194 D1
Haslingden BB4 .... 85 A3
Parkinson Terr BB8 .... 172 B2
Parkinson Way 1 FY4 .. 130 C1
Park La
Brierfield BB9 .... 148 C5
Caton LA2 .... 237 B5
Garstang PR3 .... 204 A4
Great Harwood BB6 .... 124 D6
Holmes PR4 .... 56 B2
Horwich BL6 .... 32 D3
Kirkham PR4 .... 114 A7
Maghull L31 .... 5 F3
Middleforth Green PR1 ..... 96 E3
Oswaldtwistle BB5 .... 103 E3
Preesall FY6 .... 200 B3
Wennington LA2 .... 238 E8
Parkland Cl FY5 .... 175 C1
Parkland Gr LA3 .... 216 E2
Parklands
Skelmersdale WN8 .... 18 D2
Southport PR9 .... 35 E8
Parklands Ave PR1 .... 96 A4
Parklands Cl PR1 .... 96 A4
Parklands Dr PR2 .... 117 E8
Parklands Gr PR2 .... 117 E8
Parklands High Sch
PR7 .... 43 A8
Parklands The PR3 .... 181 D3
Parklands Way BB2 .... 81 B8
Parkland View BB11 .... 127 E2
Park Lane Dr L31 .... 6 B2
Park Lee Rd BB2 .... 101 E2
Park Link L39 .... 15 B1
Park Lo BB2 .... 101 A7
Park Mews BB7 .... 231 B3
Park Mill Pl PR1 .... 118 A1
Park Pl
Blackburn BB2 .... 101 B3
Blackburn, Feniscowles
BB2 .... 80 D7
24 Preston PR1 .... 97 A7
Walton-le-D PR5 .... 97 E4
PARK PLACE 101 F3
Park Prim Sch BB8 .... 171 F5
Park Rd
Accrington BB5 .... 104 A6
Adlington PR7 .... 30 F6
Bacup OL13 .... 87 F1
Barnoldswick BB18 .... 196 B1
Blackburn BB2 .... 101 E3
Blackpool FY1 .... 130 D3
Burnley BB10 .... 128 E1
Chorley PR7 .... 43 C8
Coppull PR7 .... 42 E1
Darwen BB3 .... 65 B6
Edgworth BL7 .... 48 E5
Formby L37 .... 11 E1
Fulwood PR2 .... 118 A4
Gisburn BB7 .... 231 B3
Great Harwood BB6 .... 124 D5
Haslingden BB4 .... 67 F7
Kirkham PR4 .... 113 F4
Lancaster LA1 .... 215 A8
Leyland PR25 .... 60 A7
Longshaw WN5 .... 10 F1
Lytham St Anne's FY8 ...... 89 E6
Mellor Brook BB2, PR5 ... 121 A1
Middleforth Green PR1 ..... 96 D4
Newchurch BB4 .... 86 F1
Ormskirk L39 .... 15 E5
Padiham BB12 .... 126 C8
Poulton-le-F FY6 .... 153 E4
Ramsbottom BL0 .... 49 F3
Rishton BB1 .... 124 C1
Silverdale LA5 .... 224 D4
Southport PR9 .... 35 D8
Southport PR9 .... 53 D1
Thornton FY5 .... 176 B1
Park Rd W PR9 .... 53 C1
Park Road Ind Est OL13 ... 87 F1
Park Sch FY3 .... 130 E4
Parkside
Morecambe LA4 .... 217 C3
Preston, Holme Slack
PR1 .... 118 B3
Preston, Lea PR2 .... 116 D2
Whitworth OL12 .... 71 D2
Park Side BB18 .... 195 A8
Parkside Ave
Chorley PR7 .... 43 C8
Skelmersdale WN8 .... 8 D8
Parkside Cl
Garstang PR3 .... 181 A7
Todmorden OL14 .... 109 B1
Parkside Cres WN5 .... 10 F6
Parkside Ct
6 Morecambe LA4 .... 217 C3
Southport PR9 .... 53 D1
Parkside Dr PR6 .... 61 B6
Parkside La PR3 .... 181 A7
Parkside Rd
Lytham St Anne's FY8 ...... 90 A7
Nelson BB9 .... 149 B8
Todmorden OL14 .... 109 B1
Parkside View FY5 .... 176 A4
Park Sq LA1 .... 215 A8
Park St
Accrington BB5 .... 104 C6
Barnoldswick BB18 .... 196 B1
Barrowford BB9 .... 170 D4
Chorley PR7 .... 61 C1
Clitheroe BB7 .... 166 E7
Eccleston PR7 .... 41 C6
Great Harwood BB6 .... 124 D5
Haslingden BB4 .... 85 B3
Haslingden, Bridge End
BB4 .... 67 F7
Lytham St Anne's FY8 ...... 91 B3
Morecambe LA4 .... 217 E6
Parks The LA4 .... 217 E7
Parkstone Ave
Carleton FY6 .... 153 B5
Thornton FY5 .... 153 D8
Park Stone Rd PR3 .... 137 C3
Park Street E BB9 .... 170 E4
Parksway FY6 .... 199 D5
Park Terr
Blackburn BB1 .... 101 D7
Great Harwood BB6 .... 124 D6
Parkthorn Rd PR2 .... 95 C8
Park View
Accrington BB5 .... 104 A7
Carnforth LA5 .... 223 D3
Gisburn BB7 .... 231 B3
Middleforth Green PR1 ..... 96 D4
Newchurch BB4 .... 86 F1
Padiham BB12 .... 126 C8
Park View Ave PR2 .... 117 B2
Parkview Cl 5 LA3 .... 217 C3
Park View Cl
Nelson BB9 .... 148 B7
Rawtenstall BB4 .... 85 F5
Park View Ct 2 FY4 ..... 110 C6
Parkview Flats FY8 .... 89 D6
Park View Rd FY8 .... 91 B4
Park View Terr
Abbey Village PR6 .... 80 C1
Salterforth BB18 .... 194 D7
Park Wall Rd L29, L38 ...... 4 B2
Parkway
Blackpool FY3 .... 131 A6
Shevington Moor WN6 ...... 29 A2
Park Way
Colne BB8 .... 171 C6
Formby L37 .... 11 F1
Middleforth Green PR1 ..... 96 D4
Park Wlk PR2 .... 118 A4
Parkwood BL7 .... 47 D2
Parkwood Ave BB12 .... 127 D7
Parkwood Ct 6 BB4 .... 85 E2
Park Wood Dr BB4 .... 85 E2
Parkwood Mews 1
BB9 .... 170 F2
Parliament St
Burnley BB11 .... 128 B5
11 Colne BB8 .... 171 E5
19 Darwen BB3 .... 82 A1
Lancaster LA1 .... 218 D1
Morecambe LA3 .... 216 E4
Up Holland WN8 .... 10 C7
Parlick Ave PR3 .... 140 B7
Parlick Rd
Fulwood PR2 .... 119 A2
Garstang PR3 .... 181 B6
Parramatta St 8 BB4 ...... 86 A2
Parr Cottage Cl PR7 ...... 41 C7
Parr La PR7 .... 41 C7
Parrock Cl PR1 .... 96 E3
Parrock Par 10 BB4 .... 86 A7
Parrock Rd BB9 .... 170 C2
Parrock St
Barnoldswick BB18 .... 196 B2
19 Nelson BB9 .... 170 E1
11 Rawtenstall BB4 .... 86 A7
Parrox Fold FY6 .... 200 A5
Parrox La PR4 .... 114 E2
Parr's La L39 .... 15 D1
Parrys Way FY6 .... 153 E4
Parsley Cl FY2 .... 152 F3
Parsonage Ave PR3 .... 141 D3
Parsonage Brow WN8 ..... 10 A8
Parsonage Cl
3 Bury BL9 .... 33 A2
Morecambe LA3 .... 217 C2
Up Holland WN8 .... 10 A7
Parsonage Cotts 10
BB7 .... 166 E8
Parsonage Dr BB9 .... 148 C5
Parsonage Gdns PR4 ...... 57 A5
Parsonage La PR3 .... 185 C1
Parsonage Rd
Blackburn BB1 .... 123 A4
Up Holland WN8 .... 10 A7
Parsonage St
Bury BL9 .... 33 A3
2 Church BB5 .... 103 E5
Colne BB8 .... 171 C4
Parson La BB7 .... 166 E8
Parson's Brow 4 PR7 .... 43 C7
Parson's Bullough Rd PR6,
BL6 .... 44 E5
Parsons Cl LA1 .... 214 F4
Parth St BL9 .... 33 D1
Partnership Way BB1 .... 102 D2
Partridge Ave FY5 .... 176 A4
Partridge Dr BB5 .... 104 F1
Partridge Hill 4 BB12 ... 146 D1
Partridge Hill St 5
BB12 .... 146 D1
Part St PR8 .... 35 B6
Pashmire Brow BB7 .... 143 E6
PASSMONDS 52 B1
Passmonds Cres OL11,
OL12 .... 52 B1
Past La
Lane Ends, Bay Gate
BB7 .... 230 A5
Lane Ends BB7 .... 230 A7
Pasture Barn BB8 .... 195 F2
Pasture Cl
Barnoldswick BB18 .... 196 C4
Burnley BB11 .... 127 E3
Pasture Dr
Bonds PR3 .... 181 D6
Foulridge BB8 .... 194 D1
Pasture Field FY6 .... 153 B6
Pasture Field Cl PR26 ..... 76 C1
Pasturegate BB11 .... 127 E3
Pasturegate Ave BB11 .... 127 E4
Pasture Gr BB7 .... 144 A7
Pasture La
Barrowford BB9 .... 170 C5
Hest Bank LA5 .... 220 E4
Pasturelands BB4 .... 106 A1
Pasturelands Dr BB7 .... 144 A3
Pastures The
Blackburn BB2 .... 101 A8
Grimsargh PR2 .... 139 D1
Morecambe LA3 .... 216 F1
Southport PR9 .... 54 D5
Paterson St BB2 .... 101 E3
Pathfinders Dr LA1 ...... 214 E4
Patience St 11 OL12 ...... 52 C1
Patmos St BL0 .... 50 D6
Paton St OL12 .... 52 D3
Patrick Ave BB12 .... 145 D2
Patrick Cres BB4 .... 86 C2
Patten St
Blackburn BB1 .... 102 C5
Colne BB8 .... 171 D4
Preston PR1 .... 96 F8
Patterdale Ave
Blackburn BB1 .... 102 C3
Blackpool FY3 .... 130 F2
Fleetwood FY7 .... 198 D1
Oswaldtwistle BB5 .... 103 D5
Thornton FY5 .... 176 B3
Patterdale Cl
Burnley BB10 .... 148 C4
Southport PR8 .... 21 B3
Patterdale Cres L31 .... 5 E2
Patterdale Rd LA1 .... 218 F1
Patterson Ct 8 FY8 .... 91 C3
Pattison Cl OL12 .... 52 D3
Paulhan St BB10 .... 148 B2
Paul's La
Hambleton FY6 .... 177 C2
Southport PR9 .... 53 F3
Pavey Cl FY4 .... 110 F8
Pavilion Cl 2 OL12 .... 52 F2
Pavilions The
Blackpool FY4 .... 110 D4
Bury BL9 .... 33 D2
Preston PR2 .... 96 C7
Pavilion View PR26 .... 58 B2
Paxton Pl WN8 .... 9 C4
Paxton St BB5 .... 104 B6
Paynter Cl
Barrow BB7 .... 166 D1
Clayton-le-M BB5 .... 125 A2
PAYTHORNE 231 C6
Paythorne Ave BB10 .... 128 D5
Paythorne Cl FY3 .... 153 B1
Peabody St BB3 .... 82 A2
Peacehaven WN8 .... 17 E1
Peace Pl FY5 .... 176 B4
Peace St BB11 .... 127 D5
Peachtree Cl PR2 .... 118 D6
Peacock Cres LA2 .... 220 E1
Peacock Dr PR3 .... 204 D1
Peacock Hall Rd PR25 .... 59 D7
Peacock Hill Cl PR2 ..... 119 C7
Peacock La LA2 .... 220 E1
Peahall La PR3 .... 202 A4
Pear Ave BL9 .... 33 C3
Pearfield PR25 .... 77 A2
Pearl Ave 6 FY2 .... 152 E1
Pearl Brook Ind Est BL6 ... 32 B3
Pearl St
Accrington BB5 .... 103 F5
Blackburn BB1 .... 122 F1
Pear Pl 3 OL14 .... 109 B1
Pearson St
Blackburn BB2 .... 101 D4
Bury BL9 .... 33 B3
Pear St 4 OL14 .... 109 B1
Pear Tree Ave PR7 .... 42 F3
Pear Tree Cl 2 PR5 .... 97 E2
Pear Tree Cres PR5 .... 97 E2
Pear Tree Croft PR4 ...... 75 A8
Pear Tree Ctyd PR4 ...... 115 E2
Pear Tree La PR7 .... 60 E3
Peartree Rd PR26 .... 58 B3
Pear Tree Rd PR6 .... 78 B3
Pear Tree Sch PR4 .... 114 A5
Pear Tree St 7 PR5 .... 97 E2
Peart St BB10 .... 148 B2
Pebble Ct FY5 .... 175 C3
Pechell St 5 PR2 .... 117 C1
Pedder Ave LA3 .... 213 C1
Pedder Dr LA3 .... 213 D1
Pedder Gr LA3 .... 213 D1
Pedder La FY6 .... 177 B1
Pedder Rd LA3 .... 213 C1
Pedders Gr PR2 .... 96 A8
Pedders La PR2 .... 96 A8
Pedder's La
Blackpool FY4 .... 110 D7
Preston PR2 .... 117 A1
Pedder St
Morecambe LA4 .... 217 A5
Preston PR2 .... 96 E8
Pedders Way PR2 .... 96 A8
Peebles Gr BB11 .... 127 D3
Peel Ave
Blackpool FY3 .... 130 D7
Heysham LA3 .... 212 E6
Lancaster LA1 .... 218 D2
Ramsbottom BL0 .... 50 A5
PEEL BANK 103 E7
Peel Bank Rd BB5 .... 103 B4
PEEL BROW 50 D7
Peel Brow BL0 .... 50 D6
Peel Brow Sch BL0 .... 50 D6
Peel Cl BB2 .... 81 E8
Peel Cres LA1 .... 214 D8
Peel Ct FY4 .... 111 D6
Peel Dr OL13 .... 88 B1
Peel Gdns BB8 .... 171 C5
Peel Hall Rd BL0 .... 50 B2
Peel Hall St PR1 .... 118 B1
PEEL HILL 111 E7
Peel Hill FY4 .... 111 E7
Peel Ho LA1 .... 218 C1
Peel Leisure & Ret Pk
BB1 .... 101 F4
Peel Mount
Blackburn BB1 .... 102 F4
Ramsbottom BL0 .... 50 A4
Peel Mount Cl BB1 .... 102 F4
Peel Park Ave
Accrington BB5 .... 104 D7
Clitheroe BB7 .... 166 F7
Peel Park Cl
Accrington BB5 .... 104 D7
Clitheroe BB7 .... 166 F7
Peel Park Prim Sch
BB5 .... 104 D7
Peel Pl BB9 .... 170 F6
Peel Rd
Blackpool FY4 .... 111 F4
Colne BB8 .... 171 B4
Fleetwood FY7 .... 198 F3
Skelmersdale WN8 .... 9 E5

Peel St
Accrington BB5 104 C6
Adlington PR6 31 B8
Blackburn BB2 101 C2
Chorley PR7 43 C7
Clitheroe BB7 166 E8
Haslingden BB4 85 A3
6 Oswaldtwistle BB5 103 D3
Padiham BB12 126 D8
Preston PR2 96 E8
Rawtenstall BB4 86 C2
Southport PR8 35 F6
Peel Twr* BL8 49 F5
Peel Wlk L31 5 B2
Peerart Ct 4 BB8 171 C4
Peers Clough Rd BB4 86 F7
Peet Ave L39 15 D4
Peet's La PR9 54 A1
Pegbank La LA6 241 A8
Peg's La FY8 91 B8
Peg Way PR4 92 F6
Pelham Ave 3 FY3 130 E8
Pelham St 3 BB1 102 A6
Pelican Cl FY6 200 B4
Pemberton Dr LA4 217 F5
Pemberton Pl LA4 217 F5
Pemberton St BB1 122 E1
Pembroke Ave
Blackpool FY2 152 B3
Morecambe LA4 217 D6
Pembroke Cl BL6 32 A4
Pembroke Ct
Blackpool FY2 152 B3
13 Darwen BB3 82 A1
14 Rochdale OL12 52 F1
Pembroke Pl
Chorley PR7 43 B6
Leyland PR25 60 A8
Pembroke Rd FY8 90 D4
Pembroke St
Accrington BB5 104 D6
Bacup OL13 87 F1
Blackburn BB2 101 E3
11 Burnley BB10 148 B1
Pembury Ave PR1 96 F3
Penarth Ct PR2 116 F3
Pendle Ave
Bacup OL13 88 A3
Chatburn BB7 190 E5
Clayton-le-M BB5 124 F4
Lancaster LA1 211 B6
Pendle Bridge BB12 147 F3
Pendle Bsns Ctr 10 BB9 148 E8
Pendlebury Cl PR4 75 B8
Pendle Cl
Bacup OL13 88 A2
Blackpool FY3 152 F1
Pendle Com High Sch BB8 171 B2
Pendle Com Hospl BB9 170 E1
Pendle Ct
Barnoldswick BB18 196 C3
5 Clitheroe BB7 166 F8
Kirkham PR4 114 A6
Longridge PR3 140 A7
Skelmersdale WN8 9 D3
Pendle Dr
Blackburn BB2 101 F2
Horwich BL6 32 C5
Ormskirk L39 16 A6
Whalley BB7 144 A7
Pendle Fields
Fence BB12 147 D7
Rimington BB7 231 B1
Pendle Heritage Ctr* BB9 170 E4
Pendle Hill Cl PR2 119 C7
Pendle Ho BB1 101 F5
Pendlehurst St BB11 127 E4
Pendle Ind Est BB9 148 F7
Pendlemist View 1 BB8 171 C3
Pendle Pl
Lytham St Anne's FY8 91 C4
Skelmersdale WN8 9 D4
Pendle Rd
Brierfield BB9 148 A5
Clayton-le-W PR25 77 D1
Clitheroe BB7 167 A7
Downham BB7 191 D3
Great Harwood BB6 124 F6
Lancaster LA1 218 B3
Pendle Row BB12 169 C5
Pendle St E BB7 145 F7
Pendle St W BB7 145 F7
Pendleside BB9 148 B8
Pendleside Cl BB7 145 F7
Pendle St
Accrington BB5 104 A5
Barrowford BB9 170 C3
Blackburn BB1 102 A5
Nelson BB9 170 D1
Padiham BB12 126 D8
Pendle Terr BB7 191 E8
PENDLETON 167 B4
Pendleton Ave
Accrington BB5 103 F4
Rawtenstall BB4 86 A4
Pendleton Rd
Pendleton BB7 167 A2
Wiswell BB7 144 F8
Pendle Trad Est BB7 190 C4
Pendle Vale Coll BB9 171 A2
Pendle View
Barley BB12 169 C6
Brockhall Village BB6 143 C6
Clayton-le-M BB5 125 A3
Foulridge BB8 194 E1
Grindleton BB7 190 B7
Higham BB12 146 F6
Huncoat BB5 125 F2
West Bradford BB7 189 D7
Pendle View Prim Sch BB8 171 B1
Pendle Way BB12 127 E6
Pendle Way 7 BB9 148 E8
Penfold L31 5 E1
Pengarth Rd BL6 32 C4
Penguin St PR1 118 B2
Penhale Cl LA3 212 E6
Penhale Ct LA3 212 E6
Penhale Gdns LA3 212 E6
Penhill Cl 4 FY2 130 D8
Penistone St 6 BB12 127 D6
Penketh Pl WN8 9 C5
Pennine Ave PR7 60 D1
Pennine Cl
8 Blackpool FY1 130 C4
Horwich BL6 32 C5
Pennine Cres BB9 148 C5
Pennine Gdns PR3 181 A7
Pennine Gr BB12 146 C2
Pennine Pl WN8 9 B6
Pennine Rd
Bacup OL13 88 A2
Chorley PR6 43 E8
Horwich BL6 32 C5
Pennines The PR2 118 A7
Pennine View
Dolphinholme LA2 226 A8
Fleetwood FY7 199 B4
Glasson LA2 209 E4
Great Eccleston PR3 156 C5
Kirkham PR4 114 C5
Morecambe LA4 217 B4
Pennine Way
Barnoldswick BB18 196 A2
Brierfield BB9 148 C5
Great Eccleston PR3 156 C5
Stalmine FY6 177 D7
Pennington Ave L39 15 E6
Pennington Ct
Heysham LA3 212 E6
4 Ormskirk L39 15 F6
Pennington La WN2 30 E1
Penn St BL6 32 C3
Pennyfarthing La 7 FY5 176 A2
Penny House La BB5 104 C7
PENNYLANDS 17 E1
Penny Lodge View BB4 105 F3
Penny's Hospital Almshouses 35 LA1 214 F8
Penny St
Blackburn BB1 101 F5
Lancaster LA1 214 F7
3 Preston PR1 97 A8
Pennystone Rd FY2 152 B4
Penny Stone Rd LA2 219 C7
Penrhos Ave FY7 198 E1
Penrhyn Rd LA1 218 A2
Penrith Ave
Cleveleys FY5 175 D4
Heysham LA3 212 F8
Southport PR8 21 C3
Penrith Cres
Colne BB8 171 B3
Maghull L31 5 E2
Penrith Rd BB8 171 A3
Penrod Way LA3 212 D6
Penrose Ave FY4 130 F1
Penrose Pl WN8 9 E4
Penshaw Cl 6 BB1 122 E1
Penswick Ave FY5 175 E1
Pentland Rd L33 1 A4
Penwell Fold WN8 9 E8
Penwortham Broad Oak Prim Sch PR1 96 C2
Penwortham Brow PR1 96 C6
Penwortham Ct PR1 96 D4
Penwortham Girls' High Sch PR1 96 C5
Penwortham Hall Gdns PR1 96 E3
PENWORTHAM LANE 96 F2
Penwortham Middleforth CE Prim Sch PR1 96 D3
Penwortham Prim Sch PR1 96 A5
Penwortham Residential Pk PR1 96 D4
Penwortham St Teresa's RC Prim Sch PR1 96 A5
Penwortham Way
Farington PR26, PR4 76 D7
Kingsfold PR1 96 C1
Pen-Y-Ghent Way BB18 196 A2
Penzance St BB2 101 B2
Peplow Rd LA3 213 A8
Pepper La WN6 29 B3
Perch Pool La PR9 36 F4
Percival Ct 2 PR8 35 A6
Percival St
Accrington BB5 103 F5
Blackburn BB1 101 F7
Darwen BB3 81 F3
Percliff Way BB1 102 B7
Percy Rd LA1 214 F6
Percy St
Accrington BB5 104 D6
Blackburn BB2 101 B2
Blackpool FY1 130 C7
Bury BL9 33 B3
9 Chorley PR7 43 D7
Colne BB8 171 E6
Fleetwood FY7 198 F4
Nelson BB9 148 E7
Oswaldtwistle BB5 103 B5
Preston PR1 97 A8
Ramsbottom BL0 50 B5
Shawforth OL12 71 E6
Peregrine Dr BB3 81 D3
Peregrine Pl PR25 76 D2
Peridot Cl BB1 122 F2
Perimeter Rd L33 1 E2
Peronne Cres BB1 102 D5
Perpignan Way 16 LA1 214 F8
Perryn Pl WN6 29 F1
Perry St BB3 82 B2
Pershore Gdns FY3 131 B8
Pershore Gr PR8 21 A4
Pershore Rd FY8 90 B5
Persia St BB5 103 F6
Perth Cl FY5 152 F7
Perthshire Gr PR7 60 F6
Perth St
Accrington BB5 104 B4
Blackburn BB2 101 C3
Burnley BB11 127 D5
Lancaster LA1 215 A7
8 Nelson BB9 170 F1
Peter Birtwistle Cl BB8 171 E5
Peterfield Rd 1 PR1 96 E2
Peter Grime Row BB5 125 F2
Peterhouse Sch PR9 54 B3
Peter La LA5 225 E1
Peter Martin St 2 BL6 32 B4
Petersan Ct PR6 61 C3
Peters Ave L40 25 E4
Petersbottom La LA2 239 E4
Peter St
9 Barrowford BB9 170 D4
Blackburn BB1 102 A6
Blackpool FY1 130 D5
Chorley PR7 43 C8
Colne BB8 171 E4
5 Lancaster LA1 214 F7
Rawtenstall BB4 86 A2
Petre Cres BB1 103 B8
Petrel Cl BB1 101 D8
Petre Rd BB5 124 F2
Petunia Cl PR25 77 E2
Petworth Rd PR8 21 B6
Pharos Ct 8 FY7 199 B5
Pharos Gr 2 FY7 199 B5
Pharos Pl FY7 199 B5
Pharos St FY7 199 B5
Pheasantford Gn BB10 128 B8
Pheasantford St BB10 128 B8
Pheasant Wood Dr FY5 175 F5
Philip Ave PR4 114 B4
Philip Dr PR8 21 F6
Philips Rd
Blackburn BB1 102 B8
Weir OL13 88 A7
Philip St
Barnoldswick BB18 196 B2
Darwen BB3 82 B1
Phillip's Cl L37 11 F2
Phillips La BB8 171 B3
Phillip's La L37 11 F2
Phillip St FY4 130 F2
Phillipstown BB4 86 E4
Phoenix St
8 Lancaster LA1 218 D1
Rochdale OL12 52 C1
Phoenix Way BB11 127 C5
Phyllis St OL12 52 B1
Physics Ave LA1 211 B7
Piazza The LA1 215 C7
Piccadilly LA1 214 F3
Piccadilly Cl LA1 214 F3
Piccadilly Gr LA1 214 F3
Piccadilly Rd BB11 127 E5
Piccadilly Sq 2 BB11 127 E5
Piccadilly St BB4 85 B3
Pickard Cl BB18 196 D4
Pickard St LA1 214 F6
Pickering Cl FY8 90 B7
Pickering Fold BB1 82 B7
Pickering St 1 BB9 148 B5
Pickerings The 2 PR5 77 C8
Pickles Dr L40 25 D4
Pickles St BB12 127 D7
Pickmere Ave FY4 110 E8
Pickmere Cl FY5 176 A4
Pickthorn Cl LA1 218 B4
PICKUP BANK 83 A2
Pickup Fold 3 BB3 65 C7
Pickup Fold Rd BB3 65 C7
Pickup Rd BB1 103 A8
Pickup St
Accrington BB5 103 F5
11 Bacup OL13 87 F2
Blackburn BB1 102 A5
Clayton-le-M BB5 124 F3
Picton St BB2 81 B8
Pierce Cl
Lancaster LA1 214 D7
Padiham BB12 146 C1
Piercefield Ct L37 12 A5
Piercefield Rd L37 11 F5
Pier Ct FY8 89 D7
PIERCY 86 F2
Piercy Higher Mount BB4 86 F3
Piercy Mdw BB4 86 F3
Piercy Mount BB4 86 F3
Piercy Rd BB4 86 F3
Piercy Terr BB4 86 F3
Pier Ho 3 BB1 101 F3
Pierpoint Il FY8 89 D7
Pier St FY1 130 B3
Pierston Ave FY2 152 C1
Pike Ct FY7 198 C2
PIKE HILL 128 E5
Pikelaw Pl WN8 9 C5
PIKE LOWE 79 E1
Pikestone Ct 9 PR6 43 E8
Pike View BL6 32 D4
Pilgrim St BB9 148 F6
Pilgrims Way LA3 217 E3
Pilkington Dr BB5 125 A3
Pilkington Rd PR8 35 D5
Pilkington St
6 Blackburn BB1 101 E4
14 Ramsbottom BL0 50 B5
Pilkington Tech Ctr L40 17 C6
PILLING 201 C6
Pilling Ave
Accrington BB5 104 E2
Lytham St Anne's FY8 90 C7
Pilling Cl
Chorley PR7 43 D6
Southport PR9 53 F5
Pilling Cres FY3 131 A8
Pilling Ct FY3 153 A1
Pilling Field BL7 47 E1
Pilling La
Chorley PR7 43 D6
Maghull L31 5 A5
Pilling Lane FY6 200 B7
PILLING LANE 200 B6
Pilling Pl WN8 9 C5
Pilling St John's CE Prim Sch PR3 201 C6
Pilling St
Haslingden BB4 85 B6
3 Rawtenstall BB4 69 F8
Pilmuir Rd BB2 101 E1
Pilot St BB5 104 B7
Pimbo La WN8 9 F3
Pimbo Rd WN8 9 C5
PIMHOLE 33 A1
Pimhole Bsns Pk BL9 33 A1
Pimhole Rd BL9 33 B2
Pimlico BB7 189 F3
Pimlico Link Rd BB7 190 C2
Pimlico Rd BB7 189 F2
Pinch Clough Rd BB4 86 F5
PINCOCK 42 C8
Pincock Brow PR7 42 C8
Pincock St PR7 42 C8
Pinder Cl BB7 189 B4
Pinder St BB9 170 F2
Pine Ave
Blackpool FY1 130 E2
Much Hoole PR4 74 D4
Ormskirk L39 15 F7
Pine Cl
Fulwood PR2 118 F4
Halton LA2 219 C6
Newburgh WN8 27 A1
Rishton BB1 103 B8
Skelmersdale WN8 17 F1
Pine Cres
Blackpool FY3 131 C2
Oswaldtwistle BB5 103 F3
Poulton-le-F FY6 153 E2
Pine Crest L39 15 B2
Pine Dr L39 15 F6
Pine Gr
Chorley PR6 61 D3
Clitheroe BB7 166 D7
Garstang PR3 204 C1
Ormskirk L39 15 F7
Southport PR9 35 D7
Pine Lake Resort* LA6 240 A3
Pine St N BL9 33 B3
Pine St S BL9 33 B2
Pines Cl PR5 78 C4
Pine St
7 Bacup OL13 88 A1
Blackburn BB1 102 A7
Burnley BB11 128 B5
Bury BL9 33 B2
Darwen BB3 65 B8
Haslingden BB4 85 C3
Lancaster LA1 218 C1
Morecambe LA4 217 C4
Nelson BB9 148 F8
Pines The
Leyland PR26 59 A8
Southport PR8 34 F6
Pineway PR2 117 C4
Pine Way PR4 114 B7
Pine Wlks PR2 116 C1
Pinewood
Blackburn BB2 80 F8
Skelmersdale WN8 18 D3
Pinewood Ave
Blackpool FY2 152 E4
Broughton PR3 137 C3
Caton LA2 237 C3
Formby L37 11 D1
Hest Bank LA5 220 F2
Knott End-on-S FY6 200 A5
Morecambe LA4 217 F6
Thornton FY5 153 B7
Pinewood Cl
Formby L37 11 D
Lancaster LA2 214 E
Southport PR8 36 C
Pinewood Cotts 1 LA2 239 D
Pinewood Cres
Leyland PR25 59 E
Lytham St Anne's FY8 90 D
Orrell WN5 10 E
Ramsbottom BL0 50 B
Pinewood Dr
Accrington BB5 104 E
Nelson BB9 149 A
Pinewood Rd PR1 97 A
PINFOLD 23 F
Pinfold
Barrowford BB9 170 E
Longton PR4 75 A
Pinfold Cl
Fulwood PR2 118 E
Southport PR8 21 B
Pinfold La
Inskip PR4 157 C
Lancaster LA1 218 D
Longridge PR3 140 B
Pinfold L40 23 F
Southport PR8 21 B
Pinfold Pl
5 Kirkham PR4 113 F
Nelson BB9 171 B
Skelmersdale WN8 9 D
Pinfold Prim Sch L40 24 A
Pinfold St PR1 97 E
Pingle Croft PR6 78 A
Pingwood La L33 1 A
Pink Pl BB2 101 B
Pink St BB12 127 C
Pinnacle Dr BL7 47 E
Pinner La BB4 85 F
Pinners Cl BL0 50 B
Pintail Cl
Leyland PR26 76 A
5 Rochdale OL12 52 E
Pintail Way FY8 90 E
Pioneer Cl BL6 32 C
Pioneer St BL6 32 C
Piper Cotts 4 LA4 217 C
Piper Lea BB4 87 A
Piper's La LA6 240 C
Pippin Bank OL13 87 F
Pippin Bank Mill OL13 87 F
Pippin St
Burscough L40 25 A
Thorpe Green PR6 78 E
PIPPIN STREET 78 E
Pit Hey Pl WN8 9 C
Pittman Ct PR2 118 E
Pittman Way PR2 118 C
Pittsdale Ave FY3 131 A
Pitts House La PR9 36 E
Pitt St
Lancaster LA1 214 F
11 Padiham BB12 126 D
Preston PR1 96 E
Southport PR9 35
Pitville St BB3 81
Place-de-Criel 12 BB9 148 D
Place The FY1 130 E
Plainmoor Dr FY5 152 F
Plain Pl BB2 101
Plane St
Bacup OL13 87
Blackburn BB1 102 A
Planet Earth Ctr* OL14 88 F
Plane Tree Cl BB11 127 D
Plane Tree Rd 7 BB1 102 A
Plantain Wlk LA3 217 E
Plantation Ave
Arnside LA5 224 C
Knott End-on-S FY6 199 E
Plantation Gr LA5 224 C
Plantation La LA2 232 D
Plantation Rd
Accrington BB5 104 E
Blackburn BB2 101 E
Burscough L40 25 E
Edgworth BL7 48
Plantation Sq BB5 104 D
Plantation St
Accrington BB5 104 D
Bacup OL13 70
Burnley BB10 128 A
6 Nelson BB9 170
Rawtenstall BB4 86
Plantation The BD23 236
Plantation View
Bacup OL13 87
Ramsbottom BL0 50 C
Plant St
Oswaldtwistle BB5 103 D
Preston PR2 117
Platform Gall The* BB7 166
Platt Cl BB5 104
Platten Gr LA4 217
Platt La WN1 30
Platts La L40 25
Platts Lane Ind Est L40 25
Platt St FY1 130
Pleasant Gr FY5 176
Pleasant Pl 4 BB11 127
Pleasant St
Blackpool FY1 130
Haslingden BB4 85
3 Lytham St Anne's FY8 91

leasant View
Bacup OL13 70 C7
15 Barnoldswick BB18 196 B2
Billington BB7 144 B4
Blackpool FY4 111 A4
Coppull PR7 42 F2
Earby BB18 197 C1
Hoddlesden BB3 82 F1
Leyland PR26 76 C3
Newchurch BB4 86 F1
Tockholes BB3 81 A1
Withnell PR6 80 A1
LEASINGTON 100 C1
leasington Ave PR3 181 D6
leasington Cl
Blackburn BB2 101 B4
Blackpool FY4 111 A8
leasington Gr BB10 128 D5
leasington La BB2 80 C8
leasington Old Hall Nature Reserve* BB2 100 D3
leasington St BB2 101 B4
leasington Sta BB2 100 C1
leasure Island* FY8 89 E5
leck Farm Ave BB1 101 E8
LECKGATE 122 D1
leckgate Fold BB1 122 E1
leckgate High Sch BB1 122 D1
leckgate Rd BB1 122 E1
leck Pl FY6 153 B6
leck Rd BB5 104 C6
lessington Ct PR3 140 A7
levna Rd PR1 97 C8
lex La L39 14 C5
lex Moss La L39 13 D8
lock Gn PR7 43 C5
lough La L40 17 A4
loughlands The 2 PR2 116 E1
loughmans Ct 1 PR2 139 D1
lover Cl FY5 176 A5
lover Dr
Bury BL9 33 B4
Heysham LA3 212 F5
lover St
Burnley BB12 127 D6
Preston PR1 118 B1
lovers Way FY3 131 B6
lover View 2 BB12 127 D6
lox Brow PR4 57 A6
lumbe St BB11 128 A5
lumpton Ave FY4 110 F5
lumpton Field PR4 136 E2
lumpton La
Great Plumpton PR4 112 E7
Shirdley Hill L39 22 E2
lumpton Rd PR2 117 C2
lumtree Cl PR2 118 C6
lunge Rd BL0 68 E3
lungington Rd PR1, PR2 117 E2
lymouth Ave FY7 175 C8
lymouth Gr PR6 43 E8
lymouth Rd FY2, FY3 152 E1
oachers Trail FY8 90 D7
oachers Way FY5 176 A4
ochard Pl 4 FY5 175 F1
ocklington St BB5 104 D2
oets' Rd BB12 126 F7
oint 65 Bsns Ctr BB1 102 B6
ointer Ct LA1 214 F6
ointer Gr LA2 219 D7
ointer The LA1 214 F6
oland St BB5 103 F5
olefield PR2 117 E7
ole La BB3 65 C8
ole St
Preston PR1 97 A8
Standish WN6 29 E1
olice St BB3 82 A1
olice Yd 18 LA2 239 D8
ollard Pl LA1 218 E4
ollard Row BB12 169 F1
ollards La BL9 50 C2
ollard St
Accrington BB5 104 C7
Burnley BB11 127 D5
4 Nelson BB9 170 E1
6 Preston PR1 96 E8
ollux Gate FY8 90 C4
olperro Dr PR4 93 A6
omfret St
Blackburn BB2 101 D3
Burnley BB11 127 E6
ompian Brow PR26 57 E6
ond Cl PR4 57 A5
ond Gdns FY6 153 B6
ond St LA5 223 D2
ond Terr LA5 223 D2
ont St BB9 148 D7
ontville Residential Sch L39 15 D3
ool Ct FY7 198 D1
oole Rd PR2 118 A4
oole St BB1 102 C5
ool Foot La FY6 154 E4
OOL HEY 36 B3
ool Hey La PR8, PR9 36 B3
oolhill Cl FY5 152 E7
ool House Com Prim Sch PR2 117 A6
ool House Ct PR2 117 A6
ool House La PR2 117 A5
ool La PR4 93 A4
oolside PR4 93 C6

Poolside Wlk PR9 54 C4
Pool St PR9 54 D5
Poorsland Barn BB7 229 C7
Poot Hall OL12 52 F3
Pope La
Fulwood PR2 119 A3
Kingsfold PR1 96 C2
White Stake PR4 76 B8
Pope Wlk PR1 96 D3
Poplar Ave
Bamber Bridge PR5 97 F1
Blackpool FY3 130 D5
Bury BL9 33 B3
Euxton PR7 60 C4
Great Harwood BB6 124 D6
Horwich BL6 32 E1
Kirkham PR4 114 A4
Longton PR4 75 B8
Poulton-le-F FY6 153 E2
4 Rochdale OL12 52 C1
Warton PR4 92 D6
Poplar Bank PR9 53 D1
Poplar Cl
Bamber Bridge PR5 97 F1
Oswaldtwistle BB5 103 F3
Rishton BB1 103 B8
Poplar Ct FY8 89 E5
Poplar Dr
Coppull PR7 42 F1
Freckleton PR4 93 A5
Higher Penwortham PR1 96 C5
Longridge PR3 140 A8
Skelmersdale WN8 17 F1
Poplar Gr
Bamber Bridge PR5 97 F1
Fulwood PR2 119 A4
Ramsbottom BL0 50 D7
Poplar St
2 Blackburn BB1 102 A7
Chorley PR7 43 D6
Haslingden BB4 85 B3
Nelson BB9 170 F1
Southport PR8 35 E6
Poplars The
Adlington PR7 30 F6
Burscough L40 25 E2
Poplar Terr BB4 85 F6
Poppy Ave PR6 61 D2
Poppy Cl PR8 35 B2
Poppyfield PR4 116 F6
Poppyfields PR4 73 E4
Poppy La L39 16 B1
Porritt Ave LA1 214 D8
Porritt Ct FY8 89 E6
Porritt St
Bury BL9 33 B4
Bury, Free Town BL9 33 A4
Porritt Way BL0 50 C7
Portal Gr BB12 127 B6
Porter Pl 2 PR1 97 A6
Porter St E 4 PR4 113 F6
Porters Row FY6 177 C7
Porter St
Accrington BB5 103 F5
Preston PR1 118 B1
Portfield Bar BB7 144 F3
Portfield La BB6 144 F3
Portfield Rd BB7 144 E4
Porthcawl Ct PR2 116 F3
Portland Cotts PR6 62 D8
Portland Ct FY4 111 A1
Portland Dr LA3 217 B2
Portland Ind Est 12 BL9 33 A4
Portland Pl BL6 32 C3
Portland Rd
Blackpool FY1 130 D4
Langho BB6 123 C8
Portland St
Accrington BB5 104 A6
Barrowford BB9 170 D3
Blackburn BB2 101 C3
Bury BL9 33 A4
1 Chorley PR6 43 D8
Colne BB8 171 F5
Darwen BB3 65 B6
Lancaster LA1 214 F7
Nelson BB9 148 D8
Preston PR1 96 D7
Southport PR8 35 B5
Portman St PR1 118 B1
Portree Cl PR2 118 C5
Portree Cres BB1 102 D3
Portree Rd FY2 152 E5
Port Royal Ave LA1 214 C8
PORTSMOUTH 108 F1
Portsmouth Ave BB10 148 E2
Portsmouth Cl 7 FY5 175 F4
Portsmouth Dr PR6 43 E8
Portway FY2 152 E6
Port Way
Heysham LA3 212 D5
Preston PR2 96 C7
Postern Gate Rd LA2 232 A8
Post Horse La LA2 238 B7
Post La PR4 92 F6
Post Office Ave 1 PR9 35 B7
Post Office Bldgs 18 BB18 196 B2
Post Office Row
St Michael's on W PR3 157 C7
Tunstall LA6 241 D4
Westhouse LA6 242 E4
Post Office Yd 8 BB8 171 E5
Pot Gn BL0 50 A3
POT HOUSE 82 C3
Pot House La
Darwen BB3 82 C3
Oswaldtwistle BB5 103 F2

Potter La
Coupe Green PR5 98 D5
Samlesbury PR5 119 E2
Potter Pl WN8 9 D5
POTTERS BROOK 207 B5
Potter St 5 BL9 33 A3
Poulton Ave
Accrington BB5 104 A8
Lytham St Anne's FY8 90 B8
Poulton Cres PR5 98 D3
Poulton Ct PR9 35 F7
Poulton Dr FY6 153 F3
Poulton Gdns FY6 153 F3
Poulton Gr 4 FY7 199 A4
Poulton Ind Est FY6 154 A3
POULTON-LE-FIELD 153 E2
Poulton-le-Fylde Sta FY6 153 D4
Poulton-le-Sands CE Prim Sch LA4 217 B6
Poulton Old Rd FY3 152 F1
Poulton Plaiz Holiday Pk FY6 153 C2
Poulton Rd
Blackpool FY3 130 E8
Carleton FY6 153 C5
Fleetwood FY7 198 F4
Morecambe LA4 217 B5
Southport PR9 35 F7
Poulton Sq 11 LA4 217 B6
Poulton St
Fleetwood FY7 199 A4
Kirkham PR4 114 B5
Preston PR2 117 C1
Powder House La LA1, LA4 218 A4
Powderworks La L31 6 C3
Powell Ave FY4 110 D8
Powell St
Barnoldswick BB18 196 B3
Burnley BB11 127 E4
Darwen BB3 82 A2
Powis Dr PR4 57 A8
Powis Rd PR2 96 B8
Powys Cl BB4 85 B1
Poynter St 4 PR1 118 C1
Poynton St BL9 33 A1
Prairie Cres BB10 148 B2
Pratt St BB10 148 B1
PREESALL 200 A3
Preesall Cl
Lytham St Anne's FY8 90 B7
Preston PR2 116 E1
Southport PR9 53 F4
Preesall Fleetwood's Charity CE Prim Sch FY6 200 B3
Preesall Mill Ind Est FY6 200 B2
Preesall Moss La FY6 200 D2
PREESALL PARK 200 C1
Preesall Rd PR2 116 E1
Preese Gdns PR4 156 A1
Preese Hall PR4 132 D5
Premier Way FY6 153 F3
Prenton Gdns FY5 153 A7
Prescot Cl BL9 33 A1
Prescot Gn L39 15 D3
Prescot Pl
Blackpool FY3 131 A2
Thornton FY5 176 C2
Prescot Rd L31, L39 6 D6
Prescott Ave L40 39 A3
Prescott Rd WN8 9 F4
Prescott St BB10 128 C5
Presfield Sch PR9 54 A3
Press Rd FY8 89 D8
Prestbury Ave
Blackpool FY4 110 C5
Southport PR8 21 B5
Prestbury Cl BL9 33 A1
Prestbury Dr LA3 217 B2
PRESTON 96 C8
Preston Beck BB18 197 B2
Preston College Park Campus PR1 117 F2
Preston Coll Fulwood Campus PR2 117 F5
Preston Ent Ctr 6 PR1 117 F1
Preston Grange Prim Sch PR2 119 A4
Preston Greenlands Com Prim Sch PR2 118 E3
Preston Lancaster New Rd PR3 181 B4
Preston Lancaster Old Rd PR3 181 D2
Preston Lancaster Rd
Bilsborrow PR3 159 A6
Cabus PR3 204 C5
Forton LA2, PR3 207 C5
Galgate LA2 211 A5
Preston New Rd
Blackburn BB2 101 B5
Blackpool FY3, FY4 131 C2
Clifton PR4 94 C7
Freckleton PR4 93 D7
Little Plumpton PR4 112 C6
Mellor Brook BB2, PR5 120 D1
Samlesbury PR2, PR5 119 E1
Southport PR9 54 B4
Preston Nook PR7 41 C5
Preston Old Rd
Blackburn BB2 80 D8
Blackpool FY3 131 A2
Clifton PR4 115 C1
Freckleton PR4 93 C6

Preston Rd
Charnock Richard PR7 42 C4
Chorley PR6, PR7 61 C2
Clayton Brook PR5, PR6, PR7 78 B4
Grimsargh PR2, PR3 139 E2
Inskip PR4 135 D7
Leyland PR25 77 B2
Longridge, New Town PR3 140 A5
Longridge PR3 140 E6
Lucas Green PR6 61 C4
Lytham St Anne's FY8 91 D4
Ribchester PR3 141 B5
Southport PR9 35 E8
Standish PR7, WN6 29 D5
Preston St
Carnforth LA5 223 D2
1 Chorley PR6 61 D1
Darwen BB3 81 F3
Fleetwood FY7 199 B4
Kirkham PR4 114 B5
16 Rochdale OL12 52 C1
Preston Sta PR1 96 E7
Preston Tech Ctr PR1 96 D8
Preston Temple PR6 61 C4
Prestwich St BB11 127 E5
Prestwood Pl WN8 9 F4
Pretoria St 2 OL12 52 C1
PRETTYWOOD 33 E2
Price Cl LA1 218 C3
Price St
9 Blackpool FY1 130 B1
Bury BL9 33 A1
Prickshaw OL12 52 B6
Prickshaw La OL12 52 B6
Priestfield Ave BB8 171 B5
Priesthouse Cl L37 12 A3
Priesthouse La L37 12 A3
PRIEST HUTTON 240 C4
Priestield FY5 153 A7
Priestley Nook 4 BB5 104 C5
PRIMET BRIDGE 171 C3
Primet Bridge BB8 171 C4
Primet Bsns Ctr 4 BB8 171 B4
Primet Hill BB8 171 C4
Primet Hts 2 BB8 171 B3
Primet St BB8 171 C4
PRIMROSE 166 D6
Primrose Ave FY4 110 D6
Primrose Bank
1 Bacup OL13 70 C8
Blackburn BB1 101 F6
Blackpool FY2 152 F6
Read BB12 145 D2
Primrose Cl
Blackburn BB2 101 B2
Formby L37 12 B5
Hesketh Bank PR4 73 E4
Southport PR9 54 C6
Primrose Cotts
Calder Vale PR3 182 E7
Middleton LA3 213 A2
Primrose Ct
1 Blackburn BB1 101 F5
6 Lancaster LA1 215 A7
Morecambe LA4 217 B5
Primrose Dr
2 Blackburn BB1 101 F5
Bury BL9 33 D4
Cold Row FY6 177 D4
Primrose Gr PR1 118 C3
PRIMROSE HILL 14 F8
Primrose Hill
Colne BB8 171 F5
Mellor BB1, BB2 122 A3
3 Preston PR1 97 B7
Primrose Hill Prim Sch PR7 60 B4
Primrose Hill Rd PR7 60 B4
Primrose La
Preston PR1 118 C3
Standish WN6 29 D2
Primrose Rd
Clitheroe BB7 166 D6
Preston PR1 118 C3
Primrose Row PR7 59 F1
Primrose St
Accrington BB5 104 A4
9 Bacup OL13 70 C8
Brierfield BB9 148 B5
Burnley BB10 148 C1
Chorley PR6 43 D8
Clitheroe BB7 166 D7
Darwen BB3 65 B8
Lancaster LA1 215 A7
6 Morecambe LA4 217 B5
Primrose Terr
Blackburn BB2 101 B2
Blackpool FY4 111 A4
1 Darwen BB3 65 B8
Langho BB6 143 C1
Primrose Way
Carleton FY6 153 B6
Church BB5 103 E7
Primula Dr BB3 82 A7
Prince Ave LA5 223 E1
Prince Charles Gdns PR8 34 F4
Prince Lee Mdws BB3 65 B8
Princes Cres LA4 217 E7
Princes Ct
Higher Penwortham PR1 96 B6
4 Morecambe LA4 217 E6
18 Ramsbottom BL0 50 C6
Princes Dr PR2 117 E6

Princes Gdn PR8 35 E6
Princes Gdns LA4 217 E5
Prince's Pk WN6 19 F4
Princes Rd
Higher Penwortham PR1 96 B6
Lytham St Anne's FY8 90 D4
Prince's Rd PR5 97 E5
Princes Reach PR2 96 A7
Princess Alexandra Way LA3 212 D5
Princess Ave
Clitheroe BB7 189 F1
Kirkham PR4 113 F6
Lancaster LA1 214 F6
Poulton-le-F FY6 153 D3
Princess Ct 5 FY1 130 B3
Princess Gdns BB2 80 D7
Princess Par FY1 130 B6
Princess Rd
Adlington PR6 31 B8
Cleveleys FY5 175 C2
Princess St
Accrington BB5 103 F6
17 Bacup OL13 87 F2
2 Bamber Bridge, Lostock Hall PR5 77 B7
10 Bamber Bridge PR5 77 F8
Blackburn BB2 101 C2
Blackpool FY1 130 B3
Burnley BB12 126 B8
Chorley PR7 43 D6
Church BB5 103 E6
Colne BB8 171 C4
Great Harwood BB6 124 D5
Haslingden BB4 85 B2
Leyland PR25 77 B1
Nelson BB9 148 D7
Preston PR1 97 B7
26 Rochdale OL12 52 F1
Whalley BB7 144 C5
Whitworth OL12 52 C8
Princes St
Rishton BB1 124 B1
Southport PR8 35 A6
Prince's St BB2 101 D4
Princess Way
Burnley BB12 127 F7
Euxton PR7 60 E2
Prince St
Britannia OL13 71 D7
11 Burnley BB11 127 E5
Darwen BB3 81 F1
Ramsbottom BL0 50 C6
Princes Way
Cleveleys FY5 175 C1
Fleetwood FY7 198 D3
Princeton Sq FY8 90 D7
Princeway FY4 110 C7
Pringle Bank LA5 223 D6
Pringle Ct PR3 181 C7
Pringle St BB1 102 A3
Pringle Wood PR3 137 C2
Prinny Hill Rd BB4 85 A3
Printers Fold BB12 126 E6
Printshop La BB3 65 A6
Prior's Cl BB2 101 A6
Priorsgate 3 LA3 217 C2
Prior's Oak Cotts PR1 96 C6
Priors Wlk BB7 230 C1
Priorswood Pl WN8 9 F4
Priory Chase BB9 148 F8
Priory Cl
Blackburn BB1 102 E4
Burscough L40 25 D5
Formby L37 12 B2
Higher Penwortham PR1 96 C6
6 Lancaster LA1 214 E8
Leyland PR25 77 C2
Morecambe LA3 217 C2
Newchurch BB4 86 E2
Pleasington BB2 100 C2
Tarleton PR4 57 A6
Priory Cres PR1 96 C6
Priory Ct
7 Blackpool FY1 130 C5
Burnley BB11 128 B2
Lytham St Anne's FY8 89 E7
Priory Dr BB3 65 C8
Priory Gate FY4 110 C5
Priory Gdns
Scorton PR3 204 E6
Southport PR8 34 F4
Priory Gr L39 15 D4
Priory Grange
Darwen BB3 65 C8
Southport PR8 35 A4
Priory Hospl Preston The PR4 136 A1
Priory La
Higher Penwortham PR1 96 C6
Hornby LA2 238 B7
Priory Mews
Lytham St Anne's FY8 90 D7
Southport PR8 34 F6
Priory Nook WN8 10 C7
Priory Pl BB3 65 C8
Priory Rd WN8 10 C7
Priory Sports & Tech Coll PR1 96 A5
Priory St
5 Nelson BB9 170 F1
Preston PR2 96 D8
Priory Way BB18 196 A2

Priory Wlk 6 LA1 215 A8
Pritchard St
Blackburn BB2 101 E2
Burnley BB11 127 E5
Private La BB4 68 C8
Procter Moss Rd
Lower Green Bank LA2 232 B3
Quernmore LA2 215 D1
Procter's Brow LA2 239 B5
Procter St BB2 101 F3
Proctor Cft BB8 172 B2
Proctor Cl BB9 148 F5
Proctor Rd L37 11 C4
Progress Ave BB1 102 A7
Progress Bsns Pk PR4 114 A4
Progress Ct FY3 131 B8
Progress Rd BB9 170 F3
Progress St
Chorley PR6 43 E8
Darwen BB3 82 B1
Progress Way FY4 111 B6
Promenade
Blackpool, Bispham FY2 152 B6
Blackpool FY1, FY4 130 B5
Cleveleys FY5 175 C5
Knott End-on-S FY6 199 E6
Southport, Ainsdale-on-S PR8 20 F6
Southport PR9 35 B8
Promenade N FY5 175 C3
Promenade Rd FY7 199 A5
Promenade S FY5 175 C2
Prospect Ave
Bamber Bridge PR5 77 B8
Darwen BB3 81 E2
Hest Bank LA2 220 E1
Prospect Bldgs 5 BB9 148 D8
Prospect Ct
Catterall PR3 181 D2
Longridge PR3 140 B6
Prospect Dr LA2 220 E1
Prospect Farm Cvn Pk BB8 171 D3
Prospect Gdns BB3 81 E2
Prospect Gr LA4 217 C4
Prospect Hill
Haslingden BB4 85 A2
4 Rawtenstall BB4 86 A3
Prospect Pl
7 Middleforth Green PR1 96 E4
Preston PR2 117 B1
Skelmersdale WN8 9 F5
Prospect Rd BB4 86 A3
Prospect St
Great Harwood BB6 124 D5
Lancaster LA1 215 A7
Newchurch BB4 86 F1
Prospect Terr
Bacup OL13 70 E7
10 Barrowford BB9 170 D4
Belthorn BB1 82 F6
Brinscall PR6 63 A8
Clow Bridge BB11 106 B4
Huncoat BB5 125 E2
Newchurch BB4 86 F1
Prospect View
Bamber Bridge PR5 77 A7
9 Rawtenstall BB4 86 A3
Provence Ave BB6 143 C6
Providence St BB1 102 A8
Prudy Hill FY6 153 D4
Prunella Dr BB3 82 A7
Pudding La OL14 109 C2
Pudding Pie Nook La PR3 137 F4
Puddle House La FY6 131 F8
PUDSEY 109 B2
Pudsey Rd OL14 109 B2
Pump House La PR26 58 F6
Pump St
Blackburn BB2 101 D4
Burnley BB11 127 E6
Clitheroe BB7 166 D8
Preston PR1 97 A8
Punnell's La L31 4 F5
Punstock Rd BB3 81 F1
Pupil Learning Ctr (New Summerseat Ho) BL0 50 B2
Purbeck Dr BL6 32 F1
Purlbrook Ct BL6 32 B4
Pye Busk LA2 239 E8
Pye Busk Cl LA2 239 E8
Pye's Cotts L39 5 E7
Pygon's Hill La L31 5 D6

Q

Quail Holme Rd FY6 199 D5
Quaker Brook La PR5 99 A3
Quakerfields BB3 82 A2
Quaker La BB3 82 A2
Quakers' Pl WN6 29 E1
Quakers Terr WN6 29 D3
Quakers View BB9 148 A5
Quality Row BB7 164 E1
Quarlton Dr BL8 49 B3
Quarrybank 3 FY5 152 F8
Quarry Bank
Garstang PR3 181 C6
Haslingden BB4 84 F1
Quarry Bank St 3 BB12 127 C7
Quarry Dr L39 15 C1
Quarry Farm Ct BB7 190 D5
Quarry Hill OL12 52 E3
Quarry Hill Nature Reserve* BB9 148 F6
Quarry Mount L39 16 A6
Quarry Mount Mews LA1 215 A7
Quarry Rd
Brinscall PR6 62 F7
Caton LA2 237 E3
Chorley PR6 43 E6
Halton LA2 219 C6
Lancaster LA1 215 A7
Quarryside Dr L33 1 A3
Quarry St
13 Accrington BB5 104 C5
Blackburn BB1 101 F5
Hapton BB11 126 C2
Padiham BB12 146 D1
Ramsbottom BL0 50 D6
Rochdale OL12 52 E1
Shawforth OL12 71 E6
Quayle Ave FY4 110 E8
Quayside
5 Blackburn BB1 101 F4
Fleetwood FY7 199 B3
Quayside Ct PR2 96 A8
Quays The L40 25 E5
Quay W FY8 89 E5
Quebec Ave FY2 152 E3
Quebec Rd BB2 101 B8
Queen Anne St
4 Haslingden BB4 85 A3
Southport PR8 35 B7
Queen Charlotte Villas PR8 21 C5
Queen Elizabeth Cres BB5 104 D5
Queen Elizabeth Ct LA4 217 A5
Queen Elizabeth's Gram Sch BB2 101 C6
Queen Elizabeth's Gram Sch (Annexe) BB2 101 D6
Queen Ho BB4 86 D1
Queen Mary Ave FY8 90 A5
Queen Mary Terr BB7 144 B7
Queen St E 3 PR7 43 D6
Queens Ave L37 11 E5
Queensberry Rd BB11 127 E5
Queensborough Rd BB5 104 B7
Queensbury Rd FY5 175 C2
Queen's Cl
Clitheroe BB7 166 E7
Poulton-le-F FY6 153 E3
Queenscourt Ave PR1 96 E2
Queen's Cres PR4 114 B4
Queens Croft L37 11 D2
Queens Ct
Fulwood PR2 117 E3
Ormskirk L39 15 E4
Queen's Ct FY2 152 B2
Queens Ctyd 7 PR9 35 C8
Queensdale Cl PR5 97 E4
Queens Dr
Fulwood PR2 117 D6
Longridge PR3 140 A7
Morecambe LA4 217 E6
Staining FY3 131 E5
Queen's Dr
Carnforth LA5 223 E1
Oswaldtwistle BB5 103 F3
Queens Drive Prim Sch PR2 117 D5
Queens Garth BD23 197 B5
Queensgate
Chorley PR7 43 B7
Nelson BB9 148 D7
Queens Gn L39 13 F5
Queen's Gr PR7 43 C8
Queens Hotel Ct PR9 35 B8
Queens Jubilee Nature Trail* PR8 34 E5
Queen's Lancashire Regiment Mus The* PR2 118 B4
Queen's Lancashire Way BB11 127 F6
QUEEN'S PARK 102 B4
Queens Park Cl BB1 102 A3
Queen's Park Rd
Blackburn BB1 102 A3
Burnley BB10 128 C7
Queens Pl
Kirkham PR4 113 F7
Ramsbottom BL9 50 C2
Queen's Prom FY2 152 B5
Queen Sq LA1 214 F7
Queens Rd
Clitheroe BB7 166 E7
Orrell WN5 10 C5
Southport PR9 35 C8
Queen's Rd
Accrington BB5 104 C7
Blackburn BB1 102 B3
Burnley BB10 148 B2
Chorley PR7 43 C8
Darwen BB3 65 B6
Formby L37 11 D2
Fulwood PR2 117 E3
Lytham St Anne's FY8 89 F5
Walton-le-D PR5 97 E4
Queens Rd W BB5 104 A7
Queens Ret Pk PR1 97 B7
Queens Sq 1 FY1 130 B5
Queen's Sq
Hoddlesden BB3 82 F1
Poulton-le-F FY6 153 D3
7 Rawtenstall BB4 86 A2
Queen St
12 Accrington BB5 104 C6
Bacup, Rockliffe OL13 87 F2
5 Bacup, Stacksteads OL13 70 C8
4 Bamber Bridge PR5 77 B7
Barnoldswick BB18 196 B1
Barrowford BB9 170 D4
Blackpool FY1 130 B6
Burnley BB11 127 F5
Burnley, Harle Syke BB10 148 F2
Bury BL9 33 A2
Carnforth LA5 223 D1
Clayton-le-M BB5 124 F3
Clitheroe BB7 166 C8
Colne BB8 171 C4
Darwen BB3 81 F2
Fleetwood FY7 199 A4
Great Harwood BB6 124 D5
Hoddlesden BB3 82 F1
Horwich BL6 32 B3
Lancaster LA1 214 F7
Lytham St Anne's FY8 91 A3
Morecambe LA4 217 B5
Nelson BB9 170 E1
Ormskirk L39 15 E4
Oswaldtwistle BB5 103 E4
Padiham BB12 126 C8
Preston PR1 97 B7
Ramsbottom BL0 50 B6
Rawtenstall BB4 86 A2
Whalley BB7 144 C5
Queen's Terr
3 Bacup OL13 70 E8
Blackburn BB2 101 B1
Fleetwood FY7 199 C5
QUEENSTOWN 130 D7
Queen Street Mill Textile Mus* BB10 148 F2
Queensway
Bamber Bridge PR5 97 E1
Blackburn BB2 81 A8
Blackpool FY4 110 C7
Brinscall PR6 62 F8
Church BB5 103 F7
Clitheroe BB7 166 E7
Euxton PR7 60 E2
Higher Penwortham PR1 96 B6
Leyland PR25 59 E7
Lytham St Anne's FY4, FY8 111 B2
Newchurch BB4 86 E1
Poulton-le-F FY6 153 D3
Preston PR2 116 F2
Shevington WN6 19 F4
Waddington BB7 189 B4
Warton PR4 92 E7
Queensway Cl PR1 96 B6
Queensway Ct FY8 111 A1
Queensway Ind Est FY8 111 A2
Queens Wlk FY5 175 D4
Queen Vera Rd 4 FY1 130 B5
Queen Victoria Ctr LA4 217 B5
Queen Victoria Rd
Blackpool FY1 130 C2
Burnley BB10 148 B1
Queen Victoria St BB2 101 B2
Quenby Cnr FY6 153 B3
QUERNMORE 232 A6
Quernmore Ave FY3 131 A3
Quernmore Brow LA2 232 B5
Quernmore CE Prim Sch LA2 232 A7
Quernmore Dr
Glasson LA2 209 E4
Kelbrook BB18 195 A5
Quernmore Ind Est PR4 93 C6
Quernmore Rd
Caton LA2 237 B2
Kirkby L33 1 A3
Lancaster LA1, LA2 215 D7
Quernmore Wlk L33 1 A3
Quillet The LA5 224 F3
Quins Croft PR25 76 F2
Quin St PR25 77 A1
Quinton Cl PR8 21 A4

R

Rabbit La
Burscough L40 24 F4
Cow Ark BB7 187 F6
Raby Sq 12 LA4 217 B6
Raby St
4 Morecambe LA4 217 B5
1 Rawtenstall BB4 86 A2
Rachel Ho 5 BL9 33 C3
Radburn Brow PR6 78 B3
Radburn Cl PR6 78 B3
Radcliffe Ct BB12 127 A6
Radcliffe Rd FY7 198 F2
Radeclyffe St BB7 189 E1
Radfield Ave 17 BB3 65 A8
Radfield Head BB3 64 F8
Radfield Rd BB3 64 F8
RADFORD 65 A8
Radford Bank Gdns 13 BB3 65 A8
Radford Bank Ho 14 BB3 65 A8
Radford Gdns BB3 65 A7
Radford St BB3 65 A8
Radley Ave FY3 130 E8
Radnor Ave
Burnley BB12 127 A7
Cleveleys FY5 175 F1
Radnor Cl BB5 103 C4
Radnor Dr PR9 53 F3
Radnor St
Accrington BB5 104 B7
5 Preston PR1 96 E8
Radway Cl FY5 152 F7
Radworth Cres FY4 131 B1
Raeburn Ave BB11 127 E3
Raedale Ave BB10 148 B4
Raeside Ct FY8 90 A4
Raglan Rd
Burnley BB11 127 E5
Morecambe LA3 216 E3
Raglan St
8 Colne BB8 171 D4
4 Nelson BB9 148 D8
Preston PR2 117 D2
Raikes Hill 2 FY1 130 C5
Raikes Hill Dr LA2 218 C8
Raikes Mews 6 FY1 130 C5
Raikes Par FY1 130 C5
Raikes Rd
Great Eccleston PR3 156 C5
Preston PR1 118 C1
Thornton FY5 153 E8
Rail Cl WA11 8 F2
Railgate
Britannia OL13 71 C8
Whitworth OL13 88 C1
Railton Ave BB2 81 A8
Railway App L39 15 F5
Railway Ave PR9 54 F5
Railway Cotts
Coppull PR7 42 F1
Preston PR4 116 C3
Salwick PR4 115 C4
Railway Crossing La LA1 214 C5
Railway Gr 5 BB1 102 A7
Railway Path L39 15 E4
Railway Pl LA2 209 F5
Railway Rd
Adlington PR6, PR7 31 A7
Blackburn BB1 101 E5
Brinscall PR6 63 A8
Chorley PR6 61 D1
Darwen BB3 82 A1
Haslingden BB4 85 B4
Ormskirk L39 15 F5
Skelmersdale WN8 8 E8
Railway St
Bacup OL13 70 B8
23 Barnoldswick BB18 196 B2
Brierfield BB9 148 B5
Burnley BB11 127 F7
Chorley PR7 43 D7
Foulridge BB8 194 D1
Lancaster LA1 214 F6
Leyland PR25 77 B2
Nelson BB9 148 E7
Ramsbottom BL0 50 C6
Ramsbottom, Summerseat BL0, BL9 50 C2
Southport PR8 35 B5
Railway Terr
Brierfield BB9 148 B5
Entwistle BL7 48 B8
Great Harwood BB6 124 C4
10 Kirkham PR4 113 F6
Rawtenstall BB4 85 F1
Simonstone BB12 125 E8
Southport PR8 35 A5
Railway View
5 Accrington BB5 104 C6
Billington BB7 144 B4
Blackburn BB2 101 B2
Brierfield BB9 148 B6
Croston PR26 58 A2
3 Darwen BB3 65 B8
Railway View Ave BB7 189 E1
Railway View Rd BB7 189 E1
RAINFORD JUNCTION 8 F2
Rainford Rd L39, WA11 8 C4
Rainford Sta WA11 8 F2
RAINHALL 196 D3
Rainhall Cres BB18 196 D3
Rainhall Rd BB18 196 B2
Rake 4 BL0 50 B6
Rake Fold BL0 50 A6
RAKE FOOT 86 A7
Rake Foot BB4 85 B3
RAKE HEAD 70 A7
Rakehead La OL13 70 B8
Rakehouse Brow LA2 232 F2
Rake La PR4 92 D5
Rakes Bridge BB3 82 A7
Rakes House Rd BB9 170 E2
Rakes La BD23 231 F5
Rakes Rd LA2 237 E4
Rake The LA2 232 E1
Rake Top Ave BB12 146 F6
Raleigh Ave FY4 110 B5
Raleigh Cl FY8 110 D1
Raleigh Rd PR2 117 E6
Raleigh St BB12 126 E7
Ralph St BB5 104 C8
Ralph's Wife's La PR9 54 E6
Ramparts The LA1 218 E2
Ramper Gate FY5 175 D2
Ramsay Ct FY6 199 D5
RAMSBOTTOM 50 C
Ramsbottom Cottage Hospl BL0 50 C
Ramsbottom Heritage Ctr* BL0 50 C
Ramsbottom La BL0 50 C
Ramsbottom Rd
Hawkshaw BL8, BL7 49 A
Horwich BL6 32 C
Ramsbottom St BB5 104 E
Ramsbottom Sta* BL0 50 C
Ramsbottom Stubbins Prim Sch BL0 68 D
Rams Clough La BB5 84 A
Ramsden St LA5 223 D
Ramsey Ave
Bacup OL13 88 A
Blackpool FY3 130 D
Preston PR1 118 D
Ramsey Cl FY8 110 D
Ramsey Gr BB10 148 C
Ramsey Rd BB2 101 D
Ramsgate Cl PR4 92 E
Ramsgate Rd FY8 90 A
Ramsgreave Ave BB1 122 D
Ramsgreave Bsns Pk BB1 122 E
Ramsgreave Dr BB1 122 D
Ramsgreave Rd BB1 122 E
Ramsgreave & Wilpshire Sta BB1 122 F
Ramshill Ave FY6 153 E
Ramson Ct 3 LA3 217 E
Ranaldsway PR25 59 D
Randall St 10 BB10 148 E
Randal St BB1 101 E
Randolph St 21 BB1 102 A
Ranelagh Dr PR8 21 F
Range High Sch L37 2 C
Ranger St BB5 104 E
Rangeway Ave FY4 110 C
Ranglet Rd PR5 78 B
Rangletts Ave PR7 43 C
Ranglit Ave PR2 116 C
Rankin Ave PR4 73 F
Rankin Cl BB18 196 C
Rankin Dr BB3 82 E
Ranlea Ave LA4 218 A
Ranleigh Dr
Newburgh WN8 27 A
Skelmersdale WN8 18 A
RANN 82 E
Rannoch Dr BB2 100 F
Ranslett Ct L37 12 A
Rantreefold Rd LA2 239 C
Rapley La PR4 136 A
Ratcliffe Fold 5 BB4 85 B
Ratcliffe St
Darwen BB3 65 B
10 Haslingden BB4 85 B
Ratcliffe Wharf La PR3 207 B
Rathbone Rd L38 2 F
Rathlyn Ave FY3 130 E
RATHMELL 236 F
Rathmell CE Prim Sch BD24 236 E
Rathmell Cl FY3 153 B
Rathmill Sike BB7 230 B
Rathmore Cres PR9 54 B
Rathmore Gdns FY2 152 E
Ratten La PR4 95 D
RATTEN ROW 156 B
Raven Ave BB4 68 A
Raven Cl PR7 42 F
Raven Croft BB4 68 B
Ravendale Cl OL12 52 A
Ravenglass Ave L31 5 D
Ravenglass Cl
Blackburn BB2 102 A
Blackpool FY4 110 E
Kirkham PR4 114 A
Ravenhead Dr WN8 10 A
Ravenhead Way WN8 9 F
Ravenhill Dr PR7 61 C
Raven Meols Hills Nature Reserve* L37 2 B
Raven Meols La L37 11 F
Raven Meols Lo L37 11 E
Ravenoak La BB10 129 B
Raven Pk BB4 68 B
Raven Rd BB2 101 B
Ravens Cl LA1 218 C
Raven's Cl FY3 131 B
Ravens Close Brow LA2 241 F
Ravenscroft L37 11 F
Ravenscroft Ave L39 15 E
Ravenscroft Cl BB1 123 A
Ravenscroft Way BB18 196 C
Ravens Gr BB10 148 C
Raven St
3 Nelson BB9 170 F
Preston PR1 118 C
Ravens The L37 11 F
Ravensthorpe PR7 61 A
Ravenswing Ave BB2 101 B
Ravenswood
Fulwood PR2 118 E
Great Harwood BB6 124 B
Ravens Wood BB2 101 B
Ravenswood Ave FY3 131 B
Ravenwood Ave FY4 110 D
Rawcliffe Dr PR2 95 E
Rawcliffe Rd
12 Chorley PR7 43 C
Ratten Row PR3 156 C

Rawcliffe St
Blackpool FY4 110 B8
Burnley BB11 128 A6
Rawlinson Ct PR9 35 D8
Rawlinson Gr PR9 53 F1
Rawlinson La PR6 43 E1
Rawlinson Rd PR9 53 E1
Rawlinson St
1 Darwen BB3 65 B6
13 Horwich BL6 32 B4
5 Kirkham PR4 113 F6
Rawson Ave BB5 104 A4
Rawsons Rake BL0, BL8 50 A6
Rawson St 12 BB10 148 B1
Raws St BB11 128 A6
Rawsthorne Ave
Edenfield BL0 68 D2
Haslingden BB4 85 B2
Rawstorne Cl PR4 93 A6
Rawstorne Cres PR4 95 E1
Rawstorne Rd PR1 96 B5
Rawstorne St BB2 101 C4
Rawstron St OL12 71 C1
RAWTENSTALL 86 B1
Rawtenstall Cribden House Com Specl Sch BB4 85 E1
Rawtenstall Newchurch CE Prim Sch BB4 86 E1
Rawtenstall Rd BB4 85 C1
Rawtenstall St Anne's CE Prim Sch BB4 86 F3
Rawtenstall St Paul's Constable Lee CE Prim Sch BB4 86 A4
Rawtenstall Sta BB4 85 F1
Rawtenstall Water Prim Sch BB4 87 A8
Rawthey Rd 5 LA1 218 B2
Raybourne Ave FY6 153 C3
Raygill Ave BB11 127 D3
Raygill Pl 3 LA1 218 B2
Ray La PR3 181 F4
Raylees BL0 50 C4
Raymond Ave FY2 130 D8
Raynor St BB2 101 D5
Rays Dr LA1 214 F3
Ray St BB9 148 A5
READ 145 D2
Reading Cl 14 BB1 102 A4
Read St John's CE Prim Sch BB12 145 D2
Read's Ave FY1 130 C4
Reads Ct 7 FY1 130 C4
Read St 2 BB5 125 A1
Reaney Ave 3 FY4 110 E7
Record St BB18 196 B1
Rectory Cl
Chorley PR7 43 C8
Croston PR26 58 C2
Darwen BB3 65 C8
Newchurch BB4 86 E1
Tarleton PR4 57 A5
Rectory Gdns LA2 206 C5
Rectory Hill BL9 33 D4
Rectory La
Bury BL9 33 D4
Standish WN1, WN6 30 A1
Rectory Paddock LA2 219 C6
Rectory Rd
Blackpool FY4 130 E1
Burnley BB12 127 F7
Southport PR9 54 A1
RED BANK 43 E5
Red Bank BL9 33 E6
Red Bank Rd FY2 152 C4
Red Barnes L37 11 F5
Red Bridge La LA5 224 F4
Redcar Ave
Cleveleys FY5 175 F5
Fulwood PR2 117 A4
Redcar Cl PR8 35 F3
Redcar Rd
Blackpool FY1 130 B8
Lancaster LA1 215 B3
Red Cat La L40 25 E7
Redcliffe Gdns L39 15 E3
Red Court Cvn Pk LA5 223 D1
Redcross St N OL12 52 F1
Redcross St OL12 52 F1
Red Cross St 5 PR1 96 E7
Red Delph La WA11 8 E1
Redearth Rd BB3 65 A8
Redearth St BB3 65 A8
Rede Ave FY7 198 C2
Redeemer CE Prim Sch The BB2 81 D7
Redeswood Ave FY5 152 E8
Redfearn Wood OL12 52 B2
Red Fold L39 15 C2
Redgate
Formby L37 12 A2
Ormskirk L39 15 D5
Redgate Cl BB11 128 B3
Redgate Dr L37 12 B2
Redgate Prim Sch L37 12 A2
Redgrave Ct BB12 127 A6
Redhill PR4 95 C1
Redhill Gr PR6 61 E3
Redhills Dr PR8 35 F3
Redhouse Cl BB5 125 A2
Red House La PR7 41 B6
Redisher Cl BL0 49 F3
Redisher Croft BL0 49 F3
Redisher La BL8 49 E3
Red La
Colne BB8 171 B7
Eccleston PR7 41 E6
Redlam BB2 101 B3
Redlam Brow BB2 101 C3
Red Lees Ave BB10 128 F4
Red Lees Rd BB10 129 A2
Red Lion Cl L31 5 C1
Red Lion Sh Ctr L31 5 D1
Red Lion St
Burnley BB11 128 A5
Earby BB18 197 C2
Redman Rd BB10 148 B4
Red Marsh Dr FY5 176 C3
Red Marsh Ind Est FY5 176 C3
Redmayne Dr LA5 223 F2
Redmayne St 3 PR1 97 D8
Redness Cl BB9 148 E6
Red Rake BB1 101 C7
Red Rose Ct BB2 101 D4
Red Rose Lo FY4 130 F1
Redruth Dr
Carnforth LA5 223 C1
Crag Bank LA5 221 C8
Redruth St BB12 127 D6
Red Sands L39 15 D3
Redsands Dr PR2 118 D5
RED SCAR 119 B5
Red Scar Ind Est PR2 119 B5
Red Scar St BB8 171 C4
Redshank Dr LA3 212 F6
Red Shell La BB1, BB5 83 B7
Red Spar Rd BB10 148 D3
Redstart Pl 9 FY5 175 F1
Redvers Rd BB3 81 E5
Redvers St
Burnley BB10 148 B1
Lancaster LA1 214 D8
Redvers Terr FY1 130 B8
Redwell Fisheries LA6 237 D8
Redwing Ave
1 Cleveleys FY5 175 F4
Great Harwood BB6 124 B6
Redwing Dr PR7 42 F5
Redwing Rd BL8 49 F2
Redwood Ave
Leyland PR25 76 E1
Maghull L31 5 C3
Redwood Chase PR4 113 E4
Redwood Cl
Blackpool FY4 110 C4
Rochdale OL12 52 B3
Redwood Dr
Chorley PR7 43 D6
Longridge PR3 140 A8
Morecambe LA4 217 E5
Ormskirk L39 15 D4
Rawtenstall BB4 68 F8
Redwood Gdns FY5 176 E2
Redwood Hts LA1 215 C7
Reedfield
Burnley BB10 148 C4
Clayton Brook PR5 78 C4
Reedfield Pl PR5 78 A6
REEDLEY 148 B4
Reedley Dr
Burnley BB10 148 C4
Burnley, Reedley BB10 148 B4
Reedley Farm Cl BB10 148 B5
Reedley Gr BB10 148 B3
Reedley Prim Sch BB10 148 C4
Reedley Rd BB9, BB10 148 C5
Reedmace Wlk 10 LA3 217 B2
Reed Row BB8 171 D3
Reeds Brow WA11 9 C1
Reeds Cl BB4 86 A6
REEDS HOLME 85 F5
Reedsholme Cl BB4 86 A6
Reeds La BB4 86 A6
Reed St
Bacup OL13 88 A3
Burnley BB11 128 A4
Reeds The
Lancaster LA1 218 C1
Ormskirk L39 15 D6
Reedy Acre Pl FY8 90 F4
Reedyford Cott BB9 170 D2
Reedyford Rd BB9 170 E2
Reedymoor La BB8 194 C1
Reedy Moor Terr BB8 194 C1
Reeford Gr BB7 166 D7
Rees Pk L40 25 F3
Reeth Way 3 BB5 103 F4
Reeval Cl BB18 197 C2
Reeveswood PR7 41 B6
Regal Ave FY4 110 E6
Regal Ct PR8 21 D5
Regal Terr 5 LA1 218 D3
Regency Ave PR5 77 D8
Regency Cl
Kirkham PR4 113 E5
Whalley BB7 144 A7
Regency Gdns
Blackpool FY2 152 D2
Euxton PR7 60 D1
Southport PR8 34 E4
Southport PR9 53 D1
Regent Ave
Colne BB8 171 E6
Lytham St Anne's FY8 90 D6
Regent Cl
Padiham BB12 126 C7
Southport PR8 34 F4
Regent Ct
4 Blackpool FY1 130 B6
Fulwood PR2 117 E5
Lytham St Anne's FY8 89 D8
12 Southport PR9 35 C8
Regent Dr PR2 117 D4
Regent Gr PR2 117 E5
Regent Mews PR8 34 F4
Regent Park Ave LA3, LA4 216 F3
Regent Park Gr LA4 217 A4
Regent Pk PR2 117 E5
Regent Pl BB9 170 E2
Regent Rd
Bamber Bridge PR5 97 D4
Blackpool FY1 130 C5
Chorley PR7 43 C7
Church BB5 103 F7
6 Leyland PR25 77 A1
Morecambe LA3 216 F3
Southport PR8 34 F4
Regent Rd E FY1 130 C5
Regents Cl BB2 100 C2
Regent St
4 Bacup OL13 88 A2
Blackburn BB1 101 E5
Brierfield BB9 148 B5
Coppull PR7 42 E1
Haslingden BB4 85 B3
Lancaster LA1 214 E7
Longridge PR3 140 A7
Nelson BB9 170 F2
Preston PR1 96 F6
Ramsbottom BL0 50 A5
Rochdale OL12 52 F1
Waddington BB7 189 B4
Regents Terr FY6 153 E3
Regents View BB1 122 E1
Regentsway 8 PR5 77 E8
Regents Way PR7 60 D2
Regiment Dr PR7 60 F6
Reginald St BB8 171 C5
Reigate PR6 61 F3
Reiver Rd PR26 76 C3
Renacres Hall Hospl (private) L39 23 B5
Renacres La L39 23 B5
Rendel St BB12 127 C7
Rendsburg Way 15 LA1 214 F8
Renfrey Cl L39 15 E8
Rennie Cl PR3 181 D6
Rennie Ct LA1 214 E5
Rennie St BB10 128 C5
Renshaw Dr
Bamber Bridge PR5 97 E2
Bury BL9 33 C3
Renshaw St 8 BB10 148 B1
Renwick Ave FY4 110 D8
Repton Ave
Blackpool FY1 130 C8
Morecambe LA4 217 F4
Reservoir Rd FY5 176 C3
Reservoir St
Burnley BB11 127 F4
Darwen BB3 81 F1
Reta Dr FY5 176 A3
Retford Rd L33 1 A2
REVIDGE 101 C7
Revidge Rd BB1, BB2 101 C7
REVOE 130 C3
Revoe Com Prim Sch FY1 130 C3
Revoe St FY1 130 C3
Rewe Cl 6 BB2 81 C8
Rexington Bldgs BB11 127 C5
Reynolds St
Burnley BB11 127 E3
Lancaster LA1 218 C1
Rhoda St BB9 170 F1
Rhoden Rd
Leyland PR26 76 C1
Oswaldtwistle BB5 103 D2
Rhodes Ave
Blackburn BB1 101 D8
Haslingden BB4 68 A7
Rhodesway PR5 98 E2
Rhuddlan Cl BB4 85 B1
Rhuddlan Gdns FY5 176 D2
Rhyddings Bsns & Ent Sch BB5 103 E4
Rhyddings St BB5 103 E4
Rhyddings The BL9 33 E7
Rhyl Ave BB1 101 E7
Rhyl St FY7 199 B5
Ribble Ave
Burnley BB10 148 C2
Darwen BB3 81 E4
Freckleton PR4 93 A6
Great Harwood BB6 124 E6
Grindleton BB7 190 B7
Maghull L31 5 E2
Southport PR9 54 C4
Whalley BB7 144 A7
Ribble Bank PR1 96 B6
Ribble Bank St PR1 96 E7
Ribble Brook Ho PR1 117 F1
Ribble Bsns Pk BB1 102 B8
Ribble Cl
Freckleton PR4 93 A6
Middleforth Green PR1 96 E4
3 Preston PR1 96 E6
Withnell PR6 80 A1
Ribble Cres
Kirkham PR4 114 B5
5 Preston PR5 97 C6
Ribble Ct 2 PR1 96 D6
Ribble Discovery Ctr* FY8 90 C3
Ribble Dr
Baldingstone BL9 50 F1
Hesketh Bank PR4 73 E4
West Bradford BB7 189 D7
Ribble Hall PR1 117 F1
Ribble Ho
Blackburn BB1 101 F5
11 Preston PR1 97 D8
Ribble La BB7 190 D6
Ribble Lo 10 FY8 91 A3
Ribble Point FY8 90 C3
Ribble Rd
Blackpool FY1 130 C4
Fleetwood FY7 198 F4
Leyland PR25 59 D8
Shevington Moor WN6 29 B2
Ribblesdale Ave
Accrington BB5 104 B8
Clitheroe BB7 189 E2
Wilpshire BB1 123 A7
Ribblesdale Cl
Blackpool FY4 111 A8
Kirkham PR4 114 A5
Ribblesdale Ct
Gisburn BB7 231 B3
5 Morecambe LA4 217 B5
Ribblesdale Dr
Forton PR3 207 B3
Grimsargh PR2 139 C1
Ribblesdale High Sch Tech Coll BB7 166 E7
Ribblesdale Pk BB7 231 B4
Ribblesdale Pl
Barrowford BB9 170 E6
Blackburn BB2 101 C5
Chorley PR7 43 B7
Preston PR1 96 F6
Ribblesdale Rd PR3 141 E3
Ribblesdale St BB10 128 B8
Ribblesdale View BB7 190 E5
Ribbleside Cvn Pk PR3 142 A4
Ribble St
Blackburn BB1 101 E6
Britannia OL13 71 A8
Lytham St Anne's FY8 89 D6
Padiham BB12 126 D8
Preston PR1 96 E7
Ribble Steam Rly* PR2 95 E7
Ribble Steam Rly Mus* PR2 95 E7
RIBBLETON 118 E2
Ribbleton Ave PR2 118 E2
Ribbleton Avenue Inf Sch PR1 118 D2
Ribbleton Avenue Meth Jun Sch PR1 118 D2
Ribbleton Dr BB5 104 C8
Ribbleton Gr BB7 144 A7
RIBBLETON HALL 119 B2
Ribbleton Hall Cres 2 PR2 118 F3
Ribbleton Hall Dr PR2 118 F3
Ribbleton Hospl PR2 118 F2
Ribbleton La PR1 118 C1
Ribbleton Pl 6 PR1 97 B8
Ribbleton St 8 PR1 97 B8
Ribbleton Trad Est 10 PR1 97 B8
Ribble View BB7 189 F4
Ribble View Cl PR4 92 F6
Ribble Way BB7 166 C8
RIBBY 113 D4
Ribby Ave
Kirkham PR4 113 F5
Wrea Green PR4 113 C4
Ribby Pl
Blackpool FY4 131 B1
Preston PR2 116 F1
Ribby Rd
Kirkham PR4 113 F4
Wrea Green PR4 113 C4
Ribby-with-Wrea CE Prim Sch PR4 113 B4
RIBCHESTER 141 D3
Ribchester Ave
Blackpool FY4 131 B1
Burnley BB10 128 D5
Ribchester Rd
Copster Green BB1 142 A1
Dinckley BB6, PR3 142 C4
Lytham St Anne's FY8 91 D4
Wilpshire BB1 122 E6
Ribchester St Wilfrid's CE Prim Sch PR3 141 E3
Ribchester Way BB9 148 D4
Rice Gr FY1 130 D8
Richard Burch St 2 BL9 33 A3
Richard Durning's Endowed Prim Sch L40 27 D7
Richardson Cl PR4 93 C6
Richardson St FY1 130 B4
Richards Rd WN6 29 B3
Richard's St 7 PR4 113 F6
Richard St
Brierfield BB9 148 B5
Burnley BB11 128 B5
Shuttleworth BL0 50 E7
7 Weir OL13 88 A7
Richards Way 3 FY5 175 F1
Richard's Way FY8 110 E2
Richards Wlk 7 LA1 218 B1
Richard Thornton's CE Prim Sch LA6 242 B3
Richmond Ave
Accrington BB5 104 B5
Barnoldswick BB18 196 A3
Burnley BB10 128 F4
Burscough L40 25 E3
Cleveleys FY5 175 E2
Haslingden BB4 85 C2
Richmond Ave *continued*
Lancaster LA1 218 D4
Morecambe LA4 217 D4
Wrea Green PR4 113 B3
Richmond Cl
Brinscall PR6 62 E8
Hightown L38 2 F2
Richmond Cres BB1 102 E5
Richmond Ct
8 Blackpool FY1 130 B7
Burscough L40 25 E3
Chorley PR7 43 C6
Leyland PR26 76 B1
Richmond Gr L31 5 E3
Richmond Hill 23 BB1 101 E5
Richmond Hill La PR3 207 D2
Richmond Hill St BB5 104 B5
Richmond Ho
Chorley PR7 43 C6
9 Lancaster LA1 218 D3
11 Preston PR1 97 A7
Richmond Ind Est BB5 104 B5
Richmond Mews L40 25 E3
Richmond Pk BB3 82 A2
Richmond Rd
Accrington BB5 104 A4
Barnoldswick BB18 196 A3
Barrowford BB9 170 C1
Blackpool FY1 130 B7
Chorley PR6 43 E6
Eccleston PR7 41 C7
Lytham St Anne's FY8 89 E6
Southport PR8 34 F2
Richmond St
Accrington BB5 104 A5
Burnley BB11 127 E5
Horwich BL6 32 B3
2 Preston PR1 97 B7
Richmond Terr
17 Blackburn BB1 101 E5
Clitheroe BB7 166 D7
Darwen BB3 82 A2
Rickard Rd BB9 148 E6
Ridding La BB7 144 B5
Riddings Ave BB10 128 F6
Riddings La BB7 144 C6
Ridehalgh La BB10 149 F2
Ridehalgh St BB8 171 B3
Riders Gate BL9 33 F4
RIDGE 218 F2
Ridge Ave BB10 128 D6
Ridge Cl PR9 54 C5
Ridge Ct
Burnley BB10 128 C7
Longridge PR3 140 C8
Ridgeford Gdns PR2 117 D5
Ridge Gr LA3 212 F8
Ridge La
Lancaster LA1 218 E1
Lancaster, Ridge LA1 219 A2
Roughlee BB12 169 F4
Ridgemont PR2 117 C6
Ridge Prim Sch LA1 218 F1
Ridge Rd
Burnley BB11 128 B6
Chorley PR6 43 E7
Ridge Row BB10 128 D6
Ridge Sq LA1 218 F1
Ridge St
Barnoldswick BB18 196 B2
Lancaster LA1 218 E1
Ridgeway
Barrowford BB9 170 C3
Great Harwood BB6 124 B6
Ridge Way PR1 96 E4
Ridgeway Ave BB2 82 A8
Ridgeway Dr
Maghull L31 5 E3
Thornton FY5 153 D8
Ridgeways BB4 85 C2
Ridgeway The
Fleetwood FY7 198 D3
Nelson BB9 148 D7
Ridgmont Cl BL6 32 F3
Ridgmont Dr BL6 32 F3
Ridgway BL6 31 C2
Ridgway Ct FY8 90 A7
Ridgwood Ave FY3 130 E5
Riding Barn St BB5 103 F7
Riding Cl
Barnoldswick BB18 196 C2
Haskayne L39 13 F4
Riding Head La BL0 50 F8
Riding La L39 13 E4
Riding St
Burnley BB11 127 E5
Preston PR1 117 F1
Southport PR8 35 B6
Ridings The
Burnley BB12 127 D8
Lucas Green PR6 61 C6
Southport PR9 54 A3
Ridley La
Barber's Moor PR26 58 D3
Maghull L31 5 D1
Mawdesley L40 40 F2
Ridley Rd PR2 117 C2
Ridley St 2 FY3 130 D5
Rifle St BB4 85 B2
Rigby Ave BL6 31 C2
Rigby Cl PR4 93 C6
Rigby Rd
Blackpool FY1 130 B3
Maghull L31 5 B3

294 Rig–Ros

Rigby St
Colne BB8 171 C5
Nelson BB9 148 D8
Preston PR1 97 C8
Rigg Ho 10 LA1 218 D2
Rigg La
Quernmore LA2 232 B7
Whitechapel PR3 184 B1
Rigg St BB9 148 E8
Riley Ave FY8 89 F5
Riley Cl PR25 60 A8
Riley Ct FY8 89 F4
RILEY GREEN 79 E8
Riley Green Switch Rd BB2, PR5 79 F7
Riley St
Accrington BB5 104 B4
Bacup OL13 87 F5
Brierfield BB9 148 B5
Burnley BB11 128 B4
Earby BB18 197 B2
RIMINGTON 191 F8
Rimington Ave
Accrington BB5 104 A3
Burnley BB10 128 D5
Colne BB8 171 C6
Rimington Cl BB2 101 F2
Rimington Cvn Pk BB7 231 B1
Rimington La BB7 191 D7
Rimington Pl
Lytham St Anne's FY8 90 B6
Nelson BB9 171 B1
Rimmer Gn PR8 36 D1
Rimmer's Ave
Formby L37 11 E6
Southport PR8 35 B6
Ring Dyke Way FY8 91 A4
Ring Lows La OL12 52 F4
RING O'BELLS 26 B2
Ring O'Bells La L40 26 B2
Rings St BB4 106 A2
Ringstone Cres BB9 149 B8
Ringstones La LA2 239 D4
Ringtail Ct L40 25 B4
Ringtail Ind Est L40 25 B2
Ringtail Pl L40 25 B4
Ringtail Rd L40 25 B4
RINGTON 153 B6
Rington Ave FY6 153 B6
Ringway
Chorley PR7 43 A7
Cleveleys FY5 175 E4
Ring Way PR1 96 F7
Ringwood Ave BL0 50 A4
Ringwood Cl
Accrington BB5 125 B1
Lytham St Anne's FY8 90 F3
Ringwood Rd PR1 118 C2
Ripley Cl L31 5 E1
Ripley Ct LA1 214 F6
Ripley Dr FY8 90 B6
Ripley St Thomas CE High Sch LA1 214 F6
Ripon Ave 1 LA1 218 D4
Ripon Brook PR1 118 F1
Ripon Cl
Cleveleys FY5 175 E5
Great Eccleston PR3 156 C5
Southport PR8 35 F3
Ripon Hall Ave BL0 50 B4
Ripon Pl LA3 212 E6
Ripon Rd
Blackpool FY1 130 D4
Lytham St Anne's FY8 90 D5
Oswaldtwistle BB5 103 C5
Ripon St
Blackburn BB1 102 B4
Nelson BB9 148 D7
Preston PR1 117 E2
Ripon Terr PR1 118 F1
Risedale Dr PR3 140 B7
Risedale Gr BB2 81 A7
Rise The LA5 221 B6
RISHTON 124 C2
Rishton Meth Prim Sch BB1 124 B1
Rishton Rd
Clayton-le-M BB5 124 E3
Wilpshire BB1 123 C5
Rishton St FY1 130 C4
Rishton Sta BB1 103 A8
RISING BRIDGE 85 A8
Rising Bridge Rd BB4, BB5 85 A7
Ritherham Ave FY5 175 D3
River Bank Terr BB5 125 E6
River Cl L37 12 B1
River Dr BB12 126 D8
River Hts PR5 77 C8
River Lea Gdns BB7 166 F8
Rivermead Ct PR3 204 C1
Rivermead Dr PR3 181 C8
Rivermeade PR8 35 D4
River Par PR1 96 D6
River Rd
Thornton FY5 176 D4
Thornton, Stanah FY5 176 E3
Riversedge Rd PR25 59 C8
Rivers Edge The OL12 71 C1
Riversgate FY7 198 F4
Riverside
Bamber Bridge PR5 77 E7
Clitheroe BB7 166 B8
Hightown L38 2 F4
Riverside *continued*
Preston PR1 96 E5
Riverside Ave PR26 76 E4
Riverside Bsns Ctr BB9 170 E1
Riverside Chalet Pk FY6 154 D4
Riverside Cl
Halton LA2 219 C6
Leyland PR26 76 E4
Riverside Cres PR26 58 A2
Riverside Ct OL12 71 D4
Riverside Cvn Site PR9 55 D3
Riverside Dr
Hambleton FY6 177 B1
Ramsbottom BL0 50 B2
Riverside Fold BB12 169 E5
Riverside Ind Est BB5 124 D2
Riverside Ind Pk PR3 181 C2
Riverside Lofts LA1 218 C1
Riverside Mews
Padiham BB12 126 F6
Whitewell Bottom BB4 86 F4
Riverside Mill 3 BB8 171 B4
Riverside Park Ind Est LA1 218 F4
Riverside Pk BB4 86 F4
Riverside Rd PR1 96 E5
Riverside Terr 4 BB18 197 B1
Riverside View BB5 124 E4
Riverside Wlk BB4 68 A7
Riversleigh Ave
Blackpool FY1 152 C1
Lytham St Anne's FY8 90 E3
Riversleigh Ct FY8 90 E3
Rivers St WN5 10 E6
River St
Bacup OL13 87 F1
Blackburn BB1 101 F4
Colne BB8 171 D4
Darwen BB3 81 F2
Lancaster LA1 218 C1
Preston PR1 96 E7
Ramsbottom BL0 50 C6
Trawden BB8 172 C3
Rivers View Fold LA2 226 A8
Riversway
Blackpool FY3 130 F6
4 Lancaster LA1 218 D2
Poulton-le-F FY6 153 F5
Preston PR2, PR4 95 D8
Riversway Bsns Village PR2 96 A8
Riversway Dr BB3 81 F6
Riversway Enterprise Workshops PR2 95 E8
Riversway Managed Workshops 1 PR2 95 F8
Riversway Motor Pk PR2 95 D8
River View
Glasson LA2 209 E5
Tarleton PR4 57 A8
Riverview Ct LA4 217 B3
River Way BB9 170 D4
Riverway Cl PR5 77 D8
RIVINGTON 44 F2
Rivington Ave
Adlington PR6 31 B7
Blackpool FY2 152 D5
Rivington & Blackrod High Sch (Lower) BL6 32 B4
Rivington & Blackrod High Sch (Upper) BL6 32 B6
Rivington Cl
Poulton-le-F FY6 153 D3
Southport PR8 35 A3
Tarleton PR4 56 F8
Rivington Ctry Pk* BL6 32 A8
Rivington Dr
Burscough L40 25 E3
Up Holland WN8 10 C7
Rivington Hall Cl BL0 50 C4
Rivington La
Adlington PR6 31 D6
Horwich BL6 32 A7
Rivington BL6 44 F1
Rivington Park Ind Sch BL6 32 B6
Rivington Pl PR7 29 D6
Rivington Prim Sch BL6 44 F1
Rivington Rd
Belmont BL6, BL7 46 B4
Chorley PR6 61 E1
Rivington St
Blackburn BB1 102 B4
Blackrod BL6 31 D2
Rochdale OL12 52 F1
Rivington View PR6 61 E1
Rixton Gr FY5 176 B4
ROACH BRIDGE 98 F6
Roach Bridge Cotts PR5 98 E6
Roach Rd PR5 99 B4
Roach St BL9 33 C1
Road La OL12 52 D4
Robbin's Bridge L31 5 E5
Roberts Ct
Leyland PR25 59 F8
Warton LA5 223 D6
Robertson Ct FY7 198 F1
Roberts St
2 Chorley PR7 43 C7
Nelson BB9 148 F8
7 Rawtenstall BB4 86 A3
Robert St
Accrington BB5 104 C7
Barnoldswick BB18 196 B2
Blackburn BB2 101 E3
Colne BB8 171 E5
15 Darwen BB3 81 F2
Great Harwood BB6 124 D6
43 Lancaster LA1 214 F8
Newchurch BB4 86 F2
Oswaldtwistle BB5 103 D3
Ramsbottom BL0 68 C1
Robin Bank Rd BB3 82 A2
Robin Cl PR7 42 D3
Robin Cres LA3 212 F6
Robin Croft LA2 241 A1
Robin Hey PR26 76 B1
Robin Hill Dr WN6 29 B2
Robin Hill La WN6 29 C3
ROBIN HOOD 28 C4
Robin Hood La WN6 28 B3
Robin House La BB10 149 C4
Robin La
High Bentham LA2 239 D8
Hill Dale WN8 27 C5
Rimington BB7 231 B1
Robin Rd BL0 50 B2
Robins Cl FY6 153 A4
Robins La
Blackpool FY6 153 A4
Carleton FY6 153 A6
Robinson Ct BB18 196 A3
Robinson Fold BB18 196 A3
Robinson La BB9, BB10, BB12 148 A4
Robinson St
Blackburn BB1 102 B7
Burnley BB10 128 A8
Chatburn BB7 190 E5
Colne BB8 171 C5
Foulridge BB8 194 D1
Fulwood PR2 117 D3
15 Horwich BL6 32 B4
Robin St PR1 118 D1
Robson St BB9 148 B6
Robson Way FY3 153 A2
ROBY MILL 19 B3
Roby Mill WN8 19 B3
ROCHDALE 52 C2
Rochdale Girls Sch OL12 52 F1
Rochdale Infmy OL12 52 F1
Rochdale Old Rd BL9 33 D4
Rochdale Rd
Bacup OL13 88 A1
Britannia OL13 71 B8
Bury BL9 33 B2
Edenfield BL0 68 F2
Ramsbottom BL0 51 B7
Rochester Ave
Cleveleys FY5 175 F4
Morecambe LA4 217 D3
Rochester Cl 3 OL13 88 A7
Rochester Dr BB10 148 C3
Rochford Ave FY5 175 E1
Rock Bridge Fold BB4 86 E5
Rock Brow PR3 163 B7
Rockburgh Cres PR4 75 A5
Rockcliffe Ave OL13 87 E1
Rockcliffe Dr OL13 87 E1
Rockcliffe Rd OL13 87 F1
Rockcliffe St 5 BB4 86 A3
Rockcliffe Villas OL13 70 E8
Rockfield Gdns 2 L31 5 C2
Rockfield Rd BB5 104 D6
Rockfield St BB2 101 E3
Rock Fold BL7 47 F1
Rock Gdns PR5 99 B3
Rock Hall Rd BB4 85 B3
Rockhaven Ave BL6 32 C4
Rockingham Rd FY2 152 D3
Rock La
Burnley BB11 128 B3
Tockholes BB3 81 A3
Trawden BB8 172 C3
ROCKLIFFE 88 A2
Rockliffe La OL13 88 A1
Rockliffe Rd OL13 87 F1
Rockliffe St BB2 101 E2
Rock m' Jock LA2 237 B3
Rockmount BB7 189 F3
Rock St
Accrington BB5 104 E2
Clitheroe BB7 166 E8
18 Haslingden BB4 85 B3
Horwich BL6 32 B3
Shuttleworth BL0 50 E7
Thornton FY5 176 B4
Rock Terr
Bolton BL7 47 F1
Pendleton BB7 167 B4
13 Rawtenstall BB4 86 A7
Rock Villa Rd PR6 61 C8
Rockville BB9 170 E5
Rockville Ave FY5 152 F8
Rock Water (Bird Conservation Ctr)* BB10 129 C2
Rockwood Cl BB10 148 E3
Roddlesworth La PR6 63 E8
Roddlesworth Nature Trail* BB3 64 B8
Roddlesworth Visitor Ctr* BB3 64 B8
Rodhill La BB7 230 B3
Rodney Ave FY8 110 E1
Rodney St
Blackburn BB2 101 C3
3 Preston PR1 96 F8
Rodwell Wlk FY3 130 F8
Roebuck Cl BB2 101 D3
Roebuck Prim Sch PR2 117 D2
Roebuck St PR2 117 C2
Roeburndale Cres LA3 213 A8
Roeburndale Rd LA2 238 B1
Roeburn Dr LA3 217 F2
Roeburn Hall PR1 96 E8
Roeburn Pl LA1 218 C2
Roeburn Terr LA2 238 D6
Roedean Ave LA4 217 F4
Roedean Cl
Maghull L31 5 D2
Thornton FY5 176 A2
Roe Greave Rd BB5 103 D3
Roehampton Cl 11 FY5 176 A2
Roe Hey Dr PR7 42 F2
Roe La PR9 35 E8
ROE LEE 122 E1
Roe Lee Ind Est BB1 122 F1
Roe Lee Park Prim Sch BB1 122 F2
Roe Lee Pk BB1 122 F2
Roe-Park Mews PR9 35 D8
Roe St OL12 52 C1
Rogerley Cl FY8 91 A4
Rogersfield BB6 123 B8
Rolleston Rd BB2 101 B4
Roman Cres LA2 237 C3
Roman Mus* PR3 141 E3
Roman Rd
Blackburn BB1, BB2 82 B8
Preston PR1 97 B7
Whittlestone Head BB3 66 A4
Roman Way
Cleveleys FY5 175 F1
Clitheroe BB7 167 A8
Kirkham PR4 114 C4
Red Scar PR2 119 C6
Roman Way Ind Est PR2 119 C6
Rome Ave BB11 127 C4
Romford Rd PR1 118 C2
Romford St 2 BB12 127 C7
Romiley Dr WN8 17 F2
Romney Ave
Barrowford BB9 170 D3
Blackpool FY4 130 D1
Burnley BB11 127 E3
Fleetwood FY7 198 E3
Romney St BB9 148 D7
Romney Wlk BB1 102 C4
Romsey Ave L37 12 B2
Rona Ave 4 FY4 110 F6
Ronald St
Blackburn BB1 102 C5
Burnley BB12 127 A5
Ronaldsway
Nelson BB9 171 B2
Preston PR1 118 D3
Ronaldsway Cl OL13 88 B1
Ronbury Cl 1 BB9 170 C1
Roney St BB2 101 C5
Ronwood Cl PR4 155 F1
Ronwood Ct PR2 96 B8
Roocroft Sq BL6 31 C2
Roods The LA5 223 E6
Rookery Ave WN6 19 E8
Rookery Cl
Chorley PR7 43 A6
Kingsfold PR1 96 F2
Rookery Ct PR1 96 F1
Rookery Dr PR1 96 F2
Rookery Rd
Barnoldswick BB18 196 C3
Southport PR9 53 F1
Rook St
Barnoldswick BB18 196 B2
Colne BB8 171 D5
Nelson BB9 170 E1
Preston PR1 118 B1
3 Ramsbottom BL0 50 C6
Rookwood PR7 41 B6
Rookwood Ave PR7 61 C2
Rooley Moor Rd
Bacup OL12, OL13 70 C4
Rochdale OL12 52 A3
Rochdale, Spotland Fold OL12 52 C1
Rooley St OL11, OL12 52 C1
Rooley View OL13 87 E1
Roosevelt Ave LA1 214 D7
Roots La PR4 135 E2
Ropefield Way OL12 52 E3
Rope Wlk PR3 181 C7
Rosary Ave FY4 130 E1
Roscoe Ave FY5 176 D2
Roscoe Lowe Brow PR6 31 D7
ROSEACRE 134 D6
Roseacre FY4 110 C5
Roseacre Cl BB4 86 F4
Roseacre Dr PR4 156 A1
Rose Acre La LA5 225 F2
Roseacre Pl
Lytham St Anne's FY8 90 B8
5 Preston PR2 116 E1
Roseacre Prim Sch FY4 110 C5
Roseacre Rd
Roseacre PR4 134 D6
Wharles PR4 134 F4
Rose Ave
Blackpool FY1 130 D2
Burnley BB11 127 E4
Fulwood PR2 117 C3
Rosebank
8 Blackpool FY5 152 F8
Clayton-le-M BB5 125 A3
Edenfield BL0 68 D1
2 Preston PR2 116 C1
Rose Bank
Lancaster LA1 215 A5
Rawtenstall BB4 86 A3
Rosebank Ave 3 FY4 110 C5
Rose Bank St OL13 87 F3
Rosebay Ave BB2 80 D8
Rosebay Cl L37 12 A3
Roseberry Ave PR4 116 E5
Roseberry Cl BL0 50 C3
Rosebery Ave
Blackpool FY4 110 B6
Lancaster LA1 215 A5
Lytham St Anne's FY8 90 B4
Morecambe LA4 217 C4
Rosebery St
Burnley BB10 148 B2
Southport PR9 36 A6
Todmorden OL14 109 C1
Rosebowl View L40 24 B4
Rose Cl PR25 77 E2
Rose Cotts
Low Bentham LA2 239 B8
Preesall FY6 200 C3
Rose Cres
Skelmersdale WN8 17 E1
Southport PR8 21 C2
Rosecroft Cl L39 15 E6
Rose Ct
Blackburn BB2 101 B6
1 Fleetwood FY7 198 F4
Haslingden BB4 85 B5
Rosedale Ave
Blackpool FY4 131 A2
Heysham LA3 213 A8
Rosedale St BB4 85 F5
Rosedene LA2 218 D7
Rosedene Cl PR4 116 E5
Rosefinch Ct FY3 131 B2
Rosefinch Way FY3 131 B3
Rose Fold
Middleforth Green PR1 96 D4
Thornton FY5 176 B4
Rose Fold Cotts PR1 96 D4
Rosegarth LA2 218 D7
Rose Gdns PR4 73 E4
Rose Gr LA2 210 F4
ROSE GROVE 127 B6
Rosegrove Cvn Pk FY6 200 A6
Rosegrove Inf Sch BB12 127 A6
Rosegrove La BB11 127 B5
Rose Grove Sta BB11 127 B5
ROSEHILL 65 C7
ROSE HILL 127 F3
Rose Hill
Euxton PR7 60 C4
Ramsbottom BL0 50 B6
Southport PR8, PR9 35 D6
Rosehill Ave
Burnley BB11 127 E4
12 Nelson BB9 170 F1
Rose Hill Ave BB1 102 A4
Rosehill Bsns Pk 1 PR9 35 D6
Rosehill Dr L39 15 C2
Rosehill Mans L39 15 C2
Rosehill Mt BB11 127 E4
Rosehill Rd
Burnley BB11 127 F3
Nelson BB8 171 A2
Rose Hill Rd BB2 100 C1
Rose Hill St
Bacup OL13 87 F2
Darwen BB3 65 B8
Rawtenstall BB4 106 A1
Rose Hill Terr 7 BB3 65 B8
Rose La PR1 118 C3
Roseland Ave BB9 148 C6
Roseland Cl L31 5 B4
Rose Lea PR2 118 D6
Roselea Dr PR9 54 C4
Roselyn Ave FY4 110 C5
Rosemary Ave
Blackpool FY4 110 C5
Cleveleys FY5 175 F3
Rosemary Ct
Formby L37 11 F3
1 Kingsfold PR1 96 C2
Rosemary La
Formby L37 11 F2
Haskayne L39 14 B4
8 Lancaster LA1 214 F8
Swillbrook PR4 136 A1
Rosemeade Ave PR5 77 B8
Rosemede Ave FY4 130 F2
Rosemount OL13 88 A4
Rose Mount BB4 86 F1
Rosemount Ave
Barnoldswick BB18 196 A3
Burnley BB11 127 E4
Knott End-on-S FY6 200 A5
Rosendale Cl 5 OL13 88 B3
Rosendale Cres OL13 88 B3
Rose Path L37 12 A2
Rose Pl
Accrington BB5 104 B4
Ormskirk L39 15 D2
Rose St
Accrington BB5 104 B4
Bacup OL13 87 F2
6 Blackburn BB2 101 E3
Darwen BB3 82 B1

Rose St *continued*
Leyland PR25 77 B3
10 Morecambe LA4 217 B6
Newchurch BB4 86 E2
14 Preston PR1 97 A7
Rose Terr
Bacup OL13 70 F8
Preston PR2 117 B2
Rose Vale St BB4 86 B2
Roseway
Blackpool FY4 110 C5
Lytham St Anne's FY8 90 B6
Poulton-le-F FY6 153 C3
Preston PR2 117 A1
Rosewood PR4 116 E5
Rosewood Ave
Blackburn BB1 101 F8
Burnley BB11 127 E3
Haslingden BB4 85 C3
Higher Walton PR5 98 C3
Rosewood Cl
Chorley PR7 43 D6
Lytham St Anne's FY8 90 E4
1 Thornton FY5 176 D1
Rosewood Ct PR5 98 B3
Rosewood Dr PR5 98 B3
Rosewood Pk BB1 101 F8
Rosewood Prim Sch BB11 127 E3
Roshaw PR2 139 C1
Rosklyn Rd PR6 43 E7
Rosley St BB8 172 B5
ROSSALL BEACH 175 D5
Rossall Cl
Coupe Green PR5 98 E3
Fleetwood FY7 175 D8
Padiham BB12 126 D6
Rossall Ct
Cleveleys FY5 175 C5
Fleetwood FY7 198 E3
Rossall Dr PR2 117 C4
Rossall Gate FY7 175 C8
Rossall Gdns FY5 175 D4
Rossall Grange La FY7 198 D3
Rossall Hospl FY7 175 C8
Rossall La FY7 175 E7
Rossall Rd
Blackpool FY3 130 D7
Chorley PR6 61 E1
Cleveleys FY5 175 D3
Fulwood PR2 117 C4
Lancaster LA1 218 A2
Lytham St Anne's FY8 90 D4
Rossall Sch FY7 175 C6
Rossall St PR2 117 C1
Rossall Terr BB2 101 E1
Rossendale Ave
Burnley BB11 127 E2
Lancaster LA1 211 B8
Morecambe LA4 217 C6
Rossendale Ave N FY5 176 B2
Rossendale Ave S FY5 176 B1
Rossendale General Hospl BB4 85 D2
Rossendale Mus* BB4 85 E2
Rossendale Rd
Burnley BB11 127 C3
Lytham St Anne's FY8 90 A7
Rossendale Sch BL0 51 A7
Rosser Ct 18 BB9 148 E8
Rossett Ave FY4 131 C1
Rossetti Ave BB11 127 F3
Rossington Ave FY2 152 E5
Rosslyn Ave FY6 200 A6
Rosslyn Cres FY6 200 B5
Rosslyn Cres E FY6 200 B5
Rossmoyne Rd LA1 215 A4
Ross St
Brierfield BB9 148 B5
Darwen BB3 65 A6
Rostle Top Rd 6 BB18 197 B1
Rostrevor Cl 4 PR26 76 B1
Rostron Cres L37 11 E1
Rostron Rd BL0 50 B6
Rostron's Bldgs BB4 86 D1
Rothay Ave FY7 198 D2
Rothbury Pl FY8 91 C4
Rotherhead Cl BL6 31 F2
Rotherwick Ave PR7 43 B7
Rothesay Cres LA3 212 D5
Rothesay Rd
Blackburn BB1 102 D3
Brierfield BB9 148 C6
Heysham LA3 212 D5
Rothley Ave PR8 21 A4
Rothsay Rd LA3 212 E5
Rothwell Ave BB5 104 C4
Rothwell Cl L39 15 D5
Rothwell Cres PR2 118 F4
Rothwell Ct PR25 77 A2
Rothwell Dr
Fleetwood FY7 198 D3
Ormskirk L39 15 B2
Southport PR8 21 A4
Rothwell Lo 5 PR2 118 F4
Rothwell Rd PR6 31 B7
Rothwell St BL0 50 B6
Rotten Row
Caton LA2 237 D3
Southport PR8 34 F6
Rough Hey Gate BB5 103 F2
Rough Hey Ind Est PR2 119 B7
Rough Hey Pl PR2 119 B7
Rough Hey Rd PR2 119 B7
Rough Heys BB5 104 A2
Rough Heys La FY4 110 E7
Rough Hill La BL9 33 E4
Rough Lea Rd FY5 175 D2
ROUGHLEE 170 B5
Roughlee CE Prim Sch BB12 169 F4
Roughlee Gr BB10 128 D5
Roughlee Old Hall BB9 170 A5
Rough Lee Rd BB5 104 C4
Roughlee St BB9 170 D2
Roughlee Terr BB11 106 B4
Roughwood Dr L33 1 A4
Round Acre
Bamber Bridge PR1 97 A1
Nab's Head PR5 99 E7
Round Barn BL7 66 B3
Roundell Rd BB18 196 C3
Roundel St BB10 148 B2
Roundhay FY4 110 F8
ROUNDHILL 84 E6
Roundhill La BB4 85 A7
Round Hill Pl BB10 128 E1
Roundhill Rd BB4, BB5 84 E6
Roundhill View BB5 85 A8
Roundhouse The 44 LA1 214 F8
Round Mdw PR26 76 C1
Round Meade The L31 5 C2
Roundway FY7 175 C8
Roundway Down PR2 117 C7
Roundway The L38 2 F3
Round Wood PR1 96 C7
Roundwood Ave BB10 148 A4
Rowan Ave
Fulwood PR2 119 A4
2 Horwich BL6 32 E1
Oswaldtwistle BB5 103 D2
Rowan Bank LA2 219 C7
Rowan Cl
Blackburn BB1 123 B1
Bonds PR3 181 D6
Burscough Bridge L40 25 F6
Clifton PR4 115 D1
Higher Penwortham PR1 96 B3
Rochdale OL12 52 B3
Rowan Croft PR6 78 B1
Rowan Dr BL9 33 B3
Rowangate PR2 118 C7
Rowan Gr
Burnley BB10 128 C6
Chorley PR6 61 C3
Rowan Ho PR7 42 F6
Rowan La WN8 18 B4
Rowans The
6 Adlington PR6 31 A8
Aughton L39 6 A7
Poulton-le-F FY6 153 A2
Rowan Tree Cl BB5 104 D7
Rowberrow Cl PR2 118 D6
Rowen Pk BB2 101 B8
Rowland Ave BB9 149 A8
Rowland Cl FY5 175 F2
Rowland La FY5 175 F2
ROWLANDS 50 D2
Rowlands Rd BL9 50 D2
Rowland St BB5 104 A5
Rowley La BB10 128 D6
Rowley Trad Est FY8 89 D7
Rowntree Ave FY7 198 F3
Roworth Cl PR5 97 E3
Rowsley Rd FY8 89 D7
Row The
Garstang PR3 226 C2
Heapey PR6 62 D3
Silverdale LA5 224 E3
Rowton Heath PR2 117 C7
Roxburgh Rd FY4 111 A6
Roxton Cl BL6 32 B5
Royal Albert Cotts LA1 214 E4
Royal Ave
Blackpool FY3 130 F3
Fulwood PR2 117 E6
Kirkham PR4 114 B4
Leyland PR25 59 E7
Royal Bank Rd FY3 130 E3
Royal Beach Ct FY8 89 D7
Royal Birkdale Golf Links PR8 34 D3
Royal Blackburn Hospl BB1 102 B2
Royal Brook Ho 7 PR1 118 A1
Royal Cl L37 12 A1
Royal Cres L37 12 A1
Royal Cross Prim Sch PR2 116 E1
Royal Ct
Burnley BB10 148 F3
11 Lancaster LA1 214 F7
Royal Dr PR2 117 D3
Royal Fold LA3 212 E8
Royal Gdns BL0 50 A3
Royal Lancaster Infmy LA1 214 F7
Royal Lytham & St Anne's Golf Course FY8 90 B5
ROYAL OAK 6 F4
Royal Oak Ave BB1 122 E1
Royal Oak Bldgs 16 FY4 130 B1
Royal Oak Cotts BB9 170 B4
Royal Oak Mdw LA2 238 B8
Royal Pk PR8 34 E4
Royal Pl FY8 90 C8
Royal Preston Hospl The PR2 117 F6
Royal Rd LA4 217 C6
Royals The FY8 90 A6
Royal Terr PR8 35 A7
Royal Troon Ct PR4 114 A4
Royalty Ave PR4 96 A1
Royalty Gdns PR4 76 A8
Royalty La PR4 76 A8
Royalty Mall LA4 217 A5
Royal Umpire Cvn Pk PR26 58 E3
Royds Ave
Accrington BB5 104 C3
Morecambe LA3 216 D2
Royds Gr LA3 216 D1
Royds Rd OL13 70 A7
Royds St
Accrington BB5 104 C4
Bury BL9 33 D4
Lytham St Anne's FY8 89 E5
Roylen Ave FY6 153 B5
Royle Rd
4 Burnley BB12 127 F6
Burnley BB12 127 F7
Chorley PR7 43 C8
Royles Brook Cl 9 FY5 176 B3
Royles Ct FY5 176 B2
Royle St 1 FY1 130 B1
Roynton Rd BL6 32 B7
Royshaw Ave BB1 101 E8
Royshaw Cl BB1 101 E8
Roy St OL14 109 A1
Royston Cl BL8 49 F1
Royston Rd FY6 153 F5
Royton Dr PR6 61 C5
Ruby St
Blackburn BB1 122 F2
Ramsbottom BL0, BL9 50 C3
Ruddington Rd PR8 35 E2
Rudd St BB4 85 A3
Rudman St OL12 52 E2
Rudyard Ave WN6 29 E2
Rudyard Dr BB3 65 D8
Rudyard Pl
Blackpool FY3 130 F7
Lytham St Anne's FY8 89 E8
Ruecroft Cl WN6 19 D8
Ruff La L39, L40 16 B4
RUFFORD 39 C3
Rufford Ave L31 5 E3
Rufford CE Sch L40 39 B4
Rufford Cl PR7 43 B3
Rufford Cotts L40 38 C6
Rufford Dr PR9 54 F5
Rufford New Hall L40 39 B5
Rufford Old Hall* L40 39 C5
Rufford Park La L40 39 A5
Rufford Rd
Bispham Green L40 39 F1
Lytham St Anne's FY8 90 D5
Southport PR9 54 C4
Rufford Sta L40 39 D4
Rufus St PR1 118 C2
Rugby Ave BB5 104 C7
Rugby Cl WN5 10 E5
Rugby Dr WN5 10 F8
Rugby St 9 FY4 130 D1
Rumley's Fold BB11 127 E2
Runcorn Ave FY2 152 F2
Rundle Rd PR2 117 D3
RUNNEL BROW 26 B4
Runnel The L39 23 B1
Runnymede Ave FY5 175 D2
Runriggs The FY5 176 B1
Runshaw Ave WN6 19 E8
Runshaw Coll PR7 60 E4
Runshaw Hall PR7 60 A5
Runshaw Hall La PR7 60 A5
Runshaw La
Euxton PR7 60 B3
Runshaw Moor PR7 59 E3
RUNSHAW MOOR 59 E4
Runshaw Sixth Form Coll PR25 60 B6
Rupert St
Carnforth LA5 223 D3
Nelson BB9 148 C7
Rochdale OL12 52 C1
RUSH BED 86 A6
Rushbed Cotts BB4 86 A6
Rushbed Dr BB4 86 A6
Rushden Rd L32 1 A1
Rushes Farm Cl BB5 103 C4
Rushey Cl BB4 86 A6
Rush Hey Bank BB11 107 D8
Rushley Dr LA2 220 D1
Rushley Mount LA2 220 D1
Rushmoor Cl BB4 106 A1
Rushton Ave BB18 197 B1
Rushton Cl BB9 171 B2
Rushton St
5 Bacup OL13 70 E8
Barrowford BB9 170 D3
Great Harwood BB6 124 B4
Rushworth Bldgs OL13 70 C8
Rushworth St E 6 BB10 148 B1
Rushworth St W 14 BB10 148 B1
Rushy Field BB5 124 F5
Rushy Hey PR5 77 A7
Rushy Hill View 18 OL12 52 C1
Ruskin Ave
9 Blackpool FY1 130 B2
Colne BB8 171 D6
Leyland PR25 77 A1
Oswaldtwistle BB5 103 C5
Padiham BB12 126 E7
Ruskin Ave *continued*
Thornton FY5 176 A3
Ruskin Cl PR4 56 F6
Ruskin Dr LA4 217 E6
Ruskin Gr
Bolton-le-S LA5 221 A5
Hapton BB11 126 C4
Ruskin Ho LA1 218 C4
Ruskin Pl BB9 170 F2
Ruskin Rd
Freckleton PR4 93 B6
2 Lancaster LA1 218 D3
Ruskin St
Burnley BB10 148 A2
Preston PR1 97 B6
Rusland Ave FY4 131 D1
Rusland Dr PR5 98 E4
Ruslands Gdns LA4 217 C4
Russell Ave
Blackpool FY5 152 D8
Colne BB8 171 E6
Leyland PR25 60 C8
Preston PR1 98 A8
Southport PR9 36 A7
Russell Ct
Burnley BB11 128 B4
Lytham St Anne's FY8 89 F6
Southport PR9 54 B4
Russell Dr LA4 218 A4
Russell Mews 40 LA1 214 F8
Russell Pl BB6 124 B5
Russell Rd
Carnforth LA5 223 E1
Southport PR9 36 A6
Russell Sq PR6 61 D1
Russell Sq W 6 PR6 61 D1
Russell St
Accrington BB5 104 C5
Bacup OL13 87 F4
Blackburn BB2 101 E3
39 Lancaster LA1 214 F8
6 Nelson BB9 148 D8
Russell Terr BB12 126 D7
Russia St BB5 103 F6
Rutherford Pl FY8 110 B4
Ruthin Cl BB1 101 E7
Ruthin Ct PR2 116 F3
Ruthin Dr FY5 176 D2
Ruth St
Edenfield BL0 68 D2
Whitworth OL12 71 D1
Rutland Ave
1 Bamber Bridge PR5 97 D3
Blackburn BB1 102 E4
Burnley BB12 127 A6
Cleveleys FY5 175 E3
Fleetwood FY7 198 F3
Freckleton PR4 93 C7
Lancaster LA1 215 A5
Poulton-le-F FY6 153 C3
Rutland Cl
Clayton-le-M BB5 124 F3
Garstang PR3 181 B8
Rutland Cres L39 15 E7
Rutland Ct FY8 90 D5
Rutland Pl 8 BB12 126 D7
Rutland Rd
Lytham St Anne's FY8 90 D5
Southport PR8 35 D5
Rutland St
Accrington BB5 103 F5
Blackburn BB2 101 B3
Colne BB8 171 F5
1 Nelson BB9 170 F1
Preston PR1 97 C8
Rutland Wlk BB4 68 A8
Ryan Cl PR25 76 E1
Ryburn Ave
Blackburn BB2 101 B6
Blackpool FY4 130 E1
Ryburn Rd L39 15 E4
Rycliffe St BB12 146 C1
Rydal Ave
Bamber Bridge PR5 97 D2
Blackpool FY1 130 C3
Darwen BB3 65 A8
Fleetwood FY7 198 E4
Formby L37 11 D3
Freckleton PR4 93 A6
Kingsfold PR1 96 C3
Orrell WN5 10 F7
Poulton-le-F FY6 153 D3
Thornton FY5 176 B1
Rydal Cl
5 Accrington BB5 125 D1
Blackrod BL6 31 C3
Burnley BB10 148 C4
Fulwood PR2 118 C4
Padiham BB12 146 C1
Rydal Ct LA4 217 B5
Rydal Gr
Knott End-on-S FY6 199 F6
1 Morecambe LA3 216 D2
Rydal Mount BB1 82 F6
Rydal Pl
Chatburn BB7 190 C3
Chorley PR7 43 C6
Colne BB8 172 A5
Rydal Rd
Blackburn BB1 102 A7
Hambleton FY6 177 C2
Haslingden BB4 68 C8
Hest Bank LA5 220 F4
Lancaster LA1 215 A8
Lytham St Anne's FY8 89 E8
Morecambe LA3 216 D2
Preston PR1 118 D2
Rydal St BB10 148 A2
Ryddingwood PR1 96 B6
Ryde Cl BB4 85 C1
Ryden Ave
Cleveleys FY5 175 D3
Leyland PR25 77 C1
Ryden Rd BB1 122 D6
Ryder Cl L39 15 C2
Ryder Cres
Ormskirk L39 15 C1
Southport PR8 21 E7
Ryding Cl PR26 76 E3
Rydinge The L37 12 A6
Ryding's La PR9 55 D8
Rydings The BB6 143 A1
Ryecroft PR6 62 A7
Ryecroft Ave FY6 177 C1
Ryecroft La BL7 46 C5
Ryecroft Pl FY6 177 C2
Ryefield PR6 62 A7
Ryefield Ave
Haslingden BB4 85 B2
Kingsfold PR1 96 D2
Ryefield Ave W BB4 85 A2
Ryefield Pl BB4 85 B2
Rye Gdns BB2 81 D6
Rye Gr 3 BB12 126 D7
Ryeground La L37 12 A5
Ryeheys Rd FY8 89 E8
RYELANDS 218 C2
Ryelands Cres PR2 95 E8
Ryelands Prim Sch LA1 218 B2
Ryelands Rd LA1 218 C2
Rye Moss La L37 4 B8
Rye St PR1 118 A1
Ryknild Way LA3 217 F3
Ryland Ave FY6 153 C3
Rylands Rd PR7 43 B7
Rylands St BB10 148 B1
Ryldon Pl FY4 131 A2
Rylstone Dr
Barnoldswick BB18 196 A2
Morecambe LA3 216 D1
Rymer Gr PR4 75 B8
Rymers Gn L37 11 E4
Ryscar Way FY2 152 F6
Rysdale Cres LA4 217 C4
Ryson Ave FY4 130 F1

S

SABDEN 145 F8
Sabden Brook Ct BB7 146 A8
Sabden Pl FY8 90 C7
Sabden Prim Sch BB7 145 F8
Sabden Rd
Higham BB12 146 F6
Padiham BB12 146 B4
Whalley BB7 145 A4
Saccary La BB1, BB2 122 A4
Sackville Gdns BB9 148 A5
Sackville St
Barnoldswick BB18 196 B1
Blackpool FY4 110 C6
Brierfield BB9 148 B5
10 Burnley BB11 127 F5
Chorley PR6 43 E7
Nelson BB9 148 F7
Sacred Heart RC Prim Sch
Blackburn BB2 101 B6
Chorley PR6 43 E7
Church BB5 103 F6
Colne BB8 171 D7
Preston PR2 117 C1
Thornton FY5 176 B3
Saddle Lo 11 PR2 118 F4
Saddler Nook La LA6 241 C8
Saddlers Mews 5 BB7 166 E8
Sadlers Row FY8 90 D7
Sadler St 3 BB5 103 E5
Saer Cl FY7 198 D3
Saffron Cl 4 BB9 170 C1
Sagar Dr PR4 93 A6
Sagar Fold
Colne BB8 171 F5
Ormskirk L39 6 D8
Sagar Holme Terr BB4 86 E5
Sagar La OL14 109 D3
Sagar St
Eccleston PR7 41 C6
Nelson BB9 148 E8
Sage Cl FY2 152 F3
Sage Ct PR1 96 C2
Sage La PR1 118 B3
Sahara Fold 1 BB1 102 A7
St Aidan's Ave
Blackburn BB2 101 D2
Darwen BB3 65 B8
St Aidan's CE Prim Sch
Bamber Bridge PR5 97 F1
Blackburn BB2 101 C2
St Aidan's CE Tech Coll FY6 200 B3
St Aidan's Cl BB2 101 C1
St Aidans Pk 9 PR5 97 E2
St Aidan's Rd 8 PR5 97 E2
St Alban's Ct 2 BB1 101 F6
St Alban's Pl PR7 43 D5
St Alban's RC Prim Sch BB1 101 F6
St Albans Rd
Morecambe LA4 217 F6
Rishton BB1 103 A8

St Alban's Rd
Blackpool FY1 130 D4
Darwen BB3 81 E4
Lytham St Anne's FY8 89 F7
St Ambrose Terr [5] PR25 77 B2
St Andrew's Ave
Cleveleys FY5 175 D2
Preston PR2 117 B2
St Andrew's CE Prim Sch
Oswaldtwistle BB5 103 D4
Preston PR2 117 B1
Ramsbottom BL0 50 B5
St Andrews Cl
[3] Colne BB8 171 C3
Euxton PR7 60 D4
Lancaster LA1 215 C8
St Andrew's Cl
Leyland PR25 60 A7
Oswaldtwistle BB5 103 D4
Ramsbottom BL0 50 C4
St Andrews Ct
Lytham St Anne's FY8 89 E7
Southport PR8 35 B6
St Andrew's Ct FY5 175 D2
St Andrew's Ct [1] BB5 103 D3
St Andrews Gate FY8 89 D7
St Andrews Gr LA4 217 D6
St Andrew's Maghull CE Prim Sch L31 5 D1
St Andrew's Pl
Blackburn BB1 101 D6
Southport PR8 35 B6
St Andrews Rd BB6 143 C6
St Andrew's Rd PR1 118 A2
St Andrew's Rd N FY8 89 E7
St Andrew's Rd S FY8 89 F6
St Andrew's St
Blackburn BB1 101 D6
[4] Burnley BB10 148 B1
St Andrews Way PR25 60 A8
St Anne & St Joseph's RC Prim Sch BB5 104 D5
St Anne's Ave LA4 217 F5
St Annes Cl
[5] Blackburn BB1 101 F3
[4] Church BB5 103 E5
St Anne's Cl
Caton LA2 237 D3
Formby L37 11 F6
St Anne's Coll & Jun Sch FY8 89 E5
St Anne's Cres BB4 86 F3
St Annes Ct FY4 130 C1
St Anne's Ct WN6 19 F5
St Anne's Dr BB12 147 D7
St Anne's on-the-sea Sta FY8 89 E7
St Anne's Path L37 11 F6
St Anne's Pl [18] LA1 214 F8
St Anne's RC Prim Sch
Blackburn BB2 101 D4
Leyland PR25 59 D8
Ormskirk L39 15 E4
St Annes Rd
Blackpool FY4 110 D7
[4] Chorley PR6 43 E7
Great Eccleston PR3 156 C5
Horwich BL6 32 C4
Southport PR9 53 F4
St Anne's Rd
Formby L37 11 F6
Leyland PR25 77 C3
Ormskirk L39 15 D4
St Anne's Rd E FY8 89 F7
St Anne's Rd W FY8 89 E6
St Anne's St
Padiham BB12 126 C7
Preston PR1 118 A2
St Anne's Way BB12 147 D7
St Ann's Ct BB7 166 B8
St Ann's Sq BB7 166 C8
St Ann's St [4] BB2 101 E3
St Anthony's Cl PR2 117 C4
St Anthony's Cres PR2 117 C4
St Anthony's Dr PR2 117 C4
St Anthonys Pl PR4 114 A4
St Anthony's Pl [7] FY1 130 C7
St Anthony's RC Prim Sch PR2 117 C4
St Anthony's Rd PR1 118 A2
St Antony's RC Prim Sch BB1 102 C3
St Augustine of Canterbury RC Prim Sch BB12 127 B6
St Augustine's RC High Sch Billington BB7 144 A4
St Augustine's RC Prim Sch PR1 97 A7
St Austell Dr BL8 49 F2
St Austell Pl LA5 221 C8
St Austin's Pl PR1 97 A7
St Austin's Rd PR1 97 A7
St Barnabas' Pl PR1 118 A1
St Barnabas' & St Paul's CE Prim Sch BB2 101 D5
St Barnabas St
Blackburn BB2 101 C5
[2] Darwen BB3 65 B6
St Bartholomewis CE Prim Sch OL12 52 C8
St Bartholomew's Parish CE Prim Sch BB6 124 C6
St Bede's Ave FY1 130 B1
St Bedes Cl L39 15 D3
St Bedes Pk BB3 81 E5
St Bede's RC High Sch
Blackburn BB2 81 A8
Lytham St Anne's FY8 91 C4
Ormskirk L39 15 D4
St Bee's Cl BB2 101 F1
St Benet's Cl PR5 97 D1
St Bernadettes RC Prim Sch LA1 215 B4
St Bernadette's RC Prim Sch FY2 152 D5
St Bernard Ave FY3 130 F7
St Bernard's RC Prim Sch PR2 116 C1
St Bernard's Rd FY6 199 E6
St Brides Cl BL6 32 A4
St Catherine Cl FY3 153 B1
St Catherine's CE Prim Sch BL6 32 A3
St Catherines Cl [4] PR25 77 C2
St Catherines Ct
Horwich BL6 32 B3
[26] Lancaster LA1 214 F8
St Catherine's Dr PR2 117 C4
St Catherine's RC Prim Sch PR25 77 C2
St Catherines Way PR5 77 C7
St Cecilia's RC Tech Coll PR3 140 A6
St Cecilia St BB6 124 D5
St Celia's Way LA4 217 E6
St Chad's Ave BB7 190 D5
St Chad's CE Prim Sch FY6 153 D3
St Chads Cl FY6 153 D2
St Chad's Dr LA1 218 B3
St Chad's RC Prim Sch PR6 61 F6
St Chad's Rd
Blackpool FY1 130 B2
Preston PR1 118 C1
St Charles' RC Sch BB1 124 B1
St Charles' Rd BB1 124 B1
St Christines Ave PR25 77 C4
St Christopher's CE High Sch BB5 104 A7
St Christopher's Rd PR1 118 A2
St Christopher's Way LA4 217 D6
St Clair Dr PR9 54 A1
St Clair Rd BL8 49 F3
St Clares Ave PR2 118 A6
St Clare's RC Prim Sch PR2 117 F7
St Clemance Ct [19] BB9 170 D3
St Clements Ave PR25 77 C3
St Clement's Ave FY3 130 E5
St Clements Cl [3] BB1 102 B4
St Clements Ct BB9 170 C3
St Clement St BB1 102 B4
St Crispin Way BB4 85 A2
St Cuthbert's CE Prim Sch
Darwen BB3 81 E3
Halsall L39 23 B1
St Cuthberts Cl BB3 81 E3
St Cuthbert's Cl
[1] Fulwood PR2 117 D3
[1] Lytham St Anne's FY8 91 A3
Southport PR9 54 A2
St Cuthbert's Ct [6] FY8 91 A3
St Cuthbert's RC Prim Sch FY4 110 C8
St Cuthbert's Rd
Bamber Bridge PR5 97 A1
Preston PR1 118 A2
Southport PR9 54 A2
St Cuthbert St BB10 148 C2
St David's Ave
Blackburn BB2 80 E7
Cleveleys FY5 175 D2
St David's Gr FY8 89 D8
St David's Rd
Leyland PR25 77 C2
Preston PR1 118 A2
St David's Rd N FY8 89 D8
St David's Rd S FY8 89 F6
St David's Wood BB5 104 D7
St Deny's Croft [4] BB7 189 E1
St Edmund Hall Cl BL0 50 C4
St Edmund's RC Prim Sch WN8 17 F1
St Edmund's Rd FY4 130 E1
St Edmund's St BB6 124 D5
St Edward's RC Prim Sch BB3 81 E4
SS John Fisher & Thomas More RC High Sch BB8 171 B2
SS Peter & Paul RC Prim Sch L40 40 F2
St Frances Cl [4] BB1 101 F3
St Francis Cl PR2 118 A7
St Francis of Assisi RC Prim Sch WN8 9 D7
St Francis RC Prim Sch PR3 161 A2
St Francis' Rd BB2 101 A2
St Gabriel Cl WN8 19 C3
St Gabriel's Ave BB1 122 F3
St Gabriel's CE Prim Sch BB1 122 E2
St George Ct FY1 130 D6
St George's Ave
Blackburn BB2 101 B1
St George's Ave *continued*
Cleveleys FY5 175 D2
Lytham St Anne's FY8 89 E7
St George's CE High Sch FY4 111 A8
St George's CE Prim Sch PR7 43 E5
St Georges Cl BB8 171 C3
St George's Ct [10] PR7 43 D7
St George's La
Cleveleys FY5 175 D2
Lytham St Anne's FY8 89 E6
St Georges Pk PR4 113 E6
St George's Pl PR9 35 B7
St George's Quay LA1 218 C1
St Georges Rd BB9 148 F7
St George's Rd
Blackpool FY4 110 C6
Formby L37 11 E4
Hightown L38 2 F5
Lytham St Anne's FY8 89 E6
Preston PR1 118 A2
St George's Sh Ctr [8] PR1 96 F7
St George's Sq
Burnley BB10 148 C1
Lytham St Anne's FY8 89 D7
St George's St PR7 43 C7
St Georges Terr BB3 81 F1
St George's Terr BB4 70 A6
St Gerrard's Rd PR5 97 A1
St Giles St [7] BB12 146 C1
St Giles Terr [6] BB12 146 C1
St Gregory Rd PR1 118 B2
St Gregory's Pl PR7 43 C5
St Gregory's RC Prim Sch
Chorley PR7 43 C5
Maghull L31 5 C4
Preston PR1 118 B3
St Helens Cl BB5 103 F3
St Helen's Cl PR3 181 A2
St Helens Rd L39 16 A2
St Helen's Rd
Clayton Green PR6 78 C1
Overton LA3 209 E8
St Helens Well PR4 57 A5
St Helier Cl BB2 81 C8
St Helier's Pl PR3 137 A7
St Heliers Rd FY1 130 C1
St Hilda's Cl PR7 43 C4
St Hilda's Rd FY8 89 D8
St Hilda's Way PR7 43 C4
St Hubert's Rd BB6 124 C4
St Hubert's St BB6 124 D5
St Ignatius' Pl [6] PR1 97 A8
St Ignatius' RC Prim Sch PR1 97 A8
St Ignatius' Sq [5] PR1 97 A8
St Ives Ave
Blackpool FY1 130 E3
Freckleton PR4 93 A6
St Ives Cres PR2 117 A4
St Ives Rd BB1 102 D4
St James CE Prim Sch BB3 82 A7
St James' CE Prim Sch
Blackburn, Brookhouse BB1 101 E7
Darwen BB3 82 B2
St James Cl
Bamber Bridge PR5 77 B8
Church BB5 103 E7
[3] Haslingden BB4 85 B3
Ormskirk L40 16 C3
St James' Cres BB3 82 B2
St James Ct
[1] Bamber Bridge PR5 77 B8
Blackburn BB1 101 E7
Heysham LA3 212 E7
[9] Lancaster LA1 214 E8
Standish WN6 29 D2
St James Ho BB5 104 B5
St Jamesí St BB4 69 E8
St James' Lanehead CE Prim Sch BB10 148 D2
St James Lo
Leyland PR26 59 B8
Lytham St Anne's FY8 90 A5
St James Mews BB5 103 E7
St James Pl
[4] Padiham BB12 126 D8
Southport PR8 35 B5
St James' RC Prim Sch
Orrell WN5 10 D4
Skelmersdale WN8 18 B4
St James Rd
Blackpool FY4 110 C6
Church BB5 103 E7
Orrell WN5 10 D4
St James' Rd [10] BB18 196 B2
St James Row BB4 86 A3
St James's CE Prim Sch BB7 166 E7
St James's Dr LA6 240 B7
St James's Fold BB1, BB3 82 B7
St James's Gdns PR26 59 B8
St James's La [7] BB11 128 A6
St James's Pl
Blackburn BB1 101 E7
[9] Chorley PR6 43 E7
St James Sq [15] OL13 87 F3
St James' Sq [11] BB18 196 B2
St James's Rd
Blackburn BB1 101 E7
Preston PR1 117 F2
St James's Row [13] BB11 127 F6
St James's St
Burnley BB11 127 F6
Burnley BB11 128 A6
[8] Chorley PR6 43 E7
Clitheroe BB7 166 E7
St James St
Bacup OL13 87 F2
[7] Brierfield BB9 148 B5
[1] Rawtenstall BB4 86 A3
Southport PR8 35 B6
St James' St
Accrington BB5 104 B5
Blackburn BB2 101 C1
St Jame's Terr PR5 99 E7
St James-the-Less RC Prim Sch BB4 85 F3
St Jerome's RC Prim Sch L37 11 C3
St John Ave FY7 198 D2
St John Bosco RC Prim Sch L31 5 B2
St Johnís St BB4 69 F8
St John Rigby RC Sixth Form Coll WN5 19 F2
St Johns Ave
Kirkham PR4 113 F4
Smallwood Hey PR3 201 C5
St John's Ave
Darwen BB3 65 B8
Morecambe LA3 216 E2
Poulton-le-F FY6 153 E5
Silverdale LA5 224 C3
Thornton FY5 176 D1
St John's CE & Meth Prim Sch PR6 62 E7
St John's CE Prim Sch
Blackpool FY1 130 C5
Great Harwood BB6 124 C4
Higham BB12 147 A6
Nelson BB9 149 B8
Southport PR9 54 C5
St John's CE Prim Sch, Cliviger BB10 108 B6
St Johns Cl PR6 61 B7
St John's Cl
Accrington BB5 104 E2
[6] Rawtenstall BB4 86 A7
Read BB12 145 D2
St Johns Ct
Fulwood PR3 137 F1
[17] Ramsbottom BL0 50 C6
Southport PR8 21 D4
St John's Ct
[5] Bacup OL13 87 F3
[8] Blackpool FY1 130 C5
[6] Burnley BB12 127 C6
[6] Lytham St Anne's FY8 91 C3
St John's Gn PR25 76 E1
St John's Gr
Morecambe LA3 216 E2
Silverdale LA5 224 C3
St John Southworth RC Prim Sch BB9 148 D7
St John's Pl
Nelson BB9 149 A8
[16] Preston PR1 97 A7
St John's RC Prim Sch
Burscough L40 25 E2
Poulton-le-F FY6 153 E4
Skelmersdale WN8 18 C1
St John's Rd
[5] Burnley BB12 127 C6
Morecambe LA3 216 D2
Padiham BB12 126 C7
Southport PR8 34 F1
Walton-le-D PR5 97 D5
St John's Sh Ctr [18] PR1 97 A8
St John's St
Darwen BB3 65 B8
Great Harwood BB6 124 C4
Lytham St Anne's FY8 91 C3
St John's Stonefold CE Prim Sch BB5 85 A7
St John St
Bacup OL13 87 F3
Colne BB8 171 E5
Horwich BL6 32 B3
St John's Terr LA3 217 C2
St John Stone RC Prim Sch PR8 21 D2
St Johns Wood FY8 90 E3
St John The Baptist RC Prim Sch
Burnley BB10 148 C3
Padiham BB12 126 C7
St John Vianney's RC Prim Sch FY1 130 E2
St John with St Augustine CE Prim Sch BB5 104 C7
St John with St Michael CE Prim Sch OL12 71 E5
St Joseph & St Bede RC Prim Sch BL9 33 B4
St Josephs Cl FY3 130 E5
St Joseph's Con Ctr WN8 19 B2
St Josephs Convent Sch BB12 127 A8
St Josephs Pl PR6 61 D1
St Joseph's RC High Sch & Sports Coll BL6 32 E1
St Joseph's RC Prim Sch
Bacup OL13 70 D8
Barnoldswick BB18 196 B3
Chorley PR6 61 D2
Darwen BB3 65 A8
Gregson Lane PR5 98 E1
Hurst Green BB7 164 F1
St Joseph's RC Prim Sch *continued*
Kirkham PR4 113 F7
Lancaster LA1 218 D3
Preston PR1 118 C1
Ramsbottom BL0 50 B6
Shevington Moor WN6 29 A3
Withnell PR6 80 A1
St Joseph's Terr [1] PR1 118 C1
St Judes Ave PR25 77 C4
St Jude's Ave PR5 97 D1
St Katherines Dr BL6 31 C3
St Kentigern's RC Prim Sch FY3 130 D5
St Kitts Cl BB3 81 E6
St Laurence's CE Prim Sch PR7 61 C1
St Lawrence Ave BB2 101 B8
St Lawrence's Ave PR3 137 B8
St Lawrence St BB6 124 C5
St Leger Ct [11] BB5 104 C5
St Leonard Ct [6] LA1 218 E1
St Leonard's Ave BL6 32 F1
St Leonards CE Prim Sch BB2 121 A5
St Leonard's CE Prim Sch
Bamber Bridge PR5 97 C4
Langho BB6 143 E2
Padiham BB12 146 C1
St Leonard's Cl PR2 117 A3
St Leonard's Ct FY8 89 D8
St Leonard's Gate LA1 214 F8
St Leonard's Rd FY3 131 A3
St Leonard's Rd E FY8 89 E8
St Leonard's Rd W FY8 89 D8
St Leonard's St [8] BB12 146 C1
St Louis Ave FY3 130 F7
St Lucia Cl BB3 81 F6
St Luke & St Philip's CE Prim Sch BB2 101 D3
St Luke's Bldg [2] PR8 35 D6
St Luke's CE Prim Sch
Formby L37 11 D1
Lancaster LA1 218 D3
Slyne LA2 218 C8
St Luke's Church Rd L37, L38 2 C8
St Lukes Ct [2] LA1 214 E8
St Luke's Ct [1] FY4 110 C6
St Luke's Dr
Formby L37 11 C2
Orrell WN5 10 E4
St Luke's Gr PR9 35 E7
St Luke's Pl [9] PR1 118 C1
St Luke's Rd
Blackpool FY4 110 C6
Southport PR9 35 D7
St Margarets Cl PR2 117 A4
St Margaret's Ct
[1] Blackburn BB1 102 B5
[1] Fleetwood FY7 199 A4
St Margaret's Gdns BB11 126 C4
St Margaret's Rd
Bolton-le-S LA5 221 B6
[1] Leyland PR25 77 C2
Morecambe LA4 217 D6
St Margarets Way BB1 102 B5
St Maria Goretti RC Prim Sch PR2 118 F5
St Marie's RC Prim Sch
Kirkby L33 1 A3
Standish WN6 29 E2
St Mark's CE Prim Sch L40 23 D8
St Mark's Pl
Blackburn BB2 101 B4
[1] Blackpool FY3 130 E8
St Mark's Pl E [5] PR1 96 D8
St Mark's Pl W [4] PR1 96 D8
St Mark's Rd
Blackburn BB2 101 B4
Preston PR1 96 D8
St Marlow Ave [3] PR25 77 C3
St Martins Cl FY6 153 B5
St Martin's Ct FY5 175 F2
St Martin's Dr BB2 80 D8
St Martin's Rd
Blackpool FY4 110 C6
Lancaster LA1 215 A7
Preston PR1 118 A2
St Mary CE Prim Sch BB2 121 D2
St Mary Cl FY3 153 B1
St Mary Magdalene's RC Prim Sch BB12 127 D8
St Mary Magdalen's CE Prim Sch BB5 104 B2
St Mary Magdalen's RC Prim Sch PR1 96 E4
St Mary & St Andrew's RC Prim Sch PR3 137 A5
St Mary & St Michael RC Prim Sch PR3 181 C6
St Mary's Ave
Bamber Bridge PR5 97 D1
Barnoldswick BB18 196 D3
St Mary's CE Prim Sch
Eccleston PR7 41 C6
Hawkshaw BL8 49 B2
Spen Brook BB12 169 C3
St Marys Cl
Blackburn BB1 102 B5
Longridge PR3 140 A8
[8] Preston PR1 97 C8

St Mary's Cl PR5 97 D1
St Mary's Coll BB1 101 E7
St Mary's Ct
Clayton-le-M BB5 124 F2
Mellor BB2 121 E2
Preston PR1 97 B8
Rawtenstall BB4 85 F2
St Mary's Dr BB6 143 D1
St Mary's Gate
Burnley BB11 128 B5
Euxton PR7 60 C3
St Mary's Gdns
Mellor BB2 121 E2
Southport PR8 21 F7
St Mary's Par LA1 214 E8
St Mary's Rawtenstall CE Prim Sch BB4 85 F3
St Mary's RC Coll FY3 130 F7
St Mary's RC High Sch PR5 97 F1
St Mary's RC Prim Sch
Accrington BB5 103 F4
Bacup OL13 88 B2
Burnley BB10 128 B6
Chipping PR3 185 E3
Chorley PR7 43 A7
Claughton PR3 182 D1
Clayton-le-M BB5 124 F3
Fleetwood FY7 199 A5
Great Eccleston PR3 156 B5
Haslingden BB4 85 C2
Horwich BL6 32 D2
Langho BB6 143 C1
Morecambe LA4 217 C6
Osbaldeston BB2 121 D4
Sabden BB7 145 F7
St Mary's RC Prim Sch Scarisbrick L40 24 A7
St Mary's Rd
Bamber Bridge PR5 97 E1
Great Eccleston PR3 156 B5
Heysham LA3 212 E8
St Mary's & St Benedicts RC Prim Sch PR5 97 E1
St Mary's & St Joseph's RC Prim Sch BB2 101 F3
St Mary's St N 7 PR1 97 B8
St Mary's St
6 Clitheroe BB7 189 E1
Nelson BB9 148 C8
Preston PR1 97 B8
St Mary's Terr 6 BB4 86 A2
St Mary's Way BB4 86 A2
St Marys Wharfe BB1 101 F3
St Mary's Wlk 16 PR7 43 C8
St Matthew's CE Prim Sch BB1 101 F4
St Matthew's CE Sch PR1 97 D8
St Matthew's Ct 9 BB11 127 E5
St Matthew St BB11 127 E5
St Michael & All Angels CE Prim Sch BB8 171 E8
St Michael Rd L39 5 F7
St Michael & St John's RC Prim Sch BB7 166 E8
St Michael's CE High Sch PR7 61 C1
St Michael's CE Prim Sch PR4 114 B5
St Michaels Cl
Fulwood PR2 117 D3
Normoss FY3 131 A8
St Michael's Cl
Blackburn BB2 80 E7
Bolton-le-S LA5 221 A4
Chorley PR7 61 B1
Southport PR9 53 F3
St Michael's Cres LA5 221 A4
St Michael's Ct
Barrowford BB9 170 C2
1 Blackburn BB1 101 F6
St Michael's Gr
Bolton-le-S LA5 221 A4
Morecambe LA4 217 C4
St Michael's La LA5 221 A4
ST MICHAEL'S ON WYRE 157 C7
St Michael's-on-Wyre CE Prim Sch PR3 157 C6
St Michaels Pk L39 6 A7
St Michael's Pl
Bolton-le-S LA5 221 A4
Newsham PR3 137 B5
St Michaels Rd
Blackpool FY2 152 D3
Kirkham PR4 114 C5
St Michael's Rd
Duncombe PR3 158 D4
4 Leyland PR25 77 C3
Preston PR1 118 A2
St Michael's St BB1 101 F7
St Michaels Terr PR26 58 B2
St Michael with St John CE Prim Sch BB1 101 E6
St Mildred's Way LA3 212 E6
St Monica's Way FY4 131 D1
St Nicholas Arcs 13 LA1 214 F8
St Nicholas' Ave BB7 145 F8
St Nicholas CE Prim Sch BB5 103 F7
St Nicholas' CE Prim Sch FY4 111 A4
St Nicholas Cres LA5 221 B6
St Nicholas Gr PR4 113 B4
St Nicholas La LA5 221 A6
St Nicholas Rd
Blackpool FY4 111 B5
Church BB5 103 F7
St Ogg's Rd LA4 217 C3
St Oswald Ho LA1 215 A6
St Oswald's Cl
Blackburn BB1 102 E4
Preston PR1 118 C2
St Oswalds Ct PR7 29 E8
St Oswald's RC Prim Sch
Accrington BB5 104 A3
Coppull PR7 29 D8
Longton PR4 75 B8
St Oswald's Rd BB1 102 E4
St Oswald St LA1 215 A6
St Patrick's Pl PR5 97 E4
St Patrick's RC Prim Sch
Heysham LA3 213 A8
Southport PR9 54 A2
Walton-le-D PR5 97 E4
St Patrick's Rd N FY8 89 E7
St Patrick's Rd S FY8 89 F6
St Patrick's Wlk LA3 212 E7
St Paul's Ave
Blackburn BB2 101 D5
Lytham St Anne's FY8 90 B4
Preston PR1 118 A1
St Paul's CE Prim Sch
Bury BL9 33 B4
Nelson BB9 148 D6
Oswaldtwistle BB5 103 E4
St Pauls Cl PR26 76 F7
St Paul's Cl
Adlington PR6 31 A8
Clitheroe BB7 166 C8
St Paul's Ct
5 Burnley BB11 127 F5
12 Oswaldtwistle BB5 103 E4
10 Preston PR1 97 A8
St Paul's Dr
Caton LA2 237 D3
Lancaster LA1 214 F5
St Pauls Mans 4 PR8 35 A6
St Paul's Pas PR8 35 A6
St Paul's RC Prim Sch BB2 80 D8
St Paul's Rd
Blackpool FY1 130 B8
Lancaster LA1 214 F5
Nelson BB9 148 E6
Preston PR1 118 A1
1 Rishton BB1 124 A1
St Paul's Sq
Preston PR1 97 A8
Southport PR8 35 A6
St Paul's St
Blackburn BB2 101 D5
Bury BL9 33 A3
Clitheroe BB7 166 C8
Oswaldtwistle BB5 103 E4
4 Ramsbottom BL0 50 C6
Southport PR8 35 A6
St Paul's Terr
Clitheroe BB7 166 C8
Hoddlesden BB3 82 E2
St Paul's Villas BL9 33 A3
St Paul's Wlk 4 FY8 90 C4
St Peter & St Paul's CE Prim Sch BB1 124 A2
St Peter's Ave
Formby L37 11 D4
Haslingden BB4 85 B2
St Peter's CE Prim Sch
Accrington BB5 104 A2
Burnley BB11 128 A6
Chorley PR6 61 E2
Fulwood PR2 117 F7
Heysham LA3 212 E7
St Peter's Cl
Darwen BB3 65 B8
Formby L37 11 D4
Salesbury BB1 122 D6
St Peter's Ctr 8 BB11 128 A6
St Peters Mews 16 LA1 215 A8
St Peter's Pl
Fleetwood FY7 199 B4
7 Haslingden BB4 85 B2
St Peter's RC Cath* LA1 215 A8
St Peter's RC High Sch Visual Arts Coll WN5 10 F7
St Peter's RC Prim Sch
Blackburn BB2 101 B2
Lytham St Anne's FY8 91 C5
Newchurch BB4 86 E2
St Peter's Rd
Lancaster LA1 215 A8
Newchurch BB4 86 E2
Southport PR8 35 A3
St Peter's Sq 8 PR1 96 E8
St Peter's St
Chorley PR6 61 E1
1 Preston PR1 96 F8
St Peter St
Blackburn BB2 101 E4
2 Rishton BB1 124 A1
St Philip's CE Prim Sch
Nelson BB9 148 E8
Southport PR8 35 C5
St Philip's Ct BB2 101 C3
St Philip's Rd PR1 118 A2
St Philip's St
Blackburn BB2 101 B3
13 Nelson BB9 170 E1
St Philip St BB10 148 A1
St Pius X Prep Sch PR2 117 E4
St Richard's RC Prim Sch WN8 17 D1
St Saviour's Cl PR5 77 F7
St Saviours Ct OL13 87 F1
St Silas's CE Prim Sch BB2 101 B6
St Silas's Rd BB2 101 B6
St Stephenís Rd WN6 29 C1
St Stephen's Ave
8 Blackburn BB1 102 A7
Blackpool FY2 152 B2
St Stephen's CE Inf Sch BB1 102 B7
St Stephen's CE Jun Sch BB1 102 B7
St Stephen's CE Prim Sch BB11 128 B4
St Stephen's CE Sch PR1 96 E6
St Stephens Rd PR4 113 F4
St Stephen's Rd
9 Blackburn BB1 102 A7
Hightown L38 2 F4
Preston PR1 118 B2
St Stephen's St 2 BB11 128 B4
St Stephen's Tockholes CE Prim Sch BB3 81 A3
St Stephen's Way BB8 171 F6
St Teresa's Ave FY5 175 D1
St Teresa's RC Inf Sch PR8 35 A4
St Teresa's RC Prim Sch
Cleveleys FY5 175 D1
Preston PR1 118 E1
Up Holland WN8 19 B1
St Theodore's RC Sports Coll & Sixth Form BB10 128 B7
St Theresas Ct 2 PR4 114 B5
St Theresa's Dr PR2 117 C4
St Thomas CE Prim Sch
Blackburn BB1 102 B5
Maghull L31 5 D4
St Thomas' CE Prim Sch
Bury BL9 33 B1
Lytham St Anne's FY8 89 F6
St Thomas Cl
Blackpool FY3 153 B1
Haslingden BB4 68 A7
St Thomas Ct 4 BL9 33 A2
St Thomas More Wlk LA1 214 D8
St Thomas' Pl PR1 117 F1
St Thomas Rd PR4 114 A4
St Thomas' Rd
Lytham St Anne's FY8 89 F6
Preston PR1 118 A2
St Thomas's Ct WN8 10 C7
St Thomas's Rd
Chorley PR7 43 C8
Rawtenstall BB4 86 A7
St Thomas's Sq 4 PR7 43 C8
St Thomas St BB1 102 B4
St Thomas' St PR1 117 F1
St Thomas the Martyr CE Prim Sch WN8 10 B7
St Veronica's RC Prim Sch BB4 68 B7
St Vincent Ave FY1 130 E3
St Vincent RC Prim Sch OL12 52 A1
St Vincents Cl BB3 81 F6
St Vincents Rd PR2 117 F5
St Vincent's Way PR8 35 A4
St Walburga's Rd FY3 130 F7
St Walburge Ave PR2 96 E8
St Walburges Gdns 8 PR2 96 D8
St Wilfredís Dr OL12 52 D4
St Wilfrid's CE High Sch & Tech Coll BB2 101 D3
St Wilfrid's CE Prim Sch LA2 219 C7
St Wilfrid's Pk LA2 219 C7
St Wilfrid's Rd WN6 29 F1
St Wilfrid St 3 PR1 96 F7
St Wilfrid's Terr PR3 140 A7
St Wilfrid's Way WN6 29 E1
St Williams RC Prim Sch PR3 201 E4
St Wulstan's RC Prim Sch BB6 124 C5
St Wulstan's & St Edmund's RC Prim Sch FY7 198 E3
St Wyburn Ct PR8 34 F5
Salcombe Ave FY2 152 F2
Salcombe Dr PR9 54 A5
Salcombe Rd FY8 110 C1
Salem Mews LA3 212 E8
Salem St BB4 85 B3
Salerno St BB11 127 C4
SALESBURY 122 D6
Salesbury CE Prim Sch BB1 122 D7
Salesbury View BB1 122 F4
Sales's La BL9 51 B3
Salford BB1 101 E5
Salford Ct PR8 21 C5
Salford Rd
Galgate LA2 211 A3
Southport PR8 21 C5
Salford St BL9 33 A4
Salisbury Ave
5 Grimsargh PR2 139 D1
Knott End-on-S FY6 199 E5
Salisbury Cl 1 LA3 217 B2
Salisbury Ct
Knott End-on-S FY6 199 E5
Lancaster LA1 214 D8
Salisbury Rd
Blackpool FY1 130 D4
Brinscall PR6 62 F8
Darwen BB3 81 E3
Horwich BL6 32 F1
Lancaster LA1 214 D8
Preston PR1 96 D7
Salisbury St
3 Chorley PR7 43 D7
Colne BB8 171 E5
Great Harwood BB6 124 E6
15 Haslingden BB4 85 B3
5 Preston PR1 118 D1
Southport PR9 36 A6
Sallowfields WN5 10 D5
Sally Barn Cotts BB4 68 E8
Sally's La PR9 54 A2
Salmesbury Ave FY2 152 E2
Salmesbury Hall Cl BL0 50 B5
Salmons Leap PR4 113 E4
Salmon St PR1 97 C7
Salop Ave FY2 152 C4
Saltash Rd FY5 176 B5
Salt Ayre La
Lancaster LA1 218 B1
Morecambe LA1 217 F1
Saltburn St BB12 127 B6
SALTCOTES 91 D5
Saltcotes Pl FY8 91 D4
Saltcotes Rd FY8 91 D7
Salter Fell Rd LA1 218 B2
Salterford La BB10 129 A4
SALTERFORTH 194 D7
Salterforth La
Barnoldswick BB18 196 E2
Salterforth BB18 194 D7
Salterforth Prim Sch BB18 194 D8
Salterforth Rd BB18 197 A1
Salter St PR1 117 F1
Salthill Gdns BB7 189 F1
Salthill Ind Est BB7 190 A2
Salthill Rd BB7 189 F1
Salthill View BB7 189 F1
Salthouse Ave FY1 130 C3
Salt Marsh Cl FY6 177 B1
Salt Marsh La FY6 177 B1
Saltpit La L31 5 E1
Salt Pit La L40 40 F3
Salus St BB10 148 C1
SALWICK 115 E3
Salwick Ave FY2 152 D5
Salwick Cl PR9 53 F5
Salwick Pl
Lytham St Anne's FY8 90 A8
Preston PR2 116 E1
Salwick Rd PR4 135 B3
Salwick Sta PR4 115 C5
Sambourn Fold PR8 21 A5
SAMLESBURY 119 E1
Samlesbury Aerodrome BB2, PR5 120 F3
SAMLESBURY BOTTOMS 99 D6
Samlesbury CE Sch PR5 119 D1
Samlesbury Hall* PR5 120 E2
Samuel's Ct LA1 215 A8
Samuel St
Bury BL9 33 A3
Preston PR1 97 D8
Sanctuary The 5 FY4 110 C5
Sandbank Gdns OL12 71 C2
Sandbeds La LA2 238 A8
Sand Beds La BL0, BB4 69 B5
Sandbridge Ct PR3 181 C8
Sandbrook Gdns WN5 10 D5
Sandbrook Rd
Orrell WN5 10 C5
Southport PR8 21 D4
Sandbrook Way PR8 21 C3
Sandcastle Waterpark* FY4 110 A8
Sanderling Cl
6 Cleveleys FY5 152 F8
Lytham St Anne's FY8 90 E7
Sanderling Rd L33 1 A3
Sanders Gr LA4 217 A4
Sanderson La PR7 28 A8
Sanderson St 9 BL9 33 A3
Sandersons Way FY4 110 F8
Sandfield 4 FY5 176 A2
Sandfield Cotts L39 15 D2
Sandfield Ho 6 LA1 215 A3
Sandfield Pk L39 15 D2
Sandfield Rd OL13 88 A1
Sandfield St 11 PR25 77 B1
Sandford Dr L31 5 D2
Sandford Rd WN5 10 C5
Sandgate
Blackpool FY4 110 D5
Chorley PR7 43 D5
Lytham St Anne's FY8 89 C7
SANDHAM'S GREEN 111 C8
Sandham St 7 PR6 43 D8
Sandhams Way FY4 111 D8
Sandheys Dr PR9 53 F1
Sandhills L38 2 F3
Sandhills Ave FY4 110 B5
Sandhills Cl BB18 194 E8
Sandhill St BB3 65 B5
Sandholme La PR3 82 A4
Sandholme Villas BB18 197 A1
Sandhurst Ave
Blackpool FY2 152 C5
Lytham St Anne's FY8 89 E7
Sandhurst Cl
Formby L37 11 C1
9 Kirkham PR4 113 F5
Sandhurst Ct FY8 89 D6
Sandhurst Grange FY8 89 E7
Sandhurst St BB11 128 B6
Sandhurst Way L31 5 B5
Sandicroft Ave FY6 177 C1
Sandicroft Pl FY6 200 B4
Sandicroft Rd FY1 152 C1
Sandilands Gr L38 2 F3
Sandiway Ct PR9 35 E8
Sandiway Dr BB10 148 F3
Sandiways L31 5 E1
Sandiways Cl FY5 153 C8
Sand La LA5 223 C4
Sandon Pl FY4 110 C4
Sandon Rd PR8 34 F1
Sandon St
Blackburn BB2 101 C3
Darwen BB3 82 B2
Sandon Terr BB2 101 C3
Sandown Cl PR4 113 E5
Sandown Ct
31 Preston PR1 97 A7
10 Southport PR9 35 C8
Sandown Rd
Haslingden BB4 85 C2
Lancaster LA1 215 B3
Thornton FY5 176 B1
Sandpiper Cl
8 Blackburn BB1 101 F6
Normoss FY3 131 B6
Sandpiper Cres PR5 98 A2
Sandpiper Ct FY5 175 C2
Sandpiper Pl 7 FY5 175 F1
Sandpiper Sq 5 BB11 127 C5
Sandridge Ave PR7 43 B7
Sandridge Pl FY4 110 B4
Sandringham Ave
Leyland PR25 77 C1
Thornton FY5 176 B1
Sandringham Cl
Adlington PR7 30 E6
5 Barrowford BB9 170 C1
Blackburn BB1 122 E1
Tarleton PR4 57 A6
Whalley BB7 144 A7
Sandringham Ct
Lytham St Anne's FY8 90 D4
3 Morecambe LA4 217 A4
Southport PR9 35 B8
Sandringham Dr
Brinscall PR6 62 F8
Ramsbottom BL8 50 A1
Sandringham Gr 2 BB4 85 A1
Sandringham Lo 2 FY5 175 D2
Sandringham Park Dr PR4 76 A8
Sandringham Rd
Bamber Bridge PR5 97 D3
Chorley PR7 43 B8
Darwen BB3 81 E4
Eccleston PR7 41 C7
Formby L37 11 E1
Horwich BL6 32 E2
Lytham St Anne's FY8 90 A5
Morecambe LA4 217 A4
Southport, Ainsdale PR8 21 C5
Southport PR8 34 E3
Sandringham Way PR4 116 E6
Sands Cl BB1 124 B2
Sandsdale Ave PR2 118 C5
SAND SIDE 205 D2
Sandside Cvn & Camping Pk LA5 220 F5
Sandside Dr LA4 217 C3
Sands Rd BB1 124 B2
Sands The
Blackpool FY4 110 B4
Whalley BB7 144 C5
Sands Way FY1 130 C3
Sandwell Ave FY5 176 C2
Sandwell Brow PR3 204 E7
Sandwich Cl BB1 102 C4
Sandwick Cl PR2 117 E7
Sandy Bank Rd BL7 48 D5
Sandy Bank Terr BB4 69 D8
Sandybeds Cl BB5 104 D2
Sandybrook Cl PR2 118 E5
Sandy Brook Ho PR2 117 F7
Sandy Cl
Cleveleys FY5 175 C3
Newburgh WN8 27 A2
Sandycroft PR2 118 F2
Sandyfields PR4 116 E6
Sandyforth Ave FY5 176 B3
Sandyforth La PR4 117 A8
Sandygate BB11 127 F6
Sandy Gate La PR4 137 B2
Sandyhall La BB9 170 A2
Sandy La
Accrington BB5 104 E5
Adlington PR7 30 F6
Barrowford BB9 170 D2
Bispham Green L40 39 F2
Blackburn BB3 81 E6
Blackpool FY4 111 A4
Brindle PR5, PR6 79 C6

Sandy La *continued*
Brinscall PR6 62 E8
Clayton Green PR6 78 C3
Cottam PR4 116 D7
Fleetwood FY7 175 D7
Hambleton FY6 177 C1
Hightown L38 3 A3
Holmeswood L40 38 D5
Leyland PR25 60 A8
Maghull, Holt Green L39 6 B6
Maghull, Lydiate L31 5 C5
Mawdesley L40 40 A1
Newburgh WN8 26 F1
Ormskirk L40 16 D7
Orrell WN5 10 D4
Out Rawcliffe PR3 178 F1
Pleasington BB2 100 C2
Preesall FY6 200 B4
Skelmersdale WN8 17 D1
Sollom L40 39 A8
Thorpe Green PR6 78 E4
Sandy La Ctr WN8 17 D1
SANDYLANDS 216 E2
Sandylands Arc LA3 216 D3
Sandylands Com Prim Sch LA3 216 E3
Sandylands Prom LA3 216 D3
Sandy Pl 7 PR25 60 A8
Sandy Way L40 38 D4
Sanfield Cl L39 15 E6
Sangara Dr BB3 81 F7
Sangness Dr PR8 35 E3
Sanraya Ave FY4 111 F6
Sansbury Cres BB9 171 A2
Santon Cl PR4 114 A7
Sanvino Ave PR8 21 D5
Sapphire St BB1 122 F1
Sarah La PR26 57 F5
Sarahs Fold FY6 177 C7
Sarah St
Britannia OL13 71 C8
Darwen BB3 82 B1
Edenfield BL0 68 E3
Sark Gdns BB2 101 F1
Sarmatian Fold PR3 141 D3
Sarscow La PR26 58 E2
Saswick Ct PR4 134 B7
Saul's Dr LA5 224 A8
Saul St PR1 96 F8
Saunder Bank BB11 128 A5
Saunder Height La BB4 86 E3
Saunders Cl BB4 86 A7
Saunders' La
Hutton PR4 95 D2
New Longton PR4 95 E1
Saunders Mews PR7 43 C3
Saunders Rd BB2 101 C5
Saunders St PR9 53 C1
Savick Ave PR2 116 D1
Savick Cl PR5 77 F8
Savick Ct PR2 117 D4
Savick Rd PR2 117 D4
Savick Way PR2 116 E3
Saville Ave FY6 153 B6
Saville Rd
Blackpool FY1 130 C1
Maghull L31 5 C3
Saville St PR7 43 C5
Savon Hook L37 12 B1
Savoy Ave 1 LA3 217 C2
Savoy St
Accrington BB5 103 F5
4 Preston PR1 96 E7
Sawdon Ave PR8 35 E3
SAWLEY 230 C1
Sawley Abbey* BB7 230 C1
Sawley Ave
Accrington BB5 104 D7
Blackpool FY4 110 D5
Lytham St Anne's FY8 90 C6
Read BB12 145 D1
Sawley Cl BB3 65 C8
Sawley Cres PR2 118 F2
Sawley Dr BB6 124 E6
Sawley Rd
Chatburn BB7 190 E6
Grindleton BB7 190 C8
Sawley BB7 230 C1
Sawmills Ind Est FY1 130 D6
Sawrey Ct BB5 124 E2
Sawthorpe Wlk FY6 153 B3
Sawyer St 5 OL12 52 F1
Saxby Gr FY4 130 F1
Saxenholme PR8 34 F5
Saxifield St BB10 148 E3
Saxon Cl
Oswaldtwistle BB5 103 C5
Thornton FY5 153 C8
Saxon Hey PR2 117 C3
Saxon Hts LA3 212 F5
Saxon Lo
Southport PR8 34 F5
Southport PR8 35 A5
Saxon Rd PR8 34 F5
Saxon St BB10 128 A7
Scafell Ave LA4 217 D5
Scafell Cl BB12 127 C8
Scafell Rd
Lancaster LA1 218 E2
Lytham St Anne's FY8 111 A2
Scaffold La L38 3 D4
SCAITCLIFFE 104 B5
Scaitcliffe St BB5 104 B5
Scale Farm Rd LA1 218 A2
SCALE HALL 218 A2
Scale Hall La
Lancaster LA1 218 B2
Newton-w-S PR4 115 A2
Scarborough Rd
Blackburn BB2 102 A1
Lytham St Anne's FY8 111 A1
Scar End Cl OL13 88 A8
Scargill Rd LA5, LA6 221 F1
SCARISBRICK 23 E7
Scarisbrick Ave
Parbold WN8 27 C2
Southport PR8 35 A7
Scarisbrick Cl L31 5 E3
Scarisbrick Ct PR8 35 C6
Scarisbrick Ho 3 L39 15 F5
Scarisbrick New Rd PR8 35 D5
Scarisbrick Pk L40 24 A6
Scarisbrick St
Ormskirk L39 15 E6
Southport PR9 35 B7
Scarlet St PR6 43 E7
Scarlett Dr PR4 95 F2
Scarlett St BB11 127 E5
Scarr Dr OL12 52 F3
Scarr La BB2 101 A6
Scarr Terr OL12 71 D2
Scarsdale Ave FY4 110 C5
Scar St BB2 101 B3
SCARTH HILL 16 B1
Scarth Hill La L39 16 A2
Scarth Hill Mans L39 15 E2
Scarth La BB12 126 B5
Scarth Pk WN8 9 C7
Scawfell Rd PR7 43 B5
Sceptre Way PR5 78 B6
Schleswig St PR1 97 A8
Schleswig Way PR26 59 C7
Schofield Ave FY3 131 B7
Schofield Cl BB4 85 F2
Schofield Rd BB4 85 F2
Schofield St
Darwen BB3 81 F2
Haslingden BB4 68 A6
2 Rawtenstall BB4 69 E8
Schola Green La
Morecambe LA4 217 B5
Morecambe, West End LA4 217 B4
Scholars Ct FY8 89 E5
Scholars Gn PR2 116 C1
Scholars Way 14 BL9 33 A4
Scholefield Ave BB9 148 E5
Scholefield La BB9 148 F5
Scholes Bank BL6 32 A5
Scholes St BB3 81 F2
Scholey Head La BB10 108 A8
School Ave L37 11 F3
School Brow PR6 61 B7
School Cl
Ormskirk L39 15 C1
Southport PR8 35 B2
School Ct
Bolton BL7 47 E2
Edenfield BL0 68 D2
School Field PR5 78 B5
School Fields BB18 197 B3
Schoolfold PR4 73 E4
School Hillocks Cotts 4 PR5 77 A8
School Ho The BB10 148 D2
Schoolhouse Fold BB11 126 C3
School House Gn L39 15 F5
School House Gr L40 25 D5
Schoolhouse La LA2 219 D7
School House La BB5 104 B1
School House Mews 7 PR6 43 E7
School La
Bamber Bridge PR5 97 F2
Blackburn BB1 82 D8
Brinscall PR6 62 E8
Burnley BB11 128 A7
Burscough Bridge L40 25 F5
Catforth PR4 136 A4
Earby BB18 197 B2
Edgworth BL7 48 D8
Euxton PR7 60 D3
Farington PR5 76 F7
Formby L37 11 F3
Forton LA2, PR3 207 B3
Freckleton PR4 93 C7
Hammerton Mere BB7 235 E3
Haskayne L39 13 F4
Inskip PR4 157 D1
Kirkham PR4 114 B5
Laneshaw Bridge BB8 172 E6
Leyland, Moss Side PR26 59 A8
Leyland PR25 77 A1
Longton PR4 75 A8
Lytham St Anne's FY8 91 A3
Maghull L31 6 A1
Mawdesley L40 40 C1
Mereclough BB10 129 A1
Newton-w-S PR4 115 A2
Ollerton Fold PR6 79 F4
Out Rawcliffe PR3 178 F2
Over Kellet LA6 237 B8
Pilling PR3 201 C6
Preesall FY6 200 B3
Simonstone BB12 145 F1
Skelmersdale WN8 17 E1
Standish WN6 29 D1
Up Holland, Roby Mill WN8 19 B3
Up Holland WN5, WN8 10 C7
Westhead L40 16 E3
School La *continued*
Winmarleigh PR3 203 F6
Wray LA2 238 D6
SCHOOL LANE 97 F2
School Rd
Blackpool FY4 111 B5
Heysham LA3 212 E7
Hightown L38 2 F4
Thornton FY5 153 C8
School St
Accrington BB5 104 B6
Bacup OL13 70 B8
Bamber Bridge PR5 97 F2
Bury BL9 33 B1
Colne BB8 171 D4
Darwen BB3 82 A1
Great Harwood BB6 124 C4
Horwich BL6 32 C3
Kelbrook BB18 195 A6
Leyland PR25 77 B2
Nelson BB9 148 C8
Preston PR1 96 E7
Ramsbottom BL0 50 B5
Rawtenstall BB4 86 A8
Rishton BB1 124 B1
Walmer Bridge PR4 74 F5
Whitewell Bottom BB4 86 F4
School Terr
Salterforth BB18 194 D8
Whitworth OL12 71 C1
School View BL7 48 D8
School Villas LA2 211 B5
Schwartzman Dr PR9 55 A6
SCORTON 204 E6
Scorton Ave FY3 130 F7
Scorton CE Prim Sch PR3 204 E6
Scorton Hall Pk PR3 204 E6
Scorton Ho LA1 215 A2
Scotch Green La PR3 160 A6
SCOTFORTH 215 A3
Scotforth Ct 1 LA1 215 A3
Scotforth Rd
Lancaster LA1 215 A4
Preston PR1 97 C8
Scotforth St Paul's CE Prim Sch LA1 215 A4
Scotland Bank Terr BB2 81 C8
Scotland La BL9 33 D8
Scotland Pl 11 BL0 50 C6
Scotland Rd
Carnforth LA5 223 E3
15 Nelson BB9 170 D1
Scotshaw Brook Ind Est BB3 81 E7
Scotswood Ave FY4 110 D6
Scott Ave
Accrington BB5 104 E2
Morecambe LA4 216 F3
Simonstone BB12 145 E2
Scott Cl
Blackpool FY4 110 F8
Maghull L31 5 D1
Oswaldtwistle BB5 103 D5
Scott Dr L39 15 F7
Scott Gr LA4 217 A4
Scott Laithe La BB7 230 E3
Scott Mews FY4 110 F8
Scott Park Rd BB11 127 E4
Scott Rd LA3 216 F3
Scott St
Clayton-le-M BB5 124 F3
Nelson BB9 170 D1
Padiham BB12 126 F7
Southport PR9 36 A7
Scott's Wood PR2 117 D7
SCOUT 86 E2
Scout Bottom Ind Est BB4 86 F3
Scout Rd
Bolton BL7 47 A1
Edenfield BL0 69 A2
Newchurch BB4 86 F3
Scowcroft Dr LA4 217 E5
Scow Croft La PR6 62 D4
Scriffen La LA2 211 D3
SCRONKEY 201 E3
Scudamore Cres 6 FY4 130 D1
Seabank Rd
Fleetwood FY7 199 A5
Southport PR9 35 B8
Seaborn Dr LA4 217 E6
Seaborn Gr LA4 217 D6
Seaborn Rd LA4 217 D6
Seabourne Ave FY4 110 B7
Seabrook Dr FY5 152 E8
Seacole Cl BB1 102 B1
Seacrest Ave FY1 130 C8
Seacroft Cres PR9 54 B5
Seafield L37 12 A2
Seafield Rd
Blackpool FY1 130 B8
Lytham St Anne's FY8 90 F3
Southport PR8 21 C6
Seafore Cl L31 5 B4
Sealand Ave L37 11 E2
Sealand Cl L37 11 D2
Seascale Cl BB2 102 A1
Seasiders Way FY1 130 B3
Seathwaite Ave
Blackpool FY4 131 C1
Morecambe LA3 216 E2
Seathwaite Way BB5 104 E8
Seaton Ave FY5 175 E4
Seaton Cres FY8 89 C8
Seaton Pl WN8 17 E3
Seaton Way PR9 54 A5
Seattle Ave FY2 152 E2
Sea View
Lancaster LA1 215 A5
Longridge PR3 161 D2
Walmer Bridge PR4 74 F5
Sea View Cl LA2 218 B8
Sea View Dr LA2 218 B8
Seaview Way FY7 199 B3
Sea Wall FY7 198 C3
Seawell Ave LA3 216 D2
Second Ave
Blackpool FY4 110 C7
Bury BL9 33 D4
Church BB5 104 A8
Preesall Park FY6 200 D1
Second Terr LA3 209 B4
Sedbergh Ave FY4 130 F1
Sedbergh Cl 2 BB5 104 D5
Sedbergh Jun Sch LA2 239 B8
Sedberg St PR2 117 D3
Sedburgh St BB10 148 C2
Seddon Pl WN8 17 E3
Sedge Ct 8 LA3 217 B2
Sedgefield PR4 74 E8
Sedgeley Mews PR4 93 A6
Sedgfield Cl FY4 110 F6
Sedgley Ave PR4 93 A6
Sedgwick St PR1 118 A1
Sedum Gdns BB5 125 E2
Sedwell Cl FY8 90 F4
Seedall Ave BB7 166 D7
Seedhill Terr 13 BB9 170 D1
SEED LEE 78 C7
Seedlee Rd PR5 78 A6
Seed St
Blackpool FY1 130 C6
Preston PR1 96 F8
Sefton Ave
4 Burnley BB11 127 E5
Orrell WN5 10 D5
Poulton-le-F FY6 153 D1
Sefton Cl
Clayton-le-M BB5 125 A3
Darwen BB3 65 C6
Orrell WN5 10 D5
Sefton Ct FY8 89 D7
Sefton Dr
Bury BL9 33 A6
Lancaster LA1 218 B2
Sefton Gdns L39 6 D7
Sefton Ho L40 25 F3
Sefton La BL6 32 E1
Sefton Rd
Bamber Bridge PR5 97 D3
Formby L37 11 E2
Lytham St Anne's FY8 89 F7
Morecambe LA3 216 E3
Orrell WN5 10 D5
Sefton St
Brierfield BB9 148 B5
Colne BB8 171 F5
Southport PR8 35 C5
Sefton Terr 3 BB11 127 E5
Sefton View WN5 10 D5
Segar's La PR8, L39 22 B4
Segar St
19 Great Harwood BB6 124 C5
Kirkham PR4 113 F6
Selborne Mews BB2 101 B3
Selborne St
Blackburn BB2 101 B3
Preston PR1 97 B6
Selbourne Rd FY1 130 D6
Selbourne Terr BB18 197 C2
Selby Ave
Blackpool FY4 110 D5
Cleveleys FY5 175 F4
2 Lancaster LA1 218 D4
Selby Cl BB5 104 E3
Selby Dr L37 12 B2
Selby Pl WN8 17 D2
Selby Rd PR4 113 F5
Selby St
Colne BB8 171 C5
Nelson BB9 148 E7
Preston PR1 117 D1
Seldon St
11 Colne BB8 171 D4
15 Nelson BB9 170 E1
Selkirk Cl 6 BB1 102 A4
Selkirk Dr PR5 97 D2
Selkirk St BB11 127 D4
Sellers St PR1 118 C1
Selous Rd BB2 101 B3
Selside Dr LA4 217 B3
Selworthy Rd PR8 34 E3
Senior Ave FY4 130 F1
Seniors Dr FY5 175 F3
Senset Well La LA5 223 E5
Sephton Dr L39 15 F7
Sephton St 7 PR5 77 A8
Sergeant St 11 PR5 77 F8
Serpentine Rd BB11 127 F4
Serpentine The
3 Lytham St Anne's FY8 91 A3
Ormskirk L39 6 D8
Sett End Rd W BB1 102 C1
Sett End Road N BB1 102 D2
Settle La BB7 231 B7
Settle Pl FY8 90 C7
Settle Terr BB10 148 C2
Seven Acres PR5 78 C5
Seven Hos BB1 102 D4
Sevenoaks PR7 43 C4
Sevenoaks Ave PR8 21 B5
Sevenoaks Ct 2 FY5 152 F8
Sevenoaks Dr FY5 152 F8
Seven Sands PR4 95 A1
SEVEN STARS 59 D7
Seven Stars Prim Sch PR25 59 D7
Seven Stars Rd PR25 59 D7
Seventh Ave FY4 110 C6
Seven Trees Ave BB1 102 A8
Severn Ave FY7 175 D8
Severn Ct LA3 217 F2
Severn Dr PR5 97 D2
Severn Hill PR2 117 C8
Severn Ho 10 PR1 97 D8
Severn Rd FY4 110 B7
Severn St PR3 140 A7
Seville Ct FY8 90 D3
Seymour Ave LA3 212 F7
Seymour Ct PR1 117 D2
Seymour Dr L31 5 E3
Seymour Gr LA3 212 F7
Seymour Rd
Blackpool FY1 130 C2
Fulwood PR2 117 C3
Lytham St Anne's FY8 90 D4
Seymour St
Chorley PR6 43 E8
2 Fleetwood FY7 198 F4
5 Lancaster LA1 215 A8
Shacklady Rd L33 1 A4
Shackleton Rd PR4 114 B2
Shackleton St
Burnley BB10 128 B8
Todmorden OL14 109 C1
Shade La PR7 43 D1
Shade Row FY6 200 B3
SHADSWORTH 102 D3
Shadsworth Bsns Pk BB1 102 C1
Shadsworth Cl BB1 102 C4
Shadsworth Inf Sch BB1 102 D4
Shadsworth Jun Sch BB1 102 C2
Shadsworth Rd BB1 102 C3
Shady La
Clayton-le-W PR5, PR25 77 E3
Slyne LA2 218 C8
Shaftesbury Ave
Blackpool FY2 152 C2
Burnley BB11 127 F3
Cleveleys FY5 175 D5
Darwen BB3 81 E3
Great Harwood BB6 124 E6
Higher Penwortham PR1 96 B6
New Longton PR4 75 F8
Normoss FY3 131 B6
Southport PR8 22 A8
Shaftesbury Cl FY8 90 D5
Shaftesbury Ct FY2 152 C2
Shaftesbury Gr PR8 35 A1
Shaftesbury Pl
Chorley PR7 43 B8
Lancaster LA1 214 F4
Shaftesbury Rd PR8 35 A1
Shakeshaft St 11 BB1 102 A4
Shakespeare Ave BB6 124 B4
Shakespeare Ctr The PR8 35 B5
Shakespeare Prim Sch FY7 198 E4
Shakespeare Rd
Fleetwood FY7 198 E4
Lancaster LA1 218 C4
Preston PR1 118 D1
Shakespeare St
Padiham BB12 126 D7
Southport PR8 35 B5
Shakespeare Terr PR6 61 D2
Shakespeare Way BB2 101 C3
Shalbourn Rd FY8 90 A4
Shale St BB12 127 D6
Shalgrove Field PR2 117 C7
Shallow Valley Ct 9 BB5 103 E5
Shalom Lo FY8 89 F5
Shannon Sq BB10 148 C2
Shannon St FY1 130 B3
Shanter Cl OL12 71 E6
Shap Cl
Accrington BB5 104 E3
Barrowford BB9 170 D4
Shap Ct FY7 198 D1
Shap Gr BB10 148 A3
Shard La FY6 154 B8
Shard Rd FY6 154 B6
Shards Ct 17 LA1 218 D2
Sharley Fold PR3 140 B7
Sharman Ave FY8 110 F1
SHARNEYFORD 88 C5
Sharneyford Prim Sch OL13 88 C5
Sharoe Bay Ct PR2 117 F6
SHAROE GREEN 117 E6
Sharoe Green La PR2 117 F7
Sharoe Green Pk PR2 118 A5
Sharoe Mount Ave PR2 117 F7
Sharow Gr FY1 130 D3
Sharpe's Ave LA1 215 A5
Sharpes Mill LA1 214 F7
Sharples Ct PR3 140 A8
Sharples Gn BL7 48 D6
Sharples Mdw BL7 48 D6
Sharples St
Accrington BB5 103 F5
Blackburn BB2 101 D3

Sharp St
1 Barrowford BB9 170 D3
Burnley BB10 148 B1
Sharratts Path PR7 42 F4
Sharrock St 7 PR8 35 B7
Shawbridge Ct BB7 166 F8
Shaw Bridge St 4
BB7 166 F8
Shawbrook Cl
Euxton PR7 60 C5
Hapton BB11 126 C4
Shaw Brook Cl BB1 103 A8
Shaw Brook Rd PR25 59 E6
Shaw Brow PR6 61 B7
Shawbury Cl BL6 31 D1
Shaw Cl
Blackburn BB2 101 D5
Shirdley Hill L39 23 A6
Shawcliffe La BB6, BB7 144 B2
SHAWCLOUGH 52 C2
Shawclough Cl OL12 52 D3
Shawclough Com Prim Sch
OL12 52 E3
Shawclough Dr OL12 52 D3
Shawclough Mews BB4 86 F3
Shawclough Rd OL12 52 C3
Shaw Clough Rd BB4 86 F3
Shaw Clough St BB4 86 F3
Shawclough Way OL12 52 D3
Shaw Cres L37 12 B3
Shawes Dr PR6 31 C7
SHAWFIELD 52 A2
Shawfield 4 BB4 85 F1
Shawfield La OL12 52 A2
SHAWFORTH 71 D6
SHAW GREEN 59 D2
Shaw Hall Cvn Site L40 24 B4
Shawhead Cotts BB8 195 E1
Shaw Hill PR6 61 B7
Shaw Hill Dr PR6 61 B6
Shaw Hill St PR7 43 C7
Shaw La
Haskayne L39 13 E6
Nether Kellet LA6 221 F4
Todmorden OL14 109 C3
Shaw Rd
Blackpool FY1 130 B1
Horwich BL6 32 B5
Shaw's Ave PR8 35 A1
Shaws Garth L39 23 A6
Shaw's La PR3 201 A3
Shaw Sq 4 BB18 197 B2
Shaw's Rd PR8 35 A1
Shaw St
Blackburn BB2 101 D5
Bury BL9 33 B3
Colne BB8 171 D4
Haslingden BB4 85 B6
2 Lancaster LA1 215 A8
2 Preston PR1 118 A1
Shay La
Longridge PR3 139 F6
Slaidburn BB7 229 B7
Shay Lane Ind Est PR3 139 F5
Shays Dr BB7 167 A7
Shay The 10 FY5 152 F7
Shear Bank Cl BB1 101 D6
Shear Bank Gdns BB1 101 D6
Shear Bank Rd BB1 101 D6
Shear Brow BB1 101 D7
Shearwater Dr BB1 101 F6
Sheddon Gr BB10 128 E5
Shed St
Colne BB8 171 C4
Oswaldtwistle BB5 103 D3
Whitworth OL12 71 D1
Sheep Gap OL12 52 B1
Sheep Gn BB4 85 B3
Sheep Hill Brow PR6 78 A3
Sheephill La PR4 76 A7
Sheep Hill La
Clayton Green PR6 78 B3
Clayton-le-W PR6, PR25 77 F2
Sheep House La BL6 45 A3
Sheffield Dr PR2 116 D1
Sheldon Ave WN6 29 E2
Sheldon Ct 1 PR1 117 F1
Shelfield La BB10 149 F7
Shelfield Rd BB9 171 B1
Shelley Cl
Blackpool FY2 152 F6
Bolton-le-S LA5 221 A5
Coppull PR7 29 F8
Shelley Dr
Accrington BB5 104 E2
Eccleston PR7 41 D5
Ormskirk L39 15 D6
Shelley Gdns BB6 124 B4
Shelley Gr
Blackpool FY5 152 D8
Darwen BB3 82 C1
Southport PR8 35 F6
Shelley Mews PR2 117 D1
Shelley Rd PR2 117 C2
Shellfield Rd PR9 54 A4
Shellingford Cl WN6 19 D7
Shelton Dr PR8 21 A4
Shenley Way PR9 54 D5
Shenstone Rd FY3 130 F7
Shepherd Rd FY8 90 A7
Shepherd Rd N FY8 90 A8
Shepherd's Ave PR3 181 D4
Shepherds Cl
Blackrod BL6 31 C3
Ramsbottom BL8 49 F1
Shepherds Gn BB4 87 A8
Shepherd's La L39 14 E5
Shepherd St
Bacup OL13 87 F3
Bury BL9 33 A1
Darwen BB3 65 A7
9 Lytham St Anne's FY8 91 B3
Preston PR1 97 A7
Shepherds Way PR6 43 D8
Sheppard St FY1 130 B4
Sheraton Pk PR2 117 A6
Sherborne Lo 9 PR2 118 F4
Sherbourne Cl FY6 153 C5
Sherbourne Cres PR1 118 B3
Sherbourne Ct FY6 153 C5
Sherbourne Rd
Accrington BB5 104 E3
Blackpool FY1 130 C7
Hambleton FY6 177 C2
Sherbourne St 5 PR6 43 D7
Sherburne Ave 4 PR4 113 F5
Sherburn Rd PR1 96 E3
Sherburn Sch PR1 118 A3
Sherdley Rd PR5 77 B7
SHERFIN 85 B7
Sherfin Nook BB5 85 B7
Sherfin Side BB5 85 B7
Sheridan Rd BB8 172 D6
Sheridan St
Burnley BB10 148 E2
6 Nelson BB9 170 F2
Sheriff St OL12 52 E1
Sheringham Ave FY5 152 D7
Sheringham Way FY6 153 E3
Sherrat St WN8 17 D1
Sherringham Rd PR8 34 E2
Sherrington Ct PR8 35 A3
SHERWOOD 118 A6
Sherwood Ave
Blackpool FY3 130 E8
Ormskirk L39 15 C2
Sherwood Ct BB10 128 C5
Sherwood Dr WN8 18 D3
Sherwood Ho PR8 21 C5
Sherwood Lo PR8 34 F5
Sherwood Pl
Chorley PR6 43 D8
2 Cleveleys FY5 175 F1
Sherwood Prim Sch
PR2 118 A7
Sherwood Rd
Blackburn BB1 102 B3
Lytham St Anne's FY8 90 C6
Sherwood Way
Accrington BB5 125 A1
Fulwood PR2 118 A7
Shetland Cl
Blackburn BB1 102 C3
Wilpshire BB1 122 F7
Shetland Rd FY1 130 C2
SHEVINGTON 19 F5
Shevington Com Prim Sch
WN6 19 F6
Shevington Cswy PR26 58 B2
Shevington La WN6 29 B1
SHEVINGTON MOOR 29 B2
Shevington Moor WN6 29 A2
Shevington's La L33 1 A6
SHEVINGTON VALE 19 E7
Shevington Vale Prim Sch
WN6 19 E8
Shilton St BL0 50 B5
Shipley Cl FY3 153 B1
Shipley Rd FY8 90 B7
Shipper Bottom La BL0 50 D5
Shirdley Cres PR8 21 C3
SHIRDLEY HILL 22 F6
Shire Bank Cres PR2 117 E5
Shireburn Ave BB7 166 C7
Shireburn Cotts BB7 164 E1
Shireburn Cvn Pk BB7 189 B1
Shireburne Holiday Pk
BB7 166 B8
Shireburn Rd L37 11 D5
Shire La BB7 142 D8
SHIRESHEAD 207 E3
Shireshead Cres LA1 215 A2
Shires The BB2 81 D6
Shirewell Rd WN5 10 E5
Shirley Cres FY2 152 D6
Shirley Gdns BB3 80 F2
Shirley Hts FY6 153 D4
Shirley La PR4 95 A1
Shop La
Accrington BB5 104 D5
Higher Walton PR5 98 B4
Maghull L31 5 C1
SHORE 109 C2
Shore Ave BB10 148 F2
Shore Cl LA5 224 B2
Shore Cotts LA5 224 B3
Shorefield Mount BL7 47 E1
Shore Fields 4 FY3 131 A8
Shorefields Cvn Pk
LA3 208 E7
Shore Gn
Cleveleys FY5 175 F3
Silverdale LA5 224 B2
Todmorden OL14 109 C2
Shore New Rd OL14 109 B1
Shore Rd
Blackpool FY5 152 C8
Hesketh Bank PR4 73 C4
Heysham LA3 212 D6
Silverdale LA5 224 B2
Southport PR8 21 B6
Shoreside Prim Sch
PR8 21 B4
Shore The LA5 220 F5
SHOREY BANK 82 A2
Shorey Bank BB11 128 A6
Shorrock La BB2 101 B1
Shorrocks Ave PR3 157 C8
Shorrock St BB3 65 A8
Short Clough Cl BB4 86 A6
Short Clough La BB4 86 A6
Shorten Brook Dr BB5 125 E6
Shorten Brook Way
BB5 125 E6
Short La PR3 137 F5
Shortlands Dr LA3 212 E7
Shortlands The BB12 146 C2
Shortridge Rd FY4 110 F8
Short St
Bacup OL13 70 B8
Colne BB8 171 D4
Showfield BB10 129 B6
Showley Brook Cl BB1 122 F4
Showley Ct BB1 122 E6
Showley Rd BB1 122 A6
Shrewsbury Cl PR4 114 C5
Shrewsbury Dr
Lancaster LA1 215 B5
Thornton FY5 176 A2
Shropshire Dr BB1 122 F6
Shuttle Cl BB5 104 A6
SHUTTLEWORTH 50 E8
Shuttleworth Coll
BB12 127 A7
Shuttleworth Mead Bsns
Pk BB12 126 B7
Shuttleworth Rd PR1 117 F2
Shuttleworth St
Burnley BB10 148 B2
Earby BB18 197 B2
6 Padiham BB12 126 C8
Rishton BB1 124 B2
Shuttling Fields La PR5 98 B2
Sibbering Brow Preston Rd
PR7 42 C7
Siberia Mill BB10 148 F3
Sibsey St LA1 214 F7
Siddow's Ave BB7 166 D7
Sidebeet La BB1 102 E7
Sidegarth Gate LA2 237 C7
Sidegarth La LA2 237 D7
Side La BB7 192 C7
Sidford Ct FY3 130 F8
Sidgreaves La PR4 116 B4
Siding La
Kirkby L33 1 C7
Rainford WA11 8 C1
Siding Rd FY7 199 A3
Sidings Bsns Pk The
BB7 144 C6
Sidings Rd LA3 212 F2
Siding St OL13 70 C8
Sidings The
Britannia OL13 71 A8
5 Colne BB8 171 C4
Darwen BB3 65 B7
Low Bentham LA2 239 C8
Whalley BB7 144 C6
Sidmouth Ave BB4 85 C2
Sidmouth Rd FY8 110 C1
Sidney Ave
Becconsall PR4 73 F3
Blackpool FY2 152 E2
Sidney Rd PR9 35 F8
Sidney Terr 4 LA1 215 A8
Siemens St BL6 32 C2
Signal Ho BB5 103 F4
Silbury Cl BB2 82 A8
Silcock's Cotts FY5 176 F1
Silk Mill La PR3 160 B3
Silloth Cl BB2 101 F1
Silly La LA2 239 D2
Silsden Ave PR2 118 D5
Silsden Cl FY3 153 B1
Silver Birch Way L31 5 B5
Silverburn 4 FY8 90 A8
SILVERDALE 224 C3
Silverdale
Becconsall PR4 73 F3
Blackpool FY2 152 E6
Southport PR8 34 E4
Silverdale Ave
Fleetwood FY7 198 D1
Heysham LA3 212 F7
Silverdale Cl
Blackburn BB2 81 F8
Burnley BB10 148 B3
Clayton-le-M BB5 124 E2
Coupe Green PR5 98 E4
Leyland PR25 60 B6
Silverdale Ct PR8 35 E4
Silverdale Dr PR2 118 E5
SILVERDALE GREEN 224 D3
Silverdale Moss Rd
LA5 224 D7
Silverdale Rd
Arnside LA5 224 C8
Chorley PR6 43 E7
Lytham St Anne's FY8 90 C7
Yealand Redmayne LA5 225 E4
Silverdale St John's CE
Prim Sch LA5 224 C3
Silverdale Sta LA5 224 F3
Silvermere Cl 20 BL0 50 B5
Silver Ridge Cvn Pk
LA7 225 E8
Silversmiths Row FY8 90 D7
Silver St
Clifton PR4 115 D1
Hurst Green BB7 164 E1
8 Preston PR1 97 A6
Ramsbottom BL0 50 C6
Silverstone Gr L31 5 B4
Silverthorne Dr PR9 53 F1
Silverwell St BL6 32 B4
Silverwood Ave FY4 110 D8
Silverwood Cl FY8 90 E4
Silverwood Ct 1 FY4 110 D8
Silvester Rd PR7 43 C6
Silvia Way FY7 198 E4
Simfield Cl WN6 29 D1
Simmonds Way BB9 148 B7
Simmons Ave PR5 97 B3
Simmons' St BB2 101 D5
Simmons Way BB5 125 A3
Simms Cl BL0 50 A5
SIMONSTONE 145 E1
Simonstone Bsns Pk
BB12 125 F7
Simonstone La BB12 125 E8
Simonstone Rd BB12,
BB7 145 F6
Simonstone St Peter's CE
Prim Sch BB12 145 F1
Simonswood Ind Pk L33 1 B6
Simonswood La
Kirkby L33 1 A2
Royal Oak L39 6 F3
Simonswood Wlk L33 1 A2
Simpson Cl BB18 196 D3
Simpson Ct 26 PR1 97 A7
Simpson St
Blackpool FY4 110 B8
Hapton BB12 126 C4
Oswaldtwistle BB5 103 D3
9 Preston PR1 96 F8
Simpson Street Ind Units
BB12 126 C5
Sinclair Ct FY8 90 B7
Sineacre La L33, L39 1 E8
SINGLETON 154 E1
Singleton Ave
Horwich BL6 32 C5
Lytham St Anne's FY8 90 B8
Read BB12 145 D2
Singleton CE Prim Sch
FY6 154 E1
Singleton Cl PR2 117 F7
Singleton Ct 4 FY1 130 B4
Singleton Hall FY6 154 E3
Singleton Rd
Weeton Camp PR4 132 E6
Weeton PR4 132 F4
Singleton Row 14 PR1 96 F8
Singleton St 3 FY1 130 B3
Singleton Way PR2 117 F7
Sion Brook Ho PR2 118 F4
Sion Cl PR2 118 F4
Sion Hill PR2 118 F4
Sir Frank Whittle Way
FY4 110 D4
Sir John Thursby Com Coll
BB10 148 D1
Sir Simon's Arc 27 LA1 214 F8
Sir Tom Finney Way PR1,
PR2 118 B3
Sir William Hartley Ct
BB8 172 C6
Six Acre La PR4 75 C6
Six Arches Cvn Pk
PR3 204 D8
Sixfields 13 FY5 152 F7
Sixpenny La L37 21 D1
Sixth Ave
Blackpool FY4 110 C7
Bury BL9 33 D4
Sizehouse St 22 PR1 96 F8
Size House Village 6
BB4 85 B2
Sizergh Ct LA1 214 D7
Sizergh Rd LA4 217 E5
Sizer St PR1 117 F1
Size St OL12 71 D1
Skaithe The BB7 229 C7
Skeffington Rd PR1 118 C1
Skeleron La BB7 192 B6
SKELMERSDALE 18 A1
Skelmersdale & Ormskirk
Colls (Westbank Campus)
WN8 9 B8
Skelmersdale Rd L39,
WN8 8 B7
Skelmersdale Sports Ctr
WN8 9 C7
Skelshaw Cl BB1 102 A3
Skelton St BB8 171 E5
Skelwith Rd FY3 131 B2
Skerryvore Res Pk
FY4 110 D6
SKERTON 218 C4
Skerton 1 LA1 218 D2
Skerton Com High Sch
LA1 218 D2
Skerton Com Prim Sch
LA1 218 D2
Skerton Ct LA1 218 D2
Skerton Ho 6 LA1 218 D2
Skiddaw Cl BB12 147 C1
Skiddaw Rd
Blackpool FY4 110 F8
Lancaster LA1 218 E2
Skiddaw St BB1 102 A5
Skip La PR4 95 B3
SKIPPOOL 153 F6
Skippool Ave FY6 153 E5
Skippool Rd FY5 153 E7
Skipton Ave
Carleton FY6 153 C5
Southport PR9 54 C6
Skipton Cl
Bamber Bridge PR5 97 F2
Skipton Cl *continued*
Blackpool FY4 130 F1
Skipton Cres PR2 118 E5
Skipton Gate LA6 242 C2
Skipton Old Rd
Colne BB8 172 C7
Foulridge BB8 194 E2
Skipton Rd
Barnoldswick BB18 196 D4
Colne BB8 171 E6
Earby BB18 197 B3
Foulridge BB8 194 E2
Lytham St Anne's FY8 90 B6
Trawden BB8 172 B3
Skipton Road Bsns Ctr
BB18 196 B3
Skipton St
2 Morecambe LA4 217 A5
Nappa BB7 231 D7
Ski Rossendale* BB4 85 E3
SKITHAM 179 B4
Skitham La PR3 179 D4
Skull House La WN6 19 D8
Skull House Mews
WN6 19 C8
Skye Cl OL10 33 F1
Skye Cres BB1 102 C3
Slack BB12 146 F6
Slack Booth BB8 172 C1
Slackey La PR9 54 C4
Slack Gate OL12 52 F8
Slack La LA2 209 C1
Slack's La PR6 44 B2
Slackwood La LA5 224 E2
Slade La BB12 146 C1
Sladen St OL12 52 F1
Slade St PR1 96 E7
SLAIDBURN 229 C7
Slaidburn Ave
Burnley BB10 128 D5
Rawtenstall BB4 86 A4
Slaidburn Brennands Prim
Sch BB7 229 C7
Slaidburn Cres PR9 54 B5
Slaidburn Dr
Accrington BB5 104 A4
Lancaster LA1 215 A3
Slaidburn Heritage Ctr*
BB7 229 C7
Slaidburn Ind Est PR9 54 B5
Slaidburn Pl PR2 119 A2
Slaidburn Rd
Fulwood PR2 119 A2
Lowgill LA2 239 E4
Waddington BB7 189 A6
Waddington, Newton Fells
BB7 229 C2
Slaidburn Wlk 5 FY3 131 A8
Slape La LA6 240 C8
Slate La WN8 17 C2
Slater Ave
Colne BB8 171 D6
Horwich BL6 32 C4
Slater La
Leyland, Moss Side
PR26 59 B8
Leyland, Seven Stars
PR25 59 D8
Slater Rd FY5 175 C2
Slater St BB2 101 C1
Slinger Rd FY5 175 C3
Slip Inn La 29 LA1 214 F8
Slipper Lowe Brow BB3 64 A5
Sliven Clod Rd BB4 105 E2
Sluice La L40 39 B3
SLYNE 218 D8
Slyne Cvn Pk LA2 218 D8
Slyne Hall Hts LA2 221 A1
Slyne Rd
Bolton-le-S LA2, LA5 221 A2
Lancaster LA1 218 D3
Morecambe LA4 218 A5
Slynewoods LA2 218 F7
Smalden La BB7 230 A3
Smalley Croft PR1 96 F3
Smalley St
Burnley BB11 128 B4
Standish WN6 29 E1
Smalley Thorn Brow
BB6 123 F6
Smalley Way BB2 101 E2
Small La
Bescar L40 37 E1
Ormskirk, Clieves Hills
L39 15 A3
Ormskirk L39 15 F4
Small La N L39 23 E2
Small La S L39 14 D6
Smallshaw Ind Est
BB11 127 C5
Smallshaw La BB11,
BB12 127 B5
Smallshaw Rd OL12 52 A4
SMALLWOOD HEY 201 B5
Smallwood Hey Rd
PR3 201 C5
Smeaton St BL6 32 C2
Smethurst Hall Pk WN5 10 C2
Smethurst Hall Rd BL9 33 F4
Smethurst Rd WN5 10 C2
Smirthwaite St BB11 127 D5
Smith Ave PR4 73 F1
Smith Brow BL6 31 C3
Smith Cl PR2 139 C1
Smith Croft PR26 59 B8

SMITH GREEN 211 C3
Smithills Cl PR6 61 E1
Smithills Hall Cl BL0 50 C5
Smith La BL7 47 F1
Smith Rd FY5 175 D2
Smith's La PR4 57 A1
Smith St
Adlington PR7 30 F6
13 Bamber Bridge PR5 77 F8
Barnoldswick BB18 196 A1
Burnley BB12 127 E6
Bury BL9 33 A3
Chorley PR7 43 D6
Colne BB8 171 C4
3 Kirkham PR4 113 F5
Nelson BB9 148 F8
Ramsbottom BL0 50 B5
Skelmersdale WN8 17 D1
Whittle-le-W PR6 61 C8
Worsthorne BB10 129 B5
Smithy Bridge St 9
BB5 103 D3
Smithy Brow
Abbeystead LA2 232 F1
Haslingden BB4 85 B4
Newburgh WN8 27 A1
Wrightington Bar WN6 28 C8
Smithy Brow Ct BB4 85 B4
Smithy Cl
Brindle PR6 78 F5
Formby L37 12 B4
Garstang PR3 181 C8
Stalmine FY6 177 C7
Smithy Ct PR4 74 E2
Smithy Cvn Pk PR3 204 A5
Smithyfield Ave BB10 128 F6
Smithy Fold
Rochdale OL12 52 C1
Wrea Green PR4 113 B4
Smithy Glen Dr WN5 10 E4
Smithy Gn L37 12 B4
Smithy La
Aughton L39 6 A6
Brindle PR6 78 F6
Claughton PR3 182 B2
Foulridge BB8 171 B8
Haskayne L39 14 A6
Heysham LA3 212 E6
Holmeswood L40 38 C6
Hurlston Green L40 24 B3
Lytham St Anne's FY8 90 C6
Mawdesley L40 40 C2
Much Hoole PR4 74 E2
Preesall FY6 200 B3
Staining FY3, FY6 131 E6
Stalmine FY6 177 C7
Westhouse LA6 242 E4
Smithy Lane Ends L40 24 D6
Smithy Mews 9 FY1 130 C7
Smithy Row BB7 164 E1
Smithy St
2 Bamber Bridge PR5 77 E8
9 Haslingden BB4 85 B3
7 Ramsbottom BL0 50 C6
Smithy Wlk L40 25 E5
Smythe Croft PR9 54 A2
Snaefell Rd BB2 101 E1
Snape Gn
Scarisbrick PR8 23 D8
Southport PR8 36 E1
SNAPE GREEN 36 E1
Snape La LA5 225 F1
Snape Rake La PR3 183 D4
Snape St BB3 81 F3
Snapewood La PR3 204 B3
Snell Gr BB8 171 F6
Sniddle Hill La BB3 64 E8
Snipe Cl
Cleveleys FY5 175 F5
Normoss FY3 131 B6
Snipewood PR7 41 B6
Snoballey L40 24 B4
Snodworth Rd BB6 123 D7
Snowden Ave LA3 216 D3
Snowden St 1 BB12 127 B6
Snowdon Ave BB1 101 E7
Snowdon Cl FY1 130 D3
Snowdon Dr BL6 32 C5
Snowdon Rd FY8 111 A2
Snowdrop Cl
Clayton-le-W PR25 77 E2
Haslingden BB4 67 F8
Snow Hill PR1 96 F8
Snowhill La PR3 204 F6
Snowshill Cres FY5 152 F7
Snow St BB1 101 F6
Sod Hall La PR4 76 A5
Sollam's Cl 4 PR5 97 F2
SOLLOM 57 B2
Sollom La PR4 57 B2
Solway Ave BB2 100 F1
Solway Cl
Blackpool FY2 152 C6
Middleforth Green PR1 96 E3
Somerby Rd LA4 217 C4
Somerford Cl BB12 127 D7
Somersby Cl PR5 97 E3
Somerset Ave
Blackpool FY1 130 D3
Chorley PR7 61 C1
Clitheroe BB7 189 F2
Darwen BB3 81 F3
Lancaster LA1 215 A6
Wilpshire BB1 122 F6
Somerset Cl BB5 103 F3
Somerset Ct FY1 130 D3
Somerset Dr PR8 21 C3
Somerset Gr
Church BB5 103 F7
6 Rochdale OL11 52 A1
Somerset Pk PR2 117 B7
Somerset Pl BB9 171 A1
Somerset Rd
Leyland PR25 77 B2
Preston PR1 118 A1
Rishton BB1 124 A1
Somerset St BB11 128 A4
Somerset Wlk BB4 68 B8
Somerton Cl WN6 29 D1
Sorrel Cl
Cleveleys FY5 175 F5
Knott End-on-S FY6 200 A6
Sorrel Ct 2 PR1 96 C2
Soudan St BB10 148 B2
SOUGH
Darwen 65 B7
Earby 195 A8
Sough La
Belthorn BB1 83 A7
Blackburn BB1, BB5 102 F2
Earby BB18 195 A7
Sough Rd BB3 65 B7
Soulby Cl 3 BB2 101 C1
South Ave
Barnoldswick BB18 196 B3
Chorley PR7 43 D6
Cleveleys FY5 175 C4
Morecambe LA4 217 C5
New Longton PR4 75 F8
Southbank Ave FY4 111 A7
Southbank Rd PR8 35 C5
Southbourne Ave FY6 153 C2
Southbourne Rd FY3 131 A2
Southbrook Rd PR25 76 F1
Southcliffe BB6 124 B6
Southcliffe Ave BB12 127 C7
South Cliff St 5 PR1 96 E6
South Clifton St FY8 91 B3
South Cross St BL9 33 A1
Southdene WN8 27 B2
Southdown Dr FY5 153 D8
Southdowns Rd PR7 43 D6
South Dr
Appley Bridge WN6 28 C2
Fulwood PR2 117 E7
Inskip PR4 135 C8
Lancaster LA1 211 B6
Padiham BB12 126 E8
South East Dr LA1 211 B7
South End PR1 96 E5
Southern Ave
Burnley BB12 127 C7
Preston PR1 97 C6
Southern Cl PR3 140 A6
Southern Ct BB12 127 C8
Southern Par PR1 97 B6
Southern Rd PR8 35 A6
Southey Cl PR2 117 F7
Southey St 2 BB11 127 E6
SOUTHFIELD 149 B6
Southfield PR4 74 E3
Southfield Cotts BB10 149 B6
Southfield Dr
New Longton PR4 75 F7
Poulton-le-F FY3 131 C8
West Bradford BB7 189 F5
Southfield Gdns PR4 74 E3
Southfield La BB8, BB10 149 C7
Southfield Rd BL0 50 A2
Southfield Sq BB9 148 F8
Southfield St BB9 148 F7
Southfield Terr BB8 172 E6
Southfleet Ave FY7 198 E1
Southfleet Pl FY7 198 E1
Southfold Pl FY8 91 A4
Southgate
Fleetwood FY7 175 D8
Fulwood PR2 117 D5
Morecambe LA3 217 E2
Preston PR1 117 F1
Whitworth OL12 52 C7
Southgates PR7 42 D3
South Gr
Barton PR3 137 B8
Fulwood PR2 117 E8
Morecambe LA4 217 C5
South Hey FY8 90 C6
South Holme FY8 91 B4
South King St FY1 130 C5
Southlands PR4 114 A4
Southlands Ave PR5 97 C1
Southlands Dr PR26 59 C8
South Lawn FY1 130 E2
South Meade L31 5 B1
South Meadow La PR1 96 E6
South Meadow St PR1 97 A8
South Moss Rd FY8 90 C7
South Par FY5 175 E1
South Park Dr FY3 130 F2
South Pk FY8 91 A4
SOUTHPORT 35 C3
Southport Barn Cotts BB7 230 C1
Southport Botanic Gdns* PR9 54 B2
Southport Coll PR9 35 C7
Southport Ent Ctr PR9 36 A6
Southport FC PR8 35 E5
Southport & Formby District General Hospl PR8 35 E4
Southport General Infmy PR8 35 D5
Southport Holiday Ctr PR8 20 F6
Southport New Rd
Banks PR9 54 F5
Holmes PR4 56 D3
Mere Brow PR4, PR9 55 D3
Southport Old Rd L37 12 B7
Southport Rd
Chorley PR7 43 A8
Formby L37 12 A5
Haskayne L39 14 A6
Hurlston L40 24 A2
Maghull L31, L39 5 B5
Ormskirk L39, L40 15 D8
Scarisbrick L40, PR8 23 E7
Southport PR8 36 B2
Ulnes Walton PR26, PR7 59 B2
Southport Sta PR8 35 B7
Southport Terr PR6 43 E7
South Prom FY8 89 E5
South Rd
Bretherton PR26 57 F5
Coppull PR7 42 E1
Lancaster LA1 214 F7
Morecambe LA4 217 D5
Thornton FY5 176 D3
South Ribble Ind Est PR5 97 C5
South Ribble Mus & Ex Ctr* PR25 60 A8
South Ribble St 8 PR5 97 C6
SOUTH SHORE 110 C8
South Shore Hospl FY4 110 C5
South Shore St
6 Church BB5 103 E5
Haslingden BB4 85 A3
Southside PR7 60 C3
South Sq
Blackpool FY3 130 D6
Cleveleys FY5 175 D5
South St
Accrington BB5 104 C5
Accrington, Hillock Vale BB5 104 E8
Bacup OL13 88 A3
Burnley BB11 128 A6
16 Darwen BB3 82 A1
Great Eccleston PR3 156 B5
Haslingden BB4 85 C1
Lytham St Anne's FY8 91 D4
Newchurch BB4 86 E1
Ramsbottom BL0 50 D6
16 Rawtenstall BB4 86 A3
South Strand FY7 175 E7
South Terr
Abbey Village PR6 80 C2
Ormskirk L39 15 E4
Ramsbottom BL0 68 C2
South Valley Dr BB8 171 C3
South View
2 Bamber Bridge, Lostock Hall PR5 77 A7
Bamber Bridge PR5 77 B7
Belmont BL7 46 C5
Bretherton PR26 57 F5
Cumeragh Village PR3 138 F6
Dolphinholme LA2 226 A8
Fisher's Row PR3 201 F4
4 Great Harwood BB6 124 C5
20 Haslingden BB4 85 B3
Kirkham PR4 114 A4
Moss Side FY8 112 D1
Nelson BB9 148 D7
Read BB12 145 E3
South View St OL14 109 C1
South View Terr 1 PR25 60 A8
South Villas 17 OL13 70 C8
SOUTHWARD BOTTOM 108 A8
South Warton St FY8 91 C3
Southway
Fleetwood FY7 198 D1
Skelmersdale WN8 18 B1
South Westby St 2 FY8 91 B3
South West Dr LA1 211 A7
Southwood Ave FY7 198 F3
Southwood Cl FY8 90 E4
Southwood Dr BB5 104 E3
Southworth Ave FY4 110 E7
Southworth St BB2 101 D2
Southworth Way FY5 175 E5
Sovereign Ct FY5 175 D1
Sovereign Ct FY6 154 A3
Sovereign Gate FY4 110 F5
Sow Clough Rd OL13 87 D1
Sowerby Ave FY4 110 D8
Sowerby Rd PR3 157 E3
Sowerby St 4 BB12 126 C8
SOWER CARR 177 D4
Sower Carr La FY6 177 D4
Spa Ct LA4 217 E7
Spa Fold L40 17 A4
Spa Garth BB7 166 F8
Spa La L40, WN8 17 C4
Spalding Ave PR3 181 D6
Spa Rd PR1 96 D8
Spark La L40 39 B6
Sparrable Row BB10 149 B3
Sparrowhawk Dr FY6 200 B4
Sparrow Hill WN6, WN8 28 A2
Sparth Ave BB5 124 F3
Sparth Rd BB5 124 F3
Spa St
Burnley BB12 127 E7
Spa St *continued*
Padiham BB12 126 D8
3 Preston PR1 96 D8
Speakmans Dr WN6 19 C6
Speedie Cl BB2 81 D8
Speedwell Cl FY5 175 F5
Speedwell St BB2 101 B2
Speke St BB2 101 B2
SPEN BROOK 169 D2
Spen Brook Cotts BB12 169 C2
Spenbrook Rd BB12 169 C3
Spen Brow LA2 239 B6
Spencer Ct FY1 130 C7
Spencer Fold BB12 169 F1
Spencer Gr BB6 124 B5
Spencers Dr PR4 57 A8
Spencers La WN8 9 B7
Spencer's La
Orrell WN5 10 D7
Southport L39 22 B3
Spencer St
Accrington BB5 104 D6
Burnley BB10 148 A1
Ramsbottom BL0 50 B5
14 Rawtenstall BB4 86 A7
Spen Cnr FY4 130 D1
Spendmore La PR7 42 E1
Spen Farm FY4 111 C8
Spen La PR4 114 E6
Spenleach La BL8 49 D3
Spen Pl FY4 110 F8
Spenser Cl BB10 129 C4
Spenser St BB12 126 D7
Spey Cl
Leyland PR25 59 E8
Standish WN6 29 D1
Speyside FY4 110 D7
Spindle Berry Ct 5 BB5 104 C4
Spindle Cl BB1 101 F7
Spinnakers The FY8 89 E5
Spinners Ct
Buckshaw Village PR7 60 E6
Lancaster LA1 214 F7
Spinners Gn OL12 52 F2
Spinners Sq PR5 77 E7
Spinney Apts WN8 19 C1
Spinney Brow PR2 118 D4
Spinney Cl
Lucas Green PR6 61 B6
New Longton PR4 75 F8
Ormskirk L39 15 D3
Spinney Croft PR3 140 A7
Spinney La LA5 224 C8
Spinneyside BB2 101 D3
Spinney The
Arnside LA5 224 C8
Blackburn BB2 101 A8
Burnley BB12 127 D8
Chapeltown BL7 48 C2
Chorley PR6 61 C3
Cleveleys FY5 152 F7
Formby L37 12 A5
Grindleton BB7 190 B7
Heysham LA3 213 A7
Lancaster LA1 215 B5
Poulton-le-F FY6 153 E4
Preston PR1 95 F3
Rochdale OL12 52 D3
Tarleton PR4 57 A7
Spinning Ave BB1 82 D8
Spinnings The BL0 50 C3
Spire Cl BB3 65 D8
Spiredale Brow WN6 29 F2
Spires Gr PR4 116 E5
Spodden Cotts OL12 71 D2
Spodden Fold OL12 52 C8
Spod Rd OL12 52 D1
SPOTLAND FOLD 52 C1
Spotland Tops OL12 52 B1
Spouthouse La BB5 125 F1
Spout Houses BB9 170 D8
Spout La LA2 241 F1
Spread Eagle St BB5 103 C5
Spring Ave BB6 124 C6
Springbank BB9 170 E5
Spring Bank
Appley Bridge WN6 19 C8
Garstang PR3 181 C6
11 Preston PR1 96 E7
Silverdale LA5 224 C3
Whitworth, Broadley OL12 52 D4
Whitworth OL12 71 D1
Springbank Ave FY5 176 C2
Springbank Gdns BB4 105 F2
Spring Bank Terr BB2 101 C2
Springbrook Ave FY5 152 F8
Spring Brook Ho BB5 124 F2
Springburn Cl BL6 32 D1
Spring Cl
Kirkby L33 1 A5
Ramsbottom BL0 50 B6
Southport PR8 35 A5
Spring Cres PR6 61 E5
Springcroft 1 PR25 77 D3
Spring Ct 15 BB8 171 D5
Springdale Rd BB6 123 C8
Springfield
Blacko BB9 170 D8
High Bentham LA2 239 E8
Spring Field WA11 8 E2
Springfield Ave
Accrington BB5 103 F4
Bacup OL13 88 A3
Blackburn BB2 100 E1
Earby BB18 197 C1
Springfield Ave *continued*
Kirkham PR4 113 E5
Springfield Bank BB11 128 B5
Springfield Cl
Burscough L40 25 D2
Formby L37 11 C2
Whalley BB7 144 D6
Springfield Com Prim Sch BB11 128 B4
Springfield Cres LA2 239 E8
Springfield Ct
19 Bacup OL13 88 A3
1 Blackpool FY3 130 E3
Springfield Dr
Newchurch BB4 86 E1
Thornton FY5 176 B4
Springfield Flats 8
BB3 65 A8
Springfield Gdns
Nether Kellet LA6 221 F5
Scorton PR3 204 E6
Springfield Ho 2 L37 12 A3
Springfield Ind Est 9
PR1 117 E1
Springfield Mews 2
BB5 103 D3
Springfield Rd
Adlington PR6 31 A8
Blackpool FY1 130 B6
Burnley, Burnley Wood BB11 128 A4
Burnley, Fulledge BB11 128 B5
1 Chorley PR7 43 C8
Coppull PR7 29 E8
Great Harwood BB6 124 B4
Horwich BL6 32 E1
Leyland PR25 59 D7
Lytham St Anne's FY8 89 E6
Maghull L39 5 F6
Nelson BB9 148 E6
4 Ramsbottom BL0 50 A2
Rawtenstall BB4 86 B3
Springfield Rd N PR7 29 E8
Springfield St
Blackburn BB2 101 B3
Darwen BB3 65 A8
Lancaster LA1 214 F7
Morecambe LA4 216 F4
Oswaldtwistle BB5 103 D4
Preston PR1 117 E1
Springfield Terr
Blackburn BB2 101 A1
Fleetwood FY7 176 A6
Springfield View BB11 106 C5
SPRING GARDENS 87 B8
Spring Gardens Rd
BB8 171 D4
Spring Gardens St 4
BB4 69 F8
Spring Garden St 41
LA1 214 F8
Spring Gardens Terr 3
BB12 146 C1
Spring Gdns
8 Accrington BB5 104 C5
12 Bacup OL13 88 A3
12 Darwen BB3 65 A8
Freckleton PR4 93 B8
12 Horwich BL6 32 B4
Kingsfold PR1 96 F2
Leyland PR25 59 F8
Lytham St Anne's FY8 110 F1
Rawtenstall BB4 69 F6
8 Rawtenstall, Crawshawbooth BB4 86 A7
Spring Gr BB8 172 C6
Spring Hall BB5 124 F5
SPRING HILL 103 F5
Spring Hill
6 Blackburn BB1 101 E5
Freckleton PR4 93 D7
Springhill Ave OL13 70 D8
Spring Hill Com Prim Sch BB5 104 A4
Spring Hill Com Prim Sch (Hannah St) BB5 104 B5
Spring Hill Rd
Accrington BB5 103 F4
Burnley BB11 127 F4
Springhill Villas OL13 70 D8
Spring La
Blackburn BB2 101 B3
10 Colne BB8 171 D5
Haslingden BB4 85 B4
Nab's Head PR5 99 C8
Spring Mdw
Clayton-le-W PR25 77 E1
3 Clitheroe BB7 189 E1
Mere Brow PR4 55 F2
Spring Mdws
Clayton-le-M BB5 125 A3
Darwen BB3 65 D7
Springmount BB18 197 C2
Springmount Dr WN8 27 C5
Spring Pl
Colne BB8 171 D5
Whitworth OL12 71 D3
Spring Rd WN5 10 F8
Spring Row BB8 172 C6
Springsands Cl PR2 118 E5
SPRING SIDE 86 B3
Spring Side
Rawtenstall BB4 69 F6
Whitworth OL12 71 D4
Spring Side Cotts BL7 47 A2
Springs Mews PR6 61 E6
Springs Rd
Chorley PR6 61 D2

Springs Rd *continued*
Longridge PR3 140 B8
Spring St
Accrington BB5 103 F4
Bacup OL13 87 F1
Bank Lane BL0 50 D7
Horwich BL6 32 B4
6 Leyland PR25 77 B1
Nelson BB9 148 C7
5 Oswaldtwistle BB5 103 E4
Ramsbottom BL0 50 B6
Rawtenstall BB4 86 A8
Rishton BB1 124 B2
Todmorden OL14 109 C1
Spring Terr
4 Bacup OL13 70 D8
Goodshaw Chapel BB4 105 F2
Langho BB6 143 D1
Oswaldtwistle BB5 103 D4
5 Rochdale OL11 52 A1
Spring Terr S 5 BB4 85 E2
Springthorpe St 5 BB3 65 B6
Springvale BB5 103 F4
SPRING VALE 65 C7
Spring Vale PR3 207 B3
SPRING VALE 85 A2
Springvale Bsns Pk BB3 65 B6
Spring Vale Garden Village BB3 65 C6
Spring Vale Rd BB3 65 B7
Spring View
Blackburn BB2 101 C5
Holme Chapel BB10 108 A8
Spring Villas 5 OL14 109 B1
Springwater Ave BL0 50 A3
Springwood Cl PR5 97 A3
Springwood Dr
Chorley PR7 43 E5
Rufford L40 39 A5
Spring Wood Nature Trail* BB7 144 E5
Springwood Rd BB10 128 E5
Spring Wood St BL0 50 B7
Spring Yd 5 BB8 171 D5
Sprodley Dr WN6 28 B2
Spruce Ave
Bury BL9 33 B2
Lancaster LA1 214 F4
Spruce Cl PR2 118 C7
Spruce Ct 1 BB5 104 E8
Spruce St BL0 50 B5
Spruce Way L37 11 C3
Sprucewood Cl BB5 104 D6
Spurrier St PR26 77 A4
Spymers Croft L37 12 A6
Square House La PR9 55 C6
Square La
Burscough L40 25 E3
Catforth PR4 135 F4
Square St BL0 50 C6
Square The
Bacup OL13 87 F2
Blackpool FY3 131 A2
Brinscall PR6 62 F7
Burton-in-K LA6 240 B7
Cleveleys FY5 175 D5
Cumeragh Village PR3 138 F5
Great Eccleston PR3 156 B5
Hurlston Green L40 24 B4
1 Leyland PR25 77 B2
Scorton PR3 204 E6
Waddington BB7 189 B4
Walton-le-D PR5 97 F5
Whalley BB7 144 C5
Worsthorne BB10 129 B5
Squire Rd BB9 148 F8
Squires Cl PR5 98 E2
Squires Ct
7 Blackpool FY4 110 C5
10 Lytham St Anne's FY8 91 B3
SQUIRES GATE 110 B5
Squires Gate Ind Est FY4 110 E4
Squires Gate La FY4 110 D5
Squire's Gate Rd PR2 117 C3
Squires Gate Sta FY8 110 B4
Squires Rd PR1 96 C6
Squires Wood PR2 118 D6
Squirrel Fold PR2 118 F2
Squirrel Gn L37 11 C5
Squirrel La BL6 32 A4
Squirrels Chase PR4 115 D1
Squirrel's Chase PR5 77 A7
Squirrels Cl BB5 104 E8
Stable Cl
Gisburn BB7 231 B3
Kirkham PR4 114 A6
Stable La PR6 62 A7
Stables Cl BB4 86 A6
Stables The
Leyland PR7 60 A5
Thornton FY5 176 B3
Whitworth OL12 71 C1
Stable Yd PR3 201 E5
Stack Croft PR6 78 A2
Stackhouses The 2 BB11 128 A6
Stack La OL13 71 B8
STACKSTEADS 70 B8
Stadium Ave FY4 110 E5
Staffa Cres BB1 102 D4
Stafford Ave FY6 153 D1
Stafford Cl PR4 156 A1
Stafford Moreton Way L31 5 D1
Stafford Rd
11 Preston PR1 118 A1

Stafford Rd *continued*
Southport PR8 35 A1
Stafford St
Burnley BB10 128 A7
Darwen BB3 81 F4
Nelson BB9 149 A8
Skelmersdale WN8 17 D1
STAGHILLS 86 D1
Staghills Rd BB4 86 D1
Stainburn Cl WN6 19 E6
Stainforth Ave FY2 152 E5
STAINING 131 E5
Staining Ave PR2 95 F8
Staining CE Prim Sch FY3 131 D5
Staining Old Rd FY3, FY6 131 D7
Staining Rd FY3 131 C6
Staining Rd W FY3 131 D5
Staining Rise FY3 131 E5
Stainton Dr BB12 127 E8
Stainton Gr 1 LA4 217 E4
STAKE POOL 201 E4
Stakepool Dr PR3 201 E4
Stakes Hall Pl BB2 101 C2
Stalls Rd LA3 212 F2
STALMINE 177 C7
Stalmine Ctry Pk FY6 177 D5
Stalmine Hall Pk FY6 177 C8
STALMINE MOSS SIDE 177 E7
Stalmine Prim Sch FY6 177 D7
Stamford Ave FY4 110 D7
Stamford Ct FY8 89 D8
Stamford Dr PR6 61 C5
Stamford Pl 3 BB7 189 F1
Stamford Rd
Skelmersdale WN8 17 D2
Southport PR8 35 B2
Stanagate PR4 115 C1
STANAH 176 E2
Stanah Gdns FY5 176 E2
Stanah Prim Sch FY5 176 D1
Stanah Rd FY5 176 E2
Stanalee La PR3 160 B8
Stanbury Cl
Burnley BB10 148 E2
Bury BL9 33 D1
Stanbury Dr BB10 148 E2
Stancliffe St BB2 101 C3
Standedge Cl BL0 50 C4
Standen Hall Cl BB10 148 E3
Standen Hall Dr BB10 148 D3
Standen Park Ho LA1 215 C8
Standen Rd BB7 166 F7
Standen Road Bglws BB7 166 F7
Standhouse La L39 15 C2
Standing Stone La BB8, BB9 194 A2
STANDISH 29 F2
Standish Com High Sch WN6 29 C2
Standish St Wilfrid's CE Prim Sch WN6 29 F1
Standish St
Burnley BB11 128 A6
Chorley PR7 43 D7
Standridge Clough La BB18 197 D1
Standroyd Dr BB8 172 A5
Standroyd Rd BB8 172 A5
Standside Pk WN8 8 D8
Stanford Gdns BB2 102 A1
Stanford Hall Cres BL0 50 B4
Stangate L31 5 B2
Stang Top Rd BB9 169 F6
STANHILL 103 B4
Stanhill La BB5 103 C4
Stanhill Rd BB1, BB5 102 F4
Stanhill St BB5 103 C3
Stanhope Ave LA3 217 E3
Stanhope Ct LA3 217 F3
Stanhope Rd 1 FY1 130 C7
Stanhope St
Burnley BB12 127 F7
Darwen BB3 82 A2
Preston PR1 117 E2
Stanier Pl BL6 32 C2
Stanifield Cl PR25 77 B3
Stanifield La PR5, PR25 77 C5
Stankelt Ho LA5 224 C2
Stankelt Rd LA5 224 C2
Stanlawe Rd L37 11 E6
STANLEY 17 E3
Stanley Ave
Cleveleys FY5 175 E2
Hutton PR4 95 D2
Leyland PR25 77 C4
Middleforth Green PR1 96 E5
Poulton-le-F FY6 153 D3
Southport PR8 34 F3
Stanley Cl PR3 140 B7
Stanley Croft PR4 137 B3
Stanley Ct
Accrington BB5 104 D7
Burscough Bridge L40 25 E5
Chipping PR3 185 E3
Stanley Ct BB6 124 E5
Stanley Ct PR4 114 B4
Stanley Dr
Darwen BB3 65 B5
Hornby LA2 238 B7
Stanleyfield Cl PR1 118 A1
Stanleyfield Rd PR1 118 A1
Stanley Fold PR5 76 F8
STANLEY GATE 7 E7

Stanley Gate
Fleetwood FY7 198 D3
Mellor BB2 121 E2
Stanley Gr
Higher Penwortham PR1 96 A5
Horwich BL6 32 D1
Stanley High Sch Sports Coll PR9 53 F4
Stanley Ho PR1 96 E7
Stanley Mews PR4 134 E7
Stanley Mount 6 OL13 87 F3
Stanley Park Cl FY3 130 F3
Stanley Pl
9 Chorley PR7 43 C8
Lancaster LA1 214 D8
Preston PR1 96 E7
Stanley Prim Sch FY3 131 B2
Stanley Range BB2 101 B1
Stanley Rd
Blackpool FY1 130 C4
Fleetwood FY7 198 F3
Formby L37 11 E6
Kirkham PR4 113 F7
Leyland PR25 77 C4
Lytham St Anne's FY8 90 D3
Morecambe LA3 216 E3
Up Holland WN8 10 B7
Stanley St
Accrington BB5 104 C6
Accrington BB5 104 D6
Bacup OL13 87 F4
Blackburn BB1 102 B6
Brierfield BB9 148 B6
6 Burnley BB11 127 F5
Carnforth LA5 223 D1
Colne BB8 171 D5
Kirkham PR4 114 B4
10 Leyland PR25 77 B1
Longridge PR3 140 A8
4 Morecambe LA4 217 B6
Nelson BB9 148 D8
Ormskirk L39 15 F5
Oswaldtwistle BB5 103 D3
Preston PR1 97 B8
Ramsbottom BL0 50 B5
Rochdale OL12 52 E1
Southport PR9 35 B8
Stanley Terr PR1 96 E7
Stanley Villas PR5 99 B4
Stanley Way WN8 17 E3
Stanmere Ct BL8 49 B3
Stanmore Ave FY4 110 F6
Stanmore Dr LA1 214 E5
Stannanought Rd WN8 18 E2
Stanner Lo FY8 110 F2
Stanning Cl PR25 59 E8
Stanrose Cl BL7 47 E1
Stansfeld St BB2 101 C3
Stansfield Ave L31 5 F1
Stansfield Cl 7 BB9 170 D4
Stansfield Rd BB4 69 E8
Stansfield St
2 Bacup OL13 70 C8
Blackpool FY1 130 C1
Burnley BB11 127 B5
7 Darwen BB3 65 A8
Nelson BB9 148 E8
Stansfield Terr 6 OL14 109 B1
Stansford Ct PR1 96 D4
Stansted Rd PR7 43 A7
Stansy Ave LA3 216 E1
Stanthorpe Wlk BB10 148 A1
STANWORTH 80 C4
Stanworth Brow PR6 80 A5
Stanworth Rd BB9 148 D8
Stanworth St BB10 129 B5
Stanworth Terr PR6 80 B4
Stanzaker Hall Dr PR3 158 D7
Stapleton Rd L37 11 D1
Star Bank OL13 70 D7
Starbeck Ave FY4 130 D1
Starfield Cl FY8 91 A4
Starkie St
Blackburn BB1 101 F5
Burnley BB11 127 E5
Darwen BB3 65 B8
12 Leyland PR25 77 B1
Preston PR1 96 F6
Star La BL6 31 F3
Starr Gate FY4 110 B4
Starrgate Dr PR2 116 E1
Star St
Accrington BB5 103 F5
Darwen BB3 82 B1
Startifants La PR3 184 F4
Startifants Lane End PR3 185 A5
Startley Nook PR4 76 B6
States Rd FY8 90 B6
Statham Rd WN8 17 E3
Statham Way L39 15 E4
Station App
Burscough Bridge L40 25 E5
Ormskirk L39 15 F5
Station Ave WN5 10 D5
Station Bldgs LA5 223 D2
Station Brow PR25 77 B2
Station Cl
Rishton BB1 103 A8
Wilpshire BB1 122 F4
Station Cotts LA6 241 D2
Station Ct
Bacup OL13 88 A1
Hornby LA2 238 B7
Station La
Burton-in-K LA6 240 B7

Station La *continued*
Nateby PR3 203 B1
Newsham PR3 137 A5
Scorton PR3 204 D7
Station Par OL14 108 F1
Station Rd
Adlington PR7 31 A6
Bamber Bridge PR5 77 E8
Banks PR9 54 F5
Barnoldswick BB18 196 B2
Blackpool FY4 110 B8
Blackrod BL6 31 E1
Caton LA2 237 C3
Chapeltown BL7 48 C4
Clitheroe BB7 166 E8
Coppull PR7 42 F1
Croston PR26 58 B3
Fleetwood FY7 199 A4
Foulridge BB8 194 D1
Great Harwood BB6 124 D5
Haskayne L39 13 E7
Haslingden, Bridge End BB4 68 A7
Haslingden, North Hag BB4 85 B4
Hesketh Bank PR4 73 F3
Hest Bank LA2 220 D1
High Bentham LA2 239 D7
Hoghton PR5 99 B2
Holme Mills LA6 240 B8
Hornby LA2 238 B7
Huncoat BB5 125 E2
2 Kirkham PR4 113 F5
Lancaster LA1 214 E8
Lytham St Anne's FY8 91 B3
Maghull, Lydiate L31 5 A6
Morecambe LA4 217 B5
New Longton PR4 75 F8
Ormskirk L39 15 F6
Padiham BB12 126 C8
Parbold WN8 27 C2
Poulton-le-F FY6 153 E4
Ramsbottom BL8 49 F1
Rimington BB7 191 E8
Rishton BB1 124 A1
Rufford L40 39 D4
Salwick PR4 115 C4
Singleton FY6 132 C8
Southport PR8 21 C5
Thornton FY5 176 D1
Todmorden OL14 109 C1
Walmer Bridge PR4 74 D4
Whalley BB7 144 C5
Whitworth, Broadley OL12 52 C5
Whitworth OL12 71 D3
Wrea Green PR4 113 B4
Station Road Ind Est BB6 124 E5
Station Sq FY8 91 A3
Station Terr
Abbey Village PR6 80 C2
Blackpool FY4 110 B8
Station View BB6 143 D1
Station Way
Garstang PR3 181 C8
Hornby LA2 238 B7
Station Yd BB18 197 A2
Staunton St LA5 223 D3
Staveley Ave L40 25 E4
Staveley Gr FY7 198 D2
Staveley Pl PR2 116 E2
Staveley Rd
Skelmersdale WN8 17 E3
Southport PR8 21 D4
STAYNALL 177 A4
Staynall La FY6 177 B4
Stead St BL0 50 C6
Sted Terr BB1 101 E6
Steeley La PR6 43 D7
Steeple View PR2 96 D8
Steer St BB10 148 B1
Steeton Rd FY3 153 B1
Stefano Rd 1 PR1 97 C8
Steiner's La BB5 103 E7
Steiner St BB5 104 A6
Stephenage Pk PR1 97 A2
Stephendale Ave PR5 78 B8
STEPHEN MOOR 235 F1
Stephens Gr LA3 209 D8
Stephenson Dr BB12 127 C7
Stephenson St
2 Chorley PR6 43 E7
Horwich BL6 32 B2
Stephenson Way L37 12 C3
Stephen St
Blackburn BB2 101 B2
Lytham St Anne's FY8 89 E7
Step Row OL13 87 F5
Sterling Pl OL10 33 F1
Sterndale Ave WN6 29 E2
Stevant Way LA3 217 F2
Stevenson Ave 2 PR25 77 C3
Stevenson St E BB5 104 A5
Stevenson St W BB5 103 F5
Steward Ave LA1 215 B5
Stewart Cl LA5 224 B8
Stewart Ct 9 LA1 218 D2
Stewart St
Blackburn BB2 81 D8
Burnley BB11 128 B4
11 Preston PR1 96 D8
Stiles Ave PR4 95 C1
Stiles The L39 15 E5
Stirling Cl
Chorley PR6 43 E7
Clitheroe BB7 166 C6
1 Leyland PR25 77 C1

Stirling Ct
8 Blackpool FY1 130 D7
Lane Bottom BB10 149 B4
Southport PR9 54 A2
Stirling Dr BB1 101 F4
Stirling Ind Est BL6 32 C2
Stirling Rd
Blackpool FY3 130 D7
Lancaster LA1 215 A7
Stirling St BB2 101 B1
STOCK 231 F4
Stockbridge Cotts BB7 164 E3
Stockbridge Dr BB12 126 E8
Stockbridge Rd BB12 126 D7
Stock Cl OL12 52 E2
Stockclough La BB2 80 D6
Stockdale Cres PR5 77 F8
Stockdove Way FY5 175 E3
Stockdove Wood FY5 175 E3
Stockholm St BB11 127 B5
Stockley Cres L39 7 E6
Stockley Dr WN6 19 E8
Stockpit Rd L33 1 D2
Stocks Cl PR6 79 B1
Stocks Ct
Heskin Green PR7 41 E3
5 Poulton-le-F FY6 153 D3
Stocksgate OL12 52 B2
Stocks La
Barnoldswick BB7 193 A7
Carleton FY6 153 A3
Heskin Green PR7 41 E3
Stocks Lane End PR3 181 D2
Stocks Park Dr BL6 32 C3
Stocks Rd PR2 117 C2
Stocks Resr & Gisburn Forest Walks* BB7 235 E3
Stocks St 7 PR1 96 E8
Stockwood Cl BB2 101 A8
Stockydale Rd FY4 111 A6
STODDAY 214 C2
Stoke Ave FY1 130 D2
Stokes Hall Ave PR25 60 A8
Stoneacre Dr PR6 44 A1
Stonebarn Dr L31 5 C3
Stonebridge Cl 6 PR5 77 C8
Stone Bridge La BB5 103 E3
Stonebridge Terr PR3 140 A7
Stonechat Cl FY3 131 B6
Stone Cl BL0 50 A4
Stonecroft BB9 170 E6
Stone Croft PR1 96 D2
Stonecroft Rd PR25 59 D7
Stonecrop WN6 28 D1
Stonecross Cl BB5 103 E5
Stone Cross Gdns PR3 181 D2
Stone Edge Rd BB9 170 E6
Stone Edge View BB9 170 E6
Stonefield
Longton PR4 74 F8
Middleforth Green PR1 96 E4
Stonefield Cotts BB2 100 B2
Stone Fold BB5 85 B8
Stonefold Ave PR4 95 C1
Stonegate Fold PR6 44 B1
Stone Hall La
Skelmersdale WN8 18 F4
Up Holland WN8 19 A5
Stonehill Cres OL12 52 A3
Stonehill Dr OL12 52 B3
Stone Hill Dr BB1 123 A1
Stone Hill La OL12 52 A2
Stonehill Rd OL12 52 B3
Stoneholme Ind Est BB4 86 A8
Stoneholme Rd BB4 86 A8
Stone Holme Terr BB4 86 A8
Stonehouse Gn PR6 78 B3
Stoneleigh Cl PR8 21 C4
Stoneleigh Ct LA5 224 C3
Stonemasons Ct FY3 130 E7
Stone Mill Cotts BL7 48 D4
Stone Moor Bottom BB12 126 C6
Stone Pits BL0 68 E3
Stone Row Head LA1 215 C8
Stoner Rd PR7 30 F7
Stones Bank Rd BL7 47 B5
Stones La PR3 181 E3
Stone St
Haslingden BB4 84 F2
Rawtenstall BB4 69 F8
Stone Trough Brow BB18 194 F4
Stoneway Rd FY5 175 E1
Stonewell 17 LA1 214 F8
Stoney Bank Rd BB18 197 C2
Stoney Brow WN8 19 B1
Stoney Butts PR2 95 D8
Stoneycroft BB10 129 A5
Stoneycroft Ave BL6 32 D4
Stoneycroft Cl BL6 32 D5
Stoney Croft Dr LA5 223 E6
Stoney Ct BB8 194 E1
Stoneygate
Cleveleys FY5 175 F1
17 Preston PR1 97 A7
Stoneygate La WN6 28 B2
STONEYHOLME 127 F8
Stoneyholme Com Prim Sch BB12 127 F8
Stoney Holt PR25 77 E1
Stoneyhurst Ave
Burnley BB10 128 D5

Stoneyhurst Ave *continued*
Thornton FY5 153 D8
Stoneyhurst Ht BB9 148 D4
Stoney La
Adlington PR7 30 E4
Bamber Bridge PR5 77 C6
Foulridge BB8 194 E1
Freckleton PR4 93 B5
Galgate LA2 211 B3
Hambleton FY6 177 C2
Longridge PR3 161 C7
Parbold WN6, WN8 27 E4
Stoney Royd OL12 71 D1
Stoney St BB11 128 B4
Stony Bank PR6 79 A6
Stonybutts [9] BB1 101 E5
Stonycroft Ave FY4 110 C5
Stonycroft Pl [2] FY4 110 C5
Stony Fold Brow BB3 64 A5
Stonygate La PR3 141 D6
Stony Hill Ave FY4 110 C5
Stonyhurst PR7 43 C4
Stonyhurst Cl
Blackburn BB2 101 D4
Padiham BB12 126 E6
Stonyhurst Coll BB7 165 A3
Stonyhurst Coll Gdns* BB7 165 A2
Stonyhurst Rd BB2 101 D4
Stony La
Cockerham PR3 206 F2
Hollins Lane PR3 207 D3
Todmorden OL14 109 E2
Stoopes Hill BB18 197 C2
Stoops Fold BB2 121 E2
Stoops La BB7 191 F8
Stoop St BB11 127 C5
Stopes Brow BB1, BB3 82 A4
Stopford Ave FY2 152 E2
Stopford Ct [1] BB5 124 F3
Stopgate La L33 1 C7
Stopper La BB7 192 B7
STOPPER LANE 192 A8
Store St
Blackburn BB3 82 A7
[17] Haslingden BB4 85 B3
Horwich BL6 32 C4
Storey Ave LA1 214 D8
Storey Hall LA1 214 E5
Storey Inst LA1 214 E8
Stork Cl FY5 175 F1
Stork St BB3 65 D8
Storrs La LA5 225 B4
Storwood Cl WN5 10 E5
Stott St
[1] Nelson BB9 148 D8
Rochdale OL12 52 F1
Stour Lo PR2 117 C6
Stourton Rd PR8 21 C4
Stourton St BB1 124 A2
Stout St BB2 101 D4
Straight Up La PR9 36 D8
Strait La LA2 232 F1
Straits BB5 103 E4
Straits La BB12 145 D2
STRAITS THE 76 D1
Straits The PR5 99 B2
Strand Rd PR1 96 D7
Strand St W PR2 96 C8
Strands Farm Ct LA2 238 B7
Strand The
Blackpool FY1 130 B6
Fleetwood FY7 175 D8
Horwich BL6 32 D3
Strange St BB11 128 B4
Strang St [9] BL0 50 C6
Strang Stee [6] BB7 166 E8
Stransdale Cl [5] PR3 181 B7
Stratfield Pl [5] PR25 77 B1
Stratford Cl
Lancaster LA1 218 C3
Southport PR8 21 A6
Stratford Dr PR2 117 D4
Stratford Pl
Blackpool FY1 130 E2
[2] Fleetwood FY7 198 E4
Stratford Rd
Chorley PR6 43 D8
Lytham St Anne's FY8 90 B7
Stratford Way
[7] Accrington BB5 104 A7
Colne BB8 171 F5
Strathaven Pl [5] OL10 33 F1
Strathclyde Rd BB1 102 A4
Strathdale FY4 110 F7
Strathmore Cl BL0 50 C4
Strathmore Gr PR7 43 B7
Strathmore Rd PR2 117 E3
Strathyre Cl FY2 152 F5
Stratton Ct BB9 148 E6
Stratton Gr BL6 32 B5
Strawberry Bank [1] BB1 101 D5
Strawberry Fields PR7 61 B3
Strawberry Mews [1] LA3 212 F8
Streatly Wlk BB2 82 A8
STREET 226 A6
Street The PR6 44 E3
Strellas La LA5 221 C1
Stretton Ave FY4 110 E8
Stretton Dr PR9 35 F8
Stretton Rd BL0 50 A2
Strickens La PR3 182 C6
Strickland Dr LA4 217 E5
Stricklands La PR1 96 E4
Strickland's La FY6 177 D6
Strike La PR4 93 B8
Strine The L40, PR4 57 A1
Stromness Gr [3] OL10 33 F1
STRONGSTRY 68 C2
Strongstry Rd BL0 68 C2
Stronsay Pl FY2 152 F6
Stroyan St BB10 128 C5
Strutt St [2] PR1 118 B1
Stryands PR4 95 C1
Stuart Ave
Bacup OL13 70 D8
Morecambe LA4 217 D6
Stuart Cl
[14] Darwen BB3 82 A1
Fulwood PR2 118 E3
Stuart Pl FY3 153 A1
Stuart Rd
Fulwood PR2 118 E3
Thornton FY5 176 C2
Stuart St
Accrington BB5 104 B7
[5] Barnoldswick BB18 196 C2
STUBBINS
Catterall 181 F2
Ramsbottom 68 B1
Stubbins La
Catterall PR3 181 F2
Ramsbottom BL0 50 C8
Sabden BB7 146 A7
Stubbins St BL0 68 C1
Stubbins Vale Cvn Pk BB7 146 A7
Stubbins Vale Rd BL0 68 C1
Stubbins Vale Terr BL0 68 B1
Stubbylee La OL13 70 F8
Stubley Holme OL14 109 A1
Stubley La OL14 109 B1
Studfold PR7 61 B2
Studholme Ave PR1 96 E2
Studholme Cl [8] PR1 96 E2
Studholme Cres PR1 96 E2
Studley Ct PR9 53 D1
Stump Cross La BB7 230 F5
Stump Hall Rd BB12 146 F7
Stump La PR6 43 D8
Stunstead Cotts BB8 172 C2
Stunstead Rd BB8 172 C3
Sturgess Cl L39 15 F7
Sturminster Cl [5] PR1 96 E2
Styan St FY7 199 A4
STYDD 141 E4
Stydd La PR3 141 E4
Sudell Ave L31 5 F2
Sudell Cl BB3 82 C1
Sudell Cross [20] BB1 101 E5
Sudell La L31, L39 5 E6
Sudell Prim Sch BB3 82 B1
Sudell Rd BB3 82 B1
Sudellside St BB3 82 B1
Suffolk Ave BB12 127 A6
Suffolk Cl PR25 59 E6
Suffolk Rd
Blackpool FY3 131 A2
Preston PR1 118 A1
Southport PR8 22 A8
Suffolk St BB2 101 C2
Sugar Stubbs La PR9 55 C4
Sugham La LA3 212 F8
Sulby Cl PR8 34 F3
Sulby Dr
Fulwood PR2 118 F5
Lancaster LA1 214 F6
Sulby Gr
Fulwood PR2 119 A5
Morecambe LA4 217 E6
Sulby Rd BB2 101 E1
Sullivan Dr BB2 102 A1
Sullom Side La PR3 182 C5
Sullom View PR3 181 C6
Sultan St BB5 104 D7
Sulyard St LA1 214 F8
Summerdale Dr BL0 50 B2
Summerer Gr PR4 132 F6
Summerfield
Leyland PR25 76 F3
Thornton-in-C BD23 197 A5
Summerfield Cl PR5 97 B2
Summerfield Dr LA2 218 C7
Summerfields
Coppull PR7 29 F7
Lytham St Anne's FY8 89 C8
Summerhill LA2 239 D7
SUMMERSEAT 50 C2
Summerseat La BL0 50 A2
Summerseat Meth Prim Sch BL9 50 D2
Summerseat Sta* BL9 50 C2
Summersgill Rd LA1 218 B2
Summer St
Horwich BL6 32 B4
Nelson BB9 148 C7
Skelmersdale WN8 18 A4
Summerton Wlk BB3 82 A2
Summer Trees Ave PR2 116 D3
Summerville [4] FY4 110 C6
Summerville Ave FY3 131 E5
Summerville Wlk [4] BB2 101 D5
Summerwood Cl FY2 152 D1
Summerwood La L39 23 C1
Summit Cl BL9 33 F4
Summit Dr PR4 93 C6
Summit St BL9 33 F4
Summit The BD23 197 A5
Summit Works BB11 127 E2
Sumner Ave L39 13 F4
Sumner Rd L37 11 F3
Sumners Barn PR2 118 E6
Sumner's La PR26 40 A7
Sumner St
Blackburn BB2 101 E3
Leyland PR25 77 A1
Sumpter Croft PR1 96 E2
Sumpter Ct PR1 96 F2
Sunacre Ct [6] LA3 216 E3
Sunbank Cl OL12 52 D2
Sunbury Ave PR1 96 D3
Sunbury Dr PR8 21 B4
Suncliffe Rd BB9 148 D4
Suncourt PR8 34 F6
SUNDERLAND 209 B4
Sunderland Ave
Cleveleys FY5 175 F4
Hambleton FY6 177 D2
Sunderland Dr LA3 217 A2
Sunderland St BB12 127 B6
Sunfield Cl FY4 111 A7
Sunnindale Ave BB4 87 A1
Sunningdale PR4 137 B3
Sunningdale Ave
Blackpool FY4 131 A2
Fleetwood FY7 175 D7
Hest Bank LA2 220 D1
Sunningdale Cl PR4 114 A4
Sunningdale Cres LA2 220 D1
Sunningdale Ct FY8 90 A6
Sunningdale Dr
Buckshaw Village PR7 60 E6
Thornton FY5 153 D8
Sunningdale Gdns
Burnley BB10 148 D3
Formby L37 11 E3
Sunningdale Pl PR4 135 C8
Sunny Bank
Kirkham PR4 113 F5
Middleforth Green PR1 96 F3
Sunny Bank Ave
Blackpool FY2 152 C4
Newton-w-S PR4 115 A2
Sunny Bank Cl BB4 68 A6
Sunny Bank Cotts BB4 67 F5
Sunnybank Dr BB5 103 C2
Sunnybank Gdns BB2 101 E1
Sunny Bank Ind Est FY6 177 D1
Sunny Bank Mill PR4 113 F5
Sunny Bank Prep Sch BB11 127 E4
Sunnybank Rd LA5 221 A5
Sunny Bank Rd BB2 101 E1
Sunnybank St
Darwen BB3 82 A1
[8] Haslingden BB4 85 A3
Sunny Bank Terr [11] OL14 109 B1
SUNNY BOWER 123 B1
Sunny Bower Cl BB1 123 B1
Sunny Bower Rd BB1 123 B1
Sunny Brow PR7 43 A2
Sunnycliff Ret Pk LA3 217 D1
Sunny Dr WN5 10 F6
Sunnyfield Ave
Holme Chapel BB10 108 A8
Morecambe LA4 217 E6
Sunnyfield La BB3 66 A8
Sunnyfields L39 16 A5
Sunnyhill PR2 118 C5
Sunnyhill Cl BB3 81 D2
SUNNYHURST 81 D2
Sunnyhurst BB3 81 D1
Sunnyhurst Ave FY4 110 D6
Sunnyhurst Cl BB3 81 D2
Sunnyhurst La BB3 81 D2
Sunnyhurst Rd BB2 101 D4
Sunnyhurst Res Pk FY4 110 D6
Sunnyhurst Wood Visitor Ctr* BB3 81 D2
Sunny Lea St BB4 85 F5
Sunnymede Dr L31 5 D3
Sunnymede Sch PR8 34 F6
Sunnymede Vale BL0 50 A3
Sunnymere Dr BB3 81 E2
Sunny Rd PR9 54 A2
Sunnyside
[5] High Bentham LA2 239 D8
Ormskirk L39 6 C7
Southport PR8 34 F3
Sunnyside Ave
Billington BB7 144 B4
[1] Blackburn BB2 80 E8
Ribchester PR3 141 D3
Warton PR4 92 E6
Wilpshire BB1 123 A7
Sunnyside Camp Site LA3 217 A2
Sunnyside Cl
Freckleton PR4 93 B7
Lancaster LA1 214 E7
Rawtenstall BB4 86 A6
Sunnyside Ct PR9 53 C1
Sunnyside Cvn Pk PR3 158 F5
Sunnyside La LA1 214 E7
Sunnyside Terr FY6 200 C3
Sunny View PR6 80 C2
Sunset Cl L33 1 A5
Sun St
Colne BB8 171 E5
Lancaster LA1 214 F8
Nelson BB9 148 C8
Oswaldtwistle BB5 103 E4
Ramsbottom BL0 50 B7
Sun Terr OL14 109 B1
Super St BB5 124 E4
Surgeon's Ct PR1 96 F7
Surrey Ave
Burnley BB12 127 B7
Darwen BB3 81 F3
Surrey Cl PR9 54 C5
Surrey Rd
Barrowford BB9 170 D2
Blackburn BB1 102 D5
Surrey St
Accrington BB5 104 D6
Preston PR1 97 C8
Sussex Ave BL9 33 E1
Sussex Cl
Church BB5 103 F7
Standish WN1 30 B1
Sussex Dr
Blackburn BB1 102 A4
Garstang PR3 181 B7
Haslingden BB4 68 B8
Sussex Rd
Blackpool FY3 130 E6
Rishton BB1 102 F8
Southport PR8, PR9 35 D6
Sussex St
[25] Barnoldswick BB18 196 B2
Burnley BB11 128 B4
[1] Nelson BB9 170 E1
Preston PR1 118 A1
Sussex Wlk [10] BB1 102 A4
Sutch La L40 26 B5
Sutcliffe St
Britannia OL13 71 C8
[18] Burnley BB11 127 F6
Burnley, Harle Syke BB10 148 F3
[7] Chorley PR7 43 D7
Sutcliffe Terr BB1 82 F6
Sutherland Cl BB1 123 A7
Sutherland Rd
Blackpool FY1 130 C8
Heywood OL10 33 F1
Sutherland St BB8 171 C4
Sutherland View [2] FY1 130 C7
Sutton Ave
Burnley BB10 148 D2
Tarleton PR4 57 A8
Sutton Cres BB5 125 F1
Sutton Dr PR2 95 D8
Sutton Fold PR6 44 A1
Sutton Gr PR6 61 F4
Sutton La
Adlington PR6 31 B8
Tarleton PR4 56 F5
Sutton Pl FY1 130 C4
Sutton Rd L37 11 E1
Sutton's La L37 12 E3
Sutton St
Blackburn BB2 80 D8
Weeton Camp PR4 132 E6
Swainbank St BB11 128 B5
Swaine St BB9 148 C8
Swainson St
[11] Blackpool FY1 130 C6
Lytham St Anne's FY8 90 F3
Swain St [5] OL12 52 E1
Swainstead Raike BD24 236 E8
Swaledale LA2 211 B4
Swaledale Ave BB10 148 B4
Swalegate L31 5 C2
Swallow Ave [1] PR1 96 E4
Swallow Cl
Blackpool FY3 131 B2
Thornton FY5 176 A4
Swallow Ct
Clayton Green PR6 78 C1
Heysham LA3 212 F6
Swallow Dr
Blackburn BB1 101 E6
Bury BL9 33 B4
Swallow Field PR4 74 E3
Swallowfields
Blackburn BB1 101 E8
Cottam PR4 116 E5
Swallowfold [3] PR2 139 D1
Swallow Pk [6] BB11 127 C5
Swallow Wharf [8] LA1 218 E1
Swanage Ave FY4 110 B6
Swanage Rd BB10 148 C1
Swan Alley [2] L39 15 E5
Swan Cl L40 37 B2
Swan Delph L39 15 C2
Swan Dr FY5 175 F1
Swan Farm Cl BB3 81 F7
Swanfield Ct BB8 172 A5
Swanfield Terr BB8 172 A5
Swan La L39 5 F6
Swan Mdw BB7 189 D1
Swanpool La L39 15 C2
Swan Rd BL8 49 F2
Swansea St PR2 96 C8
Swansey La PR6 78 C1
Swan St
Blackburn BB2 101 E3
Darwen BB3 65 B6
Preston PR1 97 C8
Swan Yd [1] LA1 215 A7
Swarbrick Ave PR2 139 D1
Swarbrick Cl FY1 130 D7
Swarbrick Ct PR3 140 B7
Swarbrick St PR4 114 A4
Sweet Briar Cl
Clayton-le-M BB5 124 E4
Rochdale OL12 52 E2
Sweet Briar La OL12 52 E2
Sweetclough Dr BB12 126 F6
Swift Cl
Blackburn BB1 101 F5
Blackpool FY3 131 B3
Swift Gdns LA3 212 F5
Swiftís Fold WN8 8 D8
Swilkin La FY6 177 E6
SWILLBROOK 136 B2
Swill Brook La [1] PR1 97 C6
Swinburne Cl [2] BB5 104 E2
Swinburn Gr WN5 10 D1
Swinden Hall Rd BB9 170 E2
Swinden La BB8 171 A2
Swindon Ave [7] FY4 110 D8
Swindon St BB11 127 D5
Swinglehurst Cotts PR3 185 E3
Swinglehurst La PR3 185 E3
Swinless St BB10 128 B8
Swinshaw Cl BB4 106 A2
Swinside PR4 116 D4
SWISS CLOUGH 86 F1
Swiss St BB5 103 F6
Swithemby St BL6 32 A4
Sword Meanygate PR4 56 C6
Sycamore Ave
Blackpool FY4 110 F5
Burnley BB12 127 B7
Euxton PR7 60 D3
Garstang PR3 181 B8
Nelson BB9 149 A8
Sycamore Bglws BB7 231 C3
Sycamore Cl
Blackburn BB1 101 F8
Burnley BB12 127 C6
Elswick PR4 156 A1
Fulwood PR2 118 C6
Mawdesley L40 40 C2
Rishton BB1 103 B8
Sycamore Cres
Caton LA2 237 C3
Clayton-le-M BB5 125 A5
[1] Rawtenstall BB4 85 F1
Sycamore Ct
Chorley PR7 43 B5
Thornton-in-C BD23 197 B5
Sycamore Dr
Kirkham PR4 113 D4
Middleforth Green PR1 96 E3
[1] Skelmersdale WN8 17 E2
Sycamore Gdns
Foulridge BB8 194 D1
Heysham LA3 212 E6
Sycamore Gr
Accrington BB5 104 E3
Darwen BB3 82 B2
Formby L37 11 C1
Lancaster LA1 214 D8
Sycamore Ho PR7 42 F6
Sycamore Rd
Bilsborrow PR3 159 A5
Blackburn BB1 101 F8
Caton LA2 237 C3
Chorley PR6 61 D2
Fulwood PR2 118 E2
Sycamore Rise
Brierfield BB9 148 D5
Foulridge BB8 194 D1
Sycamore Trad Est FY4 110 F5
Sycamore Way BB18 196 A1
Sycamore Wlk [1] BL6 32 E1
Syd Brook La PR26, L40 40 E7
Sydenham Terr OL12 52 D3
Sydney Ave BB7 144 D5
Sydney St
Accrington BB5 104 C6
Accrington, Enfield BB5 125 A1
[1] Burnley BB11 127 F6
Darwen BB3 65 B7
Hoddlesden BB3 82 F1
Lytham St Anne's FY8 89 F6
Sydney Terr BB8 172 C3
SYKE 52 F4
Sykefield BB9 148 A5
Syke Hill [13] PR1 97 A7
Syke House La PR3 160 E4
Syke La OL12 52 F4
Sykelands Ave LA2 219 D7
Sykelands Gr LA2 219 D7
Syke Rd OL12 52 F4
Sykes Cl BB18 194 E8
SYKE SIDE 85 B1
Syke Side Dr BB5 125 E6
Syke St PR1 97 A7
Sylvancroft PR2 117 A5
Sylvan Dr BB11 127 B4
Sylvan Gr PR5 98 A2
Sylvan Pl LA3 212 E6
Sylvester St LA1 214 E7
Symonds Rd PR2 117 E3

T

Tabby Nook PR4 55 F2
Tabby's Nook
Newburgh WN8 27 A1
Skelmersdale WN8 18 A8
Taberner Cl WN6 29 F1
Tabley La PR4 116 E7
Tabor St BB12 127 D6
Tadema Gr BB11 127 F2
Tadlow Cl L37 11 C1
Tag Croft PR2 116 F5
Tag Farm Ct PR2 116 F5
TAGG WOOD 50 A5
Tagg Wood View BL0 50 A5
Tag La PR2 117 A4

Talaton Cl PR9 54 A5
Talbot Ave 4 BB5 124 F2
Talbot Cl
Clitheroe BB7 166 F7
Rawtenstall BB4 68 E8
Talbot Ct
11 Blackpool FY4 130 B1
3 Lytham St Anne's FY8 90 A8
Talbot Dr
Burnley BB10 148 F2
Euxton PR7 60 D2
Southport PR8 35 B6
Talbot Gr BL9 33 A6
Talbot Ho PR7 61 C2
Talbot Rd
Accrington BB5 104 A8
Blackpool FY1, FY3 130 C6
Leyland PR25 76 E2
Lytham St Anne's FY8 91 C4
Middleforth Green PR1 96 E5
Preston PR1 96 D7
Talbot Row 2 PR7 60 D1
Talbot Sq FY1 130 B5
Talbot St
Burnley BB11 128 B6
Burnley, Harle Syke BB10 148 F2
Chipping PR3 185 E3
Chorley PR6 61 E1
Colne BB8 171 D6
Fulwood PR2 117 D4
Rishton BB1 124 C1
Southport PR8 35 A6
Talbot Terr 1 FY8 91 B3
Tall Trees LA1 218 D4
Tamar Cl PR25 60 B7
Tamar St PR1 97 E8
Tamneys The WN8 17 F1
Tancaster WN8 17 E1
Tanfield Nook WN8 27 C2
Tanfields WN8 17 F1
Tanglewood PR2 118 B5
Tan Hill Dr LA1 218 D3
TANHOUSE 9 D8
Tanhouse 6 LA2 211 A4
Tan House Cl WN8 27 C3
Tanhouse La PR6 61 F6
Tan House La WN8 27 C2
Tanhouse Rd WN8 9 E7
TANNERS 50 B7
Tanners Croft 5 BL0 50 B6
Tannersmith La L40 40 F5
Tanners St BL0 50 B6
Tanner St 15 BB11 127 F6
Tanners Way FY8 90 D7
Tan Pit Cotts WN8 19 C4
Tanpits La LA6 240 B7
Tanpits Rd BB5 103 F6
Tansley Ave PR7 42 D1
Tansley Cl BL6 32 C2
Tansy La PR3 206 F4
TANTERTON 117 A6
Tanterton Hall Rd PR2 117 A6
Tanyard Cl PR7 42 D1
Tan Yard La PR3 140 C8
Tan Yd PR3 140 C8
Taper St BL0 50 B6
Tape St 2 BL0 50 B6
Tapestry St BB2 101 D1
Tarbert Cres BB1 102 D4
Tarbet St LA1 215 A7
TARDY GATE 77 B8
Tardy Gate Trad Ctr PR5 77 A8
TARLETON 57 A7
Tarleton Ave BB11 128 B4
Tarleton Com Prim Sch PR4 56 F8
Tarleton High Sch PR4 57 A7
Tarleton Holy Trinity CE Prim Sch PR4 57 A5
Tarleton Lo FY8 89 F4
Tarleton Mere Brow CE Prim Sch PR4 55 F2
Tarleton Rd PR9 36 A8
Tarleton St BB11 128 B4
TARLSCOUGH 38 D1
Tarlscough La L40 38 D1
Tarlswood WN8 17 F1
Tarnacre Hall Bsns Pk PR3 180 D1
Tarnacre Hall Mews PR3 180 D1
Tarnacre La PR3 180 E2
Tarnacre View PR3 181 C6
Tarn Ave BB5 124 F4
Tarnbeck Dr L40 40 D2
Tarnbrick Ave PR4 93 C7
TARNBROOK 233 B2
Tarnbrook Cl
Crag Bank LA5 223 C1
Hest Bank LA5 220 F2
Tarn Brook Cl BB5 125 F1
Tarnbrook Cotts PR3 201 E5
Tarnbrook Dr FY3 131 A7
Tarnbrook Rd
5 Heysham LA3 212 F8
2 Lancaster LA1 218 B2
Tarn Brow L39 15 C3
Tarn Cl PR1 95 F4
Tarn Cotts LA5 221 C6
Tarn Ct FY7 198 D1
Tarn Hows Cl 1 PR7 43 B5
Tarn La LA6 240 B6
Tarn Rd
Formby L37 11 D3
Thornton FY5 153 D7
Tarnside FY4 131 B1
Tarnside Rd WN5 10 E6
Tarnsyke Rd LA1 218 B2
Tarnwater La LA2 210 E7
Tarnway Ave FY5 153 D8
Tarradale PR4 94 F1
Tarragon Dr FY2 152 F4
Tarry Barn La BB7 167 A3
Tarvin Cl
Burnley BB10 148 F3
Southport PR9 54 D5
Taskers Croft BB7 144 F8
Tasker St 13 BB5 104 C6
TATHAM 238 D8
Tatham Ct FY7 198 C1
Tatham Fells CE Prim Sch LA2 239 C4
Tattersall Sq BB4 86 F3
Tattersall St
5 Blackburn BB2 101 E4
Haslingden BB4 85 B6
Oswaldtwistle BB5 103 D4
2 Padiham BB12 126 D8
Tatton St BB8 171 B3
Tauheedul-Islam Girls' High Sch BB1 101 E6
Taunton Rd BB2 101 B5
Taunton St
8 Blackpool FY4 130 D1
Preston PR1 118 D1
Tavistock Dr PR8 21 B6
Tavistock St BB9 170 F1
TAWD BRIDGE 9 B7
Tawd Rd WN8 9 C8
TAWD VALLEY PARK 18 A2
Taybank Ave FY4 110 D7
Taydale Cotts BB10 148 E3
Taylor Ave
Blackburn BB2 81 C7
Newchurch BB4 86 F2
Ormskirk L39 16 A5
Taylor Cl BB2 101 C3
Taylor Ct 1 BB4 85 A3
Taylor Gr LA4 217 F6
Taylor Holme Ind Est OL13 70 B8
Taylor St W 4 BB5 104 B6
Taylor's Bldgs BB6 143 D1
Taylors Cl FY6 153 C5
Taylor's Ind Est PR3 201 E5
Taylor's La
Fisher's Row PR3 201 D6
Holmes PR4 56 D3
Taylor's Meanygate PR4 56 A7
Taylors Pl 18 OL12 52 F1
Taylor St
Barnoldswick BB18 196 A2
Blackburn BB2 101 D3
Brierfield BB9 148 B6
Burnley BB10 128 A8
Bury BL9 33 A3
Chorley PR7 43 B5
Clitheroe BB7 166 F8
Darwen BB3 65 A8
Haslingden BB4 85 B6
Horwich BL6 32 B3
Preston PR1 96 D6
6 Rawtenstall BB4 86 A3
Rochdale OL12 52 F1
Skelmersdale WN8 17 C1
Whitworth OL12 52 D8
Taymouth Rd 5 FY4 111 A6
Tay St
Burnley BB11 127 D5
3 Preston PR1 96 D6
Taywood Cl FY6 153 F4
Taywood Rd FY5 176 A4
Teak St BL9 33 B2
Teal Cl
Blackburn BB1 101 D8
Leyland PR25 59 D7
Ormskirk L39 15 C2
Thornton FY5 176 A4
Teal Ct FY3 131 B6
Teal La FY8 90 E7
Teanlowe Ctr FY6 153 D3
Tears La WN8 26 F1
Teasel Wlk 6 LA3 217 B2
Tebay Ave
Cleveleys FY5 175 D4
Kirkham PR4 114 C5
Tebay Cl L31 5 F2
Tebay Ct LA1 218 C4
Tedder Ave
Burnley BB12 127 B6
Southport PR9 36 A7
Teenadore Ave 1 FY4 110 E7
Tees Ct FY7 198 D2
Teesdale 8 LA2 211 A4
Teesdale Ave FY2 130 D8
Tees St PR1 118 C2
Teil Gn PR2 118 E6
Telford St
Burnley BB12 127 C7
Horwich BL6 32 D2
Telletholme Ind Est L40 25 B3
Temperance St 8 PR6 43 E8
Temple Cl 2 BB1 102 B4
Temple Ct
11 Preston PR1 96 F7
Yealand Redmayne LA5 225 D5
Temple Dr BB1 102 B4
Templegate Cl WN6 29 F2
Templemartin 2 WN8 17 F2
Temple St
10 Blackpool FY1 130 B5
Burnley BB11 128 B5
Colne BB8 171 E6
Temple St *continued*
Nelson BB9 148 F8
Templeton Cl BB3 82 A2
Temple Way PR6 61 D3
Tenby 2 WN8 17 E2
Tenby Cl BB1 101 E7
Tenby Gr 6 OL12 52 C1
Tenby Rd 7 PR1 97 A6
Tenby St OL12 52 C1
Tennis St BB10 128 A8
Tennyson Ave
Chorley PR7 43 C6
Lytham St Anne's FY8 91 D4
Oswaldtwistle BB5 103 C4
Padiham BB12 126 E7
Read BB12 145 D2
Thornton FY5 176 A3
Warton PR4 92 D6
Tennyson Cl LA5 221 A5
Tennyson Dr
Blackpool FY2 152 F6
Longshaw WN5 10 D1
Ormskirk L39 15 D6
Tennyson Mill Ct PR1 118 D1
Tennyson Pl
Bamber Bridge PR5 97 D2
Great Harwood BB6 124 B4
Tennyson Rd
Blackpool FY3 130 F7
Colne BB8 171 D5
Fleetwood FY7 199 A4
Preston PR1 118 D1
Tennyson St
Burnley BB11 127 D5
Burnley, Harle Syke BB10 148 F3
6 Hapton BB12 126 C4
Ten Row LA2 209 E5
Tensing Ave FY2 152 D5
Tensing Rd L31 5 D1
Tenterfield St
23 Preston PR1 96 F8
6 Rawtenstall BB4 69 F8
Tenterheads 8 BB4 69 F7
Terance Rd 2 FY4 110 E8
Tern Gr LA3 212 F5
Terrace Row BB7 144 C4
Terrace St PR1 118 C1
Terrace The 8 LA2 239 B8
Terra Cotta Bldgs BB4 107 A1
Terry St BB9 171 A2
Tetbury Cl 6 BB2 80 E8
Teven St 5 PR5 97 E1
Teversham WN8 17 F2
Teviot 5 WN8 17 E2
Teviot Ave FY7 198 D3
TEWITFIELD 240 A4
Tewkesbury 4 WN8 17 E2
Tewkesbury Ave FY4 110 D5
Tewkesbury Cl BB5 104 E3
Tewkesbury Dr FY8 91 D5
Tewkesbury St BB2 101 B1
Thames Ave BB10 148 C3
Thames Dr WN5 10 F7
Thames Ho 8 PR1 97 D8
Thames Prim Sch FY4 110 B7
Thames Rd FY4 110 B7
Thames St PR4 114 F2
Thane Row BB11 107 D7
Thanet WN8 17 F2
Thanet Lee Cl BB10 128 E1
Thealby Cl WN8 17 E2
Theatre St PR1 96 F7
THE GREAVES 214 F6
Thelma St BL0 50 B6
Thermdale Cl 3 PR3 181 B7
Thetis Rd LA1 214 C8
Thickrash Brow LA2 239 D7
Third Ave
Blackpool FY4 110 C7
Bury BL9 33 D4
Preesall Park FY6 200 C1
Thirlmere Ave
Burnley BB10 148 A2
Carleton FY6 153 C4
Colne BB8 171 F6
Fleetwood FY7 198 C1
Formby L37 12 A2
Haslingden BB4 68 C8
Horwich BL6 32 C2
1 Orrell WN5 10 F7
Padiham BB12 146 C2
Up Holland WN8 10 B7
Thirlmere Cl
2 Accrington BB5 125 D1
Adlington PR6 31 B8
6 Blackburn BB1 101 F6
Knott End-on-S FY6 199 F6
Longton PR4 75 B8
Maghull L31 5 E2
Thirlmere Ct LA1 218 F1
Thirlmere Dr
Darwen BB3 82 C2
Longridge PR3 139 F5
Morecambe LA4 217 A4
Southport PR8 21 B3
Withnell Fold PR6 79 D2
Thirlmere Gr LA4 217 B4
Thirlmere Rd
Blackpool FY4 110 C7
Blackrod BL6 31 C3
Burnley BB10 128 E5
Chorley PR7 43 B6
Hightown L38 3 A4
Lancaster LA1 218 F2
Preston PR1 118 F1
Thirlmere Way BB4 106 A1
Thirsk WN8 17 E2
Thirsk Ave FY8 90 B7
Thirsk Gr FY1 130 D2
Thirsk Rd LA1 215 B4
Thistle Break LA3 213 A7
Thistle Cl
Chorley PR6 43 E8
Cleveleys FY5 175 F5
Hesketh Bank PR4 73 E4
Thistlecroft PR2 117 A5
Thistle Ct L40 25 F6
Thistlemount Ave BB4 86 F1
Thistle St 15 OL13 87 F2
THISTLETON 133 D8
Thistleton Mews 3 PR9 35 C8
Thistleton Rd
Elswick PR4 155 C1
Preston PR2 95 E8
Thomas Gr LA4 217 B5
Thomason Fold BL7 48 D6
Thomas St
Blackburn BB2 101 D4
Brierfield BB9 148 A5
Burnley BB11 128 A5
Colne BB8 171 C4
7 Haslingden BB4 85 A3
6 Lytham St Anne's FY8 91 B3
Nelson BB9 148 E7
7 Oswaldtwistle BB5 103 D3
4 Preston PR1 97 B7
Todmorden OL14 109 C1
Whitworth OL12 71 D2
Thomas's Weind PR3 181 C7
Thompson Ave L39 16 B5
Thompson Dr BL9 33 C3
Thompson St
Blackburn BB2 101 C4
Darwen BB3 65 B7
Horwich BL6 32 A3
8 Kirkham PR4 113 F6
Padiham BB12 126 D7
Preston PR1 118 D1
Thompson Street Ind Est BB2 101 C4
Thonock Rd LA4 217 D3
Thorburn Dr OL12 52 B7
Thornbank FY3 131 B7
Thorn Bank OL13 88 A2
Thornbank Dr PR3 181 D2
Thornbeck Ave L38 2 F3
Thornber 1 WN8 17 F2
Thornber Ct BB10 148 C1
Thornber Gr FY1 130 D3
Thornber St BB2 101 C3
Thornbridge Ave L40 25 E3
Thornbury WN8 17 F2
Thornby 3 WN8 17 F2
Thorncliffe Dr BB3 65 D8
Thorn Cres 7 OL13 88 A2
Thorncross 7 FY5 152 F8
Thorndale 4 WN8 17 F2
Thorn Dr OL13 88 A2
Thorne St BB9 171 A2
Thorneybank Ind Est BB11 126 C2
Thorney Bank St 7 BB11 127 F5
Thorneycroft Cl FY6 153 B5
THORNEY HOLME 169 E5
Thorneyholme RC Prim Sch BB7 228 C5
Thorneyholme Rd BB5 104 C8
Thorneyholme Sq BB12 169 E5
Thorneylea
Blackburn BB2 81 D7
Whitworth OL12 71 D1
Thornfield
Bretherton PR26 57 F7
Lancaster LA1 214 F5
Much Hoole PR4 74 E3
Thornfield Ave
Fulwood PR2 118 F3
Longridge PR3 140 A8
Newchurch BB4 86 E1
8 Rawtenstall BB4 69 F8
Thornton FY5 153 D8
Thornfield Cvn Pk FY3 131 D5
Thorngate PR1 96 B4
Thorngate Cl PR1 96 B4
Thorn Gdns OL13 88 A2
Thorn Gr
Blackpool FY1 130 E2
Colne BB8 171 F6
Thornham Ct FY3 130 E5
Thornhill L39 6 B8
Thornhill Ave
Knott End-on-S FY6 200 A5
Rishton BB1 103 A8
Thornhill Cl
Blackpool FY4 110 F5
Ormskirk L39 6 B8
Thorn Hill Cl BB1 102 A5
Thornhill Rd
Chorley PR6 61 E2
Leyland PR25 59 D8
Ramsbottom BL0 50 A1
Thornhill St BB12 127 A6
Thorn La PR3 140 B2
Thornlea Dr OL12 52 B2
Thornleigh Cl 10 FY5 176 A2
Thornleigh Dr LA6 240 C7
Thornley Ave BB1 102 C6
Thornley Pl PR2 119 A3
Thornley Rd PR2 119 A3
Thornpark Dr 3 PR2 116 D1
Thorns Ave LA2 220 D1
Thorn St
Bacup OL13 88 A2
Burnley BB10 128 A8
Clitheroe BB7 166 D8
Great Harwood BB6 124 D6
Preston PR1 118 C1
Ramsbottom BL0 50 C3
Rawtenstall BB4 85 F5
Sabden BB7 146 A7
Thorns The L31 5 B2
Thornthwaite Rd PR4 116 D4
THORNTON 176 C3
Thornton WN8 17 F2
Thornton Ave
Fulwood PR2 117 B4
Lytham St Anne's FY8 90 B8
Morecambe LA4 217 C6
Thornton Cl
Accrington BB5 104 A8
Blackburn BB2 81 F8
Rufford L40 39 C4
Thornton Cleveleys Baines Endowed Prim Sch FY5 176 C1
Thornton Cleveleys Manor Beach Prim Sch FY5 175 D3
Thornton Cleveleys Red Marsh Sch FY5 176 B3
Thornton Cleveleys Royles Brook Prim Sch FY5 176 A2
Thornton Cres
Burnley BB10 128 E5
2 Morecambe LA4 217 C5
Thornton Ctr FY5 176 C1
Thornton Dr
Coupe Green PR5 98 D4
Leyland PR26 76 E4
Thornton Gate FY5 175 C4
Thornton Gr 1 LA4 217 C5
Thornton Hall Mews FY5 153 E7
Thornton Hts BD23 197 A5
THORNTON-IN-CRAVEN 197 A6
Thornton in Craven Com Prim Sch BD23 197 B6
THORNTON IN LONSDALE 242 F4
Thornton La
Ingleton LA6 242 F5
Morecambe LA4 217 C6
Thornton Manor Ct BD23 197 A5
Thornton Pl FY5 176 A4
Thornton Prim Sch FY5 176 B3
Thornton Rd
Burnley BB10 128 E5
Morecambe LA4 217 C6
Southport PR9 35 F7
Thorntrees Ave
Newsham PR3 137 B5
Preston PR2 116 D1
Thorn View BL9 33 C3
Thornway Ave FY5 153 D8
Thornwood WN8 17 F2
Thornwood Cl
5 Blackburn BB1 122 E1
Lytham St Anne's FY8 90 E4
Thoroughfare The LA5 223 D5
Thoroughgood Cl L40 25 D2
Thorough Way PR3 203 E7
Thorpe WN8 17 F2
Thorpe Ave LA4 217 F4
Thorpe Cl PR1 117 F1
THORPE GREEN 78 E4
Thorpe St BL0 50 B5
Thorvald Gdns LA4 217 F4
Thrang Brow La LA5 225 C6
Threagill La LA5 223 F5
Three Brooks Way BB5 103 D2
Threefields PR2 117 A5
Three Lane Ends PR6 62 C4
Three Nooks PR5 78 C5
Three Oaks Cl L40 26 B2
Three Point Bsns Pk BB4 85 A2
Three Pools PR9 54 C3
Three Rivers Pk BB7 189 D7
Three Tuns La L37 11 F3
Three Turns PR3 142 A8
Threlfall PR7 60 F2
Threlfall Rd FY1 130 D1
Threlfall's La PR9 53 F2
Threlfall St 1 PR2 117 C1
Threshers Ct PR3 207 C2
Threshfield Ave LA3 212 F8
Thrimby Ct LA4 217 B4
Thrimby Pl LA4 217 B4
Thropps La PR4 75 D6
Throstle Cl BB12 128 A7
Throstle Gr LA2 218 D8
Throstle Mill OL13 87 F2
Throstle Nest La PR3 203 C4
Throstle Nest Mill Bsns Ctr BB9 170 E1
Throstle St
Blackburn BB2 101 C4
7 Nelson BB9 170 E1
Throstle Way 8 FY5 175 F1
Throstle Wlk LA2 218 D8
Throup Pl BB9 170 E2
Thrum Fold OL12 52 D3

Thrum Hall La
Rochdale, Lower Healey OL12 . . . 52 E3
Rochdale OL12 . . . 52 D3
Thrush Dr BL9 . . . 33 B4
Thrushgill Dr LA2 . . . 219 D7
Thrush St OL12 . . . 52 C1
Thurcroft Dr WN8 . . . 17 E2
Thurland Ct 2 LA4 . . . 217 A3
Thurland Mill Cotts LA6 . . . 241 D3
Thurnham Glasson Christ Church CE Prim Sch LA2 . . . 209 E4
Thurnham Mews 7 LA1 . . . 214 F7
Thurnham Rd PR2 . . . 95 E8
Thurnham St LA1 . . . 214 F7
Thursby Ave FY4 . . . 110 D6
Thursby Cl PR8 . . . 21 B3
Thursby Pl 13 BB9 . . . 170 F2
Thursby Rd
Burnley BB10 . . . 148 C1
Nelson BB9 . . . 170 F2
Thursby Sq BB10 . . . 128 A8
THURSDEN . . . 149 D2
Thursden Ave BB10 . . . 148 F3
Thursden Pl BB9 . . . 171 B1
Thursfield Ave FY4 . . . 110 E8
Thursfield Rd BB10 . . . 128 B5
Thursford Gr BL6 . . . 31 D1
Thursgill Ave 3 LA4 . . . 217 C3
Thurston WN8 . . . 17 E2
Thurston Rd PR25 . . . 77 A1
Thurston St BB11 . . . 128 B6
Thurtell Cotts LA2 . . . 237 B3
Thwaite Brow La LA5 . . . 221 B6
Thwaite La LA2 . . . 239 C5
Thwaites Ave BB2 . . . 121 E2
Thwaites Cl BB1 . . . 102 D2
Thwaites Rd BB5 . . . 103 C4
Thwaites St BB5 . . . 103 C3
Thyme Cl FY2 . . . 152 F3
Tiber Ave BB11 . . . 127 C4
Tiber St PR1 . . . 97 B7
Tibicar Dr E LA3 . . . 216 D1
Tibicar Dr W LA3 . . . 216 D1
Tib St 18 BL0 . . . 50 B5
Tiger The PR25 . . . 76 D2
Tilbury Gr WN6 . . . 19 D7
Tilcroft WN8 . . . 17 E2
Timber Brook PR7 . . . 61 A2
Timberhurst BL9 . . . 33 D2
Timber St
Accrington BB5 . . . 104 C5
Bacup OL13 . . . 87 F1
Brierfield BB9 . . . 148 B6
Timbrills Ave BB7 . . . 145 F8
Timms Cl L37 . . . 11 F5
Timms La L37 . . . 11 F5
Tincklers La PR7 . . . 41 A6
Tinedale View BB12 . . . 146 D1
Tinker Brook Cl BB5 . . . 103 D2
Tinkerfield PR2 . . . 117 E7
Tinker's La LA2 . . . 226 B7
Tinklers La BB7 . . . 229 E7
Tinline St BL9 . . . 33 A2
Tinniswood PR2 . . . 117 B1
Tinsley Ave PR8 . . . 35 E3
Tinsley's La PR8 . . . 36 A1
Tintagel WN8 . . . 17 E2
Tintagell Cl BB2 . . . 80 C7
Tintern Ave
Chorley PR7 . . . 43 D5
Rochdale OL12 . . . 52 E2
Tintern Cl
Accrington BB5 . . . 104 E2
Read BB12 . . . 145 D1
Tintern Cres BB1 . . . 102 B8
Tintern Dr L37 . . . 12 B2
Tippet Cl BB2 . . . 102 A1
Titan Way PR26 . . . 76 B2
Tithebarn Gate FY6 . . . 153 D4
Tithebarn Hill LA2 . . . 209 E5
Tithe Barn La
Knowley PR6 . . . 62 A4
Runshaw Moor PR25, PR7 . . . 59 F5
Scorton PR3 . . . 204 E5
Tithebarn Pl FY6 . . . 153 D4
Tithebarn Rd PR8 . . . 35 E7
Tithebarn St
Poulton-le-F FY6 . . . 153 D4
Preston PR1 . . . 97 A8
Up Holland WN8 . . . 10 B7
Tittington Brow BB7 . . . 229 C2
Tiverton Ave WN8 . . . 17 E2
Tiverton Cl PR2 . . . 117 F8
Tiverton Dr
Blackburn BB2 . . . 81 C8
Burnley BB10 . . . 148 F3
TOCKHOLES . . . 81 A2
Tockholes Rd
Darwen BB3 . . . 81 E2
Tockholes BB3 . . . 81 A3
Todber Cvn Pk BB7 . . . 231 C1
Todd Carr Rd BB4 . . . 86 F1
Todd Hall Rd BB4 . . . 84 F4
Todd La N PR5 . . . 97 C2
Todd La S PR5 . . . 77 C8
Todd's La PR9 . . . 55 A6
Tod Holes La BD23 . . . 236 E4
Todmorden Old Rd OL13 . . . 88 B5
Todmorden Rd
Bacup OL13 . . . 88 B4
Todmorden Rd *continued*
Burnley BB11 . . . 128 B3
Cockden BB10 . . . 149 B1
Lytham St Anne's FY8 . . . 89 C8
Toll Bar Bsns Pk 13 OL13 . . . 70 D8
Toll Bar Cres LA1 . . . 214 F3
Toll Bar Ct LA6 . . . 240 C7
Tollgate PR1 . . . 96 E4
Tollgate Cres L40 . . . 25 C2
Tollgate Rd L40 . . . 25 B3
Tolsey Dr PR4 . . . 95 D2
Tom Benson Way PR2, PR4 . . . 116 F4
Tom La BB4 . . . 86 F2
Tomlinson Rd
Heysham LA3 . . . 212 F6
Leyland PR25 . . . 76 F2
Preston PR2 . . . 117 C2
Tomlinson St BL6 . . . 32 B3
TONACLIFFE . . . 52 C6
Tonacliffe Prim Sch OL12 . . . 52 C6
Tonacliffe Rd OL12 . . . 52 C6
Tonacliffe Terr OL12 . . . 52 C7
Tonacliffe Way OL12 . . . 52 C6
Tongbarn WN8 . . . 17 E2
TONG END . . . 71 C2
Tong End OL12 . . . 71 C2
Tong La
Bacup OL13 . . . 88 B2
Britannia OL13 . . . 71 C8
Whitworth OL12 . . . 71 D1
Tongues La FY6 . . . 200 C6
TONTINE . . . 10 D5
Tontine WN5 . . . 10 C5
Tontine Rd WN5, WN8 . . . 10 C6
Tontine St BB1 . . . 101 E5
Toogood La WN6 . . . 28 D6
Tootell St PR7 . . . 43 B6
Tootle La L40 . . . 39 A3
Tootle Rd PR3 . . . 140 B8
Top Acre PR4 . . . 95 C1
Top Acre Rd WN8 . . . 9 C7
Topaz St BB1 . . . 122 F2
Topaz Way PR6 . . . 43 E6
Top Barn La BB4 . . . 86 E1
Topiary Gdns PR3 . . . 181 D4
Top Locks L40 . . . 26 A4
Top of Fawna Rd PR3 . . . 163 D1
Top Of Heap OL10 . . . 33 F2
TOP OF RAMSGREAVE . . . 122 C3
Top of Wallsuches BL6 . . . 32 F4
Top o' th' Croft BB2 . . . 81 D8
TOP O' TH' LANE . . . 78 F3
TOPPING FOLD . . . 33 D3
Topping Fold Rd BL9 . . . 33 C3
Topping St
Blackpool FY1 . . . 130 B5
Bury BL9 . . . 33 A3
Toppings The PR3 . . . 181 C6
Top Row BB7 . . . 145 F8
Tor Ave BL8 . . . 49 F2
Torcross Cl PR9 . . . 54 A5
Tor End Rd BB4 . . . 67 F6
Tor Hey Mews BL8 . . . 49 F2
Tormore Cl PR6 . . . 62 A3
Toronto Ave
Blackpool FY2 . . . 152 E3
Fleetwood FY7 . . . 198 E2
Toronto Rd BB2 . . . 101 C8
Torquay Ave
Blackpool FY3 . . . 131 A2
Burnley BB10 . . . 148 D2
Torra Barn Cl BL7 . . . 47 E3
Torrentum Ct FY5 . . . 176 C1
Torridon Cl BB2 . . . 100 F1
TORRISHOLME . . . 218 A4
Torrisholme Com Prim Sch LA4 . . . 217 F5
Torrisholme Rd LA1 . . . 218 B3
Torrisholme Sq 8 LA4 . . . 217 F4
Torside Gr FY6 . . . 153 B3
Torsway Ave FY3 . . . 130 F6
Torver Cl BB12 . . . 127 B8
Tor View
Haslingden BB4 . . . 85 C1
Rawtenstall BB4 . . . 86 A1
Tor View Rd BB4 . . . 85 C1
Tor View Sch BB4 . . . 68 D8
TOSSIDE . . . 236 C2
Totnes Cl FY6 . . . 153 C5
Totnes Dr PR9 . . . 54 A5
Tottenham Rd BB3 . . . 81 F6
Tottington Rd BL7, BL8 . . . 48 F2
Tottleworth BB6 . . . 124 C3
Tottleworth Rd BB1 . . . 124 C2
Toulmin Cl PR3 . . . 181 D2
Tourer Terr L40 . . . 24 B4
Towbreck Gdns FY6 . . . 131 E8
Tower Ave
Lancaster LA1 . . . 211 B7
Ramsbottom BL0 . . . 50 A5
Tower Bldgs 11 PR9 . . . 35 C8
Tower Cl FY5 . . . 176 A4
Tower Cotts 3 LA3 . . . 212 E7
Tower Ct
Chapeltown BL7 . . . 48 C4
Lancaster LA1 . . . 214 F7
Tower Dene Sch PR9 . . . 53 F2
Tower End L37 . . . 11 C5
Tower Gn PR2 . . . 117 F7
Tower Hill
Clitheroe BB7 . . . 189 F1
Ormskirk L39 . . . 16 A5
Tower Hill Rd WN8 . . . 10 B6
Tower La PR2 . . . 117 F7
Tower Nook WN8 . . . 10 A5
Tower Rd
Blackburn BB2 . . . 100 E2
Darwen BB3 . . . 65 B8
Towers Ave L31 . . . 5 C2
Towers Ct BB2 . . . 101 D3
Tower St
13 Bacup OL13 . . . 87 F2
Blackpool FY1 . . . 130 B5
Chapeltown BL7 . . . 48 C4
Oswaldtwistle BB5 . . . 103 C5
Todmorden OL14 . . . 109 A1
Tower View
Belthorn BB1 . . . 83 A5
Blackpool FY2 . . . 152 D2
Blackrod BL6 . . . 31 C3
Darwen BB3 . . . 82 C1
Higher Penwortham PR1 . . . 96 C7
TOWN BENT . . . 103 D2
Town Brook Ho 5 PR1 . . . 117 E1
Town Brow PR25 . . . 77 F2
TOWN CENTRE . . . 18 C1
Towneley Ave BB5 . . . 125 F2
Towneley Cl LA1 . . . 214 D7
Towneley Hall (Art Gall & Mus)* BB11 . . . 128 C2
Towneley High Sch BB11 . . . 128 C4
Towneley Ho PR3 . . . 140 A7
Towneley Par PR3 . . . 140 A7
Towneley Rd PR3 . . . 140 A7
Towneley Rd W PR3 . . . 140 A7
Towneley St BB10 . . . 148 B1
TOWN END . . . 155 C8
Town End
Bolton-le-S LA5 . . . 221 A3
Kirkham PR4 . . . 114 A5
Slaidburn BB7 . . . 229 C7
3 Thornton FY5 . . . 176 A2
Town End Cl L39 . . . 15 D4
Town End Fold LA5 . . . 223 C5
Townfield Ave BB10 . . . 128 F6
Townfield Cl PR4 . . . 74 F7
Townfield La LA2 . . . 218 C7
Townfields 1 BB11 . . . 128 B5
Towngate
Eccleston PR7 . . . 41 B7
Foulridge BB8 . . . 194 D1
Leyland PR25 . . . 60 A8
Leyland PR25 . . . 77 A1
Leyland, Wade Hall PR25 . . . 59 F7
Town Gate BB6 . . . 124 C5
Towngate Works L40 . . . 40 E2
TOWN GREEN . . . 6 D7
Town Green Ct L39 . . . 6 C8
Town Green Gdns L39 . . . 6 C8
Town Green La L39 . . . 6 C8
Town Green Sta L39 . . . 6 C8
Town Hall Sq 8 BB6 . . . 124 C5
Town Hall St
16 Blackburn BB2 . . . 101 E5
9 Great Harwood BB6 . . . 124 C5
TOWN HEAD . . . 196 A1
Town Head BB18 . . . 196 A1
Town Hill Bank BB12 . . . 146 D1
Town House Rd BB9 . . . 149 B8
Town La
Coppull PR7 . . . 42 C1
Heskin Green PR7 . . . 41 C2
Much Hoole PR4 . . . 74 D1
Southport PR8 . . . 35 E3
Whittle-le-W PR6 . . . 61 D6
Town Lane (Kew) PR8 . . . 35 E3
Townlea Cl PR1 . . . 96 A3
Townley Ave FY4 . . . 110 E8
Townley La PR1 . . . 95 D4
Townley St
Brierfield BB9 . . . 148 B5
Burnley, Harle Syke BB10 . . . 148 F3
Chorley PR6 . . . 43 D7
Colne BB8 . . . 171 E6
Morecambe LA4 . . . 217 B6
Town Rd PR26 . . . 58 B2
TOWNSEND FOLD . . . 68 E8
Townsend St
Haslingden BB4 . . . 85 A3
Rawtenstall BB4 . . . 69 F8
Townsfield LA5 . . . 224 C4
Townshill Wlk PR4 . . . 114 A6
Townside Gate PR3 . . . 156 B5
Townsley St BB9 . . . 148 E6
TOWN'S MOOR . . . 101 E3
Townsmoor Ret Pk 7 BB2 . . . 101 E3
Townsway PR5 . . . 77 C8
Town View BB1 . . . 101 F4
Town Wlk BB1 . . . 101 F4
Towpath Wlk 2 LA5 . . . 223 D1
Tow Scar Rd LA6 . . . 242 F6
Toxhead Cl BL6 . . . 32 A3
Tracks La WN5 . . . 10 D3
Trafalgar Cl PR2 . . . 117 D3
Trafalgar Ct PR8 . . . 34 F3
Trafalgar Ho BB11 . . . 127 E6
Trafalgar Mall 3 BB9 . . . 148 E8
Trafalgar Rd
Blackpool FY1 . . . 130 B2
Lancaster LA1 . . . 215 A6
Southport PR8 . . . 34 E3
Trafalgar St
Burnley BB11 . . . 127 F5
Chorley PR6 . . . 61 C1
Lytham St Anne's FY8 . . . 89 F7
Trafford Gdns BB7 . . . 166 D1
Trafford St PR1 . . . 117 E2
Tramway La PR5 . . . 78 B6
Tranmere Ave LA3 . . . 216 D1
Tranmere Cres LA3 . . . 216 D1
Tranmere Rd FY4 . . . 130 E1
Tranmoor PR4 . . . 74 F6
Trans Brittania Enterprise Est BB11 . . . 127 B3
Trap Hill L37 . . . 11 C2
Trapp La BB12 . . . 145 F2
Trash La
Rimington BB7 . . . 231 B1
Tockholes BB3 . . . 81 B2
Travellers Ct BB7 . . . 231 C3
Travers Lo 8 PR2 . . . 118 F4
Travers Pl PR2 . . . 96 C8
Travers St BL6 . . . 32 D1
Travis St BB10 . . . 128 A8
TRAWDEN . . . 172 C2
Trawden Cl BB5 . . . 104 C4
Trawden Cres PR2 . . . 118 E4
Trawden Forest Prim Sch BB8 . . . 172 C2
Trawden Rd BB8 . . . 172 B4
Traylen Way OL12 . . . 52 A1
TREALES . . . 114 D6
Treales CE Prim Sch PR4 . . . 134 E2
Treales Rd PR4 . . . 115 B6
Trecastle Rd L33 . . . 1 A4
Tredgold St BL6 . . . 32 C2
Treen Cl PR9 . . . 54 B6
Treesdale Cl PR8 . . . 34 F4
Treetops Ave BL0 . . . 50 A3
Treetop Villas PR9 . . . 53 F4
Trefoil Cl FY5 . . . 176 A5
Tremellen St BB5 . . . 104 A6
Trengrove St 7 OL12 . . . 52 C1
Trent Ave L31 . . . 5 F2
Trent Cl
Burscough Bridge L40 . . . 25 F5
Morecambe LA3 . . . 217 F2
Trent Rd
Blackpool FY4 . . . 110 B7
Nelson BB9 . . . 149 A8
Trent St
Longridge PR3 . . . 139 F7
Lytham St Anne's FY8 . . . 91 D3
Tresco Cl BB2 . . . 101 B1
Tretower Way FY5 . . . 176 D2
Trevarrick Ct BL6 . . . 32 E2
Trevelyan Dr WN5 . . . 10 D1
Trevor Cl BB1 . . . 101 F7
Trevore Dr WN1 . . . 30 B1
Trevor Rd
Burscough L40 . . . 25 E4
Southport PR8 . . . 21 C4
Triangle The
Accrington, Hillock Vale BB5 . . . 104 E8
Fulwood PR2 . . . 117 E4
Trident Pk BB1 . . . 102 C8
Trident Way BB1 . . . 102 C8
Trigge Ho PR7 . . . 61 C2
Trigg La PR6 . . . 62 D5
Trillium Way BB3 . . . 82 A7
Trinity CE Sch WN8 . . . 17 F1
Trinity Cl
Brierfield BB9 . . . 148 C5
Freckleton PR4 . . . 93 B7
Padiham BB12 . . . 126 D6
Trinity Ct 3 BB1 . . . 101 F6
Trinity Fold 20 PR1 . . . 96 F8
Trinity Gdns
Southport PR8 . . . 35 A6
Thornton FY5 . . . 176 A3
Trinity Gn BL0 . . . 50 B2
Trinity Mews PR9 . . . 35 C7
Trinity Pl 24 PR1 . . . 96 F8
Trinity Rd PR7 . . . 43 B7
Trinity & St Michael's CE/ Meth Prim Sch PR26 . . . 58 C2
Trinity St Peter's CE Prim Sch L37 . . . 12 A5
Trinity St
15 Bacup OL13 . . . 70 C8
Blackburn BB1 . . . 101 F6
Oswaldtwistle BB5 . . . 103 D3
Trinity Student Village PR1 . . . 96 F8
Trinity Twrs 6 BB11 . . . 127 E6
Trinity Wlks PR4 . . . 57 A5
Trinket La LA2 . . . 238 E6
Tristan Ave PR4 . . . 75 A5
Troon Ave
Blackburn BB1 . . . 102 C3
Thornton FY5 . . . 153 D8
Troon Cl PR7 . . . 60 D4
Troon Ct PR1 . . . 96 A6
TROUGH GATE . . . 71 D8
Trough of Bowland* BB7 . . . 227 F7
Trough Rd BB7 . . . 228 B5
Troughton Cres 1 FY4 . . . 110 E8
Trout Beck BB5 . . . 124 F4
Troutbeck Ave
Fleetwood FY7 . . . 198 D2
Forton PR3 . . . 207 B3
Maghull L31 . . . 5 E2
Troutbeck Cl
Burnley BB12 . . . 127 B8
Hawkshaw BL8 . . . 49 B2
Troutbeck Cres FY4 . . . 111 D8
Troutbeck Dr BL0 . . . 50 C7
Troutbeck Pl PR2 . . . 118 E5
Troutbeck Rd
Chorley PR7 . . . 43 B5
Lancaster LA1 . . . 218 E1
Troutbeck Rd *continued*
Lytham St Anne's FY8 . . . 110 D1
Trout St
8 Burnley BB10 . . . 128 A8
Preston PR1 . . . 97 C7
Trower St PR1 . . . 97 B6
Troy St BB1 . . . 101 F7
Trumacar Com Prim Sch LA3 . . . 212 E5
Trumacar La LA3 . . . 212 E5
Trumacar Terr LA3 . . . 212 E5
Truman Ave LA1 . . . 214 C7
Trumley Ct LA3 . . . 217 A2
Trundle Pie La L39 . . . 14 C6
TRUNNAH . . . 176 B3
Trunnah Gdns FY5 . . . 176 B3
Trunnah Rd FY5 . . . 176 B3
Truro Ave PR9 . . . 54 B5
Truro Pl 8 PR1 . . . 118 D1
Truro St 7 FY4 . . . 130 D1
Truscott Rd L40 . . . 25 D4
Tucker Hill BB7 . . . 189 E1
Tucker's Hill Brow WN2 . . . 31 B1
Tudor Ave
Preston, Lea PR2 . . . 116 D1
Preston PR1 . . . 118 F1
Tudor Cl
Carleton FY6 . . . 153 A4
1 Cleveleys FY5 . . . 175 F1
Darwen BB3 . . . 82 A2
Langho BB6 . . . 143 D1
Preston PR2 . . . 116 D1
Tudor Croft PR5 . . . 77 C7
Tudor Ct
Lytham St Anne's FY8 . . . 89 D8
Ormskirk L39 . . . 15 F6
Tudor Dr PR4 . . . 114 B2
Tudor Gate FY8 . . . 90 B8
Tudor Gdns L38 . . . 2 F4
Tudor Gr 2 LA4 . . . 217 E6
Tudor Mans PR8 . . . 34 F6
Tudor Pl FY4 . . . 110 B6
Tudor Rd
Bamber Bridge PR1 . . . 97 A2
Lytham St Anne's FY8 . . . 89 D8
Southport PR8 . . . 21 B6
Tuer St PR25 . . . 76 F2
Tulip Gr OL12 . . . 52 E3
Tulketh Ave PR2 . . . 117 B1
Tulketh Brow PR2 . . . 117 C1
Tulketh Com Sports Coll PR2 . . . 117 B4
Tulketh Cres PR2 . . . 117 C1
Tulketh Rd PR2 . . . 117 B1
Tulketh St PR8 . . . 35 B7
Tunbridge Pl 7 PR1 . . . 118 D1
Tunbridge St 4 PR1 . . . 118 D1
Tunbrook Ave PR2 . . . 139 E1
Tunley Holme PR5 . . . 78 C5
Tunley La WN6 . . . 28 E5
Tunley Moss WN6 . . . 28 E4
Tunnel St
Burnley BB12 . . . 127 D6
5 Darwen BB3 . . . 65 C7
TUNSTALL . . . 241 E4
Tunstall Dr BB5 . . . 125 B1
Tunstall Ho 10 LA1 . . . 215 A3
Tunstall St LA4 . . . 217 A5
Tunstead Ave BB12 . . . 125 E8
Tunstead Cres OL13 . . . 87 C1
Tunstead La BB4, OL13 . . . 87 B1
Tunstead Mill Terr 3 OL13 . . . 70 B8
Tunstead Rd OL13 . . . 70 C8
Tunstill Fold BB12 . . . 169 F1
Tunstill St BB10 . . . 148 B1
Turbary Rd LA6 . . . 242 E7
Turbary The PR2 . . . 117 C3
Turflands PR26 . . . 58 B1
Turf Mdw BB4 . . . 106 A2
Turf Moor Football Gd (Burnley FC) BB10 . . . 128 B6
Turf St BB11 . . . 128 B6
Turkey Red Ind Est BB5 . . . 84 F8
Turkey St
Accrington BB5 . . . 104 D7
Out Rawcliffe PR3 . . . 178 A1
Turks Head Yd 22 PR1 . . . 97 A7
TURN . . . 69 A1
Turnacre L37 . . . 12 B6
Turnberry WN8 . . . 17 D2
Turnberry Ave FY5 . . . 153 D8
Turnberry Cl
Kirkham PR4 . . . 114 A4
Morecambe LA4 . . . 217 D6
Turnberry Way PR9 . . . 54 D5
Turnbridge Rd L31 . . . 5 C3
Turnbury Cl PR7 . . . 60 D4
Turncroft Rd BB3 . . . 65 B8
Turner Ave PR5 . . . 77 A7
Turner Fold BB12 . . . 145 D3
Turnerford Cl 4 BL7 . . . 47 E1
TURNER GREEN . . . 120 C2
Turner's Pl OL12 . . . 52 E3
Turner Rd BB9 . . . 148 B8
Turner St
3 Bacup OL13 . . . 70 C8
4 Barnoldswick BB18 . . . 196 C2
Clitheroe BB7 . . . 166 E7
3 Preston PR1 . . . 118 A1
Rochdale OL12 . . . 52 E1
Turney Crook Mews 9 BB8 . . . 171 D5
Turnfield PR2 . . . 116 F6
Turning La PR8 . . . 36 A1
Turn La BB3 . . . 64 F8
Turnpike BB4 . . . 86 F1
Turnpike Fold LA2 . . . 218 D5

Turnpike Gr BB5 103 C5
Turnpike Rd L39 15 A2
Turnpike The PR2 117 D6
Turn Rd BL0 50 E8
Turnstone FY3 131 B6
TURPIN GREEN 77 B1
Turpin Green La PR25 77 B1
Turton Belmont Com Prim Sch BL7 46 C5
TURTON BOTTOMS 48 D4
Turton Dr PR6 61 E1
Turton & Edgworth CE/ Meth Prim Sch BL7 48 D5
Turton Gr BB10 128 D6
Turton Hollow Rd BB4 86 A8
Turton Rd BL8 49 B1
Turton Twr* BL7 48 C3
Tuscan Ave BB11 127 C5
Tuscany Gr BB6 143 C6
Tuson Croft PR4 74 F8
Tuson Dr PR2 96 E8
Tuson Ho 2 PR1 96 E2
Tustin Ct PR1 96 C8
Tuxbury Dr FY5 153 D8
Tuxford Ct 1 FY8 90 D6
Tuxford Rd FY8 90 C6
Tweed St
Blackburn BB2 81 D8
4 High Bentham LA2 239 D8
5 Lytham St Anne's FY8 89 E6
Nelson BB9 149 A8
Tweed Street Ct 3 LA2 239 D8
Tweedys Ct PR3 185 C4
Twemlow Par
Heysham LA3 212 F8
Morecambe LA3 216 D1
Twenty Acre La PR4 75 B1
Twickenham Pl 4 FY8 90 D6
Twig La L31 5 E1
Twinegate OL12 52 E3
Twine Valley Ctry Pk* BL0 51 A8
Twine Wlk LA6 242 C3
Twin Lakes Ind Est PR26 58 A3
Twistfield Cl PR8 34 F5
Twist Moor La PR6 63 B8
TWISTON 192 A4
Twiston La BB7 191 D5
Twitter La BB7 189 A3
Two Acre La PR1 96 C1
Two Brooks La BL8 49 B2
Two Laws Rd BD22 174 C1
Two Saints Pl 8 L39 15 E5
Twyford Cl L31 5 E1
Twyn Ghyll Cvn Site BB7 231 B6
Tyldesley Rd FY1 130 B3
Tyne Ave 4 FY3 130 D4
Tyne Cl FY5 175 E5
Tynedale Pl FY3 153 A1
Tynedale Rd FY3 153 B1
Tyne St
1 Bamber Bridge PR5 97 F1
4 Preston PR1 96 D6
Tynwald Rd BB2 101 E1
Tyrer Rd L39 15 F7
Tyrer's Ave L31 5 B5
Tyrers Cl L37 11 F2
Tyrone Ave FY2 152 D2
Tyseley Gr BB18 197 A1
Tythebarn St BB3 82 B1

U

Udale Pl 1 LA1 218 C2
Uggle La LA1 214 F3
Uldale Cl
Nelson BB9 148 E6
Southport PR8 21 B3
Ullswater Ave
Accrington BB5 125 D1
Fleetwood FY7 175 D8
Morecambe LA4 217 D4
Orrell WN5 10 F7
Rochdale OL12 52 C1
Thornton FY5 176 B1
Ullswater Cl
Blackburn BB1 101 F6
Hambleton FY6 177 C2
3 Rishton BB1 124 A1
Ullswater Cres
Carnforth LA5 221 E8
Thornton FY5 176 B1
Ullswater Rd
Blackpool FY4 110 C7
Burnley BB10 128 F5
Chorley PR7 43 B6
Fulwood PR2 118 C4
Lancaster LA1 215 A8
Ullswater Way BB4 106 A1
ULNES WALTON 59 A2
Ulnes Walton La PR26 59 A6
Ulpha Cl BB12 127 B8
Ulster Rd LA1 215 B5
Ulster St BB11 127 D5
Ulverston Cl
Blackburn BB2 102 A1
Maghull L31 5 E2
Ulverston Cres FY8 90 C7
Ulverston Dr BB1 124 A1
Underbank Cl 3 OL13 87 F3
Underbank Ho 1 OL13 87 F3
Underbank Rd
Haslingden BB4 84 F3
Rising Bridge BB5 85 A7
Underbank Rd *continued*
Thornton FY5 176 F1
Underbank Way 2 BB4 85 A3
Under Billinge La BB2 100 F4
Underley St BB10 148 C3
Under Wood PR2 117 C3
Unicon Pk BB4 84 F3
Union Cl WN5 10 E5
Union Ct 13 OL13 70 C8
Union La PR3 178 C7
Union Pas 6 PR4 114 A5
Union Rd
Oswaldtwistle BB5 103 D3
Rawtenstall BB4 85 D2
Union St
Accrington BB5 104 B6
Bacup, Rockliffe OL13 87 F2
Bacup, Stacksteads OL13 70 C8
Blackburn BB2 101 E3
6 Bolton BL7 47 D2
Brierfield BB9 148 B5
Chorley PR7 43 C8
Clitheroe BB7 166 C8
Colne BB8 171 E5
Darwen BB3 82 A1
Haslingden BB4 85 A3
5 Morecambe LA4 217 A5
10 Preston PR1 96 F8
Ramsbottom BL0 50 C6
Rawtenstall BB4 86 A3
Southport PR9 35 C8
Whittle-le-W PR6 61 C8
Whitworth OL12 52 C8
Union Terr
Clow Bridge BB4 106 A4
Rawtenstall BB4 86 B2
Unit Rd PR8 21 D5
Unity St
3 Barnoldswick BB18 196 C2
Blackburn BB2 101 E2
Kelbrook BB18 195 A6
Unity Trad Est BB2 101 D4
Unity Way BB4 85 F3
Univ of Central Lancashire PR1 96 E8
Univ of Central Lancashire Avenham Bldg PR1 97 A6
Univ of Cumbria LA1 215 B6
Univ of Lancaster LA1 211 B7
Unsworth Ave FY6 200 A4
Unsworth St OL13 70 D7
Up-Brooks BB7 190 A1
Up-Brooks Ind Est BB7 190 A1
UP HOLLAND 10 B6
Up Holland High Sch WN5 10 C4
Upholland Rd WN5 10 D2
Upholland Roby Mill CE Prim Sch WN8 19 B3
Upholland Sta WN8 9 F4
Uplands Chase PR2 117 B6
Uplands Dr BB12 147 D7
Upper Ashmount BB4 86 C1
Upper Aughton Rd PR8 35 B4
Upper Cliffe (Bersham Dr) BB6 124 C6
Upper George St 23 OL12 52 F1
Upper Hill Way BB18 194 B7
Upper Lune St FY7 199 B5
Upper Mead BL7 47 F1
UPPER THURNHAM 210 B2
Upper Westby St FY8 91 A3
Upphall La LA6 240 C4
Uppingham WN8 17 D1
Uppingham Dr BL0 50 B7
Upton Ave PR8 21 B6
Upton Barn L31 5 C2
Upwood Cl FY2 152 E5
Urban View PR6 62 F8
Ushers Mdw LA1 214 E7
Usk Ave FY5 176 D2

V

VALE 109 C1
Vale Ave BL6 32 A3
Vale Cl WN6 19 E8
Vale Coppice
Horwich BL6 32 A3
Ramsbottom BL0 50 C3
Vale Cotts BL6 31 F2
Vale Cres PR8 21 C2
Vale Croft WN8 10 A6
Vale Ct BB5 125 F1
Vale Gr L32 1 A1
Vale Ho 9 BL7 47 D2
Vale House Cl BB7 144 C5
Vale La L40 17 F5
Vale Mill Ct BL0 68 D5
Valentia Rd FY2 152 D3
Valentines La PR2, PR4 116 E4
Valentines Mdw PR4 116 E4
Vale Rd LA1 218 C3
Vale Royal PR4 114 C5
Vale St
Bacup OL13 88 A3
Blackburn BB2 101 E2
Darwen BB3 81 F2
Haslingden BB4 85 B4
Vale Terr
Calder Vale PR3 182 E8
Newchurch BB4 86 F3
Vale The
Appley Bridge WN6 19 D8
Vale The *continued*
Bamber Bridge PR5 97 B2
Fulwood PR2 117 F5
Valeway Ave FY5 152 D8
Valley Cl BB9 171 A1
Valley Ctr The 4 BB4 86 A2
Valley Dr
Barnoldswick BB18 196 D4
Padiham BB12 126 D8
Valley Forge Bsns Pk BB9 170 D2
Valley Gdns
2 Earby BB18 197 B2
Padiham BB11 126 F4
Valley Hts BB8 171 E5
Valley Mill Ct BB8 172 E6
Valley Mill La BL9 33 A1
Valley Rd
Barnoldswick BB18 196 C2
Earby BB18 197 B2
Higher Penwortham PR1 96 D5
Hoghton PR5 99 F3
Longridge PR3 140 C7
Wilpshire BB1 122 F5
Valley St BB11 127 B4
Valley Terr BB12 145 E1
Valley View
Bamber Bridge PR5 97 A3
Chorley PR6 43 E7
Fulwood PR2 118 A4
Whitworth OL12 71 D4
Valligates BB1 102 B7
Vance Rd FY1 130 B4
Vancouver Cres BB2 101 C8
Vandyck Ave BB11 127 E2
Vardon Rd BB2 101 B2
Varley St
Colne BB8 171 F6
2 Darwen BB3 82 A1
Preston PR1 118 A2
Varlian Cl L40 16 C3
Vaughan Cl L37 11 D4
Vaughan Rd PR8 35 B4
Vaughan St BB9 148 F7
Vauxhall St BB2 101 B3
Vauze Ave BL6 31 D1
Vauze House Cl BL6 31 D2
Veevers St
Brierfield BB9 148 A6
7 Burnley BB11 127 F6
Padiham BB12 126 D8
Velvet St BB2 81 D8
Venables Ave BB8 171 F6
Venice Ave BB11 127 C4
Venice St BB11 127 D5
Ventnor Pl PR2 117 A4
Ventnor Rd
Blackpool FY4 110 B6
1 Chorley PR7 43 B6
Haslingden BB4 85 C1
Venture Ct BB5 125 D5
Venture Cvn Pk LA4 217 B3
Venture Rd FY7 176 A6
Venture St OL13 88 A3
Venture Works L33 1 C1
Verax St OL13 87 F1
Verbena Cl BB3 82 A7
Verbena Dr FY6 199 F6
Vermont Gr FY5 152 E8
Verna St 15 BL0 50 C6
Vernon Ave
Blackpool FY3 130 E3
Warton PR4 92 E6
Vernon Cres LA2 211 A3
Vernon Ct
4 Galgate LA2 211 A4
Southport PR8 35 D5
Vernon Lo FY8 89 F5
Vernon Pk 3 LA2 211 A4
Vernon Rd
Laneshaw Bridge BB8 172 D6
Lytham St Anne's FY8 110 E1
Ramsbottom BL8 50 A1
Southport PR9 36 A8
Vernon St
Blackburn BB2 101 E4
Darwen BB3 82 B1
Nelson BB9 148 E7
Preston PR1 117 F1
Verona Ave BB11 127 C5
Verona Ct 6 FY5 176 A2
Veronica St BB3 81 E4
Verulam Rd PR9 54 B3
Vesta St 6 BL0 50 B6
Vevey St PR25 77 A1
Viaduct Rd PR5 99 F2
Vicarage Ave
5 Burnley BB12 126 B8
Caton LA2 237 C3
Cleveleys FY5 175 D3
Vicarage Cl
Adlington PR6 31 A8
Burton-in-K LA6 240 C7
Euxton PR7 60 D3
Formby L37 11 D4
Fulwood PR2 117 F4
Lytham St Anne's FY8 89 F7
2 Morecambe LA3 217 C2
Ormskirk L40 16 B3
Wrea Green PR4 113 B4
Vicarage Ct BB3 82 A3
Vicarage Dr BB3 65 C8
Vicarage Fold BB7 144 F7
Vicarage Gdns L40 25 D4
Vicarage La
Accrington BB5 104 E1
Banks PR9 54 F7
Blackpool FY4 130 E1
Vicarage La *continued*
Burton-in-K LA6 240 C7
Churchtown PR3 181 A2
Fulwood PR2 117 F4
Newton-w-S PR4 115 A3
Ormskirk L40 16 C3
Rawtenstall BB4 85 F2
Samlesbury PR5 119 E1
Wilpshire BB1 122 F6
Vicarage Rd
Barnoldswick BB18 196 C3
Blackrod BL6 31 D2
Formby L37 11 D4
Kelbrook BB18 195 A6
Nelson BB9 148 D7
Orrell WN5 10 D4
Poulton-le-F FY6 153 E3
Vicarage Rd W BL6 31 C2
Vicarage St 3 PR6 61 D1
Vicarage Wlk L39 15 E5
Vicar La LA6 241 C2
Vicarsfields Rd PR25 60 A7
Vicar St
Blackburn BB1 101 F5
Great Harwood BB6 124 C4
Viceroy Ct 3 PR8 35 A6
Vickers Dr WN8 9 E8
Vickers Ind Est LA3 217 C2
Vickers Way LA3 217 C2
Victor Ave LA4 217 E6
Victoria Apartments 20 BB12 146 C1
Victoria Ave
Accrington BB5 104 D2
2 Blackburn BB2 80 E8
Brierfield BB9 148 B6
Chatburn BB7 190 E5
Lancaster LA1 214 F5
Victoria Bldgs
Darwen BB3 82 E3
Formby L37 11 E5
9 Low Bentham LA2 239 B8
1 Preston PR1 96 F7
Victoria Bridge Rd PR8 35 C6
Victoria Bsns & Ind Ctr BB5 104 B4
Victoria Cl BB7 144 A7
Victoria Cross 4 BB1 101 E6
Victoria Ct
7 Blackburn BB1 101 E5
Broughton PR3 137 C2
Chatburn BB7 190 D5
Croston PR26 58 B3
Fulwood PR2 117 E3
Horwich BL6 32 C3
Padiham BB12 126 E7
Skelmersdale WN8 17 D1
4 Southport PR8 34 F4
Victoria Dr BB4 85 B2
Victoria Gdns BB9 170 C2
Victoria Lo BB12 145 D2
Victoria Mans
Blackpool FY3 131 A6
Preston PR2 96 A7
Victoria Mews
7 Clitheroe BB7 166 D7
9 Earby BB18 197 B2
Morecambe LA4 217 C6
Southport PR9 35 D7
Victoria Mill BB18 197 B2
Victorian Lanterns BL9 50 C2
Victoria Par
Morecambe LA4 217 C6
Preston PR2 117 B1
7 Rawtenstall BB4 69 E8
Victoria Park Ave
Leyland PR25 59 D7
Preston PR2 116 D1
Victoria Park Dr PR2 116 D1
Victoria Pk WN8 17 C1
Victoria Pl
Halton LA2 219 C6
6 Lancaster LA1 214 F7
Victoria Quay PR2 96 A7
Victoria Rd
Barnoldswick BB18 196 C2
Earby BB18 197 B2
Formby L37 11 D5
Fulwood PR2 118 A4
Horwich BL6 32 C2
Ince Blundell L38 3 E3
Kirkham PR4 113 F5
Lytham St Anne's FY8 89 F5
Ormskirk L39 15 C2
Padiham BB12 126 E7
Pleasington BB2 100 C1
Poulton-le-F FY6 153 E4
Preston PR5 97 D5
Victoria Rd E FY5 176 B1
Victoria Rd W FY5 175 E2
Victoria Sq FY5 175 D2
Victoria St
Accrington BB5 104 B5
Bacup OL13 70 D8
Bamber Bridge PR5 77 B8
Barrowford BB9 170 D3
25 Blackburn BB1 101 E5
Blackpool FY1 130 B5
Blackrod BL6 31 D2
1 Burnley BB11 127 F5
Burscough Bridge L40 25 E5
Carnforth LA5 223 D1
Chorley PR7 43 D7
Church BB5 103 E6
Clayton-le-M BB5 124 F2
Clitheroe BB7 166 D7
22 Darwen BB3 82 A1
7 Earby BB18 197 B2
Victoria St *continued*
Fleetwood FY7 199 B5
Great Harwood BB6 124 D5
Haslingden BB4 85 A3
Longridge PR3 140 A7
Lytham St Anne's FY8 91 C3
Morecambe LA4 217 A5
Nelson BB9 148 D8
Oswaldtwistle BB5 103 D3
Preston PR1 117 E1
Ramsbottom BL0 50 B6
Rawtenstall, Lower Cloughfold BB4 86 C1
Rawtenstall, Waterfoot BB4 69 E8
Rishton BB1 124 B1
22 Rochdale OL12 52 F1
Southport PR9 35 B8
Todmorden OL14 109 C1
Wheelton PR6 62 A7
Whitworth OL12 52 C8
Victoria Terr
Abbey Village PR6 80 B2
12 Bamber Bridge PR5 77 A8
Billington BB7 144 A4
Calder Vale PR3 182 E8
2 Chorley PR6 61 D1
Glasson LA2 209 F5
5 Leyland PR25 60 A8
Mellor Brook BB2 121 C3
Tockholes BB3 80 F2
Wheelton PR6 62 A7
Victoria Way
Formby L37 11 D5
Rawtenstall BB4 86 C2
Southport PR8 34 F7
Victoria Wharf LA1 218 C1
Victoria Works Ind Est BB11 127 B5
Victor St BB5 124 F3
Victory Ave PR9 36 A7
Victory Bvd FY8 91 D3
Victory Cl BB9 148 E8
Victory Ctr The 2 BB9 148 E8
Victory Rd FY1 130 C6
Victrex Rd FY5 176 D4
Viewfield Mews BB2 101 B5
View Rd BB3 81 E5
View St PR7 41 C7
Vihiers Cl BB7 144 C6
Viking Cl PR8 35 A4
Viking Way LA3 212 F5
Village Cl WN8 8 D8
Village Croft PR7 60 D3
Village Ct OL12 71 C1
Village Dr PR2 118 F2
Village Green La PR2 116 F6
Village Row PR8 21 C5
Village The FY6 154 E1
Village Way
Blackpool FY2 152 D5
Hightown L38 2 F4
Skelmersdale WN8 8 D8
Villas Ct LA1 214 E7
Villas Rd L31 6 B2
Villas The PR4 116 E5
Villa Way PR3 181 C6
Villiers Ct PR1 117 E2
Villiers St
Burnley BB11 127 C5
Bury BL9 33 A3
Padiham BB12 126 D7
Preston, Maudlands PR1 117 D2
Preston PR1 117 E2
Vincent Ct BB2 81 D8
Vincent Rd BB9 148 F8
Vincent St
Blackburn BB2 81 D8
Colne BB8 171 F6
8 Lancaster LA1 215 A7
Vincit St BB10 128 C8
Vine Ct FY2 152 C1
Vinery The PR4 75 F8
Vine St
6 Accrington BB5 104 A6
Brierfield BB9 148 B5
Chorley PR7 61 C1
Lancaster LA1 214 F6
Oswaldtwistle BB5 103 C3
Preston PR1 96 D8
Ramsbottom BL0 50 A4
Viola Cl WN6 29 D2
Violet Ct BB1 101 F6
Violet St BB10 148 A1
Virginia Ave L31 5 D3
Virginia Gr L31 5 C3
Virginia St PR8 35 C6
Viscount Ave BB3 82 A6
Viscount Dr LA1 214 E4
Vivary Way BB8 171 B5
Vivian Dr PR8 35 A2
Vulcan Rd PR4 114 B1
Vulcan St
4 Nelson BB9 170 F1
Southport PR9 35 C7

W

Wackersall Rd 3 BB8 171 B3
WADDINGTON 189 C4
Waddington Ave BB10 128 D6
Waddington Ct FY8 90 C6

Waddington Hospl (Almshouses) BB7 ..... 189 B5
Waddington Rd
Accrington BB5 ..... 104 D6
Clitheroe BB7 ..... 189 E1
Fulwood PR2 ..... 119 A2
Lytham St Anne's FY8 ..... 90 C7
West Bradford BB7 ..... 189 D5
Waddington St
Earby BB18 ..... 197 B2
3 Padiham BB12 ..... 126 D8
Waddington & West Bradford CE Prim Sch
BB7 ..... 189 C5
Waddow Gn BB7 ..... 166 C8
Waddow Gr BB7 ..... 189 C4
Waddow View BB7 ..... 189 B4
Wade Brook Rd PR26 ..... 58 F6
WADE HALL 59 E7
Wades Croft PR4 ..... 93 C6
Wades Ct FY3 ..... 152 F1
Wade St BB12 ..... 146 D1
Wadham Rd PR1 ..... 97 B6
Wagon Rd LA2, PR3 ..... 226 B8
Wagstaff Cl BB2 ..... 81 C8
Waidshouse Cl BB9 ..... 148 E6
Waidshouse Rd BB9 ..... 148 E6
Wain Ct BB2 ..... 101 B4
Waingap Cres OL12 ..... 52 D8
Waingap Rise OL12 ..... 52 F4
Waingap View OL12 ..... 52 D7
Waingate
Grimsargh PR2 ..... 139 C1
Rawtenstall BB4 ..... 86 B3
Waingate Cl BB4 ..... 86 B3
Waingate Ct PR2 ..... 139 C1
Waingate La BB4 ..... 86 B3
Waingate Rd BB4 ..... 86 B3
Waitholme La LA5 ..... 240 A7
Wakefield Ave LA4 ..... 217 D6
Wakefield Dr LA1 ..... 215 A4
Wakefield Rd FY2 ..... 152 E4
Walden Rd BB1 ..... 122 F4
Waldon St PR1 ..... 97 E8
Waldron WN8 ..... 8 D8
Walesby Pl FY8 ..... 90 D5
Wales Rd BB4 ..... 86 F1
Wales Terr BB4 ..... 86 F1
Walgarth Dr PR7 ..... 43 B7
Walkdale PR4 ..... 95 D2
Walkden Barn Cotts
BB5 ..... 103 A1
Walkden Cotts L39 ..... 1 E8
Walker Ave 1 BB5 ..... 104 A4
Walker Cl L37 ..... 11 F2
WALKER FOLD 164 C8
Walker Gr LA3 ..... 212 F7
Walker La PR2 ..... 117 B6
Walker Office Pk BB1 ..... 82 C8
Walker Park Ind Est
BB1 ..... 82 C7
Walker Pl PR1 ..... 97 B7
Walker Rd BB1 ..... 82 C7
Walkers Hill FY4 ..... 111 A7
WALKER'S HILL 111 A7
Walkers Ind Est LA3 ..... 212 F3
Walker St
Blackburn BB1 ..... 101 F4
Blackpool FY1 ..... 130 B6
Clitheroe BB7 ..... 166 F8
Preston PR1 ..... 96 F8
Walker Way FY5 ..... 176 B4
WALK MILL 107 F8
Walk Mill Pl BB10 ..... 128 E1
Walk The
Hesketh Bank PR4 ..... 73 C4
Southport PR8 ..... 35 A5
Wallace Hartley Mews 1
BB8 ..... 171 D5
Wallace La PR3 ..... 207 C4
WALLBANK 52 B7
Wallbank Dr OL12 ..... 52 C7
Wallbrook Ave WN5 ..... 10 D1
Wallcroft St WN8 ..... 8 E8
Walleach Farm Cvn Pk
BL7 ..... 48 E6
Walled Garden The
PR6 ..... 61 B6
Wallend Rd PR2 ..... 95 D7
Waller Ave FY2 ..... 152 C5
Waller Hill BB8 ..... 194 D1
Wallets Wood Ct PR7 ..... 43 A5
Walletts Rd PR7 ..... 43 B6
Walling's La LA5 ..... 224 B4
Wall La PR3 ..... 155 E5
Wall St
Blackpool FY1 ..... 130 C7
Newchurch BB4 ..... 86 E2
Wallstreams Ct BB10 ..... 129 B5
Wallstreams La BB10 ..... 129 B5
Wallsuches BL6 ..... 32 F4
WALMER BRIDGE 74 F5
Walmer Ct PR8 ..... 34 F4
Walmer Gn PR4 ..... 74 F5
Walmer Rd
Lytham St Anne's FY8 ..... 89 F8
Southport PR8 ..... 35 A3
Walmersley Old Rd BL9 ..... 50 F2
Walmersley Rd BL9 ..... 50 E2
Walmsgate BB18 ..... 196 B2
Walmsley Ave BB1 ..... 103 B8
Walmsley Bridge La
Bilsborrow PR3 ..... 159 E8
Claughton PR3 ..... 182 E1
Walmsley Brow BB7 ..... 144 B4
Walmsley CE Prim Sch
BL7 ..... 47 E1
Walmsley Cl
Church BB5 ..... 103 E6
Garstang PR3 ..... 181 C7
Walmsley Ct BB5 ..... 124 F1
Walmsley St
Darwen BB3 ..... 82 B2
Fleetwood FY7 ..... 199 A4
18 Great Harwood BB6 ..... 124 C5
Rishton BB1 ..... 124 B1
Walney Cl 8 PR2 ..... 116 C1
Walney Gdns BB2 ..... 101 F1
Walney Pl FY3 ..... 131 A7
Walnut Ave
Bury BL9 ..... 33 C3
Haslingden BB4 ..... 85 C3
Walnut Cl PR1 ..... 96 B3
Walnut St
Bacup OL13 ..... 87 F3
3 Blackburn BB1 ..... 102 A7
Southport PR8 ..... 35 C4
Walpole Ave FY4 ..... 110 B5
Walpole St
Blackburn BB1 ..... 101 F4
9 Burnley BB10 ..... 148 B1
Walro Mews PR9 ..... 54 A3
Walsden Gr BB10 ..... 128 C6
Walshaw La BB10 ..... 148 D2
Walshaw St BB10 ..... 128 B8
Walsh Fold BL7 ..... 48 D2
Walsh St
Blackburn BB2 ..... 101 E2
Horwich BL6 ..... 32 B4
Walter Ave FY8 ..... 111 A2
Walter Pl FY8 ..... 111 A2
Walter Robinson Ct
FY3 ..... 130 D6
Walter St
5 Accrington BB5 ..... 104 B6
Blackburn BB1 ..... 102 A4
Brierfield BB9 ..... 148 B5
Darwen BB3 ..... 65 B5
Huncoat BB5 ..... 125 E2
Oswaldtwistle BB5 ..... 103 D3
Walter Street Prim Sch
BB9 ..... 148 B5
Waltham Ave FY4 ..... 110 D5
Waltham Cl BB5 ..... 104 E3
Waltham Ct LA2 ..... 219 C7
WALTHEW GREEN 19 C3
Waltho Ave L31 ..... 5 E1
Walton Ave
Higher Penwortham
PR1 ..... 96 B3
Morecambe LA4 ..... 217 F5
Walton Cl OL13 ..... 88 A1
Walton Cottage Homes
BB9 ..... 171 A1
Walton Cres BB2 ..... 102 A1
Walton Gn PR5 ..... 97 C4
Walton Gr LA4 ..... 217 F5
Walton Hts 18 BB8 ..... 171 D4
Walton La BB9 ..... 171 A1
WALTON-LE-DALE 97 D4
Walton-le-Dale Art Coll & High Sch PR5 ..... 97 F2
Walton-le-Dale Com Prim Sch PR5 ..... 97 D2
Walton's Par PR1 ..... 96 E7
Walton St
Accrington BB5 ..... 125 A1
Adlington PR7 ..... 31 A6
Barrowford BB9 ..... 170 E4
Colne BB8 ..... 171 D4
8 Nelson BB9 ..... 170 E1
Southport PR9 ..... 35 C8
WALTON SUMMIT 78 B7
Walton Summit Ctr
PR5 ..... 78 A6
Walton Summit Rd PR5 ..... 78 A7
Walton View PR1 ..... 97 D8
Walverden Ave 4 FY4 ..... 110 D8
Walverden Cres 3
BB9 ..... 148 F8
Walverden Prim Sch
BB9 ..... 148 F8
Walverden Rd
Brierfield BB9 ..... 148 D5
Lane Bottom BB10 ..... 149 B4
Walverden Terr BB9 ..... 148 F7
Wanes Blades Rd L40 ..... 26 E5
Wanishar La L39 ..... 14 A5
Wanless Villas BB18 ..... 194 D6
Wansbeck Ave FY7 ..... 198 D2
Wansbeck Ho FY7 ..... 198 D2
Wansfell Rd BB7 ..... 166 C7
Wanstead Cres FY4 ..... 130 E1
Wanstead St PR1 ..... 97 E8
WAPPING 196 A2
WARBRECK 152 D1
Warbreck Ct FY2 ..... 152 B1
Warbreck Dr FY2 ..... 152 B2
Warbreck Hill Rd FY2 ..... 152 D1
Warburton Bldgs 3
BB4 ..... 84 F1
Warburton St 1 BB4 ..... 84 F1
Warbury St PR1 ..... 118 E1
Warcock La OL13 ..... 88 B3
Ward Ave
Cleveleys FY5 ..... 175 D3
Formby L37 ..... 11 D2
Oswaldtwistle BB5 ..... 103 C3
Warde St 10 BB9 ..... 148 E8
Ward Green Cross
PR3 ..... 141 A7
Ward Green La PR3 ..... 141 A7
Wardle Ct PR6 ..... 61 C6
Wardle Dr FY5 ..... 175 F3
Wardle St OL13 ..... 70 D8
Wardley's La FY6 ..... 177 A3
Ward's End PR1 ..... 97 A7
Ward St
Bamber Bridge PR5 ..... 77 B7
Belmont BL7 ..... 46 C5
5 Blackpool FY1 ..... 130 B1
Burnley BB11 ..... 127 E6
Chorley PR6 ..... 43 E7
Great Harwood BB6 ..... 124 C5
Kirkham PR4 ..... 114 A4
Wareham Cl BB5 ..... 125 B1
Wareham Rd FY3 ..... 152 F1
Wareham St BB1 ..... 102 A7
Warehouse La BB8 ..... 194 D1
Warehouse The 7
PR1 ..... 117 E1
Waring Dr FY5 ..... 176 A2
Warings The
Heskin Green PR7 ..... 41 E4
Nelson BB9 ..... 148 E6
Warkworth Terr 13
OL13 ..... 88 A3
Warley Ave LA3 ..... 217 E4
Warley Dr LA3 ..... 217 E4
Warley Rd FY1 ..... 130 C8
Warley Wise La BB8 ..... 195 F3
Warmden Ave BB5 ..... 104 E3
Warmden Gdns BB1 ..... 102 A7
Warne Pl LA1 ..... 218 B1
Warner Rd PR1 ..... 118 D1
Warner St
Accrington BB5 ..... 104 C5
Haslingden BB4 ..... 85 B3
Warpers Moss Cl L40 ..... 25 F5
Warpers Moss La L40 ..... 26 A5
Warren Ave N FY7 ..... 198 F4
Warren Ave S FY7 ..... 198 F4
Warren Cl LA2 ..... 218 C8
Warren Ct PR8 ..... 34 E5
Warren Dr
Barrowford BB9 ..... 170 C3
Blackpool FY5 ..... 152 E7
Britannia OL13 ..... 71 C8
Slyne LA2 ..... 218 C8
Warren Fold BB7 ..... 142 F8
Warren Gn L37 ..... 11 D3
Warren Gr
Blackpool FY5 ..... 152 E8
Heysham LA3 ..... 212 E5
Warrenhouse Rd L33 ..... 1 B4
Warrenhurst Ho 1
FY7 ..... 198 F3
Warrenhurst Rd FY7 ..... 199 A4
Warren Manor FY5 ..... 152 E8
Warren Rd
Heysham LA3 ..... 212 E5
Southport PR9 ..... 36 A8
Warrenside Cl BB1 ..... 123 A4
Warren St FY7 ..... 199 B4
Warren The
Blackburn BB2 ..... 101 A7
Fulwood PR2 ..... 118 E6
Warrington St BB1 ..... 102 A8
Warrington Terr BB6 ..... 144 D8
Warth La
Ingleton LA6 ..... 242 F2
Rawtenstall BB4 ..... 69 D8
WARTON
Carnforth 223 D5
Lytham St Anne's 92 D6
Warton Archbishop Hutton's Prim Sch
LA5 ..... 223 D5
Warton Ave LA3 ..... 212 E6
WARTON BANK 92 C4
Warton Crag Nature Reserve* LA5 ..... 223 C6
Warton Old Rectory*
LA5 ..... 223 D5
Warton Pl PR7 ..... 43 A8
Warton Rd LA5 ..... 223 D2
Warton St
Lytham St Anne's FY8 ..... 91 C3
2 Preston PR1 ..... 96 E6
Wartonwood View 1
LA5 ..... 223 D1
Warwick Ave
Accrington BB5 ..... 104 B7
Clayton-le-M BB5 ..... 124 F3
Cleveleys FY5 ..... 175 F4
Darwen BB3 ..... 81 E3
Lancaster LA1 ..... 215 A5
Morecambe LA4 ..... 217 F6
Warwick Cl
Church BB5 ..... 103 F7
Fulwood PR2 ..... 117 E4
Ramsbottom BL8 ..... 50 A1
Southport PR8 ..... 35 B4
Warwick Dr
Barnoldswick BB18 ..... 196 F1
Brierfield BB9 ..... 148 D5
Clitheroe BB7 ..... 189 F2
Padiham BB12 ..... 126 D7
Warwick Pl
Fleetwood FY7 ..... 199 A5
Normoss FY3 ..... 131 B8
Warwick Rd
Bamber Bridge PR5 ..... 97 D4
Blackpool FY3 ..... 130 D7
Eccleston PR7 ..... 41 C7
Leyland PR25 ..... 59 E7
Lytham St Anne's FY8 ..... 89 F6
Warwick St
Adlington PR7 ..... 30 F6
Church BB5 ..... 103 F7
Haslingden BB4 ..... 85 B3
Warwick St *continued*
Longridge PR3 ..... 140 A8
Nelson BB9 ..... 148 E7
Preston PR1 ..... 96 F8
Southport PR8 ..... 35 B4
Wasdale Ave
Blackburn BB1 ..... 102 C3
Maghull L31 ..... 5 F2
Wasdale Cl
Leyland PR25 ..... 60 B6
Padiham BB12 ..... 146 C1
Wasdale Gr PR3 ..... 139 F5
Wasdale Rd FY4 ..... 111 A8
Washbrook Cl BB7 ..... 166 D1
Washbrook Way L39 ..... 15 E4
Washburn Ct LA3 ..... 217 F2
Washington Ave
Blackpool FY2 ..... 152 E2
3 Morecambe LA4 ..... 217 B5
Washington Cl LA1 ..... 214 D7
Washington Ct FY2 ..... 152 E2
Washington Dr LA5 ..... 223 E6
Washington Hall Fire Brigade Training Ctr
PR7 ..... 60 F2
Washington La PR7 ..... 60 F2
Washington St BB5 ..... 104 C6
Wash La BL9 ..... 33 B2
Waste La LA2 ..... 226 C7
Wastwater Dr 4 LA4 ..... 217 E4
Watchyard La L37 ..... 12 A4
WATER 87 A8
WATERBARN 70 A8
Waterbarn La OL13 ..... 70 B8
Waterbarn St BB10 ..... 148 B1
Waterdale FY2 ..... 152 E5
WATERFALL 101 C2
Waterfall Mills BB2 ..... 101 B2
Waterfall Terr BL7 ..... 46 C5
Waterfield Ave BB3 ..... 65 B6
Water Fold BB4 ..... 87 A8
Waterfold Bsns Pk BL9 ..... 33 B1
Waterfold La BL9 ..... 33 C1
WATERFOOT 69 E8
Waterfoot Ave
Blackpool FY3 ..... 130 E6
Southport PR8 ..... 21 B3
Waterfoot Bsns Ctr 6
BB4 ..... 86 F2
Waterfoot Prim Sch
BB4 ..... 69 F8
Waterford Cl
Adlington PR6 ..... 44 A1
Fulwood PR2 ..... 118 C5
Waterford St BB9 ..... 170 F1
Waterfront 2 BB1 ..... 101 F3
Waterfront Marine & Ind Est FY8 ..... 91 E3
Water Head PR2 ..... 117 B3
Waterhead Cres FY5 ..... 152 C6
Waterhouse Gn PR6 ..... 61 B7
Waterhouse Nook BL6,
PR7 ..... 31 A5
Watering Pool La PR5 ..... 97 B1
Water La
Edenfield BL0 ..... 68 D2
Preston PR2 ..... 117 D1
Southport PR9 ..... 54 D5
Waterleat Glade FY6 ..... 131 E8
WATERLOO 81 B8
Waterloo Cl BB2 ..... 81 B8
Waterloo Prim Sch
FY4 ..... 130 D1
Waterloo Rd
Blackpool FY4 ..... 130 D1
Burnley, Burnley Wood
BB11 ..... 128 B4
Burnley, Fulledge BB11 ..... 128 B5
Clitheroe BB7 ..... 166 F8
Kelbrook BB18 ..... 195 A6
Preston PR2 ..... 117 C1
Southport PR8 ..... 34 E2
Waterloo St
Accrington BB5 ..... 125 A1
Chorley PR7 ..... 61 C1
Waterloo Terr PR2 ..... 117 C1
Watermans Cl BL6 ..... 32 C4
Water Mdws BB2 ..... 81 D7
Watermede WN5 ..... 10 E3
Waters Edge
3 Blackburn BB1 ..... 101 F4
Whalley BB7 ..... 144 C4
Water's Edge PR2 ..... 116 F3
Waters Edge Gn PR3 ..... 181 C6
Waterside FY2 ..... 152 D2
WATERSIDE
Brierfield 147 F6
Colne 171 E4
Darwen 82 E3
Waterside LA1 ..... 218 D1
Waterside Cl PR3 ..... 181 B7
Waterside Ind Est BB8 ..... 171 E4
Waterside Mews BB12 ..... 126 D8
Waterside Pl LA4 ..... 217 B3
Waterside Rd
Colne BB8 ..... 171 D4
Haslingden BB4 ..... 85 A2
Ramsbottom BL0, BL8,
BL9 ..... 50 C3
Waterside Terr
10 Bacup OL13 ..... 87 F3
Darwen BB3 ..... 82 E3
WATERSLACK 224 E6
Waterslack Rd LA5 ..... 224 E6
Waters Reach
Cleveleys FY5 ..... 175 C3
Lytham St Anne's FY8 ..... 90 D3
Water St
9 Accrington BB5 ..... 104 C6
Adlington PR7 ..... 31 A6
1 Bamber Bridge PR5 ..... 97 F2
4 Bolton, Egerton BL7 ..... 47 D2
Brindle PR6 ..... 78 F5
Chorley PR7 ..... 61 C1
Clayton-le-M BB5 ..... 124 F5
1 Colne BB8 ..... 171 E5
Earby BB18 ..... 197 B2
Great Harwood BB6 ..... 124 C5
Hapton BB12 ..... 126 C4
Lancaster LA1 ..... 218 D1
Nelson BB9 ..... 148 E8
8 Ramsbottom BL0 ..... 50 B5
Rawtenstall BB4 ..... 86 A8
Ribchester PR3 ..... 141 E3
Whitworth OL12 ..... 52 C8
Worsthorne BB10 ..... 129 B5
Waterworks Cotts L39 ..... 6 F4
Waterworks Rd L39 ..... 16 A6
Watery Gate La PR3,
PR4 ..... 156 D3
Watery La
Darwen BB3 ..... 65 B6
Garstang PR3 ..... 204 E1
Lancaster LA1 ..... 218 B3
Preston, Fishwick PR1 ..... 97 E7
Preston PR2 ..... 96 B8
Watery Lane Ind Est
BB3 ..... 65 B6
Watford St 5 BB1 ..... 101 E6
Watkin La PR5 ..... 77 B7
Watkin Rd PR6 ..... 61 B8
Watkins Cl BB9 ..... 148 C4
Watling Cl LA3 ..... 217 E3
Watling Gate BB6 ..... 143 C6
Watling St BL8 ..... 49 A1
Watling Street Rd
Fulwood, Brookfield
PR2 ..... 118 E5
Fulwood PR2 ..... 118 B3
Watson Ct FY4 ..... 110 D7
Watson Gdns OL12 ..... 52 D2
Watson Mews FY4 ..... 110 D8
Watson Rd FY4 ..... 110 C7
Watson St
Blackburn BB2 ..... 101 B2
8 Oswaldtwistle BB5 ..... 103 E4
Watton Beck Cl L31 ..... 5 F2
Watts Cl L33 ..... 1 A4
Watts St BL6 ..... 32 C2
Watt St
Burnley BB12 ..... 127 C7
Sabden BB7 ..... 145 F7
Wavell Ave PR9 ..... 36 B7
Wavell Cl
Accrington BB5 ..... 104 F1
Southport PR9 ..... 36 B7
Wavell St BB12 ..... 127 C6
WAVERLEDGE 124 B4
Waverledge Bsns Pk
BB6 ..... 124 B4
Waverledge Rd BB6 ..... 124 B4
Waverledge St BB6 ..... 124 C4
Waverley WN8 ..... 17 D1
Waverley Ave
Blackpool FY1 ..... 130 C8
Fleetwood FY7 ..... 198 D3
Waverley Cl
Brierfield BB9 ..... 148 D4
Read BB12 ..... 145 D1
Waverley Dr
New Longton PR4 ..... 75 F7
Tarleton PR4 ..... 57 A6
Waverley Gdns PR2 ..... 118 E2
Waverley Pl BB2 ..... 101 B5
Waverley Rd
Accrington BB5 ..... 104 E3
Blackburn BB1 ..... 102 F4
Preston PR1 ..... 118 D1
Wilpshire BB1 ..... 122 E4
Waverley St
1 Burnley BB11 ..... 127 E6
Southport PR8 ..... 35 A7
Waxy La PR4 ..... 93 C7
Wayfarers Arc PR8 ..... 35 B7
Way Gate FY5 ..... 175 D5
Wayman Rd FY3 ..... 130 D6
Wayoh Croft BL7 ..... 48 D6
Wayside FY6 ..... 199 D5
Way The LA3 ..... 217 F3
Weald The PR4 ..... 116 D5
Weasel La BB3 ..... 81 B2
Weatherhill Cres BB9 ..... 148 E5
Weaver Ave L40 ..... 25 F5
Weaver's Brow PR6 ..... 43 F5
Weavers Cl FY8 ..... 90 D7
Weaver's Croft BB7 ..... 144 A4
Weavers Ct
Blackburn BB2 ..... 101 C5
Buckshaw Village PR7 ..... 60 E6
Trawden BB8 ..... 172 B2
Weavers Mews BB3 ..... 81 F1
Weavers Triangle Ctr The*
BB11 ..... 127 F5
Webber Ct BB11 ..... 127 A3
Webber Rd L33 ..... 1 C1
Webb St BL6 ..... 32 C3
Weber St BB4 ..... 86 D1
Webster Ave FY4 ..... 110 E7
Webster Gdns PR4 ..... 75 A4
Webster Gr LA4 ..... 218 A4
Webster St PR2 ..... 117 C1
Wedgewood Rd BB5 ..... 125 F1
Wedgwood Ct FY8 ..... 90 A1
WEETON 132 F1

Weeton Ave
Blackpool FY4 110 E5
Cleveleys FY5 175 D3
Lytham St Anne's FY8 90 A8
WEETON CAMP 132 D5
Weeton Pl 4 PR2 116 E1
Weeton Prim Sch PR4 132 E6
Weeton Rd
Great Plumpton PR4 112 F7
Kirkham PR4 113 C8
Weeton Camp FY6, PR4 132 E7
Weeton PR4 132 F2
Weeton St Michael's CE Prim Sch PR4 132 E1
Weets View BB18 196 C3
Weind The PR3 156 B5
WEIR 88 A7
Weir Bottom OL13 88 A7
Weirden Cl PR1 96 C1
Weir La OL13 88 A7
Weir St BB2 101 E4
Welbeck Ave
Blackburn BB1 102 B8
Blackpool FY4 130 E1
Fleetwood FY7 198 F3
Welbeck Cl 8 PR5 97 E1
Welbeck Gdns FY7 198 F3
Welbeck Ho 4 FY7 198 F4
Welbeck Rd PR8 35 A4
Welbeck Terr PR8 35 A4
Welbourne WN8 17 D1
Welburn Cl WN5 10 E5
Welburn Wlk FY5 176 D2
Welbury Cl 5 BB18 197 B2
Weldale 5 PR8 34 F4
Weld Ave PR7 43 C5
WELD BANK 43 C5
Weldbank La PR7 43 C5
Weldbank St PR7 43 C5
Weld Blundell Ave L31 5 B5
Weld Dr L37 11 D4
Weldon Dr L39 15 F4
Weldon St BB11 127 E5
Weld Par 2 PR8 34 F4
Weld Rd PR8 34 F5
Welland Cl FY2 152 E4
WELL BANK 85 A3
Wellbrow Dr PR3 140 B8
Wellbrow Terr OL12 52 D2
Wellcross Rd WN8 10 B6
Well Ct
Clitheroe BB7 189 F1
Standish WN6 29 E1
Wellesley St BB12 126 F6
Wellfield PR4 94 F1
Well Field BB5 125 A2
Wellfield Ave PR25 76 F1
Wellfield Bsns & Ent Coll PR25 76 F1
Wellfield Bsns Pk PR1 96 D8
Wellfield Dr BB12 127 D7
Wellfield La L40 16 C3
Wellfield Methodist & Anglican Church Sch BB12 127 D8
Wellfield Rd
Bamber Bridge PR5 77 A7
Blackburn BB2 101 C6
Preston PR1 96 D8
Wellfold BB7 166 F8
Wellgate BB7 166 F8
Wellhead BB8 172 B4
Well Head Rd BB12 169 A3
Wellhouse Rd BB18 196 B2
Wellhouse Sq 20 BB18 196 B2
Wellhouse St BB18 196 B2
Wellington Ave PR25 60 B8
Wellington Cl WN8 9 E8
Wellington Ct
7 Accrington BB5 104 C5
3 Burnley BB10 128 B5
Wellington Fold 3 BB3 82 A1
Wellington Mews BL7 48 D4
Wellington Pl PR5 97 D2
Wellington Rd
Blackburn BB2 101 C3
Blackpool FY1 130 B2
Chapeltown BL7 48 D4
Lancaster LA1 215 A5
Preston PR2 117 C1
Wellington St
Accrington BB5 104 C5
Barnoldswick BB18 196 B1
Chorley PR7 61 C1
Clayton-le-M BB5 124 F2
Great Harwood BB6 124 C4
Kirkham PR4 113 F5
Lytham St Anne's FY8 91 D3
16 Nelson BB9 170 D1
Preston PR1 96 D8
19 Rochdale OL12 52 F1
1 Southport PR8 35 A6
Wellington Street St Johns BB1 101 D6
Wellington Terr LA4 217 B5
Well La
Brinscall PR6 62 F7
Haskayne L39 13 E6
Little Eccleston PR3 155 D6
Warton LA5 223 E5
Yealand Redmayne LA5 225 E3
Wellogate Gdns FY4 110 D6
Well Orch PR5 78 B5
Wellow Pl FY8 90 C5
Well St N BL0 68 C2
Well St W 6 BL0 50 B5
Wells Cl
Morecambe LA3 217 B2
Wells Cl *continued*
Thornton FY5 176 A2
Wells Fold Cl PR6 78 C1
Well Springs 2 BB3 82 C1
Wells St
Haslingden BB4 85 B3
9 Preston PR1 118 D1
Well St
Burnley BB12 126 B8
Newchurch BB4 86 F3
Rishton BB1 124 B2
Well Terr 1 BB7 189 F1
Welsby Rd PR25 59 D8
Welwyn Ave PR8 21 E6
Welwyn Pl FY5 175 E1
Wembley Ave
Blackpool FY3 130 E8
Higher Penwortham PR1 96 B5
Poulton-le-F FY6 153 E3
Wembley Ct PR1 96 B5
Wembley Rd FY5 176 B4
Wemyss Cl 1 LA3 212 E7
Wendover Rd FY6 153 A6
Wenlock Cl BL6 32 C6
Wenning Ave
High Bentham LA2 239 D7
Maghull L31 5 E2
Wenning Ct LA3 217 F2
Wenning Pl LA1 218 C2
Wenning St BB9 148 F7
WENNINGTON 241 E1
Wennington Hall Sch LA2 241 E1
Wennington Rd
Southport PR9 35 F7
Wray LA2 238 D6
Wennington Sta LA2 238 E8
Wensley Ave FY7 198 E1
Wensley Bsns Pk BB2 101 B4
Wensley Cl BB11 127 E3
Wensleydale Ave FY3 131 A7
Wensleydale Cl
Maghull L31 5 B2
Thornton FY5 153 D8
Wensley Dr
Accrington BB5 104 D5
Lancaster LA1 218 D3
WENSLEY FOLD 101 C4
Wensley Fold CE Prim Sch BB2 101 B5
Wensley Pl PR2 118 D4
Wensley Rd BB2 101 B4
Wentcliffe Dr BB18 197 B1
Wentworth Ave
Fleetwood FY7 175 D7
Inskip PR4 135 C8
Wentworth Cl
Higher Penwortham PR1 96 A6
Southport PR8 21 C4
Wentworth Cres LA3 217 B2
Wentworth Ct PR4 114 B4
Wentworth Dr
Broughton PR3 137 C3
Euxton PR7 60 D4
Lancaster LA1 215 C7
Thornton FY5 153 D8
Wentworth Mews FY8 90 A6
Wentworth Pl PR3 137 C3
Werneth Cl PR1 96 F1
Wescoe Cl WN5 10 E5
WESHAM 114 A6
Wesham Cross PR4 113 F7
Wesham Hall Cl PR4 114 A6
Wesham Hall Rd PR4 114 A6
Wesham Park Hospl PR4 113 F7
Wesleyan Row BB7 166 E8
Wesley Cl LA2 239 D8
Wesley Ct
3 Fleetwood FY7 199 B5
16 Great Harwood BB6 124 C5
Wesley Dr LA3 212 F7
Wesley Gr 5 BB12 127 D7
Wesley Mews FY4 111 A7
Wesley Pl
Bacup OL13 87 E1
Higham BB12 146 F6
Wesley St
Bamber Bridge PR5 77 F8
Blackburn BB1 101 F7
Brierfield BB9 148 B6
Church BB5 103 F6
Oswaldtwistle BB5 103 E5
8 Padiham BB12 126 D8
Sabden BB7 145 F8
Southport PR8 35 B7
Wesley Terr 1 OL13 88 A7
Wesley Way LA2 239 D8
Wessex Cl
Accrington, Hillock Vale BB5 104 F8
Standish WN1 30 B1
West Ave
Barnoldswick BB18 196 B2
Fulwood PR2 117 A6
Lancaster LA1 211 A6
West Bank PR7 43 C8
Westbank Ave FY4 111 A7
West Bank Ave FY8 90 E3
West Beach FY8 91 A2
Westboro Cl LA3 216 D1
Westbourne BB4 68 A8
Westbourne Ave
Blackpool FY1 130 C1
Burnley BB11 127 D3
Wrea Green PR4 113 B3
Westbourne Ave S BB11 127 E3
Westbourne Ct FY6 199 D5
Westbourne Dr LA1 214 D7
Westbourne Gdns PR8 34 D4
Westbourne Pl LA1 214 D8
Westbourne Rd
Chorley PR7 43 B6
Cleveleys FY5 175 D5
Knott End-on-S FY6 199 D5
Lancaster LA1 214 D7
Middleton LA3 213 A2
Southport PR8 34 D4
Warton LA5 223 C4
WEST BRADFORD 189 F5
West Bradford Rd
Clitheroe BB7 189 F4
Grindleton BB7 190 A6
Waddington BB7 189 C5
West Bridge L31 5 C1
Westbrook Cres PR2 117 A3
Westbury Cl
Blackpool FY5 152 C7
Burnley BB10 148 E2
Westbury Gdns BB1 102 C4
WESTBY 112 E4
Westby Ave FY4 110 E5
Westby Cl FY4 111 D7
Westby Ct FY6 153 D2
Westby Gr FY7 199 B5
Westby Pl PR2 116 F1
Westby Rd
Lytham St Anne's FY8 89 E8
Westby PR4 112 E5
Westby St FY8 91 B3
Westby Way FY6 153 D2
West Cliff PR1 96 E6
Westcliffe BB6 124 B6
West Cliffe FY8 91 C3
Westcliffe Ct PR8 34 F5
Westcliffe Dr
Blackpool FY3 130 E8
Morecambe LA3 217 A2
Westcliffe Gr LA3 217 A2
Westcliffe Rd PR8 34 F5
Westcliffe Residential Cvn Pk LA3 217 A2
Westcliffe Wlk BB9 148 E7
Westcliff Prim Sch FY5 152 C6
West Cliff Terr PR1 96 E6
West Close Ave BB12 146 F5
West Close Rd BB18 196 B3
Westcote St 6 BB3 65 B6
West Craven Bsns Pk BB18 197 B3
West Craven Dr BB18 197 B3
West Craven High Tech Coll BB18 196 C1
West Cres
Accrington BB5 104 B8
Broughton PR3 137 C3
Westcroft PR4 74 E3
West Ct FY5 175 C5
Westdene PR9 53 D1
West Dene WN8 27 B2
West Dr
Clayton-le-W PR25 77 D3
Cleveleys FY5 175 E3
Inskip PR4 135 C8
Kirkham PR4 113 E7
Lancaster LA1 218 B2
Whalley BB7 144 A7
West Dr W FY5 175 D3
West End
Great Eccleston PR3 156 A5
Higher Penwortham PR1 96 B6
WEST END
Morecambe 217 B3
Oswaldtwistle 103 C5
Westend Ave PR7 29 D8
West End Bsns Pk BB5 103 B5
West End La PR4 92 B5
West End Prim Sch
Morecambe LA3 216 F4
Ormskirk L39 15 E7
Oswaldtwistle BB5 103 C5
West End Rd LA4 217 A4
Westend Residential Pk PR4 113 D5
West End Terr PR8 35 A7
Westerdale Dr PR9 55 B5
Westerlong PR2 116 D1
Western Ave
Burnley BB11 127 E4
Leyland PR7 60 D7
Western Ct OL13 70 B8
Western Dr PR25 76 D2
Western Rd OL13 70 C8
West Exchange St 7 BB8 171 D4
Westfield
Bamber Bridge PR5 77 A8
1 Nelson BB9 170 D1
Westfield Ave
Blackpool FY3 153 A1
Fleetwood FY7 198 E2
Normoss FY3 131 B7
Read BB12 145 D1
Westfield Cl BB7 144 A7
Westfield Ct FY5 176 B4
Westfield Dr
Bolton-le-S LA5 221 A6
Fulwood PR2 118 E4
Gregson Lane PR5 98 D1
Leyland PR25 76 E1
Warton PR4 92 F5
Westfield Dr *continued*
West Bradford BB7 189 E6
Westfield Gr LA4 217 A4
Westfield Hamlet LA5 221 C2
Westfield Rd FY1 130 D1
West Field Rd BB18 196 A4
Westfields PR26 58 A2
Westgate
Barnoldswick BB18 196 A1
Burnley BB11 127 E6
Fulwood PR2 117 D5
Leyland PR25 59 F8
Morecambe LA3, LA4 217 C3
Read BB12 145 C1
Skelmersdale WN8 8 D8
Whitworth OL12 52 B7
West Gate FY7 198 D4
Westgate Ave
Morecambe LA3 217 B2
Ramsbottom BL0 50 A2
Westgate Cl OL12 52 B7
Westgate Cvn Pk LA3 217 A2
Westgate Dr WN5 10 D5
Westgate La LA6 242 E5
Westgate Park Rd LA4 217 C3
Westgate Prim Sch LA4 217 B3
Westgate Rd FY8 110 C4
Westgate Trad Ctr 2 BB11 127 F6
West Gdns 1 OL13 70 B8
WEST GILLIBRANDS 8 E8
West Gillibrands Ind Est WN8 8 E8
West Hall La LA6 241 C7
Westham St LA1 215 A7
Westhaven PR9 35 D8
Westhaven Cres L39 15 C1
WESTHEAD 16 D4
Westhead Ave L33 1 A1
Westhead Cl L33 1 A1
Westhead Lathom St James' CE Prim Sch L40 16 E4
Westhead Rd PR26 58 B2
Westhead Wlk
1 Fleetwood FY7 198 F2
Kirkby L33 1 A1
West Hill BB9 170 D4
Westholme Ct PR9 53 C1
Westholme Sch (Boys) BB2 101 A6
Westholme Sch (Lower) BB2 101 A5
Westholme Sch (Middle) BB2 101 A6
Westholme Sch (Upper) BB2 100 E6
Westhoughton Rd PR6, PR7 30 F8
WESTHOUSE 242 E5
West Ing La BD23 231 D5
West La
Downham BB7 191 A4
Formby L37 11 F6
West Lancashire Light Rly* PR4 73 F2
Westland Ave BB3 64 F8
Westlands PR26 59 C7
Westlands Ct FY5 153 B8
West Lane Hill LA2 239 D6
Westleigh Rd PR2 116 F1
West Leigh Rd BB1 101 C8
West Lo FY6 177 C1
West Mdw PR2 116 E3
West Meade L31 5 B2
Westminster Ave LA4 216 F4
Westminster Cl
Accrington BB5 104 E3
Darwen BB3 81 E3
11 Morecambe LA3 217 B2
Read BB12 145 D1
Westminster Dr PR8 21 A4
Westminster Pl
Eccleston PR7 41 A8
Hutton PR4 95 D1
Westminster Rd
Blackpool FY1 130 C8
Chorley PR7 43 C7
Darwen BB3 81 E3
Morecambe LA3, LA4 216 E3
Westmoor Gr LA3 212 E5
Westmoreland Rd PR8 35 D5
Westmoreland St BB9 148 C8
Westmorland Ave
Blackpool FY1 130 D3
Cleveleys FY5 175 D4
Westmorland Cl
Darwen BB3 65 C6
Higher Penwortham PR1 96 B4
Leyland PR25 59 E7
Westmorland Sch PR7 43 C5
Westmorland St BB11 127 D5
West Moss La FY8 111 E1
West Mount WN5 10 F6
Weston Pl 4 FY1 130 D1
Weston St 9 PR2 96 D8
Westover Ave LA5 223 E5
Westover Cl L31 5 C1
Westover Gr LA5 223 E5
Westover Rd
Maghull L31 5 C1
Warton LA5 223 E5
Westover St LA4 217 B5
West Paddock PR25 59 E8
West Park Ave PR2 116 F2
West Park Cl WN8 8 D8
West Park Dr FY3 130 E4
West Park La PR2 117 A2
West Park Rd BB2 101 C6
West Pennine Bsns Pk OL13 87 F5
WEST PIMBO 9 D4
West Pimbo Ind Est WN8 9 D4
West Pk PR9 53 D1
West Rd
Fulwood PR2 117 F3
Lancaster LA1 214 E8
Thornton FY5 176 C3
Westside FY4 110 F8
West Sq PR4 75 A8
West St
9 Blackpool FY1 130 B5
Burnley BB10 128 C8
Chorley PR7 43 C7
Colne BB8 171 E4
Great Harwood BB6 124 C4
Lancaster LA1 214 F5
Morecambe LA3 216 E4
7 Nelson BB9 170 D1
Padiham BB12 126 B8
7 Ramsbottom BL0 50 B5
Rawtenstall BB4 69 E8
Southport PR8 35 A7
West Strand PR1 96 D8
West Street Com Prim Sch BB8 171 E4
West View
Bacup, Lane Head OL13 88 A4
Bacup, Waterbarn OL13 70 B8
Bamber Bridge PR5 77 E7
Blackburn BB2 101 B4
Blackpool FY1 130 C3
Carnforth LA5 223 D3
Clitheroe BB7 166 D7
Elswick PR4 155 F1
Garstang PR3 181 C7
Glasson LA2 209 E5
Grindleton BB7 190 B8
Haslingden, Bridge End BB4 68 A7
Haslingden, North Hag BB4 85 B4
Hollins Lane PR3 207 D2
Holme Chapel BB10 108 A8
Kirkham PR4 113 F7
Longton PR4 75 A8
4 Newchurch BB4 86 F1
1 Ormskirk L39 15 F5
Oswaldtwistle BB5 103 E4
Parbold WN8 27 C2
Preston PR1 118 C2
Ramsbottom BL0 68 C2
Waddington BB7 189 B4
Wheelton PR6 62 A7
West View Ave 8 FY1 130 B2
West View Pl BB2 101 B6
West View Rd
1 Morecambe LA4 217 A5
Whitewell Bottom BB4 86 F5
West View Terr
Billington BB7 144 A4
Padiham BB12 126 C7
1 Preston PR1 96 D8
Tockholes BB3 81 A2
Westway
Burnley BB11 127 D6
Freckleton PR4 93 A6
Fulwood PR2 118 A4
Hightown L38 2 F4
Maghull L31 5 C2
West Way
Chorley PR7 61 A2
Fleetwood FY7 175 D8
Westway Ct PR2 118 B4
Westwell Gr 2 FY1 130 C4
Westwell Rd 4 PR6 61 D1
Westwell St
Darwen BB3 81 E4
14 Great Harwood BB6 124 C5
West Wlk BL7 47 D2
Westwood Ave
Blackpool FY3 130 E4
2 Fleetwood FY7 198 E3
Poulton-le-F FY6 153 E3
Rishton BB1 124 A1
Westwood Cl PR8 35 E3
Westwood Ct BB1 102 A6
Westwood Mews FY8 91 A3
Westwood Prim Sch PR5 78 C4
Westwood Rd
Burnley BB12 127 C8
Clayton Brook PR5, PR6 78 C4
Leyland PR25 77 A2
Lytham St Anne's FY8 91 A3
Westwood St BB5 104 B7
Wetherall St PR2 117 D1
Wetherby Ave FY4 110 B5
Wetherby Ct BL6 32 A4
Wetherfield Cl LA1 218 E4
Weymouth Rd FY3 130 F3
Weythorne Dr BL9 33 F4
WHALLEY 144 B5
Whalley Abbey* BB7 144 B5
WHALLEY BANKS 144 D3
Whalley Banks BB2 101 D4
Whalley Banks Trad Est BB2 101 D4
Whalley CE Prim Sch BB7 144 C5

Whalley Cres
Darwen BB3 82 B1
Staining FY3 131 E5
Whalley Dr
Formby L37 12 A2
Ormskirk L39 6 D8
Rawtenstall BB4 86 A4
Whalley Gdns OL12 52 B1
Whalley Ind Pk BB7 144 D8
Whalley La FY4 111 A8
Whalley New Rd BB1 122 F1
Whalley Old Rd
Billington BB6, BB7 144 B3
Blackburn, Bank Hey BB1 123 B1
Blackburn, Cob Wall BB1 102 A7
Whalley Pl FY8 90 B6
Whalley Range BB1 101 F6
Whalley Range Bsns Pk 14 BB1 101 F6
Whalley Rd
Accrington BB5 104 B7
Bank Lane BL0 50 E7
Barrow BB7 166 D2
Billington BB6, BB7 143 F3
Burnley BB12 126 B8
Clayton-le-M BB5, BB6 124 F5
Clitheroe BB7 166 D5
Heskin Green PR7 41 D4
Hurst Green BB7 165 B1
Lancaster LA1 218 D4
Langho BB6 143 D1
Mellor Brook BB2 121 C3
Read BB12 145 C1
Rochdale OL12 52 B1
Sabden BB7 145 D6
Turner Green BB2, PR5 120 C2
Wilpshire BB1, BB6 123 B7
WHALLEYS 18 B5
Whalleys Rd WN8 18 B5
Whalley St
2 Bamber Bridge PR5 97 F2
Blackburn BB1 101 E6
Burnley BB10 148 A1
5 Chorley PR7 43 C7
5 Clitheroe BB7 166 D8
Whalley Sta BB7 144 B6
Whalley Terr BB3 81 B6
Wham Bottom La OL12 52 D4
Wham Brook Cl BB5 103 B5
Wham Hey PR4 76 A7
Wham La
New Longton PR4 76 A7
Walmer Bridge PR4 75 D4
Whams La LA2 207 D7
Wharfdale Ave BB10 148 B4
Wharfe Ct LA3 217 F3
Wharfedale
Blackpool FY4 110 F7
Galgate LA2 211 B4
Wharfedale Ave
Fulwood PR2 118 E5
Thornton FY5 176 B3
Wharfedale Cl
Blackburn BB2 80 D7
Leyland PR25 60 A7
Wharfedale Ct FY6 153 C3
Wharfedale Rd LA1 214 D8
Wharf Ho 8 BB2 101 B1
Wharf St
Blackburn BB1 101 F5
Lytham St Anne's FY8 91 C3
Rishton BB1 124 C1
WHARLES 134 F4
Wharton Ave FY5 176 D1
Whave's La PR6 79 D4
Wheatacre WN8 8 E8
Wheatcroft Ave BB12 147 D8
Wheatfield PR26 59 A8
Wheatfield Cl 1 FY5 152 F7
Wheatfield Ct 8 LA1 214 E8
Wheatfield St
Lancaster LA1 214 E8
Rishton BB1 124 B2
Wheathead La BB9 170 B8
Wheatholme St BB4 86 B2
Wheat La L40 26 A4
Wheatlands Cres FY3 131 C2
Wheatley Cl
3 Burnley BB12 127 D7
Fence BB12 147 D7
Wheatley Dr PR3 140 B8
Wheatley Gr BB9 170 C3
WHEATLEY LANE 169 F1
Wheatley Lane Methodist Prim Sch BB12 147 E8
Wheatley Lane Rd
Barrowford BB9 170 B2
Fence BB12 147 E8
Wheatsheaf Ave PR3 140 A7
Wheatsheaf Wlk
4 Ormskirk L39 15 E5
Standish WN6 29 D1
Wheat St
1 Accrington BB5 104 A6
Padiham BB12 126 D7
Wheel La PR3 201 A6
WHEELTON 62 A7
Wheelton La PR25 77 A3
Wheelwright Cl BB7 231 B3
Wheelwrights Wharf L40 23 F4
Whelan Cl BB2 81 D7
Whernside FY4 110 F7
Whernside Cl BB18 196 A2
Whernside Cres PR2 118 D5
Whernside Gr LA5 223 F2
Whernside Rd LA1 218 B3
Whernside Way PR25 77 C1
Whewell Row BB5 103 C5
Whimberry Cl 1 PR6 43 E8
Whimbrel Dr FY5 176 A4
Whin Ave LA5 221 B6
Whinberry Ave BB4 86 A1
Whinbrick Cotts PR4 113 B6
Whin Dr LA5 221 B6
Whinfell Dr LA1 215 A3
Whinfield Ave
7 Chorley PR6 61 D1
Fleetwood FY7 198 E2
Whinfield La PR2 96 A8
Whinfield Pl
Blackburn BB2 101 A6
Preston PR2 96 A8
Whinfield St 9 BB5 125 A1
Whin Gr LA5 221 B6
Whin La PR3 155 B8
WHIN LANE END 155 A8
Whinney Brow La PR3 207 C3
Whinneyfield La PR4 136 D2
Whinney Fold LA5 224 B2
Whinney Heys Rd FY3 131 A6
Whinney Hill Rd BB5 125 C1
Whinney La
Blackburn BB2 101 C8
Euxton PR7 60 E3
Langho BB6 143 D1
Mellor BB2 122 B2
Whinny Clough Ct 1 PR2 117 B1
WHINNY HEIGHTS 102 A2
Whinny La FY6 199 E4
Whinnysty La LA3 216 D1
Whinpark Ave FY3 131 A6
Whinsands Cl PR2 118 D5
Whins Ave BB7 145 E7
Whinsfell View LA4 217 B5
Whins La
Read BB12 145 E3
Wheelton PR6 62 A8
Whins The BB7 145 E7
Whipney La BL8 49 E1
Whipp Ave BB7 166 D7
Whitaker Gn 8 BB4 85 E2
Whitaker St BB5 104 B7
Whitbarrow Sq 8 LA1 215 A8
Whitburn WN8 17 D1
Whitburn Rd L33 1 A4
Whitby Ave
Fulwood PR2 116 F5
Southport PR9 54 D6
Whitby Dr BB2 102 A1
Whitby Pl PR2 116 F5
Whitby Rd
Lytham St Anne's FY8 111 A1
Morecambe LA4 217 C5
Whiteacre WN6 29 A2
Whiteacre La BB6 144 E8
White Acre Rd BB5 104 E2
Whiteacres Cl BB11 127 E4
White Ash Est BB5 103 D4
White Ash La BB5 103 D3
White Ash Sch BB5 103 C4
Whitebeam Cl
Cleveleys FY5 175 F5
Higher Penwortham PR1 96 B3
Whitebeck La LA6 240 B4
WHITEBIRK 102 C6
White Birk Cl BL8 49 F2
Whitebirk Dr BB1 102 C8
Whitebirk Ind Est BB1 102 B8
Whitebirk Rd BB1 102 D5
White Bull St 4 BB12 127 C6
White Carr La
Bury BL9 51 A1
Cleveleys FY5 153 A8
Hollins Lane PR3 207 E4
Treales PR4 134 C2
WHITECHAPEL 160 D7
Whitecoats Dr FY8 91 D4
Whitecrest Ave 3 FY5 175 F4
Whitecroft Ave 8 BB4 85 B2
Whitecroft Cl BB4 85 B2
Whitecroft La BB2 121 E2
Whitecroft Mdws BB4 85 B2
Whitecroft View BB5 104 E2
White Cross Ind Est LA1 214 F7
White Cross St LA1 214 F7
WHITEFIELD 148 C8
Whitefield Cl
Hightown L38 2 F2
Rufford L40 39 C3
Whitefield Inf Sch BB9 148 C8
Whitefield Mdw 5 PR5 97 F1
Whitefield Pl LA3 217 C2
Whitefield Prim Sch PR1 96 A4
Whitefield Rd PR1 96 A4
Whitefield Rd E PR1 96 B4
Whitefield Rd W PR1 96 A4
Whitefield St BB12 126 C4
Whitefield Terr BB11 128 B3
Whitefriar Cl PR2 117 A5
Whitegate LA3 217 D3
Whitegate Bsns Ctr LA3 217 D3
Whitegate Cl BB12 126 E7
Whitegate Dr FY3 130 E3
White Gate Fold PR7 42 E3
Whitegate Gdns BB12 126 E7
Whitegate Lo 5 FY1 130 E3
White Gates 5 BL7 47 E1
White Gr BB8 171 C6
Whitehalgh La BB6 143 C1
WHITEHALL 65 B5
Whitehall Ave WN6 19 E8
Whitehall Ct 3 FY8 89 E6
Whitehall La
Blackrod BL6 31 D3
Grindleton BB7 230 A1
Whitehall Rd
Blackburn BB2 101 B7
Darwen BB3 65 A5
Whitehall St
Darwen BB3 65 B5
Nelson BB9 170 F1
Rochdale OL12 52 F1
Whitehaven Cl
Blackburn BB2 102 A1
Southport PR8 21 B3
Whitehaven St 7 BB11 127 E5
Whitehead Cl FY3 131 D5
Whitehead Dr PR26 76 E3
Whitehead St
Blackburn BB2 101 C5
21 Rawtenstall BB4 86 A3
Whitehey WN8 8 E8
Whitehey Rd WN8 8 E8
White Hill Cl OL12 52 D4
Whitehill Rd FY4 111 E6
WHITEHOLME 152 E7
Whiteholme Dr FY6 153 B6
Whiteholme Pl 3 PR2 116 E1
Whiteholme Rd FY5 152 F7
White Horse Cl BL6 32 C5
White Horse La PR3 158 E1
Whitehough Outdoor Education Ctr BB12 169 E6
Whitehough Pl BB9 171 B1
Whitehouse Ave L37 12 A3
Whitehouse La L37 12 A3
White House La
Bescar L40 37 C1
Lane Heads PR3 156 E4
Whitehouse Residential Pk Homes PR3 204 C6
White Lea PR3 204 C1
Whiteledge Rd WN8 9 B6
White Lee Ave BB8 172 C2
White Lee La PR3 183 C2
Whitelees Way FY6 153 D3
Whitelens Ave 4 PR2 116 C1
Whiteley Ave BB2 101 A1
White Leys Cl BB18 196 F1
Whiteleys La L40 16 D2
Whiteley St BB4 85 C1
Whitelow Rd BL0 50 E5
WHITE LUND 217 D2
White Lund Ave LA3 217 C2
White Lund Rd LA3 217 C2
White Lund Trad Est LA3 217 D2
Whitely Gr L33 1 A6
White Mdw PR2 116 E3
Whitemoor Rd BB8 194 C2
Whitemoss OL12 52 B2
Whitemoss Ave FY3 131 B7
Whitemoss Bsns Pk WN8 8 F6
White Moss La FY6 177 E4
White Moss Rd WN8 8 C7
White Moss Rd S WN8 8 D7
Whitendale 8 LA1 218 A2
Whitendale Cres BB1 102 A3
Whitendale Dr
Bamber Bridge PR5 77 F8
Hest Bank LA5 220 F2
Whitendale Hall PR1 117 F1
Whitepits La LA2 239 D5
Whiterails Dr L39 15 D6
Whiterails Mews L39 15 D6
Whiteray Rd 9 LA1 218 B2
White Rd BB2 101 B6
Whiteside Fold OL12 52 A1
Whiteside St 7 FY1 130 C6
Whiteside Way FY5 175 E3
White St
2 Burnley BB12 127 B6
Colne BB8 171 B4
WHITE STAKE 76 B8
Whitestock WN8 8 E8
Whitethorn Cl PR6 78 A2
Whitethorne Mews FY5 153 C8
Whitethorn Mews FY8 111 A2
Whitethorn Sq 4 PR2 116 D1
White Walls Cl BB8 171 A3
Whitewalls Dr BB8 171 A4
Whitewalls Ind Est
Colne BB8 171 A3
Nelson BB9 170 F2
WHITEWELL 228 D2
WHITEWELL BOTTOM 86 F5
Whitewell Cl PR3 181 D3
Whitewell Dr BB7 166 C7
Whitewell Pl 11 BB1 101 F6
Whitewell Rd
Accrington BB5 104 D8
Dunsop Bridge BB7 228 C4
Whitewell Vale BB4 86 F2
Whitewood Cl FY8 90 E4
Whitley Ave
4 Blackpool FY3 130 D5
Cleveleys FY5 175 E5
Whitley Rd WN8 19 D3
Whitmoor Cl 7 LA4 217 B5
Whitmore Dr PR2 119 A2
Whitmore Gr PR2 119 A2
Whitmore Pl PR2 119 A2
Whitpark Gr BB12 127 D7
Whitstone Dr WN8 9 D7
Whittaker Ave FY3 130 E7
Whittaker Cl BB12 127 B8
Whittakers La BB7 189 F8
Whittaker St BB2 101 C5
Whittam Ave FY4 130 E1
Whittam Cres BB7 144 B6
Whittam Ct BB10 129 B6
Whittam Rd
Chorley PR7 43 B5
Whalley BB7 144 B6
Whittam St BB11 127 F5
Whitters La PR3 203 D2
Whittingham Dr BL0 50 C3
Whittingham La
Goosnargh PR3 138 C5
Grimsargh PR2 139 B2
Whittingham Rd PR3 139 F7
WHITTINGTON 241 D7
Whittle Cl BB7 189 F1
Whittle Ct BB12 127 E7
Whittle Dr L39 15 E7
WHITTLEFIELD 127 D7
Whittlefield Prim Sch BB12 127 D7
Whittle Gn PR4 136 E3
Whittle Hill
Bolton BL7 47 E3
Woodplumpton PR4 136 E3
WHITTLE HILLS 61 C8
Whittle La WN6, WN8 27 F4
WHITTLE-LE-WOODS 61 C7
Whittle-le-Woods CE Prim Sch PR6 61 B8
Whittle Pk PR6 78 B2
Whittles St OL13 71 B8
Whittle St
Haslingden BB4 85 A2
Rawtenstall BB4 86 A3
WHITTLESTONE HEAD 65 F4
Whitton Mews 5 BL6 32 B4
Whittycroft Ave BB9 170 E6
Whittycroft Dr BB9 170 E6
Whitwell Ave 4 FY4 110 C5
Whitwell Cl WN6 29 D2
Whitwell Gdns BL6 32 B5
WHITWORTH 71 D1
Whitworth Com High Sch OL12 52 C8
Whitworth Dr PR7 43 A7
Whitworth Heritage Mus* OL12 71 C1
Whitworth Rake OL12 52 D8
Whitworth Rd OL12 52 F2
Whitworth Sq OL12 52 D8
Whitworth St
Horwich BL6 32 C2
Kirkham PR4 113 F6
Whitworth Water Ski Ctr* OL12 71 C2
Whitworth Way BB18 196 C4
Wholesome La
Bescar PR9 37 E3
New Longton PR4 75 E5
Whytha Rd BB7 192 D6
Wickentree Holt OL12 52 A1
Wicken Tree Row BB12 145 F3
Wickliffe St 9 BB9 170 F1
Wicklow Ave FY8 91 E5
Wicks Cres L37 11 C4
Wicks Gdns L37 11 D3
Wicks Gn L37 11 C3
Wicks Green Cl L37 11 C3
Wicks La L37 11 D3
Wickworth St BB9 149 A7
Widford Wlk BL6 31 E1
Widgeon Cl FY5 175 F4
Widow Hill Ct BB10 148 D1
Widow Hill Rd BB10 148 D1
Wigan La
Adlington PR7, WN1 30 D7
Chorley PR7 43 E2
Wigan Rd
Bamber Bridge PR5 77 E7
Euxton PR7, PR25 60 C5
Ormskirk L39 16 A5
Skelmersdale WN8 8 F8
Westhead L40 16 E4
Wigeon Row FY8 90 E7
Wiggins La L40 38 B6
WIGGLESWORTH 236 F4
Wight Moss Way PR8 35 D3
Wignalls Mdw L38 2 F3
Wignall St 8 PR1 118 C1
Wigston Cl PR8 21 B4
Wigton Ave PR25 59 D7
Wilbraham St PR1 118 C1
Wilcove WN8 17 F1
WILDERSWOOD 32 D5
Wilderswood Ave BL6 32 C4
Wilderswood Cl PR6 78 C2
Wilderswood Ct BL6 32 C4
Wilding's La FY8 90 B8
Wild La FY4 111 D4
Wildman St
3 Blackpool FY3 130 D7
Preston PR1 117 E2
Wildoaks Dr FY5 153 D8
Wilds Pl BL0 50 B5
Wildwood Cl BL0 50 A4
Wild Wood Rise OL14 109 C1
Wilfield St BB11 127 E6
Wilford St FY3 130 E7
Wilfred Dr BL9 33 B4
Wilfred St BB5 104 C4
Wilfrid's Pl WN6 29 F1
Wilkie Ave BB11 127 E2
Wilkinson Ave FY3 130 E4
Wilkinson Mount 6 BB18 197 B2
Wilkinson St
Bamber Bridge PR5 77 B8
Barrowford BB9 170 C2
Clow Bridge BB11 106 B4
Haslingden BB4 85 B4
Higham BB12 146 F5
Nelson BB9 148 E7
Wilkinson Way
Blackburn BB1 102 C1
Knott End-on-S FY6 199 F5
Wilkin Sq 7 BB7 166 E8
Willacy La PR4 135 E3
WILLACY LANE END 135 E3
Willacy Par LA3 216 E2
Willard Ave WN5 10 D3
Willaston Ave BB9 170 E8
Willerby Way PR3 204 A5
Willey La LA2 206 D6
William Griffiths Ct BB2 101 B2
William Henry St 6 PR1 97 C8
William Herbert St 13 BB1 101 F6
William Hopwood St 8 BB1 102 A4
Williams Ave LA4 218 A6
Williams Dr BB2 102 A1
Williams La PR2 118 C7
Williamson Park Butterfly Ho* LA1 215 B7
Williamson Rd LA1 215 A8
Williams Pl 2 BB9 148 F8
Williams Rd BB10 128 B8
William St
Accrington, Enfield BB5 125 A1
Accrington, Lower Fold BB5 104 C7
11 Bamber Bridge PR5 77 A8
Blackburn BB2 101 E2
3 Blackpool FY3 130 E7
Brierfield BB9 148 B6
Britannia OL13 71 C8
Carnforth LA5 223 D3
Colne BB8 171 E4
11 Darwen BB3 82 A1
5 Earby BB18 197 B1
Horwich BL6 32 A3
17 Nelson BB9 170 E1
Ramsbottom BL0 68 C1
Whitworth OL12 71 C1
William Thompson Rec Ctr BB11 128 A5
William Young Cl PR1 118 C2
Willis Rd BB2 101 A2
Willis St 6 BB11 127 E5
Willoughby Ave FY5 175 D2
Willoughby St 6 BB1 101 E6
Willow Ave BB4 86 A4
Willow Bank
Bilsborrow PR3 159 A5
Darwen BB3 65 A6
Willowbank Ave FY4 110 E6
Willowbank Cotts PR26 58 B2
Willowbank Ct FY6 153 B5
Willowbank Holiday Home & Touring Pk PR8 21 B2
Willow Bank La BB3 81 F1
Willow Brook
8 Accrington BB5 104 B6
Shirdley Hill L39 23 A6
Willow Chase PR4 113 D4
Willow Cl
Adlington PR6 31 B8
Bamber Bridge PR5 77 A8
Barrowford BB9 170 B1
Clayton-le-M BB5 124 E3
Forton PR3 207 B3
Gregson Lane PR5 98 E1
Higher Penwortham PR1 96 A4
Knott End-on-S FY6 200 A6
Thornton FY5 176 D1
Willow Coppice PR2 116 E3
Willow Cres
Burscough Bridge L40 25 F6
Clayton-le-W PR25 77 D3
Fulwood PR2 118 E2
Willowcroft Dr FY6 177 B1
Willow Ct
Poulton-le-F FY6 154 A3
Standish WN6 29 E2
5 Thornton FY5 176 D1
Willow-Dale FY5 176 D1
Willowdene FY5 175 E1
Willow Dr
Barrow BB6 144 D8
Charnock Richard PR7 42 D3
Freckleton PR4 93 A5
Garstang PR3 204 C1
Kirkham PR4 114 B2
Nelson BB9 149 A8
Poulton-le-F FY6 131 D8
Skelmersdale WN8 17 E1
Wrea Green PR4 113 C4
Willow End L40 25 F
Willow Field PR6 78 C
Willow Field Chase PR5 99 B
Willowfield Rd LA3 213 A
Willow Gn
5 Ormskirk L39 15 F
Preston PR2 96 A
Rufford L40 39 A

Willow Gr
Blackpool FY3 153 A1
Formby L37 11 F4
Goosnargh PR3 138 D6
Hambleton FY6 177 B2
Lancaster LA1 215 B8
Morecambe LA4 217 F6
Southport PR9 35 E7
West Bradford BB7 189 D7
Willow Grove Cvn Pk
PR3 156 A5
Willowgrove Pk FY6 200 B4
Willowhey PR9 53 F4
Willow Hey
8 Haslingden BB4 84 F1
Skelmersdale WN8 17 F1
Tarleton PR4 57 A7
Willow La LA1 214 C7
Willow Lane Com Prim Sch
LA1 214 D8
Willow Lo FY8 90 C7
Willowmead Pk FY8 112 F2
Willowmead Way OL12 52 A2
Willow Mill LA2 237 C3
Willow Mount BB1 122 F3
Willow Pk
Oswaldtwistle BB5 103 C2
Southport PR8 35 A5
Willow Pl PR4 155 F1
Willow Rd
Chorley PR6 61 E2
Wymott PR26 58 F6
Willows Ave
Cleveleys FY5 175 E1
Lytham St Anne's FY8 90 E3
Willows La
Accrington BB5 104 A3
Kirkham PR4 113 F5
Willows Park La PR3 140 B8
Willows RC Prim Sch The
PR4 113 F5
Willow St
Accrington BB5 104 B6
Blackburn BB1 102 A7
Burnley BB12 127 E6
Bury BL9 33 B2
Clayton-le-M BB5 124 E3
Darwen BB3 81 F1
Fleetwood FY7 199 A4
Great Harwood BB6 124 C4
Haslingden BB4 85 B3
Rawtenstall BB4 69 E8
Willows The
Chorley PR7 43 B4
Coppull PR7 29 E8
Kirkham PR4 113 E4
Lytham St Anne's FY8 90 E3
Mawdesley L40 40 C2
Mellor Brook BB2 121 C3
Southport PR8 34 F6
Whitworth OL12 52 C5
Willow Tree Ave
Broughton PR3 137 D3
Rawtenstall BB4 85 E2
Willow Tree Cres PR25 76 D1
Willow Tree Gdns 3
FY5 176 D1
Willow Trees Dr BB1 122 C1
Willow Way PR4 75 F7
Willow Wlk WN8 18 B4
Wills Ave L31 5 C2
Willshaw Rd FY2 152 B1
Wilmar Rd PR25 77 C2
Wilmcote Gr PR8 21 B4
Wilmore Cl BB8 171 C5
Wilmot Rd PR2 118 E3
WILPSHIRE 122 E5
Wilpshire Banks BB1 122 F4
Wilpshire Rd BB1 123 E4
Wilsham Rd WN5 10 E5
Wilson Cl PR4 57 A7
Wilson Dr PR4 155 F1
Wilson Fold BB12 127 B6
Wilson Fold Ave BL6 32 F1
Wilson Gr LA3 212 E8
Wilson's Endowed CE Prim
Sch LA6 237 B8
Wilson Sq FY5 152 D7
Wilson St
Blackburn BB2 101 D2
Bury BL9 33 A1
Clitheroe BB7 166 E7
Foulridge BB8 194 D1
Horwich BL6 32 A4
Wilton Cl
Blackburn BB2 100 F8
Lancaster LA1 218 E4
Wilton Ct BB2 100 F7
Wilton Gr PR1 96 A4
Wilton Par FY1 130 B7
Wilton Pl 3 PR25 77 B1
Wilton St
Barrowford BB9 170 D3
Brierfield BB9 148 B5
Burnley BB10 148 B1
Wiltshire Ave BB12 127 B7
Wiltshire Dr BB4 68 B8
Wiltshire Mews PR4 116 D5
Wilvere Ct FY5 152 C7
Wilvere Dr FY5 152 C8
Wilworth Cres BB1 122 E2
Wimberley Banks BB1 101 F7
Wimberley Gdns 7
BB1 101 E6
Wimberley Pl 8 BB1 101 E6
Wimberley St BB1 101 E7
Wimbledon Ave FY5 152 D7
Wimbledon Ct FY5 152 D6
Wimborne FY8 89 F5
Wimborne Cl BL6 32 F1
Wimborne Pl FY4 110 B6
Wimbrick Cl L39 15 D4
Wimbrick Cres L39 15 D3
Winchcombe Rd FY5 152 E7
Winchester Ave
Accrington BB5 104 C7
5 Blackpool FY4 130 D1
Chorley PR7 43 E4
Lancaster LA1 215 B5
Morecambe LA4 217 D6
Winchester Cl
Morecambe LA3 217 B2
4 Orrell WN5 10 F7
Winchester Dr FY6 153 B6
Winchester Rd
Longshaw WN5 10 D2
Padiham BB12 126 D6
Winchester St BB1 102 A3
Winchester Way 2
PR3 181 B7
Winckley Ct 12 PR1 96 F7
Winckley Rd
Clayton-le-M BB5 124 F2
Preston PR1 96 E6
Winckley Sq PR1 96 F7
Winckley St 10 PR1 96 F7
Winder Garth LA6 240 B1
Winder La PR3 207 B2
Windermere Ave
Accrington BB5 125 D1
Burnley BB10 148 A2
Clitheroe BB7 166 C7
Colne BB8 171 F6
Fleetwood FY7 175 D8
Leyland PR25 77 A3
Morecambe LA4 217 D4
Windermere Cl 4
BB1 101 F6
Windermere Cres PR8 21 C3
Windermere Ct 4
LA4 217 D4
Windermere Dr
Adlington PR6 44 B1
Darwen BB3 82 C3
Maghull L31 5 E2
Rainford WA11 8 F2
Ramsbottom BL0 50 C7
Rishton BB1 124 A1
Windermere Ho PR1 96 B4
Windermere Rd
Bacup OL13 88 A3
Blackpool FY4 110 C8
Bolton-le-S LA5 221 A4
Carnforth LA5 221 E8
5 Chorley PR6 43 E7
Fulwood PR2 118 C4
Hightown L38 3 A4
Lancaster LA1 215 B8
Orrell WN5 10 F8
Padiham BB12 146 C2
Preston PR1 119 A1
Windermere Sq FY8 110 F2
Windermere St 4 OL12 52 F2
Windfield Cl L33 1 A6
Windflower Dr PR25 77 E3
Windgate
Much Hoole PR4 74 E2
Tarleton PR4 57 B5
Windgate Fold PR4 57 A5
Windham Pl LA1 218 A3
Windholme 6 LA1 218 A2
Windle Ash L31 5 C2
Windle Cl FY4 110 B4
Windmill Animal Farm*
L40 38 B4
Windmill Ave
Kirkham PR4 114 C4
Ormskirk L39 15 F5
Windmill Cl FY3 131 E5
Windmill Cotts BB2 121 C1
Windmill Ct 9 LA1 215 A3
Windmill Cvn Site FY4 111 E8
Windmill Ho
1 Blackpool FY4 110 F6
Southport PR9 53 F2
Windmill Hts WN8 10 A8
Windmill La PR6 79 B7
Windmill Pl 3 FY4 110 F6
Windmill Rd WN8 9 F7
Windmill St LA1 214 D8
Windmill View PR4 114 A6
Windrows WN8 17 F1
Windrush Ave BL0 50 A2
Windrush The OL12 52 C4
Windsor Ave
Adlington PR7 30 F6
Blackpool FY4 110 B8
Church BB5 104 A8
Clitheroe BB7 166 C7
Fulwood PR2 117 B2
Haslingden BB4 85 A1
Lancaster LA1 215 B5
Longridge PR3 139 F7
Middleforth Green PR1 96 C3
Morecambe LA4 217 A3
Newchurch BB4 86 E1
New Longton PR4 96 A1
Thornton FY5 176 B2
Windsor Cl
Blackburn BB1 102 B3
Burscough L40 25 E3
Chorley PR7 43 B7
Leyland PR25 59 D7
Ramsbottom BL8 50 A1
Read BB12 145 D2
Windsor Ct
Poulton-le-F FY6 153 E3
Southport PR8 34 E4
Windsor Dr
Brinscall PR6 62 E8
Fulwood PR2 117 D6
Horwich BL6 32 E2
Windsor Gdns PR3 181 B7
Windsor Gr LA4 217 A4
Windsor Lo 3 FY8 90 D4
Windsor Pl
Barnoldswick BB18 196 D3
1 Fleetwood FY7 199 B5
Windsor Rd
Bamber Bridge PR5 97 D3
Blackburn BB2 101 B6
Blackburn, Knuzden Brook
BB1 102 E4
Chorley PR7 43 B7
Darwen BB3 81 F3
Eccleston PR7 41 C7
Formby L37 11 F1
Garstang PR3 181 B7
Great Harwood BB6 124 D5
6 Kirkham PR4 113 F5
Lytham St Anne's, Ansdell
FY8 90 D4
Lytham St Anne's FY8 90 A5
Morecambe LA3 216 F3
Normoss FY3 131 B7
Southport PR9 35 D7
Up Holland WN8 10 A8
Windsor St
Accrington BB5 104 C6
Burnley BB12 127 C6
Colne BB8 171 E5
Nelson BB9 149 A7
Windsor Terr FY7 199 B5
Windy Bank BB8 171 E5
Windy Harbour Holiday Ctr
FY6 154 F5
Windy Harbour Rd
Singleton FY6 155 A4
Southport PR8 21 E7
Windyhill 36 LA1 214 F8
Windy Hill LA2 239 E8
Windy St PR3 185 E3
Winery La PR5 97 C5
WINEWALL 172 C4
Winewall La BB8 172 C5
Winewall Rd BB8 172 B5
Wingate Ave
Blackpool FY5 152 D7
Morecambe LA4 217 C4
Wingate Pl FY5 152 D8
Wingates 2 PR1 96 C3
Wingate-Saul Rd LA1 214 E7
Wingrove Rd FY7 198 F2
Winifred Ave BL9 33 F4
Winifred La L39 6 B8
Winifred St
Blackpool FY1 130 B4
Ramsbottom BL0 50 B5
Rochdale OL12 52 B1
WINMARLEIGH 203 E4
Winmarleigh CE Prim Sch
PR3 203 E5
Winmarleigh Rd
Lancaster LA1 215 A2
Preston PR2 117 B1
Winmarleigh St 3
BB1 102 C5
Winmarleigh Wlk BB1 102 C4
Winmoss Dr L33 1 A5
Winnipeg Cl BB2 101 B8
Winnipeg Ct FY2 152 E3
Winnipeg Pl FY2 152 E3
Winscar Wlk FY6 153 B3
Winsford Cres FY5 152 C8
Winsford Wlk BB11 127 B5
Winslow Ave FY6 153 B5
Winslow Cl 7 PR1 96 E2
Winsor Ave PR25 60 B8
Winstanley Coll WN5 10 F3
Winstanley Gr 1 FY1 130 C5
Winstanley Rd
Orrell WN5 10 F3
Skelmersdale WN8 8 F8
Winster Cl PR5 98 E4
Winster Ct BB5 124 E2
Winster Pk LA1 218 A2
Winster Pl FY4 131 D1
Winsters The WN8 17 F1
Winster Wlk LA1 218 A2
Winston Ave
Cleveleys FY5 175 F2
Lytham St Anne's FY8 90 B6
Winston Cres PR8 35 E2
Winston Rd BB1 101 D7
Winterburn Rd BB2 81 C7
Winter Gardens Arc 12
LA4 217 A5
Winter Hey La BL6 32 B3
Winter Hill Cl PR2 119 C7
Winterley Dr BB5 125 E1
Winterton Rd BB3 82 A2
Winthorpe Ave LA4 217 D3
Winton Ave
Blackpool FY4 131 A1
Fulwood PR2 117 F6
Winton Gn BL6 32 F1
Winward Cl BB3 81 F6
Wiseman Cl LA4 217 C4
Wiseman St BB11 127 F6
Wisp Hill Gr LA2 219 D6
Wisteria Dr BB3 82 B7
WISWELL 144 F7
Wiswell Cl
Burnley BB10 148 E2
Rawtenstall BB4 86 A4
Wiswell La BB7 144 D6
Wiswell Shay BB7 144 E7
Witham Cl WN6 29 D1
Witham Rd WN8 17 D1
Withens Rd L31 5 D3
Witherslack Cl 7 LA4 217 B3
Withers St BB1 101 F4
Withgill Piggery Cotts
BB7 165 E6
Within Gr BB5 104 D8
WITHIN GROVE 125 E1
Withington La PR7 41 E2
Within Lea PR5 77 E8
Withins Field L38 2 F3
Withins La L37 4 A7
WITHNELL 80 B1
WITHNELL FOLD 79 C3
Withnell Fold PR6 79 C2
Withnell Fold Old Rd
PR6 79 E1
Withnell Fold Prim Sch
PR6 79 C3
Withnell Gr PR6 61 E1
Withnell Rd FY4 110 B8
Withy Ct PR2 117 E3
Withy Grove Cl PR5 97 F1
Withy Grove Cres PR5 97 F1
Withy Grove Rd PR5 97 F1
Withy Par PR2 117 E4
Withy Trees Ave PR5 97 F1
Withy Trees Cl PR5 97 F1
Witney Ave BB2 80 E8
Wittlewood Dr BB5 125 B1
WITTON 101 B3
Witton Ave FY7 198 E1
Witton Ctry Pk* BB2 100 F4
Witton Ctry Pk Visitor Ctr*
BB2 100 F3
Witton Gr FY7 198 E1
Witton Par BB2 101 C3
Witton Park High Sch
BB2 101 A4
Witton St PR1 97 B8
Woborrow Rd LA3 212 E8
Woburn Cl BB5 104 E3
Woburn Gn PR25 77 B2
Woburn Rd FY1 130 C7
Woburn Way PR3 181 D2
Wold The PR6 62 A3
Wolfenden Gn BB4 69 F8
Wollaton Dr PR8 35 F3
Wolseley Cl PR25 60 A8
Wolseley Pl 20 PR1 97 A7
Wolseley Rd PR1 96 E5
Wolseley St
Blackburn BB2 101 D1
Lancaster LA1 215 A8
Wolsey Cl FY5 175 E3
Wolsley Rd
Blackpool FY1 130 B1
Fleetwood FY7 198 F4
Wolverton WN8 8 F8
Wolverton Ave FY2 152 B2
Woodacre Rd PR2 119 A2
Woodale Laithe BB9 170 C3
Wood Bank
Haslingden BB4 67 F6
Kingsfold PR1 96 C3
Woodbank Ave BB3 81 E2
Woodbank Ct 3 FY5 152 F7
Woodbine Gdns BB12 127 C7
Woodbine Rd
Blackburn BB2 101 B6
Burnley BB12 127 C6
Woodbine Terr OL14 109 B1
Woodbridge Gdns OL12 52 C2
Woodburn Cl BB2 101 A8
Woodbury Ave
Blackburn BB2 101 D2
Fence BB12 147 D7
Woodchat Ct PR7 42 F5
Wood Cl BB9 170 A5
Wood Clough Platts
BB9 148 A5
Woodcock Cl
Bamber Bridge PR5 98 A2
Thornton FY5 176 A5
Woodcock Est PR5 77 B6
Woodcock Fold PR7 41 C7
Woodcock Hill Rd BB2 100 B3
Woodcote Cl L33 1 A4
Woodcourt Ave BB11 127 D3
Woodcrest BB1 122 F5
Woodcroft
Appley Bridge WN6 19 E6
Skelmersdale WN8 8 F8
Woodcroft Ave BB4 85 F5
Woodcroft Cl PR1 96 C2
Woodcroft St BB4 85 F5
Wood End
Brierfield BB12 147 F3
Kingsfold PR1 96 C1
Wood End Rd PR6 78 B2
Woodfall PR7 61 B2
Woodfield PR5 78 C6
Woodfield Ave
Accrington BB5 104 D3
3 Blackpool FY1 130 B2
Rochdale OL12 52 E2
Woodfield Cl PR1 96 B4
Woodfield Ct FY5 176 B1
Woodfield Rd
Blackpool FY1 130 B2
Chorley PR7 61 C1
Ormskirk L39 15 D3
Woodfield Rd *continued*
Thornton FY5 176 D1
Woodfields
Hurst Green BB7 165 B3
Simonstone BB12 145 E3
Woodfield Terr BB9 148 C5
Woodfield View BB7 144 C5
Woodfold PR1 96 B3
Woodfold Cl BB2 121 C3
Woodfold Hall BB2 100 B7
Woodfold La PR3 204 C5
Woodfold Park Farm
BB2 100 B8
Woodfold Pl BB2 101 B5
Woodford Copse PR7 43 A7
Woodgate LA3 217 F2
Woodgate Ave BL9 33 D4
WOODGATE HILL 33 D4
Woodgate Hill Rd
Bury BL9 33 C3
Bury, Woodgate Hill BL9 33 D4
Woodgate Pk LA3 217 F2
Woodgates Rd BB2 100 F5
Wood Gn
Kirkham PR4 114 B7
Leyland PR25 76 E2
Wood Green Dr FY5 152 F8
Woodgrove Rd BB11 128 B3
Woodhall Cres PR5 98 E4
Woodhall Gdns FY6 177 C2
Woodhart La PR7 41 C5
Woodhead Cl
Ramsbottom BL0 50 C4
Rawtenstall BB4 87 A2
Woodhead Rd BB12 145 D2
WOODHEY 50 B3
Wood Hey Gr OL12 52 F4
Woodhey High Sch BL0 50 A3
Woodhey Rd BL0 50 A3
Woodhill Ave LA4 217 A3
Woodhill Cl LA4 217 A3
Woodhill La LA4 217 A4
WOOD HOUSE 229 B8
Wood House La BB7 229 A8
Woodhouse Rd FY5 153 E8
Woodhurst Dr WN6 29 D1
Wood La
Edenfield BL0 68 D2
Haskayne L37, L39 13 D1
Heskin Green PR7 41 E3
Hoscar L40 26 E5
Mawdesley L40 40 D5
Parbold WN8 27 D2
Wrightington Bar WN6,
PR7 28 E8
Woodland Ave
Bacup OL13 87 F5
Bescar L40 23 F7
Thornton FY5 176 B2
Woodland Cl
Hambleton FY6 177 D1
Wrea Green PR4 113 B3
Woodland Cres FY6 200 A6
Woodland Ct BB3 82 D1
Woodland Dr
Clayton-le-M BB5 124 F5
Poulton-le-F FY6 153 E1
Standish WN6 29 E2
Woodland Gr
Blackpool FY3 130 E4
Bolton BL7 47 D2
Higher Penwortham PR1 96 B5
Woodland Pk BB7 144 C5
Woodland Pl BB3 81 F7
Woodland Rd OL12 52 C2
Woodlands Ave
Bamber Bridge PR5 98 A2
Blackburn BB2 100 E1
Fulwood PR2 118 E2
Kingsfold PR1 96 E2
8 Kirkham PR4 113 F5
Woodlands Cl
Blackburn BB1 102 B4
Formby L37 11 D2
Newton-w-S PR4 114 F3
Ormskirk L39 16 A4
Rawtenstall BB4 86 D1
Southport PR9 35 D8
Woodlands Cnr BB1 101 D6
Woodlands Com Prim Sch
WN8 18 C2
Woodlands Cres PR3 137 B5
Woodlands Ct 5 FY8 90 D4
Woodlands Dr
Fulwood PR2 117 E8
Kirkham PR4 114 B7
Leyland PR25 76 F1
Morecambe LA3 216 E2
Shevington WN6 19 F4
Silverdale LA5 224 C4
Warton PR4 92 C5
West Bradford BB7 189 D7
Whalley BB7 144 C5
Woodlands Gr
Darwen BB3 81 D2
Grimsargh PR2 139 E1
Morecambe LA3 216 E2
Padiham BB12 146 B1
Woodlands Mdw PR7 43 C3
Woodlands Prim Sch
L37 11 D3
Woodlands Rd
Edenfield BL0 68 D2
Formby L37 11 D3
Lancaster LA1 218 E4

Woodlands Rd continued
Lytham St Anne's FY8 . . . . . .90 D4
Nelson BB9 . . . . .148 E8
Woodlands Sch FY3. . . . . . .130 E4
Woodlands The
Brockhall Village BB6 . . 143 C6
Garstang PR3 . . . . .181 B8
6 Preston PR2 . . . . .116 E1
Ring o'Bells L40. . . . . . . .26 A3
Southport PR8 . . . . .21 C5
Woodlands View
Lytham St Anne's FY8 . . . . . .90 D5
Over Kellet LA6 . . . . .237 B8
Woodlands Way
Longton PR4 . . . . .74 F8
Newsham PR2 . . . . .137 B5
Woodland Terr OL13 . . . .87 F4
Woodland View
Bacup OL13 . . . . .87 F4
Brinscall PR6 . . . . .62 F7
Great Harwood BB6 . . 124 C6
Wood Lark Dr PR7 . . . . . .42 F5
Wood Lea Bank 9 BB4 . .69 F8
Woodlea Chase BB3 . . . . .65 C3
Woodlea Cl PR9 . . . . .54 D5
Woodlea Gdns BB9 . . . .148 D5
Woodlea Jun Sch PR25 . .59 F8
Woodlea Rd
Blackburn BB1. . . . . .102 B4
Leyland PR25. . . . . .59 F8
Wood Lea Rd BB4 . . . . . . .69 F8
Woodlee Rd PR4. . . . . . . .73 F2
Woodleigh Cl L31. . . . . . . .5 B5
Woodley Ave
Accrington BB5 . . . . .104 C4
Thornton FY5 . . . . .176 D1
Woodley Park Rd WN8 . . .18 B4
Woodmancote PR7 . . . . . .61 B2
Woodman La LA6. . . . . . .241 F6
Woodmoss La PR8, L40 . .36 E2
WOODNOOK. 104 B4
Wood Nook 2 BB4 . . . . . .86 A7
Woodnook Prim Sch
BB5 . . . . .104 C4
Woodnook Rd WN6 . . . . . .19 E8
Wood Park Rd FY1. . . . . .130 E1
Woodpecker Hill 3
BB11 . . . . .127 C5
WOODPLUMPTON. 136 E2
Woodplumpton La
PR3 . . . . .137 C2
Woodplumpton Rd
Burnley BB11. . . . . .127 F1
Fulwood PR2 . . . . .117 C3
Woodplumpton, Moor Side
PR4. . . . . .136 D4
Woodplumpton PR6 . . .136 E2
Woodplumpton St Anne's
CE Prim Sch PR4 . . . . .136 D2
Woodridge Ave FY5. . . . .152 C8
WOOD ROAD 50 C1
Wood Road La BL8, BL9. . .50 C1
Woodrow WN8. . . . . .8 E8
Woodrow Dr WN8. . . . . . . .27 A1
Woodroyd Dr BL9. . . . . . . .33 C3
Woodruff Cl FY5. . . . . . . .175 F5
Woodrush LA4. . . . . .217 F6
Woods Brow BB2 . . . . . .120 D5
Wood's Brow PR3. . . . . . .141 B6
Woods Cl L39. . . . . .14 A4
Woods End PR1 . . . . .97 B6
Woodsend Cl BB2. . . . . . . .82 A8
WOODSFOLD. 135 E6
Woods Gn PR1 . . . . .96 E6
Woodside
Blackpool FY4 . . . . .111 E7
Chorley PR7. . . . . .43 E4
Euxton PR7 . . . . .60 C3
Haslingden BB4 . . . . .85 C1
Leyland PR25. . . . . .77 C4
Woodside Cl
Clayton Green PR6 . . . . . .78 B3
Fulwood, Cadley PR2. . . .117 E4
Fulwood, Ribbleton PR2. .118 E3
New Longton PR4 . . . . . . .75 F7
Rishton BB1. . . . . .102 F8
Southport PR8 . . . . .21 B3
Woodside Cl
Huncoat BB5 . . . . .125 F1
Up Holland WN8 . . . . .10 C8
Woodside Cres BB4. . . . . .86 D1
Woodside Dr
Blackpool FY3 . . . . .131 A5
Ramsbottom BL0. . . . . . . .50 A5
Woodside Gr BB2. . . . . . . .81 A8
Woodside Pk FY6. . . . . . .200 D1
Woodside Pk Cvn Pk
FY6. . . . . .200 D1
Woodside Rd
Accrington, Hillock Vale
BB5. . . . . .104 E8
Huncoat BB5 . . . . .125 F1
Simonstone BB12 . . . . . .145 E2
Woodside Terr BB8 . . . .148 C8
Woods La PR3, PR4. . . . .135 E8
Wood's La PR3 . . . . .180 A6
Woodsley Cl BB12 . . . . . .127 B5

Wood St
Blackpool FY1 . . . . .130 B5
Brierfield BB9 . . . . .148 B5
Burnley BB10. . . . . .128 A8
Church BB5 . . . . .103 E5
Colne BB8 . . . . .171 E4
Darwen BB3. . . . . .81 F1
Fleetwood FY7. . . . . .175 E8
Great Harwood BB6 . . . .124 E5
Hapton BB12. . . . . .126 C4
Horwich BL6. . . . . .32 C3
1 Lancaster LA1. . . . . . .214 F8
Lytham St Anne's FY8 . . . .89 E6
Poulton-le-F FY6 . . . . . . .154 A3
Ramsbottom BL0. . . . . . . .50 B5
Woodstock Ave FY5. . . . .153 C8
Woodstock Cl 8 PR5 . . . .77 C8
Woodstock Cres BB2. . . . .80 E8
Woodstock Dr PR8. . . . . . .21 F8
Woodstock Gdns FY4 . . .110 B7
Woodstock St 12 OL12 . . .52 C1
Wood Street Livesey Fold
PR5. . . . . .81 F2
Wood Terr
Chatburn BB7 . . . . .190 E5
Simonstone BB12 . . . . . .145 F2
Woodtop **1** BB11. . . . . . .127 D5
WOOD TOP. 85 E1
WOODVALE. 21 B2
Woodvale
Darwen BB3. . . . . .81 F1
Leyland PR25. . . . . .59 A8
Woodvale Ct PR9 . . . . .55 A5
Woodvale Rd
Clayton Green PR6 . . . . . .78 B3
Southport PR8 . . . . .21 D2
Wood View
Blackburn BB2. . . . . .100 F1
Burton in L LA6 . . . . .242 C3
Wood View La LA6 . . . . .177 C7
Woodville Rd
Adlington PR6 . . . . .43 F1
Blackburn BB1. . . . . .102 A7
Brierfield BB9 . . . . .148 C6
2 Chorley PR7 . . . . .43 C8
Kingsfold PR1. . . . . .96 D2
Woodville Rd W 6 PR1 . .96 C2
Woodville St
Lancaster LA1. . . . . .215 A8
Leyland PR25. . . . . .77 B2
Woodville Terr
Darwen BB3. . . . . .65 B6
Lytham St Anne's FY8 . . . .90 F3
Woodward Rd L33 . . . . . . .1 D4
Woodway PR2 . . . . .117 C4
Woodwell La LA5 . . . . . . .224 C1
Wookey Cl PR2 . . . . .118 D6
Wooley La BB5 . . . . .104 F2
Woolman Rd FY1 . . . . . . .130 C4
Woolpack BB8. . . . . .171 E3
Woolton St BB1 . . . . .102 B5
Woome La BB7 . . . . .166 D7

Worcester Ave
4 Accrington BB5 . . . . . .104 A7
Garstang PR3 . . . . .181 B8
Lancaster LA1. . . . . .215 B5
Leyland PR25. . . . . .60 B8
Worcester Gdns PR4 . . . .116 D5
Worcester Pl PR7 . . . . .43 E3
Worcester Rd
Blackburn BB1. . . . . .102 C5
Blackpool FY3 . . . . .131 A3
Worden Brook Cl PR7. . . .60 E6
Worden Cl PR25 . . . . .59 F7
Worden La PR25. . . . . .60 A7
Worden Pk* PR25 . . . . . . .59 F7
Worden Rd PR2 . . . . .117 D3
Wordens The PR25. . . . . . .60 B7
Wordsworth Ave
Blackpool FY3 . . . . .131 B2
Bolton-le-S LA5 . . . . . . .221 A5
Longshaw WN5 . . . . .10 D1
5 Lytham St Anne's FY8. . .91 D4
Orrell WN5. . . . . .10 F6
Padiham BB12 . . . . .126 E7
Thornton FY5. . . . . .176 A2
Warton PR4 . . . . .92 E6
Wordsworth Cl
Ormskirk L39. . . . . .15 D6
Oswaldtwistle BB5 . . . . .103 C4
Wordsworth Ct 1 FY8 . . . .90 C4
Wordsworth Dr BB6. . . . .124 B4
Wordsworth Gdns BB3. . .82 B1
Wordsworth Ho LA1 . . . .218 C4
Wordsworth Pl PR25. . . . . .97 D2
Wordsworth Rd
Accrington BB5 . . . . .104 A4
Colne BB8 . . . . .171 D5
Wordsworth St
Burnley, Harle Syke
BB10. . . . . .148 F2
Burnley, Whittlefield
BB12. . . . . .127 C6
6 Hapton BB12 . . . . .126 C4
Wordsworth Terr PR6. . . .61 D2
Workshop Rd LA3. . . . . . .212 F2
Worrall St 1 OL12. . . . . . .52 D2
Worsicks Cotts FY6 . . . . .154 E1
Worsley Ave FY4. . . . . . . .110 C7

Worsley Cl FY6. . . . . .199 E5
Worsley Ct 13 BB5 . . . . . .103 E4
Worsley Rd FY6. . . . . .90 C5
Worsley St
Accrington BB5 . . . . .104 D4
Rising Bridge BB5 . . . . . . .85 A8
Worsten Ave BB2 . . . . . . .101 C1
WORSTHORNE. 129 B5
Worsthorne Prim Sch
BB10 . . . . .129 A6
WORSTON. 190 D2
Worston Cl
Accrington BB5 . . . . .103 F4
Rawtenstall BB4 . . . . .86 A4
Worston La BB6 . . . . .124 F6
Worston Pl BB2 . . . . .101 C5
Worswick Cres 3 BB4 . . .86 A2
Worswick Gn BB4. . . . . . . .86 B2
Worthalls Rd BB12. . . . . .145 D1
Worthing Cl PR8. . . . . .34 F3
Worthing Rd PR2 . . . . . . .117 A4
Worthington Rd FY4 . . . .111 B4
Worthy St PR6. . . . . .43 E7
Wove Ct PR1 . . . . .117 E2
Wraith St BB3 . . . . .65 A8
WRANGLING THE 101 D3
WRAY 238 D6
Wray Cres
Wrea Green PR4 . . . . . . .113 C4
Wymott PR26. . . . . .58 F6
Wray Ct LA1 . . . . .218 C4
Wray Gr FY5. . . . . .158 D2
WRAYTON 241 E3
Wray with Botton Endowed
Prim Sch LA2 . . . . .238 D6
Wraywood Ct FY7. . . . . . .198 C1
WREA GREEN 113 B3
Wren Ave PR1. . . . . .96 E5
Wren Cl
Carleton FY6 . . . . .153 A4
Thornton FY5 . . . . .153 D8
Wren Dr BL9 . . . . .33 B4
Wren Gr FY3 . . . . .130 E2
Wrennalls La PR7. . . . . . . .41 B5
Wren St
Burnley BB12. . . . . .127 C6
Nelson BB9 . . . . .148 F8
Preston PR1. . . . . .118 B2
WRIGHTINGTON. 28 D4
WRIGHTINGTON BAR . . .28 F7
Wrightington Hospl
WN6. . . . . .28 D2
Wrightington Mossy Lea
Prim Sch WN6 . . . . .28 F6
Wright St W 3 BL6. . . . . . .32 B4
Wrights Fold PR25. . . . . . .60 C8
Wright St
Chorley PR6. . . . . .43 E8
Horwich BL6 . . . . .32 B4
6 Kirkham PR4. . . . . . . .113 F6
Southport PR9 . . . . .35 C7
3 Weir OL13. . . . . .88 A7
Wrights Terr PR8 . . . . .35 B3
Wrigleys Cl L37. . . . . .11 F5
Wrigleys La L37 . . . . .11 F5
Written Stone La PR3 . . .162 E1
Wroxham Cl BB10. . . . . . .148 D2
Wroxton Cl FY5. . . . . .152 F7
Wycherley Rd OL12 . . . . . .52 B2
Wychnor PR2. . . . . .117 B7
Wycollar Cl BB5 . . . . .104 C4
Wycollar Dr BB2 . . . . .101 A6
Wycollar Rd BB2. . . . . . . .101 B6
WYCOLLER 173 A3
Wycoller Ave BB10. . . . . .128 D5
Wycoller Ctry Pk*
BB8 . . . . .173 B3
Wycombe Ave FY4 . . . . . .110 B6
Wyfordby Ave BB2 . . . . . .101 A7
Wyke Cop Rd PR8, PR9 . . .36 D2
Wykeham Gr OL12 . . . . . . .52 B1
Wykeham Rd FY8 . . . . .91 B4
Wyke La PR8, PR9 . . . . . . .36 E6
Wyke Wood La PR9 . . . . . .36 F7
Wyllin Rd L33 . . . . .1 A2
WYMOTT. 58 F6
Wymundsley PR7 . . . . .61 A2
Wyndene Cl PR3 . . . . .140 C8
Wyndene Gr PR4 . . . . .93 B6
Wyndham Gdns FY4 . . . .110 D6
Wyndham Pl LA4 . . . . . . .217 F6
Wynfield PR5. . . . . .97 F2
Wynnstay Ave L31 . . . . . . .5 D3
Wynnwood Ave 1
FY1. . . . . .130 D8
Wynotham St BB10 . . . . .148 C1
Wyre Ave PR4 . . . . .114 B5
Wyre Bank PR3 . . . . .157 B6
Wyre Cl
Great Eccleston PR3 . . . .156 C5
Morecambe LA3. . . . . . . .217 F2
Wyre Cres BB3 . . . . .81 D4
Wyre Ct
Fleetwood FY7. . . . . .198 E3
Poulton-le-F FY6 . . . . . . .154 A3
Wyredale Ct FY7. . . . . . . .198 F3
Wyredale Rd FY6 . . . . .89 C8
Wyre Estuary Cctry Pk*
FY5. . . . . .176 E3
Wyrefields FY6 . . . . .154 A3

Wyre Gr FY1. . . . . .130 C3
Wyre Ho LA1 . . . . .214 F7
Wyre La PR3 . . . . .204 D1
Wyre Rd FY5. . . . . .153 F6
Wyresdale Ave
Accrington BB5 . . . . .104 A8
Blackpool FY2 . . . . .152 D4
3 Morecambe LA3 . . . . .216 E1
Poulton-le-F FY6 . . . . . . .153 C3
Southport PR8 . . . . .35 D4
Wyresdale Cres
Fulwood PR2 . . . . .118 D4
Glasson LA2. . . . . .209 E4
Scorton PR3. . . . . .204 E7
Wyresdale Ct LA1. . . . . . .215 B7
Wyresdale Dr PR25 . . . . . .60 B6
Wyresdale Gdns LA1. . . .215 B7
WYRESDALE PARK 204 E7
Wyresdale Rd
Knott End-on-S FY5 . . . .199 D5
Lancaster LA1. . . . . .215 B6
Quernmore LA2 . . . . .232 A6
Wyreside PR3 . . . . .155 E8
Wyre Side Cl PR3 . . . . . . .181 C8
Wyreside Dr FY6. . . . . . . .177 B2
Wyreside Ecology & Visitor
Ctr* FY5 . . . . .176 E3
Wyreside Hall LA2 . . . . . .226 B7
Wyre St
Fleetwood FY7. . . . . .198 F3
Kirkham PR4 . . . . .113 F6
Lytham St Anne's FY8 . . . .90 A7
Padiham BB12 . . . . .126 D8
Preston PR2. . . . . .117 C1
Wyre Vale Pk PR3 . . . . . .204 B1
Wyre View
1 Fleetwood FY7 . . . . . .199 B5
Knott End-on-S FY5 . . . .199 E5
Wytham St 6 BB12 . . . . .126 D7
Wythburn Ave BB2. . . . . . .80 E8
Wythburn Cl BB12 . . . . . .127 B8
Wythorpe Croft LA4. . . . .217 B4
Wyvern Way FY6. . . . . . . .153 C5

X

XL Bsns Pk WN8 . . . . .17 C3

Y

Yale St BL7 . . . . .48 D4
Yardley Ctr L33 . . . . .1 C1
Yardley Rd L33 . . . . .1 C1
Yare St 7 BB8 . . . . .69 F8
Yarlside La BD23. . . . . . . .231 E4
Yarmouth Ave BB4 . . . . . . .85 C2
Yarm Pl BB11. . . . . .128 A6
Yarraville St BB4. . . . . .86 A2
Yarrow Ave L31. . . . . .5 F2
Yarrow Cl
Croston PR26. . . . . .58 B2
Withnell PR6 . . . . .80 A1
Yarrow Gate PR7. . . . . .43 E6
Yarrow Gr BL6. . . . . .32 B4
Yarrow Mill PR6 . . . . .43 E6
Yarrow Pl PR25 . . . . .59 D8
Yarrow Rd
Chorley PR6. . . . . .43 E6
Leyland PR25. . . . . .59 D8
Yarrow Valley Pk* PR7. . . .43 A2
Yarrow Wlk 8 LA3. . . . . . .217 B2
Yarwood St BL9. . . . . .33 A2
Yates Fold BB2 . . . . .101 F2
Yates St
Blackpool FY1 . . . . .130 B6
Chorley PR7. . . . . .43 B5
Yeadon Gr PR7 . . . . .43 A7
Yeadon Way FY4 . . . . . . .110 D7
Yealand Ave LA3 . . . . . . .212 F6
Yealand CE Prim Sch
LA5. . . . . .225 E3
YEALAND CONYERS 225 F1
Yealand Dr LA1 . . . . .215 A4
Yealand Gr LA1 . . . . .223 E2
Yealand Rd LA5. . . . . .225 E2
YEALAND
REDMAYNE 225 E4
YEALAND STORRS. 225 E3
Yeargate Ind Est BL9. . . . .33 D2
Yellow Hall BB10 . . . . .15 A6
Yellow House La PR8 . . . . .35 A6
Yenham La LA3. . . . . .213 E1
Yerburgh Rd BB2 . . . . . . .121 E2
Yewbarrow Cl BB12 . . . . .147 C1
Yew Ct FY7 . . . . .198 F3
Yewdale WN8. . . . . .18 A1
Yewdale Ave LA3 . . . . . . .212 F6
Yew Gn PR4 . . . . .114 B7
Yewlands Ave
4 Bamber Bridge PR5 . . . .97 F1
Heskin Green PR7 . . . . . . .41 F3
5 Leyland PR25. . . . . . . .77 A1
Yewlands Cres PR2 . . . . .117 E6
Yewlands Dr
Burnley BB10. . . . . .148 B3
Fulwood PR2 . . . . .117 E6

Yewlands Dr continued
Garstang PR3 . . . . .204 C1
2 Leyland PR25 . . . . .77 A1
Yew St
10 Blackburn BB1. . . . . .102 A7
2 Bury BL9. . . . . .33 C3
Yewtree Ave PR2 . . . . . . .119 A4
Yew Tree Ave
Euxton PR7 . . . . .60 C4
Grimsargh PR2 . . . . .139 C2
Yewtree Cl PR7 . . . . .43 C3
Yew Tree Cl
Garstang PR3 . . . . .181 B8
Newton-w-S PR4 . . . . . . .114 F3
Wilpshire BB1 . . . . .122 E6
Yew Tree Dr
Blackburn BB2. . . . . .122 B1
Low Bentham LA2 . . . . . .239 C8
Oswaldtwistle BB5 . . . . .103 F3
Yew Tree Gdns
Silverdale LA5 . . . . .224 C2
Stalmine FY6 . . . . .177 C8
Yewtree Gr PR5. . . . . .77 A7
Yew Tree Gr BB4 . . . . .68 F8
Yew Tree Rd
Blackpool FY3 . . . . .153 A1
Ormskirk L39. . . . . .15 E7
YORK 123 D8
York Ave
Cleveleys FY5 . . . . .175 D2
Fleetwood FY7. . . . . .198 F3
Fulwood PR2 . . . . .117 E4
Haslingden BB4 . . . . .68 B8
Preston PR8. . . . . .35 A5
York Cl
4 Bamber Bridge PR5 . . . .97 C3
Clayton-le-M BB5. . . . . .124 F3
Formby L37 . . . . .11 F6
Leyland PR25. . . . . .59 E7
York Cres BB1 . . . . .122 F3
York Dr
Great Eccleston PR3 . . . .156 C5
Kirkham PR4 . . . . .114 B2
Ramsbottom BL0. . . . . . . .50 A4
Yorke St 2 BB11 . . . . .127 F5
York Fields BB18. . . . . . . .196 B1
York Gdns PR8 . . . . .35 A5
York Pk PR3 . . . . .181 B7
York Ho LA1 . . . . .215 A5
York La BB6 . . . . .123 D8
York Manor PR8 . . . . .35 A5
York Pl
Accrington BB5 . . . . .104 B7
Adlington PR6 . . . . .31 A8
Morecambe LA4. . . . . . . .217 C5
York Rd
Blackpool FY2 . . . . .152 B4
Formby L37 . . . . .12 A3
Lancaster LA1. . . . . .215 A5
Langho BB1, BB6. . . . . . .123 D6
Lytham St Anne's FY8 . . . .89 F5
Southport PR8 . . . . .34 F4
Yorkshire Cl PR7. . . . . .60 F6
Yorkshire St E LA4. . . . . .216 F4
Yorkshire St W LA3 . . . . .216 E4
Yorkshire St
Accrington BB5 . . . . .104 C4
16 Bacup OL13. . . . . .87 F3
Blackpool FY1 . . . . .130 B3
Burnley BB11. . . . . .128 B6
Huncoat BB5 . . . . .125 E2
8 Nelson BB9 . . . . .148 E8
York St
Accrington BB5 . . . . .104 B7
Bacup OL13 . . . . .87 F3
Barnoldswick BB18 . . . . .196 B1
Blackburn BB2. . . . . .101 E3
Blackpool FY1 . . . . .130 B3
Bury BL9 . . . . .33 A2
Chorley PR7. . . . . .43 D7
Church BB5 . . . . .103 E6
Clitheroe BB7 . . . . .189 F1
Colne BB8 . . . . .171 F5
Great Harwood BB6 . . . .124 D5
Nelson BB9 . . . . .148 F8
Oswaldtwistle BB5 . . . . .103 C3
Rawtenstall BB4 . . . . .86 A7
Rishton BB1. . . . . .124 A1
York Terr
Blackburn BB2. . . . . .80 D8
Southport PR9 . . . . .35 C8
York View BB3 . . . . .81 B6
Young Ave PR25 . . . . .77 C1
Young St
Blackburn BB2. . . . . .101 B2
Ramsbottom BL0. . . . . . . .50 B6

Z

Zama St 9 BL0. . . . . .50 A4
Zebudah St BB2 . . . . .101 C2
Zetland St
Preston PR1. . . . . .97 C7
Southport PR9 . . . . .35 D7
Zion Rd BB1. . . . . .102 A8
Zion St
Bacup OL13 . . . . .88 A3
Colne BB8 . . . . .171 D4